FOR REFERENCE

Do Not Take From This Room

DELPHI PUBLIC LIBRARY

222 East Main Street
Delphi, Indiana 46923
765-564-2929

CRITICAL SURVEY OF

Long Fiction

Fourth Edition

CRITICAL SURVEY OF

Long Fiction

Fourth Edition

Volume 8
Ousmane Sembène—Jules Verne

Editor
Carl Rollyson
Baruch College, City University of New York

SALEM PRESS
Pasadena, California   Hackensack, New Jersey

Editor in Chief: Dawn P. Dawson

Editorial Director: Christina J. Moose	*Research Supervisor:* Jeffry Jensen
Development Editor: Tracy Irons-Georges	*Research Assistant:* Keli Trousdale
Project Editor: Judy Selhorst	*Production Editor:* Joyce I. Buchea
Manuscript Editor: Desiree Dreeuws	*Design and Graphics:* James Hutson
Acquisitions Editor: Mark Rehn	*Layout:* William Zimmerman
Editorial Assistant: Brett S. Weisberg	*Photo Editor:* Cynthia Breslin Beres

Cover photo: John Updike (Frank Capri/Hulton Archive/Getty Images)

Some of the essays in this work, which have been updated, originally appeared in the following Salem Press publications: *Critical Survey of Long Fiction, English Language Series* (1983), *Critical Survey of Long Fiction, Foreign Language Series* (1984), *Critical Survey of Long Fiction, Supplement* (1987), *Critical Survey of Long Fiction, English Language Series, Revised Edition* (1991; preceding volumes edited by Frank N. Magill), *Critical Survey of Long Fiction, Second Revised Edition* (2000; edited by Carl Rollyson).

∞ The paper used in these volumes conforms to the American National Standard for Permanence of Paper for Printed Library Materials, Z39.48-1992 (R1997)

Library of Congress Cataloging-in-Publication Data

Critical survey of long fiction / editor, Carl Rollyson. — 4th ed.
    p. cm.
Includes bibliographical references and index.
    ISBN 978-1-58765-535-7 (set : alk. paper) — ISBN 978-1-58765-536-4 (vol. 1 : alk. paper) —
ISBN 978-1-58765-537-1 (vol. 2 : alk. paper) — ISBN 978-1-58765-538-8 (vol. 3 : alk. paper) —
ISBN 978-1-58765-539-5 (vol. 4 : alk. paper) — ISBN 978-1-58765-540-1 (vol. 5 : alk. paper) —
ISBN 978-1-58765-541-8 (vol. 6 : alk. paper) — ISBN 978-1-58765-542-5 (vol. 7 : alk. paper) —
ISBN 978-1-58765-543-2 (vol. 8 : alk. paper) — ISBN 978-1-58765-544-9 (vol. 9 : alk. paper) —
ISBN 978-1-58765-545-6 (vol. 10 : alk. paper)
  1. Fiction—History and criticism. 2. Fiction—Bio-bibliography—Dictionaries. 3. Authors—Biography—Dictionaries. I. Rollyson, Carl E. (Carl Edmund)
  PN3451.C75 2010
  809.3—dc22

2009044410

First Printing

CONTENTS

COMPLETE LIST OF CONTENTS

VOLUME 1

VOLUME 2

VOLUME 3

VOLUME 4

VOLUME 5

Volume 6

Volume 7

VOLUME 8

VOLUME 9

VOLUME 10

WORLD LONG FICTION (continued)

NORTH AMERICAN LONG FICTION

GENRE OVERVIEWS

RESOURCES

INDEXES

PRONUNCIATION KEY

Foreign and unusual or ambiguous English-language names of profiled authors may be unfamiliar to some users of the *Critical Survey of Long Fiction*. To help readers pronounce such names correctly, phonetic spellings using the character symbols listed below appear in parentheses immediately after the first mention of the author's name in the narrative text. Stressed syllables are indicated in capital letters, and syllables are separated by hyphens.

VOWEL SOUNDS

Symbol	*Spelled (Pronounced)*
a	answer (AN-suhr), laugh (laf), sample (SAM-puhl), that (that)
ah	father (FAH-thur), hospital (HAHS-pih-tuhl)
aw	awful (AW-fuhl), caught (kawt)
ay	blaze (blayz), fade (fayd), waiter (WAYT-ur), weigh (way)
eh	bed (behd), head (hehd), said (sehd)
ee	believe (bee-LEEV), cedar (SEE-dur), leader (LEED-ur), liter (LEE-tur)
ew	boot (bewt), lose (lewz)
i	buy (bi), height (hit), lie (li), surprise (sur-PRIZ)
ih	bitter (BIH-tur), pill (pihl)
o	cotton (KO-tuhn), hot (hot)
oh	below (bee-LOH), coat (koht), note (noht), wholesome (HOHL-suhm)
oo	good (good), look (look)
ow	couch (kowch), how (how)
oy	boy (boy), coin (koyn)
uh	about (uh-BOWT), butter (BUH-tuhr), enough (ee-NUHF), other (UH-thur)

CONSONANT SOUNDS

Symbol	*Spelled (Pronounced)*
ch	beach (beech), chimp (chihmp)
g	beg (behg), disguise (dihs-GIZ), get (geht)
j	digit (DIH-juht), edge (ehj), jet (jeht)
k	cat (kat), kitten (KIH-tuhn), hex (hehks)
s	cellar (SEHL-ur), save (sayv), scent (sehnt)
sh	champagne (sham-PAYN), issue (IH-shew), shop (shop)
ur	birth (burth), disturb (dihs-TURB), earth (urth), letter (LEH-tur)
y	useful (YEWS-fuhl), young (yuhng)
z	business (BIHZ-nehs), zest (zehst)
zh	vision (VIH-zhuhn)

OUSMANE SEMBÈNE

Born: Ziguinchor, Senegal, French West Africa
(now in Senegal); January 1, 1923
Died: Dakar, Senegal; June 10, 2007

PRINCIPAL LONG FICTION

Le Docker noir, 1956 (*Black Docker*, 1987)
Ô pays, mon beau peuple!, 1957
Les Bouts de bois de Dieu, 1960 (*God's Bits of
Wood*, 1962)
L'Harmattan, livre I: Référendum, 1964
*"Vehi-Ciosane: Ou, Blanche-Genèse," suivi du
"Mandat,"* 1965 (novellas; *"The Money-
Order" with "White Genesis,"* 1972)
Xala, 1973 (novella; English translation, 1976)
Le Dernier de l'empire, 1981 (*The Last of the
Empire*, 1983)
"Niiwam," suivi de "Taaw," 1987 (*"Niiwam,"
and "Taaw": Two Novellas*, 1991)
Guelwaar, 1996 (adaptation of his screenplay)

OTHER LITERARY FORMS

In addition to his novels, Ousmane Sembène (sehm-
BEH-neh) wrote short stories, collected as *Voltaïque*
(1962; *Tribal Scars, and Other Stories*, 1974), titled for
the final piece, which is narrated mainly by a man from
the Upper Volta. These stories, regarded by some as
Sembène's best work, explore the same themes found in
his novels: the reactionary influences of Islam and po-
lygamy, historical and cultural contexts vis-à-vis Western civilization, cultural displacement, union activities
and the betrayal of national leaders, and the defiance of
established authority.

Sembène is also known for his success in cinema, in-
cluding *Borom-Sarret* (1962) and *Ceddo* (1977). Several
of his films won prizes in international competition.
Again, the themes of the films resemble those of the nov-
els and, in fact, four are based on published fiction: *La
Noire de . . .* (1966; also known as *Black Girl*), on "The
Promised Land" in *Tribal Scars*; *Niaye* (1964), on *White
Genesis*; *Mandabi* (1968; also known as *Le Mandat* and
The Money Order), on *The Money-Order*; and *Xala*
(1974; also known as *Impotence*), on the book of that

name. Inversely, Sembène's fiction after 1962 shows the
effects of cinematographic technique.

ACHIEVEMENTS

Ousmane Sembène was a remarkable anomaly among
Francophone African writers. Unlike his fellow countryman Léopold Senghor, for example, one of the select
few during the colonial period who rose in the French educational system and went on for advanced degrees in
Paris, Sembène spent his first thirty years as a member
of the working class. He began as a fisherman, like his
father, and later turned mason, mechanic, dockworker,
and union leader. Though he attended school briefly as a
child, he is largely self-educated. His struggle against
prejudice and poverty developed in him not only a strong
work ethic but also a suspicion of any established authority—social, political, or religious—that discriminated
against the common person. This principle guided him
throughout his career.

Given this background, one must admire Sembène's
dedication and achievement. He began writing his first
novel at the age of twenty-nine, while still a docker in
Marseilles. Each of his works is essentially a defense of
individual human integrity. Sembène never forgot his
own background as he focused on the heroism of ordinary people or on the ineptitude and insensitivity of authority figures who abuse them. When he realized that
fiction was not reaching the people, he turned to film, as
writer, producer, and director. By using Wolof, the language spoken by the majority of Senegalese, he was able
to participate in the education of even the illiterate
among the population. He pushed vigorously for social
change in the face of the entrenched conservatism of Islam and tribal custom. He was, in particular, a proponent
of women's rights, a sensitive subject in a polygamous
society. Sembène's willingness to take on such controversial topics and his ability to do so with skill and humor put him in the forefront of African novelists and
filmmakers. Nevertheless, in English-speaking countries, he has not received the recognition he deserves;
only some of his novels have been translated into English.

BIOGRAPHY

Ousmane Sembène was born on January 1, 1923, at Ziguinchor in the Casamance region of Southern Senegal, an area of tropical rain forest rather than savannah, six hundred kilometers from Dakar and cut off from that major city and the rest of Senegal by the Gambia. Sembène's father, a fisherman, spoke Wolof, the predominant language of the country, and his mother spoke Diola, the language of the Casamance. Sembène's early life was thus spent among the people and sets the tone for his entire career. His second novel relies heavily on his childhood experiences among fishermen and farmers in the Casamance, and several of his other stories are also set in the region.

At the age of eight, Sembène left the Casamance briefly to live with an uncle in Dakar, and when that did not work out, he was sent to Marsassoum to live with another uncle, Abdou Bahmane Diop, a Muslim scholar and teacher. He was responsible for Sembène's early education. Sembène attended school in Marsassoum, but before he could receive his diploma, he was dismissed from the school, apparently for striking the director with his fist. This was not the only time that Sembène would demonstrate a penchant for violence and a disrespect for authority.

Between 1938 and 1940, before World War II was to begin affecting this French colony, Sembène was at loose ends. Rather than return to Ziguinchor as a fisherman, excluded from public schools, he made his way in Dakar as a mechanic, then as a mason. His intellectual development continued, however, though the means may not have seemed auspicious. He and his friends attended the cinema almost every evening—for the most part cheap Western melodramas, no doubt, but one film, Leni Riefenstahl's *Les dieux du stade* (the French title of a 1938 German film about the Olympic Games in Berlin), seems to have been a turning point in his career. He became conscious of race, of being an African. The very fascination with film was to have its consequences as well. Even his early novels show the effects of melodramatic character, structure, and scene. In addition, he was trying to continue his education by attending evening classes, and he flirted briefly with the self-effacement of Islamic mysticism, which he was later to deplore as a barrier to social change.

According to Paulin Vieyra, Sembène experienced the prevailing sentiments about the war during the early 1940's—the tendency to support the French side, then to admire the power of Germany after the Occupation. He also must have sensed the injustice in the unequal treatment of blacks during the harshness of the war economy. He frequented union meetings but at the same time associated with youth who kept in touch with African tradition through the playing of tam-tams and by listening to the songs of the griot (storyteller). That was to change with the arrival of Charles de Gaulle in Dakar in 1942. Sembène joined the French colonial army and fought in Chad, North Africa, and Baden-Baden, West Germany. He failed, however, to get an honorable discharge. He did not submit easily to military discipline and supposedly struck an officer. He left the army in 1946.

After the war, back in Dakar, Sembène participated in the famous rail strike of 1947-1948, which he celebrated in his third novel. With nothing to do once the strike was ended, he traveled to Marseilles as a stowaway. By autumn, 1948, he was in Paris, where he worked for three months as a mechanic for Citroën, but the weather and the fast pace chased him back to Marseilles, where he became a docker and a union leader and organizer. His first novel, *Black Docker*, draws from these experiences. During this time, he became interested in African American literature, especially in the Jamaican Claude McKay, Harlem's "poet of anger," whose novel *Banjo* (1929) is also about black dockworkers in Marseilles. He began to notice that black literature had been written primarily by non-Africans, and he came under the influence of the newly established *Présence africaine*. In 1950, he joined the French Communist Party and attended classes for party initiates. He remained in the party until the independence of Senegal.

Between 1950 and 1960, Sembène traveled in Europe, the Soviet Union, China, and North Vietnam. He also began his writing career with the publication of his first three novels. In 1960, Sembène returned to Africa after an absence of twelve years. After a brief tour of that continent, including the countries of Mali, Niger, Ivory Coast, and Congo, he began to realize that he could not reach a large African audience through his fiction alone. In 1961, he received a grant to study film in the Soviet Union. Since that time, Sembène had a dual career: He wrote and directed numerous films, won prizes at various international film festivals, was named president of the film association in Senegal, and worked toward establishing an African film industry. In spite of his preoccupation with film, Sembène continued to write fiction. In fact, there seemed to be little conflict between the two occupations; his fiction furnished scripts for his films, while his study of cinematographic technique contributed to his management of fictional structures, including an expertise in dialogue—a feat not achieved by many African writers.

The transformation of fiction into film provided one solution to the problem of language. Sembène addressed the problem in another way by helping create the newspaper *Kaddu*, written entirely in Wolof (and advertised rather obviously by a street vendor in the film *Xala*). This direct communication with the people, together with the critical and often satiric attacks that form the substance of his work, took Sembène out of the purely cultural field and placed him in the political arena. Sembène died, after a long illness, on June 10, 2007 at his home in Dakar, Senegal.

ANALYSIS

What is most obvious about Ousmane Sembène is his social conscience. His novels, based on a Marxist-Socialist ideology, have an essentially political function. They have a contemporary setting and are concerned with Africa's transition from a traditional tribal mentality to a cosmopolitan one. Two issues that receive considerable attention are the plight of women in a polygamous, Islamic society and the plight of the ordinary person trapped and enslaved by the capitalist elite. In fact, given his Socialist leanings, Sembène emphasizes the inequalities of class as much as those of race. This distinguishes him from other Francophone writers, such as Senghor, whose insistence on the uniqueness of the African—his intuitive, emotional nature vis-à-vis the rationality of the Caucasian—subordinates political and social realities in an attempt to define and glorify cultural phenomena. The rejection of negritude as a realistic or useful principle, seen especially in his last novel, aligns Sembène with Anglophone writers such as Chinua Achebe and Wole Soyinka, though they do not share his ideological emphases.

In spite of his Marxism, Sembène consistently creates romantic heroes. Perhaps the novel form dictates such dominant personalities; perhaps Sembène has not found a way to reconcile form with content—though, as Gerald Moore has argued, there is detectable a shift from heroic individualism to communal action between *Black Docker* and *God's Bits of Wood*. Yet even in this third novel, Sembène obviously admires the special powers of Bakayoko. Perhaps, instead, Sembène is simply not an orthodox adherent to the concept of anonymity in the Socialist state. Certainly, the personality of the author himself plays a dominant role, and though one cannot identify the creator with his creations, the choice of heroes seems to follow the pattern of Sembène's own life. The protagonists of the first three novels are all political activists, engaged in one way or another with the struggle for recognition and independence.

Beginning with *L'Harmattan, livre I: Référendum*, however, the central characters are more ambivalent and

Ousmane Sembène. (AP/Wide World Photos)

retiring. This may reflect only the tendencies within the society, but it probably relates to Sembène's own withdrawal from direct political activity and his assumption of the authorial role—a conflict anticipated as early as the first novel. One must also admit that Sembène is more or less critical of such political neutrality, while at the same time generating considerable sympathy for the ambivalent character. It is not easy to generalize about Sembène's protagonists, but his first three are essentially working-class men of a revolutionary stamp who rise to a kind of prominence through their own efforts, while the later heroes have already achieved status in society but have lost their integrity or have failed to make their influence felt in the world of politics and social realities. All of these male protagonists, with the exception of El Hadji in *Xala* (and even he eventually obtains one's sympathy and rises through his humiliation above the members of his class), are presented as superior types.

What is noticeable about the protagonist in every novel, including the fallen hero El Hadji, is a recurring trait that must originate in Sembène's own personality—a resistance to authority. To some extent, one must expect this motif in novels of a Marxist persuasion. Embedded as it is in the character of his heroes, however, this insistence on individual freedom is not so much ideological as personal and psychological. What Sembène creates are men and women with strong egos that defy any manipulation of the social or intellectual life. It is not Marxism, therefore, that is actually at the root of Sembène's novels, but a stubbornness and a pride in the integrity of the individual that no political system—capitalist, Socialist, or whatever—has the right to violate.

BLACK DOCKER

Black Docker, Sembène's first novel, bears a superficial resemblance to Albert Camus's *L'Étranger* (1942; *The Stranger*, 1946) with its alienated, misunderstood hero, convicted of murder in a tense trial scene, subjected to prejudice, and left alone in prison at the end, wrestling with his soul. It is as though Sembène were looking for a model to guide him in this first literary attempt. In any case, *Black Docker* is clearly exploratory in structure, purpose, and theme. Rather than follow a simple chronological pattern, Sembène begins in medias res, at the time of Diaw Falla's trial: first the reactions of

his mother back in Senegal; of his pregnant mistress, Catherine; and of his fellow dockers; then the trial itself, which is carried to the moment of the jury's decision. At this point, Sembène returns to the past to give a picture of Diaw's dual life as docker at the port of Marseilles and as aspiring novelist.

Diaw's first role gets him involved in a confrontation with his white employers, and his second brings frustrating rejections by the publishing establishment, until the promises of a well-known white woman novelist lead him to deception and murder, as she publishes the novel under her own name and he, in an attempt to get his due, accidentally kills her. Sembène then returns to the trial scene, where the jury declares Diaw guilty and sentences him to life imprisonment. The novel closes with a philosophical letter from Diaw to an uncle in Senegal.

In addition to this melodramatic structuring to gain suspense, Sembène makes several attempts to capture local color, especially the African district in Marseilles. There are also scenes of physical violence and love, but the most dramatic, perhaps, is the trial itself, which climaxes with Diaw's reciting from memory the final chapter of his prizewinning novel to demonstrate to an incredulous audience that he is indeed the author. Such melodramatic coloring surely owes something to Sembène's longtime fascination with Western cinema. The protagonist himself is both a leader of the working men and a sensitive intellectual. Yet one must admit that the main source for this hero is not the movies but the life of the novelist himself. Sembène is, among other things, exploring the autobiographical potential in fiction.

Various details of Diaw's life identify him as a fictional variation of his creator: born in a fishing village, son of a fisherman, reared and educated by an uncle who taught him French, and in his early life an indolent boy of the streets, a compound of gentleness, stubbornness, and violence. What is most obvious is Sembène's own experience as a docker in Marseilles, during which time he, like Diaw, began writing his first novel. Diaw's two novels, indeed, resemble Sembène's. In the first, Africans stage an escape from a slave ship; Sembène's own first novel is symbolically an attempt by Diaw and others to escape from slavery within the white society of France. Diaw's second novel anticipates Sembène's subsequent fiction, in that it is set in Africa, not in France, and focuses on the confrontation between the old and the new in contemporary African societies.

Furthermore, within *Black Docker* is stated a theory of the novel that seems to fit both Diaw's and Sembène's authorial intentions. One of Diaw's friends cautions him about his duties as a writer: He must have a cause, that is, he must be a spokesman for his people; he must see things as they are; and he must have the courage to speak his mind. Later, when Diaw is out of work, he understands the warning. He vows to avoid the naïve, to acknowledge life for what it is, a battle. This is also an implicit acknowledgment of an earlier warning, that individuals like Diaw who rise above their class eventually forget and hence betray the people. Sembène is obviously making a commitment to remain a spokesman for the ordinary person. This novel is the first installment of that commitment.

In spite of its melodramatic devices—which Sembène never completely abandons—*Black Docker* is a novel of ideas. It espouses a Marxist ideology, attacking the capitalistic establishment, the entrenched social prejudices against black (and white) dockers, the legislative and judicial processes, the penal system and penal code, and in particular the manipulative education of youth to accept blindly the old ideological assumptions. The theorizing goes beyond social criticism to a wistful, paradisiacal dream for the future, a world in which everyone's work is pleasurable, so that physical labor does not condemn the mind to dullness. In his final letter home, Diaw wishes for the son he leaves behind a sense of beauty and freedom, human dignity, and thoughts unsullied by false values and prejudice. *Black Docker* does not anticipate such a paradise in the near future.

It does, however, contain Sembène's defiance of any authority that presumes to control his mind. The novel is an attack on slavery in all of its forms. Moore may be right in seeing a conflict between the romantic form and the Marxist content—though he is probably interpreting Sembène's Marxism too rigidly—but he surely is wrong to say that Diaw's individualism reveals itself as a desire for fame. Diaw turns to authorship as a social tool and as an escape from the brutalizing effect of manual labor under white masters. Diaw's striking out against his white employer on the docks and his confrontation with Ginette, who expropriated his manuscript, are violent, physical symbols of his defiance. The recitation from his novel in a court of justice is his intellectual defiance against the whole racist society.

Ô PAYS, MON BEAU PEUPLE!

The circumstances in Sembène's second novel, *Ô pays, mon beau peuple!* (oh country, my beautiful people!), resemble those of the first, but with significant variations. The struggle continues between Africans and the white establishment, but now on African, not on French, soil. Sembène returns to his native Senegal, a symbolic shift in setting that he will maintain, with one minor exception, in all of his subsequent fiction. The uncontrolled and destructive violence of Diaw gives way to the purposeful (if romanticized) combativeness of Faye Oumar. The latter has a white wife, whom he loves and respects, rather than a mulatto mistress, whom Diaw is slow to admit into his inner life—suggesting not only a complete rejection of racism but also a public and private commitment to one woman. Oumar's personal and social goals are more clearly unified than Diaw's, and though the white authorities defeat them both, Diaw's suffering as a scapegoat is essentially personal, while Oumar's, being sacrificial, has meaning for a whole community.

The structure of *Ô pays, mon beau peuple!* is not nearly as complex as that of *Black Docker*. It follows a basically chronological pattern. Oumar, after fighting in the French colonial army during World War II, returns home with a French wife, Isabelle, to Ziguinchor-Casamance, Senegal. Part 1 deals with their adaptation to the provincial environment, the building of a private home somewhat apart from the family compound and the community, Oumar's return to fishing as a livelihood, and finally the antagonisms between Oumar and his family because of his white wife and his changed mentality. Sembène again establishes suspense, but in a more direct manner. In the opening pages, Oumar defends African passengers aboard a riverboat against the physical and verbal abuse of a white merchant. Since striking a white man under any circumstances is still felt to be taboo, an ominous cloud hangs over Oumar's life. This scene also announces the dominant motif in Sembène's work, the obsession with personal freedom. It is felt as well in Oumar's rebellion against his father's traditional authority.

In part 2, as the rainy season begins, Oumar violates family tradition and turns farmer. His home has become a rendezvous for the young people in the community to discuss political and social issues. He again has a direct confrontation with the white community, as he instigates a strike among female dockworkers. The relationship with his mother improves as his wife begins learning her language and demonstrates a respect for the African people. Oumar himself has come to be accepted by whites and blacks as a powerful force in the community.

In part 3, two years pass. The hot season brings locusts that destroy most of the crops. Oumar offers free seeds to all farmers for replanting and begins discussion of a farmers' cooperative. The white merchants and political leaders, sensing loss of control over the market, have Oumar killed. His death promises to unite the local populace as the novel ends. This chronological narrative thus has a cyclic structure appropriate to the agrarian setting. The cycle of hot and wet seasons, the planting and harvesting, and the sterility, then pregnancy, of Isabelle all provide a background for Oumar's cyclic return to his native land. At the end, the anticipated return of the dry season, the harvest, and the birth of Isabelle's child correspond to Oumar's rebirth into legend. All is not auspicious, however, as a threat inevitably hangs not only over the harvest but also over Isabelle's pregnancy and hence, by symbolic extension, over the future unity of the people.

Thus, Sembène, like other African novelists, adapts the myth of the cyclic return in a novel about the "been-to" and, in addition, makes of it a basic structural pattern. It harmonizes with other mythic and romantic elements characteristic of Sembène's novels. There are scenes of local color: the boat trip up the river to Ziguinchor, the long walk through the forest to a traditional village of the interior, and the elders under the palaver tree. Oumar and Isabelle build their house in a paradisiacal setting near the Casamance River, and much of Oumar's work as fisherman and farmer has an edenic quality; certainly, his vision of the future is a romantic ideal. Oumar himself is, even more than Diaw, a romantic protagonist, but, like Diaw, he is modeled on his creator, not only in the specifics of his birth and early life in the Casamance, his career in the army and his travel, his association with a white woman, and his experience as a mechanic but also in his personality and his goals.

This authorial personality is given epic dimensions. He resembles the gallant knight or the star of the cowboy Westerns. When he instigates the strike on the wharf, he melodramatically takes on all the white workers by standing with his back to a building, fighting off the opposition with a makeshift weapon, and taking a bullet in the leg. Sembène, aware of the melodrama, even has one of his characters make the film-star allusion. Later, in an "uncivilized" village, Oumar resembles a backwoodsman facing an Indian tribe as he uses his wits to win an intellectual combat with the king's councillors, then demonstrates wizardry by shooting a crow with his rifle. Sembène also places Oumar in the presence of sophisticated white businessmen and politicians to test his intellectual superiority and awareness. His mythic dimension becomes clear at the end, when his death makes him part of local legend. This insistence on the mythic suggests that *Ô pays, mon beau peuple!* is not simply a stage in Sembène's development of the Marxist novel, and that Oumar is not, as Moore argues, an unsympathetic individualist, arbitrarily transformed into a romantic hero, who fails to subordinate himself to the collective interest.

Sembène is clearly sympathetic to Oumar from the very beginning. His alienation from various elements in the society stems not primarily from his own lack of tact but from the provincial ignorance and ill will of others, including his own father, whose Muslim faith renders him totally intolerant of Oumar's liberal attitudes. Like Diaw in *Black Docker*, Oumar considers religious orthodoxy itself an inhibiting force. It is one among many traditions that breed prejudice and therefore enslave the mind. It is such prejudice and intolerance that characterize the white establishment's condescending attitude toward the African and dictate the African's resistance to change. It is within this context that one must see Sembène's obsession with personal freedom, his rebellion against the capitalistic authorities that restrict it, and his use of the romantic hero as the vehicle for change. The essential quality of this Marxist hero—the measure of his commitment to the collective good—is his rejection of the hero status and his recognition that he is not indispensable. In *Ô pays, mon beau peuple!* this is

Sembène's resolution of the apparent conflict between individual and social ideals.

GOD'S BITS OF WOOD

Though Western formalistic critics might judge *God's Bits of Wood* harshly for its episodic structure and its social functionalism, many regard it as Sembène's masterpiece. It is his best-known novel—with the possible exception of *Xala*—and it is his only long novel that has appeared in English. It is less autobiographical than Sembène's first two novels, taking as its subject a historical event, the railway strike in the Western Sudan (Senegal-Mali) between October 10, 1947, and March 19, 1948.

Both Diaw and Oumar lead a docker strike, and Oumar has plans for a farmers' cooperative, but this is the first time that Sembène's Marxist ideology is actualized in an uprising of the proletariat. Sembène is obviously attempting to write a Socialist novel in which the collective populace is the protagonist. This in itself dictates the novel's episodic structure. He develops stories about several individuals and families in the cities of Bamako, Thiès, and Dakar, intertwining their various adventures. The first two-thirds of the novel moves slowly as the strike is declared and the tension mounts. Conflicts erupt among the strikers, between the strikers and the traditional social elements, and between the Africans and the French authorities. The climax, triggered by the irrational killing of two African children, is the march of the women of Thiès to Dakar that leads to the successful conclusion of the strike.

Thus, Sembène for the first time merges a Marxist ideology with what appears to be an appropriate structure. The epic dimension of the structure, however, once again reveals that romance and heroic individualism are essential ingredients of Sembène's social philosophy. The scenes of local color indicate a progression in technique, as the idyllic scenes of *Ô pays, mon beau peuple!* give way to a harsher reality. The most striking scenes, perhaps, are the camera-like panning of the slums of Thiès, scenes of torture in the detention camp, and the gruesome vignette of Sounkaré, the old watchman, eaten by rats. This is not quite realism, however; rather it is naturalism tinged with sentiment and pathos. The same technique is evident in the creation of character. While Sembène always balances virtues with weaknesses, the latter have the effect of arousing sympathy rather than simply establishing objectivity and realism, and in certain characters the weaknesses or limitations do not override the heroic qualities. Furthermore, that the characters are from the working class or from the ordinary people does not deny the heroism but romanticizes it.

Sembène's attraction to the heroic personality is felt as strongly in this novel as in the first two. As collective as the march of the women may be, it still has its leader, Penda, a prostitute who discovers herself in her new social role and who dies a martyr as the women enter the city of Dakar. Maïmouna, the blind mother of twin babies, one of whom is trampled to death during the strike, becomes a symbol of spiritual strength; other women as well perform heroic acts as they break out of their traditional subservient roles. The wise man, Fa Keïta, is too old to become an active member of the strikers, but it is his traditional wisdom that prevails in the trial of a strikebreaker and his experience in the detention camp that reveals not only his exceptional courage but also the possibility of change within the old order. This tremendous capacity for change, so important in Sembène's conception of human nature, is evident also in the young girl N'Deye Touti, who represents the African youth's vain attraction to superficial Western values and conveniences. She undergoes a spiritual baptism to become a dedicated patriot in the African cause. These representatives of the people are thus romantic heroes in their own right.

The most important of them, however, attains the stature of the main protagonist, in spite of his late entrance in the novel. In the early part of the narrative, Bakayoko is a creature of legend. In the opening chapter, Sembène introduces Bakayoko's family, including the precocious and avant-garde Ad'jibid'ji, his stepdaughter and protégé, a representative of the new order. Periodically, his name appears in conversation and his character as an epic figure emerges from recollections, especially those of N'Deye Touti, his young and naïve admirer. His absence is almost as strongly felt as his presence.

Sembène creates suspense as the people (and hence the reader) look forward to the return of their spiritual leader. His specific role is to deliver speeches throughout the country and, through his rhetoric and magnetic personality, to raise money and to keep the collective community enthusiastically behind the strike. When Bakayoko does finally make his appearance, Sembène takes pains to show that the legend is also a fallible human being, but Bakayoko's personal coldness and relative indifference to family are only the negative side of his total commitment to the strike. It is obvious that he is not actually lacking in emotion and that the rejection of sentimentality, which continues a motif begun in *Black Docker*, is the result of a conscious facing of social realities. Furthermore, once the strike is over, Bakayoko relaxes and begins a reintegration into his family. In spite of his familial irresponsibility and his lack of social graces, the society and the author regard him as a superior personality.

In fact, as Soyinka argues, Bakayoko functions as a kind of secular deity, replacing the outmoded deities of the past. He possesses confidence, power, and a divine vision that foresees the future. This mythic conception of Bakayoko is only one element in a total epic structure. Sembène raises the struggle of the people beyond realism to symbolic action. Bakayoko himself identifies the strike as an initiation ritual. Individual scenes work not only realistically but also symbolically. The deprivation of water is not a simple physical phenomenon; it calls into question basic assumptions about social and familial roles. Ad'jibid'ji discovers, moreover, that even water is less powerful than the mind. The riddle she poses at the beginning of the novel—What can purify water?—she herself answers at the end with the word "spirit."

God's Bits of Wood is a novel of spiritual transformation, which is the key to Sembène's motif of personal freedom. One character specifically calls slavery a mental state. It is, in the terms of this novel, a state of illusion, a judgment of the world and of people according to prejudice and provincial custom. The main weakness in the novel, the characterization of the French, nevertheless has this virtue: It is a vehicle for the blindness and ignorance that inhibit freedom. What lies behind even the Marxist ideology, then, is the idea that illusions must give way to a perception of realities and that this transformation will give rise to heroic action.

WHITE GENESIS

Beginning in 1963, Sembène's interests turned to film, to the temporary eclipsing of the long novel. The three short novels that he published during that time, *White Genesis* with *The Money-Order*, in 1965, and *Xala*, eight years later, all became movie scripts. The two earlier works anticipate major motifs in the third. In *White Genesis*, the emphasis is on social responsibility.

The narrator (Sembène) is a kind of wandering griot who insists that the African storyteller must expose the full truth about his society. Hence this "true history" is from the colonial era of incest, suicide, and patricide in a small, disintegrating village in the Niaye region of Senegal. The chief of the village has committed incest with his daughter. Though the truth is known, public acknowledgment does not come until the young girl's mother, Ngone, the heroine of the story, commits suicide, and the chief's son, out of ambition, provokes his mad brother to kill their father. Significantly, it is the local griot in the village who persuades the elders to disown the instigator, thus admitting the truth of what has happened. What begins as a sordid episode becomes instead a story of nobility and courage. Ngone in various ways rejects traditional subservience, in the name of humanity, and recognizes the rights of the young mother and her child, who leave the village for Dakar to prepare for the "genesis" of the new world. The local griot himself reiterates the principle that no one can "travel" who has not stood up for truth in his own country.

THE MONEY-ORDER

In *The Money-Order*, the scene shifts to the city of Dakar and the emphasis shifts to the contrast between the old and the new in contemporary Senegal—specifically, to a reversal of values with the introduction of a money economy. The protagonist, Ibrahima Dieng, receives a money order from a nephew in Paris. Accustomed to being treated with respect and solicitude in a familial environment where it is the women who are the realists, the naïve Dieng discovers, in his attempt to cash the money order, that every human act now has a price attached to it. Eventually, his own wealthy cousin absconds with the money. After the experience, Dieng comments philosophically in a letter to his nephew that money is not the essence of life or even security, but rather loneliness and alienation. It kills one's humanity. Dieng's tendency is to turn to Allah for refuge, but at the end, he is faced with the incredible charge that he himself is responsible for changing the state of things.

XALA

In *Xala*, Sembène concentrates for the first time on the situation in postindependence Senegal. The setting is Dakar. The Chamber of Commerce has just become a totally African institution, and one of its members, El Hadji Abdou Kader Beye (the name itself is a sign of his pretension) is about to take a third wife, a symbol of his social status. The story is about his sudden impotence (*xala*) on his wedding night and his gradual loss of wealth and prestige as he spends all of his time and money on local Marabouts to determine the cause and the cure. Sembène touches on the overindulged male in the other two short novels, but in *Xala* he notes its insidious carryover into the public world of modern Dakar. A former revolutionary who has lost his social conscience, El Hadji has totally repudiated the ordinary people. Though actually only a small businessman, the real power still being in the hands of foreign-controlled interests, he regards himself as a secure member of the elite, until the disaster strikes and his artificial world crumbles about him. His impotence has both spiritual and political implications.

Here, as in Sembène's other novels, there is an emphasis on the sustaining strength of women. The third wife's aunt, Bineta, uses repugnant but strong-willed tactics to control the self-conscious and helpless El Hadji. The first wife, Adja, retains her dignity and loyalty as she watches the decline of her husband's fortunes. Her daughter, Rama, is Sembène's feminist representative of the militant younger generation.

There are, however, strong male figures in the novel as well; they belong not to the elite but to the lower class or to those who live on the fringes of society. El Hadji's chauffeur, Modu, proves to possess natural eloquence and a genuine affection for his employer. It is Modu's intervention that finally leads to the cure, and it is the marabout living isolated from the centers of power whose sorcery first breaks the curse.

Finally, it is the beggar, whose chant furnishes the chorus throughout the novel and whom El Hadji has specifically singled out as a public nuisance, who not only is responsible for the curse but also must exorcize it. In the climactic scene, he leads the entire crippled, blind, and beggared population on a march to El Hadji's door. They invade the premises and assume ownership rights to all the property. The beggar explains that El Hadji's rise in society was on the backs of the people. He had falsified records and sold land that belonged not to him as son of the chief but to the entire clan. Furthermore, the beggar diagnoses El Hadji's disease as a leprosy that infects the entire country. Because of this public theft, the beggar has cursed him with impotence and now demands his humiliation.

The novel closes with El Hadji standing naked, being spit upon by all the people he has cheated of their rightful share to the public wealth. In this novel, then, instead of the forces of resistance or the innocent victims, Sembène chooses as his protagonist a representative of the establishment who deprives the people of their personal dignity. By the end, however, El Hadji is beginning to recapture a certain measure of his former manhood. He delivers a polemic against the other members of the Chamber who have voted him out, and his dignified submission to the ritualistic humiliation promises an end to physical and spiritual impotence. The degree of credibility that Sembène grants to the power of sorcery is not clear, but whatever its literal reality, it functions here as a symbol of psychological retribution. Yet El Hadji is also, in a sense, a sacrificial victim with a capacity for change. Faced with the reality of his guilt, he is on the verge of the spiritual transformation that concludes most of Sembène's novels.

Thomas Banks

OTHER MAJOR WORKS

SHORT FICTION: *Voltaïque*, 1962 (*Tribal Scars, and Other Stories*, 1974).

SCREENPLAYS: *Borom-Sarret*, 1962; *Niaye*, 1964; *La Noire de . . .*, 1966 (also known as *Black Girl*); *Mandabi*, 1968 (adaptation of his novella; also known as *Le Mandat* and *The Money Order*); *Taaw*, 1970; *Emitaï*, 1972; *Xala*, 1974 (adaptation of his novella; also known as *Impotence*); *Ceddo*, 1977; *Camp de Thiaroye*, 1987; *Guelwaar*, 1992; *Faat Kiné*, 2000.

NONFICTION: *Ousmane Sembène: Interviews*, 2008 (Annett Busch and Max Annas, editors).

BIBLIOGRAPHY

Agho, Jude, and Francis Oseghale. "'Wonder Women': Towards a Feminization of Heroism in the African Fiction—A Study of the Heroines in Buchi Emecheta's *Second Class Citizen* and Sembène Ousmane's *God's Bits of Wood*." *LWATI: A Journal of Contemporary Research* 5 (2008): 181-191. A feminist analysis of Sembène's novel—along with a novel by Nigerian author Buchi Emecheta—demonstrating how his depiction of heroic female characters challenges male-dominated African culture.

Hawkins, Peter. "Marxist Intertext, Islamic Reinscription? Some Common Themes in the Novels of Sembène Ousmane and Aminata Sow Fall." In *African Francophone Writing: A Critical Introduction*, edited by Laïla Ibnlfassi and Nicki Hitchcott. Oxford, England: Berg, 1996. Hawkins's essay comparing the novels of Sembène with those of Aminata Sow Fall, another Senegalese writer, is included in this survey of African francophone writing from 1950 through the late 1990's.

Murphy, David. *Sembène: Imagining Alternatives in Film and Fiction*. Trenton, N.J.: Africa World Press, 2000. A study of Sembène's fiction and films, stressing the common themes of these works. Among other topics, Murphy analyzes Sembène's representation of colonialism, neocolonialism, African women, and the African city.

O'Brien, Sara Talis, and Renée Schatteman. *Voices from the Continent: A Curriculum Guide to Selected West African Literature*. Trenton, N.J.: Africa World Press, 2003. Provides literary criticism and anthropological and historical research that can be used to teach students about Sembène's novel *God's Bits of Wood* and other West African literature.

Tsabedze, Clara. *African Independence from Francophone and Anglophone Voices: A Comparative Study of the Post-Independence Novels by Ngugi and Sembène*. New York: Peter Lang, 1994. A comparative study of fiction by Sembène and Kenyan author Ngugi wa Thiong'o, focusing on the two writers' representations of African independence and of neocolonial exploitation.

Willey, Ann Elizabeth. "Language Use and Representation of the Senagalese Subject in the Written Work of Ousmane Sembène." In *A Call to Action: The Films of Ousmane Sembène*, edited by Sheila Petty. Westport, Conn.: Praeger, 1996. Although most of the essays in this book analyze Sembène's film career, Willey's article discusses his novels, some of which he adapted for the screen.

RAMÓN JOSÉ SENDER

Born: Chalamera de Cinca, Spain; February 3, 1901
Died: San Diego, California; January 15, 1982
Also known as: Ramón José Sender Garcés; Ramon Sender

PRINCIPAL LONG FICTION

Imán, 1930 (*Earmarked for Hell*, 1934; better known as *Pro Patria*, 1935)
Siete domingos rojos, 1932, 1973 (*Seven Red Sundays*, 1936)
La noche de las cien cabezas, 1934
Mr. Witt en el cantón, 1936 (*Mr. Witt Among the Rebels*, 1937)
El lugar del hombre, 1939 (*A Man's Place*, 1940)

O. P.: Orden público, 1941
Epitalamio del prieto Trinidad, 1942 (*Dark Wedding*, 1943)
Crónica del alba, 1942-1966 (3 volumes, 9 parts; volume 1 translated as *Before Noon: A Novel in Three Parts*, 1957; includes *Crónica del alba*, 1942 [*Chronicle of Dawn*, 1944]; *Hipogrifo violenta*, 1954 [*Violent Griffin*, 1957]; *La quinta Julieta* [*The Villa Julieta*])
La esfera, 1947, 1969 (originally as *Proverbio de la muerte*, 1939; *The Sphere*, 1949)
El rey y la reina, 1949 (*The King and the Queen*, 1948)

El verdugo afable, 1952 (*The Affable Hangman*, 1954)

Mosén Millán, 1953 (also known as *Requiem por un campesino español*, 1960; *Requiem for a Spanish Peasant*, 1960)

Los cinco libros de Ariadna, 1957, 1977

Emen hetan, 1958

Los laureles de Anselmo, 1958

El mancebo y los heroes, 1960

En la vida de Ignacio Morel, 1969

OTHER LITERARY FORMS

By the end of 1981, first editions of Ramón José Sender's books, exclusive of an anthology of selections from his works, numbered ninety-six. At the time of his death early in 1982, Destino, the Barcelona publishing house, had scheduled for publication two new novels by Sender; an additional manuscript of a novel, appropriately titled "Toque de Queda" ("Taps"), was found among his papers, ready for publication.

Depending on one's criteria for the determination of literary genre (in Sender's case, a task made all but impossible by the author's disdain for such classifications and his deliberate attempts, at times, to blur traditional genre distinctions), Sender's total production of ninety-nine books (including the three unpublished novels) could be described as including sixty-four novels or novellas, seven collections of short stories, five works of drama, two volumes of poetry, and twenty-one books of essays, personal narratives, and journalistic articles. Almost all of this last category consists of material published earlier in newspaper articles or in Sender's literary column, "Los libros y los días" (books and days), which was syndicated in Spanish-language newspapers throughout Latin America from early in the 1950's until the author's death. More than eight hundred articles appeared in "Los libros y los días."

ACHIEVEMENTS

Ramón José Sender surely ranks as one of the greatest Spanish novelists of the twentieth century. Marcelino Peñuelas, the Spanish critic, places him "at the head of the Spanish novelists of our time" and adds, in case there is any doubt, that he means by this to exalt Sender above Pío Baroja, generally held to be the preeminent Spanish

novelist of the twentieth century. Few, if any, Spanish writers of all history, except for Miguel de Cervantes and Benito Pérez Galdós, have had their novels so widely translated as has Sender.

Sender's first novel, *Pro Patria*, was translated into ten major languages; by 1970, his novels had appeared in more than eighty foreign translations, according to Peñuelas. Thirteen of his novels have appeared in English, all in both British and American editions. In January, 1936, his first historical novel, *Mr. Witt Among the Rebels*, was awarded the National Prize for Literature, at that time regarded as Spain's highest literary award. In 1966, the first three-volume edition of his monumental autobiographical novel, *Crónica del alba* (chronicle of dawn), received the City of Barcelona Prize. In 1969, Sender won the lucrative Planeta Prize from the Planeta publishing house for his rather mediocre novel *En la vida de Ignacio Morel* (in the life of Ignacio Morel).

BIOGRAPHY

Ramón José Sender, whose full name is Ramón José Sender Garcés, was born in the village of Chalamera de Cinca, in the Aragonese province of Huesca, on February 3, 1901. His father was town clerk of both Chalamera and the nearby town of Alcolea de Cinca. Both his parents' families had long-standing roots in Alcolea, and the Sender family returned there in 1903, moving next to Tauste (Aragon) in 1908 or 1909. A composite of both Alcolea and Tauste can be recognized as the scene of three of the author's finest novels, *A Man's Place*, *Crónica del alba*, and *Requiem for a Spanish Peasant*. His deep attachment to his native region and pride in his Aragonese heritage never left him.

From his earliest years, Sender rebelled against the authoritarian attitude of his father, a strict Catholic whose efforts to force his views upon the future novelist seem to have been decisive in determining Sender's lifelong rebellion against the existing order of things, including his rejection of the Roman Catholic Church. Sender's attitude of rebellion and protest is evident in all of his writings, both journalistic and literary. His protests against the dictatorship of Primo de Rivera in 1927 led to his imprisonment for three months in Madrid, an experience that he novelized in *O. P.*

Difficulties with his father apparently led to Sender's

being sent to a Catholic boarding school in Reus (Catalonia) for the academic year 1913-1914, a year that forms the basis for his novel *Violent Griffin*, which later became the second of the three parts of the first volume of his monumental three-volume autobiographical novel *Crónica del alba*. Only volume 1 of the series has appeared in English translation (as *Before Noon: A Novel in Three Parts*, 1957), and its first part initially appeared separately under the same title as the series—*Chronicle of Dawn*.

From 1914 to 1917, Sender attended the Institute of Zaragoza. During the next school year, he worked as a pharmacy clerk in Alcañiz while meeting, through special arrangements with the Institute of Teruel (in Teruel), the remaining requirements for his high school diploma. During the next three years, from 1918 to 1921, he worked on the editorial staff of *La tierra*, a small newspaper in Huesca published by the Association of Farmers and Ranchers of Upper Aragon.

Upon his return in 1924 from fourteen months of service in the Spanish army in the ill-fated Moroccan War, Sender joined the editorial staff of the prestigious liberal newspaper *El sol* in Madrid. Following the success of his first novel, *Pro Patria*, Sender left *El sol* to devote himself full-time to freelance journalistic writing and to writing novels. During the next six years, he published six novels in addition to nearly two hundred articles in the newspaper *La libertad* and numerous articles in *Solidaridad obrera*, the organ of the Confederación Nacional de Trabajo (National Labor Federation) in Barcelona.

During the Spanish Civil War, Sender served in the republican army, rising to the rank of *comandante* (major). His wife was executed by Nationalist forces in Zamora on October 10, 1936. Late in 1938, Sender, seeing that the republican cause was hopeless, fled to France and from there to Mexico City in March of 1939. From Mexico, he entered the United States on a Guggenheim Fellowship in 1942, becoming a naturalized U.S. citizen in 1946 and remaining in the United States until his death in 1982.

From 1947 until 1963, Sender was a professor of Spanish at the University of New Mexico in Albuquerque; from 1965 until 1971, he was a visiting professor of Spanish literature at the University of Southern Califor-

nia. Upon retirement in 1971, he moved to San Diego, California, where he lived until his death.

Sender remained an outspoken enemy of the Nationalist regime in Spain, and it was not until June of 1974 that he returned to his native land, his first visit since his self-imposed exile in 1938. During this three-week stay, he was warmly received and highly praised by the Spanish literary community.

ANALYSIS

Though marked by great diversity, Ramón José Sender's vast novelistic production over five decades reveals a remarkable unity of vision. In substance, one finds that there are continuing, basic Senderian concepts and themes, found in large measure in his first novel, *Pro Patria*, as well as in his posthumously published works. In them all, one finds the author's deep concern with social justice, with the struggle of the individual for self-realization, for love, and for an ideal that gives transcendent value to life. Sender's writings serve as a vehicle for ceaselessly probing certain immutable problems of existence: the question of death or human mortality; the enigma of evil in the individual and in the world at large; the possibility of an ultimate basis for moral judgments; and the function of the mysterious and the nonrational in life. Ordinary realism is in a Senderian novel only the starting point or the springboard for reaching out for transcendent meaning, for discovery of the marvelous and the mysterious, for brief flights of poetic fantasy, and for a constant metaphysical-religious-lyric questioning of the ultimate nature of reality. Sender's novels usually move on three distinct levels: the realistic, the poetic, and the philosophical-religious.

Though neither an orthodox believer in God nor an atheist, Sender reveals in his novels a deep faith in and reverence toward humanity; in *The Sphere*, he elaborates his belief that the essential part of humanity is imperishable, believing (along with Benedict de Spinoza) that "man is an integral part of the infinite intellect of God." An offense to humanity thus becomes an offense to God. Humanity, both its individual persons and in the abstract, is squarely in the center of Sender's novelistic universe. Though his short stories, theatrical pieces, essays, and poetry have received very little critical attention, they all exhibit the same basic view of humans and explore the same fundamental questions to be found in his novels.

Sender's style is that of the author speaking directly and personally to the reader in simple, clear, unaffected language, even when passages of the harshest realism are interrupted with flights of lyric fantasy or dialectical probing of philosophical-religious problems (from which inconclusive and eclectic syntheses are derived; Sender is never dogmatic except to reiterate the impossibility of humanity arriving at absolute truth—at least in this life). In a taped interview at the University of Southern California on June 7, 1966, Sender named four Spanish authors as having greatly influenced him: Fernando de Rojas, Francisco de Quevedo y Villegas, Ramón María del Valle-Inclán, and Baroja. Sender, like Baroja, is a writer of substance, always with something worthwhile to say, and openly disdainful of mere style; he also is preoccupied with social, moral, and metaphysical problems.

The influence of Valle-Inclán can be seen in Sender's occasional juxtaposition of the grotesque and the lyrically innocent and in the use of tragicomedy. His bitter social satire, his tendency to caricature and his austere humor (never far removed from sadness) may owe something to Quevedo, the seventeenth century writer of *Los sueños* (1627; *The Visions*, 1640) and the celebrated picaresque novel, *Historia de la vida del buscón* (1626; *The Life and Adventures of Buscon*, 1657). Sender's peculiar fusion of realistic and nonrealistic elements (fantasy, dreams, hallucinations, the mysterious, the marvelous, the magical, and so on) recalls not only the two levels of realism and fantasy in *La Celestina* (1499; *The Rogue*, 1634) of Rojas but also those in the greatest Spanish novel of all, Miguel de Cervantes' *Don Quixote de la Mancha* (1605, 1615).

Francisco Carrasquer calls Sender's first novel, *Pro Patria*, a "provisional anticipatory synthesis of all of Sender's work" and adds that it is such a great novel "that one cannot understand how a first work like it did not definitely consecrate its author." Peñuelas also calls it a "great novel," and he told Sender, "You have a few novels the equal of *Imán* [*Pro Patria*], but none better." Until recently, critics have tended to regard the work as simply a realistic account of the Moroccan War much in the style of Erich Maria Remarque's *Im Westen nichts Neues* (1929, 1968; *All Quiet on the Western Front*,

1929, 1969), published one year earlier in Germany. *Pro Patria*'s fantastic, poetic, philosophical, and symbolic dimensions were long overlooked, but masterful studies of the work by both Carrasquer and Peñuelas have helped to correct this misapprehension.

PRO PATRIA

Pro Patria tells the story of the Spanish military campaign to suppress the rebellion of the Moorish leader Abd-el-Krim in 1921 in Spanish Morocco. The story is told from the perspective of Viance, a Spanish private who attracts misfortune (hence the book's Spanish title, *Imán*, meaning "magnet"), alternating with that of a Spanish journalist, Antonio, and that of an omniscient narrator.

Harsh realism is especially evident in the first of the book's three major divisions, "The Camp—The Relief." In the tone and atmosphere set here for the rest of the narrative, there is an implied denunciation of the utter stupidity and uselessness of war, perhaps not only of the specific Spanish campaign but also of war in general—whether the novel is a pacifist work is subject to debate.

In the second division, "Annual—The Catastrophe," the suffering of Viance from hunger, thirst, and exhaustion reaches the limits of human endurance while the Spanish forces are routed. Through it all, however, Viance, though a common soldier (and symbolic of the Spanish masses), engages in some metaphysical-lyric probing of the meaning of his experience and of human life. Lying in the stinking belly of a horse, hiding from the Moors, he senses "that his own matter is alike to that which encircles him, that there is only one kind of matter, and that all of it is animated by the same blind impulses, obedient to the same law." One dark night inclines Viance "to believe in some kind of justice . . . [in] A kind of bright and translucent justice implicit in all things."

In the third and last division, "Escape—War—Discharge—The Peace of the Dead," Viance escapes from his Moorish captors and returns to the Spanish forces, only to receive inhuman treatment from them and finally to be discharged, a bitter, disillusioned man contemplating suicide. The book's social protest arises from the action itself; Viance's officers treat him as the upper classes have for centuries in Spain treated the lower classes. Because Sender's military service in Morocco occurred two years or more after the crushing defeat of the Spaniards at Annual, the events recorded are not autobiographical but are rather a composite of what the young author heard from others combined with his own vivid imagination.

MR. WITT AMONG THE REBELS

The first of several historical novels published by Sender over four decades, *Mr. Witt Among the Rebels* portrays an insurrection against the First Spanish Republic in the province of Cartagena in 1873; the action occurs in Murcia and, strangely enough, it seems to foreshadow the Civil War, which was to erupt July 18, 1936, almost immediately after the appearance of the novel. Fused with the outer events of the revolution is the private, inner story of Mr. Witt, a balding English engineer of fifty-three, stationed in Cartagena and married to Milagritos, a charming and vivacious Spaniard eighteen years younger than he; the two contrast sharply in temperament and character. Events from the outside world invade the calm and quiet of their domestic life; Milagritos, passionate and nonreflective, wholeheartedly abandons herself to the uprising, while Mr. Witt, logical, reflective, and timid, retreats further into his private world: His "world" and that of the revolution are the two main poles between which the novel is built.

The characterizations of both Mr. Witt and Milagritos are superb, an admirable study in contrasting human psychology. In the end, the uprising is utterly crushed; though Milagritos knows that during the insurrection her husband acted perfidiously, she suspects that his actions were motivated by jealousy, a jealousy that confirms his love for her. Accordingly, she pardons him, and the two resume normal relations. The objective and the subjective, the outer and the inner, are found here in delicate and subtle balance; a serene work, *Mr. Witt Among the Rebels* is probably Sender's best historical novel and surely one of his finest works.

CRÓNICA DEL ALBA

The monumental *Crónica del alba* narrates the author's life from the age of ten to his mid-thirties, the time of the Spanish Civil War. The first part, bearing the title of the novel as a whole—*Chronicle of Dawn*—appeared in 1942 and was well received; it and the second part, *Violent Griffin*, are regarded by Peñuelas as superior to the remaining parts.

The novel is essentially a study in idealism, a returning to one's origins to discover the sources of the idealism that led republican officers such as the protagonist José Garcés (obviously the author's alter ego) to risk their lives in defense of the Second Spanish Republic. José, nicknamed Pepe (Sender himself was called Pepe by members of his family), discovers love in the form of his sweetheart, Valentina, an embodiment of his idealistic values. Though Pepe's grandiose dreams as a ten-year-old boy in the "dawn" of life contrast sharply with the cruel realities of defeat that José the mature man suffers at the end of the series (the "noon" of life), his devotion to Valentina remains firm. Lying ill in a concentration camp in Algiers as the Civil War ends, José writes his autobiography in a desperate attempt to remain a man "of substance." "In a man," he explains, "substance is faith." Purportedly, he gives the three notebooks in which he has written his autobiography to Sender the author, then dies.

Following a chronological order, the series follows José's life from childhood through adolescence, young manhood, and into maturity; through it all, he seeks to live up to the grandiose ideals he had conceived as a child, especially as Valentina's sweetheart. An ancient document found in a castle by the young José declared that the men most needed to ensure the greatness of Spain were saints, poets, and heroes, though "there can be no true saint without a touch of the poet, nor, finally, any of the three without some of the virtues of the others."

In the last volume, Valentina assumes in memory the force of a pure ideal, no longer an entity of flesh and blood but a mysterious influence, a dream, a secret nostalgia for some "lost paradise." It is a longing made all the more poignant by the harsh realities of civil war.

THE SPHERE

A revision and considerable augmentation of an earlier novel, *Proverbio de la muerte*, *The Sphere* could properly be called a new novel; its first Spanish edition appeared in 1947; its definitive edition, slightly augmented and retouched from the first edition, was published in 1969. Sender regarded it as his most serious work; in it, he presents his lifelong belief in the spheroidal nature of all reality. The title of the novel is itself a metaphor of the author's monistic conception of total reality.

While crossing the Atlantic on the way to the Western Hemisphere after having escaped from Spain at the end of the Civil War, Saila, Sender's alter ego, observes that nature is composed of an infinite number of spheres or spheroids. This is true in the infinitely small (atoms), and in the infinitely large (planets, suns, the entire universe). By analogy with observable physical phenomena, Saila imagines that moral life is likewise "spherical," unified but showing two sides or two faces. As day is the other side of night and sound the other side of silence, so hate is the other side of the hate-love sphere, good the other side of evil; even death is only the complementary side of life. Thus, Saila reasons, death does not exist, and this idea becomes the fundamental thesis of the book.

To support his thesis of the nonexistence of death, Sender elaborated in *The Sphere*—and in other works as early as *La noche de las cien cabezas* (the night of one hundred heads), for example—his theory of *hombría* and the "persona." The "persona" is the human mask, the individualization of one's personality, which begins at birth, or soon thereafter, and grows throughout life—human self-consciousness. It is temporal and fears death. On the other hand, *hombría*, or "man-ness," is a mystical essence that endows humans with eternal worth; it is a person's essential self and lives in the unconscious. Upon the death of the individual, it joyfully returns to its source, the Great All or the Great Nothing.

Overladen with metaphysical musings and poetic and symbolic meaning, *The Sphere* loses the reader in a labyrinth of levels, dimensions, and meanings to the detriment of narrative force and direction. As a novel, it fails if a novel is to be judged by traditional criteria—narrative interest, character creation, sense of place, and so on. Perhaps such criteria should not be applied; nevertheless, *The Sphere* is notable for its originality and density of ideas, and it is a key work in understanding Sender's self-made philosophy or what, in all seriousness, amounted to his private religion.

Requiem for a Spanish Peasant

Requiem for a Spanish Peasant (originally titled *Mosén Millán*) is perhaps the most widely read of Sender's novels, at least in the Spanish-speaking world, where it has undergone numerous reprintings in Mexico, Argentina, and Spain; an English-Spanish bilingual edition was issued by Las Americas in New York in 1960. A short novel, it is probably Sender's most perfectly constructed work.

In an unnamed Aragonese village, Mosén Millán, a priest, waits in the sacristy to perform a requiem Mass for Paco, a peasant unjustly executed one year earlier by Nationalist forces in the early days of the Spanish Civil War. This period of waiting while the church bell tolls, calling the villagers to the Mass, lasts about twenty minutes and constitutes the novel's primary plane of action. On this plane, nothing happens except for the arrival of the three men most responsible for Paco's execution, the coming and going of the acolyte (who occasionally recites fragments of a ballad recounting Paco's life and death), the discovery of Paco's colt in the sanctuary and its subsequent ejection, and in the end the priest's moving to the chancel and beginning the Mass—with no one except the acolyte and the dead man's chief enemies (all wealthy) present, while the villagers absent themselves in mute protest against the priest's role, ambiguous and unintentional as it may have been, in the events that led to Paco's execution.

While waiting in vain for people to come to the Mass, the priest in a series of flashbacks reconstructs the story of Paco—the second plane of action—his baptism, childhood, adolescence, marriage, protest against an unjust feudal landholding system, capture, and execution. Past and present are thus skillfully woven together while the ballad recited by the acolyte and interspersed throughout the narrative comes to create what Peñuelas calls a third plane, a legendary one beyond the confines of time.

The structure of *Requiem for a Spanish Peasant*, with the priest and his memories as the focal point, provides it with remarkable unity and compactness; past and present are tightly but unobtrusively interwoven; the classical unities of time, place, and action are almost totally observed; social protest is implicit in the events themselves, related in a sober and objective tone, making such protest all the more effective. Here the author's realism is at its best, and Paco emerges as both an individual and a symbol of the Spanish masses; what happened to him in essence happened throughout Spain during the Civil War. At the same time, Mosén Millán, for whom the events of the narrative constitute a deep personal tragedy, likewise comes to embody the inertia of the Spanish Church and its tragically misguided intervention in secular affairs and lack of social conscience. The ballad, composed anonymously by the villagers, is a projection of the author's idealistic faith in the cause of a just social order. Noble also is the book's vivid and memorable portrayal of the life and customs in a Spanish village early in the twentieth century, its humor—the rough humor of country folk—and its psychological realism in the characterization of Mosén Millán.

Sender was a highly individualistic author who never adhered to any literary movement (nor to any political movement or party, despite some flirtation with the communists in the early 1930's) but who did not hesitate to take whatever seemed useful to him from any and all literary and philosophical movements (existentialism, for example), absorbing and adapting them to his own peculiar mode of expression. The voluminous totality of his production surprises and impresses not only by its great diversity but also by its amazing consistency and unity in outlook and vision as well as its unmistakable style and manner. In a sense to be taken with adequate caution, Sender, like other great writers, wrote only one novel, though he wrote it in more than sixty versions, each revealing a different angle or perspective on that reality called life, the enigma of human existence.

Charles L. King

OTHER MAJOR WORKS

SHORT FICTION: *Novelas ejemplares de Cíbola*, 1961 (*Tales of Cibola*, 1964); *Cabrerizas Altas*, 1965; *Las gallinas de Cervantes, y otras narraciones parabólicas*, 1967.

POETRY: *Las imagenes migratorias*, 1960; *Libro armilar de poesía y memorias bisiestas*, 1974.

NONFICTION: *Viaje a la aldea del crimen*, 1934; *Counter-attack in Spain*, 1937; *Hernán Cortés*, 1940; *Mexicayotl*, 1940; *Examen de ingenios: Los noventayochos*, 1961; *Valle-Inclán y la dificultad de la tragedia*, 1965; *Ensayos sobre el infringimiento cristiano*, 1967; *Tres ejemplos de amor y una teoria*, 1969; *Ensayos del otro mundo*, 1970; *El futuro comenzó ayer*, 1975.

BIBLIOGRAPHY

Devlin, John. *Spanish Anticlericalism: A Study in Modern Alienation*. New York: Las Americas, 1966. Sender is included in this study of anticlerical Spanish literature from the nineteenth and twentieth centuries. Includes a bibliography.

Eoff, Sherman Hinkle. "Ramón J. Sender: *The Sphere* (1949) and *El lugar del hombre* (1939)." In *The Modern Spanish Novel: Comparative Essays Examining the Philosophical Impact of Science on Fiction*. New York: New York University Press, 1961. An analysis of two of Sender's novels, *The Sphere* and *A Man's Place*, is included in this study of Spanish literature.

Hart, Stephen M. *Sender: "Réquiem por un campesino español."* Reprint. 1990. London: Grant & Cutler, 1996. A brief guide to *Requiem for a Spanish Peasant* designed to introduce the novel to graduate and undergraduate students. Includes a revised bibliography.

King, Charles L. *Ramón J. Sender*. New York: Twayne, 1974. An introductory overview to Sender's life, with analysis of his writings. One of the volumes in the Twayne World Authors series. Includes a bibliography.

Lough, Francis. *Politics and Philosophy in the Early Novels of Ramón J. Sender, 1930-1936: The Impossible Revolution*. Lewiston, N.Y.: Edwin Mellen Press, 1996. An analysis of novels published in the early to mid-1930's, in which Sender expressed his concern with the historical background of Spain's social and political problems and with the morality of the anarchists, communists, and other revolutionaries.

Perriam, Chris, et al., eds. *A New History of Spanish Writing, 1939 to the 1990's*. New York: Oxford University Press, 2000. This history of almost sixty years of Spanish writing includes a chapter, "Representing Ordinary Histories: Ramón José Sender and Ignacio Aldecoa," in which Sender's work is discussed.

Trippett, Anthony M. *Adjusting to Reality: Philosophical and Psychological Ideas in the Post-Civil War Novels of Ramon J. Sender*. London: Tamesis Books, 1986. Trippett's analysis of Sender's work focuses on three novels: *The Affable Hangman, Emen hetan*, and *Crónica del alba*. Includes a bibliography.

MARY LEE SETTLE

Born: Charleston, West Virginia; July 29, 1918
Died: Ivy, near Charlottesville, Virginia;
       September 27, 2005
Also known as: Mrs. Charles Palmer

PRINCIPAL LONG FICTION

The Love Eaters, 1954
The Kiss of Kin, 1955
O Beulah Land, 1956
Know Nothing, 1960
Fight Night on a Sweet Saturday, 1964
The Clam Shell, 1971
Prisons, 1973
Blood Tie, 1977
The Scapegoat, 1980
The Killing Ground, 1982 (revision of *Fight
       Night on a Sweet Saturday*)
Celebration, 1986
Charley Bland, 1989
Choices, 1995
*I, Roger Williams: A Fragment of
       Autobiography*, 2001

OTHER LITERARY FORMS

In addition to her novels, Mary Lee Settle wrote several nonfiction books. Her juvenile works, *The Story of Flight* (1967) and *Water World* (1984), the latter being a parallel history of humanity's exploration of the sea, are not as significant as her autobiographical *All the Brave Promises: Memories of Aircraft Woman Second Class 2146391* (1966) or her historical study *The Scopes Trial: The State of Tennessee vs. John Thomas Scopes* (1972). *All the Brave Promises* describes Settle's experiences as an American volunteer in the Women's Auxiliary Air Force of the Royal Air Force (RAF) in 1942 and 1943. *The Scopes Trial*, like *All the Brave Promises*, deals with human responses to a historical confrontation. In *Addie* (1998), Settle examines her life as it is framed by her ancestors, including her grandmother, Addie Tompkins.

ACHIEVEMENTS

As late as 1978, when she won the National Book Award for fiction for *Blood Tie*, critics were calling Mary Lee Settle an "unknown" writer. With the earlier publication of four of her historical novels, some of them had praised her for the research-based realism that resulted in works more respectable than the typically lurid products of that genre. Critics, however, found Settle's complexity sometimes confusing, pointing out the changes in point of view, the flash-forwards and flashbacks, and sometimes the assumption that the reader knew the history of her characters as well as the writer did. There was a lack of agreement as to whether her characters were well developed. After the completion of the Beulah Quintet (consisting of *O Beulah Land*, *Know Nothing*, *Prisons*, *The Scapegoat*, and *The Killing Ground*) in 1982, however, critics recognized the depth and scope of her vision, arguing that Settle's structural complexity was justified by her aim: to present the truth about human relationships in their historical context. To her early champions, among them Malcolm Cowley and George Garrett, were added numerous other critics who saw evidence of her considerable talent in her contemporary works as well as in the historical novels. To them, the award for *Blood Tie* was a belated recognition rather than an unexpected one.

When *Celebration* was published in 1986, Settle received praise, rather than blame, for her stylistic and technical feats, and she was no longer faulted for her characterization. Settle's reputation was established as that of a skillful, serious writer whose approach to her material was justified by her purpose: to document her own search and that of her characters for, as critic Peggy Bach put it, "their own personal past and the taproot that was cut." Settle's lifetime achievement was formally recognized in 1994, when the American Academy of Arts and Letters awarded her its Academy Award in Literature.

BIOGRAPHY

Mary Lee Settle was born in Charleston, West Virginia, on July 29, 1918. She attended Sweet Briar College from 1936 to 1938. An aspiring actor, during the winter of 1938-1939 she worked as a model for several major modeling houses. In the summer of 1939 she married Rodney Weathersbee, the father of her only son, Christopher. When the war broke out, her husband joined the Canadian army and the couple separated, divorcing in 1946. Settle's marriage later that year to Douglas Newton ended in divorce in 1956. Settle served in the RAF Women's Auxiliary Air Force during World War II. She then became a freelance writer and journalist, working briefly as an editor for *Harper's Bazaar* and later as English correspondent for *Flair*.

After writing several plays, still unpublished, Settle turned to fiction, publishing her first novel in 1954. She was awarded Guggenheim Fellowships in 1957-1958 and in 1959-1960. In 1965 her play *Juana La Loca* was given an Off-Broadway production. In 1980, Settle was instrumental in founding the now-prestigious PEN/Faulkner Award for Fiction, raising funds to ensure its continuance; she would remain a member of the PEN/Faulkner board throughout the rest of her life.

In 1987 Settle converted to Roman Catholicism. Though at various times she had lived in Italy, Greece, England, and Turkey as well as in the United States, she finally made a permanent home at Ivy, Virginia, near Charlottesville, the home of the University of Virginia, where she taught from time to time. In 1978, Settle had married writer and historian William Littleton Tazewell; he died in 1998. On September 27, 2005, Settle died of lung cancer at her home in Ivy.

ANALYSIS

Whether her works are set in the present or in the past, in Europe or in West Virginia, Mary Lee Settle's preoccupations are always the same: the quest for freedom and the pursuit of love in a threatening, changing social environment. Like a Greek dramatist, she employs a background of ordinary people who ignore the issues and the dangers of their time and place, who accept their intellectual and social prisons, blindly assuming that all is for the best, no matter what persons or what ideals they betray. In contrast to this chorus are a few exceptional people who are incapable of that blind and easy acceptance. Whatever the social cost, they insist on honesty. Whatever the political and economic cost, they seek freedom. Their ideals are ultimately democratic, for they will not judge others by narrow social standards or limit their associations by social formulas. Because they are

uncompromising, they are destined to be misunderstood, ridiculed, deserted, even betrayed, but they may also be followed, admired, and loved.

Most of Settle's novels fall into three categories: the southern novels, such as her first two published works, *The Love Eaters* and *The Kiss of Kin*, as well as *The Clam Shell* and *Charley Bland*; the Beulah Quintet, five historical novels published between 1956 and 1982, out of chronological order; and the European novels, the award-winning *Blood Tie*, set in contemporary Turkey, and *Celebration*, set in London but tracing the past lives of its characters to Kurdistan, Hong Kong, and Africa. Settle's final work, *I, Roger Williams*, is a historical novel, though it was not linked to the Beulah Quintet except thematically. Like all of her previous novels, *I, Roger Williams* revisits the past in a search for social reform and personal redemption.

THE LOVE EATERS

The Love Eaters is set in Canona, West Virginia, among the country-club people who will appear again in the final novel of the Beulah Quintet, *The Killing Ground*—Anne Randolph Potter, for example, the drawling Virginian, and her "real American" husband, George Potter. The men work, talk, and drink; the women decorate their homes, plan community projects, talk, and drink. With her fine ear for dialogue, Settle captures their sterile lives by carefully recording that talk, the beauty-shop gossip blaring under the hair dryers, the brief exchanges between husbands and wives, between mothers and daughters, between men in the country-club locker room. The marriages in Canona have become the routine relationships of people who live politely in the same houses, like the Potters and their friends the Dodds, Jim and Martha. Because she was tired of the meaningless talk, Martha married Jim, and when she feels alone in their silent home, she reminds herself that she got exactly what she wanted. What Jim himself wanted was a quiet routine; knowing this, Martha has not even permitted herself to bear him a child.

The bored women of the Canona Country Club have brightened their lives by organizing an acting company, and it is through this venture that one of the two disrupting forces in *The Love Eaters* comes to Canona. As the novel opens, the itinerant director Hamilton Sacks descends from the train, accompanied by his devoted mother. Sacks is a physical and emotional cripple who delights in "playing" the people he meets as if he were playing to an audience, as indeed he is, and who has no sense of moral responsibility for the effects his wicked hints may have on their lives. The second disrupting force comes, ironically, through the placid Jim Dodd. Through a letter, he has learned the whereabouts of his son by a previous marriage, about whom he had never told his childless present wife. With the arrival of charming, slender, handsome, and, above all, lovable Selby Dodd in Canona, the lives of Jim and Martha are changed forever.

In Settle's modern version of Seneca the Younger's play *Phaedra* (c. 40-55 C.E.; English translation, 1581), the passion of a menopausal woman, trapped in the aimless days and nights of a society that thinks in stereotypes and in a marriage whose value has been its placid silence, is no more surprising than the fact that George Potter keeps the local beautician as his mistress. Martha's upcountry old mother is familiar with the yearnings of middle-aged women, familiar enough to warn that infatuations with young men, while not surprising, are generally unwise. Martha is not the only one who is taken with Selby Dodd, who, as Hamilton comments, lives on love and, without exerting himself, attracts women of all ages, as well as men such as Hamilton; Martha's contemporary Anne Randolph Potter and her seventeen-year-old daughter, Sally Bee Potter, vie for Selby from the first time they meet him. There is, then, very little shock in speculations about Martha's feelings. It is Martha who inflicts the punishment on herself, and her emphasis is not on the immorality of incestuous feelings or fear of a heroic husband—for neither moral rectitude nor heroism is common in Canona society—but on her own need for Selby's physical and emotional love. As Hippolytus, Selby is neither morally outraged nor committed to a young princess. He trifles with Sally Bee Potter under the same rules that she observes in teasing him, but no love is involved, for Selby, like Hamilton, is too narcissistic to love anyone but himself and too opportunistic to be troubled by morality. Because his long-range plans include acquiring as much of Jim's property as possible, however, Selby cannot afford to risk angering Jim, and his pose must remain that of loving son and considerate stepson.

The differences between the traditional tragic characters in this account of a stepmother's passion for her stepson and Settle's characters, who lack the tragic stature and the rigid moral sense of those in the earlier versions of the story, indicate the diminished standards of modern society, which imprisons its members within patterns that have no moral dimension but merely the force of mindless custom. At the end of the novel, Martha at least briefly takes responsibility for Selby's death, but instead of dying, she loses her mind. Jim, too, escapes from reality; having made his dead son into a hero, he waits for Martha to become her old self.

THE KISS OF KIN

In *The Kiss of Kin*, the imprisoning society is a southern family, brought together for a funeral. Into this society comes Abraham Passmore, summoned to claim his inheritance and determined also to discover the wrong that his father's people once did to his mother. By the end of the novel, Abraham has forced the members of the family to admit the truth, but it is obvious that they will not therefore become honest. Only the cousin who leaves with him has been forced by the day's events to reject the family, as well as her similarly dishonest Yankee lover, in order to find her own freedom.

While entertaining, *The Kiss of Kin* is too clearly an adaptation of the light comedy that Settle had first written. Like *The Love Eaters*, it is skillfully constructed, hilariously satirical, accurate in dialogue; avoiding authorial comment, it depends on dramatic scenes and on the meditations of the few sensitive characters to comment on the society that is its target. At this point, Settle made an important turn in her literary career. She produced the first of the Beulah Quintet novels, which plunged into the historical past to find the roots of that southern society realized in her first two novels.

O BEULAH LAND

Settle's first two historical novels were written in chronological order. *O Beulah Land* is set in what was later to be West Virginia at the time of the French and Indian War; *Know Nothing*, in the 1840's and 1850's. It is significant that each of these novels takes place just before a momentous historic event—in the first case, the American Revolution; in the second, the Civil War. In both of them, exceptional people understand the issues of their time and respond heroically. Others either insist on living in a changeless world, clinging to a familiar pattern, or blindly refuse to admit that change is inevitable.

In *O Beulah Land*, a massacre results from the insistence of two Englishmen, at opposite ends of the social scale, that the New World pattern is no different from the pattern of the Old World. "Squire" Josiah Devotion Raglan steals, as he did in England; the arrogant British commander is rude, as he could afford to be in England. Unfortunately, the American Indians, whose tomahawk is stolen and whose pride is offended, are not governed by Old World rules, and the massacre is the outcome. Significantly, Hannah Bridewell, a transported prostitute and thief, survives captivity by the American Indians and reaches safety in the arms of a frontiersman, Jeremiah Catlett. Adapting to the New World, they create a marriage outside the church, which has not yet come to the wilderness, and later defend their home through the justifiable murder of the blackmailing Squire, who once again has miscalculated in the New World.

In the Lacey family, Settle again contrasts the selfish and the blind with those perceptive, freedom-loving individuals who refuse to enslave themselves to an old pattern. Sally Lacey, the spoiled, pretentious wife of Jonathan Lacey, refuses to adapt to frontier life. Failing in her lifelong crusade to make over her homely neighbors, Sally at last goes mad. In contrast, the printer Jarcey Pentacost has lost his shop rather than tailor his efforts to the values of a community already stagnating; for him, the frontier means freedom.

KNOW NOTHING

In *Know Nothing*, although the historical background is very different, the descendants of the characters in *O Beulah Land* must choose between enslavement to old patterns that no longer suit the changing country and emerging new patterns. Another Sally Lacey and her husband, Brandon, must move west because the plantation economic system has failed them. Unable to adapt, Brandon kills himself, and Sally retreats permanently into the contemplation of her heredity. Other casualties of inherited patterns are Johnny Catlett, who cannot escape from his role as slave owner and finally as Confederate officer; Lewis Catlett, the prisoner of his religious obsession, whose abolitionism, the result of his mother's influence, has in it no grain of compassion; Melinda

Lacey and Sara Lacey, both trapped in miserable marriages from which, in a society that does not permit divorce, only death can release them. Already in *Know Nothing*, the same kind of social prisons from which American immigrants escaped have been established in the New World, and the quest for freedom has become more and more difficult.

FIGHT NIGHT ON A SWEET SATURDAY

In 1964, the Viking Press published *Fight Night on a Sweet Saturday*, which was to have been the concluding work in the "Beulah Trilogy." In that book, Hannah McKarkle, who is named for the heroic Hannah of *O Beulah Land*, comes to Canona, West Virginia, originally to see her brother and then to investigate his death. During her visit, she begins to explore the past of her family and of her region, thus, in a sense, becoming Mary Lee Settle herself. Unfortunately, the publishers so cut *Fight Night on a Sweet Saturday* that Settle found the relationships obscured. Eventually, she was to add two volumes to the Beulah works, *Prisons* and *The Scapegoat*, and to rewrite *Fight Night on a Sweet Saturday*, creating the novel published as *The Killing Ground*.

PRISONS

Still pursuing the democratic ideal, Settle returned to Great Britain, where she tracked down a chance reference to John Lilburne, the leader of a group of radicals, a number of whom were executed by the forces of Oliver Cromwell, who were averse to the "Leveling" principles of true egalitarians. It is the story of one of these executed radicals that Settle tells in her seventeenth century novel *Prisons*, which becomes the first novel in the Beulah Quintet, viewed chronologically. Its hero, the brave, idealistic Johnny Church, enmeshed in amoral public policy, refuses to save his own life by becoming Cromwell's agent among the men who see Johnny as a natural leader. It is the descendants of Johnny Church, both literal and spiritual, who continue to fight for freedom in Settle's historical and contemporary novels.

THE CLAM SHELL

Meanwhile, Settle had published another novel set in the contemporary South, *The Clam Shell*, which is set among the same country-club crowd as *The Love Eaters*. In Canona in 1966, Anne Randolph Potter, "Plain" George Potter, and their friends are involved in their usual rituals. This time, however, the disrupting influence is one of their own friends, the woman protagonist, who watches them watching football, drinking, and reminiscing. Unlike Martha Dodd, she learned young that she was unable to fit the mold of her friends in Canona, just as she could not fit the mold of the Virginia finishing school to which she was sent. Musing on her youth, remembering her unjust treatment at the finishing school, she realizes that she long ago ceased wishing to be accepted by mindless, restrictive upper-class Virginia or West Virginia society. Like Abraham Passmore, she is content to be an honest exile.

In literary quality, *The Clam Shell* is one of Settle's less effective novels. Satirical and often angry, it divides its characters into two groups: those who understand life and those who, from dullness or from choice, choose not to understand but, instead, to persecute those who do.

BLOOD TIE

After this simplistic novel came one of Settle's best, *Blood Tie*, a contemporary work set on a Turkish island. The protagonist—idealistic, innocent Ariadne—has come to Ceramos to recover from a midlife divorce. There she becomes acquainted with a group of expatriates, the sensationalist Basil, a German archaeologist, a Jewish bar owner, a wealthy American girl, and Central Intelligence Agency (CIA) agent Frank Proctor. None of the expatriates understands the language well enough to realize the disapproval, contempt, and ridicule with which they are viewed by the natives, nor have they any idea of the intrigue with which they are surrounded. The archaeologist, for example, does not guess that a hunted university student is hiding in the sacred caverns that he cannot find.

As the Turks manipulate the expatriates for gain, the expatriates utilize one another and the Turks for the sensations they seek. Through the corruption walks Ariadne, mothering the spoiled American girl and the mute Turkish child, struggling with her sense of rejection and with her own troublesome sexuality, unintentionally shocking the Turks, who misinterpret her actions. When she and the other expatriates at last leave the island, the chief of police praises her because, of all the visitors, only Ariadne tried to see the Turks as individuals rather than as background figures in an exotic environment. Although Ariadne does not know it, she has made a differ-

ence to the troubled, mute child, for at last he is able to speak.

THE SCAPEGOAT

In *The Scapegoat*, published three years after *Blood Tie*, Settle again creates complex characters who have a moral sense. Foolish, innocent, and idealistic though they may be, such individuals do provide some hope for the future. Like its predecessors in the Beulah Quintet, *The Scapegoat* takes place at a time of confrontation, on a single day, June 7, 1912, when the hostility between British mine owners and their hired thugs on one hand and the miners with their union leaders on the other results in armed conflict. In the middle of the conflict are the mine owners, Beverley and Ann Eldridge Lacey, who hope to keep their mine, their home, and their friendships apart from the approaching violence. Ironically, the idealism of their daughter Lily Ellen Lacey, home from college, leads directly to the violence. Her friendship with a young striker is exploited to inflame both the strikebreakers and the strikers. As the day develops, basically good people do evil. To save her son, Lily's friend sacrifices a new immigrant, the "scapegoat" of the title; to help the friend escape, Lily and Beverley take advantage of the death of the scapegoat, thus in a sense participating in the guilt.

In her later books, however, Settle deals more realistically with guilt, seemingly recognizing that in this world every act is tainted. Rather than expecting her exceptional characters to be flawless and fully cognizant of the situation in which they are placed, Settle is more compassionate toward the well-meaning, even if, like Lily, they unintentionally play into the hands of clearly evil forces. Granted, ignorance cannot exempt one from guilt. Lily's service as a nurse in World War I, which results in her death, is a course deliberately chosen because she must take responsibility for her tragic blindness. Nevertheless, Settle seems in her later works to be castigating fewer characters for their blindness and permitting more of them the possibility of redemption.

THE KILLING GROUND

In the final volume of the Beulah Quintet, *The Killing Ground*, Settle's writer Hannah McKarkle sums up what she has learned of history. In clash after clash, people struggle for freedom. Often, as Johnny Church learned in the English Civil War, as the Laceys saw in the American mine wars, both sides in a confrontation seek power, and it is a third group that must struggle for real freedom. Whatever its pretensions, every society is made up of many who are blind, often for their own comfort, and of many who, though perceptive, are unprincipled. Because of that convenient or deliberate blindness, the rebels, the seekers for freedom, must always struggle, first to see the truth and then, and only then, to act upon it.

Because critics were becoming aware of Settle's themes by the time *The Killing Ground* was published, they were able to see justification for the shifts in point of view and the movements back and forth in time that can make her work difficult. In *The Scapegoat*, for example, Settle tells her story through the eyes of several different characters, whose testimony, weighed and judged by the reader, can add up to objective truth. Similarly, in *Blood Tie*, the mutual misunderstandings between the Turkish and the expatriate populations are dramatized by frequent changes in point of view, often revealing opposite interpretations of events and statements. Thus, the thematic emphasis on the pursuit of truth is exemplified by Settle's own method of revealing the truth.

Moreover, because, as William Faulkner believed, the truth of any one moment involves the past of an individual, a community, a people, and because the human mind never lives purely in present consciousness, it was now becoming evident to critics that Settle's frequent shifts in time are also a technical expression of a thematic emphasis. In a comic novel such as *The Kiss of Kin*, the thrust of the work is toward the revelation of a single element in the past, and therefore the dramatic technique is effective. In a complicated novel such as *The Killing Ground* or *Blood Tie*, however, in which characters attempt to understand the present while always being conscious of the past, the shifts in time are both effective and thematically necessary.

CELEBRATION

Settle's increasing technical mastery and her developing theme of redemption are both evident in *Celebration*. The six chapters of the novel alternate between London and three distant areas where various characters once lived: Kurdistan, Hong Kong, and Africa. The process through which the main characters must go is that of the Mass: an honest facing of the past, the acceptance of guilt, repentance, redemption, and joy. Each of the char-

acters has crossed what Settle terms "the Styx," directly confronting death and despair. For Teresa Cerrutti, it was the death of her husband in Malakastan, followed by her own surgery for cancer. For Noel, Lord Atherton, it was a disastrous encounter with a Chinese lover in Hong Kong. For Ewen Stuart McLeod, it was the betrayal by his uncle, who trapped him in an unsavory African expedition and involved him in the murder of innocent people.

The movement toward a joyful future is suggested in the fourth of Settle's chapters, when her major characters and their friends together watch the first moon landing, which is an affirmation of humankind's possibilities. That chapter, however, is followed by the darkest account in the novel, Ewen's African adventure, revealing humanity at its treacherous, murderous worst. Ewen's life was saved by the black Roman Catholic priest Pius Deng, who is also now in London, one of the friends.

In the final chapter, there is a celebration of death and of life. The priest is killed by London muggers, but as the guilt-stricken youngest of them comments, he died in a state of grace. Furthermore, the commitment for which he had hoped, the marriage of Ewen and Teresa, concludes the novel. Under the influence of the saintly Pius and through their ever-increasing love for one another, the London friends have made the Styx not a river of death, but one of life.

CHARLEY BLAND

In *Charley Bland*, Settle returns once more to the class tensions between the country-club people and the intellectuals, both surrounded by the poor of Appalachia, this time in the decades just after World War II. Characters in the novel suggest ghosts of Settle's own biography as well as their counterparts in *The Love Eaters* and *The Clam Shell*. In fact, some of them are the same characters. Also as in *The Clam Shell*, the central figure, a young novelist, finds herself drawn back into the world of small-town society, only to learn that she can never be part of that world again. Her life in postwar England and France has expanded her vision so greatly that she and the country clubbers no longer speak the same language.

Like others of Settle's characters, she is shaped by her origins as the daughter of a well-to-do mine owner. Thus, although her father once lost his money and although she has long felt freed from any obligations to her remote, unloving mother, when her mother tries to arrange a match between her daughter and the eligible Charley Bland, she feels powerless to resist the arrangements. Bland's family have always been both friends and rivals of her own, and Bland himself is almost a southern stereotype—the irresistibly charming bachelor, a "devil with women" whose only flaw appears to be that he drinks too much.

The intended love affair occurs, and the narrator finds herself moving into old patterns of social life she thought she had left long before. Even as she enjoys the romance, however, she recognizes that Charley Bland is more deeply flawed than he first appeared, partly because his alcoholism is much more serious than anyone admits and partly because he has no intention of defying his mother, who intends to use him as her protector and her source of entertainment as long as she lives. The narrator is only one in his long series of romances. At the same time, the narrator gradually realizes that the people she used to know intend to freeze her out of their world. It is a world she is ready to leave again but that she will leave with great pain, because she loves its mountains and hollows, its seasons, and the language of its people.

CHOICES

Choices takes the form of a memoir of Melinda Kregg Dunston, who looks back on the eighty-two years of her life to examine the choices that have shaped it. They have been the choices of one whose compassion has always moved her to support the oppressed, first through her Red Cross work in support of striking coal miners (the source of her family's wealth), later her fight against Fascism in Spain in 1937, and later still in her involvement in the Civil Rights movement. These are issues that engaged Settle's own passions as an unapologetic liberal in a conservative community. This novel emphasizes the potency of the choices a person such as Dunston can make, choices that bring one through danger to a heightened recognition of the beauty and fragility of life.

I, ROGER WILLIAMS

Like her earlier work *Prisons*, Settle's final novel dramatizes the political and religious conflicts that tore England apart during the seventeenth century. However, while both books deal with the struggle for freedom of speech, in *I, Roger Williams* the author approaches her theme very differently. The title character of this novel is a famous man, known to every schoolchild as the founder of Rhode Island. Moreover, as the work's subtitle—*A Fragment of Autobiography*—indicates, this is more than a historical novel; it is an attempt to write in the spirit and the voice of the protagonist. Settle's achievement is even more impressive because in order to accomplish this task, she has to show how Williams's thought processes developed over the course of eighty-five years.

The novel begins in 1676, when Williams is seventy-three. He has just seen the town he founded go up in smoke, burned down by young warriors of the Native American tribe whose friendship he had treasured for so many years. Williams himself has lost everything, including his beloved library. However, he also feels a deep sense of remorse, for he had become a captain of the militia, fighting against the very tribe he still thinks of as his family. As he looks back on his life, Williams recalls his first exposure to the horrors of religious persecution, when at the age of eight he saw a man burned for heresy. More formative experiences were to come. At fourteen, because of his gift for languages, Williams was made an assistant to the great jurist Sir Edward Coke, and during the next five years he saw enough of life at the corrupt court of King James I to question a system in which birth and money, combined with a total lack of moral principles, gave a few people complete power over the rest.

Because his continuing insistence on the rule of law made Coke a prime target for his enemies, he feared for Williams; to ensure the young man's safety, Coke placed Williams in Charterhouse School and then at Cambridge University. Finally Coke had Williams ordained a priest of the Church of England. At first Williams identified with the Puritans, who remained in the Church but intended to cleanse it. Shortly after his marriage to Mary Barnard, however, he became a Separatist, denying the validity of the Church that had ordained him. In 1630, the couple joined a group emigrating to the Massachusetts Bay Colony, but as a Separatist, Williams was soon forced to leave Boston for Salem. Eventually his radical opinions, including his insistence that the native tribes, not the king, owned the land, caused Williams to be branded a traitor and banished. Williams remembers his flight through the snowy wilderness and the kindness of the Narragansetts, who saved his life. Eventually he bought land from them and established a settlement in Providence, Rhode Island, and later he obtained a charter for the colony of Rhode Island, which guaranteed religious freedom to everyone.

I, Roger Williams ends in 1683. Providence has been rebuilt and is thriving. Moreover, Williams has made peace with himself and his deity. He now sees that he has often been as intolerant as those he criticized. Not only did he take up arms against his friends the Narragansetts, but also throughout his life he has often displayed hostility toward those who did not share his views or at least made it difficult for them to remain his friends. As he approaches death, Williams can see that he has indeed accomplished a great deal in his lifelong battle for freedom. However, his most important achievement has come in his final years, when by admitting his own flaws he has made himself worthy to meet his God.

In her works, Mary Lee Settle always stresses the need for personal honesty, for emotional and political freedom, and for a democratic acceptance of others on an individual basis. In her early southern novels, she emphasizes the stagnant, snobbish, superficial society that broke the weak and drove the strong into exile. In the Beulah Quintet and in the European novels, however, while still castigating the cruel, the selfish, and the blind, Settle increasingly emphasizes the possibility of expiation or of redemption. It is appropriate that her final book, which celebrates a heroic struggle against tyranny, should end with the hero's victory over his own intransigent spirit.

Rosemary M. Canfield Reisman
Updated by Ann D. Garbett

OTHER MAJOR WORKS

NONFICTION: *All the Brave Promises: Memories of Aircraft Woman Second Class 2146391*, 1966; *The Scopes Trial: The State of Tennessee vs. John Thomas Scopes*, 1972; *Turkish Reflections: A Biography of a Place*, 1991 (with an introduction by Jan Morris); *Addie*, 1998; *Spanish Recognitions: The Roads to the Present*, 2004; *Learning to Fly: A Writer's Memoir*, 2007.

CHILDREN'S LITERATURE: *The Story of Flight*, 1967; *Water World*, 1984.

BIBLIOGRAPHY

Appalachian Heritage 34, no. 1 (Winter, 2006). Special issue devoted to Settle's fiction includes articles on specific works, discussion of the author's recurring themes, and information on such matters as her years with *The Paris Review*.

Garrett, George. *Understanding Mary Lee Settle*. Columbia: University of South Carolina Press, 1988. Seminal work discusses Settle's major fiction, with special attention to the Beulah Quintet. Also includes chapters on *Blood Tie*, *Celebration*, and some nonfiction.

McKinney, Irene, ed. *Backcountry: Contemporary Writing in West Virginia*. Morgantown, W.Va.: Vandalia Press, 2002. Collection of selections from the works of twenty-three writers helps to place Settle's work within a regional context. Editor's introduction discusses the impact of ideas of place and of home on Appalachian writers.

Miller, Danny L., Sharon Hatfield, and Gurney Norman, eds. *An American Vein: Critical Readings in Appalachian Literature*. Athens: Ohio University Press, 2005. Includes two substantial essays on Settle, one focusing on Jeremiah Catlett and the other analyzing the use of autobiographical elements in her works, especially in the Beulah Quintet.

Perry, Carolyn, and Mary Louise Weaks, eds. *The History of Southern Women's Literature*. Baton Rouge: Louisiana State University Press, 2002. Includes a succinct discussion of Settle's life and works by Loretta Martin Murrey. Supplemented with an informative appendix titled "The Study of Southern Women's Literature," bibliography, and index.

Rosenberg, Brian. *Mary Lee Settle's Beulah Quintet: The Price of Freedom*. Baton Rouge: Louisiana University Press, 1991. Examines the quintet as a single fiction instead of as a series of related novels. Provides analysis of the work and also discusses its critical reception.

Settle, Mary Lee. "Wrestling with the Angel." Interview by Brian Rosenberg. In *Appalachia and Beyond: Conversations with Writers from the Mountain South*, edited by John Lang. Knoxville: University of Tennessee Press, 2006. Settle discusses the experiences that inspired several of her works, explains how she developed her personal philosophy, and expresses her disapproval of the present-day publishing industry.

Stephens, Mariflo. "Mary Lee Settle: The Lioness in Winter." *Virginia Quarterly Review* 74 (Fall, 1996):

581-589. A novelist records her acquaintance with Settle, including material about Settle's life, politics, and writing. Stephens asserts that politics inspired negative critical responses to Settle's novel *Choices*.

MARY WOLLSTONECRAFT SHELLEY

Born: London, England; August 30, 1797
Died: London, England; February 1, 1851
Also known as: Mary Wollstonecraft Godwin

PRINCIPAL LONG FICTION

Frankenstein: Or, The Modern Prometheus, 1818
Valperga: Or, The Life of Castruccio, Prince of Lucca, 1823
The Last Man, 1826
The Fortunes of Perkin Warbeck, 1830
Lodore, 1835
Falkner, 1837
Mathilda, 1959 (wr. 1819)

OTHER LITERARY FORMS

Mary Wollstonecraft Shelley was a prolific writer, forced into copiousness by economic necessity. Punished by Sir Timothy Shelley, father of her husband, Percy Bysshe Shelley, for her violation of his moral codes with his son, Mary Shelley was denied access to the Shelley estate for a long time after her husband's death. Her own father, William Godwin, was eternally in debt himself and spared her none of his troubles. Far from helping her, Godwin threw his own financial woes in her lap. It fell to Mary to support her son by writing, in addition to her novels, a plethora of short stories and some scholarly materials. The stories were mainly available to the public in a popular annual publication called the *Keepsake*, a book intended for gift giving. Her stories were firmly entrenched in the popular gothic tradition, bearing such titles as "A Tale of Passion," "Ferdinand Eboli," "The Evil Eye," and "The Bride of Modern Italy." Her scholarly work included contributions to *The Lives of the Most Eminent Literary and Scientific Men* in

Lardner's Cabinet Encyclopedia (1838). She attempted to write about the lives of both her father and her husband, although these efforts were never completed. She wrote magazine articles of literary criticism and reviews of operas, an art form that filled her with delight. She wrote two travel books, *History of a Six Weeks' Tour Through a Part of France, Switzerland, Germany, and Holland* (1817) and *Rambles in Germany and Italy* (1844). Shelley edited two posthumous editions of her husband's poetry (1824 and 1839), and she wrote several poetic dramas: *Manfred*, now lost, *Proserpine* (pb. 1922), and *Midas* (pb. 1922). She wrote a handful of poems, most of which were published in *Keepsake*.

ACHIEVEMENTS

Mary Wollstonecraft Shelley's literary reputation rests solely on her first novel, *Frankenstein*. Her six other novels, which are of uneven quality, are very difficult indeed to find, even in the largest libraries. Nevertheless, Shelley lays claim to a dazzling array of accomplishments. First, she is credited with the creation of modern science fiction. All subsequent tales of the brilliant but doomed scientist, the sympathetic but horrible monster, both in high and mass culture, owe their lives to her. Even Hollywood's dream factory owes her an imaginative and economic debt it can never repay.

Second, the English tradition is indebted to her for a reconsideration of the Romantic movement by one of its central participants. In her brilliant *Frankenstein* fantasy, Mary Shelley questions many of the basic tenets of the Romantic rebellion: the Romantic faith in humankind's blissful relationship to nature, the belief that evil resides only in the dead hand of social tradition, and the Romantic delight in death as a lover and restorer.

Finally, Shelley created one of the great literary fictions of the dialogue with the self. The troubled relationship between Dr. Frankenstein and his monster is one of the foundations of the literary tradition of "the double," doubtless the mother of all the doubles in Charles Dickens, Robert Louis Stevenson, and even in Arthur Conan Doyle and Joseph Conrad.

BIOGRAPHY

Born Mary Wollstonecraft Godwin, Mary Shelley lived the life of a great Romantic heroine at the heart of the Romantic movement. She was the daughter of the brilliant feminist Mary Wollstonecraft and the equally distinguished man of letters William Godwin. Born of two parents who vociferously opposed marriage, she was the occasion of their nuptials. Her mother died ten days after she was born, and her father had to marry for the second time in four years to provide a mother for his infant daughter. He chose a rather conventional widow, Mary Jane Clairmont, who had two children of her own, Jane and Charles.

In her childhood, Shelley suffered the torments of being reared by a somewhat unsympathetic stepmother; later, she led the daughter of this extremely middle-class woman into a life of notoriety. The separation traumas in her early years indelibly marked Shelley's imagination: Almost all of her protagonists are either orphaned or abandoned by their parents.

Shelley's stormy early years led, in 1812 and until 1814, to her removal to sympathetic "foster parents," the Baxters of Dundee. There, on May 5, 1814, when she was seventeen years old, she met Percy Bysshe Shelley, who was then married to his first wife, Harriet. By March 6, 1815, Mary had eloped with Shelley, given birth to a daughter by him, and suffered the death of the baby. By December 29, 1816, the couple had been to Switzerland and back, had another child, William, and had been married, Harriet having committed suicide. Mary Shelley was then nineteen years old.

By the next year, Mary's stepsister, Jane Clairmont, who called herself Claire Clairmont, had had a baby daughter by Lord Byron, while Mary was working on *Frankenstein*, and Mary herself had given birth to another child, Clara.

The network of intimates among the Shelley circle rapidly increased to include many literati and artists. These included, among others, Leigh and Marianne Hunt, Thomas Love Peacock, Thomas Jefferson Hogg, and John Polidori. The letters and diaries of the Shelleys from this period offer a view of life speeded up and intensified, life at the nerve's edge.

While the Shelleys were touring Switzerland and Italy, they sent frantic communications to their friends, asking for financial help. Mary issued frequent requests for purchases of clothing and household items such as thread. There were also legal matters to be taken care of concerning publishing, Percy Shelley's estate, and the custody of his children from his previous marriage.

The leaves of the letters and diaries are filled with urgent fears for the safety of the Shelley children and the difficulties of what was in effect an exile necessitated by the Shelleys' unorthodox lifestyle. In 1818, Clara Shelley died, barely a year old, and in 1819, William Shelley died at the age of three. Five months later, a son, Percy Florence, was born, the only child of the Shelleys who would grow to maturity.

In 1822, Mary Shelley's flamboyant life reached its point of desolation. Percy Shelley, while sailing with his close friend Edward Williams in his boat *Ariel*, drowned in the Gulf of Spezia. Mary's letters and diaries of the time clearly reveal her anguish, her exhaustion, and her despair. Her speeding merry-go-round suddenly and violently stopped.

Literary historians find themselves in debate over this point in Mary Shelley's life. Her letters and diaries record unambiguous desolation, and yet many scholars have found indications that Percy Shelley was about to leave her for Jane Williams, the wife of the friend with whom he drowned. There is also some suspicion that Mary's stepsister had recently given birth to a baby by Percy Shelley, a rumor that Mary Shelley denied. Because of Percy Shelley's mercurial nature, such speculations are at least conceivable. Against them stands Mary's diary, a purely private diary, which suggests that she would have no reason to whitewash her marriage among its confidential pages.

Mary's tragedy did not prompt warmth and help from her estranged father-in-law. He refused to support his grandson, Percy Florence, unless Mary gave the child to a guardian to be chosen by him. This she would not do, and she was rewarded for her persistence. Her son became heir to the Shelley estate when Harriet Shelley's son died in 1826. After the death, Mary's son became Lord Shelley. Just as important, however, was the warm relationship that he maintained with Mary until her death. Mary Shelley's life ended in the tranquil sunshine of family affection. Her son married happily and had healthy children. Mary seems to have befriended her daughter-in-law, and, at the last, believed herself to be a truly fortunate woman.

ANALYSIS

Mary Wollstonecraft Shelley's six novels are written in the gothic tradition. They deal with extreme emotions, exalted speech, the hideous plight of virgins, the awful abuses of charismatic villains, and picturesque ruins. The sins of the past weigh heavily on their plot structures, and often include previously unsuspected relationships.

Shelley does not find much use for the anti-Catholicism of much gothic fiction. Her nuns and priests, while sometimes troublesome, are not evil, and tend to appear in the short stories rather than in the novels. She avoids references to the supernatural so common in the genre and tends instead toward a modern kind of psychological gothic and futuristic fantasy. Like many gothic writers, she dwells on morbid imagery, particularly in *Frankenstein* and *The Last Man*. Graphic descriptions of the plague in the latter novel revolted the reading public that had avidly digested the grotesqueries of Matthew Gregory Lewis's *The Monk: A Romance* (1796; also known as *Ambrosio: Or, The Monk*).

With the exception of *Frankenstein*, Shelley's novels were written and published after the death of her husband; with the exception of *Frankenstein*, they appear to be attempting to work out the sense of desolation and abandonment that she felt after his death. In most of her novels, Shelley creates men and particularly women who resign themselves to the pain and anguish of deep loss through the eternal hope of love in its widest and most en-

compassing sense. Reconciliation became Shelley's preponderant literary theme.

FRANKENSTEIN

Frankenstein is Shelley's greatest literary achievement in every way. In it, she not only calls into the world one of the most powerful literary images in the English tradition, the idealistic scientist Victor Frankenstein and his ironically abominable creation, but also, for the one and only time, she employs a narrative structure of daring complexity and originality.

The structure of *Frankenstein* is similar to a set of Chinese boxes, of narratives within narratives. The narrative frame is composed of the letters of an arctic explorer, Robert Walton, to his sister, Mrs. Saville, in England. Within the letters is the narrative of Victor Frankenstein, and within his narrative, at first, and then at the end within Walton's narrative, is the firsthand ac-

Mary Wollstonecraft Shelley. (Library of Congress)

count of the monster himself. Walton communicates to England thirdhand then secondhand accounts of the monster's thoroughly unbelievable existence. Here, it would seem, is the seminal point of Joseph Conrad's much later fiction, *Heart of Darkness* (1902): the communication to England of the denied undercurrents of reality and England's ambiguous reception of that intelligence. In *Frankenstein* as in *Heart of Darkness*, the suggestion is rather strong that England cannot or will not absorb this stunning new perception of reality. Just as Kurtz's fiancé almost a century later cannot imagine Kurtz's "horror," so Mrs. Saville's silence, the absence of her replies, suggests that Walton's stunning discovery has fallen on deaf ears.

The novel begins with Walton, isolated from his society at the North Pole, attempting to achieve glory. He prowls the frozen north "to accomplish some great purpose"; instead, he finds an almost dead Victor Frankenstein, who tells him a story that, in this setting, becomes a parable for Walton. Frankenstein, too, has isolated himself from society to fulfill his great expectations, and he has reaped the whirlwind.

Frankenstein tells Walton of his perfect early family life, one of complete kindness and solicitude. It is a scene across which never a shadow falls. Out of this perfection, Victor rises to find a way of conquering death and ridding himself and humankind of the ultimate shadow, the only shadow in his perfect middle-class life. Like a man possessed, Frankenstein forges ahead, fabricating a full, male, human body from the choicest corpse parts he can gather. He animates the creature and suddenly is overwhelmed by the wrongness of what he has done. In his success, he finds utter defeat. The reanimated corpse evokes only disgust in him. He abandons it in its vulnerable, newborn state and refuses to take any responsibility for it.

From that day, his life is dogged by tragedy. One by one, all his loved ones are destroyed by the monster, who at last explains that he wanted only to love his creator but that his adoration turned to murderous hate in his creator's rejection of him. Ultimately, Frankenstein feels that he must destroy the monster or, at the very least, die trying. He succeeds at both. After Frankenstein's death in the presence of Walton—the only man other than Frankenstein to witness the monster and live—the monster mourns the greatness that could have been and leaves Walton with the intention of hurling himself onto Frankenstein's funeral pyre.

The critical task regarding this fascinating work has been to identify what it is that Frankenstein has done that has merited the punishment that followed. Is the monster a kind of retribution for people's arrogant attempt to possess the secrets of life and death, as in the expulsion from Eden? Is it the wrath of the gods visited on people for stealing the celestial fire, as in the Prometheus legend, a favorite fiction of Percy Shelley? Or is this a rather modern vision of the self-destructiveness involved in the idealistic denial of the dark side of human reality? Is this a criticism of Romantic optimism, of the denial of the reality of evil except as the utterly disposable dead hand of tradition? The mystery endures because critics have suggested all these possibilities; critics have even suggested a biographical reading of the work. Some have suggested that Victor Frankenstein is Shelley's shrewd insight into her husband's self-deceived, uncritical belief in the power of his own intelligence and in his destined greatness.

VALPERGA

Valperga, Shelley's second novel, has a fairy-tale aura of witches, princes, maidens in distress, castles, and prophecies. The author uses all these fantasy apparatuses but actually deflates them as being part of the fantasy lives of the characters that they impose on a fully logical and pragmatic reality. The novel pits Castruccio, the Prince of Lucca, a worldly, Napoleonic conqueror, against the lost love of his youth, the beautiful and spiritual Euthanasia. Castruccio's one goal is to gain power and military dominion, and since he is enormously capable and charismatic, not to mention lucky, he is successful. Nevertheless, that he gains the world at the price of his soul is clearly the central point of the novel.

To gain worldly sway, he must destroy Valperga, the ancestral home of his love, Euthanasia. He must also turn Italy into an armed camp that teems with death and in which the soft virtues of love and family cannot endure. His lust for power raises to predominance the most deceitful and treacherous human beings because they are the ones who function best in the context of raw, morally unjustified power.

In the midst of all this, Castruccio, unwilling to recognize his limits, endeavors to control all. He wants to continue his aggrandizing ways and have the love of Euthanasia. Indeed, he wants to marry her. She reveals her undying love for him, but will only yield to it if he yields his worldly goals, which he will not do. As his actions become more threatening to her concept of a moral universe, Euthanasia finds that she must join the conspirators against him. She and her cohorts are betrayed, and all are put to death, with the exception of Euthanasia. Instead, Castruccio exiles her to Sicily. En route, her ship sinks, and she perishes with all aboard. Castruccio dies some years later, fighting one of his endless wars for power. The vision of the novel is that only pain and suffering can come from a world obsessed with power.

Surely the name Euthanasia is a remarkable choice for the novel's heroine. Its meaning in Shelley's time was "an easy death"; it did not refer to the policy of purposefully terminating suffering as it does today. Euthanasia's death is the best one in the story because she dies with a pure heart, never having soiled herself with hurtful actions for the purpose of self-gain. Possibly, the import of Shelley's choice is that all that one can hope for in the flawed, Hobbesian world of *Valperga* is the best death possible, as no good life can be imagined. It is probable that this bleak vision is at least obliquely connected with the comparatively recent trauma of Percy Shelley's death and Mary Shelley's grief and desolation.

THE LAST MAN

The degenerating spiral of human history is the central vision of *The Last Man*. Set in the radically distant future of the twenty-first century, this novel begins with a flourishing civilization and ends with the entire population of the world, save one man, decimated by the plague. Lionel Verney, the last man of the title, has nothing to anticipate except an endless journey from one desolate city to another. All the treasures of humankind are his and his alone; all the great libraries and coffers are open only to him. All that is denied to him—forever, it seems—is human companionship.

The novel begins before Lionel Verney's birth. It is a flashback narrated by Lionel himself, the only first-person narrator possible in this novel. Lionel describes his father as his father had been described to him, as a man of imagination and charm but lacking in judgment. He was a favorite of the king, but was forced out of the king's life by the king's new wife, a Marie Antoinette figure. The new queen, depicted as an arrogant snob, disapproves of Verney's father and effects his estrangement from the king by working on her husband's gullible nature.

Verney's father, in ostracized shame, seeks refuge in the country, where he marries a simple, innocent cottage girl and thus begets Lionel and his sister Perdita. Verney's father can never, however, reconcile himself to his loss of status and dies a broken man. His wife soon follows, and Lionel and Perdita live like wild creatures until chance brings the king's son, Adrian, into their path. Their friendship succeeds where the aborted friendship of their fathers failed, despite the continued disapproval of the queen.

What is remarkable to the modern reader is that Shelley, having set her story two hundred years in the future, does not project a technologically changed environment. She projects instead the same rural, agrarian, hand- and animal-driven society in which she lived. What does change, however, is the political system. The political system of *The Last Man* is a republican monarchy. Kings are elected, but not at regular intervals. The bulk of the novel concerns the power plays by which various factions intend to capture the throne by election rather than by war.

Adrian and Lionel are endlessly involved with a dashing, Byronic figure named Lord Raymond, who cannot decide whether he wants life in a cottage with Perdita, or life at the top. Ultimately, Raymond, like the protagonist of *Valperga*, wants to have both. He marries Perdita and gives up all pretensions to power, but then returns with her to rule the land. Power does not make him or his wife happy.

Despite the sublimation of the power process into an electoral system, the rage for power remains destructive, degenerating finally into war. The plague that appears and irrevocably destroys humankind is merely an extension of the plague of people's will to power. Not only Raymond and Perdita but also their innocent children, Lionel's wife, Iris, and Adrian's sister, who stayed home to eschew worldly aspirations, are destroyed. No one is immune.

Lionel's survival carries with it a suggestion of his responsibility in the tragedy of humankind. His final exile in a sea of books and pictures suggests that those who commit themselves solely to knowledge and art have failed to deal with the central issues of life. In simply abdicating the marketplace to such as Lord Raymond, the cultivators of the mind have abandoned humanity. Through Lionel, they reap a bitter reward, but perhaps the implication is that it is a just reward for their failure to connect with their fellow human beings.

A number of critics consider *The Last Man* to be Mary Shelley's best work after *Frankenstein*. Like *Frankenstein*, this novel rather grimly deals with the relationship between knowledge and evil. Its greatest drawback for modern audiences, however, is its unfortunate tendency to inflated dialogue. Every sentence uttered is a florid and theatrical speech. The bloated characterizations obscure the line of Shelley's inventive satire of people's lemminglike rush to the sea of power.

THE FORTUNES OF PERKIN WARBECK

The Fortunes of Perkin Warbeck attempts to chronicle the last, futile struggles of the House of York in the Wars of the Roses. Perkin Warbeck was a historical character who claimed to be Richard, the son of Edward IV of England. Most scholars believe that Richard died in the tower with his brother Edward; Perkin Warbeck claimed to be that child. Warbeck said that he had survived the tower, assumed another identity, and intended to reclaim the usurped throne held by Henry VII.

Shelley's novel assumes that Perkin was indeed Richard and documents his cheerless history from his childhood to his execution in manhood by Henry VII. The novel attempts to explore once more man's fruitless quest for power and glory. Richard is an intelligent, virtuous young man who finds true companionship even in his outcast state, and the love of a number of women, each different, utterly committed, and true. He is unable, however, to forsake the dream of conquest and live simply. As he presses onward to claim the throne, he suffers a series of crushing losses, not one of which will he yield to as a revelation of the wrongheadedness of his quest. His rush toward the throne achieves only the death of innocent persons. When he is executed at the end of the novel, his wife Katherine is given the last words. She needs to find a way of continuing to live without him. She is urged by his adherents to forsake the world, and for his sake to live a reclusive life. Although Katherine

appears only briefly in the interminable scenes of war and the grandiose verbiage through which the reader must trudge, her appearance at the end of the novel and her refusal to forsake the world in her grief are the most impressive moments in the work.

In refusing to retreat from the world, Katherine commits herself to the only true value in the novel, love, a value that all the senseless suffering of Richard's quest could not destroy. Katherine, as the widow of the gentle but misguided warrior, becomes a metaphor for the endurance of love in a world that has its heart set on everything but love. Her final, gracious words are a relaxing change from the glory-seeking bombast of the action, "Permit this to be, unblamed—permit a heart whose sufferings have been and are, so many and so bitter, to reap what joy it can from the strong necessity it feels to be sympathized with—to love." Once again, Shelley's basic idea is an enthralling one, but her execution of her plan includes a grandiose superfluity of expression and incident.

LODORE

Lodore and Shelley's last novel, *Falkner*, form a kind of reconciliation couplet to end her exploration of loss and desolation. Reward for persistence in loving through the trials of death and social obliquity is her final vision. In *Lodore*, an extremely long parade of fatal misunderstandings, the central image is the recovery of a lost mother. The novel begins veiled in mystery. Lord Lodore has exiled himself and his fairylike, delicate daughter, Ethel, to the forests of Illinois in far-off America. Lord Lodore is without his wife, who has done something unnamed and perhaps unnameable to provoke this unusual separation. Reunion with her is the central action of the plot.

Lord Lodore is a perfect gentleman amid the cloddish but honest American settlers. His one goal is to produce the perfect maiden in his daughter, Ethel. Father and daughter are entirely devoted to each other. A series of flashback chapters reveal that Lady Lodore, very much the junior of Lord Lodore, had been overly influenced by her mother, who had insinuated herself between husband and wife and alienated her daughter's affections from Lord Lodore. Lord and Lady Lodore lived what life they had together always on the brink of rapprochement, but utterly confounded by the wiles of the mother-in-law, who managed to distort communicated sentiments to turn husband and wife away from each other, finally effecting a radical separation that neither Lord nor Lady Lodore wanted.

The American idyll ends for Ethel and her father when Ethel is about fifteen years old. The unwanted attentions of a suitor threaten Ethel's perfect life, and her father moves his household once more. Lodore thinks of reestablishing the bond with his estranged wife but is killed in a duel hours before departing for England. His last thoughts of reconciliation are buried with him, because the only extant will is one recorded years ago when he vindictively made Lady Lodore's inheritance dependent on her never seeing Ethel again. Ethel returns to England shaken and abandoned, but not to her mother. Instead, she lives with Lodore's maiden sister.

Ethel is wooed and won by a gentleman, Edward Villiers, coincidentally one of the few witnesses to her father's death and many years older than herself. The marriage of this truly loving couple is threatened because Edward, reared in luxury, is in reduced financial circumstances owing to the irresponsibility of his father, one of the few truly despicable characters in the novel.

Much suffering ensues, during which Edward and Ethel endeavor to straighten out priorities: Which is more important, love or money? Should they part to give Ethel a chance at a more comfortable life, or should they endure poverty for love? They choose love, but Edward is taken to debtor's prison, Ethel standing by for the conjugal visits that the prison system permits.

Through a series of chance encounters, Lady Lodore, now a seemingly shallow woman of fashion, becomes aware of Ethel's needs and of her need to be a mother to the young woman. Telling no one but her lawyer what she intends, she impoverishes herself to release Edward from prison and to set the couple up appropriately. She then removes herself to a humble country existence, anticipating the blessings of martyrdom. She is, however, discovered, the mother and daughter are reunited, and Lady Lodore is even offered an advantageous marriage to a rich former suitor who originally was kept from her by the machinations of his sisters.

Lodore includes many particulars that are close to the biographical details of the author's life: the penury and social trials of her marriage to Shelley, the financial irre-

sponsibility of her father, and the loss of her mother. Shelley's familiarity with her material appears to have dissolved the grandiose pretensions of the previous novels, which may have sprung from her distance from their exotic settings and situations. *Lodore* has the force of life despite its melodramatic plot. If it were more widely available, it would be a rich source of interest for historians and literary scholars. It contains an interesting image of America as envisioned by the early nineteenth century European. It also contains a wealth of interest for students of women's literature.

FALKNER

If *Lodore* offers a happy ending with the return of a long-lost mother, then *Falkner* finds contentment in the restoration of an estranged father. Here, the father is not the biological parent, but a father figure, Rupert Falkner. The plot is a characteristic tangle of gothic convolutions involving old secrets and sins, obdurate Catholic families, and the pure love of a young girl.

The delightful Elizabeth Raby is orphaned at the age of six under severe circumstances. Because her fragile, lovely parents were complete strangers to the little town in Cornwall to which they had come, their death left Elizabeth at the mercy of their landlady. The landlady is poor, and Elizabeth is a financial burden. The landlady keeps her only because she suspects that the now decimated, strange little family has noble connections. Thus begins a typical Shelley fiction—with abandonment, innocence, and loss of love.

The plot is set in motion by a mysterious stranger who identifies himself as "John Falkner." Falkner undertakes the guardianship of Elizabeth, not only because of her charm but also because of an unfinished letter found in the family cottage. This letter connects Elizabeth's mother to one "Alithea." The reader comes to learn that Falkner was Alithea's lover, that he carries the guilt of her ruin and death since Alithea was a married woman, and that her husband continues to bear his wife's seducer a vindictive grudge. Happily, for the moment, Alithea's husband believes that the seducer was surnamed Rupert. Alithea's husband was and is an unsuitable mate for a sensitive woman, and the marriage was one from which any woman would have wanted to flee. Alithea's infraction was only against the letter of the marriage bond, not its spirit.

The vindictive husband has conceived a hatred for Alithea's son, Gerard, on account of Alithea's connection with "Rupert." Elizabeth, Falkner's ward, coincidentally meets and forms an attachment to Gerard. Falkner repeatedly attempts to separate them because of his guilty feelings. Their attachment blooms into a love that cannot be denied, and Falkner is forced to confess all to Gerard after the boy saves Falkner's life. He is the infamous Rupert, Rupert Falkner.

With the revelation comes the separation of Elizabeth and Gerard, she to stand loyally with Falkner, he to defend his father's honor. For the first time in his life, Gerard finds himself on his father's side, but familiarity breeds contempt. Gerard wants to fight a manly duel for honor, while his father wants to crush Falkner for economic gain in the legal system. Gerard finds this an inexcusable pettiness on his father's part. He then joins Elizabeth to defend Falkner in court. To do this, they will need to go to America to bring back a crucial witness, but the witness arrives and saves them the voyage: Falkner is acquitted. The legal acquittal is also metaphorical: In comparison with the ugly sins of greed, the sins of passion are pardonable.

Elizabeth, the reader knows, is also the product of an elopement in defiance of family, a sin of passion. The proud Catholic family that once spurned her decides to acknowledge Elizabeth. Gerard and Elizabeth, both wealthy and in their proper social position, marry. Falkner will have a home with them in perpetuity.

Once again, Shelley's fictional involvement in the domestic sphere tones down her customary floridity and affords the reader fascinating insights into the thinking of the daughter of an early feminist, who was indeed an independent woman herself. It can only clarify history to know that such a woman as Mary Shelley can write in her final novel that her heroine's studies included not only the "masculine" pursuits of abstract knowledge but also needlework and "the careful inculcation of habits and order . . . without which every woman must be unhappy—and, to a certain degree, unsexed."

Martha Nochimson

OTHER MAJOR WORKS

SHORT FICTION: *Mary Shelley: Collected Tales and Stories*, 1976.

PLAYS: *Midas*, pb. 1922; *Proserpine*, pb. 1922.

NONFICTION: *History of a Six Weeks' Tour Through a Part of France, Switzerland, Germany, and Holland*, 1817 (with Percy Bysshe Shelley); *Lardner's Cabinet Cyclopaedia*, 1838 (numbers 63, 71, 96); *Rambles in Germany and Italy*, 1844; *The Letters of Mary Shelley*, 1980 (2 volumes; Betty T. Bennett, editor).

MISCELLANEOUS: *Mary Shelley's Literary Lives, and Other Writings*, 2002 (Nora Crook, editor).

BIBLIOGRAPHY

Baldick, Chris. *In Frankenstein's Shadow: Myth, Monstrosity, and Nineteenth-Century Writing*. Oxford, England: Clarendon Press, 1987. Analyzes the structure of modern myth as it adapted and misread Shelley's novel before the release of the 1931 film adaptation. Focuses on the novel *Frankenstein* as itself a monster that is assembled, speaks, and escapes like its protagonist. Includes footnotes, illustrations, an appendix summarizing the novel's plot, and an index.

Bennett, Betty T., and Stuart Curran, eds. *Mary Shelley in Her Times*. Baltimore: Johns Hopkins University Press, 2000. Collection of essays presents an examination of Shelley and her works in the full context of her life and times. Addresses all of Shelley's writings rather than concentrating only on her best-known novel.

Fisch, Audrey A., Anne K. Mellor, and Esther H. Schor, eds. *The Other Mary Shelley: Beyond "Frankenstein."* New York: Oxford University Press, 1993. Valuable collection of critical essays illuminates Shelley's major and less well-known works, including her novels *The Last Man* and *Valperga*. The essays by Mary Jean Corbett, Mary Favret, Morton D. Paley, and Esther H. Schor are particularly recommended.

Garrett, Martin. *Mary Shelley*. New York: Oxford University Press, 2003. Biography provides a general overview for readers new to Shelley's work. Discusses Shelley's early, formative years and includes a rich collection of illustrations and excerpts from diaries and letters.

Hoobler, Dorothy, and Thomas Hoobler. *The Monsters: Mary Shelley and the Curse of "Frankenstein."* New

York: Little, Brown, 2006. Biography describes Shelley's creation of *Frankenstein* and demonstrates how the themes of this novel corresponded to the events of Shelley's life.

Mellor, Anne K. *Mary Shelley: Her Life, Her Fiction, Her Monsters.* London: Methuen, 1988. Argues against trends of analysis that subordinate Shelley to her husband, Percy Bysshe Shelley. Extends feminist and psychoanalytic criticism of *Frankenstein* to include all of Shelley's life and work, arguing that her stories are creations of the family she never enjoyed. Includes illustrations, chronology, ample notes, bibliography, and index.

Morrison, Lucy, and Staci Stone. *A Mary Shelley Encyclopedia.* Westport, Conn.: Greenwood Press, 2003. Reference volume contains alphabetically arranged and cross-referenced entries providing information about Shelley's family, friends, homes, works, characters, literary influences, and themes, among other topics.

Smith, Johanna M. *Mary Shelley.* New York: Twayne, 1996. Devotes a chapter to Shelley's biography, then divides Shelley's work into categories for closer discussion. More descriptive than analytical, this is an accessible introduction to Shelley's literary career. Includes selected bibliography.

Spark, Muriel. *Mary Shelley.* London: Constable, 1988. Revision of Spark's *Child of Light*, published in 1951, reassesses the view that Shelley craved respectability after her husband's death. Skillfully narrates Shelley's life and then analyzes her writings. Includes illustrations, selected bibliography, and index.

Sunstein, Emily. *Mary Shelley: Romance and Reality.* Boston: Little, Brown, 1989. One of the most complete biographies of Shelley available. Chapter notes explicitly identify key primary sources of information about Shelley's life and work, and an appendix provides detailed listings of works definitively identified as Shelley's as well as works that might be attributed to her.

CAROL SHIELDS

Born: Oak Park, Illinois; June 2, 1935
Died: Victoria, British Columbia, Canada; July 16, 2003
Also known as: Carol Ann Warner

PRINCIPAL LONG FICTION

Small Ceremonies, 1976
The Box Garden, 1977
Happenstance, 1980
A Fairly Conventional Woman, 1982
Swann: A Mystery, 1987
A Celibate Season, 1991 (with Blanche Howard)
The Republic of Love, 1992
Happenstance, 1993 (contains *Happenstance* and *A Fairly Conventional Woman*)
The Stone Diaries, 1993
Larry's Party, 1997
Unless, 2002

OTHER LITERARY FORMS

Carol Shields began her writing career as a poet with the publication of *Others* in 1972 and *Intersect* in 1974; she would return to her poetic roots with 1992's *Coming to Canada*. Shields wrote in various genres; in addition to composing novels and poetry, she was a short-story writer, an essayist, a playwright, a literary critic, and a biographer. Shields collaborated on a number of projects across genres with other writers. She coauthored the novel *A Celibate Season* with Blanche Howard, cowrote the drama *Anniversary* (pr., pb. 1998) with Dave Williamson, and edited two essay anthologies with Marjorie Anderson, *Dropped Threads: What We Aren't Told* (2001) and its sequel, *Dropped Threads 2: More of What We Aren't Told* (2003). Long an admirer of the British novelist Jane Austen, Shields researched and wrote a literary biography of the author that was published in 2001 to great acclaim.

ACHIEVEMENTS

The success that Carol Shields experienced as a novelist is remarkable given that she did not publish her first novel until she was forty, although her talent as a writer was apparent much earlier. In 1965 she received recognition from the Canadian Broadcasting Corporation (CBC) for a poem she entered in a contest; by the mid-1970's, she had published two volumes of poetry. It was her first novel, *Small Ceremonies*, however, that captured the attention of critics and the reading public. In the three decades of her career as a novelist, her works met with both popular and critical approval. *Small Ceremonies* won the Canadian Authors' Association Award for the Best Novel of 1976. Shields's popular *The Stone Diaries* was short-listed for the Booker Prize, won the National Book Critics Circle Award in 1994, and received the Pulitzer Prize in 1995. Her other award-winning novels include *Larry's Party*, recipient of the Orange Prize for women's fiction, and *Swann: A Mystery*, recipient of the Arthur Ellis Award for Best Canadian Mystery. Her final novel, *Unless*, was nominated for the Booker Prize and the Orange Prize and won the Ethel Wilson Fiction Prize. In other genres, Shields received the CBC Prize for Drama in 1983, and her biography *Jane Austen* was awarded the Charles Taylor Prize for Literary Non-Fiction in 2002. In recognition of her talents as an author, Shields was named a fellow of both the Guggenheim Foundation and the Royal Society of Canada. In 2003 she received an honorary doctorate from the University of Manitoba.

BIOGRAPHY

Carol Shields was born Carol Ann Warner in Oak Park, Illinois, on June 2, 1935, the third and youngest child of Robert Warner and Inez Warner (née Selgren). Her father supervised a candy company, and her mother taught grade school. Carol grew up in a household in which books were treasured by her parents and her older twin siblings; she taught herself to read before she began formal schooling. After completing her studies at Oak Park High School in 1953, she left Illinois to attend Hanover College in Indiana. She spent her junior year abroad, studying in England at the University of Exeter, where she met and fell in love with Donald Shields. Following her graduation from Hanover, they married and

returned to England so that Donald, a civil engineer, could enter a doctoral program at the University of Manchester. Their union produced four children, a son and three daughters.

In 1963, Shields and her family settled in Toronto, Canada, where in 1971 the transplanted American became a Canadian citizen. In the midst of raising a family and running a household, Shields carved out time for her writing. In 1964 she submitted a poem to the Young Writers Competition, sponsored by the Canadian Broadcasting Corporation, and won. Encouraged by her success, Shields continued to write and to submit her work for publication. Her poems appeared in print in various Canadian journals, and several were broadcast on CBC programs. Her output as a poet resulted in the publication of two collections of poetry: *Others* in 1972 and *Intersect* in 1974. In 1973, Shields began graduate studies at the University of Manitoba and found part-time employment as an editorial assistant at the journal *Canadian Slavic Papers*. She completed her master of arts degree in 1975; her master's thesis was a study of female sexuality and social roles in works by nineteenth century Canadian author Susanna Moodie.

Following her graduation, Shields obtained teaching positions at a number of universities, including the University of Ottawa, the University of British Columbia in Vancouver, and the University of Manitoba in Winnipeg. She continued to write poetry but found greater success as a writer of novels. Beginning with her 1976 debut novel, *Small Ceremonies*, and ending with the publication of *Unless* in 2002, Shields would experience twenty-five years of increasing acclaim as a novelist. In her final years, aware that she had terminal cancer, Shields wrote at a prodigious rate, completing several works, including *Unless* and her Austen biography. She died of cancer on July 16, 2003.

ANALYSIS

Critics generally divide Carol Shields's novels into two groups: those novels written prior to her Pulitzer Prize-winning *The Stone Diaries* and those following. Shields's first four novels, *Small Ceremonies*, *The Box Garden*, *Happenstance*, and *A Fairly Conventional Woman*, are domestic in focus and realistic in style. Set in her adopted Canada, they trace the lives of ordinary

Carol Shields. (© Neil Graham)

women in commonplace circumstances who are striving to discover who they are through relationships with other people in their lives. The search for identity is a common theme in these works. The titles of the works suggest the insularity of the women's lives through words like "small," "box," and "conventional." What marks Shields's early work is the contrast between the quiet personalities and lives of her protagonists and the strong impression they make on readers, who see versions of their own lives, those of ordinary women, represented on the pages.

Shields's later novels bear trademarks of postmodernism, a literary style characterized by fragmentation and multiple narrative voices. Whereas modern novelists quest after meaning in their works, postmodern writers question the very possibility of creating meaning through words. Shields's use of multigeneric forms and multiple, competing narrators places her within this movement. Even prior to *The Stone Diaries*, her 1987 novel *Swann* exhibited traits of postmodernism. In

Swann, the questionable circumstances surrounding the title character's death are relayed by four separate narrators, and the final chapter is written as a script. Using this unconventional format, Shields unravels the mystery genre even as she reconstructs the murder of Swann, a once obscure Canadian poet made famous in death. *Swann* is a precursor to *The Stone Diaries*, a novel that, in its unconventional approach to chronicling the life of Daisy Goodwill, deconstructs the genre of fictional autobiography. Increasingly, in her later works, including *Larry's Party* and *Unless*, Shields became more emboldened in the use of structures and styles associated with postmodernism.

SMALL CEREMONIES

While at the University of Manitoba, Shields was encouraged by her professors to try her hand at fiction in addition to literary criticism. Her first novel, *Small Ceremonies*, published in 1976, manages to blend both elements. Inspired by Shields's scholarly thesis, the novel features a narrator who, mirroring her creator, conducts research on Canadian author Susanna Moodie in order to write a literary biography of Moodie's life. Although classified as realistic fiction, the novel nevertheless hints at the more postmodern forms that emerge in Shields's later works. Present already is the metatextual element: Shields writes about a writer who writes about a writer.

Clearly this novel draws on autobiographical elements. Similar to Shields at the time, the novel's protagonist, Judith Gill, is a literary scholar who is married with children. Reminiscent of Shields's relocation to England during her husband's graduate studies, Gill's husband's sabbatical takes his family to Birmingham and to the residence of a family that has traveled to Greece. These parallel circumstances offer a family living abroad in the home of a family living abroad. The novel begins with the Gill family recently returned to Canada and traces events across three seasons, autumn through spring. A central theme in the novel is identity, both personal and national. In the process of researching the life of Susanna Moodie, Gill examines her own. Both inquiries lead to reflections on what it means to be a writer, mother, wife, Canadian, and traveler abroad. Gill contemplates the effects of life abroad on her family's return to Canadian life and on her writing. In another connection between author and character, Shields has Gill step aside from her scholarly book on Moodie to attempt to write a novel.

The Stone Diaries

In *The Stone Diaries*, Shields's multilayered narration reinvents the fictional biography. The story of Daisy Goodwill is told at intervals in the first and the third person. Wherever Daisy leaves off telling her version of events, or is unable to speak for herself, a second narrator steps in and continues her story. In this manner, Shields blends together biography and autobiography in a fictional setting to create a hybrid genre. Witnessing is a major motif in the novel, beginning with the neighbors who view Daisy's birth and her mother's resultant death. Shields suggests that a person's life is too complex for a single voice to be sufficient—to acknowledge a life, there must be outside observers. The third-person narrator, in addition to recounting scenes from Daisy's life, offers commentary on that life and on the nature of autobiography. The metatextual elements that emerge—an autobiography that explores the nature of autobiography—are a continuation of techniques that Shields began employing in *Small Ceremonies*.

Divided into ten chapters, *The Stone Diaries* records life stages. Chapter titles such as "Birth," "Childhood," "Marriage," "Love," and "Illness and Decline" progress until "Death" is reached. The novel ends with the nondescript eulogy delivered at Daisy's funeral, one that appears to negate her existence. This last testimonial to Daisy's life offers little that is memorable. We learn from the minister that she was a wife, a mother, and a citizen, but who Daisy was when she was not filling these roles is omitted. From her own account, what gave her the greatest satisfaction in life was not marriage or children but writing a gardening column, a job taken from her and given to a man. In the final verdict of her life, Daisy becomes simultaneously an everywoman and a no woman. The novel is unsettling as it leaves readers with little comprehension of the value of Daisy's life. There remains a sense that it was worth more than what was recorded. The character's own dissatisfaction with the remembrances accorded her is clear in her dying thought, "I am not at peace." In her chronicle of Daisy, Shields manages to create a fictional biography about the invisibility of most women's lives.

Unless

In her final novel, one written with knowledge of her own impending death, Shields returns to the life of a woman writer, the subject of her first novel. In *Unless*, Shields expands the scope and intensifies the depth of her inquiry. The lead character, Reta Winters, despite her facility with words, which has allowed her to pen a successful first novel and begin a second, finds herself unable to communicate with friends and, more painfully, with her reclusive college-age daughter. Complicating matters is an envious editor who insists she rewrite her female heroine into the background of her second novel in order to elevate the status of a minor male character. *Unless* explores the role of women in modern society and culture, and the pain that often accompanies women's efforts to achieve visibility and voice. Critics consider *Unless* to be Shields's most postmodern and most feminist work.

Dorothy Dodge Robbins

Other major works

SHORT FICTION: *Various Miracles*, 1985; *The Orange Fish*, 1989; *Dressing Up for the Carnival*, 2000; *Collected Stories*, 2004.

PLAYS: *Departures and Arrivals*, pr., pb. 1990; *Thirteen Hands*, pr., pb. 1993; *Fashion, Power, Guilt, and the Charity of Families*, pr., pb. 1995 (with Catherine Shields); *Anniversary: A Comedy*, pr., pb. 1998 (with Dave Williamson); *Thirteen Hands, and Other Plays*, 2002.

POETRY: *Others*, 1972; *Intersect*, 1974; *Coming to Canada*, 1992.

NONFICTION: *Susanna Moodie: Voice and Vision*, 1976; *Jane Austen*, 2001.

EDITED TEXTS: *Dropped Threads: What We Aren't Told*, 2001 (with Marjorie Anderson); *Dropped Threads 2: More of What We Aren't Told*, 2003 (with Anderson and Catherine Shields).

Bibliography

Atwood, Margaret. "A Soap Bubble Floating over the Void." *Virginia Quarterly Review* 81, no. 1 (Winter, 2005): 139-142. Tribute to Shields characterizes her as intelligent, witty, and observant, a writer equally capable of creating images of intense joy and images of despair.

Besner, Neil K., ed. *Carol Shields: The Arts of a Writing Life*. Winnipeg, Man.: Prairie Fire Press, 2003. Collection of essays takes an anecdotal, rather than critical, approach to Shields's life as a writer, connecting her fiction to events in her own life. Focuses primarily on Shields's poetry and novels.

Ciabattari, Jane. "The Goodbye Girl." Review of *Unless*, by Carol Shields. *Los Angeles Times*, May 12, 2002. Assesses the novel in terms of its postmodern conceits. Includes discussion of its metatextual format (a novel about a woman writing a novel about a woman writing a novel) and its juxtaposition of fact and fiction.

Eden, Edward, and Dee Goertz, eds. *Carol Shields, Narrative Hunger, and the Possibilities of Fiction*. Toronto, Ont.: University of Toronto Press, 2003. Collection of essays addresses Shields as a complex and significant author. Presents critical examination of Shields's oeuvre in relation to realist and postmodern narratives. Includes extensive annotated bibliography.

Schwartz, Lynn Sharon. "The Allures of Form." Review of *Dressing Up for the Carnival*, by Carol Shields. *New Leader* 83, no. 2 (May/June, 2000): 35-37. Compares the stories in the collection *Dressing Up for the Carnival* to Shields's novels *The Stone Diaries* and *Larry's Party* and asserts that the stories are rich in ideas but insufficient in character development, a trademark of the novels.

Stovel, Nora Foster. "'Because She's a Woman': Myth and Metafiction in Carol Shields's *Unless*." *English Studies in Canada* 32, no. 4 (December, 2006): 51-73. Examines the blend of feminism and modernism in *Unless*, a novel about a woman on the margins of society. Categorizes the novel as Shields's most experimental in form and most daring in content.

Weese, Katherine. "The 'Invisible Woman': Narrative Strategies in *The Stone Diaries*." *Journal of Narrative Theory* 36, no. 1 (Winter, 2006): 90-120. Applies feminist theories to the complex narrative techniques used in *The Stone Diaries* to reveal a main character who is simultaneously central to and distant from her own story.

MIKHAIL SHOLOKHOV

Born: Kruzhilino, Russia; May 24, 1905
Died: Kruzhilino, Russia, Soviet Union (now in Russia); February 21, 1984
Also known as: Mikhail Aleksandrovich Sholokhov

PRINCIPAL LONG FICTION

Tikhii Don, 1928-1940 (partial translation *And Quiet Flows the Don*, 1934, also known as *The Don Flows Home to the Sea*, 1940; complete translation *The Silent Don*, 1942, also known as *And Quiet Flows the Don*, 1967)

Podnyataya tselina, 1932, 1960 (translation of volume 1 *Virgin Soil Upturned*, 1935, also known as *Seeds of Tomorrow*, 1935; translation of volume 2, *Harvest on the Don*, 1960; complete translation *Virgin Soil Upturned*, 1979)

Oni srazhalis za rodinu, 1943-1944 (serial), 1971 (book; *They Fought for Their Country*, 1959)

Sud'ba cheloveka, 1956-1957 (novella; *The Fate of a Man*, 1958)

OTHER LITERARY FORMS

Mikhail Sholokhov (SHAWL-eh-kawf) published collections of short stories, *Donskiye rasskazy* and *Lazorevaya Step*, in 1926. In 1931, *Lazorevaya Step* was expanded to include *Donskiye rasskazy* and was translated in 1961 as *Tales from the Don*. His short stories form volume 1 of his complete works, *Sobranie sochinenii* (1956-1960; *Collected Works in Eight Volumes*, 1984), which were first published in Moscow in eight volumes; war stories and essays form volume 8. They also are available in English as *One Man's Destiny, and Other Stories, Articles, and Sketches, 1923-1963*

(1967) and *At the Bidding of the Heart: Essays, Sketches, Speeches, Papers* (1973).

ACHIEVEMENTS

Mikhail Sholokhov occupies a unique place in Soviet literature as the author of *The Silent Don*, the greatest novel to be published in the Soviet Union. He has been compared to Leo Tolstoy in his creation of a national epic, to Fyodor Dostoevski in his portrayal of Grigorii Melekhov, and to Nikolai Gogol and Anton Chekhov in his evocations of the steppe. In 1965, he was permitted by Soviet authorities to receive the Nobel Prize in Literature, a privilege denied to Boris Pasternak, who wrote a more profoundly philosophical novel. In addition, Sholokhov held numerous positions of honor in the Communist Party and the Union of Soviet Writers. He won the Stalin and Lenin prizes for literature (1941, 1960) and received honorary degrees from Western and Soviet universities.

In his two major works, *The Silent Don* and *Virgin Soil Upturned*, Sholokhov succeeds in bringing to life the Cossack world that he knew so well. Shrouded in legends, scorned for their barbarity, the Cossacks were little known to the Russians and totally unknown to Western readers. Sholokhov speaks in their dialect, clothes his characters in colorful Cossack traditions, and arms the soldiers with a spirit of courage and adventure. Part 1 of *The Silent Don* in particular and much of *Virgin Soil Upturned* shows them in their daily occupations, their celebrations and their interaction, much in their colorful and often crude language. Through his fictitious characters, all modeled on his own friends and acquaintances, the image of a people emerges.

Particularly in *The Silent Don*, Sholokhov skillfully combined Socialist Realism and art. Officially promulgated in 1934, Socialist Realism required that literature served the ideals of the Communist Party and portrayed a positive Soviet citizen. Early Soviet critics—with the exception of Aleksandr Serafimovich and Maxim Gorky—could not understand that *The Silent Don*, with its vacillating hero and its objective portrayal of both Reds and Whites, was a true proletarian novel, and they tried desperately to block its publication. Eventually, however, the critics accepted it because it showed the triumph of the Revolution through suffering and violence

on both sides. Yet it was the artistic qualities of the novel, already evident in Sholokhov's early short stories, and to be continued in *Virgin Soil Upturned*, that won millions of readers in the Soviet Union and abroad. The humanness of suffering, the tenderness of love, and the uncertainty of truth touched them.

It was not without difficulty that Sholokhov acquired this reputation. Particularly in *The Silent Don*, the censors mercilessly changed and deleted some of his most brilliant passages. Joseph Stalin asked that the hero of *The Silent Don*, Grigorii Melekhov, accept Communism, but Sholokhov refused, saying that this was against the artistic conception of the work. Although *Virgin Soil Upturned* received less criticism, the death of Davydov was a concession to Stalin's wishes, since Sholokhov had planned a suicide. Yet the changes imposed on Sholokhov or accepted by him did not dim the original ideas that he had researched and reflected on painstakingly from 1925 to 1940 for *The Silent Don*, and from 1930 to 1960 for *Virgin Soil Upturned*. Outspoken like his Cossack hero Grigorii, Sholokhov says that an artist must follow his heart. He did not hesitate to criticize the inefficiency of the Soviet system and to express the depth of human suffering that accompanied the Revolution. On the other hand, as a dutiful Communist, he said that one's heart must follow the party. This was a difficult reconciliation, yet Sholokhov seems to have effected it more successfully than any other writer in the Soviet Union.

It should be noted, however, that ever since the publication of the first part of *The Silent Don*, Sholokhov's authorship of this masterwork, which clearly stands above the rest of his production, has been questioned. Among those to raise this charge was Aleksandr Solzhenitsyn, who believed that the actual author was a Cossack officer named Fyodor Krykov, who had written several books about the Don region before his death in the Civil War. This charge against Sholokhov has yet to be conclusively proved or disproved.

BIOGRAPHY

Born on May 24, 1905, in the Cossack village of Kruzhilino near Veshenskaya, Mikhail Aleksandrovich Sholokhov was himself not a true Cossack. His father, Aleksandr Mikhailovich, did not marry his mother,

Anastasiya Danilovna Chernikova, until 1912, when Sholokhov's birth was legitimated and the Cossack status he had held from his mother's first husband was abrogated. Nevertheless, he grew up in the customs and traditions of the Cossack world that he was later to convey with such realism to his readers. His early education in his native village was minimal when he left for a year in Moscow in 1914. Financial reasons precluded his continuing, but he was subsequently enrolled in an eight-year *Gymnasium* (college-preparatory secondary school) in Boguchar. The German invasion of 1918 marked the end of his formal education but did not interrupt his love of reading and writing.

In the years between 1918 and 1922, Sholokhov worked for the new Soviet regime in many capacities, especially grain-requisitioning, and wrote plays for young people. His home was in an area controlled by the Whites. He saw much violence, participated in it himself, and was twice at the point of being killed. This experience is reflected especially in the violence and objectivity of *The Silent Don*, where Grigorii broods confusedly on the injustices committed by both sides.

In 1922, Sholokhov married Maria Petrovna Gromoslavskaya, the daughter of a well-to-do and long-established Cossack family. She was to prove an ideal "comrade" for him. The couple, who would have four children, moved to Moscow, where Sholokhov began his first serious commitment to literature. He published a number of short stories, uneven in literary value but extremely popular. In their vividness of language, diversity of speech, and lively dialogue, they anticipate the achievements of his mature fiction. Never at home in the capital, or in any city, Sholokhov returned to Kruzhilino in 1924.

Sholokhov began working on his masterpiece, *The Silent Don*, in 1925, amid innumerable difficulties with the censors. It was only the intercession of Aleksandr Serafimovich, editor of the monthly *Oktyabr'*, that permitted publication of the initial segment of the novel. Serafimovich's support, however, did not prevent the many attacks on the novel and on Sholokhov himself, who was first accused of plagia-

rism in 1929-1930. Later, Gorky's intervention, and ultimately Stalin's, permitted him to complete publication of the novel. Sholokhov worked on *The Silent Don* almost constantly from 1925 to 1930, the most productive years of his career. He interrupted *The Silent Don* in 1930 to begin *Virgin Soil Upturned*. In 1932, he gained admission into the Communist Party, and in 1934 he was elected to the presidium of the Union of Soviet Writers. He visited Sweden, Denmark, Great Britain, and France as a representative of the Writers' Union. His success did not prevent him from speaking out fearlessly against the bureaucracy, which ultimately placed him in a dangerous position, especially in 1938, when he narrowly escaped liquidation. His personal friendship with Stalin saved him, and he always remained loyal to his friend, even after Stalin's death.

During World War II, in which he experienced much personal suffering, including the loss of his manuscripts, Sholokhov became a war correspondent. His writings as a reporter are not his best; nevertheless, after the war he

Mikhail Sholokhov. (Library of Congress)

devoted himself mainly to journalism, with the exception of volume 2 of *Virgin Soil Upturned*; *They Fought for Their Country*, an unfinished novel in a war setting; and a very successful novella, *The Fate of a Man*. In the postwar era, he enjoyed unparalleled success in the Soviet Union, receiving many prizes, the most notable of which was the Nobel Prize in Literature in 1965. He became a staunch defender of party policies, attacking such dissidents as Pasternak, Solzhenitsyn, Yuli Daniel, and Andrei Sinyavsky, all of whom are superior to him as writers. Typical of his attacks on the West was an invective against Harry S. Truman, then-president of the United States.

Until his death in 1984, Sholokhov lived in the village where he was born. He hunted and fished, traveled widely in Europe, the United States, and Japan, and enjoyed his substantial wealth and international reputation.

ANALYSIS

The critic Herman Ermolaev has observed that Mikhail Sholokhov's art embraces the epic, the dramatic, the comic, and the lyric; to this one might justly add the tragic, at least in *The Silent Don*. Helen Muchnic, for example, sees in the character of Grigorii the fatal flaw that marks the heroes of Greek tragedy: Grigorii is doomed by his failure to recognize the greatness of Bolshevism. His error lies in his independence. Like Oedipus, Grigorii cannot *not* know the truth, but unlike Sophocles' hero, Sholokhov's is destined never to know clearly. Even Soviet critics noted the tragic element in *The Silent Don*, and in 1940, Boris Emelyanov compared *The Silent Don* to Aeschylus's *The Persians* (472 B.C.E.), since both were written from the viewpoint of the vanquished. *The Silent Don* is of epic proportions because of its length and its scope in time (1912-1922) at a crucial period in Western history, World War I and the Soviet Revolution. It was serialized in *Oktyabr'* and *Novy mir* from 1928 to 1940. Volume 1 was published by Moskovskii Rabochii in 1928, volume 2 in 1929; Khudozhestvennaya Literatura published volumes 3 and 4 in 1933 and 1940 respectively.

THE SILENT DON

The novel is the story of the fall of a people seen through some of its most representative families: Melekhov, Korshunov, and Koshevoi in particular. Often

compared to Tolstoy's *War and Peace* (1865-1869), *The Silent Don* unfolds a vast panorama of people and world-shaking events, and 1917 is to Sholokhov what 1812 was to Tolstoy. Yet Sholokhov is no Tolstoy. He lacks Tolstoy's depth of vision, moral intensity, and psychological analysis. Sholokhov's choice of a secluded and anachronistic prerevolutionary society places *The Silent Don* in the category of the primitive and popular epics, as David Stewart demonstrates through his analysis of action, character, language, and meaning in the novel.

Early in his career, Sholokhov was attracted to the theater, and thus it is not surprising that in both of his novels dialogue and action are of extreme importance. Sholokhov uses lively and spirited conversation, filled with dialectical and sometimes crude Cossack expressions, and often incorrect Russian. In fact, the major part of the novels is dialogue rather than narrative, and important events come to light through the characters rather than through the author. Sholokhov does not write reflective philosophical works. Grigorii Melekhov's search for truth is less evident in his thoughts than in his actions, as he vacillates constantly between Red and White, and between his wife, Natalia, and his mistress, Aksinia. Collectivization is not a well-thought-out plan in *Virgin Soil Upturned* but rather a process that occurs because each farmer moves in that direction.

Both people and nature are actors in Sholokhov's works, and he moves effortlessly and harmoniously from one to the other. The poetic evocations of nature that make up at least one-fourth of *The Silent Don* and a good part, though less, of *Virgin Soil Upturned* show Sholokhov's lyric mastery at its height. Most are placed at strategic positions, such as the beginning and end of chapters, and convey the union of people with nature. In somewhat pantheistic exultation, Sholokhov rejoices with nature in its cycle of birth, death, and resurrection. As one might expect from the titles of his novels, the Don mirrors human hopes and sorrows. Sholokhov's books convey the feel of the earth—the Russian soil—and evoke the rhythm of nature.

Nature is frequently associated with love in Sholokhov's fiction. Ermolaev, who has studied the role of nature in Sholokhov, identifies floral blooming with Aksinia; Easter, the spring, and rain, with Natalia. In Grigorii and Aksinia, one finds perhaps the tenderest love story in Soviet literature. Their passionate and fatal love recalls Anna Karenina or Dmitri Karamazov. As with Sholokhov's poetic lyricism, his love stories are close to the earth and show the deep bond of human beings with nature. The tenderness of maternal love also plays an important role in Sholokhov's works, as seen in the tender farewell of Ilinichna for her dead son, Piotra, and contrasts sharply with the brutality and violence of war.

Sholokhov's humorous vein is more evident in *Virgin Soil Upturned* but is not absent from *The Silent Don*, where one might cite Panteleimon Melekhov's wit. *Virgin Soil Upturned* abounds in comic characters and scenes: Shchukar's endless stories, the exuberance of the induction into the party, the initial reactions to collectivization at the village meetings. Sholokhov's dialogue is brisk and witty; his colloquial and dialectical language, always appropriate to the speaker, lightens the heavy subject and makes both novels highly readable.

Indeed, Sholokhov's style is brisk and light; the chapters, composed of short vignettes, leave the reader momentarily in suspense, for Sholokhov knows where to break his tale. His rapid transitions from humor to violence, from love to war, from nature to humanity, show the all-encompassing unity of life and the complexity of the Revolution and its effects. He shows the stark reality of war, the atrocities of both Reds and Whites, and humankind's inhumanity to others. On the other hand, he portrays the tenderness of love and the exultation of nature, as in his beautiful apostrophe to the steppe that rivals Gogol. He works in a linear manner, without flashbacks or foreshadowing, much in the tradition of the nineteenth century or indeed the ancient and medieval epic. He portrays life and love, the endless rhythm of birth and death, as seen in one great epoch, the Soviet Revolution.

The Silent Don was first conceived as an epic of the Don and of the role of the Don Cossacks in the Revolution, and Sholokhov projected the title *Donshchina*, later abandoning it because of its archaic allusions. The story begins in 1912 and ends in 1922. It shows the peaceful agrarian life of the Don Cossacks in the small village of Tatarsk. The domineering patriarch Panteleimon Melekhov and his independent and passionate son, Grigorii, clash often, especially in regard to Grigorii's liai-

son with the bewitching Aksinia. Neither the father's wrath and the arranged marriage with the beautiful and virtuous Natalia Korshunova, daughter of the prosperous Miron, nor the abuse by Aksinia's husband, Stepan Ashtakov, can break the liaison. The two lovers, defying all convention, finally choose to live together as hired help on the estate of Listnitsky.

The calm of the Cossack existence, broken only by such outbursts of passion, is shattered by mobilization in Tatarsk in 1914. Grigorii is called into battle, where his attraction and repulsion toward killing and violence are first evident. The war provides Grigorii's first contact with Bolshevism, for which he also feels both an attraction and repulsion. On leave in Tatarsk because of a wound, he learns of Aksinia's unfaithfulness and returns to his wife, who later gives birth to twins.

Like World War I, the Revolution is portrayed through the eyes of the soldiers and villagers and evoked through images of nature: "Above blood-soaked White Russia, the stars wept mournfully." The desertion of the troops, Kornilov's arrest, and the fall of Kerensky are moments of confusion to the Don Cossack soldiers. Grigorii embraces Bolshevism and becomes an officer but is incapable of the cold dedication exemplified by Bunchuk, whose brief idyll with the Jew Anna Pogudko softens the drama, and by Mishka Koshevoi, Grigorii's former friend and henceforth implacable enemy.

When Grigorii joins the Whites, his position becomes more dangerous. The violence grows more senseless and immediate, with victims such as Miron Korshunov and Piotra Melekhov, the latter killed by Mishka Koshevoi. Family tragedies also cloud Grigorii's existence and confuse his values. His sister-in-law, Daria, commits suicide; his wife, Natalia, dies as the result of an abortion after learning of Grigorii's return to Aksinia; his father dies of typhus. Parallel to Grigorii's uncertainty is Mishka's advance in the Soviet ranks and in coldheartedness. Even his marriage to Grigorii's sister, Dunia, does not dull his determination to kill Grigorii, which the reader surmises will occur when Grigorii returns home, having lost Aksinia to a stray bullet. Only his son, Mishatka, remains, and the implacable march of history will destroy the unwilling Grigorii, born to greatness at a point in history when only conformity can save him.

In 1930, Sholokhov interrupted his work on *The Silent Don* to address a contemporary problem: collectivization. He published part 1 of *Virgin Soil Upturned* in 1932, practically without any censorship difficulties. Part 2 was not completed until 1960 and is radically different in spirit. This novel is much more concentrated in scope, since it covers only the period between 1930 and 1932, has fewer characters, and is confined to the small Cossack village of Gremyachy Log. Although it does not have the epic sweep of *The Silent Don*, it is an on-the-spot documentary of a crucial phase in Soviet history.

VIRGIN SOIL UPTURNED

Also unlike *The Silent Don*, *Virgin Soil Upturned* has no main tragic character. Stewart observes that the heroes are dissolved by the party, so that the real hero is perhaps the collective people at Gremyachy Log. The logical hero is Siemion Davydov, a former factory worker and sailor, who was mobilized in 1930 to organize collective farms. He becomes chair at Gremyachy Log and manifests the zeal and inefficiency typical of early Soviet leaders. He is a colorless but not unlikable character. His death at the end of part 2 is far less tragic than Grigorii's return to Tatarsk. Although he shows his human side in his love affairs with Nagulnov's former wife, Lukeria, and with a gentle, shy seventeen-year-old, Varia Kharlamova, he is not convincing as a lover.

Siemon's associate, the passionate and impulsive Makar Nagulnov, secretary of the Gremyachy Log Party nucleus and still secretly in love with his former wife, is more attractive. Even better portrayed is Andrei Razmiotov, chair of the village Soviet. His one passion is his deceased wife, Yevdokia, and the novel ends as he visits her grave and wistfully mourns her absence. Stewart, however, regards Kondrat Maidannikov as the novel's most convincing character: A "middling Cossack," Kondrat joins the collective farm because he believes in it, yet his instincts draw him to his own property. He does not join the party until he has reflected carefully. In his simplicity, he is the most philosophical and intellectually convinced Communist in the novel.

The plot of the story is simple: the gradual conversion of the village to the collective farm. The beginning reflects Sholokhov's portrayal of violence and brutality, as entire kulak families are deported. Although collectivization is presented as voluntary, those who withdraw after reading Stalin's pronouncement are left with no animals and inferior land. The end of part 1 is indecisive though promising. In part 2, collectivization is complete, and a revolt is suppressed. Thus, this volume becomes mainly a series of sketches and stories, mostly in a humorous vein. It seems to be the work of a writer who has totally accepted party policies, writing about an accomplished fact no longer questioned.

Actually Sholokhov's best creative period ended before World War II, and part 2, written in 1960, weakens what promised to be a powerful, though limited, novel. Nevertheless, Sholokhov's treatment of collectivization has not been surpassed, and his wit and lyricism make *Virgin Soil Upturned* a valuable contribution to literature.

Irma M. Kashuba

OTHER MAJOR WORKS

SHORT FICTION: *Donskiye rasskazy*, 1926; *Lazorevaya Step*, 1926, 1931 (1931 edition includes *Donskiye rasskazy; Tales from the Don*, 1961); *Early Stories*, 1966.

NONFICTION: *Pisatel i vozhd*, 1997; *Pisma*, 2003.

MISCELLANEOUS: *Sobranie sochinenii*, 1956-1960 (8 volumes; *Collected Works in Eight Volumes*, 1984); *One Man's Destiny, and Other Stories, Articles, and Sketches, 1923-1963*, 1967; *At the Bidding of the Heart: Essays, Sketches, Speeches, Papers*, 1973.

BIBLIOGRAPHY

Clark, Katerina. "Socialist Realism in Soviet Literature." In *The Routledge Companion to Russian Literature*, edited by Neil Cornwell. New York: Routledge, 2001. Clark's essay includes discussion of *The Silent Don* and *Virgin Soil Upturned*, placing these novels within the broader context of Soviet Social Realism.

Ermolaev, Herman. *Mikhail Sholokhov and His Art*. Princeton, N.J.: Princeton University Press, 1982. A study of Sholokhov's life and art, philosophy of life, and handling of style and structure, with a separate chapter on the historical sources of *The Silent Don* and another on the question of plagiarism. Includes maps, tables of similes, notes, and a bibliography.

Klimenko, Michael. *The World of Young Sholokhov: Vision of Violence*. North Quincy, Mass.: Christopher,

1972. The introduction discusses the Sholokhov canon as well as his life and his critics. Other chapters explore the genesis of Sholokhov's novels, vision of life, heroes, and treatment of revolution. Includes a bibliography.

Medvedev, Roy. *Problems in the Literary Biography of Mikhail Sholokhov.* New York: Cambridge University Press, 1977. A piercing examination of *The Silent Don*, exploring the issue of Sholokhov's authorship of the novel and how it poses problems for his literary biography.

Mukherjee, G. *Mikhail Sholokhov: A Critical Introduction.* New Delhi: Northern Book Centre, 1992. A bilingual study, in both English and Russian. Mukherjee analyzes the major novels and other writings

of Sholokhov, considering them in relation to Soviet literature and ideology, and he discusses Sholokhov's critical reception.

Scammell, Michael. "The Don Flows Again." *The New York Times Book Review*, January 25, 1998. Scammell's review of a new translation of Sholokhov's best-known novel provides a useful overview of the writer's life and literary reputation, including an update on new evidence supporting Sholokov's claim to be the author of the book.

Stewart, David Hugh. *Mikhail Sholokhov: A Critical Introduction.* Ann Arbor: University of Michigan Press, 1967. Found in most university libraries, this is an accessible overview of Sholokhov and his works. Includes a bibliography.

HENRYK SIENKIEWICZ

Born: Wola Okrzejska, Poland; May 5, 1846
Died: Vevey, Switzerland; November 15, 1916
Also known as: Henryk Adam Alexander Pius Sienkiewicz

PRINCIPAL LONG FICTION

Na marne, 1872 (*In Vain*, 1899)
Ogniem i mieczem, 1883-1884 (serial), 1884 (book; *With Fire and Sword: An Historical Novel of Poland and Russia*, 1890)
Potop, 1884-1886 (serial), 1886 (book; *The Deluge: An Historical Novel of Poland, Sweden, and Russia*, 1891)
Pan Wołodyjowski, 1887-1888 (serial), 1888 (book; *Pan Michael: An Historical Novel of Poland, the Ukraine, and Turkey*, 1893; also known as *Fire in the Steppe*, 1992)
Bez dogmatu, 1889-1890 (serial), 1891 (book; *Without Dogma*, 1893)
Rodzina Połanieckich, 1895 (*Children of the Soil*, 1895)
Quo vadis, 1895-1896 (serial), 1896 (book; *Quo Vadis: A Narrative of the Time of Nero*, 1896)

Krzyżacy, 1897-1900 (serial), 1900 (book; *The Knights of the Cross*, 1900; also known as *The Teutonic Knights*, 1943)
Na polu chwały, 1903-1905 (serial), 1906 (book; *On the Field of Glory*, 1906)
Wiry, 1908-1910 (serial), 1910 (book; *Whirlpools: A Novel for Modern Poland*, 1910)
Dzieła, 1948-1955 (60 volumes)

OTHER LITERARY FORMS

There can be no doubt that it was Henryk Sienkiewicz's success as an author of historical novels that led the Swedish Academy to select him as the recipient of the Nobel Prize in Literature in 1905. He was at the same time, however, a prolific writer of short stories, many of which continue to be ranked among the finest ever written in the Polish language. One of his masterworks in this genre is titled "Janko myzikant" (1879; "Yanko the Musician," 1893). In this story, a young peasant boy named Yanko is so obsessed with the beauty of music that he is unable to resist the temptation of stealing a violin from the manor house of the local squire. When caught, he is beaten so severely that he dies. The underlying irony of this tale stems from the fact that those who live in the manor house consider themselves to be patrons of the arts and frequently travel to Italy for the purpose of discovering and assisting young artists.

Equally popular is "Latarnik" (1882; "The Lighthouse Keeper of Aspinwall," 1893), the plot of which centers on the fate of an aged Polish exile who finally succeeds in being hired as a lighthouse keeper on the island of Aspinwall near the Panama Canal Zone. One day he receives a parcel of Polish books that includes a copy of Adam Mickiewicz's *Pan Tadeusz: Czyli, Ostatni Zajazd na litwie historia Szlachecka zr. 1811 i 1812 we dwunastu ksiegach wierszem* (1834; *Pan Tadeusz: Or, The Last Foray in Lithuania, a Tale of Gentlefolk in 1811 and 1812, in Twelve Books in Verse*, 1917). He becomes so engrossed while reading this patriotic national epic that he forgets to light the beacon and, having caused a ship to run aground, is fired for his negligence. As is the case with most of Sienkiewicz's short stories, those two works were first published in periodicals and subsequently incorporated into editions of his collected works, the first of which appeared while he was still in his early thirties. For this reason, the numerous collections of his short stories in English translation have no Polish-language counterparts as such and have actually been gathered together in accordance with the personal preferences of the individual translators themselves.

Throughout his adult life, Sienkiewicz was an inveterate traveler, and he wrote two works during his trips abroad that are still capable of holding the modern reader's attention. The first of these is titled *Listy z podróży do Ameryki* (1876-1878, serial; 1896, book; *Portrait of America: Letters*, 1959). These letters, arising from a journey to the United States, were commissioned by a Polish periodical and record Sienkiewicz's first-hand impressions of the United States—chiefly of New York City, the Plains states, and California. The Polish author's views are, it should be noted, far more balanced than those to be found in Charles Dickens's *American Notes* (1842), in which life in the United States is depicted in largely negative terms. Later in his career, Sienkiewicz traveled throughout East Africa and wrote *Listy z Afryki* (1891; letters from Africa). In these reports, the role of European colonization is judged to be generally beneficial for the indigenous peoples, but Sienkiewicz is highly critical of the Arabs, who ruthlessly exploited the native populace in this region. Both the American and the African journals are, in short, valuable historical records pertaining to everyday life in a bygone era.

ACHIEVEMENTS

Henryk Sienkiewicz is both a literary and a political phenomenon in his homeland. In order to appreciate the twofold significance of his major novels, it is necessary to recall the troubled state of Polish national life throughout the nineteenth century. Poland had been partitioned by Russia, Prussia, and Austria during the latter part of the eighteenth century and had completely disappeared from the map of Europe. The largest portion of Poland, including Warsaw itself, came under the control of the Russians, and Sienkiewicz was destined to spend his entire life as an involuntary subject of the czar. Two full-scale insurrections against the Russians, the first occurring in 1831 and the second in 1863, ended in defeat, and their failure served only to intensify the oppressive policies of the czarist officials. Both of these revolts were largely inspired by Romantic idealists. After the debacle of 1863, the Polish intelligentsia appeared to wash its collective hands of the doctrines of Romanticism and rapidly embraced the scientifically oriented philosophy of positivism as the best solution to the problems confronting the nation. The adherents of positivism in Poland openly abandoned the quixotic quest for national independence by means of political conspiracy and armed insurrection and focused their energies on promoting organic economic development in the various Polish territories as well as on expanding educational opportunities available to the masses. The transition from Romanticism to positivism signaled a rejection of the feudal values cherished by the landowning gentry and the adoption of the ideals of capitalism championed by the middle class.

For the positivists, writers had a moral obligation to tackle contemporary social problems in their works, and Sienkiewicz's early writings were duly composed in accordance with this stricture. Before long, however, his own ancestral heritage and aristocratic temperament came to the fore, and in 1882 he began work on a historical trilogy that would dramatize Polish military exploits of the seventeenth century. The first volume bears the title *With Fire and Sword*; the other two are *The Deluge* and *Pan Michael*. These three novels are collectively designated the "Trilogia" (trilogy). Sienkiewicz's decision to write about the seventeenth century stemmed from his desire to depict a period in Polish history during which the country successfully defended its national existence against the attacks launched by a combination of powerful enemies. Unlike the positivists, who tended to dwell on the failures of Poland's ruling classes, Sienkiewicz chose to emphasize the valorous feats achieved by Polish arms. The inspirational intent of the author is explicitly acknowledged in his brief postscript to the final volume of the trilogy, in which he asserts that the entire series was written "for the sake of the strengthening of hearts." Public response to these novels was so enthusiastic that sentiment for the cause of Polish independence increased immeasurably throughout the land, and Sienkiewicz soon found himself regarded as his nation's foremost champion, both at home and abroad.

After the publication of the trilogy, Sienkiewicz wrote a pair of moderately successful novels on contemporary themes and then went on to compose two additional historical novels of major stature. The first deals with the persecution of Christians in Rome during the reign of the Emperor Nero and is titled *Quo Vadis*. It soon became an international best seller of unprecedented magnitude and remains Sienkiewicz's most popular novel among the reading public outside the author's native land. In the second of these works, Sienkiewicz returns to the annals of Polish history and depicts Poland's struggle against an aggressive military order of Teutonic monks who are ultimately defeated in the year 1410 at the Battle of Greenwold. This novel bears the title *The Knights of the Cross*. Most Polish critics consider it to be superior to *Quo Vadis* in terms of literary merit, and a few even go as far as to prefer it to the trilogy itself. In 1905, Sienkiewicz was awarded the Nobel Prize in Literature, and he took the occasion to thank the members of the Swedish Academy for recognizing the fact that Poland, though physically enslaved, lived on in spiritual freedom. The abiding popularity of his works in present-day Poland is ample testimony that Sienkiewicz is still capable of strengthening the hearts of his countrymen, as he did during his own lifetime.

Henryk Sienkiewicz. (© The Nobel Foundation)

BIOGRAPHY

Henryk Adam Alexander Pius Sienkiewicz's paternal ancestors were Lithuanian Tatars who had traditionally followed a military vocation. His great-grandfather, Michael, was baptized in 1740 and subsequently admitted to the ranks of the gentry (*Szlachta*) in 1775 through an act of the national diet by way of recognition of the family's military service on behalf of the Polish Commonwealth. Despite this honor, he and his descendants continued to remain impoverished. His own father, Józef, managed to advance himself both socially and financially in 1843 by marrying Stefania Cieciszowska, a young woman from a well-established household of landowners who were generally conceded to be members of the aristocracy. Sienkiewicz was born on May 5, 1846, on an estate that belonged to his mother's parents. This estate (as well as the nearby village) was named Wola Okrzejska and was located near Siedlice, a city in Russian-occupied Poland approximately fifty miles to the east of Warsaw. Sienkiewicz had one brother and four sisters, and when he was nine years old, his parents purchased an estate of their own in the province of Mazovia. A few years later, they sold the estate and bought an apartment house in the Warsaw suburb of Praga in order to supplement their modest financial resources from rental payments made by the tenants. They also hoped to give their children the educational advantage of attending schools in the city that had once been the nation's capital.

Sienkiewicz became an avid reader quite early in life. While still at Wola Okrzejska, he immersed himself in popular Romantic poetry extolling the virtues of gallant knights and fair ladies and thus acquired an abiding affection for the institution of chivalry. He also developed an intense desire to travel through reading Daniel Defoe's *Robinson Crusoe* (1719) and Johann David Wyss's *The Swiss Family Robinson* (1812) and even dreamed of settling on an uninhabited island when he grew up. During the time that he attended secondary school in Warsaw, he frequently neglected his studies to read the historical romances of Sir Walter Scott and Alexandre Dumas, *père*. Except for the areas of literature and history, Sienkiewicz's scholastic achievements were relatively modest. Despite his aptitude for literary and historical studies, however, he never seriously considered becoming a writer during his adolescent years.

When the time arrived for him to matriculate at the newly founded University of Warsaw, then called Szkoła Główna (Central Academy), he readily acceded to his mother's wishes and entered the Faculty of Law in 1866. Soon after, he switched to medicine and finally to history and literature. Students at the University of Warsaw in those years were imbued with a philosophy known as positivism, which was based on the ideas espoused by the French thinker Auguste Comte (1789-1857), and Sienkiewicz himself soon became a confirmed, if only transient, adherent of this social doctrine. Unable to obtain much financial assistance from his parents, Sienkiewicz was obliged to earn funds through employment as a private tutor while still working toward a degree. For reasons that are still unclear, Sienkiewicz terminated his studies at the University of Warsaw in 1871 without bothering to take the final examinations and abruptly embarked on a career as a freelance writer and journalist.

Within a year, Sienkiewicz was finding success in his new career. His first novel, *In Vain*, dealt with student life and was serialized in a biweekly periodical. At about the same time, he became a feature writer for a newspaper named *Gazeta Polska* and contributed numerous sketches, literary essays, and reviews to its *feuilleton* section. On assignment for *Gazeta Polska*, he went to Vienna in 1873. In the following year, he undertook longer trips abroad, to Obstend and Paris, for personal motives. Upon returning to Warsaw in 1875, Sienkiewicz became acquainted with the famous Polish actor Helena Modjeska and her circle of friends. It was within this circle that the utopian idea of founding a Polish Socialist community in California was first proposed. Both Sienkiewicz and Modjeska had personal reasons for wishing to leave Poland—an unhappy love affair on his part and a weariness with the backstage intrigues of the theater world on hers. The worsening political situation in Poland, moreover, made the prospect of leaving the country doubly attractive. When their plan was made public, the *Gazeta Polska* commissioned Sienkiewicz to write a series of articles devoted to his impressions of the New World. He therefore set out in advance of the main party, which was to include Modjeska and her husband as well as her teenage son from a previous marriage.

Less than a month after he left Liverpool for New York, Sienkiewicz had crossed the continent and arrived in San Francisco on March 16, 1876. After a brief stay, he moved on to Southern California and eventually chose a site near Anaheim as the best location for the colony. Modjeska and her small party arrived in September, 1876. The project ran into difficulties almost immediately, owing largely to the group's collective inexperience with the methods of farming, and was abandoned after only a few months. Modjeska thereupon decided to resume her former vocation. Unlike Sienkiewicz, she chose to remain abroad and managed to have a successful stage career in the United States as well as in Great Britain, where she fulfilled her lifelong ambition to play Shakespearean roles in English in the bard's own country. Her son, Ralph Modjeski, went on to become one of the foremost bridge engineers in the United States, by serving as the chairman of the board of consulting engineers for the San Francisco-Oakland Bay Bridge, which was completed in 1936.

After a lengthy sojourn in France and Italy, Sienkiewicz returned to Poland in April, 1879, and gradually assumed his activities as a journalist. The two years spent in the United States were by no means unproductive with respect to his literary development. His impressions of the United States were published in *Gazeta Polska* on a regular basis from 1876 to 1877. In addition, the American experience provided Sienkiewicz with the material for a number of short stories whose locale is the American West—most of which, however, were written after his return to Europe. While still in California, he also wrote a group of satiric sketches about rural life in Poland that was originally published in installments by the *Gazeta Polska* and that now constitutes the novel titled *Szkice węglem* (charcoal sketches). Inspired by the tenets of positivism, this work depicts events in a benighted Polish village, the plight of which, the author intimates, stems ultimately from the indifference of the local gentry toward the welfare of the peasants, whose recent emancipation has left them totally unprepared to cope with the ensuing changes in their way of life. A clear signal that Sienkiewicz was already turning away from the doctrines of positivism may, however, be seen in the short story called "Niewola Tatarska" (1880; "Tartar Captivity," 1897). Here he offers his readers a chivalric account of life in the Old Polish Commonwealth that ran counter to the negative assessments of the positivist historians and their allies in the literary establishment. Critical disapproval notwithstanding, the general public was delighted.

On August 18, 1881, Sienkiewicz married an attractive young lady named Maria Szetkiewicz who was known to have a tubercular condition. Despite the chronic illness of his wife, he was to find great happiness in this brief marriage. A son, Henryk Józef, was born in July, 1882; a daughter, Jadwiga, in December, 1883. Maria's health took a sudden turn for the worse shortly thereafter, and she died on October 19, 1885. Throughout this entire period, so full of joy and sorrow, Sienkiewicz somehow managed to maintain a productive professional life both as a journalist and as a writer of fiction. Not long after his marriage, he accepted an appointment as editor of a newly founded Warsaw daily called *Słowo*. At the same time, he engaged in extensive historical research in preparation for writing a series of three

novels based on the military upheavals in seventeenth century Poland. The project was to take him six years to complete.

With Fire and Sword, the first volume in the trilogy, was published in installments in *Słowo* as well as in the Kraków newspaper *Czas*. Sienkiewicz was thus able to reach readers in both the Russian and the Austrian occupied areas of Poland. The next two volumes, *The Deluge* and *Pan Michael*, were serialized simultaneously, not only in Warsaw and Kraków but also in Poznań—the largest city in the Polish territories annexed by Germany. There it was published by *Dziennik Pozna ski*. This arrangement had the advantage of allowing the author to receive three separate royalty payments. When subsequently published in book form, each of these works became a best seller. Now that he had become the most popular writer in Poland, Sienkiewicz resigned the post of editor for *Słowo* in 1887.

In his next two novels, Sienkiewicz returned to the contemporary scene. The first, *Without Dogma*, constitutes an attack on fin de siècle decadence. The novel is written in diary form, and its hero is a highly cultivated aristocrat who is completely unproductive and purposeless, owing to his intellectual incapacity to believe in anything whatsoever. The second novel, *Children of the Soil*, is considerably more positive in tone. Its protagonist, a member of a family named Polaniecki, is a philistine businessman of noble ancestry who, despite his numerous shortcomings, manages to advance the welfare of his own family as well as that of his countrymen.

Both of these novels were received more warmly abroad than in Poland. Polish readers apparently desired additional historical romances from the undisputed master of this genre, and Sienkiewicz duly responded to the public's wishes with his next novel. Its topic, however, caught his readers by surprise. Instead of another work based on Polish history, Sienkiewicz chose to re-create the events surrounding the persecution of Christians in Rome during the reign of the emperor Nero. He did, however, return to the realm of Polish history in his succeeding novel, a work published in 1900 whose title has been variously translated as *The Knights of the Cross* and *The Teutonic Knights*. Like the trilogy itself, each of these historical novels proved to be enormously successful with the readership in Poland. *Quo Vadis*, moreover, went on to become an unprecedented international favorite and was eventually translated into more than thirty different languages.

Sienkiewicz's devoted admirers looked forward to honoring him on the twenty-fifth anniversary of his literary debut. Strictly speaking, this commemoration should have taken place in 1898, but Sienkiewicz himself requested that it be postponed until 1900 so that it would not interfere with the centennial celebrations to be held in homage of the poet Adam Mickiewicz, who was born in 1798. On the occasion of his own jubilee, Sienkiewicz was presented with a small estate that was purchased from donations made by the public at large. The estate, called Oblegorek, was situated approximately one hundred miles due south of Warsaw near the city of Kielce.

On May 5, 1904, Sienkiewicz married a distant relative named Maria Babska, who was herself a writer. The marriage seems to have been contracted in a spirit of deep friendship rather than one of passionate love, but the arrangement provided Sienkiewicz with a comfortable domestic environment. In the following year, the Swedish Academy selected him to be the recipient of the Nobel Prize in Literature. It is, however, ironic that at the time he became a Nobel laureate, his creative powers were already on the wane. Although he continued to write, his only true success thereafter was a work of children's literature titled *In Desert and Wilderness*, in which an English girl and a Polish boy, having been abducted from their parents, undergo an unending chain of adventures in Egypt and the Sudan.

The outbreak of World War I interrupted Sienkiewicz's work on a novel dealing with the fate of the Polish legions that formed an important part of the Grande Armée of Napoleon during the ill-fated invasion of Russia in 1812. Moving from Oblegorek to Vevey in neutral Switzerland, Sienkiewicz abandoned his literary activities in order to serve as chairman of the Central Swiss Committee for Victims of War in Poland. This organization, whose chief sponsor was the Polish pianist and composer Ignacy Jan Paderewski, succeeded in raising large sums of money to alleviate the suffering of their compatriots back in war-torn Poland. On November 15, 1916, Sienkiewicz died of arteriosclerosis and thus was denied the privilege of witnessing the restoration of Pol-

ish independence in the aftermath of the Allied victory over the Central Powers in 1918. In the fall of 1924, however, his ashes were transferred from Switzerland to Poland and interred in the crypt of Saint John's Cathedral in Warsaw. This church, although subsequently rebuilt, was totally destroyed by the Germans in the fall of 1944 as part of their punitive demolition of the city of Warsaw after the failure of the uprising of the Polish Home Army. Even during the period 1945-1989, when Poland was under Communist domination, Sienkiewicz continued to remain one of the official cultural heroes of his nation, and the dissemination of his writings is actively promoted today throughout the Republic of Poland.

ANALYSIS

Some degree of familiarity with Polish history is essential for an appreciation of Henryk Sienkiewicz's *The Knights of the Cross* and the three novels that form the trilogy. Most translators of these works have, accordingly, provided extensive historical introductions for the benefit of the uninitiated reader. With respect to *The Knights of the Cross*, the most useful introduction is surely the one written by Alicia Tyszkiewicz to accompany the translation she published in 1943 under the title *The Teutonic Knights*. Those about to embark on a reading of this work in any one of its various translations can also find an exceptionally clear survey of medieval Polish history in the third chapter of James Michener's bestselling novel *Poland* (1983).

THE KNIGHTS OF THE CROSS

Because of the wedge-shaped black crosses embroidered on their white mantles, the members of the Order of Teutonic Knights were always referred to by the Poles as *krzyżacy*, or Knights of the Cross. (The term *krzyżacy* is derived from *krzyż*, the Polish word for "cross," and its literal meaning is "those of the cross.") This order was founded in Palestine around 1190, during the Third Crusade. Thirty-five years after its founding, it was formally invited by Duke Conrad of Mazovia, in an act of utter folly, to settle along the eastern shores of the Baltic Sea. Its official mission was to subdue a heathen people called the Prussians, who were closely related to the Lithuanians both culturally and linguistically. The Teutonic Knights succeeded in subduing the Prussian tribes within fifty years, chiefly by following a policy of extermination, and then sought to expand their realm at the expense of the Lithuanians under the pretext of spreading Christianity to this still-pagan people. They also turned on their Polish hosts, despite the fact that Poland had already converted to Christianity in the tenth century. An alliance between the Kingdom of Poland and the Grand Duchy of Lithuania was clearly in the interests of both countries, and in 1386 the Polish Queen Jadwiga and the Lithuanian Grand Duke Jagiełło were wed. Both nations were thus joined in a personal union. As one of the conditions for his elevation to the Polish throne, Jagiełło agreed to abandon paganism and to impose Christianity on his Lithuanian subjects.

The inevitable confrontation with the Teutonic Knights occurred on the morning of July 15, 1410, when a combined force of 46,000 Poles, Lithuanians, and assorted allies joined battle with 32,000 of the enemy on the fields near the little village of Grunwald in East Prussia. By day's end, half of the Teutonic Knights lay dead and the other half were in captivity. Although the Order continued to exist until it was secularized in the aftermath of the Protestant Reformation, its power to expand had been effectively checked. The victory of Poland and Lithuania at Grunwald was the subject of one of the most famous historical paintings by the Polish artist Jan Matejko (1838-1893). How deeply the crushing defeat of the Teutonic Order continued to rankle the sensitivity of the Germans over the succeeding centuries may be inferred from the concerted effort made by the Nazis to locate the whereabouts of this huge canvas after their conquest of Poland in September, 1939.

Prior to this date, Matejko's painting had been the centerpiece of the collection housed in the Polish National Art Museum in Warsaw. Fearing for its destruction at the hands of the Germans, the curator had the canvas removed from its frame and rolled up so that it could fit into a crate made of solid oak. This crate was then placed in a concrete vault five feet underground at a secret location in eastern Poland. The German authorities offered a reward of two million Reichsmarks (a sum equivalent to $750,000 in terms of the currency exchange rates in effect at that time) as well as safe passage out of Poland to a neutral country to anyone who would reveal the location of Matejko's painting. Today the Grunwald picture is on permanent display in the fortified medieval castle at Marienburg that was built by the Teutonic Knights to serve as their central administrative headquarters. Marienburg, moreover, reverted to its previous Polish name of Malbork at the end of World War II.

Sienkiewicz's *The Knights of the Cross* has the Battle of Grunwald as its climax and may be considered the literary counterpart of Matejko's renowned historical canvas. Parts of the book were, in fact, read publicly by Sienkiewicz himself while standing beside the painting that had been his constant inspiration in the course of writing the novel. In addition to presenting a graphic description of the battle itself, Sienkiewicz offers his readers a brilliant pageant of medieval society as it existed in northeastern Europe around 1400. The cast of characters is predominantly fictive, but there are a few historical figures in the novel. King Jagiełło and Queen Jadwiga, however, play relatively minor roles. The historical figures and the fictive characters, it should be noted, function independent of each other for the most part. Neither of these groups plays a significant role in determining the fortunes of the other.

The fictive plot that runs parallel to the historical events described in the novel centers on a young Polish knight, Zbyszko, and his relationship with two women. He falls in love with a delicate beauty named Danusia and marries her. At the same time, he maintains a strong friendship with Jagienka, a warrior maiden who is very much like him in terms of robust health and vivacious demeanor. Danusia, who happens to be the daughter of the powerful Polish magnate Jurand, is kidnapped by members of the Teutonic Order shortly after her marriage to Zbyszki in an attempt to wrest political concessions from her father. While in captivity, Danusia is mistreated to such a degree that she dies directly following her rescue by Zbyszko. After a long period of mourning, Zbyszko decides to marry Jagienka, who really should have been his first choice in matrimony from the outset. As for Jurand himself, he, too, falls into the clutches of the Teutonic Knights and is subjected to bestial treatment. Sometime after his release, his erstwhile tormentors become his prisoners. Instead of avenging himself by retaliating in kind, Jurand chooses to pardon them. In this way, Sienkiewicz is underscoring his belief that the

Polish gentry had more affinity with the ideals of Christianity than did the monks belonging to the Order of the Teutonic Knights. The degree of haughtiness, cruelty, and lust for power attributed to the Teutonic Knights by Sienkiewicz might once have appeared somewhat excessive, but the traumatic events that occurred in Poland and in much of Eastern Europe in the course of World War II have done much to enhance the plausibility of his portrayal.

The alliance between the Kingdom of Poland and the Grand Duchy of Lithuania that made the victory at the Battle of Grunwald possible was to continue over the next two centuries, despite many periods of acute political tension. In 1569, moreover, the two countries agreed to a charter, known as the Union of Lublin, that united them in a single political entity called the Polish Commonwealth. The Commonwealth was a multinational state whose territories extended from the Baltic Sea in the north to the Black Sea in the south. In addition to incorporating the Poles and the Lithuanians within its borders, the Commonwealth comprised large numbers of Byelorussians, Ukrainians, Cossacks, and Tatars. The viability of such an oddly constituted state was put to the test in the seventeenth century through a series of domestic insurrections and foreign invasions, and it is these trials that furnish the historical background for the works that form Sienkiewicz's trilogy.

The central event in each of these three novels involves the heroic defense of a Polish city that is under siege by the enemy. The historical incidents depicted in the trilogy span a period of approximately twenty-five years. Each novel covers a different war and takes place in a different part of the Commonwealth. The first volume, *With Fire and Sword*, deals with the Cossack rebellion in the Ukraine between the years 1647 and 1649. The second volume, *The Deluge*, tells the story of the Swedish attempt to add Poland to the personal domain of the Swedish king, Charles Gustavus, in the mid-1660's. The third volume, *Pan Michael*, although beginning with the year 1669, focuses on the struggles with the Turks and the Tatars during the years 1672 and 1673. Many of the characters that are introduced in *With Fire and Sword* reappear in the successive novels of the trilogy. Some personages that make their first appearance in *The Deluge* are, likewise, carried over into the plot of

Pan Michael. A major character in one novel may be demoted to playing a minor role in another, and the reverse may also occur. The fictive and the historical figures in the trilogy, it should be noted, interact far more than is the case in *The Knights of the Cross*.

WITH FIRE AND SWORD

The historical events that constitute the narrative framework of Sienkiewicz's *With Fire and Sword* occurred in the course of the Polish-Cossack wars that were waged on the steppes of the Ukraine. Under the inspired leadership of Bohdan Chmielnicki, the Cossacks initially scored a number of impressive victories over Polish forces. The long-suffering Ukrainian peasants, sensing an opportunity to throw off the yoke of foreign oppression, joined the Cossacks and began a savage massacre of Polish landowners and Catholic clergy. Jews also perished by the tens of thousands, because they usually served as administrators and overseers on the Polish estates.

Retribution on the part of Poland came in the person of a powerful prince named Jarema Wiśniowiecki, whose army checked the advances of the Cossacks and restored Polish authority over large sections of the Ukraine. Both Chmielnicki and Prince Jarema play major roles in the plot of *With Fire and Sword*. As portrayed in the novel, the Polish commander is a man of noble character whose courage and patriotism are largely responsible for his nation's triumph over the Cossacks and their Tatar auxiliaries. Sienkiewicz does, however, permit this hero's virtue to be tested. As a result of his military successes in the Ukraine, Prince Jarema soon found himself in a position to make the entire region subservient to his personal rule and was sorely tempted to sacrifice his country's interests for the sake of his own private ambitions. Midway through the novel, Prince Jarema engages in a debate with his conscience that takes the form of a lengthy monologue, which he delivers while kneeling beneath a crucifix during a nocturnal prayer vigil. As dawn breaks, he resolves to remain loyal to the Commonwealth, even though he disapproves of many of its policies pertaining to the suppression of the insurrection in the Ukraine.

Despite the prominence of the historical figures in *With Fire and Sword*, they do not overshadow the fictive characters and their private adventures. The most memorable fictive personality in the novel is an old warrior named Zagloba, whose droll appearance and ribald speech have led critics to categorize him as the Polish Falstaff. Zagloba's antics provide much welcome comic relief in a novel filled with grim scenes. The chief nonfactual narrative involves a love triangle. Jan Skrzetuski, an adjutant of Prince Jarema, falls in love with an orphaned princess named Helena. The two soon agree to marry, but a Cossack officer named Bogun abducts Helena in the hope of persuading her to become his own bride. She is eventually rescued by Jan's loyal retainer Jendzian. Before the two lovers can be reunited, however, the city of Zbaraż is besieged by thousands of Cossacks and Tatars. Prince Jarema is in charge of the small Polish garrison within the city and finally decides to let Jan make an attempt to slip through enemy lines in order to summon aid from the Polish king, Jan Kazimierz. The royal army is duly dispatched, and the heroic defenders of Zbaraż are at last relieved after having withstood the determined attacks of Chmielnicki's troops for more than six weeks.

The decisive victory over the Cossacks did not occur until two years later, at the Battle of Beresteczko (1651), and Sienkiewicz skips over the intervening period to give his readers an account of this crucial confrontation in the final chapter of the novel. Bogun is among the Cossack prisoners who are taken at Beresteczko, and Prince Jarema turns him over to Jan for punishment. Jan, who married Helena after the siege of Zbaraż had been lifted, chooses to be magnanimous in victory and pardons the Cossack officer.

THE DELUGE

The next two novels in the trilogy have a narrative structure similar to that employed in *With Fire and Sword*. Both feature fictive love triangles in which the heroine is first abducted and then rescued. The chief historical figure in *The Deluge* is a Polish hetman named Stefan Czarniecki, whose tireless energy and soldierly talent contributed greatly to the ultimate expulsion of the Swedish invaders from the territory of the Commonwealth. He did not, however, participate in the key military engagement of the Swedish-Polish conflict: namely, the defense of the fortified Pauline monastery of Jasna Góra (Bright Hill). Jasna Góra, which is located within the city of Czestochowa, was founded in 1382.

Two years later, it came into possession of an icon depicting the Virgin Mary and the infant Jesus that is reputed to have been painted by Saint Luke the Evangelist. (This work is now referred to as the Black Madonna because of the dark hue that distinguishes the face and hands of each subject.) When the Polish garrison within the monastery put up a heroic defense and finally forced the Swedes to lift the siege and depart, the credit for this signal victory was assigned to the miraculous powers of the icon itself. Believing themselves to be under the special protection of the Virgin Mary, the Polish people took heart and rallied to the nation's cause.

PAN MICHAEL

In contrast, the siege of Kamieniec that is depicted in the closing chapters of *Pan Michael* ends in a defeat for the Polish defenders and a triumph for the Turkish invaders. The eponymous hero of the novel is a fictive personage named Pan Michael Wołodyjowski. (The designation "Pan" is a polite form of address in Polish that is analogous to the use of "Mister" and "Sir" in English.) Rather than surrender to the Turks, he chooses to perish in the ruins of the city when it is finally overrun. The novel, nevertheless, ends on a positive note, because among those who attend the ceremony accompanying Pan Michael's interment in a nearby monastery church is the hetman Jan Sobieski, the future king of Poland who was destined to lead a contingent of twenty thousand Polish soldiers to fight against the Turkish forces that were besieging the city of Vienna in the summer of 1683. Sienkiewicz himself was later to write a novel with Jan Sobieski as its protagonist, *On the Field of Glory*. This novel proved to be a great disappointment to almost everyone, for Sienkiewicz inexplicably failed to depict the victory at Vienna and chose to restrict himself to relating events that occurred during the winter of 1682-1683.

QUO VADIS

Quo Vadis, like the other historical novels by Sienkiewicz, has a cast of fictive and historical personages. This time, however, the non-Polish reader is on familiar ground with respect to the historical background, because the work is set in ancient Rome circa 64 C.E. Among the well-known figures are the Apostles Peter and Paul as well as Nero and Petronius. Petronius was the author of the Satyricon (first century C.E.) and enjoyed the reputation of being the arbiter of elegance throughout Rome. He was also a great favorite of the Emperor Nero, who made him the director of entertainment at his court. It is his fictive nephew, Vinicius, who falls in love with a foreign princess named Lygia. (Her name indicates that she belongs to the tribe known as the Lygians, who inhabited the heartland of Poland in ancient times.) Lygia, it soon becomes known, is a member of the clandestine Christian community in Rome. Vinicius makes several attempts to obtain Lygia's sexual favors by force, but he is foiled each time by Christians who take it upon themselves to watch out for Lygia's welfare. As he gets to know the Christians and their doctrines better, Vinicius finds himself gradually transformed into an adherent of the teachings of Jesus. Now that they share a common faith, Lygia agrees to marry Vinicius. The couple's plans, however, are interrupted by the persecution of Christians that began in the aftermath of the fire that destroyed Rome.

Nero decides to put Rome to the torch in the hope that this personal experience with catastrophe will enable him to compose an immortal epic poem celebrating the city's destruction. In order to divert suspicion from himself, he subsequently accuses the Christians of having set the fires and has them hunted down all over Rome. Petronius does his best to dissuade the emperor, but to no avail. Both Saint Peter and Saint Paul are to become martyrs on the same day. At first, Saint Peter attempts to escape the persecutions that are decimating his followers by fleeing from Rome along the Appian Way. Before long, he sees a radiant figure coming toward him whom he recognizes as Jesus and asks, "Quo vadis, Domine?" ("Where are you going, Master?"). Jesus replies, "If you desert my people, I am going to Rome to be crucified a second time." Thoroughly ashamed of his moral weakness, Saint Peter turns about and retraces his steps. Back in Rome, he himself is crucified. Lygia, for her part, narrowly escapes martyrdom. After being arrested and imprisoned, she is stripped of her clothing and tied to the back of a huge bull that is released into the arena. Her faithful servant, a giant named Ursus, manages to break the bull's neck with his bare hands. The spectators are so overwhelmed by the feat that they insist on freedom for both Lygia and Ursus. Lygia then joins Vinicius in an escape to Sicily. Having lost the favor of Nero for his defense of the Christians, Petronius is obliged to commit suicide at the request of Nero—an act that he performs with great style at a banquet held in his home. Sienkiewicz concludes the novel with a brief epilogue in which Nero's own suicide is depicted in a manner that underscores the cowardly nature of the emperor.

All of Sienkiewicz's historical novels are primarily works in which action is stressed at the expense of psychological development of character. The fact that each of them was first serialized in a periodical greatly influenced the structure of the narrative, for Sienkiewicz felt obliged to conclude every installment with an episode that kept the reader in suspense. The historical accuracy of these works has been the subject of considerable debate. Some historians defend their accuracy; others find fault with it. No one, however, has ever accused Sienkiewicz of failing to research his topic thoroughly or of neglecting to include sufficient data within the novels themselves. More important is the fact that Sienkiewicz possessed the narrative skills and the stylistic gifts needed to create works that quicken the spirit and comfort the heart.

Victor Anthony Rudowski

OTHER MAJOR WORKS

SHORT FICTION: "Szkice w glem," 1877 ("Charcoal Sketches," 1897); *Yanko the Musician, and Other Stories*, 1893 (includes "Yanko the Musician" and "The Lighthouse Keeper of Aspinwall"); *Lillian Morris, and Other Stories*, 1894; *Hania*, 1897 (includes "Tartar Captivity" and "Charcoal Sketches"); *For Daily Bread, and Other Stories*, 1898; *Let Us Follow Him, and Other Stories*, 1898; *Sielanka: A Forest Picture, and Other Stories*, 1898; *Life and Death, and Other Stories*, 1904; *Tales*, 1931; *Western Septet: Seven Stories of the American West*, 1973; *The Little Trilogy*, 1995.

NONFICTION: *Listy z podróży do Ameryki*, 1876-1878 (serial), 1896 (book; *Portrait of America: Letters*, 1959); *Listy z Afryki*, 1891.

CHILDREN'S LITERATURE: *W pustyni i w puszczy*, 1910 (serial), 1912 (book; *In Desert and Wilderness*, 1912).

BIBLIOGRAPHY

Coleman, Arthur Prudden, and Marion Moore Coleman. *Wanderers Twain: Modjeska and Sienkiewicz—*

A View from California. Cheshire, Conn.: Cherry Hill Books, 1964. Describes the trip that Sienkiewicz and Helena Modjeska made to Anaheim, California, in 1876. The chapters on Sienkiewicz's early years in Poland are most informative for students of his fiction.

Giergielewicz, Mieczyslaw. *Henryk Sienkiewicz*. 1968. Reprint. New York: Hippocrene Books, 1991. Good introductory volume begins with a section on historical background, as Sienkiewicz's fiction is tied so closely to the fate of Poland and of Central Europe in the eighteenth and nineteenth centuries. Also provides biographical material, particularly on his experience as a journalist, and discusses his stories as well as his epic novels. Includes chronology, notes, and annotated bibliography.

Krżyanowski, Jerzy, ed. *The Trilogy Companion: A Reader's Guide to the Trilogy of Henryk Sienkiewicz*. New York: Hippocrene Books, 1991. Several essays in this collection, including some by the editor, provide information about the settings, historical background, and translations of *With Fire and Sword*, *The Deluge*, and *Pan Michael*. Includes glossaries of the principal characters, place-names, and linguistic and historic terms used in the trilogy.

Lednicki, Waclaw. *Henryk Sienkiewicz: A Retrospective Synthesis*. The Hague: Mouton, 1960. Lednicki met the novelist on several occasions and uses his personal experience to provide insightful and well-balanced comments on Sienkiewicz's significance.

Modjeska, Helena. *Memories and Impressions: An Autobiography*. New York: Macmillan, 1910. Modjeska, an actor who knew Sienkiewicz in Warsaw and accompanied him to Anaheim, California, provides insight into his character and literary sensibility.

Phelps, William Lyon. *Essays on Modern Novelists*. New York: Macmillan, 1910. Although brief, Phelps's essay on Sienkiewicz is an excellent place to begin for an assessment of the novelist's place in world literature.

Scodel, Ruth, and Anja Bettenworth. *Whither "Quo Vadis": Sienkwiecz's Novel in Film and Television*. Malden, Mass.: Wiley-Blackwell, 2009. Analyzes four films and a television version of *Quo Vadis*, describing how these adaptations modified the novel and its sources. Discusses the depiction of gender and ethnicity, politics, the Roman people, and religion in the adaptations, explaining how these portrayals reflected the historical and ideological concerns of their own times.

LESLIE MARMON SILKO

Born: Albuquerque, New Mexico; March 5, 1948
Also known as: Leslie Marmon

PRINCIPAL LONG FICTION

Ceremony, 1977
Almanac of the Dead, 1991
Gardens in the Dunes, 1999

OTHER LITERARY FORMS

Leslie Marmon Silko's first published book is a collection of poems called *Laguna Woman: Poems* (1974). Her earliest published works were short stories, published in magazines, most of which were later included in *Storyteller* (1981). This book defies genre classification by including short fiction, poetry, retellings of traditional stories, and family photographs, all linked by passages of commentary and memoir. Her interest in images interacting with words led Silko to produce a film in 1980 with Dennis Carr titled *Estoyehmuut and the Gunnadeyah* (Arrowboy and the Destroyers). In shooting the film in Laguna, New Mexico, using pueblo residents and elders instead of professional actors, Silko documented a time and place that no longer exist.

Silko's nonfiction works include *The Delicacy and Strength of Lace: Letters Between Leslie Marmon Silko and James Wright* (1986; edited by Ann Wright), and

Yellow Woman and a Beauty of the Spirit: Essays on Native American Life Today (1996), a collection of essays. In *Sacred Water: Narratives and Pictures* (1993), she self-published her essay on water interwoven with her Polaroid photographs. The first edition was hand sewn and glued by Silko; a subsequent edition was conventionally bound.

ACHIEVEMENTS

The publication of Leslie Marmon Silko's first novel, *Ceremony*, along with N. Scott Momaday's winning of the 1969 Pulitzer Prize for *House Made of Dawn*, marked the beginning of a surge in publishing by Native American authors—the Native American renaissance of the late 1960's and early 1970's. Yet just as her works defy genre classification, Silko transcends the category of Native American writer. Her earlier works draw heavily on her own experiences and the traditional stories of Laguna Pueblo; later works move beyond the pueblo while maintaining a strong connection with the Southwest and with traditional and autobiographical materials. Her first two novels, *Ceremony* and *Almanac of the Dead*, are experimental in form, testing the limits of the novel as a genre and format. Indeed, Silko once said that she loves working in the novel form because its flexibility imposes so few limitations on the writer. Her third novel, *Gardens in the Dunes*, adheres more closely to conventional novel form, but like the previous two, it is highly political, reflecting Silko's activism.

Silko's books, particularly *Ceremony* and *Storyteller*, are widely taught in colleges and universities; her short fiction and poetry are widely anthologized. Her works have been translated into Italian and German and are popular internationally, both in translation and in the original English.

Silko's works in fiction, nonfiction, and poetry earned her a National Endowment for the Arts Discover Grant (1971), *The Chicago Review* Poetry Award (1974), the Pushcart Prize for Poetry (1977), a MacArthur Prize Fellowship (1981), the *Boston Globe* prize for nonfiction (1986), a New Mexico Endowment for the Humanities "Living Cultural Treasure" Award (1988), and a Lila Wallace-Reader's Digest Fund Writers Award (1991). Her story "Lullaby" was selected as one of twenty best short stories of 1975.

BIOGRAPHY

Leslie Marmon Silko was born to Leland (Lee) Howard Marmon and Mary Virginia Leslie in 1948. Her extended mixed-heritage family (Laguna, Mexican, white) had a rich history of tribal leadership and a rich tradition of storytelling. Growing up at Laguna Pueblo, Silko rode horses, hunted, and was free to explore the land of her ancestors, land that was inextricably tied to the traditional stories told by her aunts and grandmother.

In 1964, Silko entered the University of New Mexico. In 1966, she married Richard Chapman and gave birth to Robert William Chapman. During her sophomore year, she took a creative writing class. Despite the success of a short story written for that class, "The Man to Send Rainclouds," which was published first in *New Mexico Quarterly* and then in Kenneth Rosen's anthology of Native American writing as the title piece, Silko did not yet see herself primarily as a writer. After receiving her bachelor of arts degree in 1969, she entered the University of New Mexico law school in the American Indian Law Fellowship program. During the same year, she separated from and eventually divorced Chapman.

In 1971, Silko left law school. Convinced that the American justice system was inherently unjust, and believing that her own role was to call attention to this injustice by telling stories, she entered graduate school in English at New Mexico. She soon left to teach at Navajo Community College. During the same year, she married John Silko (whom she would also later divorce) and gave birth to her second child, Cazimir Silko.

Leaving the Southwest for the first time, Silko moved with her husband and children to Ketchikan, Alaska, in 1973. The impact of the Alaskan landscape and climate can be seen in her short story "Storyteller," written during this time, and it resurfaces in *Almanac of the Dead*. She also began writing *Ceremony* while in Alaska, recreating her beloved southwestern landscape.

Silko returned to Laguna for a short time before moving to Tucson in 1978, where she taught at the University of Arizona. She eventually settled on a ranch outside Tucson, enjoying the physical labor of ranch life. In 1981, the year in which *Storyteller* was published, Silko was awarded the MacArthur Prize Fellowship. Sometimes called the genius award, the MacArthur Prize provided five years of financial support, allowing her, for the first time, to devote all of her efforts to writing. While writing *Almanac of the Dead*, she became incensed about Arizona politics, leading her to paint a mural of a snake with political graffiti on the outside wall of her Stone Avenue office. Though later owners painted over the mural, it was well received by the people of the neighborhood and was important both in helping Silko (who describes herself as a "frustrated painter") to overcome writer's block and to develop further her technique of combining images with words. After the publication of *Almanac of the Dead* in 1991, Silko's desire for independence from the publishing world and her experiments with photography (in part inspired by her father, a professional photographer) led her to self-publish *Sacred Water: Narratives and Pictures*.

ANALYSIS

Leslie Marmon Silko once stated that she tries to write a very different book every time. Indeed, her novels are as different from one another as they are from her books in other genres. Despite such diversity, however, Silko's novels share certain common traits. All draw heavily on her personal experiences, but they are not conventionally autobiographical. Although only *Ceremony* deals exclusively with Native American themes and characters, Native American themes and characters are central in the other novels as well.

Silko was so attuned to the political situation in northern Mexico that, in *Almanac of the Dead*, published two years before the Zapatista uprising in Chiapas, her description of an uprising in northern Mexico seems prophetic. Silko's work makes use of her eclectic reading on topics as diverse as the Gnostic gospels and orchid collecting.

Silko uses very little dialogue, yet her characters are richly drawn through the use of an omniscient narrator who reveals their inner thoughts and reactions. Her descriptions are vivid and detailed. Though predominantly serious, all of Silko's novels display her wry, ironic sense of humor. An important recurring theme in all of Silko's novels is the conflict between the "destroyers," those whose disregard for the land leads them to exploit it and its people for profit, and those who are in touch with and respect the land. Although those in touch with the land are usually the indigenous people who have not separated themselves from nature, indigenous people can be destroyers, and whites can be in touch with the land.

CEREMONY

In *Ceremony*, Tayo, a young veteran of mixed Laguna and white ancestry, returns from World War II with what would now be called post-traumatic stress disorder. When the U.S. Veterans Administration (V.A.) hospital sends him home to the pueblo uncured, his family asks the tribal healer, old Ku'oosh, to perform the traditional ceremony for reincorporating warriors into the community. The ceremony is only partially successful; Tayo is still deeply disturbed, blaming himself for his cousin and friend Rocky's death and turning to alcohol along with a group of friends who are also veterans. After a fight with his friend Emo, Tayo is sent back to the V.A. hospital, but his treatment is no more successful than it was the first time.

Betonie, a Navajo medicine man who uses unconventional methods, is more successful. He conducts a Navajo healing ceremony for Tayo that sets him on the

Leslie Marmon Silko. (Courtesy, University Press of Mississippi)

road to recovery. When Tayo leaves, Betonie says that to complete the ceremony Tayo must recover the spotted cattle that Tayo and his Uncle Josiah had planned to raise but that had presumably wandered off in Tayo's absence after Josiah died. Tayo discovers that the cattle were stolen by white ranchers and realizes that he had believed the lie that only Indians and Mexicans stole because whites did not need to steal. With the help of Ts'eh, a mysterious woman who turns out to be the spirit of the sacred mountain, Tayo takes the cattle home.

Meanwhile, Emo has become one of the destroyers, a participant in witchery, and he convinces the rest of the group to cooperate in his plan to kill Tayo. Warned by Ts'eh, Tayo is able to resist the witchery. He returns home and tells his story to the elders in the kiva, who recognize Ts'eh as the spirit who brings rain and healing to their drought-stricken land. Tayo's separation from his community, in part caused by the war but also caused by his rejection as an illegitimate "half-breed," was symptomatic of a larger rift in the community. His healing demonstrates that things must change, that the new must be incorporated into the old, and that the "half-breed" can act as a mediator between the old traditions and the new world. Much of *Ceremony* is told in flashbacks. Traditional Laguna stories are woven throughout, set off from the text. The language is lyrical, and the message is of healing and conciliation.

Almanac of the Dead

When Silko read from this novel at the time of its publication, she announced, "This book attempts to crush linear time." It succeeds by repeatedly shifting time frames. Silko interweaves an enormous cast of characters involved in multiple subplots. They tell the story, in an indeterminate time in the not-too-distant future, of a spontaneous uprising across the Americas of dispossessed indigenous peoples who move throughout the novel toward an apocalyptic convergence on Tucson.

Lecha and Zeta are twins, mixed-blood Yaquis, who have been given pieces of an old Mayan book (the almanac of the title). Unlike the Mayan codices, this book has stayed in the hands of the people. As they work to transcribe the pieces, they discover that the Mayans foretold the coming of the white European invaders—and foretold their demise as well. Seese, a young white woman

whose baby has been kidnapped, consults Lecha, who is a psychic, and stays to work for her. Sterling, an old man who is exiled for revealing tribal secrets, also comes to work at the twins' ranch.

Other characters include Allegria, a mercenary architect, and her husband, Menardo, who live near Mexico City; the Tucson branch of the Blue family, mafiosi who dominate the Tucson real estate market; the Indian twin brothers Tacho and Wacah, who embody the mysterious power of twins and lead the people north toward Tucson; and Marxist Mexican revolutionaries Angelita (La Escapia) and El Feo. Their stories intertwine as they converge on Tucson, where the Barefoot Hopi warns that the familiar way of life on earth will end unless the destroyers change their ways and respect the earth. "Ecowarriors" to the north threaten a suicide bombing of a dam. The novel ends as all are poised on the brink of revolution.

Gardens in the Dunes

In an unpublished interview, Silko described her third novel as "full of flowers and light." Set in the time immediately following the stock market crash of 1893, *Gardens in the Dunes* tells the story of Indigo and Sister Salt. The young sisters are the last of the Sand Lizards, a fictional tribe based loosely on the Colorado River tribes that were wiped out around the beginning of the twentieth century. After a Ghost Dance they are attending is raided by the police, the girls are separated from their mother as they flee. Later, their grandmother dies and Indigo is captured by the police. She is sent to boarding school in Riverside.

There Indigo is befriended by Hattie and Edward, a wealthy couple who live near the school. Before marrying Edward, Hattie attended Harvard University until her unconventional thesis proposal on the Gnostic gospels was rejected. Edward is a professional plant collector who sells rare specimens to wealthy buyers. They take Indigo along on their European trip during the school's summer break. Indigo sees the Jesus of the European churches as another manifestation of Wovoka, the prophet of the Ghost Dance. Edward's scheme to steal citron cuttings fails; Hattie, disgusted by his greed, divorces him and vows to help Indigo find her family.

Meanwhile, Sister Salt is befriended by Big Candy, who fathers her baby, the "little black grandfather."

When Big Candy's preoccupation with wealth causes him to neglect Sister Salt and the baby, she and the Chemehuevi twins leave to farm land that the twins acquired from an aunt. The sisters are reunited, returning to the old gardens. Indigo plants the seeds and bulbs she collected on her journey, mixing the impractical but beautiful flowers with the traditional food crops. As in earlier works, Silko emphasizes the need to live in harmony with the land, the dangers of capitalism, and the need to use the new along with the old.

Robin Payne Cohen

OTHER MAJOR WORKS

SHORT FICTION: *Yellow Woman*, 1993.

PLAY: *Lullaby*, pr. 1976 (with Frank Chin).

POETRY: *Laguna Woman: Poems*, 1974.

NONFICTION: *The Delicacy and Strength of Lace: Letters Between Leslie Marmon Silko and James Wright*, 1986; *Sacred Water: Narratives and Pictures*, 1993; *Yellow Woman and a Beauty of the Spirit: Essays on Native American Life Today*, 1996; *Conversations with Leslie Marmon Silko*, 2000 (Ellen L. Arnold, editor).

MISCELLANEOUS: *Storyteller*, 1981 (includes poetry and prose).

BIBLIOGRAPHY

Allen, Paula Gunn. "The Feminine Landscape of Leslie Marmon Silko's *Ceremony*." In *Studies in American Indian Literature: Critical Essays and Course Design*. New York: Modern Language Association of America, 1983. Interprets Silko's *Ceremony* from a feminist perspective and sees it as divided into two kinds of characters: earth spirits in harmony with the earth and spirit destroyers. Allen maintains that this is a novel of feminine life forces and the mechanistic death force of witchery; the women are equitable with the land, the life force, a thesis that is central to Native American culture. Allen analyzes the main characters and the causes for Tayo's illness from a Jungian perspective; she discusses Silko's poetry and the storyteller tradition that underpins her fiction. Includes a brief and helpful bibliography of Silko's work and of criticism about her fiction.

Barnett, Louise K., and James L. Thorson, eds. *Leslie Marmon Silko: A Collection of Critical Essays*. Albuquerque: University of New Mexico Press, 1999. These essays cover the entire range of Silko's work through *Almanac of the Dead*, offering biographical information on Silko as well as an extensive bibliography of primary and secondary sources complete with a helpful bibliographical essay.

Chavkin, Allan, ed. *Leslie Marmon Silko's "Ceremony": A Casebook*. New York: Oxford University Press, 2002. Collection of essays offers readings of Silko's novel from a variety of theoretical perspectives and provides background information on Native American culture. Includes an interview with Silko.

Fitz, Brewster E. *Silko: Writing Storyteller and Medicine Woman*. Norman: University of Oklahoma Press, 2004. Fitz analyzes *Almanac of the Dead* and several of Silko's short stories, focusing on the relationship between the written word and oral storytelling tradition of Silko's family and Laguna culture.

Krupat, Arnold. "The Dialogic of Silko's *Storyteller*." In *Narrative Chance: Postmodern Discourse on Native American Indian Literature*, edited by Gerald Vizenor. Albuquerque: University of New Mexico Press, 1989. Discusses *Storyteller* from the point of view of the work of literary theorist Mikhail Bakhtin and Native American autobiography.

Larson, Charles R. *American Indian Fiction*. Albuquerque: University of New Mexico Press, 1978. Views Silko as an author who is very aware of her cultural and ethnic identity and as a writer of "authentic" Native American novels. Provides an in-depth analysis of *Ceremony*, summarizes the plot, and discusses the experimental structure of the novel. Relates the story in *Ceremony* to the Grandmother Spider motif and myth. Discusses the poems included in *Ceremony*, asserting that they act as a second persona in the novel, as a medicine man.

Nelson, Robert M. *Leslie Marmon Silko's "Ceremony": The Recovery of Tradition*. New York: Peter Lang, 2008. Nelson focuses on the Navajo and other Native American texts that form the backbone of Silko's novel, describing how she adapts and relates these texts to her narrative.

Owens, Louis. "The Very Essence of Our Lives: Leslie Silko's Webs of Identity." In *Other Destinies: Un-*

derstanding the American Indian Novel. Norman: University of Oklahoma Press, 1992. Owens examines Native American novels written between 1854 and the 1990's, focusing on the common themes of self-discovery and cultural recovery. He analyzes *Ceremony* as a search for identity through memory and returning home.

Salyer, Gregory. *Leslie Marmon Silko*. New York: Twayne, 1997. A critical study of Silko's work, describing how her fiction has been influenced by her Laguna background and by Native American stories. Includes a bibliography and an index.

Teuton, Sean Kicummah. "Learning to Feel: Tribal Experience in Leslie Marmon Silko's *Ceremony*." In *Red Land, Red Power: Grounding Knowledge in the* *American Indian Novel*. Durham, N.C.: Duke University Press, 2008. Teuton's analysis of *Ceremony* is included in his study of Native American literature in the late 1960's and 1970's. Examines how these books used historical memory and oral tradition to create a more "enabling knowledge" of the lives and possibilities of American Indians.

Wiget, Andrew. *Native American Literature*. Boston: Twayne, 1985. Wiget offers an analytical overview of *Ceremony* and compares the novel to N. Scott Momaday's *House Made of Dawn*. He maintains that *Ceremony* explores the death of, or threats to, traditional Native American values and ways and sets the human struggle against mythic Native American legends. Includes a brief but useful bibliography.

FRANS EEMIL SILLANPÄÄ

Born: Hämeenkyrö, Finland, Russian Empire (now in Finland); September 16, 1888

Died: Helsinki, Finland; June 3, 1964

PRINCIPAL LONG FICTION

Elämä ja aurinko, 1916

Hurskas kurjuus, 1919 (*Meek Heritage*, 1938)

Nuorena nukkunut, 1931 (*The Maid Silja*, 1933; also known as *Fallen Asleep While Young*, 1939)

Miehen tie, 1932

Ihmiset suviyössä, 1934 (*People in the Summer Night*, 1966)

Elokuu, 1941

Ihmiselon ihanuus ja kurjuus, 1945

OTHER LITERARY FORMS

In addition to his novels, Frans Eemil Sillanpää (SIHL-ahn-pah) published several volumes of short stories dealing with the topics that preoccupied him throughout his career. These topics include the Finnish Civil War of 1918 and the role of humans as integral parts of nature. He also wrote a number of causeries, which might best be characterized as autobiographical self-examinations. The collections from the 1920's are considered among the finest in twentieth century Finnish literature, while the short stories from the following decades are less significant. In 1953, Sillanpää produced a series of radio programs devoted to his memoirs, which were expanded and published in three volumes later in the 1950's, forming the last of his published works.

ACHIEVEMENTS

Frans Eemil Sillanpää belongs primarily to the great epic tradition in Finnish literature that began with Aleksis Kivi (1834-1872), combining a realistic depiction of rural life with a mystical awareness of nature. While Sillanpää's fiction reflects the influence of the nineteenth century realistic novel, largely unaffected by the currents of modernism, his blend of lyricism with an almost naturalistic emphasis on the power of instinct (prompting comparisons with the British novelist D. H. Lawrence) introduced a new and distinctive voice in Finnish literature. Several of Sillanpää's novels became international best sellers, and in 1939 he became the first Finnish writer to receive the Nobel Prize in Literature.

BIOGRAPHY

The son of a crofter and farmhand, Frans Eemil Sillanpää spent only a few years in grade school before he entered the *Gymnasium* (college-preparatory secondary school) of Tampere, from which he graduated in 1908. During his last years at the *Gymnasium*, while supporting himself through private tutoring, he read at the public library the works of Knut Hamsun, Selma Lagerlöf, and the great Russian writers Leo Tolstoy and Fyodor Dostoevski. At the University of Helsinki, Sillanpää studied natural sciences, particularly biology, for four years, and he was influenced by the philosophical theories of Ernst Haeckel and Friedrich Wilhelm Ostwald. Financial problems and failing health, however, forced him to give up his studies and return to his family home. During these years, August Strindberg and Maurice Maeterlinck became his favorite writers; later, Swedish neo-Romanticist Erik Axel Karlfeldt had the greatest artistic influence on him.

During the summer of 1914, Sillanpää visited the Baltic Exhibition in the Swedish city of Malmö, and from there he went to Copenhagen, Denmark. From both cities he sent travel letters home to the Finnish newspaper *Uusi Suometar*, together with some short stories written while he had attended the *Gymnasium* of Tampere, his first published works. After marrying Sigrid Maria Salomäki in 1916, Sillanpää moved to Helsinki. Gradually he came to be regarded as the grand old man of Finnish literature, but his life was disrupted by the death of his wife in 1939. A short and unhappy second marriage was one of the causes of his mental collapse in 1940, which forced him to spend three years in a hospital. In 1939, Sillanpää was awarded the Nobel Prize in Literature.

ANALYSIS

Frans Eemil Sillanpää's writings are rooted in his home region, the area around Tampere. Its people—crofters and farmhands—its animals, its changing seasons, and its natural surroundings constitute his fictional world. Only seldom did Sillanpää depart from this milieu to depict city life and the higher social classes, and then frequently with satire. His characters are for the most part passive beings governed by their instincts who, without intellectual insight, yield to blind fate.

Frans Eemil Sillanpää. (© The Nobel Foundation)

These characters are analyzed either undramatically and with cool objectivity or with concern and compassion, framed by descriptions of nature showing superb poetic inspiration.

Together with this duality in narrative attitude, readers find, on the stylistic level, a fluctuation between harsh, realistic expression and suggestive, lyric sequences of the highest sophistication, almost imperceptibly following the rhythms of nature. Sillanpää did not regard life from a psychological or metaphysical standpoint; rather, he treated it as a totality that includes all living things—humans, animals, and nature. This biological monism elevates his humble and tragic characters above their sufferings, breaks the pattern of decay and catastrophe, and lends them a heroic stature either through resignation or through a realization of their affinity with an ever-revitalizing nature.

ELÄMÄ JA AURINKO

Sillanpää's first novel, *Elämä ja aurinko* (life and the sun), turned out to be very different from all previous Finnish fiction. Animated nature was described with a hitherto unseen precision, counterbalanced by evocative sensitivity, together reflecting the undercurrents of the human mind: The internal and the external, the self and surrounding nature, merged in a unique and refined pattern. Into the magic world of a few summer months—and of rather secondary importance—is placed a love story describing the short-lived affairs of a peasant student who has returned to his village, with both a young girl of his own social background and, at the same time, a mature, upperclass woman.

MEEK HERITAGE

In Sillanpää's next novel, *Meek Heritage*, the narrative structure has been tightened and the characters have been given firm and precise contours. *Meek Heritage* was written immediately after the Finnish Civil War and reflects the author's discouraging experiences with both the communist and the anticommunist factions. It concentrates entirely on the destiny of the main character, containing few lyric descriptions of nature or philosophical reflections.

The novel is mainly about the life of Juha Toivola before the war. It tells of his childhood during the famine of the 1860's as a penniless orphan and the abuses to which he is subjected by relatives and other people for whom he works. He marries almost unthinkingly, leases a small piece of land, drifts because of his poverty into the Socialist movement, joins the Red Guard, and is shot by mistake at the end of the war. The book, however, is no novel of indignation and social accusation. Everything goes wrong for Juha because he is unable to take care of himself. He never commits any dishonest act; he simply falls prey to the whims of fate in a world in which dreariness and evil can be found everywhere. He remains, in spite of his spinelessness and filthiness, a pitiful yet valuable representative of humanity, worthy of protection.

Meek Heritage is considered the classic description of the Finnish Civil War and one of the literary catalysts in the process of national reconciliation. Twelve years went by—a period in which Sillanpää established his profile as a short-story writer—before he published his second masterpiece, *The Maid Silja*, his longest and most widely read novel.

THE MAID SILJA

In *The Maid Silja*, the narrative, too, is disrupted by exquisite descriptions of the Finnish summer. Sillanpää tells of the extinction of an old peasant family, the last years in the lives of an old man and his daughter. Like Juha in *Meek Heritage*, they, too, are unable to protect themselves, but unlike him, they are intellectually and emotionally mature. Somewhat idealized—and not without sentimentality—is the portrait of the girl Silja, who is placed in an everyday reality in which she does not belong and who finds escape from this reality mainly in her romantic fantasies. Her first and only erotic experience, with a student, becomes both the climax and the turning point in her life. He abandons her, her latent tuberculosis surfaces, and after hardship and suffering, she dies the following spring. The dramatic events are, however, presented not as tragic but rather as the entry into blissful peace. The story is enveloped in a chiaroscuro atmosphere, a manifestation of the inner strength of humankind when facing death—the author's demonstration of the spirit's victory over matter.

MIEHEN TIE

Greater epic breadth distinguishes the novel *Miehen tie* (the way of man), which, in contrast to Sillanpää's previous works, focuses on determined and hardworking human beings. The weak farmer, Paavo, must make many mistakes, including an unsuccessful marriage, before he is united with the strong-willed Alma, his youthful love and a direct contrast to the vulnerable Silja. Alma, who defies all conventional moral concepts, is from the outset aware that she and Paavo, by nature, are destined for each other—the influence of Lawrence has been suggested—and here we find Sillanpää's moral message: The peasant family is able to survive because of its acceptance of this fate. The otherwise somewhat robust character delineation and narrow realism of this novel alternates with poetic passages in which humans and nature fuse.

PEOPLE IN THE SUMMER NIGHT

In *People in the Summer Night*, the description and the mystique of nature again dominate. The action takes place during a few days and nights of summer and offers a cross section of human destinies from birth to death, either peaceful or violent. Here, Sillanpää allows a number of separate events and characters to appear as apparently insignificant and transitional elements of what proves to be an invisible and timeless totality.

ELOKUU *and* IHMISELON IHANUUS JA KURJUUS

In part as a result of his severe illness, Sillanpää's bright and optimistic mood in his early works yielded to a dark pessimism in his late novels. *Elokuu* (August), through its portrayal of a failing writer who succumbs to daydreams and alcoholism, presents a relentless study of human destruction. Related in topic and atmosphere is Sillanpää's last novel, *Ihmiselon ihanuus ja kurjuus* (life's beauty and mystery), the protagonist of which is a successful poet who is haunted by the tragic realization of having reached his peak artistically—perhaps a reflection of Sillanpää's own doubts.

In his last works, Sillanpää does not, with the same ease as earlier, offer an escape from disillusionment and decay through resignation, heroism, or consolation in nature. This skepticism adds a new dimension to his oeuvre and indicates that his pantheistic harmony is only tentative. The late works exhibit a tension between idealized Romanticism and brutal naturalism, with greater psychological nuances, a more complex narrative technique, and frequent changes in point of view; Sillanpää increasingly enhances the action with his own comments.

Sillanpää is a master in Finnish literature. His works are living classics, accessible in translation to a wide audience and still highly readable despite their period flavor.

Sven H. Rossel

OTHER MAJOR WORKS

SHORT FICTION: *Ihmislapsia elämän saatossa*, 1917; *Rakas isänmaani*, 1919; *Enkelten suojatit*, 1923; *Hiltu ja Ragnar*, 1923 (novelette); *Maan tasalta*, 1924; *Töllinmäki*, 1925; *Rippi*, 1928; *Kiitos hetkistä, Herra*, 1930; *Virran pohjalta*, 1933; *Viidestoista*, 1936; *Erään elämän satoa*, 1948.

NONFICTION: *Poika eli elämäänsä*, 1953; *Kerron ja kuvailen*, 1955; *Päivä korkeimmillaan*, 1956.

BIBLIOGRAPHY

Ahokas, Jaakko. *A History of Finnish Literature*. 1973. Reprint. London: Routledge/Curzon, 1997. There are many references to Sillanpää in this overview of Finnish literature, but the majority of them are in chapter 8, "Literature in Finnish Between the Two World Wars."

Alho, Olli, et al., eds. *Finland: A Cultural Encyclopedia*. Helsinki: Finnish Literature Society, 1997. An encyclopedic introduction to the culture of Finland, including its literature. Essays by close to eighty scholars and other contributors. Includes maps and an index.

Crouse, Timothy. "Past Present." *The Nation*, October 1, 1990. A portrait of Sillanpää, containing biographical information and a discussion of some of his works, including the novels *People in the Summer Night* and *Meek Heritage*.

Envall, Markku. "Earlier Authors Continue: Koskenniemi and Sillanpää." In *A History of Finland's Literature*, edited by George C. Schoolfield. Lincoln: University of Nebraska Press, in cooperation with the American-Scandinavian Foundation, 1998. One of the few English-language books that contains information about Sillanpää. This history of Finnish literature includes a chapter discussing Sillanpää's work, placing it within the broader context of Finnish fiction.

Laitinen, Kai. "F. E. Sillanpää, Life and Sun: The Writer and His Time." *Books from Finland* 22, no. 2 (1988). An overview of Sillanpää's life and writings.

Stark, Tuula. "Frans Eemil Sillanpää." In *The Nobel Prize Winners: Literature*, edited by Frank N. Magill. Vol. 2. Pasadena, Calif.: Salem Press, 1987. Provides a brief but thorough study and analysis of Sillanpää's works.

ALAN SILLITOE

Born: Nottingham, England; March 4, 1928

PRINCIPAL LONG FICTION

Saturday Night and Sunday Morning, 1958
The Loneliness of the Long-Distance Runner,
　　1959 (novella)
The General, 1960
Key to the Door, 1961
The Death of William Posters, 1965
A Tree on Fire, 1967
A Start in Life, 1970
Travels in Nihilon, 1971
The Flame of Life, 1974
The Widower's Son, 1976
The Storyteller, 1979
Her Victory, 1982
The Lost Flying Boat, 1983
Down from the Hill, 1984
Life Goes On, 1985
Out of the Whirlpool, 1987
The Open Door, 1989
Last Loves, 1990
Leonard's War, 1991
Snowstop, 1993
The Broken Chariot, 1998
The German Numbers Woman, 1999
Birthday, 2001
A Man of His Time, 2004

OTHER LITERARY FORMS

With his short-fiction collection *The Loneliness of the Long-Distance Runner* (1959), Alan Sillitoe (SIHL-ih-toh) reinforced the critical acclaim and popular recognition earned by his first novel, *Saturday Night and Sunday Morning*. The collection's title novella is now regarded as the archetypal Sillitoe narrative about a working-class protagonist fighting an indifferent, oppressive society. Sillitoe has continued to publish novellas and short stories of high quality and notable originality.

While his prose works have carried on his sympathetic portrayal of working-class life, his steady output of poetry reflects significant changes in mood and theme over five decades. His early collection *The Rats, and Other Poems* (1960) is strident political-protest verse, with brief, vivid echoes of the fiction's dark themes. His later poems develop hopeful themes: the definition of love in a postromantic age, the possibility of individual happiness amid political upheaval and oppression, and the consolation of nature. Sillitoe believes that he will ultimately be remembered for his poetry rather than his fiction. He has also written several works of nonfiction, including his autobiography *Life Without Armor* (1996) and a memoir of his 1967 travels to Russia titled *Gadfly in Russia* (2007), as well as works of juvenile fiction, plays, and screenplays.

ACHIEVEMENTS

Alan Sillitoe is one of the most successful of England's "Angry Young Men," who dramatically changed post-World War II literary culture. For their stark depiction of working-class life, Sillitoe's first novel and his first story collection received prizes: the Author's Club Award in 1958 for *Saturday Night and Sunday Morning* and the Hawthornden Prize in 1960 for *The Loneliness of the Long-Distance Runner*. In 1975, Sillitoe became a fellow of the Royal Geographic Society for his work in travel writing.

His critical and popular acclaim begin to wane in the 1970's, when, after a half dozen books, Sillitoe showed little ability to go beyond the sociological themes and alienated heroes of his early work. His reputation rebounded a decade later, however, with the publication of *Her Victory*. In this and subsequent works, Sillitoe displays an enlarged gallery of characters, a facility for different narrative forms, and an awareness that young rebels remain interesting even as they age and adapt. Sillitoe continues to experiment in his fiction, as is evident in his novels *The Widower's Son*, *Her Victory*, *Last Loves*, *The German Numbers Woman*, and, in a return to his saga of the Seaton family, *Birthday*.

BIOGRAPHY

Alan Sillitoe was born in Nottingham, England, on March 4, 1928, one of five children in a working-class family. In the economic depression of the 1930's, Sillitoe's father could not find steady work; the family survived by taking odd jobs, receiving public assistance, and doing without. Educated in local schools until he was fourteen, Sillitoe worked at several factory jobs during the years of World War II. These experiences convinced him that only personal rebellion and political revolution could change life for millions of Great Britain's workers. In 1946 he began a tour of duty with the Royal Air Force in Malaysia as a radio operator. There he began to read literature and witnessed a war between Communist insurgents and the Malaysian government. A routine physical examination before his discharge from the service revealed that Sillitoe had tuberculosis. To pass the time in his hospital bed, he began writing a novel and poems.

Although he destroyed his earliest drafts, Sillitoe continued to write. After his discharge from the air force, he lived, worked, and wrote in France, Spain, and Italy for a decade. This long sojourn was partly for his health and partly a rejection of England. While living in Majorca, he wrote *Saturday Night and Sunday Morning* and *The Loneliness of the Long-Distance Runner*. He also was befriended and inspired by the writers Robert Graves and Ted Hughes. In 1959, Sillitoe married Ruth Fainlight, an American poet, with whom he had two children.

In the 1960's, Sillitoe traveled in the Soviet Union in the hope of finding that life for workers in a socialist society was better. Though his travels generated many poems and a book, he did not find the Soviet Union's system to be the political or economic solution to his complaints about Great Britain. Later, Sillitoe visited Israel and found much to admire. He also traveled to and lived in Tangier and Spain. He occasionally teaches writing, dividing his time between London and France. He has made a truce with his native land, signaled by his commentary in two books of photographs that celebrate Nottinghamshire and England's southeast coast.

ANALYSIS

Great Britain began the twentieth century a political and economic power. By 1950, two world wars and a Great Depression later, it had lost its colonial empire, its industrial leadership, and its identity as an ordered, cultured community of mutually respectful social classes. To many young British writers of the postwar era, Great Britain seemed a doomed society, led by an archaic aristocracy and blighted by decaying industrial cities. That the nation seemed apathetic about its plight and lethargic about change angered them. Venting their frustration in plays, novels, poems, and short stories that were radically different from the social comedy and reflective character study typical of British literature, a new generation of writers that included John Braine, Kingsley Amis, John Osborne, and John Wain became known as

Alan Sillitoe. (Getty Images)

the Angry Young Men. Alan Sillitoe's first works immediately identified him as one of the angriest and most artful of this group. While other writers satirized the privileges of the upper class or traced the dead-end ambitions of the middle class, Sillitoe expressed the proletarian point of view. Unsparingly he threw light on the daily life of the factory worker and welfare recipient; ingeniously he reported this life—which he knew so well—through their eyes and in their words. He made Nottingham the emblem of postwar Britain.

Many critics and readers recognized immediately that *Saturday Night and Sunday Morning* and *The Loneliness of the Long-Distance Runner* were original contributions to English literature. Not only were Sillitoe's emotional intensity and subject matter distinctive, but also his narrative method fit his subject and theme perfectly. Employing as first-person narrator an articulate though not necessarily educated young worker, Sillitoe created a modified stream-of-consciousness technique. Retaining the essentials of standard written English, Sillitoe altered diction, syntax, and logic to reflect the speaker's knowledge, values, and emotions. Although critics have sometimes found his plots uneven and the public has occasionally regarded his themes as tendentious, no reader of his works can fail to appreciate the immediacy of scene and intimacy of character created by Sillitoe's method.

THE LONELINESS OF THE LONG-DISTANCE RUNNER

The main character of the novella *The Loneliness of the Long-Distance Runner*, known only by his last name, Smith, is the archetypal Sillitoe protagonist. A few weeks out of the Essex Borstal (a corrections facility for teenage offenders), he recounts the story of his arrest and incarceration. After conviction for robbing a bakery cash till, the lean, restless Smith becomes, at the warden's urging, a long-distance runner. Every day at dawn he runs five miles, outside the prison, not to win a race in the Borstal games, as the warden wants, but for his own sense of freedom.

As Smith runs, he thinks. He thinks with anger of the "In-laws" who run the Borstal and impose society's rules on "Out-laws" such as he, who work at menial jobs and get nowhere. He thinks with pride of his ability to outfox the detective investigating the bakery robbery until mere accident (a sudden rainstorm flushed the stolen money hidden in a drainpipe) linked him to the crime. He thinks with contempt of the warden, who may be tempting him to run away and thereby get into worse trouble; Smith is confident that "I can see further into the likes of him than he can see into the likes of me." He recalls with pride the cunning way in which he bettered the warden.

At the competition, Smith easily outdistances the other Borstal boys until he is in sight of the finish line. Then he runs in place, simply marking time, until the other runners pass him and the warden apoplectically sees victory snatched away. Although this deliberate loss costs him his running privileges and earns for him extra chores, Smith has no doubt that frustrating the In-laws is a triumph for all Out-laws. While running provided him the pleasure of being alone and free to imagine sometimes that he was "the first man" and sometimes "the last man" on Earth, Smith sacrifices such pleasure because "it's war between them and me." In this war, victory is control of fate; by his cunning, Smith is sure that he controls his fate more than the In-laws do.

Smith concludes with a boast that he has resumed stealing since his release; he is more successful and will be harder to catch. His unrelenting rebelliousness at the end of the novella leaves many readers at a disturbing impasse. Does Sillitoe mean only to cheer Smith's assertion of his own worth and indict society's inability to affect Smith's worldview? What does the future bode for the alienated individual battling an entrenched system? What happens to Smith as he matures? Does Sillitoe's vision extend beyond the terrible elation of proving dignity by spitting back?

SATURDAY NIGHT AND SUNDAY MORNING

Arthur Seaton, the twenty-four-year-old protagonist of *Saturday Night and Sunday Morning*, provides one answer. Unmarried, Arthur lives at home with his parents and siblings in a crowded neighborhood where no one has any privacy. He works in a bicycle factory, but his pleasure in craftsmanship is ruined by the bosses who worry about productivity, schedules, and the like. Arthur lives for the freedoms of the weekend: Saturday pub crawls punctuated by fights and drunken revelry; Sunday-morning lovemaking in the bed of Brenda, whose husband works nights at the factory. Through alcohol and sex Arthur asserts that he is alive and thumbs his nose at "them," those who control society and begrudge him and his class even a meager share of the wealth.

Throughout the novel, Arthur teeters willingly on the brink: Brenda becomes pregnant, and he helps her through a self-induced abortion; he seduces Brenda's sister Winnie; he tries to date a single girl, Doreen, even as he woos the married sisters; he teases an annoying neighbor by shooting her with an air rifle. Not until Winnie's husband beats him badly does Arthur stop to reflect upon himself. His only visitor during his convalescence is Doreen, and Arthur gradually discovers in her a woman with whom he can converse frankly and imagine the possibility of engagement and marriage.

In the final scene, as Arthur fishes and looks toward the future, he decides that life is good. Though a man, like a fish, may be hooked and dragged from the river of life by powerful outside forces, he can enjoy the passions and sensations of existence. Arthur determines not to weaken before life: He will make the world hear from him yet.

Saturday Night and Sunday Morning has been highly praised for its evocation of Nottingham and of the rhythms of industrial life. Critics have judged its protagonist to be as fully realized as Smith in *The Loneliness of the Long-Distance Runner* and have been pleased by the resolution, even if temporary, in Arthur Seaton's life.

KEY TO THE DOOR

Sillitoe returns to the Seaton world in *Key to the Door*, which recounts how the world hears not from Arthur but from his older brother Brian. Divided into four parts, the novel traces Brian's life from birth through age twenty-one. The first two parts contrast life in the city of Nottingham during the Depression with life on a farm belonging to Brian's grandfather. In Nottingham, Brian experiences privation and turmoil as his parents, Harold and Vera Seaton, struggle without hope or help to survive. At the farm, Brian experiences peace; he learns sympathy for other people and discovers the world of books. Eventually, however, the farm is gobbled up by the city's sprawl.

The third and fourth parts of the novel contrast Brian's factory work in Nottingham during World War II with his postwar military service in Malaysia. Brian is ill suited to soldiering; he wears his uniform rarely and prefers chasing women. He is hostile, in fact, to his country's foreign policies and openly proclaims himself a socialist. His factory experiences justify his position: Forced to perform dangerous work and seeing how bosses treat their employees, Brian becomes convinced that workers are always exploited under capitalism.

When he goes mountain climbing on Gunong Barat with five friends, Brian alone is strong enough to make it to the summit, but he chooses not to go alone. The view from where his friends must rest is magnificent enough. When Communist guerrillas attack the Malaysian government, British forces intervene against the insurgents. Valuing political solidarity, Brian only fires into the air and refuses to kill a guerrilla, even though his own life is threatened. Brian returns to England convinced that the world must listen to so-called radicals or face revolution. His new awareness is the key to the door of economic and political change.

Critics generally have praised the first part of this novel, which expands readers' knowledge of the Seaton family's world, but have found the second part devoid of literary interest. As a statement of Sillitoe's commitment to socialism and proletarian revolution, it is unequivocal. Few readers sense that Brian's conversion is well motivated; they might follow him into anger and frustration with understanding, but not into revolution.

WILLIAM POSTERS TRILOGY

The protagonist of *The Death of William Posters*, Frank Dawley, seems to be simply an older Brian Seaton. Frank acts out the implications of Brian's political commitment. Trapped in an unhappy marriage and routine job, Frank realizes that his life requires radical restructuring. He leaves Nottingham, has a brief though serious affair with a nurse, and makes contact with an old friend, painter Arthur Handley, who shares Frank's political sympathies. Through him Frank meets Myra Bassingfield and Shelley Jones. Through Myra, Frank evolves a new understanding about love; through Shelley, an ideological mercenary, Frank develops a commitment to bring about social change through violence. Shelley helps Frank outgrow his "Bill Posters" mentality. William Posters is Frank's name for Everyworker, derived from the signs on city walls that threaten, "Bill Posters will be prosecuted." William Posters symbolizes society's exploitation, but Shelley shows Frank that Posters is an image of despair that only hinders revolutionary violence. Frank joins Shelley in fighting on the side of Algerian rebels and, in an ambush of government mercenaries, imaginatively slays Posters as well.

Two subsequent novels, *A Tree on Fire* and *The Flame of Life*, follow Frank's revolutionary career in Algeria and upon his return to England. In his native country, Frank joins a group driven by a mystical vision of a cleansing civil war that will create a reinvigorated, socialist Great Britain. When the group splinters into factions, their plot fails.

The William Posters trilogy is generally perceived as a failure, both artistically and philosophically. Frequent, repetitious arguments over political issues slow down the novels' plots, and the protagonist's failure to succeed, though he clearly believes in the right (that is, the author's) ideas, creates thematic confusion. The trilogy does not offer any convincing or engaging answers to the questions raised by Sillitoe's earlier works: What hope for Smith? How will the world hear of Arthur Seaton? What next for Brian Seaton?

THE OPEN DOOR

The Open Door, which picks up the story of Brian Seaton at age twenty-one, articulates the vision Sillitoe struggled unsuccessfully to capture in the William Posters trilogy. Like *Key to the Door*, *The Open Door* has strong autobiographical overtones. Perhaps it supplies the answers about Smith and the Seatons more convincingly because it offers what Sillitoe has lived rather than what he has abstractly concluded.

Upon his return from Malaysia, Brian is diagnosed with tuberculosis. Confined for long periods to a hospital bed, he spends his time reading great books and listening to classical music. At last he has time to educate himself. He instructs himself in French from a school primer. No longer feeling connected to his wife, Pauline, whom he married before entering the service, he becomes involved first with one nurse, Rachel, and later with a second, Nora. He sees them as providing him an education of the heart even as great literature educates his head. Brian begins to write; though dissatisfied enough to destroy his first efforts, he decides to become a writer. In search of kindred spirits, he joins the Nottingham literary society, only to find its members' commitment to

art superficial and self-indulgent. After Lillian, another consumptive patient who had become Brian's lover, commits suicide, Brian decides to go to France alone to dedicate himself to writing.

The Open Door relies less on dramatic plot than do other Sillitoe novels, yet it presents a satisfying portrait of Brian's growth as a writer. Sillitoe's tour de force in the novel is an account that Brian composes of the ascent of Gunong Barat recounted in *Key to the Door*. The passage is a brilliant rendering of a budding writer's effort—powerful and trite, original and derivative by turns. Even Nottingham, so vividly realized in previous books, is blurred as Sillitoe concentrates on depicting Brian's development as a storyteller. Though still disliking England for the nation's continued exploitation of its working class, Brian remains apolitical. No longer does revolution seem a desirable or necessary path to change.

The Open Door echoes a theme of several Sillitoe novels published after the Posters trilogy that inquire into the power of storytelling to blur, pleasingly and persuasively, the lines between reality and fantasy, between caring and alienation, between solitude and community. Narrative itself is the answer to the questions about Smith, Arthur, and Brian. As long as each can speak in his authentic voice, Smith faces no impasse, Arthur knows another of life's good things, and Brian needs no gun to make the world listen.

THE GERMAN NUMBERS WOMAN

The German Numbers Woman follows the lives of Howard and Richard. Howard, now in his sixties, was blinded in his twenties as the result of an injury he sustained during a World War II bombing raid over Germany. Married to the long-suffering Laura, he obsessively listens to communications on his radio. Richard also listens to radio transmissions, but for a different reason: He sells tidbits of information about weather and ship movements to his boss, a drug smuggler. Richard, who also works as part of the boat crew on drug-smuggling missions, meets Howard accidentally and shares his interest in radio communications.

Howard, the central figure of the novel, has turned inward. Laura, his link to the outer world, reads to him, cooks for him, plans their travel, and protects him. Howard immerses himself in arcane wireless messages: weather reports, ship and airplane routes, the incessant droning of number codes from the woman he dubs The German Numbers Woman, and snatches of spoken communication between ships. His rich fantasy world revolves around the characters he imagines from these messages. Stumbling upon a conversation on the radio late one night, he becomes fascinated by the two women involved—Judy, a young Englishwoman, and Carla, her Spanish lover.

Howard becomes increasingly unhappy with his life. Guessing that Richard is involved in a smuggling mission, Howard uses coercion to come aboard as the radio man. Howard's complex and contradictory reasons for wanting to join the trip include his need to feel independent and competent again. He repeatedly sees himself as a split personality—a young man of impulsive action whose life was sent into stasis as a result of his injury and an old man who depends on his wife for his very existence. Joining the smugglers is his way of asserting his independence and competence as a skilled radio operator, an adventurer, and a member of a crew. He also sees himself as an exemplar of morality—a testimony to the moral fiber developed through his role in the Royal Air Force in World War II. He feels obligated to stop the illegal and immoral drug trade that jeopardizes the youth of England and Europe. He reveals information about the trip to police through a taped Morse code message and transmits the boat's estimated arrival time to police. Finally, he sees the trip as an opportunity to meet Judy, the voice on the radio. He has become obsessed with meeting her and has deduced that she is part of the same drug run as Richard.

Howard, both smug and conflicted, agonizes over his roles as snitch, coconspirator, and lover. The plot comes together, albeit in a somewhat implausible and melodramatic fashion, with Howard wounded, the drug lord dead, Richard imprisoned, and the drug deal thwarted. The concluding chapter finds Howard married to the twenty-eight-year-old Judy, his sight recovered, living in a quaint rural English village, and parents to a young son, Arnold. Howard has gone back to his twenties to recreate the life he lost because of his blindness. In a dialectic forged through crisis, he has reunited his two disparate selves into his new life with Judy.

More significant than its convoluted drug-smuggling conspiracy and adventure is the way in which *The Ger-*

man Numbers Woman develops the concept of the difficulties of communication through the image of the wireless radio. Mysterious and incomplete messages wreak havoc, not only through garbled and cryptic radio transmissions influenced by sunspots and weather but also through the misinterpreted, hooded communications between people. Mistrust, lies, and deception corrode nearly all of the relationships in the novel. Sillitoe reinforces this sense of covert meaning by alternating quickly between characters' points of view and by emphasizing the multiple meanings and implications inherent in every conversation.

BIRTHDAY

Birthday continues Sillitoe's story of the brothers Brian and Arthur Seaton, begun in *Saturday Night and Sunday Morning* and *Key to the Door*. Some forty years later, Arthur is in his sixties and married to Avril, and Brian is approaching seventy. The central event of the story is the seventieth birthday of Brian's first love, Jenny. The novel pieces together the stories of Seaton family and friends—marriages, children, divorces, and deaths. Brian, a television scriptwriter, lives alone in London after two failed marriages. The sixty-year-old Arthur, the former rogue and womanizer, now lives happily with his soul mate Avril in an ordered, disciplined, and tranquil household.

Arthur, however, is forced to confront the devastating death of his beloved Avril from cancer. Her impending death allows Sillitoe to develop the bond between Brian and Arthur while also contrasting the two brothers. The novel presents the notion of death as a blackness into which all humans fall, with no prospect of consciousness after death. Late in the novel, however, Sillitoe mitigates this bleak view of death by speculating that Vera Seaton is looking down on her family from beyond the grave, that Grandfather Merton, dead for many years, approves of Arthur's life, and that the dead continue to haunt the world, evidenced by the ghost story told by Arthur's son, Harold. Harold's story suggests not only life after death but also a continuation of the Arthur Seaton storytelling tradition.

Brian, as the central figure of the novel, returns to the Nottingham of his youth and to the love of his youth, Jenny. The novel serves as an elegy not only for Avril but also for Nottingham. Buildings are gone, streets are crime-ridden, residents stay home and watch television instead of going to the pubs, and the mines are closed. Jenny, now a widow, speculates with Brian about what their life together would have been like. Fatalistically and unromantically, they assume that they would have been no happier, but they spend time together enjoying each other's company, reliving old experiences, and attempting to atone for past mistakes.

The novel ends with an elaborate and stunning example of Brian's usual wanderlust. He left Nottingham as a youth, and the final pages of the novel describe in exquisite detail the survival equipment that he has packed in his automobile trunk in the event of any possible emergency he might face as he travels to the remote corners of the world. He can leave in an instant and be totally self-sufficient. Arthur embraces his Nottingham heritage and family, while Brian acknowledges that he is inevitably destined to leave his hometown and travel the world.

Robert M. Otten
Updated by Ann M. Cameron

OTHER MAJOR WORKS

SHORT FICTION: *The Ragman's Daughter*, 1963; *A Sillitoe Selection*, 1968; *Guzman Go Home, and Other Stories*, 1968; *Men, Women, and Children*, 1973; *The Second Chance, and Other Stories*, 1981; *The Far Side of the Street*, 1988; *Collected Stories*, 1995; *Alligator Playground: A Collection of Short Stories*, 1997; *New and Collected Stories*, 2003.

PLAYS: *All Citizens Are Soldiers*, pr. 1967 (adaptation of Lope de Vega's play *Fuenteovejuna*; with Ruth Fainlight); *Three Plays*, 1978.

POETRY: *Without Beer or Bread*, 1957; *The Rats, and Other Poems*, 1960; *A Falling out of Love, and Other Poems*, 1964; *Love in the Environs of Voronezh, and Other Poems*, 1968; *Shaman, and Other Poems*, 1968; *Poems*, 1971 (with Ted Hughes and Ruth Fainlight); *Barbarians, and Other Poems*, 1974; *Storm: New Poems*, 1974; *Snow on the North Side of Lucifer*, 1979; *More Lucifer*, 1980; *Sun Before Departure*, 1984; *Tides and Stone Walls*, 1986; *Collected Poems*, 1993.

SCREENPLAYS: *Saturday Night and Sunday Morning*, 1960 (adaptation of his novel); *The Loneliness of the Long-Distance Runner*, 1961 (adaptation of his novella);

Che Guevara, 1968; *The Ragman's Daughter*, 1974 (adaptation of his novel).

NONFICTION: *The Road to Volgograd*, 1964; *Raw Material*, 1972; *Mountains and Caverns: Selected Essays*, 1975; *The Saxon Shore Way: From Gravesend to Rye*, 1983 (with Fay Weldon); *Nottinghamshire*, 1986 (with David Sillitoe); *Every Day of the Week*, 1987; *Leading the Blind: A Century of Guidebook Travel, 1815-1914*, 1996; *Life Without Armor*, 1996; *A Flight of Arrows: Opinions, People, Places*, 2003; *Gadfly in Russia*; 2007.

CHILDREN'S LITERATURE: *The City Adventures of Marmalade Jim*, 1967; *Big John and the Stars*, 1977; *The Incredible Fencing Fleas*, 1978; *Marmalade Jim at the Farm*, 1980; *Marmalade Jim and the Fox*, 1984.

BIBLIOGRAPHY

Atherton, Stanley S. *Alan Sillitoe: A Critical Assessment*. London: W. H. Allen, 1979. Focuses on the revolutionary spirit of Sillitoe's first novels, but discusses his lesser works as well.

Hanson, Gillian Mary. *Understanding Alan Sillitoe*. Columbia: University of South Carolina Press, 1999. Provides biographical information and discusses such aspects of Sillitoe's fiction as the search for identity in his love stories and his depictions of women. Includes bibliography and index.

Hitchcock, Peter. *Working-Class Fiction in Theory and Practice: A Reading of Alan Sillitoe*. Ann Arbor, Mich.: UMI Research Press, 1989. Provides a good examination of the writer's themes and execution.

Hutchings, William. "Proletarian Byronism: Alan Sillitoe and the Romantic Tradition." In *English Romanticism and Modern Fiction*, edited by Allan Chavkin. New York: AMS Press, 1993. Discusses the romantic aspects that can be found in Sillitoe's seemingly antiromantic fiction.

Kalliney, Peter. "Cities of Affluence: Masculinity, Class, and the Angry Young Man." *Modern Fiction Studies* 47 (Spring, 2001): 92-117. Examines the class element in Sillitoe's work and discusses the ways in which gender dynamics illustrate class dynamics.

Minogue, Sally, and Andrew Palmer. "Confronting the Abject: Women and Dead Babies in Modern English

Fiction." *Journal of Modern Literature* 29, no. 3 (Spring, 2006): 103-125. Presents a discussion of the treatment of the topic of abortion in the modern English novel, including Sillitoe's work.

Penner, Allen Richard. *Alan Sillitoe*. Boston: Twayne, 1972. Provides an informative midcareer overview of Sillitoe's work. Includes a brief biographical chapter and a helpful bibliography.

Sawkins, John. *The Long Apprenticeship: Alienation in the Early Work of Alan Sillitoe*. New York: Peter Lang, 2001. Focuses on the protagonists of *Saturday Night and Sunday Morning* and *The Loneliness of the Long-Distance Runner*, arguing that their resistance

to conformist society makes them representatives of a long-standing literary tradition.

Slack, John S. "A Sporting Chance: Sports, Delinquency, and Rehabilitation in *The Loneliness of the Long-Distance Runner*." *Aethlon: The Journal of Sport Literature* 17, no. 2 (Spring, 2000): 1-9. Presents an investigation of the role of sports in Sillitoe's novel.

Tucker, John L. "Alan Sillitoe." In *British Writers, Supplement 5*, edited by Jay Parini. New York: Charles Scribner's Sons, 1999. Provides an overview of Sillitoe's work, with an emphasis on the tradition of working-class writing and the picaresque.

IGNAZIO SILONE

Born: Pescina dei Marsi, Italy; May 1, 1900
Died: Geneva, Switzerland; August 22, 1978
Also known as: Secondo Tranquilli

PRINCIPAL LONG FICTION

Fontamara, 1930, 1933 (revised 1958; English translation, 1934, revised 1960)

Pane e vino, 1937 (revised as *Vino e Pane*, 1955; first pb. as *Brot und Wein*, 1936; *Bread and Wine*, 1936, revised 1962)

Il seme sotto la neve, 1942 (first pb. as *Der Samen unterm Schnee*, 1941; *The Seed Beneath the Snow*, 1942)

Una manciata di more, 1952 (*A Handful of Blackberries*, 1953)

Il segreto di Luca, 1956 (*The Secret of Luca*, 1958)

La volpe e le camelie, 1960 (*The Fox and the Camellias*, 1961)

OTHER LITERARY FORMS

While known primarily for his novels, Ignazio Silone (see-LOH-nay) also wrote short stories, sketches, essays, and plays. The essays and plays are considered to be among his finest works. Silone's essays are, for the

most part, autobiographical in character and apologetic in tone. His most famous essay, "Uscita di sicurezza" ("Emergency Exit," which first appeared in English in 1949), was published in Italian in 1951. The essay recounts the author's personal odyssey from early allegiance to the Communist Party, through his opposition to the Fascist regime in Italy and eventual exile in Switzerland, to a dramatic break with the Italian Socialist Party in the years following the reestablishment of democracy. Despite its intention to defend the author's controversial political stances, the essay is free of polemical rhetoric and is distinguished by the simple and direct manner of expression that marks the style of Silone's novels as well. This essay also appeared in 1965 in a collection with the same name.

The plays, though they often employ the same themes as the novels, lack their dramatic intensity and complex symbolic development. *La scuola dei dittatori* (pb. 1938; *The School for Dictators*, 1938), a satire, seems foreign to the usual tone of Silone's work. *Ed egli si nascose* (pb. 1944; *And He Did Hide Himself*, 1946), which elaborates a single strand of the plot of the novel *Bread and Wine*, falls short of the latter work's rendering of the complexities of human relationships. *L'avventura di un povero cristiano* (pb. 1968; *The Story of a Humble*

Christian, 1971), the last work of the Silone canon, comes closest to realizing the dramatic promise of its form. This may perhaps be explained by the extraordinary traits of its hero, Pope Celestine V, whose unprecedented gesture of renouncing his position makes him a particularly engaging and enigmatic figure. Silone used the inherently intriguing features of his central character to great advantage in this, his final play. Yet all of his plays seem less than perfectly suited to the demands of theatrical production and may with some justice be accurately described as prose narratives cast in dialogue form.

One of the most notable features of Silone's fiction is his near indifference to the technical experimentation that characterized much of twentieth century European fiction. He confessed that during the earlier years of his literary career, he was little interested in aesthetics, and he has been widely criticized on this point. However, a study of the entire corpus of his works reveals that he was increasingly concerned with the formal demands of his art, a fact exemplified by his decision to revise and reissue versions of three of his earlier novels in the 1960's. Silone often spoke of his novels as parables, a term well suited to the simplicity and clarity with which they present their themes and ideas. On balance, Silone's novels represent triumph of literary realism in an age that seems all too anxious to abandon this traditional perspective. His novels insist on the coordination of simple story, believable characters, and symbolic meaning. Perhaps the literary credo that lies behind this amalgam is suggested by the sentiments of the aged priest Don Benedetto in *Bread and Wine*. Truth, he remarks, always appears simple and crude when compared to the elegant veneer of hypocrisy. In these terms, Silone has consistently chosen the way of truth for his novels.

ACHIEVEMENTS

The most curious fact of Ignazio Silone's literary reputation is that he has been highly regarded almost everywhere except in his native Italy. He received the honorary degree of doctor of letters from Yale, Toulouse, and Warwick universities and was a member of the French Legion of Honor, yet Silone has been severely criticized on both literary and political grounds by his countrymen.

Silone's political commitments and his devotion to

literary realism place him at odds with the main currents of twentieth century Italian literature. Turning his back to the models of aestheticism, eroticism, and Hermetism, which have to a great extent dominated modern letters in Italy, he was determined to make of literature a means to awaken the social conscience of his contemporaries. Such an aim is likely to stir opposition and controversy, for it often requires touching the raw nerves of national pride. Silone's writings reflect an era of economic distress, political repression and instability, and military failure. Further, Silone was dedicated to examining the causes, effects, and remedies of this chaotic social scene through a vision of rural Italian life. This vision, with its constant reference to Abruzzi mountain villages, is anything but an appeal to the glory of twentieth century Italian culture: Silone's characters embody values antithetical to urban industrialized Italy. In this sense, he would seem to be quite reactionary, yet he does not propose a return to an idyllic past.

The humble people of the land who populate his fiction are sometimes backward and unimaginative, and their dependence upon the past is often portrayed as a tremendous handicap. The fidelity to a simple code of compassion and personal integrity, which appealed so strongly to Silone, found its fullest expression in those characters that lived close to the land. The virtues of the Silone hero, be it Bernardo Viola, Pietro Spina, or Luca Sabatini, point not toward the past but toward a timeless world where, by a difficult and even dangerous sort of ascesis, the trials of life in an imperfect world may be endured if not overcome.

The choice of peasants to portray this set of values, the *cafoni* of the author's native Abruzzi, met with resistance from Italian literati; in a similar way, Silone's disavowal of political parties cost him the support of many partisan readers. By remaining faithful to his own understanding of the terms of an ageless and universal struggle for human dignity, Silone effectively abdicated the claim to literary ingenuity and political propriety that his own culture expected of him, yet the success with which he fashioned his universal message from the most provincial details of Italian life is indicated precisely by the acclaim given Silone outside his own land, where, though the *cafoni* he wrote about were total strangers, they were nevertheless recognized as authentic representations of heroic resistance to adverse fate and human injustice. It is this particularized portrayal of humankind's resilience and indomitability that constitutes Silone's greatest achievement.

BIOGRAPHY

Born Secondo Tranquilli in a village of the rugged Abruzzi region of central Italy, Ignazio Silone (a pseudonym he later used to protect his family from Fascist persecution) could never totally separate the image of its rugged topography from his view of human destiny. Again and again its mountains and valleys, as well as the harshness of life this terrain breeds, serve as the background for the struggles of his characters. The Abruzzi was a link between the medieval origins and the modern dilemmas of Italian culture, and the course of Silone's own life runs parallel to the region's emergence from a religious past into a secular and politicized present.

Partly because of poor health in his youth, Silone was educated close to home in religious schools, and although he abandoned rather early any thoughts of entering the priesthood, he seems never to have forgotten the lessons of faith that were no doubt inculcated during this period of his life. He later referred to his commitment to Socialist causes as a matter of "faith," and the roots of this secular *via fidei* can be traced to the era of World War I, when Silone became the secretary of a syndicalist peasant movement, the Federation of Land Workers of the Abruzzi.

The year 1917 found Silone in Rome, where he was again associated with liberal causes through his selection as secretary of the Socialist Youth of Rome. His career as political journalist began with editorial duties on the Socialist weekly *Avanguardia* in 1918, and by 1921, he was respected enough to be chosen as a delegate to the conference in Moscow that organized the Italian Communist Party. During the 1920's, Silone was a member of the central committee of the Italian Communist Party, but in 1930, he broke ties with the party, feeling that its dogmatism and its dependence on Moscow's directives compromised the ideals he held for social reform in Italy. In the same year, three warrants for his arrest were issued by the Fascist special tribunal, and Silone fled to Switzerland, where he lived until the autumn of 1944, after the fall of the Fascists.

Ignazio Silone. (Library of Congress)

In these years of exile, Silone wrote a number of cultural and political essays, a play, and three novels, including what is perhaps his most famous work, *Bread and Wine*. Upon his return to Italy, he served as a member of the Italian constituent assembly from 1946 to 1948 and as a member of the executive committee of the Italian Socialist Party until 1947. In addition, he founded and edited the liberal journal *Tempo presente*. Silone's outspoken criticism of the postwar Italian Communist Party and its leader, Palmiro Togliatti, earned for him the wrath of many Italian intellectuals.

Having finally left the Italian Socialist Party, Silone maintained an independent political stance through the Cold War years, one that again put him at odds with other "committed" European writers. The Soviet invasion of Hungary in 1956 moved Silone to condemn both the Soviets and the Americans, the latter for failing to come to the aid of the Hungarian people. On this issue, he clashed sharply with Jean-Paul Sartre, and the two were never fully reconciled. Silone's fierce independence in political issues and in response to current affairs won for him no friends among Italian intellectuals, who sought, with considerable success, to exclude Silone from his country's political life after 1950. These same years of enforced isolation produced two highly acclaimed novels, *A Handful of Blackberries* and *The Secret of Luca*, as well as writings that eventually would appear in *Uscita di sicurezza* (1965; *Emergency Exit*, 1968), a retrospective volume of essays (which includes the previously released "Emergency Exit") on the writer's experiences before and during the Fascist years.

Judging by the tone of the works written in this latter phase of his literary career, Silone seems to have accepted his exclusion from public life with equanimity. There is a quiet dignity in both his public pronouncements and his writing that is impressive, a dignity not unlike that exhibited by many of the humble inhabitants of the Abruzzi who fill the pages of his fiction. Like Pope Celestine V in Silone's final work, the author appears to have been resigned to paying a price for fidelity to his own principles and beliefs.

The final measure of Silone's separation from the world of politics and public intellectual life is suggested by the poverty and the obscurity in which he died. His cremation was attended only by his wife of thirty-four years, Darina, by a single friend from Italy, and by a handful of consular officials and journalists.

ANALYSIS

Although the literary canon of Ignazio Silone may be divided into several fairly distinct phases or periods, a number of themes and motifs serve to unite his works into a single vision of life. One of the most obvious of these is the use of Abruzzi villages as the setting for his fiction. A second common element is a fascination with the idea of the hero as a solitary figure who must strive to restore communion with his fellow human beings. Yet another may be found in the persistent motif of the hero's return to his native region, an experience that triggers a flood of ambivalent emotion in more than one Silone character. Finally, the symbolic role of women and the emphasis accorded to acts of self-sacrifice and renunciation also help to unify Silone's works. Taken together, these elements create a peculiarly Silonean frame of reference in which the vicissitudes of history and circumstance test the capacity of the human spirit to endure and prevail.

FONTAMARA

Fontamara, Silone's first novel, portrays the injustices suffered by a mountain village at the hands of the Fascist state. In one sense, the entire village is the hero of this work, with its collective sorrows and bewilderment serving as the focal point of the action. While the emphasis rests on this common tragedy, the novel also reveals its author's interest in the reactions of individuals caught up in the aggregate patterns of human fate. Thus, the fortunes of the village of Fontamara are interwoven with the private destiny of one of its sons, Bernardo Viola. Viola's hopes for a better life, a life enriched by love and freedom from poverty, are dashed on the rocks of the times in which he lives. Having journeyed to Rome to seek his fortune, Viola is betrayed by the false promise of urban life under Fascism and, upon hearing of the death of the woman he loves in Fontamara, he confesses to crimes he has not committed in order to allow a young revolutionary to go free.

Viola's personal sacrifice, though certainly noble, is less than redemptive as far as Fontamara is concerned. The young revolutionary who has been freed because of Viola's sacrifice makes his way to Fontamara and sets up a clandestine newspaper, which the villagers decide to call *What Must We Do?* When the authorities trace the paper to Fontamara, the village is attacked and many of its inhabitants murdered by Fascist militiamen. The few survivors are described at the end of the novel as asking the same question that had served as the title for their newspaper: "What can we do?" The novel thus closes on a highly ambiguous note, for the villagers' query is never answered. This ambiguity deepens the tragedy that befalls the village and Viola, who ends his own life in a jail cell. *Fontamara* thus portrays the defeat of human hope on both the collective and the individual levels. It seems content with alerting readers to the dangers of Fascism and to the tragic triumph of history over human desire. The bleakness of *Fontamara* presents a challenge to Silone's basic faith in the resilience of the human spirit, and it was only in his later works that he could clearly respond to the haunting question with which this early text ends.

BREAD AND WINE

In *Bread and Wine*, his second novel, Silone discovered resources on which he could draw for the remainder of his literary career. These resources were both thematic and technical: The title of the novel suggests the power latent in the communion of humankind and the dynamics of literary symbols that point beyond the present moment to a better future.

Pietro Spina, the novel's hero, returns in disguise to his native Italy from exile in Belgium. Because he is still a hunted man, Spina assumes the identity of a priest and calls himself Paolo Spada. As a "priest" of the secular gospel of brotherhood and social reform, Spina feels himself bonded to the lives of the humble rural folk through breaking bread and drinking wine with them. As the plot progresses, the terms of this secular Eucharist become more and more explicit, until in the episode of the funeral meal for a young Socialist, Luigi Murica, who has been killed by the Fascist authorities, the full meaning of the novel's title is revealed. The many grapes needed to make wine and the ears of grain necessary for the production of bread speak of the merging of individual human lives into a common identity. It is the strength of this new corporate identity that provides the hope that beyond the present misery lies a brighter future.

This dominant theme is even hinted at by the novel's time scheme, a span of approximately nine months, to which the period needed for the maturation of grapes and grain and that allotted for human gestation correspond. The motif of gestation applies to subtle changes undergone by Spina himself during the novel. The limitations of his devotion to political principle are suggested by the hero's growing interest in people rather than in doctrine and by the episode of the apparent suicide of the embittered revolutionary Uliva in Rome. For belief in causes, Silone substitutes a compassion rooted in the experience of human solidarity. Lest the novel seem blindly optimistic, however, the fate of the old Don Benedetto, priest and teacher of Spina, is included. Don Benedetto attempts to maintain his faith and personal integrity in the face of the progressive corruption of Church and state and is finally murdered when he drinks poisoned sacramental wine while saying Mass. The figurative implications of the old priest's death mitigate the hope inspired by the novel's central image of communion by reminding the reader that wine also symbolizes blood, sorrow, and death.

In the novel's two most prominent women, Bianchina Girasole and Christina Colamartini, Silone presents both the two sides of human nature, body and soul, and a dual vision of Italy dominated by Fascism. Bianchina, a rural girl who eventually becomes a prostitute in Rome, represents the physical degradation endured by the oppressed Italian people. Christina, the daughter of an aristocratic old family, is devoured by wolves after following Spina into the mountains as he tried to escape capture by government authorities; her fate represents the death of the human spirit under Fascism. At the close of the novel, then, the promise of human solidarity suggested by the image of communion is imperiled. Spina's flight to the mountains may be read as an allusion to Moses on the mountain or Christ at Golgotha, but in fact the text of *Bread and Wine* is silent concerning his fate. This ambiguous closure, though it recalls the end of *Fontamara*, also transcends it, for Spina, unlike Viola, is still alive and thus may return to reestablish his communion with the peasants of the Abruzzi. For this reason, and for many others, *Bread and Wine* is a more satisfying and affirmative novel than *Fontamara*.

THE SEED BENEATH THE SNOW

The Seed Beneath the Snow is designed as a sequel to the message of *Bread and Wine*. It picks up the thread of Pietro Spina's story but does not address the question of what happened to him after his flight to the mountains. The reader knows only that Spina has survived and is searching for a means by which the promise of human solidarity may be sustained. As in the previous novel, the direction of this hope is implied by the metaphor of its title. The respect for the earth and agrarian life, which is implicit in Silone's earlier fiction, evolves into a complex reverence in *The Seed Beneath the Snow*.

In addition to Spina, this novel focuses on two figures, each of whom is rather extraordinary. The first is "Aunt" Euremia, a strange old woman whose supposed wealth is coveted by the inhabitants of the village where she lives. She is a skewed version of Silone's image of Italy as woman, and her sexual indeterminacy suggests again the distorted nature of this nation under fascism. The "wealth" of Euremia consists of chests full of her own excrement, which may be taken as another sign of the corruption of Italian culture.

The second figure is the village deaf-mute, Infante, whom Spina tries to teach to speak. The first word he attempts to have Infante pronounce is "manure," which provides a curious link with the figure of Euremia. In dedicating himself to Infante, Spina suppresses his love for Donna Faustina. This sacrifice seems to come to naught when Infante, who has murdered his own brutal father, must flee the village to avoid arrest. In one final, dramatic gesture of self-sacrifice, Spina himself confesses to the crime, and the novel ends with the police leading him away. The grand hope with which the novel began has thus been reduced to a single gesture of sacrifice, the value of which is at best questionable.

The "seed" of new life does not bear the sort of fruit that the reader might have expected from *The Seed Beneath the Snow*, but it does anticipate Silone's later interest in gratuitous gestures of self-sacrifice, which stand at the center of works such as *The Secret of Luca* and *The Story of a Humble Christian*. In a sense, *The Seed Beneath the Snow* brings to a close that phase of Silone's thought that emphasized a radical reordering of individual lives and of society according to the prophetic hope for political reform. Hereafter, Silone's hope is more circumscribed, focusing on gestures of the individual rather than grand movements that seek to change society as a whole.

A HANDFUL OF BLACKBERRIES

A Handful of Blackberries, published more than a decade after the appearance of *The Seed Beneath the Snow*, reveals the contours of Silone's new priorities. Its hero, Rocco de Donatis, returns to his native Abruzzi and becomes a leader in the local Communist Party. He gradually loses faith in its promises, however, as did the author himself at one point in his life, and turns instead to the twin virtues of love and endurance, the first exemplified by Stella, a Jewish refugee—whom he marries—and the second by the figure of the old peasant Lazzaro. Lazzaro, whose name associates him with the Lazarus who was raised from death in the Bible, represents the new life, which has been the object of the quest of Silone's heroes since the novel *Bread and Wine*.

Metaphorically, Lazzaro is associated with that bread which sustains human hope, for he is at one point in the novel compared to a cart loaded with wheat in a starving village. In him, symbolically, the reader may see the fruit of the seed planted in the Pietro Spina novels. The figure of Lazzaro is also the embodied answer to the question posed at the end of *Fontamara*. What must be done is to root oneself in the enduring virtues of the earth itself, in its serene endurance and fruitfulness, drawing from it a sustenance more real than that provided by any commitment to abstract political ideals. The emblem of this simple manner of living is found in the novel's title: The handful of blackberries suggests a humble rural meal rather than a sacramental feast of bread and wine, and the modulated symbolic overtones of this new image are in keeping with the character of the final phase of Silone's works. Rocco de Donatis has adopted the virtues of Lazzaro's life as the novel ends; he is shown passing his days quietly in the company of friends while serving in a movement whose goal is to improve the lot of farm laborers. The same rhythms of provincial life, which seemed tantamount to imprisonment in *Fontamara*, lend to life its true worth in *A Handful of Blackberries*. Such is the transformation of thought that distinguishes Silone's final works.

THE SECRET OF LUCA

The culmination of the evolution of Silone's vision of life may be observed in his last major novel, *The Secret of Luca*. The plot of the novel centers on Andrea Cipriani, a young man recently released from prison after serving twelve years for anti-Fascist activities, and his attempt to understand the aged Luca Sabatini, who has also been released from prison after having spent forty years there for a crime he did not commit.

Both men return to the mountain village of Cisterna, and Cipriani begins his search for the truth behind Luca's refusal to testify in his own defense at his trial years earlier. The only other villager who seems at all concerned about Luca is the priest Don Serafino. The rest of the people seem to resent the old convict's very presence. Luca's secret involves his devotion to a woman whom he could never possess, and his suffering stems from his steadfast refusal to compromise her reputation. Here again is the act of gratuitous self-sacrifice, an act akin to Pietro Spina's confession to Infante's crime in *The Seed Beneath the Snow* and to Bernardo Viola's confession for the sake of the young revolutionary in

Fontamara. Yet Luca's motives are purer than those of his precursors by just so much as love is superior to despair and desperation. In this novel, Silone seems to discern beauty and truth in two contradictory modes of human existence: the integrity of love and the enigma of sacrifice. In the case of Luca, these forms of truth intersect. The old man's virtue stands as a mute rebuke to the selfishness and pettiness of his fellow villagers, and they smart from it.

Luca stands as an emblem of the power of renunciation to purify the human spirit; in him, the reader can glimpse some of Silone's own willingness to sacrifice public acclaim to remain true to his principles in the latter part of his career. With Luca, as with Lazzaro in *A Handful of Blackberries*, Silone accomplished what he could not do with Pietro Spina, the hero of the first phase of his literary vision. These older men seem to have returned from the mountain having seen the promised land of social justice and human dignity, which seems to have eluded Spina. They realize, as perhaps Spina did not, that the kingdom sought by the Silone hero, like the Kingdom of God in the Gospel of Luke, lies within the human spirit. The heroes of Silone's final works possess quiet and determined spirits, and these spirits produce the seeds of virtue that may be planted in the lives of those who recognize the Lucas and Lazzaros of this world. In this way only, spirit by spirit, can the field of human society bear the long-awaited harvest of brotherhood, which was the central concern of Silone's life and art.

No discussion of Silone's writing would be complete without reference to the author's revision of his first three novels some twenty years after their original dates of publication. Silone commented that he wished to render these novels more enduring works of art by deleting elements that he felt in retrospect to be too subjective or dated. This impulse bears witness to Silone's development as an artist. The changes made in his works preserve their original thematic emphases for the most part. The structure of *Bread and Wine* is changed by the division of its plot into twenty-nine short chapters instead of the twelve of the earlier version, but the effect on the action is minimal. Of greater import is the suppression of the murder of the old priest Don Benedetto, a modification that relieves the darkened atmosphere of

the novel's final chapters. The revisions of *Fontamara* and *A Seed Beneath the Snow* are of similar character and effect.

Perhaps the most suggestive remark contained in the author's "Note on the Revision of *Bread and Wine*" is the one dealing with the reversal of the words of the title from *Pane e vino* in 1937 to *Vino e pane* in 1955. Silone states that it is his impression that wine plays a larger role than bread in the new version of his novel. While his words may be taken in a number of ways, they certainly point to the author's sensitivity to the symbolic import of his writing. One possible reading of his emphasis on wine is that while *pane* could easily summon up thoughts of collectivist worker and peasant slogans from the 1930's, *vino* may more readily suggest the cup of personal destiny from which every human being must drink alone. Hence, Silone may be alluding once more to ascendency of the solitary hero in his later work.

Be this as it may, the author's note to the revised version of *Fontamara* contains a passage in which he compares himself to certain monks in the Middle Ages who spent their whole lives painting the figure of Christ over and over again. Like these monks, Silone's portrait of humankind becomes more delicate and finely detailed with each successive canvas. This devotion is another dimension of Silone's personal integrity. Never satisfied with seeing life darkly in the mirror of art, he constantly strove to create an image of truth beheld face-to-face.

Paul Reichardt

OTHER MAJOR WORKS

SHORT FICTION: *Viaggio a Parigi: Novelle*, 1993 (first pb. as *Die Reise nach Paris*, 1934; *Mr. Aristotle*, 1935).

PLAYS: *La scuola dei dittatori*, pb. 1938 (*The School for Dictators*, 1938); *Ed egli si nascose*, pb. 1944 (*And He Did Hide Himself*, 1946); *L'avventura di un povero cristiano*, pb. 1968 (*The Story of a Humble Christian*, 1971).

NONFICTION: *Memoriale dal carcere svizzero*, 1979 (wr. 1942; *Memoir from a Swiss Prison*, 2006); *Uscita di sicurezza*, 1965 (essays; *Emergency Exit*, 1968).

MISCELLANEOUS: *Romanzi e saggi*, 1998-1999 (2 volumes).

BIBLIOGRAPHY

Holmes, Deborah. *Ignazio Silone in Exile: Writing and Antifascism in Switzerland, 1929-1944.* Burlington, Vt.: Ashgate, 2005. Focuses on Silone's fifteen-year exile in Switzerland. Holmes discusses the influence of German antifascist émigrés and Swiss socialists upon Silone's work, Silone's role in Zurich's intellectual community and the Swiss leftist press, and the reception and rewriting of *Bread and Wine.*

Krieger, Murray. "Ignazio Silone: The Failure of the Secular Christ." In *The Tragic Vision: Variations on a Theme in Literary Interpretation.* New York: Holt, Rinehart and Winston, 1960. Krieger provides a probing study of *Bread and Wine.*

Leake, Elizabeth. *The Reinvention of Ignazio Silone.* Buffalo, N.Y.: University of Toronto Press, 2003. Silone, a hero among Italian liberals and a onetime high-ranking member of the Communist Party, was revealed in 1996 to have secretly supported the Italian Fascist Party. Leake reevaluates Silone's fiction from a psychoanalytic perspective, demonstrating how his novels reflect his struggles with this duplicity.

Mooney, Harry J., Jr., and Thomas F. Staley, eds. *The Shapeless God: Essays on Modern Fiction.* Pittsburgh, Pa.: University of Pittsburgh Press, 1968. Chapter 2, "Ignazio Silone and the Pseudonyms of God," is chiefly a study of *Bread and Wine,* but there are illuminating references to Silone's other novels as well.

Origo, Iris. *A Need to Testify: Portraits of Lauro de Bosis, Ruth Draper, Gaetano Salvemini, Ignazio Silone.* 1984. Reprint: New York: Helen Marx Books, 2002. Origo's memoir about four of her friends who were opposed to Italian Fascism provides a brief but particularly penetrating portrait of Silone. Includes notes but no bibliography.

Paynter, Maria Nicolai. *Ignazio Silone: Beyond the Tragic Vision.* Buffalo, N.Y.: University of Toronto Press, 2000. Critical study focusing on the controversies surrounding Silone and his writing. Paynter analyzes his intellectual and political convictions and assesses his development as a writer. Includes a bibliography and an index.

Scott, Nathan A., Jr. "Ignazio Silone: Novelist of the Revolutionary Sensibility." In *Rehearsals of Discomposure: Alienation and Reconciliation in Modern Literature: Franz Kafka, Ignazio Silone, D. H. Lawrence, T. S. Eliot.* New York: Columbia University Press, 1952. Scott offers a wide-ranging overview of Silone's fiction within the broader context of European literature.

Sipe, A. W. Richard. "Will the Real Priest Please Stand Up: Ignazio Silone." In *The Serpent and the Dove: Celibacy in Literature and Life.* Westport, Conn.: Praeger, 2007. A study of religious celibacy, focusing on historic figures who were celibate and on literary accounts of celibacy, including those of Silone.

Slonim, Marc. Afterword to *Bread and Wine,* by Ignazio Silone. New York: New American Library, 1963. Slonim provides a useful introduction to the novel, explaining the circumstances in which it was written, analyzing its characters, and discussing Silone's politics and artistic achievement.

GEORGES SIMENON

Born: Liège, Belgium; February 13, 1903
Died: Lausanne, Switzerland; September 4, 1989
Also known as: Georges Joseph Christian Simenon;
Georges Sim; Christian Brulls

PRINCIPAL LONG FICTION

Au pont des Arches, 1921 (as Georges Sim)
Au rendez-vous des terreneuves, 1931 (*The Sailors' Rendezvous*, 1940)
Le Charretier de la "Providence," 1931 (*The Crime at Lock 14*, 1934; also known as *Maigret Meets a Milord*, 1963)
Le Chien jaune, 1931 (*A Face for a Clue*, 1939; also known as *Maigret and the Yellow Dog*, 1987; also known as *The Yellow Dog*, 1940)
Un Crime en Hollande, 1931 (*A Crime in Holland*, 1940)
La Danseuse du Gai-Moulin, 1931 (*At the "Gai-Moulin,"* 1940)
La Guinguette à deux sous, 1931 (*The Guinguette by the Seine*, 1940)
M. Gallet, décédé, 1931 (*The Death of Monsieur Gallet*, 1932; also known as *Maigret Stonewalled*, 1963)
La Nuit du carrefour, 1931 (*The Crossroad Murders*, 1933; also known as *Maigret at the Crossroads*, 1964)
Le Pendu de Saint-Pholien, 1931 (*The Crime of Inspector Maigret*, 1933; also known as *Maigret and the Hundred Gibbets*, 1963)
Pietr-le-Letton, 1931 (*The Strange Case of Peter the Lett*, 1933; also known as *Maigret and the Enigmatic Lett*, 1963)
Le Relais d'Alsace, 1931 (*The Man from Everywhere*, 1941)
La Tête d'un homme, 1931 (*A Battle of Nerves*, 1939)
L'Affaire Saint-Fiacre, 1932 (*The Saint-Fiacre Affair*, 1940; also known as *Maigret Goes Home*, 1967)
Chez les Flamands, 1932 (*The Flemish Shop*, 1940)

L'Écluse numéro un, 1932 (*The Lock at Charenton*, 1941)
Le Fou de Bergerac, 1932 (*The Madman of Bergerac*, 1940)
Liberty Bar, 1932 (English translation, 1940)
L'Ombre chinoise, 1932 (*The Shadow in the Courtyard*, 1934; also known as *Maigret Mystified*, 1964)
Le Passager du "Polarlys," 1932 (*The Mystery of the "Polarlys,"* 1942; also known as *Danger at Sea*, 1954)
Le Port des brumes, 1932 (*Death of a Harbour Master*, 1941)
Le Coup de lune, 1933 (*Tropic Moon*, 1942)
Les Fiançailles de M. Hire, 1933 (*Mr. Hire's Engagement*, 1956)
Les Gens d'en face, 1933 (*The Window over the Way*, 1951)
Le Haut Mal, 1933 (*The Woman in the Gray House*, 1942)
La Maison du canal, 1933 (*The House by the Canal*, 1948)
L'Homme de Londres, 1934 (*Newhaven-Dieppe*, 1942)
Le Locataire, 1934 (*The Lodger*, 1943)
Maigret, 1934 (*Maigret Returns*, 1941)
Les Suicidés, 1934 (*One Way Out*, 1943)
Quartier Nègre, 1935
Les Demoiselles de Concarneau, 1936 (*The Breton Sisters*, 1943)
L'Assassin, 1937 (*The Murderer*, 1949)
Le Blanc à lunettes, 1937 (*Talatala*, 1943)
Faubourg, 1937 (*Home Town*, 1944)
Chemin sans issue, 1938 (*Blind Alley*, 1946)
L'Homme qui regardait passer les trains, 1938 (*The Man Who Watched the Trains Go By*, 1945)
Monsieur la Souris, 1938 (*The Mouse*, 1950)
Les Inconnus dans la maison, 1940 (*Strangers in the House*, 1951)
Il pleut, bergère . . . , 1941 (*Black Rain*, 1949)

Le Voyageur de la Toussaint, 1941 (*Strange Inheritance*, 1950)

Les Caves du Majestic, 1942 (*Maigret and the Hotel Majestic*, 1977)

Cécile est morte, 1942 (*Maigret and the Spinster*, 1977)

La Maison du juge, 1942 (*Maigret in Exile*, 1978)

Oncle Charles s'est enfermé, 1942 (*Uncle Charles Has Locked Himself In*, 1987)

La Veuve Couderc, 1942 (*Ticket of Leave*, 1954; also known as *The Widow*, 1955)

Félicie est là, 1944 (*Maigret and the Toy Village*, 1978)

L'Inspecteur cadavre, 1944 (*Maigret's Rival*, 1979)

Signé Picpus, 1944 (*To Any Lengths*, 1958)

L'Aîné des Ferchaux, 1945 (*Magnet of Doom*, 1948)

La Fuite de Monsieur Monde, 1945 (*Monsieur Monde Vanishes*, 1967)

Trois Chambres à Manhattan, 1946 (*Three Beds in Manhattan*, 1964; also known as *Three Bedrooms in Manhattan*, 2003)

Le Clan des Ostendais, 1947 (*The Ostenders*, 1952)

Lettre à mon juge, 1947 (*Act of Passion*, 1952)

Maigret à New York, 1947 (*Maigret in New York's Underworld*, 1955)

Maigret se fâche, 1947 (*Maigret in Retirement*, 1976)

Maigret et son mort, 1948 (*Maigret's Special Murder*, 1964)

La Neige était sale, 1948 (*The Snow Was Black*, 1950; also known as *The Stain in the Snow*, 1953; also known as *Dirty Snow*, 2003)

Pedigree, 1948 (English translation, 1962)

Les Vacances de Maigret, 1948 (*Maigret on Holiday*, 1950; also known as *No Vacation for Maigret*, 1953)

Les Fantômes du chapelier, 1949 (*The Hatter's Ghosts*, 1956)

Le Fond de la bouteille, 1949 (*The Bottom of the Bottle*, 1954)

Maigret chez le coroner, 1949 (*Maigret at the Coroner's*, 1980)

Mon Ami Maigret, 1949 (*My Friend Maigret*, 1956)

La Première Enquête de Maigret, 1949 (*Maigret's First Case*, 1958)

Les Quatre Jours du pauvre homme, 1949 (*Four Days in a Lifetime*, 1953)

L'Amie de Mme Maigret, 1950 (*Madame Maigret's Own Case*, 1959; also known as *Madame Maigret's Friend*, 1960)

L'Enterrement de Monsieur Bouvet, 1950 (*The Burial of Monsieur Bouvet*, 1955)

Maigret et la vieille dame, 1950 (*Maigret and the Old Lady*, 1958)

Les Volets verts, 1950 (*The Heart of a Man*, 1951)

Maigret au "Picratt's," 1951 (*Maigret in Montmartre*, 1954)

Maigret en meublé, 1951 (*Maigret Takes a Room*, 1960)

Maigret et la grande perche, 1951 (*Maigret and the Burglar's Wife*, 1969)

Les Mémoires de Maigret, 1951 (*Maigret's Memoirs*, 1963)

Une Vie comme neuve, 1951 (*A New Lease on Life*, 1963)

Maigret, Lognon, et les gangsters, 1952 (*Inspector Maigret and the Killers*, 1954; also known as *Maigret and the Gangsters*, 1974)

Le Révolver de Maigret, 1952 (*Maigret's Revolver*, 1956)

Antoine et Julie, 1953 (*The Magician*, 1955)

Feux rouges, 1953 (*The Hitchhiker*, 1955; also known as *Red Lights*, 1975)

Maigret a peur, 1953 (*Maigret Afraid*, 1961)

Maigret et l'homme du banc, 1953 (*Maigret and the Man on the Bench*, 1975)

Maigret se trompe, 1953 (*Maigret's Mistake*, 1954)

Crime impuni, 1954 (*The Fugitive*, 1955)

Le Grand Bob, 1954 (*Big Bob*, 1954)

L'Horloger d'Everton, 1954 (*The Watchmaker of Everton*, 1955)

Maigret à l'école, 1954 (*Maigret Goes to School*, 1957)

Maigret chez le ministre, 1954 (*Maigret and the Calame Report*, 1969)

Maigret et la jeune morte, 1954 (*Maigret and the Dead Girl*, 1955)

Les Témoins, 1954 (*The Witnesses*, 1956)

Les Complices, 1955 (*The Accomplices*, 1964)

Maigret et le corps sans tête, 1955 (*Maigret and the Headless Corpse*, 1967)

Maigret tend un piège, 1955 (*Maigret Sets a Trap*, 1965)

Un Échec de Maigret, 1956 (*Maigret's Failure*, 1962)

En cas de malheur, 1956 (*In Case of Emergency*, 1958)

Le Petit Homme d'Arkangelsk, 1956 (*The Little Man from Archangel*, 1966)

Maigret s'amuse, 1957 (*Maigret's Little Joke*, 1957)

Dimanche, 1958 (*Sunday*, 1960)

Maigret voyage, 1958 (*Maigret and the Millionaires*, 1974)

Les Scrupules de Maigret, 1958 (*Maigret Has Scruples*, 1959)

Une Confidence de Maigret, 1959 (*Maigret Has Doubts*, 1968)

Maigret et les témoins récalcitrants, 1959 (*Maigret and the Reluctant Witnesses*, 1959)

Maigret aux assises, 1960 (*Maigret in Court*, 1961)

Maigret et les vieillards, 1960 (*Maigret in Society*, 1962)

L'Ours en peluche, 1960 (*Teddy Bear*, 1971)

Betty, 1961 (English translation, 1975)

Maigret et le voleur paresseux, 1961 (*Maigret and the Lazy Burglar*, 1963)

Le Train, 1961 (*The Train*, 1964)

Maigret et le client du samedi, 1962 (*Maigret and the Saturday Caller*, 1964)

Maigret et les braves gens, 1962 (*Maigret and the Black Sheep*, 1976)

La Porte, 1962 (*The Door*, 1964)

Les Anneaux de Bicêtre, 1963 (*The Patient*, 1963; also known as *The Bells of Bicêtre*, 1964)

La Colère de Maigret, 1963 (*Maigret Loses His Temper*, 1964)

Maigret et le clochard, 1963 (*Maigret and the Bum*, 1973)

La Chambre bleue, 1964 (*The Blue Room*, 1964)

Maigret et le fantôme, 1964 (*Maigret and the Apparition*, 1975)

Maigret se défend, 1964 (*Maigret on the Defensive*, 1966)

La Patience de Maigret, 1965 (*The Patience of Maigret*, 1966)

Le Petit Saint, 1965 (*The Little Saint*, 1965)

Le Confessional, 1966 (*The Confessional*, 1968)

Maigret et l'affaire Nahour, 1966 (*Maigret and the Nahour Case*, 1967)

La Mort d'Auguste, 1966 (*The Old Man Dies*, 1967)

Le Chat, 1967 (*The Cat*, 1967)

Le Voleur de Maigret, 1967 (*Maigret's Pickpocket*, 1968)

L'Ami de l'enfance de Maigret, 1968 (*Maigret's Boyhood Friend*, 1970)

Maigret à Vichy, 1968 (*Maigret in Vichy*, 1969)

Maigret hésite, 1968 (*Maigret Hesitates*, 1970)

La Main, 1968 (*The Man on the Bench in the Barn*, 1970)

La Prison, 1968 (*The Prison*, 1969)

Maigret et le tueur, 1969 (*Maigret and the Killer*, 1971)

Novembre, 1969 (*November*, 1970)

La Folle de Maigret, 1970 (*Maigret and the Madwoman*, 1972)

Maigret et le marchand de vin, 1970 (*Maigret and the Wine Merchant*, 1971)

La Cage de verre, 1971 (*The Glass Cage*, 1973)

La Disparition d'Odile, 1971 (*The Disappearance of Odile*, 1972)

Maigret et l'homme tout seul, 1971 (*Maigret and the Loner*, 1975)

Maigret et l'indicateur, 1971 (*Maigret and the Informer*, 1972)

Les Innocents, 1972 (*The Innocents*, 1973)

Maigret et Monsieur Charles, 1972 (*Maigret and Monsieur Charles*, 1973)

OTHER LITERARY FORMS

Georges Simenon (see-muh-NOHN) is known primarily for his fiction. Throughout his career as a novelist, however, he frequently displayed mastery of shorter forms as well, both with and without the presence of his famous character Inspector Maigret. Originally published for the most part in periodicals, his short stories and novellas have been collected in such volumes as *Les Dossiers de l'Agence O* (1943), *Nouvelles exotiques* (1944), and in English translation as well. In his late thirties, erroneously informed by his doctors that he had but a short time to live, Simenon began writing his autobiography as a memoir for his infant son. At the urging of the eminent novelist André Gide (1869-1951), he soon abandoned the project, incorporating its best portions into the novel *Pedigree*, published in 1948. After publicly renouncing the practice of fiction shortly before his seventieth birthday, Simenon published his recollections in *Mémoires intimes* (1981; *Intimate Memoirs*, 1984).

ACHIEVEMENTS

Georges Simenon is among the most prolific fiction writers of his generation. During fifty years of sustained creative activity, he published upward of three hundred novels under his own name, exclusive of lesser efforts for which he employed a variety of pseudonyms. Although best known for his novels featuring Inspector Maigret of the Paris police, Simenon in fact published more titles outside the detective genre and was justly acclaimed both in France and abroad for his keen analysis of human character in mainstream fiction.

Simenon was a gifted student of human nature and a born raconteur whose keen powers of observation, linked to a highly retentive memory, have furnished the world with a vast array of memorable characters both within and outside the mystery genre. Incredibly, the sheer quantity of Simenon's work had little, if any, negative effect on its quality; throughout most of his career, Simenon was taken seriously, as a "serious" novelist, by general readers and critics alike.

Heir apparent to the tradition of French naturalism that flourished a quarter of a century before his birth through the works of Émile Zola, Guy de Maupassant, and Edmond and Jules de Goncourt, Simenon brought the best features of naturalism into the twentieth century. Unlike some other novelists and playwrights of his own generation, who pretended to "psychological realism" by parroting forth, as if undigested, the latest insights of Sigmund Freud and Carl Jung, Simenon evolved throughout his career a mode of psychological observation and recording that is all the more credible, and convincing, for its lack of cant or visible erudition. In most of his novels, Simenon appears to be suggesting that it is unnecessary to read Freud or Jung to gain an understanding of the criminal or psychotic mind, that all one need do is observe others closely, with understanding and compassion.

Maigret, among the most convincing and memorable of modern fictional detectives, is an "instinctive" psychologist who solves many initially baffling murders by focusing his attention on the victims, attempting to figure out what they might have done to invite violent death. In the non-Maigret novels, it is Simenon himself, as unseen and frequently omniscient narrator, who portrays apparently "normal" characters driven to sudden crime and violence by inevitable forces that they themselves can barely comprehend. Seldom, in either type of novel, does the action appear forced or the characters' behaviors unconvincing—a fault that hampers, if only infrequently, even the finest narratives of Zola and Maupassant.

It can be argued that Simenon's Maigret has contributed as much to the development of the mystery novel as did Sherlock Holmes himself, implicitly awarding to psychology the role in detection that Arthur Conan Doyle, writing a half century earlier, had attributed to the then-innovative scientific method. To Simenon and Maigret, as to their contemporary readers, it is usually more important (as well as entertaining) to understand *why* a crime was committed than precisely *how* it was done.

Of perhaps equal importance is Simenon's role in helping to create, through his Maigret novels, the subgenre of detective fiction known as the police procedural, now widely read and written the world over. Departing from the frequently romantic private detective whose dazzling insights make law officers look like buffoons, Simenon and his many followers in the subgenre focus instead on the grueling routines of police work itself, featuring career detectives whose profiles often fall far short of the heroic. Maigret is a case in point—a portly, balding, dedicated civil servant in late middle age with a durable, affectionate, but unfortunately childless marriage. Assisted in his many investigations by a recurring cast of subordinates and his voluble physician friend, Pardon, Maigret puts in long and frequently fruitless hours in his efforts to look at and through the crime to the mind of the criminal. Among the least judgmental of fictional detectives, Maigret on occasion comes to "understand" the crime so well that he either lets the perpetrator go free or agrees to testify in the person's defense.

At the risk of belaboring the obvious, it is perhaps appropriate to observe that the main difference between Simenon's Maigret novels and his "mainstream" works (by far the larger part of his production) is that in the latter, Maigret does not appear. Without Maigret's avuncular presence to tie up the loose ends of the characters' lives, the loose ends remain untied—frequently with disastrous results. As Lucille Frackman Becker has observed, the

> reassuring presence of Maigret . . . convinces us that there is an order, a structure, and a meaning to life. In the other novels, there is no Maigret to whom the protagonist can confess, there is no one to understand or with whom to communicate, leaving him immured in his solitude, stifled and suffocated by repressed confessions.

Indeed, the usual and highly credible atmosphere is one of utter solitude, alienation, and estrangement in which the characters, fully comprehensible to the author and hence to the reader, are just as fully incomprehensible to one another.

Among twentieth century French novelists, perhaps only the Nobelist François Mauriac—a possible source for some of Simenon's novelistic predicaments—has rendered as convincingly as Simenon the heart-wrenching predicaments of cross-purposes and unheard cries for help that often reverberate through life and love. In Mauriac's fictional universe, however, there is always the promise, secured only by the author's personal religious faith, of a better life to come in the next world. In those of Simenon's novels without Maigret, by contrast, hell on earth is most often simply hell. In his own de-

fense, Simenon argued with some justice that in the twentieth century the novel came to fulfill much the same function that tragedy did for the ancient Greeks. People's destinies are played out in repeated dialogue between author and audience, the one compelled to exorcise inner demons and the other to see its best hopes and worst fears replicated in the characters' behavior. After readers are thus reassured—presumably by a catharsis similar to that emerging, in Aristotle's view, from the viewing of a classical tragedy—they are able to address themselves to life with renewed vigor, aware of their limitations but better suited to savor the sights, sounds, and smells of everyday life.

Literary critics have most often reproached Simenon, like Zola before him, for his lack of literary style. Advised early in his career by the novelist Colette, then serving as one of his editors, to pare his work down to the barest essentials, Simenon soon perceived that his most effective style was one that favored the literal over the figurative, the concrete over the abstract. Over the years, that decision served him well, especially in the creation of plausible atmospheres in which to place his often hapless characters.

BIOGRAPHY

Born in 1903 in Liège, Belgium, the elder of two brothers, Georges Joseph Christian Simenon enjoyed an urban childhood that was sufficiently middle class that he recalled being disgruntled when his mother felt herself obliged to take in boarders in order to make ends meet. The failing health of his father, an insurance clerk, obliged the young Simenon to cut short his formal education and join the workforce at about age sixteen. After false starts as apprentice to a pastry cook and subsequently as a salesclerk, Simenon found steady work as a journalist at a still-precocious age and thereafter earned his living through writing, either as a journalist or as a secretary-speechwriter. Married in 1923 to Régine Renchon, Simenon later in that year began selling short stories to newspapers and soon expanded to the novel as well, publishing more than two hundred potboilers under various pseudonyms between 1925 and 1934, by which time his own name, thanks in part to Maigret, was beginning to ensure brisk sales.

According to Becker, Simenon originally attempted

Georges Simenon. (AP/Wide World Photos)

the erroneous belief that he was soon to die of a respiratory ailment; after revision, those memoirs would form the basis of the major novel *Pedigree*, completed during 1943 but not published until five years later. Toward the end of the hostilities, Simenon traveled extensively in North America and met the Canadian Denise Ouimet, who, after his divorce in 1950, would become his second wife. Residing first in Arizona, Simenon settled in northern Connecticut following his marriage to Ouimet; there he would write a number of his best-remembered novels, many with American settings and characters.

After returning to Europe in 1955, Simenon spent most of his time in the Lausanne area of Switzerland, where he was to die in 1989. Around 1972, Simenon renounced the writing of fiction, preferring instead to record on tape the most salient excerpts of his photographic memory. In 1981, he published his massive autobiography, *Intimate Memoirs*, notable for its sensational disclosures with regard to his unconventional sex life and his obsession with the suicide of his daughter, Marie-Jo. Despite its self-advertised candor, it is a strangely unrevealing work; Simenon the man remains elusive.

ANALYSIS

Named by the highly regarded André Gide as the greatest modern French novelist, Georges Simenon indeed compiled an enviable record of achievement, producing a body of work equally remarkable for its quality as for its quantity. The apprenticeship he served in writing his so-called potboilers appears to have served him well, allowing him to write fluently while maintaining rigorous standards of content and characterization. Simenon's demonstrated proficiency in the mystery genre alone would no doubt suffice to secure his position in the history of modern letters; nevertheless, he further confirmed his reputation with a solid list of mainstream titles valued for their psychological insights.

Simenon's prodigious accomplishment may be explained, at least to a point, by acknowledging that his fictional universe remains essentially the same regardless of whether Maigret is involved in the action; in both types of novel, the true protagonists are hounded, uncommunicative creatures with little more than the most marginal knowledge of what makes them behave as they

the detective novel "as a bridge between the popular potboilers he had been writing and the more serious literary efforts to which he aspired but for which he did not consider himself ready." His proposal accepted by the publisher Fayard, Simenon contracted in 1929 to write eighteen Maigret novels, which in time would expand to eighty-three in addition to shorter Maigret adventures. Curiously, Simenon's talent and fame as a mainstream novelist developed almost simultaneously with his reputation as a mystery writer, with several examples of each type of novel published annually throughout the 1930's to generally good sales and reviews.

In the mid-1930's, Simenon traveled extensively throughout the world; the "exotic" novels resulting from these voyages are justly famous among readers and scholars, although they constitute a small fraction of his literary output and depend more heavily on character than on atmosphere for their overall effect. Shortly after the outbreak of World War II, already involved in refugee relief work, Simenon began writing his memoirs in do. The main difference, as Becker has observed, lies in the thoughtful, reconciling presence of Maigret, who functions almost as a psychoanalyst in "solving" the mystery of behavior to the satisfaction of characters and readers alike; in the mainstream novels, the characters remain in their own private hells, understood (if at all) only by the narrator and his reader. Rarely, and then with remarkable effect, does Simenon surprise the reader with his conclusions; even then, as elsewhere in Simenon's novels, the denouement soon appears inevitable, amply prepared for by what he has revealed of the characters' makeup and motivations.

MAIGRET NOVELS

By his own admission, Simenon "discovered" Maigret at a time when, still unsure of his skills as a novelist, he was seeking a viewpoint character who could move about in space and time as the conventional narrator (or novelist) could not; eventually, he settled on a policeman as ideally suited to his needs and proposed the Maigret series, initially planned for eighteen volumes. The result, by now almost legendary, was one of the most durable characters in the history of detective fiction, further established by his omnipresent pipe, his childless wife, and cold meals ordered "to go" during the late-night hours from the obliging Brasserie Dauphine. Modeled on Simenon's own pensive, easygoing father, Maigret is on occasion so appealing that he makes the prospect of crime seem nearly attractive to the reader. The eminent playwright Jean Anouilh paid indirect homage to Maigret with *L'Arrestation* (pr., pb. 1975; *The Arrest*, 1978), in which an aging gangster, mortally wounded in a motor accident, is fortunate enough, in his final moments, to have his entire life explained to him by an even older inspector who has devoted his own career to studying the gangster's lifestyle and habits. Habitual criminals are, however, rather rare quarry for Maigret; more commonly, the crimes with which he deals are perpetrated by inhabitual offenders, seemingly normal people suddenly propelled toward violence by an accumulation of privation or resentment.

Maigret's murderers frequently kill for love or for its cherished memory. In *Maigret and the Loner*, one of Simenon's later Maigret adventures, more than twenty years elapse before a lovesick painter avenges his girlfriend's murder with the apparently gratuitous killing of his erstwhile rival, who has since become a homeless derelict. To Maigret, as to his creator, the painter could not possibly have behaved otherwise, his crime having long since been predetermined. Indeed, Maigret solves easily half of his initially baffling mysteries by reconstructing the lives of the victims in search of signs of irregularity or stress that could have engendered violence. Simenon himself claimed that, upon study of the evidence, "there are at least eight crimes in ten in which the victim shares to a great extent the responsibility of the murderer." Similar cases abound throughout Maigret's career, from nagging spouses and sadistic lovers to the "public enemy" Fumal in *Maigret's Failure*, who himself victimized so many people that Maigret is hard put to choose among them as he reluctantly searches for Fumal's killer.

Occasionally, as in *Maigret Sets a Trap*, the identity of the murderer is known early in the novel, lacking only Maigret's deductive analysis to render the case against him (or her) conclusive. Identified by a police "plant" and hemmed in by circumstantial evidence, the admittedly unlikely mass murderer, a mild-mannered interior decorator named Moncin, eludes conviction only because an additional, identical murder was committed after he was taken into custody. As Maigret, following a hunch, delves deeper into Moncin's life and career, he finds a spoiled and highly intelligent man dominated by his wife and mother, who compete ceaselessly for top billing in his life. Either woman, Maigret reasons, would have had both motive and capacity to commit the "decoy" murder; in fact, it was the wife who did it, thus scoring a final, irrefutable "point" against her husband's mother.

STRANGERS IN THE HOUSE

Generally similar in theme and subject matter to the novels featuring Maigret, Simenon's mainstream titles likewise abound in ill-adjusted characters who live in quiet desperation, occasionally bursting out in violence. The expository method employed is frequently similar to that of the detective novel, with one or more characters attempting to solve the mystery in their lives. A case in point is that of Loursat in *Strangers in the House*, an intriguing novel perhaps even more timely in the twenty-first century than when it first appeared. A once-promising attorney, Loursat has responded to his wife's desertion by hiding out for years, bottle in hand, in the sanctuary of his personal library. A gunshot and the discovery of a body in his attic one night forces his attention to the fact that his adolescent daughter, Nicole, who lives in the same house but whom he has seen only at mealtimes, is in fact the leader of a housebreaking ring and that their accumulated loot is stored in Loursat's own attic. The dead man proves to have been a criminal who was blackmailing Nicole's band. Nicole's lover, Émile Manu, a poor young man who proves a convenient but innocent suspect, is arrested. As Loursat—his professional instincts and sense of justice awakened from long dormancy by what he knows is an unjust arrest—attempts to track down the real killer, he proceeds as well toward a long-overdue assessment of his own strengths and weaknesses; in time, Loursat discovers the true murderer and obtains Manu's freedom, proceeding thereafter to resume the life and career that he had abandoned years earlier.

UNCLE CHARLES HAS LOCKED HIMSELF IN

Such happy endings are rare in Simenon's work; more frequently, the self-knowledge reached through deduction is then used for self-serving means, with little prospect of true liberation. Such is the case in *Uncle Charles Has Locked Himself In*, in which deduction leads a petty embezzler toward the even greater satisfaction of "invisible" blackmail.

Mild-mannered and unprepossessing, like many of the criminals ferreted out by Maigret, "Uncle" Charles Dupeux has for years nursed a grudge against his overbearing employer and brother-in-law, Henri, occasionally feeding that grudge with small thefts that, carefully managed, have grown into a considerable fortune; presumably, he will one day make his "break," supported by the embezzled nest egg. Before that can happen, however, Charles discovers that Henri is being blackmailed, and with good cause: Henri, although not legally responsible for his late partner's early death, in fact conspired to bring it about. Armed with this knowledge, Charles retreats to the attic, where he keeps his hoard of stock certificates, trying to decide how best to use what he has learned. To Henri's consternation, he refuses a generous offer for his silence, knowing that Henri does not even suspect him of embezzlement. Instead, Charles prefers "the revenge of the underdog"—to hold over Henri's de-

tested head the potential threat of exposure and thus avenge himself, albeit in secret, for what he regards as years of exploitation.

THE WITNESSES

Yet another of Simenon's memorable character studies is *The Witnesses*, which recalls the Maigret series as it carefully considers the often fragile foundations of justice. *The Witnesses* presents the tale of two men, the judge and the accused, and of circumstances that might, on occasion, be assessed as "circumstantial evidence." Little but the judicial bench, indeed, separates Judge Lhomond from Lambert in the dock; both men have notoriously bad marriages and have lately been prone to irregular behavior. As Lhomond successfully enjoins his jury to allow for "reasonable doubt" in Lambert's case, he is sure that the man would be convicted were not he, Lhomond, sitting on the bench that day.

TROPIC MOON

Simenon's exotic novels of the 1930's, although few in number, contain some of his best-remembered insights and descriptions; as elsewhere in his work, however, the setting is of interest to Simenon almost solely for its effects on human behavior. Joseph Timar, the ill-starred protagonist of *Tropic Moon*, arrives in the Congo only to find that the company that hired him is about to go bankrupt, that his job lies ten days upriver, and that his predecessor is still in place, having threatened to kill anyone who might be sent in to replace him. Soon thereafter, somewhat corrupted by an older woman of his acquaintance, Timar goes more than a little mad; aboard the ship that has been sent to fetch him home, he confidently declares that "there is no such place as Africa."

QUARTIER NÈGRE

Hardly more fortunate is the engineer Dupuche of *Quartier Nègre*, who, like Timar, discovers upon arriving at the site of a new job that his position has been abolished as a result of the firm's bankruptcy. Set in Panama, *Quartier Nègre* is perhaps even richer in atmosphere than *Tropic Moon*. In any case, both novels resulted in lawsuits against Simenon by residents of the Congo and Panama, respectively, who considered themselves ill represented in his works. Unlike Timar, Dupuche never leaves the tropics. Necessarily separated from his wife, who finds employment while he does not, Dupuche gradually but definitively goes native, residing in a tumbledown shack with his black mistress and their several children until he eventually dies, still young, of a tropical disease. Somewhat more fortunate is Ferdinand Graux, the title character of *Talatala*, who survives both the heat and his infatuation with a wanton Englishwoman long enough to rebuild his life and career with the help of his wife, Emmeline.

PEDIGREE

Unique among Simenon's many works outside the detective genre is the novel *Pedigree*, successfully mined by many of his critics in search of clues to his life and technique. Covering scarcely sixteen years in the life of Simenon's alter ego Roger Mamelin, *Pedigree* memorably chronicles the sights, sounds, and smells of Liège during the author's youth, adding unforgettable portraits of "Roger's" parents, aunts, and uncles. Implicit throughout the novel is the author's satiric attack on his German-descended mother and her representation of the lower-middle class, which would sooner starve than eat the cheap, abundant food favored by "peasants." Included as well are detailed portraits of his mother's boarders, many of whom had already appeared, or would soon appear, with slight fictional disguise, in Simenon's novels. Of Roger's parents, the ailing father is by far the more wise and sympathetic, if less forceful and therefore less significant; later, in *Lettre à ma mère* (1974; *Letter to My Mother*, 1976), the septuagenarian Simenon would give even fuller vent to his resentment of his mother. In any case, it is clear from *Pedigree* that were it not for the influence of his mother, Simenon would never have had the determination and perseverance to become a writer and that without his father, he would never have acquired the patience, skill, and compassion that made his work as successful as it is.

SUNDAY

Among Simenon's later novels, *Sunday* is one of the most memorable and impressive, rivaled perhaps only by *The Old Man Dies*. As befits its title, the events of the novel take place on a particular Sunday, the day that Émile, an accomplished chef, has selected in advance for the murder of his wife, Berthe, who is also his employer. Impotent in marriage, released from his affliction only in the arms of a wild and uncultured young waitress, Émile remains unaware of his abiding dependence on the domineering Berthe. So great, in fact, is Berthe's hold on Émile that when he learns that she has outsmarted him, feeding to his young mistress the poisoned lunch intended for herself, he meekly heeds her suggestion that he is already late for the regional soccer match. By the time he returns, all traces of the girl and his act will be gone, and everything will be restored to order.

THE OLD MAN DIES

In *The Old Man Dies*, similarly concerned with the running of a restaurant, the heir apparent, Antoine, is portrayed initially as an unsympathetic character, but he divides with his brothers, upon their father's death, a supposed "legacy" that is in fact wholly composed of his own funds. The true legacy, Simenon implies, is the restaurant itself, a business long since spurned by Antoine's brothers.

Simenon still stands virtually unchallenged in the territory that he claimed as his own between the two world wars. Faulted by some observers for his essentially negative, deterministic view of human nature and by others for his implied derogation of women and marriage, Simenon nevertheless remains among the most accomplished observers and chroniclers of his generation, his own legacy a challenge to any aspiring successors.

David B. Parsell

OTHER MAJOR WORKS

SHORT FICTION: *Les 13 coupables*, 1932 (*The Thirteen Culprits*, 2002); *Les Dossiers de L'Agence O*, 1943; *Les Nouvelles Enquêtes de Maigret*, 1944 (*The Short Cases of Inspector Maigret*, 1959); *Nouvelles exotiques*, 1944; *Maigret et l'inspecteur malchanceux*, 1947 (also known as *Maigret et l'inspecteur malgracieux*); "La Pipe de Maigret," 1947 ("Maigret's Pipe," 1977); *Un Noël de Maigret*, 1951 (*Maigret's Christmas*, 1951).

NONFICTION: *Le Roman de l'homme*, 1958 (*The Novel of Man*, 1964); *Quand j'étais vieux*, 1970 (*When I Was Old*, 1971); *Lettre à ma mère*, 1974 (*Letter to My Mother*, 1976); *Mémoires intimes*, 1981 (*Intimate Memoirs*, 1984); *Mes apprentissages: Reportages, 1931-1946*, 2001.

BIBLIOGRAPHY

Assouline, Pierre. *Simenon: A Biography*. Translated by Jon Rothschild. New York: Alfred A. Knopf, 1997. Presents a wealth of biographical information, providing an honest and often unflattering portrait of the writer.

Becker, Lucille Frackman. *Georges Simenon, Revisited*. New York: Twayne, 1999. Begins with a biographical chapter and then analyzes Simenon's novels, which are divided into novels of crime and detective, novels of crime and deviance, and exotic novels. Also discusses Simenon's "gift of narration" and reviews the film versions of his novels. Includes notes and bibliography.

Bresler, Fenton. *The Mystery of Georges Simenon*. Toronto, Ont.: General, 1983. Well-written, informative biography gives a strong sense of Simenon's roots and the development of his literary career. Includes conversations between Bresler and Simenon.

Carter, David. *The Pocket Essential Georges Simenon*. Harpenden, England: Pocket Essentials, 2003. Concise guide to Simenon's prolific body of fiction includes discussion of his Maigret mystery novels, the adaptation of his fiction to film, and critical opinions of the author.

Eskin, Stanley. *Simenon: A Critical Biography*. Jefferson, N.C.: McFarland, 1987. Provides a comprehensive narrative of Simenon's life and a meticulous analysis of his work, accompanied by detailed and helpful notes and a bibliography.

Franck, Frederick. *Simenon's Paris*. New York: Dial, 1970. Basically a book of illustrations of Paris, but informative in that it reveals a good deal about the way Simenon chose locations for his fiction.

Freeling, Nicolas. "Georges Simenon." In *Criminal Convictions: Errant Essays on Perpetrators of Literary License*. Boston: D. R. Godine, 1994. Examines how Simenon's works question the meaning of redemption and suffering. Part of a collection of essays in which Freeling, a crime novelist, analyzes the crime writing of other authors.

Marnham, Patrick. *The Man Who Wasn't Maigret: A Portrait of Georges Simenon*. London: Bloomsbury, 1992. Accessible and thorough study of Simenon's turbulent life and times is based in part on Marnham's analysis of Simenon's voluminous memoirs. Includes bibliographical references and index.

Raymond, John. *Simenon in Court*. New York: Harcourt Brace and World, 1968. Classic work provides an excellent overview of Simenon's fiction.

Simenon, Georges. "The Art of Fiction: Georges Simenon." Interview by Carvel Collins. *The Paris Review* 9 (Summer, 1993): 71-90. The author discusses both his career and his fictional methods in this wide-ranging interview.

WILLIAM GILMORE SIMMS

Born: Charleston, South Carolina; April 17, 1806
Died: Charleston, South Carolina; June 11, 1870

PRINCIPAL LONG FICTION

Martin Faber: The Story of a Criminal, 1833
Guy Rivers: A Tale of Georgia, 1834
The Partisan: A Tale of the Revolution, 1835
The Yemassee: A Romance of Carolina, 1835
Mellichampe: A Legend of the Santee, 1836
Pelayo: A Story of the Goth, 1838
Richard Hurdis: Or, The Avenger of Blood, a Tale of Alabama, 1838
The Damsel of Darien, 1839
Border Beagles: A Tale of Mississippi, 1840
Confession: Or, The Blind Heart, 1841
The Kinsmen: Or, The Black Riders of the Congaree, 1841 (revised as *The Scout*, 1854)
Beauchampe: Or, The Kentucky Tragedy, a Tale of Passion, 1842
Count Julian: Or, The Last Days of the Goth, a Historical Romance, 1845
Helen Halsey: Or, The Swamp State of Conelachita, a Tale of the Borders, 1845

The Lily and the Totem: Or, The Huguenots in Florida, 1850

Katharine Walton: Or, The Rebel of Dorchester, 1851

The Sword and the Distaff: Or, "Fair, Fat, and Forty," 1852 (revised as *Woodcraft*, 1854)

Vasconselos: A Romance of the New World, 1853

The Forayers: Or, The Raid of the Dog-Days, 1855

Charlemont: Or, The Pride of the Village, 1856

Eutaw: A Sequel to the Forayers, 1856

The Cassique of Kiawah: A Colonial Romance, 1859

OTHER LITERARY FORMS

William Gilmore Simms wrote extensively in all major literary genres. He began as a poet and achieved his first widespread fame in the northern United States with his long poetic work *Atalantis: A Story of the Sea* (1832). Although he continued to write and publish his verse throughout his lifetime and, indeed, felt himself to be a good poet, his reputation has never rested on his poetic abilities. Still, his poetry is not without interest, for Simms often reveals a sharp eye for natural detail in his descriptions, especially of the southern landscape. His accomplishments as a writer of short fiction only began to be appreciated in the late twentieth century.

Simms's emphasis on realism can be seen in such works as "The Hireling and the Slave," and his wonderful command of folk humor can be found in such literary "tall tales" as "Bald-Head Bill Bauldy" and "How Sharp Snaffles Got His Capital and Wife." Longer stories such as "Paddy McGann" contain further elements of the tall tale and folklore. Simms was not a good dramatist; he wrote a number of aborted plays and, in the case of *Pelayo*, adapted a failed drama into novel form. His best play is considered to be *Michael Bonham: Or, The Fall of Bexar, a Tale of Texas* (pb. 1852), which deals with the Texas war for independence.

In his nonfiction works, Simms often turned to the history of the South. Of his four major biographies, two—*The Life of Francis Marion* (1844) and *The Life of Nathanael Greene* (1849)—grew out of his abiding interest in the Revolutionary War in the South; both men also appeared as characters in his novels. His historical writings include *The History of South Carolina* (1840), a general history of the state, beginning with its settlement; *South-Carolina in the Revolutionary War* (1853), which concentrated on that part of the state's history that he so often used in his fiction; and his contemporary account of the Civil War, *Sack and Destruction of the City of Columbia, S.C.* (1865), an inspired example of reporting.

Although Simms was not always accurate or unbiased, he was a surprisingly good historian. He collected sources throughout his life and made use of private recollections and memories. His work provides a storehouse of information often overlooked by more standard historical works. Simms's combination of the factual and the imaginative in his historical romances is one of his strongest and most appealing traits.

ACHIEVEMENTS

Although during his lifetime William Gilmore Simms's popularity as a novelist ranked second only to that of James Fenimore Cooper, his reputation steadily diminished after his death, so that by the beginning of the twentieth century he was little more than a footnote in literary histories. With the University of South Carolina Press publications of *The Letters of William Gilmore Simms* (1952-1956; five volumes, Mary C. Simms Oliphant, editor) and the first volumes of *The Centennial Edition of the Writings of William Gilmore Simms* (1969-1975; sixteen volumes, John C. Guilds and James B. Meriwether, editors), however, there has been a growing interest in his work. Still, Simms's contributions to the development of American literature in the first half of the nineteenth century have been much underrated. Put simply, Simms was the most important antebellum southern man of letters. He created a body of work that is awesome in size and scope. More than eighty separate volumes were published during his life, and ongoing research is uncovering more of his writings hidden in forgotten periodicals or under various pseudonyms.

When, in 1832, Simms first traveled to New York City, he was determined to establish himself as a writer of national importance. He made the necessary publishing connections and paid homage to the leading Northern literary figures. The publication of his poetic work *Atalantis* in that year was enthusiastically received, but it and his short novel *Martin Faber*, published the following year, were still apprenticeship pieces that followed patterns set down by others. With *Guy Rivers*, *The Yemassee*, and *The Partisan*, Simms not only staked out his own literary territory but also publicly placed himself in competition on a national level. Simms was an ardent supporter of the idea that America must produce its own unique brand of writing, inspired by its own land and people and experiences. Simms's own interest lay in the South, but, as he explained in the preface to *The Wigwam and the Cabin* (1845), by mastering sectional material, the writer could still be of national importance, since no single writer could adequately depict the United States as a whole.

It was in his commitment to the South that Simms achieved his greatness. He saw the South as a land of exciting potential. He loved its rawness as well as its manners, its violence as well as its vitality. Its heritage was rich, he felt, but largely unknown to people both inside and outside the region. Thus Simms, with his passion for history and folklore, set out to reveal this past to southerners and northerners alike, to correct the historical picture he found so lacking. In his romances, he helped to define the popular image of the South from precolonial times up to the American Civil War. Northerners, Simms maintained, had no right to feel superior to their southern brethren, but southerners had all too often been remiss in preserving and appreciating their own heritage.

As the political disputes between North and South intensified, Simms became a protector of a way of life he felt was being threatened. In this time of trouble, he maintained that the past held lessons for the present: The courageous spirit of the pioneer and the partisan soldier could still inspire, the inherent nobility of the manor-born ladies and gentlemen could still instruct. Thus, Simms's tales of an earlier era, marked by characters of indomitable strength, could be seen as examples for his own time.

The sheer quantity of Simms's work remains staggering and his overall achievement approaches the heroic. Although he sometimes bemoaned the lack of appreciation and support he received in the South, most of his contemporaries, despite occasional carping, freely awarded him the laurels of leadership. A less courageous and confident person would never have faced the challenges that Simms invited. Before the war, he sought, through his own example, to impart a sense of dignity to the southern artist. For the five years he lived after the war, he struggled to rekindle the pride of a defeated people, in the middle of his own great personal tragedy. As a critic and an editor, as a poet and a writer of fiction, he worked at first with energy and enthusiasm, later out of a kind of desperation against the inevitable, but he never stinted in his devotion to art and to a world that came to lie in ruins around him.

BIOGRAPHY

William Gilmore Simms was born in Charleston, South Carolina, on April 17, 1806, the second son and only surviving child of William Gilmore and Harriet Ann Augusta Singleton Simms. Simms's father came from Ireland after the American Revolution and established a successful mercantile business in Charleston. His mother's family, the Singletons, had lived in the port city for generations. Her grandfather, Thomas Singleton, was one of the Charleston citizens arrested by the British authorities during their occupation and, despite his advanced age, sent in exile to St. Augustine; her father, John Singleton, had fought as a soldier on the side of the patriots.

Simms's mother died in 1808, and shortly thereafter, his father, grief-stricken at the loss of his wife, left Charleston to journey westward, placing his only child in the care of his late wife's mother, Mrs. Gates (she had remarried in 1800 after the death of John Singleton in 1799). The elder Simms went on to lead what must have seemed an incredibly exciting life to his impressionable son; the boy heard tales of his father's fighting under Andrew Jackson in the Indian Wars in Florida and later at the Battle of New Orleans in the War of 1812 before settling in Mississippi, then the edge of the frontier. Thus, Simms the boy grew up surrounded by legends and dreams of almost mythical characters—the Revolutionary War heroes on the Singleton side of the family, and the pioneer-soldier he saw in his own father. Both romantic threads would run throughout Simms's writings. In addition, growing up in historic Charleston allowed him to visit sites of revolutionary incidents in and near the city. His unflagging interest in history (especially that of South Carolina but also of foreign lands) provided a foundation for his wilder imagination, and his writings would always contain a solid understructure of fact.

Although tradition has held that Simms grew up in genteel poverty in Charleston, feeling ostracized by that aristocratic city's more prominent citizens, his father had, in fact, left him substantial property holdings, and Simms was recognized early for his achievements. Still, it is equally clear that Simms was sensitive to slight—partly because of boyhood loneliness after the loss of his immediate family—and his enormous artistic energy no doubt fed on this partial uncertainty.

In 1812, at the age of six, Simms began school in Charleston. He entered the College of Charleston when he was ten, and at twelve he began work in a local apothecary shop. He was already writing poetry and drama. By the age of sixteen, he had published verse in a Charleston newspaper; at age seventeen he was editing a juvenile periodical, the first of many editorships he would undertake in his lifetime. The next year, 1824 to 1825, Simms spent with his father in Mississippi. Together they ranged into the wilderness, where Simms met and carefully observed the types of frontiersmen (rascals and rogues among them) and American Indians that would people his romances.

When Simms returned to Charleston in 1825, he set about establishing himself as a writer. His first volume of verse, *Monody on the Death of Gen. Charles Cotesworth Pinckney* (1825), made him a prominent local talent. In 1826, he married Anna Malcolm Giles. The next year Simms was admitted to the bar and published his second and third volumes of poetry. In 1828, he became editor of the *Southern Literary Gazette*; in 1829, his fourth volume of verse appeared, and his fifth followed in 1830. Also in 1830, he became co-partner in Charleston's *City Gazette*. In this role he figured as a leading opponent to the Nullification Controversy, which was dividing South Carolina into two very fractious parties. Simms's opposition brought him into serious disfavor with many important citizens, and it was an experience that he would remember with a mixture of anger and regret.

The year 1832 was a decisive one for Simms. His wife, Anna, died in February. Overtaxed by emotional and professional demands, Simms gave up his legal practice (never a foremost interest), sold the *City Gazette*, and journeyed to New York City, determined to make his way in earnest as a literary man. In New York, he formed what was to be a lifelong friendship with James Lawson. Simms would use Lawson's home as his northern base until the Civil War finally intervened; Lawson would be among the first to help Simms in the dark days after the war as well. With Lawson's encouragement and advice, Simms published his sixth volume of poetry, *Atalantis*, in 1832. When it proved extremely popular with the Northern audience, Simms followed it with his first novel, *Martin Faber*, and his first collection of short fiction, *The Book of My Lady*, both in 1833. With the publication of *Guy Rivers* in 1834 and of *The Parti-*

William Gilmore Simms. (Getty Images)

san and *The Yemassee* in 1835, Simms had announced his literary directions, as these three books were the first of his border, revolutionary, and colonial romances, respectively.

The next twenty or so years were generally good ones for Simms. In 1836, he married Chevillette Eliza Roach, the daughter of a prominent land owner in South Carolina. As part of his marriage inheritance, Simms obtained Woodlands plantation, which became his most prized retreat, an emblem of all he saw best in the southern way of life. The demands of his lifestyle made it necessary that Simms publish as much and as often as possible, but because of the laxity of copyright laws he often received far less than he was due for what he did write. Simms would travel to New York about once a year to confer with his publishers (for a time new works by Simms came out annually) and to visit old friends. He enjoyed his growing reputation as spokesman for the South. Although he was always interested in politics and acted as an informal adviser to a number of political leaders in South Carolina, he served only one term in government, as a member of the South Carolina House of Representatives from 1844 to 1846. His most notable literary position during this time was as editor of the *Southern Quarterly Review* from 1849 to 1854.

Beginning in the 1850's, Simms became a leading voice in the call for the South's secession from the Union and in the defense of slavery. He is too often remembered for the attitudes struck in these pronouncements, so at odds with modern understanding, at the expense of his more important creative works. As a public figure, Simms attracted the opprobrium aimed at the South as war became inevitable. His 1856 lecture tour of the North on the role of the South in the American Revolution had to be cut short when Simms enraged his audiences with his vigorous and even pugnacious arguments against the Union stand. He welcomed the final break and was confident of Southern victory, but as the war progressed, he came to see the specter of defeat.

The last years of Simms's life were tragic. In 1862, Woodlands was partially burned but was rebuilt through the subscriptions of appreciative South Carolinians. In 1863, his second wife died, a devastating blow to Simms, who had also lost nine of his children. In 1865, Woodlands was again set ablaze, this time by stragglers

from General Sherman's army. Simms lost in this conflagration his private library of ten thousand volumes, considered to be the finest in the South at the time.

During the five years remaining to him after the war, Simms worked as never before, as editor of two newspapers—the *Columbia Phoenix* and the *Daily South Carolinian*—and as the author of still more poems, addresses, short fiction, and serialized novels. Despite his own almost inconceivable losses, Simms did what he could to bring about the resurrection of the South. When he died on June 11, 1870, a world and a way of life had clearly passed with him.

ANALYSIS

As early as 1835, in the preface to *The Yemassee*, William Gilmore Simms attempted to define his goals as a writer. He distinguished his full-length fiction as romances rather than novels. Following definitions already in vogue, Simms described the novel as picturing ordinary people in everyday situations, both domestic and common. These works he traced to Samuel Richardson and Henry Fielding. The romance, on the other hand, he saw as the modern-day equivalent to the ancient epic, drawing its inspiration and power from both drama and poetry. The romance (as practiced by writers such as Sir Walter Scott, Edward Bulwer-Lytton, and James Fenimore Cooper) was of "loftier origins" than the novel. Its characters were individuals caught up in extraordinary, uncertain, even improbable events. As Simms saw it, the writer of a romance was not as bound by strict logic as was the novelist; indeed, the romancer's ingenuity in plotting was often a strong point in the work. As critics have pointed out, a number of Simms's supposed literary sins—stock characters, absurd resolutions, inflated dialogue—resulted from the Romantic tradition in which he worked rather than from a lack of art or skill.

REALISM

To categorize Simms simply as a writer of romances is, however, somewhat misleading, and later studies emphasized the strong sense of realism that is found in his work. During his lifetime, Simms was regularly accused of exceeding the bounds of propriety. He answered these objections on numerous occasions. In his "Advertisement" to *Mellichampe*, for example, he insisted that his purpose was to "adhere as closely as possible, to the features and the attributes of real life." Thus, although he endeavored to invest his stories with noble characters involved in stirring adventures, he wished to write neither "a fairy tale, [n]or a tale in which none but the colors of the rose and rainbow shall predominate."

This sense of realism, which must have seemed uncouth in Simms's own time, has come to be recognized as one of his strongest traits. He was clearly influenced by the "realism" of the legends and frontier tales of his youth and in the writings of the southern and southwestern humorists. Augustus Baldwin Longstreet's *Georgia Scenes* was published in 1835, the same year as *The Yemassee* and *The Partisan*. (Simms would himself write several brilliant tall tales such as "Bald-Head Bill Bauldy" and "How Sharp Snaffles Got His Capital and Wife.") Simms's sense of realism did not apply only to "low" characters and their exploits, however, as has often been implied. Simms would modify the nobility, the wisdom, even the courage of his "model characters," his aristocrats, if the story warranted it. His heroes could learn, could fail, could grow; and his villains were often surprisingly complex, capable of unexpected decency and courageous deeds.

Underlying all of Simms's romances was a strong awareness of history, of what had actually happened at the time and place about which he wrote. Simms felt free to bend fact to the demands of art, but not to misrepresent the essential truth of the situation. The *facts* of history, he said, standing by themselves, carried little weight, but the artist—the creative writer—by giving *shape* to the facts, could give them life and meaning. Thus, it is the writer who is the true historian, and it was as an "artist-historian" that Simms wrote most of his romances.

As all commentators on Simms like to point out (and as Simms himself was aware), he usually wrote too rapidly and carelessly. He simply produced too much for the good of his own reputation. His faults are often glaring, but they are usually the result of haste and little or no revision. Simms could write with clarity and precision, but he could also sacrifice both for blood and thunder. Simms was a storyteller, and his books, for all their length, keep a steady pace. When he turned his hand to psychological interpretations of characters, when he tried to "analyze the heart," he often did so with the concomitant loss of energy and drive. In his best works,

however, he was able to combine complexity of character with a compelling story.

REVOLUTIONARY WAR NOVELS

Simms wrote eight romances dealing with the Revolutionary War in the South, and as a group they represent his best work. The novels cover the period from 1775, when the first open warfare began, to 1783, when the British abandoned Charleston and the soldiers returned home to a new and difficult way of life. The internal chronology of the novels does not correspond to the sequence of their composition. *Joscelyn: A Tale of the Revolution*, which was meant to be the "opening scene" in Simms's "grand drama" of the South's seven-year war of Revolution, was one of the very last works he wrote, and the only one of the eight never to appear in book form during his lifetime. It appears as volume 16 of *The Centennial Edition of the Writings of William Gilmore Simms*. *Joscelyn* is set around the Georgia-South Carolina border and describes the early conflicts between those who joined in the growing freedom movement and those who remained loyal to the crown. It also shows that people on both sides of the issue could be motivated by cruelty as well as courage, by selfishness as well as honor.

THE PARTISAN, MELLICHAMPE, and KATHARINE WALTON

Simms conceived of the three novels *The Partisan*, *Mellichampe*, and *Katharine Walton* as a trilogy, with developing characters and overlapping plots, although each was also meant to stand as an independent work. These books cover the events of 1780, following the fall of Charleston to the British. *The Partisan* is a big, sprawling book that Simms later described as a "ground-plan," a setting of the stage for the works to come. It introduces numerous characters, both historical—Francis Marion, Lord Cornwallis, Sir Banastre Tarleton, Horatio Gates, Baron de Kalb—and fictional—Major Robert Singleton, Colonel Richard Walton and daughter Katharine, Lieutenant Porgy—who return in later works in the series. *The Partisan*'s story lines include the development of Marion's guerrilla forces in the swamps of South Carolina, the growth of love between Singleton and Katharine Walton, and the agony of Colonel Walton's decision to align himself with the rebel cause. The novel closes with a detailed description and analysis of the Battle of Camden (August, 1780), wherein Gates and the Southern Continental Army were soundly defeated by Cornwallis.

Mellichampe is set in the fall of 1780. It put less emphasis on the large historical picture and was more clearly intended as a work of fiction, although here again the facts of the war are not forgotten. In *Mellichampe*, Simms expands his description of Marion's role in the war, develops several minor characters found in *The Partisan*, and illustrates the "excesses of patriotism" and the necessity of honor in times of conflict. The third book of this trilogy, *Katharine Walton*, again takes up the story of Colonel Walton, his daughter, and Robert Singleton. It is set largely in Charleston during the last months of 1780 and describes the social life and attempts at rebellion in the captured city at this very trying time.

The Scout

The next in the series is *The Scout*, which moves into the central region of South Carolina. It is, in some ways, the most "romantic" and melodramatic of the novels. Its plot of feuding brothers and mysterious outriders is heavy with conventions, but in its description of the marauding outlaw bands that terrorized the backcountry and in its discussion of Nathanael Greene's siege of the British fort at Ninety-Six (upstate South Carolina) in the summer of 1781, *The Scout* is an impressive and absorbing story.

The Forayers and *Eutaw*, which were first conceived as one book, follow the retreat of the British from Ninety-Six to Charleston and present the events leading to the climactic battle at Eutaw Springs, South Carolina, in September, 1781, which effectively ended British rule in the state, although the battle itself was a draw.

Woodcraft

The last of the Revolutionary War novels is *Woodcraft*, which begins in December, 1782, after the British evacuation. Its theme is the readjustment of soldiers to domestic life, and its main character is Lieutenant Porgy, the wastrel aristocrat soldier whom many feel to be Simms's most successful character. Porgy appears in five of the eight novels, but his most important role is in *Woodcraft*. Basically a comic character (Porgy is often compared to William Shakespeare's Falstaff, although such comparisons rarely go beyond surface descriptions), this fat soldier confronts the challenges of peace

after the adventures of war. Born of the landed gentry, Porgy is known to have wasted his inheritance as a young man, and despite his courage and wit, he is not one of Simms's noble heroes. He is, however, among the most likable and (with reservations) the most admirable of Simms's characters, and it is his mood of reconciliation (after one final battle) and acceptance that presides over this last book. Some critics hold *Woodcraft* to be Simms's best work (although *The Forayers* and *Eutaw* might be better choices), and it certainly shows Simms at his most relaxed and amiable.

Guy Rivers

Commonly listed under the category of Simms's border romances are *Guy Rivers*, *Richard Hurdis*, *Border Beagles*, *Beauchampe*, *Helen Halsey*, *Charlemont*, "Voltmeier: Or, The Mountain Men," and "The Cub of the Panther." These works lack the specific historical overview of the Revolutionary War novels—they are closer to Simms's own time and are not as likely to be built around identifiable events—but they do give excellent descriptions of the frontier of the Old South—the customs, speech patterns, and lifestyle of settlers, outlaws, and adventurers. The first of these, *Guy Rivers*, was Simms's first full-length novel as well. Set in the mountainous region of Georgia, where gold was being mined in the early nineteenth century, the story centers on the conflict between Guy Rivers, a notorious outlaw (though once a respected lawyer) and Ralph Colleton, a young South Carolinian whose own frustrations with love and family have led him to the frontier. There he meets Mark Forrester, a native of the region who helps Ralph in his "natural" education. Colleton foreshadows such later Simms heroes as Robert Singleton, Ernest Mellichampe, and Willie Sinclair (in *The Forayers* and *Eutaw*), while Forrester anticipates Thumbscrew Witherspoon in *Mellichampe* and Supple Jack Bannister in *The Scout*, woodsmen who teach the young aristocrats the need for clear thinking and honorable actions. Rivers is the melodramatic villain of the type that would chew the scenery and threaten feminine virtue in a number of Simms's works: Barsfield in *Mellichampe*, Edward Conway in *The Scout*, Captain Inglehardt in *The Forayers* and *Eutaw*.

Richard Hurdis

Richard Hurdis, the second of the border novels, is perhaps the best of them. Set in Alabama, the story is loosely based on the outrages of John Murrell and his outlaw gang, which roamed throughout Alabama and Mississippi. Simms apparently had met witnesses to or even participants in some of this gang's doings while visiting his father in Mississippi as a boy. The plot is somewhat similar to that of *The Scout*. In each novel, two brothers—one virtuous and one criminally inclined—find themselves at odds; both books are concerned with the attempts to bring outlaw bands to justice. In a sense, *Border Beagles* is a continuation of *Richard Hurdis*; a tale of bandits on the Mississippi frontier, it is generally considered a less effective story than its predecessor.

BEAUCHAMPE

Beauchampe was Simms's retelling of the notorious Beauchampe-Sharpe Kentucky tragedy, a murder case in which Beauchampe killed Warham Sharpe, the seducer of Margaret Cooper, whom Beauchampe had married. In 1856, Simms returned to this story in *Charlemont*, which detailed the events leading up to the tragedy in *Beauchampe*. Thus, *Beauchampe*, although published first, was, in Simms's words, the "sequel" to *Charlemont*. Simms's last two border romances were both published in magazines in 1869. "Voltmeier" was published again in 1969 as volume 1 of *The Centennial Edition of the Writings of William Gilmore Simms*. "Voltmeier" and "The Cub of the Panther" were drawn from Simms's personal observations and experiences during trips into the mountainous regions of North Carolina, and they contain some of his best writing.

THE YEMASSEE *and* THE CASSIQUE OF KIAWAH

Simms dealt with the settling of South Carolina in the early eighteenth century in two important works, *The Yemassee* and *The Cassique of Kiawah*. *The Yemassee* was Simms's most popular novel and, because of its American Indian theme, was immediately compared to the works of Cooper. The novel described the 1715 Yemassee Indian War against the colonists. Simms's tale concentrates on two main characters: Governor Charles Craven (a historical figure), who takes the disguise of Gabriel Harrison for much of the book, and Sanutee, the chief of the Yemassee. Simms illustrates Sanutee's problem with sympathy and understanding—the Native American had originally welcomed the settlers and then found himself and his tribe threatened by

them—but the novel finally argues in favor of the whites and the advanced civilization they bring with them.

Despite *The Yemassee*'s popularity—it is still the work for which Simms is best remembered—the novel is not as impressive as *The Cassique of Kiawah*, a much later and more mature work, which deals with similar material but has received little critical attention. It has been argued that Simms's picture of the American Indian was more realistic than Cooper's. He avoided the idea of the "noble savage," but often imbued his Native Americans with traits of courage and dignity. In addition to these two novels, Simms used colonial and American Indian material in several of his shorter works found in *Carl Werner* (1838) and *The Wigwam and the Cabin*.

PELAYO, COUNT JULIAN, THE DAMSEL OF DARIEN, *and* VASCONSELOS

Simms's interest in European history, especially in Spanish history, dated back to his childhood and formed the basis for four foreign romances. *Pelayo* had been conceived when Simms was seventeen as a drama on the conquest of Spain by the Moors. The play was never performed, and the material later grew into a novel. *Count Julian* was the sequel to *Pelayo*, but its publication was delayed for a number of years because its manuscript was lost for a time. *The Damsel of Darien* was inspired by the adventures of explorer Vasco Núñez de Balboa, while *Vasconselos* concerned itself with Hernando de Soto's explorations in the New World. Most critics and readers would agree that these works are among Simms's weakest.

MARTIN FABER *and* CONFESSION

Simms's first novel, *Martin Faber*, recounts the first-person confessions of the title character, who has seduced and murdered one girl and married another, whom he then begins to suspect of adultery. Faber tells his story in prison, just before his execution. The book is a short and emotional work, and it was quickly linked to William Godwin's *Things as They Are: Or, The Adventures of Caleb Williams* (1794), although its antecedents could also be found in numerous gothic romances.

Simms returned to this type of story in *Confession*, which, in his introduction, Simms linked to Godwin. *Confession* was the reworking of an idea Simms had played with as a younger writer. He explained that he had forgotten the work before he found the manuscript by accident years later. As he reread it, he was "led away" by the psychological aspects of the tale. *Confession* tells of Edward Clifford, a young lawyer who is consumed by jealousy of his wife. Convinced of the worst, Clifford kills the entirely virtuous woman; when he later discovers the truth, he condemns himself to a life of wandering and self-recrimination. The similarities to Shakespeare's *Othello, the Moor of Venice* (pr. 1604) are obvious, although Simms maintained that the materials were "gathered from fact."

The same interests in crime, guilt, and retribution are found throughout his other works—he was always intrigued by the psychological complexities of sinners and criminals—and it could be argued that *Beauchampe* and *Charlemont* might better be placed in this group than among the border tales. These psychological novels, however, are not the works for which Simms is remembered. Although his constantly inquiring imagination was stirred by these situations, he was the master of scope and action rather than the kind of close analysis these topics demanded. The twists and entanglements of plot that could be overridden in his more sweeping works became all too obvious when related at a slower, more concentrated pace.

In his lasting works, Simms's long undervalued contribution to America's literary heritage is clearly evident. His was the voice of the South—the maker of its romances, the singer of its legends, the keeper of its history, and the defender of its traditions. More than any other writer, he embodied his time and place: its grandeur, its courage, and its wrongheadedness.

Edwin T. Arnold III

OTHER MAJOR WORKS

SHORT FICTION: *The Book of My Lady*, 1833; *Carl Werner*, 1838; *The Wigwam and the Cabin*, 1845; *Southward Ho!*, 1854.

PLAY: *Michael Bonham: Or, The Fall of Bexar, a Tale of Texas*, pb. 1852.

POETRY: *Monody on the Death of Gen. Charles Cotesworth Pinckney*, 1825; *Early Lays*, 1827; *Lyrical, and Other Poems*, 1827; *The Vision of Cortes*, 1829; *The Tri-Color*, 1830; *Atalantis: A Story of the Sea*, 1832; *Areytos: Or, Songs of the South*, 1846; *Poems Descriptive, Dramatic, Legendary, and Contemplative*, 1853.

NONFICTION: *The History of South Carolina*, 1840; *The Geography of South Carolina*, 1843; *The Life of Francis Marion*, 1844; *Views and Reviews in American Literature, History, and Fiction*, 1845; *The Life of Captain John Smith*, 1846; *The Life of Chevalier Bayard*, 1847; *The Life of Nathanael Greene*, 1849; *South-Carolina in the Revolutionary War*, 1853; *Sack and Destruction of the City of Columbia, S.C.*, 1865; *The Letters of William Gilmore Simms*, 1952-1956 (5 volumes; Mary C. Simms Oliphant, editor).

MISCELLANEOUS: *The Centennial Edition of the Writings of William Gilmore Simms*, 1969-1975 (16 volumes; John C. Guilds and James B. Meriwether, editors).

BIBLIOGRAPHY

Busick, Sean R. *A Sober Desire for History: William Gilmore Simms as Historian*. Columbia: University of South Carolina Press, 2005. Busick argues that Simms is best understood as a historian, and he describes Simms's efforts to record and comprehend American history and to preserve the past. Among other topics, he addresses Simms's ideas about the relation of fiction to history.

Frye, Steven. "Metahistory and American Progressivism: Cultural Dialogics in Simms's *The Yemassee*." In *Historiography and Narrative Design in the American Romance: A Study of Four Authors*. Lewiston, N.Y.: Edwin Mellen Press, 2001. Frye analyzes romances by Simms and three other nineteenth century American writers, describing how these novels employ various techniques and models for writing history.

Guilds, John Caldwell. *Simms: A Literary Life*. Fayetteville: University of Arkansas Press, 1992. Guilds has attempted to rescue Simms from obscurity, editing several twentieth century editions of Simms's novels, as well as collections of essays about the southern author. In this account of Simms's life and writing, Guilds maintains that Simms's historical fiction provides an "epic study" of the United States and should be recognized as the work of a major writer.

_____, ed. *"Long Years of Neglect": The Work and Reputation of William Gilmore Simms*. Fayetteville: University of Arkansas Press, 1988. The twelve essays in this collection address Simms as novelist, poet, historical philosopher, humorist, lecturer, and literary critic.

Guilds, John Caldwell, and Caroline Collins, eds. *William Gilmore Simms and the American Frontier.* Athens: University of Georgia Press, 1997. Collection of essays analyzing the frontier motif in Simms's works, including the novels *Guy Rivers* and *Border Beagles.*

Johanyak, Debra. "William Gilmore Simms: Deviant Paradigms of Southern Womanhood?" *Mississippi Quarterly* 46 (Fall, 1993): 573-588. Discusses the portrayal of women in Simms's fiction. Johanyak claims that just as intellectual, independent, or masculinized women are repeatedly destroyed by seducers in Simms's work, readers are encouraged to view them as deviant and as contributing to their own downfall.

Mayfield, John. "'The Soul of a Man': William Gilmore Simms and the Myths of Southern Manhood." *Journal of the Early Republic* 15 (Fall, 1995): 477-500. An examination of southern men in Simms's fiction. Mayfield argues that both as literary figures and as paradigms, Simms's characters are failures, being stereotypes with little to offer.

Watson, Charles S. *From Nationalism to Secessionism: The Changing Fiction of William Gilmore Simms.* Westport, Conn.: Greenwood Press, 1993. Watson closely analyzes Simms's work to demonstrate his changing political opinions. From 1825 until 1848, Simms was a nationalist, creating patriotic romances; however, as the United States edged closer to Civil War, he became a secessionist, as evidenced by his later works.

Wimsatt, Mary Ann. *The Major Fiction of William Gilmore Simms: Cultural Traditions and Literary Forms.* Baton Rouge: Louisiana State University Press, 1989. Focusing on Simms's novels, Wimsatt provides one of the most useful discussions of Simms's work, re-evaluating many of the misconceptions and dismissive attitudes about his fiction. She makes use of biographical as well as historical information, and she discusses Simms's novels within the context of twentieth century critical formulations about the romance genre.

CLAUDE SIMON

Born: Tananarive (now Antananarivo), Madagascar; October 10, 1913
Died: Paris, France; July 6, 2005
Also known as: Claude-Eugène-Henri Simon

PRINCIPAL LONG FICTION

Le Tricheur, 1945
Gulliver, 1952
Le Sacre du printemps, 1954
Le Vent: Tentative de restitution d'un rétable baroque, 1957 (*The Wind: Attempted Restoration of a Baroque Altarpiece*, 1959)
L'Herbe, 1958 (*The Grass*, 1960)
La Route des Flandres, 1960 (*The Flanders Road*, 1961)

Le Palace, 1962 (*The Palace*, 1963)
Histoire, 1967 (English translation, 1968)
La Bataille de Pharsale, 1969 (*The Battle of Pharsalus*, 1971)
Les Corps conducteurs, 1971 (*Conducting Bodies*, 1974)
Triptyque, 1973 (*Triptych*, 1976)
Leçon de choses, 1975 (*The World About Us*, 1983)
Les Géorgiques, 1981 (*The Georgics*, 1989)
L'Invitation, 1987 (*The Invitation*, 1991)
L'Acacia, 1989 (*The Acacia*, 1991)
Le Jardin des plantes, 1997 (*The Jardin des Plantes*, 2001)
Le Tramway, 2001 (*The Trolley*, 2002)

OTHER LITERARY FORMS

In addition to his novels, Claude Simon (see-MOHN) published *La Corde raide* (1947; the tightrope), a journal containing various impressions of the Spanish Civil War and World War II as well as reflections upon painting and writing; *Orion aveugle* (1970; blind Orion), an art edition that includes portions of his novel *Conducting Bodies* along with reproductions of several paintings mentioned in the text; and *Femmes* (1966; women), a series of commentaries on paintings by Joan Miró.

ACHIEVEMENTS

One of the foremost members of a group of avant-garde writers in France usually designated by the term New Novelists, Claude Simon successfully merged critical theory with the practice of writing. In so doing, he extended the limits of the novel while at the same time elaborating a unique fictional universe. He referred to his novels as a "field of investigation"; that is to say, he constantly experimented with new modes of narrative discourse, not with a particular and ultimate form in mind but as a means of exploring diverse perspectives on the relationship between reality and its representation. By conceiving of the novel as production rather than product, by refusing to allow the text to become transparent and self-erasing as it progresses toward an inevitable resolution—as tends to be the case in the traditional, realistic novel—Simon obliged readers to change their habits. His novels require an active participation by the reader in the shaping of the text.

Unlike some of the New Novelists, Simon did not reduce the novel to an arid linguistic game or a treatise on narrative technique. His works, no matter how experimental, are never mere pretexts for the founding of a new science of the novel. He was able to combine brilliantly his aesthetic preoccupations with themes and images that probe the nature of the human condition and exert a compelling attraction upon those readers who are willing to undergo the demanding apprenticeship that his novels require.

The protagonists of Simon's fictional universe find that once the complacent order of their everyday lives is disrupted, they are forced to confront fundamental questions regarding the human condition and the role of language in shaping, or distorting, their comprehension of reality and, ultimately, of their own identity. Simon's doubt about the ability of words to seize the nature of experience gives rise to a literary language that can be extraordinarily rich, sensual, and evocative. This flow of language tends to create its own order out of the chaos of existence. Although Simon's audience is a limited one, drawn largely from the university, he provided these "happy few" with compelling insights into the character of existence and the process of fiction-making. For his efforts, he was granted the Nobel Prize in Literature in 1985.

BIOGRAPHY

Claude-Eugène-Henri Simon was born on October 10, 1913, in Tananarive, the capital city of the island of Madagascar, then a French possession. He left Madagascar at a young age and spent his childhood in Perpignan, a small city in the eastern Pyrenees. His father, an army officer, was killed in World War I. In 1924, Simon entered the Lycée Stanislas in Paris, where he completed his secondary education. He decided to prepare himself for a career as a painter and studied under André Lhôte.

As a young man traveling in Europe during the 1930's, Simon found himself in Spain at the time of the Civil War and participated in the conflict on the republican side. At the beginning of World War II, he was drafted into a cavalry regiment. In May, 1940, he took part in the Battle of the Meuse, in which France suffered a crushing defeat. He was captured by the Germans and placed in a prisoner-of-war camp, from which he escaped in November. Thereafter he lived in Paris, spending part of his time in the Perpignan region, where he was once a wine grower.

Although he began writing in the early 1940's, Simon did not publish his first novel, *Le Tricheur*, until 1945. In 1960, he received the Prix de l'Express for *The Flanders Road* and in 1967 the Prix Médicis for *Histoire*. In 1963, his only theatrical work, *La Séparation*, based on *The Grass*, was produced in Paris but met with little success.

After his Nobel Prize win in 1985, Simon published photographic collections, autobiographical novels, and a work of nonfiction based on a writers' conference. In interviews, Simon said that he preferred to think of his novels as reflections of a lived reality, rather than as direct transcriptions of a life. He continued to write, collect art, and live in Paris for most of the year and in Perpignan in the summers until his death on July 6, 2005 in Paris.

ANALYSIS

Most of Claude Simon's critics divide the evolution of his novels into three principal phases: an initial period, consisting largely of traditional novels and ending with two transitional works, *The Wind* and *The Grass*; a middle period, commencing with *The Flanders Road* and concluding with *Conducting Bodies*; and a third period, beginning with *Triptych*, which includes *The Georgics*. These divisions, although somewhat arbitrary, are based on Simon's developing formal concerns.

Thematically, there is considerable unity among Simon's novels. Indeed, it is this thematic material, with its psychological, social, and cultural richness, that—combined with Simon's experimentation with the novelistic form—separates him from other New Novelists whose works often serve as pretexts for the demonstration of a particular theory of novel writing. Simon's novels are not confined within a prison of solipsistic self-reflection that reduces all the elements of fiction to metaphors of its own creation.

At the heart of Simon's universe lies a fundamental absurdity—a tension between the inherent disorder of reality and those means by which the human consciousness attempts to impose upon it a logic and coherence. War, sexual desire, and, to a lesser extent, avarice are the violent forces that tend to shatter the specious order of everyday existence and thus reveal its underlying chaos. Simon's vision of reality is pessimistic: Matter is in a constant state of mutation; the passage of time ineluctably undermines human activity; history seems to mock the human desire for progress, for it offers only patterns of cyclic repetition that reduce human beings to actors playing out predetermined roles; eroticism becomes a means of provisionally escaping from time and history.

A crucial aspect of the absurdity of the human condition lies in the attempt to discern the reality of experience and hence establish a definitive identity. The intrusion of human consciousness into the world results in the transformation of perceptions into images. No sooner does a given perception take place than it becomes a mental im-

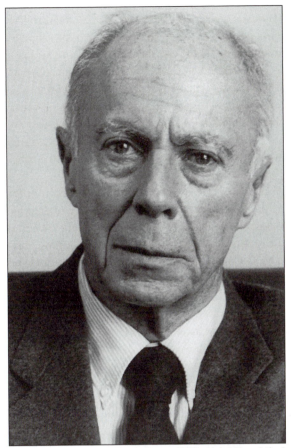

Claude Simon. (© The Nobel Foundation)

age, stripped of its original spatiotemporal coordinates and shaped by and connected with other images by a variety of associative processes. Thus, if knowledge of the real is essentially subjective, a creative representation, the self becomes an imaginary construct. A crucial complication arises from the use of language as a tool of discovery. For Simon, there is an inevitable "slippage" between word and thing. Experience is filtered through the order of language and thus becomes the material of fiction.

Simon's early novels differ from those of his middle and recent periods in that their largely traditional plot structure, character development, and language create a coherence that is not consonant with Simon's view of reality—style and vision are not integrated. With *The Wind* and notably the novels of his middle period, *The Flanders Road*, *The Palace*, *Histoire*, *The Battle of*

Pharsalus, and *Conducting Bodies*, the central narrative consciousness becomes aware not only of the nature of experience, such as Simon depicts it, but also of the inadequacy of the means by which one attempts to seize its reality and that of the self immersed in it. This awareness converges with the search for new forms by the novelist. Thus, one finds in these novels, among other characteristics, the dissolution of chronology and plot, the fragmentation of character, and an unstable narrative perspective.

These novels are also marked, to varying degrees, by the proliferation of language: an abundance of descriptive terms to circumscribe a given phenomenon, syntactic dislocation to accommodate various associative links as well as appositions and rectifications, frequent use of the present participle to detemporalize actions and transform them into states. The inevitable generation of fictions transforms the novel into a mode of knowledge. Other media are frequently used to put into sharper relief the illusory movement of the text. Frequent references to paintings and other kinds of "stills" as well as to the cinema reflect upon the nature of that movement through the animation of the isolated, static image. Like the optical illusion created by the movement of frames in a film, a painting or postcard is narrated and is transformed into a text with its complex web of associations. This process has been compared to the reconstruction of a fossil, where a few bare bones may evoke an entire epoch. Other literary texts may also serve as part of the cultural inventory by which fictions are generated and in which the narrative consciousness attempts to locate itself.

In the phase of Simon's writing that comprises *Triptych*, *The World About Us*, and *The Georgics*, the central narrative consciousness disappears and is replaced by the text constituting itself as tissue through the interweaving of several stories. The proliferating language of Simon's middle phase gives way to more coherently structured intersecting sequences that serve as elements of a particular story as well as associative junction linking one story to another.

Simon's departure from traditional modes of narration has resulted in the need for a more active participation by the reader, who must create (rewrite), through the process of reading, those patterns and structures that are suggested by the text. Only through this difficult but ultimately rewarding participation can the reader share with the writer the conception of the novel as a means of exploring the shifting, complex relationships between self, world, and word.

THE WIND

Although *The Wind* bears many resemblances to Simon's earlier, more traditional fiction, it poses, both thematically and stylistically, several of the questions regarding narrative perspective, temporality, the elusive nature of reality, and the structuring role of language that would henceforth preoccupy the author.

The novel's title refers to the ceaselessly blowing wind that characterizes the climate of the unnamed town in southern France where the events of the novel take place. More than a simple indication of local color, the wind functions as a metaphor of the destructive passage of time—its ceaseless activity, its erosive power, its effect of intermingling disparate elements. Its pervasive presence underlines the transitoriness of the characters' lives and their futile attempts to impose a coherence upon reality.

The novel's subtitle—*Attempted Restoration of a Baroque Altarpiece*—adumbrates the narrator's failure to adequately restore the past. The notion of an altarpiece suggests that the reconstitution in question will be an artistic endeavor that will leave the past still mysterious and even mystical. One can apply the term "baroque" to the sort of fiction that Simon produces in *The Wind* and also in his later novels. In this context, one can think of the baroque as the dynamic tension that exists between product and production, between the completed work of art as an illusion and the processes that engendered it and that tend to undermine that illusion.

The mysterious past that the anonymous narrator of the novel attempts to restore has as its locus the protagonist of the story, Antoine Montès. He is a thirty-five-year-old man whose development seems to have been arrested during his childhood. Like Fyodor Dostoevski's Prince Myshkin in *Idiot* (1868; *The Idiot*, 1887), a novel to which *The Wind* is indebted, Montès is an innocent, an almost saintlike figure to whom people are mysteriously attracted. He is incapable of comprehending the complex and sometimes sinister events that swirl around him and for which his presence acts as a catalyst.

The naïveté of Montès makes it even more difficult for the narrator to reconstitute the story of what transpired during the seven months that Montès had recently spent in the town.

Montès returns to the town where he was conceived in order to claim his deceased father's estate—a valuable but rather dilapidated farm. Montès arrives in town as an obvious eccentric. His shabby, ill-fitting clothes are covered by an even shabbier, stained raincoat. Around his neck hangs an expensive camera—he is a photographer by profession—and he carries with him a worn leather briefcase stuffed with documents and letters of various sorts.

He quickly discovers that claiming his inheritance is more difficult than he had expected. The resident steward of the property ties up the estate in litigation. Montès is compelled to spend most of his time in legal affairs and is forced to take a room in a seedy hotel. There he falls in love with a maid named Rose—if love is indeed the term one can apply to the curious affection he feels for the woman. Rose lives with a Gypsy boxer named Jep, who has fathered her two children. Montès's involvement with Rose is further complicated when he discovers that she is concealing the loot from a jewel theft in which Jep was involved. She is persuaded to give the jewels to Montès for safekeeping, an act that leads to her death. She is stabbed by Jep, who in turn is shot dead by the police.

Also living at the hotel is a traveling salesman named Maurice. He tries in vain to obtain the jewelry and is forced to settle for an attempt at blackmail. He steals a letter written to Montès by his young cousin Cécile. The letter asks for a rendezvous with Montès, whom Cécile, having broken her engagement, is apparently attempting to seduce so she can get a share of the property. Cécile's sister Hélène snatches the letter from Maurice before he can extort money from her father, Montès's uncle, a gentleman farmer living in a crumbling house, surrounded by the portraits of his illustrious military forebears.

With Rose dead, her two daughters in an orphanage, and the case against the steward lost, Montès is obliged to sell the property and leave town. Once his disturbing presence is removed, the town resumes its former patterns of existence as if nothing had ever happened. Rose

is replaced by another maid, Cécile returns to her fiancé, the steward occupies the farm. The narrator is left behind, as it were, to try to piece together what has taken place. He begins to suspect that the melodrama he has established in his attempt to reconstitute the past is but an illusion, based, in part, upon his inherent desire to give an order and coherence to events and personalities that would by their very nature otherwise elude him. He is also aware that his means of ordering the past—language—is suspect. He compares language to a thick sauce by means of which one holds together the disparate components of a dish and renders them edible. The logic of grammar and syntax restructures and domesticates reality. The disparity between the order of language and the disorder of reality is also manifested in certain stylistic traits that in later novels, particularly in *The Flanders Road*, would become characteristic of Simon's writing. Among them one can note a proliferation of descriptive terms used to "capture" a given phenomenon and the frequent use of the temporally indeterminate present participle.

THE FLANDERS ROAD

The publication of *The Flanders Road* placed Simon in the first ranks of the New Novelists, bringing him the critical attention he had hitherto not enjoyed. It remains the best known of his novels. The protagonist of the novel is a young man named Georges. As a soldier in World War II, he is a victim of the rout of the French army by vastly superior German forces. His cavalry unit is decimated, and its leader, Captain de Reixach, Georges's aristocratic cousin, is killed. Georges is captured and placed in a German prisoner-of-war camp along with two of his comrades, Blum, a Jew suffering from tuberculosis, and Iglésia, a jockey formerly in the employ of de Reixach. Two years after the end of the war, Georges has a brief affair with Corinne, de Reixach's beautiful wife, now remarried. During the course of a night of lovemaking in a hotel room, Georges, his memory stimulated by the presence of Corinne, attempts to recapture the events of the war and, in so doing, determine his own identity.

Two questions emerge as leitmotifs in Georges's search for the past. One concerns the circumstances of de Reixach's death. Was he simply a casualty of the war, surprised in a German ambush, or had he sought to expose himself to death after having discovered that his wife had been unfaithful with Iglésia? The second question is more fundamental, encompassing the doubt about the Captain's death and the whole of Georges's enterprise: "How do we know?"

Georges is faced with the problem of separating fact from fantasy. He must somehow reconstitute his perceptions of the war, such as they took place at the time, freeing them from the network of mental images in which they are bound. Furthermore, he must in some way also find a language that will not transform his experiences into fictions. This search upon which Georges has embarked can result only in failure.

War reveals to Georges the tyranny of time and history. In a previous novel, *The Grass*, Simon compared the process of history to the continuous showing of a film—the same pattern of events returning at regular intervals. In *The Flanders Road*, the story of a de Reixach ancestor who served as a general in one of the revolutionary armies exemplifies this view of history as cyclic. He reputedly shot himself, perhaps as a result of a disastrous military defeat—all wars resemble one another—perhaps as a result of discovering his wife's adultery with one of his domestics. History would, then, have made de Reixach one of its victims—he had but to act out his role. This kind of repetition also blurs the reality of any specific event, which comes to mirror countless similar occurrences.

The nature of time is conveyed through the central symbol of the novel, the horse. Simon described the shape of the novel as taking the form of an ace of clubs that one draws with a continuous line, passing through the same point three times. That point is represented in the novel by a decomposing horse on the side of the road, slowly sinking into the mud of Flanders so that—its matter transmuted—it will, in turn, nourish the grass that will sustain other horses. Georges envies the horse, for it has escaped from time and history.

He seeks an analogous escape in his lovemaking with Corinne. He compares her to an earth mother in whose womb he wishes to be engulfed. Eroticism, however, offers but a temporary "death," a brief moment of ecstasy during which the individual self in time is dissolved and merges with the Other. Georges's search for oblivion in Corinne's body marks his frustration at his inability to

seize the reality of her person. During his imprisonment, he and his two comrades fantasized about Corinne, thereby transforming her into a mythical creature. Now, in the presence of the actual woman, he is unable to separate truth from invention and thereby determine the real cause of de Reixach's death. Ultimately, the text itself becomes the locus of desire as Georges seeks meaning through the textualization of his memories.

Georges's father, apparently a professor of literature, comes from an illiterate peasant family and, as befits that background, puts enormous faith in the magical power of language to capture reality. Georges does not share his father's confidence in language. He sees language as an instrument that distorts reality, transforming it into fictions and imposing a specious order upon it. As for the self, it is fragmented in the stories that language tells about it. Moreover, as Georges perceives, language is incapable of arresting time—as soon as it is evoked, the present slips into the past and becomes yet another memory. He depicts language as a solitary voice that is drowned out by the sound of horses' hoof beats—the inexorable passage of time.

The style of *The Flanders Road* reflects Georges's inability to resolve the questions he has raised and thus objectively recall the past. Its most salient feature is its dense flow of proliferating observations and images. In the attempt by the narrating consciousness to capture reality adequately, each perception or event becomes surrounded by words that attempt to circumscribe it. Parenthetical statements, appositions, and rectifications abound, as well as such qualifiers as "perhaps" and "doubtless." Traditional punctuation and paragraph and chapter divisions fail to segment the narration logically and, in so doing, manifest their artificiality. Words branch in a variety of directions, linking diverse subjects and moments—most notable in this regard is the constant shifting between the vocabulary of riding and that of sexual activity. One finds in the text—and it is a trait already discernible in *The Wind*—an unusually high frequency of present participles. These forms, which carry no mark of duration and person, create a mythical present, transforming activities into states. They suggest in their accumulation, and hence detachment from the subject, that the protagonist is not the shaper of events but the medium or theater through which they pass.

The reader participates in the urgency of Georges's quest for truth and in the processes by which language transforms reality. In the absence of chronology and other guides that permit the reader of the traditional novel to recognize the ultimate meaning of what is related and organize its disclosure, the reader of *The Flanders Road* is obligated to discover in his or her rewriting of the text the multiple possibilities of meaning that can emerge from the chaos of Georges's defeat.

THE BATTLE OF PHARSALUS

In *The Battle of Pharsalus*, Simon plunges his readers into an inter-and intratextual battle. Only fragments of plots, characters, and settings remain to remind one that it is the varied assemblages of these elements and not their sustained development within a dramatic structure that constitutes the substance and interest of this novel. These assemblages yield possible meanings that are unstable and dissolve into other structures. Each signified, thus constructed and deconstructed, occasions a signifier that will tend toward yet another signified.

The last part of the novel contains a section in which the reader discovers the narrator in his room—though one is not certain of that identification—surrounded by a number of objects, a kind of inventory, which may have served to arouse the narrator's imagination and memory. Among them are a Larousse dictionary (an encyclopedia as well as a lexicon—the second section of the novel is titled "Lexicon"), a frieze depicting a battle from antiquity, and a pack of Gauloise cigarettes with its emblem of a winged helmet. The predominant color of the objects in the room is yellow. From the window of the room, one can see railroad tracks and agricultural machinery. All of these elements will appear in multiple variations in the text. Present as well, but only in the narrator's mind, is a variety of literary texts and paintings. The latter, mostly of battle scenes, are by such famous artists as Nicolas Poussin, Caravaggio, Piero della Francesca, and Pieter Brueghel the Elder. More important will be the presence in the novel of two literary texts, among others: Paul Valéry's "Le Cimetière marin" (1920; "The Graveyard by the Sea") and Marcel Proust's *À la recherche du temps perdu* (1913-1927; *Remembrance of Things Past*, 1922-1931).

The specific historical reference in the novel's title is to the site in Thessaly where Caesar defeated Pompey in 48 B.C.E. In 1897, the same locality served as a battleground in a war between Greece and Turkey. The narrator visits the battlefield, only to find there a soccer game between some Greek boys (another kind of battle) and, nearby, the rusting hulk of a McCormick threshercombine.

To evoke one war, such as the one between Caesar and Pompey, is, for Simon, to evoke all wars. References to the Spanish Civil War and World War II amplify the theme of history's lack of progress, despite the inexorable corruption of time. The image of a Greek—or Roman—warrior appears frequently in the novel, and the arms he bears proliferate in metonymic variations—javelins, swords, lances, arrows. There will be sexual warriors as well, brandishing their "spears"; *Pharsalus*, the reader is reminded, contains the letters *p-h-a-l-u-s*. Contrasted with the weapons of war is the McCormick thresher-combine, the modern plowshare into which the soldiers' swords might be beaten.

The violence of war is played against the violence of sex. The text indicates a sexual relationship between the narrator and a model, who apparently consorts with other men and may be another aspect of the Corinne of *The Flanders Road*. His jealousy is given full expression when, having discovered his mistress in bed with another man, he is left to hammer on her locked door in frustration. The story of Swann and Odette in *Remembrance of Things Past* is the intertextual counterpoint to the narrator's love affair. Just as the relationship between Charles Swann and Odette served as a negative model for that of the protagonist Marcel with Albertine, the narrator's uncle, named Charles, has preceded his nephew in having an unhappy relationship with his mistress. Marcel eventually rejected love for art and withdrew from the world to write his novel. The narrator seems to have followed the same path, only to generate a novel that lacks the spatial, temporal, and psychological coherence of Proust's. One might say that Simon himself has come to grips with Proust—as perhaps all French novelists must—by reinscribing the Proustian material within a radically different text.

The poem by Valéry provides an equally rich pretext for Simon. One of the principal themes of "The Graveyard by the Sea" is the opposition between mobility and immobility, an opposition whose variants are change versus stasis, creation versus meditation. The "play" between mobility and immobility appears in Simon's numerous references to paintings as well as to photographs and postcards. They become generators of texts as, through language, they are given a temporality and movement. That movement is illusory, obtained through the magic of narration. The Valéry poem contains references to Zeno of Elea, the Greek philosopher, who, in a number of paradoxes concerning the flight of an arrow and a race between Achilles and a tortoise, maintained the impossibility of movement. Achilles, an ancient warrior, is one of the elements from the Valéry poem that Simon recirculates in his text. Another crucial element from Valéry's poem is the image of the doves, which in the original text represent white sailing ships. They reemerge as pigeons in Simon's novel and are linked to flight of various sorts—the feathered arrows of war, the soaring of memory and imagination that will be inscribed by the pen, once a quill feather.

The thresher-combine can be interpreted as a metaphor of the novel's creative processes. It serves, as a quotation from philosopher Martin Heidegger indicates, as a demonstration of "utensility"; it points to the intrusion of human consciousness in the world as a means to accomplish a task. The delving of the narrator's mind into the mass of language and culture produces a novel that functions like the machine once did: It harvests what has been generated by diverse linguistic mechanisms and binds together, if only provisionally, otherwise disparate elements. A precarious but fruitful tension is maintained between proliferating growth and its threshing-combining. One might cite as an example of this tension the presence of the color yellow, so dominant in *The Battle of Pharsalus*. The color traditionally symbolizes jealousy and, in a larger sense, the anarchy of love. It links, among other elements, a lance, pubic hair, an old woman, and the sun. Its phonic combinations, as Jean Ricardou has demonstrated in *Pour une théorie du nouveau roman* (1971; for a theory of the new novel), will associate *nuage* (cloud), *nue* (naked), *Jeanne* (the name of Joan of Arc), and *âne* (donkey). This sort of generative wordplay serves as the novel's most striking stylistic trait.

Once again, Simon asks his reader to become an ever more active reader-writer, to become part of the act of literary production. The letter *O* that designates the narrator suggests that the novel has an empty center of meaning, that it is concerned with those combinatory processes by which possible meanings are posited.

TRIPTYCH

Triptych takes its title from a term used to describe a painting that is divided into three panels, usually conveying some sort of narrative content, such as episodes from the life of a saint. Simon's novel also contains three panels, three principal narrative sequences, but—unlike the sort of painting from which the title is derived—the three stories in question are not inherently related. They merge into one another through the complex web of associations that progressively link them.

The three principal stories can be easily summarized. One story deals with two young boys who forsake their fishing, as well as a young child left in their care, in order to spy on a couple making love in a barn. A second story portrays a bridegroom who, while celebrating with his friends in a tavern, winds up behind the store, making love to the barmaid. The third story is set in the Riviera, where a middle-aged woman—perhaps an older Corinne—languishes in her hotel room. In exchange for sexual favors, she obtains the liberation of her son, who has been arrested for possession of drugs.

Each story has a different cast of characters and takes place in a different location—the first in a rural area, the second on the outskirts of a city, the third on the Mediterranean coast. As he would do in his later novels, *The World About Us* and *The Georgics*, Simon transforms these separate stories into a text. The word "text" is related to "textile"; it is a fabric of interwoven threads. In the traditional novel, the process of interweaving remains hidden and the threads all belong to the same basic design, the patterning of a single story, but such is not the case in *Triptych*. There is no longer, as there was in Simon's previous novels, a localized narrative consciousness. In *Triptych*, the changes of narrative perspective and the switching from one story to another must be ascribed to the associative powers of language to shape the overall text.

In *Triptych*, as in many of Simon's novels, there is a "play" between narrative movement and the static image that may have served as its point of departure. The action of the boys observing the couple in the barn can be linked to an engraving showing a similar scene that is hanging in the hotel room. The woman in the hotel room, lying partially nude in bed, can be found on a strip of film the two boys scrutinize; she is also the subject of a motion picture that is being filmed as well as of a motion picture that is being shown in a local theater that was once a barn. The scene between the bridegroom and the barmaid may be the subject of the novel the woman on the Riviera is reading and can also be found in a film poster. There is a fourth thread in the novel, not so prominent as the principal three, that deals with the performance of a clown in a circus and that seems to derive from a poster affixed to the wall of the barn in which the couple is making love. Given the presence of generators of one story in another story, the novel suggests a set of interlocking mirror images in which any sense of the real tends to disappear.

A shifting from one story to another, frequently within the same sentence, may cause virtually any image to accumulate multiple associations and transcend whatever meaning it may have had within a particular story frame. A rabbit killed and skinned by a peasant woman can be linked to various nude bodies. Its death throes recall and anticipate erotic activity, as do its rose and purple colors. The removal of its eyes can be connected with broader thematic concerns—seeing and not seeing. Sounds, colors, objects of varying sorts, actions, gestures may all function within such multiple contexts.

The clown's performance suggests a parodic counterpoint to what is taking place in the three principal panels. His actions and gestures mimic the violence and the lust that are present in the other stories. His painted mask, his costume, his offering of himself as a spectacle, all serve to make the reader reflect upon the illusions of reality that the text creates.

A crucial image in *Triptych*, one that can be found in several of Simon's novels, but without the same emphasis, is the film camera. Not only does the novel deal explicitly with the making and viewing of a film, but many of the descriptions, particularly the country setting in which the story of the two young voyeurs takes place, are depicted from various camera angles, with considerable attention also paid to lighting and color. The pervasive presence of the camera accentuates certain elements of Simon's literary medium: the significance of perspec-

tive, the absence of psychological commentary, the use of sequential contiguity to replace overt plotting, and the irregular movement of the narrative.

THE ACACIA

The Acacia draws once again on World War I and World War II, and the story is knit together in the narrator's mind as he remembers his family's history. There are allusions to 1880 as well as to the 1980's. Simon's narrator participates in world history at the same time as he remembers his own personal history. Images of the bloodletting of the two world wars dominate the novel, particularly the ill-fated cavalry under attack by German tanks at the Meuse in Belgium. As in *The Flanders Road* and *Histoire*, the author juxtaposes individual memories to create a collection of disparate characters, events, and scenes. Many of the same techniques are used: suppression of punctuation, page-long sentences with parenthetical statements within parenthetical statements, and sequencing of scenes and memories by association. However, with this novel, Simon becomes increasingly autobiographical. As he said in an interview with the French newspaper *Libération* in 1989, "in comparison with books like *Histoire* or *La Route des Flandres*, the fictional element has completely disappeared."

In *The Acacia*, Simon's father and mother appear; the father is an officer who dies in World War I, the mother, with son in tow, is in search of her dead husband's resting place. Simon's own experience at the Meuse in 1940 parallels the war experience of the dead father-officer. *The Acacia*, as well as *The Jardin des Plantes*, uses literary collage and juxtaposition. Collage is never far from the readers' minds when reading Simon, as he was trained as an artist and has written about art, painted, and photographed for much of his life.

THE JARDIN DES PLANTES

Indeed, in *The Jardin des Plantes*, works of art are simply listed in isolated fragments among the collage-memories of the narrator. Yet the works of art do not dominate the fragmented narrative; instead, Simon once again draws on both old and newer memories to create the image of a life filled with the most diverse and varied experiences: having brief surgery on his lung, being in the cavalry at the Meuse, participating in a writers' conference in Russia in the 1980's, making love, attending chapel as an adolescent, having an interview with a beady-eyed and uncomprehending journalist. What unites all the memories is the narrator-author; yet chronology is destroyed and a kind of temporal chaos pervades the novel. Simon not only juxtaposes memories but also uses an inventive typography: The page is split, with two competing or contemporaneous memories facing each other across a strip of white paper.

For example, Simon juxtaposes the memory of an army camp where he shaved once a week with the associated memory of going to a barbershop. The two memories are twenty or thirty years apart in real time, but they are linked by association. *The Jardin des Plantes*, like its namesake botanical garden with its myriad species of plant life, is a vast compendium of a lifetime of memories that remain uncatalogued, linked by triggering associative words or images. It is perhaps one of the best examples in any language of how memory and the mind work. Linear narrative is abandoned in favor of psychological truth. The single unifying factor is the writer's life experience.

Alain Robbe-Grillet, probably the best-known practitioner of the New Novel, states in *Pour un nouveau roman* (1963; *For a New Novel*, 1966) that "all literary revolutions are made in the name of realism." Changing concepts of reality, he maintains, require concomitant changes in the literary forms with which that reality is represented. The evolution of Simon's novels reveals their author's commitment to this continuing revolution. An integral part of Simon's exploration of the novel, his "field of investigation," has been the changing role of the reader. The latter has been transformed from a relatively passive recipient of a disturbing but fascinating vision of the human condition into a cocreator of that vision, a participant both in the narrative of an adventure and in the adventure of a narrative.

Philip H. Solomon
Updated by Margaret Krausse

OTHER MAJOR WORKS

PLAY: *La Séparation*, pr. 1963.

NONFICTION: *La Corde raide*, 1947 (journal); *Femmes*, 1966 (commentaries on painting by Joan Miró); *Orion aveugle*, 1970 (portions of *Conducting Bodies* and paintings); *La Chevelure de Bérénice*, 1983 (*Bérénice's Golden Mane*, 1998).

BIBLIOGRAPHY

Birn, Randi, and Karen Gould, eds. *Orion Blinded: Essays on Claude Simon*. London: Associated University Presses, 1981. Essays explore Simon's worldview, different critical approaches, studies of evil in his work, and links between Simon and Latin American fiction in the 1970's.

Britton, Celia, ed. *Claude Simon*. New York: Longman, 1993. A collection of articles published from 1959 to 1982. Britton has selected diverse critics who address questions of perception and memory, textual space, bricolage, intertextuality, the subject, and the problem of the referent. Covers all approaches in an extended introduction to the articles.

Duffy, Jean H. *Reading Between the Lines: Claude Simon and the Visual Arts*. Liverpool, England: Liverpool University Press, 1998. An illustrated study of the relation between Simon's fiction and the visual and plastic arts. Duffy analyzes such artists as Jean Dubuffet and Paul Cézanne in connection with Simon's frequent statements about painting and the role of art in his novels. An excellent bibliography of works on both the visual arts and on Simon also includes an extended list of interviews and short pieces he wrote for newspapers.

Duffy, Jean H., and Alastair B. Duncan, eds. *Claude Simon: A Retrospective*. Liverpool, England: Liverpool University Press, 2002. A collection of essays edited by two prominent Simon scholars, offering an overview of responses to Simon's work. Includes several analyses of Simon's novel *The Jardin des Plantes*.

Duncan, Alastair B. *Claude Simon: Adventures in Words*. 2d ed. New York: Palgrave, 2003. Designed to introduce new readers to Simon's works by placing those works within the context of French literary theory and debate of the second half of the twentieth century.

Fletcher, John. *Claude Simon and Fiction Now*. London: Calder and Boyars, 1974. Fletcher, a British critic, assesses Simon's novels in the context of modernism. Fletcher provides a study of Simonian themes and compares the writer to other modernists after World War II. Fletcher concludes with a chapter on humanism, tragedy, and the avant-garde.

Jimenez-Fajardo, Salvador. *Claude Simon*. Boston: Twayne, 1975. This early study examines Simon's novels through *Triptych*. Situates the novelist in the tradition of Marcel Proust and William Faulkner; examines the themes of Eros, death, memory, and representation.

Loubère, J. A. E. *The Novels of Claude Simon*. Ithaca, N.Y.: Cornell University Press, 1975. An eclectic, broadly based introduction to Simon's fiction. Loubère relies frequently on Simon's own statements about his fiction. Includes a bibliography and an index.

UPTON SINCLAIR

Born: Baltimore, Maryland; September 20, 1878
Died: Bound Brook, New Jersey; November 25, 1968
Also known as: Upton Beall Sinclair, Jr.

PRINCIPAL LONG FICTION

Springtime and Harvest, 1901
The Journal of Arthur Stirling, 1903
Prince Hagen, 1903
Manassas, 1904 (revised as *Theirs Be the Guilt*, 1959)
A Captain of Industry, 1906
The Jungle, 1906
The Overman, 1907
The Metropolis, 1908
The Moneychangers, 1908
Samuel the Seeker, 1910
Love's Pilgrimage, 1911
Sylvia, 1913
Sylvia's Marriage, 1914
King Coal, 1917
Jimmie Higgins, 1919
100 Percent, 1920
They Call Me Carpenter, 1922
Oil! A Novel, 1927
Boston, 1928
Mountain City, 1930
Roman Holiday, 1931
The Wet Parade, 1931
Co-op, 1936
The Flivver King, 1937
No Pasaran!, 1937

Little Steel, 1938
Our Lady, 1938
World's End, 1940
Between Two Worlds, 1941
Dragon's Teeth, 1942
Wide Is the Gate, 1943
Presidential Agent, 1944
Dragon Harvest, 1945
A World to Win, 1946
Presidential Mission, 1947
One Clear Call, 1948
O Shepherd, Speak!, 1949
Another Pamela: Or, Virtue Still Rewarded, 1950
The Return of Lanny Budd, 1953
What Didymus Did, 1954
It Happened to Didymus, 1958
Affectionately Eve, 1961

OTHER LITERARY FORMS

Between 1901 and 1961, Upton Sinclair wrote or rewrote more than forty novels, but in addition to his longer fiction, Sinclair also wrote and published a massive amount of nonfiction, including pamphlets, analyses of diverse subjects, memoirs, twelve plays, and letters by the thousands. The bibliography of his works is testimony to his amazing fluency, but no one who is so prolific can escape being uneven, and this is indeed the case with Sinclair. His career, which spanned more than six decades, was unified in one respect, however, for both his fiction and his nonfiction were devoted to a single aim—the achievement of social justice. Everything he wrote was written primarily as a means to attain the end he sought, betterment of the conditions of life for all people. Much of what Sinclair produced is thus not belletristic in any full sense, but propaganda to spread his ideas about politics and economics. In books such as *The Industrial Republic* (1907), he tries to explain how socialism will be arrived at by a natural process in the United States; the theory is based on the premise that social revolutions are bound to be benevolent. During the period following World War I to the onset of the Great Depression, most of Sinclair's writing was nonfiction. In a number of books that he called his Dead Hand series, in an ironic allusion to Adam Smith's "Invisible Hand" of laissez-faire economics, Sinclair deals with the destructive influence of capitalism on numerous American institutions: *The Profits of Religion* (1918) treats the abuses of institutional religions, showing how the established church supports the ruling classes in exchange for economic advantages; *The Brass Check: A Study in American Journalism* (1919) details the operation of class bias in American journalism; *The Goose-Step: A Study of American Education* (1923) reveals higher education's lackeylike relationship to capitalism, fostered by grants and endowments made to the universities by wealthy families and industry. In *The Goslings: A Study of the American Schools* (1924), the same kind of servile relationship with the capitalist status quo is exposed as existing in elementary and high schools, and in *Mammonart* (1925), Sinclair shows how artists and writers through history have been duped into serving oppressive economic and political power structures. Not even William Shakespeare, Fyodor Dostoevski, or Joseph Conrad was his own man according to Sinclair's ideological criticism. Although the Dead Hand series is flawed by an excess of socialist polemics, Sinclair did extensive research to produce each book, and though the case is overstated, there is a grain of truth in his analysis of the all-pervasive influence of the economic and political structure of the United States on those areas that should be most independent of such pressure—the church, the press, the educational system, the arts.

Of more interest to the general reader are Sinclair's autobiographical works *American Outpost: A Book of Reminiscences* (1932) and *The Autobiography of Upton Sinclair* (1962), which updates his life for the thirty years intervening between the two books. In his accounts of his life, Sinclair reveals himself to be an honest but self-centered idealist. He chronicles his victories and defeats through childhood, youth, and marriage as the educational experiences of a genius; he offers in generally positive and optimistic terms his lifelong belief in progress and his hatred of social inequality and social exploitation.

ACHIEVEMENTS

Upton Sinclair's literary remains weighed in at eight tons when they were collected for donation to Indiana University Library. Of modern American writers, Sinclair is among the most widely translated, his works having been published in forty-seven languages in thirty-nine countries, yet his literary reputation steadily declined after the 1940's, despite the fact that *The Jungle* was still widely read in high school and college classrooms. Moreover, Sinclair himself has historical importance for the role he played in the American radical movement.

Sinclair's recurring theme as a novelist was class conflict, the exploitation of the poor by the rich, of labor by management, of the have-nots by the haves. With few exceptions, the rich are depicted as useless, extravagant, and unprincipled, while the poor are essentially noble characters who are the victims of capitalistic society. Sinclair's literary method, which came to be called "muckraking," was intended to expose the evils of such a society. Apart from *The Jungle*, which is the best-known example of this genre, there is the Lanny Budd series— ten historical novels that trace the history of the world from 1913 to 1946. *Dragon's Teeth*, the third in the series, won the Pulitzer Prize for fiction in 1942 by virtue of its vivid portrayal of conditions in Nazi-dominated Europe. In addition to these, the most widely read of Sinclair's novels, he produced novels on almost every topic of then-current social history, including coal strikes in Colorado in *King Coal*, exploitation by the oil industry in California in *The Wet Parade*, and the legal injustices of the murder trial of Italian immigrants Nicola Sacco and Bartolomeo Vanzetti case in *Boston*. All of Sinclair's fiction was aimed at the middle-class liberal, whom he hoped to convert to his idealistic vision of a fellowship of labor. Sinclair was thus a spokesman for the progressive era of American history; a chronic protester and iconoclast, he tried to stir the conscience of his nation and to cause change. In only one case, *The Jungle*, was he successful in prompting the desired changes through legislation. As a propagandist writing in the spirit of Thomas Paine and in the idiom of Karl Marx, Sinclair made a permanent impact by what he said, if not by how he wrote, and to this day, he still serves as one of the chief interpreters of American society to other nations.

BIOGRAPHY

Upton Beall Sinclair, Jr., was born in Baltimore, Maryland, but reared in New York City. He finished high school at the age of twelve, but he was too young for college and had to wait until he was fourteen before he could enter the City College of New York. While an undergraduate, he helped support himself by writing stories and jokes for pulp magazines. In one span of a few weeks, he turned out fifty-six thousand words, an incredible feat even for a prolific prodigy such as Sinclair. In 1898, after taking his B.A. from CCNY, Sinclair enrolled as a special student in the Graduate School of Columbia University; he withdrew, however, after a professor told him, "You don't know anything about writing." In 1900, Sinclair married Meta Fuller and began work on his first novel, *Springtime and Harvest*, which was written in Canada. Shortly afterward, in 1902, he joined the Socialist Party. The reception of his early fiction gave Sinclair little critical encouragement, and the works gained him very little cash—his first four novels brought him less than one thousand dollars, and the threat of poverty put a strain on his marriage. In 1905, Sinclair, with Jack London, formed the Intercollegiate Socialist Society, an indication of his growing political radicalism.

Sinclair's first fame came with his fifth novel, *The Jungle*; he was even invited to the White House by President Theodore Roosevelt to discuss the book. With the thirty thousand dollars that *The Jungle* earned for him, Sinclair founded a utopian community, Helicon Colony, in New Jersey. In 1907, an arsonist burned down the colony and Sinclair's fortune with it. This was the first actual persecution that Sinclair had experienced for professing unpopular views. In private life, he faced further difficulties; his wife divorced him in 1911; he remarried in 1913 and moved West with his new wife, Mary Kim-

brough, in 1915. Continuing to write at a furious pace, Sinclair became a publisher during World War I with the *Upton Sinclair Magazine*. He also issued a series of tracts on the effects of capitalism, objecting to its effects on education, art, journalism, and literature.

Not all of Sinclair's energies went into writing. He was instrumental in creating the League for Industrial Democracy and the American Civil Liberties Union. Three times he ran for the California state legislature and three times for governor, usually on the Socialist Party ticket but also as a Democrat. In *I, Governor of California and How I Ended Poverty* (1933), he set forth his platform, "End Poverty in California" or "E.P.I.C.," which explained the Depression as a result of private ownership and the economic insanity of limited production. His ideas found a large degree of public acceptance in the early days of the New Deal, and he came close to

Upton Sinclair. (Library of Congress)

being elected despite the mudslinging of his opponent. Some critics believe that the chief reason for Sinclair's decline as a novelist was his involvement in electoral politics in the 1930's. His novels of that decade are about specific political situations. *The Flivver King* attacks Ford Motor Company and makes a case for labor unions. "Little Steel" is a story about the organization of steel-mill owners against unions. "Pasaram!" is another short story from the 1930's about the brave fight in the Spanish Civil War against right-wing dictators.

During World War II, Sinclair began the historical record of his times in the Lanny Budd series. The novels in this ten-book series show the metamorphosis of the hero, Lanny, from an espouser of socialist causes to an anti-Communist, a change that reflected Sinclair's own changed sympathies.

By the decade of the 1950's, Sinclair had entered semiretirement, during which he nevertheless managed to expand his autobiography and finish six books, including a clever parody of Samuel Richardson's epistolary novel *Pamela: Or, Virtue Rewarded* (1740-1741), titled *Another Pamela: Or, Virtue Still Rewarded*, and a biography of Jesus. In these years, Sinclair finally settled his quarrel with the status quo. In his old age, he came to approve of the American establishment's foot-dragging on civil rights and supported American intervention in Vietnam. The old radical had, like so many before him, softened his position.

ANALYSIS

Upton Sinclair was a prodigy as a writer and wrote with great fluency and consequent unevenness. For him, the essential purpose of literature was to expose social evils and promote change; his end as a writer was the improvement of the condition of humankind. His literary reputation is thus not really germane to what he was trying to do as a writer. His fiction has more relevance when it is regarded in a political and historical light rather than as literature per se. As the social and economic issues of Sinclair's time recede into history, so does interest in those of his books that were simply propaganda.

Although Sinclair was regarded as a literary rebel for his iconoclastic attacks on the economic, intellectual, and political institutions of the United States, he was not in any way an avant-garde writer in terms of style and

structure. His subject was society rather than the individual human consciousness. It is necessary in any analysis of Sinclair's fiction to admit at once the defects in his writing. Most of it is journalistic in quality rather than belletristic. In fact, Sinclair deliberately wrote against the genteel tradition in American letters. He employed his rhetoric for practical results rather than to achieve poetic effects. His polemics were couched in fictional form because he believed the novel to be a particularly effective medium for his idealistic radicalism.

Sinclair's first four novels were produced between 1900 and 1904. These early works were awkward but full of passionate idealism. In *Prince Hagen* and *The Overman*, which were written before Sinclair discovered socialism, there is already a conflict between the pure-minded and the corrupt oppressors, but no solutions for the problems are proposed. The ideology of socialism provided him with solutions, although Sinclair was not a traditional Socialist; to him, socialism was the purest expression of the American Dream. He did not see himself as an overthrower of American values but as a writer who was helping his fellow citizens return to a vision of human alliance.

MANASSAS

Prior to *Manassas*, Sinclair's fiction had been based on personal experience. In this novel about the American Civil War, a young Southerner, Alan Montague, the son of a Mississippi plantation owner, becomes a supporter of the abolition of slavery. The protagonist is present at many historic moments—the raid at Harper's Ferry, the bombardment of Fort Sumter—and encounters many historical figures, such as Abraham Lincoln, Jefferson Davis, Frederick Douglass, and John Brown. *Manassas* differed from Sinclair's early books in that it was more realistic and objective. As a work of art, however, *Manassas* is not remarkable. The plot is often an inert review of historical facts, the characterizations are shallow, and the story is too filled with coincidence to be plausible. Despite its flaws, *Manassas* marked a turning point in Sinclair's career. In this novel, he revealed attitudes that pointed toward his development as a writer of exposés.

THE JUNGLE

In 1904, Sinclair was asked by the editor of *The Appeal*, a radical newspaper, to write a novel about wage slavery and the oppressive conditions of industrial workers that would show that their plight was analogous to that of the blacks in the Old South. Responding to this offer, Sinclair spent two months in the meatpacking houses of Chicago talking to the workers; he visited the plants also as an official tourist, and in disguise as a worker. The impressions and information Sinclair gathered from this experience were extremely distressing to him. His personal reaction to the corruption he saw was outrage; it is his identification with the exploited workers and his naturalistic descriptions of the oppressive industrial conditions that make *The Jungle* so gripping.

As Sinclair explains in his memoirs, *American Outpost*, he returned to his farm in New Jersey after he had collected his data on the meatpacking industry in Chicago and started writing the novel on Christmas Day, completing it in the summer of 1905 after less than six months' work. Although it was published in serial form as it was being written, Sinclair had trouble finding a publisher for the book; it was refused by five houses before Doubleday and Company took it after their lawyers made a careful investigation to avoid any possible libel suits. When *The Jungle* was published in February, 1906, the public was horrified, not by the novel's account of the conditions of the workers as Sinclair and his socialist friends expected, but by the naturalistic descriptions of the slaughterhouses and the evidence of criminal negligence in meat inspection. *The Jungle*, like most of Sinclair's fiction, straddles genres; it is partly a novel and partly exposé journalism. Sinclair's purpose in writing the book was to protest the exploitation of the workers and to recommend socialism as a corrective ideology to capitalism; the revelations of unsanitary packing-plant procedures were only a means to those ends.

Hardly a dozen pages of this long novel are explicitly concerned with the repugnant details of the slaughter-house, yet what remains in the reader's mind long after the plot line and thematic intentions fade are the scenes of grinding up poisoned rats, children's fingers, and carcasses of steers condemned as tubercular for canning meats; and the rendering of hogs dead of cholera for a fine grade of lard. Most dramatic of all, however, was Sinclair's report that men who worked in the cooking room occasionally fell into the boiling vats and were returned to the world transubstantiated into Durham's Pure Leaf Lard. The vividness of the author's descriptions had two effects: The first was an immediate drop in meat sales across the United States and Europe; the second was a summons to the White House to detail the abuses in the meat industry for President Theodore Roosevelt. The outraged public brought pressure to bear on politicians, and the U.S. Congress enacted the Federal Pure Food and Drug Act of 1906.

The sensational revelations of *The Jungle* have drawn attention from the book's literary qualities. *The Jungle* has been compared to the polemical late works of Leo Tolstoy and to the naturalistic fiction of Émile Zola because of its pessimistic determinism. The setting is the grim slums of Chicago and the gory stockyards. The novel tells the story of a group of recent Lithuanian immigrants who have been lured to the United States from their Old World villages with the promise of high wages.

Jurgis Rudkus, the novel's principal character, comes to the stockyard district, along with several of his friends and relatives, expecting to realize the American Dream, little aware that they have entered a jungle. Unable to speak English, the immigrants are exploited by almost everyone in power—the politicians, the police, the landlords, and the "Beef Trust" bosses. Jurgis has to pay his foreman part of his low salary to keep his job. He is cheated by a crooked real estate agent, who sells him a house with a hidden clause that allows the mortgage company to foreclose on him. After Jurgis and his family lose their house, they are further afflicted with misery. Jurgis loses his job after he is blacklisted, and he serves a jail term for slugging his wife's lascivious boss, who has compromised her honor. In turn, his father dies of disease, his wife and infant son die in childbirth, and, finally, he loses his last son in a drowning accident. Jurgis is left without anything; alone and in ill health, he is a broken man. He becomes a hobo, a petty criminal, and a strikebreaking scab—the lowest form of degradation for him.

In his extremity, Jurgis for the first time reflects on how unjustly he has been treated by society, which he begins to regard as his enemy, but his views are inchoate. One day, by chance he hears a Socialist speak. The lecture transforms his conception of the world; socialism is like a revelation, for now there is a way by which the workers of the world can win respect. With Jurgis's conversion, the novel as a narrative ends for all practical purposes. The last chapters are devoted to socialist propaganda and socioeconomic analysis. The optimistic conclusion of the novel contrasts sharply with the pessimistic naturalism of the first chapters. Ironically, and to Sinclair's disappointment, the novel's promotion of socialism and its protest against wage slavery did not win the hearts and minds of his audience, but his realistic portrayal of conditions in the meatpacking industry (as he once remarked) surely turned the stomach of the nation.

The Jungle will never be placed in the first rank of American fiction because of its mixture of fictional and journalistic elements, its unresolved contradictions in theme, and its melodramatic plot and bifurcated structure. Sinclair tried to do too many things at once, and he was only partially successful. Most readers think that the true significance of Sinclair's achievement in *The Jungle* lies in the uncensored presentation of the conditions of working-class life. Only Stephen Crane in *Maggie: A Girl of the Streets* (1893) had dealt with slum subjects with such integrity, and Sinclair had no models to follow in depicting this stratum of society. In his firsthand observations and deep compassion for the oppressed, he was breaking new ground for literary treatment, which Theodore Dreiser would follow to different purposes.

Following the success of *The Jungle* was difficult for Sinclair. He spent the next eight years trying to repeat what he had done with his first and best "muckraking" book. He produced a number of novels focused on specific problems, but at the other end of the social scale. *The Metropolis* is an exposé of conspicuous consumption among upper-class New York socialites. It is a poor book by Sinclair's own admission and is remarkable only for the absence of socialistic sermons by the author. Sinclair, like F. Scott Fitzgerald, apparently believed that money sets the very wealthy quite apart from the rest of society, but, rather than seeking rapport with his wealthy characters, as Fitzgerald did, Sinclair hoped to reform them. Another novel of this period, *The Money Changers*, is a story of the machinations of a high financier, obviously patterned on J. P. Morgan; the story tells of the exploits of Dan Waterman, the elderly head of the Steel Trust, who creates a panic on Wall Street purely for personal revenge against a rival steel magnate. Although *The Money Changers* is not very good fiction, it

does have an interesting premise, suggesting a connection between sexual desire and the drive for financial power.

Another novel of this period that deserves mention for its subject is *Love's Pilgrimage*; neofeminist in theme, this work examines the pressures on Sinclair's own marriage because of his male insensitivity to his wife's personal, sexual, and intellectual needs. The novel is also interesting for the insight it offers into Sinclair's personality, for he implies that the divorce his first wife sought was deserved because he prudishly withheld from sexual relations on the theory that it would decrease his creative energy.

KING COAL

In 1914, Sinclair remarried and began living in California. The transition in his life resulted in a change in his writing. In the West, Sinclair was drawn back to the problems of the proletariat by labor strife in the Colorado coal mines. As a result of the attempt by the United Mine Workers to organize the miners, the governor of Colorado had called up the state militia to break up strikes. In 1914, in the town of Ludlow, National Guard troops fired into a camp of strikers and their families, killing eleven women and two children. This shocking event outraged Sinclair as nothing had since he had witnessed the brutal conditions of the stockyards.

Following the methods he had used to collect background material for *The Jungle*, he went to Colorado, visited the miners and their families, and talked with the mining officials and labor leaders. His direct contact with the working-class people stirred his emotions and gave him a more realistic point of departure for his next novel, *King Coal*, than any he had employed since *The Jungle*. In fact, *King Coal* was an attempt to repeat the same sort of muckraking performance that had succeeded so well in the former case. Unfortunately for Sinclair, *King Coal* did not create the response aroused by *The Jungle*, a fact largely resulting from the lag time in the publication of the novel. When *King Coal* appeared in 1917, the events in Ludlow were three years old and yesterday's news. The United States had just entered World War I, and the nation's mind was on "doughboys" rather than on coal miners.

The poor reception of *King Coal* was a great disappointment to Sinclair, because he knew he had produced the kind of novel he wrote best. *King Coal*, while not as powerful as *The Jungle*, has the rhetorical strength and the factual validity of the earlier book. Sinclair tells the story of a rich young man named Hal Warner, who impersonates a coal miner in order to investigate working conditions in the western coal camps. He becomes a union sympathizer and labor agitator after he becomes convinced that the mine owners are denying the miners their legal rights and are cheating them out of their wages by rigged scales. After witnessing the futility of getting justice for working men inside the legal system, the miners go on a wildcat strike. Hal convinces his coworkers to join the union, and the novel ends with the lines drawn between labor and management while Hal returns to college, vowing to continue his fight for the working people of America.

Although *King Coal* is not as powerful in its naturalistic details as *The Jungle* and lacks the pessimistic determinism of that novel, it is in the opinion of most critics Sinclair's second-best effort at muckraking. If very few Americans responded to Sinclair's account of the dangers of cave-ins, coal dust, and explosions, this result may be because they were never exposed to such perils, whereas all were subject to health hazards as a result of unsanitary food processing. For this reason, the exposé of negligence in Chicago meatpacking plants had a much more profound and practical effect than the exposé of the inhuman conditions in the coal camps of Colorado.

BOSTON

Between World War I and the start of the Depression, Sinclair wrote two remarkable novels based on topical social or political situations. *Oil!* delves into the Teapot Dome and other oil scandals of Warren G. Harding's presidential administration and thus has considerable historical significance as well as being one of Sinclair's most readable books. *Boston*, on the other hand, represents Sinclair's best use of a contemporary event for fictional purposes. This novel enfolds the drama of the Sacco and Vanzetti case, but it also encompasses the whole of Boston society, suggesting that the city itself was responsible for what happened in that tragic case. The central character is again from the upper classes, an elderly Back Bay aristocrat, Cornelia Thornwell, wife to a governor. Full of vitality and intelligence, she thinks

that she has spent her life as an artificial adornment to a great family. She determines late in life to emancipate herself from the mores and manners of the mansion and moves out to board with the Brini family, who are honest Italian mill hands, and starts to earn her own living in a factory.

At this point, Vanzetti enters the story. During a strike in the mill, he plays an important role in keeping up the workers' spirits. He also prevents them from organizing, because as an anarchist, Vanzetti does not support unions. Afterward, Vanzetti and his friend Sacco are marked as "anarchist wops" by the police. They are picked up as suspects in a payroll robbery, and in the midst of the deportation mania of the postwar period, the city's reason and sense of justice are beclouded. The courts, judge, jury, and prosecutor seem determined to make the foreigners pay—if not for the crime, then for their politics. The climax of the novel comes when the cogs of justice bring the proletarian saints, Vanzetti and Sacco, to the electric chair with many doubts about their guilt still lingering.

Through a blending of fact and fiction, Sinclair is able to record a complex and tragic story of social injustice, although the story of the runaway grandmother does get lost in the final pages as the historical facts dominate the plot. As a novel, the two-volume *Boston* is too long except for readers with some special interest in the Sacco and Vanzetti case. As usual, Sinclair was writing for a mass audience, and the novel employs many stock characters and a melodramatic plot; furthermore, a statement of socialist doctrine forms a coda to the novel. Sinclair does, however, create a convincing portrait of Vanzetti. It is in Sinclair's account of the death of this man of dignity and intelligence that the novel gains its greatest power.

LANNY BUDD SERIES

The major literary effort of Sinclair's career was launched just before the outbreak of World War II: a ten-novel series offering a fictionalized history of the Western world in the first half of the twentieth century. The series is unified by its central character, Lanny Budd, and is known collectively by his name. One of the Lanny Budd novels, *Dragon's Teeth*, won for Sinclair a Pulitzer Prize in 1943. A chronicle of Germany's slide into Nazism, *Dragon's Teeth* is a scrupulous study of the fateful years between 1930 and 1934 and reflects an extensive research effort on Sinclair's part. In fact, several critics claimed that if the book were stripped of its fictional ingredient, it might well serve as a history text.

Sinclair creates an air of impending doom as he shows how quickly Europe was led to the abyss. His protagonist, Lanny Budd, is a neutral observer traveling the Continent with his millionaire wife, Irma, who is especially obtuse about economics, politics, and national traits. She is a foil to the sensitive and intelligent Lanny, who is aware of the coming crisis. Irma and her upper-class female friends refuse to believe that their smug routine of bridge and dinner parties will be disrupted. The reader in 1942 received these opinions with a great deal of dramatic irony. Meanwhile, Lanny grows increasingly concerned about the absence of morality in the political climate of Germany. Lanny has rather improbable meetings with the bigwigs of the Nazi regime. He goes hunting with Hermann Göring, has cocktails with Joseph Goebbels, and a discussion with Adolf Hitler about the Jewish question. His interest in this topic is not merely academic, since his sister is married to one of Germany's most prominent Jews. The Jews in Germany, however, are like Irma's circle; they refuse to face the realities of Nazism. The novel ends with Lanny's contriving to help his brother-in-law escape the dragon's teeth of the Nazi menace, closing the story on an exciting climax, somewhat like that of a cliffhanger film of the 1940's.

Sinclair continued the adventures of Lanny Budd, interweaving fiction with fact as he related the sequence of world events in *World's End*, which covers the years 1913 to 1919. *Between Two Worlds* deals with the events between the Treaty of Versailles and the stock market crash of 1929; the author then covers the Nazi "Blood Purge" of 1934 to the Spanish Civil War in *Wide Is the Gate*; the annexation of Austria, the invasion of Czechoslovakia, and the Munich pact in *Presidential Agent*; the fall of France in *Dragon Harvest*; and America's entry into the war in *A World to Win*. The years of Allied setbacks, 1941-1943, are covered in *Presidential Mission*; *One Clear Call* and *O Shepherd, Speak!* deal with the Normandy Invasion and the defeat of the German military machine; and in the sequel to the series, *The Return of Lanny Budd*, Sinclair brings events up to 1949 and the

onset of the Cold War between the United States and the Soviet Union.

As a whole, this group of novels is interesting, in part simply because the series surveys a dramatic period of history in considerable detail. Throughout the series, Sinclair's careful research is evident, but the popularity of these novels was also a result of their appeal to patriotism. America's role as the savior of civilization is increasingly emphasized in the later novels in the series. During this period, Sinclair's confidence that progress was represented by socialism and communism was shaken by the example of the Soviet Union. Like so many early twentieth century political radicals, he became an anticommunist in the 1950's.

Sinclair was a propagandist first and a novelist second, if propaganda is defined as an "effort directed systematically toward the gaining of support for an opinion or course of action." He wrote millions of words trying to change, improve, or expose oppressive conditions. Because Sinclair so obviously used literature for ulterior purposes and because he was so prolific, serious critics have unduly neglected him; on the other hand, he has been overrated by those foreign critics who delight in finding indictments of the United States by American writers. As time puts Sinclair's contribution to American literature into perspective, it seems certain that he will never be regarded as a great novelist, but he will fairly be judged an honest, courageous, and original writer.

Hallman B. Bryant

OTHER MAJOR WORKS

PLAYS: *Plays of Protest*, pb. 1912; *Hell: A Verse Drama and Photo-Play*, pb. 1923; *The Millennium*, pb. 1924; *The Pot Boiler*, pb. 1924; *Singing Jailbirds*, pb. 1924; *Bill Porter*, pb. 1925; *Wally for Queen!*, pb. 1936; *Marie Antoinette*, pb. 1939; *A Giant's Strength*, pr., pb. 1948.

NONFICTION: *Our Bourgeois Literature*, 1904; *The Industrial Republic*, 1907; *The Fasting Cure*, 1911; *The Profits of Religion*, 1918; *The Brass Check: A Study in American Journalism*, 1919; *The Book of Life, Mind, and Body*, 1921; *The Goose-Step: A Study of American Education*, 1923; *The Goslings: A Study of the American Schools*, 1924; *Letters to Judd*, 1925; *Mammonart*, 1925; *Money Writes!*, 1927; *Mental Radio*, 1930; *Ameri-*

can Outpost: A Book of Reminiscences, 1932; *I, Governor of California and How I Ended Poverty*, 1933; *The Way Out—What Lies Ahead for America?*, 1933; *The EPIC Plan for California*, 1934; *I, Candidate for Governor, and How I Got Licked*, 1935; *What God Means to Me*, 1936; *Terror in Russia: Two Views*, 1938; *Expect No Peace!*, 1939; *The Cup of Fury*, 1956; *A Personal Jesus*, 1952; *My Lifetime in Letters*, 1960; *The Autobiography of Upton Sinclair*, 1962.

CHILDREN'S LITERATURE: *The Gnomobile: A Gnice Gnew Gnarrative with Gnonsense, but Gnothing Gnaughty*, 1936.

BIBLIOGRAPHY

Arthur, Anthony. *Radical Innocent: Upton Sinclair*. New York: Random House, 2006. Presents a well-researched, balanced, and thorough portrait of Sinclair that tracks the ups and downs of his career and personal life. Includes sixteen pages of black-and-white photographs.

Bloodworth, William A. *Upton Sinclair*. Boston: Twayne, 1977. Short, sympathetic, yet balanced literary biography examines Sinclair's place in American literary radicalism and the writer as social activist. Includes bibliography and index.

Colburn, David R., and George E. Pozzetta, eds. *Reform and Reformers in the Progressive Era*. Westport, Conn.: Greenwood Press, 1983. Collection of essays includes discussion of Sinclair's position as a muckraker and his role in inspiring Progressive reforms. Notes that, unlike other journalistic writers, Sinclair was personally and ideologically committed to reform.

Dell, Floyd. *Upton Sinclair: A Study in Social Protest*. New York: AMS Press, 1970. Treatment of Sinclair's career analyzes the apparent discrepancy between the author's literary position in the United States and his position throughout the rest of the world. Descriptions of personal incidents and psychological insights are intertwined with evaluations and interpretations of specific works.

Harris, Leon. *Upton Sinclair: American Rebel*. New York: Thomas Y. Crowell, 1975. Traces Sinclair's rise from obscurity to fame and his subsequent decline in popularity. Provides interesting information regarding source materials for some of his novels. Includes photographs, extensive notes, a list of Sinclair's books, and an index.

Mattson, Kevin. *Upton Sinclair and the Other American Century*. Hoboken, N.J.: John Wiley & Sons, 2006. Combines biography with a history of the American Left to place Sinclair's life and works within the context of the social, cultural, economic, and political events that surrounded them. Includes notes and index.

Mitchell, Greg. *The Campaign of the Century*. New York: Random House, 1992. Excellently researched work details Sinclair's 1934 California gubernatorial campaign from August to November, stressing the media's key role in defeating Sinclair and ushering in a new era of media politics. Includes notes.

Mookerjee, R. N. *Art for Social Justice: The Major Novels of Upton Sinclair*. Metuchen, N.J.: Scarecrow Press, 1988. Mookerjee, a critic of writers of the 1930's, provides a reevaluation of *The Jungle*, *King Coal*, *Oil!*, *Boston*, and the Lanny Budd series, describing the pioneering role Sinclair played in creating the "documentary novel." Includes a selected bibliography.

Scott, Ivan. *Upton Sinclair: The Forgotten Socialist*. Lewiston, N.Y.: Edwin Mellen Press, 1997. Sound scholarly biography draws extensively on the Sinclair collection at the Lilly Library at Indiana University. In his introduction, Scott makes a good case for Sinclair's importance.

Yoder, Jon A. *Upton Sinclair*. New York: Frederick Ungar, 1975. Like some other critics, Yoder attributes Sinclair's "meager reputation" in part to his socialistic views. Five chapters in this volume examine various facets of the novelist's life and career. Includes chronology, notes, bibliography, and index.

ISAAC BASHEVIS SINGER

Born: Leoncin, Poland; July 14 or November 21, 1904
Died: Surfside, Florida; July 24, 1991
Also known as: Isaac Bashevis; Isaac Warshawsky; Tse

PRINCIPAL LONG FICTION

Der Sotn in Gorey, 1935 (*Satan in Goray*, 1955)
Di Familye Mushkat, 1950 (*The Family Moskat*, 1950)
Der Hoyf, 1953-1955 (*The Manor*, 1967, and *The Estate*, 1969)
Shotns baym Hodson, 1957-1958 (*Shadows on the Hudson*, 1998)
Der Kuntsnmakher fun Lublin, 1959 (*The Magician of Lublin*, 1960)
Der Knekht, 1961 (*The Slave*, 1962)
Sonim, de Geshichte fun a Liebe, 1966 (*Enemies: A Love Story*, 1972)
Der Bal-Tshuve, 1974 (*The Penitent*, 1983)
Neshome Ekspeditsyes, 1974 (*Shosha*, 1978)
Reaches of Heaven: A Story of the Baal Shem Tov, 1980
Der Kenig vun di Felder, 1988 (*The King of the Fields*, 1988)
Scum, 1991
The Certificate, 1992
Meshugah, 1994

OTHER LITERARY FORMS

The first work that Isaac Bashevis Singer published when he moved to the United States was the novel known as "Messiah the Sinner," which was serialized in 1936 but was never published as a book. It was serialized in three Yiddish daily papers: *Der Vorwärts* (the *Jewish Daily Forward*, in New York), the *Warshanahaint* (in Warsaw), and the *Pariser Haint* (in Paris). Singer himself considered this work a "complete failure" and never attempted to translate it. In addition to his novels, Singer wrote several memoirs: *Mayn Tatn's Bes-din Shtub* (1956; *In My Father's Court*, 1966), *A Little Boy in Search of God: Mysticism in a Personal Light* (1976), *A*

Young Man in Search of Love (1978), and *Lost in America* (1980). He also wrote more than one hundred stories and numerous books for children. He wrote two works on Hasidism, one in collaboration with the artist Ira Moskowitz titled *The Hasidim* (1973). His Yiddish translations of works by such noted authors as Stefan Zweig, Knut Hamsun, Erich Maria Remarque, and Thomas Mann are well regarded, as are his many literary essays and reviews. Several of Singer's short stories have been adapted as plays; "Yentl der Yeshive Bocher" ("Yentl, the Yeshiva Boy"), which was written in Yiddish in the 1950's, became a Broadway play in 1975 and a film (*Yentl*) in 1983.

ACHIEVEMENTS

Isaac Bashevis Singer has been acclaimed by some critics as a genius and referred to by others as one of the greatest writers of the modern world. In the aftermath of the Holocaust, which resulted in the obliteration of central and eastern European Jewry, the works of Isaac Bashevis Singer stand as monuments to a vibrant and vital world. Singer's writing does not idolize this community: He depicts it in its totality, in its full humanity. His people are saints and sinners, believers and heretics, fools and scholars, avaricious merchants and ineffectual rabbis, patient wives and termagants. His imaginative world includes demons, elves, dybbuks, and magicians, mystical figures from a lost folk culture. However, Singer's fiction does more than recall a world destroyed by the Holocaust. The power of his work, while remaining thoroughly Jewish, transcends the boundaries of cultural and religious ethnicity to raise questions about life that have been translatable across the changing contexts of twentieth century thought.

Singer's works are written in Yiddish, the language of the shtetl—the eastern European village or town. For Singer, Yiddish is more than the vernacular of the people of the central and eastern European Jewish community. It is, as he stated in his Nobel Prize lecture, "the wise and humble language of us all, the idiom of a frightened and hopeful humanity." His Yiddish reflects the influence of three languages, Yiddish, Hebrew, and Aramaic, and contains frequent allusions to rabbinic and talmudic lore. The richness of his prose and its texture, pace, and rhythm are not easy to capture in translation. Singer worked with his translators and participated in the editing. All of his major works first appeared in serial form in the *Forward* (originally a daily, the *Jewish Daily Forward*, then a weekly) prior to their translation and rendition into book form except for his first novel, *Satan in Goray*, which was serialized in the magazine *Globus* in Warsaw in 1934.

One of the outstanding characteristics of Singer's tales is his use of demoniac imagery. This motif does not represent a love of the bizarre, the occult, or the gothic, although Singer is interested in these aspects. His demons figuratively portray the evil side of human nature; moreover, Singer believed that supernatural powers—both good and evil—do exist, and he affirmed his ultimate faith in Providence.

Singer's vision is optimistic when it concerns cosmic matters but pessimistic in dealing with humanity. He differs from his Yiddish literary contemporaries or predecessors in that most have been secularists who relinquished the past in favor of the Enlightenment. Most Yiddish writers after the 1940's portrayed an idealized and sentimental view of the shtetl. Singer could not accept this tradition. He maintains that the greatest gift of God is freedom of choice. Where there is no evil, there is also no freedom. He is aware that good does not always triumph, so his Jews are not all good. His characters share the traits and illusions of all humankind.

Singer is a supreme storyteller. For him, the suspense, the adventure, the age-old pleasures of narrative are paramount. He leaves explanations and interpretations to his readers and critics. Singer achieved a popular success unusual for a writer of his distinction: His works have become best sellers and have been translated into fifty-eight languages. He won the National Book Award twice, three of his works were named Newbery Honor Books, and he was awarded the Nobel Prize in Literature in 1978. A number of his works have been dramatized and widely performed; some have also been made into motion pictures. He was an engaging and popular figure on the campuses of colleges and universities and a favorite of interviewers; he served as writer-in-residence at Oberlin College, at the University of California, and at

Bard College. In 1989, the American Academy and Institute of Arts and Letters bestowed on Singer its highest award, its Gold Medal.

BIOGRAPHY

Isaac Bashevis Singer was born in Leoncin, Poland. There has long been some uncertainty as to the date of his birth; in *Isaac Bashevis Singer: The Magician of West Eighty-sixth Street* (1979), biographer Paul Kresh quotes Singer as stating that November 21 was, as far as he knew, "more or less" the actual date of his birth. For many years, however, he had celebrated July 14 because his parents had told him that was his birthday to cheer him up after they moved.

He was the third child in a family of four siblings, who included an older sister, Hinde Esther, an older brother, Israel Joshua, and a younger brother, Moishe. His parents were Pinchas Mendel Singer, a Hasidic rabbi from Tomoszov, and Bathsheba Zylberman, the daughter of the *Mitnagid*—the opposing sect—rabbi of Bilgoray. The couple seemed to be mismatched. Pinchas Mendel, a gentle, pious, spiritual man, was an ardent follower of Hasidism. Bathsheba, a learned, strong-minded woman, was a rationalist and a pragmatist. Israel Joshua, eleven years Singer's senior, inherited his mother's rationalism; Moishe, two years Singer's junior, inherited his father's piety. The confluence of parental legacies—the mysticism of Singer's father and the rationalism of his mother—was Singer's inheritance, reflected in the tensions of his fictive characters: conflicts between the heart and the head, the sacred and the profane, the spiritual and the secular.

Four years after Singer's birth, the family moved to Warsaw, to an apartment on Krochmalna Street. Rabbi Pinchas Mendel became the rabbi of Krochmalna Street, and the Singer home served as its *bet din*, or rabbinic court. Singer's memoirs *In My Father's Court* and *A Day of Pleasure: Stories of a Boy Growing Up in Warsaw* (1969) and the novels *Shosha* and "Yarme and Kayle" (serialized in the *Forward* in 1977 but never published in book form) re-create the intricate life that existed on this cobblestoned shtetl street, a "literary gold mine" to which Singer regularly returns.

In 1917, World War I forced Singer, his mother, and his younger brother to flee the city. They went to

Bilgoray, where they stayed for four years. The visit was crucial in his development as a writer. The village of Bilgoray, far removed from the bustle of cosmopolitan Warsaw, appeared to be untouched by modernity. Young Singer witnessed Old World spirituality unblemished by the encroaching Enlightenment. This experience remained with him as an eternal reminder of his rootedness—indeed, humankind's rootedness—in the past, in history, in that which transcends human nature. Bilgoray plays an important role in many of his works; Singer once said that he could never have written *Satan in Goray* without having been there. In Bilgoray, he studied the Talmud and modern Hebrew, which in turn he taught in private homes. He also studied the Kabbalah, read the works of philosopher Baruch Spinoza, and studied German and Polish. He became immersed in the rural Hasidic folk culture that would permeate his work.

In 1921, Singer entered a rabbinical seminary in Warsaw. He remained for a year and then went back to Bilgoray and supported himself by teaching Hebrew. Shortly afterward, he joined his parents in Dzikow, a shtetl close to Bilgoray, where his father had accepted a position as a rabbi. He found this village stifling and depressing, and he was delighted when his older brother, who was coeditor of the *Literarische Bleter*, offered him a job as proofreader for the journal. In 1923, Singer moved back to Warsaw to take up this new position. His family was settled in Dzikow, and he never saw his mother or younger brother again.

Singer's brother Israel Joshua was also a writer and served as Singer's mentor. He was the person who exerted the greatest influence on the young Singer, encouraging him when he began to write and instructing him in the rules of good storytelling. Although Isaac was given to mysticism, Israel Joshua was a realist who became part of the Jewish Enlightenment, the *Haskalai*, which was overtaking the shtetl at the beginning of the twentieth century. This situation had caused friction in the Singer home, especially with their father, who was a traditionalist. Joshua—no one called him by his first name—moved out of the house, becoming an artist and then a writer. Singer often visited his brother and discovered, in his studio, a whole new world. He describes the experience of going from his father's house to his

Isaac Bashevis Singer. (AP/Wide World Photos)

brother's studio in *In My Father's Court*, saying: "It is just one step from the study house to sexuality and back again. Both phases of human existence have continued to interest me." Through his brother, he was introduced to secular literature. Singer lived, for the most part, in his brother's literary shadow. He used pseudonyms for his early writings; some stories were signed "Isaac Bashevis" (a form of his mother's first name in Yiddish) to distinguish his works from those of Joshua, while some were signed "Isaac Warshawsky" ("man of Warsaw").

In 1925, Singer made his fiction debut in Yiddish with a short story, "Oyf der elter" (in old age), which won a prize in *Literarishe bleter*'s literary contest. It was published under the pseudonym "Tse." In 1935, it was reprinted in the *Jewish Daily Forward*. His second published story, "Nerot" (candles), appeared in 1925 in *Ha-*

yon. In 1932, Singer edited, with Aaron Zeitlin, a magazine called *Globus*, which printed several of Singer's short stories and in 1933 serialized his first novel, *Satan in Goray*, which was published in book form by the Warsaw PEN Club in 1935. In these early years, Singer also began a series of translations into Yiddish, which by 1935 included Hamsun's *Pan* and *Victoria*, Remarque's *All Quiet on the Western Front*, and Mann's *The Magic Mountain.*

Singer fell in love with Runya, the mother of his only child, Israel, who was born in 1929, the year of Singer's father's death. Runya was an avid communist and wanted to live in Russia. She and Singer quarreled heatedly, frequently about political issues. Runya finally took their child and left for Russia in 1934. She was expelled shortly thereafter and went to join her mother in Palestine. Once settled there, she sent their son to Kibbutz Bet Alpha. He changed his name to Israel Zamir—the Hebrew equivalent of Singer. Singer did not see his son until 1955, when Zamir decided to visit his father; this episode is described in the short story "The Son" in the collection *A Friend of Kafka, and Other Stories* (1970).

Joshua Singer emigrated to the United States with his family in 1933 and found a job on the Yiddish daily, the *Jewish Daily Forward*. He urged his brother to do likewise. With the shadow of Adolf Hitler extending over most of Europe, Singer did not need much coaxing, and in 1935 he followed his brother. He never returned to Poland. Singer's acclimation to America was difficult. English was a strange language to him, and Yiddish, his mother tongue and his literary language, did not seem to have a future in America. *Lost in America* records this transitional period. He reviewed plays for the *Jewish Daily Forward* but could not resume his writing. At the urging of his Warsaw friend Aaron Zeitlin, he completed a novel, begun in Warsaw, known as "Messiah the Sinner." It was not a success.

In 1937, Singer met Alma Haimann Wasserman at a summer resort in the Catskill Mountains in New York State. She had emigrated from Germany the previous year. Theirs was an attraction with "telepathic qualities," Singer would reminisce in his later years. They married on February 14, 1940. For many years, Alma supported Singer's writing by working in sales positions in New York department stores. She tended to all their financial concerns and served as one of his translators.

The "greatest misfortune" of his life, according to Singer, was the death of his brother Joshua in 1944. In the dedication to the English version of *The Family Moskat*, he extols his brother as his "spiritual father and master." Singer's family sagas, *The Family Moskat*, *The Manor*, and *The Estate*, are efforts to emulate his brother's work; critics agree that they do not represent the best of Isaac Bashevis Singer and are not typical of his work. However, these novels do present a historical overview of Jewish life in Poland, beginning with the Polish uprising of 1863 in *The Manor* and culminating in the catastrophe of the Holocaust during World War II in *The Family Moskat*.

In 1943, *Satan in Goray, and Other Tales* was published in New York in Yiddish, and in the mid-1940's Singer's fiction began appearing regularly. In 1945, "Gimpel Tam" ("Gimpel the Fool"), perhaps Singer's most famous story, was published in *Yidisher kemfe*. In the 1950's a range of Singer's work—long and short novels, a novella, and a collection of short stories—was brought before an English-speaking public. The May, 1953, publication of "Gimpel the Fool," translated by Saul Bellow in the *Partisan Review*, was a crucial breakthrough for Singer. Thereafter, his work appeared widely in English in magazines such as the *Partisan Review*, *Commentary*, *The New Yorker*, *Harper's*, and *Esquire*. In 1960 Singer began his long affiliation with the publishing house of Farrar Straus Giroux. With the publication by *The New Yorker* of "The Slaughterer" in 1967, later collected in *The Séance, and Other Stories* (1968), Singer began his exclusive association with that magazine that lasted until his death.

At the suggestion of a friend, Elizabeth Shub, Singer started writing children's books; the first, *Zlateh the Goat, and Other Stories*, appeared in 1966. He published more than fifteen books for children. Singer's books for children are not written with the left hand; indeed, the format is particularly congenial to certain aspects of his genius. His children's books have been extremely popular and have won numerous prizes; they have been translated into a dozen languages in addition to the usual English, French, Spanish, Japanese, and Hebrew. Singer worked with a variety of translators, including his wife, Alma, and his nephew, Joseph.

ANALYSIS

An oft-quoted line from Isaac Bashevis Singer's story "Gimpel Tam" ("Gimpel the Fool") epitomizes the author's theory of fiction and his worldview: "No doubt the world is entirely an imaginary world, but it is only once removed from the real world." His approach to his material is both imaginative and historical. Sometimes these strains run concurrently; at other times, one is subdued by the other. Through his use of the supernatural, he imaginatively portrays the Jewish community from the seventeenth to the twentieth century.

Singer's concern is not only with Jewish destiny but also with the destiny of any individual. He believes that the soul is a battleground for good and evil impulses. His use of the fantastic suggests the tenuous line between reality and fiction; it also provides what Singer termed a "spiritual stenography" of human behavior. He suggests that the perversions in which humans engage are otherworldly, that people are not always in control of their actions. Although individuals have freedom of choice, this freedom may be illusory because the forces of evil, if allowed to prevail, can be stronger than the forces of good. Ultimately, however, a desire for good can triumph if people can exert all their efforts to that end. The struggle between good and evil, between the spiritual and sensual, supplies the tension in his works. Singer contends that humankind cannot be separated from its passions; they are one and the same. His early novels, especially *Satan in Goray* and *The Magician of Lublin*, illustrate the problem of passions ruling the individual. Singer's solution to human problems is a return to one's ancestral heritage.

SATAN IN GORAY

Singer's first novel, *Satan in Goray*, written while he was still in Poland, is a gothic tale, commingling the historical with the phantasmagoric, the mysticism of Hasidism with the influences of Fyodor Dostoevski and Edgar Allan Poe, the sacred with the profane. The work is historical, contemporary, and prophetic. Its vision is dark, its tone harsh, and it deals with eternal conflicts: between good and evil, between predestination and freedom of choice.

Two historical events constitute the background of this novel: The first is the Cossack rebellion (1648-1649) led by Bogdan Chmielnicki against the Polish landowners, which resulted in the destruction of 100,000 Jews.

This was a period of Jewish history remembered for its tremendous loss of life and for its acts of absolute barbarism, surpassed only by the Holocaust of World War II. The second is the messianic movement known as Shabbeteanism, after its originator Shabbetai Zvi (1626-1676). Historically, these movements converged when Shabbetai Zvi, in Smyrna, Turkey, proclaimed himself messiah in the year 1648, the time of the Chmielnicki massacres.

For Singer, however, historical events are important only in their effects upon individuals. His interest, at all times, lies with the passions that govern individuals and engage them in a continuous struggle. In this early work, Singer presents the shtetl of Goray in the aftermath of the Chmielnicki pogrom and indicates how the spiritual decline of the community is related to its physical destruction. The action of the novel takes place in the year 1666 as the survivors of the massacre move back to Goray and attempt to resume their lives. The village, however, cannot be resuscitated. Its people are maimed; its leaders are ineffectual; all are vulnerable. Singer focuses on what happens to people during a time of utmost vulnerability. He presents a good but misguided community, easily led astray by promises of redemption and the cessation of their earthly travails. The community has suffered much, and its prospects for the future are bleak. Its roads and its earth are drenched with the blood of recently murdered people. Life appears meaningless. The inhabitants move about sluggishly. It would seem that the guardian of Israel slumbers, while her adversaries are on the alert.

The work is divided into two parts. The first deals with the struggle between good and evil as represented by the opposing factions within the community. Rabbi Benish Ashkenazi, the spiritual leader of this enervated community, one of its last survivors to return, represents the forces of good within the shtetl. His is the voice of traditionalism. He was a strong leader before the events of 1648. He did not allow the study of the Kabbala, with its promise of messianic redemption and with the asceticism of its adherents. At present, he can resume certain rabbinic functions within the community, he can deal with legal matters, but he cannot handle the spiritual and social problems of the villagers. He cannot control the dissension within his family; likewise, he cannot control the growing dissension in Goray. In both situations, he retreats into his own chambers and ultimately is concerned only with his own salvation. Meanwhile, rumors of the new messiah have filtered into the secluded village, injecting into it a vitality heretofore absent, resurrecting the shtetl as only messianism can. It is, however, a destructive messianism, one that must be preceded by absolute evil, an abrogation of societal restraints, an immersion in sexual perversity and religious heresy. Part 1 ends with the rabbi's leaving town, after being wounded in a battle with Satan, because he does not want to be buried in Goray. He fears that the evil that has overtaken Goray will contaminate even the dead.

Part 2 concerns the spiritual decline of the community through lack of leadership and perversions of the Law in the name of Shabbeteanism. The battle has been lost. Once the rabbi leaves, total chaos ensues. Part 2 begins with Rechele's marriage to an impotent ascetic—who is also a believer in Shabbeteanism—and ends with her death, after the dybbuk (a form of satanic possession) in her body was exorcised. In the interim, the community gets a new leader, Reb Gedaliya, an emissary who proclaims the news of the crowning of the messiah. He is a ritual slaughterer by trade, a charlatan by profession. One of Singer's many perverted religious functionaries, his lust for blood is exceeded only by his lust for Rechele, who is the innocent victim of life's misfortunes. Gedaliya persuades the community that its redemption can take place only upon the abandonment of traditional Jewish life. Singer vividly portrays the manner in which the community loses sight of the relationship between traditional Judaism and redemption and the depths of moral turpitude into which it has plunged. Ultimately, evil—the dybbuk—is exorcised, together with the remaining Shabbeteans, and good returns to Goray. The novel ends in the spirit of a morality tale with these words: "Let none attempt to force the Lord. . . . The Messiah will come in God's own time."

Satan in Goray is a bleak tale in which the forces of good and evil fight for the human soul; humankind, maimed, vulnerable, and misguided, easily succumbs to the passions of lust and perversity. Critics have seen this work as adumbrating events that were soon to take place in Europe. The strength of this early novel lies in its use of demonology and the supernatural, which became a distinctive feature of Singer's fiction.

THE MAGICIAN OF LUBLIN

Written in 1958, serialized in 1959, and published in English in 1960, *The Magician of Lublin* also deals with human passions, but it is not overcast with the gloom of past events. It reflects an expansiveness often missing in Singer's works. Its focus is not on the Jewish community itself but on the individual in a timeless context. Singer's magician-protagonist is well cast. On a literal level, he is representative of the artist. On a symbolic level, every person may be seen as a magician, living life, like Yasha Mazur, the novel's protagonist, "as if walking the tightrope merely inches from disaster." The variegated personality of the hero, "religious and heretical, good and evil, false and sincere," and the lack of dates in the work lend themselves to a symbolic interpretation. Singer focuses on the single individual and the choices he or she makes. In *Satan in Goray*, historical events negate options. In *The Magician of Lublin*, Singer removes the encumbrances of history and allows his hero to make conscious decisions that determine the progress of his life.

Yasha Mazur is a complex person, vital, exuberant, intense—above all, a man with a personal destiny. Unlike Jacob, the protagonist of *The Slave*, for example, who is a good person, motivated to do right no matter what the circumstances are, Yasha has an intricate personality. It engages him constantly in a struggle of opposing forces. In *Satan in Goray*, the opposing forces are presented as two distinct elements within the community. The triumph of one necessitates the removal of the other. When evil was victorious, Rabbi Benish Ashkenazi had to leave Goray. In *The Magician of Lublin*, however, these forces exist within the individual, enduring aspects of human nature. Yasha Mazur's entire life is a battle. He can never conquer the evil drive. He can only negotiate with it, appease it, or in some other way deal with it, so that it remains dormant. He never knows, however, when it will awaken to begin another round.

Yasha Mazur was reared in a pious Jewish home, studied the Talmud until his father died—his mother died when he was seven—and then joined the circus. He maintains a home in Lublin with his wife, Esther, but roams the Polish countryside as a "circus performer and hypnotist." As an artist or magician, he moves in various worlds, assumes various guises or personalities, and has a different mistress in each world. He aspires to higher things: He is a successful artist and would like to perform in Warsaw, in the summer theater of the prestigious Saxony Gardens. He is barred from doing so because he is Jewish. The closest he comes to achieving this goal is at the apartment of the middle-class Gentile Emilia, located on a street opposite the Saxony Gardens. Yasha's relationship with Emilia focuses the tensions of the work. He thinks he is in love with her, but she refuses the role of mistress. She wants to be his wife. To marry her, Yasha would have to divorce Esther, convert to Christianity, and procure great wealth to maintain the facade he has established in his courting of Emilia. These are formidable decisions that will determine his future.

Singer establishes the dichotomy of predestination and free will early in the work in the contrasting attitudes toward life represented by Yasha and his wife. Esther is a religious woman, married twenty years to Yasha; they have no children. Her entire life consists of making a home for a husband who returns to it only on holidays. She loves him but regrets, at times, not having married someone more stable. The thought of changing her life, however, never crosses her mind. She is a strong believer in Providence and accepts her fate as a lonely woman.

Yasha, although he says that "everything is fate," realizes that he shapes his own destiny in all his choices. He is a magician who consorts with thieves, but he refuses to use his powers for evil purposes. He will not become a thief. When he finally attempts it, out of a desperate need to support Emilia, he fails and injures himself. The man who is so agile that he can walk a tightrope to the awe of his audience becomes a shlemiel and bungles a simple act of burglary. Although he is Jewish by birth, he is a nonbeliever—or says he is—by choice. He does not pray, because God does not answer the prayers of his supplicants: his "gifts" are "plagues, famines, poverty, and pogroms." Nevertheless, to become a Christian for Emilia is a difficult choice for him. He is a libertine, yet he considers the institution of marriage sacred and cannot easily make the decision to break up his home for his new infatuation. He is faced with the dilemma of choosing "between his religion and the cross, between Esther and Emilia, between honesty and crime." These choices will "seal his destiny." He finally chooses to remain with his own religion and decides also that traditionalism is more meaningful than assimilationism.

Yasha is aware that life is the most powerful seductress. He returns to his home and builds for himself a doorless brick prison, which frees him from temptation and allows him to meditate on his past actions, yet he discovers that as long as he is alive, he cannot shut out the world. As an artist or a magician, he went out into the world, succumbing to carnal pleasures, drinking, eating, loving unrestrainedly. Having come to the realization that "there must be discipline," he undergoes the transformation from sinner to saint. As an ascetic, in the confines of his self-imposed banishment, considered by all a "holy man," the world comes to him. Even his past love writes him a letter. Yasha's imprisonment has been only partially successful. He has turned his intense feelings in another direction, moving from the sensual to the spiritual. In this work, Singer suggests that people cannot escape their essence: They and their passions are one. *The Magician of Lublin* presents a positive outlook even though it concludes (as does Singer's novel *Shosha*) in a dark cell or room.

ENEMIES

Singer's novels *Enemies* and *Shosha* directly address the most tragic time of Jewish history, the Holocaust. *Enemies*, ironically subtitled *A Love Story*, is Singer's only novel set in the United States; it deals specifically with survivors of the Holocaust. In *Shosha*, Singer returns for another nostalgic look at the destroyed world in which he grew up and attempts to capture the spirit of his people as the perimeters of death close in on them.

Like *The Magician of Lublin*, *Enemies* is written on two levels. It fills a gap in Singer's canon. Until this work, Singer's literary aim was to re-create the destroyed world of eastern European Jewry, to present the pulsating life that existed specifically in his native Poland. *Enemies* acknowledges the destruction of his fictive world and deals with problems confronting those who survived. In a note that precedes the work, Singer asserts that although he has lived with survivors for years, this work is in no way typical of the Holocaust experience. The novel presents the "exceptional case," he says, unique to an individual who is a victim both of his own personality and of his persecutors. Certainly, this can be said of all victims, and the novel, despite his abjuration, is a moving depiction of the varied problems many survivors have encountered. Singer's note cautions the reader against a rigorous historical interpretation. The Holocaust serves as a framework within which Singer presents his perennial concern: humankind battling its adversaries in the dark of night, in the fashion of Jacob and the angel. In the biblical narrative, Jacob is not overcome; he walks away, at daybreak, limping but unvanquished. Singer's hero also walks away, but not as a victor.

Enemies bears a similarity to *Satan in Goray* both in its focus on an individual who lives a tormented life, burdened with the knowledge of the tragic destruction of all that is meaningful to him, and in its use of the supernatural. In this work, the spiritual powers that represent the forces of good and evil also reflect a movement away from traditionalism. In addition, they indicate the extent to which the characters, through their previous experiences, have lost touch with reality. *Enemies* also has affinities with *The Magician of Lublin*: The multiple personalities of the protagonist are reflected in his relationships with three strikingly different women.

Enemies is a ghostly story. Herman Broder, the protagonist, is defined through his actions in the Holocaust. He spent those years hiding in a hayloft and has acquired a negative identity in the Holocaust's aftermath. Now, as a survivor, he is psychologically warped and socially maimed. He lacks the courage to commit suicide, hides behind schizophrenia to "deaden" his consciousness, and assumes the guise of a demon. In New York, Broder becomes a ghostwriter for a rabbi. He shuns contact with others to preserve his anonymity and lives a life of haunting duplicity with his second wife and his mistress. The tensions in his spiritual juggling act are intensified by the appearance of his wife from the Old World—he had assumed her to be dead. Ultimately, he disappears, vanishing like a ghost.

The work is divided into three parts. Part 1 establishes the diverse personalities of Herman Broder, "a fraud, a transgressor—a hypocrite," as he sees himself, and the complications they create. Broder's current life in New York is eclipsed by the terrifying experiences of his past. He lives in Brooklyn with his second wife, Yadwiga, the Polish woman who worked for his family before the war and who hid him in a hayloft during the Nazi occupation. He married her in gratitude for saving his life, but his relationship with her is deceitful. She

does not know about his professional life or about his mentally disturbed mistress, Masha, who shares with him her experience of the Holocaust. He spends as much time with Masha as he does with Yadwiga, always telling Yadwiga that, as a book salesman, he must go out of town to sell books.

The tangled web of Broder's relationships is further complicated when his first wife, Tamara, who has survived being shot twice—one bullet still lodged within her—comes to New York and seeks him out. Part 1 ends with an additional complication when Masha claims to be pregnant and Broder promises to marry her.

Part 2 attempts a resolution of the problems. Through Broder's conversations with Masha and Tamara, much of the Holocaust experience is re-created. Like Elie Wiesel and other writers of the Holocaust, Singer points out that the full enormity of the Holocaust can never be expressed, because words are inadequate to the task. That which is related, however, is extremely powerful. Singer deals with the theological, social, and philosophical problems, both individual and universal, that confront humankind in coming to terms with the Holocaust. While presenting the myriad issues with which survivors have been faced—equivocal attitudes toward faith, a missing spouse who turns up after the other has remarried, disorientation in a new environment, reestablishing an identity that was nonexistent for a time, relating to people as human beings within a society rather than as individuals competing for survival—Singer indicates that the individual is also his or her own victim, governed by passions he or she cannot or will not control. Broder would not have married Yadwiga if he had thought that Tamara were alive. Now, however, he wants to hold on to all three women. They satisfy different needs: Yadwiga cares for him and worships him with a childlike simplicity; Masha fulfills his sexual desires and fires his imagination with her nightlong storytelling; Tamara is his wife, to whom he feels committed.

When the intricacies of his life seem overwhelming, he resorts to traditionalism as a life-sustaining measure, yet he cannot maintain his resolve to be a good Jew. He is a weak person by nature, and the impact of the Holocaust has left him without a will, without the power to make meaningful choices and decisions. He is, as he tells Tamara, a "corpse." His only alternative is to vanish.

Herman Broder joins Singer's other eternal wanderers, the most famous of whom is Gimpel the Fool. The epilogue, in an almost Darwinian statement, attests the insignificance of the individual in the larger scheme of things by confirming Herman Broder's disappearance and suggesting that life nevertheless continues for those who can battle their enemies successfully.

SHOSHA

Shosha is narrated in the first person, unusual in Singer's novels that have been translated into English. Originally appearing in the *Forward* under the title *Neshome Ekspeditsyes* (soul expeditions) in 1974, it is considered a fictionalized and expanded version of the memoir *A Young Man in Search of Love*, which appeared almost simultaneously in 1978. A beautifully wrought work, it is one of the most poignant of all of Singer's novels. Set in Poland in the 1930's, the novel portrays the plight of the Jewish community, overcast with the gloom of the Nazi invasion, yet it brims with the lives, loves, and hopes of its characters. It combines realism with humor and pathos. It is another nostalgic glance at a decimated world, but it is not a gloomy work. It is, as the Yiddish title indicates, the journey of the author's soul, in an affectionate tribute to the vitality of the shtetl, and stands in defiance of his statement at the end of the work: "Time is a book whose pages you can turn forward, not back." *Shosha* presents a marvelous picture of Warsaw before the war, focusing on its Yiddish cultural and intellectual life, its writers, artists, philosophers, actors, critics, and dilettantes, as well as its simple people. Within this historical framework, Singer presents his protagonist's life in Poland at the time of greatest stress, a time when Jewish life and culture were disintegrating.

In *Shosha*, the conflict between good and evil that animates all of Singer's works takes the form of the relationship between victim and persecutor. All of the characters are concerned with their immediate gratification. They arouse the reader's sympathy because they become victims of their own blindness and naïveté. In their determination to live normally, they love, argue, philosophize, celebrate holidays. They write plays about dybbuks and talk about dybbuks within themselves. They do not recognize the external evil, the phantom that surrounds them or pursues them.

The first part of the novel charts the circular movement of the protagonist as he attempts to reestablish a sense of belonging, transporting the reader to the halcyon days of the narrator's childhood and moving forward to the period preceding the destruction of the shtetl by Hitler. The ancestors of the protagonist, Aaron Greidinger, have lived in Poland for seven hundred years. Krochmalna Street, already familiar to Singer's public through his memoir *In My Father's Court*, is not only a place housing his father's judiciary but also the scene of the narrator's first love, for Shosha—his neighbor, his playmate, his first audience—who believes and trusts him implicitly and unconditionally.

The work delineates the maturation of the narrator, as the serenity of his youthful universe is quickly replaced by the turmoil of world events with their disquieting effect upon the Jews of Poland. The first twenty years of his life pass rapidly as he moves from Krochmalna Street and attempts to define himself as a writer. In Warsaw, the Writers' Club becomes the focal point for the intellectuals, much as the synagogue was the focal point of the traditional Jewish community. It is through the people whom he meets at the Writers' Club that Aaron Greidinger works out his role as writer and lover.

Greidinger's destiny and identity are intimately bound to his youth on Krochmalna Street, and after twenty years, he returns to the area and visits Shosha and her mother. He is amazed that Shosha has changed only slightly during the years: She and Greidinger are the same age, but she looks like a child. Greidinger falls in love with her immediately. He explains to Betty Slonim, the Yiddish actor from America for whom he is writing a play, that he sees himself in Shosha. Shosha represents the naïveté and gentleness of his childhood, a phase of his life that he wants to recapture and repossess. She is Krochmalna Street. She is the shtetl. She is the traditionalism that refuses to keep in step with modernity but is beautiful nevertheless. She also represents the sources of his creativity, the childlike wonder that Singer the writer still possesses in old age. Part 1 ends with Greidinger's movement back in time, his failure as a playwright, his proposal to Shosha, and his spending most of his time in the small apartment on Krochmalna Street as the political situation worsens for the Jews in Poland.

Part 2 develops the protagonist's affirmation of his

unity with his people. It is Yom Kippur, a day of judgment and reckoning for all Jews. The war is getting closer, Poles are more outspoken in their anti-Semitism, and Greidinger spends the day with Shosha, fasting. He marries Shosha two months later during the festival of Hanukkah. By doing so, he forgoes the opportunity to leave Warsaw before the Germans enter. He will not forsake Shosha, knowing that she could not survive by herself during these times. His writing career has improved; he is writing novels that have been accepted by his publisher. Part 2 concludes with the war imminent but with everyone presenting reasons for not leaving Warsaw prior to the German invasion. The epilogue ties the loose ends together. It takes place thirteen years later, during Greidinger's trip to Israel, where he meets his Warsaw friend, Haiml. While seated in the dark, each tells the story of what happened to his family, his friends, and how he escaped. Shosha died, as expected, because in her fragility she could not keep ahead of the march of malevolence pursuing her and overtaking Europe.

THE KING OF THE FIELDS

Singer's last novel to be published before his death in 1991 was *The King of the Fields*, set in prehistoric Poland, a violent, animalistic place where tribes of cave-dwelling hunters struggle against Poles who cultivate the land. Singer seems to have dipped into a nightmare world so embedded in the past as to be unrelated to the present, yet the hellish qualities of this Stone Age Poland and the brutality of its inhabitants conjure up the Poland of the Holocaust—a wilderness of corruption, a wasteland for humanity.

SCUM

Scum, written in the late 1960's and published in English the year of Singer's death, re-creates pre-Holocaust Warsaw at the beginning of the twentieth century. Max Barabander, a thief turned businessman, returns to Singer's famous Krochmalna Street after decades in Argentina. His son has died, and his grieving wife ignores him; he has become impotent. His journey backward to Krochmalna Street is his attempt to journey toward renewed health, or at least toward a new life.

Barabander becomes involved both with Shmuel Smetena, the central figure in Krochmalna Street mobster activities, and with a saintly rabbi whose daughter, Tsirele, he wants to marry. He poses as a grieving widower to win Tsirele while working with Shmuel Smetena's mistress on a scheme to seduce unsuspecting young women and ship them off to an Argentinian brothel. The project has a restorative effect on Max's virility, but when the web of lies he must weave begins to unravel, he is exposed as bereft of moral character, one for whom life—his or another's—is devoid of meaning. His only dreams are of "shady deals." *Scum* is Singer's version of the underworld; the literal underworld of gangsters mirrors the underworld of demons and dybbuks that make no appearance in this novel. When human beings are such scum, there seems to be no need for the Evil One.

THE CERTIFICATE

The Certificate, serialized in the *Forward* in 1967, was published posthumously in 1992. Its protagonist, David Bendinger, an eighteen-year-old would-be writer, arrives in Warsaw in 1922 with an unfinished novel, an essay on Spinoza and the Kabbala, and a collection of prose poems. Like so many of Singer's males, David soon finds himself involved with three women: Sonya, his old girlfriend; Minna, a woman whom he agrees to marry in order to obtain immigration papers for Palestine; and Edusha, his Marxist landlady. Like the youthful Singer, whom he resembles, David turns every event, no matter how seemingly insignificant, into an occasion for philosophical musing. Unlike Max Barabander of *Scum*, David Bendinger dreams of more than shady deals, and he believes that those around him have worth. No matter how complicated his life becomes, he dreams of writing and he thinks of God.

MESHUGAH

Meshugah, which means crazy, was first called *Lost Souls*, a title that connects this novel with *Shosha*, which was first called *Neshome Ekspeditsyes* (soul expeditions). Serialized in the *Forward* in the early 1980's and appearing in English in 1994, the novel brings Aaron Greidinger, the protagonist of *Shosha*, into a post-Holocaust 1950's setting. This most Singer-like character is a Polish exile who serializes novels in Yiddish for the *Forward*. While Aaron has his series of women, his primary mate, Miriam Zalkind, who is writing her dissertation on his work, juggles her own set of men. All are "lost souls" harboring memories of the Holocaust, mourning loved ones, contemplating suicide. Aaron discovers that the real truth of human suffering defies the power of writing—the world is meshugah.

SHADOWS ON THE HUDSON

Shadows on the Hudson was originally serialized in Yiddish twice a week in the *Forward* between January, 1957, and January, 1958. Singer had long wanted this novel to be published in English, but the project was undertaken only years after his death. It is set in the 1940's in Manhattan, and the lives of its characters are, like those in *Meshugah*, overshadowed by the Holocaust. As bleak as *Scum* but without its sordid underworld, *Shadows on the Hudson* deals with characters who strive for some sense and meaning in a world that continuously trips them up. Hertz Dovid Grein rotates among wife, mistress, and lover, always yearning for the one who is not there. His lover, Anna, juggles him along with her first and second husbands. His mistress, Esther, marries another, divorces, flees with Grein, and, in turn, flees him.

In the second part of this three-part novel, these chaotic couplings seem to be headed for resolution in a return to the past and traditional values. Grein returns home to his wife and to orthodoxy, Anna returns to her first husband, Esther marries, and even Anna's long-widowed father marries and has a son. The hope that a retreat from the secular will result in a return to meaning is demolished in part 3, however, when the new couplings are undone and the newborn child is recognized as severely retarded. The shadows of the Holocaust stretch over the Hudson and into the future. What saves this novel, and much of Singer's fiction, from a darkness too intense to bear is his extraordinary ability to create comic situations from the bleakest of moments. Whether caricaturing secondary characters or rendering outlandish a protagonist's rationalization of his or her latest sexual exploit, Singer's comic touch lightens his vision. Except in a few novels such as *Scum* and *The King of the Fields*, there is a redemptive quality in the very need his characters display for meaning and for love.

Singer occupies a unique place in the literary world. His works transcend the barriers of age, education, and culture, and they appeal to all peoples. Singer was a chronicler, historian, spiritualist, and moralist, and his writings are informed by a deep compassion for men and women who are, after all, only human. Singer may admit to a pessimistic view of humankind, but it is a sympathetic rather than a cynical pessimism. Throughout the darkness of his presentation, there flickers a spark of faith in the basic goodness of humankind, the promise of a universal and eternal light.

L. H. Goldman
Updated by Grace Farrell

OTHER MAJOR WORKS

SHORT FICTION: *Gimpel the Fool, and Other Stories*, 1957; *The Spinoza of Market Street*, 1961; *Short Friday, and Other Stories*, 1964; *The Séance, and Other Stories*, 1968; *A Friend of Kafka, and Other Stories*, 1970; *A Crown of Feathers, and Other Stories*, 1973; *Passions, and Other Stories*, 1975; *Old Love*, 1979; *The Collected Stories of Isaac Bashevis Singer*, 1982; *The Image, and Other Stories*, 1985; *The Death of Methuselah, and Other Stories*, 1988.

PLAYS: *The Mirror*, pr. 1973; *Shlemiel the First*, pr. 1974; *Yentl, the Yeshiva Boy*, pr. 1974 (with Leah Napoli); *Teibele and Her Demon*, pr. 1978.

NONFICTION: *Mayn Tatn's Bes-din Shtub*, 1956 (*In My Father's Court*, 1966); *The Hasidim*, 1973 (with Ira Moskowitz); *A Little Boy in Search of God: Mysticism in a Personal Light*, 1976; *A Young Man in Search of Love*, 1978; *Isaac Bashevis Singer on Literature and Life*, 1979 (with Paul Rosenblatt and Gene Koppel); *Lost in America*, 1980; *Love and Exile*, 1984; *Conversations with Isaac Bashevis Singer*, 1985 (with Richard Burgin); *More Stories from My Father's Court*, 2000.

TRANSLATIONS: *Romain Rolland*, 1927 (of Stefan Zweig's biography); *Di Vogler*, 1928 (of Knut Hamsun's novel); *Victoria*, 1929 (of Hamsun's novel); *All Quiet on the Western Front*, 1930 (of Erich Maria Remarque's novel); *Pan*, 1931 (of Hamsun's novel); *The Way Back*, 1931 (of Remarque's novel); *The Magic Mountain*, 1932 (of Thomas Mann's novel); *From Moscow to Jerusalem*, 1938 (of Leon Glaser's memoir).

CHILDREN'S LITERATURE: *Zlateh the Goat, and Other Stories*, 1966; *The Fearsome Inn*, 1967; *Mazel and Shlimazel: Or, The Milk of a Lioness*, 1967; *When Shlemiel Went to Warsaw, and Other Stories*, 1968; *A Day of Pleasure: Stories of a Boy Growing Up in Warsaw*, 1969; *Elijah the Slave*, 1970; *Joseph and Koza: Or, The Sacrifice to the Vistula*, 1970; *Alone in the Wild Forest*,

1971; *The Topsy-Turvy Emperor of China*, 1971; *The Wicked City*, 1972; *The Fools of Chelm and Their History*, 1973; *Why Noah Chose the Dove*, 1974; *A Tale of Three Wishes*, 1975; *Naftali the Storyteller and His Horse, Sus, and Other Stories*, 1976; *The Power of Light: Eight Stories*, 1980; *The Golem*, 1982; *Stories for Children*, 1984.

BIBLIOGRAPHY

Allentuck, Marcia, ed. *The Achievement of Isaac Bashevis Singer*. Carbondale: Southern Illinois University Press, 1969. Collection of eleven essays addresses various aspects of Singer's work. Most of the essays focus on themes in individual novels, but the collection also includes pieces on Singer's memoirs and children's stories as well as examinations of "The Spinoza of Market Street" and "Gimpel the Fool."

Farrell, Grace, ed. *Critical Essays on Isaac Bashevis Singer*. New York: G. K. Hall, 1996. Collection of essays provides an extensive introduction to Singer's critical reception and the issues that have preoccupied him and his critics. Includes both contemporary reviews and essays on a wide range of topics, including Leslie Fiedler's "I. B. Singer: Or, The Americanness of the American Jewish Writer."

_____. *Isaac Bashevis Singer: Conversations*. Jackson: University Press of Mississippi, 1992. Collection of interviews with Singer enables readers to draw connections among the writer's philosophy of life, his perspective on literature, and his mode of living.

Hadda, Janet. *Isaac Bashevis Singer: A Life*. New York: Oxford University Press, 1997. Examines both the forces of family and the social environment that influenced Singer, uncovering the public persona to reveal a man who was more complex than many had previously understood.

Kresh, Paul. *Isaac Bashevis Singer: The Magician of West Eighty-sixth Street*. New York: Dial Press, 1979. Provides a lively account of Singer's first seventy-five years, incorporating refreshing quotes and anecdotes, creating a delightful sense of intimacy for the reader. Careful attention to facts clarifies the often ambiguous details of Singer's works in terms of creation, translation, publication, and reissue. Includes photographs, bibliography, and index.

Mulbauer, Asher Z. *Transcending Exile*. Miami: Florida International University Press, 1985. Presents a thoughtful contemplation of exile in the works of three writers: Joseph Conrad, Vladimir Nabokov, and Singer. The discussion of Singer focuses on three novels—*Shosha*, *The Slave*, and *Enemies*—and also is mindful of thematic parallels to Singer's short stories.

Noiville, Florence. *Isaac B. Singer: A Life*. Translated by Catherine Temerson. New York: Farrar, Straus and Giroux, 2006. For those unfamiliar with Singer, this concise, easy-to-read biography serves as an excellent introduction to the man and his works. Noiville gleans information from interviews with Singer's wife, son, friends, and colleagues as well as his memoir *In My Father's Court*. Focuses on Singer's life struggles, his relationships with others, and the adversity he had to overcome as a Jewish writer.

Qiao, Guo Qiang. *The Jewishness of Isaac Bashevis Singer*. New York: Peter Lang, 2003. Analyzes Singer's work and finds a unique place for the writer within American Jewish literature. Addresses Singer's depiction of past and present Jewish assimilation in both Poland and the United States, examines Singer's narrative strategies, and compares the Jewish identity and Jewish historical consciousness in works by Singer, Saul Bellow, Bernard Malamud, and Philip Roth.

Sinclair, Clive. *The Brothers Singer*. London: Allison & Busby, 1983. Presents a fascinating examination of Singer and his work in the context of one of the most important personal and literary relationships of the author's life. Effectively interweaves biography and literary analysis, conveying a deep understanding of the lives and works of Isaac and Joshua Singer.

Wolitz, Seth L., ed. *The Hidden Isaac Bashevis Singer*. Austin: University of Texas Press, 2001. Collection of essays covers such topics as Singer's use of Yiddish language and cultural experience, themes that persist throughout his writing, his interface with other times and cultures, his autobiographical work, and a translation of a previously unpublished "gangster" novel.

ANDREI SINYAVSKY

Born: Moscow, Russia, Soviet Union (now in
Russia); October 8, 1925

Died: Fontenay-aux-Roses, France; February 25,
1997

Also known as: Andrei Donatovich Sinyavsky;
Abram Tertz

PRINCIPAL LONG FICTION

Sad idzie, 1959 (in Polish; in Russian as *Sud
idyot*, 1960; as Abram Tertz; *The Trial
Begins*, 1960)

Lyubimov, 1963 (in Polish; Russian translation,
1964; as Tertz; *The Makepeace Experiment*,
1965)

Kroshka Tsores, 1980 (novella; *Little Jinx*, 1992)

Spokoynoy nochi, 1984 (*Goodnight!*, 1989)

OTHER LITERARY FORMS

Andrei Sinyavsky (sihn-YAHV-skee) is the author
of an important book-length essay, *Chto takoe sotsialisticheskii realizm* (1959; *On Socialist Realism*,
1960), published under the pseudonym Abram Tertz, in
which he maintains with some humor that realism is not
the proper medium for the mythmaking inherent in a
communist society. Because he believed that the grandiose neoclassicism inherited from eighteenth century Russian literature had also become inadequate, Sinyavsky
proposed that the more appropriate genre would be fantasy, and he himself became a writer of fantasy. His collection *Fantasticheskie povesti* (1961; *Fantastic Stories*,
1963; also known as *The Icicle, and Other Stories*,
1963), including a novella and several short stories, is
surrealistic, an excursion into the literature of the absurd.
Mysli vrasplokh (1966; as Tertz; *Unguarded Thoughts*,
1972), a collection of aphorisms, came as a revelation to
Sinyavsky's Western readers, disclosing for the first
time his profound faith as a Russian Orthodox believer.

In addition to these works, all of which were signed
with the pen name Abram Tertz and published abroad
before his arrest, Sinyavsky has published a number of
important critical studies, including an introductory essay to Boris Pasternak's *Stikhotvoreniya i poemy* (1965,

1976; verses and poems); an analysis of the nineteenth
century writer Nikolai Gogol, *V teni Gogolya* (1975; in
the shadow of Gogol); and a book on the poet Alexander
Pushkin, *Progulki s Pushkinym* (1975; walks with Pushkin). Sinyavsky's *Golos iz khora* (1973; *A Voice from
the Chorus*, 1976), largely composed of letters that he
wrote to his wife during his six years in a labor camp, is
in the tradition initiated by Fyodor Dostoevski and continued by such twentieth century writers as Aleksandr
Solzhenitsyn. The essay "Literaturnii protess v Rossii"
(literary process in Russia), published in the dissident
journal *Kontinent* in 1976, is both a savage analysis of
the Soviet mind and an extraordinary literary manifesto
that transcends its occasion. Finally, Sinyavsky's *Little
Jinx*, with the Yiddish word *tsores* in the original title,
serves as a reminder that he identifies with Jews as alienated people outside the normal parameters of Soviet existence.

ACHIEVEMENTS

The true identity of the elusive writer Abram Tertz (a
pen name taken from the hero of an underworld ballad)
became known to readers in the Soviet Union and the
West only after his arrest in 1965 and subsequent imprison-
onment. Tertz turned out to be the gifted and sophisticated critic Andrei Sinyavsky. Prior to this catastrophe,
Sinyavsky had mastered the extremely difficult task of
keeping his two voices, that of the writer Tertz and the
critic Sinyavsky, separate. Writing as Tertz, Sinyavsky
produced fantastic stories and short novels, as well as the
famous essay *On Socialist Realism*, a devastating critique of officially tolerated literary practice.

So accomplished a writer was Sinyavsky that his
achievements were considered far superior to those of
his contemporaries, and it was even thought for a time
that Tertz might be the brilliant prose writer Yury Olesha,
from the 1920's. Writing during a period when Russian
prose had only just begun to emerge from the stultifying limitations of Socialist Realism, Sinyavsky managed
to continue the earlier ornamentalist prose tradition of
Andrey Bely, Alexey Remizov, and, ultimately, Gogol.

The sophistication of Sinyavsky's worldview is equal

to that of his style, for he presents society with all of its inherent contradictions, limitations, and absurdities, a far cry from the narrow vision peculiar to Socialist Realism and official Soviet ideology. With his stylistic brilliance and metaphysical depth, Sinyavsky has rightly come to be considered one of the finest Russian authors of the post-Stalin period.

BIOGRAPHY

Andrei Donatovich Sinyavsky was born in Moscow in 1925 and grew up there. He served in the Russian army during World War II. After the war, he was a student at the philological faculty of Moscow State University, one of the nation's most prestigious institutions of higher learning. He eventually became a candidate of philological sciences, a degree equivalent to a doctorate in the United States, and he obtained a position as a senior staff member with the Gorky Institute of World Literature in Moscow. Sinyavsky immediately came to be regarded as a gifted critic; his book on postrevolutionary Russian poetry, *Poeziya pervykh let revolyutsii, 1917-1920* (1964), coauthored with A. Menshutin, was considered one of the best studies of its time. His interests extended beyond literature to the plastic arts, and he collaborated with I. N. Golomshtok on a work about Pablo Picasso, *Pikasso* (1960).

Simultaneously with his activities as a critic, Sinyavsky pursued a secret career as a fantasy writer, using the name Abram Tertz; it was the revelations of de-Stalinization in 1956 that converted him from establishment critic to dissident author. Madame Hélène Peltier-Zamoyska, daughter of the French naval attaché in Moscow, had become close friends with Sinyavsky when they were students together at Moscow State University, and it was she who arranged for the publication of the works of "Tertz" in the West. In spite of Sinyavsky's discretion, he was unmasked in 1965. He was tried in February, 1966, with fellow dissident writer Yuli Daniel, who had achieved fame in the West and notoriety in the Soviet Union as Nikolay Arzhak. Sinyavsky was sentenced to six years in prison, spending the time in a labor camp in Mordovia. He left the Soviet Union for France in 1973, thereafter teaching at the Sorbonne. The fine works that he has published since his departure attest Sinyavsky's continued development as a writer.

ANALYSIS

Any attempt to analyze Andrei Sinyavsky's fiction must take the essay *On Socialist Realism* into account, for the ideas developed in that essay provide the basis for his fictional works. Socialist Realism has been defined in the Soviet Union as a depiction of "reality in its revolutionary development," the favored official medium being an anemic descendant of the so-called critical realism of the nineteenth century. This realism, Sinyavsky believes, is inadequate for expressing the heroic purpose, a purpose essential to the ideology forming the basis for the Soviet state. The neoclassicism of the eighteenth century, normally the ideal vehicle for the purpose of the autocratic state, could not be used for contemporary Soviet literature; the debunking of the Stalinist myth and absence of a figure of similar stature robbed the Russians

Andrei Sinyavsky. (AP/Wide World Photos)

of anyone or anything to glorify. The only remaining method possible is one based on hypothesis instead of purpose, and that method has to be fantasy. It is with this premise in mind that Sinyavsky has approached the novel.

THE TRIAL BEGINS

Sinyavsky's first novel, *The Trial Begins*, is set in Moscow during the last days of Joseph Stalin. It is ostensibly a realistic novel dealing with such well-known phenomena of the time as the "doctors' plot," which resulted in the stepped-up persecution of the Jews, the terrifying inner workings of the secret police, and the mass panic immediately following the death of Stalin. Sinyavsky's principal characters include the public prosecutor Vladimir Petrovich Globov, his idealistic son, Seryozha, and Seryozha's friend, Katya. Globov's second wife, Marina, and Yuri Karlinsky, a defending attorney, eventually manage to become lovers behind Globov's back. Globov's former mother-in-law, Yekaterina Petrovna, is an old Bolshevik idealist.

Globov is scheduled to prosecute the gynecologist S. Y. Rabinovich, who performed an illegal abortion, but the woman in question is Globov's beautiful and sexy but soulless wife, Marina. Rabinovich is Jewish, and his predicament is a transparent reference to Stalin's anti-Semitic campaign in the 1950's. Globov's life is complicated further by the fact that his adolescent son, Seryozha, has written a notebook calling for a new Communist society that will be free of the corruption that has stained the old one, a society in which those in the highest offices would earn the lowest wages, money would be abolished, and everyone would receive "according to his needs." Seryozha shares his ideas with Katya and gives her the notebook. She takes it to Karlinsky for advice, protesting against Seryozha's orthodoxy that a noble end should be served by noble means; Karlinsky counters that power corrupts, with the noble means soon forgotten. After she leaves, he gives vent to his jealous rage against Marina's husband, deciding to strike at him by blowing the whistle on his son, Seryozha. Seryozha is eventually tried and sent to a labor camp, where he is joined by Rabinovich. Finally given the opportunity to consummate his affair with Marina, Karlinsky proves to be impotent. Katya is trampled to death in the mass stampede following Stalin's funeral.

At first glance, *The Trial Begins* appears to be a realistic work that reveals corruption and evil in the Soviet Union, a critique of the system in the tradition of Vladimir Dudintsev's *Ne khlebom yedinym* (1956; *Not by Bread Alone*, 1957) or Ilya Ehrenburg's *Ottepel* (1954; *The Thaw*, 1955). Appearances, however, are deceiving, and *The Trial Begins* stands apart from its fellows by virtue of Sinyavsky's use of fantasy.

The Trial Begins is introduced by a narrator, one of a series of Sinyavsky's quirky, neurotic narrators. He bears a close resemblance to Yury Olesha's hero Kavalerov in the novel *Zavist* (1927; *Envy*, 1936), and it is easy to see why a number of Western critics initially assumed that the novelist and critic known as Tertz was actually Olesha. Tertz's narrator, similar to but not identical with Tertz himself, is the author of the manuscript that constitutes the major portion of the novel. He is a writer, the generic, nonconformist Soviet writer.

The narrator is victimized in the middle of the night by two secret police agents, Vitya and Tolya, who work as a team and bear a strong resemblance to Thompson and Thomson from Hergé's series of children's books on the young French reporter Tintin. Vitya and Tolya, like Thompson and Thomson, are the enemies of freedom and originality, and their purpose is to destroy art. One of them scoops all the letters and punctuation marks off the page and crushes one caught trying to escape. The manuscript they have confiscated is *The Trial Begins*, but the characters and events in the work come to life as if they had been written by an omniscient, not a first-person, narrator. The narrator himself disappears from the story, not to surface again until the end, when he is shown in prison camp with his invented characters Rabinovich and Seryozha. Thus, the body of the novel is sandwiched between the reader's introduction to the narrator at the beginning and the reader's final, sad view of him at the end.

The most fantastic element of the frame technique used by Sinyavsky is that two characters who are part of the body of the novel—that is, part of the manuscript written by the convict author—actually appear with him in prison at the conclusion of the story. The reader is then left with the uneasy sensation that the manuscript has taken over and somehow become actuality, that the omniscient and first-person narrators might possibly be the same individual. The implications of this confusing situation are enormous.

Beneath the surface of an apparent protest novel, a novel peppered with such peculiar events as the appearance of the hand of God to the narrator at the beginning or Marina's gift of liqueur-filled chocolates to Seryozha at the end, other factors are at work. Sinyavsky's novel is only superficially about political events and the illicit love affair between Karlinsky and Marina. It is actually about art, specifically about literature and the intricacies involved in the writing of fiction. As such, it follows in the tradition of Russian works that are consciously but obliquely about literature or art, works such as Olesha's *Envy*—a tradition that ultimately extends back to the subtle plays and short stories of Pushkin.

Sinyavsky is, of course, concerned with political abuses and is clearly against the overwhelming domination of all aspects of Soviet life by Stalin's dictatorship, but he is primarily preoccupied with artistic freedom. The arrest, to which any citizen was subject at any time, without warning, was a commonplace of Soviet life during the Terror of the 1930's and then again after World War II. Sinyavsky's account of the narrator's arrest uncannily anticipates his own later arrest and imprisonment; it is the fictional arrest that sets in motion the events of the novel, for only through the narrator's arrest do the police (and the readers) learn of the existence of the formerly secret manuscript. The apparent fragility of the narrator's creation is touchingly depicted in the opening scene, when an escaping letter is destroyed like a bug. The author of the manuscript is himself fragile, easily trapped by the state and sent to prison.

This leads to the realization that there is yet another layer of fantasy operative here, for the entire novel—including both the frame story and the manuscript—actually resurfaces and is subsequently published; the manuscript of the story is only a larger portion of the real manuscript that exists in the form of Sinyavsky's novel. The captured letters have escaped after all, coming to new life in print. The captured narrator, an unfortunate prisoner who is the product of Sinyavsky's imagination, achieves new life within his larger, real novel. If straightforward art cannot appear, Sinyavsky suggests, then the writer must resort to the art of circumlocution. If a literary work is helpless in a police state, then an entire manuscript can be incorporated into another work, and that novel can somehow escape the predatory actions of official limitation. It is through the cunning of fantasy that art survives at all. This is fitting, because fantasy itself is the product of the artistic imagination, an answer to the superficial strictures enforced by politics. The survival of art is the answer to the state, because the actual reality envisioned by art is of a different order from that of the apparent reality of a political system; the boundary between the visible and the hidden is nowhere better demonstrated than in the encounter between the awesome hand of God and the tiny fist of Stalin in Sinyavsky's initial frame segment. The relative disparity between them is but a symbol of the enormous gulf separating apparent and absolute values, be they religious or aesthetic.

THE MAKEPEACE EXPERIMENT

Fantastic elements are more easily discernible in *The Makepeace Experiment* than in *The Trial Begins*. The Russian title of Sinyavsky's second novel is *Lyubimov*, the name of the town that provides the setting for the incredible events of the novel. *The Makepeace Experiment* was published three years after *The Trial Begins*, and Sinyavsky's greater expertise as a novelist is reflected in the more intricate characterization, fantastic plot, and convoluted narration.

Like his nineteenth century predecessors, Sinyavsky abandons the setting of Moscow in favor of the small, remote town of Lyubimov. It has the flavor of the innumerable squalid hamlets peppering Gogol's prose masterpieces, but it is especially reminiscent of the town in Mikhail Saltykov's novel *Istoriya odnogo goroda* (1869-1870; *The History of a Town*, 1981). *The Makepeace Experiment*, however, is only ostensibly a story of rural life. As circumstances of the plot make amply clear, the events taking place there are actually a microcosm of the larger politico-historical world. Lyonya Tikhomirov's dictatorship (his name means "peaceful world"), the fruitful result of his ability to apply mass hypnosis to the populace of an entire town, bears a certain resemblance to the larger one bedeviling Russians in hundreds of small towns all across the Soviet Union. Lyonya, however, has heeded the idealism of Seryozha in *The Trial Begins*, for this dictatorship is devoid of corruption, greed, and coercion. Through the magic wand of

Lyonya's hypnotic powers, the locals believe that toothpaste has changed into fish paste, the local river runs with champagne for thirty minutes, and ordinary bottled water, the sort normally avoided by most of the residents, seems to have turned into grain alcohol and in fact causes the death of one drinker.

Lyonya's aristocratic ancestor, Samson Samsonovich Proferantsov, owned a leather-bound book from India titled *The Magnet of the Soul*. Having accidentally acquired the book, Lyonya masters the contents and sets out to acquire the two things he desires: mind control over the citizens of Lyubimov and the love of the previously indifferent beauty Serafima Petrovna Kozlova. He celebrates his wedding to Serafima simultaneously with his formal installment as official leader of the town of Lyubimov; for a while, events run smoothly, and Serafima is his willing slave. Lyonya has audiences directly with his citizens, attempting to please all of those under his jurisdiction, and they turn Stakhanovite for the dubious reward of ersatz luxuries. He has an elaborate alarm system installed to foil incursions from the outside, using his magnetic powers to baffle would-be enemies, but he becomes increasingly bored with the obedient Serafima and is exhausted by the heavy demands of his office.

Unwilling to be left out of the action, the original owner of the book asserts himself. He scrambles Lyonya's magnetic powers, and our hero's every thought turns into a command subconsciously transmitted to the residents of Lyubimov. A young man silently commanded to "drop dead" collapses and dies of a heart attack; an old woman rides her broom, having become a witch in accordance with Lyonya's desires. The entire utopian society falls apart, and Lyonya escapes in the end, enabling his town to return to normal.

It is in *The Makepeace Experiment* that Sinyavsky introduces a Jewish character for the first time—Serafima Petrovna. The narrator gossips to Lyonya about her ethnic origins and, in the end, the reader learns that she really is part Jewish and that Kozlov was only the name of her first husband. She had kept the existence of her husband and small daughter secret from Lyonya, and there is a hint that these scandalous facts are all related to her Jewishness. Having warned Lyonya that his intended is not really "Russian," the narrator allows himself a di-

gression about Jews. He admires them; they are survivors. They are scattered in society like indissoluble specks, like "raisins" or "black pepper" but never salt. They have Jewish eyes, sad eyes with *tsores* (trouble); Proferantsov calls them "desert eyes."

Sinyavsky's intense interest in Jews extends even to his selection of a Jewish pseudonym, Abram Tertz, a choice that must be regarded as highly unusual for a Russian writer. There are various reasons for his singular interest. In the first place, Sinyavsky resembles Olesha in regarding the writer as a foreign element in society, particularly Soviet society. The writer is like the Jew in his cosmopolitanism, his resultant separation from the mainstream, and his awareness of "trouble." Sinyavsky even flavors his writing with a Jewish accent when describing the Jewish woman who had once been part of his life, a stylistic touch that does not come across in the English translation.

Sinyavsky, however, has yet another complex reason for his apparent obsession: his sense of history. The Jews encountered in Russian society are a reminder that "history did not begin today and it is still not known how it will end." Those desert eyes are sad because of "historical memories." The Jews—and, by extension, the writer—are somehow outside the deterministic orthodoxy that history has evolved along certain lines from the beginning of time. Official Soviet history centers on the concept that the October Revolution was the great break from the capitalism dominating nineteenth century Europe, an economic and political structure giving way to the socialism and eventual communism that will someday grace the Soviet Union. Sinyavsky counters this supposition through his narrator Proferantsov, stating that no one knows how history will end. This incredible statement flies in the face of Marxist orthodoxy, for the presumed final result is the withering away of the state with the triumph of communism. Reality, says Sinyavsky, is unpredictable and cannot be controlled, and he underlines this firmly by his use of fantasy and multiple narrators.

The seeming ordinariness of life gives way at the conclusion of the novel to the ramblings of the narrator Proferantsov, for *The Makepeace Experiment* is a frame story introduced and ended by a chatty writer, in a genre ultimately going back to Pushkin's stories. The narrative here is complicated by the presence of a second narrator, Samson Samsonovich Proferantsov himself, who intrudes into Proferantsov's story in the form of corrective footnotes; it is an irritating practice that does not endear him to his descendant.

By such devices, Sinyavsky makes it impossible for his readers to maintain that "willing suspension of disbelief" so crucial to the flow of most fictional works. He constantly reminds us that we are reading a work of fiction and have entered an artificial world. He underscores this unreality with his pterodactyl, a creature rumored by Dr. Linde, one of the novel's several eccentrics, to inhabit the swampy woods outside town. The pterodactyl indeed exists; it appears to Colonel Almazov, commander of the forces sent to storm the town, during his final drugged moments and seems to speak perfect French. What better witness to this impossible horror than the supporter of state power, a man who would never allow for the oddities of events outside the orthodox conception of reality. The scene between the two is the high point of the novel, the sort of confrontation for which Sinyavsky himself pushed in creating a fantastic world as rival to the rigidity of the real one.

Sinyavsky's fiction provides an excellent illustration of the sort of fantasy he advocated in his theoretical writing. Serving as an antidote to the rigidity of Socialist Realism, it is a reminder that Russian literature still has room for the incredible and unorthodox. Fantasy for Sinyavsky is a vehicle for addressing crucial questions, for it is by circumventing the real world that he is able to deal with such issues as the role and methods of the writer, the meaning of history, and the problems and inequities of the dictatorship that provided the setting for his works. As both artist and thinker, he must be accounted one of the most interesting and significant of contemporary Russian authors.

Janet G. Tucker

OTHER MAJOR WORKS

SHORT FICTION: *Fantasticheskie povesti*, 1961 (*Fantastic Stories*, 1963; also known as *The Icicle, and Other Stories*, 1963).

NONFICTION: *Istoriya russkoy sovetsky literatury*, 1958, 1961; *Chto takoe sotsialisticheskii realizm*, 1959 (as Abram Tertz; *On Socialist Realism*, 1960); *Pikasso*, 1960 (with I. N. Golomshtok); *Poeziya pervykh let revolyutsii, 1917-1920*, 1964 (with A. Menshutin); *Mysli vrasplokh*, 1966 (as Tertz; *Unguarded Thoughts*, 1972); *For Freedom of Imagination*, 1971 (essays); *Golos iz khora*, 1973 (*A Voice from the Chorus*, 1976); *Progulki s Pushkinym*, 1975 (*Strolls with Pushkin*, 1993); *V teni Gogolya*, 1975; *"Opavshie list'ya" V. V. Rozanova*, 1982; *Soviet Civilization: A Cultural History*, 1990; *Ivan-durak: Ocherk russkoi narodnoi very*, 1991 (*Ivan the Fool: Russian Folk Belief—A Cultural History*, 2007); *The Russian Intelligensia*, 1997.

BIBLIOGRAPHY

Fenander, Sara. "Author and Autocrat: Tertz's Stalin and the Ruse of Charisma." *Russian Review* 58 (April, 1999): 286-297. Examines Sinyavsky in his role as both cultural critic and the provocateur Abram Tertz; claims that by turning the discredited Joseph Stalin into a double for himself, Sinyavsky/Tertz reveals both the artistry of Stalinism and the mythical privileged place of the writer in Russian culture.

Frank, Joseph. "The Triumph of Abram Tertz." *The New York Review of Books*, June 27, 1991. A brief biographical and critical discussion of the events of Sinyavsky's life and the nature of his fiction. Notes the importance of his trial for having his works published outside the Soviet Union.

Genis, Alexander. "Archaic Postmodernism: The Aesthetics of Andrei Sinyavsky" and "Postmodernism and Sots-Realism: From Andrei Sinyavsky to Vladimir Sorokin." In *Russian Postmodernism: New Perspectives on Post-Soviet Culture*, by Mikhail Epstein, Alexander Genis, and Slobodanka Vladiv-Glover. Translated and edited by Vladiv-Glover. New York: Berghahn Books, 1999. These two essays about Sinyavsky's postmodernist writings are included in this examination of Russian fiction, poetry, art, and spirituality after the demise of the Soviet Union.

Grayson, Jane. "Back to the Future: Andrei Siniavskii and Kapitanskaia Dochka." In *Reconstructing the Canon: Russian Writing in the 1980's*, edited by Arnold B. McMillin. Amsterdam: Harwood Academic, 2000. This discussion of Sinyavsky's work is included in a collection of essays examining Soviet writers whose work appeared during the 1980's, a decade in which artists were allowed greater freedom of expression.

_____. "Picture Windows: The Art of Andrei Siniavskii." In *Russian Literature, Modernism, and the Visual Arts*, edited by Catriona Kelly and Stephen Lovell. New York: Cambridge University Press, 2000. Grayson's examination of Sinyavsky's work is included in a collection of essays about the influence of the visual arts on Russian modernist literature, focusing on collaborations between writers and artists, designers, and theater and film directors.

Kolonosky, Walter F. *Literary Insinuations: Sorting Out Sinyavsky's Irreverence*. Lanham, Md.: Lexington Books, 2003. Kolonosky's examination of Sinyavsky's writing focuses on the satire in his work, exploring how the writer uses allegory, parody, and irony to criticize abuses and foolishness.

Lourie, Richard. *Letters to the Future: An Approach to Sinyavsky-Tertz*. Ithaca, N.Y.: Cornell University Press, 1975. Lourie analyzes Sinyavsky's novels, short stories, and other work, placing them within the context of Soviet history and Slavic literature. Compares Sinyavsky's "philosophical satire" to the work of Nikolai Gogol. Includes notes, a bibliography, and an index.

Mathewson, Rufus W., Jr. *The Positive Hero in Russian Literature*. 1975. Reprint. Evanston, Ill.: Northwestern University Press, 1999. Mathewson includes an analysis of Sinyavsky's writing in this examination of the "positive hero," a character who sets an example for readers' behavior. Describes how this model character was a longstanding source of controversy in Russian literature.

Sandler, Stephanie. "Ending/Beginning with Andrei Sinyavsky/Abram Tertz." In *Commemorating Pushkin: Russia's Myth of a National Poet*. Stanford, Calif.: Stanford University Press, 2004. Sandler analyzes Russia's complex relationship with Alexander Pushkin, describing how his work has influenced Sinyavsky and other Russian writers and how his legacy is reflected in museums and other Russian cultural institutions.

Theimer Nepomnyashchy, Catherine. "Sinyavsky/Tertz: The Evolution of the Writer in Exile." *Humanities in Society* 7, no. 314 (1984): 123-142. After providing a brief overview of Sinyavsky's career during his first decade in the West, the author goes on to detail Sinyavsky's concerns with the role of the writer in relationship to reality and society at large. Concludes with a discussion of *Little Jinx*.

JOSEF ŠKVORECKÝ

Born: Náchod, Czechoslovakia (now in Czech Republic); September 27, 1924

Also known as: Josef Václav Škvorecký

PRINCIPAL LONG FICTION

Zbabělci, 1958 (*The Cowards*, 1970)

Legenda Emöke, 1963 (novella; *Emöke*, 1977)

Bassaxofon, 1967 (novella; *The Bass Saxophone*, 1977)

Konec nylonoveho véku, 1967

Faráňův konec, 1969 (with Evald Schorm)

Lvíče, 1969 (*Miss Silver's Past*, 1974)

Tankový prapor, 1969 (*The Republic of Whores: A Fragment from the Time of the Cults*, 1993)

Mirákl: Politická detektivka, 1972 (*The Miracle Game*, 1991)

Konec poručíka Borůvky, 1975 (*The End of Lieutenant Boruvka*, 1989)

Prima sezóna, 1975 (*The Swell Season: A Text on the Most Important Things in Life*, 1982)

Příběh inženýra lidských duší, 1977 (*The Engineer of Human Souls: An Entertainment on the Old Themes of Life, Women, Fate, Dreams, the Working Class, Secret Agents, Love, and Death*, 1984)

Návrat poručíka Borůvky, 1981 (*The Return of Lieutenant Boruvka*, 1990)

Scherzo capriccioso: Veselý sen o Dvořákovi,
　　1983 (*Dvořák in Love: A Light-Hearted*
　　Dream, 1986)
Nevěsta z Texasu, 1992 (*The Bride of Texas*,
　　1995)
Nevysvětlitelny pšríbšeh: Aneb, Vyprávšení
　　Questa Firma Sicula, 1998 (*An Inexplicable*
　　Story: Or, The Narrative of Questus Firmus
　　Siculus, 2002)
Two Murders in My Double Life, 1999
Obyčejné životy, 2004 (*Ordinary Lives,* 2008)

OTHER LITERARY FORMS

Josef Škvorecký (shkwor-EHT-skee) has published
books on jazz, such as *Talkin' Moscow Blues* (1988),
and films, such as *All the Bright Young Men and Women:
A Personal History of the Czech Cinema* (1971). He also
is known for publications concerning literature and politics.

ACHIEVEMENTS

During the Communist-dominated regime in Czechoslovakia, Josef Škvorecký did not receive proper recognition for his achievements, except for the Writers'
Union Annual Award for *Konec nylonoveho véku* in
1967. Ironically, in 1990, Czech president Václav Havel
awarded the Order of the White Lion, the Czech Republic's highest award for foreigners, to Škvorecký and his
wife, the former singer and actor Zdena Salivarová, for
their promotion of Czech literature through their publishing firm. Most appreciation for Škvorecký's work as
a writer came from his adopted home in Canada and
from the United States. In 1980, the University of Oklahoma awarded him the Neustadt International Prize
for Literature. He received the Canadian Governor-
General's Award for best fiction in English, the first
translation so honored, for *The Engineer of Human Souls*
in 1985.

Beyond the official prizes, Škvorecký has won recognition for his promotion of Czech literature. His early
novels defied the Soviet insistence on Socialist Realism,
and his creation of character Danny Smiricky provided
Czechoslovaks with an often comic antihero, one clever
enough to exist under authoritarian rule. Škvorecký's
supple use of the Czech language subverts the empty
communist slogans ponderously translated into Czech.
He is a highly visible champion of Czech literature in
speeches and written commentary, serving as a bridge
between the cultures of his native and adopted countries.

BIOGRAPHY

Josef Václav Škvorecký was born in 1924. Much of
Škvorecký's life is evident in his fiction: Significant
events are recalled in several works. While he was attending the local *Gymnasium* (college-preparatory secondary school) from 1935 to 1943, he developed what
would become a lifelong appreciation for jazz and began
his study of English, reading American authors in translation. During the Nazi occupation, he was a forced laborer in a Messerschmitt factory, an experience that is
described in *The Cowards* and *The Engineer of Human
Souls*. He earned a doctorate in philosophy from Charles
University in Prague in 1951. His writing career started
auspiciously; he won a university prize for his short stories. He taught at a girls' school in Horice (described in
The Miracle Game) for a year, and in 1951, he was inducted into the army, serving two years in a tank division.

By 1948, Škvorecký was a member of the Prague underground group of writers and artists, reacting against
the Soviet occupation and control of Czechoslovakia,
which took place in 1945. Between 1948 and 1949
he worked on his first novel, *The Cowards*, which was
not published for ten years. He had abandoned *Konec
nylonoveho véku* during this time; it was unpublished but
perhaps privately circulated because of the oppressive
censorship of the Soviet regime. Although *The Cowards*
was popularly received in 1958, the book was banned,
and Škvorecký lost his post as deputy editor in chief of
the magazine *Světová Literatura*. Škvorecký, however,
had established himself as a worthy essayist, critic, and
translator, particularly of modern American literature giants Ernest Hemingway, John Steinbeck, and William
Faulkner.

With the arrival of the Soviet tanks in 1968,
Škvorecký and his wife, Zdena, whom he had married in
1957, emigrated to Canada and settled in Toronto.
Škvorecký joined the faculty of the University of Toronto as a writer-in-residence and a member of the English Department. In 1971 the Škvoreckýs founded

Josef Škvorecký. (Getty Images)

Sixty-Eight Publishers, a conduit for the publications of Czech literature, including Škvorecký's own works. Now free to devote himself to writing, Škvorecký began an amazingly productive period. He also began to broadcast for the U.S. government-run radio network Voice of America, not only speaking about Czech literature but also reviewing publications by British and American writers. No longer just a symbol of dissidence, he emerged as a significant figure in international literature.

ANALYSIS

Josef Škvorecký deliberately challenges readers by creating a complex structure for his novels. He shifts episodes, conversations, and images around, then groups them to give some meaning to the individual's struggle to rise above the confusion of modern life. Škvorecký deliberately places incidents and characters at random to keep readers alert. His fragmentation gives emphasis to

the term "postmodern." It is an oversimplification to dismiss him as just an autobiographical novelist. The Danny Smiricky novels may echo some important episodes in Škvorecký's life, but Škvorecký clearly states the artist's right to embellish, to embroider, to transpose.

Above all, Škvorecký brings a special humor to his writing; he once commented that he never intended to write satire, but he found himself producing fiction "indistinguishable" from it. He enjoys playing with language, a fact that is best appreciated by those who can read his original Czech.

Perhaps Škvorecký's most successful use of humor is in his creation of a pertinent incident that is often inherently comic and demonstrates a theme or idea. This is evidenced in *The Engineer of Human Souls*, with Škvorecký's description of the arrival of a paranoid messenger carrying a banned book into Toronto Union Station to deliver it to an unfamiliar receiver, Danny. The whole passage can be extracted from the novel and used as a short story with an obvious theme: the difference between the East and the West.

Škvorecký's novels are novels of ideas; they are neither didactic nor propagandistic. He faced criticism for not championing the reformers and ideologies made popular during the Prague Spring of 1968, but he purposefully created an apolitical hero in Danny, who does not espouse one truth over others. Again, Škvorecký challenges readers to not only construct his novels but also examine critically their own thinking.

THE MIRACLE GAME

The Miracle Game is an excellent example of Škvorecký's method of writing, as it spans a twenty-year period while avoiding a linear chronology. The novel involves crucial years in Czechoslovak history, from the Soviet occupation to the Prague Spring. In it, Škvorecký satirizes the authoritarian control over the Czechoslovaks, particularly Danny Smiricky's fellow artists. Danny is a jazz-loving adolescent, a member of the tank corps, and a mature writer of innocuous musical comedies. He is distracted from ideological warfare. He is on the fringe of the writers' groups and manages to view the "intellectuals" from an "inferior" perspective. One of the miracles of the book's title is the Prague Spring itself, but Danny does not side with any new, strong position, and he prefers to watch disputes from the sidelines. Škvorecký does not miss the opportunity for satire, particularly at the writers' conference, featuring delegates who actively support Socialist Realism, the Communist Party's view of "good" literature. The satire against authoritarianism is also evident in the hilarious episode of the matriculation exams for the students at Danny's school.

If the Prague Spring represents a Marxist miracle, the Roman Catholic Church, the other dominant force in Czechoslovakia, can boast of a miracle of its own. A statue of Saint Joseph in a remote chapel moves during morning mass, apparently bowing, possibly toward the West. In the search for the truth about the miracle, the novel borrows from Škvorecký's detective fiction. Was the statue's movement a scheme to undermine the Church? Did Father Doufal, the priest saying mass at the time, "manufacture" the miracle, as the authorities claimed? Was another culprit involved? For more than twenty years the veracity of the miracle is debated. After an inspiring visit to a sanatorium, Danny seems close to learning the solution; the "answer," when revealed, however, is ambiguous. The cynical Danny cannot make the leap of faith needed to accept the apparent truth. Readers are forced to make their own choice.

THE ENGINEER OF HUMAN SOULS

The declaration (often attributed to Soviet leader Joseph Stalin) that a writer must be the "engineer" directing humanity toward acceptance of Marxist ideology almost demands Škvorecký's satire. Not only is Škvorecký conscious of the artist's independence, but also he questions the right of any entity to impose its version of truth on the rest of society. This premise echoes throughout Škvorecký's fiction and is brought to fruition in this, the richest of his novels of ideas.

The book is the fifth and last in the saga of Danny Smiricky, but it is not merely a sequel to *The Miracle Game*. Danny is safely ensconced as a faculty member at the University of Toronto, still apolitical, still passive, more reflective—a modern hero caught between the past and the need to adapt to a new culture. He still defies rules and annoys political ideologues, never losing his sense of humor.

The fragmentation of the novel is eased by naming the seven chapters for some of Škvorecký's favorite authors: Edgar Allan Poe, Nathaniel Hawthorne, Mark Twain, Stephen Crane, F. Scott Fitzgerald, Joseph

Conrad, and H. P. Lovecraft. They are featured on Danny's syllabus for his course, and allusions to their work lend substance to the narrative.

Readers are again amused as Danny challenges his students with solemn declarations of Conrad's prescience in detecting the evils of communist dominance in the figure of Kurtz in *Heart of Darkness* (1902). Škvorecký, however, does not skirt the agony of the past; old friends Benno, Prema, and Vrata die, and another former friend languishes in Israel. The letters written to Danny over twenty-five years are the richest of the fragments that comprise the novel; they underscore Danny's greatest skill—listening.

Characters may move rapidly through the narrative, but they leave a resonant impact, especially the earnest publisher, Mrs. Santner, the predatory Dotty, and the homesick Veronika. Danny's old and new friends remind readers that Škvorecký writes for two audiences, Czechs and North Americans. Though Škvorecký (and Danny) cannot return to the past, as Veronika did, he must make peace with the present.

DVOŘÁK IN LOVE

Beginning with the title of the book, *Dvořák in Love* presents the reader with challenges that are often unsettling. The Czech title, *Scherzo capriccioso*, was deemed too obscure for readers, but the English translation is misleading. As a scherzo, the book should yield a sprightly transition of time and place, but even these characteristics are denied in the reader's confrontation of numerous characters and incidents. Škvorecký omits a unifier—a first-person narrator—and thus places the burden of assembly on the reader.

Most editions of the work provide a chronology of Antonín Dvořák's life, signaling that Škvorecký is not producing the traditional biographical novel. By not entering Dvořák's consciousness, Škvorecký simplifies the process of introducing a contradictory, complex character, an earthy genius; Dvořák is viewed only externally. The apparently plotless novel actually focuses on three love triangles: Dvořák's love for Josephine Čermáková and for her sister, Anna, whom he later married; his devotion to Josephine despite her marriage to Count Kounic; and Dvořák's daughter's attraction to two suitors.

Škvorecký helps to link parts of the novel with poetic

devices, such as imagery and symbolism; above all, he uses music as a running thread. An amber field, a circling butterfly, and a reference to Dvořák's famous *Stabat mater* introduce the novel. Echoes of these devices resound to the last pages. The focus on America and its music is another theme: Dvořák is lured to New York to direct the National Conservatory of Music, meeting music critic James Huneker, black violinist Will Marion Cook, and Harry T. Burleigh, who brought spirituals to the concert stage. As American music inspired Dvořák, he, in turn, affected jazz and, by extension, even influenced popular pianist George Gershwin's music. The novel is both scherzo and elegy, Škvorecký's tribute to a fellow artist and countryman.

THE BRIDE OF TEXAS

Although it may seem unusual for a Czech émigré to focus on a segment of American history in a novel, Škvorecký became intrigued with his discovery of the records of Czechoslovak soldiers who had fought in the Union Army during the American Civil War. Most of the characters are real, but Škvorecký uses dramatic license to add some significant fictional characters. Most of the Czechoslovak soldiers are real émigrés who served under General William Tecumseh Sherman; Škvorecký places them in one division, allowing for exchanges of stories and a camaraderie based on a common language. They are distinguished by their reasons for leaving home; most were beckoned by the promise of freedom and economic opportunity. Škvorecký views the war from their point of view, but he defends Sherman's intensity in the afterword, because he was impressed with Sherman's efforts to end the war.

Škvorecký introduces a semifictional character, Lorraine Tracy, a writer of romances and friend of General Ambrose Burnside, to examine the general's role in the prosecution of Copperhead Clement Vallandigham. Tracy, an abolitionist, provides insight into the slavery issue, with the help of her black maid Jasmine. The central fictional characters are Cyril Toupelik and his sister Lida, who fled Moravia. Lida, the bride of the title, represents the materialistic desire for a new life with her determination to marry a rich husband. Cyril is an idealist, determined to locate and marry the slave Dinah.

While Škvorecký employs a common structural pattern in the novel. He assembles flashbacks, anecdotes, and other narratives, introducing a poetic strain in his descriptive prose, which is marked with the stately repetition of such phrases as "turpentine forest on fire." Furthermore, Škvorecký manages to make the novel a tribute to his past and present: Czechoslovak history as viewed through the difficulties of Czechs dominated by Austria and Hungary and their own upper classes, as well as an appreciation of America for giving Czechs refuge and an opportunity to succeed.

Elizabeth R. Nelson

OTHER MAJOR WORKS

SHORT FICTION: *Smutek poručíka Borůvky*, 1966 (*The Mournful Demeanour of Lieutenant Boruvka*, 1973); *Hříchy pro pátera Knoxe*, 1973 (*Sins for Father Knox*, 1988); *Povídky tenorsaxofonisty*, 1993 (*The Tenor Saxophonist's Story*, 1997); *When Eve Was Naked: A Journey Through Life*, 2000 (also known as *When Eve Was Naked: Stories of Life's Journey*, 2002).

NONFICTION: *O nich—o nás*, 1968; *All the Bright Young Men and Women: A Personal History of the Czech Cinema*, 1971; *Jiří Menzel and the History of the "Closely Watched Trains,"* 1982; *Talkin' Moscow Blues*, 1988.

MISCELLANEOUS: *The Bass Saxophone*, 1977 (includes the essay "Red Music," *The Bass Saxophone*, and *Emöke*); *Headed for the Blues: A Memoir with Ten Stories*, 1996.

BIBLIOGRAPHY

Coetzee, J. M. "Josef Skvorecky." In *Stranger Shores: Literary Essays, 1986-1999*. New York: Viking Press, 2001. Coetzee, a novelist who has won the Nobel Prize in Literature and two Man Booker Prizes, discusses work by Škvorecký and other writers in this collection of his literary criticism.

Meyer, Bruce. "In Pursuit of Eden: The Displacement and Relocation of Vision in Josef Skvorecky's Fiction." In *Floating the Borders: New Contexts in Canadian Criticism*, edited by Nurjehan Aziz. Toronto, Ont.: TSAR, 1999. This study of Škvorecký's fiction is included in a collection of essays discussing Canadian authors of diverse ethnic and cultural backgrounds. Explores how this diversity challenges the traditional definition of Canadian literature.

O'Brien, John, ed. "Special Issue: Mario Vargas Llosa and Josef Škvorecký." *Review of Contemporary Fiction* 17, no. 1 (Spring, 1997): 78-158. Contains brief but perceptive essays, a limited select bibliography, an interview with and a previously unpublished short story by Škvorecký, and two essays on *The Bride of Texas*.

Solecki, Sam. *Prague Blues: The Fiction of Josef Škvorecký—A Critical Study*. Toronto, Ont.: ECW Press, 1990. The best starting point for a study of Škvorecký. Solecki has an appreciation for Škvorecký's work and is extremely perceptive. Includes a good bibliography.

_____, ed. *The Achievement of Josef Škvorecký*. Toronto, Ont.: University of Toronto Press, 1994. A collection of essays that focus on the major works. Includes an essay on the literary scandal surrounding the publication of *The Cowards*. Features an extensive bibliography.

Trensky, Paul I. *The Fiction of Josef Škvorecký*. New York: St. Martin's Press, 1991. Trensky describes how Škvorecký's work was influenced by his opposition to, and exile from, the former communist government in Czechoslovakia. Trensky offers a good perspective on the earlier works.

JANE SMILEY

Born: Los Angeles, California; September 26, 1949

Also known as: Jane Graves Smiley

PRINCIPAL LONG FICTION

Barn Blind, 1980
At Paradise Gate, 1981
Duplicate Keys, 1984
The Greenlanders, 1988
A Thousand Acres, 1991
Moo, 1995
The All-True Travels and Adventures of Lidie Newton, 1998
Horse Heaven, 2000
Good Faith, 2003
Ten Days in the Hills, 2007

OTHER LITERARY FORMS

In addition to her novels and novellas, Jane Smiley has written numerous book reviews, short stories, and nonfiction essays. Her stories have appeared in *The Atlantic Monthly*, and five are included in *The Age of Grief: A Novella and Stories* (1987). Among the most notable of her nonfiction essays is "Say It Ain't So, Huck: Second Thoughts on Mark Twain's 'Master-piece,'" which first appeared in *Harper's* in January, 1996; this work produced a storm of controversy, as in it Smiley questions the primacy of Mark Twain's *Adventures of Huckleberry Finn* (1884) in American fiction, arguing that critics have been evasive about the racism present in Twain's work and that Harriet Beecher Stowe's *Uncle Tom's Cabin* (1852) offers a more frank and open approach to racism.

Smiley has published in a variety of genres, including biography and literary history. Her nonfiction works include a collection of essays titled *Catskill Crafts: Artisans of the Catskill Mountains* (1988). Smiley's lifelong interest in horses is reflected in her chronicle of the careers of two racehorses she owned in *A Year at the Races: Reflections on Horses, Humans, Love, Money, and Luck* (2004). Her biography *Charles Dickens* (2002) has been widely praised for its nonpedantic approach, and in *Thirteen Ways of Looking at the Novel* (2005), Smiley analyzes the novel writer's craft by examining one hundred important novels.

Two of Smiley's fiction works have been made into motion pictures. The film version of *A Thousand Acres* was released in 1997, and an adaptation of the novella *The Age of Grief*, titled *The Secret Lives of Dentists*, was released in 2002.

ACHIEVEMENTS

Jane Smiley is a prolific writer with three O. Henry Awards (1982, 1985, and 1988) to her credit. *The Age of Grief* received a nomination for the National Book Critics Circle Award in 1987, and *A Thousand Acres* garnered several prestigious literary prizes, including the Pulitzer Prize for fiction, the National Book Critics Circle Award, the Midland Authors Award, and the Heartland Prize, all in 1992. Smiley has also enjoyed other honors, such as a Fulbright Fellowship, which took her to study in Iceland (1976-1977). She has twice been the recipient of fellowships from the National Endowment for the Arts (1978, 1987).

Critics have generally praised Smiley for the fine craftsmanship and psychological subtlety of her fiction and have noted her competence in handling complex and varied historical, sociological, and scholarly issues. In 2001, Smiley was inducted into the American Academy of Arts and Letters, and in 2006 she received the PEN USA Lifetime Achievement Award for Literature.

BIOGRAPHY

Although she writes extensively and convincingly about the American rural landscape and agricultural themes, Jane Graves Smiley grew up a city girl in St. Louis, Missouri, among gifted writers and storytellers. Her mother, Frances Nuelle (Graves) Smiley, held a newspaper job, and her father, James La Verne Smiley, was a West Point graduate and career military man. Smiley attributes much of her literary success to the fact that she grew up in a family that loved to tell its own history; listening to this history engendered in Smiley a lifelong fascination with character motives and plots.

Smiley attended Vassar College, from which she received her B.A. in 1971. The rest of her education was completed at the University of Iowa, including her M.F.A., her M.A., and her Ph.D. She began her working life humbly in a teddy-bear factory, but at Iowa State University she rapidly progressed from assistant professor in 1981 to distinguished professor in 1992.

Smiley retired from teaching in 1996 and settled in Northern California to pursue writing full time and to enjoy horseback riding. She has been married and divorced three times; she has two daughters (Phoebe Silag and Lucy Silag) and one son (Axel James Mortenson).

At six feet, two inches, Jane Smiley is affectionately known as the tallest woman in American fiction. Perhaps her height contributes to the fact that she is not easily intimidated. Rather, she is plainspoken and, by her own admission, sometimes "too hard to take." Although she considered teaching at other colleges, her immense self-confidence and lack of conformity proved off-putting to prospective employers. At Iowa State, however, she enjoyed prodigious popularity among faculty and students alike. Students flocked to her creative-writing class, where she refrained from either criticism or praise, regarding each student's work as a mode for educational analysis.

ANALYSIS

The hallmark of Jane Smiley's work is variety: Among her novels are a mystery (*Duplicate Keys*), an epic (*The Greenlanders*), a tragedy (*A Thousand Acres*), a comedy (*Moo*), and a romance (*The All-True Travels and Adventures of Lidie Newton*). All her works, with the exception of a few short stories, are consistent in craftsmanship, meticulous attention to detail, and evidence of careful, scholarly research. Certain themes recur in her fiction, such as the relationship between power and love, the ecological consequences of farming with chemicals, the successes and failures of capitalism, and simple human fallibility. Smiley consistently refuses to offer tidy solutions to complex human conflicts; her characters move gradually toward the light but receive no moments of blinding epiphany. Her vision can best be described as tragicomic: Her most tragic tales have moments of biting humor, and her most comic tales contain a melancholic strain.

THREE NOVELLAS

Some of Jane Smiley's finest work can be found in her three novellas *The Age of Grief*, *Ordinary Love*, and *Good Will*. All these works are finely crafted stories of family life and marriage. The novella, with its compactness and intensity, seems to be the ideal form for Smiley's rich talent for examining the psychological subtleties of ordinary human life. Without the encumbrances of subplots and multiple characters, Smiley is able to do what she does best: examine one theme deeply and meditatively.

A theme shared by these three novellas is that human

Jane Smiley. (Stephen Mortensen/Courtesy, Knopf)

fallibility prevents people from achieving their visions of marital and family bliss. Dave and Dana, the couple at the center of *The Age of Grief*, seem to have everything that should make a marriage happy—love (at least at the beginning of their marriage), a successful joint dental practice, an equitable arrangement for child care, and even good looks. Their marriage survives an extramarital affair, which neither of the two openly acknowledges or seems to understand. Dave, the narrator, is left with little more knowledge of his marriage than he had before; he is even perplexed about exactly what marriage is, other than something too small to contain the complexities of two individuals.

Ordinary Love and *Good Will*, which were published together, are intended to be paired works, one from the point of view of a mother and one from the point of view of a father. Smiley sees one of these narratives as essentially masculine, with its linear plot, and one as essentially feminine, with a plot that relies on revealing what is hidden. *Ordinary Love* is the story of a woman who helped create and then destroy a perfect family. The protagonist, a middle-aged woman, reveals an extramarital affair that destroyed her marriage to her children's father, only to have her children, now adults, almost vengefully reveal tales of physical abuse, abandonment, and sexu-

ally inappropriate behavior suffered in the presence of their father.

Good Will is the story of a man who created his own Eden on a Pennsylvania farm. His family also seems perfect in this idyllic setting, where he and his wife grow their own food, make their own clothes, and rely on bartering their trades and services rather than earning money to accumulate worldly goods. However, Bob Miller, the protagonist, is intent on creating his world, including his wife and son, in his own image, a vision that—as history has shown—must fail. This novella and *Ordinary Love* are both rooted in the theme that fulfillment of desire does not necessarily bring human happiness.

A THOUSAND ACRES

Of all Smiley's novels, *A Thousand Acres* has enjoyed the greatest literary and popular acclaim, not only receiving a Pulitzer Prize and the National Book Critics Circle Award but also remaining on *The New York Times* paperback best-seller list for twenty-nine weeks. The literary appeal of this novel is due in part to its plot, a feminist revision of William Shakespeare's drama *King Lear* (pr. c. 1605-1606). Its popular appeal may be attributed to growing awareness of issues of child sexual abuse in the United States. Motivated by the question of what could have caused King Lear's daughters to feel such anger, Smiley chooses to retell this classical tragedy through the eyes of one of his daughters.

A Thousand Acres is set on a farm in Zebulon County, Iowa, and centers on Lawrence Cook and his three daughters, Ginny, Rose, and Caroline. Ginny and Rose correspond to the characters of Lear's "evil" older daughters, Goneril and Regan, whereas Caroline plays the part of Lear's "good" youngest daughter, Cordelia. True to the *King Lear* plot, Lawrence Cook proposes to divide his kingdom, a one-thousand-acre farm, among his three daughters. The two older daughters, farm wives themselves, accept, while the youngest daughter, a lawyer living in Des Moines, refuses. A nearby farmer, Harold Clark, takes the part of the earl of Gloucester, with his two rivalrous sons, Loren and Jess. After the land transaction takes place, Lawrence Cook apparently goes mad (although he could be faking insanity to get his land back); Harold Clark loses his eyesight in a farm chemical accident; Ginny and Rose commit adultery with the same man, Jess Clark; and Ginny tries unsuccessfully to poison Rose. Although Smiley's retelling of Shakespeare's tragedy may rob King Lear of his majesty, as Christopher Lehmann-Haupt has complained, the novel more than adequately restores the dignity of women silenced by incest and patriarchal suppression.

The story is narrated from the point of view of Ginny Cook Smith, a woman who, in the beginning, caters to her father's every whim without ever offering her own opinion. Rose is no less servile than Ginny, but she is more visibly angry. Smiley allows the subplot of this *King Lear* story to unfold gradually, not revealing the issue of incest until at least halfway through the novel. Suddenly Ginny's self-conscious physical awkwardness and Rose's vitriolic anger begin to make sense when Rose reveals her memory of their father having sex with both of them. Ginny at first denies Rose's revelation, having completely repressed this horrific childhood memory. Ironically, as Ginny makes the bed that her lover, Jess, will sleep in—her own childhood bed—she begins to recalls bits and pieces of this incestuous relationship, such as the balding spot on her father's head and the way his knees forced hers apart. Ginny, knowing that she cannot bear to recall this memory in full, consciously chooses not to, but Rose dwells on the memory, determined until her dying day not to forgive the unforgivable.

A second theme in the novel, that of poisoning, is closely allied with the theme of incest. The women of Zebulon County have been poisoned by agricultural chemicals used as either pesticides or fertilizers. Three women—Ginny and Rose's mother, Jess Clark's mother, and Rose herself—succumb to cancer. Ginny is rendered infertile, suffering five miscarriages as a result of drinking the well water. When Ginny discovers that Rose has stolen her lover, Jess Clark, she devises an elaborate scheme to poison Rose with hemlock-laced sausages, determined that Rose should die from her own gluttonous appetites. Ginny's scheme is thwarted with

Rose's conversion to vegetarianism, but on another level, Rose is already poisoned by her hatred and inability to forgive her father. Smiley never suggests that Rose should forgive her father; nevertheless, Rose's lack of the ability to forgive clearly poisons all her relationships, including her relationship with Ginny.

Moo

Smiley, who enjoys experimenting with different genres, decided that she would write two novels with agricultural themes: a tragedy set on a farm (*A Thousand Acres*) and a comedy set at a university (*Moo*). The midwestern university setting of *Moo* is suspiciously similar to Iowa State University, where Smiley taught for fifteen years, but she has denied that she used Iowa State directly as a model. *Moo* is a satire of academic life with a rich array of characters, including administrators, faculty members, students, a secretary, a governor, and a few community members.

Most notable among the novel's characters are Dr. Lionel Gift, a corrupt distinguished professor whose goal is to profit from gold mining beneath the last remaining virgin cloud forest in the Western Hemisphere; Arlen Martin, a Texas billionaire who conspires with Dr. Gift; Mrs. Walker, a lesbian secretary with amazing powers to subvert university finances for what she considers worthy projects; Tim Monohan, a self-centered writer who thinks that his talents are wasted at Moo U.; Cecilia Sanchez, a woman from Los Angeles with Costa Rican roots who, unable to adjust to life in the Midwest, develops an insatiable passion for Chairman X, a Marxist vegetarian and Dr. Gift's sworn enemy; Helen Levy, a language professor who abandons her academic ambitions for the sensual pleasures of cooking, gardening, and sex; Loren Stroop, a paranoid farmer-inventor who actually does invent a machine that may save the university; Orville T. Early, the governor, who remains an offstage but menacingly stupid presence with his constant schemes for budgetary cuts; and, finally, Earl Butz, a hog who must carry not only his seven-hundred-pound weight but also the weight of the central metaphor of the novel. Hidden away near the center of the university, Earl Butz is an expensive agricultural experiment with the sole purpose of seeing just how big a hog might grow if allowed to eat continuously. Like Earl Butz, many of the novel's characters are single-mindedly pursuing one greed or another, whether it is greed for food, sex, power, fame, or money.

Smiley has described *Moo* as a "slippery slope" novel that warns what can happen when there is no clear separation between the university and the corporate world. The university becomes corrupt and loses its educational focus, supporting only profit-making research and technical education. Land-grant universities are especially culpable, with their support of the destructive tendencies of large-scale agriculture. Some critics have expressed disappointment with Smiley's refusal to cut the university down to size in *Moo*, but most have praised the gentleness of this satire. Clearly, Smiley loves the university too much to engage in any really vicious satirical attacks on the institution. The university is composed of people, and these people are just like people everywhere: fallible, needy, sometimes sad, and often comical or absurd.

HORSE HEAVEN

Since the publication of *Moo*, Smiley has continued to experiment with a variety of subjects and literary genres. In *Horse Heaven*, her version of the ever-popular horse novel, she traces the careers of several horses, trainers, riders, owners, and others involved with the thoroughbred horse business. In this novel, dedicated in part to the memory of the German-bred horse Terson, the human characters represent a range of personalities, but the focus seems largely on the stallion Limitless and the filly Residual, though probably the most appealing animals are the indomitable gelding Justa Bob and Eileen, the Jack Russell terrier.

Written before the death of Kentucky Derby winner Barbaro brought public attention to the fragility of thoroughbred horses' legs, and before news reports of former racehorses being slaughtered for food, this novel also portrays the fates of horses that have become too old, too slow, or too difficult to succeed in the sports for which they were bred, such as racing, jumping, or dressage. Smiley's memoir, *A Year at the Races*, develops many of the same ideas in factual terms, based on her experiences as owner of two racehorses.

GOOD FAITH

Smiley has portrayed events in the news in some of her novels while continuing to experiment with form, such as the use of a first-person narrator in *Good Faith*

and the use of a frame story in *Ten Days in the Hills*. In *Good Faith*, Smiley places individuals' private turmoil in the larger context of public events as she addresses the scandals of the 1980's, especially those with continuing relevance. Joe Stratford, the protagonist and first-person narrator, is typical of Americans caught up in the get-rich-quick schemes of the era, most notably land speculation and trading in T-bill futures, junk bonds, and commodities such as gold and silver. Like the United States as a whole, Joe and his friends lose both their money and their innocence in these ventures.

The novel's title has particular significance for Joe, who is initially a successful Realtor specializing in houses built by a large-scale builder (Gordon Baldwin) and an upscale builder (Gottfried Nuelle). Professionally, Joe operates within the Realtor's ethical code, keeping "good faith" with his clients, both sellers and buyers. Though lonely, dissatisfied, and somewhat dishonest in his personal relationships, Joe is content with his career until Bobby (Gordon's son) introduces him to Marcus Burns, apparently a hugely successful wheeler-dealer. The most naïve character in the novel, Joe seemingly is the one most damaged, financially and psychologically, by his friendship with Marcus, who does not keep good faith with him.

When Gordon brings Joe and Marcus into a scheme to create an upscale housing development, manipulation by other characters begins. Gordon's son-in-law, Hank, describes Marcus as "just a bullshit artist," but Joe invests all his savings, and Gordon mortgages everything he owns, despite drainage problems with the land. Marcus's schemes seem validated, however, when Jim Crosbie takes over as head of Portsmouth Savings and Loan, the financial institution backing the project.

Various characters assess Marcus accurately. Both Hank and Marcus's sister, Jane, warn Joe that Marcus cannot be trusted, but Marcus dismisses Hank as a tree hugger and Jane as a pathological liar, and Joe—who has never had a close male friend in adulthood—ignores warnings of a possible downturn in real estate values, choosing to work full time for Marcus and entrust all his finances to Marcus's company. Even when he realizes that his telephone and utility bills have not been paid as promised, Joe still believes Marcus is his best friend.

Throughout *Good Faith*, Smiley uses houses symbolically. Joe initially sees his life and his condominium as sterile; he prefers the warmth he sees at the Baldwins' and the peace at his parents' home. His appreciation of the craftsmanship of Gottfried's houses adds to his success in selling them, as does his ability to identify with the buyers in Gordon's various developments. Likewise, Joe's friendship with two characters named David is based in part on their shared enthusiasm for restoring old houses. Moreover, Joe can understand another character's obsession with the exotic hillside house he cannot afford to possess, perhaps because it seems to parallel Joe's obsession with Felicity (Gordon's daughter).

The women in Joe's life serve a similar function. Although his ex-wife is not really a character in *Good Faith*, Joe cannot escape her influence until he becomes involved with Marcus and emotionally involved with Felicity. Felicity describes Joe as "transparent," well-meaning, and kind, but she wants to test the limits of his kindness. Joe admires Gordon's wife, Betty, who responds to financial ruin with equanimity, but overall his experiences result in a new appreciation for his own mother and his family's old-fashioned values.

TEN DAYS IN THE HILLS

Family also plays an important role in *Ten Days in the Hills*, Smiley's homage to Giovanni Boccaccio's *Decameron: O, Prencipe Galeotto* (1349-1351; *The Decameron*, 1620). Like its model, this novel is primarily a frame story for a series of individual stories told by ten people visiting two houses. The novel begins in March, 2003, on the day after the Academy Awards ceremony, at the somewhat secluded home of Max, once a famous Hollywood director. Nine visitors, diverse in age and ethnicity, assemble. Most are closely related to Max in some way: Elena, his current lover; Zoe, his ex-wife; Isabel, Max and Zoe's daughter; Delphine, Zoe's mother; Stoney, Max's agent; and Charlie, Max's lifelong best friend. The remaining three are friends of Max's friends: Cassie, Delphine's longtime confidant; Simon, Elena's son; and Paul, Zoe's current lover-healer. As Cassie observes, everyone in Hollywood is family.

The most significant metaphor in the novel, however, is the war in Iraq, which has just begun. The attitudes of the visitors gathered at Max's home parallel the range of American public opinion on the war in 2003: Elena vehemently opposes the war, Charlie defends it, the others range from neutrality to disheartened opposition to indifference, and Cassie becomes the judge of their debates. For ten days, however, these ten people avoid their political conflicts by watching old movies and telling stories, often about their personal or family histories. Other stories involve politics, current events, specific motion pictures, film directors, actors, and writers. In essence much of it is gossip, even when the teller is describing something personal or arguing about politics. The novel's dust jacket warns that the book is not intended for children, probably because Smiley follows Boccaccio's example in "collecting" stories in which sexuality is repeatedly emphasized.

On the seventh day of the gathering, the characters are placed in a different setting, as they agree to move to an exotic house (also in the Hollywood Hills) belonging to Mike, a wealthy Russian who wants Max to direct a remake of *Taras Bulba*. Here the stories become more confessional, as eventually several conflicts are aired and some are resolved.

Nancy E. Sherrod
Updated by Charmaine Allmon Mosby

OTHER MAJOR WORKS

SHORT FICTION: *The Age of Grief: A Novella and Stories*, 1987; *"Ordinary Love" and "Good Will": Two Novellas*, 1989.

NONFICTION: *Catskill Crafts: Artisans of the Catskill Mountains*, 1988; *Charles Dickens*, 2002; *A Year at the Races: Reflections on Horses, Humans, Love, Money, and Luck*, 2004; *Thirteen Ways of Looking at the Novel*, 2005.

BIBLIOGRAPHY

Carden, Mary Paniccia. "Remembering/Engendering the Heartland: Sexed Language, Embodied Space, and America's Foundational Fictions in Jane Smiley's *A Thousand Acres*." *Frontiers: A Journal of Women's Studies* 18, no. 2 (1997): 181-202. Examines how in the novel Smiley challenges agrarian ideologies that serve to silence women.

Farrell, Susan Elizabeth. *Jane Smiley's "A Thousand Acres": A Reader's Guide*. New York: Continuum, 2001. Provides a good, close look at Smiley's award-winning novel. Addresses such subjects as father-daughter relationships, King Lear as a legendary character, and rural families and farm life. Includes bibliographical references.

Humphreys, Josephine. "Perfect Family Self-Destructs." Review of *"Ordinary Love" and "Good Will,"* by Jane Smiley. *The New York Times Book Review*, November 5, 1989. Discusses Smiley's artistry in the novellas and praises her provocative investigation into the roles of power, imagination, and desire in family life.

Kakutani, Michiko. "Hollywood Decameron, Without All the Fun." Review of *Ten Days in the Hills*, by Jane Smiley. *The New York Times Sunday Book Review*, February 13, 2007. Mixed review of Smiley's Hollywood novel finds it less effective in its characterization than her earlier work.

Leslie, Marina. "Incest, Incorporation, and King Lear in Jane Smiley's *A Thousand Acres*." *College English* 60, no. 1 (January, 1998): 31-50. Presents a scholarly comparison of *King Lear* and *A Thousand Acres*, with an emphasis on Shakespearean criticism that recognizes incest themes in *King Lear*.

Nakadate, Neil. "Jane Smiley." In *American Novelists Since World War II, Sixth Series*, edited by James R. Giles and Wanda H. Giles. Vol. 227 in *Dictionary of Literary Biography*. Detroit, Mich.: Gale Group, 2000. Provides an informative general overview of Smiley's career and writing.

_____. *Understanding Jane Smiley*. Columbia: University of South Carolina Press, 1999. Takes a close look at most of Smiley's novels through *The All-True Travels and Adventures of Lidie Newton*. Includes bibliography and index.

Olson, Catherine Cowen. "You Are What You Eat: Food and Power in Jane Smiley's *A Thousand Acres*." *Midwest Quarterly* 40, no. 1 (1998): 21-33. Focuses on how food reflects Ginny's rebellion and submission under patriarchal rule in *A Thousand Acres*.

Sheldon, Barbara H. *Daughters and Fathers in Feminist Novels*. New York: Peter Lang, 1997. Examines Smiley's *A Thousand Acres* as well as novels by Gail Godwin, Mary Gordon, and other feminist writers.

Smiley, Jane. "The Adventures of Jane Smiley." Interview by Katie Bacon. *The Atlantic Monthly*, May 28, 1998. Smiley addresses the influences that shaped *The All-True Travels and Adventures of Lidie Newton* and also discusses such topics as her controversial 1996 *Harper's* essay comparing Twain's *Adventures of Huckleberry Finn* unfavorably to Stowe's *Uncle Tom's Cabin*, her interest in the unresolved question of race in American life, her belief that all of her writing is on some level historical fiction, and her continually evolving perspective on the family drama as literary subject.

ZADIE SMITH

Born: London, England; October 27, 1975
Also known as: Sadie Smith

PRINCIPAL LONG FICTION

White Teeth, 2000
The Autograph Man, 2002
On Beauty, 2005

OTHER LITERARY FORMS

Zadie Smith is known for her short fiction as well as her novels. She first came to the attention of the publish-

ing world with the short story "The Newspaper Man" in the 1997 *May Anthologies*, the annual collection of work by students at Oxford and Cambridge. Her short stories have appeared in *Granta* and *The New Yorker* as well as in anthologies. Smith has edited and written introductions to several collections of short stories.

ACHIEVEMENTS

As a clever and inventive writer and a woman of mixed race, Zadie Smith became a symbol of a new multiethnic strain of British writing. *White Teeth* won a host of awards, including the *Guardian* First Book Award—a Commonwealth Writers' Prize—and the Whitbread Book of the Year Award, both in 2000. *White Teeth* was translated into more than twenty languages and was adapted for television. *The Autograph Man* won the *Jewish Quarterly Review*'s Wingate Literary Prize in 2003. Also in 2003, Smith was included in *Granta* magazine's list of twenty Best Young British Novelists. *On Beauty* was short-listed for the 2005 Booker Prize, and it won the Orange Prize for fiction in 2006.

BIOGRAPHY

Zadie Smith was born Sadie Smith on October 27, 1975, in the Willesden area of North London, the daughter of a British father and a Jamaican mother. Later she would draw on this North London setting and her own multicultural ethnicity in her novels. She changed her name to the more exotic-sounding Zadie as a child pursuing the performing arts of tap dancing and jazz singing. She was fascinated with old Hollywood movie musicals, another source she would draw upon in her novel *The Autograph Man*. Smith attended Hampstead Comprehensive School until the age of eighteen and King's College, Cambridge University, from 1994 to 1997, graduating with a degree in English literature.

While at Cambridge, Smith published short stories in the *May Anthologies*, the annual collection of work by students at Oxford and Cambridge. While still a university student, she was offered an advance of £250,000, approximately $400,000, for her first two books. The size of the advance for such a young, unknown writer put her name in the news even before her first book was published.

White Teeth, Smith's first novel, was published in January, 2000, when Smith was twenty-four years old. The book, a saga of three families in multicultural north London, was an instant best seller, and Smith became a literary celebrity.

Smith was writer-in-residence at the Institute of Contemporary Arts in London from 2000 to 2001 while writing her second novel, *The Autograph Man*. This novel was not as well-received as *White Teeth*, more than likely because it was impossible to live up to the media attention that had attended the first novel. One of the themes of *The Autograph Man* is an exploration of the nature of fame and celebrity, possibly in reaction to Smith's experience after the publication of *White Teeth*.

In 2002-2003, Smith lived in the United States, teaching, studying, and writing as a fellow at the Radcliffe Institute for Advanced Study at Harvard University. While there, she began work on literary essays.

Smith's third novel, *On Beauty*, a transatlantic campus novel, was published in 2005. Set in London and on the campus of a fictional American university, the novel depicts the disintegration of the marriage of Howard Belsey, a liberal, white art-history professor married to a vibrant African American woman, and his collision with his ultraconservative Anglo-Caribbean archrival, Monty Kipps.

In 2004, Smith married poet and novelist Nicholas Laird. The two met while students at Cambridge.

ANALYSIS

Zadie Smith is recognized for her wide-ranging, panoramic novels, deeply plotted with an extensive cast of characters. A primary theme of her work is multicultural identity. Most of her characters identify with more than one culture, country, and ethnicity. Irie Jones, the principal character of *White Teeth*, is the daughter of a working-class, white, British father and a Jamaican mother living in multiracial North London. Alex-Li Tandem, the protagonist of *The Autograph Man*, is a Chinese-Jewish North Londoner, and the Belseys of *On Beauty* are an interracial couple.

Smith is noted for her vivid descriptive style for settings and mannerisms, and she is especially noted for her ear for speech. Nonlinear plot development emphasizes coincidence, ambiguity, and unpredictability. Humor and irony abound in her use of language and social satire, which occasionally shades into farce. Smith's work is not easily categorized. It is a hybrid: part popular culture and part dense literary writing. Critical reception has been mixed, perhaps because each book is so different from those that came before, because the scope of her work is vast, and because expectations have been so shaped by the amount of publicity associated with Smith.

WHITE TEETH

White Teeth is a complex and multilayered novel, with a wide cast of characters and a twisting plot ranging over many years and several continents. The story follows the fortunes of two best friends, World War II buddies Archie Jones, a white working-class man married for the second time to the much younger Clara, a Jamaican woman; and Samad Iqbal, a Bangladeshi who works at an Indian restaurant in London and marries the much younger Alsana. Their children, Irie Jones and the twin Iqbal brothers, Magid and Millat, are friends in multicultural North London.

Samad, concerned that his boys are losing their cultural heritage, sends Magid to be raised by relatives in Chittagong. Irie and Millat, caught smoking marijuana in the schoolyard, agree to be tutored by classmate Joshua Chalfen in order to avoid harsher consequences. The Jewish, Catholic, atheist Chalfens are a stereotypical white liberal family, delighted to welcome such multicultural diversity into their home. Irie Jones has an unrequited desire for Millat, and Joshua Chalfen has an unrequited love for Irie.

Marcus Chalfen is a genetic engineer who is working on a project called FutureMouse. The many threads of the novel come together at the event that introduces FutureMouse to the public. All the living characters are present: the senior Joneses and Iqbals; Irie who has embraced her Jamaican ancestry by returning to live with her grandmother and decided to go to university under the influence of the educated Chalfens; Joshua Chalfen, who has defied his father by becoming an animal-rights activist; Magid, who has become Marcus's protégé and publicist; and Millat, whose militant Islamic group has determined to disrupt the event. Coincidences abound, chance meetings occur, and all attempts to control outcomes fail; the event ends in chaos, and FutureMouse escapes.

The novel ends with a snapshot of the future: On December 31, 1999, Irie Jones and Joshua Chalfen, now lovers, are in Jamaica with Irie's grandmother. Irie's daughter, now seven years old, is with them. Just before the FutureMouse unveiling, Irie had slept first with Millat, then gone directly to Magid, ensuring that, since the twins have exactly the same genetic material, the child's father will never be known. Thus, the child carries all the threads of multiple ethnicities in one body,

Zadie Smith. (Roderick Field)

and the novel ends on a note of hope on the eve of the millennium.

The book, a youthful first novel, has been criticized for this optimistic view of multicultural Britain, which is perhaps an unrealistic view. Nevertheless, the wide scope of the book, with its rich twists and turns of plot, its abundance of sharply defined characters and the sometimes unexpected connections among them, and its social observation, humor, and language, all combine to make the novel technically impressive and popular with readers.

THE AUTOGRAPH MAN

The Autograph Man is set in a fictional North London suburb called Mountjoy. The novel opens with a prologue in which the young Alex-Li Tandem attends a wrestling match with his father, Li-Jin, and his two friends, Mark Rubenfine and Adam Jacobs. They meet Joseph Klein, who introduces the boys to autograph collecting. At the end of the prologue, Alex's father collapses and dies of a brain tumor just at the moment the boys are rushing forward to get the autograph of the wrestler Big Daddy. Throughout most of the novel, the inability to face the death of his father and escaping reality by collecting autographs are Alex's predominant character traits.

Book 1 is set fifteen years later in Mountjoy. Alex has become a professional autograph dealer. He especially desires the autograph of 1950's Hollywood film star Kitty Alexander, to whom he has written weekly for thirteen years. The four boys of the prologue are still close friends. Alex lives a superficial life and seems unable to connect with other people. He is obsessed with the cult of celebrity. The brittle shallowness of this life is presented with satirical and sometimes ribald humor. Book 1 ends as Alex finally receives Kitty Alexander's autograph in the mail.

Book 2 is set in New York, where Alex is attending an autograph fair and trying to find Kitty at her return address in Brooklyn. When he finds her living in genteel poverty he persuades her to return with him to London so that he can make her rich by auctioning some of her rare autographs and letters. Because a television news story wrongly reports Kitty's death, Alex makes even more money than he imagined. Throughout book 2, Alex grows in self-knowledge, and he gives his commission on the sale of Kitty's letters to a dying fellow autograph man as evidence of his character development. In the final scene of book 2 and in the epilogue, Alex finally acknowledges his connection to his father, a living hero, and elevates him above the artificial heroes of Hollywood films.

Like *White Teeth*, *The Autograph Man* observes and satirizes the subcultures of North London's multicultural inhabitants, but Smith's second novel is both narrower in scope and deeper in exploration of character than her first. It is inventive in form and clever in its wide range of references to both popular and literary culture.

ON BEAUTY

On Beauty's cast of characters includes the members of the liberal Belsey family—the Englishman, Howard, who is white and married to Kiki, an African American, and their three children, Jerome, Zora, and Levi. They are joined by the conservative Anglo-Caribbean Kipps family, made up of Monty, Carlene, and their children, and a host of other students and academics at fictional Wellington College.

As the novel opens, the Belsey's oldest son, Jerome, while spending a summer in London, has come under the influence of Howard Belsey's academic and philosophical archrival, Monty Kipps. The antagonism between the two men is intellectual and academic; they are both art historians specializing in Rembrandt and have radically different approaches to interpreting the artist's work.

Howard is an antihero. He is sometimes amusing but his morals are too loose to make him a likeable character. His affairs with a colleague and with Monty's daughter are reminiscent of Howard Kirk in Malcolm Bradbury's *The History Man* (1975). Howard's approach to art is purely theoretical; he has spent his career deconstructing others' ideas of good and beauty to the ultimate detriment of his own soul.

Monty is not above reproach either; he is having an affair with his graduate assistant while his devoted wife is dying of an unnamed disease. The two rivals' worlds and families collide when Monty is invited to give a lecture at Wellington. Ultimately, both men lose their wives, and Howard's valued intellect "deconstructs" along with his personal life. There is no redemption in the ambiguous ending.

In another ambitious novel filled with witty observation and commentary on academia, family life, politics, and pop culture, Smith has created a transatlantic campus satire in the tradition of Bradbury's *Stepping Westward* (1968), and a novel of manners containing clashes of culture and class in the tradition of E. M. Forster's *Howards End* (1910). She adds multiethnic elements that are uniquely her own.

Susan Butterworth

OTHER MAJOR WORKS

SHORT FICTION: *Piece of Flesh*, 2001.
EDITED TEXT: *The Book of Other People*, 2008.

BIBLIOGRAPHY

Childs, Peter. "Zadie Smith: Searching for the Inescapable." In *Contemporary Novelists: British Fiction Since 1970*. New York: Palgrave Macmillan, 2005. Childs offers accessible analyses of twelve late twentieth century and early twenty-first century British novelists. Also includes a chapter on his reading of Smith's *White Teeth* and *The Autograph Man*.

Dawson, Ashley. *Mongrel Nation: Diasporic Culture and the Making of Postcolonial Britain*. Ann Arbor:

University of Michigan Press, 2007. Includes the chapter "Genetics, Biotechnology, and the Future of 'Race' in Zadie Smith's *White Teeth*."

Head, Dominic. "Zadie Smith's *White Teeth*: Multiculturalism for the Millennium." In *Contemporary British Fiction*, edited by Richard J. Lane, Rod Mengham, and Philip Tew. Malden, Mass.: Blackwell, 2003. Focuses on the multicultural aspects of Smith's novel *White Teeth*. Part of a collection surveying the reception and literary status of contemporary British fiction.

Phillips, Caryl. "The Pioneers: Fifty Years of Caribbean Migration to Britain" and "*White Teeth* by Zadie Smith." In *A New World Order: Essays*. New York: Vintage Books, 2002. Phillips's essays in this collection foreground Smith's position as an Anglo-Caribbean writer.

Squires, Claire. *Zadie Smith's "White Teeth": A Reader's Guide*. New York: Continuum International, 2002. An accessible slim volume that illuminates *White Teeth* for general readers rather than literary critics or advanced students of literature.

Walters, Tracey L., ed. *Zadie Smith: Critical Essays*. New York: Peter Lang, 2008. A comprehensive collection of essays solely devoted to Smith. Section 1 discusses postcolonial and postmodernist readings of Smith. Section 2 discusses racial identity and race mixing in Smith's work.

TOBIAS SMOLLETT

Born: Dalquhurn (now Renton), Scotland;
March 19, 1721 (baptized)
Died: Antignano (now in Italy); September 17, 1771
Also known as: Tobias George Smollett

PRINCIPAL LONG FICTION

The Adventures of Roderick Random, 1748
The Adventures of Peregrine Pickle: In Which Are Included Memoirs of a Lady of Quality, 1751
The Adventures of Ferdinand, Count Fathom, 1753
The Adventures of Sir Launcelot Greaves, 1760-1761
The Expedition of Humphry Clinker, 1771

OTHER LITERARY FORMS

Tobias Smollett combined his medical practice with an active and varied career as a man of letters. His earliest, though unsuccessful, effort was as a playwright with *The Regicide: Or, James the First of Scotland, a Tragedy* (pb. 1749), published by subscription a full ten years after fruitless attempts at having it staged in London. Two other disappointments followed with his inability to secure a production for *Alceste* (pb. 1748-1749), a combination of opera, tragedy, and masque, and with the rejection of his first comedy, *The Absent Man* (wr. 1751), which was never produced or published. Both of these works have now been lost. His only success on the stage came finally with *The Reprisal: Or, The Tars of Old England* (pr. 1757), a comedy; this farce was produced by David Garrick at the Theatre Royal, Drury Lane.

Smollett's deep moral energy surfaced in two early verse satires, "Advice: A Satire" (1746) and its sequel, "Reproof: A Satire" (1747); these rather weak poems were printed together in 1748. Smollett's poetry includes a number of odes and lyrics, but his best poem remains "The Tears of Scotland." Written in 1746, it celebrates the unwavering independence of the Scots, who had been crushed by English troops at the Battle of Culloden.

As Smollett's literary career grew, his hackwork for publishers increased with translations. His most popular work among these projects was *A Complete History of England* (1757-1758) and its sequel, *Continuation of the Complete History of England* (1760-1765). He took great pride in his achievements as a historian and as a historical editor of *A Compendium of Authentic and Entertaining Voyages* (1756). A diversity of interests from medicine to politics prompted the writing of numerous pamphlets and essays. *An Essay on the External Use of Water* (1752) was a farsighted proposal for the improvement of public hygiene at Bath that caused a furor among the resort's staff and patrons.

Though his health was rapidly deteriorating from overwork, Smollett completed a thirty-five-volume edition of *The Works of M. de Voltaire* (1761-1774). In the hope that a warm climate would improve his health, he traveled to France and Italy, and on returning to England he published *Travels Through France and Italy* (1766). His didactic observations instructed his readers to accept England, for all its faults, as the best nation for securing happiness on Earth. His last nonfiction works were *The Present State of All Nations* (1768-1769) and the political satire *The History and Adventures of an Atom* (1749, 1769). Editor Lewis M. Knapp offers the best modern edition of the *Letters of Tobias Smollett* (1970).

ACHIEVEMENTS

Tobias Smollett cannot be said to have added dignity to the art of the novel in the manner of Henry Fielding's imitation of the epic, nor can it be argued that he gave form to the genre as did Samuel Richardson, yet the eighteenth century novel cannot be discussed without giving full attention to Smollett's stylistic virtuosity and satiric intent.

Smollett successfully challenged Richardson's and Fielding's substantial popular reputation by providing "familiar scenes in an uncommon and amusing point of view." In *The Adventures of Roderick Random* (commonly known as *Roderick Random*), his first novel, he displayed a thorough understanding of the distinction between the novel and the romance, of which Samuel Johnson would speak in *The Rambler* essays (1750-1752). Borrowing from Latin comedy and Elizabethan drama, Smollett created caricatures of human beings with the dexterity of William Hogarth and Thomas Rowlandson. Though his characters lack the psychological depth of those of Richardson, they possess breathtaking energy and evocative power.

Only in the late twentieth century did Smollett's role in the development of the English novel become fully

appreciated. Criticism of that time emphasized the wrongheadedness of viewing Smollett's satiric energy as a deviation from Fielding's epic ambitions for the novel. Instead, Smollett is seen at the beginning of another tradition. Sir Walter Scott and Charles Dickens both valued Smollett's work; Dickens acknowledged his debt to Smollett's picaresque realism and comic characterization in *Pickwick Papers* (1836-1837, serial; 1837, book). Among modern novelists, the savage comedy of writers as various as Evelyn Waugh and Joseph Heller is in Smollett's tradition rather than that of Fielding or Richardson.

Smollett's works continue to provoke critical inquiry. The Oxford English Novels series has published all five of his novels, and the University of Delaware has published its *Bicentennial Edition of the Works of Tobias Smollett*, with *The Expedition of Humphry Clinker* (commonly known as *Humphry Clinker*) appearing in 1979.

BIOGRAPHY

Tobias George Smollett was born at Dalquhurn, Dumbartonshire, in western Scotland, and baptized on March 19, 1721. He was the son of Archibald Smollett, a lawyer, who suffered from ill health, and Barbara Cunningham Smollett, a woman of taste and elegance but no fortune. Smollett's grandfather, of whom the boy was especially proud, had been knighted by King William in 1698 and had become an influential member of the landed gentry as a local Whig statesman. When Smollett's father died only two years after his son's birth, the family suffered from lack of money.

Smollett's education, for all of his family's financial deterioration, was of superior quality though erratic. He entered Dumbarton Grammar School in 1728, remaining for five years, and received the traditional grounding in the classics. His matriculation to Glasgow University (though officially unrecorded) was interrupted when he became a Glasgow surgeon's apprentice while still attending university medical lectures. In the fall of 1739, Smollett was released from his apprenticeship to go to London; now eighteen, he had some reputation as a writer of earthy satires and doggerel. While traveling to London, Smollett carried the manuscript of a tragedy, *The Regicide*, which, he soon realized, would provide no entrée for him with the London theater managers. He is described at this time as "attractive, entertaining as a *raconteur*, and blessed with self-assurance." His future as a London man of letters uncertain, Smollett received advice from a number of Scottish physicians suggesting he continue practicing medicine. On March 10, 1740, he received a medical warrant from the navy board and embarked on the HMS *Chichester* as a surgeon's second mate.

The author's naval experience, material used later for *Roderick Random*, began during the outbreak of war with Spain and continued through the bloody Carthagena, West Indies, expedition of 1741. Smollett returned to England in 1742 but was drawn back to Jamaica, where he resided until 1744. While living on the island, he met Anne Lassells, the daughter of an established family of planters; they married in 1743.

Smollett, on the advice of his wife's family, returned to London alone, where he set up a practice as a surgeon on Downing Street in May, 1744. Having never lost hope of a literary career, he worked on improving his fluency in Spanish and then began translating Miguel de Cervantes' *Don Quixote de la Mancha* (1605, 1615); his translation was published in 1755. The years from 1747 to 1750 were marked by considerable literary activity, numerous changes in residence, various trips abroad, a widening circle of acquaintances, and the birth of his only child, Elizabeth, in 1747.

In January, 1748, *Roderick Random* was published; this was followed by the impressive translations of Alain Le Sage and Cervantes, and in 1749, *The Regicide* was printed. The success of *Roderick Random* was instantaneous and prolonged, with sixty-five hundred copies sold in twenty-two months; it was to rival the popularity of Fielding's *Joseph Andrews* (1742). The success of *Roderick Random*, which was written in less than six months, became a kind of revenge on the theater managers of London. During this period, Smollett made plans to produce *Alceste*, his opera (George Frideric Handel was contracted for the music), but this effort was to fail; only a lyric from this work survives. Furthermore, Smollett's failure at drama was a continuing source of frustration throughout his career.

In June, 1750, Smollett purchased his medical degree from Marischal College, Aberdeen, and in the same

month moved his family to Chelsea, a fashionable London suburb. It became an ideal home for him, where both his medical practice and his writing flourished; he remained there for thirteen years until forced abroad by his health in 1763. It was in Chelsea that he wrote *The Adventures of Peregrine Pickle* (commonly known as *Peregrine Pickle*), a work of nearly 330,000 words composed at top speed in anticipation of a trip to Paris. On February 25, 1751, his second novel was published to laudatory reviews and wide popularity.

Smollett's involvement with various periodicals began during the 1750's, first as a book reviewer for the *Monthly Review* and later as editor and proprietor of the *Critical Review*. Smollett joined Oliver Goldsmith in launching the *British Magazine* (the *Monthly Repository* beginning in 1760), remaining as coeditor until 1763. With a final venture, Smollett gained public notoriety and untold enemies by agreeing to write the *Briton*, a political effort in support of Lord Bute's ministry. Of Smollett's various journalistic efforts, only the work in the *Critical Review* is exceptional; as a literary periodi-

Tobias Smollett. (Getty Images)

cal, it remains one of the most significant of the last half of the eighteenth century.

In the early 1750's, Smollett was driving himself to escape debt. Publishing a medical paper, *An Essay on the External Use of Water*, brought him little money, and in February, 1753, his third novel, *The Adventures of Ferdinand, Count Fathom* (commonly known as *Ferdinand, Count Fathom*), was published with poor financial results. The book attracted few readers, and Smollett was forced to borrow money and to supplement his medical fees with further hackwork. The years of hack writing began in earnest with *A Complete History of England*, a translation of Voltaire's writings, a geographical reference work, and several digests of travel.

The period from 1756 to 1763 destroyed Smollett's health, but his reputation as a critic and a successful writer became unquestioned. Unfortunately, this frantic production hardly kept him from debtor's prison. Returning to the novel in the *British Magazine*, Smollett published "the first considerable English novel ever to be published serially"—*The Adventures of Sir Launcelot Greaves* (commonly known as *Sir Launcelot Greaves*). In monthly installments from January, 1760, to December, 1761, the novel gave the six-penny periodical substantial popularity.

In the middle of this literary hard labor, Smollett was imprisoned for three months, having been convicted of libeling an Admiral Knowles in an article in the *Critical Review*. On his release in early 1761, Smollett continued fulfilling his contracts with certain booksellers but also traveled extensively, possibly to Dublin, even though troubled by asthma and tuberculosis. In addition to these difficulties, his spirit was nearly broken by the illness and death of his daughter in April, 1763. This final shock caused him to cut all his London ties and move his family to the Continent, hoping to calm his wife and cure his ailments in the mild climate of the south of France and Italy. He spent two years abroad, returning to England in July, 1765; the literary result of his tour was *Travels Through France and Italy*. Though ill health plagued him, he sought for the third time a consulship but was rejected; in 1768 he left England for the last time.

Arriving in Pisa, Italy, Smollett visited with friends at the university, finally settling at his country villa in Antignano, near Leghorn, in the spring of 1770, where he completed his masterpiece, *Humphry Clinker*. Immediately following its publication, he received the rave notices of friends and critics concerning the novel, but he had little time to enjoy the praise. On September 17, 1771, he died from an acute intestinal infection and was buried at the English cemetery at Leghorn.

ANALYSIS

Tobias Smollett not only is a great comic novelist but also a morally exhilarating one—a serious satirist of the brutality, squalor, and hideous corruption of humankind. His definite moral purposes are firmly grounded in the archetypal topic of all novelists—people's unceasing battle for survival in the war between the forces of good and evil. Smollett insists that people defy "the selfishness, envy, malice, and base indifference of mankind"; in such a struggle, the hero will ultimately prevail and will be rewarded for his (or her) fortitude.

RODERICK RANDOM

The principal theme of Smollett's first novel, *Roderick Random*, is the arbitrariness of success and failure in a world dominated by injustice and dishonesty. Smollett's decision to use realistic detail as a guise for his satire produces a lively and inventive work; moreover, the hero, Roderick, is not a mere picaro nor a passive fool but an intent satiric observer "who recognizes, reacts, and rebukes." The novel is organized in a three-part structure. The initial stage reveals Roderick's numerous trials as a young man; he loses his innocence during the years of poverty in Scotland, of failure in London, and of brutal experience in the Navy. The middle of the narrative embodies "the lessons of adversity" as the hero declines into near collapse. In a final brief section, Roderick recovers his physical and moral equilibrium and promotes the simple human values of friendship, love, and trust as the only viable bases for a satisfying existence.

Roderick's problem is both to gain knowledge of the world and to assimilate that knowledge. M. A. Goldberg, in *Smollett and the Scottish School* (1959), finds that "at first his responses are dictated by his indignation, by passions . . . eventually, he learns . . . to govern the emotions with reason." The struggle between these two forces is central to an understanding of eighteenth century England and its literature. In Smollett's first novel, good sense seems a sufficient defense against the sordid viciousness of the world. Good sense, however, can only be achieved, or learned, when the hero can control his pride and passionate nature, which are inextricably linked. Equilibrium, an orderly existence, arises paradoxically from the ashes of his random adventures. This understanding develops as the hero pursues the happiness he thinks he deserves but can never fully attain; as a good empiricist, Roderick gathers knowledge from each reversal, finally achieving a "tranquillity of love" with the prudent Narcissa.

In *Roderick Random*, the hero's search for happiness differs significantly from the quest of the traditional picaro. While gaining an education and suffering the rebukes of others, Roderick remains good and effectual, unlike Don Quixote, who is powerless against cruelty. Roderick's youthful ferocity contributes to the practicality of the satire. Smollett's approach to correcting the ills of society is to allow no attack or insult to go unavenged. A thorough whipping of a bully or the verbal punishment of a pedant lifts the book beyond the picaresque and advances it past the formal verse satire. The center of the satiric discussion implicates the surroundings and not the hero, thus permitting Smollett to offer a long list of evil, self-centered figures who provide an excellent contrast to the goodness and charity of the ill-served protagonist. Only his faithful servant, Strap; his uncle, Tom Bowling; and the maid, Narcissa, join him in opposing his neglectful grandfather, the scoundrel Vicar Shuffle, the tyrannical Captain Oakum, the dandiacal Captain Whiffle, and the rapacious Lord Strutwell.

The last section of the novel provides the hero with the riches of his long quest: family, wealth, and love. The moral of the adventures follows as Roderick's recently discovered father "blesses God for the adversity I had undergone," affirming that his son's intellectual, moral, and physical abilities had been improved "for all the duties and enjoyments of life, much better than any education which affluence could bestow." The felicity of this final chapter provides a conventional ending, but the crucial point is that Roderick, having completed a rigorous education in the distinctions between appearance and reality, is now deserving of these rewards.

PEREGRINE PICKLE

The protagonist of Smollett's long second novel, *Peregrine Pickle*, reminds one of Roderick in every as-

pect, except that Peregrine is an Englishman, not a Scot. The supporting players are improved; among the novel's outstanding comic creations are Commodore Hawser Trunnion and the spinster, Grizzle Pickle. Often described as the best picaresque novel in English, *Peregrine Pickle* satirizes the upper classes of mid-eighteenth century England. Rufus Putney argues in "The Plan of *Peregrine Pickle*" (1945) that Smollett

> meant to write a satire on the affectations and meannesses, the follies and vices that flourished among the upper classes in order that his readers might learn with Peregrine the emptiness of titles, the sordidness of avarice, the triviality of wealth and honors, and the folly of misguided ambition.

The novel begins by sketching Peregrine's social and emotional background and introducing other principal characters. Following this introductory section, Smollett's protagonist describes his adolescence and education at Winchester and Oxford, where he becomes addicted to coarse practical jokes and to satisfying his overbearing pride. Here the hero meets Emilia, a beautiful orphan with whom he falls in love; because of his capricious nature, however, he cannot remain long with her. Having become alienated from his parents, Peregrine departs on the Grand Tour with the best wishes of his guardian, Trunnion.

Peregrine returns from France an unprincipled, arrogant rogue whose every action supports his vanity. After numerous incidents including the death of Trunnion and his replacement with the eccentric Cadwallader Crabtree as Peregrine's mentor, the hero tests the virtue of Emilia and is rebuffed. The remainder of the novel observes the long distress, the eventual imprisonment, and the final rehabilitation of the protagonist, who by now is convinced of the fraud and folly of the world. As Putney mentions, only after matriculating to the "school of adversity," which reduces his pride and vanity, can Peregrine hope to achieve wealth, marry his true love, triumph over his enemies, and retire to the country. Adversity teaches him to distinguish between the complex vices of the urban sophisticates and the simpler but more substantial pleasures of generosity and love in a rural retreat. Despite its picaresque vigor and satisfactory resolution, the novel suffers from a confusion of purposes: Peregrine's arrogance undermines the credibility of his role as a satirist of high society. Thus, Smollett's satiric intentions are blunted by his aspirations to a novel of character.

FERDINAND, COUNT FATHOM

Ferdinand, Count Fathom is remembered today for its dedication, in which Smollett gives his famous definition of the novel, and for its place as the first important eighteenth century work to propose terror as a subject for a novel. In *The Novels of Tobias Smollett* (1971), Paul-Gabriel Boucé finds that the major defect of the novel is the author's "mixture of genres, without any transition brought about by unfolding of the story or the evolution of the characters." Fathom's dark cynicism informs the majority of the work, with the last ten chapters unraveling into a weak melodrama; nevertheless, Smollett's satire remains effective as a bitter denunciation of the hypocrisy and violence of elegant society. As an early contribution to the literature of terror, the novel probes the emotions of a young, virtuous girl who undergoes isolation, deprivation, and sadistic brutality at the hands of a rapacious creature. The figure of Fathom is used to undercut sentimental conventions and show their uselessness when civilized norms are forgotten.

SIR LAUNCELOT GREAVES

Sir Launcelot Greaves completed serialization in December, 1761, and was published as a book in March, 1762. Because of its serial publication, the novel's structure suffers from the frequent contrivance of artificial suspense. Modern criticism, however, has pointed to an underlying thematic unity based on a series of variations on the theme of madness, with minute investigation into the physical, psychological, and moral aspects of the disorder. Greaves, the quixotic hero, launches a noble crusade for reform. His hopeless demand that a corrupted world listen to reason embraces Smollett's social idealism. If moral intention were the only measure of a novel's worth, then the didactic power of *Sir Launcelot Greaves* would guarantee its success; unfortunately, the delicate balance of the genre remains disordered by the force of an overobvious moral preoccupation.

HUMPHRY CLINKER

Smollett's last novel, *Humphry Clinker*, appeared in the bookstalls on June 15, 1771; Smollett had written the three volumes over a five-year period. It is his master-

piece, and it remains among the great English novels. The work was inspired by the epistles of Christopher Anstey's witty and popular *New Bath Guide* (1766).

Using the epistolary method instead of the travel narrative of the early novels, Smollett characterizes his correspondents by means of their wonderfully individual letter-writing styles. Old Matthew Bramble of Brambleton Hall, Wales, travels with his household through Gloucester, Bath, London, Scarborough, Edinburgh, Cameron (Smollett country), Glasgow, Manchester, and home again. Squire Bramble suffers various physical complaints, and his ill health makes him sensitive to the social ills surrounding him on his journey. Bramble searches for a recovery but finds himself becoming worse, not better, yet his compassionate nature remains undiminished. The journey was begun so that Bramble might distract his young niece, Lydia Melford, from a strolling actor named Wilson. The party also includes Tabitha, his aging, narrow-minded, old-maid sister; her malapropic maid, Winifred Jenkins, the classic example of the illiterate servant; and the modishly cynical nephew, Jery. En route, they adopt, much to Tabitha's delight, a Scottish veteran of American Indian warfare, Obadiah Lismahago. Soon, they add Humphry Clinker to the party as a new footman; he turns out to be the natural son of Matthew.

There are three major plots to develop, and numerous minor episodes, all of which hinge on the characteristic picaresque device of the journey; Smollett exchanged the rogue hero for a group of picaros—Bramble and nephew Jery—who analyze and observe society. Through careful stages in letter after letter, Matthew's character is revealed to the reader, who learns to trust him as a reliable observer of society's foibles; in this respect *Humphry Clinker* is much stronger than *Peregrine Pickle*, where the satire was blunted by the protagonist's unreliability.

Smollett's satire strikes not individuals but categories of people and assorted social institutions; in particular *Humphry Clinker* is an exposé of the false attitudes and disordered life of the eighteenth century nouveaux riches. His conservative political views are displayed in Bramble's rages against an unrestricted press, politically biased juries, and the ignorance of the mob, and, as in *Peregrine Pickle*, he contrasts the folly and depravity of urban life with idealized pictures of the country.

Smollett's achievement in *Humphry Clinker* depends on his skillful use of the picaresque and epistolary traditions. His last novel is also distinguished by a warmth and tolerance not found to such a degree in his earlier works. Bramble's cynicism never becomes obnoxious to the reader; the brutality of Roderick is muted here. Smollett allows his hero to accept human society, despite "the racket and dissipation." Finally, for all his burlesque of Samuel Richardson's epistolary method, Smollett's characterization of Lydia has a depth and intensity that raises her above mere romantic convention.

In contrast to many critical reports, *Humphry Clinker* ends on a buoyant note of pure happiness, a happiness that fulfills the eighteenth century dictum of conformity to the universal order. Smollett's novels embrace moral and virtuous methods for pursuing one's goals. Passions and reason must remain in balance, and within this harmony, nature and art can moderate the demands of vice and folly.

Paul J. deGategno

OTHER MAJOR WORKS

PLAYS: *The Regicide: Or, James the First of Scotland, a Tragedy*, pb. 1749; *The Reprisal: Or, The Tars of Old England*, pr. 1757.

NONFICTION: *The History and Adventures of an Atom*, 1749, 1769; *An Essay on the External Use of Water*, 1752; *A Compendium of Authentic and Entertaining Voyages*, 1756; *A Complete History of England*, 1757-1758; *Continuation of the Complete History of England*, 1760-1765; *Travels Through France and Italy*, 1766; *The Present State of All Nations*, 1768-1769; *Letters of Tobias Smollett*, 1970 (Lewis M. Knapp, editor).

TRANSLATIONS: *The Adventures of Gil Blas of Santillane*, 1748 (of Alain René Le Sage's novel); *The History and Adventures of the Renowned Don Quixote*, 1755 (of Miguel de Cervantes' novel); *The Works of M. de Voltaire*, 1761-1774 (35 volumes); *The Adventures of Telemachus, the Son of Ulysses*, 1776 (of François de Salignac de La Mothe-Fénelon's novel).

BIBLIOGRAPHY

Beasley, Jerry C. *Tobias Smollett: Novelist*. Athens: University of Georgia Press, 1998. Beasley devotes separate chapters to an analysis of each of Smollett's five novels, which he interprets as "exercises in the visual imagination," written by an author who believed the private, interior life could be defined by the externally visible.

Bold, Alan, ed. *Smollett: Author of the First Distinction*. New York: Barnes & Noble Books, 1982. A collection of essays about Smollet's work, with four essays discussing general issues and five concentrating on each of the major novels. Includes a bibliography and an index.

Brack, O. M., Jr, ed. *Tobias Smollett, Scotland's First Novelist*. Newark: University of Delaware Press, 2007. Collection of essays on both the fiction and nonfiction, including a discussion "On the External Uses of Water in *The Expedition of Humphrey Clinker*" and a comparison of novels by Smollett and Henry Fielding.

Bulckaen, Denise. *A Dictionary of Characters in Tobias Smollett*. Nancy, France: University Press of Nancy, 1993. A useful way to keep track of the multitude of characters in Smollett's fiction. Each character is identified; chapter and page number of the character's first appearance are also cited. There is also an index of the main categories of characters.

Gibson, William. *Art and Money in the Writings of Tobias Smollett*. Lewisburg, Pa.: Bucknell University Press, 2007. Gibson analyzes Smollett's novels and nonfiction writing, focusing on issues of aesthetics, commercialism, luxury, and taste, to describe how these works provide insights into the eighteenth century art world.

Grant, Damian. *Tobias Smollett: A Study in Style*. Totowa, N.J.: Rowman & Littlefield, 1977. As the title suggests, Grant ignores questions of realism and moral purpose to concentrate on what he regards as Smollett's three styles: comic, passionate, and, to a lesser extent, lyrical.

Lewis, Jeremy. *Tobias Smollett*. London: Jonathan Cape, 2003. An appreciative look at Smollett's life, written by an acclaimed biographer. Includes a bibliography and an index.

Spector, Robert D. *Smollett's Women: A Study in an Eighteenth-Century Masculine Sensibility*. Westport, Conn.: Greenwood Press, 1994. Organized differently from most books on Smollett, with chapters on society, personality, and literary tradition; heroines, fallen women, and women as victims; and the comic and the grotesque. Includes notes and a bibliography.

_____. *Tobias George Smollett*. 1968. Rev. ed. Boston: Twayne, 1989. The first chapter of the book quickly surveys Smollett's minor works; the rest of the book is a consideration of his novels. Contains an annotated bibliography of secondary criticism.

C. P. SNOW

Born: Leicester, England; October 15, 1905
Died: London, England; July 1, 1980
Also known as: Charles Percy Snow; Baron Snow

PRINCIPAL LONG FICTION

Death Under Sail, 1932, 1959
New Lives for Old, 1933
The Search, 1934, 1958
Strangers and Brothers, 1940 (reissued as *George Passant*, 1972)
Strangers and Brothers, 1940-1970 (collective title for *Strangers and Brothers*, 1940, and the following 10 novels)
The Light and the Dark, 1947
Time of Hope, 1949
The Masters, 1951
The New Men, 1954
Homecomings, 1956 (also known as *Homecoming*)
The Conscience of the Rich, 1958
The Affair, 1960
Corridors of Power, 1964
The Sleep of Reason, 1968
Last Things, 1970
The Malcontents, 1972
In Their Wisdom, 1974
A Coat of Varnish, 1979

OTHER LITERARY FORMS

Reflecting his various careers and interests, C. P. Snow published, in addition to his novels, a number of books, including the literary biographies *Trollope: His Life and Art* (1975) and *The Realists* (1978), as well as

many reviews and articles. He had some interest in the drama, encouraging the staging of his novels *The Affair*, *The New Men*, and *The Masters*. He wrote a full-length play, *A View over the Bridge*, which was produced in London in 1950, and collaborated with his wife, Pamela Hansford Johnson, on six one-act plays published in 1951: *Spare the Rod*, *The Pigeon with the Silver Foot*, *Her Best Foot Forward*, *The Supper Dance*, *To Murder Mrs. Mortimer*, and *Family Party*.

ACHIEVEMENTS

C. P. Snow's accomplishments, in general, were many and varied; his achievement was more limited as a novelist and yet probably more long lasting. Snow the scientist and Snow the public figure cannot, however, be divorced from Snow the writer. Just as his novels drew upon his experiences in his nonliterary careers, so were his sociopolitical ideas presented in his novels. Yet, there is less of the detail of "doing" science, less of the specificity of the public life than one might have expected from Snow's background had he been more of a naturalistic novelist, and there is less ideological content than might have been anticipated from one with Snow's strong views had he been more of a propagandist.

Snow was, rather, a realistic novelist, using his particular knowledge, background, and political ideology not primarily for their own sake, but in the service of his art. This art was conventional, relatively old-fashioned. Snow had limited patience with James Joyce and the literary avant-garde. As a *roman-fleuve*, *Strangers and Brothers* has a few interesting features, but it certainly lacks the subtlety that Snow admired in Marcel Proust. Snow did little to advance novelistic techniques; his own craftsmanship shows scant development over the course of a long writing career. His style has frequently been described as dull or pedestrian; Edmund Wilson found his novels "unreadable."

Snow implicitly defended his own style in discussing that of Anthony Trollope, praising his predecessor for using language that was often intentionally made flat in order to be clear. Snow's style is certainly more serviceable than inspired. His imagery is limited and repetitious. Unity and impact are achieved through the recurrence of a limited number of images, such as those of lighted windows and rivers, but the impact is gained at the expense of a degree of monotony.

If Snow's style and imagery are little more than adequate, his plot construction is only somewhat more skillful. Unlike Trollope, whom Snow admired and to whom he has frequently been compared, Snow uses plots that are usually suspenseful; one reads his books partly to see how they will come out. This element of suspense, going back to his first published novel, a whodunit, no doubt helps explain his having attracted a fairly wide and loyal audience, many of whom were not regular readers of novels. Snow's plots, however, are seldom particularly ingenious or original; essentially, they are a means to the revelation of character.

It is in characterization that Snow's prime virtue as a novelist lies; yet his characterizations excel only within certain limits. These limits arise from his subject matter. As has been frequently noted, Snow is particularly effective in dealing with "man in committee." This focus, related to the election, by thirteen fellows, of a new head of their college, is central to Snow's most highly praised novel, *The Masters*. A similar focus is present in a number of his other novels, most strongly in *The Affair*. The men operate in committees because of the nature of their work—they are professionals involved in their careers, as academics, businessmen, scientists, civil servants. This work—not the physical labor described in a proletarian novel but the work of "The New Men," the professional, bureaucratic, technological, managerial classes—is presented with knowledgeable detail to be found in hardly any other novelist. Snow's work, in effect, filled a vacuum.

Snow filled another void in his treatment of love and sex. While these topics have hardly been ignored by novelists, Snow's consideration of the social dimensions of a love affair or a marriage—the effect, for example, of a particular passion upon a man's career, such as Jago's protective love, in *The Masters*, for his wife—is rare among modern novelists. For Snow, the passion per se is never the central concern.

Snow's concern is character; the conditions of work, the politicking in committee, the impact of love—all these are used to reveal character in action. Thus, Snow is fundamentally a very traditional novelist, even though his distinctive reputation rests upon his having been a kind of contemporary social psychologist, carefully observing particular segments of modern society. While he is likely to continue to be read for some time for the picture of parts of society that his special experience allowed him to present, he may well still be read when this picture, encrusted by time, is of only historical interest. If his novels do survive, it will be because, while dealing with the time-bound particulars of their age, they were able to rise to an understanding of fundamental human motivation and thus to enjoy the longevity of true art.

Biography

Charles Percy (C. P.) Snow was born on October 15, 1905, in the Midland city of Leicester, the second of four sons. His background was similar to that of his fictional persona, Lewis Eliot. Snow's family had risen to the lower levels of the middle class; his father worked as a clerk in a shoe factory. Like Eliot's father, who led a choir, Snow's father played the organ in church; when he was no longer able to do so, he died soon after, at the age of eighty-four.

In school, Snow specialized in science; after graduation he worked as a laboratory assistant while he prepared for the examination that won him a scholarship, in 1925, at the University College of Leicester. He graduated in 1927 with first class honors in chemistry and received a grant that allowed him to proceed to a master of science degree in physics in 1928. Subsequently, he gained a scholarship to Cambridge, where he entered Christ's College as a research student in physics, published a paper on the infrared investigation of molecular structure, and, in 1930, received a doctorate and was elected a fellow of Christ's College, a post he held until 1950; he served there as a tutor from 1935 until 1945.

C. P. Snow. (The Granger Collection, New York)

Like the fictional Lewis Eliot, whose law career hinged on his doing well in examinations and receiving scholarships, Snow must have worked hard (as did the hero of *The Search*) and must have been driven by ambition. His lifelong friend, William Cooper (H. S. Hoff; 1910-2002) wrote novels about the life of the young people in Leicester in which the young Snow appears in fictional form; this work helps confirm the autobiographical quality of Snow's *Time of Hope*. Snow himself suggests the autobiographical aspect of *The Conscience of the Rich*, writing that when he was "very poor and very young," he "was taken up by one of the rich patrician Anglo-Jewish families."

Just as Lewis Eliot changes careers, and as the narrator of *The Search* turns from science to writing, Snow also did not rest in the comfort of being a rising young scientific don. He later wrote that since age eighteen or so he knew that he wanted to be a writer, and while an undergraduate he wrote a novel, never published, called "Youth Searching." He had gone into science because it offered a practical possibility for a poor boy. Although he did good scientific work at Cambridge and published some significant papers, according to Cooper in *C. P. Snow* (1959), when some of Snow's scientific research went wrong through oversight, he abandoned scientific experimentation and turned more to his writing.

Snow had already published his first novel, *Death Under Sail*, a detective story, in 1932; he looked on it as practice for his later, more serious fiction. The next year he published *New Lives for Old*, combining his interest in science and politics in a work of science fiction. Worried that it would hurt his scientific career, he published this novel anonymously; it has never been reprinted. The first of his "serious" novels, *The Search*, appeared in 1934; like the Lewis Eliot series, it had a significant autobiographical element.

Snow did not move away from science to a complete commitment to literature at this time; rather, he became involved in administration, starting at his college. In 1939, he was appointed to a committee of the Royal Society that was organizing scientists for the war effort. This position led to a career in civil service; during World War II, he worked with the ministry of labour, being responsible for scientific personnel; after the war, he recruited scientists for government service. Beginning in 1944, he was associated with the English Electric Company, becoming a member of its board of directors in 1947. He was a civil service commissioner from 1945 until 1960.

Snow's public life led to public honors; in 1943 he was made a Commander of the British Empire, and he was knighted in 1957. In 1964, when the Labour Party resumed power, Snow was made a life peer—Baron Snow, of the City of Leicester—and served for two years as parliamentary secretary of the ministry of technology.

During these years of public service, Snow was, of course, also living a personal life. He married the novelist Pamela Hansford Johnson in 1950. Like Margaret Davidson in the *Strangers and Brothers* series, she had been previously married, and like Lewis Eliot, Snow became a stepfather before having a son of his own, Philip Hansford Snow, born in 1952. Lady Snow has written autobiographically; her accounts are especially interesting in suggesting the similarities and differences between her children and the fictional children presented, especially in *Last Things*, by Snow.

Both the public and the personal sides of Snow's life were reflected in the *Strangers and Brothers* series, the idea for which occurred to him, he wrote, on January 1, 1935, while he was in France. It is difficult to determine the degree to which the whole series was worked out in advance. It would seem that Snow developed early certain controlling themes, such as "possessive love" and the idea of the "resonance" of experience upon the narrator, Lewis Eliot, while remaining flexible regarding the number and nature of the volumes that would make up the series. The first volume, *Strangers and Brothers*, which was to give the title to the whole series, appeared in 1940. It was followed in 1947 by *The Light and the Dark*. The subsequent nine volumes of the series appeared at roughly two-year intervals. They continued to draw directly on his own life, including his eye operations, his cardiac arrest, his interest in the Moors murder case, and his experience in parliament.

The course of Snow's simultaneous literary and public careers brought him increased recognition and honors, including numerous honorary degrees, and appointment as rector of the University of St. Andrews, Scotland. (Like Lewis Eliot, he postponed the first of his eye operations in order to attend this academic installation.) They also involved him in notable controversy, the most famous resulting from his Cambridge lectures in 1959, later published as *The Two Cultures and the Scientific Revolution* (1959). Snow's position, which included a criticism of intellectuals' general lack of understanding of modern science, provoked much discussion and a strong attack, renewed in 1961 by the noted Cambridge literary critic, F. R. Leavis. In 1960, Snow, while on one of his trips to the United States, stirred up another controversy by his lectures at Harvard. In those lectures, he criticized some of the military-scientific decisions made by Winston Churchill's government during World War II.

In his later years, Snow continued to speak out on public policies. He remained a controversial figure, but he gradually acquired the image of an elderly, liberal sage, even if his sagacity was frequently questioned by both the political Left and Right. Following the completion of the *Strangers and Brothers* series, he revised it for an Omnibus edition and continued his writing, publishing *The Malcontents, In Their Wisdom*, and ending his career, as he began it, with a detective story of sorts, *A Coat of Varnish*. His remarkably full life ended on July 1, 1980.

ANALYSIS

Characterization is the foundation of C. P. Snow's fiction. While theme and idea, as one might expect from a writer as political and engagé as was Snow, are important to his work, and while plot is nearly always a major source of interest, character is fundamental. It was his special approach to characterization, at once limited and complex, that allowed him to employ theme and plot, as well as style and imagery, in its service and that made certain subject matter particularly appropriate. Consequently, his works have their own distinctive and satisfying unity.

In his study of Trollope, a writer whom he valued highly and with whom he identified in a number of ways, Snow speaks interestingly of characterization. He defines character as persona, distinguishes it from inherent, individual nature, and considers personality to be a fusion of nature and character. These distinctions are certainly relevant to Snow's own work. His starting interest is in "characters," that is, an individual's personal qualities that are conditioned by, and expressed in, social experience. Yet, recognizing that this character interacts with "nature," Snow, in attempting to represent a rounded picture of personality, must demonstrate the interaction. His fiction, then, is simultaneously concerned with showing people their character in social situations, indicating their nature or personal psychology, and presenting the interplay of the two, the social character and the private nature. All people have, in differing proportions, both a private and a social side to their personalities; all are both strangers and brothers.

Given this approach, it is not difficult to understand why Snow dealt frequently with "man in committee," or why he balanced this social material with presentation of individual passions, such as Lewis Eliot's for Sheila. Work and careers, seen in relation to individual nature and love and sex, were the two poles to which his subject matter flowed. As the social side of personality developed, Snow was able to suggest its changing formation.

One observes, for example, Walter Luke's evolution from a brash young scientist to Lord Luke of Salcombe; his persona, but not his basic nature, changes with the years. Because an individual's nature is inherent (like his or her physiology), it is taken as a *donnée*, and its effects are dealt with. It is, for example, a given fact that Roy Calvert is a kind of "manic-depressive"; the reader discovers what the results of this nature will be, both for Calvert himself and for those with whom he interacts.

It was convenient for Snow that this approach to character was quite appropriate to the type of plotting that he apparently preferred. Most of his novels pose a question: "What will Martin decide?" "Who will be elected master?" "Will Roger Quaife succeed?" The reader, in attempting to anticipate the answer, and Snow, in providing and justifying it, must consider the personalities involved. This consideration requires some understanding of the characters' public personae, their social interactions, and their private passions. Plot, a strong element in its own right, is based on character.

Imagery also consistently reinforces Snow's binocular view of personality. The light of brotherhood wages a never-ending Manichaean conflict with the dark of private estrangement. Windows may be lit, inviting people to "come home" to social involvement, but they often walk the dark streets, locked out in their lonely individuality.

Much of Snow's style also reflects his view of personality. E. A. Levenston, in a careful study of Snow's sentence structure (*ES*, 1974), has noticed the prevalence of qualifying "interrupters." Many of these are a result of Snow's comparing the particular to the general, one person's qualities to many people's. Expressions such as "very few men, George least of all" or "Roy was not a snob, no man was less so," run throughout his work.

Thus, Snow was consistent in his craft. If this consistency imposed some limitations on his achievements, it also provided a valuable unity to his whole literary corpus.

Death Under Sail

For reasons that he later described as "obscure," Snow "signalled" that he intended to abandon his scientific career by writing "a stylised, artificial detective story very much in the manner of the day." *Death Under*

Sail is a competent example of this form; it remains quite readable and in some ways foreshadows his more significant work. Told in the first person (curiously, for a book by a twenty-six-year-old, the narrator is sixty-three), it employs light and dark and also water imagery; it includes a political discussion regarding class society being justified through the ranks of the elite being open to talent; and it is concerned with friendship and the generation gap. More important, the plot hinges on character. While the novel's characterization is relatively superficial, it involves both social character, as seen in the interaction of a small group (the narrator, the detective, and the suspects), and the individual psychology of concealed motives. It is thus typical of Snow's novels, most of which have the element of a suspense story based on the two sides, public and private, of personality.

New Lives for Old

Snow's second published novel, *New Lives for Old*, is the weakest of his canon, but it is not without its virtues. The story involves the discovery of a rejuvenating process and the subsequent questions of whether the process will be suppressed, its effects on the love lives of some of the characters, and the political implications of the discovery. These three questions are not well unified; instead of integrating the love interest and the politics, in this one instance Snow treats them as essentially separate stories, at the expense of both. The love story in the middle section becomes tedious; in the last section of the book Snow, atypically, lets a political interest stifle the story. The first part of the book, however, is fairly successful. Here, the plot is related to character, social interactions, private motivations, and moral decisions. Snow is doing what he does best. The falling-off of the work after its relatively effective beginning, however, justifies his decision not to have it reprinted; it is now a difficult book to obtain.

The Search

Snow's third published novel, *The Search*, was slightly revised and reprinted twenty-four years after its first appearance. It is generally superior to the first two novels and more easily related to the *Strangers and Brothers* series, especially *Time of Hope* and *Homecoming*. Although Snow warns the reader, in his preface to the 1958 edition, that the book's narrator and protagonist, Arthur Miles, is "not much like" Snow himself, clearly there is an autobiographical element in the story of a poor boy's using his talent, determination, and scholarships to make a career in science, later to abandon it to turn to writing. The book was praised for its accurate picture of what it is like to be a scientist; in fact, very little scientific activity per se is present. Rather, professional concerns, ambitions, the relation between love and career, and the decisions made by men in committees constitute the basic material of the book. The protagonist might just as easily be a barrister as a scientist. Indeed, *The Search*, while a worthwhile book in its own right, can be seen as a trying out of the material that Snow was to go on to develop in his series.

The defects of *The Search* result primarily from attempting to try out too much at once; the book's construction becomes somewhat confused. The virtues arise from Snow's basing his work on personal experience; he employed, more thoroughly than in his first two published novels, his skill in showing the interconnections of the personal and public aspects of personality.

The favorable reception given to *The Search* certainly encouraged Snow to continue his career as a novelist; within a year of its publication, he conceived of the series on which his reputation rests. He must have made various plans for the series as a whole; the first volume, however, did not appear until 1940, six years after *The Search*. Writing a *roman-fleuve*, as opposed to a series of individual novels, presents an author with certain problems and various opportunities. While Snow avoided some of the pitfalls, such as narrative inconsistency, he failed to take advantage of some of the potentialities of the form. The overall pattern of this series is more blurred than it need have been. This is indicated by the order in which the books were published; it is not the essentially chronological order of the Omnibus edition, published after the series was concluded. While this authorial rearrangement must be accepted, the fact that Snow did not originally insist on it suggests a certain random quality to the series' organization as first conceived of and executed. Furthermore, proposed systems of classification of the books within the series—as, for example, novels of "observed experience" and of "direct experience," or novels dealing with individuals, groups, or a mixture of both—while useful, fail to make clear a compelling pattern.

Indeed, the individual volumes of the series, with the possible exception of the final *Last Things*, stand on their own and easily can be enjoyed separately. That is not to say that nothing is gained by reading them all in the order that they appear in the Omnibus edition. As compared, however, to a work such as Anthony Powell's *roman-fleuve*, *A Dance to the Music of Time* (1951-1975), *Strangers and Brothers* fails to develop the potential cumulative effect of a series.

The series form does allow the overlapping of incident and the "resonance" between events as seen and felt by the narrator, Lewis Eliot. Snow has an interesting concept here but he does too little with it. The reader does not, as in some of the novels of Joyce Cary, see the same events through different eyes; rather, one is given different accounts by a relatively consistent Eliot. The result is that events described for the second time sometimes bore the reader; at other times the reader feels cheated by the inadequacy of the first account. Only occasionally does the technique work well, as, for example, in the two accounts, in *The Light and the Dark* and *The Masters*, of Roy Calvert's giving of a self-damning paper to Winslow. The first account omits material in order to focus on Calvert; subsequently, as one learns of the larger implications of the act, it takes on new meaning.

STRANGERS AND BROTHERS SERIES

More obvious benefits of a series novel are present in *Strangers and Brothers*. The reader observes more characters, over a longer period of time, than would normally be possible in a single volume. Snow, however, possibly in the interest of verisimilitude, does relatively little with his opportunity. Roy Calvert is killed off, George Passant's change is not traced; one does see more of Martin Eliot and Francis Getliffe, but their developments, such as they are, have little drama. There is little in Snow corresponding to the surprises that Powell gives the reader when, for example, his villain, Widmerpool, makes one of his sudden appearances. Only quite rarely does Snow make effective use of surprise, as when the elderly Hector Rose is found to have acquired a younger, sexy wife.

The time span of the series does, however, allow Snow to present the succession of generations, and he does a fine job of suggesting how childhood experiences affect parents as they react to their own children and their friends' children. The parents' point of view is an important part of human experience, infrequently treated in fiction; here again, in presenting parental love, Snow effectively filled a vacuum.

A more fundamental aspect of the *roman-fleuve* is the development of the narrator. Lewis Eliot does change, both in his attitudes and in his style, becoming more ironic in the later volumes. Looking back on earlier events, such as his support of Jago in *The Masters*, he recognizes his errors. While Eliot's development adds interest to the whole series, it would be difficult to maintain that this interest is central.

There are two final aspects of a series novel that make *Strangers and Brothers* something other than eleven separate books—repetition and thematic development. The former is a two-edged device. Any reader of the whole series will be struck by the frequent repetition of certain phrases, sententious remarks, images, and tricks of style, and can readily assemble a list. Are the values of the repetition—interesting variations on a theme and a sense of continuity—greater than the drawback—monotony? In Snow's case, it is something of a tossup. On balance, although many readers may be inclined to say "Oh no! Not another lighted window," the recurring images of light and darkness do form a pattern that unifies the series and reinforces its themes.

Finally, there is theme. Snow himself, in a note preceding *The Conscience of the Rich*, indicated the importance of recurring themes, including "possessive love" and love of, and renunciation of, power. The list could be easily expanded; as has been indicated, the title of the series itself points to a fundamental thematic concern. By seeing these various themes dramatized through different characters in differing circumstances, and learning Lewis Eliot's reactions, the reader certainly gains a perspective that would be impossible in a single volume. Thematic perspective, then, provides the most convincing justification for Snow's series. It is a sufficient justification; the whole is greater than the sum of the parts. That Snow's strength lay more in characterization than thematic presentation may account for the occasional failures of the series.

A brief discussion of three of the eleven novels of the series may serve to suggest aspects of the volumes considered as individual works. *Time of Hope* is both an early novel and one that focuses on Lewis Eliot; *The Masters*, generally the most highly regarded of the series, is from the middle period and has a "collective hero"; *Corridors of Power*, a later novel, centers on a protagonist other than Eliot.

TIME OF HOPE

Time of Hope was the third volume in the series; in terms of internal chronology, however, it comes first, dealing with the years 1914 to 1933, during which Lewis Eliot matures from a boy of nine years to an established barrister, who is involved in an "impossible" marriage. Strongly unified by its plot, it is perhaps the most emotionally moving volume of the whole series, and one of the more successful.

Indicative of Snow's central concern for the interconnections of the public and private aspects of character, the title refers to both the hope for a better society that Eliot shares with George Passant's group, and the hero's private ambitions. Asked what he wants from life, Eliot, in a phrase he returns to much later in the series, replies that he wants to see a better world, spend his life not unknown, and gain love.

The suspense in the novel is based on the question of whether Eliot will succeed, whether he will at least be started on the road to realizing these hopes. The conflict and tension behind this question provide the angst that contrasts to the hope. The book begins with a "homecoming," dreaded by the young Eliot. (In a clear parallel with Proust, Snow picks this up at the start of the very last volume of the series.) Just as he had reason to fear this first homecoming, Eliot later dreads subsequent returns to the woman he manages to marry. Eliot's success is mingled with failure. Through a combination of his nature, which gives him the drive to struggle, and his social character, which wins him the help of Passant, Eliot's personality wins through on the public level: He succeeds in becoming a barrister. On the personal level, however, while he "succeeds" in marrying Sheila, his possessive love evokes no response; his marriage is personally disastrous and a handicap to his career.

Snow in *Time of Hope* thus successfully utilizes his approach to character and his recurring themes in a self-contained story, but one that also prepares for subsequent volumes. His techniques in this volume are typical of the series: The imagery of light and darkness prevails; secondary characters, such as Herbert Getliffe, the barrister under whom Eliot trains, are well drawn; the nature of a major character is presented as a *donneé*. Not being shown what makes her the strange person she is, one must take Sheila's problems as given. Fortunately for the story, it is easier to do so than to accept Calvert's inherent depression in *The Light and the Dark*. As a bildungsroman, *Time of Hope* is more conventional than the majority of the volumes in the series. Consequently, it is both one of the more satisfactory of Snow's novels and one of the less distinctively interesting.

THE MASTERS

While *Time of Hope* has a clear protagonist, *The Masters*, the first volume in the revised series, has no one hero. Snow is particularly good at dealing with interactions within a group, and *The Masters* has been the most highly regarded of his novels. The title refers to two "masters" or heads of a college; after the first one dies, a new one must be elected. It is on this election, involving the votes of thirteen fellows of the college, that the plot centers. The election comes down to two candidates, Jago and Crawford. While Lewis Eliot, now one of the fellows, supports Jago, and while the reader's sympathies are involved on this side, Snow is careful to avoid making the choice one between good and evil. There are very few outright villains in Snow's novels, and Crawford is certainly not one. Politically on the left, but personally not so well suited for the mastership, he is contrasted to Jago, whom Eliot finds less appealing politically but much more appealing as a man. Thus, the issue is essentially between personal nature and public character. The different fellows line up on this basis, thereby reflecting their own natures and characters; their ultimate votes demonstrate the balance of these two aspects of personality.

Interestingly, given Snow's famous dispute, following the publication of *The Masters*, over "the two cultures," the literary and the scientific, one might see Jago, a scholar of English literature, as the humanists' candidate, and Crawford, a member of the Royal Society, as the scientists'. Snow, opposed to the split between the "cultures," does not have the fellows vote on the basis of this split. Walter Luke, a scientist, judges by nature and sticks with Jago. Francis Getliffe, also a scientist, although recognizing Jago's virtues, is motivated by "public" principle and supports Crawford. Eustace Pilbrow, a literary scholar, agrees with Getliffe. Nightingale, another scientist, jealous of Crawford's professional success, initially supports Jago. Paradoxically, Despard-Smith, because he identifies with Jago, supports Crawford.

Having established the initial lineup of votes, Snow skillfully shows the interactions of motives that cause some of them to shift. One particularly important consideration is the question of Jago's wife; her character, thought to be unsuitable for that of a master's spouse, becomes an issue in the election. The personal issue here involves another form of "possessive love" and sets up a "resonance" for Eliot, who is ambivalently trapped in his marriage to Sheila. Snow handles the development of the plot and the suspense leading to the election quite effectively. In bringing so many insightful changes on the interactions of the personalities within a small group, Snow wrote what may be his own masterpiece.

In the later volumes of the series, Eliot moves from college to national and international political maneuvers; the implications are that there is not that much difference. Nevertheless, the "Tolstoyan" view of history—that individuals are secondary to the larger forces of history, which is explicitly mentioned more than once in the series—is more pronounced in the later volumes. Snow suggests that with other people, probably the same policies would be carried out, the same forces would operate. Thus, the mechanisms of politics are of primary interest, but to understand them, one must understand the people who work and are worked by them. As Snow once said, one must understand how the world "ticks" if one is to change it for the better.

CORRIDORS OF POWER

Corridors of Power, the ninth volume in the series, gives the reader a picture of how the high-level decision making that he also described in *The New Men* and questioned in *Science and Government* (1961) does operate. However deterministic its underlying historical philosophy, the novel supports the statement of one of its characters that what is important is how something is done, who it is done by, and when it is done.

The story centers on Roger Quaife, a politician committed to an "enlightened" view of the use of atomic weapons. Once again, one sees both the public and private side of a protagonist, the nature and character that interact to form Quaife's personality; again, however, the nature is essentially a *donneé*—Quaife is to be taken as found. Ostensibly happy in his marriage, Quaife has a mistress; she is a factor, although not a decisive one, in his political career. Snow is quite good at showing the interactions of career considerations and more personal feelings within the triangle composed of Quaife, his wife, Caro, and his mistress, Ellen. Sex is seen as a relationship, social as well as emotional and physical. In order to present this relationship, however, verisimilitude must be stretched a bit, because Lewis Eliot, the narrator, has to be in places and hear confidences from which one would expect him to be barred. Not only does Eliot learn much about private lives, but also he is rather surprisingly ubiquitous at political councils. Here, in describing some of the behind-the-scenes maneuvers, Snow is quite effective, as he is with the presentation of secondary characters, such as the member of Parliament, Sammikins, and the important civil servant, Hector Rose.

After the completion and revision of the *Strangers and Brothers* series, Snow not only worked on biographical studies—Trollope, *The Realists*, and *The Physicists* (1981)—but also continued his novel writing. Although the final volume in the series, *Last Things*, was diffuse in plotting, he returned, in his final novels, to the use of a strong plot line. Both *The Malcontents* and *A Coat of Varnish* are forms of the whodunit, and *In Their Wisdom*, like *The Sleep of Reason*, maintains the reader's interest in the outcome of a law case.

THE MALCONTENTS

The Malcontents received generally poor reviews. It does have obvious weaknesses; the dialogue, usually one of Snow's stronger points, is somewhat unconvincing. Well attuned to the talk of his cohorts, Snow's ear for the speech of contemporary youth was less acute. A more serious defect is related to the mystery-story requirement of providing a goodly number of suspects. Too many characters are introduced at the beginning; the reader has an initial problem in differentiating them, and the book gets off to a slow start. Once the story is under way, however, the narrative interest is strong.

It involves the interaction of a group of seven young people, planning to take action against the establish-

ment. One of them is known to be an informer. Typically for a Snow novel, to appreciate fully the narrative one must consider the formative aspects of each individual's personality. Class background, family relations, ideological positions, and love interests all enter in. Diffused through seven characters, however, Snow's analysis of these factors is somewhat superficial, with the exception of Stephen Freer, whose relationship to the older generation is presented with sensitivity. An underlying sympathy for the ends, if not the means, of the young radicals informs much of the book. This sympathy, while somewhat Olympian, avoids being patronizing and becomes one of the novel's virtues.

IN THEIR WISDOM

In Their Wisdom is a more successful work. Again, to develop narrative interest, a problem is posed. In this instance, it involves an argument over a will and the results of a trial over the disputed legacy. Just as the reader's sympathy is involved, in *The Masters*, on Jago's side, here there is no question of whom to support in the contest. Julian, a selfish and opportunistic young man, is Snow's closest approach to a clear villain. By simplifying some of the characters, Snow is able to devote more attention to the others. Jenny is particularly interesting, different from characters in Snow's earlier books. In showing her life of genteel poverty and the effect on her of the trial and its outcome, Snow once again effectively intertwines the personal and the public.

A COAT OF VARNISH

Snow's last novel, *A Coat of Varnish*, was a return to the detective-story genre of his first book. A less pure example of this genre than *Death Under Sail*, however, it is somewhat unsatisfactorily considered simply as a mystery. The title refers to a line within the book, to the effect that civilization is a thin coat of varnish over barbarism, a notion relevant also to *The Sleep of Reason*. A fairly interesting cast of characters is introduced, but none of them is treated with the depth of analysis of which Snow was capable. Here, character is secondary to plot, and plot itself is used to comment on society. To try to work out who is guilty, one must understand motives: money, sex, and power. In understanding these motives, one gains, Snow expects, an understanding of society. Although this is one of Snow's weaker novels, certainly not ending his career triumphantly, it does manage a degree of fulfillment of the Horatian formula, to delight and to instruct.

Perhaps one should ask for no more. Throughout his career as a novelist, Snow, although with varying degrees of success, never failed to provide a number of intelligent readers with these twin satisfactions. This may not put him in the ranks of a Leo Tolstoy or a Proust; it is, nevertheless, no small accomplishment.

William B. Stone

OTHER MAJOR WORKS

PLAYS: *A View over the Bridge*, pr. 1950; *Family Party*, pb. 1951 (with Pamela Hansford Johnson); *Her Best Foot Forward*, pb. 1951 (with Johnson); *The Pigeon with the Silver Foot*, pb. 1951 (with Johnson); *Spare the Rod*, pb. 1951 (with Johnson); *The Supper Dance*, pb. 1951 (with Johnson); *To Murder Mrs. Mortimer*, pb. 1951 (with Johnson); *The Public Prosecutor*, pr. 1967 (with Johnson; adaptation).

NONFICTION: *Richard Aldington: An Appreciation*, 1938; *Writers and Readers of the Soviet Union*, 1943; *The Two Cultures and the Scientific Revolution*, 1959 (revised as *Two Cultures and a Second Look*, 1964); *The Moral Un-neutrality of Science*, 1961; *Science and Government*, 1961; *A Postscript to Science and Government*, 1962; *Magnanimity*, 1962; *C. P. Snow: A Spectrum—Science, Criticism, Fiction*, 1963; *Variety of Men*, 1967; *The State of Siege*, 1969; *Public Affairs*, 1971; *Trollope: His Life and Art*, 1975; *The Realists*, 1978; *The Physicists*, 1981.

BIBLIOGRAPHY

De la Mothe, John. *C. P. Snow and the Struggle of Modernity*. Austin: University of Texas Press, 1992. Chapters on Snow's view of literature, science, and the modern mind and on his career as writer and public intellectual. Includes extensive notes and a bibliography.

Eriksson, Bo H. T. *The "Structuring Forces" of Detection: The Cases of C. P. Snow and John Fowles*. Stockholm, Sweden: Almqvist & Wiksell, 1995. Originally written as a doctoral thesis, this book compares mystery and detective fiction by Snow and novelist John Fowles. Includes a bibliography and an index.

Heptonstall, Geoffrey. "Venturing the Real: The Significance of C. P. Snow." *Contemporary Review* 290 (Summer, 2008): 224-232. A discussion of Snow's life and work. Heptonstall describes Snow's fiction as "the territory of reason in age of excess," speaking "for decency in a culture of outrage."

Karl, Frederick S. *C. P. Snow: The Politics of Conscience*. Carbondale: Southern Illinois University Press, 1963. A generally useful study of Snow that analyzes his novels up to and including *The Affair*.

Ramanathan, Suguna. *The Novels of C. P. Snow: A Critical Introduction*. London: Macmillan, 1978. A sympathetic and recommended assessment of Snow that discusses all of his novels except his two earliest works. Notes Snow's "imaginative impulse," his understanding of the changing social scene in England over a span of fifty years, and the gradual change in his outlook from hopefulness to doom.

Shusterman, David. *C. P. Snow*. Rev. ed. Boston: Twayne, 1991. A competent, brief study of Snow, including his early life, the controversies surrounding his nonfiction, and his literary output. Contains an analysis of the *Strangers and Brothers* series of novels, noting their interest apart from their literary value. Includes a chronology and a select bibliography.

Snow, Philip. *A Time of Renewal: Clusters of Characters, C. P. Snow, and Coups*. New York: Radcliffe Press, 1998. A memoir by Snow's younger brother. Philip Snow was a character in three of his brother's novels, and his book discusses his brother's work. Includes illustrations, an index, and a bibliography.

Thale, Jerome. *C. P. Snow*. New York: Charles Scribner's Sons, 1965. Considered an excellent secondary source on Snow that is both readable and informative. Presents Snow's work up to and including 1964. Discusses his nonfiction writings, among which are his two controversial works, *The Two Cultures and the Scientific Revolution* and *Science and Government*.

ALEKSANDR SOLZHENITSYN

Born: Kislovodsk, Russia, Soviet Union (now in
    Russia); December 11, 1918
Died: Moscow, Russia; August 3, 2008
Also known as: Aleksandr Isayevich Solzhenitsyn

PRINCIPAL LONG FICTION

Odin den' Ivana Denisovicha, 1962 (novella;
    One Day in the Life of Ivan Denisovich,
    1963)
Rakovy korpus, 1968 (*Cancer Ward*, 1968)
V kruge pervom, 1968 (*The First Circle*, 1968)
Avgust chetyrnadtsatogo, 1971, expanded version
    1983 (*August 1914*, 1972; expanded version
    1989, as *The Red Wheel*)
Lenin v Tsyurikhe, 1975 (*Lenin in Zurich*, 1976)
Krasnoe koleso, 1983-1991 (includes *Avgust
    chetyrnadtsatogo*, expanded version 1983
    [*The Red Wheel*, 1989]; *Oktiabr'
    shestnadtsatogo*, 1984 [*November 1916*,
    1999]; *Mart semnadtsatogo*, 1986-1988;
    Aprel' semnadtsatogo, 1991)

OTHER LITERARY FORMS

Although the literary reputation of Aleksandr Solzhenitsyn (sohl-zheh-NEET-seen) rests largely on his
long prose works, this prolific writer experimented in
numerous genres. The short story "Matryona's House"
is an excellent example of Solzhenitsyn's attention to detail as well as his reverence for old Russian values as exemplified by the peasant woman Matryona and her
home. In addition to his short stories, in 1964 Solzhenitsyn published *Etyudy i krokhotnye rasskazy*, a collection of prose poems (translated in *Stories and Prose
Poems by Alexander Solzhenitsyn*, 1971), each of which
generally conveys a single message by focusing on a solitary image. Solzhenitsyn also composed the long poem
Prusskie nochi (1974; *Prussian Nights*, 1977), which he
committed to paper only after his release from prison.
Drama, as well, interested Solzhenitsyn from his early
years as a writer. His dramatic trilogy was written between 1951 and 1954, but the plays were never published or staged in the Soviet Union. Solzhenitsyn's ea-

gerness to experiment with different genres and to mesh
them makes him an unusually interesting writer. Fairy
tales, film scenarios, drama, poetry, and prose are continually found interwoven in Solzhenitsyn's works. A
particularly striking example of his desire to mix genres
is his history of the Stalinist labor camps, *Arkhipelag
GULag, 1918-1956: Opyt khudozhestvennogo issledovaniya* (1973-1975; *The Gulag Archipelago, 1918-1956:
An Experiment in Literary Investigation*, 1974-1978).

ACHIEVEMENTS

The publication of Aleksandr Solzhenitsyn's first
work, *One Day in the Life of Ivan Denisovich*—in Russian in 1962 and in English in 1963—sent shock waves
throughout both the East and the West. Suddenly a new
voice was heard in the Soviet Union, shattering the long,
oppressive decades of silence and revealing forbidden
truths of Stalinist society. In his preface to *One Day in
the Life of Ivan Denisovich*, Aleksandr Tvardovsky, an
established Soviet poet and editor of the journal *Novy
mir*, notes that the talent of the young writer is as extraordinary as his subject matter. Tvardovsky states that *One
Day in the Life of Ivan Denisovich* is a work of art. The
decision to make this comment is revealing, for, from the
outset, it has been difficult, if not impossible, for readers
both in the East and in the West to evaluate Solzhenitsyn
as an artist apart from his political views. Solzhenitsyn
became a symbol of hope. Born after the Russian Revolution, educated in the Soviet system, and tempered by
war and the Stalinist camps, he was in every sense a Soviet man. With the publication of *One Day in the Life of
Ivan Denisovich*, he also became a Soviet writer published in the Soviet Union—a writer who, through the
actions and words of a simple peasant, unmasked decades of terror and tyranny.

Solzhenitsyn's focus on the peasant in *One Day
in the Life of Ivan Denisovich* and in the short story
"Matryona's House" contributed to the tremendous up-
surge and success of the village theme in contemporary
Soviet literature. "Village prose," as the movement has
been called, treating the concerns of the Soviet Union's
vast rural population, represents one of the dominant and

interesting trends in the 1960's and 1970's. Solzhenitsyn's initial success undoubtedly encouraged other writers to turn to such subjects as a means of speaking the truth, a means of "acceptable" protest.

The nomination of Solzhenitsyn for the Lenin Prize in 1964 demonstrates the height of popularity and prestige that the author attained in his own country. Although he was not to receive his country's highest literary honor, six years later, in 1970, he was accorded worldwide recognition when he received the Nobel Prize in Literature. In his Nobel lecture, Solzhenitsyn stressed the writer's responsibility to the truth, a responsibility that he took seriously throughout his career. Solzhenitsyn took it upon himself to record—in both his fiction and his nonfiction works—events that would otherwise be lost to the world. His history of the Stalinist camps (*The Gulag Archipelago*) as well as his writings on the prerevolutionary politics of Russia (such as *August 1914*, *Lenin in Zurich*, and *November 1916*) and on the workings of the Soviet literary machine in *Bodalsya telyonok s dubom* (1975; *The Oak and the Calf*, 1980) will serve as historical sources for future generations. Solzhenitsyn's works had been translated into more than forty languages only ten years after his first publication. Popularity and politics aside, Solzhenitsyn will be remembered as a master of Russian prose whose works are among the finest of the twentieth century. His preoccupation with the profound issues confronting humankind and his search for a literary means to express these themes mark him as a great writer.

BIOGRAPHY

Aleksandr Isayevich Solzhenitsyn was born in Kislovodsk, a city in the north Caucasus, on December 11, 1918, one year after the Russian Revolution. His father, whose studies at the university were interrupted by World War I, died in a hunting accident six months before his son was born. Solzhenitsyn's mother, Taisiya Zakharovna Shcherbak, worked as an office clerk throughout Solzhenitsyn's childhood, earning very little money. In 1924, Solzhenitsyn and his mother moved to Rostov-on-Don, a city at that time of nearly a quarter million people. Because of financial considerations and the poor health of his mother, Solzhenitsyn was to continue his education there until he graduated in 1941 from the University of Rostov-on-Don, specializing in mathematics and physics. From an early age, Solzhenitsyn dreamed of being a writer. Having displayed a natural talent for math and finding no adequate literary institution in Rostov-on-Don, however, Solzhenitsyn studied mathematics and physics. Nevertheless, in 1939, Solzhenitsyn decided to pursue his literary interests and began a two-year correspondence course in literature at the Moscow Institute of History, Philosophy, and Literature while continuing his studies in mathematics and physics. He finished this course of study in 1940, the same year that he married Natal'ya Alekseyevna Reshetovskaya (the apparent prototype of Nadya in *The First Circle*). Reshetovskaya, a specialist in physical chemistry and biochemistry, taught at the Agriculture Institute in Rostov-on-Don. On October 18, 1941, Solzhenitsyn was drafted into the Soviet army; he hardly saw his wife for the next fifteen years.

Solzhenitsyn served in the army in various capacities, working his way up to battery commander. He was a decorated and inspiring leader, but his army duty was cut short in February, 1945, when he was summoned to his commanding officer's quarters and arrested. The charges, as was typical throughout the Stalinist era, were not made clear to Solzhenitsyn at that time. Later, he determined that he had been arrested for oblique, derogatory remarks concerning Joseph Stalin and his mismanagement of the war that he had made in a personal journal and in a letter to a friend. Upon his arrest, he was taken to the Lubyanka, the notorious prison in Moscow. On July 7, 1945, after four months of interrogation, he was sentenced to eight years of hard labor. Solzhenitsyn's novella *One Day in the Life of Ivan Denisovich*, his novel *The First Circle*, and his multivolume work *The Gulag Archipelago* are all based on his firsthand experience of the Stalinist labor camps. He, like countless other Soviet citizens, was sentenced, under section 58 of the Soviet penal code, for counterrevolutionary crimes. Solzhenitsyn spent the beginning of his term at Butyrka, a Moscow prison, laying parquet floors, as does Nerzhin, the protagonist of *The First Circle*. Later in 1946, because of his training in mathematics and physics, he was transferred to a *sharashka* (a prison where scientists work on special projects for the state) very similar to the one depicted in *The First Circle*. After one year in the *sharashka*, Solzhenitsyn was sent to a labor camp in northern Kazakhstan. During his stay there, he had a tumor removed; the prisoner was not told that it was malignant.

In February, 1953, Solzhenitsyn was released from prison only to enter perpetual exile (a common Stalinist practice) in Kok-Terek, Kazakhstan. There, Solzhenitsyn taught mathematics until his health deteriorated so severely that, in 1954, he was permitted to travel to Tashkent for treatment. In Tashkent, he was admitted to a clinic where he was treated for cancer and where he gathered material for his novel *Cancer Ward*. After his treatment, he returned to Kok-Terek to teach and began working on the play *Olen'i shalashovka* (pb. 1968; also known as *Republika truda*; *The Love Girl and the Innocent*, 1969) as well as *The First Circle*. In June, 1956, as a result of the "thaw" that followed Stalin's death in 1953, Solzhenitsyn was released from exile, and he moved to Ryazan, where he taught physics and mathematics until the end of 1962. In Ryazan, he saw his wife for the first time in many years. She had remarried and had two children from her second marriage. In that same year, Reshetovskaya left her second husband and reunited with Solzhenitsyn.

Solzhenitsyn and his wife stayed in Ryazan, where they both taught and where Solzhenitsyn continued to write in secret. In 1961, upon hearing Aleksandr Tvardovsky's speech to the Twenty-second Party Congress, in which he called for writers to tell the whole truth, Solzhenitsyn, in a bold move, sent his novella *One Day in the Life of Ivan Denisovich* to Tvardovsky's then-liberal journal *Novy mir* (new world). The literary battles waged for the publication of this work and subsequent works by Solzhenitsyn are documented by the author in *The Oak and the Calf* and by Vladimir Lakshin in *Solzhenitsyn, Tvardovsky, and "Novy Mir"* (1980). The response to the novel made Solzhenitsyn an immediate celebrity, and he was nominated for the Lenin Prize in 1964. The political tide was beginning to turn, however, and with it the possibilities for the future publication of Solzhenitsyn's works.

At this time, Solzhenitsyn's unpublished works were already being circulated in samizdat (a self-publishing underground network for literary, philosophical, and political works) and were being smuggled abroad. In 1964,

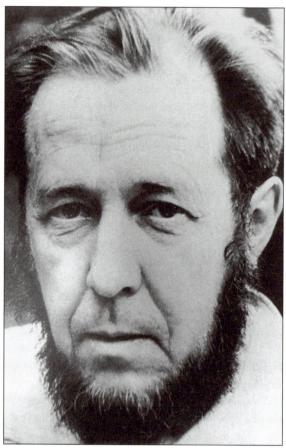

Aleksandr Solzhenitsyn. (© The Nobel Foundation)

his prose poems appeared in the West German journal *Grani* (facets). By 1966, when Solzhenitsyn's "Zakhar-the-Pouch" appeared in the Soviet press, the political and artistic tensions were further intensified by the highly publicized trials of Andrei Sinyavsky and Yuli Daniel. That same year, permission to publish *Cancer Ward* in the Soviet Union was denied. Finally, in 1968, both *The First Circle* and *Cancer Ward* were published in the West without authorization from Solzhenitsyn.

The following year, Solzhenitsyn was expelled from the Union of Soviet Writers, a fatal blow to his career in the Soviet Union, for without membership, publication there was impossible. The situation was quite serious in 1970, when Solzhenitsyn was awarded the Nobel Prize in Literature. The author did not travel to Sweden to accept the prize at that time for fear that he would not be allowed to return to his country. From that point on,

Solzhenitsyn, recognizing the impossibility of publication within his own country, authorized the publication of some of his works abroad. Personal attacks as well as attacks from the Soviet press continued to mount, and, in 1974, after ignoring two summons from the State Prosecutor's Office, Solzhenitsyn was arrested and taken to Lefortovo prison. There he was interrogated, charged with treason, and placed on a plane. Only upon landing was he informed that he had been exiled. Six weeks later, Solzhenitsyn was joined in Zurich by his second wife, Natal'ya Svetlova (he had divorced Reshetovskaya in 1973), their three sons, and his stepson.

In October of 1974, the U.S. Senate conferred honorary citizenship on Solzhenitsyn (an honor bestowed only twice before—on the Marquis de Lafayette and Sir Winston Churchill). He soon settled in Vermont, where he continued to write, deliver occasional lectures, and promote the publication of materials dealing with the Soviet Union.

Living by choice in his Vermont isolation, Solzhenitsyn turned his attention to the past, writing historical works centered on the early twentieth century. His antipathy toward his adopted country was matched only by his lack of contact with his native land and his failure to stay in touch with the evolution of that complex country. He eventually returned to Russia in 1994, a few years after the collapse of the Soviet Union. Somewhat to his surprise, instead of revisiting the land of the evil gulags and oppressed but saintly people, Solzhenitsyn arrived in a consumerized, highly commercial country striving to compete in European and global contexts. The gulags were remembered only by the oldest and were largely dismissed as uninteresting by the young. Irony had dealt Russian history a new blow by reinstating Russian Orthodoxy and removing secular saintliness—including the monastic, agrarian ideals propounded by Solzhenitsyn, Russia's self-conscious prophet.

Undaunted by his lack of popularity, Solzhenitsyn continued to pursue his platform with the support of many respectable nationalist factions. He tried to reach out to Russians of the post-Soviet era through a television talk show on which he propounded his ideals of a special Slavic nationality and its mission in the world. The program lasted only a few months, however, as objections to his verbosity and unwillingness to listen prevailed. On August 3, 2008, Solzhenitsyn died in Moscow after suffering heart failure.

ANALYSIS

Aleksandr Solzhenitsyn and his novels are better appreciated and understood when the author's vision of himself as a writer is taken into consideration; he believed that a great writer must also be a prophet of his or her country. In this tradition of the great Russian novelists Leo Tolstoy and Fyodor Dostoevski, Solzhenitsyn sought to discover a place for the individual in history and in art. Solzhenitsyn viewed art, history, life, and people as continually interacting, forming a single pulsing wave that creates a new, vibrant, and oftentimes disturbing vision of reality and the future. From his first publication, *One Day in the Life of Ivan Denisovich*, to his cycle of historical novels, *Krasnoe koleso*, Solzhenitsyn concentrated on people's ability to survive with dignity in environments that are fundamentally inhumane. Whatever the situation of his protagonist—whether in a Stalinist prison camp, a hospital, the army, or exile—Solzhenitsyn demands from that character a certain moral integrity, a code of behavior that separates him or her from those who have forsaken their humanity. It is the ability or inability to adhere to this code that renders the protagonist triumphant or tragic.

Given the importance of the interrelationship of history, art, and life in Solzhenitsyn's works, it is not surprising that the works are often preoccupied with the larger issues confronting humanity. For the most part, Solzhenitsyn's novels are concerned less with action and plot than with ideas and ethical motivation. Radically different characters are thrown together into artificial environments, usually state institutions, which are separated from society as a whole and are governed by laws and codes of behavior that are equally estranged from society. Such institutions serve as a means of bringing together and equalizing people who would normally not have contact with one another; previous status and education become meaningless. Physical survival itself is usually at issue—prisoners and soldiers struggle for food, patients for treatment, and "free" people for continued freedom and integrity. For Solzhenitsyn, however, physical survival is not the only issue, or even the primary one. Several of his characters, including

Alyosha in *One Day in the Life of Ivan Denisovich* and Nerzhin in *The First Circle*, actually welcome the prison camp experience, for they find their time in camp to be conducive to reflection on fundamental questions.

Nerzhin, like many of the other *zeks* (prisoners in the Stalinist camps), is also aware that, in contrast to the "free" members of Stalinist society, prisoners are allowed greater opportunity to speak their minds, to debate issues freely and openly, and to come to terms with the society and state that have imprisoned them. The freedom that some of the prisoners enjoy, the freedom that the ill-fated patients experience in the *Cancer Ward*, is the freedom encountered by those who have nothing left to lose. As the author indicates through one of the prisoners in *The First Circle*, society has no hold over a person once it has taken everything from him or her. Solzhenitsyn repeatedly returns to the theme of materialism as a source of manipulation and a potential evil in people's lives. According to Solzhenitsyn, those who maintain material ties can never be entirely free, and therefore their integrity can always be questioned and tested. Worldly possessions per se are not evil, nor is the desire to possess them, nor does Solzhenitsyn condemn those who do have or desire them. He is skeptical of their value, however, and ultimately holds the conscience to be humankind's single treasured possession.

Solzhenitsyn's insistence on integrity extends beyond the life of the individual. Solzhenitsyn asserts that because a person has only one conscience, he or she must not allow that conscience to be compromised on a personal level by justifying personal actions or the actions of the state by insisting that the end, no matter how noble, justifies the means. This single observation is the foundation of Solzhenitsyn's attack on the Soviet state. A brilliant, perfect Communist future is not motivation or justification enough for a secretive, censor-ridden socialist state, not in Stalin's time or in the author's lifetime. In Solzhenitsyn's view, corrupt means cannot produce a pure end.

Detractors of Solzhenitsyn in both the East and the West have claimed that his writings are too political and generally unconcerned with stylistic matters. Given the life and the times of the man, these objections fail to be particularly persuasive. Solzhenitsyn's language is rich and textured, and both a glossary (Vera Carpovich, *Solzhenitsyn's Peculiar Vocabulary*, 1976) and a dictionary (Meyer Galler, *Soviet Prison Camp Speech*, 1972) of his language have been produced. Prison slang, camp jargon, political slogans, colloquialisms, and neologisms all mesh in Solzhenitsyn's texts. His attention to language is often voiced by his characters, such as Ignatich in "Matryona's House" or Sologdin in *The First Circle*, and his prose is sprinkled with Russian proverbs and folk sayings that often summarize or counteract lengthy philosophical debates. A further indication of his concern for language can be seen in his insistence on commissioning new translations of many of his works, which were originally issued in hurried translations to meet the worldwide demand for them.

On another stylistic level, Solzhenitsyn employs two narrative techniques that enhance his focus on the exchange of ideas and debate as a means of attaining truth: *erlebte rede*, or quasi-direct discourse, and polyphony. Quasi-direct discourse involves the merging of two or more voices, one of these voices usually being that of a third-person narrator and the other the voice of the character depicted. Through this device, Solzhenitsyn draws the reader as close as possible to the thoughts, perceptions, and emotions of the character without interrupting the narrative with either direct or indirect speech. Similarly, polyphony, a term introduced by the Soviet critic Mikhail Bakhtin in regard to Dostoevski's narrative and structural technique and a term that Solzhenitsyn himself applied to his own novels, is employed in order to present more empathetically a character's point of view. Polyphony allows each character in turn to take center stage and present his or her views either directly or through quasi-direct discourse; thus, throughout a novel, the narrative focus continually shifts from character to character. The third-person omniscient narrator serves as a linking device, seemingly allowing the debates to continue among the characters alone.

In addition to these literary techniques, Solzhenitsyn's prose, particularly in *The First Circle*, is permeated with irony and satire. A master of hyperbole and understatement, Solzhenitsyn is at his best when caricaturing historical figures, such as Vladimir Ilich Lenin and Joseph Stalin, to name but two. Solzhenitsyn further deepens the irony by underscoring small physical and verbal gestures of his targets. The target need not be as powerful as Lenin or Stalin to draw the author's fire, and there are touches of self-irony that provide a corrective to Solzhenitsyn's occasionally sanctimonious tone.

ONE DAY IN THE LIFE OF IVAN DENISOVICH

Not all of Solzhenitsyn's works are dependent on irony and satire. *One Day in the Life of Ivan Denisovich* is striking for its restraint, verbal economy, and controlled tone. This *povest'*, or novella, was originally conceived by the author in 1950-1951 while he was in the Ekibastuz prison. The original draft, written in 1959 and titled "One Day in the Life of a Zek," was significantly revised, politically muffled, and submitted to *Novy mir*.

Set in a labor camp in Siberia, *One Day in the Life of Ivan Denisovich* traces an ordinary day in the life of a prisoner. The author reveals through a third-person narrator the stark, grim world of the *zek* in meticulous detail, including the daily rituals—the searches, the bed checks, the meals—as well as the general rules and regulations that govern his daily existence: little clothing, little contact with the outside world, little time to himself. Every detail of Ivan Denisovich's day resounds in the vast, cold emptiness of this remote camp. As György Lukács noted of the novel, "Camp life is represented as a permanent condition"; into this permanent condition is thrust a common person who quietly and simply reveals the essence of retaining one's dignity in a hopeless, inhumane environment.

Uncharacteristic of Solzhenitsyn's works, the tone of *One Day in the Life of Ivan Denisovich* is reserved, solemn, and dignified; irony surfaces only occasionally. The tone is probably somewhat attributable to the editing of Tvardovsky, whose language is felt here. Throughout the work, which is uninterrupted by chapter breaks, the focus remains on Ivan Denisovich and the passage of this one day. Secondary characters are introduced only insofar as they touch his day, and flashbacks and background information are provided only to deepen the reader's understanding of Ivan Denisovich's present situation. Unlike Solzhenitsyn's later novels, which focus largely on an institution's impact on many different individuals, *One Day in the Life of Ivan Denisovich* focuses on one man. Criticism of the camps is perceived by the reader, who slowly observes and absorbs the daily steps of this man. Only after Solzhenitsyn has revealed the drudgery of that one day, one almost happy day, does he place it in

its context, simply stating that "there were three thousand six hundred and fifty-three days like this in his sentence, from reveille to lights out. The three extra ones were because of leap year."

CANCER WARD

Unlike its predecessor, *Cancer Ward* directly reveals the constant intense emotional pressure of its characters and its themes. Solzhenitsyn fixed upon the idea of writing this novel at his discharge from the Tashkent clinic in 1955. He did not begin writing the novel until 1963, and only after a two-year hiatus did he return to serious work on *Cancer Ward*. In 1966, having finished the first part of the work, Solzhenitsyn submitted it to the journal *Novy mir*; it was rejected by the censor. Meanwhile, Solzhenitsyn completed the novel, which soon began to circulate in samizdat. Eventually, *Cancer Ward* was smuggled to the West and published, first in excerpts and later in its entirety. It was never published in the Soviet Union.

On the surface, *Cancer Ward* depicts the lives of the doctors, patients, and staff of a cancer clinic. The two protagonists of the novel, Pavel Rusanov and Oleg Kostoglotov, are socially and politically polar opposites: Rusanov is a member of the Communist Party, well established, living a comfortable life with a wife and a family; Kostoglotov is a former prisoner who arrives at the hospital with no one and nothing. Because of the cancer that has afflicted them both, they find themselves in the same ward with an equally diverse group of patients. The novel is largely plotless and focuses on the contrasting attitudes of the patients in regard to the institution, their treatment, and life and death, as well as other philosophical and political issues.

The one plot line that runs through the novel centers on Kostoglotov, who, having been imprisoned and consequently deprived of female companionship for years, becomes an avid "skirt chaser," pursuing both his doctor, Vera Gangart, who ironically falls victim to the very cancer in which she specializes, and a young medical student, Zoya. Kostoglotov throughout the novel continually objects to the secrecy that surrounds his treatment and demands that he has a right to know. In a twist characteristic of Solzhenitsyn, Zoya informs Kostoglotov that the X-ray treatment that he is receiving will temporarily render him impotent. This serves as another reminder to Kostoglotov that, as in prison, his fate, his manhood, and in fact his life are beyond his control and in the hands of yet another institution. Throughout *Cancer Ward*, the abuses, idiocies, and tragedies of Soviet medical care are revealed, as terminally ill patients are released believing they are cured, patients are misdiagnosed, and hospitals prove to be poorly staffed and supplied.

Unfortunately, *Cancer Ward* suffers from its near absence of plot, its heavy-handed dialogues and debates, and its lack of focus, either on a genuine protagonist or on an all-encompassing theme. The reader feels little sympathy for Rusanov, a Communist Party member, or for Kostoglotov, despite the fact that he has been unjustly imprisoned and is a victim of cancer. Kostoglotov is generally impatient, intolerant, and at times completely insensitive to others. Nevertheless, he does grow in the course of the novel. In a discussion with Shulubin, another patient in the ward, Kostoglotov dismisses Shulubin's warning that happiness is elusive and only a mirage, but when he is finally dismissed from the clinic, Kostoglotov, wandering the streets free from prison and free from cancer, realizes that an appetite can be more easily stimulated than satisfied. By the conclusion of the work, Kostoglotov understands Shulubin's warning and abandons his dreams of love with Vera and Zoya.

Despite the work's significant shortcomings, there are scenes in *Cancer Ward* that remain unforgettable for their sensitivity and poetry. One such scene involves the two adolescents Dyomka and Asya. Dyomka is to lose his leg; Asya, a breast. Asya, a seventeen-year-old, worries about her appearance in a swimsuit and her future with men, lamenting that no man will ever touch her breast. In an act of both hope and despair, Asya asks Dyomka to kiss her breast before, as the narrator observes, it is removed and thrown into the trash. Throughout the novel, compassion, sensitivity, poetry, and philosophy are shamelessly interrupted by the reality of the cancer ward. The sharp contrast between the human spirit of hope and the ominous presence of death and destruction in the form of cancer simultaneously underscores the fragility of human existence and the immortality of the human spirit. It is this spirit that is admired and celebrated in this novel and that is also a feature of Solzhenitsyn's finest work, *The First Circle*.

THE FIRST CIRCLE

The First Circle, like *Cancer Ward*, is largely autobiographical, based in this case on Solzhenitsyn's experiences in the *sharashka*. The author began writing the novel while in exile in Kok-Terek in 1955. Between 1955 and 1958, Solzhenitsyn wrote three redactions of the novel, none of which has survived. After 1962, he wrote four additional redactions of the novel, the last of which appeared in 1978. The novel was first published abroad in 1968 and, like *Cancer Ward*, was never published in the Soviet Union. The 1978 redaction differs from the sixth redaction (the edition used for all foreign translations) largely in the addition of nine chapters. The discussion below is based on the sixth redaction.

The First Circle masterfully combines all of Solzhenitsyn's finest assets as a writer. It is by far the most artistic of his novels, drawing heavily on literary allusions and abounding with literary devices. The title itself is a reference to Dante's *La divina commedia* (c. 1320; *The Divine Comedy*, 1802), alluding to the first circle of Hell, the circle designated for pagan scholars, philosophers, and enlightened people, where the pain and the suffering of Hell are greatly diminished. The *sharashka*, as Lev Rubin indicates in the chapter "Dante's Idea" (chapter headings are particularly revealing in this novel), is the first circle of the Stalinist camps. Unlike Ivan Denisovich, who is in a hard-labor camp, the *zeks* in the *sharashka* have adequate food and livable working conditions. The *zeks* inhabiting the *sharashka* thus have a great deal to lose, for if they do not conform to the rules governing the *sharashka*, they may fall from the first circle into the lower depths of the Stalinist camps.

Three of the four protagonists of the novel, Gleb Nerzhin, Lev Rubin, and Dmitri Sologdin, face a decision that may endanger their continued stay at the *sharashka*. Each must decide whether he is willing to work on a scientific project that may result in the imprisonment of other citizens or whether he will retain his integrity by refusing to work on the project, consequently endangering his own life. The debates and discussions that permeate this novel are thus well motivated, playing a significant role in revealing the character and philosophies of these prisoners while drawing the reader deeply into their lives and minds. The tension of the novel arises as the reader attempts to determine whether each prisoner will act in accordance with his conscience. Placed in a similar situation, Innokenty Volodin, a free man and the fourth protagonist of the novel, decides to risk imprisonment by warning a fellow citizen that he may be in danger. Volodin decides to follow his conscience in the first chapter of the novel; in his case, suspense depends on the questions of whether he will be caught and punished for his actions and whether he will continue to endorse the decision that he has made.

The First Circle is a novel of characters and choices; the choices that must be made by nearly all the characters, primary and secondary, are of compelling interest to the reader, for each choice functions as an echo of another person's choice. The overall impact of nearly every character (free and imprisoned) being faced with a life-threatening decision based on moral issues vividly demonstrates the inescapable terror of the time. Furthermore, the multidimensional aspects of this novel—the wide range of characters from virtually every social stratum, the numerous plots, the use of polyphony, the shifting to and from radically different settings, the views of peasant and philosopher, the plethora of literary allusions, the incredible richness of the language—show the sophistication and remarkable depth of the author.

AUGUST 1914

Solzhenitsyn's historical works were first seen with the publication of *August 1914* in the West in Russian in 1971 and its English translation in 1972. This book was a greatly shortened variant of the intended whole book, and it was met with general perplexity. Paralleling the "literary experimentation" style of his nonfiction work *The Gulag Archipelago* (published in English 1974-1978), Solzhenitsyn casts his figures as embodiments of historical situations and ethical issues. Whereas in *The Gulag Archipelago* he wrote from personal experience, in *August 1914* he tries to reconstruct a past of which he was not a part, with varying results. The book's chapter on Lenin, deliberately withheld from publication in the first edition, was published separately in Paris in 1975 as *Lenin v Tsyurikhe* and translated in 1976 as *Lenin in Zurich*. Solzhenitsyn had expanded and reworked it after his 1974 exile. Many other chapters were written and added in 1976 and 1977.

KRASNOE KOLESO

August 1914 was republished in English in 1989, this time in its entirety. It was identified as a section, or "knot," of Solzhenitsyn's historical series *Krasnoe koleso* (words that translate into English as "the red wheel"). Confusingly, this version was published under the title *The Red Wheel* rather than *August 1914*. By the time of the 1989 translation, Solzhenitsyn had published two more knots of *Krasnoe koleso* in Russian, *Oktiabr' shestnadtsatogo* (1984; translated as *November 1916* in 1999) and *Mart semnadtsatogo* (1986-1988). A fourth knot, *Aprel' semnadtsatogo*, appeared in 1991. That same year the Soviet Union collapsed. The "evil empire" that had formed the fulcrum for the critical leverage of Solzhenitsyn's prose was gone, and Solzhenitsyn became a prophet without a cause. The work, while historical in nature and presumably impervious to the vagaries of political change, settled into Russian literary history almost like an anachronism. It had a very limited readership.

The structure of the work was intended to reveal the nature of Russia's history as Solzhenitsyn believed it to be. Unlike the first publication (*August 1914*), *The Red Wheel* and *Krasnoe koleso* as a whole used a framework composed of "knots," nodes at which historical events are compressed. Solzhenitsyn's philosophy, responding to Tolstoy's from *Voyna i mir* (1865-1869; *War and Peace*, 1886), conforms to the proposition that history is shaped not so much by great people as by all people striving to make the proper ethical choices when forced to take part in significant events. Tolstoy's ideas, however, are revealed in the narration; Solzhenitsyn uses narrative structure instead of describing the idea, leaving the narration in large measure beyond the ordinary means of artistic forms. His intention was to reveal the "full column" of historical actors, yet such a structure tends to obscure history at the same time that it loses literary form through diffusion of the plot.

Solzhenitsyn created an enormous role for himself as a prophet of Russian history with his first novella, *One Day in the Life of Ivan Denisovich*. In his later life, history granted him only a piece of the past. *Krasnoe koleso* fell outside the interest of the Russian readership it was intended to instruct. Moreover, Solzhenitsyn's ambitions and personal interests came under hostile scrutiny by the Russian literati, who questioned his motivation for returning to Russia in 1994. Solzhenitsyn remained unmoved by the criticism, however, and continued to work as before, motivated from within, defiant of the exterior world.

Suzan K. Burks
Updated by Christine D. Tomei

OTHER MAJOR WORKS

SHORT FICTION: *Dlya pol'zy dela*, 1963 (*For the Good of the Cause*, 1964); *Dva rasskaza: Sluchay na stantsii Krechetovka i Matryonin dvor*, 1963 (*We Never Make Mistakes*, 1963); *Krokhotnye rasskazy*, 1970; *Rasskazy*, 1990.

PLAYS: *Olen'i shalashovka*, pb. 1968 (also known as *Respublika truda*; *The Love Girl and the Innocent*, 1969); *Svecha na vetru*, pb. 1968 (*Candle in the Wind*, 1973); *Dramaticheskaya trilogiya-1945: Pir Pobediteley*, pb. 1981 (*Victory Celebrations*, 1983); *Plenniki*, pb. 1981 (*Prisoners*, 1983).

POETRY: *Etyudy i krokhotnye rasskazy*, 1964 (translated in *Stories and Prose Poems by Alexander Solzhenitsyn*, 1971); *Prusskie nochi*, 1974 (*Prussian Nights*, 1977).

SCREENPLAYS: *Tuneyadets*, 1981; *Znayut istinu tanki*, 1981.

NONFICTION: *Les Droits de l'écrivain*, 1969; *A Lenten Letter to Pimen, Patriarch of All Russia*, 1972; *Nobelevskaya lektsiya po literature 1970 goda*, 1972 (*The Nobel Lecture*, 1973); *Solzhenitsyn: A Pictorial Autobiography*, 1972; *Arkhipelag GULag, 1918-1956: Opyt khudozhestvennogo issledovaniya*, 1973-1975 (*The Gulag Archipelago, 1918-1956: An Experiment in Literary Investigation*, 1974-1978); *Iz-pod glyb*, 1974 (*From Under the Rubble*, 1975); *Pis'mo vozhdyam Sovetskogo Soyuza*, 1974 (*Letter to Soviet Leaders*, 1974); *Amerikanskiye rechi*, 1975; *Bodalsya telyonok s dubom*, 1975 (*The Oak and the Calf*, 1980); *Warning to the West,* 1976; *East and West*, 1980; *The Mortal Danger: How Misconceptions About Russia Imperil America*, 1980; *Kak nam obustroit' Rossiiu? Posil'nye soobrazheniia*, 1990 (*Rebuilding Russia: Reflections and Tentative Proposals*, 1991); *Russkii vopros*, 1994 (*The Russian Question: At the End of the Twentieth Century*, 1994); *Invisible Allies*, 1995; *Dvesti let vmeste, 1795-1995*, 2001.

MISCELLANEOUS: *Sochineniya*, 1966; *Six Etudes by Aleksandr Solzhenitsyn*, 1971; *Stories and Prose Poems by Alexander Solzhenitsyn*, 1971; *Mir i nasiliye*, 1974; *Sobranie sochinenii*, 1978-1983 (10 volumes); *Izbrannoe*, 1991.

BIBLIOGRAPHY

Bloom, Harold, ed. *Aleksandr Solzhenitsyn*. Philadelphia: Chelsea House, 2001. Collection of critical essays includes analyses of *One Day in the Life of Ivan Denisovich*, the representation of detention in works by Solzhenitsyn and Fyodor Dostoevski, and Solzhenitsyn's experiences as a creative artist in a totalitarian state.

Ericson, Edward E. *Solzhenitsyn and the Modern World*. Washington, D.C.: Regnery Gateway, 1993. Examines the reputation of Solzhenitsyn in the West in an attempt to clear up previous misunderstandings. Argues that Solzhenitsyn was never antidemocratic and that his criticisms of the West were made in the spirit of love, not animosity.

_____. *Solzhenitsyn: The Moral Vision*. Grand Rapids, Mich.: Wm. B. Eerdmans, 1980. Presents an analysis of Solzhenitsyn's work from the perspective of the author's Christian vision. Begins with discussion of Solzhenitsyn's theory of art, as enunciated in his Nobel Prize lecture, and then devotes chapters to his major novels as well as to his short stories and prose poems.

Ericson, Edward E., and Alexis Klimoff. *The Soul and Barbed Wire: An Introduction to Solzhenitsyn*. Wilmington, Del.: ISI Books, 2008. Two major Solzhenitsyn scholars provide a detailed biography of the writer and analyses of all of his major fiction.

Feuer, Kathryn, ed. *Solzhenitsyn*. Englewood Cliffs, N.J.: Prentice-Hall, 1976. Collection of thirteen essays includes discussions of Solzhenitsyn's uses of structure and symbolism, the theme of war in his works, and epic and dramatic elements in the works. Also provides an evaluation of the English-language translations of his writings.

Klimoff, Alexis. *"One Day in the Life of Ivan Denisovich": A Critical Companion*. Evanston, Ill.: Northwestern University Press, 1997. Useful guide for readers encountering Solzhenitsyn's novel for the first time. Provides primary source materials, a discussion of the novel within the context of Solzhenitsyn's body of work and of Russian literary tradition, and an annotated bibliography.

Lakshin, Vladislav. *Solzhenitsyn, Tvardovsky, and "Novy Mir."* New York: Oxford University Press, 1980. Presents an insider's view of the publication history of *A Day in the Life of Ivan Denisovich*, involving Aleksandr Tvardovsky, a poet and the editor of the journal *Novy mir.*

Mahoney, Daniel J. *Aleksandr Solzhenitsyn: The Ascent from Ideology.* Lanham, Md.: Rowman and Littlefield, 2001. Focuses on Solzhenitsyn's political philosophy and its impact on twentieth century thinking. Presents analysis of Solzhenitsyn's writings to demonstrate how they represent the political condition of humankind in the modern world.

Medina, Loreta, ed. *Readings on "One Day in the Life of Ivan Denisovich."* San Diego, Calif.: Greenhaven Press, 2001. Collection of critical essays is designed to assist students and other readers of the novel. Contributors interpret the novel from a variety of perspectives and provide biographical information about Solzhenitsyn.

Moody, Christopher. *Solzhenitsyn.* 2d rev. ed. New York: Barnes & Noble Books, 1976. Discussion of Solzhe-

nitsyn's literary works to 1975 takes an essentially negative view, in contrast to the generally favorable reception of his early work.

Pearce, Joseph. *Solzhenitsyn: A Soul in Exile.* New York: HarperCollins, 1999. Generally uncritical biography chronicles Solzhenitsyn's evolution from pro-Marxist youth to anti-Soviet writer and, finally, to literary anachronism after the demise of the Soviet Union. Features exclusive personal interviews with Solzhenitsyn, previously unpublished poetry, and rare photographs.

Scammell, Michael. *Solzhenitsyn.* New York: W. W. Norton, 1984. Exhaustive and lively biography deals with practically all important aspects of Solzhenitsyn's life, but does not discuss his writings in detail.

Thomas, D. M. *Alexander Solzhenitsyn: A Century in His Life.* New York: St. Martin's Press, 1998. Personal portrait of the writer provides insights into Solzhenitsyn's struggle with Joseph Stalin and his successors as well as the author's relationships with the two women who provided strong support for his efforts to expose the evils of the Communist regime. Imaginative, well-documented, and at times combative biography includes a discussion of Solzhenitsyn's return to Russia in 1994.

SUSAN SONTAG

Born: New York, New York; January 16, 1933
Died: New York, New York; December 28, 2004
Also known as: Susan Rosenblatt

PRINCIPAL LONG FICTION

The Benefactor, 1963
Death Kit, 1967
The Volcano Lover, 1992
In America, 2000

OTHER LITERARY FORMS

Although two of her novels achieved popular and critical success, Susan Sontag was best known as an es-

sayist who took on controversial topics such as art, war, disease, and politics. She first made her reputation as a cultural commentator with *Against Interpretation, and Other Essays* (1966), a study of avant-garde art, including drama, film, literature, and other cultural events. She expanded her range of subject matter in *Styles of Radical Will* (1969), which included not only influential essays on science fiction and pornography but also a travel journal of her trip to Hanoi during the Vietnam War. Her reputation as an essayist reached its apogee in her widely debated book *On Photography* (1977), which evoked simultaneously her fascination with photographs and her distrust of them as purveyors of knowledge about the human condition. Sontag later revised some of her views on photography in the well-received *Regarding the Pain of Others* (2003). She also authored a highly praised collection of experimental short fiction, *I, Etcetera* (1978). Her long short story "The Way We Live Now," published originally in *The New Yorker* in 1986 and then in 1991 published on its own in a special edition featuring hand-colored engravings by Howard Hodgkin, has come to be considered one of the classic accounts of the acquired immunodeficiency syndrome (AIDS) epidemic. Her one play, *Alice in Bed* (pb. 1993), devoted to the life of Alice James, the sister of novelist Henry James and psychologist William James, is representative of Sontag's increasing interest in feminist issues in the latter part of her career.

ACHIEVEMENTS

Although Susan Sontag's early novels received some praise for their daring experimental narratives, many critics considered them derivative of the French New Novel as developed by Nathalie Sarraute and Alain Robbe-Grillet. Sontag herself discounted her early long fiction, although it has remained in print and continues to elicit critical commentary.

What might be called Sontag's second career as a novelist began with the best-selling *The Volcano Lover*, an account of the Admiral Nelson-Emma Hamilton romance set against the revolution in Naples and the avid aesthetic sensibility of Emma's husband, Sir William Hamilton, the British ambassador. That Sontag should have turned to the historical novel astounded but also delighted reviewers, many of whom praised her ability to fuse her intellectual and artistic interests with a love story. Sontag's achievement, however, is probably best honored for the distinctive narrative voice she crafted—one that reflected her own sensibility even as it plumbed the lives of historical figures. Also noteworthy is Sontag's use of first-person narratives at the end of her novel in order to give voice to some of the female victims of the eighteenth century revolution.

Sontag's fourth novel, *In America*, won the National Book Award for fiction. While certain critics deemed this work inferior to *The Volcano Lover*, Sontag's impressive grasp of nineteenth century American history and her development of her main character (modeled on a Polish

Susan Sontag. (Annie Leibovitz/Courtesy, Farrar, Straus and Giroux)

actress who immigrated to America) won her many new readers. The novel also reflects Sontag's continuing experiments with narrative voice—in this case she introduced the novel with an autobiographical prologue, calling attention to the highly personal nature of her story and the way the novelist identifies with her characters.

BIOGRAPHY

Susan Sontag was born Susan Rosenblatt in New York City in January, 1933, the daughter of Jack Rosenblatt, a trader-merchant based in China, and Mildred Jacobsen, a teacher and business partner of her husband. Sontag's father died in China when she was only five years old. She felt his loss keenly and wrote about it in an autobiographical story, "Project for a Trip to China," in *I, Etcetera*.

Sontag's restless mother moved the family briefly to Florida and then to Arizona in the hope of curing her daughter's asthma. Sontag received her early education in Tucson, where her mother met and married air force captain Nathan Sontag. Susan adopted his last name at the age of twelve.

The Sontags (Nathan, Mildred, and Susan's younger sister, Judith) moved to Southern California after World War II. Sontag attended North Hollywood High School, wrote for the school newspaper, and cultivated an intense interest in music, dance, theater, and literature. A precocious student, she attended the University of California at Berkeley for a year and then transferred to the University of Chicago, receiving her undergraduate degree before she was nineteen and marrying a sociology professor, Philip Rieff.

After graduate study at the University of Connecticut and Harvard and a year in Paris, Sontag divorced Rieff in 1959, deciding to live on her own in New York City with their only child, David. She earned a living teaching at Columbia University and other New York-area schools while pursuing her ambition to write fiction. Although her first novel attracted a prestigious publisher, her work did not receive the approbation she craved, and with the relative failure of a second effort in 1967, she turned primarily to writing deft and provocative cultural and political essays that vaulted her to the center of attention in the New York media market and in Europe, where her books were translated into several languages.

Gifted with the knack for aphorism, Sontag was eminently quotable. Critics often borrowed her lines or referred to her opinions when formulating their own arguments. A tall, striking woman, Sontag glamorized the role of public intellectual, a role few women of her time could equal in a realm dominated by men.

Sontag's first love was always fiction, however, and by the late 1980's, she was determined to return to novels that would give her the kind of freedom lacking in the essay format. After years of false starts on works of fiction, she gradually regained her confidence, first in the short-story form and then in the novel, even as her essay writing (especially the pieces in *Under the Sign of Saturn*, 1980) became more personal and novelistic. While Sontag never entirely abandoned the essay form—she was committed to maintaining her role as public intellectual—she continued to project long, ambitious works of fiction, none of which, unfortunately, came to fruition

after her burst of success with *The Volcano Lover* and *In America*. Shortly after the publication of the latter, she had a recurrence of cancer, a second debilitating disease after a traumatic bout with breast cancer in the 1970's, a period of ill health that led to her writing the classic long essay *Illness as Metaphor* (1978), which has become a staple of literature classes and courses in medicine.

A third occurrence of cancer (a form of leukemia in part caused by treatment for uterine cancer) gradually diminished her capacity to work. Although she pursued heroic efforts to find a cure (including a bone-marrow transplant), Sontag succumbed to her illness on December 28, 2004, at Memorial Sloan-Kettering Cancer Center in New York City.

ANALYSIS

Susan Sontag's career as a novelist can be divided into two distinct phases. Early on, she produced work considered to be experimental in the European tradition of the New Novel or *nouveau roman*. Thus *The Benefactor* and *Death Kit* were interpreted as rejections of the American realist school. In other words, Sontag was not concerned so much with the manners and mores of contemporary society as she was with literature itself; that is, she pursued a form of narrative that was self-reflexive, turned back on itself, in which the narrator made the idea of "reality" itself problematic, a fiction. Perhaps the best example of her technique is to be found in *Death Kit*, in which Sontag leaves the reader wondering if Diddy really did murder a railroad worker or if the entire action of the novel is taking place in his mind. This doubt as to the reality of Diddy's experiences is a way of exploring the radically subjective way people perceive reality. Similarly, *The Benefactor* focuses on the consciousness of its narrator, Hippolyte. To a great extent, he makes his world by fictionalizing it, transforming his friends and family into projections of his sensibility.

After publishing these two early novels and a similarly constructed collection of short stories, *I, Etcetera*, Sontag by her own account lost confidence in her ability to write fiction. Reviews of her novels had been mixed, and, aside from this lack of encouragement, it may be that the kind of fiction she was writing proved to be a dead end—that is, as soon as she established the radical subjectivity of her main characters and narrators, contriving an energetic and engaging narrative that would fully engage with the world seemed beyond her reach. Her novels were enervating rather than inspiriting.

After two decades of writing essays that were very much engaged with social and political reality, Sontag's turn to historical fiction made sense—even though it was surprising given the nature of her earlier novels. As she noted in several interviews, history itself became an exciting study for her, and she came to appreciate how much ideas are shaped by historical context and not only by the sensibilities of those who hold those ideas. Thus *The Volcano Lover* and *In America* became the perfect vehicles for an exhilarating collation of radical individual perspectives and the forces of history.

THE BENEFACTOR

In *The Benefactor*, Hippolyte attempts to live through his dreams, which are often nightmares in which he is dominated and tortured. His dreams are the art he makes of his life, and his desire is to make his life conform to the immediacy and sensuousness of dreams. Like Sontag's idea of art, Hippolyte's dreams are self-contained, which is to say that like Sontag he fancies himself to be self-invented, and, also like the early Sontag, he prefers to obscure the details of his past. Not even his last name is divulged.

Sohnya Sayres observes that this youthful first novel tries too hard to reject autobiography. Other critics have noted that the details about Hippolyte's family and background are quite vague. By making her narrator a sixty-one-year-old man, Sontag may be, in Sayres's words, "hiding from a complex set of feelings" as much as she is exploring them.

DEATH KIT

Diddy, the protagonist of *Death Kit*, narrates his life in the third person. The book is his artifice. He inhabits his dreams as much as Hippolyte lives in his. It eventually becomes clear that the "events" of the novel are actually Diddy's hallucinations in the final minutes of his life (he has committed suicide). Diddy's death dream is an attempt to repeat his life and to get it right the second time. His tragedy is the human condition; human beings do not get the chance to live again. Critics who like the novel have admired its form and language, but even they have expressed regret that Diddy is never believable as a fully created character. In effect, the novel fails the test

of good fiction because many of its readers are unable to identify with its main character.

THE VOLCANO LOVER

The Volcano Lover was a major breakthrough for Sontag, lifting her out of the hermetic shell of her earlier fiction. The novel closely channels the consciousness of Sir William Hamilton, a neoclassical man, the vivid romantic behavior of his wife, Emma, and the bold actions of Admiral Horatio Nelson as naval hero. Each of them has a sense of greatness and grandeur, with Nelson serving as the apex of their hero worship even as he sees his heroism reflected in their unstinting devotion. Sontag understands that theirs is a combined quest for fame and glory.

Sontag admitted in an interview that *The Volcano Lover* was the only one of her books she really liked, the only one that fulfilled her ambitions as a writer. In it she finally fuses in brilliant fashion the techniques of her fiction and her nonfiction. It is also her most autobiographical work, finally releasing a pent-up romanticism.

IN AMERICA

In Sontag's final novel, *In America*, a group of Poles travel to Anaheim, California, in 1876 to establish a utopian community. Their leader is Maryna Zaleska, Poland's greatest actress, who has forsaken her career to create a farming commune. She is aware of the likelihood of failure, but the romance of starting anew, the challenge of succeeding where communities such as Brook Farm failed, is too enticing not to pursue. She takes with her a devoted husband, Bogdan, a young son, Piotr, and the young writer Ryszard, who aspires to win her love.

The novel is inspired by the career of Helena Modjeska (originally Modrzejewska), Poland's renowned actress, who did indeed immigrate to the United States in 1876 and settled in Anaheim with her husband, Count Karol Chapowski; their fifteen-year-old son, Rudolf; Henryk Sienkiewicz, a future Nobel Prize-winning writer; and a group of friends. While relying on the historical record, Sontag also indulged her freedom to invent characters and scenes, including an opening section, "Zero," that is the culmination of her efforts to deal with her own biography in the realm of fiction. "Zero" contains numerous references to events in her life (her marriage, her trips to Sarajevo, and her upbringing in Arizona and California).

Although Sontag won the National Book Award for *In America*, critical opinion has been deeply divided on the novel's merits. Several critics have deemed the novel a farrago of historical research and bland psychological commentary, whereas others have praised its panoramic quality and dazzling array of devices, including diaries, letters, dialogue, and interior monologues. Still others have expressed admiration for the range of Sontag's social observations and the variety of her characters while also noting their regret that her intrusive intellectual side (her ideas) slows the narrative and undermines passages that are not deeply imagined.

Carl Rollyson

OTHER MAJOR WORKS

SHORT FICTION: *I, Etcetera*, 1978.

PLAY: *Alice in Bed: A Play in Eight Scenes*, pb. 1993.

SCREENPLAYS: *Duet for Cannibals*, 1969; *Brother Carl*, 1972; *Promised Lands*, 1974; *Unguided Tour*, 1983.

NONFICTION: *Against Interpretation, and Other Essays*, 1966; *Trip to Hanoi*, 1968 (journalism); *Styles of Radical Will*, 1969; *On Photography*, 1977; *Illness as Metaphor*, 1978; *Under the Sign of Saturn*, 1980; *AIDS and Its Metaphors*, 1989; *Conversations with Susan Sontag*, 1995 (Leland Poague, editor); *Where the Stress Falls*, 2001; *Regarding the Pain of Others*, 2003; *At the Same Time: Essays and Speeches*, 2007 (Paolo Dilonardo and Anne Jump, editors); *Reborn: Journals and Notebooks, 1947-1964*, 2008 (David Rieff, editor).

EDITED TEXTS: *Selected Writings*, 1976 (by Antonin Artaud); *A Barthes Reader*, 1982; *Homo Poeticus: Essays and Interviews*, 1995 (by Danilo Kiš).

MISCELLANEOUS: *A Susan Sontag Reader*, 1982.

BIBLIOGRAPHY

Kennedy, Liam. *Susan Sontag: Mind as Passion*. Manchester, England: Manchester University Press, 1995. Offers a sound introduction to Sontag's work, although best approached after reading Sayre's biographical introduction or Rollyson's *Reading Susan Sontag* (see below).

Poague, Leland, ed. *Conversations with Susan Sontag*. Jackson: University Press of Mississippi, 1995. Indispensable collection of Sontag's important inter-

views provides insights into the author's approach to her fiction. Includes a comprehensive introduction and a detailed chronology of Sontag's life and work as well as bibliography and index.

Poague, Leland, and Kathy A. Parsons, comps. *Susan Sontag: An Annotated Bibliography, 1948-1992*. New York: Garland, 2000. Compiled with Sontag's cooperation (she gave Poague access to her private archives), this impressive work of scholarship is an indispensable way to chart the development of her career.

Rollyson, Carl. *Female Icons: Marilyn Monroe to Susan Sontag*. Lincoln, Nebr.: iUniverse, 2005. Includes several scholarly articles on Sontag's identity as a modernist writer, her relationship to popular culture, and the role biography plays in understanding the development of her fiction and nonfiction.

_____. *Reading Susan Sontag: A Critical Introduction to Her Work*. Chicago: Ivan R. Dee, 2002. Contains summaries and critiques of Sontag's fiction and nonfiction, discussions of her interviews, and a glossary of the artists and concepts that appear in her body of work. Intended specifically for undergraduate students and first-time readers of Sontag's sometimes difficult subjects and complex prose style.

Rollyson, Carl, and Lisa Paddock. *Susan Sontag: The Making of an Icon*. New York: W. W. Norton, 2000. The only biography of Sontag discusses not only her work but also the way she shaped her career as a public intellectual. Draws on the archives of Sontag's publisher and on interviews with many of Sontag's friends and associates. Includes extensive notes and photographs.

Sayres, Sohnya. *Susan Sontag: Elegiac Modernist*. New York: Routledge, 1990. Scholarly exploration focuses on Sontag's relationship to modernism and the modernist writers who preceded her. Serves as an accessible introduction to Sontag at midcareer.

Seligman, Craig. *Sontag and Kael: Opposites Attract Me*. New York: Counterpoint, 2004. Well-received critical appreciation probes Sontag's sensibility as a critic in juxtaposition to the sensibility of Pauline Kael (best known for her film reviews). Explores both Sontag's strengths and her weaknesses.

WOLE SOYINKA

Born: Ijebu Isara, near Abeokuta, Nigeria; July 13, 1934

Also known as: Akinwande Oluwole Soyinka

PRINCIPAL LONG FICTION

The Interpreters, 1965
Season of Anomy, 1973

OTHER LITERARY FORMS

Wole Soyinka (sho-YIHN-kah) is best known as a dramatist. He has written more than twenty plays in various modes, including *The Swamp Dwellers* (pr. 1958), *The Lion and the Jewel* (pr. 1959), *A Dance of the Forests* (pr. 1960), *Madmen and Specialists* (pr. 1970; revised pr., pb. 1971), and *Death and the King's Horseman* (pb. 1975). He is also a filmmaker. He has published several collections of poetry, including *Idanre, and Other Poems* (1967), *A Shuttle in the Crypt* (1972), and *Mandela's Earth, and Other Poems* (1988), and the long poem *Ogun Abibiman* (1976). His nonfiction prose includes impressive books of criticism such as *Myth, Literature, and the African World* (1976) and *Art, Dialogue, and Outrage: Essays on Literature and Culture* (1988). His autobiographical works examine various aspects of his life experiences: his prison years in *"The Man Died": Prison Notes of Wole Soyinka* (1972), his early life in *Aké: The Years of Childhood* (1981), and the influence of his father in *Ìsarà: A Voyage Around "Essay"* (1989). In addition, he has translated the 1938 Yoruba novel *Ogboju ode ninu igbo irunmale*, by D. O. Fagunwa, as *Forest of a Thousand Daemons: A Hunter's Saga* (1968).

ACHIEVEMENTS

Wole Soyinka is perhaps the most talented and versatile writer to have emerged during the literary flowering in Africa beginning in the 1950's. He is, without doubt, the finest dramatist; he is also an accomplished poet and has written two novels so experimental that critics are not yet sure what to make of them. While tapping numerous twentieth century fictional devices, the novels are based on his own cultural heritage, combining ritual, myth, comedy, and hard realism in a new configuration. He draws from the Yoruba mythology of his native region but makes contact with a larger public by frequent references and parallels to myths and literatures of other cultures. Not only his literary achievements but also his championing of individual freedoms have gained for him recognition both in his native Nigeria and abroad. He has received numerous awards, including first prize at the Dakar Negro Arts Festival in 1960, the John Whiting Drama Prize in 1966, the Jock Campbell Award for Fiction in 1968, and the Nobel Prize in Literature in 1986.

BIOGRAPHY

Wole Soyinka was born Akinwande Oluwole Soyinka on July 13, 1934, at Abeokuta, in western Nigeria. A Yoruba by birth, he studied Yoruba mythology and theology and made it the basis of his literary themes. His formal education, however, was British. He attended primary and secondary schools in Abeokuta and Ibadan, began his undergraduate work at University College, Ibadan, and received his bachelor of arts degree with honors in English (1957) at the University of Leeds. He would continue to be associated with various universities throughout his academic and literary career, holding lectureships, delivering papers at academic meetings, and publishing critical reviews and articles. His career as a dramatist began at Leeds and continued with his establishment of acting companies in Lagos and Ibadan. Aside from the theater and his own literary endeavors, he has been a political activist; the Nigerian authorities detained him in prison during the Biafran War, from August, 1967, to October, 1969. Individual freedom and social responsibility are themes in his earliest work, but his commitment to social justice became even more intense after his prison experiences and the Nigerian atrocities during the war.

After winning the Nobel Prize in 1986, Soyinka received the honorary title of Order of Commander of the Federal Republic of Nigeria. Just a few years later, however, in 1994, he was forced to flee the country when his criticism of the new military dictator General Sani

Abacha made him once again a target for political imprisonment. Tensions had been rising in Nigeria after the military annulled the democratic elections of 1993, and when Soyinka's vocal opposition group learned that he was soon to be arrested, he was forced into exile. In the following years Soyinka held appointments at both Harvard and Emory universities in the United States while continuing his biting criticism of Abacha, as evidenced in the 1996 publication of *The Open Sore of a Continent: A Personal Narrative of the Nigerian Crisis*, a political tract that exposes the abuses of Abacha's regime. This work led in 1997 to Abacha's transparently false treason charges against Soyinka for his alleged participation in a series of bombings across Nigeria. Not until Abacha's death in 1998 was Soyinka able to return to Nigeria, and then only after Abacha's successor dropped the treason charges and openly courted Soyinka and other exiled dissidents to come home.

ANALYSIS

Like other novelists in Africa during the years just before and after independence, Wole Soyinka faced the question of ethnic and cultural identity. The now notorious negritude movement, begun in the 1930's, had attempted to promote a pan-African identity by distinguishing between two mentalities: the rational, methodical, categorical tendency of the industrialized Westerner and the emotional spontaneity of the African still in tune with the rhythms of nature. Many, including Soyinka, came to see this definition as a sign of cultural dependence—the African described by contrast to the dominant European culture. In his most famous remark on the subject, Soyinka declared that "the tiger does not proclaim his tigretude!" Soyinka presumably meant that Africans need not be defensive about their identity; at any rate, Soyinka has proclaimed unabashedly, in all of his works, including his two novels, the indigenous source of his themes and inspiration.

As Soyinka makes clear in his book of criticism *Myth, Literature, and the African World*, his own cultural heritage is Yoruba. Drawing from its fascinating and complex mythology, Soyinka concentrates on two central events. One is the disintegration of primal oneness, which he calls Orisa-nla. In the beginning, only Orisa-nla existed, with his servant Akunda; in a moment of revolution or treachery, depending on the point of view, Akunda rolled a boulder down the back of Orisa-nla, shattering him into the fragments that became the human race and the gods of the Yoruba pantheon; god and humanity were thenceforth separated from one another. Among these individuated gods, two stand out, Obatala and Ogun, as aspects of the original oneness. Soyinka uses human representations of them both in his novels. Obatala appears as the titular leader of a traditional community. While not actively pursuing the rejuvenation of society, he tries to hold things together: "He is the embodiment of the suffering spirit of man, uncomplaining, agonised, full of the redemptive qualities of endurance and martyrdom."

Wole Soyinka. (© The Nobel Foundation)

Soyinka also includes a third human figure in the novels, a woman, who appears as the fertility principle inherent in Orisa-nla and promises continuity.

The most important god for Soyinka, however, is Ogun, whose story is central to the plots in the two novels and whose complex character makes him the most complete symbol of the original oneness. Most simply, he is the god of creation and destruction, and he is incarnate in humankind. After the original disintegration, Ogun took on the task of entering the abyss that separated humankind from the gods and building a bridge across the primeval gulf to reunite them. To accomplish this task, he had to "die," to risk total disintegration of the personality (thus repeating the original fragmentation) and to reintegrate himself through an act of the will. Ogun's success was his grand triumph that humanity must strive to emulate. Ogun's cautionary tale does not, however, end here. At the call of human beings, he reluctantly descended to aid them, but his gift of "Promethean" fire—Ogun is the god of the forge—gave humankind the power of destruction as well as creation. During his sojourn among people, Ogun, as god of wine and of war, then experienced his most shameful moment, the massacre in battle, while in a drunken rage, of both friends and enemies. This destructive power of the will repeated the drunken act of Akunda and symbolizes the ever-present threat of humankind's own destructiveness. It is especially Ogun's personality and social roles that provide for Soyinka a rationale for contemporary events. Ogun's story proclaims the will as the crucial ethical faculty, individual heroism as the dynamic factor in social change, and the communal function of the heroic act as its sanction.

THE INTERPRETERS

Soyinka's first novel, *The Interpreters*, is a dark comedy. The settings are the capital city of Lagos, the university city of Ibadan, and the surrounding lagoons, at a time soon after Nigeria's independence, in the early 1960's. Soyinka presents a directionless society seen mainly through the eyes of a few university-educated observers who have just returned from abroad to take up their roles, which they have yet truly to discover, in the new state. What they see is an assortment of professional people holding on to or seeking status and power; their attractive public image is but a disguised sleaziness, a combi-

nation of Old World corruption and Victorian hypocrisy. Moving through this structured society are various lost people seeking stability: an American black man who is gay, an evangelical preacher, a thief, and occasional transients from outside Africa. The novel traces the lives of the five interpreters—Egbo, Sagoe, Kola, Sekoni, and Bandele—as they get in touch with themselves and their society. What sets them apart, in particular, is their refusal to accept wholesale imported Western values and mores, as well as a vague sense that an indigenous worldview should mold the new state. The problem is to get in touch with it and revive it. Soyinka does not offer any hope of immediate success.

Of all the interpreters, Egbo and Sekoni are most closely associated with the Ogun experience. Sagoe, Kola, and Bandele do not share the risky heroism of Ogun's nature but seem closer to the passive, suffering attitude of the god Obatala, though it is difficult and undesirable to make such identifications with any allegorical rigidity. Sagoe, the newspaper reporter whose experiences give insight into the corrupt practices of business and politics and into the religious void of modern Nigeria, suffers in the first part of the novel from inebriation and a morning hangover. He has developed the absurd "Philosophy of Voidancy," a solipsistic return to original oneness, a passive loss of identity. A recurring childhood memory perpetuates a Western, Manichaean split between divine and human nature. He finally agrees to abandon his philosophy and commit himself to his fiancé, Dehinwa, but Sagoe never displays any deep internal struggle.

Kola is a painter who is intellectually aware of Yoruba tradition; he spends several months finishing his huge canvas, a symbolic representation of the Yoruba pantheon using contemporary models. Kola gradually recognizes his own inadequacy as an artist—Ogun is Soyinka's divine symbol of the true artist—and is almost ready to accept his role as simply a teacher of art. The painting itself would suggest, at least in the eyes of Egbo, an inadequate conception of human struggle and redemption. Kola presents Ogun (Egbo) not in his creative role as architect of order but as a drunken murderer. Bandele is the clearest image of the god Obatala. Throughout the novel, he tries to mediate among the various interpreters and to judge and encourage ethical behavior. He also tries to live a life of compromise, to prevent a complete split between the intellectuals and the rest of society. In the end, he continues his role of judge—as the traditional Oba—but strikes out at the society itself, ensuring a split, as he sarcastically accuses the hypocritical professional class of burying its own children.

Soyinka measures human character against divine behavior after the original fragmentation. Only Ogun, among all the gods, risked the loss of individuation in the abyss of transition. Egbo, the grandson and heir of a village chief, is on the edge of the abyss. The novel places two choices before him: between the power and privileges of the Osa chiefdom and a life in a modern state, and between a sensuous life with Simi, a nationally famous and beautiful courtesan, and a New World university student, a feminist rebel pregnant with his child. While he has not made either choice definitively at the end of the novel, he leans toward contemporary demands. Such a commitment would be a denial of African heritage as superficially perceived but an assertion of it in essential terms. The university student is herself a heroine, defying artificial conventions of the day and committed to her child and to her education in spite of bitter rejection by the professional elite. She is also the only person with whom Egbo has shared his religious commitment to the Yoruba gods; their night of love takes place in his sacred retreat under the bridge crossing the Ogun River. Egbo has at least three initiation experiences, all sexual, described as symbolic leaps into the abyss of death and rebirth: twice during his first night with Simi and once during his more mature "venturing" with the unnamed student girl. By the end of the novel, he knows, though he has not yet made the decision, that "he could not hold her merely as an idyllic fantasy, for the day rose large enough and he was again overwhelmed by her power of will."

While Egbo's Ogun experience is still on the level of "idyllic fantasy," Sekoni's has a degree of fulfillment and a tragic finality. Like Egbo, at the beginning of the novel he perceives the sacred through physical reality. Egbo calls the fleshy black dancer at the Club Cabana "the exaltation of the Black Immanent." For Sekoni, she is a symbol of the original oneness: It would be profane, he says in his stuttering excitement, "t-t-to bring her in

c-c-conflict." In moments of inspiration, as he comes into contact with spiritual reality, his language breaks down and his stuttering increases. Sekoni's first profession is engineering. His dream is to harness the powers of nature. A flashback has him returning home aboard ship, imagining the ocean as "a deafening waterfall defying human will," and his creative fingers as shapers of bridges, hospitals, derricks, and railroads.

The sea, however, proves to be too strong; the bureaucracy at home gives him a desk job and then allows him to build a rural power plant only to have it condemned by an expatriate expert. The failure drives him insane. When he is released from the mental hospital, he goes on a pilgrimage to Jerusalem (not to Mecca, as his devout Muslim father would have wished), and by putting his fingers through the broken walls of the city, he has a mystical experience. Soyinka's description of it suggests an identification between the Jewish and the African diasporas, the disintegration of traditional community, and, by implication, a repetition of the original fragmentation of Orisa-nla. Sekoni returns to Nigeria as an inspired artist. His one great work, a sculpture that he calls *The Wrestler*, seems a race against time. Using Bandele as a model and a rough incident with a bouncer at the Club Cabana as the inspiration, Sekoni depicts what appears to be Ogun just beginning to relax after subduing the forces of chaos in the abyss. Kola admires and envies Sekoni's genius, his ability to create "that something which hits you foully in the stomach."

When Ogun grants such powers, however, he demands a sacrifice in return. In a symbolic scene, with obvious mythological references and a typical Soyinka setting, Sekoni dies in an automobile accident during a raging storm, near a bridge that spans a precipice. As god of the forge, Ogun is associated with automobiles and bridges and with the metal that draws down lightning from the heavens. On that chaotic night, the "dome" of heaven "cracked," and, like Ogun in the abyss, Sekoni loses his identity, literally, except as he survives in his sculpture. His death leaves the other interpreters drained of energy, searching desperately for a myth that will convince them of rebirth. That Sekoni is not reborn seems to provoke estrangement. At the end, the four remaining interpreters are no longer a close-knit group: They experience "a night of severance, every man . . . going his way." The Ogun paradigm would suggest that, since everyone is an incarnation of Ogun, the interpreters are facing the transition experience.

SEASON OF ANOMY

Like *The Interpreters*, *Season of Anomy* has as its major theme the reestablishment of cultural and spiritual continuity. Bandele's searing rebuke of his peers, that they are burying their own children, applies even literally to the generation in power in Soyinka's second novel. The ruling Cartel (a conglomerate of business, political, and military leaders) use their positions to exploit the country (a fictionalized Nigeria) and to intimidate, suppress, and massacre in order to maintain control. The novel's main antagonist is the innocuous-appearing community of Aiyéró, headed by the wise Pa Ahime, which perpetuates the traditional African values of community and harmony with nature. Ahime resembles the Obatala personality in his passive, suffering role as priest. Beneath his surface calm dwell "doubts upon doubts, thicker than the night" about African ideals ever overcoming the forces of exploitation. He himself, however, does not struggle actively against the forces outside the community. The conflict in the novel begins when Ofeyi, the novel's protagonist and the Ogun personality in its artistic, creative aspect, goes out into the larger world to combat the Cartel. Ofeyi is at first a propagandist jingle writer for the Cocoa Corporation, an ally of the Cartel; under the influence of Ahime and his own vision of a new Africa, however, he uses his position to undermine the corporation, until he has to resign under fire. The novel, then, presents a conflict between these two forces, creation and destruction, but the plot is a tracing of Ofeyi's growing commitment to his cause, his debate in particular over using either peaceful or military means, his eventual acceptance of violence, and his personal and communal quest for Iriyise, his mistress, whom Soyinka develops as a goddess of fertility, an aspect of Orisa-nla, who gave birth to the Yoruba pantheon. Ofeyi travels into the center of the Cartel's massacres in order to rescue Iriyise from the enemy prison and carry her, though comatose, safely back to the refuge of Aiyéró.

While the novel often operates on a realistic level—with its vivid pictures of war, for example—its language is infused with ritual and myth. Ofeyi's actions take on a ritualistic meaning and, as in ritual and myth, detailed, causal explanations are not always forthcoming. The novel does not follow a clear chronological line; it oscillates between the communal life in Aiyéró and the outside world and between the inner life of Ofeyi, his memories and reflections, and public action.

The novel tries to make sense of the chaotic events through which Ofeyi moves. It judges the Cartel according to traditional values and myths. In particular, it condemns an exploitation that forgets the obligation of one generation to another. Ofeyi's subversive jingles accuse the Cocoa Corporation of milking the country dry: "They drained the nectar, peeled the gold/ The trees were bled prematurely old/ Nor green nor gold remained for the next generation." The proverb that defines the Cartel, one of its own choosing, damns it: "The child who swears his mother will not sleep, he must also pass a sleepless night." The mother (the Cartel), accusing the child of the crime, fails to acknowledge that the child is restless and screams for attention because the mother has not been nurturing him. The Cartel fails in its function of ensuring continuity from one generation to the next. Aiyéró, on the other hand, through its rituals and myths, maintains the three necessary connections, between generations, between the living and the dead, and between gods and humanity. Aiyéró is not a pastoral paradise; it has a reputation for its boatbuilding, uses hydroelectric power, and manufactures guns. Soyinka's notion of the idyllic community is not backward. Still, its communal ideal suggests strongly its allegorical representation of the divine world attempting to reestablish ties with the fragmented human race to achieve wholeness.

Ogun's transitional journey is the paradigm for the novel's plot and theme. Individual scenes and incidents reinforce the idea. Ofeyi's main concern is whether his actions will make any impact on history: whether the attempt to create order out of chaos is hopeless and whether his own personal contribution will soon be covered in obscurity. When he is still debating his role, sitting in a canoe on the pond that the people of Aiyéró use as a retreat for reflection, Ofeyi watches the wake quickly disappear as the waters resume their calm cover. Even "this simple rite of passage," he says, seems a meaningless challenge. Beneath the pond are centuries of history—"Slaves, gold, oil. The old wars"—and his efforts seem doomed to join them. The oil could be a promise for the future; like Ogun, Ofeyi regards resources as the raw materials of creativity. As he contemplates the Cartel's exploitation of them, he determines, through an act of the will, that victory requires "only the rightful challenger."

The novel's central symbol of the new Nigeria, as conceived by Ahime and Ofeyi, is the dam at Shage, which will, when completed, span the river into Cross-river, the region most antagonistic to Aiyéró's ideas and known for its xenophobia. Mainly Aiyéró men, living outside their native community, are engaged on the project, and Ofeyi, as ideologue, has been its inspiration. It, like Iriyise's dance performed for the workers on the construction site, celebrates the harmonious creation of power—hydroelectric power—out of natural forces. Later, however, after the Cartel has begun to react to the initiatives of the Aiyéró men and has begun to repress them, Ofeyi passes by Shage Dam on the way to Cross-river. The site is abandoned, the dam only partially finished, and dead bodies—perhaps the men of Aiyéró—lie floating in the artificial lake. The Cartel has begun its massacres. When Ofeyi first sees the crane with its rope suspended over the lake, he recalls a similar scene in Scotland and remembers his reaction to the unfinished bridge there. It seemed to him then that all unfinished things were sublime—a Western romantic notion to which he had clung until this day at Shage Dam. Now he reevaluates that experience, according to the myth of his own culture: "It all remained unfinished, and not sublime." Ofeyi as the Ogun personality cannot accept the chaos of the abyss as the end of the creative effort. The goal must be to restore order, not aesthetically admire the incomprehensible.

When Ofeyi arrives at the bridge that will carry him into Cross-river, he, like Egbo in *The Interpreters*, bathes himself in the purifying waters. Unlike Egbo, however, he then takes the final plunge into the abyss. He enters Cross-river in search of Iriyise. As he experiences at first hand the horrors of war, he moves deeper and deeper into enemy territory and ends in Temoko Prison. He is there not because he is forced to be but because he wills to be. In the final symbolic act of the abyss, he is knocked unconscious, loses his "individuation," and then wills himself back to life. This unrealistic mythical event accompanies his simultaneous rescue of Iriyise from the prison.

Their return to Aiyéró with Ahime and Demakin (the warrior aspect of Ogun) means a temporary defeat for society but a victory for Ofeyi, whose will has overcome the recurring temptation of passivity.

A common complaint against Soyinka, in spite of the high acclaim he receives for his artistry and his patriotism, is his failure to speak realistically to the issues confronting African societies. Not only does his complex, allusive style encourage elitism, but his characters also are intellectuals whose problems and solutions have little direct relationship to the larger society. Whereas Western audiences, especially critics, might be attracted to such a highly individualistic aesthetic, African readers and critics might wish for a voice that is closer to their pitch, that seems to echo their complaints.

Certainly, many would wish fervently that one who is perhaps the most talented literary figure on the continent could use his gift to effect real and visible change. Nevertheless, three things must be said about Soyinka as an African spokesman. First, his novels have as their underlying theme the freedom of the individual and the use of that freedom in the interests of society. Second, he insists on African roots and traditional African concepts as rationales and sanctions for human behavior. Finally, Soyinka does not indulge in experimentation for its own sake, nor does he employ fiction merely as a medium for presenting the tensions of contemporary conflict; rather, by incorporating ritual and myth in his novels, he seeks to suggest the very communal sense that must ultimately hold the society together.

Thomas Banks
Updated by Harland W. Jones III

OTHER MAJOR WORKS

PLAYS: *The Swamp Dwellers*, pr. 1958; *The Invention*, pr. 1959 (one act); *The Lion and the Jewel*, pr. 1959; *A Dance of the Forests*, pr. 1960; *The Trials of Brother Jero*, pr. 1960; *The Strong Breed*, pb. 1963; *Three Plays*, 1963; *Five Plays*, 1964; *Kongi's Harvest*, pr. 1964; *The Road*, pr., pb. 1965; *Madmen and Specialists*, pr. 1970 (revised pr., pb. 1971); *The Bacchae*, pr., pb. 1973 (adaptation of Euripides' play); *Jero's Metamorphosis*, pb. 1973; *Collected Plays*, 1973-1974 (2 volumes); *Death and the King's Horseman*, pb. 1975; *Opera Wonyosi*, pr. 1977 (adaptation of Bertolt Brecht's play *The Three-*

penny Opera); *Requiem for a Futurologist*, pr. 1983; *A Play of Giants*, pr., pb. 1984; *Six Plays*, 1984; *From Zia, with Love*, pr., pb. 1992; *The Beatification of Area Boy: A Lagosian Kaleidoscope*, pb. 1995; *Plays: Two*, 1999.

POETRY: *Idanre, and Other Poems*, 1967; *Poems from Prison*, 1969; *A Shuttle in the Crypt*, 1972; *Ogun Abibiman*, 1976; *Mandela's Earth, and Other Poems*, 1988; *Early Poems*, 1997; *Samarkand and Other Markets I Have Known*, 2002.

RADIO PLAYS: *Camwood on the Leaves*, 1960 (pb. 1973); *A Scourge of Hyacinths*, 1990 (pb. 1992).

NONFICTION: *"The Man Died": Prison Notes of Wole Soyinka*, 1972 (autobiography); *Myth, Literature, and the African World*, 1976; *Aké: The Years of Childhood*, 1981 (autobiography); *Art, Dialogue, and Outrage: Essays on Literature and Culture*, 1988; *Ìsarà: A Voyage Around "Essay,"* 1989; *The Credo of Being and Nothingness*, 1991; *Orisha Liberated the Mind: Wole Soyinka in Conversation with Ulli Beier on Yoruba Religion*, 1992; *Wole Soyinka on "Identity,"* 1992; *"Death and the King's Horseman": A Conversation Between Wole Soyinka and Ulli Beier*, 1993; *Ibadan: The Penkelemes Years—A Memoir, 1946-1965*, 1994; *The Open Sore of a Continent: A Personal Narrative of the Nigerian Crisis*, 1996; *Seven Signposts of Existence: Knowledge, Honour, Justice, and Other Virtues*, 1999; *The Burden of Memory, the Muse of Forgiveness*, 1999; *Conversations with Wole Soyinka*, 2001 (Biodun Jeyifo, editor); *Climate of Fear: The Quest for Dignity in a Dehumanized World*, 2005; *You Must Set Forth at Dawn: A Memoir*, 2006.

TRANSLATION: *Forest of a Thousand Daemons: A Hunter's Saga*, 1968 (of D. O. Fagunwa's novel).

BIBLIOGRAPHY

Adelugba, Dapo, ed. *Before Our Very Eyes: Tribute to Wole Soyinka, Winner of the Nobel Prize for Literature*. Ibadan, Nigeria: Spectrum, 1987. Collection of sixteen essays is divided into two parts, the first devoted to personal tributes and the second to analytical essays on the author's writings. Brian Crow's essay on Soyinka's romanticism is particularly informative.

Coger, Greta M. K. *Index of Subjects, Proverbs, and Themes in the Writings of Wole Soyinka*. Westport,

Conn.: Greenwood Press, 1988. Valuable key to references and allusions in much of Soyinka's work. Includes an introduction that provides brief discussion of connections among works, descriptions of topics of interest to Soyinka, and commentary on Soyinka's use of Yoruba proverbs and rituals.

Jeyifo, Biodun. *Wole Soyinka: Politics, Poetics, and Postcolonialism*. New York: Cambridge University Press, 2004. Focuses on the connection between Soyinka's works and his involvement in radical political activity, describing how Soyinka uses literature and the theater for political purposes.

_____, ed. *Conversations with Wole Soyinka*. Jackson: University Press of Mississippi, 2001. First publication of transcripts of Soyinka's recorded interviews with Henry Louis Gates, Jr., Anthony Appiah, Biodun Jeyifo, and others. Soyinka's remarks in these interviews help to clarify obscure aspects of his work.

_____, ed. *Perspectives on Wole Soyinka: Freedom and Complexity*. Jackson: University Press of Mississippi, 2001. Collection of critical essays on the author's work over three decades offers analyses of Soyinka's writings from several schools of critical theory, from feminism to phenomenology. The essays also discuss Soyinka's postcolonial politics and aestheticism.

Jones, Eldred Durosimi. *The Writing of Wole Soyinka*. Rev. ed. London: Heinemann, 1988. Standard general introduction to Soyinka's work is still a useful resource. Contains lucid analyses of all the major works and helpful information about Soyinka's background.

Maduakor, Obi. *Wole Soyinka: An Introduction to His Writing*. New York: Garland, 1986. Helpful critical study is designed to clarify difficult aspects of Soyinka's works. Separate sections examine his poetry, his fictional and autobiographical prose, his five metaphysical plays, and his literary essays.

Maja-Pearce, Adewale, ed. *Wole Soyinka: An Appraisal*. Portsmouth, N.H.: Heinemann, 1994. Collection of essays primarily by African writers addresses topics such as Soyinka's fiction, poetry, and drama and the African culture from which he writes. His Nobel lecture is the lead entry, and the book also contains an interview with Soyinka.

Okome, Onookome, ed. *Ogun's Children: The Literature and Politics of Wole Soyinka Since the Nobel.* Lawrenceville, N.J.: Africa World Press, 2002. Collection of essays compares and contrasts Soyinka's earlier works with those written after he received the Nobel Prize in Literature. Includes bibliography.

Wright, Derek. *Wole Soyinka Revisited.* New York: Twayne, 1992. Provides an introductory overview of Soyinka's work, critical studies of his works, biographical information, and a chronology of his life and works. Includes bibliography and index.

MURIEL SPARK

Born: Edinburgh, Scotland; February 1, 1918
Died: Florence, Italy; April 13, 2006
Also known as: Muriel Sarah Camberg

PRINCIPAL LONG FICTION

The Comforters, 1957
Robinson, 1958
Memento Mori, 1959
The Bachelors, 1960
The Ballad of Peckham Rye, 1960
The Prime of Miss Jean Brodie, 1961
A Muriel Spark Trio, 1962 (includes *The Comforters, Memento Mori*, and *The Ballad of Peckham Rye*)
The Girls of Slender Means, 1963
The Mandelbaum Gate, 1965
The Public Image, 1968
The Driver's Seat, 1970
Not to Disturb, 1971
The Hothouse by the East River, 1973
The Abbess of Crewe: A Modern Morality Tale, 1974
The Takeover, 1976
Territorial Rights, 1979
Loitering with Intent, 1981
The Only Problem, 1984
A Far Cry from Kensington, 1988
Symposium, 1990
The Novels of Muriel Spark, 1995
Reality and Dreams, 1996
Aiding and Abetting, 2000
The Finishing School, 2004

OTHER LITERARY FORMS

In addition to her novels, Muriel Spark produced a sizable amount of work in the genres of poetry, the short story, drama, biography, and criticism. Her volumes of poetry include *The Fanfarlo, and Other Verse* (1952) and *Going Up to Sotheby's, and Other Poems* (1982). Her first collection of short stories, *The Go-Away Bird, and Other Stories*, appeared in 1958; among her several other collections are *The Stories of Muriel Spark* (1985) and *All the Stories* (2001). *Voices at Play*, a collection of short stories and radio plays, appeared in 1961, and her play *Doctors of Philosophy* was first performed in London in 1962 and published in 1963. Spark's literary partnership with Derek Stanford resulted in their editing *Tribute to Wordsworth* (1950), a collection of essays on the centenary of the poet's death; *My Best Mary: The Selected Letters of Mary Shelley* (1953); and *Letters of John Henry Newman* (1957). Spark also edited *The Brontë Letters* (1954). Among her works of nonfiction, Spark produced a study of Mary Wollstonecraft Shelley, *Child of Light: A Reassessment of Mary Wollstonecraft Shelley* (1951, revised as *Mary Shelley*, 1987), and *The Essence of the Brontës: A Compilation of Essays* (1993).

ACHIEVEMENTS

Critical opinion about Muriel Spark's status as a novelist is sharply divided. In general, her work is less highly valued by American critics; Frederick Karl, for example, dismissed her work as being "light to the point of froth" and said that it has "virtually no content." English critics such as Frank Kermode, Malcolm Bradbury, and David Lodge, on the other hand, consider Spark a major contemporary novelist. Kermode complimented her on being "obsessed" with novelistic form, called *The Mandelbaum Gate* a work of "profound virtuosity," and described Spark as a "difficult and important artist." Bradbury, who regarded Spark as an "interesting, and a very amusing, novelist" from the beginning of her career, later added his assessment that she was also a "very high stylist" whose work in the novella shows a precision and economy of form and style. In a reassessment of *The Prime of Miss Jean Brodie*, Lodge commented on the complex structure of the novel and Spark's successful experimentation with authorial omniscience.

Spark was known for being able to combine popular success with critical acclaim. In 1951, she received her first literary award, the *Observer* Story Prize for the Christmas story "The Seraph and the Zambesi." A radio drama based on *The Ballad of Peckham Rye* won the Italia Prize in 1962, and in the same year she was named a fellow of the Royal Society of Literature. In 1965, Spark received the prestigious James Tait Black Memorial Prize for Fiction for *The Mandelbaum Gate*. *Mary Shelley* received a Stoker Award in 1987. Spark was made Dame Commander of the Order of the British Empire in 1993, and in 2001 she received an honorary doctor of literature degree from the University of London. In 2004, she was presented with the Edinburgh International Book Festival Enlightenment Award.

BIOGRAPHY

Muriel Spark was born Muriel Sarah Camberg in Edinburgh, Scotland, on February 1, 1918, of a Jewish father, Bernard Camberg, and an English mother, Sarah Uezzell Camberg. She attended James Gillespie's School for Girls in Edinburgh, an experience that later formed the background for *The Prime of Miss Jean Brodie*. She lived in Edinburgh until 1937, when she married S. O. Spark and moved to Africa. During the next two years she gave birth to her son, Robin, and divorced Spark, who had become abusive and was showing signs of mental illness. She moved into an apartment with a young widow and her child and wrote poems and plays while waiting for the long process of her divorce to conclude. Her life in Rhodesia and South Africa provided background material for some of her earliest successful short stories, such as "The Portobello Road"

and "The Seraph and the Zambesi." The onset of World War II interfered with her plans to return to Scotland, and she worked at a number of jobs before managing to book passage home in 1944; because there were travel restrictions for children, her son was unable to join her for a year and a half.

During her sojourn as young divorcée awaiting the arrival of her child, Spark moved to London to find work; there she lived at the Helena Club, which had been endowed by Princess Helena, the daughter of Queen Victoria, for "ladies from good families of modest means who are obliged to pursue an occupation in London." Spark's experiences at the Helena Club with other young women earning their living in a big city became the background for her novel *The Girls of Slender Means*.

From 1944 to 1946, Spark worked in the Political Intelligence Department of the British Foreign Office, an experience she later drew upon when writing *The Hothouse by the East River*. Her interest in poetry led to her serving as general secretary of the Poetry Society in London from 1947 to 1949 and as editor of the *Poetry Review*; in 1949, she introduced a short-lived journal titled *Forum Stories and Poems*. In the 1950's, she began a successful career as a critic and editor that included books on William Wordsworth, Mary Wollstonecraft Shelley, Emily Brontë, John Masefield, and John Henry Newman; she collaborated on several of these works with her literary partner and friend Derek Stanford.

The major turning point in Spark's career as a writer occurred in 1954, when she converted to Roman Catholicism. Brought up in the Presbyterian religion, she said that she had "no clear beliefs at all" until 1952, when she became "an Anglican intellectually speaking," although she did not formally join the Anglican Church until late in 1953. The Church of England was, however, a halfway house for Spark, who was an Anglo-Catholic for only nine months before her conversion to Roman Catholicism. She later stated that the writings of John Henry Newman were an important factor in her move to the Catholic Church.

Spark's conversion initially caused her a great deal of emotional suffering, and she said that her mind was, for a period of time, "far too crowded with ideas, all teeming in disorder." This feeling of mental chaos gave way later to what she called "a complete reorganization" of her mind that enabled her to begin writing fiction. Several persons encouraged her to produce a novel, among them Graham Greene and representatives of the publishing house Macmillan and Company, which was looking for new writers at the time; the result was *The Comforters*.

In 1961, Spark traveled to Jerusalem to research the background for *The Mandelbaum Gate*, and in 1964 she moved from her home in London to New York City. She lived for less than a year in an apartment close to the United Nations building, a location that later became the setting for *The Hothouse by the East River*. In 1967, she was awarded the Order of the British Empire and left England to settle in Italy. In 1982, after fifteen years in Rome, she moved to Tuscany. Spark lived and worked in Italy until her death in Florence on April 13, 2006.

ANALYSIS

Muriel Spark frequently used the word "minor" to describe her achievement as a novelist, a term that, in her vocabulary, is not as derogatory as it may at first appear. Believing that the artist is by definition a "minor public servant," Spark claimed that she chose to write "minor novels deliberately." This characterization of the artist and of her own intentions as a writer reflects her concerns about the novel as a form and the creative process in general, issues that are present throughout her work. She admitted that while writing her first novel, *The Comforters*, she had difficulty resigning herself to the fact that she was writing a novel, a genre that, in her opinion, was a "lazy way of writing poetry." For Spark at that time, poetry was the only true literature, while the novel was an "inferior way of writing" whose "aesthetic validity" was very much in doubt. Although she apparently revised her earlier low estimation of the novel, she said that she always considered herself a poet rather than a novelist and believed that her novels are "the novels of a poet."

Spark's distrust of the novel form also resulted from her suspicions about fiction's relationship to truth; she said that she was interested in "absolute truth" and that fiction is a "kind of parable" from which a "kind of truth" emerges that should not be confused with fact. The truth that the novel can embody is similar to her definition of

Muriel Spark. (© Jerry Bauer)

"legend" in *Emily Brontë: Her Life and Work* (1953). Speaking of the literary legends that surround a writer such as Brontë, Spark said that these stories, though not literally true, are "the repository of a vital aspect of truth" that should be accorded respect in their own right. It is imperative, however, for writers and readers to discriminate among types of truth and between life and art, a discrimination that Charmian Colston, the aged novelist in *Memento Mori*, is capable of making. She tells another character that "the art of fiction is very like the practice of deception," and, when asked if the practice of deception in life is also an art, replies, "In life . . . everything is different. Everything is in the Providence of God." Spark, who was careful to maintain this distinction in her statements about her work, described her own novels as a "pack of lies."

Caroline Rose in *The Comforters*, who shares this distrust of fiction, struggles against being a character in a novel because she resents being manipulated by the novelist. At one point, she describes the author of the fiction as an "unknown, possibly sinister being." The writer's "sinister" nature results from his or her ability to create fictions that are imaginative versions and extensions of the truth rather than the truth itself; perhaps more important, the novelist deprives his or her characters of their free will and independence. As Patricia Stubbs observed, Spark perceived a parallel between God and the novelist, and the act of creating fiction is, in a sense, "dabbling in the devil's work."

As a result, Spark's novels are filled with would-be artists and artist figures, people who attempt to create fictions in real life and consequently bring about discord and mischief. In *The Prime of Miss Jean Brodie*, Miss Brodie begins to view the people around her as characters in a story she is creating and attempts to bring about sexual pairings and heroic deeds in her self-made "plot," with disastrous results. Both Alec Warner in *Memento Mori* and Dougal Douglas in *The Ballad of Peckham Rye* are involved in "research" into the lives of the people around them; Douglas carries his curiosity about others a step further, fictionalizing an autobiography for an actor and later becoming the author of "a lot of cock-eyed books."

In two later novels, *The Public Image* and *Territorial Rights*, fictions are devised even more consciously— and are potentially more dangerous. In *The Public Image*, film actor Annabel Christopher is, for the most part, merely the product of a clever publicity campaign, with its accompanying lies, distortions, and omissions. After her husband's suicide, she becomes the victim of his well-planned attempt to destroy her career, for he has left behind a group of letters that would impugn her sexual morality and destroy her carefully devised "public image." In *Territorial Rights*, Robert Leaver stages his own kidnapping and sends threatening letters filled with truth and lies to his family and friends. In addition, he leaves fragments of a "novel" he is supposedly writing that contain a sensational mixture of fact and fiction that could hurt many of the people around him. Just as these characters are guilty of trying to manipulate reality by inserting carefully constructed "fictions" into the lives of real people, Sir Quentin Oliver in *Loitering with Intent* overtly plagiarizes a fictional model to accomplish his ends. Af-

ter reading Fleur Talbot's novel *Warrender Chase*, he begins to orchestrate the lives of the members of the Autobiographical Association according to its plot, an action that causes Fleur to complain, "He's trying to live out my story."

The ubiquitous "listening devices" and spying present in Spark's fiction are another aspect of her fascination with the process of creating fictions. Dougal Douglas, the artist-to-be, sells tape recorders to African witch doctors; the abbey in *The Abbess of Crewe* is bugged; and Curran in *Territorial Rights* has a sudden moment of paranoia in a restaurant when he wonders if his fellow diners are all spies armed with "eavesdropping devices." As the servants in *Not to Disturb* realize, recording and preserving experience allows the person doing the recording to alter and, in a sense, to create reality. Armed with tape recorders and cameras, they are busy creating their own version of the events of an evening that culminates in the deaths of the Baron and Baroness Klopstock and their secretary; the servants are artist figures, manipulating the plot of the story that they will soon sell to the public media. Spark sees the novelist, like the "typing ghost" who plagues Caroline Rose in *The Comforters*, as an eavesdropper who spies on his or her characters and then manipulates their actions in order to create a fiction; she peoples her novels with characters who are also engaged in this process.

Because Spark is so intent upon acknowledging her fiction as fiction, most of her novels are consciously artificial in both form and content. She never had a desire to be a realistic novelist or to write the "long novel"; she said she grew bored writing her only lengthy novel, *The Mandelbaum Gate*, because of its length. Rather, she claimed to speak in a "kind of shorthand" in which the narrative voice is curiously impersonal. Not surprisingly, in several novels, among them *Not to Disturb* and *The Driver's Seat*, she experimented with her own version of the New Novel. In Spark's fiction, however, unlike that of many of the antinovelists, all details, no matter how arbitrary they at first appear, are ultimately significant. In fact, a word that appears throughout her statements about fiction and in her novels is "economy." In *The Takeover*, the narrator mentions the "intuitive artistic sense of economy" that characterizes the creative person, and Spark emphasized her belief that the artist should carefully select only the most appropriate details in order to create meaning.

At the same time, Spark held the belief that it is "bad manners to inflict emotional involvement on the reader"; in her novels, the narrators' witty detachment from the subject matter signifies Spark's goal of creating art that remains distanced from the human suffering it presents. Literature, according to Spark, should not continue to sympathize with the victims of violence and tyranny; art should instead abandon sentimental depictions of the human condition so that it can "ruthlessly mock" the forces that cause the individual to suffer. Spark asserted that art needs "less emotion and more intelligence" and should aspire to become an art of satire and ridicule. The world, for Spark, is essentially absurd, and "the rhetoric of our time should persuade us to contemplate the ridiculous nature of the reality before us, and teach us to mock it."

THE COMFORTERS

Spark's first novel, *The Comforters*, reflects the two pivotal experiences of her life: her conversion to Roman Catholicism and her change as a writer from poet to novelist. Spark said that to overcome her aesthetic skepticism about the novel form, she needed "to write a novel about somebody writing a novel." In addition, she believed that *The Comforters* resulted from the "complete reorganization" of her mind that followed her religious conversion and that its theme is "a convert and a kind of psychic upheaval." Caroline Rose, the novel's central character, is in the process of coming to terms with both these issues. A recent convert to Catholicism who dislikes many of her fellow Catholics, Caroline is writing a book called *Form in the Modern Novel* and trying to understand why she has begun to overhear a disembodied "novelist," complete with typewriter, who is writing a novel about her and her friends.

The Comforters is about the battle between the author and her characters, a battle in which Caroline struggles to preserve her free will in the face of the novelist's desire to control the events of the story. Caroline finds the experience of being "written into" someone else's narrative painful, just as her friend Laurence Manders protests that "I dislike being a character in your novel" when he discovers that Caroline is writing fiction that includes the story of their relationship. Caroline believes that it is her "duty" to "hold up the action" of the novel, to "spoil" it,

and she asserts her right to make her own decisions, finding, however, that this is usually impossible; the predetermined "plot" of the novelist prevails.

Caroline remains unaware, however, that she in turn is capable of affecting the novel as it is being written. The narrator admits that Caroline's "remarks" continue to interfere with the book and that she does not realize her "constant influence" on the story's development. From Caroline's perspective, she has only partial knowledge of the plot, and she complains that the voices she overhears only give her "small crazy fragments" of a novel in which there may be other characters whom she does not know. In this sense, Caroline is a surrogate for Spark the novelist, a character who "discovers" the plot, as does its creator, while it is being written. As a result, *The Comforters* concludes with Caroline leaving London to write a novel that apparently will be *The Comforters*.

Spark would appear to be working out both the technique and the morality of writing fiction in her first novel. Caroline's fascination with "form in the modern novel" is also Spark's fascination, and Spark writes a story about the problems involved in writing a story: *The Comforters* is about the struggle between the novelist's will to impose form and the continued growth and development of the characters, who begin to become independent entities in the narrative, insisting on the right to break free of the restraints of plot and situation. One of the reasons Caroline Rose gives for opposing the novelist is that Caroline "happens to be a Christian"; Spark, as a Catholic, is uneasy with the idea of the novelist "playing God" and depriving her characters of choice.

The Comforters is also about Catholicism and the recent convert's attempts to find an identity as a Catholic. Georgina Hogg, the Catholic in the novel whom Caroline particularly despises, symbolizes Caroline's (and Spark's) reservations about individual Catholics. These reservations are not, it should be emphasized, about Catholicism as a religion. Rather, Mrs. Hogg represents a Catholicism that, in the hands of a certain type of individual, becomes simply dogma. Mrs. Hogg, who lacks insight or any true feeling about her religion, uses her sense of self-righteousness to impinge on the people around her. In the novel, she is called a "sneak," a "subtle tyrant," and a "moral blackmailer," and she is indeed guilty of all these accusations. At one point in the story, Caroline decides that Mrs. Hogg is "not a real-life character . . . merely a gargoyle"; she is so lacking in identity that she literally "disappears" when there are no other people around to perceive her existence. As several characters observe, Georgina Hogg "has no private life," a phrase that ironically underscores her lack of substance as a character and as a Catholic.

Mrs. Hogg's lack of identity is a major theme of the novel and a problem that several other characters share. Helena Manders, when she has a sudden sense of how "exhilarating" it is to be herself, actually perceives her personality as belonging to someone else. Eleanor Hogarth, as Caroline realizes, has completely lost contact with her true personality because she has for so long been satisfied with mimicking others, adopting other roles to play. Caroline's auditory hallucinations are another aspect of this problem, for she feels that her free will as an individual is being taken from her: Is she Caroline Rose, or simply a character in someone else's novel? At the same time, she is obsessed with the identity of what she calls the "typing ghost," at one point making a list titled *"Possible identity"* in which she speculates about who the typist-novelist may be—Satan, a hermaphrodite, a woman, or a Holy Soul in Purgatory.

The characters' lack of identity is related to their isolation and inability to communicate with one another. "Is the world," asks Caroline, "a lunatic asylum then? Are we all courteous maniacs discreetly making allowances for everyone else's derangement?" Although she rejects this idea, *The Comforters* certainly depicts a world in which individuals search for an identity while remaining locked into a very subjective set of preconceptions about everything external to them. The way out of this trap, at least for Caroline, is to write a novel, the novel that Spark has actually written. *The Comforters* represents Spark's successful confrontation with and resolution of the issues of Catholicism, creativity, and the novel as a genre. Her interest in the novel as a form and the process of creating fictions continued throughout her career as a novelist.

THE PRIME OF MISS JEAN BRODIE

In an interview, Spark said that the eponymous protagonist of *The Prime of Miss Jean Brodie* represents "completely unrealised potentialities," a descriptive phrase that reflects the same ambiguity with which she is treated in the novel. The story of an Edinburgh schoolmistress and her effects on the lives of six of her pupils, *The Prime of Miss Jean Brodie* concentrates on the relationship between Jean Brodie and Sandy Stranger, the student who eventually "betrays" her. Like many other characters in Spark's fiction, Miss Brodie begins to confuse fact and fiction, and it is when Sandy perceives that her teacher has decided that Rose Stanley must begin an affair with art teacher Teddy Lloyd that Sandy realizes that Jean Brodie is no longer playing a game or advancing a theory: "Miss Brodie meant it." As David Lodge notes in his article on the novel in *The Novelist at the Crossroads* (1971), Sandy and Jenny intuitively understand when their fiction, a made-up correspondence between Miss Brodie and music teacher Gordon Lowther, should be buried and forgotten; unlike her students, Jean Brodie does not know when fantasies should be discarded.

In addition to seeing herself as an artist figure who can manipulate the lives of her students and lovers, Jean Brodie is guilty, in Sandy's eyes, of serious religious and political errors. Although she has not turned to religion at the time, a very young Sandy is frightened by her vision of all the "Brodie set" in a line headed by their teacher "in unified compliance to the destiny of Miss Brodie, as if God had willed them to birth for that purpose." Later, Sandy is horrified to discover that her former teacher "thinks she is Providence" and that she can see the beginning and the end of all "stories." Jean Brodie's lack of guilt over any of her actions results from her assurance that "God was on her side"; she elects herself to grace with an "exotic suicidal enchantment" that drives her to the excesses that eventually result in her forced retirement.

Jean Brodie's view of herself as "above the common moral code," a phrase she applies to Rose, her chosen surrogate for an affair with Teddy Lloyd, is related to her political views as well. An early admirer of Italian premier Benito Mussolini and German chancellor Adolf Hitler whom Sandy later characterizes as a "born fascist," she sees herself as duty-bound to shape the personalities and the destinies of the young girls around her. "You are mine," she says to her "set," whom she has chosen to receive what she calls the "fruits of her prime," which will remain with the girls "always," a prophecy that is partially true.

The complexity of *The Prime of Miss Jean Brodie* lies in the fact that Jean Brodie is not simply a villainous character who oversteps her bounds as a teacher and begins to exert a potentially corruptive force on the young people entrusted to her. Although she flirts with fascism (after the war she calls Hitler "rather naughty"), she at the same time encourages a fierce individualism in her chosen students, who, as the headmistress of the Marcia Blaine School for Girls sadly learns, are totally lacking in "team spirit." She makes good her promise to "put old heads on young shoulders" and creates the "capacity for enthusiasm" for knowledge that remains with several of her students for life. The lecture to her girls on her theory of education—"It means a leading out. To me education is a leading out of what is already there in the pupil's soul. . . . Never let it be said that I put ideas into your heads"—is, like the portrait of Jean Brodie that Spark presents in the novel, open to several interpretations. Although in the later years of her prime, Miss Brodie does attempt to put "ideas" into the girls' heads, at the same time she bequeaths to her students a knowledge of and sensitivity to art, culture, and ideas that would have been impossible in a more conventional educational situation.

Just as *The Prime of Miss Jean Brodie* is about "unrealised potentialities," Miss Brodie also communicates to her students a knowledge of the unlimited potential inherent in all experience. In her late thirties, Jenny Gray has an experience that reawakens a memory of her "sense of the hidden possibility in all things" that she felt as an eleven-year-old student under the tutelage of Jean Brodie. More important, however, is the teacher's influence on Sandy Stranger. In his book on Spark, Derek Stanford says that "truth, for Muriel Spark, implies rejection," and Sandy laments in the novel that she has had nothing, particularly in the religious realm, to react against or reject. Jean Brodie finally provides this catalyst, and Sandy's decision to "put a stop" to her results from a variety of reasons: her moral indignation over Miss Brodie's "plans" for Rose and Joyce Emily, sexual jealousy of Teddy Lloyd's continued infatuation with her teacher, and her awakening sense of Christian morals.

As an adult, however, Sandy acknowledges that Jean Brodie was her most important formative influence and in a sense responsible for the course her life has taken. Her conversion to Catholicism and taking of the veil are the result of her affair with Teddy Lloyd, an affair she instigates in order to subvert Jean Brodie's plans. Although Spark does not indicate the exact subject of the psychological treatise that has made Sandy famous, other than the fact that it concerns the nature of "moral perception," its title, "The Transfiguration of the Commonplace," reveals that it in some way deals with the mind's ability to alter everyday reality. Clearly, this topic owes a debt to Jean Brodie's communication to her students of the endless "possibilities" that surrounded them and is a reflection of Jean Brodie's constantly changing nature in the novel. The narrator observes that, unlike her colleagues, Miss Brodie is in a "state of fluctuating development"; like her students, her "nature was growing under their eyes, as the girls themselves were under formation." One element of Jean Brodie's "prime" is her nonstatic personality, and the problem, of course, is the direction in which the changes take place. As the narrator notes, "the principles governing the end of her prime would have astonished herself at the beginning of it."

In *The Prime of Miss Jean Brodie*, Spark is at the height of her powers as a novelist, and nowhere else in her fiction is she more in control of her subject. The flash-forwards that occur throughout the novel cause the reader to concentrate on the characters' motivations and interrelationships rather than on any intricacies of the plot, and Spark makes use of the principle of "economy" that she so values on almost every page, providing only the most telling details of the story while refraining, for the most part, from any authorial interpretation. In fact, the idea of economy is an important thematic element in the book. Sandy is first fascinated by the economy of Jean Brodie's fusing her tales of her dead lover, Hugh, with her current associations with Gordon Lowther and Teddy Lloyd, and later she is angered and intrigued by the economy of the art teacher's paintings, which make Jean Brodie's students resemble their teacher. When Sandy betrays Miss Brodie to the headmistress, she uses this principle after concluding that "where there was a choice of various courses the most economical was the best." Both in form and style, *The Prime of Miss Jean*

Brodie shows Spark utilizing her own "intuitive artistic sense of economy."

THE DRIVER'S SEAT

In *The Driver's Seat*, Spark writes her revisionist version of the New Novel. She said that she disagreed with the philosophical tenets of the antinovel, and she adopted many of its techniques to prove the invalidity of its philosophy. Although *The Driver's Seat* initially appears to be filled with randomly chosen, objectively described phenomena, ultimately the novel denies the entire concept of contingency. As Frank Kermode has observed, Spark's fiction is not about any kind of "brutal chaos" but rather presents a "radically non-contingent reality to be dealt with in purely novelistic terms." Every event, every description becomes, in the light of the ending of *The Driver's Seat*, significant.

The novel concerns a young woman named Lise who leaves her home in northern Europe to travel south. Spark carefully fails to specify which cities are involved in order to create the same impersonal, anonymous air in the novel that characterizes Lise's world in general. The purpose of her journey is to find a man to murder her, and in this story Spark inverts the typical thriller: The "victim" relentlessly stalks her murderer and finally "forces" him to act. Lise, who has abandoned the sterile loneliness of her former existence symbolized by her apartment, which "looks as if it were uninhabited," takes control of her life for the first time and decides to take the most dramatic final step possible. In the opening scene, she shouts at a salesgirl who attempts to sell her a dress made of nonstaining fabric because, having already decided that she is to be stabbed to death, she wishes for clothing that will provide the more lurid touch of bloodstains. At the conclusion of the scene, Lise again shouts at the salesgirl "with a look of satisfaction at her own dominance over the situation," and the remainder of the novel is about Lise's carefully planned murder and the trail of information and clues she leaves for Interpol all across Europe.

Unlike Caroline Rose in *The Comforters*, whose response to being a character in a novel is to write a novel about characters in a novel, Lise actually wrests control of the plot from the narrator, who is forced to admit ignorance of Lise's thoughts and intentions. "Who knows her thoughts? Who can tell?" asks the narrator, who is even unsure as to whether or not Lise tints her hair or the reason she attracts so much attention. As a result, the narrator is forced to give only external information, but this information is, as the reader begins to realize, all pertinent to the outcome of the novel. Only at the conclusion, after Lise's death, does the narrator seem privy to the interior knowledge accessible to the omniscient author.

One of the most important themes in *The Driver's Seat* is, as in many other Spark novels, the inability of people to communicate with one another. In the majority of the conversations, no logical connections are made between the participants, who remain isolated in their own worlds of obsessional concerns. It would even appear that the more sane the individual, the less likely it is that any communication can take place. Instead, it is the more psychotic characters who are capable of nonverbal, intuitive understanding. Lise realizes immediately, as does Richard, that he is the man who is capable of murdering her, and he initially avoids any conversation with her. The three men who do converse with her—Bill, Carlos, and the sickly looking man on the plane—are not, as she phrases it, "her type"; this is because they attempt to communicate verbally with her. As Lise says of the salesman in the department store, "Not my man at all. He tried to get familiar with me. . . . The one I'm looking for will recognize me right away for the woman I am, have no fear of that." The verb "sense," which is used several times in the novel, signifies the subterranean, psychotic apprehension of other people that is the only perception taking place in *The Driver's Seat*.

Although most of Mrs. Friedke's conversations with Lise have the same illogical, uncommunicative structure that characterizes the other dialogues, Mrs. Friedke does momentarily enter Lise's realm of supernatural perception. She buys a paper knife for her nephew Richard similar to the one Lise decides against purchasing at the beginning of her journey, and this gift becomes the weapon Richard uses to murder Lise. She also prophetically insists that "you and my nephew are meant for each other . . . my dear, you are the person for my nephew." It is at this point that Lise reveals how she will recognize the man for whom she is searching. In a phrase that tells a great deal about her past life, she says that she will know him not as a feeling of "presence" but as a "lack of absence."

Malcolm Bradbury has observed that Spark's fiction "conveys significant absences, a feeling of omission, and so has considerable resemblances to a good deal of contemporary art, including the *nouveau roman*." Lise's search for a "lack of absence" is a statement about the emptiness and lack of meaning in her own existence and the type of novel Spark has chosen to write about her: The form of the antinovel is used to comment both on the psychosis of the main character and on the failure of the New Novel to deal with the ultimate significance of phenomena. In the New Novel, the present tense frequently signifies the meaninglessness and ephemerality of events; in *The Driver's Seat*, the present tense is used to create a world of terrifying inevitability in which the smallest details become integral elements in Lise's carefully plotted death.

Spark called *The Driver's Seat* "a study, in a way, of self-destruction" but also admitted that the novel was impossible for her to describe. She said that she became so frightened while writing the story that she was forced to enter a hospital in order to complete it. The fear the novel inspired in her—and many readers—cannot be explained simply by Lise's self-destructiveness; Lise's decision to assert herself, to play God with her life independent of any control by the novelist or a higher power, also contributes to the frightening dimension of the novel. Spark, who expressed a belief that "events are providentially ordered," creates a character who decides to become providence and the author of her own story; unlike Jean Brodie, who mistakenly thinks she can see the "beginning and the end" of all stories, Lise successfully orchestrates the novel's conclusion.

LOITERING WITH INTENT

In *Loitering with Intent*, Spark's heroine, novelist Fleur Talbot, frequently quotes from Benvenuto Cellini's *The Autobiography of Benvenuto Cellini* (wr. 1558-1562): "All men . . . who have done anything of merit, or which verily has a semblance of merit . . . should write the tale of their life with their own hand." *Loitering with Intent* is the fictional autobiography of its "author," Fleur Talbot, and a meditation by Spark on her own career as a novelist; it is, in addition, a meditation on the creative process and the relationship between fiction and autobiography. Spark shows that she has come a long way from her early distrust of the novel: *Loitering*

with Intent is a paean to the artistic, fiction-making sensibility. Although the habitual tension between life and art and the danger of confusing the two are still present in this novel, Spark comes down firmly on the side of art, defending it against individuals who would seek to "steal" its myth and pervert its truth.

Fleur Talbot frequently comments on "how wonderful it is to be an artist and a woman in the twentieth century." At the conclusion, she admits that she has been "loitering with intent"; that is, she has used her observations about the people and events around her as fictional material, taking joy in both the comic and the tragic occurrences in the lives of the individuals who become characters in her own "autobiography." "I rejoiced in seeing people as they were," she says, and the word "rejoice" occurs many times in the novel as Fleur repeatedly uses Cellini's phrase, saying that she "went on her way rejoicing." In her later life she is accused by her friend Dottie of "wriggling out of real life," but Fleur makes no apologies for the way in which she handles the relationship between her life and her creativity; instead, *Loitering with Intent* calls into question the use "real" people make of the fictions of others.

Fleur becomes the secretary of Sir Quentin Oliver, head of the spurious Autobiographical Association he has formed in order to bring people together to compose their memoirs. Like the character of Warrender Chase in the novel Fleur is in the process of completing, Sir Quentin begins to exert a devastating influence on the association's members, psychologically manipulating them not for blackmailing purposes but for the enjoyment of pure power. Instead of encouraging them to fictionalize their autobiographies, as Fleur attempts to do, Sir Quentin begins to fictionalize their lives with tragic results. Fleur says,

> I was sure . . . that Sir Quentin was pumping something artificial into their real lives instead of on paper. Presented fictionally, one could have done something authentic with that poor material. But the inducing them to express themselves in life resulted in falsity.

Fiction, when acknowledged as fiction, can help the individual to comprehend reality more clearly, as Fleur notes when she tells a friend that she will have to write several more chapters of *Warrender Chase* before she will be able to understand the events of the Autobiographical Association. In the same way, she says that one can better know one's friends by picturing them imaginatively in various situations. Sir Quentin, however, inserts "fictions," frequently stories and events taken from Fleur's novel, into the lives of the association's members.

The relationship between Sir Quentin and Fleur symbolizes the battle between life and art that is waged in *Loitering with Intent*, for Fleur accuses him of "using, stealing" her myth, "appropriating the spirit" of her legend, and trying to "live out the story" she creates in *Warrender Chase*. Although she believes that it is wrong for Sir Quentin to take her "creation" from her, she in turn believes that he may well be a creation of hers, particularly when he begins to resemble her character Warrender Chase as the story progresses. She takes pride in saying that she could almost "have invented" Sir Quentin and that at times she feels as if she *has* invented him; in fact, this feeling so persists that she begins to wonder if it is Warrender Chase who is the "real man" on whom she has partly based the fictional character of Sir Quentin. From Fleur's point of view, this kind of inversion of life and art is necessary and productive for the artistic process and is not dangerous because it results in a bona fide fiction that acknowledges itself as fiction; Sir Quentin's appropriation of her "myth," however, is dangerous because he refuses to acknowledge the fictiveness of his creation. One irony of this situation is editor Revisson Doe's refusal to publish *Warrender Chase* because it too closely resembles the activities of the Autobiographical Association: Sir Quentin's literal and figurative theft of Fleur's novel almost results in its never becoming a work of art available to the public.

The relationship between life and art has another dimension in *Loitering with Intent*. In this novel, Spark is also concerned with the psychic potential of the artist, the ability of the creative imagination to foresee the future in the process of creating fictions. Just as Fleur remarks that writing a novel or imagining her friends in fictional situations helps her to understand them better, so does the artist often predict the future while constructing a work of art. At the end of the novel, Dottie admits that Fleur had "foreseen it all" in *Warrender Chase*, and the events of *Loitering with Intent* do bear an eerie resemblance to the plot of Fleur's first novel. In her book on Emily Brontë, Spark says that "poetic experience is . . . such that it may be prophetic." In *Loitering with Intent*, Fleur uses reality as raw material for her novel, while Sir Quentin attempts to use art to tamper with the lives of real people; at another level, however, Fleur's poetic imagination perceives and creates future events.

Loitering with Intent also permits Spark to look back on her life as a novelist and defend many of her fictional techniques. Fleur's philosophy of art is, to a great degree, Spark's philosophy, and Fleur's descriptions and explanations of her craft could easily be addressed by Spark directly to her readers. Like Spark, Fleur is a believer in economy in art, observing "how little one needs . . . to convey the lot, and how a lot of words . . . can convey so little." Fleur does not believe in authorial statements about the motives of her characters, or in being "completely frank" with the reader; in fact, "complete frankness is not a quality that favours art." She defends herself against the charge of writing novels that are called "exaggerated" by critics and states that her fiction presents "aspects of realism." The novel, she believes, is not a documentary transcription of reality but should always seek to transform its subject. "I'm an artist, not a reporter," she informs her readers.

Fleur also answers the critics who in the past have accused Spark of treating her material in a flippantly detached manner. She says that she treats the story of Warrender Chase with a "light and heartless hand," which is her method when giving a "perfectly serious account of things" because to act differently would be hypocritical: "It seems to me a sort of hypocrisy for a writer to pretend to be undergoing tragic experiences when obviously one is sitting in relative comfort with a pen and paper or before a typewriter." At one point in the novel, Spark even challenges the "quality" of her readers, having her narrator remark that she hopes the readers of her novels are of "good quality" because "I wouldn't like to think of anyone cheap reading my books."

The most significant theme of *Loitering with Intent*, however, is joy: the joy the artist takes in the everyday reality that contributes to the imaginative act and the euphoria the artist feels in the act of creation. Spark has indeed traveled a great distance from her early suspicions of the fiction-making process and of the novel as form.

THE ONLY PROBLEM

In three novels published after *Loitering with Intent—The Only Problem, A Far Cry from Kensington*, and *Symposium*—Spark continues to play variations of her characteristic themes. *The Only Problem* centers on the problem of evil: How can a just God "condone the unspeakable sufferings of the world"? Spark's protagonist, Harvey Gotham, an eccentric Canadian millionaire, wrestles with this question in a treatise on the biblical book of Job. Harvey's study is repeatedly interrupted as a consequence of the escapades of his young wife, Effie, who joins a terrorist group, kills a French policeman, and is herself eventually shot and killed by the police during a raid on a terrorist hideout. The intrusion of these events helps Harvey to appreciate the ultimate inscrutability of the human condition.

In this novel, Spark again celebrates the fiction-making process: In contrast to scholars who attempt to rationalize Job's story or abstract the philosophical issues from it, Harvey recognizes the unique power of the story itself. *The Only Problem* is thus a "commentary" on the book of Job that remains true to the spirit of the original.

A FAR CRY FROM KENSINGTON

A Far Cry from Kensington, like *Loitering with Intent* and *The Girls of Slender Means*, draws on Spark's experiences in post-World War II London. *A Far Cry from Kensington* is a retrospective first-person narrative; from the vantage point of the 1980's, the narrator recalls events that took place in 1954 and 1955. She was then in her late twenties, a war widow who had married at age eighteen a man whom she had met only a month before. Throughout the narrative other characters address her as Mrs. Hawkins (her married name) rather than by her given name, and she is regarded as a reliable confidant— in part, she suggests, because she was then rather fat. As Mrs. Hawkins loses weight, she acquires a first name, Nancy, and gradually becomes Nancy in her own eyes and those of others. Some of her neighbors and office peers worry that she is ill and wasting away, especially the superstitious war refugee Wanda, who believes there is a curse on her. William, a medical student who lives in the flat next to Nancy, begins to see her as a woman, not

merely as a confidant and a doer of good works. Nancy and William begin an affair and ultimately get married.

As Mrs. Hawkins loses weight and gains a personal life of her own, she is less willing to fill the needs of others. She says to the reader,

> My advice to any woman who earns the reputation of being capable, is not to demonstrate her ability too much. You give advice; you say, do this, do that, I think I've got you a job, don't worry, leave it to me. All that, and in the end you feel spooky, empty, haunted. And if you then want to wriggle out of so much responsibility, the people around you are outraged. You have stepped out of your role. It makes them furious.

Spark shows how the transformation of Mrs. Nancy Hawkins evokes resentment from those around her for services not rendered, services others never should have expected.

The backdrop of the story is the London publishing scene, especially its dubious fringe. The narrator's encounters with a variety of publishers and literary hangers-on are deftly sketched; also figuring in the plot are devotees of "radionics," a pseudoscience employing a device similar to Wilhelm Reich's orgone box. In particular, Mrs. Hawkins jousts with a hack writer and an adept of radionics, Hector Bartlett, whom she dubs a *pisseur de copie*. Initially, this conflict might seem to be merely a matter of aesthetics, and Bartlett—with his absurd pretensions and truly awful writing—merely a figure of comedy, yet he is shown to be an agent of evil, responsible for the death of a troubled woman. Unsettled by this mixture of nostalgia and satire, light comedy and metaphysical probing, the reader is never allowed to become comfortable. Evidently, this is Spark's intention.

SYMPOSIUM

Symposium, which focuses on a dinner party in the Islington district of London, offers a similarly unsettling mixture for which the reader is duly prepared by an epigraph from Plato's *Symposium* that suggests the interdependence of comedy and tragedy. The novel features an omniscient narrator who tells of the robbery of two of the dinner guests prior to the beginning of the main story, then injects flashbacks and parallel happenings as the dinner, which constitutes the body of the story, progresses. Spark's technique owes something to that used by Virginia Woolf in *Mrs. Dalloway* (1925); her juxtaposition of a gala dinner party and a murder that is occurring simultaneously also remind the reader of W. H. Auden's 1939 poem, "Musée des Beaux Arts."

At the beginning of the novel, many characters are introduced and described; some prove to be unimportant and are never mentioned again. Spark seems to be deliberately confusing the reader by obscuring the main focus of the novel, perhaps in imitation of real-life events, in which often the most important elements are initially obscure and only become clear with time. Neither the guests nor those who serve them are what they seem. The butler and his attractive young assistant, an American graduate student who has been employed by several of the guests and is admired for working his way through school, are members of a burglary ring that observes houses and files away conversations spoken at society parties about valuable possessions. Among the guests are a newly married young couple; the bride is a fresh, appealing Scottish girl who is so innocent and kind she appears to be too good for this world. In time the reader will come to see this young lady in a different light.

As *Symposium* progresses, the plot grows denser and darker, although an overlay of superficial dinner conversation pervades the novel. There is talk of the "evil eye" (reminiscent of the occult machinations of Hector Bartlett in *A Far Cry from Kensington*). The concept is absurd, and yet as the narrative develops there is evidence that one of the women present at the party genuinely possesses this maleficent power. In this novel, more than ever, Spark manipulates her characters with detachment: The reader is always aware that this is a performance. If Spark's novels are coolly ironic entertainments, however, they are also oblique parables that explore with obsessive persistence the nature of evil.

Reality and Dreams

Crises relating to aging, love, and money fill *Reality and Dreams*, which tells the story of film director Tom Richards, who at the beginning of the novel is in a Catholic hospital, recovering from a fall he took from a camera crane on the set of the motion picture he was directing. As his bedside visitors keep reminding him, he is lucky to be alive. Richards moves between lucidity and dream during his recovery, confusing his life with the action of

his film. He makes a vow to himself and gives orders to his lawyer that reflect this confusion. Richards's life is already a complex one, even without the influx of dream-induced ideas, because of complicated family relations and a somewhat open marriage.

After a difficult recovery, Richards is able to resume the director's chair on his film, *The Hamburger Girl*. He had a glimpse, in a recreational park, of a plain-looking French girl bent over a stove in cramped quarters, cooking hamburgers. The image had a strangely powerful effect on him, leading not only to the movie but also to the vow he made during his recovery, which he remembers only intermittently.

As important as his directorial and authorial duties are, family matters soon come to take over Richards's life, involving his wife, Claire, and his two daughters. The beautiful Cora is his daughter by his previous marriage. His daughter with Claire is the unattractive, difficult, and socially maladroit Marigold.

Matters of economics, too, come to dominate events. While Richards is in recovery, several members of his extended family are "made redundant," or laid off from their jobs. As Richards resumes active life, the made-redundant individuals find their ways into his schedule, sometimes seeking help. Richards himself makes some of the actors in his employ redundant, and then begins to sense that he, himself, has become redundant. When Marigold decides to undertake the writing of a book about redundancy and then mysteriously disappears, Richards reaches a crisis point in his life, although he only partially realizes it. Marigold's disappearance makes headlines. To their surprise, her absence forces the wandering, impulsive Richards and his wife to reassess their lives.

In *Reality and Dreams*, love and money seem to be inseparable topics. Fear of their loss is paralleled by similar fears about aging. While Richards never acknowledges these fears, he dwells on the notion that the century itself has grown old and frequently repeats lines of a dour nature from the poetry of T. S. Eliot.

Reality and Dreams lacks some of the inspired invention of Spark's earlier novels, but it has compelling complexity, with characters who lift themselves off the page despite the short shrift Spark gives their outward appearances or even their inward thoughts. Spark's motif of the individual ambitious to control others, often through writing, appears in Richards himself, who has thoughts of God when aloft in his treacherously dangerous crane and who keeps trying to shape reality to suit the vision that has arisen from his glimpse of the seemingly quite ordinary "hamburger girl."

AIDING AND ABETTING

Whereas *Reality and Dreams* seems expertly crafted yet less vital than the best of Spark's novels, *Aiding and Abetting* is a vigorous work that embodies a number of familiar motifs while striking into fresh territory. The action of the novel circles around a quartet of unusual characters, two of them having distinct criminal pasts. These two characters are based on real-life personalities, although Spark has fictionalized their lives.

The seventh earl of Lucan, who went by the name "Lucky" Lucan, disappeared from view on November 7, 1974, the day his wife was taken to the hospital with a severe head wound and their nanny was found murdered and bundled into a mail sack. Wanted on charges of murder and attempted murder, Lucan managed to evade capture for a quarter century. Eventually he was officially pronounced dead, although miscellaneous unconfirmed reports had surfaced of his appearance in various parts of the world.

In *Aiding and Abetting*, Lucan shows up in the office of Parisian psychiatrist Dr. Hildegard Wolf, seeking her services. Wolf is startled by his claim to be Lucan, for another man had recently appeared in her office making the same claim. Of similar appearance, this other patient goes under the name of Robert Walker.

Wolf herself has a secret past, having once postured as a holy stigmatic capable of faith healing under the name Beate Pappenheim. She collected money for the assistance of the poor, then absconded with the funds. To Wolf's discomfort, both Lucan and Walker know her secret and threaten to unveil it. It becomes evident that the two men are acting together and are doing so because of their need for money. Although Wolf has difficulty pinpointing their identities, she believes one of them to be the real Lucan, while the other is his double.

Wolf's romantic partner of the previous five years, antiques restorer Jean-Pierre Roget, has known nothing of her past. Learning of it now, he accepts this as he has accepted everything else about his lover. When she sud-

denly disappears, hoping to avoid the exposure threatened by the murderer and his double, Roget suddenly becomes the figure around whom the other characters must operate and with whom they must deal.

As suggested by the title, the giving of assistance to criminals recurs throughout *Aiding and Abetting*. The aristocratic Lucan was appalled by the idea of being brought low by mere civil justice. His friends, of like mind, aided in his concealment and escape in 1974 and assisted with funds during his life on the run. In other countries, Lucan found help from others of aristocratic, antidemocratic leanings; in Mexico, one such friend gave him Walker to act as his double. Walker became Lucan's main source of aid. The two, soon inseparable out of necessity, would come to distrust and hate each other. Roget aids the fugitive Hildegard Wolf/Beate Pappenheim, once given the chance, and he finds himself in the odd position of doing the same for the Lucan and Walker, in finding a solution to the convoluted situation of multiple criminals threatening to expose one another.

While Roget is the character in the novel to devise the solution, Hildegard Wolf remains the central character and main imaginative invention in *Aiding and Abetting*. Although running from her past, she simultaneously embraces it, believing that despite her deceptions she had somehow effected some miracle cures as the "holy stigmatic." Unlike Lucan, who found shelter and safety through his fellow aristocrats, Wolf avoided discovery in a convent in Avila, where she was noted for her devotion.

Consistent with others of Spark's novels in its incisive portrayals, ironies, and religious motifs, *Aiding and Abetting* stands securely on its own, with its exploration of duplicity, greed, and the criminal personality. With its complex symmetries, it ranks among the most rewarding of Spark's novels.

Angela Hague; Isabel Bonnyman Stanley
Updated by Mark Rich

OTHER MAJOR WORKS

SHORT FICTION: *The Go-Away Bird, and Other Stories*, 1958; *Voices at Play*, 1961 (with radio plays); *Collected Stories I*, 1967; *Bang-Bang You're Dead, and Other Stories*, 1981; *The Stories of Muriel Spark*, 1985;

Open to the Public: New and Collected Stories, 1997; *All the Stories*, 2001 (also known as *The Complete Short Stories*).

PLAY: *Doctors of Philosophy*, pr. 1962.

POETRY: *The Fanfarlo, and Other Verse*, 1952; *Collected Poems I*, 1967; *Going Up to Sotheby's, and Other Poems*, 1982; *All the Poems of Muriel Spark*, 2004.

NONFICTION: *Child of Light: A Reassessment of Mary Wollstonecraft Shelley*, 1951 (revised as *Mary Shelley*, 1987); *Emily Brontë: Her Life and Work*, 1953 (with Derek Stanford); *John Masefield*, 1953; *Curriculum Vitae*, 1992 (autobiography); *The Essence of the Brontës: A Compilation with Essays*, 1993.

CHILDREN'S LITERATURE: *The Very Fine Clock*, 1968; *The Small Telephone*, 1993.

EDITED TEXTS: *Tribute to Wordsworth*, 1950 (with Derek Stanford); *My Best Mary: The Selected Letters of Mary Shelley*, 1953 (with Stanford); *The Brontë Letters*, 1954 (also known as *The Letters of the Brontës: A Selection*); *Letters of John Henry Newman*, 1957 (with Stanford).

BIBLIOGRAPHY

Apostolou, Fotini E. *Seduction and Death in Muriel Spark's Fiction*. Westport, Conn.: Greenwood Press, 2001. Examines social structures that have limiting and destructive effects on characters as they operate in Spark's novels.

Bold, Alan. *Muriel Spark*. London: Methuen, 1986. Discusses the relationship between Spark's personal background and the development of her characters, particularly links between her religious experience and the religious facets of her fiction. Presents some biographical information on Spark and then discusses her novels in chronological order. Includes an extensive bibliography.

Cheyette, Bryan. *Muriel Spark*. Jackson: University Press of Mississippi, 2001. Critical study examines Spark's novels in terms of her life, with special focus on her conversion to Catholicism.

Hynes, Joseph, ed. *Critical Essays on Muriel Spark*. New York: G. K. Hall, 1992. Comprehensive collection of reviews, essays, and excerpts from books on Spark's fiction presents discussion by both her detractors and her admirers. Includes a survey and critique of criticism of her works.

McQuillan, Martin, ed. *Theorizing Muriel Spark: Gender, Race, Deconstruction*. New York: Palgrave, 2002. Wide-ranging collection of readable essays presents discussion of Spark's characters, themes, and social constructs. Includes an interview with Spark and a bibliography on her works.

Maley, Willy. *Muriel Spark for Starters*. Edinburgh: Capercaillie Books, 2008. Provides an introductory survey of Spark's entire literary output as well as information about her life. Designed for the general reader.

Montgomery, Benilde. "Spark and Newman: Jean Brodie Reconsidered." *Twentieth Century Literature* 43 (Spring, 1997): 94-106. Insightful essay discusses the influence of John Henry Newman on the tension between Jean Brodie and Sandy Stranger in *The Prime of Miss Jean Brodie*, arguably Spark's most enduring novel.

Page, Norman. *Muriel Spark*. New York: St. Martin's Press, 1990. Provides biographical information as well as criticism and interpretation of Spark's works. Includes bibliography and index.

Randisi, Jennifer Lynn. *On Her Way Rejoicing: The Fiction of Muriel Spark*. Washington, D.C.: Catholic University of America Press, 1991. Argues that Spark's vision is metaphysical, combining piety and satire, deception and anagogical truth. Discusses the tension between mysticism and satire in Spark's novels and stories.

Walker, Dorothea. *Muriel Spark*. Boston: Twayne, 1988. Informative study examines the main themes of Spark's work, with emphasis given to the wit and humor of her characters. Includes an extensive bibliography.

CHRISTINA STEAD

Born: Rockdale, New South Wales, Australia; July
    17, 1902
Died: Sydney, New South Wales, Australia; March
    31, 1983
Also known as: Christina Ellen Stead

PRINCIPAL LONG FICTION

Seven Poor Men of Sydney, 1934
The Beauties and Furies, 1936
House of All Nations, 1938
The Man Who Loved Children, 1940, 1965
For Love Alone, 1944
Letty Fox: Her Luck, 1946
A Little Tea, a Little Chat, 1948
The People with the Dogs, 1952
Dark Places of the Heart, 1966 (also known as
    Cotter's England)
The Little Hotel, 1973
Miss Herbert: The Suburban Wife, 1976
I'm Dying Laughing: The Humourist, 1986

OTHER LITERARY FORMS

Christina Stead began her career with a volume of
short stories, *The Salzburg Tales* (1934), and she contributed short stories to both literary and popular magazines. A posthumous collection, *Ocean of Story: The Uncollected Short Stories of Christina Stead*, was published
in 1985. Her volume *The Puzzleheaded Girl* (1967) is a
collection of four novellas. Her other literary output includes reviews and translations of several novels from
the French. She also edited two anthologies of short stories, one with her husband, William Blake.

ACHIEVEMENTS

Christina Stead is considered to be in the first rank of
Australian novelists; in 1974, she received Australia's
Patrick White Award. One of Stead's novels, *The Man
Who Loved Children*, received particular critical acclaim. Stead resisted critics' attempts to represent her as
a feminist writer, but she has received attention from
feminist critics for her depictions of women constricted
by their social roles.

BIOGRAPHY

Christina Ellen Stead was born in Rockdale, New
South Wales, on July 17, 1902. Her parents were David
George Stead, a naturalist and fisheries economist, and
Ellen Butters Stead. After her mother died of a perfo-
rated appendix when Christina was two years old, her father married Ada Gibbons, a society woman, and they
had six children to whom Stead became big sister. Stead
trained at the Sydney Teachers College, where she became a demonstrator in experimental psychology. As a
public school teacher, she taught abnormal children and
administered psychological tests in the schools. Stead
suffered voice strain, however, and she later saw this as a
symptom of her being unfit for the work. Like Teresa
Hawkins in *For Love Alone*, Stead studied typing and
shorthand to embark on a business career.

In 1928, Stead left Sydney, sailing on the *Oronsay* for
England. She worked as a grain clerk and as a bank clerk
in London and Paris, experiences that became background for her novel about finance, *House of All Nations*. By that time, Stead had met the economist and
writer William Blake (born William Blech), whom she
married in 1952. Stead settled in the United States from
1937 to 1946, publishing several novels and working for
a time as a writer with the Metro-Goldwyn-Mayer film
studio in Hollywood. At the end of World War II, Stead
returned to Europe with Blake, living in various places
on the Continent and returning to England when she
feared that she was losing her feel for the English language. In 1968, Stead's husband died, and a few years
later, in 1974, she returned to live with one of her brothers in Australia. She died in Sydney on March 31, 1983,
at the age of eighty.

ANALYSIS

Christina Stead was preeminently a novelist of character. She identified herself as a psychological writer, involved with the drama of the person. Her stories develop
out of the dynamics of characters asserting their human
energy and vigor and developing their wills. Stead established personality and communicated its energy and vitality through her creation of a distinctive language for

each character. This individuating language is explored in the characters' dialogues with one another (Sam Pollit talking his fantastic baby talk to his children), in their interior monologues (Teresa Hawkins, walking miles to and from work, meditating on her need to find a life beyond the surface social conventions), and in letters (the letter to Letty Fox from her former lover, who wants his money back after she has had an abortion). The language establishes the sense of an individual person with obsessions and characteristic blindnesses. One gets to know the quality of the mind through the texture of the language. As Christopher Ricks has noted of Stead's accomplishment, she re-creates the way people talk to themselves "in the privacy of [their] skulls." Ricks's phrase gives a sense of how intimately and deeply the language belongs to the person: It is in the skull and the bone.

In her novel *Letty Fox*, Stead has Letty sum up her adventures to date by saying, "On s'engage et puis on voit." The statement (roughly translated as "one gets involved and then one sees") is an existentialist one that reconciles what critics see as two forces in Stead's fiction: a preoccupation with character that links Stead to nineteenth century novelists and an analysis of social, psychological, and economic structures behind individual lives that links her to her contemporaries.

The phrase "On s'engage et puis on voit" also sums up Stead's method. First, she immerses the reader in the particular atmosphere of the character's mind and world; only then does she lead the reader to see a significance behind the individual passion. The phrase implies that one cannot see clearly by being disengaged, looking down on the human spectacle with the detachment of an objective physical scientist. Instead, one must become part of the experience, seeing it as a participant, in order to understand its reality. Some of the constant preoccupations of Stead's characters include family, love, marriage, money, and individual power.

THE MAN WHO LOVED CHILDREN

Stead's masterpiece, most critics agree, is her larger-than-life depiction of a family, *The Man Who Loved Children*. Out of print for twenty-five years, the book enjoyed a second life because of a partly laudatory review by the poet Randall Jarrell; Jarrell's review was included as an introduction when the novel was reissued in 1965.

The Man Who Loved Children immerses its readers in the life of the Pollit family, in its swarming, buzzing intimacy. The father, Sam Pollit, is a garrulous idealist who advocates eugenics for the unfit but who fantasizes for himself babies of every race and a harem of wives who would serve his domestic comfort. On the surface, Sam's passions are his humanitarian ideals and his love for his children, but his underlying passion is what Geoffrey Chaucer said women's was—his own way or his own will. Sam is an egotistical child himself; he sees only what he wants to see. His characteristic talk is his overblown, high-sounding rhetoric expressing schemes to right the world and the fanciful, punning baby talk, whining and wheedling, that he uses with the children.

Henny, wife to Sam and stepmother to Louisa, is Sam's compulsive antagonist, worn down with childbearing and the struggle to manage her overextended household. Henny's passion is to survive, to fight dirt and debt and the intermittent sexuality that involves her in continual childbearing. Henny's characteristic talk is insult and denunciation, castigating with graphic details and metaphors the revolting sights, sounds, smells, tastes, and touches that assault her. Stead emphasizes Henny's eyes in descriptions of the fierce eyeballs in her sockets and her mouth in descriptions of her incessantly drinking tea and mouthing insults.

Stead's way of explaining the unbridgeable gap between the minds and sensibilities of the marriage partners is to say that they have no words in common. Sam's abstraction can never communicate with Henny's particularity. They have no words that they understand mutually, and so for most of the book the two characters communicate with each other only through messages relayed by the children or by terse notes concerning household necessities. In spite of that essential gap, a sixth child is conceived and born to the couple during the course of the novel, and the resources of the household are further strained, finally to the breaking point.

What brings the family to destruction is a complex of causes, many of which are fundamentally economic. The death of David Collyer, Henny's once rich father, is a blow to the family's fortunes. The Pollits lose their home, and Henny's creditors no longer expect that her father will pay her debts. Collyer's death also leaves Sam without a political base in his government job, and

Sam's enemies move to oust him. The money crisis is intensified by Sam's refusal to fight for his job. Instead, he retires to their new ramshackle home to do repairs and to play with the children. Sam grandly waits to be exonerated while Henny struggles to keep the family fed and clothed.

Another cause of the breakup of the family is the birth of Sam and Henny's newest baby. Part of the trouble is economic: The new child means more expenses when Henny had promised her money-conscious eldest son Ernie that there would be no more children. The birth also brings an anonymous letter charging falsely that the child is not Sam's because Sam has been away in Malaya for several months. The letter, filled with spite, probably has been sent by one of Henny's disappointed creditors, but it exacerbates the mutual resentment of the couple and drives them closer and closer to serious violence against each other. (The pregnancy not only invades Henny's body and multiplies her worries but it also costs her her lover, who deserts her when he hears of the pregnancy. Henny is more than ever in Sam's power.)

A pivotal character in the fierce struggle between the parents is Louisa, eldest daughter of Sam and stepdaughter of Henny. Louisa's emergence from childhood upsets the hierarchy of the household. The "man who loved children" does not love them when they question his authority and threaten his position as "Sam the Bold," leader of the band of merry children. In retaliation, Sam calls Louisa names from "Loogoobrious" to "Bluebeak." In disputing Sam's ability to make it rain (his cosmic power), Louisa and Ernie—who is quick to jump in with what he has learned in school about evaporation—introduce norms from the world outside the family.

By the end of the novel, the family tears itself apart. Sam is unconsciously comparing himself to Christ and seeing Nature as his bride, while he says that women are "cussed" and need to be "run" and that he will send Henny away and keep the children. When Louisa asks for freedom to be sent to her dead mother's relatives in Harpers Ferry, Sam says that he will never let her leave, that she must not get married but must stay and help him with the children and his work. The quarreling between the parents increases until Louisa thinks that they will kill each other. The quarrels become physical battles, and Henny screams to the children to save her from their

father. In despair, Ernie makes a dummy out of his clothes and hangs himself in effigy. Sam teases and humiliates the children, insisting that they stay up all night and help him boil down a marlin, an image that is reminiscent of Henny, with its staring eye, deep in its socket, and the wound in its vitals.

Louisa sees the two parents as passionate and selfish, inexorably destroying each other and the children, completely absorbed in their "eternal married hate." To save the children, Louisa considers poisoning both parents. Sam provides both the rationale, that the unfit should make room for the fit, and the means, cyanide that he ghoulishly describes as the bringer of death. Louisa succeeds in getting the grains of cyanide into only one large cup of tea when Henny notices what she has done and drinks it, exonerating Louisa and saying "damn you all." Even with Henny dead and Louisa's confession of her plan and its outcome, Sam refuses to believe her and refuses to let her go. Louisa's only escape is to run away, thus seizing her freedom.

The power of *The Man Who Loved Children* derives in part from the archetypal nature of the conflicts—between parents and children for independence; between man and woman, each for his or her own truth and identity; and between parents for their children, their objects of greatest value. The power also results from the particularity of the characterization, the metaphors that Stead employs to communicate the nature of each family member, and the astounding sense of individual language mirroring opposed sensibilities.

LETTY FOX *and* FOR LOVE ALONE

The epigraph to another Stead novel, *Letty Fox*, says that one can get experience only through foolishness and blunders. The method that Letty follows in her adventures puts her in the stream of picaresque heroes; the novel's subtitle, *Her Luck*, makes more sense with reference to the notion of a submission to experience, to one's fate, than it does with reference to the common meaning of "luck" as "good fortune." Letty's "luck" is that she survives and learns something about the ways of the world.

Stead once said that in *For Love Alone*, the novel that preceded *Letty Fox*, she wrote about a young girl of no social background who tries to learn about love, and readers did not understand the story. In *Letty Fox*, she thus gave American readers a story that they could understand: the story of a modern American girl searching for love and trying to obtain status through marriage.

In both novels, the social structure tells young women that they have no valid identity except through the men they marry. In *For Love Alone*, Teresa Hawkins, like her friends, fears becoming an old maid. Even though Letty Fox has had a series of lovers and a series of responsible, interesting jobs, she does not feel validated without the security of marriage. This firmly held conventional belief is belied by Letty's own family situation. Her beloved father, Solander, has a mistress, Persia, with whom he has lived faithfully for many years. The family women wonder how Persia can hold Solander without a paper and without a child. On the other hand, Mathilde, Letty's mother, has the marriage title but little else. She has three daughters—Letty, Jacky, and the much younger Andrea, conceived in a late reconciliation attempt—but Persia has Solander.

Like the picaresque hero, on her own, Letty learns the ways of the world. She truly loves Luke Adams, who tantalizes her with pretended concern for her youth and innocence and fans her fascination with him. She lives for a summer with a married man and has an abortion for which she must repay him. Originally confused by Lucy Headlong's interest in her, Letty refuses a lesbian affair with her. Letty sees a range of choices in the lives of the women around her: from her sister Jacky, in love with an elderly scientist, to her younger sister Andrea, sharing the early maternal experience of her friend.

Letty wants the security of marriage, but the men she knows do not want to make serious commitments. In *For Love Alone*, Teresa remarks on the short season for the husband hunt, with no time for work or extended study. In the marriage market for the comparatively long season of seven years, Letty does not catch a husband, even when her vicious cousin Edwige does.

Except in the matter of marriage, Letty trusts her own responses and takes credit for her own integrity. When her lover Cornelius is about to leave her for his mistress in Europe and his wife, Letty faces him with the truth of relationships from a woman's point of view. She tells Cornelius that she has ambition and looks. She works for men, and she is their friend. She suffers without crying for help and takes responsibility for her life. She sees men run after worthless, shiftless women and honor the formality of marriage when there is no substance to their relationships with them. All these facts might be just part of the injustice of the world, but Cornelius and many other men Letty knows also expect that she should be their lover and yet admit that there is no love involved but only a relationship of mutual convenience. Like the British poet William Blake, Letty sees prostitution as an invention of men who have tried to depersonalize the most intimate relationship between people. Letty affirms the reality of the sexual experience in its intimacy and its bonding.

With all her clear sight and all her independence, however, Letty does not feel safe and validated until she is married to her longtime friend Bill Van Week. Ironically, Letty marries Bill when he has been disinherited by his millionaire father, so the security Letty attains is not financial. In summing up her life to date, Letty does not claim total honesty, but—like a typical picaresque hero—she does claim grit. She says that with her marriage, her journey has begun. Here Stead limits the awareness of her character. At the end of the novel, Letty says that marriage gives her not social position but self-respect. In this retreat, Letty joins the social mainstream but denies her individual past experience. Self-respect is not an award; it is not issued like a diploma or a license. Letty, who may stand up very well to the practical problems of real life with Bill, is by no means liberated, and her awareness is finally limited.

DARK PLACES OF THE HEART

Dark Places of the Heart, which was published in Great Britain as *Cotter's England*, is an exploration of the influence of Nellie Cotter Cook on the people around her—her family, friends, and acquaintances. A central concern is the relationship between Nellie and her brother Tom, a jealous relationship with which Nellie seems obsessed. Like Michael and Catherine Baguenault, the brother-sister pair in *Seven Poor Men of Sydney*, Nellie and Tom seem too close to each other, too intimately attuned to each other's sensibilities. In their battles, Nellie calls Tom a man out of a mirror who weaves women into his life and then eats their hearts away. Tom calls Nellie a spider who tries to suspend a whole human being on a spindly thread of sympathy. Tom also criticizes Nellie's bent for soul saving, saying that it gets people into trouble.

The motif of hunger and starvation runs through the

novel. When Tom brings a chicken to the family home in Bridgehead, no one in the family knows how to cook it. When George goes away to Italy, he writes that Nellie should buy cookery books, a suggestion that she scorns. Seemingly exhibiting a strange kind of hunger, Nellie craves followers who will make her destiny.

Nellie and Tom's battles often center on Tom's relationships with women, which precipitate a tug-of-war between Nellie and Tom for the love of the woman in question. Many allusions and incidents in the novel suggest that Nellie's interest is lesbian. Nellie begins her luring of these women by demanding their friendship and, ultimately, by forcing them to prove their loyalty through death. Such demands literalize the existentialist definition of love, that the lover puts the beloved beyond the value of the world and his or her life, making that beloved the standard of value, the absolute. The demand is messianic, and in this novel the cost is the suicide of Caroline Wooler: After witnessing what seems to be a lesbian orgy, Caroline climbs a building under construction and jumps to her death.

Nellie views Caroline's death as a personal triumph. At the end of the novel, with her husband dead, Nellie goes with the window washer Walter to a temple, a "Nabob villa," where she explores "problems of the unknowable." Like Sam Pollit, who at his worst compared himself to Christ, Nellie Cook is drawn finally to outright mysticism, an interest that combines, in Nellie's case at least, a fascination with death, a craving for a high destiny, and an uncontrollable urge to manipulate other people. It seems that for Stead, the "dark places of the heart" make people dissatisfied with their humanity.

Kate Begnal

OTHER MAJOR WORKS

SHORT FICTION: *The Salzburg Tales*, 1934; *The Puzzleheaded Girl*, 1967; *Ocean of Story: The Uncollected Short Stories of Christina Stead*, 1985.

TRANSLATIONS: *Colour of Asia*, 1955 (of Fernand Gigon's travelogue); *In Balloon and Bathyscaphe*, 1956 (of Auguste Piccard's science memoir); *The Candid Killer*, 1956 (of Jean Giltène's novel).

EDITED TEXTS: *Modern Women in Love*, 1945 (with William Blake); *Great Stories of the South Sea Islands*, 1956.

BIBLIOGRAPHY

Adie, Mathilda. *Female Quest in Christina Stead's "For Love Alone."* Lund, Sweden: Lund University Press, 2004. Examines the quest of Teresa Hawkins in *For Love Alone*, analyzing the character from the perspectives of feminism, postcolonialism, and myth criticism. Also discusses Stead's other novels to trace the development of the female quest theme throughout the author's fiction.

Blake, Ann. *Christina Stead's Politics of Place*. Nedlands: University of Western Australia Press, 1999. Analyzes Stead's novels and short stories in order to describe how the writer creates a sense of place in her work. Includes bibliography and index.

Brydon, Diana. *Christina Stead*. New York: Macmillan, 1987. Provides a thorough examination of all of Stead's novels and discusses the critical reception of Stead's fiction. While admitting that she presents Stead's work from an essentially feminist perspective, Brydon qualifies this stance by examining Stead's fiction as about both sexes in varied social relationships. Includes an extensive bibliography.

Harris, Margaret, ed. *The Magic Phrase: Critical Essays on Christina Stead*. St. Lucia: University of Queensland Press, 2000. Collection of sixteen essays includes some that review Stead's entire career and others that concentrate on individual works. Among the novels discusses are *Seven Poor Men of Sydney* and *The Man Who Loved Children*.

Jarrell, Randall. "An Unread Book." Introduction to *The Man Who Loved Children*, by Christina Stead. New York: Holt, Rinehart and Winston, 1965. Randall, an American poet, provides the first serious and thorough critical examination of Stead's work, incorporating many of the themes on which subsequent critics would enlarge.

Lidoff, Joan. *Christina Stead*. New York: Frederick Ungar, 1982. The earliest full reading of Stead's fiction from a feminist perspective, this book concentrates on *The Man Who Loved Children* and *For Love Alone*. Includes an interview with Stead, a chronology, and an extensive bibliography.

Pender, Anne. *Christina Stead: Satirist*. Altoona, Vic.: Common Ground, 2002. Focuses on Stead's attempt to interpret the history of her own period through satire. Shows the ways in which Stead both uses and reinterprets the conventions of the genre.

Peterson, Teresa. *The Enigmatic Christina Stead: A Provocative Rereading*. Melbourne, Vic.: Melbourne University Press, 2001. Closely examines five novels and a collection of short stories to argue that Stead's work contains a subtext of lesbian sexuality and male homosexuality.

Rowley, Hazel. *Christina Stead: A Biography*. New York: Henry Holt, 1994. Transcends Stead's penchant for privacy to provide a detailed and incisive account of the writer's troubled life and contentious personality. Includes bibliographical references and index.

Williams, Chris. *Christina Stead: A Life of Letters*. Melbourne, Vic.: McPhee Gribble, 1989. Admirable study, the first full-length biography of Stead, depends in large part on previously unpublished materials, including Stead's letters and early drafts of stories, as well as on interviews with Stead's friends and family members.

WALLACE STEGNER

Born: Lake Mills, Iowa; February 18, 1909
Died: Santa Fe, New Mexico; April 13, 1993
Also known as: Wallace Earle Stegner

PRINCIPAL LONG FICTION

Remembering Laughter, 1937
The Potter's House, 1938
On a Darkling Plain, 1940
Fire and Ice, 1941
The Big Rock Candy Mountain, 1943
Second Growth, 1947
The Preacher and the Slave, 1950
A Shooting Star, 1961
All the Little Live Things, 1967
Angle of Repose, 1971
The Spectator Bird, 1976
Recapitulation, 1979
Joe Hill, 1980
Crossing to Safety, 1987

OTHER LITERARY FORMS

Wallace Stegner also published three collections of short fiction, *The Women on the Wall* (1950), *The City of the Living, and Other Stories* (1956), and *Collected Stories of Wallace Stegner* (1990); two biographies, *Beyond the Hundredth Meridian: John Wesley Powell and the Second Opening of the West* (1954) and *The Uneasy Chair: A Biography of Bernard De Voto* (1974); two collections of critical essays, *The Writer in America* (1951) and *On Teaching and Writing Fiction* (2002); a historical monograph, *The Gathering of Zion: The Story of the Mormon Trail* (1964); and three volumes of personal essays on the Western experience, *Wolf Willow: A History, a Story, and a Memory of the Last Plains Frontier* (1962), *The Sound of Mountain Water* (1969), and *Where the Bluebird Sings to the Lemonade Springs: Living and Writing in the West* (1992). Stegner also published a number of edited works, both nonfiction and fiction.

ACHIEVEMENTS

Wallace Stegner would have three distinct audiences after the start of his career: the popular magazine audience, readers interested in modern American literature, and a regional audience interested in the culture and history of the American West. From the 1930's, he published seventy-two short stories, with fifty of them appearing in such magazines as *Harper's*, *Mademoiselle*, *Collier's*, *Cosmopolitan*, *Esquire*, *Redbook*, *Atlantic Monthly*, *Inter-Mountain Review*, and *Virginia Quarterly Review*. Bernard De Voto, Van Wyck Brooks, and Sinclair Lewis recognized his talent early, and De Voto was instrumental in encouraging Stegner to continue writing. Stegner enjoyed a solid critical reputation as a regional American writer concerned largely with the problems and themes of the Western American experience.

Stegner also won numerous honors throughout his

career. He was elected to the American Academy of Arts and Sciences and the National Academy of Arts and Letters, and he was awarded fellowships by Phi Beta Kappa, the Huntington Library, the Center for Advanced Studies in the Behavioral Sciences, and the Guggenheim, Rockefeller, and Wintergreen Foundations. In 1937, he won the Little, Brown Novelette Prize for *Remembering Laughter*. He also won the O. Henry Memorial Award for short stories in 1942, 1948, and 1950, and in 1972 he received the Pulitzer Prize for fiction for his *Angle of Repose*. Other awards for his work include the Houghton Mifflin Life-in-America Award in 1945 and the Commonwealth Club Gold Medal in 1968. In 1981, he became the first recipient of the Robert Kirsch Award for Life Achievement from the *Los Angeles Times*.

As a master of narrative technique and a respected literary craftsman, Stegner had the opportunity to influence many young writers associated with the Stanford University Creative Writing Program, where he taught from 1945 to 1971. His students included Eugene Burdick, one of the authors of *The Ugly American* (1958); Ken Kesey; and Thomas McGuane. His own theory of literature was rather traditional and appears in two extended pieces of criticism, *The Writer in America* and *On Teaching and Writing Fiction*. The creative process, he believed, is basically the imposition of form on personal experience. The committed writer must discipline him- or herself to the difficult work of creation, choosing significant images from the insignificant and selecting significant actions for his or her characters. The writer must change the disorderliness of memory into symmetry without violating the reader's sense of what is true to life.

BIOGRAPHY

Wallace Earle Stegner was born on February 18, 1909, in Lake Mills, Iowa, the second son of George and Hilda Paulson Stegner. He was descended from Norwegian farmers on his mother's side and unknown ancestors on his father's side. His father was a drifter and a resourceful gambler—a searcher for the main chance, the big bonanza. In Stegner's early years, the family moved often, following his father's dream of striking it rich, from Grand Forks, North Dakota, to Bellingham, Washington, to Redmond, Oregon, to East End, Saskatchewan, where they lived from 1914 to 1921. East End left

him with memories of people and landscapes that played an important role in *The Big Rock Candy Mountain*. The family moved in 1921 to Salt Lake City, Utah, where Stegner attended high school and began college. Here, Stegner went through the pains of adolescence and, although not himself a Mormon, developed a strong attachment to the land and a sympathy for Mormon culture and values, which are reflected in his later books such as *Mormon Country* (1942), *The Gathering of Zion*, and *Recapitulation*.

From 1925 to 1930, Stegner attended the University of Utah, where he balanced his personal interests and his studies with a job selling rugs and linoleum in the family business of a close friend. By a fortunate chance, he studied freshman English with Vardis Fisher, then a budding novelist, and Fisher helped stimulate Stegner's growing interest in creative writing. In 1930, Stegner entered the graduate program at the University of Iowa, completing his master of arts degree in 1932 and his doctorate in 1935. His dissertation, "Clarence Edward Dutton: Geologist and Man of Letters," was a study of the Utah naturalist Clarence Dutton. The dissertation was revised and then published as *Clarence Edward Dutton: An Appraisal* by the University of Utah in 1936. This work fed his interest in the history of the American West and the life of the explorer John Wesley Powell, the subject of his *Beyond the Hundredth Meridian*.

Teaching English and creative writing occupied Stegner for several years, beginning with a one-year stint at tiny Augustana College in Illinois in 1934. Next, he went to the University of Utah until 1937, moving from there to teach freshman English at the University of Wisconsin for two years. He also taught at the Bread Loaf School of English in Vermont for several summers and enjoyed the friendship of Robert Frost, De Voto, and Theodore Morrison. In 1940, he accepted a part-time position at Harvard University in the English writing program. There, during the Depression, he was involved in literary debates between the literary left, led by F. O. Matthiessen, and the conservative De Voto.

In 1945, Stegner accepted a professorship in creative writing at Stanford University, where he remained for twenty-six years until his retirement in 1971. The Stanford years were his most productive; he produced a total of thirteen books in this period. In 1950, he made an around-the-world lecture tour, researched his family's past in Saskatchewan and Norway, and spent much of the year as writer-in-residence at the American Academy in Rome. He was also an active environmentalist long before ecology became fashionable. During the John F. Kennedy administration, he served as assistant to the secretary of the interior (1961) and as a member of the National Parks Advisory Board (1962).

ANALYSIS

Wallace Stegner was a regional writer in the best sense. His settings, characters, and plots derive from the Western experience, but his primary concern is with the meaning of that experience. Geographically, Stegner's region runs from Minnesota and Grand Forks, North Dakota, through Utah and northern Colorado. It is the country where Stegner lived and experienced his youth. Scenes from this region appear frequently in his novels. East End, Saskatchewan, the place of his early boyhood, appears as Whitemud, Saskatchewan, in *The Big Rock Candy Mountain*, along with Grand Forks and Lake Mills, Iowa, his birthplace. Salt Lake City figures prominently in *Recapitulation* and *The Preacher and the Slave*, the story of Joe Hill, a union martyr. *Wolf Willow*, furthermore, is historical fiction, a kind of history of East End, and *On a Darkling Plain* is the story of a much-decorated and seriously wounded veteran of World War I who withdraws from society in an isolated shack on the plains outside East End.

In a much larger sense, Stegner is concerned with the spiritual West—the West as an idea or a consciousness—and with the significance of Western values and traditions. He is also concerned with the basic American cultural conflict between East and West and with the importance of frontier values in American history. Bo Mason, modeled on Stegner's father, the abusive head of the Mason family in *The Big Rock Candy Mountain*, is an atavism, a character who may have been at home in the early frontier, who searches for the elusive pot of gold—the main chance of the Western myth. Never content with domestic life or with stability, Bo Mason, like George Stegner, moves his family from town to town always looking for an easy fortune. As a man of mixed qualities—fierce pride, resourcefulness, self-reliance, and a short, violent temper—he is ill at ease in the

Wallace Stegner. (Library of Congress)

postfrontier West, always chafing at the stability of community and family ties. He continually pursues the old Western myth of isolated individualism that preceded twentieth century domestication of the region. He might have made a good mountain man. Stegner stresses his impact on his family and community and shows the reader the basic tragedy of this frontier type trapped in a patterned world without easy bonanzas.

In *Angle of Repose*, Stegner explores the conflict between the values of self-reliance, impermanence, and Western optimism and the Eastern sense of culture, stability, and tradition. In a way, this is the basic conflict between Ralph Waldo Emerson's party of hope (the West) and the party of the past (the East). He also explores the idea of community as a concept alien to the Western myth. Indeed, community as the close-knit cooperation between individuals is shown in Stegner's work as the thing that ended the frontier. In *The Big Rock Candy Mountain* and in *Recapitulation*, there is a longing for community and a pervasive feeling that the Mason family is always outside the culture in which it exists, particularly in Utah, where Mormon culture is portrayed as innocent, solid, stable, and, as a result, attractive. Mormon life is characterized by the absence of frontier individualism and by a belief in permanence and group experience, an anomaly in the Western experience.

THE BIG ROCK CANDY MOUNTAIN

A third major concern throughout Stegner's work is his own identity and the meaning of Western identity. Bruce Mason in *The Big Rock Candy Mountain* is much concerned with his relationship as an adolescent to the Utah culture and its sense of community.

The Big Rock Candy Mountain, Stegner's fifth novel, is an obviously autobiographical account of his childhood and adolescence. A family saga, the novel follows the history of the rootless Mason family as it follows the dreams of Bo Mason, a thinly disguised version of Stegner's father, as he leads them to Grand Forks, North Dakota, to the lumber camps of Washington, then back to Iowa and up to Whitemud, Saskatchewan, and finally to Salt Lake City and Reno. Family identity problems are played out against the backdrop of an increasingly civilized and domesticated West against which the self-reliant and short-tempered character of Bo Mason stands out in stark relief. His qualities, which might have had virtues in the early settlement of the West, create family tensions and trauma that cause Bruce Mason (Stegner) to develop a hatred for his father only partially tempered by a grudging respect. Bo Mason relentlessly pursues the American Dream and the Western myth of easy success rooted in the early frontier: He endlessly pursues the Big Rock Candy Mountain.

Throughout this odyssey, the family longs for stability and community, for a place to develop roots. Even in Salt Lake City, where Bruce spends his adolescence, Bo keeps the family changing houses to hide his bootlegging business during the Prohibition period. His activities within puritanical Mormon culture only highlight the contrast between the Masons and the dominant community. Even in his later years, Bo pursues his dream in Reno by operating a gambling house.

Stegner vividly illustrates how this rootless wandering affects family members. Else, Bo's wife, representing the feminine, domesticating impulse, is a saintly character—long-suffering, gentle, and protective of her two sons. She longs for a home with permanence but never finds it. Her initial good nature and mild optimism eventually give way to pessimism as resettlements continue. Three of the family members die: Else is destroyed by cancer; Chet, the other son, who is defeated by both marriage and career, dies young of pneumonia; and Bo, with all his dreams shattered and involved with a cheap whore after Else's death, shoots himself. Only Bruce is left to make sense of his family's experiences, and he attempts to understand his place in the family saga as he strives to generalize his family's history.

In the final philosophical and meditative chapters, Stegner tries to link Bruce (and therefore himself) to history, to some sense of continuity and tradition. His family history, with its crudeness and tensions, is made to represent the history of the frontier West with its similar tensions and rough edges. Bruce, who long sought solace and identity in books, excels in school and finally follows the civilized but ironic path of going to law school at the University of Minnesota. He has, finally, reached a higher level of culture than his family ever attained. *The Big Rock Candy Mountain* has achieved a reputation as a classic of American regionalism, while it also deals with broader national themes and myths.

ANGLE OF REPOSE

Angle of Repose, published in 1971 and awarded the Pulitzer Prize for fiction, is regarded by many critics as Stegner's most finely crafted novel. The metaphoric title is a mining and geological term designating the slope at which rocks cease to fall, the angle of rest. Stegner uses it to apply to the last thirty years of the marriage of Susan Burling and Oliver Ward, two opposite personalities, after their often chaotic early married years. This ambitious work, covering four generations, is a fictionalized biography of writer and illustrator Mary Hallock Foote (1847-1930) and her marriage to Arthur De Wint Foote, an idealistic pioneer and self-educated mining engineer.

Lyman Ward, the narrator, was reared by his grandparents Susan Burling Ward and Oliver Ward, fictionalized versions of the Footes, and is a retired history professor from the University of California, Berkeley, who was crippled in middle age by a progressively arthritic condition. He has been transformed by the disease into a grotesque creature who loses first his leg and then his wife Ellen, who runs off with the surgeon who amputated Lyman's leg. Bitter and disillusioned by his wife's behavior and his son Rodman's radical idealism and contempt for the past, he retires to Grass Valley, California, to write his grandparents' biography. Here, he is assisted by Shelly Hawkes, a Berkeley dropout who shares Rodman's attitude toward history.

As Lyman reads through his grandparents' correspondence, he simultaneously recounts the development of their marriage and discovers the dynamics of their personalities. Susan Ward, cultured, educated in the East, and artistically talented, marries Oliver Ward, an idealistic mining engineer, her second choice for a husband. Without having resolved her disappointment at his lack of culture and appreciation for the arts, she marries him and begins two decades of following him through the West as he looks for professional and financial success in the unstable mining industry. The years in New Almaden, California; Leadville, Colorado; Michoacán, Mexico; and southern Idaho increasingly wear Susan down, despite brief interludes of stability and the frequent company of other Eastern scientists and engineers during her Western exile.

In Boise Canyon, Idaho, as Oliver's grand irrigation project falls apart, Susan falls into infidelity with Frank Sargent, Oliver's colorful assistant, and steals away to the countryside under the pretext of taking five-year-old Agnes Ward for a walk. Soon, Agnes's body is found floating in a nearby canal, and the day after her funeral, Frank commits suicide. Suspecting the worst, Oliver leaves his wife for two years until persuaded to return. For the remaining fifty years of their marriage, Oliver treats her with a kind silence and lack of physical affection, never truly forgiving her. Lyman learns that his grandparents' angle of repose was not the real thing, not a time of harmony but a cold truce full of human weakness. His naïve image of his grandparents based on childhood memories is undercut as he comes to understand them in a more sophisticated way. He learns to respect their strength and complexity.

Lyman's discoveries are all the more poignant because of the similarities between his grandparents' experience and his own relationship with an unfaithful wife who has broken trust, and who, it is implied, will seek a reconciliation. As in *The Big Rock Candy Mountain*, the two main characters symbolize two conflicting impulses in the settlement of the West—Oliver, the dreamer and idealist, pursuing his vision of success in a world with few amenities, and Susan, the finely cultured Easterner, yearning for stability and society. Lyman discovers links between his family's past and present and encounters universals of history such as suffering and infidelity that are more poignant to him because he discovers them in his own family history. Finally, the novel suggests that frontier values and the civilizing impulses need their own angle of repose. In essence, American experience had not yet reached its angle of rest; frontier and domestic values lie instead in a kind of uneasy truce.

RECAPITULATION

A continuation of the family saga played out in *The Big Rock Candy Mountain*, Stegner's *Recapitulation* is the moving drama of Bruce Mason's return to Salt Lake City to face his past. Toward the end of a successful career as a diplomat in the U.S. Foreign Service, Mason returns to the scene of his turbulent adolescence and the death of his family to attend his maiden aunt's funeral. Upon his arrival at the funeral home, the attendant presents him with a message to call Joe Mulder, his best friend in high school and in college at the University of Utah. Bruce was virtually a member of Joe's family for three years during the time when his father's bootlegging business threatened to jeopardize his social life.

Bruce remembers the 1920's and his adolescence before the stock market crash. Trying to find himself, he slowly remembers the time when he was an outsider in Mormon country, a time when he found many of the values that sustained him after the death of his family. Well-liked in high school by his teachers, Bruce was also picked on by the bigger boys and the less able students and acutely embarrassed by the family's house, which doubled as a speakeasy. His first major romance, with Nola, a Mormon country girl who was half American Indian, led to his first sexual encounter. Bruce was infatuated with her but knew her intellectual limits—that ideas put her to sleep and art bored her. Throughout the narrative, he recounts the disintegration of his family during his adolescence.

Stegner stresses Bruce's close relationship with Joe Mulder, but Bruce is emotionally incapable of meeting Joe because he hates being treated as The Ambassador, a visiting dignitary—a title that would only exaggerate the changes and losses of the past forty-five years. In a sense, he finds that he cannot go home again. He would have nothing in common with Joe except memories of adolescent love affairs and youthful myths. Their past could never be altered or renewed.

A second major theme in *Recapitulation* is the need to belong to some larger community. The Mormon sense of community, whatever its intellectual failings, is viewed nostalgically. Bruce envies the close-knit families of his friends. Nola's family, for example, seems like a tribe, a culture unto itself full of unspoken values and understandings. His decision to attend law school in Minnesota irrevocably removes him from Nola, Utah, and his adolescence, and ultimately from his chance to belong. When he returns to Utah, he is in the later stages of a successful but lonely adult life. His first job out of law school was in Saudi Arabia—a place without available women. He finally becomes a Middle Eastern specialist and a permanent bachelor.

Stegner ends the novel with Bruce, lonely, nostalgic, and emotionally incomplete, unable to make contact with Joe Mulder and with his past in a satisfying way. Even though the act of thinking through his past has served him therapeutically, he will continue as a diplomat, making formal contacts with people, living in the surface world of protocol, unable to connect emotionally with people. As the last of his family, he is a solitary figure with deep feelings that he is unable to express. He has, finally, partially tamed the frontier restlessness and anger of his father and risen above his family's self-destructive tendencies. Still, Bruce carries on the family's feeling of rootlessness, in a more formal, acceptable way. In the Foreign Service, he never develops roots and is shifted from one diplomatic post to another. In a more formal sense than his father, Bruce is still a drifter. Stegner ends the novel fittingly with Bruce being called back to the diplomatic service as U.S. representative to an important meeting of oil-producing nations in Caracas, Venezuela, reluctantly pulled away from his efforts to understand his past.

CROSSING TO SAFETY

Crossing to Safety introduces a new set of characters but also is about coming to terms with the past. Larry and Sally Morgan are a young couple who have moved to Madison, Wisconsin, because Larry has been given a teaching post for a year at the university there. Almost magically, they meet a personable young couple like themselves, Sid and Charity Lang, who also turn out to be very generous. In these Depression days, security is the most sought-after item, and all the young academics vie furiously for tenure. Yet, the Langs (though engaged as furiously in the contest as any) bestow on the Morgans a friendship rare in this atmosphere—wholehearted, sincere, and giving. Envy and jealousy are not part of their emotional makeup, though they do have their problems. Charity comes from an academic household (her father is a professor), and she wants the same for her family, including a professorship for her husband, who, however, really wants only to write poetry.

Stegner's portrayal of this lifelong friendship is neither idealistic nor blind. He reveals the human sides to his characters, keeping this paragon of *amicitia* from being falsely perfect. The ups and downs of their lives are relayed through flashback: Larry and Sally have come to visit the Langs because Charity is dying from cancer. Larry and Sally's life has not been without tragedy either: The summer after bearing their first child, Sally contracts polio and is permanently disabled.

Ultimately, Larry becomes a successful writer, while Sid never becomes successful either as an academic or as a poet. Belying her name—for she is a strong personality at best, harsh and unyielding at worst—Charity never really forgives Sid for his failure. Yet, Stegner concentrates on the love these people have for one another through thick and thin, creating a compelling story without resorting to tricks of subterfuge or violence to sustain the reader's interest. Stegner's great strength lies in knowing people; he knows their quirks and foibles so well that they come alive on the page without being demeaned or caricatured. In addition, his feeling for mood and setting are twin talents that infuse his writing with life, placing Stegner firmly on the short list of great American novelists.

Richard H. Dillman

OTHER MAJOR WORKS

SHORT FICTION: *The Women on the Wall*, 1950; *The City of the Living, and Other Stories*, 1956; *Collected Stories of Wallace Stegner*, 1990.

NONFICTION: *Mormon Country*, 1942; *One Nation*, 1945 (with the editors of *Look*); *Look at America: The Central Northwest*, 1947; *The Writer in America*, 1951; *Beyond the Hundredth Meridian: John Wesley Powell and the Second Opening of the West*, 1954; *Wolf Willow: A History, a Story, and a Memory of the Last Plains Frontier*, 1962; *The Gathering of Zion: The Story of the Mormon Trail*, 1964; *The Sound of Mountain Water*, 1969; *Ansel Adams: Images 1923-1974*, 1974; *The Uneasy Chair: A Biography of Bernard DeVoto*, 1974; *One Way to Spell Man*, 1982; *American Places*, 1983; *Conversations with Wallace Stegner on Western History and Literature*, 1983; *The American West as Living Space*, 1987; *On the Teaching of Creative Writing: Responses to a Series of Questions*, 1988 (Edward Connery Lathem, editor); *Where the Bluebird Sings to the Lemonade Springs: Living and Writing in the West*, 1992; *Marking the Sparrow's Fall: Wallace Stegner's American West*, 1998 (Page Stegner, editor); *Stealing Glances: Three Interviews with Wallace Stegner*, 1998 (James R. Hepworth, editor); *On Teaching and Writing Fiction*, 2002 (Lynn Stegner, editor); *The Selected Letters of Wallace Stegner*, 2007 (Page Stegner, editor).

EDITED TEXTS: *An Exposition Workshop*, 1939; *Readings for Citizens at War*, 1941; *Stanford Short Stories, 1946*, 1947 (with Richard Scowcroft); *The Writer's Art: A Collection of Short Stories*, 1950 (with Scowcroft and Boris Ilyin); *This Is Dinosaur: The Echo Park and Its Magic Rivers*, 1955; *Great American Short Stories*, 1957 (with Mary Stegner); *The Exploration of the Colorado River of the West*, 1957; *Selected American Prose: The Realistic Movement*, 1958; *Report on the Lands of the Arid Region of the United States*, 1962; *Modern Composition*, 1964 (4 volumes); *The American Novel: From Cooper to Faulkner*, 1965; *Twenty Years of Stanford Short Stories*, 1966; *The Letters of Bernard DeVoto*, 1975.

BIBLIOGRAPHY

Arthur, Anthony, ed. *Critical Essays on Wallace Stegner*. Boston: G. K. Hall, 1982. Although not an exhaustive discussion of Stegner's works, these essays cover much of his most important writing. Notes for further reference are included, as are primary and secondary bibliographical information and an index.

Benson, Jackson J. *Down by the Lemonade Springs: Essays on Wallace Stegner*. Reno: University of Nevada Press, 2001. Benson, who wrote a biography of Stegner, here provides a collection of essays about the writer. The essays include examinations of Stegner's fiction, the writer as an environmentalist, and Stegner's friendship with poet Robert Frost.

_____. *Wallace Stegner: His Life and Work*. New York: Viking Press, 1996. A biography that argues against pigeonholing Stegner as a Western writer. Focuses largely on the people and events that most influenced Stegner's art, including Robert Frost and Bernard DeVoto. Covers Stegner's teaching career and his influence on such writers as Ken Kesey, Edward Abbey, Wendell Berry, and Larry McMurtry.

Burrows, Russell. "Wallace Stegner's Version of Pastoral: The Topic of Ecology in His Work." *Western American Literature* 25 (May, 1990): 15-25. Stegner's environmentalism profoundly affected his work, and this article discusses Stegner's use of the pastoral setting in much of his fiction, both long and short. Includes bibliographical information and notes for further reference on points within the article.

Cook-Lynn, Elizabeth. *Why I Can't Read Wallace Stegner, and Other Essays*. Madison: University of Wisconsin Press, 1996. In the title essay of this collection, Cook-Lynn, a Native American, argues against Stegner's claim that Western history ended in 1890, the year of the massacre at Wounded Knee, and against his unchallenged statement that the Plains Indians have disappeared forever.

Fradkin, Philip L. *Wallace Stegner and the American West*. New York: Alfred A. Knopf, 2008. A detailed, astute biography, describing how Stegner transformed the failure of his father's homestead and other incidents of his father's life into his fiction about the American West.

Meine, Curt, ed. *Wallace Stegner and the Continental Vision: Essays on Literature, History, and Landscape*. Washington, D.C.: Island Press, 1997. A collection of papers presented at a 1996 symposium in Madison, Wisconsin. Includes essays on Stegner and the shaping of the modern West and on history, environmentalism, politics, bioregionalism, and on the art of storytelling.

Rankin, Charles E., ed. *Wallace Stegner: Man and Writer.* Albuquerque: University of New Mexico Press, 1996. A collection of essays by various critics on Stegner's life and art. Includes discussion of Stegner as a Western humanist; on Stegner the environment, and the West; and on *Angle of Repose* as literary history.

Stegner, Wallace. "The Art of Fiction: An Interview with Wallace Stegner." Interview by James R. Hepworth. *Paris Review*, Summer, 1990, 58-90. In this interview, Stegner talks about how he became a writer, as well as about writing in general. Although no references are included, this article is useful for the firsthand information it provides about Stegner through the interview process.

Stegner, Wallace, and Richard Etulain. *Conversations with Wallace Stegner.* 1983. Rev. ed. Salt Lake City: University of Utah Press, 1990. In an interview section added to the first part of this revised edition, Stegner talks about all of his work up to *Crossing to Safety.* Includes biographical information in the form of answers to interview questions and covers Stegner's view of the American literary West, Western history, and the Western wilderness.

Thomas, John L. *A Country in the Mind: Wallace Stegner, Bernard De Voto, History, and the American Land.* New York: Routledge, 2000. Chronicles the friendship of the two writers. Thomas focuses on their public lives, provides biographical sketches, and discusses how De Voto "converted" Stegner to environmentalism.

GERTRUDE STEIN

Born: Allegheny (now in Pittsburgh), Pennsylvania; February 3, 1874

Died: Neuilly-sur-Seine, France; July 27, 1946

PRINCIPAL LONG FICTION

Three Lives, 1909

The Making of Americans: Being a History of a Family's Progress, 1925 (abridged 1934)

Lucy Church Amiably, 1930

A Long Gay Book, 1932

The World Is Round, 1939

Ida, a Novel, 1941

Brewsie and Willie, 1946

Blood on the Dining-Room Floor, 1948

Things as They Are, 1950 (originally known as *Q.E.D.*)

Mrs. Reynolds, and Five Earlier Novelettes, 1931-1942, 1952

A Novel of Thank You, 1958

OTHER LITERARY FORMS

Any attempt to separate Gertrude Stein's novels from her other kinds of writing must be highly arbitrary. Stein thought the novel to be a failed literary form in the twentieth century, claiming that no real novels had been written after Marcel Proust, even including her own novelistic efforts in this assessment. For this and other reasons, it might be claimed that few, if any, of Stein's works are novels in any traditional sense. In fact, very few of Stein's more than six hundred titles in more than forty books can be adequately classified into any traditional literary forms. Her philosophy of composition was so idiosyncratic, her prose style so seemingly nonrational, that her writing bears little resemblance to whatever genre it purports to represent.

Depending on one's definition of the novel, Stein wrote anywhere between six and twelve novels, ranging in length from less than one hundred to 925 pages. The problem is that none of Stein's novels has a plot in any conventional sense, that few have conventionally developed and sustained characters, and that several seem almost exclusively autobiographical, more diaries and daybooks than anything else.

It is not any easier to categorize Stein's other pieces of writing, most of which are radically sui generis. If references to literary forms are made very loosely, Stein's work can be divided into novels, autobiographies, portraits, poems, lectures, operas, plays, and explanations. Other than her novels, her best-known works are *The Autobiography of Alice B. Toklas* (1933); *Tender Buttons* (1914); *Four Saints in Three Acts* (pr., pb. 1934); *Lectures in America* (1935); *Everybody's Autobiography* (1937); and *Portraits and Prayers*, 1934.

ACHIEVEMENTS

Whether towering or crouching, Gertrude Stein is ubiquitous in contemporary literature. A child of the nineteenth century who staunchly adhered to many of its values halfway through the twentieth, she nevertheless dedicated her creative life to the destruction of nineteenth century concepts of artistic order and purpose. In her own words, she set out to do nothing less than to kill a century, to lay the old ways of literary convention to rest. She later boasted that "the most serious thinking about the nature of literature in the twentieth century has been done by a woman," and her claim has great merit.

During the course of her career, Stein finally managed to convince almost everyone that there was indeed some point, if not profundity, in her aggressively enigmatic style. The ridicule and parody that frustrated so much of her early work had turned to grudging tolerance or outright lionizing by 1934, when Stein made her triumphant American lecture tour; for the last fifteen or so years of her life, she was published even if her editor had not the vaguest idea of what she was doing (as Bennett Cerf later admitted he had not). On the most concrete level, Stein's distinctive prose style is remarkably significant even when its philosophical dimensions are ignored. William H. Gass has observed, Stein "did more with sentences, and understood them better, than any writer ever has."

More important was Stein's influence on other leaders in the development of modernism. As a student of William James and as a friend of Alfred Alfred North Whitehead and Pablo Picasso, Stein lived at the center of the philosophical and artistic revolutions of the twentieth century. She was the natural emblem for modernism, and in her person, career, and legend, many of its salient issues converged.

In the light of more recent developments in the novel and in literary theory, it has also been argued that Stein was the first postmodernist, the first writer to claim openly that the instance of language is itself as important as the reality to which it refers. Among major writers, Ernest Hemingway was most obviously influenced by his association with her, but her genius was freely acknowledged by F. Scott Fitzgerald, Sherwood Anderson, and Thornton Wilder. William Saroyan explained her influence most directly when he asserted that no American writer could keep from coming under it, a sentiment reluctantly echoed by Edmund Wilson in *Axel's Castle* (1931), even before Stein's great popular success in the mid-1930's.

BIOGRAPHY

Gertrude Stein was born on February 3, 1874, in Allegheny, Pennsylvania, but she was seven years old before her family settled into permanent residence in Oakland, California, the city she was later to describe as having "no there there." Her birth itself was contingent on the deaths of two of her five brothers and sisters: Her parents had decided to have only five children, and only after two children had died in infancy were Gertrude and her older brother, Leo, conceived. Identity was to become one of the central preoccupations of her writing career, and the tenuous nature of her own birth greatly influenced that concern.

Stein's early years were comfortably bourgeois and uneventful. Her father, a vice president of the Union Street Municipal Railway System in San Francisco, was authoritarian, moody, and aggressive, but vacillating, and he may have helped foster her sense of independence, but he undoubtedly left her annoyed by him in particular and by fatherhood in general. Her mother barely figured in her life at all: A pale, withdrawn, ineffectual woman, she left most of the rearing of her children to governesses. By the time Stein was age seventeen, both parents had died and she had grown even closer to her immediate older brother, Leo. In 1893, she entered Harvard Annex (renamed Radcliffe College the following year), thus rejoining Leo, who was a student at Harvard. There, Stein studied with William James and Hugo Munsterberg and became involved in research in psychology. Together with the great influence exerted on her thinking by James, this early work in psychology was to provide her with both a subject and a style that

Gertrude Stein. (Library of Congress)

would continue in many forms throughout her career. She was awarded her bachelor of arts degree by Harvard in 1898, almost a year after she had entered medical school at Johns Hopkins University. Her interest in medicine rapidly waned, and she left Johns Hopkins in 1901, failing four courses in her final semester.

After leaving medical school, Stein spent two years moving back and forth between Europe and the United States. During that time, she was involved in an agonizing love affair with another young woman student at Johns Hopkins, May Bookstaver. The affair was painfully complicated, first by Stein's naïveté then by the presence of a more sophisticated rival for May's love, Mabel Haynes. The resulting lover's triangle led Stein, in an effort to understand May, to begin formulating the theories of personality that dominated her early writing.

The frustration and eventual despair of this lesbian relationship profoundly influenced Stein's view of the psychology of personality and of love. Most directly, Stein's troubled affair with May provided her with many, if not most, of the concerns of three of her books, *Q.E.D.*, *The Making of Americans*, and *Three Lives*, the first two of which she began while living in New York in the winter of 1903.

After a brief stay in New York, she lived with Leo, first in Bloomsbury in London and then, beginning in 1903, in Paris at 27 rue de Fleurus, the address she was to make so well known to the world. In Paris, Gertrude and Leo became more and more interested in painting, buying works by new artists such as Henri Matisse and Picasso. Leo's preference was for works by Matisse, while Gertrude favored the more experimental works of Picasso, marking the beginning of a distancing process that would lead to Leo's complete separation from his sister in 1913. Leo was bright and opinionated, and fancied himself by far the greater creative talent of the two, but his brilliance and energy never produced any creative or significant critical work, and he grew to resent both his sister's independent thinking and her emerging ability to write. Later in his life, he would dismiss Gertrude as "dumb" and her writing as "nonsense."

In 1907, Stein met another young American woman in Paris, Alice Toklas, and Alice began to displace Leo as the most important personal influence in Gertrude's life. Alice learned to type so she could transcribe Stein's handwritten manuscripts, beginning with portions of *The Making of Americans* in 1908. In 1909, Alice moved in with Gertrude and Leo at 27 rue de Fleurus, and by 1913, Alice had replaced Leo as Gertrude's companion and as the manager of her household. Stein later referred to her relationship with Alice as a "marriage," and few, if any, personal relationships have ever influenced a literary career so profoundly. Apart from providing Stein with the persona for her best-known work, *The Autobiography of Alice B. Toklas*, Alice typed, criticized, and valiantly worked to publish all of Stein's work for the rest of her career and for the twenty years that Alice lived after Stein's death. While it is doubtful that Alice was directly responsible for any of Stein's writing, her influence on its composition and on Stein's life was tremendous.

Gertrude and Alice spent the first months of World War I in England as houseguests of Alfred North Whitehead, returning to Paris briefly in 1914, then spending more than a year in Spain. They joined the war effort in 1917 when Stein ordered a Ford motor van from America for use as a supply truck for the American Fund for French Wounded, an acquisition that began Stein's lifelong fascination with automobiles, particularly with Fords. She and Alice drove this van, named Auntie, until the war ended, work for which she was later awarded the Medaille de la Reconnaissance Française.

Modernism had burst on the American consciousness when the Armory Show opened in New York in 1913, and this show, which had confronted Americans with the first cubist paintings, also led to the association in the public mind of Stein's writing with this shockingly new art, particularly since Stein's first periodical publications had been "Matisse" and "Picasso" in *Camera Work* the year before. Stein's mammoth, 925-page novel, *The Making of Americans*, was published in 1925, and in 1926, she lectured at Oxford and Cambridge, attempting to explain her idiosyncratic writing style. Her "landscape" novel, *Lucy Church Amiably*, appeared in 1930, but it was in 1933, with the publication of the best-selling *The Autobiography of Alice B. Toklas*, that Stein first captured the public's interest. She became front-page news the following year when her opera *Four Saints in Three Acts* was first performed and when she embarked on a nationwide lecture tour, later described in *Everybody's Autobiography* and *Lectures in America*.

Stein and Toklas spent World War II in Bilignin and then in Culoz, France. Although Stein and Toklas were both Jewish, they were never persecuted by occupying forces, owing in part to the influence of Bernard Fay, an early admirer of Stein's work who directed the Bibliothèque Nationale for the Vichy regime. When, after the war, Fay was sentenced to life imprisonment for his Vichy activities, Stein was one of his few defenders. That her art collection survived Nazi occupation virtually intact can only have been through Fay's intercession. During the war, Stein finished another novel, *Mrs. Reynolds*, and *Wars I Have Seen* (1945), an autobiographical work. Her novel *Brewsie and Willie*, a series of conversations among American soldiers, was published in 1946.

Stein died following an operation for cancer in the American Hospital in Neuilly-sur-Seine, France, on July 27, 1946. While Toklas's account of Stein's last words may be apocryphal, it certainly is in keeping with the spirit of her life. As Toklas later reconstructed their last conversation, Stein had asked her "What is the answer?" Then, when Toklas remained silent, Stein added, "In that case, what is the question?"

ANALYSIS

While Gertrude Stein's persistence finally earned her access to readers, it could never guarantee her readers who would or could take her strange writing seriously. As a result, more confusing and contradictory information surrounds her career than that of any other twentieth century writer of comparable reputation. Usually responding in any of four basic ways, readers and critics alike seemed to view her as one, a literary charlatan of the P. T. Barnum ilk, interested in publicity or money rather than in art; two, something of a naïve child-woman incapable of comprehending the world around her; three, a fiery-eyed literary revolutionary, den mother of the avant-garde; or four, an ageless repository of wisdom and genius. Ultimately, the reader's acceptance or rejection of these various categories will greatly determine his or her response to Stein's writing, which forces the reader to make as many cognitive choices as does that of any major writer.

Stein's many explanations of her writing further complicate its interpretation: Even her "explanations" frustrate as much as they reveal, explicitly setting her up in cognitive competition with her reader, a competition suggested by her favorite cryptogram, which works out to read "I understand you undertake to overthrow my undertaking." Stein proposes a rhetoric not of misunderstanding, but of anti-understanding; that is, her explanations usually argue precisely against the desirability of explaining.

As Stein bluntly put the matter, "understanding is a very dull occupation." "Understanding" has a special denotation for Stein, sometimes meaning as little as "paying attention to" or "reading." "To understand a thing means to be in contact with that thing," she proclaimed. Central to her mistrust of explanations and interpretations was her often anguished belief that her thoughts could never really be matched to anyone else's. She was deeply troubled by this doubt as she wrote *The Making of Americans*, referring in that work to "the complete realization that no one can believe as you do about anything" as "complete disillusionment in living." Starting from this assumption that no one can ever really understand what someone else says or writes because of the inherent ambiguity of language, Stein not only decided to force her readers to confront that ambiguity but also claimed it as a primary virtue of her writing. She announced triumphantly that

> if you have vitality enough of knowing enough of what you mean, somebody and sometimes a great many will have to realize that you know what you mean and so they will agree that you mean what you know, which is as near as anybody can come to understanding any one.

Stein's focus here is on relationships or process rather than on product—on the act of trying to become one with, rather than focusing on the ultimate result of that act.

Stein's thinking about understanding manifests itself in a number of distinctive ways in her writing, as do her theories of perception and of human psychology. Moreover, during the nearly fifty years of her writing career, her style developed in many related but perceptibly different stages, such as her "cubist" or her "cinema" phases. As a result, no single analysis can do more than describe the primary concerns and features of one of her stylistic periods. There are, however, three central concerns that underlie and partially account for all the stages in the development of her style. These concerns are with the value of individual words, with repetition as the basic rhythm of existence, and with the related concept of "movement" in writing. Her articulations of these central concerns all run counter to her reader's expectations about the purpose and function of language and of literature. Her writing surprised her readers in much the same way that her penchant for playing only the black keys on a piano surprised and frustrated all but the most patient of her listeners.

One of Stein's goals was to return full meaning, value, and particularity to the words she used. "I took individual words and thought about them until I got their weight and volume complete and put them next to

another word," she explained of seemingly nonsense phrases such as "toasted Susie is my ice cream," or "mouse and mountain and a quiver, a quaint statue and pain in an exterior and silence more silence louder shows salmon a mischief intender." This sort of paratactic juxtaposition of seemingly unrelated words rarely occurs in Stein's novels but represents a problem for her reader in many other ways in her writing. She frequently chose to stress or focus on a part or aspect of the object of her description that the reader normally does not consider. The "things" Stein saw and wrote of were not the "things" with which readers are familiar: Where another observer might see a coin balanced on its edge, Stein might choose either of the descriptive extremes of seeing it literally as a thin rectangle, or figuratively as the essence of money. Characteristically, her most opaque parataxis refers to essences or processes rather than to objects or static concepts.

A related quirk in Stein's style results from her intellectual or emotional attachment to particular words and phrases at certain stages of her career. As she admitted in *The Making of Americans*,

> To be using a new word in my writing is to me a very difficult thing. . . . Using a word I have not yet been using in my writing is to me a very difficult and a peculiar feeling. Sometimes I am using a new one, sometimes I feel a new meaning in an old one, sometimes I like one I am very fond of that one that has many meanings many ways of being used to make different meanings to everyone.

Stein said she had learned from Paul Cézanne that everything in a painting was related to everything else and that each part of the painting was of equal importance—a blade of grass as important to the composition of the painting as a tree. She attempted to apply these two principles to the composition of her sentences, taking special delight in using normally "overlooked" words, arguing that articles, prepositions, and conjunctions—the transitive elements in grammar—are just as important and more interesting than substantives such as nouns and verbs. Her reassessment both of the value of words and of the conventions of description resulted in what Michael J. Hoffman, in *The Development of Abstractionism in the Writings of Gertrude Stein* (1965), has described as Stein's "abstractionism." It also resulted in her including in her writing totally unexpected information in perplexing paratactic word strings.

A second constant in Stein's style is the pronounced repetition of words, phrases, and sentences, with no changes or with only incremental progressions of sounds or associations. Works such as *The Making of Americans* and *Three Lives* contain long passages in which each sentence is a light variation on some core phrase, with great repetition of words even within a single sentence. Stein termed this phenomenon "insistence" rather than repetition, citing her former teacher, James, as her philosophical authority. James's argument in his *The Principles of Psychology* (1890) that one must think of the identical recurrence of a fact in a fresh manner remarkably resembles Stein's contention that

> in expressing anything there can be no repetition because the essence of that expression is insistence, and if you insist you must each time use emphasis and if you use emphasis it is not possible while anybody is alive that they should use exactly the same emphasis.

Repetition or insistence is perhaps the central aspect of what has been called Stein's "cinema style," based on her claim that in writing *The Making of Americans* she was "doing what the cinema was doing." She added that her writing in that book was "like a cinema picture made up of succession and each moment having its own emphasis that is its own difference and so there was the moving and the existence of each moment as it was in me."

Stein's discussion of "what the cinema was doing" appears in her *Lectures in America* and also suggests the third basic concern of her writing: movement. By "movement," she referred not to the movement of a message to its conclusion or the movement of a plot or narrative, but to "the essence of its going" of her prose, a timeless continuous present in the never-ending motion of consciousness. Stein also credits Cézanne with discovering this concern, "a feeling of movement inside the painting not a painting of a thing moving but the thing painted having inside it the existence of moving." She seemed to understand Cézanne's achievement in terms of James's model of consciousness as an ever-flowing stream of thought.

Accordingly, Stein used her writing not to record a scene or object or idea (products of thought), but to try to capture the sense of the process of perceiving such things. Her subject is almost always really two things at once: whatever attracted her attention—caught her eye, entered her ear, or crossed her mind—and the mobile nature of reality, particularly as it is perceived by human consciousness. In fact, Stein was usually more concerned with the nature of her own perception and with that of her reader than she was with its objects. She wanted to escape the conventions of linguistic representation, arbitrary arrangements similar to the "rules" for perspective in painting, and to present "something moving as moving is not as moving should be." As confusing as her resulting efforts sometimes are, her concern with motion makes sense as an attempt to mimic or evoke the nature of consciousness as she understood it.

From James at Harvard and possibly from Henri Bergson in Paris, Stein had learned that the best model for human consciousness was one that stressed the processual, ever-flowing nature of experience. She added to this belief her assumption that the essence of any subject could only be perceived and should only be represented through its motion, echoing Bergson's claim that "reality is mobility." Unfortunately, this belief led her writing into one of its many paradoxes: She could only attempt to represent the continuous stream of experience through the segmented, inherently sequential nature of language. Streams flow; words do not. Instead, they proceed one by one, like the cars pulled by a train engine. While James would certainly have objected to Stein's sequential cinema model as an approximation of the stream of consciousness, her motion-obsessed writing probably suggests the flow of consciousness as well as does any literary style.

THINGS AS THEY ARE

Written in 1903 as *Q.E.D.*, but set aside until 1932 and not published until 1950, *Things as They Are* is Stein's most conventional novel. Its sentences employ no unexpected syntax or diction, its central concerns are clear, its time scheme is linear, and its characters are conventionally drawn. If anything, Stein's style in this first novel is markedly old-fashioned, including highly formal sentences that frequently sport balanced serial constructions. She writes, for example, "Adele vehemently and with much picturesque vividness explained her views and theories of manners, people and things, in all of which she was steadily opposed by Helen who differed fundamentally in all her convictions, aspirations and illusions." While its conventional style (crudely reminiscent of that of Henry James) is completely unlike that of any other Stein novel, *Things as They Are* is a very significant work for the consideration of Stein's career. Apart from convincingly refuting the suspicion of some of her detractors that Stein was incapable of rational writing, this book establishes her preoccupation with psychological typecasting and vaguely hints at the importance of repetition in her thinking and writing.

Things as They Are charts the growth, turbulence, and eventual dissolution of the relationships among three young women: Adele, the book's central consciousness, an obviously autobiographical figure; Helen Thomas, the object of Adele's love; and Mabel Neathe, Adele's calculating rival for Helen's affection. These three characters closely parallel Stein, May Bookstaver, and Mabel Haynes, and the story of their relationship is the story of Stein's first, agonizing love affair. While the novel follows these three young women for three years, not much happens. Most of the book relates conversations and correspondence between Adele and Helen, showing Adele's torment first from her not yet understood desire for Helen, then from her growing realization that she is losing Helen to Mabel. Of principal interest to the reader is Stein's self-characterization in her portrayal of Adele.

THREE LIVES

Three Lives is easily Stein's best-known and most respected piece of fiction. Technically three novellas, this work is unified by its three subjects, by its central concern with the nature of consciousness, and by its attempt to blend colloquial idioms with Stein's emerging style, here based largely on her understanding of Cézanne's principles of composition, particularly that "one thing was as important as another thing."

"The Good Anna," "Melanctha," and "The Gentle Lena" are the three sections of this work. Anna and Lena are poor German immigrants who patiently work as servants in Bridgepoint, Baltimore; Melanctha is a young black woman who discovers sexuality and love, then turns from a frustrating relationship with a sincere young

black doctor to a dissipative affair with a gambler. Because all three women are essentially victimized by their surroundings and die at the end of their stories, this work is deterministic in the naturalist tradition, but *Three Lives* marks the transition from naturalism to modernism as Stein departs from nineteenth century literary conventions. She abandons conventional syntax to try to follow the movement of a consciousness rather than of events, and she develops a new narrative style only partially tied to linear chronology. The result is an interior narrative of consciousness in which Stein's prose style serves as the primary carrier of knowledge. Through the rhythms of her characters' speech and the rhythms of her narration, Stein gives her reader a sense of the basic rhythms of consciousness for these three women—what Stein would elsewhere refer to as their "bottom natures."

Possibly Stein's most widely celebrated piece of writing, "Melanctha" recasts the anguishing love triangle of *Q.E.D.* into the conflict between Melanctha and Jeff Campbell, whose inherently conflicting "bottom natures" or personality types parallel the conflict between Helen and Adele in the earlier work. "Melanctha" has been praised by Richard Wright, among others, as one of the first realistic and sympathetic renderings of black life by a white American author, but Melanctha's race is actually incidental to Stein's central concerns with finding a style to express the rhythms of personality and the frustrating cycles of love.

THE MAKING OF AMERICANS

Although it was not published until 1925, Stein's *The Making of Americans* occupied her as early as 1903 and was in fact begun before *Q.E.D.* and *Three Lives*. This mammoth novel began as a description of the creation of Americans from a representative immigrant family: "The old people in a new world, the new people made out of the old, that is the story that I mean to tell, for that is what really is and what I really know." Stein's projected family chronicle soon lost its original focus, becoming first a history of everyone, then a study of character types rather than of characters. Leon Katz, who has worked with this book more than has anyone else, calls it "a massive description of the psychological landscape of human being in its totality."

Although the book ostensibly continues to follow events in the lives of two central families, the Herslands and the Dehnings, its real concern is almost always both larger and smaller, ranging from Stein's questions about her own life and identity to questions about the various personality types of all of humanity. As Richard Bridgman suggests, this is "an improvised work of no identifiable genre in which the creator learned by doing," one "full of momentary wonders and botched long-range schemes, lyrical outbursts and anguished confessions." Accordingly, Bridgman concludes that *The Making of Americans* is best thought of "not as a fictional narrative nor a philosophical tract, but as a drama of self-education." In a way, the book chronicles the "making" of Stein, presenting a phenomenology of her mind as it works its way through personal problems toward the distinctive "cinema style."

Underlying a great part of the writing in this book is Stein's belief that human personality consists of variations on a few basic "bottom natures" or kinds of identity that can be perceived through a character's repeated actions:

> There are then many things every one has in them that come out of them in the repeating everything living have always in them, repeating with a little changing just enough to make of each one an individual being, to make of each repeating an individual thing that gives to such a one a feeling of themselves inside them.

There are two basic personality types: "dependent independent" and "independent dependent." These are polarities identified in part by the way the person fights: the first kind by resisting, the second by attacking.

Concerns with character-typing dominate the book's first two sections, "The Dehnings and the Herslands" and "Martha Hersland" (the character most closely modeled on Stein's own life), while the third section, "Alfred and Julia Hersland," contains mostly digressions about contemporary matters in Stein's life. The fourth section, "David Hersland," becomes a meditation on the nature of aging and death ("He was dead when he was at the beginning of being in middle living."), and the final section, "History of a Family's Progress," is—even for Stein—an incredibly abstract and repetitive series of reflections on the concerns that had given rise to the novel. This final section contains no names, referring only to "some," "any," "every," or "very many."

Stein later described her efforts in this book as an attempt "to do what the cinema was doing"; that is, to give a sense of motion and life through a series of highly repetitive statements, each statement only an incremental change from the preceding one, like frames in a strip of film. One of the main effects of this technique is to freeze all action into a "continuous present." Not only do Stein's sentences exist in overlapping clusters, depending more for their meaning on their relationships to one another than on individual semantic content, but also her verbs in *The Making of Americans* are almost exclusively present participles, suspending all action in the present progressive tense. "The business of Art," Stein later explained, "is to live in the actual present, that is the complete actual present." As a result, while *The Making of Americans* does ostensibly present a history of four generations of the Hersland family, there exists in it little or no sense of the passage of time. Instead, the book presents a sense of "existence suspended in time," a self-contained world existing quite independent of the "real world," a basic modernist goal that has also become one of the hallmarks of postmodernism.

A 416-page version, abridged by Stein, was published in 1934 but has not been accepted by Stein scholars as adequately representative of the longer work. For all its difficulty, *The Making of Americans* is one of modernism's seminal works and an invaluable key to Stein's literary career.

LUCY CHURCH AMIABLY

Described by its author as "a novel of Romantic beauty and nature and which Looks Like an Engraving," *Lucy Church Amiably* shares many characteristics with Stein's best-known play *Four Saints in Three Acts* and with the several works she called "geographies." The book was Stein's response to the area around Belley, France, where she and Alice spent many summers. Stein's title plays on the existence of the church in a nearby village, Lucey. As Richard Bridgman has observed, Lucy Church refers throughout the book to both that church and to a woman who resembles a relaxed Stein. As Bridgman also notes, "the book is essentially a long, lyric diary," with Stein including in it information about the geography, residents, and flora of the surrounding area. This information appears, however, in Stein's distinctive paratactic style:

In this story there is to be not only white black tea colour and vestiges of their bankruptcy but also well wishing and outlined and melodious and with a will and much of it to be sure with their only arrangement certainly for this for the time of which when by the way what is the difference between fixed.

This novel can perhaps best be thought of as a pastoral and elegiac meditation on the nature of place.

THE WORLD IS ROUND *and* IDA, A NOVEL

In 1939, Stein's novel for children, *The World Is Round*, was published, with illustrations by Clement Hurd. The book focuses on a series of events in the lives of a nine-year-old girl, Rose, and her cousin, Willie. These events are more enigmatic than dramatic but seem to move both children through several kinds of initiations. Identity worries both Rose and Willie ("Would she have been Rose if her name had not been Rose and would she have been Rose if she had been a twin"), as does the contrast between the uncertainties of their lives and the advertised verities of existence, emblemized by the "roundness" of the world. Comprising both the children's meditations and their songs, the book is, for Stein, relatively conventional. Although its sentences are highly repetitive and rhythmic, they present a compelling view of a child's consciousness, and Stein scholars agree on the importance and success of this little-known work.

Originally intended as "a novel about publicity," *Ida, a Novel* expands many of the concerns of *The World Is Round*, extending them from Ida's birth well into her adult life. As is true of all of Stein's novels, there is not anything resembling a plot, and many of the things that happen in Ida's life are surrealistically dreamlike. "Funny things" keep happening to the young Ida, and while the nature of these things is never explained, most of them seem to involve men. Frequently, these men have nothing at all to do with her, or they only glance at her, but Ida sees them as vaguely threatening, and insofar as her novel can be said to have a central concern, it is with certain problems of sexuality. Although Stein later described Ida as having been based on the duchess of Windsor, this connection is only superficial, and Ida is better seen as another in the long line of Stein's autobiographical characters.

BREWSIE AND WILLIE

Stein's novel *Brewsie and Willie* redirected her revolutionary spirit from literary to social and economic problems. In this series of conversations among American soldiers and nurses awaiting redeployment from France to the United States after World War II, Stein pessimistically considered the future of her native land. Stein had long held that the United States was "the oldest country in the world" because it had been the first to enter the twentieth century. By 1945, she felt that America had grown "old like a man of fifty," and that its tired, middle-aged economic system had become stale and repressive.

In *Brewsie and Willie*, she describes that economic system as "industrialism," portraying a stultifying cycle of depleting raw materials for overproduction and installment buying. This cycle also locked the worker into "job thinking," making of him a kind of automaton, tied to his job, locked into debt, and, worst of all, robbed of freedom of thought. Through conversations involving Brewsie (Stein's spokesperson), Willie, and several other soldiers and nurses, Stein portrays an apprehensive generation of young Americans who see the potential dangers of postwar America but who fear they do not "have the guts to make a noise" about them. These conversations cover a wide range of subjects, from a comparison of French and American baby carriages to the tentative suggestion that the American system must be torn down before "pioneering" will again be possible.

Stein makes little or no effort in this book to differentiate the voices of her speakers, but she does rather amazingly blend her own voice with those of the soldiers. The result is a style that is characteristically Stein's but that also has the rhythm and the randomness of overheard conversation. Often overlooked, *Brewsie and Willie* is one of the most remarkable documents in Stein's writing career.

However idiosyncratic Stein's writing may seem, it must be remembered that a very strong case can be made for its substantial philosophical underpinnings. To her way of thinking, language could refuse few things to Stein, and the limitations of language were exactly what she refused to accept. She bent the language to the very uses that process philosophers such as James and

Bergson and Whitehead feared it could not be put. Her stubborn emphasis on the individual word—particularly on transitive elements—her insistent use of repetition, and her ever-present preoccupation with the essential motion of words were all part of Stein's monumental struggle with a language she felt was not accurately used to reflect the way people perceive reality or the motion of reality itself. In a narrow but profound sense, she is the most serious realist in literary history. Stein was not a philosopher—her magpie eclecticism, associational flights, and thundering *ex cathedra* pronouncements ill suited her for systematic explanation—but in her writing a wealth of philosophy appears.

Brooks Landon

OTHER MAJOR WORKS

SHORT FICTION: *As Fine as Melanctha*, 1954; *Painted Lace, and Other Pieces, 1914-1937*, 1955; *Alphabets and Birthdays*, 1957.

PLAYS: *Geography and Plays*, 1922; *Operas and Plays*, 1932; *Four Saints in Three Acts*, pr., pb. 1934; *In Savoy: Or, Yes Is for a Very Young Man (A Play of the Resistance in France)*, pr., pb. 1946; *The Mother of Us All*, pr. 1947; *Last Operas and Plays*, 1949; *In a Garden: An Opera in One Act*, pb. 1951; *Lucretia Borgia*, pb. 1968; *Selected Operas and Plays*, 1970.

POETRY: *Tender Buttons: Objects, Food, Rooms*, 1914; *Before the Flowers of Friendship Faded Friendship Faded*, 1931; *Two (Hitherto Unpublished) Poems*, 1948; *Bee Time Vine, and Other Pieces, 1913-1927*, 1953; *Stanzas in Meditation, and Other Poems, 1929-1933*, 1956.

NONFICTION: *Composition as Explanation*, 1926; *How to Write*, 1931; *The Autobiography of Alice B. Toklas*, 1933; *Matisse, Picasso, and Gertrude Stein, with Two Shorter Stories*, 1933; *Portraits and Prayers*, 1934; *Lectures in America*, 1935; *Narration: Four Lectures*, 1935; *The Geographical History of America*, 1936; *Everybody's Autobiography*, 1937; *Picasso*, 1938; *Paris, France*, 1940; *What Are Masterpieces?*, 1940; *Wars I Have Seen*, 1945; *Four in America*, 1947; *Reflections on the Atomic Bomb*, 1973; *How Writing Is Written*, 1974; *The Letters of Gertrude Stein and Thornton Wilder*, 1996 (Edward Burns and Ulla E. Dydo, editors); *Baby Precious Always Shines: Selected Love Notes Between Gertrude Stein and Alice B. Toklas*, 1999 (Kay Turner, editor).

MISCELLANEOUS: *The Gertrude Stein First Reader and Three Plays*, 1946; *The Yale Edition of the Unpublished Writings of Gertrude Stein*, 1951-1958 (8 volumes; Carl Van Vechten, editor); *Selected Writings of Gertrude Stein*, 1962; *The Yale Gertrude Stein*, 1980.

BIBLIOGRAPHY

Bowers, Jane Palatini. *Gertrude Stein*. New York: St. Martin's Press, 1993. A succinct, feminist-oriented introduction to Stein, with separate chapters on the novels, short fiction, and plays. Includes notes and a bibliography.

Brinnin, John Malcom. *The Third Rose: Gertrude Stein and Her World*. Boston: Little, Brown, 1959. Aside from its significant biographical value, this study contains provocative comments on Stein's writing, twentieth century painting, and modern intellectual and artistic movements. Includes a useful bibliography.

Curnutt, Kirk, ed. *The Critical Response to Gertrude Stein*. Westport, Conn.: Greenwood Press, 2000. While including quintessential pieces on Stein by Carl Van Vechten, William Carlos Williams, and Katherine Anne Porter, this guide to her critical reception also includes previously obscure estimations from contemporaries such as H. L. Mencken, Mina Loy, and Conrad Aiken.

DeKoven, Marianne. *A Different Language: Gertrude Stein's Experimental Writing*. Madison: University of Wisconsin Press, 1983. DeKoven's feminist study focuses on Stein's experimental work published after *Three Lives* and before *The Autobiography of Alice B. Toklas*. She argues that this period of Stein's writing is important not so much because of its influence on other writers but because of its attempt to redefine patriarchal language and provide alternatives to conventional modes of signification.

Dydo, Ulla E., with William Rice. *Gertrude Stein: The Language that Rises, 1923-1934*. Evanston, Ill.: Northwestern University Press, 2003. Dydo, a renowned Stein scholar, provides a comprehensive analysis of the letters, manuscripts, and notebooks Stein generated over a twenty-year period. Includes a bibliography and an index.

Hoffman, Michael J. *Critical Essays on Gertrude Stein.* Boston: G. K. Hall, 1986. A collection of reviews and essays, most of which appeared during and immediately after Stein's long career in letters. Diverse literary criticisms, such as new criticism, structuralism, feminism, and deconstruction are represented. Among the contributors are Sherwood Anderson, Marianne Moore, William Carlos Williams, B. F. Skinner, Katherine Anne Porter, Edmund Wilson, and W. H. Auden.

Kellner, Bruce, ed. *A Gertrude Stein Companion: Content With the Example.* New York: Greenwood Press, 1988. Kellner supplies a helpful introduction on how to read Stein. The volume includes a study of Stein and literary tradition, her manuscripts, and her various styles, and included biographical sketches of her friends and critics. Provides an annotated bibliography of criticism.

Knapp, Bettina. *Gertrude Stein.* New York: Continuum, 1990. A general introduction to Stein's life and art. Discusses her stylistic breakthrough in the stories in *Three Lives*, focusing on repetition and the use of the continuous present. Devotes a long chapter to *Tender Buttons* as one of Stein's most innovative and esoteric works.

Malcolm, Janet. *Two Lives: Gertrude and Alice.* New Haven, Conn.: Yale University Press, 2007. An account of Stein's relationship with Alice B. Toklas, in which Malcolm provides new information about the couple's lives during the German occupation of France. She explains how Stein and Toklas were allowed to survive because of their friendship with Bernard Fay, a wealthy, anti-Semitic Frenchman.

Souhami, Diana. *Gertrude and Alice.* London: Pandora, 1991. The most frank account of Stein's lesbian relationship with Toklas, this book shows Toklas's strength and how she dominated many aspects of her forty-year marriage to Stein.

Sutherland, Donald. *Gertrude Stein: A Biography of Her Work.* Westport, Conn.: Greenwood Press, 1951. The first substantial critical book on Stein's writing, this work treats Stein's radical writings as an illustration of her own modernist philosophy and aesthetics. The book also justifies the modern movement in writing and painting. Includes a useful appendix, which catalogs Stein's writing according to stylistic periods.

JOHN STEINBECK

Born: Salinas, California; February 27, 1902
Died: New York, New York; December 20, 1968
Also known as: John Ernst Steinbeck

PRINCIPAL LONG FICTION

Cup of Gold, 1929
The Pastures of Heaven, 1932
To a God Unknown, 1933
Tortilla Flat, 1935
In Dubious Battle, 1936
Of Mice and Men, 1937
The Red Pony, 1937, 1945
The Grapes of Wrath, 1939
The Moon Is Down, 1942
Cannery Row, 1945

The Pearl, 1945 (serial), 1947 (book)
Burning Bright, 1950
East of Eden, 1952
Sweet Thursday, 1954
The Short Reign of Pippen IV, 1957
The Winter of Our Discontent, 1961

OTHER LITERARY FORMS

In addition to his seventeen novels, John Steinbeck published a story collection, *The Long Valley* (1938), and a few other uncollected or separately printed stories. His modern English translations of Sir Thomas Malory's Arthurian tales were published posthumously in 1976. Three plays he adapted from his novels were published as well as performed on Broadway: *Of Mice and Men* (pr. 1937), *The Moon Is Down* (pr. 1942), and *Burning Bright* (pr. 1951). Three of the six film treatments or screenplays he wrote have been published: *The Forgotten Village* (1941), *A Medal for Benny* (1945), and *Viva Zapata!* (1952). The other three—*Lifeboat* (1944), *The Pearl* (1945), and *The Red Pony* (1949)—also were produced as films, the latter two adapted from his own novels. His nonfiction is voluminous, and much of it remains uncollected. The more important nonfiction books include *Sea of Cortez* (1941, with Edward F. Ricketts), *Bombs Away* (1942), *A Russian Journal* (1948, with Robert Capa), *Once There Was a War* (1958), *Travels with Charley: In Search of America* (1962), *America and Americans* (1966), *Journal of a Novel* (1969), and *Steinbeck: A Life in Letters* (1975; Elaine Steinbeck and Robert Wallsten, editors).

ACHIEVEMENTS

From the publication of his first best seller, *Tortilla Flat*, John Steinbeck was a popular and widely respected American writer. His three earlier novels were virtually ignored, but the five books of fiction published between 1935 and 1939 made him the most important literary spokesperson for the Depression decade. *In Dubious Battle*, *The Red Pony*, and *Of Mice and Men* established him as a serious writer, and his masterwork, *The Grapes of Wrath*, confirmed him as a major talent. During these years, his popular and critical success rivaled that of any of his contemporaries.

Although his immense popularity, public recognition, and the impressive sales of his works persisted throughout his career, Steinbeck's critical success waned after *The Grapes of Wrath*, reaching a nadir at his death in 1968, despite his Nobel Prize in Literature in 1962. During World War II, his development as a novelist faltered for many reasons, and Steinbeck never recovered his artistic momentum. Even *East of Eden*, the work he thought his masterpiece, proved a critical failure although a popular success. Steinbeck remains widely read, both in the United States and abroad, while his critical reputation has enjoyed a modest revival. Undoubtedly the appreciation of his considerable talents will continue to develop, as few writers have better celebrated the American Dream or traced the dark lineaments of the American nightmare.

BIOGRAPHY

John Ernst Steinbeck was born on February 27, 1902, in Salinas, California. The time and place of his birth are important because Steinbeck matured as an artist in his early thirties during the darkest days of the Depression, and his most important fictions are set in his beloved Salinas Valley. In one sense, Steinbeck's location in time and place may have made him a particularly American artist. Born just after the closing of the frontier, Steinbeck grew up with a frustrated modern America and witnessed the most notable failure of the American Dream in the Depression. He was a writer who inherited the great tradition of the American Renaissance of the nineteenth century and who was forced to reshape it in terms of the historical and literary imperatives of twentieth century modernism.

Steinbeck's family background evidenced this strongly American identity. His paternal grandfather, John Adolph Steinbeck, emigrated from Germany, settling in California after serving in the American Civil War. His mother's father, Samuel Hamilton, sailed around Cape Horn from northern Ireland, finally immigrating to the Salinas Valley. John Ernst Steinbeck and Olive Hamilton were the first-generation descendants of sturdy, successful, and Americanized immigrant farm families. They met and married in 1890, settling in Salinas, where the father was prominent in local business and government and the mother stayed home to rear their four children—three daughters and a son, the third child named for his father. The Steinbecks were refined, intelligent, and ambitious people who lived a quiet middle-class life in the small agricultural service town of Salinas.

Steinbeck seems to have enjoyed a happy childhood, and in fact he often asserted that he did. His father made enough money to indulge him in a small way, even to buy him a red pony. His mother encouraged him to read and to write, providing him with the classics of English and American literature. At school, he proved a popular and successful student and was elected president of his senior class. After graduation from Salinas High School in 1919, Steinbeck enrolled at Stanford University. His subsequent history belies the picture of the happy, normal young man. He was soon in academic difficulties and dropped out of college several times to work on ranches in the Salinas Valley and observe "real life." His interests were varied, but he settled on novel writing as his ambition, despite his family's insistence that he prepare for a more prosaic career. This traumatic rejection of middle-class values would prove a major force in shaping Steinbeck's fiction, both his social protest novels and his lighter entertainments such as *Cannery Row*.

Leaving Stanford without a degree in 1925, Steinbeck sojourned in New York for several months, where he worked as a laborer, a newspaper reporter, and a freelance writer. Disillusioned in all his abortive pursuits, Steinbeck returned to California, where a job as winter caretaker of a lodge at Lake Tahoe provided the time to finish his first novel, *Cup of Gold*. The novel, a romance concerned with the Caribbean pirate Henry Morgan, was published by a small press directly before the crash of 1929, and it earned the young writer little recognition and even less money. In 1930, he married Carol Henning and moved with her to Los Angeles and later to Pacific Grove, a seaside resort near Monterey, where he lived in his parents' summer house. Still supported by his family and his wife, the ambitious young writer produced the manuscripts of several novels.

A friend, Edward F. Ricketts, a marine biologist trained at the University of Chicago, encouraged Steinbeck to treat his material more objectively. Under Ricketts's influence, Steinbeck modified his earlier commitment to satire, allegory, and Romanticism and turned to modern accounts of the Salinas Valley. Steinbeck's next two novels, *The Pastures of Heaven* and *To a God Unknown*, are both set in the valley, but both still were marked by excessive sentimentality and symbolism. Both were virtually ignored by the public and the critics. Steinbeck's short fiction, however, began to receive recognition; for example, his story "The Murder" was selected to appear in *O. Henry Prize Stories of 1934*.

Tortilla Flat, a droll tale of Monterey's Mexican quarter, established Steinbeck as a popular and critical success in 1935. (Unfortunately, his parents died just before he achieved his first real success.) The novel's sales provided money to pay his debts, to travel to Mexico, and to continue writing seriously. His next novel, *In Dubious Battle*, established him as a serious literary artist and began the period of his greatest success, both critical and popular. This harshly realistic strike novel followed

directions established in stories such as "The Raid," influenced by the realistic impulse of American literature in the 1930's. Succeeding publications quickly confirmed this development in his fiction. His short novels *The Red Pony* and *Of Mice and Men* followed in 1937, his story collection *The Long Valley* in 1938, and his epic of the "Okie" migration to California, *The Grapes of Wrath*, in 1939. His own play version of *Of Mice and Men* won the Drama Critics' Circle Award in 1938, and *The Grapes of Wrath* received the Pulitzer Prize in 1940. Steinbeck had become one of the most popular and respected writers in the United States, a spokesperson for an entire culture.

In 1941, the Japanese attack on Pearl Harbor changed the direction of American culture and of Steinbeck's literary development. During the war years, he seemed in a

John Steinbeck. (© The Nobel Foundation)

holding pattern, trying to adjust to his phenomenal success while absorbing the cataclysmic events around him. Steinbeck's career stalled for many reasons. He left the California subjects and realistic style of his finest novels, and he was unable to come to terms with a world at war, though he served for a few months as a frontline correspondent. Personal developments paralleled these literary ones. Steinbeck divorced his first wife and married Gwen Conger, a young Hollywood star; no doubt she influenced his decision to move from California to New York. Steinbeck began to write with an eye on Broadway and Hollywood.

Steinbeck was forty-three years old when World War II ended in 1945; he died in 1968 at the age of sixty-six. Over those twenty-three years, Steinbeck was extremely productive, winning considerable acclaim—most notably the Nobel Prize in Literature in 1962. Yet the most important part of his career was finished. The war had changed the direction of his artistic development, and Steinbeck seemed powerless to reverse his decline.

Again, his personal life mirrored his literary difficulties. Although his only children—Tom, born in 1944, and John, born in 1946—were with Gwen, the couple were divorced in 1948. Like his first divorce, this one was bitter and expensive. In the same year, his mentor, Ricketts, was killed in a car accident. Steinbeck traveled extensively, devoting himself to film and nonfiction projects. In 1950, he married Elaine Scott, establishing a supportive relationship that allowed him to finish his epic Salinas Valley novel *East of Eden*.

Steinbeck tried again and again to write his way back to the artistic success of his earlier years, notably in *The Wayward Bus*, but his commercial success kept getting in the way. *East of Eden*, Steinbeck's major postwar novel, attempted another California epic to match the grandeur of *The Grapes of Wrath*. Although the book was a blockbuster best seller, it was an artistic and critical failure. Steinbeck himself seemed to recognize his own decline, and in his last years he virtually abandoned fiction for journalism.

Of his last novels, only *The Winter of Our Discontent* transcends mere entertainment, and it does not have the literary structures to match its serious themes. Despite the popularity of nonfiction works such as *Travels with Charley*, despite awards such as the Nobel Prize and the

United States Medal of Freedom, despite his personal friendship with President Lyndon B. Johnson as a supporter of Vietnam, Steinbeck was only the shell of the great writer of the 1930's. He died in New York City on December 20, 1968.

ANALYSIS

John Steinbeck remains a writer of the 1930's, perhaps *the* American writer of the 1930's. Although his first novel, *Cup of Gold*, was published in 1929, its derivative lost-generation posturing gives little indication of the masterpiece, *The Grapes of Wrath*, he would publish at the end of the next decade. Steinbeck developed from a Romantic, imitative, often sentimental apprentice to a realistic, objective, and accomplished novelist in only a decade. The reasons for this change can be found in the interplay between a sensitive writer and his cultural background.

A writer of great talent, sensitivity, and imagination, Steinbeck entered into the mood of the country in the late 1930's with an extraordinary responsiveness. The Depression had elicited a reevaluation of American culture, a reassessment of the American Dream: a harsh realism of observation balanced by a warm emphasis on human dignity. Literature and the other arts joined social, economic, and political thought in contrasting traditional American ideals with the bleak reality of breadlines and shantytowns. Perhaps the major symbol of dislocation was the Dust Bowl; the American garden became a wasteland from which its dispossessed farmers fled. The arts in the 1930's focused on these harsh images and tried to find in them the human dimensions that promised a new beginning.

The proletarian novel, documentary photography, and the documentary film stemmed from similar impulses; the radical novel put more emphasis on the inhuman conditions of the dislocated, while the films made more of the promising possibilities for a new day. Painting, music, and theater all responded to a new humanistic and realistic thrust. The best balance was struck by documentary photographers and filmmakers: Dorothea Lange, Walker Evans, and Arthur Rothstein in photography; Pare Lorentz, Willard Van Dyke, and Herbert Kline in film. As a novelist, Steinbeck shared this documentary impulse, and it refined his art.

IN DUBIOUS BATTLE

In Dubious Battle tells the harsh story of a violent ag-ricultural strike in the Torgas Valley from the viewpoint of two Communist agitators. Careful and objective in his handling of the material, the mature Steinbeck provided almost a factual case study of a strike. In a letter, he indi-cated that this was his conscious intention:

I had an idea that I was going to write the autobiogra-phy of a Communist. Then Miss McIntosh [Steinbeck's agent] suggested I reduce it to fiction. There lay the trouble. I had planned to write a journalistic account of a strike. But as I thought of it as fiction the thing got bigger and bigger . . . I have used a small strike in an orchard valley as the symbol of man's eternal, bitter warfare with himself.

For the first time, Steinbeck was able to combine his am-bition to write great moral literature with his desire to chronicle his time and place.

Significantly, the novel takes its title from John Mil-ton's *Paradise Lost* (1667, 1674) in which the phrase is used to describe the struggle between God and Satan, but it takes its subject from the newspapers and newsreels of the 1930's. The underlying structure demonstrates the universal struggle of good and evil, of human greed and selfishness versus human generosity and idealism. Jim, the protagonist killed at the conclusion, is obviously a Christ figure, an individual who has sacrificed himself for the group. Here, Steinbeck needs no overblown sym-bolic actions to support his theme. He lets his contempo-rary story tell itself realistically and in documentary fashion. In a letter, he later described his method in the novel: "I wanted to be merely a recording consciousness, judging nothing, simply putting down the thing." This objective, dispassionate, almost documentary realism separates *In Dubious Battle* from his earlier fiction and announces the beginning of Steinbeck's major period.

OF MICE AND MEN

Of Mice and Men was written in 1935 and 1936 and first published as a novel in 1937 at the height of the De-pression. Steinbeck constructed the book around dra-matic scenes so that he could easily rewrite it for the stage, which he did with the help of George S. Kauf-mann. The play opened late in 1937, with Wallace Ford as George and Broderick Crawford as Lennie. A film version, directed by Lewis Milestone, appeared in 1939. The success of the play and film spurred sales of the novel and created a wide audience for Steinbeck's next book, *The Grapes of Wrath*.

Like his classic story of the Okie migration from the Dust Bowl to the promised land of California, *Of Mice and Men* is a dramatic presentation of the persistence of the American Dream and the tragedy of its failure. His characters are the little people, the uncommon "common people," disoriented and dispossessed by modern life yet still yearning for a little piece of land, that little particle of the Jeffersonian ideal. Lennie is the symbol of this vis-ceral, inarticulate land-hunger, while George becomes the poet of this romantic vision. How their dream blos-soms and then dies is Steinbeck's dramatic subject; how their fate represents that of America in the 1930's and after becomes his theme. His title, an allusion to the Scottish poet Robert Burns, suggests that the best laid plans "of mice and men often gang a-gley"; so the Amer-ican vision had gone astray in the Depression decade Steinbeck documented so movingly and realistically.

THE RED PONY

The Red Pony involves the maturation of Jody Tiflin, a boy about ten years old when the action opens. The time is about 1910, and the setting is the Tiflin ranch in the Salinas Valley, where Jody lives with his father, Carl; his mother, Ruth; and the hired hand, a middle-aged cowboy named Billy Buck. From time to time, they are visited by Jody's grandfather, a venerable old man who led one of the first wagon trains to California. "The Gift," the first section of the novel, concerns Jody's red pony, which he names Gabilan, after the nearby moun-tain range. The pony soon becomes a symbol of the boy's growing maturity and his developing knowledge of the natural world. Later, he carelessly leaves the pony out in the rain, and it takes cold and dies, despite Billy Buck's efforts to save it. Thus, Jody learns of nature's cruel indifference to human wishes.

In the second part, "The Great Mountains," the Tiflin ranch is visited by a former resident, Gitano, an aged Chicano laborer reared in the now vanished hacienda. Old Gitano has come home to die. In a debate that recalls Frost's poem "The Death of the Hired Man," Carl per-suades Ruth that they cannot take Old Gitano in, but—as in Frost's poem—their dialogue proves pointless.

Stealing a broken-down horse significantly named Easter, the old man rides off into the mountains to die in dignity. Again, Jody is faced with the complex, harsh reality of adult life.

In "The Promise," the third section, Jody learns more of nature's ambiguous promises when his father has one of the mares put to stud to give the boy another colt. The birth is complicated, however, and Billy Buck must kill the mare to save the colt, demonstrating that life and death are inextricably intertwined. The final section, "The Leader of the People," ends the sequence with another vision of death and change. Jody's grandfather comes to visit, retelling his timeworn stories of the great wagon crossing. Carl cruelly hurts the old man by revealing that none of them except Jody is really interested in these repetitive tales. The grandfather realizes that Carl is right, but later he tells Jody that the adventurous stories were not the point, but that his message was "Westering" itself. For the grandfather, Westering was the source of American identity. With the close of the frontier, Westering has ended, and the rugged Westerners have been replaced by petty landholders such as Carl and aging cowboys such as Billy Buck. In his grandfather's ramblings, Jody discovers a sense of mature purpose, and by the conclusion of the sequence, he too can hope to be a leader of the people.

The Red Pony traces Jody's initiation into adult life with both realism and sensitivity, a balance that Steinbeck did not always achieve. The vision of the characters caught up in the harsh world of nature is balanced by their deep human concerns and commitments. The evocation of the ranch setting in its vital beauty is matched only in the author's finest works, such as *Of Mice and Men*. Steinbeck's symbols grow naturally out of this setting, and nothing in the story-sequence seems forced into a symbolic pattern, as in his later works. In its depiction of an American variation on a universal experience, *The Red Pony* deserves comparison with the finest of modern American fiction, especially with initiation tales such as William Faulkner's *The Bear* (1942) and Ernest Hemingway's Nick Adams stories.

Responding to a variety of social and artistic influences, Steinbeck's writing had evolved toward documentary realism throughout the 1930's. In fiction, this development is especially clear in the works *In Dubious Battle*, *Of Mice and Men*, and *The Long Valley*. Even more obvious was the movement of his nonfiction toward a committed documentation of the social ills plaguing America during the Depression decade. Steinbeck's newspaper and magazine writing offered detailed accounts of social problems, particularly the plight of migrant agricultural workers in California's fertile valleys. The culmination of this development was *Their Blood Is Strong* (1938), a compilation of reports originally written for the *San Francisco News* and published with additional text by Steinbeck and photographs by Lange originally made for the U.S. Farm Security Administration (FSA).

THE GRAPES OF WRATH

It is significant that Steinbeck first conceived of *The Grapes of Wrath* as just such a documentary book. In March, 1938, Steinbeck went into the California valleys with a *Life* magazine photographer to make a record of the harsh conditions in the migrant camps. The reality he encountered seemed too significant for nonfiction, however, and Steinbeck began to reshape this material as a novel, an epic novel.

Although his first tentative attempts at fictionalizing the situation in the agricultural valleys were heavily satiric, as indicated by the early title *L'Affaire Lettuceberg*, Steinbeck soon realized that the Okie migration was the stuff of an American epic. Reworking his material, adding to it by research in government agency files and by more journeys into the camps and along the migrant routes, Steinbeck evolved his vision. A grand design emerged; he would follow one family from the Oklahoma Dust Bowl to California. Perhaps this methodology was suggested by the sociological case histories of the day, perhaps by the haunted faces of individual families that stared back at him as he researched in FSA files.

In discussing his plans for his later documentary film, *The Forgotten Village* (1941), Steinbeck remarked that most documentaries concerned large groups of people but that audiences could identify better with individuals. In *The Grapes of Wrath*, he made one family representative of general conditions. The larger groups and problems he treated in short interchapters that generalized the issues particularized in the Joad family. Perhaps the grand themes of change and movement were suggested by the documentary films of Lorentz (later a personal friend), *The Plow That Broke the Plains* (1936) and *The River* (1938), with their panoramic geographical and historical visions. Drawing an archetypal theme from Malory, John Bunyan, John Milton, and the Bible—the ultimate source of his pervasive religious symbolism—Steinbeck made the journey of the Joads into an allegorical pilgrimage as well as a desperate race along Route 66. During this journey, the Joad family disintegrates, but the larger human family emerges. Tom Joad makes a pilgrim's progress from a narrow, pessimistic view to a transcendental vision of American possibilities. The novel ends on a note of hope for a new American Dream.

The Grapes of Wrath was a sensational best seller from the beginning. Published to generally favorable reviews in March, 1939, it was selling at the rate of more than twenty-five hundred copies a day two months later. Controversy helped spur sales. As part documentary, its factual basis was subject to close scrutiny, and many critics challenged Steinbeck's material. Oklahomans resented the presentation of the Joads as typical of the state (many still do), while Californians disapproved of the depiction of their state's leading industry. The book was attacked, banned, burned—but everywhere it was read. Even in the migrant camps, it was considered an accurate picture of the conditions experienced there. Some 430,000 copies were sold in a year; in 1940, the novel received the Pulitzer Prize and the Award of the American Booksellers Association (later the National Book Award).

Naturally, all the excitement attracted the attention of Hollywood, even though the controversy over the novel seemed to preclude a film version, or at least a faithful film version. Nevertheless, Darryl F. Zanuck produced and John Ford directed a faithful adaptation starring Henry Fonda in 1940; the film, like the novel, has become a classic, and it gave Steinbeck's vision of America in the 1930's even wider currency.

Indeed, Steinbeck's best work was filmic in the best sense of that word—visual, realistic, objective. These qualities nicely balanced the allegorical and romantic strains inherent in his earlier fiction. During World War II, however, his work, much to its detriment, began to cater to the film industry. In fact, much of his postwar writing seems to have found its inspiration in Hollywood versions of his work. His own screen adaptation of an earlier

story, *The Red Pony*, proves a sentimentalized reproduction of the original. Still, he was occasionally capable of recapturing his earlier vision, particularly in his works about Mexico—*The Pearl* and *Viva Zapata!*

THE PEARL

Mexico always had been an important symbolic place for Steinbeck. As a native Californian, he had been aware of his state's Mexican heritage. Even as a boy, he sought out Chicano companions, fascinated by their unconcern for the pieties of white culture; he also befriended Mexican field hands at the ranches where he worked during his college summers. Later, his first literary success, *Tortilla Flat*, grew from his involvement with the *paisanos* of Monterey, people who would today be called Chicanos.

For Steinbeck, Mexico was everything modern America was not; it possessed a primitive vitality, a harsh simplicity, and a romantic beauty—all of which are found in *The Pearl*. Mexico exhibits the same qualities in the works of other modern writers such as Malcolm Lowry, Aldous Huxley, Graham Greene, Hart Crane, and Katherine Anne Porter. All of them lived and worked there for some time, contrasting the traditional culture they discovered in Mexico with the emptiness of the modern world. Steinbeck also was fascinated by a Mexico still alive with social concern. The continued extension of the revolution into the countryside had been his subject in *The Forgotten Village*, and it would be developed further in *Viva Zapata!* For Steinbeck, Mexico represented the purity of artistic and social purposes that he had lost after World War II.

This sense of the writer's personal involvement energizes *The Pearl*, making it Steinbeck's best work of fiction in the years following the success of *The Grapes of Wrath*. At the beginning of the novella, the storyteller states, "If this story is a parable, perhaps everyone takes his own meaning from it and reads his own life into it." The critics have read Steinbeck's short novel in a number of ways, but strangely enough, they have not considered it as a parable of the author's own career in the postwar period. Much like Hemingway's *The Old Man and the Sea* (1952), *The Pearl* uses the life of a simple fisherman to investigate symbolically an aging artist's difficult maturation.

Steinbeck was presented with the tale during his Sea

of Cortez expedition in 1940. In his log, he recounts "an event which happened at La Paz in recent years." The story matches the basic outline of *The Pearl*, though Steinbeck made several major changes, changes significant in an autobiographical sense. In the original, the Mexican fisherman was a devil-may-care bachelor; in *The Pearl*, he becomes the sober young husband and father, Kino. Steinbeck himself had just become a father for the first time when he wrote the novella, and this change provides a clue to the autobiographical nature of the parable. The original bachelor thought the pearl a key to easy living; Kino sees it creating a better way of life for the people through an education for his baby son, Coyotito. If the child could read and write, then he could set his family and his people free from the social and economic bondage in which they toil. Kino is ignorant of the dangers of wealth, and *The Pearl* is the tale of how he matures by coming to understand them. Steinbeck, too, matured from his youthful innocence as he felt the pressures of success.

As in his best fiction of the 1930's Steinbeck fuses his universal allegory with documentary realism. Perhaps planning ahead for a screenplay, Steinbeck's prose in the novel often takes a cinematic point of view. Scenes are presented in terms of establishing shots, medium views, and close-ups. In particular, Steinbeck carefully examines the natural setting, often visually contrasting human behavior with natural phenomena. As in his best fiction, his naturalistic vision is inherent in the movement of his story; there is no extraneous philosophizing.

Steinbeck's characters in *The Pearl* are real people in a real world, but they are also universal types. Kino, the fisherman named for an early Jesuit explorer; Juana, his wife; and Coyotito, their baby, are almost an archetypal family, like the holy family in a medieval morality play. Kino's aspirations are the same universal drives to better himself and his family that took the Okies to California's Central Valley. Like the Joads, this symbolic family must struggle at once against an indifferent natural order and a corrupt social order. Unfortunately, aside from the screenplay of *Viva Zapata!* Steinbeck would never again achieve the fusion of parable and realism that energizes *The Pearl*.

In his Nobel Prize speech of 1962, Steinbeck indicated what he tried to accomplish in his work:

The ancient commission of the writer has not changed. He is charged with exposing our many grievous faults and failures, with dredging up to the light our dark and dangerous dreams, for the purpose of improvement.

No writer has better exposed the dark underside of the American Dream, but few writers have so successfully celebrated the great hope symbolized in that dream—the hope of human development. Steinbeck's best fictions picture a paradise lost but also posit a future paradise to be regained. In spite of his faults and failures, Steinbeck's best literary works demonstrate a greatness of heart and mind found only rarely in modern American literature.

Joseph R. Millichap

OTHER MAJOR WORKS

SHORT FICTION: *Saint Katy the Virgin*, 1936; *The Long Valley*, 1938.

PLAYS: *Of Mice and Men*, pr., pb. 1937; *The Moon Is Down*, pr. 1942; *Burning Bright*, pb. 1951.

SCREENPLAYS: *The Forgotten Village*, 1941; *Lifeboat*, 1944; *A Medal for Benny*, 1945; *The Pearl*, 1945; *The Red Pony*, 1949; *Viva Zapata!*, 1952.

NONFICTION: *Their Blood Is Strong*, 1938; *The Forgotten Village*, 1941; *Sea of Cortez: A Leisurely Journal of Travel and Research*, 1941 (with Edward F. Ricketts); *Bombs Away*, 1942; *A Russian Journal*, 1948 (with Robert Capa); *Once There Was a War*, 1958; *Travels with Charley: In Search of America*, 1962; *Letters to Alicia*, 1965; *America and Americans*, 1966; *Journal of a Novel*, 1969; *Steinbeck: A Life in Letters*, 1975 (Elaine Steinbeck and Robert Wallsten, editors); *Steinbeck and Covici: The Story of a Friendship*, 1979 (Thomas Fensch, editor); *America and Americans, and Selected Nonfiction*, 2002 (Susan Shillinglaw and Jackson J. Benson, editors).

TRANSLATION: *The Acts of King Arthur and His Noble Knights*, 1976.

BIBLIOGRAPHY

Astro, Richard, and Tetsumaro Hayashi, eds. *Steinbeck: The Man and His Work*. Corvallis: Oregon State University Press, 1971. One of the first full-length works published after Steinbeck's death, this superb collection of essays presents opinions which regard Steinbeck as everything from a mere proletarian novelist to an artist with a deep vision of humans' essential dignity.

Benson, Jackson D. *The True Adventures of John Steinbeck, Writer*. New York: Viking Press, 1984. Benson's biography emphasizes Steinbeck's rebellion against critical conventions and his attempts to keep his private life separate from his role as public figure. Considers Steinbeck as a critical anomaly, embarrassed and frustrated by his growing critical and popular success.

Beegel, Susan F., Susan Shillinglaw, and Wesley N. Tiffney, Jr., eds. *Steinbeck and the Environment: Interdisciplinary Approaches*. Foreword by Elaine Steinbeck. Tuscaloosa: University of Alabama Press, 1997. Collection of essays that interpret Steinbeck's work from an ecological perspective, including discussions of his friendship with marine biologist Edward Ricketts and environmentally oriented analyses of *The Grapes of Wrath*, *The Winter of Our Discontent*, and *East of Eden*.

Bloom, Harold, ed. *John Steinbeck*. New ed. New York: Bloom's Literary Criticism, 2008. Collection of essays discussing various aspects of Steinbeck's work, including analyses of *The Pearl*, *Of Mice and Men*, *The Red Pony*, *The Grapes of Wrath*, and *East of Eden*.

French, Warren. *John Steinbeck's Fiction Revisited*. New York: Twayne, 1994. This revision of a book originally published in 1961 provides a solid introduction to Steinbeck, with biographical information and analysis of his novels. Includes a bibliography.

George, Stephen K., ed. *John Steinbeck: A Centennial Tribute*. New York: Praeger, 2002. A collection of reminiscences from Steinbeck's family and friends as well as wide-ranging critical assessments of his works. One of several books published to commemorate the centenary of Steinbeck's birth.

George, Stephen K., and Barbara A. Heavilin, eds. *John Steinbeck and His Contemporaries*. Lanham, Md.: Scarecrow Press, 2007. A collection of papers from a 2006 conference about Steinbeck and the writers who influenced or informed his work. Some of the essays discuss his European forebears, particularly Henry Fielding and Sir Thomas Malory; and his American forebears, such as Walt Whitman and Sarah Orne Jewett. Other essays compare his work to Ernest Hemingway, William Faulkner, and other twentieth century American writers.

Johnson, Claudia Durst, ed. *Understanding "Of Mice and Men," "The Red Pony," and "The Pearl": A Student Casebook to Issues, Sources, and Historical Documents*. Westport, Conn.: Greenwood Press, 1997. This casebook contains historical, social, and political materials as a context for Steinbeck's three novellas, providing information about California and the West, land ownership, the male worker, homelessness, and oppression of the poor in Mexico.

McElrath, Joseph R., Jr., Jesse S. Crisler, and Susan Shillinglaw, eds. *John Steinbeck: The Contemporary Reviews*. New York: Cambridge University Press, 1996. A selection of reviews of all of Steinbeck's novels and some of his nonfiction that were published from 1929 through 1989. Includes a bibliography and an index.

Parini, Jay. *John Steinbeck: A Biography*. New York: Henry Holt, 1995. This biography provides both psychological interpretations of Steinbeck's life and sociological interpretations of his fiction. Parini criticizes Steinbeck for his insensitive social and political views, and he takes Steinbeck to task for what Parini calls his blindness to the political reality of the Vietnam War.

Shillinglaw, Susan, and Kevin Hearle. *Beyond Boundaries: Rereading John Steinbeck*. Tuscaloosa: University of Alabama Press, 2002. Writers from the United States, Japan, France, England, Thailand, and India examine Steinbeck's work and worldwide cultural influence. The essays include discussions of Steinbeck's legacy in the songs of Bruce Springsteen, his influence upon Native American writers, and his reception in the Indus Valley.

Steinbeck, Elaine, and Robert Wallsten. *Steinbeck: A Life in Letters*. New York: Viking Press, 1975. An indispensable source, this collection of letters written by Steinbeck between 1929 and his death forty years later shows a writer both well read and well disciplined. letters to his friend and publisher, Pascal Covici, shed light on the writer's working methods and are particularly revealing.

STENDHAL
Marie-Henri Beyle

Born: Grenoble, France; January 23, 1783
Died: Paris, France; March 23, 1842
Also known as: Marie-Henri Beyle

PRINCIPAL LONG FICTION

Armance, 1827 (English translation, 1928)
Le Rouge et le noir, 1830 (*The Red and the Black*, 1898)
La Chartreuse de Parme, 1839 (*The Charterhouse of Parma*, 1895)
Lucien Leuwen, 1855, 1894, 1926-1927 (wr. 1834-1835; English translation, 1950)
Lamiel, 1889, 1971 (wr. 1839-1842; English translation, 1929)

OTHER LITERARY FORMS

Stendhal also wrote short fiction, divided by later editors into two groups: his *nouvelles* written between 1829 and 1831, and the short stories *Chroniques italiennes* (1839, 1855; *The Abbess of Castro, and Other Tales*, 1926). Stendhal's nonfiction works include musical history and criticism, as in *Vies de Haydn, de Mozart, et de Métastase* (1815; *The Lives of Haydn and Mozart, with Observations on Métastase*, 1817), *Vie de Rossini* (1823; *Memoirs of Rossini*, 1824; also as *Life of Rossini*, 1956), and *Notes d'un dilettante* (1824-1827); art history and criticism, as in *Histoire de la peinture en Italie* (1817) and five subsequent volumes of art appreciation; travel diaries, including *Rome, Naples, et Florence en 1817* (1817, 1826; *Rome, Naples, and Florence, in 1817*, 1818), *Promenades dans Rome* (1829; *A Roman Journal*, 1957), *Mémoires d'un touriste* (1838; *Memoirs of a Tourist*, 1962), and *Voyage dans le midi de la France* (1838; *Travels in the South of France*, 1971); literary theory, including *Racine et Shakespeare* (part 1, 1823; part 2, 1825; *Racine and Shakespeare*, 1962); psychological theory, including *De l'amour* (1822; *Maxims of Love*, 1906); and autobiography and biography, including *Souvenirs d'égotisme* (1892; *Memoirs of an Egotist*, 1949), *Vie de Henry Brulard* (1890; *The Life of Henry Brulard*, 1925). In addition, Stendhal's works of journal-

ism (written between 1822 and 1830), his *Journal* (1888), and his *Correspondance* (1933-1934) occupy some six or seven thousand pages.

ACHIEVEMENTS

Stendhal is frequently referred to, along with Fyodor Dostoevski, as "the forerunner of the modern novel." Insofar as the highest manifestations of the novel form in the twentieth century developed, by way of Thomas Mann, James Joyce, and Marcel Proust, as an exploration of reality that goes beyond the limitations of "realism," the recognition accorded Stendhal is justified. Half a century before Sigmund Freud, Stendhal's power of psychological observation was granting as much scope to subconscious and irrational motivation as to more lucidly conceived manifestations of the compelling forces underlying all major human actions. The conversations between his characters rarely reveal more than the tip of the iceberg; what interests him is the long process of maturation in the mind (the *monologue intérieur*, or interior monologue) that precedes the spoken word.

While his contemporaries Honoré de Balzac and Charles Dickens were realists first and foremost, for Stendhal, realism was at best a means; it was never an end in itself. The result is an exact and compelling portrait of "reality" that at the same time (particularly in the case of *The Charterhouse of Parma*) is oddly off-key. All of Stendhal's full-length novels, without exception, are deeply rooted in the world that he observed about him—in Paris, in small French provincial towns, or in the cities and plains of northern Italy. Above all, his political and social depiction of the malaise of his time is penetratingly acute—one of the most profound analyses yet made of a society in a period of political reaction, in which the dominating emotion is that of fear. When the social order is so precarious and at the same time so disillusioned, then virtually every class, and every individual, lives in fear of every other: "We live," he noted— and the phrase has become proverbial—"in an era of suspicion." One of the forces that contributed to this suspicion was that newborn and newly powerful institution, the daily press; Stendhal was the first major novelist to take account of the power of the press in shaping the ideas, the prejudices, the opinions, and the destinies of ordinary people.

However precise this realism was within its own conventional limitations, Stendhal was constantly going beyond it. He was, he admitted, not only repelled but also *bored* by description. Faced with Balzac's Pension Vauquer, he would have given up after the first three lines. Frequently, having embarked on a description, he tails off into "etc., etc.," leaving the rest to his reader's imagination. In the place of description, he preferred what he called *le petit fait vrai*: "the tiny, true fact," the one minute detail of observation so singular that no fiction could have conceived it, yet so revealing that it conjures up a total picture of reality more vivid than could have been vouchsafed by a dozen pages of descriptive journalism. Thus, Fabrice, having strayed almost by accident onto the battlefield of Waterloo, observes his first corpse, already plundered by the still-living: "The corpse had dirty feet"—not the sublime magnificence of the cannonades, but the one "tiny, true fact," evoking a whole panorama of the sordid realities of nineteenth century warfare. In this, Stendhal's realism is at least halfway along the road to the techniques of the Symbolists: The significance of the phenomenon lies in what it reveals beyond itself.

Indeed, the Symbolists, beginning with Charles Baudelaire, recognized Stendhal as an ancestor—although, admittedly, more in the domain of aesthetic theory than in that of the novel. Even within the domain of the realistic novel, however, Stendhal formulated two further principles that are not without significance, even today. First, the novelist is not to be held morally responsible for the immorality of his characters: "A novel is a mirror trundled along beside a highroad"— the mirror is in no way responsible for what it reflects. Second, no person can be understood except in terms of the political conditions that alone explain his or her individuality: "Politics in a novel is like a pistol-shot fired during a concert; something crude, yet

which nonetheless *compels* attention." The shot would be awkward material, in fact, but material the novelist could ignore only at his peril.

BIOGRAPHY

Stendhal's experience of life was as rich and as varied as the range of his writings might suggest. Born Marie-Henri Beyle in Grenoble—a city that he detested all of his life as the very symbol of small-minded provinciality—on January 23, 1783, he lost his mother, Henriette Gagnon, before he was seven, a traumatic experience that left him with a classic Oedipus complex, adoring her memory and everything connected with her and loathing his father, Chérubin Beyle, and everything connected with him. The most abominated of the representatives of his father was a Jesuit priest, the Abbé Raillane, who became his tutor; never, in a single page of his subsequent writings, does Stendhal mention Jesuits without irony and contempt.

No part of Stendhal's writing is wholly separable from his biography. He lived through so many events

Stendhal. (Library of Congress)

that, by the time he became a novelist, "history," for him, meant that which he himself had experienced. He was six years old when the French Revolution broke out and eleven when the Terror struck Grenoble; during the latter, he enjoyed himself thoroughly playing cops and robbers and making a dangerous nuisance of himself to his father and to the rest of his family. In spite of everything, however, he received an excellent nonclassical education at the newly established École Centrale at Grenoble, concentrating on modern subjects, on art, and on mathematics, and in November, 1799, he set off for Paris to follow courses at the École Polytechnique, intending to qualify as a military engineer.

This early fascination—on one hand, with the precision of mathematics, and on the other, with the positive aggressivity of military science—was to endure all of his life; it is ironic, therefore, to discover that he never so much as set foot within the walls of the École Polytechnique. Instead, no sooner had he arrived in Paris than he discovered in himself a new ambition: that of becoming a dramatist, "a new Molière"—an extraordinary aberration that was to preoccupy him fruitlessly for the better part of twenty years. On top of this first wrong turn came a second: Alone in his student lodgings, freezing with cold in the depths of a Parisian winter, he developed pleurisy, with complications. Short of a miracle, it would be the end of Marie-Henri Beyle.

The miracle duly occurred. On the day before Stendhal arrived in Paris, November 10, 1799, Napoleon had seized power. Among Napoleon's ablest supporters and administrators—quickly rising to a position of enormous influence as director of the army's Ministry of Supply—was Pierre Daru, a distant cousin of Stendhal's father. The Daru family rescued their seventeen-year-old provincial relative in his distress, and when he had recovered, Pierre Daru found him a job in his own office. Stendhal was so ignorant of letters in that period that the very first time Daru dictated a memorandum to him, he misspelled the word *cela* as *cella*. Thirty years later, Julien Sorel would do the same thing in *The Red and the Black*.

At the beginning of May, 1800, Napoleon opened his second campaign against the Austrians in northern Italy by taking his army over the Saint-Bernard Pass and descending out of the blue onto the plain of Lombardy to beat the enemy at Marengo. Pierre Daru invited his young cousin to participate in the march, and Stendhal accepted with enthusiasm; thus, still in civilian clothes, and decidedly ill-balanced on an awkward "Swiss" horse (falling off horses is a chronic occupational hazard for the Stendhalian hero), Stendhal followed in the baggage train. On May 30, he came under fire for the first time; two days later, having a free evening in the little township of Ivrea, he paid for a seat to hear a third-rate opera company perform its uninspired version of Domenico Cimarosa's *Il matrimonio segreto* (1792; *The Secret Marriage*). This banal experience was a quasi-mystical revelation that changed Stendhal's life. From that moment on, not France but Italy—above all, Milan—was to be his spiritual home; Marie-Henri Beyle had embarked on the long process of his transformation into the creator of *The Charterhouse of Parma*. In his will, he ordained that his tombstone should bear the inscription, "Arrigo Beyle, Milanese." This stone may still be seen at the Cimetière Montmartre in Paris.

For the next thirty years, his life would be scarcely less adventurous. After eighteen months, he resigned his Italian commission and went back to Paris to write plays, study acting, and fall in love with an actress. The actress, Mélanie Guilbert, accepted an engagement to play in Marseilles; off went Stendhal in her wake, earning his living meanwhile as a grocer's storeman. Then he returned to the Napoleonic service, spending three years (1806-1809) as an administrator in Germany, rising in the ranks and becoming recognized as an enterprising and efficient officer, and traveling widely—to Brunswick, to Berlin, to Dresden (one night, his coach stopped at a little township called Stendhal; the name would seem to have stuck in his mind). He spent seven months in Vienna, returned to Paris, where he lived with an opera singer, and then was in Italy again in 1811.

In 1812, not the most propitious of moments, he volunteered to carry dispatches to Moscow, witnessed the fire that destroyed the city, lost most of his manuscripts, directed a supply column during the Great Retreat, by sheer willpower and hectoring forced his column over the Berezina River the day *before* the disastrous battle, and continued to supply his units as far as Königsberg—but vowed that, thereafter, he would never again experience cold. In 1813, he saw the Battle of Bautzen; in 1814, he was a senior officer in charge of defending the

Dauphine against the advancing Allies. A few weeks later, he was left with the last-minute responsibility of removing all art treasures in Paris from the reach of the oncoming Cossacks. Then came the great collapse.

With Napoleon exiled to Elba, Stendhal's career stood in ruins. He had to choose: either make his peace with the restored Bourbons or remain faithful to his hero and go into exile himself. He chose the latter course, retiring to Milan, penniless and in debt, and there spending the next seven years as a hack writer churning out what he could to help keep himself alive; *The Lives of Haydn and Mozart, with Observations on Métastase, Histoire de la peinture en Italie*, and the travel guide *Rome, Naples, and Florence, in 1817*. The latter sold well: Tourists, after a quarter of a century of political blockade, were pouring back into the peninsula; Stendhal's prospects at last were improving. He had learned Italian, and he was being accepted into young, adventurous literary circles—circles in which, by the year 1818, the word "Romanticism" was coming into fashion, but all too often in conjunction with other words, such as "liberal," *carbonaro*, and "independent Italy." It was to the echo of words such as these that, in 1818, Stendhal met the greatest and most enduring love of his life, Métilde Viscontini Dembowski, friend and protector of the poet Ugo Foscolo. Stendhal loved Métilde passionately and despairingly for three years; she did not ever grant him the least encouragement. In the end, his carbonarist sympathies became too marked for the Austrian authorities to ignore; he was expelled from Milan and, in 1821, returned to Paris. He never again saw Métilde, but her presence is felt in every book he wrote after that point. The essay *Maxims of Love* is an analysis of his feeling for her; Clélia Conti (*The Charterhouse of Parma*) and Madame de Chasteller (*Lucien Leuwen*) both bear her features; his own frustrated feeling of impotence in the presence of the woman he loved is reflected in Octave de Malivert (*Armance*); and it is no accident that the passionate heroine of *The Red and the Black* is named Mathilde.

Now, at last, things became calmer. Stendhal spent nine years in Paris, from 1821 to 1830, as a journalist, an art critic, an acknowledged authority on Italian opera—yet he always found time to be in love. One of his lovers, Clémentine Curial, caused him such despair that he seriously considered suicide; instead, he sat down and wrote his first novel, *Armance*.

Although it was a failure, *Armance* showed Stendhal his true vocation. He was no longer young, but now the creative fury took hold of him. In 1828, he got the first idea for a new novel—"Julien" it was to be called—and although it was not until January, 1830, that he started writing seriously, once he had begun, he worked quickly. "Julien" became *The Red and the Black*, and by July, Stendhal was correcting proofs. On July 28, firing broke out in the street beneath his window: The "Three Glorious Days" were putting a final end to the Bourbon regime. With joy in his heart, Stendhal went on correcting proofs.

Once the new government, that of Louis-Philippe, was established, Stendhal set out to achieve his heart's desire: a post in Italy. He was offered the consulship at Trieste, but Trieste was Austrian territory, and Prince Metternich's files recalled the fact that one Marie-Henri Beyle had already been expelled from Milan for "anti-Austrian activities." Stendhal was refused accreditation. In consolation, he was offered the post of French Consul at Civitavecchia, in the Papal States. There, in this little provincial seaport some eighty miles north of Rome, he was destined to remain for the rest of his career. With no opera, no society, and no intelligent conversation to be found in Civitavecchia, Stendhal had nothing to do but write: *Memoirs of an Egotist, Lucien Leuwen, The Life of Henry Brulard*, the first stories of *The Abbess of Castro and Other Tales*—masterpiece after masterpiece. In the late spring of 1836, he was granted leave, but, back in Paris, the creative mood did not desert him: He wrote *Memoirs of a Tourist, Travels in the South of France*, and another story found in *The Abbess of Castro and Other Tales*, "Vittoria Accoramboni." By what process of ingenuity Consul Beyle contrived to extend his original three months' leave to nearly three years is unknown; in any event, he was still in Paris when, in the last weeks of 1838, he had his greatest moment of inspiration and, in less than two months, set down on paper the entirety of *The Charterhouse of Parma*.

That, however, was virtually the end. "Exhausted," he notes repeatedly in his diaries and jottings during this time. Back in Civitavecchia, he began a new novel, *Lamiel*, but everything seemed to go wrong. In 1842, he was granted a new, short leave, in the course of which he collapsed on the sidewalk of the rue Neuve-des-Petits-Champs in Paris and died the following day, stricken down with apoplexy.

ANALYSIS

It is a primary characteristic of Stendhal as a writer of fiction that he was incapable both of devising a plot and of embroidering characters with the fantasy of his own imagination. He needed to have his fundamental story line laid out for him; only then could he set to work creatively. His genius lay not in fashioning but in refashioning his material.

ARMANCE

This is the pattern found in *Armance*. A certain Madame de Duras specialized in novels in which a pair of lovers are separated by an "insuperable" obstacle. In one of her novels, *Olivier: Ou, Le Secret* (written 1825), this obstacle takes the form of sexual impotence in the hero; the idea for the story was also used by Henri de Latouche for his *Olivier* (1826), which Stendhal reviewed. Stendhal, familiar with both works, had found his basic material; against that, however, was the fact that his whole idealistic sensibility was repulsed by the idea of setting out in black and white the unromantic physiological details of the "obstacle" that, for some four hundred pages, prevents his hero, Octave de Malivert, from marrying the beautiful, half-Russian Armance and that alone explains the hero's suicide, with the result that the uninformed reader can close the book without even so much as guessing at the mysterious "secret" that alone makes sense of the situation. It is not surprising that, on its first appearance, *Armance* was a failure.

It is precisely to this overcareful concealment of the key to the mystery that the novel owes its most significant qualities, however. If the secret had been revealed, the tale could have been little more than a medico-psychological casebook of the type popularized by Edmond and Jules de Goncourt a generation later. As it is, the sense of living with some "inexpressible misfortune" transforms Octave into one of the earliest examples of the true Romantic hero in the French novel: moody, solitary, unpredictable, bored, frustrated by the world, incapable of accepting happiness even when it is offered to him—a Byronic creature whose inner self is at

war with his outer semblance, possessed by a demon of inexplicable violence: a true "aristocrat of misfortune." In response, Armance likewise assumes similar characteristics. Already remote, inaccessible, and coldly exotic, thanks to her Russian origins, she alternates between moments of passion and moments of withdrawal, reacting to the "mystery" of her lover by retreating behind the veils of her own mystery.

Among the diaphanous nuances of this game of emotional hide-and-seek, Stendhal weaves a number of other themes characteristically his own. All of Stendhal's writings—even his studies on art and music—are to a greater or lesser degree "committed"; that is, they embody precise critical attitudes toward the political and social issues of his time. The 1820's in France were a period of intense social malaise, as the *ancien régime* aristocracy, supported by the Catholic Church, attempted to reassert its control over the country against the temporarily defeated forces of Jacobinism and liberalism. A major victory in this effort to set the clock back came in April, 1825, when the Chamber of Deputies passed an "act of indemnity" granting financial compensation to those aristocratic families who had had their lands and châteaus confiscated during the Revolution. The "reaction" was in the ascendant.

Octave has a title: He is the Vicomte de Malivert. Thus, whether he likes it or not, he is an aristocrat, confined irrevocably within the perimeters of that class. By the very fact of his name, he is stamped indelibly as a reactionary. At the same time, however, he is a highly intelligent, modern, mathematically minded young man, trained at the École Polytechnique and a political idealist into the bargain; today one would call him a progressive intellectual. Thus, in the outcome, the "insuperable" personal and sexual dilemma is transformed into a symbol of something far more significant and universal: the irreconcilable claims of commitment to himself as an individual, on one hand, and to his class, family, and inherited background, on the other. Once again, suicide would appear to be the only solution. Even that, when it comes, bears the same hallmark of "impotence." Octave remains his own divided self even in death. Lord Byron, faced with a parallel dilemma, at least got as far as Missolonghi in his flamboyant gesture of sacrificing himself to a "liberal" cause; not so Octave—a failed Byron if ever there was one. His ship, in Byron's wake, is bound for Greece, and he, to fight the Turks. He dies, however, with careful timing, immediately before the coast is sighted. Octave is indeed a Romantic hero, but he is also the first of Stendhal's antiheroes.

THE RED AND THE BLACK

It was not a novel but the verbatim newspaper report of a murder trial that provided Stendhal with the plot and the denouement he needed for *The Red and the Black*. In four consecutive issues dated from December 28 to December 31, 1827, the *Gazette des tribunaux* had carried the story of the trial and subsequent condemnation of Antoine Berthier. Berthier, twenty-five years of age, a former tutor and a former theological student, had, on July 11, 1827, entered a church in the little township of Brangues, near Grenoble, where, during the celebration of the Mass, he had drawn and fired a pistol, thereby mortally wounding one Madame Michoud, mother of three children formerly entrusted to Berthier's care and presumed at one time to have been his mistress. As the trial proceeded, more and more singular facts began to emerge, and on these, Stendhal's imagination began to "embroider." The novel, originally called "Julien," was born.

Julien Sorel, youngest son of a peasant sawmill owner and endowed with ambitions well above his station, becomes tutor to the children of Monsieur de Rênal, mayor of the little township of Verrières, in the Jura. There Julien seduces Madame de Rênal; when suspicions of the relationship are aroused, he leaves the household and enrolls in a theological seminary at Besançon to study for the priesthood. In the seminary, he is befriended by the director, the Jansenist Abbé Pirard, who recommends Julien as secretary to the Marquis de La Mole, an aristocrat of ancient lineage moving amid the highest circles of Legitimist Paris. Julien seduces the Marquis's daughter, Mathilde—with such success that when she becomes pregnant, the Marquis agrees to their marriage. All is set for the supreme realization of Julien's ambitions when the Marquis receives a letter from Madame de Rênal, revealing Julien's former relationship with herself. In a crisis of vengefulness and disillusion, Julien rides off to Verrières and shoots (but does not kill) Madame de Rênal during the celebration of the Mass. He is arrested, tried, condemned to death—and executed.

Julien Sorel is Stendhal's total "egotist," with all that that term implies: intelligence, willpower, and absolute lucidity, yet with so strong a sense of the highest ideal of his own self that no satisfaction of his ambitions or senses is acceptable, unless it should also satisfy that punctilious demand of "honor," without which he is "a mere peasant." Utterly contemptuous of his own peasant-capitalist background, of the provincial bourgeoisie of Verrières, and later even of the right-wing reactionary "high society" of Paris, nothing less than the highest aim of all can seem worthwhile to him. He would be a new Napoleon, a new Danton, yet at the same time he is only nineteen years old, uneducated, unsophisticated, and desperately timid. In the old days, under his hero, his model, Napoleon (he keeps a copy of Emmanuel, Comte de Las Cases's *Mémorial de Sainte-Hélène* hidden under the mattress of his bed—his bible), he might have risen through the ranks to become a marshal of France by the age of thirty (the "red"); but Napoleon is dead, and France, indeed the whole of Europe, lies in the grip of the reaction, controlled by the *ancien régime* aristocracy, by the right-wing bourgeoisie, and above all by the Church. As a soldier now, he would be destined to remain obscurely in the ranks for the rest of his days; but in the Church (the "black"), a man may become a bishop by the age of twenty-five, a cardinal by the age of thirty. In default of opportunity by way of the red, Julien Sorel opts, rationally and mathematically, for the black.

Not only does this situation set out the entire sociopolitical theme of the novel (a devastating condemnation of the whole state of France in the period preceding the July days of 1830, under the right-wing reaction that was perforce to follow a failed revolution), but also it introduces the second theme: hypocrisy. The nineteenth century, in the opinion of those who lived through it, was the most hypocritical century in the history of the world: To succeed, the first requirement was to pay lip service to whatever was in fashion. Thus, Julien Sorel decides to make himself a hypocrite, ruthlessly and lucidly. He is totally atheistic; he believes in no God, in nothing but himself. If the whole of society is corrupt and rotten, then he would be a fool not to profit by this corruption and this rottenness.

Into this pattern of controlled and rationalized egotism there intrude successively two women: Louise de

Rênal and Mathilde de La Mole. Each is the absolute antithesis of the other: The first is married, deeply religious, humble, and passionately adoring; the second is a Diana-huntress, a fair-haired virgin inviolate, as implacably Voltairean as Julien himself. Both are infinitely far above Julien in social status; neither can be attacked, save by the stratagems of war. With a degree of male-oriented military objectivity that profoundly shocked Stendhal's contemporaries and that is still more than a little disconcerting even today, Julien prepares his assault on one after another of these "fortresses"—and succeeds. Here, it is the red that is in the ascendant. Cold courage, icy calculation, "devotion to duty"—these are what drive Julien onward, when he would much rather retreat. In each case, when he is "victorious," he is rewarded by no pleasure whatsoever. "Is *that* all it was?" he asks himself after his first subjugation of Madame de Rênal; "she had done her duty" is the only comment that Stendhal allows Julien after his first night with the previously virginal Mathilde de La Mole.

The total cynicism of the assault and the cold, mathematical assessment of the "conquest" are, however, only a beginning. In his essay *Maxims of Love*, Stendhal had written a sentence whose originality, for its time, is easy to overlook: "Sexual intimacy is not so much the climax of happiness, as the last step before reaching it." This apparently simple statement implies the reversal of an entire psychologico-literary tradition in the treatment of the theme of love—the tradition that assumes that, between "true lovers," the physical coming-together is the beginning and the end. For Stendhal, sexual intimacy is only a single step on the road to a complete relationship. Both in the case of Louise de Rênal and in that of Mathilde de La Mole, the lovers only begin to appreciate the significance of their relationship weeks, or even months, after their first moment of physical surrender, and by then it is too late. It is at this point that the irrational begins to take over.

The sheer irrationality of the ending of *The Red and the Black* has puzzled, and continues to puzzle, innumerable commentators—simply because there is no rational explanation. Poor Antoine Berthier could no more explain his actions than could Julien Sorel. Julien, after his assault on Madame de Rênal, could easily have escaped sentence; Madame de Rênal had not died, and powerful friends were working for him. Every chance that is offered to him, however, he refuses. He condemns himself, as it were, against all the evidence. His vaulting ambition appeased at last, he positively exults in the prospect of death. At an earlier point in the novel, meeting the failed revolutionary Count Altamira, condemned to death in absentia by the government of his country, Julien had observed significantly: "A death-sentence is the only honour which cannot be bought." Perhaps this is the key. Caught in the toils of an utterly corrupt society, even the most sublime moments of his love for Madame de Rênal and for Mathilde were tainted with corruption: the corruption even of being alive in the nineteenth century in France. Alone in his cell during the final hours, Julien at last finds himself confronted with the only worthy opponent whom his pride acknowledges: himself. This is the ultimate sublimation of "egotism"—an egotism so vast and pure and perfect that it can find satisfaction in nothing less than the Absolute; because there is no Absolute in life, death is the most welcome of lovers.

LUCIEN LEUWEN

Among all of Stendhal's novels, *Lucien Leuwen* is the most immediately and overtly political. In fact, it was probably the realization that to see it in print was likely to cost him his job as French Consul in Civitavecchia that caused Stendhal finally to abandon it two-thirds of the way through. Even so, the two parts that have come down to us are longer than *The Red and the Black*. In spite of their incomplete and unpolished state, they nevertheless represent one of Stendhal's major achievements.

As usual, Stendhal "borrowed" his plot—in this case, from an unpublished "first novel" by one of his oldest friends, Madame Jules Gaulthier. Unfortunately, the original manuscript has vanished; it nevertheless seems to have supplied the material at least for part 1 of *Lucien Leuwen*.

Since July, 1830, when Stendhal had enthusiastically welcomed the Revolution, which brought in the new regime of Louis-Philippe, things had gone very wrong indeed, and, once again, the country stood on the brink of civil war. There were three factions: the aristocracy, supported by the Church (the Legitimists), who had never accepted Louis-Philippe and were conspiring with foreign powers for the return of the Bourbons; the Republicans (mainly intellectuals, but backed by the rising power of the proletariat), determined on a new and definitive revolution; and, sandwiched between the two and loved by no one, the Middle Way (*le juste milieu*), the compromise government actually in power. Early in 1834, a series of incidents had occurred in which troops had been called in by the bourgeois government to suppress rioting workers. One of these frays, known to history as the Affaire de la rue Transnonain, had caused an explosion of resentment throughout the country. The Affaire de la rue Transnonain not only signaled the beginning of real trouble for Louis-Philippe and gave the term "bourgeois" for the first time its modern, pejorative sense but also provided the spark in Stendhal's mind that set off *Lucien Leuwen*.

Lucien Leuwen himself is a bourgeois, the sophisticated and intelligent son of a fabulously wealthy banker (modeled on Baron Mayer Rothschild), who, because of his dictatorial powers in the financial world, has every ministry in his pocket. A student at the École Polytechnique, Lucien has been expelled as being suspect of Republicanism; now, to his father's indulgent amusement, he decides for a career in the army, for, like Julien Sorel, he has been brought up on the great Napoleonic legend, besides which, as a handsome young man, he appreciates the elegance of the uniform. His father's influence assures him of a commission as second lieutenant in the Lancers, and he is stationed in Nancy, a near-frontier garrison town in northeastern France.

With Lucien's arrival in that city, the themes of the novel immediately begin to take shape. Life in the army is anything but what his romantic imagination had pictured. After nearly twenty years without firing a shot at an enemy, it is boring; in consequence, it is disillusioning, barbaric, inefficient, and philistine. The officers spend their time quarreling, drinking, and seducing; its other ranks are sullen and recalcitrant, because the only time they see action is against their own countrymen "armed with cabbage-stumps." Moreover, there is no longer anything glorious about being an officer: Despised as a "policeman" employed by a corrupt government of financial speculators, the new second lieutenant is lampooned in the press by the Republican Left and systematically snubbed in the aristocratic salons of the Right. Even the latter have little to offer: This is not

intellectual, sophisticated Paris, but a remote provincial township bearing a remarkable resemblance to Grenoble—few writers in the entire European tradition have such utter contempt for provincial mediocrity as does Stendhal.

After one farcical "campaign" against the local cabbage-stumps, and a long, drawn-out, inconclusive love affair with an unapproachable Legitimist widow, Lucien is tricked somewhat melodramatically into leaving Nancy, having made himself unpopular in all quarters. Seeing him unemployed, his ever-indulgent father secures for him a post as private secretary to the Comte de Vaise, Minister of the Interior in Louis-Philippe's government. From this point onward, the satire of a corrupt democracy in action becomes progressively more ferocious. It is a society controlled exclusively by two forces: cupidity and fear—on one hand, bribery and peculation; on the other, spying and a ruthless censorship. Every chance acquaintance, in this first portrait of the modern police state, is a potential government agent; every post office clerk will open letters and report their contents to the authorities. To be observed reading a suspect article in the press may herald the end of a promising career.

Lucien is wiser now, his early idealism giving way to an utterly ruthless cynicism. (In its own way, *Lucien Leuwen* is a bildungsroman: a novel of indoctrination into the manners of a society.) In two memorable episodes, he is first required to "cover up" a failed attempt by a government agent provocateur to portray the workers as dangerous animals intent on destroying the forces of law and order (the "Kortis affair"); then, by a mixture of corruption and intimidation, to manipulate election results in favor of the regime. In the first of these enterprises, Lucien succeeds, almost with the sleekness of a modern secret agent; in the second, he fails but emerges with honor. Again, Stendhal asks the question: How can *any* idealism survive amid the unmitigated moral pollution of modern society? Can an honorable man so much as touch politics with his little finger and not be sullied? The answer is an emphatic no.

Into the fabric of this sociopolitical diatribe, which constitutes the essential element of the novel, there are woven two psychological portraits, which are among Stendhal's most fascinating. The first is that of Bathilde de Chasteller—another variation of the Métilde/Mathilde dream figure—a slightly prudish provincial widow who is the great love of Lucien's life and who alone redeems the misery of his sojourn in the garrison town of Nancy. The second, more interesting still, is the portrait of Lucien's own father, the successful banker Monsieur Leuwen, *père*.

François Leuwen is one of Stendhal's finest creations. He is the father Stendhal wished he had had; he is the father, perhaps, that every truly intelligent young man would allot to himself, were the choice his. He is the creative critic to his own son; he is generous, even indulgent; he will accept anything except incompetence or stupidity. He is a banker, but he is totally indifferent to money. For him, banking is a game, just as, later in the novel, when he chooses to indulge in politics, politics is a game. He is brilliant, witty, totally in control of his world, and, after twenty-five years of marriage, still adored by his wife. He is (in a different context) the fifty-year-old Stendhal in relation to his own heroes, for all of them—Octave, Julien, Lucien, Fabrice, Feder de Miossens—are of the age to have been his own sons. All of them, Lucien in particular, are Stendhal as he might have been, had he been born twenty or thirty years later. Leuwen, *père*, however, is sixty-five years old when the novel opens; by the end of part 2, he is dead. Seemingly, once he had vanished, Stendhal no longer had the courage to go on with his own story.

THE CHARTERHOUSE OF PARMA

Into *The Charterhouse of Parma*, the last and greatest of his completed works, Stendhal poured the entirety of his life's experience: his passionate love of Italy, his cult of energy and unexpectedness, his worship of the young Napoleon, his memories of Métilde, his confrontation of absolutes (the battlefield and the monastery), his contempt for the new, get-rich-quick bourgeoisie of modern Europe, his philosophy of egotism and of the pursuit of happiness ("la chasse au bonheur"), his irony, his cynicism, his frivolity when confronted with anything solemn or pompous, and his unquenchable idealism. The origin of the story lies in an Italian manuscript of the Renaissance titled *The Origins of the Greatness of the Farnese Family*, a summary of the manner in which Alessandro Farnese had risen, in 1534, to be elected to the throne of Saint Peter under the name of Pope Paul III.

Stendhal had had this narrative in mind for four or five years when, in 1838, some unrevealed incident recalled to him an event that, a decade or so earlier, had moved him deeply: the death of a child, Bathilde, daughter of his sometime mistress Clémentine Curial. This gave him the ending that he needed and, as was so frequently the case, the end was his true starting point. At the same time, he decided to set the story not in Renaissance Rome but in post-Napoleonic Parma. On November 4, 1838, he began to write, or rather, to dictate. By November 8, he had completed the Waterloo episode, and on that same day, he changed his hero's name from Alexandre to Fabrice. By December 26, the novel was complete; it had taken him exactly fifty-two days to write it.

Like *The Red and the Black*, *The Charterhouse of Parma* falls into two parts, the dominant themes and characters of part 2 being fleetingly, but nevertheless carefully, etched in in part 1. The story opens in 1796, the year in which Napoleon, in the first and most exhilarating of his campaigns, liberated Milan from the Austrians. Into these scenes of delirious rejoicing, Stendhal pours all the excitement of his own first discovery of Milan following the battle of Marengo. A penniless young French officer, Lieutenant Robert, is lodged in the *palazzo* of the noble del Dongo family. There he is welcomed, not by the Marquis (who, being a die-hard, pro-Austrian reactionary, has prudently retreated to his ancestral castle at Grianta on the shores of Lake Como), but by the Marquise, his wife, and by his young sister, the thirteen-year-old Gina del Dongo. This state of euphoria lasts for nearly three years, before the French are driven out once more after the Battle of Cassano, but at some point during the second year, the Marquise has given birth to a son, Fabrice. Stendhal never states, nor even specifically hints, that Fabrice's father is not the avaricious and cantankerous Marquis but rather Lieutenant Robert; nevertheless, the reader is entitled to his or her surmises. At all events, Fabrice's character, as it develops, is a judicious balance between the French and the Italian: He has, on one hand, something of the lucidly calculated egotism and the hypocrisy of a Julien Sorel and, on the other, a degree of spontaneity, of superstition, and of sheer frivolity that, in Stendhal's view, is "typically Italian," although nowhere else does he insist so markedly on these particular aspects.

Superstition and frivolity: These are the characteristics (in alliance with courage, passion, generosity, and an innate nobility of mind) that distinguish Fabrice from any other Stendhalian hero. Both traits, alternately qualities and defects, Fabrice owes to the total nullity of his education (his is a Jesuit-dominated society that is terrified by ideas, because ideas lead ineluctably to atheism and to revolution)—an education whose supreme achievement is to maintain the child in a state of perfect innocence, that is, ignorance. On the other hand, Stendhal exploits both traits for purposes of his own. The superstition (above all, the faith in omens as guides to decision making or as forewarnings of the future) will gradually evolve into a complex pattern of symbols—trees, towers, walls, prisons, and so on—which themselves form a coherent and autonomous substructure to the novel; the frivolity acquires status as a positive ethic, insofar as it is opposed to all that is humorless and self-important and bourgeois and puritanical in nineteenth century society. In *Lucien Leuwen*, the operations of high finance were redeemed by being "taken as a game"; in *The Charterhouse of Parma*, even the crude machinations of party politics become acceptable, provided that they are conceived as "a game of chess, or whist," or perhaps even as the artfully distracting intrigues of an Italian *opera buffa*.

Fabrice is sixteen years old when Napoleon escapes from Elba and begins the campaign that is to finish at Waterloo. Fabrice, in enthusiasm for his hero, escapes from his gloomy family castle and rushes off to join him as a volunteer—a disastrous impulse of emotional naïveté that culminates in the famous description of the battle itself. These fifty-odd pages offer a truly realistic description of a battle, one that, some twenty-five years later, so impressed Leo Tolstoy that it gave him the first inspiration for *Voyna i mir* (1865-1869; *War and Peace*, 1886). It is a picture of total chaos, a situation in which no one—least of all Fabrice—has the faintest idea of what is happening: "*Was* that a battle? *Did* I take part in a battle?" This, in the end, as he makes his way out of the rout, is the only question that torments him.

Back in Lombardy, Fabrice finds himself politically suspect as a result of his escapade, and, under the protection of his aunt, the Countess Pietranera, he is smuggled out of the Austrian dominions, first into Piedmont, later to Naples to study theology. This Countess Pietranera is that same Gina who, at the age of thirteen, had first appeared in the *palazzo* of the del Dongo family in the opening scene of the novel. On growing up, she has made a love match with an army officer, General Count Pietranera, subsequently killed in a duel; now an impoverished widow in her early thirties, at the same time that she takes Fabrice under her protection, she attracts the attention of a certain Count Mosca, who is scintillatingly competent, sophisticated, cynical, and middle-aged, currently the power behind the throne of Ranuce-Ernest IV, Prince of Parma. Gina is attracted to him. On his advice, she makes a purely nominal marriage with an aged courtier, the duke of Sanseverina-Texis, and Count Mosca and the new Duchess Sanseverina take up their residence at the court of Ranuce-Ernest IV, where they are eventually joined by Fabrice. Fabrice is now a fully fledged *monsignore* (a candidate for higher ecclesiastical office in the Roman Church), with pretensions to succeed, thanks to Mosca's influence, to the Archbishopric of Parma.

The first polarization of the novel is now complete. Against a brilliantly handled background of political intrigue in this comic-opera court, there evolve the emotional relationships of Stendhal's three most complex and convincing characters. Mosca is ever more deeply in love with Gina; Gina progressively falls in love with her own nephew, Fabrice; and Fabrice is in love with no one but quite prepared to have adventures with any pretty woman he meets. In the last analysis, the novel is the most subtle observation of the balance between maturity and immaturity in three completely sincere and generous individuals. Mosca, no less passionate for being past fifty, is able to observe himself lucidly, knowing exactly what he wants from life and how to get it, and is always able to defer immediate and present satisfaction in the interests of some more distant, but more rewarding, end. Gina, a woman at the very height of her maturity and powers, is deeply grateful to Mosca for the richness and excitement of the life he has made for her and is fully aware of the absurdity of falling in love with a man who is fifteen years younger than herself, and who is her own nephew at that, yet is unable to do anything about it. She is given, in consequence, to sudden violent and unpredictable actions that will shake the whole foundation of the state. Fabrice, revering in Mosca the father he might have had, is warmly attached to Gina in a kind of admiring and generous *amitié amoureuse*. At bottom, he is still an adolescent, emotionally dormant, prepared to commit the wildest extravagances for one woman one day, only to make love to another the day following.

One of Fabrice's ephemeral adventures involves him with a little *commedia dell'arte* actress called Marietta, a harmless enough amusement in all conscience, save that Marietta has a "protector," an uncouth lout named Giletti. Giletti, not without reason, becomes jealous of Fabrice, attacks him, and, in the resulting scuffle, gets himself killed. In this (given the prevailing ethos of Parma), there is nothing reprehensible for Fabrice—for a noble del Dongo to dispose of an ignominious, fifth-rate strolling player is, ordinarily, not too unusual. In the hothouse atmosphere of court intrigue that flourishes about Prince Ranuce-Ernest, however, Mosca's enemies recognize the opportunity to topple the all-powerful minister by having his favorite protégé indicted and executed for murder. Thus, Fabrice is arrested and imprisoned in the infamous Farnese Tower.

Fabrice's imprisonment at the very summit of this gigantic fortress (a magnified version of the Castel Sant'Angelo in Rome) marks the beginning of the most hallucinatory episode of the whole novel. From the window of his aerie, Fabrice can glimpse the residence of the Prison Governor, General Fabio Conti, some twenty-five feet below; there he watches the Governor's daughter, Clélia Conti, tending the bird cages on her balcony. Between them springs a love that is so exalted, so ineffable (its very impossibility on the human level carrying it into the domain of the transcendental), that the months of his imprisonment come to represent to Fabrice the most sublime moments of happiness on earth. The devoted and indefatigable Gina arranges his escape, but it takes all of Clélia's powers of persuasion to convince him that he must save his own life. Once restored to the world, he is as a being returned from another dimension, a being allowed a glimpse of Paradise and then wrenched away from it, a being forced to exchange the freedom of imprisonment for the imprisonment of freedom. All appears to him unreal and transparent. His life, his soul, his whole being is "on the other side."

Eventually, the novel draws to its (characteristically abrupt) close. Fabrice and Clélia, amid virtually insuper-

able difficulties, discover each other again. A child is born to them, a son, Sandrino, but Sandrino dies. A few weeks later, in despair and grief, Clélia dies also. Fabrice renounces the world and retires to a monastery—the Charterhouse of Parma—where his cell recalls to him the sublime moments of his imprisonment in the Farnese Tower. Then he, too, dies, and his death is followed by that of Gina, yet there is nothing tragic about these deaths.

The Charterhouse of Parma retained its singular density, perhaps, until the Russian novelists achieved its equivalent. Even absolutely minor characters—the Abbé Blanès, the astrologer-priest of Grianta, or Ferrante Palla, the brigand-poet, or "La Vivandière" (the canteen woman following the regiments at Waterloo), or Aniken, the Flemish-speaking innkeeper's daughter at Zonders, where Fabrice recuperates from his wounds—all of these and a score of others have an immediacy that makes them unforgettable. *The Charterhouse of Parma* is Stendhal's last will and testament, embracing all that he knew of good and evil in the world.

LAMIEL

The last of Stendhal's novels, *Lamiel*, left unfinished at his death, is of more interest to scholars than to the general reader. Whether Stendhal's creative powers had been exhausted by *The Charterhouse of Parma* or he was experimenting with new narrative forms that he never had time to master is not clear. As the fragments of *Lamiel* have come down to us, there are two quite distinct versions, of which the first (1839) is of greater originality than the second.

The first version of *Lamiel* is an extended novella in the picaresque tradition. It owes much to Voltaire's *contes philosophiques*—particularly to his *Zadig: Ou, La Destinée, Histoire orientale* (1748; *Zadig: Or, The Book of Fate*, 1749)—and it may well constitute an attempt to write such a tale in a setting of the year 1830. The heroine, Lamiel, an orphan adopted into a family of nouveau riche peasants in Normandy, sets out to discover "what love is all about." With a degree of cynicism redeemed only by absolute naïveté, Lamiel, after each amorous-sexual experience, echoes Julien Sorel's words after his first night with Madame de Rênal: "So *that's* all it was!" After Stendhal's death, a decade or so later, Gustave Flaubert, in *Madame Bovary* (1857; English translation, 1886), and Edmond and Jules de Goncourt, with *Germinie Lacerteux* (1865; English translation, 1887), were to tackle similar questions, albeit using a different tonality.

Stendhal's novels concern overall the revolt of the individual against the compulsive forces of conformism; his men and women are utterly and ruthlessly cynical in pursuit of their own self-realization, yet cynicism is only one element in the pattern. Through his novels, Stendhal has bequeathed a philosophy that is frequently known as Beylism and that, with its inextricable mixture of egoism and idealism, holds an appeal that increases from generation to generation. This philosophy can be summarized as follows: I am Myself, and outside Myself, there is no God, there is nothing. Consequently, my ultimate objective can only be the realization of my own potential, my "happiness." I can realize my ultimate happiness only if this happiness corresponds to the highest ideal that I can conceivably formulate *for* myself; anything less than that is mere vulgarity, sordid, nauseating, and unforgivable. Once that "sublime ideal" is achieved, then there is nothing beyond it—only time, which will destroy its perfection.

It is logical, therefore, that virtually all of Stendhal's novels and stories have the outward form of tragedies, ending in death. They are not tragedies, however. Rather, they are shot through with exaltation: records of men and women striving to realize the highest ideal of themselves in defiance of a faceless, sordid, corrupt, and materialistic society determined to reduce them to its own level of dreary mediocrity.

Richard N. Coe

OTHER MAJOR WORKS

SHORT FICTION: *Chroniques italiennes*, 1839, 1855 (*The Abbess of Castro, and Other Tales*, 1926).

NONFICTION: *Vies de Haydn, de Mozart, et de Métastase*, 1815 (*The Lives of Haydn and Mozart, with Observations on Métastase*, 1817); *Histoire de la peinture en Italie*, 1817; *Rome, Naples, et Florence en 1817*, 1817, 1826 (*Rome, Naples, and Florence, in 1817*, 1818); *De l'amour*, 1822 (*Maxims of Love*, 1906); *Racine et Shakespeare*, 1823, 1825 (*Racine and Shakespeare*, 1962); *Vie de Rossini*, 1823 (*Memoirs of Rossini*, 1824; also known as *Life of Rossini*, 1956); *Notes d'un*

dilettante, 1824-1827; *Promenades dans Rome*, 1829 (*A Roman Journal*, 1957); *Mémoires d'un touriste*, 1838 (*Memoirs of a Tourist*, 1962); *Voyage dans le midi de la France*, 1838 (*Travels in the South of France*, 1971); *Journal*, 1888; *Vie de Henry Brulard*, 1890 (wr. 1835-1836; *The Life of Henry Brulard*, 1925); *Souvenirs d'égotisme*, 1892 (wr. 1832; *Memoirs of an Egotist*, 1949); *Pensées, filosofia nova*, 1931; *Correspondance*, 1933-1934.

MISCELLANEOUS: *The Works*, 1925-1928 (6 volumes).

BIBLIOGRAPHY

Adams, Robert M. *Stendhal: Notes on a Novelist*. New York: Funk & Wagnalls, 1959. Still one of the best critical introductions, written lucidly, with a biographical chapter and discussions of Stendhal's major works. Includes an appendix identifying the "major slips, inconsistencies, oversights, and verbal faults" in Stendhal's two major novels.

Alter, Robert. *A Lion for Love: A Critical Biography of Stendhal*. New York: Basic Books, 1979. Concise work skillfully integrates an analysis of Stendhal's fiction into the story of his life. Includes illustrations, bibliography, and index.

Bell, David F. *Circumstances: Chance in the Literary Text*. Lincoln: University of Nebraska Press, 1993. Examines the realistic writing of Stendhal and Honoré de Balzac. Devotes one chapter to an analysis of *The Charterhouse of Parma*. Includes notes, bibliography, and index.

Bloom, Harold, ed. *Stendhal*. New York: Chelsea House, 1989. Collection of essays by distinguished critics addresses topics such as women in Stendhal's work, his use of autobiography, and his love plots. Includes an editor's introduction, chronology of Stendhal's life, and bibliography.

Keates, Jonathan. *Stendhal*. London: Sinclair-Stevenson, 1994. Lucid and shrewd biography emphasizes the events of Stendhal's life over analysis of his works. Includes bibliography and index.

Manzini, Francesco. *Stendhal's Parallel Lives*. New York: Peter Lang, 2004. Examines the influence of Plutarch's *Bioi paralleloi* (c. 105-115; *Parallel Lives*, 1579) on the biographical sketches and "imaginary biographies" in Stendhal's writing. Demonstrates how in *The Red and the Black* and other works Stendhal compares his themes and the lives of his characters to one another.

Richardson, Joanna. *Stendhal*. New York: Coward, McCann & Geoghegan, 1974. Sound narrative biography is supported by excellent documentation. Includes a bibliography.

Talbot, Emile J. *Stendhal Revisited*. New York: Twayne, 1993. Useful introductory work on the author, with a chapter on the man and the writer and separate chapters on Stendhal's major novels. Includes chronology, notes, and annotated bibliography.

Thesen, Doreen. *The Function of Gift Exchange in Stendhal and Balzac*. New York: Peter Lang, 2000. Focuses on scenes featuring the exchange of gifts in selected writings by Stendhal and Honoré de Balzac to demonstrate how these transactions depict society and concepts of money in early nineteenth century France.

Wood, Michael. *Stendhal*. Ithaca, N.Y.: Cornell University Press, 1971. Meticulous, scholarly study of Stendhal's style and structure is one of the standard works of Stendhal criticism in English. Includes notes and brief bibliography.

RICHARD G. STERN

Born: New York, New York; February 25, 1928
Also known as: Richard Gustave Stern

PRINCIPAL LONG FICTION

Golk, 1960
Europe: Or, Up and Down with Schreiber and Baggish, 1961
In Any Case, 1962 (also known as *The Chaleur Network*, 1981)
Stitch, 1965
Other Men's Daughters, 1973
Natural Shocks, 1978
A Father's Words, 1986
Pacific Tremors, 2001

OTHER LITERARY FORMS

In addition to his novels, Richard G. Stern has published several well-received collections of short fiction, including *Teeth, Dying, and Other Matters* (1964), *Noble Rot: Stories, 1949-1988* (1989), and *Almonds to Zhoof: Collected Stories* (2005). He has also published miscellanies that comprise essays, reviews, reflections, journal excerpts, interviews, and even a bit of poetry; these works include *The Books in Fred Hampton's Apartment* (1973) and *What Is What Was* (2002). He published a memoir, *A Sistermony*, in 1995, and he has

also written plays and has served as editor on the anthologies *American Poetry of the Fifties* (1967) and *Honey and Wax: The Powers and Pleasures of Narrative* (1966), further testimony to his wide range of abilities and interests.

ACHIEVEMENTS

Richard G. Stern's fiction has been compared to that of Saul Bellow by a number of critics. There are a number of similarities between the two writers, but the differences are, perhaps, more important. Stern does use literary and historical allusions and analogies in the manner of Bellow, but he is not a novelist of ideas as Bellow decidedly is. Stern, in contrast to Bellow, continues to exploit the resources of the traditional novel. His interest is more in character and theme than in the dialectic of ideas. This traditional stance may have limited Stern's audience and his recognition as a writer. He has, however, been the recipient of some prestigious awards. He received the Longwood Foundation Award in 1960, the Fiction Award of the National Institute of Arts and Letters in 1968, the Carl Sandburg Award for Fiction in 1979, the Award of Merit for the Novel in 1985, and the Heartland Award for nonfiction for his memoir, *A Sistermony*. He has been both a Rockefeller and a Guggenheim fellow.

The major complaint about Stern's novels is that they are too consciously allusive or mythical; they lack the confessional note and the excess of feeling so characteristic of much contemporary fiction. Marcus Klein is helpful, however, in revealing what Stern's fiction does contain: "In a time when serious American fiction has tended toward extreme personal assertion and extravagance of manner, Richard G. Stern has been composing a body of work which is notable for its detailed craftsmanship, its intricacy, and its reticencies."

BIOGRAPHY

Richard Gustave Stern was born in New York City on February 25, 1928. He graduated Phi Beta Kappa from the University of North Carolina, Chapel Hill, in 1947, and he received an M.A. from Harvard University in 1949 and a Ph.D. from the University of Iowa in 1954. From 1955 to 2004, when he retired as Helen A. Regenstein Professor of English and American Literature, he was a member of the faculty at the University of Chicago. In addition, he has been a visiting lecturer at such institutions as the University of Venice, Harvard University, and the University of Nice.

ANALYSIS

In an interview, Robert L. Raeder noted that Richard G. Stern's "books and stories seemed to lack a center, a common denominator." Stern replied that he adheres to a theory of art in which the artist "detaches" himself from his creations and rejects the romantic approach, wherein the author includes his own life, opinions, and feelings. Stern immerses himself not only in the personalities of the characters he invents but also in their occupations and milieus. Accordingly, Stern's novels explore the minds and worlds of such characters as a professor of biology, a famous sculptor, a journalist, and an aging film director. There is no trace of the author in these diverse creations, nor is there any trace of autobiography in characters who display a very limited range of perception, such as Hondorp in *Golk* or Edward Gunther in *Stitch*.

Despite this diversity, however, there are a few constants in Stern's fiction. One of these is the city. Stern's characters are constantly observing, describing, and identifying their fates with the great cities they inhabit,

Richard G. Stern. (Courtesy, Donald I. Fine, Inc.)

whether it be the New York of *Golk*, the Venice of *Stitch*, the Cambridge of *Other Men's Daughters*, or the Los Angeles of *Pacific Tremors*. Another recurring feature of Stern's novels is their lack of conclusive resolution: What happens to the main characters is a sort of ironic modulation, a subtle change of perception rather than a marked change in character or fortune. Marcus Klein has described the movement of a typical Stern novel as one in which a private man becomes involved in the public world and in the process becomes involved in "contingencies" with which he must deal. "His modest success is that he has become potentially moral."

GOLK

Stern's first novel, *Golk*, is the tale of a private and reclusive man. Hondorp, who is thrust into the public world by a chance encounter with Golk and his film crew in a bookstore. Up to this point, Hondorp has spent his time wandering around New York City and watching television at home with his father. Suddenly, he is on television and a public figure; he accepts a job with Golk's television crew and joins them in their "Golks," which are the tricks played on unsuspecting people who are filmed in absurd situations. The television program based on these secret glimpses of ordinary people becomes very successful, and the show receives a network contract. Yet Golk, the producer and planner of the show, has larger ambitions: He starts to expose senators, union officials, and bureaucrats. At this point, Golk's empire begins to crumble under the attacks by the politicians and network officials. The climactic moment comes when Hondorp and his girlfriend, Elaine, betray Golk and take over the program. They justify the betrayal with the highest of motives: It is a continuation "of Golk's work." Yet their victory—and their marriage—is short-lived; without the eccentric vision of Golk, the show flounders and is canceled. At the end of the book, everyone returns to his earlier state; Golk is now merely one of the crowd, as he "fits" everywhere; Elaine has gone back to her brutal husband; and Hondorp becomes once more the empty person he was at the beginning, with "all trace of his ambition, all desire for change gone absolutely and forever."

Most critics of the novel have emphasized Stern's satire on the invasion of privacy and the baleful influence of television. Stern, however, suggests that this reading ignores the primary thrust of the novel. According to Stern, *Golk* "deals in large part with genius and its epigones and the nature of contemporary exploitation in its great theater, post-war New York." Golk, then, is, for all of his eccentricities, an authentic original; he pushes his created form to its limits, and, in doing so, encounters the wrath of the establishment. Golk scares them, but his second-rate imitator, Hondorp, takes no risks and eventually fails to excite the audience. Even though Golk has lost his position, he remains a presence; he "fits," while Hondorp does not belong anywhere.

IN ANY CASE

Stern's next important novel, *In Any Case*, also deals with betrayal. The protagonist, Samuel Curry, discovers in a book by a French priest an accusation that his son, Bobbie, has betrayed the Chaleur Network, a group of French, English, and Americans working against the Nazis in the early 1940's. Curry is an unlikely hero; he is comfortable and established in France, and the thought

of involving himself in the murk of the recent war is repugnant to him. He first seeks out Bobbie's accuser, Father Trentemille, and confronts him, but he receives no satisfaction: Trentemille simply repeats the charges. He then tries two survivors of the "Network," one of whom defends Bobbie, while the other repeats the accusation. He has better luck with Bobbie's girlfriend in the Network, Jacqueline, who asserts her belief in Bobbie's innocence, although she can offer no proof. He has even better luck with German sources and discovers that the real traitor is an agent whose code name is Robert. Robert is described as a professional agent, one who "doesn't even have sides. He's a sphere." When Samuel Curry confronts Robert, he finds that the matter is more complicated than he had thought. He believes that Robert is a "decent" man and goes into business with him. The climax of the novel comes when Curry decides that he must expose Robert and ask Father Trentemille for a retraction. His motives for this action, however, are complex. He believes that he is punishing Robert for his own "delinquency" in rehabilitating Bobbie's name and because Robert has become a rival for Jacqueline's affections. The result of this series of betrayals is surprisingly tranquil. Robert is exposed, but he is not punished. Samuel Curry and Jacqueline marry and are living on the Riviera and expecting the birth of a child in a few months. Not only is Bobbie's name cleared but also his father and the girl he loved have united to repair the loss of his death—a very satisfying ending.

Stern has spoken of how he drew upon and altered the factual background for *In Any Case*. His source was a factual account of the work of the underground in France. Stern makes it into a moral tale in which "the discoverer finds in himself a treasonous impulse which is related to the official traitor's." This impulse begins when Curry sees the divergence between motive and result, of intention and action. "Action would be too easy a way into the current, too much a short cut to judgment." Curry's own intentions and actions during the war and in his relationship with his son hinder any judgment he might make or any action he might take. Stern's comment on his original title for the novel makes his intention clear. "The idea was that the hero always eschewed an active role because 'in any case' there was so much to be said for either side that to take sides was to simplify the issue. To seek relief in action." Curry seeks this sort of "relief" at the end of the novel when he can no longer control the complexities he discovers.

STITCH

In *Stitch*, Stern returns to the theme of "genius and its epigones." The protagonist, Edward Gunther, is an American who has left his advertising job to find himself and culture in Europe. He has, however, no sensitivity to or perception of art; he spends his time, instead, in eating, chasing women, and brooding. His wife and children are left behind in a hotel in Venice while he searches for the European experience. His opposite, the genius, is Thaddeus Stitch, an American sculptor who has lived in Italy for many years and is recovering from a prison sentence for supporting Fascism; he is obviously modeled on Ezra Pound. Stitch is now quite old and unable to create great art, but his monuments surround him on his island. Edward and Stitch are brought together by their common interest in Nina, a young American poet. Nina is the opposite of Edward; Nina is a poet, not a cultural hanger-on like Edward, and her epic poem has some of the connections with the past that Stitch's work does. Edward is measured and found wanting by these comparisons. As Stitch remembers creating or re-creating monuments of unaging intellect, and as Nina creates, Edward is literally swelling up with the weight he has gained and the assertions of his ego. His only encounter with Stitch ends with a curt dismissal from the master, and his only encounter with Stitch's art produces only pseudoinsights; he describes the island as "beautiful wreckage." Edward's personal life is also a disaster: His wife finds out about his adulteries and throws him out of the house. He finds cultural salvation in the pompous essays he writes and in the possibility of a place with a foundation. The novel comes to an end with Edward's return to the United States. He is teaching at a secondary school in Santa Barbara while waiting for a foundation position. He does hear news of those he left behind in Europe—news which unsettles him. Nina has married and had her epic poem published; Stitch remains in Venice and was the one who introduced Nina to her husband; Edward's wife has divorced him and has found a new partner. Edward is watching the funeral services for President John F. Kennedy as his dreams of finding himself and Europe fade into nothingness.

In *Stitch*, Stern takes the theme of genius and its epigones much further than he did in *Golk*. The genius of this novel is much more credible; some of the best parts of the book are the descriptions of Stitch's art. The epigone is also more credible: Edward is not merely a nullity who is suddenly placed in a position of power but also a chilling example of the cultural middleman who would not recognize an authentic work of art if he tripped over one. The debate between Edward and Nina over Stitch's art, and art in general, defines the differences between the genius and the epigone. Nina sees the problem in life and in art. "Attempts to be what we aren't. Overprizing our singularity. Egoism. Imperceptivity in situations solved long ago. Failure to adapt. The bloodline runs from the world to art's expression of it." Yet Edward never can escape his egoism, and he remains a bundle of unfulfilled and inexpressible longings.

OTHER MEN'S DAUGHTERS

Other Men's Daughters traces the changes in a relationship and a family, a theme in nearly all of Stern's fiction, especially the later works. The protagonist is a very attractive and settled man, Dr. Merriwether. He is a professor at Harvard Medical School, and he lives in Cambridge in a house passed down to him from his ancestors. He is jolted out of this settled life when a young girl, Cynthia Ryder, comes to him one day for a prescription for the Pill. They meet a few times and eventually become lovers. Dr. Merriwether—Stern emphasizes his title and position rather than his personal identity—resists for a while, but they become deeply involved. When Cynthia returns to Swarthmore, they correspond and keep the relationship alive. They manage to meet when Merriwether delivers a paper in New York and when Cynthia can come to Cambridge, but Merriwether manages simultaneously to keep his domestic life intact. This balance is upset, however, when Cynthia accompanies Merriwether to Italy, where he is reading a paper. Merriwether adds a few "speculations" to his formal paper and is then attacked by an American scientist who tells him to "go back to your child whore and let the rest of us do serious work."

The public exposure continues when *Newsweek* prints an item linking Merriwether and Cynthia; this brings Cynthia's father on the scene to confront the couple. The confrontation between Mr. Ryder and Merriwether is reminiscent of *In Any Case*; Mr. Ryder does not despise Merriwether but is, instead, drawn to the seriousness and character he sees in him. He does, however, require Cynthia to undergo psychiatric therapy and for the lovers not to meet for a period. The reaction of Merriwether's wife, Sarah, from whom he has long been emotionally estranged, is angry and bitter. Egged on by her lawyer, she starts acrimonious divorce proceedings, and Merriwether loses all of his comfort and the routines he has established over the years. There are some touching moments, such as the Merriwethers' last Christmas together and the parents' breaking the news of their divorce to the younger children; the mood moves away from bitterness once the painful process has been completed. The last chapter of the novel reunites Merriwether and Cynthia in Colorado. The new environment helps Merriwether to overcome the earlier dislocations, and he has some tender moments with his two youngest children. The last note is a very positive one. "The depth of love after loss. The way of human beings. . . . Linkage. Transmission. Evolving."

Other Men's Daughters emphasizes character and setting more than theme. Stern's portrayal of Robert Merriwether—he acquires a first name when he immerses himself in the private world of relationships—and his world is very full. Even Merriwether's scientific specialty, thirst, is exactly appropriate. Furthermore, Stern also renders Sarah's point of view with an impressive sympathy and fidelity. She reveals that the apparently perfect home and family is a facade that hides long-held feelings of resentment and hatred. In the late twentieth century, divorce may be what marriage was to Jane Austen in the nineteenth century, the essential social transaction to be represented in the novel.

NATURAL SHOCKS

Natural Shocks begins where *Other Men's Daughters* ends; the protagonist, Frederick Wursup, is a new journalist who has been divorced for three years. He now lives across from his children and former wife, and he spends much time peeping into his wife's apartment to see what is happening. This intrusion on privacy is directly related to Wursup's occupation as a journalist, and there are many examples in the book of Wursup's destructive private revelations. He recalls an interview with a famous Hollywood director for *Life* magazine and feels "disgusted" at his unwarranted invasion of the

man's privacy. His attempt to help a friend who is having political problems with a forthcoming magazine article revealing that the friend's father is on welfare only makes matters worse. A mutual friend, Knoblauch, sees a central problem in such writing: "The intimacies would be converted into publicity, benevolently but beyond recall. All but the hardest or deepest people would find that unbearable." After establishing the theme of the public revelation of private events and feelings, the novel shifts to deal with the most essential "natural shock," death. Wursup is looking for a topic on which to write, and his editor suggests that he look into the newly popular subject of death. When Wursup visits the hospital to talk to some dying patients, however, he becomes involved in the life of one of them, Cicia Buell. Because of his involvement, or the irreducible nature of death, Wursup finds it difficult to translate the interview with Cicia into his usual brand of journalism. Other shocks follow: His father and a friend commit suicide because of age or anxiety; the reason is never made clear. Wursup's wife remarries, which dislocates his sense of order. He tries to retreat to a Maine island to find some rest and peace; his idyll is interrupted, however, by the news that Cicia is dying. By the time he arrives at the hospital, she is dead, and the novel ends on a note of darkness unrelieved by any saving insight.

The themes are clear in *Natural Shocks*; death and privacy are interwoven throughout the novel. What is more difficult is coming to terms with the main character, Fred Wursup. He is an engaging and witty character, but his prying into people's lives for material for his journalism is disturbing. It is no accident that the book begins and ends with Wursup spying on his former wife's apartment. Wursup does have an epiphany: "Wursup himself had surrendered Cicia upstairs. She was almost as far away as Poppa and Mona. He'd toss off that article for Mike Schilp now. It was just another verbal turn." The people whose lives he has touched have become a product to be marketed. His recognition is, perhaps, what distinguishes him from other revealers of the private life.

A FATHER'S WORDS

A Father's Words is another investigation of domestic life, although the conflict is now not between husband and wife but between parent and children. The father, Cy

Riemer, is amicably divorced from his first wife; his four children are in their twenties and, with one exception, settled. Jack is the oldest child and the recipient of most of his father's words; he is a habitual liar and self-deceiver whose unstructured life is a constant source of dismay and disruption to his father. Cy is always encouraging his son to become respectable. When Jack is working in a "bucket shop" selling books by phone, his father suggests that he get a job in a publishing company. Jack resists the advice, however, and continues on his disorderly way. He only impinges on his father's life when he suggests that Cy accept personal advertisements for his scientific newsletter. Cy is in financial difficulty and lets Jack handle it, although he feels soiled by the ads.

Jack marries Maria Robusto, the daughter of a pornographic film king, and starts working for a commodities broker, so his father is temporarily relieved. Cy has trouble, however, with his other children. The next oldest, Jenny, has written a Ph.D. thesis on the "Wobbling" family in literature. The youngest son, Ben, has published a book called *The Need to Hurt*, which claims that human personality is formed at the fetal stage. Both works are attacks on Cy's fatherhood and his concept of family. The conflict with Jack comes to a head when Cy confronts Jack in a run-down tenement in New York. Again, Cy's words do not help, and Jack seems to give up on their relationship and on himself. "Face it, Dad. I'm finished. I'm never going to be what you want me to be."

There are, however, two important reversals at the end of the novel. First, only a few years later, Jack becomes successful; he is the creator of a television situation comedy which features an addled father who creates problems which the wise son has to solve. It is another attack on Cy's fatherhood and a curious metamorphosis of their relationship. The second reversal is that Cy has, once more and against all odds and sense, become a father. He resists at first and asks his then girlfriend, Emma, to get an abortion, but at the end he leaves Jack and looks forward to "coming home to a new family."

Cy seems, at first glance, to be an ideal parent. He encourages, instructs, and supports all of his children. Yet the words he directs toward his children to accomplish these tasks are resented by his children. Jenny accuses him of "the destructiveness that's there with the generosity and love." She believes that her father does not want

anyone to "rival" him and so he cuts down each of the children. Furthermore, the children's success is based on the defeat of the father, in Jack's television show, Jenny's thesis, or Ben's book. The theme, then, is the oppressive burden of a father's love, inevitably felt no matter how the father treats the child; each child in the novel must win his independence by supplanting the father in some way. It must be said that this conflict and its resolutions are given a witty rather than oppressive treatment by Stern. In addition, Cy does not, finally, bend under the weight of this conflict but accepts and looks forward to it.

Stern has created a body of work that is equal to that of any of his contemporaries. He was stereotyped early in his career as a follower of Saul Bellow and as a Jewish novelist. Those labels never did fit Stern, and they have become even less accurate as his work has developed. He has moved from such strongly thematic novels as *Golk* and *In Any Case* to novels that emphasize character and plot. Stern's ability to create not only credible characters but also their environment is most impressive. His novels are, as one critic has said, "in the great tradition of moral realism."

James Sullivan

OTHER MAJOR WORKS

SHORT FICTION: *Teeth, Dying, and Other Matters*, 1964; *1968: A Short Novel, an Urban Idyll, Five Stories, and Two Trade Notes*, 1970; *Packages*, 1980; *Noble Rot: Stories, 1949-1988*, 1989; *Shares, and Other Fictions*, 1992; *Almonds to Zhoof: Collected Stories*, 2005.

PLAYS: *The Gamesman's Island*, pb. 1964.

NONFICTION: *One Person and Another: On Writers and Writing*, 1993; *A Sistermony*, 1995.

EDITED TEXTS: *Honey and Wax: The Powers and Pleasures of Narrative*, 1966; *American Poetry of the Fifties*, 1967.

MISCELLANEOUS: *The Books in Fred Hampton's Apartment*, 1973; *The Invention of the Real*, 1982; *The Position of the Body*, 1986; *What Is What Was*, 2002.

BIBLIOGRAPHY

Bergonzi, Bernard. "Herzog in Venice, I." *The New York Review of Books*, December 9, 1965. Asserts that the hero of *Stitch* is modeled on Ezra Pound. Generally praises the novel but expresses uneasiness about Stern's evocation of literary myths.

Cavell, Marsha. "Visions of Battlements." *Partisan Review* 38, no. 1 (1971): 117-121. Reviews four of Stern's books and discusses Stern as a satirist whose writing is "at once gentle and biting."

Izzo, David Garrett. *The Writings of Richard Stern: The Education of an Intellectual Everyman*. Jefferson, N.C.: McFarland, 2002. Literary biography discusses the major themes in Stern's fiction and his use of fictionalized autobiography. Analyzes all of his novels and short stories through 2001.

Rogers, Bernard. Foreword to *Golk*. Chicago: University of Chicago Press, 1987. Introduction to a reprint of Stern's first novel treats his fiction in general, especially his novels. Traces through Stern's novels four of his major themes: adapting to change, handling moral responsibility, dealing with problems of fatherhood and domestic life, and handling power. Also discusses Stern's distinctive narrative voice.

Schiffer, James. *Richard Stern*. New York: Twayne, 1993. First book-length critical study of Stern includes a brief overview of his life, a survey of his novels and short stories, and discussions of his style and themes.

Stern, Richard G. "Conversation with Richard Stern." Interview by Milton Rosenberg and Elliot Anderson. *Chicago Review* 31 (Winter, 1980): 98-108. Edited transcript of a radio interview presents Stern's commentary on what he calls the change in his writing from creating stories drawn from the external world to creating ones drawn from inside himself. Stern talks about the nature of the novel, the purpose of a serious novel, his intentions in some of his own fiction, his opinion of other contemporary fiction writers, and the protagonists of his fiction.

_____. Interview by Molly McQuade. *Publishers Weekly*, January 20, 1989. Stern discusses his life, his literary career, and his career as a university professor.

LAURENCE STERNE

Born: Clonmel, Ireland; November 24, 1713
Died: London, England; March 18, 1768

PRINCIPAL LONG FICTION

The Life and Opinions of Tristram Shandy, Gent., 1759-1767 (commonly known as *Tristram Shandy*)
A Sentimental Journey Through France and Italy, 1768

OTHER LITERARY FORMS

Laurence Sterne began his literary career with political pieces in the *York-Courant* in 1741. Two years later, he published a poem, "The Unknown World," in *The Gentleman's Magazine* (July, 1743). His song "How Imperfect the Joys of the Soul," written for Kitty Fourmantel, appeared in Joseph Baildon's *Collection of New Songs Sung at Ranelagh* (1765), and a four-line epigram, "On a Lady's Sporting a Somerset," was attributed to Sterne in *Muse's Mirror* (1778). His sermons were published in three installments: two volumes in 1760, another two in 1766, and a final three volumes in 1769. A satire titled *A Political Romance* was published in 1759 but quickly suppressed. After Sterne's death, *Letters from Yorick to Eliza* appeared in 1773, and his daughter arranged for the publication of the three-volume *Letters of the Late Rev. Mr. L. Sterne to His Most Intimate Friends* (1775). These volumes include an autobiographical *Memoir* and the *Fragment in the Manner of Rabelais*. In 1935, Oxford University Press published the definitive edition of Sterne's letters, edited by Lewis Perry Curtis. The *Journal to Eliza*, composed in 1767, was not published until 1904.

ACHIEVEMENTS

When Laurence Sterne went to London in March, 1760, he was an obscure provincial parson. He rode as a guest in Stephen Croft's cart, and he brought with him little more than his "best breeches." Two months later, he returned to York in his own carriage. Robert Dodsley, who the year before had refused the copyright of *The Life and Opinions of Tristram Shandy, Gent.* (commonly known as *Tristram Shandy*) for 50 pounds, now gladly offered Sterne 250 pounds for the first two volumes, 380 pounds for the next two, as yet unwritten, and another 200 pounds for two volumes of sermons. The famous artist William Hogarth agreed to provide a frontispiece to the second edition of volume 1 and another for volume 3; Joshua Reynolds painted Sterne's portrait. Like Lord Byron, Sterne could have said that he awoke to find himself famous. As Sterne did say, in a letter to Catherine Fourmantel, "I assure you my Kitty, that Tristram is the Fashion." Despite the carpings of a few—Horace Walpole thought *Tristram Shandy* "a very insipid and tedious performance," and Samuel Richardson thought it immoral—the novel was the rage of London, inspiring so many continuations and imitations that Sterne had to sign the later volumes to guarantee their authenticity.

After the novel's initial popularity, sales did drop off. In book 8, Tristram complains that he has "ten cartloads" of volumes 5 and 6 "still unsold." Dodsley abandoned publication of the work after volume 4, and Sterne's new publisher, Thomas Becket, complained in April, 1763, that he had 991 copies of volumes 5 and 6 unsold (from a printing of 4,000). Samuel Johnson's famous comment, though ultimately incorrect, probably reflected the opinion of the day: "Nothing odd will do long. *Tristram Shandy* did not last." Even Sterne may have tired of the work; the volumes grew slimmer, and volume 9 appeared without its mate, volume 10 having, in Sterne's apt words for an obstetrical novel, "miscarried."

Tristram Shandy has lasted, however. It retains a readership, even if it has continued to justify Sterne's complaint of being "more read than understood." Some modern-day readers have made great, perhaps exaggerated, claims for the novel, seeing it as the harbinger of the works of Marcel Proust, James Joyce, and Albert Camus, who, it is said, derived from Sterne the concept of relative time, the stream of consciousness, and a sense of the absurd. Even if one discounts such assertions, there can be no question of the work's importance in the development of the novel or of *Tristram Shandy*'s place in the first rank of eighteenth century fiction.

Less has been claimed for *A Sentimental Journey Through France and Italy* (commonly known as *A Sentimental Journey*), yet this work, apparently so different from and so much simpler than *Tristram Shandy*, greatly influenced Continental, especially German, literature of the Romantic period. Though critics debate the sincerity of the emotions in the work, eighteenth century readers generally did not question Yorick's sentimentality, which contributed to the rise of the cult of sensibility exemplified by such works as Henry Mackenzie's *The Man of Feeling* (1771). Because of its brevity, its benevolence, and its accessibility, *A Sentimental Journey* has enjoyed continued popularity since its first appearance. Although lacking the stature of *Tristram Shandy*, it remains a classic.

BIOGRAPHY

Laurence Sterne was born in Clonmel, Tipperary, Ireland, on November 24, 1713. On his father's side, he could claim some distinction: His great-grandfather, Richard Sterne, had been Archbishop of York, and his grandfather, Simon Sterne, was a rich Yorkshire country squire. Roger Sterne, Laurence's father, was less distinguished. Sterne described his father as "a little smart man—active to the last degree, in all exercises—most patient of fatigue and disappointments, of which it pleased God to give him full measure." Sterne added that his father was "of a kindly, sweet disposition, void of all design." Many have seen Roger Sterne as the model for Uncle Toby Shandy. At the age of sixteen, Roger joined the Cumberland Regiment of Foot, and on September 25, 1711, he married Agnes Nuttall. Agnes, according to her son, was the daughter of "a noted sutler in Flanders, in Queen Ann's wars," whom Roger married because he was in debt to her father. Actually, she may have been the daughter of a poor but respectable family in Lancashire.

From his birth to the age of ten, Sterne led a nomadic life, wandering from barracks to barracks across Great Britain. During these years, he may have acquired some of the military knowledge that appears throughout *Tristram Shandy*, or at least that fondness for the military that marks the work. When Sterne was ten, his uncle Richard sent him to school near Halifax, in Yorkshire, and in 1733, Sterne's cousin sent him to Jesus College,

Cambridge, where his great-grandfather had been a master and where both his uncle Jaques and his cousin had gone. At Cambridge, Sterne met John Hall, who later renamed himself John Hall-Stevenson. Hall-Stevenson was to be one of Sterne's closest friends throughout his life; his library at "Crazy Castle" would furnish much of the abstruse learning in *Tristram Shandy*, and he would himself appear in both that novel and *A Sentimental Journey* as Eugenius, the sober adviser. While at Cambridge, Sterne suffered his first tubercular hemorrhage.

After receiving his bachelor's degree in January, 1737, Sterne had to choose a profession. Because his great-grandfather and uncle had both gone into the clergy, Sterne followed their path. After Sterne served briefly in St. Ives and Catton, his uncle Jaques, by then archdeacon of Cleveland and canon and precentor of the York Cathedral, secured for him the living of Sutton on the

Forest, a few miles north of York. A second post soon followed; Sterne received the prebend of Givendale, making him part of the York Cathedral chapter and so allowing him to preach his turn there.

At York, Sterne met Elizabeth Lumley, a woman with a comfortable fortune. Their courtship had a strong sentimental tinge to it. Indeed, if Sterne actually wrote to Elizabeth the letters that his daughter published after his death, his is the first recorded use of the word "sentimental," and the emotions expressed in these letters foreshadow both *A Sentimental Journey* and the *Journal to Eliza*. Even if these letters are spurious, Sterne's description of his courtship in the *Memoirs* is sufficiently lachrymose to rival the death of Le Fever in *Tristram Shandy*. Unfortunately for Sterne, he, unlike Tristram, did go on; on March 30, 1741, he married Elizabeth. The unfavorable portrait of Mrs. Shandy owes much to Sterne's less than sentimental feelings toward his wife, whom he called in March, 1760, the "one Obstacle to my Happiness."

The year 1741 was also important for Sterne because it marked his first appearance in print. His uncle Jaques was a strong Whig, and he recruited his nephew to write in support of the Whig candidate for York in that year's election. Sterne wrote, the Whig won, and Sterne received the prebend of North Newbold as a reward. The Whig success was, however, short-lived. When the Walpole government fell in 1742, Sterne wrote a recantation and apology for his part in "the late contested Election," and thereby earned the enmity of his uncle, an enmity that ended only with Jaques's death in 1759.

For eighteen years, Sterne lived as a typical provincial clergyman, attending to the needs of his parishioners and publishing two sermons. One of these, "For We Trust We Have a Good Conscience," Sterne reprints in its entirety in the second volume of *Tristram Shandy*. In 1751, he received the commissaryship of Pickering and Pocklington, despite his uncle's efforts to secure this position for Dr. Francis Topham. Sterne and Topham collided again in 1758, when Topham attended to include his son in a patent and thus secure for him a post after his own death. When

Laurence Sterne. (Library of Congress)

the dean of York Cathedral blocked the inclusion, a pamphlet war ensued. Sterne fired the final shot; his pamphlet *A Political Romance* so squashed Topham that he agreed to abandon the fray if Sterne would withdraw the work. Sterne did withdraw *A Political Romance*, but he was not finished with Topham, who was to appear in *Tristram Shandy* as Phutatorius and Didius.

A Political Romance is little more than a satiric squib, but it shows that Sterne was familiar with the works of Jonathan Swift. In its use of clothes symbolism as well as in its severity it recalls *A Tale of a Tub* (1704), and it shows that Swift's work was running in Sterne's head between 1758 and 1759. He was making other use of Swift, too. On May 23, 1759, Sterne wrote to Robert Dodsley, "With this You will receive the Life & Opinions of *Tristram Shandy*, which I choose to offer to You first." By this time, the first volume of the novel was finished. Although Dodsley refused the copyright for the sum of 50 pounds that Sterne requested, Sterne continued to write, completing a second volume and revising the first to remove "all locality" and make "the whole . . . more saleable," as he wrote to Dodsley several months later.

Salable it was. The York edition sold two hundred copies in two days when it appeared in December, 1759, and when Sterne went up to London, he was told that the book was not "to be had in London either for Love or money." Dodsley, who had been unwilling to risk 50 pounds on the copyright, now purchased it for 250 pounds, gave another 380 pounds to publish the still-unwritten volumes 3 and 4, and yet another 200 pounds for two volumes of Sterne's sermons. Sterne was honored by the great. Thomas Gray wrote to Thomas Wharton, "Tristram Shandy is still a greater object of admiration, the Man as well as the Book. One is invited to dinner, where he dines, a fortnight beforehand."

In March, 1760, Sterne also succeeded to the curacy of Coxwold, a better position than his earlier one at Sutton. In May, 1760, he therefore settled at Coxwold, renting Shandy Hall from Earl Fauconberg. Here he worked on the next two volumes of *Tristram Shandy*, which he brought to London at the end of the year. In 1761, he repeated this pattern, but he did not return to Yorkshire after delivering the manuscript of volumes 5 and 6. Having suffered a tubercular hemorrhage, he set off for the warmer, milder air of France.

There he repeated his earlier triumph in London, and he incidentally acquired materials for book 7 of *Tristram Shandy* and *A Sentimental Journey*. Sterne remained in France for almost two years; when he returned to England, he hastily wrote the next two volumes of *Tristram Shandy*, which appeared in January, 1765. In October of that year, he brought twelve sermons to London rather than more of his novel. After leaving the manuscript with his publisher, he again set off for the Continent; he would combine the adventures of this trip with those of his earlier one in writing *A Sentimental Journey*.

In June, 1766, Sterne was back in Coxwold, where he wrote what proved to be the last installment of *Tristram Shandy*. This he brought with him to London in late December; shortly after his arrival, he met Eliza Draper, the wife of an East India Company clerk twenty years her senior. Though initially unimpressed with her, Sterne was soon madly in love. When Sterne met her, she had already been in England some two years, and she was to return to India less than three months later, yet she was to color Sterne's last year of life. Before she sailed on the *Earl of Chatham* on April 3, 1767, Sterne visited her daily, wrote letters to her, drove with her, and exchanged pictures with her. After their separation, Sterne continued his letters; those he wrote between April 13 and the beginning of August, 1767, constitute the *Journal to Eliza*. When he broke off this journal with the words "I am thine—& thine only, & for ever" to begin *A Sentimental Journey*, her spirit haunted that work, too, as the Eliza upon whom Yorick calls.

By December, Sterne had finished the first half of *A Sentimental Journey* and again set off for London and his publisher. On February 27, 1768, *A Sentimental Journey*, volumes 1 and 2, appeared. Less than a month later, on March 18, Sterne died. He was buried in London on March 22; on June 8, 1769, he was reinterred in the Coxwold churchyard in Yorkshire.

ANALYSIS

Readers may be tempted to see Laurence Sterne's works either as sui generis or as eighteenth century sports that had no mate until Marcel Proust and James Joyce. In fact, Sterne was very much a product of his age. His humor owes much to such earlier writers as François Rabelais, Miguel de Cervantes, Michel Eyquem de

Montaigne, Sir Thomas Browne, and Jonathan Swift, all of whom influenced his experimentation with the form of the newly emerged novel. Even this experimentation is typical of the age. Thomas Amory's *The Life and Opinions of John Buncle Esquire* (1756-1766) may have suggested to Sterne his complete title *The Life and Opinions of Tristram Shandy, Gent.* Like *Tristram Shandy*, Amory's book is full of digressions, and its narrator is conceited.

Sterne's experimentation did go beyond the traditional; one need look no farther than the typography, the varying length of the chapters in *Tristram Shandy*—from four lines to sixty pages—or the unusual location of certain conventional elements—for example, the placing of *Tristram Shandy*'s preface after the twentieth chapter of book 3 or Yorick's writing the preface to *A Sentimental Journey* after chapter 6. At the same time, Sterne relied on the conventions of the novel. He is meticulous in his descriptions of clothing, furniture, and gesture. His characters are fully developed: They walk, sometimes with a limp, they cough, they bleed, they dance. From Swift, Daniel Defoe, and Samuel Richardson, Sterne took the first-person narrator. From Richardson, he adopted the technique of writing to the moment; from Henry Fielding, he got the idea of the novel as a comic epic in prose. From numerous sources—Rabelais, Cervantes, and Swift, to name but three—he learned of the satiric potential of the genre.

A Political Romance reveals Sterne's powerful satiric abilities, but this work has little in common with the novels. True, the personal satire of the pamphlet does persist in the novels. Sterne lampoons Dr. Burton (Dr. Slop), Dr. Richard Meade (Dr. Kunastrokius), and Francis Topham (Phutatorius, Didius) in *Tristram Shandy*; Tobias Smollett (Smelfungus) and Samuel Sharp (Mundungus) in *A Sentimental Journey*. For the most part, however, Sterne is after bigger game. As he wrote to Robert Dodsley, the satire is general; and, as he wrote to Robert Foley some years later, it is "a laughing good tempered Satyr," another distinction between the novels and the pamphlet.

The objects of this general satire are several: system-makers of all types, pedants, lawyers, doctors, conceited authors, prudes, and self-deceivers. A common thread uniting all these satiric butts is folly, the folly of believing that life should conform to some preconceived notion, of trying to force facts to fit theories rather than the other way around.

Sterne's insistence on common sense and reason is consistent with the Augustan tradition, which itself is rooted in Anglican beliefs that Sterne emphasized in his sermons as well as in his fiction. Although Sterne's satire is good-tempered, it attacks people's tendency to evil, a tendency noted in Article IX of the Thirty-nine Articles of the Anglican Church. Like his fellow Augustans, Sterne saw this tendency to evil in many spheres. Like them, therefore, he attacked these deviations from the norm as established by religion and reason (which for Sterne are the same), by nature, by tradition, and by authority. The characters in *Tristram Shandy* and Yorick in *A Sentimental Journey* (who is the only sustained character in that work) are laughable because they deviate from the norm and because they refuse to accept their limitations.

Sterne repeatedly reminds the reader of people's finiteness. Thus, death haunts the novels: In *Tristram Shandy*, Toby, Walter, Mrs. Shandy, Yorick, Trim, and Bobby are all dead, and Tristram is dying. In *A Sentimental Journey*, a resurrected Yorick sees death all around him—a dead monk, dead children, a dead ass, dead lovers. Another, less dramatic symbol of the characters' limitation is their inability to complete what they begin. *Tristram Shandy* and *A Sentimental Journey* remain fragments. Trim never finishes his tale of the King of Bohemia and his seven castles. Walter never finishes the *Tristrapaedia*. Obadiah never goes for yeast. Yorick never finishes the story of the notary. Nor can characters communicate effectively with one another: Walter's wife never appreciates his theories, Toby's hobbyhorse causes him to understand all words in a military sense, Dr. Slop falls asleep in the middle of Trim's reading, and Yorick in *A Sentimental Journey* never pauses long enough to develop a lasting friendship.

Death, the prison of the self, the petty and great disappointments of life—these are the stuff of tragedy, yet in Sterne's novels they form the basis of comedy, for the emphasis in these novels is not on the tragic event itself but rather on the cause or the reaction. Bobby's death, for example, is nothing to the reader, not only because one never meets Bobby alive but also because one quickly becomes involved in Walter's oration and Trim's hat. In *A Sentimental Journey*, Sterne focuses on Yorick's reaction to Maria rather than on her poignant tale: Consequently, one laughs at Yorick instead of crying with Maria. The prison of words that traps the characters is not the result of people's inherent isolation but rather of a comic perversity in refusing to accept the plain meaning of a statement. The tragic is further mitigated by its remoteness. Though Tristram writes to the moment, that moment is long past; Tristram's account is being composed some fifty years after the events he describes, and Yorick, too, is recollecting emotions in tranquillity. The curious order of *Tristram Shandy* and the rapid pace of *A Sentimental Journey* further dilute the tragic. Yorick dies in book 1 but cracks the last joke in book 9. Yorick has barely begun a sentimental attachment with a *fille de chambre*, or lady's maid, in Paris when he must set off for Versailles to seek a passport. Though the disappointments, interruptions, failures, and deaths recur, individually they quickly vanish from view. What remains are the characters, who are comic because they refuse to learn from their failures.

Sterne's world is therefore not tragic; neither is it absurd. In the world of the absurd, helpless characters confront a meaningless and chaotic world. For Sterne, the world is reasonable; he shares the Augustan worldview expressed so well by Alexander Pope: "All Nature is but Art, unknown to thee,/ All Chance Direction which thou canst not see." The reasonableness of the world is not, however, to be found in the systematizing of Walter Shandy or the sentimentalism of Yorick. People can live in harmony with the world, Sterne says, only if they use common sense. The comedy of these novels derives in large part from people's failure or laziness to be sensible.

TRISTRAM SHANDY

In *Aspects of the Novel* (1927), E. M. Forster writes: "Obviously a god is hidden in *Tristram Shandy* and his name is Muddle." There is no question that the muddle is present in the novel. Chapters 18 and 19 of book 9 appear as part of chapter 25. The preface does not appear until the third volume. There are black, marbled, and white pages. In book 4, a chapter is torn out and ten pages dropped. Uncle Toby begins knocking the ashes out of his pipe in book 1, chapter 21, and finishes this simple action in book 2, chapter 6. The novel begins in 1718 and ends, if it may be said to end, in 1713. Although called *The Life and Opinions of Tristram Shandy, Gent.*, the novel recounts the life of Uncle Toby and the opinions of Walter Shandy.

One must distinguish, however, between the muddle that the narrator, Tristram, creates and the ordered universe that Sterne offers. Theodore Baird has demonstrated that one can construct an orderly sequence of events from the information in *Tristram Shandy*, beginning with the reign of Henry VIII (III, xxxiii) through the wounding of Trim in 1693 (VIII, xix; II, v), the siege of Namur at which Toby is wounded in 1695 (I, xxv), the conception and birth of Tristram Shandy in 1718 (I-III), the death of Bobby (1719; IV, xxxii, and v, ii), the episode of Toby and the fly (1728; II, xii), the death of Yorick (1748; I, xii), and the composition of the novel (1759-1766). Tristram does attempt to impose some order on these events; the first five and a half books trace his life from his conception to his accident with the window sash and his being put into breeches. He then breaks off to recount the amours of Uncle Toby, which again appear essentially in sequence, with the major exception of book 7, Tristram's flight into France.

Although Tristram attempts to order these events, he fails. He fails not because life is inherently random or absurd, but because he is a bad artist. He pointedly rejects the advice of Horace, whose *The Art of Poetry* (c. 17 B.C.E.) was highly respected among eighteenth century writers. He will not pause to check facts and even refuses to look back in his own book to see whether he has already mentioned something; this is writing to the moment with a vengeance. He refuses to impose any order at all on his material, allowing his pen to govern him instead of acting the part of the good writer who governs his pen.

In governing his pen, the good writer carefully selects his material. Many a person has told a plain, unvarnished tale in less space than Tristram, but Tristram cannot decide what is important. Must one know what Mrs. Shandy said to Walter on the night of Tristram's begetting, which, incidentally, may not be the night of Tristram's begetting at all, since the night described is only eight months before Tristram's birth rather than nine—does Tristram realize this fact? Does one need so vivid an account of how Walter falls across the bed upon learning of Tristram's crushed nose? Is it true that one cannot understand Toby's statement, "I think it would not be amiss brother, if we rung the bell," without being dragged halfway across Europe and twenty-three years back in time? Such details serve the purpose of Tristram's creator by highlighting the follies of a bad writer, but they hardly help Tristram proceed with his story.

Tristram's failure to select his material derives in part from laziness. "I have a strong propensity in me to begin this chapter very nonsensically, and I will not balk my fancy," he writes (I, xxiii), for it requires intellectual effort to balk a fancy. In part, too, this failure to select reflects Tristram's belief that everything concerning himself is important. His is a solipsistic rendering of the humanist's credo, "*Homo sum, humani nihil a me alienum puto*"—I am a man, and nothing that relates to man can be foreign to me. He is confident that the more the reader associates with him, the fonder he (the reader) will become. Hence, the reader will want to know about his failure with Jenny, about his aunt Dinah's affair with the coachman, about his attire as he writes, about his casting a fair instead of a foul copy of his manuscript into the fire. Tristram sets out to write a traditional biography, beginning with a genealogy and proceeding to birth, education, youthful deeds that foreshadow later achievements, marriage, children, accomplishments, death, and burial. He becomes so bogged down in details, however, that he cannot get beyond his fifth year. The episode of Toby and the fly must substitute for a volume on education, and the setting up of his top replaces an account of his youthful deeds.

Although Tristram refuses to impose any system on his writing, he is a true son of Walter Shandy in his willingness to impose systems on other aspects of his world. He devises a scale for measuring pleasure and pain, so that if the death of Bobby rates a five and Walter's pleasure at delivering an oration on the occasion rates a ten, Walter proves the gainer by this catastrophe. Tristram has another scale for measuring his own writing; he awards himself a nineteen out of twenty for the design of the novel. Tristram attaches much significance to the way he is conceived, believing that one's conception determines his entire life. His declared method of describing character is similarly reductive, focusing strictly on the individual's hobbyhorse. He has a theory on knots, on window sashes, and on the effect of diet on writing. Tristram thus serves as a satire on systematizers as well as on bad writers.

The more obvious butt of Sterne's satire on systemmakers is Walter Shandy. The Augustan Age has also been called the Age of Reason, and Sterne recognizes the importance of reason. At the same time, the Augustans recognized that a person's reason alone is often an insufficient guide because it can be corrupted by a ruling passion, as Yorick's sermon in *Tristram Shandy* reveals. Tristram fails as an author because he trusts exclusively to his own logic instead of following conventional guidelines. Walter Shandy is another example of one who becomes foolish because of his reliance on his own reason. Like Pope's dunces, Walter is well read, and like Pope's dunces, he fails to benefit from his learning because he does not use common sense. He will look in the *Institutes of Justinian* instead of the more obvious, and more reliable, catechism—part of Sterne's joke here is that the source Walter cites does not contain what he wants. Walter will consult Rubenius rather than a tailor to determine of what cloth Tristram's breeches should be made. From his reading and reasoning he develops a host of theories: that cesarean birth is the best way of bringing a child into the world, that Christian names determine one's life, that auxiliary verbs provide a key to knowledge. Each of these theories rests on a certain logic. Walter is correct that no one would name his child Judas. From this true observation, however, he erects a most absurd theory, proving Tristram's statement that "when a man gives himself up to the government of a ruling passion,—or, in other words, when his Hobby-Horse grows headstrong,—farewell cool reason and fair discretion" (II, v). Neither Walter nor his son will rein in his hobbyhorse, and, as a result, they become ridiculous.

They may also become dangerous. While Walter is busily engaged in composing his *Tristrapaedia* that will codify his theories of child rearing, Tristram grows up without any guidance at all. Walter is willing, indeed eager, to have his wife undergo a cesarean operation because he believes that such an operation will be less harmful to the infant than natural childbirth. That such an operation will cause the death of Mrs. Shandy is a fact that apparently escapes him.

Even the benign and lovable Uncle Toby makes himself ridiculous by yielding to his hobbyhorse. Not only does this hobbyhorse lead him into excessive expense and so deprive him of money he might put to better use, but also it keeps his mind from more worthwhile occupations. Repeatedly, Sterne, through Tristram, likens Toby's garden battlefield to a mistress with whom Toby dallies; the Elizabethan sense of hobbyhorse is precisely this—a woman of easy virtue. As Tristram notes early in the novel, when "one . . . whose principles and conduct are as generous and noble as his blood" is carried off by his hobbyhorse, it is better that "the Hobby-Horse, with all his fraternity, (were) at the Devil" (I, viii). Deluding himself that he is somehow contributing to the defense of England, Toby blinds himself to the real horrors of war. Wrapped up in his military jargon, he isolates himself verbally from those around him; a bridge or a train has only one meaning for him. No less than Tristram, he is betrayed by words, but in his case as in Tristram's the fault lies not with the words but with the individual betrayed.

Nor is Toby's hobbyhorse dangerous to himself alone. It keeps him away from the Widow Wadman and so prevents his fulfilling his legitimate social responsibilities of marrying and begetting children; his hobbyhorse renders him sterile even if his wound has not. This hobbyhorse also comes close to rendering Tristram sterile, for Trim removes the weights from the window sash to make cannon for Toby's campaigns.

Each of the major characters is trapped in a cell of his own making. Tristram can never finish his book because his theory of composition raises insurmountable obstacles. The more he writes, the more he has to write. Walter's and Toby's hobbyhorses blind them to reality and prevent their communicating with each other or anyone else. The Shandy family is well named; "shandy" in Yorkshire means crackbrained. Significantly, the novel begins with an interrupted act of procreation and ends with sterility. As in Pope's *The Dunciad* (1728-1743), the uncreating word triumphs because of human folly.

Sterne's vision is not quite as dark as Pope's, however; the novel ends not with universal darkness but with a joke. Yorick, the voice of reason and moderation, remains to pull the reader back to reality. Yorick is a jester, and the role of the jester is to remind his audience of the just proportion of things as well as to make them laugh. Yorick does not put a fancy saddle on a horse that does not deserve one. He will destroy a sermon because it is too bad (unlike Tristram, who destroys a chapter because it is too good). He makes only modest claims for his sermons and is embarrassed even by these (unlike Tristram, who repeatedly proclaims himself a genius). Yorick thus offers in word and deed an example of living reasonably and happily.

Sterne offers a second consolation as well. Even though characters isolate themselves with their hobbyhorses, even though they cannot or will not understand one another's words, they can and do appreciate one another's feelings. These emotional unions are short-lived, but they are intense and sincere. Walter will continue to make fun of Toby even after promising not to, but at the moment the promise is made, the two are united spiritually and physically. Tristram and Jenny quarrel, but they also have their tender moments. Trim looks for a carriage in a book by shaking the leaves, and he mistakes fiction for reality in a sermon, but he allows his parents three halfpence a day out of his pay when they grow old. The benevolence that Sterne urged in his sermons is capable of bridging self-imposed isolation. Although one laughs at the characters in *Tristram Shandy*, one therefore sympathizes with them as well, seeing their weaknesses but also their underlying virtue. Though they have corrupted that virtue by yielding to a natural tendency to evil, they redeem themselves through their equally natural tendency to kindness.

Tristram Shandy offended many contemporary readers because of its bawdy tales; reviewers much preferred such seemingly sentimental episodes as the death of Le Fever and urged Sterne to refine his humor. *A Sentimental Journey* superficially appears to have been written to satisfy these demands. It is full of touching scenes, of tears, of charity, of little acts of kindness. Moreover, in a letter to Mrs. William James in November, 1767, Sterne describes the novel as dealing with "the gentle passions and affections" and says his intention is "to teach us to love the world and our fellow creatures better than we do." Sterne's letters, and especially his *Journal to Eliza*, reveal him as a man of feeling, and *Tristram Shandy* satirizes all aspects of human life except for benevolence.

Sterne's sermons reinforce his image as a believer in the importance of charity. As a Latitudinarian, he believed that the Golden Rule constitutes the essence of religion, that ritual and church doctrine, while important, are less significant than kindness. Because Yorick in *Tristram Shandy* is Sterne's spokesman, it is tempting to see Yorick in *A Sentimental Journey* as having the same normative function. Though the narrator of *Tristram Shandy* is a dunce and a satiric butt, can one not still trust the narrator of *A Sentimental Journey*?

No. In a famous letter to Dr. John Eustace, Sterne thanks Eustace for the gift of a curious walking stick: "Your walking stick is in no sense more shandaic than in that of its having *more handles than one*." Readers could regard *Tristram Shandy* as total nonsense, as a collection of bawdy stories, as a realistic novel, as a satire on the realistic novel, or as a satire on the follies of humankind. Sterne's second novel, too, is "shandaic." The reader can see it as a tribute to the popular spirit of sentimentality or can view it as a satire of that spirit, yet a careful reading of the book will demonstrate why Sterne wrote to the mysterious "Hannah" that this novel "shall make you cry as much as ever it made me laugh." In other words, Sterne is sporting with rather than adopting the sentimental mode.

A SENTIMENTAL JOURNEY

The object of Sterne's laughter is Yorick. The Yorick who recounts his travels is not the same normative parson as appears in *Tristram Shandy*. He is by now twice dead—dead in William Shakespeare's *Hamlet* (pr. c. 1600-1601) and dead again in *Tristram Shandy* some fifteen years prior to the events of *A Sentimental Journey*. This second resurrection may itself be a joke on the reader, who should recall Yorick's death in book 1 of the earlier novel.

This revived Yorick bears a great similarity to Tristram. He is, for one thing, a systematizer. He establishes three degrees of curses; he discovers "three epochs in the empire of a French woman" ("Paris"), he is able to create dialogues out of silence, and he derives national character not from "important matters of state" but rather from "nonsensical minutiae" ("The Wig—Paris"). Like Tristram, too, Yorick is vain. He gives a sou to a beggar who calls him "My Lord *Anglois*" and another sou for "*Mon cher et très charitable Monsieur*." He does not worry about being unkind to a monk but is concerned that as a result a pretty woman will think ill of him.

Even his style, though less difficult to follow than Tristram's, bears some similarities to that of Sterne's earlier narrator. In the midst of the account of his adventures in Versailles, Yorick introduces the irrelevant anecdote of Bevoriskius and the mating sparrows, thus combining Tristram's habit of digressing with Walter's love of abstruse learning. Yorick later interpolates an account of the Marquis d'E****, and while telling about Paris he presents a "Fragment" that does nothing to advance the story. Like Tristram, too, Yorick cannot finish his account, breaking off in midsentence. Apparently, he is more governed by his pen than governing.

Yorick also reminds the reader of the narrator in Swift's *A Tale of a Tub*, who believes that happiness is the state of being well deceived. Yorick is disappointed to learn that his small present to Le Fleur has been sufficient only to allow his servant to buy used clothes: "I would rather have imposed upon my fancy with thinking I had bought them new for the fellow, than that they had come out of the *Rue de friperie*" ("Le Dimanche—Paris"). Instead of inquiring about the history of the lady at Calais, he invents a pleasant account of her until he gets "ground enough for the situation which pleased me" ("In the Street—Calais"). He deceives himself into believing that he is accompanying a pretty *fille de chambre* as far as possible to protect her when actually he wants her company. Even his benevolence is self-deception. He conjures up images to weep over—a swain with a dying lamb, a man in the Bastille, an imaginary recipient of charity. When in this last instance he confronts the reality, his behavior is hardly benevolent, though.

Sterne is not satirizing benevolence as such. In his sermons "The Vindication of Human Nature" and "Philanthropy Recommended" he rejects the notion that people are inherently selfish and stresses his belief in humankind's natural benevolence, yet he had to look no farther than his own nose to discover that benevolence can become a hobbyhorse that can carry a person away from the path of reason. Yorick's hobbyhorse of benevolence is no less dangerous than Uncle Toby's or Walter Shandy's. Yorick will weep over a carriage, over a dead ass, or over a caged starling. He admits that he does not even need an object for his sympathy: "Was I in a desert,

I would find out wherewith in it to call forth my affection" ("In the Street—Calais"). Real human misery, however, he cannot understand. He can weep over his imagined prisoner in the Bastille, but he cannot imagine the real suffering there. He can be callous to the poor, but never to a pretty young woman.

Yorick's benevolence is thus a compound of self-deception and lust. He will give no money to the poor monk until he wants to impress a pretty woman. He gives a sou to a beggar with a dislocated hip, but he gives an unsolicited crown to a pretty *fille de chambre*, and he gives three *louis d'or* to a pretty grisette. He imagines that in offering to share his chaise with another pretty young lady, he is fighting off "every dirty passion" such as avarice, pride, meanness, and hypocrisy. Actually, he is yielding to desire.

True benevolence is guided by reason, and it is not a thing of the moment only, as Sterne points out in his sermon on the Good Samaritan. Yorick's benevolence is impulsive and short-lived. The cry of a caged starling moves him greatly: "I never had my affections more tenderly awakened," he says ("The Passport—The Hotel at Paris"). The hyperbole of the language is itself a warning of Yorick's inability to temper emotion with reason. After such a reaction, his attitude changes abruptly; Yorick buys the starling but never frees it. After tiring of it, he gives it away to another as callous as himself. At Namport, he mourns for a dead ass and praises its owner for his kindness, adding, "Shame on the world! . . . Did we love each other, as this poor soul but loved his ass— 'twould be something" ("Namport—The Dead Ass"). By the next page, Yorick is sending his postilion to the devil. Yorick goes out of his way to find the mad Maria, whom Sterne had introduced in book 7 of *Tristram Shandy*. He weeps with Maria at Moulines; she makes such an impression on him that her image follows him almost to Lyon—an entire chapter.

Yorick is humorous because, like Tristram, Walter, and Toby, he is the victim of his hobbyhorse. He gallops away from reason, failing to examine his motivation or to temper his sudden fanciful flights. In "Temporal Advantages of Religion," Sterne provides a picture of the ideal Christian traveler. "We may surely be allowed to amuse ourselves with the natural or artificial beauties of the country we are passing through," Sterne notes, but he warns against being drawn aside, as Yorick is, "by the variety of prospects, edifices, and ruins which solicit us." More important, Yorick forgets the chief end of people's earthly sojourn: "Various as our excursions are—that we have still set our faces towards Jerusalem . . . and that the way to get there is not so much to please our hearts, as to improve them in virtue." Yorick has come to France for knowledge, but he learns nothing. His benevolence is much closer to wantonness than to virtue; it is fitting that he ends his account in the dark.

In *A Sentimental Journey*, as in *Tristram Shandy*, Sterne mocks excess. He shows the folly that results from the abdication of reason. Though he introduces norms such as Yorick in *Tristram Shandy* or the old soldier in *A Sentimental Journey*, the ideal emerges most clearly from a depiction of its opposite—perverted learning, bad writing, and unexamined motives. When Sterne arrived in London in 1760, Lord Bathurst embraced him as the heir to the Augustan satirists.

Joseph Rosenblum

OTHER MAJOR WORKS

NONFICTION: *A Political Romance*, 1759; *The Sermons of Mr. Yorick*, 1760 (volumes 1-2), 1766 (volumes 3-4); *Sermons by the Late Rev. Mr. Sterne*, 1769 (volumes 5-7); *Letters from Yorick to Eliza*, 1773; *Letters of the Late Rev. Mr. L. Sterne to His Most Intimate Friends*, 1775 (3 volumes); *Sterne's Letters to His Friends on Various Occasions, to Which Is Added His History of a Watch Coat*, 1775; *In Elegant Epistles*, 1790; *Journal to Eliza*, 1904.

BIBLIOGRAPHY

Bowden, Martha F. *Yorick's Congregation: The Church of England in the Time of Laurence Sterne*. Newark: University of Delaware Press, 2007. Examines the religious environment in which Sterne wrote his novels and sermons, explicating passages from his work to demonstrate how his experience of life in rural parishes informed his novels.

Cash, Arthur Hill. *Laurence Sterne*. 2 vols. London: Methuen, 1975-1986. Considered the definitive biography of the author. The first volume follows Sterne's life to early 1760 and offers many details about his role in the religious and political affairs of

York. The second volume treats Sterne the author. Presents a realistic picture, freed from Victorian strictures and romantic glosses. Interesting appendixes provide a series of portraits and letters that were previously unpublished.

Cash, Arthur Hill, and John M. Stedmond, eds. *The Winged Skull: Papers from the Laurence Sterne Bicentenary Conference*. Kent, Ohio: Kent State University Press, 1971. Collection of essays covers a wide range of subjects, including Sterne's style, his reputation outside England, and his fictional devices. Includes some helpful illustrations.

Gerard, W. B. *Laurence Sterne and the Visual Imagination*. Burlington, Vt.: Ashgate, 2006. Study focuses on the illustrations by William Hogarth and other artists that complemented Sterne's work in the original editions. Examines the pictorial quality of Sterne's writing, describing how it inspires the visual imagination, and analyzes some of the illustrations for *Tristram Shandy* and *A Sentimental Journey*.

Keymer, Thomas, ed. *The Cambridge Companion to Laurence Sterne*. New York: Cambridge University Press, 2009. Collection of specially commissioned essays provides analyses of all of Sterne's works and their key issues of sentimentalism, national identity, and gender. Some of the essays consider Sterne's life and milieu, his literary career, and his subsequent influence on modernism; others analyze *Tristram Shandy* and *A Sentimental Journey*.

Kraft, Elizabeth. *Laurence Sterne Revisited*. New York: Twayne, 1996. Provides a short biography and then devotes individual chapters to specific works. Closes with a discussion of Sterne's changing critical reputation. Includes a selected bibliography.

New, Melvin. *"Tristram Shandy": A Book for Free Spirits*. New York: Twayne, 1994. Begins with background on the literary and historical milieu of Stern's most famous work and then explores five different methods of approaching *Tristram Shandy* in sections headed "Satire," "Heads" (viewing the work intellectually), "Hearts" (viewing it emotionally), "Joy," and "Tartuffery" (examining it as a humorous attack on hypocrisy).

Ross, Ian Campbell. *Laurence Sterne: A Life*. New York: Oxford University Press, 2001. Thorough and well-researched biography concentrates on the events of Sterne's life rather than on the analysis of his literary works. Includes bibliography and index.

Stedmond, John M. *The Comic Art of Laurence Sterne: Convention and Innovation in "Tristram Shandy" and "A Sentimental Journey."* Toronto, Ont.: University of Toronto Press, 1967. Provides helpful readings of Sterne's novels and describes how the works highlight the comic distance between aspiration and attainment that is endemic in human existence. Includes an appendix recording Sterne's direct borrowings.

Walsh, Marcus, ed. *Laurence Sterne*. New York: Longman, 2002. Sterne's works are particularly amenable to poststructuralist interpretation; this collection pulls together a stimulating group of essays that take modern theoretical approaches to the work.

ROBERT LOUIS STEVENSON

Born: Edinburgh, Scotland; November 13, 1850
Died: Vailima, near Apia, Samoa; December 3, 1894
Also known as: Robert Louis Balfour Stevenson

PRINCIPAL LONG FICTION

Treasure Island, 1881-1882 (serial), 1883 (book)
Prince Otto, 1885
Kidnapped: Being Memoirs of the Adventures of David Balfour in the Year 1751, 1886
The Strange Case of Dr. Jekyll and Mr. Hyde, 1886
The Black Arrow: A Tale of the Two Roses, 1888
The Master of Ballantrae, 1889
The Wrong Box, 1889
The Wrecker, 1892 (with Lloyd Osbourne)
Catriona, 1893
The Ebb-Tide, 1894 (with Osbourne)
Weir of Hermiston, 1896 (unfinished)
St. Ives, 1897 (completed by Arthur Quiller-Couch)

OTHER LITERARY FORMS

In addition to his novels, Robert Louis Stevenson published a large number of essays, poems, and short stories, most of which have been collected under various titles. The best edition of Stevenson's works is the South Seas Edition (32 volumes) published by Scribner's in 1925.

ACHIEVEMENTS

A man thoroughly devoted to his art, Robert Louis Stevenson was highly regarded during his lifetime as a writer of Romantic fiction. Indeed, few, if any, have surpassed him in that genre. Combining a strong intellect and a wide-ranging imagination with his ability to tell a story, he produced novels that transport the reader to the realms of adventure and intrigue. After his death, his literary reputation diminished considerably, until he was regarded primarily as a writer of juvenile fiction, unworthy of serious critical attention. With the growth of scholarly interest in popular literature, however, Ste-venson has enjoyed some reevaluation. Certainly his narrative skill speaks for itself, and it is on that base that his literary reputation should ultimately rest. Anyone who has vicariously sailed with Jim Hawkins in quest of buried treasure or sipped a potion that reduces intellect to instinct with Henry Jekyll can vouch for the success of Stevenson as a writer and agree with what he wrote in "A Gossip of Romance" (1882): "In anything fit to be called reading, the process itself should be absorbing and voluptuous; we should gloat over a book, be rapt clean out of ourselves, and rise from the perusal, our mind filled with the busiest kaleidoscopic dance of images, incapable of sleep or of continuous thought."

BIOGRAPHY

The only child of Thomas and Margaret (Balfour) Stevenson, Robert Louis Balfour Stevenson was born on November 13, 1850, in Edinburgh, Scotland. He was in poor health even as a child, and he suffered throughout his life from a tubercular condition. Thomas, a civil engineer and lighthouse keeper, had hopes that Stevenson would eventually follow in his footsteps, and the youngster was sent to Anstruther and then to Edinburgh University. His fragile health, however, precluded a career in engineering, and he shifted his efforts to the study of law, passing the bar in Edinburgh in 1875.

Even during his preparation for law, Stevenson was more interested in literature, and, reading widely in the essays of Michel Eyquem de Montaigne, Charles Lamb, and William Hazlitt, he began imitating their styles. Their influence can be seen in the style that Stevenson ultimately developed—a personal, conversational style, marked by an easy familiarity.

Between 1875 and 1879, Stevenson wandered through France, Germany, and Scotland in search of a healthier climate. In 1876, at Fontainebleau, France, he met Fanny Osbourne, an American with whom he fell in love. She returned to California in 1878, and in that same year became seriously ill. Stevenson set out immediately to follow her. Traveling by steerage, he underwent considerable hardships on his journey, hardships that proved detrimental to his already poor health. In 1880, he married Fanny and settled for a few months in a desolate mining camp in California. After a return to Scotland, the couple journeyed to Davos, Switzerland, for the winter.

Again returning to Scotland in the spring, Stevenson worked on his novel *Treasure Island*. Moving back and forth between Scotland and Switzerland was not conducive to improved health, and Stevenson decided to stay permanently in the south of France. Another attack of illness, however, sent him to Bournemouth, England, a health resort, until 1887, during which time he worked assiduously on his writing. In August of that year he sailed for America, settling at Saranac Lake in New York's Adirondacks. There he wrote *The Master of Ballantrae* in 1889. He finally settled in the islands of Samoa in the South Seas, a setting that he used for *The Wrecker* and *The Ebb-Tide*. He died there on December 3, 1894, ending a short but productive life.

ANALYSIS

By the time Robert Louis Stevenson published his first novel, *Treasure Island*, the golden age of Victorianism in England was over. The British Empire was far-flung and great, but the masses of England had more immediate concerns. The glory of the Union Jack gave small comfort to members of the working class who were barely able to keep their heads above water. If earlier novelists wrote for middle-class readers, those of the last twenty years of the nineteenth century revolted against the cultural domination of that class. Turning to realism, they dealt with the repression caused by a crushing environment. Stevenson, however, disdained moral and intellectual topics, preferring the thin, brisk, sunny atmosphere of romance. Consequently, he stands apart from such figures as Thomas Hardy, Arnold Bennett, and George Gissing.

In "A Humble Remonstrance," Stevenson spoke of the function of a writer of romance as being "bound to be occupied, not so much in making stories true as in making them typical; not so much in capturing the lineament of each fact, as in marshalling all of them to a common end." Perhaps, then, Stevenson should be seen not simply as an antirealistic writer of romance but as a writer whose conception of realism was different from that of his contemporaries.

In his study of Stevenson, Edwin Eigner points out that the novelist's heroes are drawn from real life and are usually failures. Moreover, says Eigner, "very few of the characters, whether good *or* evil, manage even to fail greatly." Stevenson himself wrote in his essay "Reflection and Remarks on Human Life" that "our business in this world is not to succeed, but to continue to fail, in good spirits." His own ill health may have caused him to see life in terms of conflict, and in his case a conflict that he could not win. This element of failure adds a somber dimension to Stevenson's romances—a note of reality, as it were, to what otherwise might have been simply adventure fiction. It is the element of adventure superimposed on reality that gives Stevenson's writing its peculiar character. A writer's stories, he remarked, "may be nourished with the realities of life, but their true mark is to satisfy the nameless longings of the reader, and to obey the ideal laws of the daydream." In doing this, the writer's greatest challenge, according to Stevenson, is to give "body and blood" to his stories. Setting, circumstance, and character must all fall into place to give a story the power to make an impression on the mind of the reader—"to put the last mark of truth upon a story and fill up at one blow our capacity for sympathetic pleasure." In this way a story becomes more than merely literature; it becomes art.

Stevenson regarded the tales of *The Arabian Nights' Entertainments* (fifteenth century) as perfect examples of the storyteller's art: tales that could captivate readers in childhood and delight them in old age. Such was the goal that he sought in his own works: to bring readers to the stories as involved spectators who do not shy away from the unpleasantries or the villainy, but find in witnessing them the same pleasure they do in witnessing the more optimistic and uplifting aspects of the piece. Perhaps this is Stevenson's greatest achievement: He illustrates with his stories a sometimes forgotten truth— "Fiction is to the grown man what play is to the child."

TREASURE ISLAND

"If this don't fetch the kids, why, they have gone rotten since my day," Stevenson wrote in a letter to Sidney Colvin on August 25, 1881. He was speaking of *Treasure Island*, the novel on which he was then at work. He need not have worried, for since its publication it has been a favorite of children everywhere—and, indeed, of many adults. Stevenson wrote the book, according to his own account, in two bursts of creative activity of about fifteen days each. "My quickest piece of work," he said. The novel was begun as an amusement for his stepson Lloyd Osbourne, then twelve years old. Upon its completion in November of 1881, it was serialized in the magazine *Young Folks*; as it did not raise the periodical's circulation to any degree, it was not considered particularly successful. The book was an altogether different story, however.

As a tale of adventure, *Treasure Island* stands as one of the best. Buried treasure has always had an aura of mystery and intrigue about it, and this case is no exception. Young Jim Hawkins is the hero of the novel; the adventure starts when Bill Bones, an old seaman, comes to Jim's father's inn, the Admiral Benbow, to wait for a one-legged seaman, who does not arrive. Bones does have two other visitors: a seaman named Black Dog, whom he chases away after a fight, and a deformed blind man named Pew, who gives him the black spot, the pirates' death notice. Bones is so frightened that he dies of a stroke. In the meantime, Jim's father has also died, leaving Jim and his mother alone. Opening Bones's locker, they find an oilskin packet that Jim gives to Squire Trelawney and Dr. Livesey.

Finding in the packet a treasure map, Trelawney and Livesey decide to outfit a ship and seek the treasure. Jim is invited to come along as cabin boy. Just before they sight the island where the treasure is supposed to be, Jim overhears the ship's cook, the one-legged Long John Silver, and some of the crew plotting a mutiny. When Silver and a party are sent ashore, Jim smuggles himself along to spy on them.

When Trelawney and Livesey learn of Silver's duplicity, they decide to take the loyal crew members and occupy a stockade they have discovered on the island, leaving the ship to the pirates. Unable to take the stockade, Silver offers a safe passage home to its defenders in return for the treasure map. The offer is refused, and, after another attack, the party in the stockade is reduced to Trelawney, Livesey, Captain Smollett, and Jim. Jim rows to the ship, shoots the only pirate on board, and then

Robert Louis Stevenson. (Library of Congress)

beaches the ship. Returning to the stockade, he finds his friends gone and Silver and the pirates in control. Silver saves Jim's life from the other pirates and reveals the treasure map, which Dr. Livesey had given him secretly when the former had come to treat some of the wounded pirates. What Silver does not know is that Ben Gunn, the lone resident of the island, has already found the treasure and moved it to his own quarters. When the pirates find no treasure, they turn on Jim and Silver, but Gunn and Jim's friends arrive in time to rescue them. The ship is floated by the tide, and Jim, his friends, and Silver leave the island. Silver jumps ship with only a bag of coins for his efforts, but the rest of the group divide the treasure. "Drink and the devil had done for the rest."

Though Jim may be the hero of the novel, it is Long John Silver who dominates the book. He is an ambiguous character, capable of murder, greed, and double-dealing on one hand and magnanimity on the other. He was Stevenson's favorite character—and the one who ultimately raises the book from a pedestrian adventure story to a timeless, mythically resonant tale that has absorbed generations of readers. The unifying theme of *Treasure Island* is people's desire for wealth. Trelawney and Livesey may be more moral in society's eyes than Silver, but their motivation is certainly no higher. As for Jim, he cannot, like Silver, give a belly laugh in the face of such a world and go off seeking another adventure. One such adventure is enough for Jim, and that one he would rather forget.

THE BLACK ARROW

Serialized in *Young Folks* in 1883, *The Black Arrow* was labeled by Stevenson as "tushery," a term he and William Henley used for romantic adventures written for the market. In a letter to Henley in May, 1883, he said, "Ay, friend, a whole tale of tushery. And every tusher tushes me so free, that may I be tushed if the whole thing is worth a tush." Stevenson had hopes, however, that *The Black Arrow* would strike a more receptive note in *Young Folks* than did *Treasure Island*, and in this respect, his hopes were realized.

Though it lacks the depth of *Treasure Island, The Black Arrow* was enormously popular in its time and does not deserve its critical neglect. Set in the fifteenth century against the background of a minor battle of the Wars of the Roses and the appearance of the infamous Richard, duke of Gloucester, the story recounts the adventures of Dick Shelton as he attempts to outwit his scheming guardian, Sir Daniel Brackley. An unscrupulous man, Sir Daniel has fought first on one side of the war and then on the other, adding to his own lands by securing the wardships of children orphaned by the war.

Planning to marry Dick to Joanna Sedley, an orphaned heiress, Sir Daniel has ridden away to take charge of the girl. In his absence, Moat House, his estate, is attacked by a group of outlaws led by a man with the mysterious name of John Amend-All, who pins a message to the church door of Moat House swearing vengeance on Sir Daniel and others for killing Dick's father, Henry Shelton.

Dick, deciding to remain quiet until he can learn more of the matter, sets out to inform Sir Daniel of the attack. In the meantime, Joanna, dressed as a boy, has eluded Sir Daniel. On his way back to Moat House, Dick

meets Joanna in the guise of "John Matcham." Unaware that Sir Daniel has planned the marriage and unaware that John is Joanna, Dick offers to help his companion reach the abbey at Holywood. They eventually arrive at Moat House, where Dick learns that John is really Joanna and that his own life is in danger. He escapes and, after a lengthy series of intrigues and adventures, saves the life of Richard of York, duke of Gloucester, and rescues Joanna from Sir Daniel, who is killed by Ellis Duckworth (John Amend-All). Dick then marries Joanna and settles at Moat House.

As an adventure story, *The Black Arrow* is thoroughly successful. The movement from episode to episode is swift, and the reader has little opportunity to lose interest. The love story between Dick and Joanna is deftly handled, with Joanna herself a delightfully drawn character. Still, the novel does not venture beyond the realm of pure adventure. Like many adventure stories, it is often contrived and trivial, but this fact does not detract from its readability.

THE STRANGE CASE OF DR. JEKYLL AND MR. HYDE

Stories and theories abound regarding the writing of *The Strange Case of Dr. Jekyll and Mr. Hyde*. In "A Chapter of Dreams" (1888), Stevenson himself gave an account of the composition of the novel, explaining that "for two days I went about racking my brain for a plot of any sort; and on the second night I dreamed the scene at the window; and a scene afterwards split in two, in which Hyde, pursued for some crime, took the powder and underwent the change in the presence of his pursuers. All the rest was made awake, and consciously." The whole, according to Stevenson, was written and revised within a ten-week period.

The novel is based on the idea of the double personality in every person, an idea with which Stevenson had long been concerned. Referring to Jekyll, he said to Will H. Low, a painter, that "I believe you will find he is quite willing to answer to the name of Low or Stevenson." Not the first to use the idea in literature, Stevenson does give it a different twist. Hyde is not the double of the sinner, a conscience as it were; rather, as one reviewer put it, Hyde is a personality of "hideous caprices, and appalling vitality, a terrible power of growth and increase."

As the story opens, Richard Enfield and Mr. Utterson,

a lawyer, are discussing the activities of a Mr. Hyde, who has recently trampled down a small child. Both friends of Dr. Henry Jekyll, they are perturbed that the latter has named Hyde as heir in his will. A year later, Hyde is wanted for a murder, but he escapes. Soon after, Dr. Jekyll's servant Poole tells Utterson of strange goings-on in his employer's laboratory. He is concerned that possibly Jekyll has been slain. Poole and Utterson break into the laboratory and find a man dead from poison. The man is Edward Hyde. A note in the laboratory contains Jekyll's confession of his double identity.

Early in life, he had begun leading a double existence: a public life of convention and gentility and a private life of unrestrained vice. Finally, he discovered a potion that transformed him physically into Edward Hyde, his evil self. Though Jekyll wanted desperately to be rid of Hyde, he was not strong enough to overcome his evil side. He finally closed himself in his laboratory, seeking a drug that would eliminate Hyde. Failing in his search, he committed suicide.

As an exploration into the darkest recesses of the human mind, *The Strange Case of Dr. Jekyll and Mr. Hyde* is skillfully constructed. Not only are Jekyll and Hyde presented in a haunting fashion, but Utterson also is a character brought clearly to life. The plot, sensational though it is, does not rely on the standard gothic claptrap to hold the reader. On the contrary, the story is subtly undertold, and the reader is drawn into the horror of it by Stevenson's penetrating imagination and his easy mastery of language and style. The reader, said one reviewer, "feels that the same material might have been spun out to cover double the space and still have struck him as condensed and close knit workmanship. It is one of those rare fictions which make one understand the value of temperance in art."

KIDNAPPED

Stevenson completed *Kidnapped* in the spring of 1886, intending it originally as a potboiler, and it surely has all the ingredients of high adventure: a stolen inheritance, a kidnapping, a battle at sea, and several murders. Having gained an interest in Scottish history from his travels through the Highlands, Stevenson used as his principal source of historical information *Trial of James Stewart* (1753), a factual account of the 1752 Appin murder trial.

Kidnapped is the story of David Balfour, whose only inheritance from his father is a letter to Ebenezer Balfour of Shaws, David's uncle. On the way to see Mr. Rankeillor, the family lawyer, to get the true story of the inheritance, David is tricked and sent off on a ship for slavery in the American colonies. He meets Alan Breck, an enemy of the monarch because of his part in a rebellion against King George, and, though David is loyal to the king, the two become fast and true friends. Escaping from the ship, they have numerous adventures, finally returning to Scotland, where David learns the truth of the inheritance. His father and uncle had both loved the same woman; when David's father married the woman (David's mother), he generously gave up his inheritance to his brother Ebenezer. Ebenezer knew that such an arrangement would not hold up legally, and thus he tried to kill David. David accepts Ebenezer's offer of two-thirds of the income from the inheritance, and, with the money, he helps Alan reach safety from the king's soldiers who are pursuing him.

Kidnapped is rich in its depiction of the Scottish Highlands, and the novel's dialogue is particularly effective. The contrast between David, a Lowlander and a Whig, and Alan, a Highlander and a Jacobite, for example, is well drawn. Ignoring their differences, the two, like Huck and Jim in Mark Twain's *Adventures of Huckleberry Finn* (1884), prove that their friendship is more important than geographical and political differences.

Whatever Stevenson thought of *Kidnapped*, his friend Edmund Gosse thought it the "best piece of fiction that you have done." Many would argue with Gosse's statement. While it perhaps has more human interest than does *Treasure Island*, it lacks the sharpness and force of Stevenson's masterpiece.

THE MASTER OF BALLANTRAE

Although not as well known as *Treasure Island* and *Kidnapped*, *The Master of Ballantrae* is considered by many to be Stevenson's best novel. Stevenson himself saw it as a "most seizing tale," a "human tragedy." Despite his preoccupation with character delineation in the story, he still regales the reader with a plethora of adventurous incidents. Set in eighteenth century Scotland, *The Master of Ballantrae* recounts the story of two brothers as they compete for title and love. When Stuart the Pretender returns to Scotland in 1745 to claim the English throne, Lord Durrisdeer decides to send one son to fight with Stuart and to keep one at home, hoping that way to make his estate secure regardless of the outcome of the struggle. James, Master of Ballantrae and his father's heir, joins Stuart, and Henry remains behind. When news of Stuart's defeat and James's death comes, Henry becomes Master of Ballantrae. He marries Alison Graeme, who had been betrothed to James.

James, however, is not dead, and, after adventures in America and France, returns to Scotland. Goading Henry and pressing his attentions on Alison, James soon angers his brother to the point of a midnight duel. Henry thinks that he has killed James, but again the latter escapes death—this time going to India. He surprises Henry once more by showing up alive at Durrisdeer. Taking his family, Henry secretly leaves for America, but James, with his Indian servant Secundra Dass, follows. Searching for treasure that he buried on his previous trip to America, James falls sick and dies, but Henry, thinking his brother able to return at will from death, goes to the grave one night and sees Secundra Dass performing strange ministrations over James's exhumed body. Although the servant is unable to revive James, Henry believes that he sees his brother's eyes flutter and dies from heart failure. Thus, both Masters of Ballantrae are united in death.

The Master of Ballantrae, perhaps more than any other of Stevenson's novels, goes beyond the bounds of a mere adventure story. Adventure is a key element in the book, but the characters of James and Henry Durie are drawn with such subtlety and insight that the novel takes on dimensions not usually found in Stevenson's works. Like Long John Silver in *Treasure Island*, James Durie is not an ordinary villain. Henry, who moves from a kind of pathetic passivity in the first part of the novel to a villainy of his own, is unable to assume the true role of Master of Ballantrae. Overmatched and possessed by James, he lacks the dash and charm and strength of personality that makes the latter the real Master of Ballantrae. "In James Durie," wrote one reviewer, "Mr. Stevenson has invented a new villain, and has drawn him with a distinction of touch and tone worthy of Vandyke." With all the attributes of a hateful fiend, James nevertheless has a wit and a courage that are captivating.

Perhaps the novel does, as Stevenson himself feared, leave the reader with an impression of unreality. Still, whatever its shortcomings, *The Master of Ballantrae* has all the trademarks of Stevenson's fiction: an intricately and imaginatively designed plot, power of style, clear evocation of scene, and lifelike characters. G. K. Chesterton wrote of Stevenson that he was the "first writer to treat seriously and poetically the aesthetic instincts of the boy." In his own way, Stevenson contributed a fair number of readable and memorable works to the English literary heritage, and that heritage is the richer for it.

Wilton Eckley

OTHER MAJOR WORKS

SHORT FICTION: *The New Arabian Nights*, 1882; *More New Arabian Nights*, 1885; *The Merry Men, and Other Tales and Fables*, 1887; *Island Nights' Entertainments*, 1893.

PLAYS: *Deacon Brodie*, pb. 1880 (with William Ernest Henley); *Admiral Guinea*, pb. 1884 (with Henley); *Beau Austin*, pb. 1884 (with Henley); *Macaire*, pb. 1885 (with Henley); *The Hanging Judge*, pb. 1887 (with Fanny Van de Grift Stevenson).

POETRY: *Moral Emblems*, 1882; *A Child's Garden of Verses*, 1885; *Underwoods*, 1887; *Ballads*, 1890; *Songs of Travel, and Other Verses*, 1896.

NONFICTION: *Edinburgh: Picturesque Notes*, 1878; *An Inland Voyage*, 1878; *Travels with a Donkey in the Cévennes*, 1879; *Virginibus Puerisque*, 1881; *Familiar Studies of Men and Books*, 1882; *The Silverado Squatters: Sketches from a Californian Mountain*, 1883; *Memories and Portraits*, 1887; *The South Seas: A Record of Three Cruises*, 1890; *Across the Plains*, 1892; *A Footnote to History*, 1892; *Amateur Emigrant*, 1895; *Vailima Letters*, 1895; *In the South Seas*, 1896; *The Letters of Robert Louis Stevenson to His Family and Friends*, 1899 (2 volumes), 1911 (4 volumes); *The Lantern-Bearers, and Other Essays*, 1988; *The Letters of Robert Louis Stevenson*, 1994-1995 (8 volumes); *R. L. Stevenson on Fiction: An Anthology of Literary and Critical Essays*, 1999 (Glenda Norquay, editor).

BIBLIOGRAPHY

Ambrosini, Richard, and Richard Dury, eds. *Robert Louis Stevenson: Writer of Boundaries*. Madison:

University of Wisconsin Press, 2006. Collection of essays includes contributions that cover the entire body of Stevenson's work. Divided into four parts: "The Pleasures of Reading, Writing, and Popular Culture," "Scotland and the South Seas," "Evolutionary Psychology, Masculinity, and *Dr. Jekyll and Mr. Hyde*," and "Textural and Cultural Crossings."

Bathurst, Bella. *The Lighthouse Stevensons*. New York: HarperPerennial, 2000. History of Stevenson's family, members of which built fourteen lighthouses along the Scottish coast during the nineteenth century. Offers a fascinating insight into the writer's family background.

Bell, Ian. *Dreams of Exile: Robert Louis Stevenson: A Biography*. New York: Henry Holt, 1992. Bell, a journalist rather than an academic, writes evocatively of Stevenson the dreamer and exile. Brief work on Stevenson's brief but dramatic life does a fine job of evoking the man and the places he inhabited but is less accomplished in its approach to the author's work.

Buckton, Oliver S. *Cruising with Robert Louis Stevenson: Travel, Narrative, and the Colonial Body*. Athens: Ohio University Press, 2007. Looks at much of Stevenson's nonfiction and his major fictional works to examine the importance of travel in his life and his writing.

Calder, Jenni. *Robert Louis Stevenson: A Life Study*. New York: Oxford University Press, 1980. Excellent study is richly documented with Stevenson's letters. Less a biography than a study of the writer's mind, it focuses on the personal values and attitudes that informed Stevenson's work.

Chesterton, G. K. *Robert Louis Stevenson*. London: Hodder & Stoughton, 1927. Classic critical study of Stevenson by a prominent novelist is still highly regarded for its insights as well as for its wit and lucidity.

Daiches, David. *Robert Louis Stevenson*. Norwalk, Conn.: New Directions, 1947. Along with J. C. Furnas (below), Daiches is credited with pioneering a positive reappraisal of Stevenson. His study is urbane and penetrating in the tradition of G. K. Chesterton (above).

Furnas, J. C. *Voyage to Windward*. New York: William Sloane, 1951. Popular and sympathetic biography is documented with unpublished letters. Furnas, who lived briefly in Stevenson's home in Samoa, traced the author's steps backward to his native Scotland. Includes an elaborate works-consulted bibliography.

Hammond, J. R. *A Robert Louis Stevenson Companion: A Guide to the Novels, Essays, and Short Stories*. London: Macmillan, 1984. Three sections cover the life and literary achievements of Stevenson and contain a brief dictionary that lists and describes his short stories, essays, and smaller works. The fourth section critiques his novels and romances, and the fifth is a key to the people and places of Stevenson's novels and stories.

Harman, Claire. *Myself and the Other Fellow: A Life of Robert Louis Stevenson*. New York: HarperCollins, 2005. Substantial biography covers the writer's early family life, his writing and travels, and his curious but successful marriage. Includes bibliography and index.

McLynn, Frank. *Robert Louis Stevenson: A Biography*. New York: Random House, 1993. Traces Stevenson's career, noting the malignant influence of his wife and stepson. Concludes that Stevenson "is Scotland's greatest writer of English prose."

Saposnik, Irving S. *Robert Louis Stevenson*. New York: Twayne, 1974. Useful critical survey of Stevenson's major works is an excellent starting point for serious study of the author's fiction. Supplemented by a helpful annotated bibliography.

ADALBERT STIFTER

Born: Oberplan, Bohemia, Austro-Hungarian
Empire (now Horní Planá, Czech Republic);
October 23, 1805
Died: Linz, Austria; January 28, 1868
Also known as: Ostade

PRINCIPAL LONG FICTION

Der Condor, 1840 (serial), 1844, 1896 (book;
The Condor, 1850)

Die Mappe meines Urgrossvaters, 1841 (serial),
1847, 1939 (book; (*My Great-Grandfather's
Note-book*, 1850)

Der Hochwald, 1842 (serial), 1844, 1852 (book;
Hochwald: A Story of the Thirty Years War,
1850)

Die Narrenburg, 1843 (serial), 1844, 1855 (book;
Crazy Castle, 1850)

Wirkungen eines weissen Mantels, 1843 (serial),
1922 (book; also known as *Bergmilch* in
Bunte Steine)

Brigitta, 1844 (serial), 1847, 1899 (book; English
translation, 1957)

Der Hagestolz, 1844 (serial), 1850, 1852 (book;
The Recluse, 1968)

Studien, 1844-1850 (6 volumes; includes *Der
Condor*, *Die Mappe meines Urgrossvaters*,
Der Hochwald, *Die Narrenburg*, *Brigitta*, and
Der Hagestolz)

Abdias, 1845 (serial), 1847, 1852 (book; *Abdias
the Jew*, 1850)

Der heilige Abend, 1845 (serial), 1940 (book;
also known as *Bergkristall* in *Bunte Steine*;
Rock Crystal, 1945)

Der arme Wohltäter, 1848 (serial; also known as
Kalkstein in *Bunte Steine*; *Limestone*, 1968)

Die Pechbrenner, 1849 (serial; also known as
Granit in *Bunte Steine*)

Pictures of Rural Life in Austria and Hungary,
1850

Der Pförtner im Herrenhause, 1852 (serial also
known as *Turmalin* in *Bunte Steine*;
Tourmaline, 1968)

Bunte Steine, 1853 (2 volumes; includes
Bergmilch, *Bergkristall*, *Kalkstein*, *Granit*,
and *Turmalin*)

Der Nachsommer, 1857 (*Indian Summer*, 1985)

Witiko, 1865-1867 (3 volumes; English
translation, 1999)

Julius, 1950

Limestone, and Other Stories, 1968 (includes *The
Recluse*, *Limestone*, and *Tourmaline*)

OTHER LITERARY FORMS

In addition to his novels and novellas, Adalbert Stifter composed a variety of essays on politics, culture, art, and education. Most of these writings remain relatively unknown, although among them are individual masterpieces that reflect the author's intellectual power and sharpness of observation. His treatises in *Wien und die Wiener in Bildern aus dem Leben* (1844; Vienna and the Viennese in representations from life), a book that he coedited with friends, reveal his strong personal bond to Austria's capital city. His political articles, many of which were commissioned by the government, underscore his devotion to the monarchy. In a deliberate effort to overcome the banality of everyday life through the use of elevated style, Stifter made important and lasting contributions to the essay as a literary genre. His most significant nonfiction works were published posthumously in *Vermischte Schriften* (1870, 2 volumes; miscellaneous writings).

Stifter placed a few short stories in periodicals; all of them are collected in *Erzählungen*. A year after his death, a three-volume collection of his letters appeared, and since then, scholars have edited other papers and the documents of his service as a public official.

ACHIEVEMENTS

Despite the critical controversy that still exists concerning the literary value of his works, especially the novels, Adalbert Stifter might well be regarded as the most important mediator of nineteenth century Austrian culture, landscape, and spirit. His first published novella, *The Condor*, was an instant success with the public.

Most of his early narratives were received with enthusiasm by readers and critics alike. In *Abdias the Jew* and other tales that were collected in *Studien* (studies), Stifter revealed a serious attitude toward literature and a commitment to the dignity and majesty of art. The refinement of his prose won for him continuing acclaim during the 1840's.

Later, critics and even serious writers of the time rejected Stifter's novellas as shallow and inconsequential. The quiet author was especially pained by the criticism of the dramatist Friedrich Hebbel, who viewed his stories as trivial, judging Stifter incapable of writing about anything of substance. Stifter's response to Hebbel, the novella cycle *Bunte Steine* (colored stones), with its famous preface, is one of the most beautiful collections of prose in all Austrian literature. *Bunte Steine*, however, was the last of his works to receive wide critical praise during his lifetime. His success declined sharply after the middle of the 1850's, because *Indian Summer* and *Witiko*, his two novels (the other works listed above are novellas), were largely misunderstood. Following his death, Stifter was forgotten until near the end of the nineteenth century.

Friedrich Nietzsche, whose aesthetic enthusiasm was especially awakened by *Indian Summer*, must be given ultimate credit for the rediscovery of Stifter. Hugo von Hofmannsthal and Thomas Mann, who in turn developed significant appreciation for the novels, also participated in the Stifter revival. *Witiko* eventually came to be viewed as the only nineteenth century prose epic in the German language that is executed in elevated style with total and uncompromising logical consistency. Dismissed as harmless curiosities by many nineteenth century critics, Stifter's novellas and novels are now recognized as monuments of a rich, deep, and highly moral spirit committed to the purity and ethical purpose of art.

BIOGRAPHY

Adalbert Stifter's childhood in a village environment was a significant formative experience for the author. The quiet rural and forest landscape of his native surroundings informs the scenery of much of his literature. From his early youth he absorbed the simple things and processes of nature as great personal revelations. In 1818, Stifter began his secondary schooling at the Ben-edictine Abbey in Kremsmünster. There, he received solid humanistic training that permanently shaped his fundamental attitudes toward life. The best pupil in his class, he concerned himself extensively with art, music, and literature. Between 1818 and 1825, he began to paint and wrote his first lyric poems. His gifts as a teacher became apparent, and he earned money by tutoring younger pupils. Later, he looked back fondly at those school years as the purest, most beautiful period of his existence.

After leaving Kremsmünster, Stifter entered the University of Vienna, where he studied law. Unable to commit himself fully to a course of public service, he ended his studies without formally completing them. Mathematics and science attracted him, and his extensive background in a variety of fields enabled him to become a successful tutor in homes of the Viennese aristocracy. Among his pupils were Princess Anna Maria von Schwarzenberg and Klemens Metternich's son, Richard.

While at the university, Stifter published a few poems under the pseudonym Ostade. His primary artistic interest, however, was in painting, which remained important to him throughout his life. It provided him with supplementary income during the early years of his marriage and gave him an orientation toward art that later had a profound impact on his writing.

Early reverence for his parents and grandparents led Stifter to view an effective life within the family as an ultimate ideal. His own lack of success in that area of endeavor had significant implications and consequences for his career. After an unsuccessful relationship with a merchant's daughter, Fanny Greipl, he married Amalie Mohaupt, a poor but beautiful girl with whom he had little in common. Their emotionally unrewarding marriage—childless, except for the daughter from Amalie's previous marriage—provided a frustrating background from which Stifter poured his heart out into his stories.

By accident, a friend read the manuscript of *The Condor* and subsequently mediated its publication. Spurred by the novella's success, Stifter began a fruitful creative period that produced some of his best prose narratives. By 1853, he had published ten books and many essays and had reached the peak of his literary popularity.

The Revolution of 1848 and its aftermath played an important role in the shaping of Stifter's mature works.

He reacted strongly to the violence that shredded the values that he held most dear. The "gentle law" that governed all that he wrote after 1850 is largely the codification of his rejection of the Revolution's destructiveness. Acceptance in 1850 of an administrative position in the Upper Austrian school system and his subsequent involvement in various civic enterprises allowed him to respond to negative influences of the political upheaval and partially realize his goals for educational and cultural reform. The major concerns that dominated his public and private life in Linz are visible in his novels.

Stifter's last years were burdened with ill health and misfortune. He was psychologically devastated by the decline of his literary reputation and by several family disasters. In 1865, he began to suffer from a liver ailment from which he never fully recovered. These physical and spiritual torments finally defeated him in January, 1868, and he attempted suicide. The ministrations of a doctor succeeded only in prolonging his misery for two additional days.

Adalbert Stifter. (Getty Images)

ANALYSIS

The basic directional principle that governs Adalbert Stifter's narrative prose is the search for order in a person's relationship to him- or herself and his or her external world. Stifter's novellas and novels document the lifelong pursuit of an artistic unity of physical experience and reality of the soul, of universal meaning derived from the perception and understanding of individual phenomena, of resolution of the pain of existence in the discovery of faith in the basic goodness of life.

In their original form, Stifter's early novellas differ markedly from his mature epics in their dynamic focus on humankind's failure to realize an effective harmony with surrounding people and things. Human passion emerges as a destructive force when uncontrolled by reason, assuming the role of a fate that condemns humans to affliction and loneliness because of guilt. Unreasoned obsession is a tragic factor in most of the narratives in *Studien*, but the sharply fatalistic conception that dominates *My Great-Grandfather's Note-book*, *Crazy Castle*, and *Brigitta* takes a somewhat different form in *Abdias the Jew*, in which fate becomes a clear manifestation of cause and effect rather than a product of unmastered feeling. The author revised these novellas, altering their initial form to temper the impact of inner compulsion on the lives of his characters, making them more visibly subject to the gentle law.

Stifter arrived only gradually at the concretely defined philosophy of life and literature for which he is best known. Nevertheless, his preface to *Bunte Steine* is commonly recognized as the key to interpretation of his oeuvre. The gentle law, as it has since become known, is a categorical rejection of the demoniac, catastrophe-oriented dramatic art of Hebbel. It ardently affirms the peace of a quietly benevolent world order and attests Stifter's conviction that the universe is governed by a calmly divine principle in which Christian and humanistic ethics merge. He asserts that the small, still miracles of existence, the flowering of plants, the rustling of the brook, the shimmer of stars are the truly great phenomena of human experience, because they most accurately reflect the actual form of God's plan. By contrast, the randomly violent outbursts of natural force in the physical world and the destructive emotions of humans are of less moment in the absolute framework. They are not typical of the overall pattern but remain products of isolated causes that are subject to far higher laws. In their revelation of tension within humans caused by the confrontation of the harmonious natural ideal with the chaos of unbridled passion, the most important novellas in *Studien* document the tragedy of human noncompliance with the dictates of the gentle law. The later works, on the other hand, offer a vision of the idyllic existence that is possible under a patiently rational humanistic order.

Central to Stifter's worldview is his perception of nature. Influenced by Jean Paul, at the beginning of his career he attempted to discover in small things the secret of humankind's being. The experience of landscape became especially meaningful as nature assumed the role not of background and scenery for the play of human events, but rather of elemental essence with independent presence, having rank equal to humankind's own. Objective examination of nature's every detail provides the individual with an unclouded knowledge of truth undistorted by passion, yielding a viable model for society and a resolution of civilization's problems. For that reason, Stifter cultivated intimate descriptions of forest and meadow, water and stone, interactions of animals and growing things with natural processes. Each of his narrations weaves together the softly majestic beauties of earth and sky, past and present, eternity and transitoriness, year and day, the physical elements, the large and the minute, everything coexisting with equal right. There is a clear rejection of urban haste and an insistent advocacy of quiet, slow, imperceptible growth apace with the peaceful change of the seasons. In nature, Stifter saw the means for personal achievement of the ultimate goal: serenity of the soul.

In *Studien*, the six-volume compilation of Stifter's early works, specific novellas stand out as especially successful. *Abdias the Jew*, the poignant tale of a North African Jew whose life is a mirror of human helplessness vis-à-vis the miracle and tragedy of natural events, is a masterpiece of description in its portrayal of a landscape that Stifter never saw. The melancholy, haunting love story *Brigitta* is perhaps the author's most penetrating interpretation of erotic suffering and fateful loneliness that arise from human imperfection. Neither of these narratives, however, is as important as *My Great-Grandfather's Note-book* within the broader spectrum of the author's creative legacy.

MY GREAT-GRANDFATHER'S NOTE-BOOK

A profoundly personal epic, *My Great-Grandfather's Note-book* is a document of cosmic feeling for existence, filled with peaks and abysses, mysteries and revelations, strengths of the earth and gratitude for ancestral heritage. This description of the life of the rural doctor Augustinus, a man who is purified through pain and work and fulfilled through love and the learning of self-control, occupied Stifter's attention from the beginning to the end of his literary career.

Portions of the novella exist in four different versions, the last of which was left unfinished at the author's death; their variations reflect the evolution of Stifter's style and of his perception of reality. The first version is informed by his ties to the literary currents of his time, especially the gushing subjectivity of the late Romantics and Jean Paul's demand for sensual individuality of presented phenomena. The pessimistic fatalism of this version, however, represents a break with the Romantics, while the characters' experiences of identity loss and the determining effect of history, origins, and social environment are related to approaches to reality taken by Georg Büchner, Heinrich Heine, and the Young Germans. In later revisions, Stifter attempted to weaken and even eliminate the dimension of gloomy determinism, thereby reducing the dramatic conflicts while advocating bourgeois ideals of propriety and balance. Carried to the extreme in the last rendition, Stifter's pursuit of these goals finally robbed the work of much of its richness and strength, replacing them with sparseness and sterility in both substance and language.

Of special importance for the character of the later narratives is the insistence on authentic, often scientifically precise descriptions of nature. The idyllic harmony of stones and flowers, soil and sky, fosters bonds of love that are shattered when the characters allow harsh internal passion to suppress the benevolent influence of the external order. The deft weaving together of physical milieu and the landscape of the soul gives warmth, vitality, and profound meaning to Augustinus's loss of Margarita's love, the eventual tempering of his spirit, and the couple's final reunion and reconciliation.

BUNTE STEINE

Impressive though Stifter's representations of landscape may be, his most successful treatments of natural models focus not on flowers, trees, and stones but rather on children as elements of nature and symbols for humankind's role in the pattern of existence. In *Bunte Steine*, a collection of novellas about—but not for—children, Stifter created visions of natural harmony that are unexcelled in their descriptive power anywhere in world literature. Experiences of the young are meticulously braided with carefully evoked beauties of setting such that each illuminates the other parabolically. The fairy-tale quality of the stories points to the miracle of the real world in its never-ending regeneration of life, as visually experienced objects of inorganic nature become metaphors for human fates.

The polished jewel of *Bunte Steine* is *Rock Crystal*, with its portrayal of a young brother and sister who become lost as they walk along a mountain path during a snowstorm. Infinite power and beauty lie in the little girl's complete trust of her companion, who leads her along, soothing away each silent doubt. The boy's inner assurance is complemented by the simple majesty and peaceful wonder of their salvation as they find refuge from the storm in a glacial cavern. *Rock Crystal* is especially remarkable for its demonstration of a capacity for observation that enabled Stifter to transform a visual encounter with children out walking, generating from it a convincing sequence of pictures that culminates within the chamber of ice. At the same time, the author's deep love for youth allowed him to penetrate the psychological dimension of his characters with fine precision.

In the other stories in *Bunte Steine*, Stifter used relationships between children and adults to lay bare the unconquerable spirit that is present in even the most humble individual. *Limestone* portrays the sacrifices of a rural parson who saves his every penny to build a school for the village children. At his death, his savings are insufficient for the task, yet the example of his love moves others to bring his dream to fruition. Autobiographical elements inform *Granit*, a poignant interpretation of a boyhood experience that Stifter had with his grandfather, while "Katzensilber," the only work written expressly for *Bunte Steine*, deals with the problems of tam-

ing a difficult girl, a figure modeled on Stifter's foster daughter, Julianne Mohaupt. Destructive passion and the overwhelming tragedy of the lonely and helpless are presented with special vividness in *Tourmaline*, an account of a developmentally disabled child who suffers for her parents' sins. Only *Bergmilch*, with its sentimental treatment of war's insanity, fails to measure up to the high standard of literary quality that otherwise typifies this cycle of novellas.

Stifter's codification of the gentle law in the preface to *Bunte Steine* was, among other things, a reaction to the effects of the Revolution of 1848 on Austrian society. The novels of his waning years document his search for valid alternatives to the intolerable changes that occurred around him.

INDIAN SUMMER

Indian Summer offers a solution in the return to an idealized version of the Austrian world as it existed before the Revolution, while *Witiko* represents a more drastic spiritual escape into an archetypal natural political order, symbolized in the birth of the Bohemian state during the twelfth century. One of the most controversial novels of the nineteenth century, *Indian Summer* is a bildungsroman that projects Stifter's personal educational ideals against the utopian framework of moral beauty experienced in an artistic paradise. The author's declared purpose was to create a portrait of life on a higher plane that would elevate the reader above normal existence and give him or her a spiritual milieu in which to experience him- or herself as a human being more purely and perfectly.

On one level, *Indian Summer* is the history of Heinrich Drendorf's development into a truly cosmopolitan person. Key events include his first, chance visit to Baron Risach's home and repeated returns during which Risach educates him in areas of experience that Stifter considered to be especially important: nature, art, society, history, and religion. Between encounters with his mentor, Heinrich is exposed to specific aspects of city life and to natural science via geological study excursions into the mountains. At the same time, Heinrich undergoes an education of another kind as he observes Risach's relationship with his companion Mathilde, the passionless, painless, quiet love of old age that serves as a model for implementation of the gentle law in the proper nurturing of the bond that grows between Heinrich and Mathilde's daughter, Natalie.

In a more general sense, *Indian Summer* is a revelation of Stifter's deepest personal longings. The title's metaphor, the love of Risach and Mathilde in the harmony of their late years, stands for the ultimate joy of founding a happy family life. At the same time, Risach's position within the sociopolitical framework of the novel illustrates Stifter's perception of the ideals of old Austria.

The novel is peculiar for its lack of conflicts, crises, and other signs of a hostile universe. Instead of true plot, *Indian Summer* offers an eternal state of being. The events of the novel can be told in a few lines, yet such a summary would hardly do justice to a massive content that magically encompasses the totality of Stifter's ideal world. Nevertheless, the absence of narrative motion, an element of structural repetitiveness, and a certain weakness of plastic representation of the characters have caused some critics to reject as boring and unreadable the author's most deliberate return to the classical idealism of Johann Gottfried Herder, Wilhelm von Humboldt, and Johann Wolfgang von Goethe.

WITIKO

In his final novel, Stifter expanded his focus from the creation of the humane individual to the evolution of the humanistic nation. *Witiko*, with its stylization of the twelfth century history of southern Bohemia into a mythic vision of the growth of a natural constitutional state, illustrates the idea that the political fate of a people depends on the transformation of humanity through the gentle law. The formative principle that governs *Witiko* is Stifter's belief that right determines the history of the world. His creative process transfigures the narrative's actual hero, the Bohemian people, through their spokesman Witiko in the retrospective light of the future.

Although Stifter was familiar with important scholarly studies concerning the era, his Witiko is not the historical personage. The story is a symbolic rendering of the life of a leader who is pledged to things of the soul and to goodness rather than to force and brutality. It describes an archetype of the struggling and protecting creator-founder, who deservingly becomes ruler because he perceives and chooses what is right and acts accordingly, thereby winning the trust and friendship of both the king and the forest people whom he comes to rule. *Witiko* weaves together the account of one man whose commitment to duty and propriety are exemplary with the panorama of national fates in which divine law is realized.

The influence of Romanticism is visible in the return to a time of strong people, unspoiled natural conditions, and unified relationships. Nevertheless, the Romantic elements are incorporated into a clear, sharply bounded material reality, in which individual and nation, physical surroundings and Christianity, politics and humanism form an ordered unity. *Witiko* is Stifter's final attempt to create theodicy through history as a religious and artistic act, presenting the divine pattern of things in the framework of historical occurrence.

Witiko is undoubtedly the least successful of Stifter's narratives. Despite the consistency of elevated style that makes it unique among German prose epics, the execution remains unconvincing. The novel's characters are like statues with realistic masks. Anachronistic embellishment of the twelfth century with features of the nineteenth century, coupled with formulaic ornamental speeches, distorts the realism of the work. Here and there, the abilities of the aging writer fail and strict art becomes painful affectation. Yet Stifter's oeuvre would be incomplete without *Witiko*. It complements *Indian Summer* to form a whole that extends the impact of the gentle law into every sphere of human endeavor.

Lowell A. Bangerter

OTHER MAJOR WORKS

SHORT FICTION: *Erzählungen*, 1869 (2 volumes; novellas and short stories)

NONFICTION: *Wien und die Wiener in Bildern aus dem Leben*, 1844 (with C. E. Langer and C. F. Langer); *Über den geschnitzten Hochaltar in der Kirche zu Kefermarkt*, 1853; *Briefe . . . Herausgegeben von Johannes Aprent*, 1869 (3 volumes); *Vermischte Schriften*, 1870 (2 volumes).

MISCELLANEOUS: *Sämtliche Werke*, 1908-1940 (25 volumes); *Selections*, 1952.

BIBLIOGRAPHY

Buckley, Thomas L. *Nature, Science, Realism: A Re-Examination of Programmatic Realism and the Works of Adalbert Stifter and Gottfried Keller*. New York:

Peter Lang, 1995. Buckley examines the aesthetics of German poetic realism, as well as works by Stifter and Keller, to describe the changing relationship between literature and science in nineteenth century Germany.

Danford, Karen Pawluk. *The Family in Adalbert Stifter's Moral and Aesthetic Universe: A Rarified Vision.* New York: Peter Lang, 1991. Danford analyzes Stifter's representation of the middle-class family in the nineteenth century, a time when the pressures of commercial society were significantly altering the traditional family structure.

Gump, Margaret. *Adalbert Stifter.* Boston: Twayne, 1974. An introduction to Stifter, providing biographical information and analysis of his novels and other works. Includes a bibliography. One of the volumes in Twayne's World Authors series.

Haines, Brigid. *Dialogue and Narrative Design in the Works of Adalbert Stifter.* London: Modern Humanities Research Association for the Institute of Germanic Studies, University of London, 1991. Haines focuses on the structure of Stifter's works, with particular attention to the interplay between the narrative and the dialogue. Although Stifter was a conservative and didactic writer, Haines concludes that he nevertheless presented a complex view of reality.

Jeter, Joseph Carroll. *Adalbert Stifter's "Bunte Steine": An Analysis of Theme, Style, and Structure in Three Novellas.* New York: Peter Lang, 1996. Jeter focuses on three of the novellas in the *Bunte Steine* saga. He demonstrates how these disparate narratives contain common themes, styles, and philosophies, evidence that Stifter intended for *Bunte Stein* to be a unified work.

Kontje, Todd, ed. *A Companion to German Realism, 1848-1900.* Rochester, N.Y.: Camden House, 2002. This collection of essays about German realist literature includes two pieces about Stifter: "Adalbert Stifter's *Brigitta*, or the Lesson of Realism" by Robert C. Holub and "From National Task to Individual Pursuit: The Poetics of Work in Freytag, Stifter, and Raabe" by Hans J. Rindisbache.

Ragg-Kirkby, Helena. *Adalbert Stifter's Late Prose: The Mania for Moderation.* Rochester, N.Y.: Camden House, 2000. Ragg-Kirkby argues that Stifter has been wrongly defined as a classicist, maintaining that his later works demonstrate that he was a modernist and precursor to Franz Kafka and other twentieth century absurdist writers. Her analysis of his later fiction pays particular attention to his last novel, *Witiko*.

Sjögren, Christine O. *The Marble Statue as Idea: Collected Essays on Adalbert Stifter's "Der Nachsommer."* Chapel Hill: University of North Carolina Press, 1972. Sjögren provides a close reading of the symbolism, characters, and other aspects of Stifter's novel *Indian Summer*. Includes a selected bibliography.

Swales, Martin, and Erika Swales. *Adalbert Stifter: A Critical Study.* New York: Cambridge University Press, 1984. A solid analysis of Stifter's work by two authors who have written extensively about German literature.

ROBERT STONE

Born: Brooklyn, New York; August 21, 1937
Also known as: Robert Anthony Stone

PRINCIPAL LONG FICTION

A Hall of Mirrors, 1967
Dog Soldiers, 1974
A Flag for Sunrise, 1981
Children of Light, 1986
Outerbridge Reach, 1992
Damascus Gate, 1998
Bay of Souls, 2003

OTHER LITERARY FORMS

Reflecting his particular interest in film, Robert Stone has written two screenplays: *WUSA* (1970), which is based on his novel *A Hall of Mirrors*, and, with Judith Roscoe, *Who'll Stop the Rain* (1978), a screen adaptation of *Dog Soldiers*. Stone has contributed short stories, articles, and reviews to such periodicals as *The Atlantic Monthly*, *Harper's Magazine*, *The New York Times Book Review*, and the *Manchester Guardian*. Notable among these pieces is "The Reason for Stories: Toward a Moral Fiction" (*Harper's*, June, 1988). A collection of Stone's short fiction, *Bear and His Daughter*, appeared in 1997.

ACHIEVEMENTS

Robert Stone received a Wallace Stegner Fellowship to Stanford University in 1962 and a Houghton Mifflin Literary Fellowship in 1967 for a promising first novel. In 1968 he won the William Faulkner Foundation Award for *A Hall of Mirrors*, a "notable first novel"; reviewers praised his narrative skill, facility for language and dialogue, and strength of characterization. *Dog Soldiers*, in turn, won the National Book Award for 1975 and established Stone's importance as a significant American novelist. In 1979 the Writers Guild of America nominated *Who'll Stop the Rain* for best script adapted from another medium. In 1982 *A Flag for Sunrise* received the John Dos Passos Prize for literature and the American Academy and Institute Award in literature; was nominated for the American Book Award, the National Book Critics Circle Award, and the PEN/Faulkner Award; and

was runner-up for the Pulitzer Prize in fiction. In 1983 Stone received a fellowship from the National Endowment for the Arts and a grant from the National Institute of Arts and Letters; in 1986 *Children of Light* brought him a five-year, $250,000 Strauss Living Award. Stone is an established artist of high caliber, a political and social critic whose skill has merited comparisons with Graham Greene, Joseph Conrad, John Dos Passos, and Nathanael West.

BIOGRAPHY

Robert Anthony Stone was born in south Brooklyn, New York, on August 21, 1937, the son of Gladys Catherine Grant, an elementary school teacher whose schizophrenia taught her son chaos and fear, and C. Homer Stone, a railway detective who abandoned his family during Stone's infancy. A product of orphanages and Catholic schools, the young Stone, having offended the Marist Brothers by his drinking and his militant atheism, joined the U.S. Navy's amphibious force before high school graduation and served as a senior enlisted journalist on Operation Deep Freeze Three in Antarctica. His childhood experiences taught him about the rootless, the psychotic, the irresponsible, and the hypocritical, while his military service prepared him to write credibly of military life, language, and style.

While attending New York University from 1958 to 1960, Stone worked as a copyboy, caption writer, and then editorial assistant for the *New York Daily News*, and on December 11, 1959, he married social worker Janice G. Burr. The Stones dropped their conventional life and ended up in New Orleans, where Stone worked at menial jobs for a while, read his own poetry to jazz accompaniment in a French Quarter bar, and moved with the beatnik crowd. His daughter was born at Charity Hospital (a son, Ian, was born later). His experiences in that city provided material for his first novel, *A Hall of Mirrors*.

The Stones became friends with Jack Kerouac and others of the emerging bohemian scene in New York City and with Ken Kesey and Neil Cassady while Stone was studying and then teaching creative writing at Stanford University in California. His involvement in the

Robert Stone. (© Jerry Bauer)

vard University, the University of California at Irvine, New York University, and the University of California at San Diego. During the 1970's he interrupted this itinerant teaching to travel to Central America three times and to write his third novel. His fourth novel grew out of his experiences with the Hollywood film scene. Stone retained his friendship with Kesey and continued to write short stories and articles for popular journals as well as novels.

After *Outerbridge Reach*, Stone published articles and reviews as well as the short-story collection *Bear and His Daughter* and two novels, *Damascus Gate* and *Bay of Souls*. Although Stone did his research for *Damascus Gate* at the Yale Divinity School Library (Stone has finally retired from teaching writing at Yale), much of the work's imagery resulted from his visits to Jerusalem, where he simply absorbed what he saw. In contrast, a Caribbean holiday inspired *Bay of Souls*. Testing new possibilities, Stone directed the documentary film *Guerrilla: The Taking of Patty Hearst* (2004) for Magnolia Pictures. He and his wife divide their time between the East Coast (Connecticut; Northhampton, Massachusetts; a New York apartment on Manhattan's Upper East Side) and Key West, Florida, where he has been featured at the annual Key West Literary Festival.

drug culture led to his joining the Merry Pranksters' bus in its 1964 cross-country trip. In *Prime Green: Remembering the Sixties* (2007) Stone evocatively ruminates on this defining period in his life, the education of a young writer beginning with his Navy days and ending with his time as a correspondent in Vietnam. Therein, Stone takes a candid look at a memorable and controversial decade and notes his regret that more that was positive from that period was not preserved in America.

Stone wrote for the *National Mirror* in New York City from 1965 to 1967 and then freelanced between 1967 and 1971. A Guggenheim Fellowship paid his way to London, England. Later, after two months spent gathering material in Saigon, South Vietnam, for his second novel, he moved on to Hollywood, California, to help write the film adaptation of *Dog Soldiers*. Next he began a teaching career as a writer-in-residence, mainly at Princeton University but also at Amherst College, Stanford University, the University of Hawaii at Manoa, Har-

Analysis

Intrigued by the exotic and by disappointed promises of wealth or adventure, Robert Stone writes as a disillusioned American romantic whose characters unsuccessfully pursue the American Dream in New Orleans, Vietnam, Southern California, Mexico, or Central America. Their failure to choose wisely and to accept responsibility, however, turns their dreams of wealth to ashes, destroys their personal lives, and creates nightmares. Their plight has paralleled that of the national culture as it has coped with shattered ideals and government corruption in the 1960's and after. In many ways, Stone's works have paralleled the concerns and obsessions of the baby-boom generation.

Throughout his work, most of Stone's characters are blind to their inner motives and to the destructive results of their acts. Converse, in *Dog Soldiers*, says, "I don't know what that guy did or why he did it. I don't know what I'm doing or why I do it or what it's like. . . . Nobody knows. . . . That's the principle we were defending over there [in Vietnam]. That's why we fought the war." Stone's characters ask one another what they are worth and find the answer depressing: "A little cinder in the wind, Pablo—that's what you are." A number of them contemplate or commit suicide.

Overall, Stone's characters are self-destructive men and women of their times, hooked on alcohol, drugs, greed, or egocentricity, paying the price of national and personal ignorance and irresponsibility. They are rootless wanderers of mind and world—sometimes violent, often at the end of their tether, engaging in various forms of sophistry, rationalization, equivocation, or indifference. There is a sense of a cultural breakdown, of misplaced dreams, of despair and loss of hope. Caught up in movements beyond their understanding, they continually betray one another without guilt and without self-knowledge.

In *A Flag for Sunrise* Stone's final image of the world is the cold, hostile one of the sea: at times delicate and beautiful, but always predatory. In fact, Stone relies on this image throughout his canon, with his metaphors and images repeatedly connecting humans to fish and the bleak bottom-of-the-ocean competition. Thereby he captures a sense of cosmic menace, nihilism, and conflict: race wars in *A Hall of Mirrors*, Vietnam and drug wars in *Dog Soldiers*, crazed killers and guerrilla warfare in *A Flag for Sunrise*, and war against inner demons in *Children of Light*. His true villains are casual, feckless individuals who act without thinking or feeling and survive at the cost of others' pain and death.

Stone is one of the most impressive novelists of his generation because of his journalist's sharp eye for detail and for short, intense, dramatic scenes; his poet's ear for dialogue; his English teacher's sense of the subtle nuances of language, images, and interlocking patterns; his imaginative drive; and, most important, his commitment to understanding and facing up to the moral ambiguities of America and Americans.

A HALL OF MIRRORS

Stone's first novel, *A Hall of Mirrors*, takes a sharp, satirical look at romantic pessimism in the face of racial prejudice and right-wing extremism in the 1960's. M. T. Bingamon, a "superpatriot" demagogue, exploits the racist fears of poor whites with the aid of Brother Jensen,

alias Farley the Sailor, a con man, philosopher, and supposed missionary, head of the Living Grace Mission. A cynical misfit and drifting disc jockey, Rheinhardt, and a naïve and idealistic social worker of wealthy southern parentage, Morgan Rainey, become pawns in Bingamon's power plot. Rheinhardt espouses Bingamon's cause to preserve his position as the rock disc jockey of radio station WUSA, while Rainey conducts a "welfare" census that brings only pain and loss to those whom he seeks to help. The final third of the novel is an apocalyptic Armageddon, a surreal and nightmarish description of the violent, racist "patriotic" rally the station sponsors and of the ensuing riot. Rheinhardt's parody of reactionary speeches sums up the illusions negated by Stone's novel: "The American way is innocence. In all situations we must and shall display an innocence so vast and awesome that the entire world will be reduced by it. American innocence shall rise in mighty clouds of vapor to the scent of heaven and confound the nations!"

Stone's characters have lost their innocence, and all is emptiness, ashes, and betrayal, as the coldhearted and cold-blooded dominate. Ultimately, Rainey is seriously wounded in the madness of the political rally, but Rheinhardt drifts on. His girlfriend, a basically decent woman brought low by circumstances and misplaced affections, is stunned by Rheinhardt's indifference and, picked up for vagrancy, commits suicide in her jail cell. Rheinhardt, Geraldine, and Rainey's private hall of mirrors reflects the American nightmare wherein civilization proves a farcical hell, dreams are distorted, and action fails.

DOG SOLDIERS

Dog Soldiers and *A Flag for Sunrise*, in turn, capture the naïve cynicism of failed upper-middle-class idealists of the 1970's and their involvement in romanticized drug dealing or revolutionary plots. *Dog Soldiers* depicts the tragic costs of the Vietnam War in its ongoing effects back home: the difficulty of telling friend from foe and the disintegration of moral certainties, loyalties, and conscience. It argues that the war poisoned American values and produced a loss of faith that infects the survivors. In the novel, former marine Ray Hicks, a drug smuggler from Vietnam, finds in the United States love, betrayal, craziness, and ambiguity. His trusted friend John Converse, a journalist on assignment to Vietnam, enlists

Hicks's aid to smuggle three kilograms of pure heroin home from Vietnam for a share of the anticipated forty-thousand-dollar profit. Converse classifies Hicks as a usable "psychopath" but does not understand that he himself has been set up from the beginning. Consequently, when Hicks contacts Converse's wife, Marge, a ticket girl for a pornographic cinema and a Dilaudid addict, he finds himself waylaid by hoods and fleeing for his life. Converse too is threatened, tortured, and then forced to deal with a less-than-honest federal "regulatory" agent, Antheil, who, in on the deal since its Vietnam origins, runs the hoods with "a certain Bohemian flair."

As Hicks and Marge flee across Southern California, they meet an array of fringe characters from Hicks's past, characters who make him conclude, "It's gone funny in the states." Hicks envisions himself a serious man, a modern samurai with a worthy illusion, riding the wave until it crashes, but his romantic obsession with Marge and his strong sense of loyalty doom him. After a confused battle scene, heightened by the sounds of Vietnam battles blasted out over loudspeakers, Hicks discovers an escape route but is badly wounded when he returns to rescue Marge and help reunite her with her husband.

The final line of Dieter, Hicks's mentor, sums up the message in all of Stone's novels: "We're in the dark ages." The self-centered, amoral Converse, dreaming of personal profit at the expense of friendship and loyalty, confirms this view when he attempts to renege on his agreement to meet Hicks in the desert on the far side of the mountains and then dumps the heroin to save himself. Converse is another of Stone's survivors: an egocentric creature who has sacrificed human feelings and human values to maintain his life. Federal agent Antheil, in turn, epitomizes moral ambiguity as he confiscates for personal profit the smuggled heroin. Ultimately, Stone demonstrates that the end result of the war's by-product, heroin, is nightmare and death—"a chain of victims."

A FLAG FOR SUNRISE

A Flag for Sunrise, set in the fictional Central American country of Tecan, attacks American interference in such countries. As it does so, it continually draws parallels with Vietnam through the memories of the central observer, Frank Holliwell, onetime Central Intelligence Agency operative, now a wandering professor. By exploring the fate of Americans whose lives become entangled in Tecanecan politics, Stone sums up the diverse motives that draw Americans into conflicts that they only vaguely understand. The end result of such involvement is inevitably negative: the importation of the worst from North American culture, support of cruel and murderous regimes, and destruction and death. The novel ends with the statement that "a man has nothing to fear . . . who understands history," yet Stone's characters continually fail to understand history in any of its contexts.

A bored and frustrated Roman Catholic nun, the beautiful Sister Justin Feeney, is ordered to close her failed mission and return to the United States, yet she self-righteously volunteers to aid the revolutionary wounded; the result is that she is senselessly battered to death by a crazed Tecanecan lieutenant. Pablo Tabor, a paranoid psychotic on a rampage of killing, finds his destiny: death underwater. A curious, burned-out drifter, anthropologist Frank Holliwell feels alive only when caught up in the mystery and the horror of conflicts in the threatening and oppressive tropics, but he cannot explain why. Holliwell finds survival of the fittest the only value but concludes that outsiders have "no business down there." Everyone is searching for what only the revolutionaries seem to have—a "flag" or purpose—but all are betrayed, tortured, and killed.

CHILDREN OF LIGHT

Children of Light depicts the selling-out in the 1980's of the dreams of the 1960's: Potential artists, novelists, and actors lose their vision and give in to crass commercialism. Stone's characters have buried themselves in drugs, fantasies, sex, and a wealthy lifestyle that leaves them unfulfilled, alienated from their marital partners, their children, and their art. Gordon Walker, once a Shakespearean actor and now a Hollywood writer, writes a screenplay adaptation of Kate Chopin's *The Awakening* (1899) and, after his wife's desertion, travels to Bahia Honda, Mexico, to recapture his past bittersweet romance with actress Lee Verger in order to rediscover who he was and what he can still be. Verger, in turn, acts out as her own reality the marital and personal conflicts of her screen character Edna Pontellier. Verger refers to herself and Walker as "Children of Light," the film generation, sitting in darkness and staring at the lighted screen. As "Children of Light," Verger and Gordon cannot distinguish between true relationships and those projected in their art. The "real" Walker and Verger are but empty shadows on the screen.

Verger has given up her medical treatment because it interfered with her acting; she has driven away her psychiatrist husband with her psychic projects and struggled to please director, producer, and press and to deal with sexual advances, blackmail, and threats. At the same time, she has puzzled over the suicide of her screen character, and eventually she accepts suicide as her own destiny. Walker, in contrast, ever the survivor—no matter the cost—returns to family and home and shoddy career. Stone provides no answers to his characters' plight; it is too late.

DAMASCUS GATE

Stone's 1998 novel *Damascus Gate* is set in Jerusalem and captures the complexities of the Middle East. An agnostic American journalist, Christopher Lucas, decides to research and write on the "Jerusalem Syndrome," a condition that causes some visitors to Jerusalem to believe that God has a mission for them, usually a crazy one. Lucas loses his skeptical detachment as he becomes involved with a number of passionate eccentrics. This involvement includes falling in love with Sonia Barnes, an African American Jew whose passions are Sufism and jazz. Lucas finds himself drawn into a plot by Christian fundamentalists and Jewish radicals to bomb all the mosques on Jerusalem's Temple Mount.

The real ambitions of *Damascus Gate* are spiritual, however. Through unexpected plot twists and half-demented characters, Stone shows how closely related nihilism and belief can be. Although the characters are obsessed with their spiritual torments, they are actually driven by outward events. *Damascus Gate* is a thriller that tantalizes readers with unanswerable spiritual questions but never descends into hopelessness. At its heart is a luminous spirituality and calm that appear to transcend conflict. The novel has received praise for its intricate plot, dazzling images, and language. Some critics have declared it Stone's best work, but others have found fault with its characters ("shallow" wrote one critic; "Indiana Jones and a bimbo" wrote another).

BAY OF SOULS

Whereas Stone's regular pattern is to examine the external signs of chaos on a broad social scale, in the shorter novel *Bay of Souls* he explores inner chaos, delineating the midlife crisis of Minnesota university professor Michael Ahearn. Ahearn's attempt at male bonding through a hunting trip provides two absurdist images: a dropped flashlight that shines on futilely and a fellow hunter cursing the darkness as he struggles ineptly to transport an unwieldy deer carcass that keeps falling out of a wheelbarrow.

Ahearn's personal disintegration begins when his twelve-year-old son unexpectedly survives a hyperthermia-induced coma, and Ahearn is unable to connect with him or cope with that miracle. He has been drinking too much, has acquaintances, not friends, and finds his life absolutely without meaning. His already strained marriage comes apart as he recklessly and obsessively indulges in an open affair with a glamorous new political science professor, Lara Purcell, who is imputed to have had a brief romance with Fidel Castro and whose former husband was an influential leftist. Ashamed, Ahearn nonetheless craves sexual servitude and degradation, responding to sadomasochistic use of collar, cocaine, loaded revolver, and personal mockery in the bedroom.

So powerful is Lara's hold over him that Ahearn abandons family and career to follow her to a remote Caribbean island, St. Trinity, where he finds himself caught up in surreal events: a voodoo funeral for Lara's brother, John-Paul, who had recently died of AIDS, with cultist rituals designed to reclaim Lara's soul. Supposedly John-Paul gave Lara's soul to a spirit woman named La Marinette, who sent it to the bottom of the bay of souls, where tradition holds it will lie in a kind of purgatory for a year, when it can either be reclaimed or passed on to heaven or hell. The wild beating of the drums mesmerizes Ahearn. He also, thanks to Lara, becomes involved in her dead brother's activities with the Medellín drug cartel; she persuades him to dive for Colombian contraband—three cases of emeralds and artwork trapped in the aft compartment of a downed Cessna. The result of a too-fast watery ascent is a near-death experience. Set against these activities is total social disorder on the island—looting, robbery, protests against rigged elections, a military junta, and other signs of a government and a society unraveling with the assistance of rebel forces and morally compromised American Special Forces troops. Afterward, the penitent returns to the sanity he fled and must deal with the terrible personal effects of his romantic obsession. Like Lara, he believes he has lost his soul in that developing-world bay of souls.

Andrew F. Macdonald and Gina Macdonald
Updated by Mary Hanford Bruce

OTHER MAJOR WORKS

SHORT FICTION: *Bear and His Daughter*, 1997

SCREENPLAYS: *WUSA*, 1970; *Who'll Stop the Rain*, 1978 (with Judith Roscoe).

NONFICTION: *Prime Green: Remembering the Sixties*, 2007.

BIBLIOGRAPHY

Bloom, James D. "Cultural Capital and Contrarian Investing: Robert Stone, Thom Jones, and Others." *Contemporary Literature* 36 (Fall, 1995): 490-507. Discusses Stone's comments on the uses and abuses of literary art in *Outerbridge Reach*, *Children of Light*, and *A Flag for Sunrise*.

Finn, James. "The Moral Vision of Robert Stone: Transcendent in the Muck of History." *Commonweal* 119 (November 5, 1993): 9-14. Article in a series on contemporary Catholic writers of fiction addresses the peculiarly moral strain of Stone's writing.

Fredrickson, Robert S. "Robert Stone's Decadent Leftists." *Papers on Language and Literature* 32, no. 3 (Summer, 1996): 315-334. Examines the characters in Stone's work who are cynical, disillusioned left-wing sympathizers and amoral leftist revolutionaries, particularly in *Dog Soldiers* and *A Flag for Sunrise*.

_____. "Robert Stone's Opium of the People: Religious Ambivalence in *Damascus Gate*." *Papers on Language and Literature* 36 (Winter, 2000): 42-57. Discusses the mix of skepticism and religious preoccupation in *Damascus Gate* in the light of the alienation of the characters throughout Stone's work.

Parks, John G. "Unfit Survivors: The Failed and Lost Pilgrims in the Fiction of Robert Stone." *CEA Critic* 53 (Fall, 1990): 52-57. Examines the defining features of Stone's fictive characters.

Solotaroff, Robert. *Robert Stone*. New York: Twayne, 1994. First book-length study of Stone's fiction provides biographical information as well as critical examination of each of the author's novels through *Outerbridge Reach*.

Stephenson, Gregory. *Understanding Robert Stone*. Columbia: University of South Carolina Press, 2002. Critical survey of Stone's first six novels and short fiction postulates an evolving vision of philosophical, political, and moral concerns. A biographical chapter emphasizes the life events that explain Stone's literary obsessions.

Stone, Robert. "Considering Chaos." Interview by David L. Ulin. *Los Angeles Times*, April 30, 2003. Stone addresses the events in his life that inspired the writing of his novel *Bay of Souls*.

_____. "An Interview with Robert Stone." Interview by David Pink and Chuck Lewis. *Salmagundi* 108 (Fall, 1995): 117-139. Stone discusses the creation and characters of *Outerbridge Reach*, his approach to and difficulty writing, and his moral, political, and artistic concerns, among other topics.

DAVID STOREY

Born: Wakefield, England; July 13, 1933
Also known as: David Malcolm Storey

PRINCIPAL LONG FICTION

Flight into Camden, 1960
This Sporting Life, 1960
Radcliffe, 1963
Pasmore, 1972
A Temporary Life, 1973
Saville, 1976
A Prodigal Child, 1982
Present Times, 1984
A Serious Man, 1998
As It Happened, 2002
Thin-Ice Skater, 2004

OTHER LITERARY FORMS

David Storey began as a novelist, but when publishers repeatedly rejected his first novel he looked to the theater, which he had visited infrequently. Storey took a nine-year break from publishing novels from 1963 to 1972. In 1966 his first fully produced play, *The Restoration of Arnold Middleton*, was performed in Edinburgh, Scotland, at the Traverse Theatre. Its critical success encouraged him to write *In Celebration* (pr., pb. 1969), *The Contractor* (pr. 1969), *Home* (pr., pb. 1970), and finally within that time period *The Changing Room* (pr. 1971). After this period, in Storey's work the two genres of prose fiction and drama are intrinsically joined through their themes, characters, and similarity of situations. Although his novels have received more critical acclaim, Storey continued writing and producing plays for many years; only in the 1990's did he return to writing fiction principally.

ACHIEVEMENTS

David Storey is a member of the limited group of writers who have received critical recognition and awards in two distinct genres, fiction and drama. Storey was honored with the Macmillan Fiction Award for his first published novel, *This Sporting Life*. The Mail on Sunday/John Llewellyn Rhys Prize followed two years later for *Flight into Camden*, and his third novel, *Radcliffe*, won the Somerset Maugham Award. After 1963, Storey stopped publishing fiction and switched to writing scripts for the theater, and his plays also soon garnered him awards. He earned the Evening Standard Award for Most Promising Playwright for his first production, *The Restoration of Arnold Middleton*, and he received the New York Drama Critics' Circle Award for Best Play three times within a span of less than five years—in 1969 for *The Contractor*; in 1970 for *Home*; and for *The Changing Room* in 1971. In 1971 he also won the Evening Standard Award for Best Play of the Year for *Home*. Storey's dramas *Home* and *The Changing Room* were both nominated for the Tony Award for Best Play, in 1971 and 1973, respectively. The 1970's was a time of critical acclaim and high recognition for Storey, both for his dramatic works and for his novels. Storey's *Pasmore* was short-listed for the 1972 Booker Prize for Fiction, and the novel won the Geoffrey Faber Memorial Prize in 1973. In 1976, Storey received the highest British honor for a novel when he was awarded the Booker Prize for Fiction for his sixth novel, *Saville*.

BIOGRAPHY

David Malcolm Storey was born in Wakefield, Yorkshire, the third son of Frank Richmond, a coal miner, and Lily Cartwright Storey. He attended Queen Elizabeth Grammar School and went on to study art from 1951 to 1953 at the Wakefield College of Art. He needed additional financial assistance to continue his education, so in 1952 he signed a fourteen-year contract with the professional Leeds Rugby League Club. In pursuit of his art, both visual and literary, he was awarded a scholarship to study at the Slade School of Fine Arts in London and graduated with a diploma in fine arts in 1956. Although he was entered into the art program, Storey has said in interviews that he choose art so he would have the time to write.

In 1956, the fledgling novelist and painter married language teacher Barbara Rudd Hamilton and, with her encouragement, arranged a release from his rugby team contract. From 1957 until 1960 he worked as a substitute teacher at seventeen different schools around London's tough East End. Storey's disillusionment and his experiences with demoralized fellow teachers and disruptive students are recurring elements in his novels and plays.

During the time when Storey was teaching he faced steady rejection in selling his first novel, *This Sporting Life*, so he decided to write a play that he titled "To Die with the Philistines." Shortly after he finished the script, he received word that the American publishing company Macmillan wanted to buy his novel while it was being published simultaneously in England by Longmans. When he won the Macmillan Fiction Award and received the seventy-five hundred dollars in monetary remuneration, he and his wife were expecting their first child (they would eventually have four) and were fifty pounds in debt. With the sale of his novel, Storey was able to quit teaching and devote his energy to writing full time. In the intervening years, in addition to more novels, he has written screenplay adaptations of *This Sporting Life* (1963) and his play *The Celebration* (1975) as well as television scripts, articles, and poetry. He has also served as associate artistic director at the Royal Court Theatre.

ANALYSIS

David Storey's writing is difficult to classify, although his critics and admirers have tried. Early in his writing career, Storey defied the category into which reviewers tried to slot him. When his first novel, *This Sporting Life*, was published, critics linked him with the emerging group of British fiction writers known as the "Angry Young Men" because the novel deals with the generation gap between a coal miner father and his newly educated son. The theme was timely, as a new rank was then emerging in English society, the educated and upwardly mobile. This new generation drove wedges into the tightly structured British class system after World War II. Storey, however, felt that it was not education itself that ignited the clash; rather, the core conflict lay in the mystical value and the quality of salvation the parents gave to education. The parents would never be able to experience what education could or could not do, so their perceptions of its benefits were flawed. Education served only as a vehicle that exacerbated the

cultural transformation of English society at the end of the twentieth century.

Among the recurring themes found in Storey's novels and dramatic writings are the psychological duplicity of a person's physical and spiritual personas, the alienation and estrangement between parents and their newly educated children, and the depression and disillusionment that arise from an unsatisfying job. Storey's prose is taut, matter-of-fact, and rich in visual imagery. The imagery adds clarity and impact to Storey's narratives; his descriptions border on the visceral and pull readers deep into the scenes, so they hear the sound of a piercing whistle, a roaring crowd, and the slash of a knife cutting across a cornstalk.

THIS SPORTING LIFE

This Sporting Life opens with the protagonist, star footballer Arthur Machin, deep inside a brutal and dangerous rugby scrum, with elbows, knees, and bodies shoving to reach the ball. The novel is written in the first person, and the reader experiences the smells of sewage mud, liniment, and leather. During the game Machin has six teeth knocked out, and he is taken to the hospital. While under either, he slips back to the beginning of his rugby career. The first five chapters move smoothly between Machin's memories as a rookie player, when he rented a room from the dowdy, washed-out widow Valerie Hammond on Fairfax Street, and the present, which is punctuated by visits to the dentist and a rowdy Christmas party at the team owner's home. The novel then moves into the present and remains there.

Machin describes himself as a "super ape," yet he searches for something more than athletic success. He joined the rugby league to escape the lot of the ordinary factory worker living in the North of England. He is a lonely man looking for a deeper meaning to his life, and he comes to believe that his landlady, Mrs. Hammond, is the woman with whom he can build something lasting, "to have something there for good . . . to make me feel whole and wanted." Mrs. Hammond rejects Machin, however; she chooses to regard this powerful battering ram of a man as a threat to her passive peace of mind, which overflows with hopelessness. She maintains her willful indifference to his exalted status as a rugby hero and refuses to show any gratitude for his kindnesses, even when he buys her expensive gifts and takes her

David Storey. (AP/Wide World Photos)

family out for Sunday rides. She fears that Machin only wants to see her give in and admit to her need for him before he abandons her.

Machin wants more than a brief sexual encounter. He needs a deeper connection, but he is conflicted by the dichotomy between his physical and spiritual selves. Even after Mrs. Hammond surrenders sexually she holds back the one thing he truly wants, emotional connection. His physicality frightens her so much that she throws him out of the house without ever realizing that Machin could provide warmth and security in her and her children's lives. After Machin leaves, she slips into a decline; she later dies with Machin sitting beside her hospital bed. Machin is left with loneliness, a dwindling joy in playing rugby, and fear about his approaching retirement, which will force him back to the obscure life he tried so hard to escape.

FLIGHT INTO CAMDEN

In *Flight into Camden* Storey again probes generational differences intensified by education and the psychological conflict between the physical and the spiritual. Margaret Thorpe tells her story in the first-person

narrative. She is an unmarried secretary at the Coal Board, and she lives a dreary existence at home with her oppressive parents. She meets a local art teacher through her older brother, a university lecturer, and begins an affair with him only to discover he is married and has children. Nevertheless, he convinces her to escape with him to London and begin a new life. Once in the city, Margaret discovers that her lover is incapable of making the final commitment. Although he instigated their flight, he did it to run away from a breakdown and a teaching job he despised. Throughout their affair, Margaret is barraged with emotional blackmail by her parents and hectoring older brother, who demand that she come to her senses and return home.

Margaret finds some success in London, which exaggerates the indecisive, cynical, and morose attitude of her lover and moves the couple into a sexless existence. Their relationship borders on a parasitic union in which neither party gains what he or she sought. In the end, Margaret finds a letter from her lover telling her that he never wants to see her again, although he still loves her, and that he has returned to his wife in Yorkshire. Margaret's attempt to move toward a liberated emotional state is stifled, and she leaves London to return to her old life. Her emotional growth is halted, and her journey ends where it began.

SAVILLE

After the publication of his first three works of fiction, Storey turned to writing drama. He wrote plays almost exclusively for a number of years until the publication of his fourth and fifth books, *Pasmore* and *A Temporary Life*, respectively, which were well received by the critics. It was *Saville*, however, his sixth and longest novel, that won him the prestigious Booker Prize for Fiction in 1976.

The novel is set in the village of Saxton, south of Yorkshire, during the 1940's and 1950's. Storey paints a richly detailed account of Colin Saville as he grows from childhood through adolescence and into manhood during a culturally turbulent time for the English class system. In this work Storey delves into the same themes explored in his earlier novels: the dysfunctional family, social class borderlines smudged by education, and the inner torment that arises from the duality of physical versus spiritual personalities.

This curiously old-fashioned coming-of-age story is filled with evocative descriptions of the harsh mining village where Colin lives. Colin does not see the oppression during his early years as his story is dispassionately told in the third-person narrative without explanations. The clarity of the images and the characters depicted reveal more to the reader than the young Colin grasps. Slowly, as he attends school, wins a scholarship, and makes friends, Colin recognizes the nascent conflicts that will force him to make hard choices. The novel's richly drawn characters include two delinquents who live in the woods in a "hut"; Bletchley, the only boy other than Colin who has climbed out of a life in the pits; Stafford, the wealthy son of the mill owner; the middle-aged Elizabeth, who serves as a surrogate mother to Colin and articulates the duality he is living; Colin's dead older brother, Andrew; and the sadistic, shallow schoolmaster who shows Colin what is permissible and what is not for a miner's son.

Storey's minimalist style dramatizes the inequities of the British class system at the end of World War II. Education carries Colin—and many others of his generation—into a world of possibilities, but first he must break free of the stifling bonds of family obligation and distorted sense of duty. Although this is the world his father, Harry, helped him to enter, once Colin is a successful teacher Harry cannot accept the change in his son. Both parents, in their separate ways, use impassioned guerrilla tactics to stop Colin from leaving them behind to enter an alien world they do not understand.

Finally, Colin breaks free, no longer an emotional hostage to the obsessive love of his family and their repressive code of behavior. In the novel's final pages, Colin understands that he carries the past within, yet as he rides the southbound train to London he sees a spiral of black smoke rise into the sky and disappear.

Modrea Mitchell-Reichert

OTHER MAJOR WORKS

PLAYS: *The Restoration of Arnold Middleton*, pr. 1966 (wr. 1959); *The Contractor*, pr. 1969; *In Celebra-*tion, pr., pb. 1969; *Home*, pr., pb. 1970; *The Changing Room*, pr. 1971; *Cromwell*, pr., pb. 1973; *The Farm*, pr., pb. 1973; *Life Class*, pr. 1974; *Mother's Day*, pr. 1976; *Sisters*, pr. 1978; *Early Days*, pr., pb. 1980; *Phoenix*, pr. 1984; *The March on Russia*, pr., pb. 1989; *Caring*, pb. 1992; *Stages*, pr., pb. 1992; *Plays*, 1992-1998 (3 volumes).

POETRY: *Storey's Lives: Poems, 1951-1991*, 1992.

SCREENPLAYS: *This Sporting Life*, 1963 (based on his novel); *In Celebration*, 1975 (based on his play).

TELEPLAYS: *Home*, 1971 (based on his play); *Grace*, 1974 (based on James Joyce's story).

CHILDREN'S LITERATURE: *Edward*, 1973.

BIBLIOGRAPHY

Adelman, Gary. "Possession and Gothic Horror: David Storey's Use of *The Idiot* in *Radcliffe*." *Journal of Modern Literature* 24, no. 1 (Fall, 2000): 181-188. Delves into the strong parallels between Fyodor Dostoevski's *The Idiot* (1868) and Storey's eerily familiar characters, theme, and events in *Radcliffe*. Discusses and examines the deeper psychological traits of the characters.

"David (Malcolm) Storey." In *Contemporary Novelists*. 6th ed. New York: St. James Press, 1996. Serves as a good starting point for students, offering an overview of Storey's fiction and touching on some of the recurring themes in his novels and dramas.

Liebman, Herbert. *The Dramatic Art of David Storey: The Journey of a Playwright*. New York: Greenwood Press, 1996. Focuses on Storey's major themes: the circumstances of madness, work, and family relationships. Also details the close similarities in themes, characters, and situations between his fiction and his drama.

Mellors, John. "Wearing of the Black." *London Magazine* 15, no. 4 (October/November, 1975): 74-86. Briefly discusses how Storey's writing style has changed, but in unforeseen and unique ways. Notes that the writing style he used in his first novel, *This Sporting Life*, does not hint at the sprawling prose in *Radcliffe* or the witty cool humor *of A Temporary Life*.

Pittock, Malcolm. "Double-Headed Talent: The Case of David Storey." *Studia Neophilologica* 70, no. 2 (December, 1998): 197-207. Discusses Storey's achievements as a dramatist and as a novelist and suggests that the two genres provide Storey with alternate styles of composition to tell of his experiences.

Wilcher, Robert. "David Storey." In *British and Irish Dramatists Since World War II*, edited by John Bull. Vol. 245, 3d ser. in *Dictionary of Literary Biography*.

Detroit, Mich.: Gale Group, 2001. Details Storey's overlapping themes and styles. Focuses on his plays but covers both his novels and his dramas, as they have influenced each other and share common themes and structures. Offers insight into a writer working in two genres.

THEODOR STORM

Born: Husum, Schleswig (now in Germany); September 14, 1817

Died: Hademarschen, Holstein, Germany; July 4, 1888

Also known as: Hans Theodor Woldsen Storm

PRINCIPAL LONG FICTION

Immensee, 1850 (revised 1851; *Immensee: Or, The Old Man's Reverie*, 1858)

Sommer-Geschichten und Lieder, 1851 (novellas and poetry)

Im Saal, 1854 (*In the Great Hall*, 1923)

Im Sonnenschein, 1854 (*In the Sunlight*, 1964)

Ein grünes Blatt, 1855 (*A Green Leaf*, 1964)

Hinzelmeier, 1857

In der Sommer-Mondnacht, 1860

Drei Novellen, 1861 (includes *Veronika*; English translation, 1964)

Auf der Universität, 1863

Im Schloss, 1863

Lenore, 1865

Zwei Weihnachtsidyllen, 1865

Drei Märchen, 1866

Von Jenseits des Meeres, 1867

In St. Jürgen, 1868 (*In St. Jurgen*, 1964)

Novellen, 1868

Sämtliche Schriften, 1868-1889 (19 volumes)

Eine Halligfahrt, 1871 (*Journey to a Hallig*, 1999)

Geschichten aus der Tonne, 1873

Zerstreute Kapitel, 1873

Novellen und Gedenkblätter, 1874

Pole Poppenspäler, 1874 (*Paul the Puppeteer*, 2003)

Viola tricolor, 1874 (English translation, 1956)

Waldwinkel, 1874

"Ein stiller Musikant," "Psyche," "Im Nachbarhaus links," 1876 (3 novellas)

Aquis submersus, 1877 (English translation, 1910; also known as *Beneath the Flood*, 1962)

Carsten Curator, 1878 (*Curator Carsten*, 1956)

Neue Novellen, 1878

Renate, 1878 (English translation, 1909)

Drei neue Novellen, 1880

Eekenhof, 1880 (novella; English translation, 1908)

Zur "Wald-und Wasserfreude," 1880

Der Herr Etatsrath, 1881

Die Söhne des Senators, 1881 (*The Senator's Sons*, 1947)

Hans und Heinz Kirch, 1883 (*Hans and Heinz Kirch*, 1999)

Zwei Novellen, 1883

Zur Chronik von Grieshuus, 1884 (*A Chapter in the History of Grieshuus*, 1908)

Ein Fest auf Haderslevhuus, 1885 (novella; *A Festival at Haderslevhuus*, 1909)

Vor Zeiten, 1886

Bei kleinen Leuten, 1887

Bötjer Basch, 1887

Ein Doppelgänger, 1887

Ein Bekenntniss, 1888

"Es waren zwei Königskinder," 1888

Der Schimmelreiter, 1888 (novella; *The Rider on the White Horse*, 1915)

The Rider on the White Horse, and Selected Stories, 1964 (includes *In the Great Hall, Immensee, A Green Leaf, In the Sunlight, Veronika, In St. Jurgen, Aquis submersus*, and *The Rider on the White Horse*)

OTHER LITERARY FORMS

Theodor Storm made his most significant contribution to German literature in his more than fifty novellas, but he is also recognized as one of the foremost German poets of the second half of the nineteenth century. *Liederbuch dreier Freunde* (1843; songbook of three friends), which he published with Theodor Mommsen and Tycho Mommsen, contains more than forty of his early poems, among them the best of the love lyrics that he dedicated to Bertha von Buchan. Additional poetry accompanied the novellas in *Sommer-Geschichten und Lieder*. His first substantial collection, *Gedichte* (1852; poems), appeared in repeatedly expanded editions in 1856, 1864, and 1885. Storm's poetry is characterized by simplicity, melodic rhythms, and beauty of form. Important themes are love, nature, and homeland.

In addition to his creative works, Storm wrote a few essays on literature, some of which appeared as introductions to editions of his own writings and anthologies of poems by earlier authors. Also of special interest for his development as a writer are the letters that he exchanged with Gottfried Keller, Theodor Fontane, Paul Heyse, and other contemporaries. The bulk of his correspondence has been collected and edited.

ACHIEVEMENTS

More than any other German writer of the nineteenth century, Theodor Storm shaped and perfected the novella as a finely conceived literary form. His well-developed sense of language and style, his artistic integrity, craftsmanship, and powerful grasp of the interrelationship between milieu and human nature enabled him to compose some of the best German novellas. An excellent representative of the period of poetic realism, he created stories that are meaningful on several levels. Besides penetrating deeply the domain of the individual and exploring problems that were especially relevant

within a specific time and social framework, he employed the portrayal of positive values in everyday life to make timeless statements about the human condition. His novellas had a profound impact on later writers, although his very personal style features characteristics that have never been imitated successfully.

With his first successful novella, Storm received public acclaim unequaled by that of any other German storyteller in the second half of the nineteenth century. *Immensee* went into its tenth printing in 1865, its sixtieth printing in 1905, and its seventy-ninth printing in 1915. Aside from the continuing popularity of this work, however, Storm enjoyed only limited literary recognition until after 1870, when the works of his maturity established him permanently among Germany's outstanding authors. After World War I, there was a new surge in the demand for his stories. Internationally, he became the most widely read of the German realists. A second significant expansion of his readership occurred after World War II, and he continued to appeal to large audiences in both of the postwar German states and in a unified Germany in the late twentieth century.

BIOGRAPHY

In 1817, the duchies of Schleswig and Holstein belonged to Denmark. For that reason, Hans Theodor Woldsen (T. W.) Storm was born a Danish citizen. Close family ties and the seafaring merchant traditions of his maternal forebears were the substance of his early life and perceptions of the world. Because the school that he attended in Husum was inferior, his parents sent him to Lübeck in 1835 to complete his secondary education. There he met Ferdinand Röse, who introduced him to the works of Johann Wolfgang von Goethe and various contemporary German poets. While completing his schooling, he became acquainted with Bertha von Buchan, whom he later asked to marry him. Their relationship, which ended with her rejection of his proposal in 1842, provided the model for his treatment of the problem of unfulfilled love in *Immensee* and other thematically related novellas.

When he left Lübeck, Storm entered law school at the University of Kiel. Somewhat disenchanted with the provincial atmosphere of the institution, he followed Röse to Berlin, where he remained for three semesters.

Upon returning to Kiel in 1839, he became a part of the intellectual circle around the Mommsens. A close productive friendship ensued. Influenced by the Mommsens, Storm began collecting materials for compilations of folk literature, developing a special fondness for fairy tales. He also wrote his first important poems in those years, many of which appeared in *Liederbuch dreier Freunde* in 1843.

Storm graduated from law school in 1842 and worked for a year in his father's legal office before opening his own practice. From the beginning of his public career until his retirement in 1879, he was successful in his work, serving variously as an attorney, judge, police chief, and administrative official. In the aftermath of the political struggle of 1848, he supported an attempt by Schleswig-Holstein to secede from Denmark. When Denmark regained control of the area in 1851, his license to practice law was revoked. He went into exile in Potsdam, where he worked as an unpaid legal assistant to the district court. In Potsdam, he became affiliated with two literary societies, Tunnel Across the Spree and Rütli, where he enjoyed close association with Theodor Fontane, Paul Heyse, and other conservative writers. Although he disliked the Prussian judicial system, Storm eventually accepted an appointment as district judge in Heiligenstadt, where he remained until 1864, when the Prussian liberation of Schleswig-Holstein from the Danes enabled him to return home.

Two years after Bertha von Buchan had rejected his proposal of marriage, Storm became engaged to his cousin, Constanze Esmarch. He married her in 1846, and they eventually had six children. Early on, Storm felt that his marriage lacked passion, and he grew attracted to another woman, Dorothea Jensen. Guilt concerning his unfaithfulness plagued Storm for years, even after Dorothea had left Husum and his own commitment to the sanctity of the family had enabled him to resolve the problem. During his life with Constanze, Storm devoted himself conscientiously to his family, even though it brought him little happiness. Constanze's death was a great blow to him, and even his second marriage, to Dorothea Jensen in 1866, did not free him from melancholy acceptance of the elusiveness of final happiness. That mood pervaded his life and his work.

After his first wife's death, Storm traveled often, visiting other authors and seeking escape from the pains of his personal life. His last years were his most productive ones. In Hademarschen, where he settled after his retirement, he devoted himself entirely to his family and his art until illness made it hard for him to write. In 1887, it was determined that he had abdominal cancer. He rallied against the disease long enough to complete his final masterpiece, *The Rider on the White Horse*.

ANALYSIS

Theodor Storm's importance for the history of the novella lies in his fusion of the objective reality of the Holstein-Friesland milieu and people with the most intimate physical and spiritual dimensions of subjective experience. No single aesthetic program or formal theory governs all of his creations. His early stories are an outgrowth of artistic attitudes that shaped his lyric poetry. Gradually, he progressed to a more resolute narrative

Theodor Storm. (The Granger Collection, New York)

technique in a psychological penetration of human problems, arriving finally at the clearly defined conception of the novella as a genre that informed his mature works. To be sure, there are characteristics of style and theme that are common to most of his prose writings. From *Immensee* through *The Rider on the White Horse*, a constant longing for the past accompanies a feeling of loss. The uncertainty of life, a plaintive yearning for immortality, an emphasis on transitoriness and death as the final end of humankind—all combine to give his fiction its unique atmosphere. There is an obvious focus on the family as the context for illumination of the dissonance between the course of isolated lives and the history of bourgeois society, the pain of humankind's power and impotence in the temporal state, the dreamworld of youth and the resignation of the old. Despite these constants, however, a valid picture of Storm's epic production is achieved only in the understanding that his narratives vary distinctly in tone, direction, mood, and statement with the identifiable stages in his literary development.

In his introduction to the anthology *Hausbuch aus deutschen Dichtern seit Claudius* (1870; house book, consisting of German poets since Claudius), Storm presented his poetic creed. This outline of his basic approach to poetry also effectively circumscribes the fundamental artistic concerns that influenced the writing of his early novellas. Storm believed that the work of literature should have the power to touch the reader directly, unreflectively. To accomplish this goal, it must appeal to the senses. Application of this principle to his prose writings yielded lyric mood pictures of situations imbued with the flow of feeling rather than the dynamics of active drama. Modeled to some extent on the works of the late Romantics, *Immensee* and other narratives of the period exhibit a musical lyricism that is quite absent from the stories written after the author's return from exile.

In contrast to the sharp objectivity of realism, Storm's earliest stories are characterized by an indefinite blurring of style and representation of life. At the same time, a clear tendency toward sensitive inwardness is present in the aestheticizing of past reality and penetration of the private sphere of bourgeois existence in idyllic portraits of static powerlessness. Poetic language is used to beau-

tify that which is ugly while masking facts that are revealed only in spiritual assimilation and effect, inner suffering, quiet resignation, and temporary overcoming. More than anything else, these writings illustrate the author's love for humanity's inner world as a unique and final reality.

Beginning in the late 1850's, Storm entered the second stage of his literary development. In novellas such as *Im Schloss* (in the castle) and *Auf der Universität* (at the university), he began to turn away from the mood sketches that he had been producing, experimenting with epic form while broadening his scope to explore the personal implications of humankind's struggle with fate in confrontation with a variety of social problems: class tensions, religious bigotry, individual isolation, and erotic conflicts. The prose tales of this period are characterized by subtler psychological insights and greater realism. The dramatic element comes to hold its own against the lyric dimension.

As he broke with the lyric novella, Storm generated new theoretical ideas concerning the nature of his chosen genre. Structure and form now had greater import. He demanded of himself polished organization of scenes while employing with greater mastery the technical possibilities of the novella. Aspects of epic integration broke through the classical structure of his portraits of feeling, and significant changes in content-orientation occurred. Instead of still lifes in which things weigh more heavily than persons, novelistic conflicts and their explanations became prominent. Portrayal of the family in its destruction, a microcosmic revelation of the cracks and tears in the fabric of middle-class life, enabled Storm to work out more sharply than before the social basis of his characters' struggles while strengthening his criticism of the patricians, the new bourgeoisie, and residual feudalism. Increased consciousness of the importance of strict form and dramatic moment for the art of the novella led ultimately to the concrete formalization of novella theory that molded his best works.

An essay that appears in his collected works under the title "Vorrede aus dem Jahre 1881" (preface from the year 1881) contains Storm's formalization of the ideas that governed his approach to the novella during his mature years. In that treatise, he made his famous pronouncement that the novella is the sister of the drama and the strictest kind of prose literature. He saw the novella as resembling dramatic art in the following ways: Like theater, the novella deals with the deepest problems of human life. Both literary forms are organized around a central conflict that demands the exclusion of everything superfluous for the sake of artistic unity.

During the final segment of his career, stress of dramatic conflict and stringency of form led Storm to create powerful novellas that are best described as fate tragedies, the most successful of which are his historical chronicles. *Aquis submersus* and *A Chapter in the History of Grieshuus* are excellent examples of this type of story, with their terse style, strength of action and plot, and plastic imagery. Not all the tragic novellas, however, focus on the past. Between 1870 and 1880, Storm also wrote a variety of tales about contemporary situations. *Hans and Heinz Kirch* is typical of a series of bourgeois portraits that focus on problems such as the clash between industry and craft or the tension between art and practical trade. Family tableaus and love idylls are included among the works of this group. The most striking of all of Storm's late novellas combine the dimension of history with deep penetration of physical and psychological reality in the subjective interpretation of human conflict with the irrational part of life. These components combine in *The Rider on the White Horse* to raise the author's greatest masterpiece to the level of a profound statement concerning the fragile nature of human existence in the social context.

One of Storm's most consistent themes is the human struggle with the lasting implications of ones own mortality and subjection to the ravages of time. *Immensee*, the first and most important novella of his lyric period, sets the pattern for later treatments of physical and spiritual transitoriness, in its exposition of Reinhardt Werner's nostalgic confrontation with the reality of his own lack of fulfillment.

IMMENSEE

Charming for its soft grace, dreamy sensuality, and sweetly flowing melancholy of renunciation, *Immensee* is a story of love lost because of weakness and indecision. On one level, it describes the immediate experience of the devastation caused by time's passing; on another, perception of the transience of life's meaning is magnified through reflection. Reinhardt and Elisabeth fall in love as children, but years of separation foster Elisabeth's decision to marry Reinhardt's friend, Erich. In his old age, Reinhardt succeeds for a while in recapturing the joy of earlier years by reliving the past in memory. Frailty of body and mind, however, cause his recollections to dim, confirming the finality of his last parting with Elisabeth at Immensee.

More than simply a sentimental portrait of romantic yearning for the lost golden age of youth, *Immensee* offers a static representation of the conflict between practical bourgeois existence and the insecurity of the spiritual, artistic domain. The competition between Erich, the landowner and businessman, and Reinhardt, the intellectual who inclines toward science and poetry, ends in favor of the former when Elisabeth submits to her mother's will. The result is unhappiness for both Elisabeth and Reinhardt. During their last meeting, Elisabeth experiences intense sorrow in the growing awareness of what has been lost, symbolizing the fact that bourgeois life without the poetic element is empty and hollow. At the same time, Reinhardt, who has remained true to his artistic inclinations, can never escape the haunting longing for middle-class security and stability that have never been his.

In mood and form, the narrative resembles a lyric poem that has dissolved into prose. Individual chapters function like stanzas in presenting the chain of situations as a series of lyric mood pictures. Special accents are created through the introduction of verse at key points, increasing the poetic effect and enhancing the imagery. Action is reduced to a minimum, disappearing behind the images that carry the weight of the author's message. Especially significant is the central thing-symbol, the water lily that floats forever out of reach on the surface of Immensee. Reminiscent of German Romanticism's blue flower of longing, Storm's lily represents the happiness that is always just beyond the fingertips, inviting but outside the grasp. It is childhood innocence that cannot be reclaimed, the opportunity that has been lost, the decision made that cannot be rescinded, the past receding slowly on the stream of time. Gleaming in its purity, the water blossom is the ultimate token of a spirit of mourning and resignation from which Storm never freed himself.

As Storm continued to concern himself with the

fragility of hope and the elusiveness of happiness, he focused his attention more concretely on the family, viewing its health and constitution as the moral basis for the state. During his middle period, he explored in substantial variety problems concerning the forces that establish and preserve the family, as well as those that destroy it. Psychological penetration of the individual's perceptions of the sacredness of life, truth, faithfulness, and social responsibility enabled him to unfold in his fiction the entire ethical hierarchy of German family life. *Auf der Universität*, the most important of the nine novellas that Storm wrote while in Heiligenstadt, illustrates the family's fundamental inability to shelter its members from destructive pressures that arise from humankind's confrontation with the surrounding world.

AUF DER UNIVERSITÄT

Like *Immensee*, *Auf der Universität* is a tale of resignation, filled with the quiet sadness of longing for a life that has been missed. In this instance, tragedy arises from the vulnerability of the person who attempts to transcend established social barriers. The story of Lore is a painful, sometimes funny inner illumination of the foundering of a girl from the lower-middle class who is unable to resist the attractions of higher society. It is filled with a mood of exotic destiny, focused on external beauty, elegance, and feminine grace that have the power to lift their owner above the crowd yet also cause loneliness and render the inexperienced victim seducible.

Early in the novella, Lore experiences personal conflict with a self-righteous bourgeoisie that publicly rejects her, subjecting her to humiliation in the actively negative attitudes of the wealthy. By making her happiness depend on externals, she leaves herself open to disaster. Her willingness to pay the price for social elevation is exploited by the unprincipled people around her. She is seduced, used, abused, but never accepted, as Storm weaves a potent indictment of a society that makes itself guilty by drawing the individual in without offering promise of permanent belonging. Especially tragic are the isolation and helplessness that arise from the loss of family ties that for a time give Lore support and strength to resist the influences that tear her down. Until the death of her parents, she is able to maintain the stability of reason, but the absence of their moral sustenance leaves her at the mercy of conditions that she does not understand. Her involvement with the worst elements of a community that neither comprehends nor responds to her needs utterly destroys her future. Consumed by the impersonal conflict between upper and lower class, she ends her own life. Lore's suicide is a renewal of Storm's lament concerning the transitoriness of all things, including beauty, as well as a fervent plea for a social rejuvenation that will provide every individual with the opportunity for self-development.

In its joining of dramatic conflict with intensity of mood, *Auf der Universität* establishes a bridge of sorts between the sentimental lyric portraits of Storm's early years and the fate tragedies that he wrote after his return from exile. The individual's struggle against restrictions imposed by social station and convention evolved into a key theme in novellas of his late period. Criticism of feudalism and its oppressive limitation of personal development and happiness provided a framework into which the author wove his treatment of timeless human problems. An especially powerful example of this particular form is the tragic love story *Aquis submersus*.

AQUIS SUBMERSUS

Heavy with symbolism and masterfully imbued with the atmosphere of its period setting, *Aquis submersus* renews and recombines motifs and concerns that dominate earlier works, to yield what Storm considered to be his finest novella. Incorporated into the account of a seventeenth century love affair between a painter and an aristocratic girl are effective elucidations of typical Storm conflicts: the artist versus society, the bourgeoisie at odds with the nobility, the tension between memory and transitoriness, the innocent pursuit of happiness juxtaposed to the guilt of betrayed responsibility. Basic situations of the narrative correspond in detail to the elements of a classical drama: the youthful love of Johannes for Katherina, their separation and the change in their relationship with the flow of time, their reunion under circumstances that inhibit the open declaration of their feelings for each other, the consummation of their love and its consequences, leading eventually to dual guilt in the negligent drowning of their child.

Events and characters are linked together in an unbreakable causal chain that symbolically begins in a portrait by an unknown painter and ends in Johannes's artistic representation of his own culpability. The painting of Katharina's ancestor symbolizes the unalterable course of fate in the recurrence of guilt and retribution as the apparent result of a family curse. Johannes's pictures of his dead son signify the reality and finality of the death of love and joy in the failed attempt to resist and escape the confines of a bourgeois existence that is trodden underfoot by an arrogant upper class.

Stylistically and structurally, *Aquis submersus* is one of Storm's great works. Storm's purposeful use of the traditional frame technique magnifies the distance in time between the external narrator and the substance of the tale, while his successful employment of archaic language forms creates a powerful medium in which sentence structure and diction combine to produce an atmosphere that is at once realistic and compelling. The dynamic rhythm of the narration reproduces the softest stirring of the characters' feelings and allows the reader to experience rich contrasts of mood and tone. Leitmotifs underscore the universality of pain and transitoriness, yet the simple descriptions of heath, forest, and pond contribute an element of timelessness and permanence that is once again clearly visible, just beyond reach.

THE RIDER ON THE WHITE HORSE

Nature and natural forces occupy a special position in Storm's most genial novellas. Earth and sea, wind and sky are eternal absolutes against which his characters measure their own strength, ultimately acknowledging their impotence. *The Rider on the White Horse*, his last and finest creation, captures in all of its variations humankind's struggle with the conditions of personal mortality, offering the spectrum of life's experience in the context of a titanic battle with the elements. The individual in conflict with society, the inability to find permanent happiness in love, the hopelessness of the quest for lasting meaning in a transitory world, the internal tension between real personality and perceived innocence, the fatally inescapable consequences of guilt, the inevitable confrontation with the irrational side of life—all of these combine in the story of Hauke Haien to yield a vividly convincing representation of the physical and spiritual essence of a people.

The frame story is divided into three parts. The account of Hauke's development from origins of pov-

erty to a position of power as administrator of the dike system is followed by the portrayal of his successful assertion of will against the narrow-minded, superstitious community in the completion of the new dike. A realistically gripping, magical description of the storm and flood that break his dominance over the villagers, destroy his family, and cause his suicide completes the narration of plot on the historical level. Another dimension is added to the novella, however, in a calculated merging of frame and internal narrative. The appearance in the frame of the ghostly white-horse rider, an omen of impending danger to a dike that has stood for decades since Hauke's death, erases the boundary between the material world and the realm of legend and myth, giving greater weight to the reality of the human encounter with the irrational.

The Rider on the White Horse is outstanding for not only its magnificent drama, its psychological penetration, its illumination of life's contradictions and paradoxes, and its profound interpretation of universal human problems but also for its beauty and power of scenic description, its precision of imagery, and its stylistic perfection. The haunting seascapes, the harshness of the land, the poetically captivating vision of the night with its shimmering, indistinct evocation of the dark side of experience are literary wonders unsurpassed in German prose. In the language of the northern German coast, in the symbols of whitened bones on the sands of a nearby reef, the enigmatic white horse, the sea itself, Storm concentrated and capsulized an art that is blood and bone of his native environment, in defiance against the final passing of everything that he held dear.

Lowell A. Bangerter

OTHER MAJOR WORKS

POETRY: *Liederbuch dreier Freunde*, 1843 (with Theodor Mommsen and Tycho Mommsen); *Sommer-Geschichten und Lieder*, 1851 (includes novellas); *Gedichte*, 1852, 1856, 1864, 1885.

NONFICTION: *Der Mörike-Storm Briefwechsel*, 1891; *Briefe an Friedrich Eggers*, 1911; *Briefe an seine Frau*, 1915; *Briefe an seine Freunde*, 1917; *Heyse-Storm Briefwechsel*, 1917-1918.

MISCELLANEOUS: *Theodor Storms Sämtliche Werke*, 1919-1924.

BIBLIOGRAPHY

Alt, A. Tilo. *Theodor Storm*. New York: Twayne, 1973. An introductory overview to Storm's life and work, containing a biography, literary analysis, a chronology, and a bibliography of primary and secondary sources.

Artiss, David. *Theodor Storm: Studies in Ambivalence—Symbol and Myth in His Narrative Fiction*. Amsterdam: Benjamins, 1978. Artiss analyzes the symbolism in Storm's fiction, including symbols of malevolence, time, and art. His study concludes with an analysis of the novel *Renate*. Includes notes, a select bibliography, and an index.

Bernd, Clifford Albrecht. *Theodor Storm: The Dano-German Poet and Writer*. New York: Peter Lang, 2003. Focuses on the Danish influences in Storm's life and works. Storm grew up in Schleswig when it was ruled by Denmark and before it was annexed to Germany; he spoke Danish and read Danish literature. Bernd describes how Storm refashioned the German novella in the style of Danish fiction.

Burns, Barbara. *Theory and Patterns of Tragedy in the Later Novellen of Theodor Storm*. Stuttgart, Germany: Heinz, 1996. Burns analyzes *Aquis submersus* and other novellas by Storm to examine his position as a tragedian. Includes a bibliography.

Downing, Eric. "Second Wives, Second Lives: The 'Ligeia Impulse' in Theodor Storm's *Viola tricolor*." In *Double Exposures: Repetition and Realism in Nineteenth-Century German Fiction*. Stanford, Calif.: Stanford University Press, 2000. Downing analyzes Storm's *Viola tricolor* and novellas by other writers that contain redundant motifs about gender, class, family, nature, and aesthetics; he describes how this repetition challenges traditional ideas about German poetic realism.

Dysart, David L. *The Role of Painting in the Works of Theodor Storm*. New York: Peter Lang, 1992. Dysart analyzes the frequent descriptions of paintings in Storm's fiction, demonstrating how these descriptions contribute to both the structure and symbolism of his work. Includes a bibliography.

Jackson, David A. *Theodor Storm: The Life and Works of a Democratic Humanitarian*. New York: St. Martin's Press, 1992. A biography, in which Jackson examines Storm's role as an advocate of democratic humanitarian traditions in nineteenth century Germany. Jackson focuses on Storm's criticism of Christianity, his view of capitalism, and his analysis of class structure.

Pizer, John David. "Guilt, Memory, and the Motif of the Double in Theodor Storm's *Aquis submersus* and *Ein Doppelgänger*." In *Ego—Alter Ego: Double and/as Other in the Age of German Poetic Realism*. Chapel Hill: University of North Carolina Press, 1998. Pizer's analysis of German poetic realism focuses on the use of the "double" motif, examining the movement's theories about the doppelgänger and the motif's function in Storm's two novels and works by other writers.

Strehl, Wiebke. *Theodor Storm's "Immensee": A Critical Overview*. Rochester, N.Y.: Camden House, 2000. A collection of critical opinion about Storm's novella, from the initial reaction after its publication in 1849 through critiques of the book in the late 1990's.

HARRIET BEECHER STOWE

Born: Litchfield, Connecticut; June 14, 1811
Died: Hartford, Connecticut; July 1, 1896
Also known as: Harriet Elizabeth Beecher;
Catharine Stowe

PRINCIPAL LONG FICTION

Uncle Tom's Cabin: Or, Life Among the Lowly,
  1851-1852 (serial); 1852 (book)
Dred: A Tale of the Great Dismal Swamp, 1856
The Minister's Wooing, 1859
Agnes of Sorrento, 1862
The Pearl of Orr's Island, 1862
Oldtown Folks, 1869
My Wife and I, 1871
Pink and White Tyranny, 1871
We and Our Neighbors, 1875
Poganuc People, 1878

OTHER LITERARY FORMS

In 1843, Harriet Beecher Stowe (stoh) gathered a number of her sketches and stories into a volume called *The Mayflower: Or, Sketches of Scenes and Characters of the Descendants of the Pilgrims* (1843). For forty years thereafter, she published short fiction and miscellaneous essays in magazines. In *A Key to Uncle Tom's Cabin* (1853), she assembled a mass of sources and analogues for the characters and incidents of her most famous novel. Her 1869 *Atlantic Monthly* article "The True Story of Lady Byron's Life" and a subsequent elaboration, *Lady Byron Vindicated* (1870), caused a sensation at the time. She also published a geography for children (1833, her earliest publication, issued under her sister Catharine's name), poems, travel books, collections of biographical sketches, and a number of other children's books.

Stowe's stories and sketches remain readable. Her best collection, *Sam Lawson's Oldtown Fireside Stories* (1872), differs from the novel *Oldtown Folks* mainly in that it has little in the way of plot. Selections from Stowe's frequently long and chatty letters can be found in the *Life of Harriet Beecher Stowe* (1889), written by her son, Charles Edward Stowe, and in more recent biographies, but hundreds of her letters remain unpublished and scattered in various archives.

ACHIEVEMENTS

Known primarily today for her antislavery novel *Uncle Tom's Cabin*, Harriet Beecher Stowe also interpreted the life of her native New England in a series of novels, stories, and sketches. Along with Ralph Waldo Emerson and Oliver Wendell Holmes, she contributed to the first issue of *The Atlantic Monthly* (November, 1857) and for many years thereafter contributed frequently to that Boston-based magazine. As an alert and intelligent member of a famous family of Protestant ministers, she understood the Puritan conscience and outlook as well as anyone in her time, and as a shrewd observer of the commonplace, she deftly registered Yankee habits of mind and speech. All of her novels feature authentic New England characters; after *Uncle Tom's Cabin* and *Dred*, she turned to settings that included all six New England states. Despite a contradictory idealizing tendency, she pioneered in realism.

One of the first American writers to apply a talent for dialect and local color to the purposes of serious narrative, Stowe exerted a strong influence on Sarah Orne Jewett, Mary Wilkins Freeman, and other regionalists of the later nineteenth century. Without a doubt, however, her greatest achievement was the novel that, beginning as an intended short serial in a Washington antislavery weekly, the *National Era*, forced the American reading public to realize for the first time not only that slavery was a national problem but also that slaves were people with hopes and aspirations as legitimate as their own. Critics as diverse as Henry Wadsworth Longfellow, Heinrich Heine, William Dean Howells, and Leo Tolstoy in the nineteenth century, and Edmund Wilson and Anthony Burgess in the twentieth, have used superlatives to praise *Uncle Tom's Cabin*.

BIOGRAPHY

Harriet Beecher Stowe was born Harriet Elizabeth Beecher on June 14, 1811, the seventh child of Lyman and Roxana Beecher. By this time her father's fame as a preacher had spread well beyond the Congregational Church of Litchfield, Connecticut. All seven Beecher sons who lived to maturity became ministers, one becoming more famous than his father. Harriet, after attending Litchfield Academy, a well-regarded school, was sent to the Hartford Female Seminary, which was founded by her sister, Catharine—in some respects the substitute mother whom Harriet needed after Roxana died in 1816 but did not discover in the second Mrs. Beecher. In later years, Harriet would consistently idealize motherhood. When Catharine's fiancé, a brilliant young man but one who had not experienced any perceptible religious conversion, died in 1822, the eleven-year-old Harriet felt the tragedy. In 1827, the shy, melancholy girl became a teacher in her sister's school.

In 1832, Lyman Beecher accepted the presidency of Lane Seminary in Cincinnati, Ohio, and soon Catharine and Harriet had established another school there. Four years later, Harriet married a widower named Calvin Stowe, a Lane professor. In the years that followed, she had seven children. She also became familiar with slavery, as practiced just across the Ohio River in Kentucky; with the abolitionist movement, which boasted several notable champions in Cincinnati, including the future chief justice of the United States, Salmon P. Chase; and with the Underground Railroad. As a way of supplementing her husband's small income, she also contributed to local and religious periodicals.

Not until the Stowes moved to Brunswick, Maine, in 1850, however, did she think of writing about slavery. Then, urged by her brother, Henry, by then a prominent minister in Brooklyn, New York, and by other family members in the wake of the U.S. Congress's enactment of the Fugitive Slave Act and spurred by a vision she experienced at a church service, she began to construct *Uncle Tom's Cabin*. Even as a weekly serial in the *National Era*, it attracted much attention, and its publication in 1852 as a book made Stowe an instant celebrity. After that year, from her new base in Andover, Massachusetts, where her husband taught, she twice visited Europe; met

Harriet Beecher Stowe. (Library of Congress)

Harriet Martineau, John Ruskin, the Brownings, and Lady Byron, among others; and saw the scope of her fame increase even further.

Stowe wrote another slavery novel, *Dred*, and then turned her literary attention to New England. The drowning of her son, Henry, a Dartmouth student, in the summer of 1857, marred for her the successes of these years. In the fall of 1862, infuriated by the lack of British support for the North in the American Civil War and skeptical that President Abraham Lincoln would fulfill his promise to issue a proclamation of emancipation, Stowe visited Lincoln, who is reported to have greeted her with the words, "So this is the little lady who made this big war." She left Washington, D.C., satisfied that the president would keep his word.

Following Calvin Stowe's retirement from Andover, the family moved to Hartford, the winters usually being spent in northern Florida. Two of the most sensational scandals of the post-Civil War era involved Stowe, the first arising when she published an imprudent and detailed account of Lord Byron's sins as revealed to her some years earlier by the now deceased widow of the poet, the second being an adultery suit brought against her brother, Henry, in which Stowe characteristically defended him to the hilt. The Byron affair in particular turned many people against her, although her books continued to be commercial successes throughout the 1870's. The most severe personal abuse ever directed at a respectable nineteenth century woman bothered Stowe far less than another personal tragedy: the alcoholism and eventual disappearance of her son, Fred, in San Francisco, California, in 1870.

In the last twenty-three years of her life, Stowe became the central attraction of the Hartford neighborhood known as Nook Farm, also the home of Charles Dudley Warner and Mark Twain, the latter moving there in part because of its Beecher connections. Her circle of friends included Annie Fields, wife of *The Atlantic Monthly* publisher; George Eliot, with whom she corresponded; and Holmes, always a staunch supporter. In her final years, her mind wandered at times, but she was still writing lucid letters two years before her death on July 1, 1896, at the age of eighty-five.

ANALYSIS

In 1869, after finishing her sixth novel, *Oldtown Folks*, Harriet Beecher Stowe began a correspondence with Eliot by sending her a copy of the novel. Although an international celebrity, Stowe wanted the approval of this younger and less famous woman who had contributed notably to a movement—literary realism—just beginning to be critically recognized. Like Stowe, Eliot came from a deeply religious background and had formed a union with an unromantic and bookish, but supportive, man. Unlike the American novelist, Eliot had rejected religion for rationalism and Romanticism for realism. Had Calvin Stowe's first wife not died, it would have been unthinkable for Harriet Beecher to live with him as Eliot did with George Henry Lewes. In life, the former Miss Beecher cheerfully married the unexciting scholar; in *The Minister's Wooing*, she would not permit her heroine Mary Scudder to marry her scholarly suitor (as

Eliot's Dorothea Brooke in *Middlemarch*, 1871-1872, was permitted to marry hers, Dr. Casaubon).

Stowe's hope, in a measure fulfilled, that Eliot would like *Oldtown Folks* may be taken as signifying her desire to be recognized as a realist, even though her own realism was strongly tinged with the Romanticism Eliot had come to despise. The young Harriet Beecher had probably learned something from John Bunyan's *The Pilgrim's Progress* (1678, 1684), but most of her other reading—*The Arabian Nights' Entertainments*, Cotton Mather's *Magnalia Christi Americana* (1702), and the works of Sir Walter Scott and Lord Byron—had little to teach an incipient realist. Nor did American literature in the 1830's, when she began to write, furnish any likely models. As a result, the reader finds in her works a mingling of realist and Romantic elements.

Stowe's settings, particularly the New England ones, ring true. She understood her cultural roots, and she proved able to recollect childhood impressions almost photographically. She possessed a keen ear for dialect and a sharp eye for the idiosyncrasies of people she scarcely seemed to have noticed until they turned up in her writing. She used the novel to probe urgent social issues such as slavery and women's rights. Although she liked nature and worked hard at describing it accurately, she disdained her native region's characteristic transcendental interpretations of it. She displayed the realist's aversion to mystery, mysticism, and the making of history into legend.

The Romantic tendencies of Stowe's fiction stand out against its realistic background. Her heroines are invariably saintly, as are certain of her black male characters such as Uncle Tom and, in *Dred*, Uncle Tiff. Her recalcitrant heroes often undergo rather unconvincing conversions. Occasionally, she introduces a mythic, larger-than-life character such as Dred. In common with most of the generation of American realists who followed her, she never renounced the heroic but sought to demonstrate its presence among humble and common people. Her heroes differ from those of Twain, Howells, and Henry James, however, in drawing their strength from a firm Christian commitment: Stowe's piety has been something of an impediment to her modern readers.

The looseness of plotting about which Stowe's critics have complained so much derives in large measure from her inability to develop convincing central characters in most of her novels. Four of her last five novels have plural nouns—words such as "neighbors" and "folks" and "people"—in their titles, but even *Uncle Tom's Cabin* is not about Uncle Tom in the sense that Charles Dickens's *David Copperfield* (1849-1850, serial; 1850, book) or Gustave Flaubert's *Madame Bovary* (1857) is about its title character. In fact, Stowe changed the title of *Dred* for a time to *Nina Gordon*, a more central character but one who dies many chapters from the end. *My Wife and I* and *Oldtown Folks* are narrated by relatively colorless central characters.

One of Stowe's most persistent and indeed remarkable narrative traits also works against her realism on occasions. As she confides at the beginning of chapter 44 of *Dred*, "There's no study in human nature more interesting than the aspects of the same subject in the points of view of different characters." That she periodically allowed this interest to distract her from the task at hand is clear. Although she experimented with different points of view—omniscient, first-person, dramatic, and circulating (the last primarily through the use of the epistolary method)—she worked before the time when novelists such as Joseph Conrad, James Joyce, and William Faulkner developed techniques capable of sustaining this kind of interest. It should be pointed out that Stowe uses the expression "points of view" in the sense of "opinions," and she is more likely to present the conflict of opinions through conversations than through living, breathing embodiments of motivating ideas.

It is as a realist before her time that Stowe is most profitably considered. Even where her realism does not serve a socially critical purpose, as it does in *Uncle Tom's Cabin* and *My Wife and I*, she makes her readers aware of the texture, the complexity, of social life—particularly the conflicts, tensions, and joys of New England community life. Understanding how people grow from their geographic, social, religious, and intellectual roots, she is able to convey the reality of isolated Maine coastal villages and the jaunty postwar Manhattan of aspiring journalists. In her best work, she depicts evil not as the product of Mephistophelean schemers or motiveless brutes but of high-minded people incapacitated by a crucial weakness, such as the irresolute Augustine St. Clare of *Uncle Tom's Cabin*, the temporizing Judge Clayton of *Dred*, and the imperceptive Dr. Hopkins of *The Minister's Wooing*.

UNCLE TOM'S CABIN

Uncle Tom's Cabin: Or, Life Among the Lowly, remains one of the most controversial of novels. Extravagantly admired and bitterly detested in the 1850's, it still arouses extreme reactions more than one-and-a-half centuries later. An early barrage of challenges to its authenticity led Stowe to work furiously at the assembling of *A Key to Uncle Tom's Cabin* the next year. In 262 closely printed, double-columned pages, she impressively documented horrors that verified "the truth of the work." This book unfortunately encouraged the development of an essentially nonliterary mass of criticism, with the result that the novel early gained the reputation of a brilliant piece of propaganda—even President Lincoln supposedly accepting the Civil War as its legacy—but unworthy of serious consideration on artistic grounds.

It did not help the novel's cause that the inevitable later reaction against this enormously popular story coincided with the effort, spearheaded by James, to establish the novel as a form of art rather than as a mere popular entertainment. A writer who strove too singlemindedly for mere verifiability did not merit consideration as an artist. In the same year that *Uncle Tom's Cabin* began appearing serially, Nathaniel Hawthorne—James's chief example of the American artist—prefaced his *The House of the Seven Gables* (1851) with a firm declaration of its imaginary basis, which contrasted sharply with his attempt to provide a "historical" one for *The Scarlet Letter* one year earlier. Hawthorne's star as a writer of fiction gradually rose: Stowe's sank. Like "Old Ironsides," the vigorous youthful poem of Stowe's staunch friend of later years, *Uncle Tom's Cabin* was relegated to the status of a work that made things happen—important historically but damned by that very fact to the region of the second-rate.

In *A Key to Uncle Tom's Cabin*, Stowe herself called *Uncle Tom's Cabin* "a very inadequate representation of slavery," but her excuse is significant: "Slavery, in some of its workings, is too dreadful for the purposes of art." She was acknowledging a problem that would continue to bedevil realists for most of the rest of the century. The most prominent spokesperson for realism, Howells, agreed with her, and until the 1890's, realists would generally exclude things considered "too dreadful." As late as 1891, Thomas Hardy induced mass revulsion by allowing his heroine to be raped in *Tess of the D'Urbervilles* (1891) while referring to her in his subtitle as "a pure woman."

Stowe sandwiched the story of Uncle Tom, the meek Christian capable of turning the other cheek even to the sadistic Simon Legree, between the resolute George and Eliza Harris's escape from slavery and the Harris family's fortuitous reunion at the end of the novel. If the plot is untidy and contrived, a number of the individual characters and episodes have remained among the most memorable in fiction. The famous scene in which Eliza crosses the Ohio River ice in early spring is "true" not because the feat had been accomplished (although Stowe knew it had) but because she makes the reader feel Eliza's desperation, the absolute necessity of the attempt, and the likelihood that a person who grew up in her hard school would develop the resources to succeed.

The meeting between Miss Ophelia and Topsy illustrates Stowe's talent for dramatizing the confrontation of stubborn viewpoints. Sold down the river by his first owner, Tom has rescued the angelic daughter of Augustine St. Clare and has been installed to the St. Clare household. Miss Ophelia, a Vermont cousin of St. Clare, has been brought south to take care of Eva, whose mother is languidly incompetent. St. Clare despises slavery but feels powerless to resist it; Ophelia's intransigent New England conscience will not permit her to acquiesce in it. After listening to a considerable amount of her antislavery rhetoric, St. Clare gives his cousin a little black girl rescued from alcoholic parents. Ophelia is revolted by Topsy, so utterly different from the golden, cherubic Eva. Topsy, shrewd and skeptical beyond her years, embodies the insidiousness of slavery itself. Neither was premeditated but simply "grow'd" and now must somehow be dealt with as found. Ophelia must find room in her heart for the little "black spider" or lose face with her cousin. Her struggle with Topsy—and with her own physical aversion—is fierce and richly comical, and its successful outcome believable.

For the modern reader, the death scenes in the novel are more of a problem. Little Eva's protracted illness and beatific death exactly pleased the taste of Stowe's time. Today, her father's senseless and sudden death as a re-

sult of his attempt to mediate a tavern brawl seems more like real life—or would if Stowe had not permitted St. Clare to linger long enough to undergo a deathbed religious conversion. Modern reaction to Stowe's climactic scene is complicated by the hostility of writers such as James Baldwin to the character of Uncle Tom, who, in dying at the hands of Legree's henchmen, wins their souls in the process. Whether or not the conversion of Sambo and Quimbo convinces today's reader, Tom's character has been firmly established, and he dies in precisely the spirit the reader expects.

Far less satisfactory is the subsequent escape of two of Legree's slaves from his clutches. Stowe did nothing beforehand to induce belief in a brutal master who could melt into helpless impassivity at the sight of a lock of his dead mother's hair. Finding it expedient to make Legree superstitious, she established this side of his character belatedly and ineptly, and she failed to understand that her conception of the power of motherhood was not universally shared.

In short, the reader's admiration is interrupted by idealistic and sentimental material that does not support Stowe's goal of depicting life as it was. Nor is this inconsistency surprising. No American had ever written such a novel: realistic in impulse and directed at a current social problem of the greatest magnitude. She had no models and could not, like Twain after her, draw on experiences as Missourian, journalist, Western traveler, and—before he wrote his greatest books—neighbor of Stowe and reader of her work.

Like Twain and Howells after her, Stowe did not banish Romanticism from her novels, but her commitment to realism is clear. Thirty years before Twain's accomplishments with dialect in *Adventures of Huckleberry Finn* (1884), and nearly two decades before Bret Harte popularized the concept of local color, Stowe used dialects—not with perfect consistency but not for the conventional purpose of humor either. For the first time in major American fiction, dialect served the purpose of generating a credible environment for a serious narrative. In the process, she changed the perceptions of hundreds of thousands of readers forever.

Within a year, the book had made Stowe internationally known. When, after several years of minor literary activity, she returned to the subject of slavery, events were unfolding that led inexorably to war. Her brother, Henry, was outraging North and South alike by holding his own mock slave auction in his Brooklyn church. John Brown was launching his personal civil war in Kansas. In the chamber of the U.S. Senate, abolitionist Charles Sumner was nearly beaten to death by a southern colleague. Stowe herself had been busy with antislavery petitions and appeals.

DRED

From this context emerged *Dred*, a more somber novel. As it opens, Nina Gordon has returned to her North Carolina plantation from New York upon the death of her father. She has dallied with several suitors but has sense enough to prefer Edward Clayton, an idealistic young lawyer from another part of her native state. After successfully prosecuting a white man who had hired and then physically abused Nina's domestic slave Milly, Clayton's ambition to counteract such abuses legally is checked when an appeals judge—a man of undoubted probity and, ironically, Clayton's own father—reverses the earlier decision on the grounds that no slave has any rights under state law. Meanwhile, Nina's attempt at benign management of her plantation is set back by the appearance of her wastrel brother Tom, who especially enjoys tormenting her able quadroon steward Harry. Although bearing a strong resemblance to George Harris of *Uncle Tom's Cabin*, Harry is different in two important ways. First, Stowe develops the frustration of this educated and sensitive man much more thoroughly. Second, Harry is, unknown to Nina, the Gordon children's half brother.

When Nina dies in a cholera epidemic, Tom asserts control over the plantation, and Clayton returns home with the resolve to press for changes in a legal code that permits a man to own and mistreat his own brother. Harry is driven to rebel and flee into the nearby swamp, where he falls under the influence of Dred, whom the author styles after the son of the famous black rebel Denmark Vesey, but who resembles even more closely that other noted rebel, Nat Turner.

What happens next exemplifies Stowe's familiarity with the clergy and her talent for controversy. Invited by his uncle to a Presbyterian ministers' conference, Clayton seeks there the moral support for legal reform. Even though he finds one minister passionately committed to

rights for slaves, the majority of the brethren turn out to be complacent trimmers, and Clayton learns that he can expect no help in that quarter. Stowe strategically places the conference between two scenes of desperation, both of which illustrate the social system's assault on the family. In the former, Uncle Tiff, the black guardian of two white children whose father is a shiftless squatter on the Gordon plantation, vows to preserve them from the corrupting influence of their slatternly stepmother and takes them to Dred's hidden fastness in the swamp. In the latter, another quadroon Gordon offshoot, Cora, confesses in court to the murder of her own two children to "save" them, as she puts it, from being sold away.

In the swamp, Tiff and the children are succored by Dred, who is one of Stowe's most bizarre creations: half Robin Hood, half self-appointed executioner for the Lord. Too mythic a hero for a realistic novel, Dred unfortunately develops quickly into a very tedious one too, ranting interminably in his guise of Old Testament prophet. Even he is no match, however, for the committed Christian Milly, although she can accomplish no more than the postponement of his planned revenge against the hated whites. When Tom Gordon organizes a party to ransack the swamp for Dred and Harry, the former is killed, and Harry and his wife, along with Tiff and his young charges, escape to the North. In an obviously Pyrrhic victory, Clayton, baffled by his neighbors in his attempt to educate the slaves on his own estate, takes them off to Canada, where they continue to work for him in their freedom.

Tiff is another saintly domestic slave, but he has no power to reclaim any Sambo or Quimbo from degradation. There are no spectacular personal conversions in *Dred* and no hope of any social one. Milly, who has had to endure the loss by death or sale of all her numerous children, seems to win a legal victory over a cruel master and a moral one over the vindictive fugitive Dred, but both turn out to be illusory. Not only the fugitive blacks but also Clayton the hero must leave the country. If *Uncle Tom's Cabin* stands as a warning to a divided society, *Dred* is a prophecy of disintegration.

THE MINISTER'S WOOING

Stowe's next two novels have much in common. Both *The Minister's Wooing* and *The Pearl of Orr's Island* are anchored in New England coastal communities, and both put Yankee manners and speech on display. Each novel boasts a saintly heroine who effects the conversion of a dashing young man with a strong affinity for the sea. Although the former novel paints Newport, Rhode Island, less colorfully than the latter does coastal Maine, *The Minister's Wooing* is a more carefully constructed novel that analyzes New England character more profoundly.

More than any other Stowe novel, *The Minister's Wooing* focuses on its principals: Samuel Hopkins, Congregationalist minister of Newport, and Mary Scudder, daughter of Hopkins's widowed landlady. In several respects, the minister is the historical Dr. Hopkins, learned protégé of the great Jonathan Edwards, eminent theologian in his own right and vigorous opponent of slavery in a town consecrated to the slave trade. In the 1780's, when the novel is set, however, the real Hopkins was in his sixties and had a wife and eight children; Stowe makes him middle-aged and a bachelor. Another celebrity of the time plays a significant role: Aaron Burr in the years before he became senator, vice president, and killer of Alexander Hamilton in a duel. Burr is depicted as a charming, unscrupulous seducer of women—a distortion of the historical Burr, no doubt, but one based on his reputation.

Stowe's motive for involving these men in her story of pious young Mary Scudder is utterly serious. As friend and student of Edwards, Hopkins represents the stern, uncompromising Puritan past. As Edwards's worldly and skeptical grandson, Burr stands for the repudiation of the past. Mary's choice is not—what would be easy for her—between Hopkins and Burr but between Hopkins and her young lover James Marvyn, who resembles Burr only in his impatience with the hard and incomprehensible doctrines of his forebears. James has grown up with Mary but has gravitated to the sea, and he is not quite engaged to her when he is reported lost in a shipwreck. Mrs. Scudder thereafter nudges Mary toward a union with the unexciting minister, himself an admirer of the young lady's ardent—if for his taste too sunny—Christianity.

Stowe neatly balances the claims of Hopkins's exacting Old Testament theology and Mary's simpler faith in the loving kindness of Jesus. In comforting the lost James's mother, long appalled by the minister's re-

morseless logic and now driven to near psychosis by her son's supposed death, Mary's cheerful faith receives its first test. She also befriends an aristocratic young Frenchwoman—Burr's intended victim—and learns of the world of adulterous intrigue. As in her previous novels, Stowe introduces a black servant who has looked on life long and maintained a practical Christianity that is proof against all temptation to despair. Having been freed by her master, Mr. Marvyn, under the minister's influence, Candace works freely for the Marvyns and venerates Dr. Hopkins, not failing, however, to draw Mrs. Marvyn gently from "the fathomless mystery of sin and sorrow" to the "deeper mystery of God's love." Meanwhile, Mary's faith deepens, Stowe probably raising more than a few Protestant eyebrows by likening her explicitly to the Virgin Mary, who "kept all things and pondered them in her heart."

In real life, Catharine Beecher's beloved did not survive his shipwreck, and Stowe's elder sister agonized long over the possibility of his having died unregenerate. In life, Henry Stowe did not miraculously escape drowning. James Marvyn, on the other hand, after a considerable interval in which he inexplicably fails to notify either Mary or his family of his survival, returns a week before Mary's scheduled wedding with the minister. After having promised herself to Hopkins, Mary will not of course renege, so it falls to Miss Prissy, her dressmaker and friend, to approach the formidable theologian with the fact—which he is incapable of divining—that James is Mary's true love. Miss Prissy is one of Stowe's well-conceived realistic characters; an incurable gossip and a hypocrite in her professed admiration for the minister's sermons, she is nevertheless willing to assume the unpleasant initiative on behalf of her friend. Apprised of the true situation, the minister releases Mary and promptly marries her to Marvyn.

As she had in her first *Atlantic Monthly* short story, Stowe depicts in this novel the psychology of bereavement; what she refuses to present is not death itself but the possibility of a good-hearted lad dying unregenerate. She demonstrates how the rigorous faith of a Hopkins can be a barrier, even a poison, to the unstable, but of the efficacy of Christianity to restore lost lambs, she can conceive no doubt. Even the heterodox Burr nearly succumbs to Mary's entreaties to reform. Stowe's less saintly believers, such as Miss Prissy, and her magnanimous skeptics, like Augustine St. Clare of *Uncle Tom's Cabin*, are more credible. As for Hopkins, willing to jeopardize his church financially and socially by his insistence that the most influential of his parishioners renounce his connections with the slave trade, his final renunciation of Mary is quite consistent with his previous rock-ribbed selflessness.

OLDTOWN FOLKS

Oldtown Folks, at which Stowe worked in the postwar years and published whole in 1869—for she refused to serialize it in the usual way—repeats many of the concerns of *The Minister's Wooing* and even reintroduces Jonathan Edwards's grandson, here known as Ellery Davenport. Longer, more varied, and much more rambling, this novel contains a considerable amount of Stowe's best writing. In the preface, her narrator, Horace Holyoke, vows to "interpret to the world the New England life and character of the early republic." Today, no one would choose a loose, leisurely narrative to achieve such an ambition, and perhaps no one but Stowe would have attempted it in the 1860's. It is no coincidence that *Oldtown Folks* attracted the attention of Perry Miller, the distinguished twentieth century interpreter of the New England tradition.

The Minister's Wooing had been a theological novel in which no one had very much fun. As if to redress the deficiency, Stowe widens her focus, invests this work with more of the engaging minor characters of *The Pearl of Orr's Island*, and shows her villagers enjoying themselves. Her twenty-seventh chapter, "How We Kept Thanksgiving at Oldtown," which has become an anthology piece in recent years, argues that Oldtown (based on her husband's hometown of Natick, Massachusetts) has fun precisely because the inhabitants take human life seriously enough "to believe they can do much with it." Sam Lawson—Stowe's most famous character outside *Uncle Tom's Cabin*—far from exemplifying the protestant work ethic, is the town idler, universally valued for his skill at "lubricating" with his humorous anecdotes and relaxed manner the "incessant steampower in Yankee life." By contrast, the character most devoted to work, Miss Asphyxia Smith, is easily the most hateful character in the book.

Sam also serves the tenuous plot interest by coming

upon two of its three principals (narrator Horace Holyoke is the other) in an abandoned house to which they had fled from Miss Asphyxia's clutches, for, like Uncle Tiff's young charges in *Dred*, Harry and Tina Percival have been successively deserted by their scalawag father and subjected to the slow death of their mother. Tina, who is adopted by Mehitabel Rossiter, a woman of no physical beauty but much strength of character and intellect, grows into a beautiful and kindhearted but willful woman—exactly the type favored by the unprincipled Davenport. Harry grows up as Horace's companion in the nearby Holyoke household.

Tina, not knowing that Davenport numbers among his previous victims Ellen Rossiter, Mehitabel's younger sister, marries him, and it appears that Stowe will not permit her protagonist the usual eleventh-hour rescue. Tina endures ten years with the erratic Davenport, generously adopting his daughter by Ellen Rossiter, but then, in a switch on the Burr story, Davenport is killed in a duel. Two years (but only three paragraphs) later, Tina and Horace marry and settle in Boston. At the end of the novel, the Horace Holyokes are discovered back in Oldtown visiting its most durable inhabitant, Sam Lawson.

Any synopsis leaves untouched the merits of *Oldtown Folks*: the interplay of its varied and vital minor characters and the development of its seduction theme. Of the former, Miss Asphyxia, "a great threshing-machine of a woman"; Horace's peppery grandmother, "a valiant old soul, who fearlessly took any bull in life by the horns, and was ready to shake him into decorum"; and Lawson, half nuisance, half good neighbor, are only three of the most memorable. As seducer, Davenport takes advantage of several factors: the intransigence of Calvinism in its death throes, embodied in brilliant but outdated theorizers such as this novel's version of Hopkins, Dr. Stern; the Calvinist legacy of neurosis, skepticism, and rebellion (Miss Rossiter, Tina, and Davenport himself); and the ineffectuality of well-intentioned observers such as Horace and Harry. Thwarted by orthodoxy, which has become a cruel instrument in the hands of its conservative defenders, and averse to the rationalism that played such a large part in the creation of the new republic, the Oldtowners are easily taken in by Davenport, who has turned the passion and intellectual energy inherited from

Edwards and the rest of his Puritan forebears to the service of selfish and worldly ends.

MY WIFE AND I *and* WE AND OUR NEIGHBORS

In *My Wife and I* and its sequel, *We and Our Neighbors*, Stowe turns to contemporary Manhattan life, a frivolous and even more worldly existence dotted nevertheless by young men and women of impulses Stowe characterizes as Christian but that may strike today's reader as more generally humanitarian. The full spectrum of views on women's rights is on display, including a conviction, expressed by a young woman struggling for the opportunity to study medicine, that "marriage ought never to be entered on as a means of support." The main business of the two novels, however, is to educate Harry Henderson for marriage and thus to provide a base of operations for his wife, who dedicates herself to neighborliness and charitable offices. Stowe retains her observant eye and spicy descriptive powers, but her narrator cannot "interpret" the Gilded Age as Horace Holyoke in *Oldtown Folks* could interpret post-Revolutionary New England.

POGANUC PEOPLE

Pink and White Tyranny, the story of a man who married and must endure a selfish and demanding woman, must rank, along with the earlier *Agnes of Sorrento*, among Stowe's weakest books. Finally, in *Poganuc People*, she returns to the milieu of *The Minister's Wooing*, *The Pearl of Orr's Island*, and her Oldtown books.

Poganuc is the Litchfield of her childhood and Dolly Cushing her closet approximation to an autobiographical heroine. The principal conflict is not between the old religion and the new worldliness but between entrenched Congregationalism and upstart Episcopalianism. The novel begins and ends at Christmas, when the liturgical and social differences between the two denominations stand out most sharply. Like Maggie Tulliver in Eliot's *The Mill on the Floss* (1860), Dolly is precocious, sensitive, and consequently often uncomfortable, but instead of developing the crises of her heroine's maturation, as does Eliot, Stowe whisks her off to a fashionable Boston marriage with a successful merchant, after which the author makes a final survey of the Poganuc people going about their business under the immemorial elms of the village.

Stowe seldom brought her psychological insights to bear on the development of her main characters, with the result that the less important ones invariably seem more convincing. Whether because her most productive years antedated the time of the realist novel and particularly the psychological novel, or because she felt too strongly the nineteenth century prohibition against a woman exploring the conflicts and repressions of her own life, Stowe left unwritten what might have constituted her richest vein of realism. She never wrote a novel expressing what it felt like to be a vocationless Harriet Beecher approaching womanhood or a Harriet Beecher Stowe struggling with sickness, poverty, and the multitudinous demands of husband and children. The woman who wrote of domesticity in her time avoided calling attention to its tensions, exactions, and restrictions. Whatever else family life meant to Stowe, it helped prepare her to do what no American novelist had done before: write powerfully and feelingly about slavery.

Robert P. Ellis

OTHER MAJOR WORKS

SHORT FICTION: *The Mayflower: Or, Sketches of Scenes and Characters of the Descendants of the Pilgrims*, 1843; *Sam Lawson's Oldtown Fireside Stories*, 1872.

POETRY: *Religious Poems*, 1867.

NONFICTION: *A Key to Uncle Tom's Cabin*, 1853; *Sunny Memories of Foreign Lands*, 1854; *Lady Byron Vindicated*, 1870; *Palmetto Leaves*, 1873.

CHILDREN'S LITERATURE: *First Geography for Children*, 1833 (as Catharine Stowe).

MISCELLANEOUS: *The Oxford Harriet Beecher Stowe Reader*, 1999 (Joan D. Hedrick, editor).

BIBLIOGRAPHY

Ammons, Elizabeth, ed. *Critical Essays on Harriet Beecher Stowe*. Boston: G. K. Hall, 1980. This useful collection contains essays on Stowe by literary critics and feminist scholars. Dorothy Berkson's essay "Millennial Politics and the Feminine Fiction of Harriet Beecher Stowe" is particularly good.

Boydston, Jeanne, Mary Kelley, and Anne Margolis. *The Limits of Sisterhood: The Beecher Sisters on Women's Rights and Woman's Sphere*. Chapel Hill:

University of North Carolina Press, 1988. A superb study of Stowe and her sisters, Catharine and Isabella. Brief but insightful essays address each woman as an individual and as a sister. Primary documents are appended to each chapter, providing excellent resources. Illustrations, careful documentation, and a detailed index make this an invaluable text.

Donovan, Josephine. *"Uncle Tom's Cabin": Evil, Affliction, and Redemptive Love*. Boston: Twayne, 1991. Places *Uncle Tom's Cabin* in literary and historical context. As her subtitle suggests, Donovan views Stowe's masterpiece as a book about evil and its redemption, taking it more or less at face value and reading it with the approach she believes Stowe intended—which has a decidedly feminist bent.

Hedrick, Joan D. *Harriet Beecher Stowe: A Life*. New York: Oxford University Press, 1994. Stowe's family kept a tight rein on her literary remains, and the only previous attempt at a full-scale independent biography, Forrest Wilson's *Crusader in Crinoline* (1941), is now very much out of date. Hedrick's book makes use of new materials, including letters and diaries, and takes fresh approaches to Stowe occasioned by the Civil Rights and women's movements.

Lang, Amy Schrager. *Prophetic Woman: Anne Hutchinson and the Problem of Dissent in the Literature of New England*. Berkeley: University of California Press, 1987. An excellent feminist study, focusing on *Uncle Tom's Cabin* and Stowe's role in the history of Puritan suppression of women who achieve public notice. Stowe's novel constitutes a culmination in this process and presents a model of women as moral superiors who represent the possibility of a future without slavery.

Riss, Arthur. *Race, Slavery, and Liberalism in Nineteenth-Century American Literature*. New York: Cambridge University Press, 2006. In his analysis of Stowe and two other writers who were involved in antebellum debates about slavery, Riss maintains that the proposition that "all men are created equal" can be an argument both for and against race-based slavery.

Robbins, Sarah. *The Cambridge Introduction to Harriet Beecher Stowe*. New York: Cambridge University Press, 2007. A concise introduction, designed to familiarize students and other readers with Stowe's work. Contains biographical information and analysis of Stowe's writings; discusses her life and work within the context of nineteenth century American literature, womanhood, racial politics, religion, and class identity. The final chapter surveys critical reception to her works in both the nineteenth and twentieth centuries.

Sundquist, Eric J., ed. *New Essays on "Uncle Tom's Cabin."* New York: Cambridge University Press, 1986. A collection of essays on Stowe's most famous novel. The introduction discusses changing literary theories as they relate to *Uncle Tom's Cabin*. The six diverse contributions by notable scholars include analyses of genre and gender issues. A selected bibliography also notes additional criticism.

Tompkins, Jane. *Sensational Designs: The Cultural Work of American Fiction, 1790-1860*. New York: Oxford University Press, 1985. Tompkins addresses *Uncle Tom's Cabin* from the perspective of "the politics of literary history." Nineteenth century popular domestic novels represent attempts to reorganize culture from a woman's perspective, and Stowe's novel is representative of "America's religion of domesticity" as empowerment of women. An excellent and influential study.

Weinstein, Cindy. *The Cambridge Companion to Harriet Beecher Stowe*. New York: Cambridge University Press, 2004. Collection of essays examining Stowe's works and literary influence, including analyses of *Uncle Tom's Cabin* and *The Pearl of Orr's Island* and discussions of race, regionalism, the law, and the American reform tradition.

AUGUST STRINDBERG

Born: Stockholm, Sweden; January 22, 1849
Died: Stockholm, Sweden; May 14, 1912
Also known as: Johan August Strindberg

PRINCIPAL LONG FICTION

Från Fjärdingen och Svartbäcken, 1877
Röda rummet, 1879 (*The Red Room*, 1913)
Jäsningstiden, 1886 (*The Growth of the Soul*, 1914)
Hemsöborna, 1887 (*The Natives of Hemsö*, 1965)
Tschandala, 1889 (in Danish), 1897 (in Swedish)
I havsbandet, 1890 (*By the Open Sea*, 1913)
Le Plaidoyer d'un fou, 1893 (in German), 1895 (in Swedish; *A Madman's Defense*, 1912; also known as *The Confession of a Fool*)
Inferno, 1897 (English translation, 1912)
Ensam, 1903 (*Alone*, 1968)
Götiska rummen, 1904
Svarta fanor, 1907
Syndabocken, 1907 (*The Scapegoat*, 1967)
Taklagsöl, 1907
Författaren, 1909

OTHER LITERARY FORMS

August Strindberg was an extremely prolific writer whose collected works total fifty-five volumes. Outside Scandinavia, he is known chiefly as a dramatist, and many of his plays—such as *Fadren* (pr., pb. 1887; *The Father*, 1899), *Fröken Julie* (pb. 1888; *Miss Julie*, 1912), and *Ett drömspel* (pb. 1902; *A Dream Play*, 1912)—continue to be performed regularly in many parts of the world. Strindberg also wrote several collections of shorter prose pieces; two volumes of short stories titled *Giftas I* (1884) and *Giftas II* (1886; *Married*, 1913; also known as *Getting Married*, 1973, which includes both *Giftas I* and *Giftas II*) are particularly well known. He also wrote and published poetry throughout his life.

ACHIEVEMENTS

August Strindberg is known throughout the world as one of the fathers of modern drama. In his native Swe-

den, and increasingly abroad as well, he is also known as a psychological novelist of considerable importance. His second novel, *The Red Room*, is considered the first modern novel in Swedish literature, and another of his novels, *The Natives of Hemsö*, is still one of the best-loved books in Sweden.

Strindberg has also appealed to the smaller audience of the literary establishment. Considered Sweden's greatest writer of belles lettres, he has remained the object of critical attention both in his homeland and abroad. All of his important works have been translated into English, and his reputation has long been securely established.

BIOGRAPHY

Johan August Strindberg was born in Stockholm, Sweden, on January 22, 1849. On the side of his father, a steamship agent, he came from a solid middle-class background; his mother, however, was the daughter of a tailor and had been a waitress before coming to the home of her future husband as his servant girl. Strindberg later somewhat romantically referred to himself as "the son of the maidservant," when in fact he was solidly anchored in the Swedish bourgeoisie.

Strindberg grew up around his father's business and early developed an appreciation for matters relating to the sea, especially the Stockholm archipelago. Unlike his several brothers, however, he was not to be prepared for a business career. In 1867, he received his matriculation certificate and soon thereafter took up residence as a student at the University of Uppsala.

Not finding academic life entirely to his liking, Strindberg was only intermittently a full-time student and for a time earned a living as a tutor and as an elementary school teacher. During that time, he wrote several insignificant plays, one of which was performed at Stockholm's Royal Dramatic Theatre in the fall of 1870. After abandoning his studies in 1872, Strindberg began pursuing a career as a writer more aggressively. The first fruit of this activity was the prose version of his drama *Mäster Olof* (pb. 1878; *Master Olof*, 1915), completed in early August of 1872. No theater would accept the play, however, and for the next few years, Strindberg made a living as a journalist and assistant at Stockholm's Library.

In the late spring of 1875, Strindberg was introduced to Siri von Essen, the young wife of Baron Carl Gustaf Wrangel, and a love affair ensued. Siri obtained a divorce in June of 1876, after which she and Strindberg were married in December of 1877. In the same month, Strindberg had a collection of short stories published.

Strindberg's breakthrough as a prose writer came in 1879 with the publication of his novel *The Red Room*. After a period of research into cultural history, he moved with his family to France, where he would spend a considerable portion of his life. In 1884, however, he briefly returned to Sweden to stand trial on the charge of blasphemy; one of the short stories in his just-published collection *Married* was found by the authorities to be disrespectful of the Sacrament of the Lord's Supper. Strindberg was acquitted, but the matter was agonizing for him. A second volume of *Married* stories followed in

1886, however, and the same year saw the publication of the first two volumes of the somewhat fictionalized four-volume autobiography *Tjänstekvinnans son: En s äls utvecklingshistoria* (1886; *The Son of a Servant: The Story of the Evolution of a Human Being*, 1966, volume 1 only).

Strindberg returned to Scandinavia in 1887 after a further stay in France, Switzerland, and Germany. This time he settled in Copenhagen, where his naturalistic drama *The Father* was soon to be performed. In the same year, he published his most popular novel, *The Natives of Hemsö*, utilizing memories from an island in the Stockholm archipelago where he had spent several summers. Before returning to Sweden in 1889, he also had established a short-lived experimental theater; had written two more plays, *Miss Julie* and *Fordringsägare* (pb. 1888; *Creditors*, 1910); and had finished the manuscript, written in French, of his novel *The Confession of a Fool*, for which his marriage to Siri had provided him with the raw material. Annoyances experienced in Denmark in the summer of 1888 formed the basis for *Tschandala*.

During the summer of 1889, Strindberg stayed on one of the islands near Stockholm and began work on another novel arising from the archipelago, *By the Open Sea*. After a break in his labors, this book was finished in the summer of 1890. Marital difficulties, which had been present for several years, led to the beginning of divorce proceedings, and his marriage to Siri was dissolved in 1891. Strindberg did not remain unmarried for long, however; early in 1893, during a visit to Berlin, he met the Austrian Frida Uhl. They were wed the following year but soon separated, and Strindberg again went to Paris.

The next three years, the so-called *Inferno* crisis, was probably the most difficult period in Strindberg's life. He wanted to conquer Paris not only as a writer but also as a scientist, and he carried on a series of chemical experiments. His experiences during this time became material for his autobiographical novel *Inferno*.

This novel inaugurated another great creative period in Strindberg's life, which produced his well-known play *Till Damaskus* (pb. 1898-1904; *To Damascus*, 1913) and, after his final return to Sweden the following year, a series of important historical dramas. In 1901, he married the young Norwegian actor Harriet Bosse; this mar-

August Strindberg. (Courtesy of the D.C. Public Library)

riage lasted until 1904. These years saw such great plays as *Dödsdansen* (pb. 1901; *The Dance of Death*, 1912) and *A Dream Play*. In 1907, after the establishment of Stockholm's Intima Teatern (intimate theater), Strindberg published a series of what he called chamber plays, the best known of which is *Spöksonaten* (*The Ghost Sonata*, 1916). He also wrote a number of prose works, including the infamous satiric novel *Svarta fanor*.

Strindberg had lived a stormy life, and his final years were no exception. A series of newspaper articles begun in April, 1910, set off the most intensive debate in Swedish literary history. Nicknamed the "Strindberg Feud," this debate resulted from both personal and philosophical differences and became particularly vicious when it was suggested that Strindberg—who, because of his radical views, had not received the Nobel Prize in Literature—ought to receive an equivalent prize from the Swedish people. The author's difficult financial situation made this particularly appropriate. The prize did not materialize, but Strindberg nevertheless succeeded in obtaining financial security through the sale of the rights to the collected edition of his works. Shortly thereafter, he became seriously ill and died from cancer of the stomach on May 14, 1912.

ANALYSIS

August Strindberg's novels constitute a striking illustration of the dialectical relationship between life and art. Strindberg truly lived for his art; he consciously ordered his life in such a manner that he might obtain material for his fiction, much of which was narrated in the first person. This has led several critics to overemphasize the bizarre aspects of his books and to hold that he was mentally ill when in reality he was only experimenting with his sanity. Such is especially the case with two intensely autobiographical novels, *The Confession of a Fool* and *Inferno*. There can be no doubt, however, that Strindberg's art also profoundly affected his life. Popular successes, such as *The Red Room* and *The Natives of Hemsö*, brought him considerable fame and enabled him to improve his standard of living, while *The Confession of a Fool*, which was a fictionalized account of his marriage to Siri von Essen, did much to seal the destruction of that marriage. In *Inferno*, Strindberg deliberately led the reading public to believe that he, the author, was

identical with the novel's vacillating and easily frightened protagonist, who with justice was considered mentally ill. Strindberg thus consciously injured his personal reputation for the sake of his art, for he knew that the aesthetic effect of the book would depend on the reader's identification of author and narrator-protagonist during the reading process. Even the lighthearted *The Natives of Hemsö*, which Strindberg thought to be his sanest book, took its toll on the personal affairs of the author. Strindberg had used as models for some of his characters certain people then living on Kymmendö, an island near Stockholm where he had spent many happy summers. His models were offended, and Strindberg was never again welcome on the island.

An important question, therefore, is what it was that drove Strindberg to exploit so ruthlessly both his own life and the lives of those who were close to him. Part of the answer has been suggested by the American Strindberg scholar Eric O. Johannesson, who has proposed that the fundamental theme of Strindberg's novels is the author's quest for identity. This quest, according to Johannesson, takes the form of an exploration of both the author's own self and the human psyche in general. There is little doubt that Strindberg's desire for truth, along with his need for recognition as a man of letters, was a powerful motivating force behind his artistic activity.

Strindberg's originality as a thinker did not, however, match his quality as an artist, and in his search for truth he relied heavily on ideas that had been generated by others. Constantly in step with the literary and intellectual avant-garde, he tested the validity of the various ideas and standpoints of his age as they became available to him. His development as a novelist thus closely parallels that of European intellectual history. He began as a realist and naturalist who in *The Red Room* criticized social conditions in Sweden. In the stylistically seminaturalistic *The Natives of Hemsö*, the social satire is absent; its humorous and detailed description of life in the skerries has made it one of Strindberg's best-loved books. *The Confession of a Fool* is likewise heavy with naturalistic detail, but there is also a strong interest in individual psychology that manifests itself in the "battle of the brains" that is taking place between Axel, the book's narrator, and his wife, Maria. The same emphasis on psychology is found in *By the Open Sea*, the protagonist of which is virtually a Nietzschean superman who succumbs only because he possesses the one fatal flaw of allowing himself to be influenced by a woman. The novel *Inferno*, with its interest in mysticism, religion, and other aspects of the supernatural, places Strindberg squarely within the neo-Romanticism of the 1890's.

Strindberg's desire for truth in all aspects of life, which also manifested itself in his quest for identity, was in part a function of the uneasiness with which he viewed his social position. The mixture of a middle-class background on his father's side and working-class origins on his mother's side created a strong tension in his life. His instincts were those of the bourgeoisie, but he felt considerable loyalty to the lower classes. At the same time, he desired upward mobility, to which he felt especially entitled because of his intellectual prowess. These tensions account for the sociological perspective present in his works.

The desire for an understanding of the self also explains the prevalence of autobiographical elements in Strindberg's novels. *The Confession of a Fool* and *Inferno* have been viewed as straightforward autobiography by many critics, and *The Red Room*, which tells about a group of artists and intellectuals of which Strindberg was a member in the late 1870's, has always been recognized as having numerous autobiographical traits. *The Confession of a Fool* and *Inferno* are first-person novels in which it is difficult to distinguish between author and narrator, and *The Red Room*, which is narrated in the third person, has a young writer as its protagonist. This among other things makes it easy to equate the narrator's point of view with that of Strindberg himself. The point of view in *The Natives of Hemsö* is that of an omniscient, detached narrator who is very similar to Strindberg, the summer guest on Kymmendö, while the fishing inspector Axel Borg, the center of consciousness in *By the Open Sea*, is a man who in most regards corresponds to the Nietzschean ideals that Strindberg advocated at the time.

It is indeed no wonder that the author was so frequently identified with his protagonists. Seemingly oblivious to the cost to his personal happiness and appallingly disrespectful of the right to privacy of those who were close to him, Strindberg consistently turned his life into art.

THE RED ROOM

Strindberg published *The Red Room* in 1879, when he had already had some minor successes as a serious writer but also had expended much effort on a variety of minor assignments for various newspapers and magazines. He was thoroughly acquainted with life among Stockholm's younger artists and intellectuals, however, and was thus well equipped for the task of writing the book.

Although the short span of narrated time in *The Red Room* (it covers only about a year and a half), together with its episodic structure, makes it difficult to fit the novel completely into the genre of the bildungsroman, the book may well be regarded from that perspective. The main character, Arvid Falk, is a young civil servant turned writer and journalist, and the book tells about his experiences while attempting to come to terms with society. Falk is a naïve idealist whose soul is larger than the destinies that Swedish life in the 1870's have to offer him, and his process of education therefore becomes one of a gradual loss of illusions. As a reporter, he gains insight into the hollowness and deceit of government, the Church, the newspaper industry, book publishing, the insurance industry, banking, charitable organizations, higher education, and the arts. Through this bildungsroman, Strindberg attempts to educate the reader in the true state of contemporary society by portraying his protagonist's education in disillusionment.

The book may also, however, be regarded as a novel experiment akin to the naturalistic novel. Strindberg does not conduct an experiment that, like the typical Scandinavian novel of a few years later, is designed to illustrate the thesis that biological inheritance and social environment determine human development and behavior; rather, *The Red Room* constitutes an experiment with ideas and standpoints. Strindberg tests the validity of the attitudes toward life that inhere in the philosophies of idealism, realism, and nihilism, and it is this process of testing that is of most interest to today's readers.

The standpoint of idealism is represented chiefly by Falk, the protagonist. In the beginning of the novel, he strikes one as a very young, indeed immature, man whose idealism manifests itself as a naïve sympathy with the oppressed and a vague desire for social justice, unaccompanied by serious commitment to specific causes. This naïve idealism is untenable, and Falk is faced with two choices: He may abandon idealism completely and turn to pessimism and nihilism, or he may subject his idealism to reflection and develop it in the direction of a considered realism, which would entail serious commitment on his part.

The pessimistic, nihilistic stance is represented by two characters, the actor Falander and the sculptor Olle Montanus. Falander is a decadent figure, a seducer of the young whose ideas are transmitted to Falk through Montanus. Montanus commits suicide, which might be a sign of Strindberg's dismissal of his philosophical outlook, but the matter is more complicated than that. Falander is a nihilist in that he attacks societal values, but he is also, as Johannesson has pointed out, a Christ figure: His destiny is to identify himself with others and to suffer with and for them through his compassion. Strindberg's later works show that he was far from finished with this character type.

In *The Red Room*, however, the philosophical possibilities represented by Falander are at least temporarily repressed. Falk's idealism becomes increasingly fanatic, and his demand becomes one of all or nothing. Eventually recognizing this as an impossible situation, he allows himself to be convinced by a more realistic friend to forget all thoughts of improving the world. He reenters polite society as a minor government official and teacher at a school for girls, living only for his coin collection, a few quietistic friends, and later, his fiancé. His end is thus that of the hero of the traditional bildungsroman; namely, apparent integration into society, represented by the acquisition of a respectable position and matrimony. One wonders, however, if this is Strindberg's final word concerning his hero. Falk has passed from a naïve and later desperate idealism to its opposite, an equally desperate quietism. The next stage could be a realistic synthesis of the two, a stance that indeed seems to be implied by Strindberg. The novel is open-ended on this point, for Strindberg's purpose is not as much to suggest answers as to pose questions. The book does so in a most effective manner.

THE NATIVES OF HEMSÖ

The Natives of Hemsö is a novel that fits rather poorly into Strindberg's largely autobiographical authorship, and it may well be regarded, as the author himself regarded it, as an "intermezzo scherzando." Its well-told story, its colorful and uncomplicated characters, and its vivid pictures of life in the Stockholm archipelago have given it the status of a Swedish classic.

The plot is simple. An enterprising farmhand named Carlsson arrives at the island Hemsö in order to help the middle-aged widow Flod put her farm in order. Marriage to the widow would make Carlsson the master of the farm, so he becomes his employer's suitor, and the two are married. Carlsson's main problem is now the widow's son Gusten, who is obviously not interested in being deprived of his inheritance. Gusten becomes a formidable antagonist, especially when Carlsson begins to mismanage the farm and spends most of his time trying to persuade his wife to make a will that would, in effect, disinherit her son. In the end, Carlsson loses in the conflict because of his weakness for one of the servant girls. His wife discovers his infidelity, catches pneumonia, and dies. Carlsson drowns accidentally, and Gusten is left as the farm's unchallenged ruler.

The novel is almost totally free of political and social ideas. It exhibits a kind of limited naturalism, however, for Strindberg depicts his characters as formed by their natural and social environment. At the same time, the book is imbued with a comic spirit, which manifests itself both in the events portrayed and in the depiction of Carlsson's character. Carlsson is uncomplicated and without inner conflicts, and his death is only another instance of the old giving way to youth in life's endless chain. He is simply a man who tried and failed, and his failure has no philosophical implications. As the book's point of view is consistently that of the community, which stands in opposition to the outsider, the ending leaves the reader with a feeling of contentment: The conflict has been resolved in accordance with the order of nature.

THE CONFESSION OF A FOOL

In *The Confession of a Fool*, Strindberg returns to his general artistic project with full force. His search for truth focuses on the human psyche and the effects of interpersonal relationships on it. When read strictly as a work of fiction, the book becomes a powerful and engaging psychological novel. Many critics, however, have found it difficult to regard the book from this perspective. Both the contemporary reading public and later scholars have been painfully aware that the novel tells in detail about Strindberg's relationship with his first wife, Siri von Essen. It can be argued that the book is a piece of autobiography, but if it is to be regarded as such, it quickly becomes clear that many of the events related have been significantly distorted. Strindberg used the experience he had gained in his relationship with Siri, but because he knew that he was writing fiction, not autobiography, he felt no obligation to adhere strictly to what had actually taken place in every instance.

A key to the understanding of both *The Confession of a Fool* and the novel *By the Open Sea* is to be found in an essay written by Strindberg in 1887 on Henrik Ibsen's drama *Rosmersholm* (pb. 1886; English translation, 1889). Titled "Själamord" ("Psychic Murder"), the essay explores the ways in which modern human beings destroy one another by a variety of means infinitely more sophisticated than old-fashioned physical violence. Today's psychic murderer uses public opinion, hypnotism, and suggestion to destroy his victim; more specifically, he makes the victim ridiculous, robs him of his ability to make a living, and, if possible, drives him insane. *The Confession of a Fool* tells the story of such a crime.

The first-person narrator of the book is a Swedish writer named Axel, who, with his wife, Maria, lives in exile somewhere in central Europe. He suspects that Maria, who he believes has done her best to isolate him from the world in order to destroy his reputation as a writer, is now trying to kill him by causing him to go insane. In order to defend himself both against the rumors that he fears his wife has spread about him and against other and more direct threats to his mind, he begins an investigation into their relationship. The book is the record of this investigation, and it is designed to serve as his final word to the world in case his wife should succeed in her design.

The novel's point of view is consistent throughout; Strindberg never departs from the perspective of his narrator. From this viewpoint, Maria becomes a villain of the highest order who no doubt has been doing everything in her power to rob her husband of his sanity. The discerning reader also understands, however, that there is a considerable difference between the story as told by the narrator and the author's version of it. Because the point of view is consistently that of the first-person nar-

rator, the views of the author can be reconstructed only through a careful reading. Such an analysis will make it clear that Maria is indeed innocent and that her husband, who can be classified only as a madman, is in the process of committing psychic suicide. The value of the novel lies in the tension between these two perspectives and the careful psychological portrayal that is necessary for their creation.

Some critics have argued that Strindberg indeed shared the perspective of his narrator and that he involuntarily revealed the fact that he, like his narrator, was insane during the period when the novel was written. This view is the result of an inability to distinguish between reliable and unreliable narrators. The narrator in *The Confession of a Fool* is insane, but he either does not know it or is unwilling to admit it. The novel's author is, of course, not in the same situation, and he has to find a means of transmitting his view to the reader. This difficult task Strindberg has handled in a sophisticated manner by creating a complex ironic structure. The novel is thus a thoroughly modern one, both in terms of the author's use of psychology and in its narrative technique.

BY THE OPEN SEA

Strindberg continues his search for truth concerning the human psyche in *By the Open Sea*, one of his most underrated novels. Set in the Stockholm archipelago, the book is nevertheless free of the comedy and lightheartedness of its predecessor in the same setting, *The Natives of Hemsö*. The author now has taken up a most solemn subject—namely, the process by which an individual may descend from superhuman strength and intelligence to complete disintegration of the personality. Although the novel's center of consciousness, the fishing inspector Axel Borg, is also the person through whose eyes most of the action is seen, the telling is done by a third-person narrator virtually indistinguishable from Strindberg himself. This makes the transmission of norms from the author to the reader more easily accomplished than in *The Confession of a Fool*, where Strindberg chose to employ a first-person narrator.

One day in spring, Borg arrives at a tiny, isolated island in the archipelago where he is to teach modern fishing techniques to the inhabitants. Borg is an outsider both geographically and socially; in addition, he views himself as a superman in the spirit of Nietzsche. As a character, he could be attractive only to those who fancy themselves to be of the same kind, and the stage is set for a constant battle between him and the natives. While they are creatures of instincts and feelings, Borg worships logic and reason. The battle thus also becomes one between two different attitudes toward life.

In the first part of the novel, Strindberg describes the intellectual virtues of his protagonist. The fishing inspector is an eminent scientist whose training and native intellect combine to make him an ideal type. Compared to him, the islanders are nothing; they do, however, have the advantage of belonging to a community, a group, while Borg is isolated. Borg's state of isolation constitutes both a strength and a weakness. It is necessary in order to keep him from too much contact with inferior minds, but his lack of access to a community of his equals tends to make him lose the ability to cope with the world of human beings.

A decisive change in Borg's mental state is brought about by his relationship with a young female summer guest. Her name is Maria, and she has a function that is similar to that of the female antagonist by the same name in *The Confession of a Fool*. The cerebral Borg, unable to repress his instincts, seeks Maria's company and, as he believes, allows his intellect to be degraded through their association. Knowing that the relationship is harmful to him, he attempts to liberate himself but discovers that he can accomplish this only by seducing the girl. He does so with the effect that the intended liberation is achieved, but the seduction is also a fatal surrender to his own bodily nature.

Maria leaves, but a new challenger has already arrived. He is a preacher, an old acquaintance of Borg, and his function is to bring the fishing inspector's fears and suppressed feelings of guilt to the surface. Borg's scientifically grounded rejection of religion immediately places him at odds with the man of God, and a battle of the brains follows. The preacher proves to be the stronger; Borg capitulates by asking him to say prayers for him and tell his folktales. At the end of the novel, Borg has receded into insanity. In a moment of clarity, he goes down to the sea, finds a boat, and sails to his death.

By the Open Sea can be read as a novel about the conflict between the conscious and the unconscious and the need to arrive at a state of balance between the two. Borg's personality unravels because the unconscious has been excluded from it. Strindberg, like Carl Jung after him, uses the male-female opposition as a metaphor to describe this conflict. When the book's perhaps trivial story is regarded from this perspective, this often underrated work reveals itself to be a powerful psychological novel.

INFERNO

Like *The Confession of a Fool*, the equally autobiographical novel *Inferno* is narrated in the first person. Because the book ostensibly tells about Strindberg's life in Paris during the years 1894 to 1897, it has been customary not to distinguish between Strindberg and the narrator and Strindberg the author. The lack of distinction between the two is strongly reinforced by the author/narrator, who at the end of the novel offers his diary as proof that the novel is factual. When this claim is taken at face value, however, it becomes clear that Strindberg's perception of reality during the period covered by the novel is such that the author would have to be regarded as mentally ill. The lack of distance between the novel's "experiencing self" and the self that later narrates the events, furthermore, indicates that Strindberg suffered from the same defects at the time of the book's composition.

The reader may accept Strindberg's claims at face value or may subject the book to a less orthodox reading. If, for example, the events of the novel are compared with those that are narrated in Strindberg's diary, it soon becomes clear that the diary strongly discredits the novel's claim to factuality. By inviting comparison with the diary, Strindberg offers the reader a clue that will lead to the reconstruction of a story that is radically different from what appears on the book's surface. The novel thus becomes a fundamentally ironic one, and its aesthetic value lies largely in the elegant way in which the irony is constructed. Strindberg's purpose is, in fact, to fool those of his readers who allow themselves to be taken in by the description of his supposed madness, while at the same time he wishes to commune secretly with those who are sufficiently perceptive to realize what he is up to. The structure of the narrative situation thus closely parallels the general structure of irony, with Strindberg being the author and most readers being victims of the irony, and with those few who really understand constituting its audience.

Such a narrative strategy entails a high degree of risk to the author, who by most readers will be considered a madman. Strindberg compensates for this risk by using his persona to express some important verities regarding his perception of his own destiny, much as the medieval fool often was able to express profound truths. Thus, the victims of the irony will simultaneously allow him to experience a sense of intellectual superiority and provide him with an audience that, despite its inferiority, is capable of being instructed. Those who reconstruct the irony and become part of his more sophisticated audience, on the other hand, allow him to feel a sense of community in his exalted intellectual station. At the same time, they have seen through the structure of norms offered to the victims and consequently also possess those truths that Strindberg offers to his least enlightened readers. *Inferno* thus places Strindberg in a position where he cannot lose in his relationship with the reader.

The truths that are expressed by Strindberg's first-person madman concern both how it feels to be losing one's sanity and an antidote against the disintegration of the personality that Strindberg, strictly on an experimental basis, began to administer to himself during the 1890's. This antidote, which was intended both to prevent any loss of mind and to enhance the writer's creative powers, consisted in a religious interpretation of life. Religion was becoming popular among both Scandinavian neo-Romantics and reformed Continental decadents, so Strindberg was in good company. His experimental religiosity was centered on a belief in supernatural powers that were guiding his life and in relationship to which he was a former rebel who was now being chastened and turned into a suffering sacrificial victim not dissimilar to the actor Falander in *The Red Room*. By viewing himself as a proxy for humanity, Strindberg was able to reinterpret his life in Paris as a myth of the human predicament. *Inferno* thus becomes both the story of humanity's passing through Hell and the exceptional individual's rise above his torments by virtue of his intellect.

Strindberg's career stands at the juncture between the nineteenth and the twentieth centuries. Rooted in a Romantic view of the world, Strindberg passed through the Scandinavian literary realism of the 1870's and the naturalism of the 1880's and ended in the neo-Romanticism of the 1890's. His oeuvre is dedicated to the search for truth, particularly with reference to the nature of his own identity. Although his dramas have influenced twentieth century theater to a greater extent than his novels have affected their genre, he is nevertheless an important figure when viewed in the context of the modern psychological novel. Above all, however, Strindberg was a man whose life, in its joy and pain, may well serve as a paradigm for modern people.

Jan Sjåvik

OTHER MAJOR WORKS

SHORT FICTION: *Svenska öden och äventyr*, 1882-1892; *Giftas I*, 1884; *Utopier i verkligheten*, 1885; *Giftas II*, 1886 (*Married*, 1913; also known as *Getting Married*, 1973; includes *Giftas I* and *Giftas II*); *Skärkarlsliv*, 1888; *Legender*, 1898 (*Legends*, 1912); *Fagervik och Skamsund*, 1902 (*Fair Haven and Foul Strand*, 1913); *Sagor*, 1903 (*Tales*, 1930); *Historiska miniatyrer*, 1905 (*Historical Miniatures*, 1913).

PLAYS: *Fritänkaren*, pb. 1870; *I Rom*, pr., pb. 1870; *Hermione*, pb. 1871; *Den fredlöse*, pr. 1871 (*The Outlaw*, 1912); *Mäster Olof*, pb. 1878 (*Master Olof*, 1915); *Gillets hemlighet*, pr., pb. 1880; *Anno fyrtioåtta*, pb. 1881 (wr. 1876); *Herr Bengts hustru*, pr., pb. 1882; *Lycko-Pers resa*, pr., pb. 1883 (*Lucky Peter's Travels*, 1912); *Fadren*, pr., pb. 1887 (*The Father*, 1899); *Marodörer*, pr. 1887; *Fordringsägare*, pb. 1888 (in Danish), pr. 1889 (in Swedish; *Creditors*, 1910); *Fröken Julie*, pb. 1888 (*Miss Julie*, 1912); *Kamraterna*, pb. 1888 (with Axel Lundegård; *Comrades*, 1912); *Hemsöborna*, pr. 1889 (adaptation of his novel); *Paria*, pr. 1889 (*Pariah*, 1913); *Den starkare*, pr. 1889 (*The Stronger*, 1912); *Samum*, pr., pb. 1890 (*Simoom*, 1906); *Himmelrikets nycklar, eller Sankte Per vandrar på jorden*, pb. 1892 (*The Keys of Heaven*, 1965); *Bandet*, pb. 1893 (in German), pb. 1897 (in Swedish; *The Bond*, 1960); *Debet och kredit*, pb. 1893 (*Debit and Credit*, 1906); *Första varningen*, pr., pb. 1893 (*The First Warning*, 1915); *Inför döden*, pr., pb. 1893 (*In the Face of Death*, 1916); *Leka med elden*, pb. 1893 (in German), pr. 1897 (in Swedish; *Playing with Fire*, 1930); *Moderskärlek*, pb. 1893 (*Mother Love*, 1910); *Till Damaskus, forsta delen*, pb. 1898 (*To Damascus I*, 1913); *Till Damaskus, andra delen*, pb. 1898 (*To Damascus II*, 1913); *Advent, ett mysterium*, pb. 1899 (*Advent*, 1912); *Brott och Brott*, pb.

1899 (*Crime and Crime*, 1913; also known as *There Are Crimes and Crimes*); *Erik XIV*, pr., pb. 1899 (English translation, 1931); *Folkungasagan*, pb. 1899 (*The Saga of the Folkungs*, 1931); *Gustav Vasa*, pr., pb. 1899 (English translation, 1916); *Gustav Adolf*, pb. 1900 (English translation, 1957); *Carl XII*, pb. 1901 (*Charles XII*, 1955); *Dödsdansen, första delen*, pb. 1901 (*The Dance of Death I*, 1912); *Dödsdansen, andra delen*, pb. 1901 (*The Dance of Death II*, 1912); *Engelbrekt*, pr., pb. 1901 (English translation, 1949); *Kaspers fet-tisdag*, pr. 1901; *Kristina*, pb. 1901 (*Queen Christina*, 1955); *Midsommar*, pr., pb. 1901 (*Midsummertide*, 1912); *Påsk*, pr., pb. 1901 (*Easter*, 1912); *Ett drömspel*, pb. 1902 (*A Dream Play*, 1912); *Kronbruden*, pb. 1902 (*The Bridal Crown*, 1916); *Svanevit*, pb. 1902 (*Swanwhite*, 1914); *Gustav III*, pb. 1903 (English translation, 1955); *Näktergalen i Wittenberg*, pb. 1904 (*The Nightingale of Whittenberg*, 1970); *Till Damaskus, tredje delen*, pb. 1904 (*To Damascus III*, 1913); *Brända tomten*, pr., pb. 1907 (*After the Fire*, 1913); *Oväder*, pr., pb. 1907 (*Storm*, 1913); *Pelikanen*, pr., pb. 1907 (*The Pelican*, 1962); *Spöksonaten*, pb. 1907 (*The Ghost Sonata*, 1916); *Abu Casems tofflor*, pr., pb. 1908; *Bjälbo-Jarlen*, pr., pb. 1909 (*Earl Birger of Bjälbo*, 1956); *Riksföreståndaren*, pr. 1909 (*The Regent*, 1956); *Siste riddaren*, pr., pb. 1909 (*The Last of the Knights*, 1956); *Stora landsvägen*, pb. 1909 (*The Great Highway*, 1954); *Svarta handsken*, pb. 1909 (*The Black Glove*, 1916); *Genom öknar till arvland, eller Moses*, pb. 1918 (wr. 1903; *Through Deserts to Ancestral Lands*, 1970); *Halländarn*, pb. 1918 (wr. 1902); *Hellas: Eller, Sokrates*, pb. 1918 (*Hellas*, 1970); *Lammet och vilddjuret: Eller, Kristus*, pb. 1918 (wr. 1903; *The Lamb and the Beast*, 1970); *Toten-Insel: Eller, Hades*, pb. 1918 (*Isle of the Dead*, 1962); *Six Plays*, 1955; *Eight Expressionist Plays*, 1965.

POETRY: *Dikter och verkligheter*, 1881; *Dikter på vers och prosa*, 1883; *Sömngångarnätter på vakna dagar*, 1884.

NONFICTION: *Gamla Stockholm*, 1880; *Det nya riket*, 1882; *Svenska folket i helg och söcken, krig och fred, hemma och ute eller Ett tusen år av svenska bildningens och sedernas historia*, 1882; *Tjänstekvinnans son: En s äls utvecklingshistoria*, 1886 (4 volumes; *The Son of a Servant: The Story of the Evolution of a Human Being*, 1966, volume 1 only); *Vivisektioner*, 1887; *Blomstermal-

ningar och djurstycken*, 1888; *Bland franska bönder*, 1889; *Antibarbarus*, 1896; *Jardin des plantes*, 1896; *Svensk natur*, 1897; *Världshistoriens mystik*, 1903; *Modersmålets anor*, 1910; *Religiös renässans*, 1910; *Världsspråkens rötter*, 1910; *Folkstaten*, 1910-1911; *Tal till svenska nationen*, 1910-1911; *Öppna brev till Intima Teatern*, 1911-1912 (*Open Letters to the Intimate Theater*, 1959); *Zones of the Spirit: A Book of Thoughts*, 1913.

BIBLIOGRAPHY

Carlson, Harry Gilbert. *Out of "Inferno": Strindberg's Reawakening as an Artist*. Seattle: University of Washington Press, 1996. Discusses Strindberg's reemergence as a major literary figure after the 1897 publication of *Inferno*, the novel that recounts some of his harrowing experiences during his six-year exile. Includes bibliography and index.

House, Poul, Sven Hakon Rossel, and Göran Stockenström, eds. *August Strindberg and the Other: New Critical Approaches*. Atlanta: Rodopi, 2002. Collection of essays (originally papers delivered in 2000 at a conference titled "Strindberg at the Millennium—Strindberg and the Other") focuses on interpreting the motif of "the other" and "otherness" in Strindberg's work. Includes analyses of his novel *A Madman's Defense* and his autobiographical prose.

Lagercrantz, Olof. *August Strindberg*. Translated by Anselm Hollo. New York: Farrar, Straus and Giroux, 1984. Thorough and accessible biography recounts the events of Strindberg's life and the circumstances in which he created his plays and novels. Includes illustrations, bibliography, and index.

Martinus, Eivor. *Strindberg and Love*. Oxford, England: Amber Lane Press, 2001. Examines Strindberg's letters and diaries, among other sources, to describe his relationships with women and how these relationships are reflected in his literary works. Includes bibliography and index.

Meidal, Bjorn. "Ola Hansson and August Strindberg." In *Poe Abroad: Influence, Reputation, Affinities*, edited by Lois Davis Vines. Iowa City: University of Iowa Press, 1999. Discussion of Strindberg and Swedish poet Ola Hansson is part of a collection of essays devoted to the examination of Edgar Allan Poe's impact and reputation outside the United States.

Robinson, Michael. *Studies in Strindberg*. Norwich: Norvik Press, 1998. Critical analysis sets Strindberg's achievements as a playwright against his accomplishments as an autobiographer, painter, letter writer, and theater director. Includes a discussion of the difficulties Strindberg encountered when he sought to place his life experiences into his literature.

_____, ed. *The Cambridge Companion to August Strindberg*. New York: Cambridge University Press, 2009. Collection of essays analyzes Strindberg's work and places it within the context of his life and times. Includes Ulf Olsson's essay "Learning to Speak: Strindberg and the Novel."

_____. *Strindberg and Genre*. Norwich, England: Norvik Press, 1991. Good selection of essays on Strindberg's writing in various genres. A majority of the essays analyze his plays, but some examine the novel *Inferno* and other nondramatic works. Includes bibliographical references and an index.

Robinson, Michael, and Sven Hakon Rossel, eds. *Expressionism and Modernism: New Approaches to August Strindberg*. Vienna: Edition Praesens, 1999. Collection of essays (most originally papers delivered at the Thirteenth International Strindberg Conference in October, 1997) provides wide-ranging examination of the literary works of Strindberg. Includes bibliography and index.

Schoolfield, George C. "Sweden: August Strindberg." In *A Baedeker of Decadence: Charting a Literary Fashion, 1884-1927*. New Haven, Conn.: Yale University Press, 2003. Chapter on Strindberg discusses his novels *The Red Room*, *The Madman's Defense*, and *By the Open Sea* as part of a larger study of Decadent literature.

Steene, Birgitta, ed. *Strindberg and History*. Stockholm: Almqvist & Wiksell International, 1992. Collection of essays is devoted to the examination of the theme of history in Strindberg's works. Includes bibliography and index.

JESSE STUART

Born: W-Hollow, near Riverton, Kentucky; August 8, 1907
Died: Ironton, Ohio; February 17, 1984
Also known as: Jesse Hilton Stuart

PRINCIPAL LONG FICTION

Trees of Heaven, 1940
Taps for Private Tussie, 1943
Foretaste of Glory, 1946
Hie to the Hunters, 1950
The Good Spirit of Laurel Ridge, 1953
Daughter of the Legend, 1965
Mr. Gallion's School, 1967
The Land Beyond the River, 1973
Cradle of the Copperheads, 1988

OTHER LITERARY FORMS

Jesse Stuart initially gained prominence as a poet. His first collection, *Harvest of Youth* (1930), contained eighty-one poems, which are considered largely juvenilia. His second collection, *Man with a Bull-Tongue Plow* (1934), was composed of 703 poems written in sonnetlike forms (Stuart did not always hold strictly to the sonnet structure). The book was a popular and critical success and brought Stuart his first recognition. His next volume of poetry, *Album of Destiny* (1944), was less well received, although Stuart considered it his best. Subsequently, he published three other books of verse: *Kentucky Is My Land* (1952), *Hold April* (1962), and *The World of Jesse Stuart: Selected Poems* (1975).

Stuart was also a prolific short-story writer. From his more than three hundred published short stories, Stuart gathered several collections, including *Head o' W-Hollow* (1936), *Men of the Mountains* (1941), *Tales from the Plum Grove Hills* (1946), *Clearing in the Sky, and Other Stories* (1950), *Plowshare in Heaven: Tales True and Tall from the Kentucky Hills* (1958), *Save Every Lamb* (1964), *My Land Has a Voice* (1966), and *The*

Best-Loved Short Stories of Jesse Stuart (1982). "Huey the Engineer," a story first published in *Esquire* (August, 1937), was later printed in an anthology, *The Best Short Stories of 1938*. It is generally agreed that Stuart's best work has been in the short story.

Stuart's biographical and autobiographical writings, which are among his most important, include *Beyond Dark Hills* (1938), *The Thread That Runs So True* (1949), *The Year of My Rebirth* (1956), and *God's Oddling* (1960). In addition, he has written several books for children, including *The Beatinest Boy* (1953), *A Penny's Worth of Character* (1954), *Red Mule* (1955), *The Rightful Owner* (1960), and *Andy Finds a Way* (1961).

ACHIEVEMENTS

As a writer, Jesse Stuart was both a spokesperson for and a popularizer of Appalachia, a region and people that have long bewildered and fascinated. In some ways, Stuart was responsible for strengthening and prolonging, if not creating, a number of the myths and stereotypes that have beleaguered this area, although Stuart insisted that he rarely exaggerated the truth. Stuart himself seems larger than life, and given that so much of his fiction is heavily dependent on his own life, it is difficult to determine where the actual leaves off and the imaginative begins. There was Stuart as the mountain boy from a large, poor family, who worked his way through school fired by a need for knowledge; then, as an educator who returned to his region and almost single-handedly (and sometimes two-fistedly) brought learning into a backward land; and finally as an extremely successful writer who scribbled poems by the bushel while plowing fields, who produced novels in a few weeks' time, and who gained a reputation as a true primitive, a writer who created as a force of nature. Still, there is no denying the impressive scope of Stuart's achievements. With boundless energy and enthusiasm, he established himself as perhaps the foremost American regionalist writer of the twentieth century.

Stuart was labeled as an original from the time of his first important work, *Man with a Bull-Tongue Plow*, in 1934. He claimed to have written these poems primarily for his own pleasure, as reflections and observations on the world of nature in which he lived; but when they were published, their vitality, apparent artlessness, and obvious sincerity captivated a large section of the literary establishment and the reading public. Stuart, the writing mountain man, was called "a modern Robert Burns," the kind of easy pigeonholing that reveals a misunderstanding of both writers. When Stuart followed the poems with a collection of stories (*Head o' W-Hollow*), a book of autobiography (*Beyond Dark Hills*), and an impressive novel (*Trees of Heaven*), he had declared himself a writer to be reckoned with.

The recognition and awards came quickly. In 1934, he received the Jeannette Sewal Davis poetry prize of one hundred dollars for *Man with a Bull-Tongue Plow* (beating out such other contenders as Ezra Pound and William Carlos Williams). In 1937, he was awarded the John Simon Guggenheim Literary Award for his poetry and short stories. In 1941, he was given the Academy of Arts and Sciences Award for *Men of the Mountains*, his second short-story collection. In 1943, his second novel, *Taps for Private Tussie*, was chosen for the Thomas Jefferson Southern Award as the best Southern novel of the year. *The Thread That Runs So True*, which detailed Stuart's experiences as a young teacher in a one-room schoolhouse, was selected by the National Educational Association as the "most important book of 1949" written on the subject of education (the president of the NEA, Jay Elmer Morgan, called it "the best book on education written in the last fifty years"). In 1954, Stuart was named poet laureate of Kentucky; in 1955, he was given the Centennial Award for Literature by Berea College. The recognition that meant the most to Stuart came in 1961, when the 1960 fellowship of the Academy of American Poets was bestowed on him for "distinguished service to American poetry."

BIOGRAPHY

Jesse Hilton Stuart was born on August 8, 1907, in W-Hollow in Greenup County, a mountainous and, at the time, relatively isolated section of Kentucky that Stuart would use as the locale for most of his writings. He was the first child of Mitchell and Martha Hilton Stuart; six other children followed, but two died in infancy from pneumonia. Stuart's father's family had lived in Kentucky for generations. They were a clannish people— "Tall Figures of the Earth," in Stuart's own words. His grandfather, Mitchell Stuart, had fought in the American Civil War, and Stuart honored this individualistic and often cantankerous old man in one of his first poems, "Elegy for Mitch Stuart," published by H. L. Mencken in *The American Mercury* in 1934. Stuart's father was a quieter man than "Mitch" Stuart; he worked as a coal miner, railroad man, and farmer, and his influence on his son was immense. Stuart used him as the prototype for some of his most impressive characters, and described his relationship with his father in his autobiographical *Beyond Dark Hills* and in *God's Oddling*, a biography of his father. His mother's family came to Kentucky from North Carolina and was apparently more "cultured"; it was she who encouraged her son to read and first supported him in his continuing quest for education.

The Stuarts moved from farm to farm throughout W-Hollow when Stuart was a boy, a way of life that gave him a sympathy for the plight of the landless. When he was seventeen years old, Stuart's enthusiasm for learning earned him the position of teacher in a one-room school, two years before he graduated from Greenup High School. Following graduation in 1926, Stuart left the mountains, working for a short time in a carnival; then undergoing military training at Camp Knox, Kentucky; and finally spending an unhappy period in the Ashland, Kentucky, steel mills. Later in 1926, he was accepted at Lincoln Memorial University (Harrogate, Tennessee), where he studied under Harry Harrison Kroll, a published writer and one of Stuart's greatest influences. While at Lincoln Memorial, with Kroll's encouragement, Stuart began writing poems, some of which were published in the school newspaper. After graduating in 1929, Stuart returned to the mountains and served a year as principal and teacher of Warnock High School. In 1930, his first book, *Harvest of Youth*, was privately published; Stuart dedicated it to Kroll.

In September of 1931, Stuart entered Vanderbilt University to undertake a master's degree in English. There he met such beginning writers as Robert Penn Warren and John Crowe Ransom, and he studied under his most important mentor, Donald Davidson. Stuart's year at Vanderbilt was a time of trial. He was working part time to support his studies, he was homesick for the mountains, and he was uncertain of his future. When he was assigned by Edwin Mims to write an autobiographical

paper, Stuart complied with a work of more than three hundred pages, which, when revised several years later, became *Beyond Dark Hills*. Mims was impressed by Stuart's talents, rough though they were, and further encouraged him to continue his writing. Still, the year was largely one of frustration, capped by a dormitory fire that destroyed most of Stuart's possessions, including his nearly finished thesis on the writings of John Fox, Jr. Stuart thus left Vanderbilt without a degree but with experience, inspiration, connections, and material that he would use in his later work.

In September of 1932, Stuart became superintendent of Greenup County schools, but after a year spent embroiled in political turmoil, resigned to become principal of McKell High School, where he incorporated many of his then-radical educational theories. While serving as principal of McKell, from 1933 to 1937, he published *Man with a Bull-Tongue Plow* and *Head o' W-Hollow*. He also began to lecture throughout the country on matters of education and literature. In 1937, Stuart received a Guggenheim Fellowship and traveled to Scotland after obtaining a year's leave of absence from McKell, but when he returned in April of 1938, he found that a new administration had reneged on the agreement. Following another year's teaching in Ohio (just across the state line), while continuing his fight with the Kentucky school authorities (during which time his life was threatened and he was once actually beaten by an assailant), Stuart quit teaching in disgust and returned to farming. On October 14, 1939, he married Naomi Deane Norris; their only child, Jessica Jane, was born in 1942.

Stuart wrote about many of these experiences in two of his major books, *Beyond Dark Hills* and *The Thread That Runs So True*. After his retirement from teaching, he devoted a greater part of his time to his career as a writer and lecturer. His first novel, *Trees of Heaven*, appeared in 1940; his second, *Taps for Private Tussie*, in 1943, proved his greatest success, financially and critically, and was a main selection of the Book-of-the-Month Club. From 1944 to 1945, Stuart served in the U.S. Naval Reserves, but continued to write. In 1954, he suffered a near-fatal heart attack after one of his many lectures and was left practically helpless for a year. Stuart described the experience in his "journal," *The Year of My Rebirth*.

Jesse Stuart. (Library of Congress)

In 1956, Stuart returned to the field of education, serving as principal once more at McKell High School for the year, a time he discussed in a late novel, *Mr. Gallion's School*. In 1960-1961, he taught at the American University in Cairo, Egypt, in part because of his desire to challenge the spread of communism in this region. In 1962-1963, he undertook a seven-month lecture tour overseas for the U.S. State Department for the same reasons. In 1966, he became writer-in-residence at Eastern Kentucky University, and he spent his last years in W-Hollow. He died in Ironton, Ohio, in February, 1984.

ANALYSIS

Jesse Stuart's works are a part of the rich literary heritage drawn from the people and traditions of the Appalachian Mountains. He is grouped with such writers as George Washington Harris, Mary Noailles Murfree, John Fox, Jr., Elizabeth Madox Roberts, James Still, Wilma Dykeman, and Harriette Arnow as creators (and sometimes debunkers) of one of America's most lasting stereotypes, the southern "hillbilly." Of these writers, Stuart surely stands at the head, for he has captured the imagination and sympathy of the reading public as has none of the rest.

There are several reasons for Stuart's abiding popularity. His writings are, for the most part, easily accessible. His main interest is in telling a story or relating an emotion, and he does so with simplicity of style and directness of approach. Indeed, Stuart's works are rarely overtly analytical; his characters are not introspective, which has led to charges of an anti-intellectual strain in his writings. Certainly, Stuart does tend to answer complex problems with easy solutions: If a person is determined, brave, and honest, Stuart suggests, the greatest challenge will be overcome. His autobiographical works especially emphasize this idea and, in truth, such solutions seem to have been borne out in Stuart's own life.

Stuart also has proven popular because of the uniqueness and inherent romance of his material. As Stuart presents them, his characters are a primitive people, in some ways unspoiled by the corruptions of the outside society, but often in need of the civilizing influences that such a society can offer through education. Thus, some of these people, such as Theopolis "Op" Akers in *The Good Spirit of Laurel Ridge*, glory in their separation from the rest of the world, while others, like so many of the Tussie clan, are desperately in need of some edifying influence. Because these characters are drawn in broad strokes and are easily labeled as "good" or "bad" (perhaps "worthy" or "worthless" would be more appropriate terms), they exist more as character types, clothed in the charm of dialect and locale, than as real people. Still, Stuart is capable of surprising subtlety in his work, a quality often overlooked by some of his critics. He can force his readers to question their initial judgments of such characters as Anse Bushman in *Trees of Heaven*, Grandpa Tussie in *Taps for Private Tussie*, and even Theopolis Akers in *The Good Spirit of Laurel Ridge*.

The land plays an all-important role in Stuart's works. He attended Vanderbilt at the time of the Agrarian and Fugitive movements (*I'll Take My Stand* was published in 1930, the year before Stuart arrived), and he came into contact with a number of its members, but Stuart never became a disciple himself. Although he agreed with many of the ideas of the movement, Stuart felt that "their farming was on paper," whereas he had farmed in order to eat. His writings, however, always reflect the importance of place in a person's life, and *Man with a Bull-Tongue Plow* is essentially a celebration of the land and one's relationship with it. He clearly admired characters such as Theopolis Akers, Deutsia Huntoon in *Daughter of the Legend*, and Tarvin Bushman in *Trees of Heaven*, who live in harmony with nature and draw their strength and their morality from the world-spirit. In Stuart's work, nature can be dangerous to the unwary, but it offers peace and wisdom to those who approach it with respect.

Perhaps Stuart's greatest strength as a writer is his fine sense of the comic. He has been linked to such humorists as Augustus Baldwin Longstreet, G. W. Harris, Mark Twain, Erskine Caldwell, and William Faulkner. His most serious books, such as *Mr. Gallion's School*, are among his weakest, while *Taps for Private Tussie*, his comic masterpiece, continues to delight. Stuart's humor is basically good-natured. He laughs at people's foibles, enjoys their foolishness, and shakes his head at absurdities. He rarely condemns. Even in a satiric work such as *Foretaste of Glory*, in which he recounts the many hypocrisies to which people are given, Stuart deals gently with his characters. His comedy derives from the tall-tale tradition and is at its best when it ventures into that region wherein the absurd and the tragic coexist.

Although Stuart achieved honor and success in almost every form of literature, he was most effective in the short story. Despite his early fame as a poet, his verse has never received the attention it warrants. His novels generally are loosely structured; they tend to be episodic and uneven as he moves from one event to the next. His plots also rely heavily on convention or cliché. Still, in his large body of writing, Stuart created a unique fictional world, peopled with characters recognizably his own. It is a world that is likely to last.

TREES OF HEAVEN

Stuart wrote *Trees of Heaven* in 1939 after returning from Europe. He married Naomi Deane Norris while writing the book, and their romance is reflected in the love story of Tarvin Bushman and Subrinea Tussie. *Trees of Heaven* is a big, rambling book, less a well-constructed novel than a conglomeration of facts, observations, tales, and characterizations built around a very simple plot. Anse Bushman is a prominent landowner and farmer, one who takes great pride in the quality of his work and the number of his possessions. Boliver Tussie is a squatter who lives on the land that Anse owns. The two men are antithetical to each other. Anse works—and drives others to work—to such a degree that labor and ownership have become obsessions to him. Boliver opts for a more relaxed, indolent approach to life, unburdened by responsibility. The conflict arises when Tarvin Bushman, the only child still living with Anse, falls in love with Subrinea Tussie, Boliver's beautiful daughter.

Through Tarvin's intervention, Anse agrees to take on the Tussies as sharecroppers, although he first compels Boliver to sign a contract specifying what he can and cannot do while living on Anse's land. The contract is an attempt to control not only the Tussies' work habits but their moral and social behavior as well. Although Boliver is offended by some of these demands, he is in no position to argue with Anse; thus, he agrees to stop drinking, to avoid dancing, and to abstain from fathering any more children until the harvest is over. Two such differing lifestyles cannot coexist peacefully, and when Anse becomes suspicious of his son's relationship with Subrinea and becomes convinced that the Tussies are taking advantage of his generosity, he evicts the family and takes their crops. After an accident, however—Anse is almost killed by a falling tree limb—he becomes wiser and more tolerant. Tarvin and Subrinea (who is already pregnant) marry, and, as the book ends, they are going to bring back the Tussies to work the land once again.

Although Anse Bushman is the central character of this novel and the one for whom the reader has the most sympathy and respect, he is by no means an entirely admirable character. His emphasis on work has driven away his other children, and his wife, Fronnie, has succumbed to premature aging. Indeed, toward the end of the book, she is clearly teetering on the edge of madness, haunted by nightmares of Anse's spiritual damnation and fearful that Tarvin will be caught up by his father's obsessions. Anse is a dictatorial old man who cannot balance his love of family with his greed for land. Still, Stuart does not present him as a villain; the reader can understand Anse and generally sides with him in his struggle against the Tussies. At the same time, the Tussies are more likable than one might expect. Their shiftlessness is a relief from Anse's discipline, but they are quite capable of hard work when the occasion demands and show a true love of the land on which they have lived for generations. In fact, Boliver Tussie is a farmer equal to Anse Bushman, although he is usually careless and negligent. The Tussies are a convincing thorn in Anse's side, but he is wrong in his attempt to impose his lifestyle on them.

It is difficult to label *Trees of Heaven* as either a Romantic or realistic novel, for it contains elements of each. The love story between Tarvin and Subrinea is idyllic and is the weakest part of the novel, while Stuart's detailed and factual discussions of farming and sheep raising interfere with the progress of the plot. The description of the Tussies and their kind—families that have become inbred over the years and that are capable of viciousness and violence—is sometimes at odds with their basically comic role in the book. The threat of bloodshed runs throughout the story, but it is generally averted through the author's manipulations.

Trees of Heaven is narrated in the present tense and is structured around the change of the seasons. Both devices give it a sense of timelessness, as if the characters, the place, and the actions were occurring in the present in their own world. The use of present tense sometimes leads to repetition and oversimplification, however, and its effectiveness is not sustained throughout the book. Still, *Trees of Heaven* is an impressive first novel, a work of considerable art and scope.

TAPS FOR PRIVATE TUSSIE

Stuart's second novel, *Taps for Private Tussie*, is generally considered to be his best. Certainly it is his most successful comic work, although the tale it tells is marked by numerous tragic events. Indeed, Stuart claimed that he wrote the story as a "sad thing" and was surprised that others laughed at the antics it described. The book is more carefully constructed than *Trees of Heaven* and is effectively held together through the use of a first-person narrator, a young boy who tells the story with an appealing mixture of naïveté and native wisdom.

Private Kim Tussie is reported killed in action during World War II, and his family sets about burying the returned body. Like the Tussies in *Trees of Heaven*, this branch of the family is also made up of squatters. At the beginning of the book, they are living in a schoolhouse abandoned for the summer. The immediate family is composed of Kim's parents; Grandpa and Grandma Tussie; his wife, Vittie; his unmarried brother, Mott; and the boy narrator, Sid. When Vittie collects Kim's ten-thousand-dollar insurance policy, the Tussies are able to fulfill their long-held dreams, First, they move from the schoolhouse (from which they are being evicted) to a "mansion," a fourteen-room house on the outskirts of town. Then they buy furniture for each of the rooms to replace that which has been destroyed on leaving the schoolhouse. Soon, as Grandma has predicted, other Tussies begin to arrive, hoping to benefit from Grandpa's "good fortune." The first of these is Uncle George, Grandpa's brother, who has been married five times. Others follow until finally there are forty-six Tussies living in the house. George and Mott have, by this time, begun vying for the attentions of Aunt Vittie, and as George grows more successful, Mott turns increasingly to drink.

After a period of communal living, the Tussies are again turned out of their home, which they have destroyed through their careless behavior, because Grandpa has lost his relief benefits, on which they had depended. With the last of the insurance money, Grandpa buys a small piece of land, and the family moves into a run-down shack for the winter. Uncle George marries Vittie; Sid is forced to begin school; and Mott sinks into dissipation. Grandpa learns the pride of ownership and plans to farm the following spring, while Sid discovers the joy of education and begins to consider his future, but these plans are upset when Mott kills two of his cousins while drunk and is himself killed by Uncle George. Grandpa then prepares for his own approaching death and confines himself to bed, awaiting the end. At this point, hope returns with the appearance of Kim himself, who was not killed after all, and who stands ready to take Grandpa's place as the head of the remaining group. Uncle George is tracked down by a posse, Sid learns that Vittie is his mother, and the novel ends with a mixture of death and regeneration.

Taps for Private Tussie is an extremely enjoyable book. Grandpa Tussie is one of Stuart's most successful and memorable characters, a good and loving man despite his weaknesses. Sid Tussie comes from a long line of boy narrators in American literature, including, most obviously, Huckleberry Finn but also those boys in the works of Sherwood Anderson, Faulkner, and Caldwell. Once again Stuart displays his sympathies for a basically unsympathetic group of people. Stuart distinguishes Sid from the Tussies through the revelation that he does not have Tussie blood and is therefore "superior" (he is smarter and more ambitious than the average Tussie). The book acts as a satire on the welfare system: Grandpa Tussie has so long depended on his relief check that he has forgotten the satisfaction of self-sufficiency; when he rediscovers it in the land, it is too late.

Stuart often shows people at their worst—fawning, lying, killing—but *Taps for Private Tussie* finally offers hope of renewal. The Kim who left for war was, as Sid remembers, vicious and hateful; the man who returns has been reborn and shows the boy kindness and understanding. Grandpa must die, but Sid will begin to live with a new sense of self.

FORETASTE OF GLORY

Foretaste of Glory was begun while Stuart served in the Navy during World War II and was developed from stories he remembered and told about his home. It was not published until 1946, and it was poorly received by the people in Greenup County, who took the book as an affront. It recounts the events of one night—September 18, 1941—in Blakesburg, Kentucky, when the night sky is set ablaze by the uncommon appearance of the aurora borealis. Most of the townspeople are convinced that the display prefigures the end of the world, the Second Coming. Stuart examines the reactions of selected characters when faced with their apparent Day of Judgment. The book is constructed in an episodic manner, although some characters do appear in more than one episode, and certain ideas are repeated as Stuart mocks social distinctions, political alliances (as in *Taps for Private Tussie*), and basic hypocrisies.

Stuart was attempting in this work to capture an overall sense of the community, in much the same manner as Anderson did in *Winesburg, Ohio* (1919). The book is a satire, for most of the characters reveal their deceits and

admit their sins as they await the arrival of the Lord, but the tone is not malicious. The author is more understanding and amused than cruel or vindictive. Although the book has been highly praised by some readers, its very concept finally limits its effectiveness. The narratives become redundant, the episodes are uneven, and the excitement is simply not sustained.

THE GOOD SPIRIT OF LAUREL RIDGE

Although Stuart considered *The Good Spirit of Laurel Ridge* his best novel, it is a flawed work. Its plot and many of its characters are unconvincing, although many readers have been charmed by its view of natural people in the natural world. The story is insubstantial.

Op Akers has lived all of his life on Laurel Ridge. His wife is dead; his daughter, Lucretia, was taken away from him when she was a child because of his drinking; and his simpleminded son, Jack, roams the land and appears only in the spring to see the butterflies. As the book begins, Op has undergone a cataract operation, and Lucretia has come to live with him as he regains his sight. Although the operation is successful, she decides to stay in the mountains with her father. A pretty girl, she is soon being courted by a local mountain swain, Hootbird Hammertight, but she is more interested in a mysterious stranger who is hiding out in the hills, a figure Op declares to be the ghost of Ted Newsome, a young man murdered for love many years ago. Op is convinced that spirits—both good and bad—inhabit this area of the mountains, and in his tales and memories he insists on the otherworldliness of Laurel Ridge.

Op's way of life has been disturbed by Lucretia's arrival, although her father comes to accept her. When, however, in a completely unrealistic plot contrivance, two other relatives—Alfred and Julia Pruitt, Lucretia's city cousins—arrive, Op finds himself pushed to the limits. Alf Pruitt is set up as a foil to Op, his city ways and suburban dread placed in stark contrast to Op's natural acceptance of life. Alf most fears the atom bomb, but modern civilization in general has driven him to distraction. Through Op's influence and in a series of mildly comic adventures, Alf learns the importance of nature, but he remains nervous and essentially unhappy.

Finally, it is revealed that the ghost "Ted Newsome" is really a soldier that Lucretia had known in the city. He is AWOL because he mistakenly believes that he has killed a man in a fight, and both he and Lucretia have come to Laurel Ridge to escape. When the military police track him down, just as he is about to be hanged by a group of angry mountaineers, the officer explains that the soldier has killed no one and that he can make amends with a brief prison sentence. Thus, he and Lucretia return to the city. Alfred and Julia also return, having benefited from their stay in the hills, although ultimately unable to adapt to such a rough way of life. Op is again left alone, at peace with himself.

The Good Spirit of Laurel Ridge is filled with the folklore of the hills, and Op Akers is a good storyteller and describer of these tales and customs. The plot, however, is so conventional and the ending such a cliché that the book's potential charm is never fully realized. Stuart's satire on the modern world, exemplified in Alf Pruitt, is much too heavy-handed and obvious to work for long. Despite its popularity, *The Good Spirit of Laurel Ridge* is not one of Stuart's better works.

DAUGHTER OF THE LEGEND

Generally considered Stuart's weakest novel, *Daughter of the Legend* in fact contains some of his best writing. Again, the plot of the novel is slight. The narrator, Dave Stoneking, a lumberjack, tells of his tragic love for Deutsia Huntoon, a Melungeon living in the mountains of eastern Tennessee. After a courtship in which Deutsia introduces Dave to a finer appreciation of nature than he has so far held, they are married and enjoy an idyllic winter together. In the spring, however, Deutsia dies in childbirth, and Dave leaves the land of the Melungeons a rather bitter man.

The book is notable for two reasons. First, in his discussion of the Melungeon people, Stuart calls for racial compassion and understanding. The Melungeons are people of mixed heritage, and when Dave marries into their race, he suffers the discriminations they have long felt. His attempts to rectify these injustices give the book a contemporary social awareness missing from many other works by Stuart. In addition, *Daughter of the Legend* includes one of Stuart's finest comic episodes in the chapter dealing with the death and burial of Sylvania, a six-hundred-pound moonshine seller. Although Stuart had written this tale as a short story years before, it fits smoothly into the novel and presents an ironic counterpoint to the more sentimental death of Deutsia.

MR. GALLION'S SCHOOL

Mr. Gallion's School is a semifictional account of Stuart's experiences as principal of McKell High School, to which he returned in 1956 following his heart attack. George Gallion is a thinly disguised version of Stuart himself. Against great odds, Mr. Gallion attempts to restore order and a sense of worth to the school. He must fight not only the defeatist attitudes of the students and teachers but also a corrupt and ineffectual political system that uses the schools as pawns in its power game. That Mr. Gallion succeeds so completely in his fight illustrates the weaknesses of the book. On a strictly realistic level, Stuart oversimplifies both the problems and the solutions. Indeed, the book often becomes a treatise on the author's theories of education.

Although Stuart has been the subject of numerous studies, he has never been accorded the kind of intensive scholarly study one might expect. This is caused, no doubt, by his reputation as a popular writer. His often romantic and sentimental picture of Appalachia has come under attack. His skills as a writer were considerable, however, and among his many publications are works that will continue to be read and admired.

Edwin T. Arnold III

OTHER MAJOR WORKS

SHORT FICTION: *Head o' W-Hollow*, 1936; *Men of the Mountains*, 1941; *Tales from the Plum Grove Hills*, 1946; *Clearing in the Sky, and Other Stories*, 1950; *Plowshare in Heaven: Tales True and Tall from the Kentucky Hills*, 1958; *Save Every Lamb*, 1964; *My Land Has a Voice*, 1966; *Come Gentle Spring*, 1969; *Come Back to the Farm*, 1971; *Votes Before Breakfast*, 1974; *The Best-Loved Short Stories of Jesse Stuart*, 1982; *New Harvest: Forgotten Stories of Kentucky's Jesse Stuart*, 2003 (David R. Palmore, editor).

POETRY: *Harvest of Youth*, 1930; *Man with a Bull-Tongue Plow*, 1934; *Album of Destiny*, 1944; *Kentucky Is My Land*, 1952; *Hold April*, 1962; *The World of Jesse Stuart: Selected Poems*, 1975.

NONFICTION: *Beyond Dark Hills*, 1938; *The Thread That Runs So True*, 1949; *The Year of My Rebirth*, 1956; *God's Oddling*, 1960; *To Teach, To Love*, 1970; *My World*, 1975; *The Kingdom Within: A Spiritual Autobiography*, 1979; *Lost Sandstones and Lonely Skies, and*

Other Essays, 1979; *If I Were Seventeen Again, and Other Essays*, 1980; *Jesse Stuart on Education*, 1992 (J. R. LeMaster, editor).

CHILDREN'S/YOUNG ADULT LITERATURE: *Mongrel Mettle: The Autobiography of a Dog*, 1944; *The Beatinest Boy*, 1953; *A Penny's Worth of Character*, 1954; *Red Mule*, 1955; *The Rightful Owner*, 1960; *Andy Finds a Way*, 1961.

BIBLIOGRAPHY

Blair, Everetta Love. *Jesse Stuart: His Life and Works.* Columbia: University of South Carolina Press, 1967. Blair opens with a brief account of Stuart's life and background. Subsequent chapters survey Stuart's novels, poetry, short stories, and other accomplishments; general discussions provide insight into particular works and overall trends.

Foster, Ruel E. *Jesse Stuart.* New York: Twayne, 1968. One of the earliest and, with a few exceptions, one of the best of the critical studies. Contains biographical information as well as extensive critiques on Stuart's work up to the date of publication.

Le Master, J. R., ed. *Jesse Stuart: Selected Criticism.* St. Petersburg, Fla.: Valkyrie Press, 1978. This collection of previously published articles discussing Stuart's work is an excellent introduction to the writer. Includes a bibliography.

Le Master, J. R., and Mary Washington Clark, eds. *Jesse Stuart: Essays on His Work.* Lexington: University Press of Kentucky, 1977. Critical perspectives on different facets and genres of Stuart's work, including novels, poetry, and short fiction, as well as his humor and use of folklore. The editors indicate that the book's primary purpose is to bring into sharper focus Stuart's use of multiple perspectives.

Miller, Danny L. "Native Writers and 'Authenticity': Emma Bell Miles and Jesse Stuart." In *Wingless Flights: Appalachian Women in Fiction.* Bowling Green, Ohio: Bowling Green State University Popular Press, 1996. Miller's examination of the changing depiction of mountain women in fictional works pub-

lished from the 1880's to the 1950's includes a discussion of Stuart's portrayal of female characters.

Miller, Danny L., Sharon Hatfield, and Gurney Norman, eds. *An American Vein: Critical Readings in Appalachian Literature.* Athens: Ohio University Press, 2005. This study of Appalachian literature contains two essays about Stuart: "Jesse Stuart and James Still: Mountain Regionalists" by Dayton Kohler and "The Changing Poetic Canon: The Case of Jesse Stuart and Ezra Pound" by Charles H. Daughaday.

Pennington, Lee. *The Dark Hills of Jesse Stuart.* Cincinnati, Ohio: Harvest Press, 1967. Pennington discusses Stuart's symbolism as it emerges in his early poetry and later through his novels. Argues that Stuart is far more than a regionalist; rather, he is an important creative writer and spokesperson not only for a region but for all humankind.

Richardson, H. Edward. *Jesse: The Biography of an American Writer—Jesse Hilton Stuart.* New York: McGraw-Hill, 1984. This inclusive study, printed in the year of Stuart's death, is sensitively written and offers invaluable reading for anyone with more than a passing interest in Stuart's life and work. Includes photographs.

Ward, William S. *A Literary History of Kentucky.* Knoxville: University of Tennessee Press, 1988. This historical survey includes a biographical and critical discussion of Stuart's work, pointing out that Stuart deals with people as individuals rather than in sociological terms.

Weaks-Baxter, Mary. "Jesse Stuart: A Farmer Singing at the Plow." In *Reclaiming the American Farmer: The Reinvention of a Regional Mythology in Twentieth-Century Southern Writing.* Baton Rouge: Louisiana State University Press, 2006. Weaks-Baxter's examination of southern literature from 1900 through 1960 includes a discussion of Stuart's works. She describes how Stuart and other writers substituted idealized descriptions of the plantation system with a new mythology that glorified the yeoman farmer.

THEODORE STURGEON

Born: Staten Island, New York; February 26, 1918

Died: Eugene, Oregon; May 8, 1985

Also known as: Edward Hamilton Waldo; E. Waldo Hunter; E. Hunter Waldo; Frederick R. Ewing; Ellery Queen; Billy Watson

PRINCIPAL LONG FICTION

The Dreaming Jewels, 1950 (also known as *The Synthetic Man*, 1957)

More than Human, 1953

I, Libertine, 1956 (as Frederick R. Ewing; with Jean Shepherd)

The King and Four Queens, 1956

The Cosmic Rape, 1958

Venus Plus X, 1960

Some of Your Blood, 1961

Voyage to the Bottom of the Sea, 1961

Alien Cargo, 1984

Godbody, 1986

OTHER LITERARY FORMS

While Theodore Sturgeon (STUHR-juhn) was not as prolific as some of the science-fiction fraternity, he wrote more than 190 short stories, 130 articles, and a number of radio and television scripts. His short fiction was assembled in many collections, ranging from *Without Sorcery: Thirteen Tales* (1948; also known as *Not Without Sorcery*) to *The Golden Helix* (1980).

ACHIEVEMENTS

Theodore Sturgeon's work was once called "the single most important body of science fiction by an American to date." A founder of modern American science fiction, he contributed to the genre's transition from underground to mainstream literature. He was the recipient of Argosy (1947), International Fantasy (1954), Nebula (1970), and Hugo (1971) awards.

BIOGRAPHY

Theodore Sturgeon was born Edward Hamilton Waldo on February 26, 1918, on Staten Island, New York. His parents were divorced and, after his mother remarried in 1929, his name was legally changed when he was adopted by his stepfather. After he graduated from high school, where his career as a gymnast was ended by rheumatic fever, he finished a term at Penn State Nautical School and then spent three years at sea. During that time he began to write, producing some forty conventional short stories for McClure's Syndicate before turning to science fiction, which he began to publish in John W. Campbell, Jr.'s *Astounding Science Fiction* in 1939.

Sturgeon recalled that science fiction was "the pornography of its day" and recounted how his stepfather discovered and destroyed his 1935 issues of *Amazing*. When he took up science fiction, Sturgeon was making a commitment to a literary form that promised little prestige and very modest financial returns. He married in the same year he launched his science-fiction career and contributed regularly to *Unknown* and *Astounding Science Fiction* in order to support his family. Although he produced highly regarded stories, such as "It" (1940) and "Microcosmic God" (1941), he had to seek employment in addition to writing to earn a living.

After operating a hotel in the British West Indies in 1940, Sturgeon worked as a door-to-door salesman, as assistant chief steward at Fort Simonds, and as a bulldozer operator. In 1942, he pursued the last of these occupations in Puerto Rico. Except for *Killdozer*, a novelette about a machine possessed by a malignant force, his literary output declined sharply between 1942 and 1944, when he returned to the United States and became a copy editor. These were difficult years for Sturgeon, financially and emotionally. Not until 1946, after his marriage ended in divorce, did he fully resume his career under the encouragement of John Campbell.

While continuing to write, Sturgeon tried his hand at running a literary agency and producing advertising copy. The first substantial public recognition for his work came in 1947 when he won a one-thousand-dollar prize for "Bianca's Hands." (The runner-up in the contest, sponsored by the British magazine *Argosy*, was Graham Greene.) "Bianca's Hands" had been written on

Sturgeon's honeymoon years earlier but had found no market because of its bizarre treatment of a "passionate human attachment." Its acceptance marked a turning point for Sturgeon, which was closely followed by the publication of the first of his many anthologies, *Without Sorcery*, with an introduction by Ray Bradbury.

As he entered the period of his greatest creativity, Sturgeon's personal life again underwent change, with a second marriage in 1949 and a third in 1951. His output of fiction was unabated, however, with *The Dreaming Jewels*, his first novel, appearing in 1950, and *More than Human*, published in 1953, winning the 1954 International Fantasy Award, a confirmation of his rank as one of America's foremost writers of science fiction. His stories continued to be anthologized in his own collections and those of others, and he engaged in a broad range of literary activity, from a hoax with Jean Shepherd, *I, Libertine*, published under the name Frederick R. Ewing, to a fictional case history of vampirism, *Some of Your Blood*, and a novel depicting an androgynous utopia, *Venus Plus X*.

As a major author of speculative fiction, Sturgeon helped to create a climate of acceptance for the genre among the general public. In his book reviews for the *National Review* (1961-1973), for example, he explained and defended his art while introducing some of contemporary science fiction's finest authors to an audience who might otherwise not have learned of them. He was involved in science fiction's growth in other media also. In 1966 he moved to Los Angeles to write for the television series *Star Trek*. Late in his life, he published little new fiction, but he continued to compile anthologies of his previous work for new audiences. He married for the fourth time in 1969. Sturgeon was living in Eugene, Oregon, at the time of his death in 1985.

Though Sturgeon deplored the "inexcusable invasions into . . . authors' most intimate motivations" by academic critics, there are nevertheless certain definite biographical influences on his work. Beverly Friend called him "a highly personal writer drawing from his own suffering for his craft." She cites his parents' divorce, his estrangement from his stepfather, his illness in adolescence, and his marital and professional problems as sources for his art.

ANALYSIS

Theodore Sturgeon once said, "All great literature is great because it is fable—because it creates typical and archetypical characters and situations which can be applied outside the work to illuminate the human condition." He repeatedly insisted that he did not undervalue the science of science fiction, but he clearly inclined toward minimizing technology as a focus for his work; rather, he concentrated on fable, often premising his work on occult matters about which science has had little to say. He said that "in teaching, reviewing, and enjoying science fiction, my emphasis is always on the fiction." This is, he explained, "because I like writers to be read and remembered and (when they can) to move people and shake them; to ignite, to increase their ability to share their visions and their joy and their terror, as well as their knowledge." Sturgeon's criteria for art were more affective than cognitive, and he generally concentrated on rites of passage rather than technological extrapolation.

Whatever Sturgeon's premise for a story—scientific, psychological, or occult—he wished the work to reflect essential human experiences: "love, and pain, and greed, and laughter, and hope, and above all loneliness." Loneliness is most significant, since he asserted that "what I have been trying to do all these years is to investigate this matter of love, sexual and asexual," and his major fictions are fables of growth toward community and maturity.

The four science-fiction novels that are the heart of Sturgeon's work (*The Dreaming Jewels*, *More than Human*, *The Cosmic Rape*, and *Venus Plus X*) develop the idea that "our strange species has two prime motivating forces: sex, of course, and worship." Throughout his writing, the latter is the more important, and Sturgeon was unwilling to see the highest self-sacrificial and altruistic acts as having any foundation in sexuality. Sturgeon's center of worship, however, is not to be found outside humanity but within humanity.

Sturgeon's first novel, *The Dreaming Jewels*, is an exploration of what it means to be human. Its premise is the creation of a "synthetic man" by the action of alien crystals that have a deep collective life of their own, apparently unrelated to the affairs of people. These crystals, seemingly without purpose, "dream" objects into existence, sometimes imperfectly, creating freaks and monsters, and sometimes—when they are mating—perfectly, creating creatures with the power of self-transformation. Such materials are better suited to psychological symbolism than scientific discussion. This is precisely the direction of Sturgeon's art; since he found "more room in inner space than in outer space," his fables are essentially paradigms of psychological growth that begin with the frustrations and alienation of youth and end in maturation and integration. On a number of occasions, he defined science fiction in terms of the derivation of the word "science" from the Latin "to know." "Science fiction is knowledge fiction," he wrote, adding that "by far most of the knowledge is psychological."

In *More than Human*, Sturgeon makes significant use of syzygy, a concept of nonreproductive union signified by a strange word. A collective identity is formed by a group of persons who retain their individuality while contributing to a gestalt that has the ultimate promise of a god. The collective person remains distinctly human, however, and the worship due it is finally worship of humanity. Here the components of the human being, conscience being the highest, are integrated and raised to the highest power. So, too, in a novel that deals directly with sexuality, *Venus Plus X*, the integration of the human personality and worship become paramount, with Sturgeon using androgyny as a symbol of wholeness and providing his utopia's inhabitants with a religion that worships the promise of humanity.

The form of Sturgeon's novels can present the critical reader with problems. Sturgeon is perhaps most at home as a writer of short stories, and his techniques of composition reflect at times an incomplete transition to the novel's demands. He seemingly pieces together sections that finally form the whole. This is not to say that the structuring of his books is unskillful, for he does finally bring to focus elements that run through them in parallel directions. Also, such a method can be seen as organic to Sturgeon's themes of integration, with loosely related parts finally encompassed in a total vision. Whatever a reader's verdict on form, however, his principal response will probably be to Sturgeon's handling of theme.

Sturgeon's work takes seriously his claim that "the best of science fiction is as good as the best of any mod-

ern literature—articulate, poetic, philosophical, provocative, searching, courageous, insightful." He once complained that though the finest science-fiction writers "open their veins into their typewriters, taking their craft and their readers seriously, they seem to be categorically disqualified from the serious attention of mainstream critics and readers." Fortunately, this is no longer the case, in part because of Sturgeon's fables of human nature.

THE DREAMING JEWELS

The reprint title of *The Dreaming Jewels* is *The Synthetic Man*, a title that more clearly reflects the subject matter of Sturgeon's first novel but also loses some of the symbolic suggestiveness of the original. Paul Williams has commented that the work is in part based on Sturgeon's resentment of his stepfather and has pointed out the significance of the dream to the creative act of writing science fiction. To this might be added the importance of jewel symbolism in the light of Sturgeon's view of science fiction as knowledge fiction.

Jewels often symbolize arcane knowledge and spiritual transformation; here they are connected with an unconscious dream power that can be brought to light for good or ill and in which reside keys to transformation and regeneration. Contesting for this power are Horty, the "synthetic man"—created by alien crystals that can bring objects, or people, into existence—and Pierre Monetre, a thoroughgoing misanthrope who would delight in the destruction of humankind. Horty's victory over Monetre (called "maneater" by his subordinates) comes about through his capacity to tap the power of the unconscious, and through the willing sacrifice of Zena, whose education of Horty to human values keeps him from becoming like the alienated Monetre.

Horty's potential alienation comes from abuse by a cruel stepfather, Armand Bluett, a figure Sturgeon has himself identified with "a lot of bitterness and hostility that I wanted to get out." Bluett's viciousness results in the accidental loss of three of Horty's fingers, and the young boy flees after bidding farewell to Kay Hallowell, a girl whose love balances Bluett's hatred. In his flight, Horty is befriended by carnival people, especially Zena, a midget, who notices the boy's sympathetic connection with his only possession, a jack-in-the-box with strange jewels for eyes. These gems prove to have had their effect on the child, gradually transforming him into a creature capable both of communicating with the inner life of the jewels and of transforming himself at will.

Horty's identity is hidden from Monetre, who owns the carnival. Zena disguises him as a girl and warns him never to reveal that he has regenerated his three lost fingers, which Monetre had treated upon his arrival. During his years with the carnival, Horty fails to grow and is only forced to leave when the owner discloses some curiosity about his hand. After leaving, he discovers his gift of transformation, which is useful when he encounters Armand Bluett, now a judge, victimizing Kay Hallowell. Horty cools off the sexually aggressive Bluett by taking Kay's place and slicing off his regenerated fingers, at which sight Bluett passes out. Horty thus becomes the woman who represents love for him so that he might perform a sacrificial mutilation that is both saving and vengeful.

In a series of improbable events, Kay comes under the power of Bluett and Monetre, who is clearly contrasted with Horty. While both are brilliantly gifted, Horty's mind, under Zena's guidance, has been shaped by "humanity and the extensions of humanity," as against Monetre's, which has been twisted by hatred and desire for power. In the confrontation between Horty and Monetre in a psychic duel, Zena sacrifices herself, instructing Horty to use his power to destroy jewel-created creatures. Since Monetre's character is so inhuman, he is assumed to be one. Ironically, Monetre is biologically human, without possessing any spirit of humanity, while Zena, a synthetic creature, sacrifices herself. In the end, however, Horty kills his adversary, resurrects Zena, who becomes his wife, and assumes Monetre's identity while traveling about trying to undo some of the harm he has done.

Sturgeon has assessed *The Dreaming Jewels* as "a rotten novel." Its chief faults are a contrived plot and a style that lacks the energy of the best of his stories of the 1940's. The use of psychological materials is compelling, however, making it one of Sturgeon's most popular works. Horty's series of transformations are representative of his possession of the secret of the unconscious, the capacity to convert revenge into sacrificial love, whose highest exemplar is Zena. The novel moves from mutilation to regeneration, from revenge to love, with Horty progressing toward wholeness by overcoming alienation and linking the transforming power of the unconscious to positive human values.

MORE THAN HUMAN

More than Human, Sturgeon's second and best novel, has at the center of its three-part structure a section titled "Baby Is Three," which was published separately a year before the novel appeared. According to Samuel Moskowitz, Sturgeon wrote a prologue and epilogue to this section to compose the novel. Like *The Dreaming Jewels*, "Baby Is Three" is about an alienated superman, fifteen-year-old Gerry Thompson, who in a strong first-person narration relates his visit to a psychiatrist, to whom he reveals his murder of his guardian, Miss Alicia Kew. Gerry also explains that he is part of a composite being, *homo gestalt*, a uniting of persons with extraordinary telepathic and telekinetic powers. Gerry has the capacity to probe the minds of others—he does this with the psychiatrist to make sure that he will not remember his visit—but he lacks human sympathy and moral awareness.

Sturgeon once said that "you cannot write stories about ideas—which is why so much hard-core, nuts-and-bolts science fiction fails as literature." In *More than Human*, however, he is fortunate in combining a powerful idea with a sure grasp of style and an effective structure. The first section of the novel, "The Fabulous Idiot," focuses on Lone (a shortened form of *alone*), who is an idiot in the root sense of the word. He is aware of himself alone. He gradually becomes aware of others, first through Miss Kew's sister, Evelyn, who along with Alicia had been the victim of a demonically sexually repressive father, and then through the Prodds, a pathetic couple who take him in and whose mentally disabled child, Baby, becomes the center of the gestalt being.

Lone becomes aware of a human community to which he has at least rudimentary obligations and of a more specialized group, composed of abandoned or runaway children, to which Gerry belongs, and that is destined to become a new being. By the end of the novel, this group has become a potential god, "not an exterior force, not an awesome Watcher in the sky, but a laughing thing with a human heart and reverence for its origins." In the book's last section, "Morality," Hip Barrows, the being's final component, its conscience, confronts and converts the ruthless Gerry; Hip sees himself as "an atom and his gestalt as a molecule. He saw these others as cells among cells, and he saw the whole design of what, with joy, humanity would become." His response is a "sense of worship." He participates in a vision not unlike that shared by many Romantic writers of the nineteenth century, what Walt Whitman's follower R. M. Bucke called "Cosmic Consciousness." Sturgeon said that the willingness of science-fiction writers to treat religious themes, "to invent and extrapolate and regroup ideas and concepts in this as in all other areas of human growth and change delights me and is a source of my true love for the mad breed." *More than Human* is Sturgeon's best illustration that such themes can be explored profitably.

More than Human, like *The Dreaming Jewels*, traces the progress of the growth and integration of the person. In each novel, characters move from alienation to wholeness, but in *More than Human*, the key conflict between misanthropy and humanity is handled with greater dramatic skill. In general a more sophisticated work in conception and structure, *More than Human* manages to present the idea of a collective entity without losing sight of individual characters or the dynamics of personality. As a speculative fiction, it deserves the praise and popularity it has enjoyed.

THE COSMIC RAPE

The Cosmic Rape also employs the gestalt theme of *More than Human*, extending the union to all of humankind, which in turn is joined to Medusa, an intergalactic composite creature. While the underlying theme of the book is essentially the same as that of *More than Human*, it is by no means as successful. Its premises are extrapolated in far less believable fashion, and its structure is not dramatically engaging. Intercut scenes, which range from the United States to Rome to Africa, are skillfully coordinated, but character development suffers in the effort to show individuals becoming a part of the whole.

In *The Cosmic Rape*, Sturgeon attempts to put love into the largest terms but, ironically, he employs a character most unlikely to initiate cosmic harmony. Dan Gurlick, a loathsome bum, has become an atom in Medusa by ingesting a sort of seed concealed in a fragment of hamburger. Through him, Medusa seeks to take over the earth telepathically. Medusa is at first thwarted,

having dealt only with collective minds elsewhere in the universe. This lack in humanity is repaired, however, as psychic unity among people appears as they cooperate in the destruction of invading machines created by Medusa. In the course of attaining collective consciousness, a variety of characters emerge from sexual repression and exploitation or social alienation to sacrifice themselves. Notable is the metamorphosis of Guido, a misfit who has turned to anarchism because his musical genius has been suppressed by a wicked stepfather.

Ultimately, Medusa is joined to the human collective mind. This connection occurs when Gurlick, himself excluded from the universal intelligence, is permitted to act out the sexual fantasies that Medusa has used to control him. What Gurlick intends as rape is welcomed by a woman now sexually liberated as a part of a larger design; likewise, the joining of humanity to Medusa is transformed from rape to consent. Medusa is in fact possessed by humanity rather than possessing it.

The Cosmic Rape extends the ideas of *More than Human* as far as they can go. Unfortunately, the extrapolation is ultimately too fanciful and the dramatic power of Sturgeon's myth of human integration is diffused. There is a sense of his recognition of this in his next book, which he calls "a tract"; the social criticism of *Venus Plus X* gives ballast to an imagination that had overextended itself.

VENUS PLUS X

Sturgeon responded to the charge that "science fiction is characteristically asexual and unaware of love in its larger and largest senses." He believed that this impression had sometimes arisen because writers of science fiction often "work in geological or astronomical time rather than in biographical or historical perspective." Sturgeon had dealt with themes of love in both cosmic and personal perspectives in his earlier novels, but in *Venus Plus X* he turned to utopian fiction to keep the action on a more human scale.

Though Sturgeon had written stories on sex before—"The World Well Lost" (1953) deals with homosexuality, for example—*Venus Plus X* is his most extended statement on sexism and sexual taboos. While the book has been praised for its pioneering study of sex roles, preceding Ursula K. Le Guin's much discussed *The Left Hand of Darkness* (1969) by nine years, *Venus Plus X* is also notable for its skillfully ironic employment of science-fiction conventions and for its handling of the symbolism of androgyny.

The novel is structured in alternating chapters of action that are connected only by theme. The first set of chapters deals with suburban life and the questions of sexual identity posed to America in the 1950's. Along with standard problems of sex-role definition for children and general sexism, there are hints of change; Herb Raile comes to realize how Western culture has degraded women and catches glimpses of the significance of androgyny in the style of a rock singer. Contrasted with suburban America is Ledom ("model" inverted), a utopia founded on the fact that its inhabitants are biologically hermaphrodites. Here, sex-role definition is no problem, and the wholeness of the human being in assuming all social duties is stressed. Against the predatory capitalism and commercialized worship of the suburbs are posed charitable religion and universal sharing.

Androgyny is used by Sturgeon as a symbol of wholeness. Like the universal human of *More than Human*, androgyny can be found in mystical thought as signifying the primordial unity of humankind. To stress this aspect of his work, Sturgeon provides the Ledomites with a religion that is an ecstatic celebration of the child. "We keep before us," says the guide to this utopia, "the image of that which is malleable and growing—of that which we have the power to improve. We worship that very power in ourselves, and the sense of responsibility which lives with it." Here again is Sturgeon's drive toward totality, a worship of human potential, yet to present this theme, he undercuts a number of science-fiction conventions to make his readers more aware of the symbolic nature of his statement.

The reader discovers that the book's nominal hero, Charlie Johns, is not a time traveler as he first believes. Ledom does not exist in the distant future as it first appears; rather, it is a society hidden from human eyes. The Ledomites wish to test the reaction of the outside world to their culture, and they use Charlie's responses as a gauge. After overcoming his initial bewilderment, Charlie embarks on a course of education, learning that Ledom's technical superiority consists in a machine that can inscribe thought patterns and has revolutionized learning, and a power supply that makes the community

self-sufficient. Charlie's approval of technology comes to a screeching halt, however, when he discovers that the hermaphroditism of Ledomites is biologically engineered. His reaction convinces utopian planners that the world is not ready for the revelation of Ledom.

Charlie now regards Ledom as a den of perversion and indicates that it ought to be destroyed. His education, however, has been limited: He has not detected the hints throughout that the whole culture is symbolic, that its essence is "transition." It has been designed to preserve human values while the outside world destroys itself. The novel's disquisition on religion, in fact, suggests that if one human generation could adopt the religion of Ledom, it would be saved. No hermaphroditism would be necessary for a sense of human wholeness.

The final emphasis given Ledom's symbolic nature is the revelation that Charlie Johns is not actually Charlie Johns at all, but merely a collection of his memories, obtained when he was dying after a plane crash and inscribed on the previously blank mind of a biological control. The plot, however, first permits Johns to attempt the standard escape from a dystopia. He finds the one girl who has not been biologically altered, and he tries to leave in what he thinks is a time machine. When he does so, the Ledomites are forced to tell him the truth. He and his girl therefore take up life somewhere between the two worlds, trying to sort out their identities, presumably overcoming the sexism of the man Charlie was, and learning from the wisdom of Ledom. At the same time, on the other side, Herb Raile is working his way slowly and painfully to gain some of Ledom's values.

In spite of some dated writing in the sections on suburbia in the 1950's, this is a book that powerfully anticipates many of the themes taken up by feminists in the 1960's and 1970's. Sturgeon also made fine use of the conventions of utopian fiction only to undercut them, which is most appropriate to his major points about the nature of dynamic evolutionary change throughout his fiction. Utopia, he wrote, "must be life-oriented and recognize that life is change, which is why utopias, be they by Plato or Thomas More, or Joanna Russ, have hidden in them the characteristics of the necropolis." He avoided this by permitting his own utopia to self-destruct, leaving behind the impact of its symbols, and providing in

Venus Plus X what Sturgeon saw in William Golding's *Lord of the Flies* (1954), "a fable of cultural structures, with a meaning—a 'moral' if you like—far greater than the narrative itself."

Henry J. Lindborg

OTHER MAJOR WORKS

SHORT FICTION: *Without Sorcery: Thirteen Tales*, 1948 (also known as *Not Without Sorcery*); *E Pluribus Unicorn*, 1953; *Caviar*, 1955; *A Way Home: Stories of Science Fiction and Fantasy*, 1955 (also known as *Thunder and Roses*); *A Touch of Strange*, 1958; *Aliens 4*, 1959; *Beyond*, 1960; *Sturgeon in Orbit*, 1964; *. . . And My Fear Is Great/Baby Is Three*, 1965; *The Joyous Invasions*, 1965; *Starshine*, 1966; *Sturgeon Is Alive and Well*, 1971; *The Worlds of Theodore Sturgeon*, 1972; *Sturgeon's West*, 1973 (with Don Ward); *To Here and the Easel*, 1973; *Case and the Dreamer, and Other Stories*, 1974; *Visions and Venturers*, 1978; *Maturity: Three Stories*, 1979; *The Stars Are the Styx*, 1979; *The Golden Helix*, 1980; *Slow Sculpture*, 1982; *Alien Cargo*, 1984; *Pruzy's Pot*, 1986; *To Marry Medusa*, 1987; *A Touch of Sturgeon*, 1987; *The [Widget], the [Wadget], and Boff*, 1989; *The Complete Stories of Theodore Sturgeon*, 1994-2005 (10 volumes).

PLAYS: *It Should Be Beautiful*, pr. 1963; *Psychosis: Unclassified*, pr. 1977 (adaptation of his novel *Some of Your Blood*).

TELEPLAYS: *The Adaptive Ultimate*, 1950's; *Mewhu's Jet*, 1950's; *Ordeal in Space*, 1950's; *The Sound Machine*, 1950's; *They Came to Bagdad*, 1950's; *Dead Dames Don't Dial*, 1959; "Shore Leave," 1966 (episode of television series *Star Trek*); "Amok Time," 1967 (episode of television series *Star Trek*); *Killdozer!*, 1974; *The Pylon Express*, 1975-1976.

RADIO PLAYS: *Incident at Switchpath*, 1950; *The Stars Are the Styx*, 1953; *Mr. Costello, Hero*, 1956; *Saucer of Loneliness*, 1957; *More than Human*, 1967 (adaptation of his novel).

NONFICTION: *Argyll: A Memoir*, 1993.

BIBLIOGRAPHY

Bleiler, Richard, ed. *Science Fiction Writers: Critical Studies of the Major Authors from the Early Nineteenth Century to the Present Day*. 2d ed. New York:

Scribner's, 1999. This reference book contains a brief but useful analytical article about Sturgeon's science fiction written by Brian Stableford.

Delany, Samuel. "Sturgeon." In *Starboard Wine: More Notes on the Language of Science Fiction*. Pleasantville, N.Y.: Dragon Press, 1984. Delany is not only one of science fiction's best authors, he is also one of its best critics, particularly in analysis of style. Here Delany explores some of the nuances of Sturgeon's language and the "realism" of Sturgeon's stories.

Diskin, Lahna F. *Theodore Sturgeon*. Mercer Island, Wash.: Starmont House, 1981. The first book-length study of Sturgeon's fiction, this volume focuses primarily on his most famous science fiction. Includes a bibliography and an index.

Gordon, Joan, and Veronica Hollinger, eds. *Blood Read: The Vampire as Metaphor in Contemporary Culture*. Philadelphia: University of Pennsylvania Press, 1997. This examination of vampire literature treats Sturgeon's novel *Some of Your Blood* as a harbinger of the more recent sympathetic vampire novels. Includes a bibliography.

Malzberg, Barry N. "Grandson of the True and the Terrible." In *The Engines of the Night*. Garden City, N.Y.: Doubleday, 1982. A brief but poignant evaluation of Sturgeon's importance in the history of science fiction.

Moskowitz, Samuel. "Theodore Sturgeon." In *Seekers of Tomorrow: Masters of Modern Science Fiction*. 1966. New ed. Westport, Conn.: Hyperion Press, 1974. This essay is a good general introduction to Sturgeon in terms of his place in science-fiction history and in what makes him unique.

Pringle, David, ed. *St. James Guide to Horror, Ghost, and Gothic Writers*. Detroit, Mich.: St. James Press, 1998. One entry examines Sturgeon's life and works. Includes a comprehensive bibliography of his writings.

Sackmary, Regina. "An Ideal of Three: The Art of Theodore Sturgeon." In *Critical Encounters*, edited by Dick Riley. New York: Frederick Ungar, 1978. Sackmary discusses the motif of threes in Sturgeon's fiction as his symbol for unity.

Stableford, Brian M. "Schemes of Salvation: The Literary Explorations of Theodore Sturgeon." In *Outside* the Human Aquarium: Masters of Science Fiction.* 2d ed., rev. and expanded. San Bernardino, Calif.: Borgo Press, 1995. Sturgeon is one of the science-fiction writers whose work is examined in this collection of essays. Includes notes, a bibliography, and an index.

Streitfield, David. "Science Fiction and Fantasy." *The Washington Post*, March 7, 1999. Streitfield discusses the renaissance of interest in Sturgeon, with the reissue of his *More than Human* and *To Marry Medusa* in paperback, as well as his collected short stories.

WILLIAM STYRON

Born: Newport News, Virginia; June 11, 1925
Died: Martha's Vineyard, Massachusetts;
    November 1, 2006
Also known as: William Clark Styron, Jr.

PRINCIPAL LONG FICTION

Lie Down in Darkness, 1951
The Long March, 1952 (serial), 1956 (book)
Set This House on Fire, 1960
The Confessions of Nat Turner, 1967
Sophie's Choice, 1979

OTHER LITERARY FORMS

Until 1990, William Styron (STI-ruhn) was among the few major modern literary figures who bear discussion in only a single genre—in his case, the novel. Except for a slight and rather odd play, *In the Clap Shack* (pr. 1972), and a collection of essays, *This Quiet Dust, and Other Writings* (1982), Styron mainly concentrated on novels. In 1990, however, *Darkness Visible: A Memoir of Madness* was widely hailed. A candid and insightful recounting of Styron's personal battle with severe clinical depression, *Darkness Visible* was an immediate popular success. *A Tidewater Morning: Three Tales from Youth* is a collection of short stories published in 1993.

ACHIEVEMENTS

Until the publication of *The Confessions of Nat Turner* in 1967, William Styron was well known in literary circles as a young novelist of great talent but largely unrealized potential. *The Confessions of Nat Turner*, riding the crest of a wave of social activism in the late 1960's and capitalizing on a national interest in black literature and history, gave Styron a major popular reputation as well as making him the center of a vitriolic controversy between academic and literary critics on one side, who tended to see the novel as an honest attempt to come to terms with history, and a small group of black critics on the other hand, who questioned, often abusively, the ability of any white writer to deal with the black experience and who called Styron's portrait of Nat Turner unflattering and inaccurate. The book and the debate it engendered made Styron a major voice in twentieth century fiction, and it made him rich.

Despite the twelve-year hiatus between the publication of *The Confessions of Nat Turner* and that of *Sophie's Choice*, Styron's reputation grew, particularly in terms of his role as an interpreter of the South. *Lie Down in Darkness* was recognized as one of the finest presentations in fiction of the modern southern family, haunted by memory, guilt, and time, and *The Confessions of Nat Turner* came to be seen as representative of the concern of southern writers with the burden of history. *The Confessions of Nat Turner* was accepted as a rhetorically beautiful evocation of the past, whatever its historical inaccuracies.

The publication of *Sophie's Choice* in 1979 cemented Styron's position as one of the major figures of contemporary literature. Although several major critics had reservations about the novel, its ambitious confrontation of a moral theme of enormous implication—the Holocaust—and Styron's compelling, lyrical prose made the novel the literary event of the year. With *Sophie's*

Choice, some of Styron's lifelong concerns as a novelist become clearer: the unanswerable problem of pain and suffering, the elusive nature of memory, and the ambiguous legacy of history.

BIOGRAPHY

William Styron was born William Clark Styron, Jr., on June 11, 1925, in Newport News, Virginia, which he later called "a very Southern part of the world." His mother, Pauline Margaret Abraham Styron, was from the North, but his father, William Clark Styron, Sr., a shipyard engineer, came from an old, if not aristocratic, land-poor Virginia family. Styron remembers his grandmother telling him as a little boy of the days when the family owned slaves, a memory he was to incorporate years later into *Sophie's Choice*. Styron's father was a "Jeffersonian gentleman," liberal in his views for a southerner, who implanted in his son much of the philosophical curiosity that characterized the young Styron's novels. His mother, a gentling influence, died when Styron was twelve years old, after a long, painful siege with cancer, an experience that was also to leave a mark on his fiction in the form of an almost obsessive concern with physical pain and suffering and the vulnerability of the flesh.

After his mother's death, Styron began "going wild," and his father sent him to an Episcopal boys' school in Middlesex County, where he was an indifferent student but a voracious reader. After graduating, he enrolled in Davidson College during World War II but soon dropped out to enlist in the U.S. Marine Corps.

Styron's stint in Officer Candidate School marked the beginning of his writing career, for while there, he enrolled in a creative writing course at Duke University under William Blackburn, whom Styron acknowledges as the most powerful formative influence on his work. One of his stories, about a southern lynching, similar in tone and execution to William Faulkner's "Dry September," appeared in a student anthology, Styron's first published fiction. At the tail end of the war, Styron was commissioned and was stationed on a troop ship in the San Francisco Bay, but the Japanese surrendered before he ever left port. Styron was to speak later of his sense of guilt at not having seen action, as well as his feeling of horror at the waste and destruction of the war and the ter-

rible, almost casual way in which life could be lost. Styron condemned the absurdity of Marine Corps life, but he praised the tough training that transformed him physically and mentally.

Styron resumed his program at Duke and graduated in 1947. He took a job in New York as an associate editor in the book division at McGraw-Hill. His senior editor and immediate superior was Edward C. Aswell, the august second editor of Thomas Wolfe and an éminence grise to rival editor Maxwell Perkins; Aswell was to appear grotesquely as "The Weasel" in an autobiographical passage in *Sophie's Choice* nearly thirty years later. The callow young Styron found McGraw-Hill humorless and confining, and after six months he was fired.

Living in a Brooklyn boardinghouse on a tiny financial inheritance from his grandmother, Styron took another creative writing course, this time from Hiram Haydn at the New School for Social Research in Manhattan. He began work on his first novel, *Lie Down in Darkness*, the story of a star-crossed upper-middle-class southern family whose failure to find love and meaning in life drives the sensitive daughter, Peyton Loftis, to insanity and suicide. The complex treatment of time in the novel and its high southern rhetoric showed the influence of Faulkner, whom Styron had been reading intensely, but *Lie Down in Darkness* was manifestly the work of a powerful and original talent.

At first, Styron found the writing of the book slow and difficult. Two years after leaving McGraw-Hill, he had written only a few pages that were usable. After Styron made drastic changes to the novel, dropping the original title (*Inheritance of Night*), eliminating the character Marcus Bonner, shifting the point of view to an omniscient narrator, and withholding the reader's knowledge of Peyton Loftis, Styron found the writing went surprisingly fast—he finished the book and saw it accepted for publication by Bobbs-Merrill before he was recalled by the Marine Corps for service in the Korean War. The novel was published in 1951. Styron was then on active reserve duty, from which he was eventually discharged for an eye problem; his experiences in the reserves became the basis for his second novel, *The Long March*.

Lie Down in Darkness was an immediate critical success and a moderate popular one, winning the presti-

William Styron. (Peter Simon)

gious Prix de Rome in 1952. At that time, Styron had decamped to Paris and fallen in with a young crowd of American expatriate intellectuals, many of whom would later make names for themselves in literature. George Plimpton and Peter Matthiessen were at the center of a moiling, motley, talented crowd that included Harold Humes, John P. C. Train, Donald Hall, and, on the fringe, writers such as James Baldwin, James Jones, and Irwin Shaw. In 1952 and 1953, the group began compiling a literary magazine, *The Paris Review*, which was to become one of the most influential literary periodicals of the postwar period. Plimpton became the first editor and Matthiessen the fiction editor, and Styron wrote the statement of purpose for the first issue. He also gave the periodical one of the first of its famous "Writers at Work" interviews. It was recorded by Matthiessen and Plimpton at Patrick's, the *Paris Review* crowd's favorite bar, and in it Styron claimed that "this generation . . . will produce literature equal to that of any other generation" and that "a great writer . . . will give substance to and perhaps even explain all the problems of the world." From the start, his ambitions were large.

Although Styron later said he drank enough brandy in bistros to develop a *crise de foie* and spent months in the summer of 1952 on a sybaritic "Ovidian idyll" on the Riviera with Humes, he also was writing at top speed during this period. In just six weeks, he wrote a novella based on his Marine Corps training-camp experience, *The Long March*, and it was accepted for publication in the fall by *discovery*, a literary magazine (Knopf would publish it as a book four years later). In 1953, he used the money from his Prix de Rome to travel in Italy, an experience that laid the groundwork for his 1960 novel of expatriates, *Set This House on Fire*. During this time he met Rose Burgunder, a Jewish poet with some family money from Baltimore, whom he soon married. They returned to the United States, to Roxbury, Connecticut, which would remain Styron's home and where he began work on the "big novel" that he planned to follow up the success of *Lie Down in Darkness*.

This big novel was *Set This House on Fire*, a sprawling account of American intellectuals living a life of self-indulgence and self-destruction in postwar Italy. The book contained fine lyrical passages of description, particularly of the physical beauty of Italy and the horrifying squalor and suffering of its people, but as Styron later admitted, the novel was seriously flawed—undisciplined and melodramatic. The reviews were very mixed, and some of them savage. Styron's former friend, Norman Mailer, called *Set This House on Fire* "a bad, maggoty novel," suggesting that Styron could "write like an angel about landscape, but like an adolescent about people." The novel was better received by Styron's European critics—it remains highly regarded in France—but Styron was wounded by his first really bad press, and he retreated to Roxbury to work on his next book, a novel he resolved to make so thoroughly a work of craftsmanship as to defy criticism.

The Confessions of Nat Turner took years to research and write, and true to Styron's expectations, it was immediately acclaimed as a masterpiece. For years, Styron had his mind on Nat Turner's 1831 slave rebellion as a subject for fiction. It had taken place close to his own Tidewater, Virginia, home, and Styron saw the suffering, the violence, and the misunderstanding of the revolt as emblematic both of the South's guilt and pain and of his personal concerns as a writer. Styron claimed that reading Albert Camus' *L'Étranger* (1942; *The Stranger*, 1946) furnished him with the technique he was to use in presenting Nat's story—the narrative persona reflecting from jail—and there is no doubt that much of the novel's perspective on black people and black problems was derived from Styron's friend, the black writer James Baldwin, who was a guest of Styron for months while he was writing *Another Country* (1962), Baldwin's first major novel about black and white relations.

Styron called *The Confessions of Nat Turner* "less a 'historical novel' than a meditation on history," but despite critical accolades, including the praise of Baldwin, who suggested that the novel might be considered the beginning of a "mutual history" of blacks and whites, Styron became the target of a group of critics who protested vehemently Styron's depiction of Nat. These critics assaulted Styron in print, accused him of racism and of attempting to demean the reputation of a great hero of black history, and hounded him at meetings, readings, and lectures. Ironically, Nat, as Styron presented him, was a strong and sensitive character, unquestionably the hero of the novel, but so volatile was the political climate of the United States in the late 1960's that for some critics, any black character who was not a warrior saint was unacceptable as a fictional creation.

The critical assaults provoked by *The Confessions of Nat Turner* left Styron bruised, but he was encouraged by the praise for the novel's powerful rhetoric and masterly structure, not to mention its enormous financial success. Of the controversy, he said, "It really had very little effect on me . . . largely because of the fact that I knew that it was politically motivated and hysterical, and that I had not violated any truth that a novelist is capable of doing." He turned to new work, first to a lengthy projected novel, tentatively titled "The Way of the Warrior," a novel that explored the psyche of a career Army officer, then to *Sophie's Choice*. While in Martha's Vineyard, Styron dreamed of Sophie, a Polish Catholic survivor of Auschwitz whom he had met in Brooklyn in 1949. He woke with a vision, seeing her name on a door; he decided that the book would focus on a mother who is forced to send her child to death.

The book began as an autobiographical reminiscence of Styron's aimless days as a junior editor at McGraw-Hill, when he found himself frustrated artistically, philosophically, and sexually. As he worked through his memories in the character of his narrator, Stingo, whose fictional background is almost identical to his own, he found his real theme: the life and eventual death by suicide of a woman who survived the Nazi concentration camps but emerged terribly scarred emotionally. This woman, the Sophie of the title, becomes the vehicle through which Stingo confronts the potential horror of life, and through her he matures.

Sophie's Choice was five years in the writing, but Styron was richly rewarded when it was finally published in 1979. A few critics, notably John Gardner, raised questions about its structure and about the sometimes jejune intrusions of the shallow Stingo, but for the most part the novel was accepted as a fine and satisfying offering by a major writer. "It has the feel of permanence," Peter Prescott wrote. The gratifyingly large sales were capped by a spectacular sale of the film rights. In 1983, Meryl Streep won an Academy Award for Best Actress for her portrayal of Sophie in that film.

In 1985, Styron was hospitalized with acute clinical depression. His struggle to overcome his suicidal feelings and to return to health are recounted in his memoir *Darkness Visible*, published five years later. Styron credited the peaceful seclusion of his hospital stay and the loving patience of his wife and grown children (three daughters and a son) as the principal factors in his recovery. After his hospitalization, Styron immediately wrote "A Tidewater Morning," a long short story that fictionalized the death of his mother. After writing *Darkness Visible*, he returned to his work on a novel set during World War II. Styron died of pneumonia in 2006 after a long period of failing health.

ANALYSIS

The informing patterns of William Styron's fiction are by no means self-evident, and they may not yield themselves readily to the casual critic. Unlike Faulkner, whom he often resembles in style and technique, his subjects are radically diverse—a doomed southern family, the intellectual jet set of American expatriates, a historical slave revolt, the horror of the Holocaust. He can shift stylistically from the direct "plain style" of *The Long March* to the purple rhetoric of sections in *Set This*

House on Fire, and he moves easily from romantic abstraction to concrete objectivity.

Styron is preeminently, almost self-consciously, a writer of "big" novels of weighty moral significance—a fictional *homme sérieux*, as the French say (which may account for some of Styron's great popularity with French critics). The eternal verities embody themselves relentlessly in Styron's writing. Death, suffering, the silence of God—grave truths lumber ponderously and insistently at the reader in each novel, mercifully relieved by flashes of humor and lyrical passages of poetic beauty, which spare Styron the gray fate of being a sort of American Thomas Mann. Still, the metaphysical predominates in Styron's books.

Strongly underlying all of Styron's novels is a concern with the past, not so much in the form of the passage of time, but rather an awareness that it is either lost or potentially reclaimable. Each of the major novels moves from the present to the past in an attempt to explain or understand how things came to be as they are. *Lie Down in Darkness*, with its relentless burrowing in the Loftis family past, looks backward to explain Peyton's death. In *Set This House on Fire*, Peter Leverett moves very deliberately into the past in pursuit of a piece of himself that is missing, and his whole purpose in dredging up the Italian incidents that form the body of the novel is to reveal the past so that he may deal with the present. Both *The Confessions of Nat Turner* and *Sophie's Choice* are historical novels concerned with the actual past and with what Robert Penn Warren has called "the awful burden of history."

Styron's fiction is historical, but in an intensely personal and psychological way. Each exploration of the past is filtered through the consciousness of a protagonist—Milton Loftis, Cass Kinsolving, Nat Turner, Sophie—and strongly colored by the neuroses of those characters. The alcoholism of Milton and Cass, Nat's brooding rage, and Sophie's aching guilt over her murdered child—at the core of each novel is psychological exploration rather than historical exposition. Historical process is only the context within which individual psychologies grope for resolution. Each of Styron's characters lives on the verge of apocalyptic catastrophe, always on the edge of mental breakdown. Each of his protagonists is close to outright insanity. Two actually commit suicide (Peyton

and Sophie); Nat essentially does; and Cass of *Set This House on Fire* is only saved from it by the thinnest of margins. His people may be constantly close to madness, yet Styron makes the reader feel that the madness is legitimate, for his characters search for meaning in a mad world, and only when they fail to find it do they become deranged. Peyton's loveless family, Nat's unjust world, and the horrors of the concentration camp for Sophie are atmospheres in which genuine sanity is difficult, if not impossible.

Perhaps the most representative Styron "hero," though, is Cass of *Set This House on Fire*, the only protagonist who is a philosopher as well as a sufferer. Cass's madness derives from his contemplation of the horror of human life and misery, and he staggers drunkenly around postwar Italy demanding a teleological answer for the chaos of existence in which God is silent; "you can shake the whole universe and just get a snicker up there."

Perhaps it is this tendency to project the struggles of his characters beyond the ordinary world and to magnify them to the borders of melodrama that gives all of Styron's novels powerful religious overtones. Some of this tendency derives from Styron's own Episcopalian background, which is strongly echoed in the style of *Lie Down in Darkness* and *Set This House on Fire* and is particularly evident in the rhetoric of Nat, who is stylistically more Anglican than Baptist. The central problem in these novels is the conspicuous absence of God from human life. Styron's world is one in which, as Cass says in *Set This House on Fire*, "God has locked the door and gone away to leave us to write letters to Him." They are unanswered. By the time Styron comes to reflecting on the horror of the Holocaust in his last book, it seems no answer is possible.

This is Styron's theme—the absence of God and the meaninglessness of life. Consistently, he approaches it through a single technique, the presentation and contemplation of pain and suffering. Styron's novels are catalogs of the slings and arrows of outrageous fortune, some physical, some mental, and some simply the result of an empathetic identification with the suffering state of humankind.

On its most elemental level, Styron's depiction of suffering is as pure physical pain. Peyton is tortured by the ache in her womb, the soldiers of *The Long March* by the agony of their exhausted bodies, Nat by the cold of his cell and the torments of his imprisonment, and Sophie by the tortures of the concentration camp. In *Set This House on Fire*, physical suffering is Styron's primary metaphor for the pain of humankind's empty relationship with the universe, and the novel is shot through with characters in various stages of suffering from "abuse of the carnal envelope."

Vivid as the physical suffering of Styron's characters is, it is nothing compared to their mental and emotional anguish. Often, this mental anguish derives from their acute sense of alienation—from one another and from God. Milton, Peyton, Cass, Nat, and Sophie writhe painfully and actively, aware of a pervasive emptiness in their lives.

LIE DOWN IN DARKNESS

The structural complexities of *Lie Down in Darkness*, combined with the florid rhetoric of the novel, obscure for many readers the essentially simple causality that underlies the book. It is the story of how and why Peyton Loftis becomes insane and kills herself, tracing the roots of her tortured madness to her father's weakness and her mother's inability to love. Peyton's father, Milton, showers her with an excessive adoration that is one facet of his alcoholic self-indulgence; he smothers his daughter with a sloppy, undemanding adulation that counterpoints his wife Helen's psychotic frigidity. Helen is only able to show love in terms of compulsive formal discharge of parental obligations, bitterly resentful of the martyr role she has chosen to play. Eventually, Peyton instinctively rejects both her father's almost unnatural affection and her mother's unnatural lack of it.

By the time Peyton cuts herself loose, however, she has been emotionally crippled, unable to accept any genuine love from a series of lovers, including the Jewish artist she marries and who might have brought her peace. She retreats deeper and deeper inside herself, watching first other people and finally the real world recede before her disintegrating mind. The last major section of the novel is her tormented, insane monologue, a brilliant tour de force reminiscent of the Benjy sections of Faulkner's *The Sound and the Fury* (1929).

When *Lie Down in Darkness* was published in 1951, it was widely hailed as a significant addition to the south-

ern school of writing led by Faulkner, Ellen Glasgow, Flannery O'Connor, and Thomas Wolfe. Thematically, *Lie Down in Darkness* is not a markedly "southern" novel. Although the Loftis family is from Tidewater, Virginia, and there are mannerisms described in the book that are definitively southern, Milton's weakness, his wife's cold rage, and their daughter's breakdown are in no way regional. The story could as easily be that of a New England family, such as Eugene O'Neill's Manions. What is actually distinctive about the tragedy of the Loftises is how much it is exclusively their own, rather than a product of the dictates of fate or society. In this respect, the novel differs from Styron's later works, in which he increasingly attributes humanity's sufferings to forces beyond the individual. While the novel is a tragedy of a single family, Styron is condemning an entire generation that lost its children. In describing her parents' generation as lost, Peyton says, "They thought they were lost. They were crazy. They weren't lost. What they were doing was losing us."

If Styron traces a source of the Loftis family's deterioration, it is perhaps in their lifestyle. On one level, *Lie Down in Darkness* is almost a novel of manners, for in keeping with the Loftises' "country club" lives, much of the novel delineates social activity—parties, dances, dinners. Emblematic of this are three scenes in which Milton, Helen, and Peyton go through the motions of conventional social rituals while they are torn by violent emotions lying beneath the facade of meaningless behavior. The first of these is a dance at the country club at which Peyton tries to play the role of belle-of-the-ball while her father makes drunken love to his mistress in a cloakroom and Helen seethes at both father and daughter in a jealous rage. Later, a Christmas dinner turns into a grotesque, painful fiasco, as Helen screams insults at her daughter while Milton slobbers drunkenly. Finally, Peyton's wedding becomes a nightmare when Milton again gets drunk and sloppy, and Helen, as always thinly concealing a bitter resentment of Peyton, finally cracks, screaming "Whore!" at her daughter. In a rage, Peyton claws her mother's face with her nails and flees the family forever.

The loss of love, or rather the failure to find it, informs the entire book. The three Loftises grope at one another in despair, reaching out to one another in their separate, psychologically crippled ways for an understanding and affection that will bring them some sort of emotional peace. That peace, though, is impossible because their psychic natures are flawed beyond redemption. Sigmund Freud spins the plot: Milton loves Peyton not wisely, but too well, as she uncomfortably senses, so his love of her must always seem unrequited, and he is destined to be deserted by her at the last; Helen suffers a patent jealous hatred for Peyton, who has a capacity for love that Helen lacks, and who is stranded between the two poles of her parents' emotional inadequacy. The result is endless pain and ultimately annihilation. As Milton wails, "It was awful not to be able to love. It was hell."

It is not hell, though, but obliteration—nothingness—that truly underlies this novel. In the opening scene, Milton meets the train that brings Peyton's body home for burial. The final scene is her throwing herself to her death from a New York City rooftop. Everything between, the whole body of the novel, is an explanation of that death, and the knowledge of Peyton's unavoidable extinction hangs heavily during the entire book. The title is taken from Sir Thomas Browne's gloomy *Hydriotaphia: Or, Urn Burial* (1658), a seventeenth century meditation on the inevitability of death, and the "darkness" of the title is that of the grave. Images of death haunt the dreams of the tortured characters, and the reader is never allowed to forget the ultimate negation implicit in the agony of life.

THE LONG MARCH

The agony of life, more than the nullity of death, became the focus of Styron's fiction following *Lie Down in Darkness*. His short novel *The Long March* serves almost as a précis for the motif of pain that came to dominate Styron's writing. Not much longer than a substantial short story, *The Long March* stands between the turgid psychological weight of *Lie Down in Darkness* and the ponderous solemnity of *Set This House on Fire* like a breath of fresh air. Short, clean, concise, and plotted without a wasted word, this unpretentious novella contains some of Styron's most disciplined and readable prose. He trimmed away all the heavy rhetorical and philosophical baggage of his "big" novels, leaving before the reader only his lean and awful central subject—pain and suffering. Appropriately, the pain here is of the most basic and primitive sort—pure physical agony. Stylistically, Styron's writing of the book in 1952 was anomalous in the development of his career, for it was at this period that he was gearing up to write *Set This House on Fire*, and the stylistic and structural complexities of *Lie Down in Darkness* were being inflated to match the ambitious range of the novel to come.

Like the best of Ernest Hemingway, *The Long March* is deceptively simple—a step-by-step account of a thirty-six-mile forced march inflicted on some Marine reserves by their mindless officers and endured by the men with varying degrees of courage or cowardice, acceptance or rejection, but mainly endured with pain. The march itself is relentlessly real for the reader on page after page, the physical pain of the characters becoming a kind of rhythmic pattern in the book. If the novel has a "message," it is embodied in the final lines, in which Captain Mannix, who has undergone the march protesting its sadistic insanity, swollen and aching, confronts a sympathetic barracks maid who asks if it hurts: "His words [were] uttered . . . not with self-pity, but only with the tone of a man who, having endured and lasted, was too weary to tell her anything but what was true. 'Deed it does,' he said."

SET THIS HOUSE ON FIRE

After the critical success of *Lie Down in Darkness* and the artistic success of *The Long March*, there followed the better part of a decade before the 1960 publication of *Set This House on Fire*. Comfortably ensconced in Roxbury, prosperous, rearing a family, and moving into the center of the New York literary world, Styron's reputation grew steadily, although his literary output did not. His house, along with Plimpton's New York City apartment, became one of the new camping grounds for the old *Paris Review* crowd, and Peter Matthiessen, James Jones, and James Baldwin were frequent visitors. Throughout the late 1950's, word of his forthcoming big novel spread as Styron gave private readings from it, and the publication of *Set This House on Fire* was eagerly awaited.

The novel was indeed big; actually, it sprawled embarrassingly. In place of the personal, family tragedy of *Lie Down in Darkness*, Styron broadened his scope by giving the suffering in this novel a universal dimension and by exploring the metaphysical bases of it. It is not a family that suffers, but the world. The reader sees this world through the eyes of Peter Leverett, a Styron surrogate, but the real protagonist is Cass Kinsolving, a sensitive, drunken American artist in Italy in the 1950's who is aghast by the suffering of humanity. Much of the story is told to Leverett (and the reader) by Cass, who looks for the ultimate implications of every grain of sand. Looking back, he tells Leverett that he remembers Italy as "an infinity of remembered pain," and he finds divine aspects even in his drunkenness: "God surely had clever ways of tormenting a man, putting in his way a substance whereby He might briefly be reached, but which in the end . . . sent Him packing over the horizon trailing clouds of terror." To achieve this broadened projection, Styron enlarges his cast of characters, heightens his rhetoric, and throws the whole show on an enormous stage.

A vast parade of people moves through *Set This House on Fire*, many of them poor, sick, or abused, the rest venal and contemptible. The action is lifted from the commonplace to the melodramatic; rape, murder, and mystery dominate. The characters, except for Leverett and Cass's wife, Poppy, are exotic. Mason Flagg is a monstrous idiot typifying Victor Hugo's Quasimodo of *The Hunchback of Notre Dame* (1831). He is the "super bastard" aesthete rich boy, whose cultivated corruption is nauseating but still rich and strange. Cass deteriorates theatrically, staggering about and raving lines from Greek tragedy, a far cry from the humdrum drunkard Milton Loftis.

Heightened rhetoric is Styron's principal method of extending the scope of *Set This House on Fire*. Much of the novel reads like gothic Thomas Wolfe, from Mason's mother's description of "the horror" of her son's expulsion from prep school to Leverett's account of one of the book's several nightmares: "an abomination made of the interlocking black wings of ravens crawling and loathsome with parasites . . . a country in cataclysm and upheaval." Cass spends much of the book in deliberate blasphemy, "raving at that black, baleful, and depraved Deity who seemed coolly-minded to annihilate His creatures," when he is not suffering from delirium tremens and seeing visions of a boiling sea, or giant spiders on Mt. Vesuvius.

This rhetoric not only complements, but makes possible, the projection of much of the novel on a dream level. Styron had done this before, in a Freudian fantasy of Helen Loftis's, in one of Peyton's lover's dreams of babies burning in hell, and in Peyton's entire closing soliloquy. In *Set This House on Fire*, though, the use of dream, vision, and hallucination is so pervasive that much of the novel approaches phantasmagoria. Leverett dreams of a malevolent fiend for several pages, and has recurrent, elaborately described nightmares; Cass is repeatedly haunted, and his drunken ordeal ends with an extended vision of disaster, a passage drawing heavily on Dante and the book of Revelation. So extensive is Styron's use of dramatic and fantastic imagery that it is often difficult to tell whether he is presenting the reader with a metaphor or a dream. At one point, when Cass describes himself first making love to a beautiful girl, then suddenly "groping for an answer on some foul black shore," it is impossible to tell whether he is just thinking or hallucinating again. Cass himself probably does not know.

Although they differ in scope and ambition, *Lie Down in Darkness* and *Set This House on Fire* are essentially the same kind of novel. Both are studies in personal alienation and deterioration. Both work through an elevated rhetoric and through psychological revelation. Although *Set This House on Fire* reaches self-consciously for transcendence and philosophical universality, the novel centers on the psychological aberrations of two characters, Cass and Mason. Similar to the tragedy of the Loftis family in *Lie Down in Darkness*, theirs are individual, not universal, tragedies. In *Lie Down in Darkness*, the tragedies are individual, but they represent the failings of a self-indulgent generation. In *Set This House on Fire*, the tragedies are also individual, yet they represent the tragedies of a hedonistic generation, a generation that was decadent and destructive.

THE CONFESSIONS OF NAT TURNER

Styron called *The Confessions of Nat Turner* "a meditation on history." Its subject is not only the character of Nat Turner but also the meaning of slavery itself—what it does to people, and to society. Like Styron's previous novels, the book is a contemplation of horror, with a protagonist who becomes a victim of that horror, but in this case, the horror is not a purely personal one. Significantly, unlike the Loftises and Cass, Nat does not deteriorate, but grows through the course of the book as his comprehension of society and life grows. Nat is the richest and most psychologically complex of Styron's characters, and the historical subject matter of the work is filtered through his sensitive consciousness to produce a visionary "meditation" on the world of slavery, dreamlike in quality and poetic in execution. Southern Virginia of the 1830's, the novel's world, is very much a projection of Nat's mind—a mind produced by that world, and savaged by it.

To develop the subtlety of Nat's mind, Styron drew on all his technical and rhetorical resources. His mastery of time shifts and dream sequences, already amply demonstrated, was enhanced in this novel, and he explored a variety of rhetorical styles, varying from rural black dialect to a high Anglican style echoing Joan Didion's *A Book of Common Prayer* (1977) for Nat's more poetic utterances. Nat's mind ranges with astonishing virtuosity over his universe—the natural world, the complexities of human relations, the elusive mysteries of God, and the bitterness of mortality. An enormously sophisticated narrative persona, Nat moves fluidly across time, contemplating the painful mystery of the past, represented by his long-dead African grandmother, and of the future, represented by his own forthcoming death. Nat tells the entire novel in flashback, remembering his abortive slave rebellion and the personal and historical events leading up to it, constantly trying to cipher out the meaning of those events.

The novel is a study of the growth of knowledge and of the growth of Nat's mind. In the introspective isolation of his anguished imprisonment, he reconstructs his lifelong struggle to understand the meaning of existence. He recalls his progression from childhood, when he had no comprehension of what slavery meant, to an early adult period when he accepted his condition either bitterly or philosophically, to a final understanding of slavery in personal, societal, and moral terms. Ironically, as Nat becomes more morally and aesthetically sensitive, he becomes more insensitive in human terms, gravitating toward an acceptance of the violence that finally characterizes his revolt. Only a sudden, visionary conversion to a God of love at the end of the novel saves him from closing the book as an unrepentant apostle of retributory cruelty.

In the process of expanding his knowledge and de-

veloping his terrible vision of deliverance from slavery by violence, Nat becomes the spokesperson for two familiar Styron themes—the complexity of human psychology and the mystery of human suffering. The most self-searching of Styron's characters, Nat exhaustively explores the ambivalence and ambiguity of his feelings about race, sex, religion, and violence. Although he casts himself convincingly as a Christian prophet, Nat is no simplistic fundamentalist, for he recognizes in his own emotional turmoil the personal depths that he can plumb with only partial understanding. His psychology is the battleground of conflicting feelings, symbolized by his powerful attraction to his master's gentle daughter and his vitriolic hatred for all she represents. When he eventually kills her, neither he nor the reader can discriminate his motives. She dies imploring, "Oh, Nat, it hurts so!" and his realization of her pain is the climax of his apprehension of the myriad pains of all humankind, particularly those of his own people. In this concern, he is representative of all Styron's protagonists.

It is almost impossible to deal with *The Confessions of Nat Turner* without mentioning the storm of controversy that followed its publication and success. A number of critics maintained that the novel was historically inaccurate (for example, it portrayed Nat as having homosexual tendencies but never mentioned that there are records indicating that the real Nat Turner had a wife). Styron was also accused of demeaning a black hero, in that his Nat has reservations about his mission and is squeamish about wholesale slaughter. The real complaint against Styron, though, most thoroughly summarized in a casebook edited by John Henrik Clarke, *William Styron's Nat Turner: Ten Black Writers Respond* (1968), was that he was a white man attempting a theme that should be the province of black writers. In answer to the historical criticism, Styron and his defenders point out that *The Confessions of Nat Turner* is a work of fiction that does not pretend to be straight history, and that it violates no factual information known to Styron at the time of writing.

The second complaint, that it degrades a black hero, is more difficult to understand. Unquestionably, Styron, like any true artist, presents his hero with his neuroses, self-doubts, and weaknesses. In the main, however, Nat is without doubt a positive and even heroic character, arguably the most admirable in all Styron's fiction. Only a critic in search of a black plaster saint *sans peur et sans reproche* (without fear and without reproach) could consider the creation of as rich and sensitive a character as Nat a slur. While Styron was researching *The Confessions of Nat Turner*, Baldwin lived in Styron's cottage, and Baldwin encouraged Styron to write the book. Although Styron never acknowledged Baldwin as the model for his Nat Turner, there are similarities in thinking and speech, and Turner's sexual ambivalence may be based on Baldwin. In any case, Styron's Turner is as much a modern intellectual who ponders the effects of slavery as a historical figure.

SOPHIE'S CHOICE

Styron's novel *Sophie's Choice* was some twelve years in the works, if somewhat less in the writing, and is in every way as ambitious a novel as *The Confessions of Nat Turner*, although its rank in the Styron canon is still in question. Having dealt in earlier novels with suicide, physical agony, existential despair, and slavery, Styron chose the Holocaust as the logical next state of human misery suitable for artistic contemplation. For a long time, Styron had been moving his narrative personae closer toward the subjects of his novels, introducing clearly autobiographical narrators in *The Long March* and *Set This House on Fire*, and making *The Confessions of Nat Turner* an intensely personal first-person narrative.

For *Sophie's Choice*, Styron turned to the confessional form plied by novelists as various as Saul Bellow and Norman Mailer and poets such as Robert Lowell. The narrator of *Sophie's Choice*, a young southerner named Stingo, is, for all intents and purposes, indistinguishable from the young Styron. A young artist manqué in New York, Stingo meets and is fascinated by Sophie, a beautiful survivor of a Nazi concentration camp who is psychologically scarred by the horror she has undergone, the most ghastly aspect of which was being forced to decide which of her two children would live and which would die. Stingo is the ultimate naïf: sexually, emotionally, morally, and artistically immature. As he comes to know Sophie, he comes to know himself. Stingo is an artist in search of a subject, as Styron evidently felt that he himself had been.

Styron's problems with finding subject matter commensurate with his talents as a technician have been pointed out by William Van O' Conner in "John Updike and William Styron: The Burden of Talent" (1964) and by other critics. Styron himself acknowledged his concern with finding a fit subject for his early fiction, but he also felt that a concern with pain had been central to his earlier work. In 1970, he said, "Consciousness of pain and suffering has informed my work. . . . I hope my present work will not be so preoccupied." At that time, he was working on his military novel "The Way of the Warrior," which he eventually abandoned to write a book that returned to the pain motif with a vengeance, along with the other leitmotif of *Sophie's Choice*, that of the artist's finding of himself.

The emotional pain of Peyton Loftis is alienation from family and love. Cass Kinsolving suffers from guilt brought on by self-hatred and contemplation of human suffering. Nat Turner's ultimate pain derives from his isolation from all humankind and God. Sophie and Stingo suffer the pain of guilt. Stingo, the apotheosis of Styron's autobiographical white, Protestant characters, feels he has not "paid his dues," suffered as others have suffered, and he learns of Sophie's anguished life with a guilty voyeurism. Sophie's guilt has a specific origin in her hideous and impossible choice to doom one of her children. She also feels ashamed that in Auschwitz she somehow "suffered less" because she was the commandant's mistress and finally survived when others died. Constantly and compulsively her mind plays over the fates of those dead—her little girl, her tortured friends, and the gassed millions whom she never knew. Even memories of her murdered husband and of her father, both of whom she despised, bring her reproach and grief. The knowledge that she did what she had to gives no relief. She says, "I see that it was—beyond my control, but it is still so terrible to wake up these many mornings with the memory of that, having to live with it . . . it makes everything unbearable. Just unbearable." Soon, she will kill herself to stop the pain.

After Sophie's death, the shattered Stingo, who had just become her lover, walks on the beach trying to find some sort of personal resolution and acceptance of a world in which horror and anguish such as Sophie's exist. Her message, though, has been clear: There is no resolution. Madness and suffering of the magnitude represented by the Holocaust can be neither accepted nor understood. Sophie, like Herman Melville's Ishmael, realizes that "there is a wisdom that is woe, and there is a woe that is madness." Stingo has come to know it, too.

With the death of Sophie, Styron seems to have come full circle in his exploration of human suffering and his search for meaning in a flawed and painful world. Both Sophie and Peyton Loftis find death to be the only release from lives so agonizing and painful as to be unbearable. In both his first novel and this one, Styron leads the reader to the edge of the grave and points to it as the goal of life—"therefore it cannot be long before we lie down in darkness, and have our light in ashes." The crucial difference between *Sophie's Choice* and *Lie Down in Darkness*, however, is the character of Stingo, who like Ishmael escapes to tell the tale. The earlier novel leaves the reader in desolation, but the latter, through Stingo, holds forth the possibility of an alternative existence, one not horribly haunted by the knowledge of pain. Stingo's life is hardly one of euphoria, but it is a tenable existence compared to Sophie's untenable one. To some degree, Stingo has paid his dues through her; he has come to know pain and evil through her sacrifice, and therefore he is sadder and wiser, but not destroyed as she is. His survival counterpoints her destruction; the novel that Stingo will write grows out of her ashes and becomes her immortality.

Sophie's Choice is not a cheerful novel, or even an affirmative one, but it is not nihilistic. Perhaps Stingo's optimism at the close is unjustified. A number of critics feel that when Stingo walks on the beach after Sophie's death and finds the morning "excellent and fair," anticipating his own promising career, Styron is simply tacking on an upbeat ending hardly defensible in view of the horror explored by the novel. Similarly, Cass in *Set This House on Fire* never satisfies his thirst for metaphysical answers to terrible questions, but simply decides to stop thirsting and take up fishing. In each of Styron's novels, characters suffer, and some suffer unto death. These tragedies reveal an unjust world, not a nihilistic one—Styron's tragedies are moral pronouncements. As moral pronouncements, the novels point to the possibility of a better way.

John L. Cobbs
Updated by Roark Mulligan

OTHER MAJOR WORKS

SHORT FICTION: *A Tidewater Morning: Three Tales from Youth*, 1993.

PLAY: *In the Clap Shack*, pr. 1972.

NONFICTION: *This Quiet Dust, and Other Writings*, 1982, expanded 1993; *Darkness Visible: A Memoir of Madness*, 1990; *Havanas in Camelot: Personal Essays*, 2008.

BIBLIOGRAPHY

Casciato, Arthur D., and James L. W. West III, eds. *Critical Essays on William Styron*. Boston: G. K. Hall, 1982. Collection of critical essays that cover all of Styron's major novels and provide a more general discussion of his works. Includes bibliographical references and an index.

Clarke, John Henrik, ed. *The Second Crucifixion of Nat Turner*. 2d ed. Baltimore: Black Classic Press, 1997. A new edition, with a new introduction by Clarke, of the book originally published in 1968 as *William Styron's Nat Turner: Ten Black Writers Respond*. The essayists in this collection argue that Styron misrepresented Turner's life and activities in *The Confessions of Nat Turner*.

Coale, Samuel. *William Styron Revisited*. Boston: Twayne, 1991. Provides a brief biography and an analysis of Styron's novels. Coale devotes a chapter to each major work and includes a selected bibliography.

Cologne-Brookes, Gavin. *The Novels of William Styron: From Harmony to History*. Baton Rouge: Louisiana State University Press, 1995. Study of the influence of the modernist movement on Styron, exploring his psychological themes and analyzing his shifting patterns of discourse. Includes an analysis of Styron's later work.

Hadaller, David. *Gynicide: Women in the Novels of William Styron*. Madison, N.J.: Fairleigh Dickinson University Press, 1996. Explores the women in Styron's fiction, particularly their deaths and the meaning of these deaths. Hadaller argues that Styron's depictions force readers to question a society that victimizes women.

Mandel, Naomi. *Against the Unspeakable: Complicity, the Holocaust, and Slavery in America*. Charlottesville: University of Virginia Press, 2006. Mandel analyzes *The Confessions of Nat Turner* and other novels that deal with unspeakable events, such as American slavery and the Holocaust. She argues that defining human suffering as unspeakable enables people to negate and forget that suffering.

Morris, Robert K., and Irving Malin, eds. *The Achievement of William Styron*. Athens: University of Georgia Press, 1975. Provides essays by various critics on Styron's fiction up to *Sophie's Choice*. The essay by Morris and Malin on Styron's career as a visionary novelist is a good introduction to his work.

West, James L. W., III, ed. *Conversations with William Styron*. Jackson: University Press of Mississippi, 1985. Collected interviews with Styron in which Styron attempts to "restore a little balance," giving his side to the many controversies that his books have created.

_____. *William Styron: A Life*. New York: Random House, 1998. The first comprehensive biography of Styron, West's extraordinary work lucidly and cogently connects events in Styron's life to his fiction. This is an essential work for anyone who wishes to understand Styron and his writing.

Zetterberg Pettersson, Eva. *The Old World Journey: National Identity in Four American Novels from 1960 to 1973*. Uppsala, Sweden: Uppsala University Press, 2005. An analysis of *Set This House on Fire* and other novels about Americans traveling to Europe that were published in the 1960's and early 1970's. Zetterberg Pettersson demonstrates how the European journey is a means of raising questions about American identity.

ITALO SVEVO

Born: Trieste, Austrian Empire (now in Italy); December 19, 1861
Died: Motta di Livenza, Italy; September 13, 1928
Also known as: Aron Hector Schmitz

PRINCIPAL LONG FICTION

Una vita, 1892 (*A Life*, 1963)
Senilità, 1898 (*As a Man Grows Older*, 1932; also known as *Emilio's Carnival*, 2001)
La coscienza di Zeno, 1923 (*Confessions of Zeno*, 1930; also known as *Zeno's Conscience*, 2001)

OTHER LITERARY FORMS

The major short stories of Italo Svevo (SVAY-voh) have been translated into English, as have the fragments of an incomplete novel, in *Further Confessions of Zeno* (1969). Eight stories written between 1910 and 1928, only three of which were published in Svevo's lifetime, were collected under the title *Corto viaggio sentimentale, e altri racconti inediti* (1949; *Short Sentimental Journey, and Other Stories*, 1966). The standard Italian edition of Svevo's work is the four-volume *Opera omnia* (1966-1969), which includes letters, plays, stories, essays, and novels.

ACHIEVEMENTS

Italo Svevo had few readers and virtually no literary reputation until he reached the age of sixty-four. He published articles, short stories, and a serialization of *As a Man Grows Older* in the Trieste newspaper *L'indipendente* (for which he also worked as an editor), brought out book editions of his first two novels at his own expense, and then for twenty-five years published nothing at all. The few local reviews that these works received were sometimes kind, but generally uncomprehending, and they were critical of Svevo's faulty Italian. These reproaches, according to the biography written by his wife, Livia Veneziani Svevo, and Lina Galli, "wounded him deeply" and increased his lack of trust in himself.

The issue of Svevo's style has not subsided. It was raised again when, after the publication of *Confessions of Zeno*, James Joyce, Valéry Larbaud, and Benjamin Crémieux brought Svevo to French attention as a master of the modern novel. Accused of having ignored one of their country's best writers, some Italian reviewers defended themselves by noting what critic Giulio Caprin called Svevo's "incredibly poor and confused language." This debate over Svevo's language must be understood in the context of his multilingual background and of traditional Italian literary expectations. The Triestine dialect Svevo spoke naturally underlies his own psychological and linguistic patterns and those of his heroes; nevertheless, he wished to be recognized as an Italian writer and thus attempted to write in the Tuscan-based language Alessandro Manzoni had chosen for his *I promessi sposi* (1840-1842; *The Betrothed*, 1951). The mature style Svevo developed amid these pressures is an antiliterary one, a kind of business Italian, neither formal nor poetic, that is quite suitable to the private, middle-class atmosphere of his novels.

After the publication of *Confessions of Zeno*, Svevo was recognized as an important figure in the development of the modern psychological novel, bearing comparison with writers such as Marcel Proust, Franz Kafka, and Joyce. His reputation has grown slowly since his death, and he is now generally credited with taking the Italian novel beyond naturalism and bringing it into the twentieth century.

BIOGRAPHY

Italo Svevo was born Aron Hector Schmitz on December 19, 1861, in the multiracial city of Trieste. Trieste was then a territory of the Habsburg Empire, despite its cultural identity with Italy. The pen name Italo Svevo ("The Italian Swabian") reflects Svevo's mixed background. His father, Francesco, was descended from German Jews and lived as a youth in Austria, Hungary, and Yugoslavia, but regarded himself as an Italian and married an Italian-speaking Jewish woman, Allegra Moravia. Francesco, who had become successful in the glassware business, sent his sons to a German boarding school to prepare them for commercial careers. In his six years in Germany, Svevo took a greater interest in literature than in commercial studies, and he read, among others, Friedrich Schiller, William Shakespeare, Nikolai Gogol, and Ivan Turgenev. When he returned to Trieste in 1878, he was secretly determined to have a literary career and wanted to study classical Italian literature in Florence. Eager to see Svevo begin his business career,

his father refused to send him to Florence but did allow him to enroll at the Istituto Superiore Commerciale Revoltella; here, Svevo again used his time to study literature instead of commerce.

In 1880, Svevo's father lost much of his money (largely because of generosity to relatives) and degenerated both mentally and physically. Svevo accepted a position as a bank clerk, which he found tedious and demeaning. Meanwhile, he read Italian classics and French novels (by Émile Zola, Gustave Flaubert, and Alphonse Daudet) in the evenings at a public library; frequented cafés and theaters with his painter friend Umberto Veruda, whose flamboyant bohemian style complemented Svevo's more timid and bourgeois manner; wrote a few articles for Italian Nationalist periodicals; and attempted to write plays.

After his favorite brother died in 1886, Svevo began his first novel, *A Life*, which he had published at his own expense. He had an affair with a woman named Giuseppina Zergol and drew on this episode for the material of his second novel, *As a Man Grows Older*. Svevo's intentions to remain a bachelor were dispelled during his mother's final illness, when he was touched by the kindness of his cousin Livia Veneziani. Livia was a practicing Roman Catholic, though a quarter Jewish by descent, and thirteen years Svevo's junior. Her wealthy family opposed the engagement but eventually relented; the couple had a civil marriage ceremony in July, 1896. The marriage was apparently an affectionate and satisfying one, though Svevo persisted in analyzing and discussing his contradictory and often unflattering feelings about his wife, and she remained a religious, loyal, loving, but socially conservative and nonintellectual woman.

Livia's parents manufactured and sold an internationally used submarine paint that her father had invented. The couple lived at her parents' house, and eventually Svevo went to work for the Veneziani firm. Throughout these years, Svevo continued writing, occasionally publishing short fiction or articles in *L'indipendente*. When *As a Man Grows Older*, again self-published in its book vowed to give up writing altogether. He took up the violin, became more involved in business, and confined his writing to diary entries, bits of self-analysis, and occasional fables or short plays. He supervised the setting up of two new paint factories, one in Murano, Italy, and the other in England. He never regarded himself as a successful businessman and seemed surprised at his usefulness to the firm. Still, this active life soothed him and helped him accept his literary disappointments.

The year 1907 was to become—in retrospect—a turning point in Svevo's literary life. Wishing to improve his English, Svevo engaged an aspiring Irish writer then living in Trieste to tutor him. The tutor was Joyce. When Svevo confided his own literary ambitions and gave Joyce a copy of *As a Man Grows Older*, he was astonished and gratified by Joyce's opinion that Svevo's novels had been unfairly neglected. Svevo, in turn, encouraged Joyce by his response to *A Portrait of the Artist as a Young Man* (1916) and became one of the several models for Leopold Bloom in Joyce's *Ulysses* (1922).

World War I brought turbulence to Trieste and a halt to business. Svevo kept the Austrians from learning the secret formula for the paint, but they did confiscate the factory. Many of his family and friends were in Italy or Switzerland, and Svevo filled the spare time by making drafts of his memoirs and reading the works of Sigmund Freud. He was fascinated by Freud's theories but doubted the efficacy or even the desirability of psychoanalytic therapy.

After the war, Trieste became part of Italy, an event that Svevo found personally liberating. He said that Italy, whose critics had ignored him before, had now come to him, and he—now an Italian citizen—again wished to write an Italian novel. At the age of fifty-eight, he outlined and began writing *Confessions of Zeno*. This novel might also have gone without praise except for the efforts of Joyce, to whom Svevo sent a copy. Within a few months, Svevo was spoken of in Paris as a great modern writer; the Italian poet Eugenio Montale read *Confessions of Zeno* in Paris and returned to proclaim Svevo's work in Italy. Translations were made; Svevo received letters from readers and invitations from literary circles. Svevo wrote several more short stories, including *Una burla riuscita* (1929; *The Hoax*, 1929), which gives an ironic view of literary fame, and began a new novel continuing the story of Zeno into old age. During this period of literary rejuve-

Italo Svevo with his wife and daughter.
(The Granger Collection, New York)

nation, Svevo's health was weakening. He often told Livia he had premonitions of his own death. An automobile accident on September 12, 1928, injured his leg and brought on a fatal heart attack.

Livia survived him until 1957, devoting herself to his works by answering letters and making arrangements with editors. Unable to register herself as an Aryan in World War II, she declared herself a Jew and spent two years hiding from the Nazis and writing a biography of Svevo.

ANALYSIS

The twenty-five-year hiatus between the writing of Italo Svevo's first novels and his third, *Confessions of Zeno*, which is probably his best and certainly his most innovative work, makes it risky to generalize about his themes and techniques. In *Confessions of Zeno*, he achieves a dimension of comedy that is unique in modern literature, a comedy akin to Shakespeare's in the inclusiveness of its sympathy and vision. This comedy is possible because Svevo allows the novel to expand to the limits of his own consciousness. Critic Naomi Lebowitz has listed three "zones" in which the Svevian consciousness moves: the bourgeois order represented by daily family life and business transactions, a zone guided by chronology, manners, and morals; the zone of desires, motivations, and "unchronological" mental activity; and third, an overarching zone of comic objectivity and lyric humor from which human life appears a mere speck within the huge realm of nature.

In all of his works, Svevo focuses on the incongruity between a man's goals and his actual possibilities, particularly on the ways in which self-deception, vanity, rationalization, and misdirected idealism prevent him from correcting this disparity. Hence, Svevo's fictional world shares an absurd, incoherent quality with those of other modern writers, such as Franz Kafka. Most of Svevo's protagonists find themselves unable to shape their own lives; they are, by bourgeois standards, inept, weak-willed, insignificant. (Svevo intended to title his first novel *Un inetto* ["the inept one"], but the publisher refused to offer a book with such an unappealing title.) In *A Life*, a book notably influenced by Zolaesque naturalism, Svevo clearly describes the business and social world Alfonso Nitti wants to enter and shows that the gap between Nitti and that world is unbridgeable. With *As a Man Grows Older*, Svevo discovers a name and a metaphor for the condition of his protagonists: senility. Emilio Brentani is not literally old, but he is detached from reality as the senile are; he adapts his perceptions to suit his illusions and makes himself comfortable. The humor in the two early novels derives almost exclusively from the ironic observations of the narrator, because Nitti and Brentani are seldom able to stand enough outside themselves to become self-aware. The ideas of fate and "Mother Nature" that Svevo makes explicit in *Confessions of Zeno* operate only as authorial imperatives in the earlier novels.

When Svevo wrote the story of Zeno Cosini, he was himself a successful businessperson and head of a family; he possessed the distancing, harmonizing perspec-

tive he had lacked before. Yet he had maintained his fascination with the mental workings of personality, a sense of the lively interior life each person carries on despite his apparent conformity with society, and he had augmented that fascination by his reading of Freud. Freud reinforced Svevo's own perceptions of mental life and provided him with names and patterns for the various negotiations a person must make between his internal and external life. Svevo's debt to Freud has been heavily emphasized by critics, partly because *Confessions of Zeno* was the first novel to make use of Freud's work. The editorial fiction of that novel (that it is a notebook kept by Zeno at the request of his analyst, Dr. S.) and the analyst's diagnosis, late in the book (that Zeno suffers from an Oedipus complex), are two obvious examples of this use. It is, however, a mistake to assume that Svevo offers a novelized presentation of Freudian theory or that Svevo's concerns were the same as Freud's. Like Freud, he was interested in the intertwining of significant psychic processes with ordinary, conscious activities, and particularly in the compulsive aspects of behavior.

Svevo differed from Freud in that he disapproved of attempts to cleanse human beings of their weaknesses. He believed that unconscious, morally unacceptable motivations often emerge in positive social or moral actions. In Zeno's case, it often happens that he does a good thing for a bad reason, such as when he proposes to Augusta out of spite over her sister Ada's engagement to Guido Speir. Though his love for Ada, or his idea that he loves her, continues to direct many of his actions, it also determines him to treat Augusta kindly, allowing her to love him in return. His marriage with Augusta is ideal for him, whereas one with Ada would have been disastrous. In suppressing his desires and hostilities, Zeno has floundered into happiness; he has found a way to live comfortably in both the bourgeois and personal zones. Svevo thus transformed the Freudian material to suit his own social and aesthetic conceptions.

Svevo also introduced the themes of psychosomatic illness and hypochondria into the novel. Zeno's body is mapped by the pains he has developed at moments of moral and emotional crisis. Throughout his life, he longs to become innocent and healthy, though the exact nature of his guilt and illnesses varies. Connections between his mind and body are clear even to Zeno himself, and what he seeks is not so much a cure as a diagnosis of his malady. Life, for Svevo, must include sickness, for sickness is part of the unpredictability and variousness of life for which death is the only "cure." The apparently healthy men in his novels, Stefano Balli and Guido Speir, for example, make little headway in the world. (Healthy, fecund women, such as Angiolina Zarri and Augusta, do survive; perhaps they are not susceptible to the modern disease of consciousness.) The trick is to take sickness as a warning from reality and use it as an adversary against which to strengthen oneself, using the available weapons of imagination, humor, and wit.

Svevo deals with the theme of disease as a universal, philosophical problem as well. There was a vague but prevalent idea in Europe at the turn of the century that society as a whole was ill, that the fin de siècle was a *mal de siècle*. This trend, Svevo thought, was a dangerous one, because it either permitted a self-consciously tragic resignation to failure or invited fanatical cures (such as Nazism was to be). Svevo asserted that imperfection was essential to life. If humans do not interfere with Mother Nature—Svevo's Darwinian overseer of the universe—too much, nature keeps life in balance. Nature's ways of doing so are surprising and unpredictable, and it has manias of its own for reproduction and for mystery.

In response to Guido's adages, Zeno comes up with his own term to describe life: It is, he says, "original." Originality may not at first seem to be a profound conception of life, but it stands out brightly and, indeed, sensibly, next to other worldviews of Svevo's era. Caught between his troublesome, old-fashioned conscience and his strange, unfathomable consciousness, modern humans—in Svevo's comic view—may yet survive and even enjoy life if they feel its originality. Life is not predictable and knowable as it was in traditional, religious, or bourgeois schemes; however, it is not hopelessly incomprehensible, as it is in the view of many modernists.

The bourgeois protagonists of Svevo's mature works live in the world not as its proprietors and not as its outcasts. They are among Mother Nature's biological experiments, and their fitness for survival depends on their ability to relinquish willful control and to adapt harmoniously. Such adaptation, as Zeno demonstrates, is possible, but it is not assured. The apocalyptic vision that concludes *Confessions of Zeno*—a startlingly accurate prediction of nuclear weapons—issues a warning of what can happen if humans use technology out of aggressive weakness. Against that possibility, Svevo's modest doctrine of originality remains a compellingly heroic one.

A LIFE

Of Svevo's two early novels, *A Life* and *As a Man Grows Older*, the second has retained far greater interest for the general reader than the first. In *A Life*, Svevo attempted to combine the naturalism he had learned from Flaubert and Zola with his own sense of the importance of individual consciousness. The protagonist of *A Life*, Alfonso Nitti, is a country boy who is unable to achieve independence from his childhood and who fails in his attempt to love and work in a sterile city environment. Nitti's incompetence and lack of direction bring him one disappointment after another; finally, without regret, he commits suicide. Nitti's life might be considered tragic except that, like Flaubert's Frédéric Moreau, Nitti is too weak a character to embody the resonance of tragedy. With *A Life*, Svevo exorcised the ghost of naturalism and cleared the way for the greater psychological penetration and more intricate form of *As a Man Grows Older*.

AS A MAN GROWS OLDER

Emilio Brentani, the protagonist of *As a Man Grows Older*, is a thirty-five-year-old insurance company clerk who once published a novel, thereby acquiring a local reputation as an intellectual. Like Nitti, he is inept and self-deluded; sheer inertia prevents him from writing again, but he considers himself to be in continual preparation for greater achievements. He lives with his unmarried sister, Amalia, who keeps house for him and leads an even narrower, more solitary life than his own. When the novel opens, Brentani has just begun a flirtation with a young woman named Angiolina Zarri. He tells himself that, because he cannot write, he will allow himself to live out the desires he might otherwise convert into art. The narrator makes it clear that Angiolina has subtly accosted Brentani, but he believes that he is himself initiating an affair with an innocent, inexperienced girl. This self-deception about their first meeting sets a pattern that plagues Brentani throughout the relationship. His attempts to assuage his guilt, to imagine Angiolina as a respectable woman, and to separate his emotions from his sexual desires form the main plot of *As a Man Grows*

Older. The reader, drawn into Brentani's thoughts, shares his confusion about what Angiolina really is for a while; gradually the discrepancies between her behavior and Brentani's ideals become ironically funny.

Angiolina is, in fact, a poor, stylish, good-natured prostitute. Yet Brentani, trapped in a society that perceives women as either wives or whores, continually misapprehends her. In the first part of the novel, he refrains from consummating his love for her and indulges in various fantasies to justify his involvement with her and consequent neglect of his sister. He convinces himself that he is doing a generous service by educating Angiolina in the ways of genteel behavior. He is enthralled by her beauty, her strong, healthy appearance, her sexuality. Both Amalia and Brentani's sculptor friend, Stefano Balli, are upset by Brentani's attachment to Angiolina. Amalia is lonely without even her brother's company; there is no social life for a respectable unmarried woman, and she has repressed her own need for love. Now, jealous of her brother, who has exposed her to the possibilities of romance, Amalia falls hopelessly in love with Balli. Entirely absorbed in his own affair, Brentani does not notice his sister's quiet suffering.

Balli is a physically imposing, sexually aggressive man, as much Brentani's opposite as Angiolina is Amalia's. He sees immediately that Brentani's adventure in love cannot end happily and resolves to "cure" his deluded friend of his infatuation. He also hopes to regain his friend's company, for Balli—though he has many mistresses (Angiolina herself is attracted to him) whom he dominates entirely—cannot do without the male friendship and admiration of Brentani. When Balli encounters Angiolina with another of her lovers, he rushes to bring Brentani to witness the betrayal. Vowing to give up Angiolina, Brentani returns home and overhears his sister speaking passionately in her dreams about her love for Balli.

Brentani breaks with Angiolina and then ineptly sets about helping Amalia by banishing Balli from the household. He rationalizes his action as a familial duty and intends to devote himself to Amalia, but the brother and sister are unable to console each other. Amalia turns secretly to alcohol, while Brentani attempts to write a novel about love but finds he cannot make it realistic. Instead, he takes up with Angiolina again, this time as a cynical lover claiming the sexual favors from her that his idealized version of her prevented him from taking before. He demeans himself by helping her compose a deceitful letter to her nominal fiancé. Returning home after writing that letter, Brentani finds Amalia delirious with fever, gravely ill. Nearly paralyzed by this crisis, he seeks help from a neighbor, Signora Chierici, and from Balli. During the long, gripping scene of Amalia's death, Balli comes to love her in his way, with an aesthete's admiration for the spectacle of her strength and goodness. Signora Chierici's compassionate care of Amalia, with whom she has been only slightly acquainted, impresses Brentani and he attempts—later—to adopt her credo of devotion to the needs of the living.

Yet, even while Amalia is dying, Brentani cannot resist his wish to keep an appointment with Angiolina. His mind, vacillating between grief and desire, seeks wildly for explanations: He tries blaming Angiolina for his sister's death, blaming himself, and making a complex analogy between the impassive destruction of the sea, for which no one is to blame, and the destruction in his own life. When he finds Angiolina dressed for another engagement, he becomes angry and calls her, for the first time, a whore. As she runs away, he throws a handful of pebbles at her, missing. Humiliated and enraged, Brentani nevertheless continues his mental drama of image-making and logic-chopping; such conversions of reality into private perception and memory are Brentani's method of psychic survival, the premature senility suggested by the novel's Italian title.

As a Man Grows Older closes on a retrospective note: Brentani's grief at Amalia's death and his love and resentment of Angiolina have been gradually replaced by a simple need for quiet and security. In his imagination, he melds the two women into one figure, a beautiful, warm-blooded, sad, thoughtful symbol of a brighter future for humanity. This image, which Joyce admired and memorized when he first read Svevo's work, appropriately causes the elements of the novel to converge within Brentani's mind; despite its patterned quartet of contrasting characters and its dramatic scenes, this novel represents a foray into Svevo's exploration of interior life. By itself, *As a Man Grows Older* is a fine example of the "well-made" novel, and it displays Svevo's novelistic skills and his acute sensitivity to the ironies of mental activity. For readers interested in Svevo's later development, it sketches a territory that Svevo returned to chart in *Confessions of Zeno*.

CONFESSIONS OF ZENO

In *Confessions of Zeno*, Svevo allows the middle-aged hero, Zeno Cosini, to narrate his own story. Thus, Zeno's voice, like Huck's in Mark Twain's *Adventures of Huckleberry Finn* (1884), provides a unified tone for the novel. With some unity established by the character's voice, Svevo is free to abandon the structure of the traditional "well-made" novel he had perfected in *As a Man Grows Older* for other, more idiosyncratic structural devices. This novel, often called the first modern Italian novel, does not present a coherent plot of events linked by cause and effect; rather, it offers Zeno's recollections and meditations about his life—his parents, his habits, his family and friends, his enterprises in business, his attempts to understand his mind. Zeno Cosini is a typical Svevian hero (or antihero) in that he finds himself helpless to act against his own desires, the plans of others, or the events of the world at large. Yet, the ironic differences between wishes and results that Svevo relentlessly exposed in *A Life* and *As a Man Grows Older* by dividing the sensibilities of the self-deluded protagonists from those of the knowing narrators are, in *Confessions of Zeno*, merged within the single—but multifarious—character of Zeno.

The Italian title of this novel, *La coscienza di Zeno*, contains a word for which there is no single equivalent in English: *Coscienza* means both "conscience" and "consciousness." Unable to render the full implications of *coscienza*, the translator instead chose the title *Confessions*, which neatly describes the form of the novel and suggests the transitional moral atmosphere of Zeno's times by its reminder of Saint Augustine's religious meditations and of Jean-Jacques Rousseau's secular autobiography. Zeno's confessions are actually a sort of memoir that he has written at the request of a psychoanalyst called Dr. S., whom he has seen about his neuroses. Later, when Zeno refuses to continue Dr. S.'s treatment, the vengeful doctor keeps and publishes Zeno's writings. The theme of a patient-analyst relationship and the theme of mental health are evident throughout the book. Dr. S.'s pronouncements, which Zeno quotes, provide a separate view of Zeno; further, the doctor's preface includes a warning that Zeno's autobiography is a mixture of truths and falsehoods and suggests that the analyst may not be entirely competent, for it is against Freudian procedure to encourage self-analysis. These contradictory opening gambits are appropriate because, in this novel, Svevo is not concerned to present a single "true" version of life, but rather to investigate the many truths of experience that even an ordinary man like Zeno Cosini may encounter.

Zeno writes his confessions from 1914 to 1915, dividing his life story into six chapters that do not adhere to a strictly chronological time scheme. The chapter titles represent concerns that have occupied Zeno during his life as a bourgeois Triestine; the events of his childhood and youth appear in a double perspective as Zeno remembers his experience but also modifies it with the distancing irony and humor of the years that have passed. The opening chapter introduces "the dance of the last cigarette"—Zeno's habit of smoking and resolving to give up smoking, which is a behavior pattern that repeats itself several times in the novel. Zeno marks significant occasions in his life, such as his father's death or a change of his field of study, by a vow to quit smoking. He chooses, by an intricate private numerology, the date and time when he will smoke his last cigarette and writes them down. Last cigarettes have, for Zeno, a better taste than others, for they represent a victory of willpower over the body's weakness and give hope of health in the future. The resolutions cannot be kept, however, because it is the act of renouncing that is satisfying. The dance of the last cigarette represents a transaction Zeno makes between his unconscious mind, Freud's id, and his conscience or ego in order to outwit the latter and secure a continuing pleasure.

Similar patterns appear in Zeno's relations with his mistress, wife, and brother-in-law. Though Zeno seldom keeps his resolutions to become well-behaved and healthy, stronger forces of moral expectation, Mother Nature, or mere chance often intervene to produce an unexpected and happy result. Thus, Zeno, like the Stoic philosopher who is his namesake, understands that the universe is paradoxical and can glory in its changeable originality even when it subverts his own intentions.

Confessions of Zeno deals, as the chapter titles suggest ("The Death of My Father," "The Story of My Marriage," "Wife and Mistress," "A Business Partnership," "Psychoanalysis"), with events that are predictably major in any middle-class life and in many realistic novels of moral education, yet it treats them, so to speak, from the underside. Zeno's quirky personality and confusion of motives and rationalizations are interwoven with the social activity of parties, funerals, weddings, business deals, births, and war. Though Zeno is driven by a desire to find himself innocent, he lives in a world where the categories of good and evil are unclear or even inverted. In trying to keep his dying father in bed as the doctor has ordered, Zeno creates the impression that he is trying to prevent his father from rising up for the air he craves; the old man struggles to his feet and strikes Zeno on the cheek as he falls to the floor. Vainly, Zeno tries to explain that he is not at fault, but his father is already dead. Thus, Zeno feels guilt for his father's death and for his own survival. He finds solace only in becoming a patriarch himself.

Life is infinitely unpredictable, however, and Zeno often receives forgiveness when he does not deserve it. When, suffering remorse over his adultery with Carla, he murmurs "Poor Cosini," his wife understands his words as a sign that he is dreading old age and death and comforts him generously. Augusta's kindness and naïveté do not demean her; they not only make Zeno love her more but also forward Mother Nature's amoral but life-sustaining purposes. Carla eventually abandons Zeno and marries her singing master (whom Zeno had chosen) because Zeno has inadvertently convinced her that he loves his wife. In Svevo's fiction, unconscious guilt and the complexes it produces are not analyzed in isolation; Svevo is interested in the social manifestations of interior life, in the ways Mother Nature reroutes infidelities back to the marriage bed. He shows that affection may survive and even thrive on the conflicting needs of conscience and consciousness. In *Confessions of Zeno*, the transforming agent, the nourishment for the flowering of affection, is humor. Thus the larger pattern of this comic novel, in which Zeno participates but which he does not wholly perceive, confounds the logic of bourgeois morality without overturning its purposes.

The ending of *Confessions of Zeno* surprises many readers. Isolated, as Svevo himself was, from his family by the war, Zeno continues the investment speculations

he began when he salvaged Guido's fortune. He buys whatever commodities are offered him, holds them, and sells them at a profit when the war creates a shortage. In an essay, Svevo wrote that war, unlike the animals' struggle for survival, destroys all sides, all that is fought for, for generations to come. Zeno's vision of the destruction of life by "spectacled man," bent on improving the world by using implements that subvert natural selection, is an appropriate culmination of the themes of health and sickness, willpower and reconciliation, that have run through *Confessions of Zeno*. The man who would blow up the earth is a weak being who does not accept his weakness. The Svevian hero, too, is weak, but he is content to find humor in his condition and satisfied by the affection and small successes that come his way.

Carol J. Sklenicka

OTHER MAJOR WORKS

SHORT FICTION: *Una burla riuseita*, 1929 (*The Hoax*, 1929); *La novella del buon vecchio e della bella fanciulla*, 1930 (*The Nice Old Man and the Pretty Girl, and Other Stories*, 1930); *Corto viaggio sentimentale e altri racconti inediti*, 1949 (*Short Sentimental Journey, and Other Stories*, 1966); *Further Confessions of Zeno*, 1969.

NONFICTION: *James Joyce*, 1950 (lecture given in 1927); *Corrispondenza*, 1953; *Saggi e pagini sparse*, 1954 (essays).

MISCELLANEOUS: *Opera omnia*, 1966-1969 (4 volumes; Bruno Maier, editor).

BIBLIOGRAPHY

Bartoloni, Paolo. *Interstitial Writing: Calvino, Caproni, Sereni, and Svevo*. Market Harborough, England: Troubadour, 2003. An examination of the literary and philosophical foundations of works by four Italian writers, with a chapter comparing Svevo and Italo Calvino. For the advanced student.

Dombroski, Robert S. "The Foundations of Italian Modernism: Pirandello, Svevo, Gadda." In *The Cambridge Companion to the Italian Novel*, edited by Peter Bondanella and Andrea Ciccarelli. New York: Cambridge University Press, 2003. This introductory overview of Italian literature includes Dombrowski's essay, which defines Svevo as a modernist writer and compares his work to that of Luigi Pirandello and Carlo Emilio Gadda.

Furbank, Philip N. *Italo Svevo: The Man and the Writer*. Berkeley: University of California Press, 1966. In one of the first major works on Svevo in English, Furbank considers Svevo to be the creator of modern Italian fiction. The book contains a biography of Svevo, followed by literary analyses of his works.

Gatt-Rutter, John. *Italo Svevo: A Double Life*. New York: Oxford University Press, 1988. Gatt-Rutter stresses the duality of Svevo's life: a writer and businessman, an atheist who converted from Judaism to Catholicism, and a socialist who was a successful capitalist. While it is short on literary criticism, this remains an excellent source on the details of Svevo's life and is based on letters and other primary sources.

Lebowitz, Naomi. *Italo Svevo*. New Brunswick, N.J.: Rutgers University Press, 1978. An excellent study that focuses on Svevo's writing rather than on his life. Lebowitz regards Svevo as the founder of modern Italian literature and as one of the great modernists, ranked with James Joyce, Franz Kafka, and William Faulkner.

Minghelli, Giuliana. *In the Shadow of the Mammoth: Italo Svevo and the Emergence of Modernism*. Toronto, Ont.: University of Toronto Press, 2002. Minghelli provides a close analysis of Svevo's novels and short stories, describing the philosophers and contemporary writers who influenced his work and exploring his contribution to modernism.

Moloney, Brian. *Italo Svevo: A Critical Introduction*. Edinburgh, Scotland: Edinburgh University Press, 1974. An excellent critical introduction to Svevo's work that includes chapters on his novels and short fiction. Includes a bibliography.

Schächter, Elizabeth. *Origin and Identity: Essays on Svevo and Trieste*. Leeds, England: Northern Universities Press, 2000. Collection of essays analyzing Svevo's three novels, examining the structure, irony, and narration of these books and other aspects of his life and fiction. The opening chapter discusses Trieste, the city where he was born and a place that figures prominently in his work.

Svevo, Livia Veneziani. *Memoir of Italo Svevo*. Marlboro, Vt.: Marlboro Press, 1990. A memoir by Svevo's widow that captures his humor and gentle nature. Includes many of his letters and an appendix with a 1927 lecture by Svevo on James Joyce.

Weiss, Beno. *Italo Svevo*. Boston: Twayne, 1987. Weiss considers Svevo to be one of the seminal figures in modern European literature. Stresses the divided nature of Svevo's life and the importance of Judaism to his life and literature. Brief biographical overview, followed by chapters on Svevo's major works.

GRAHAM SWIFT

Born: London, England; May 4, 1949
Also known as: Graham Colin Swift

PRINCIPAL LONG FICTION

The Sweet Shop Owner, 1980
Shuttlecock, 1981
Waterland, 1983
Out of This World, 1988
Ever After, 1992
Last Orders, 1996
The Light of Day, 2003
Tomorrow, 2007

OTHER LITERARY FORMS

In addition to his long fiction, Graham Swift has published numerous short stories in various magazines such as the *London Review* and *Punch*. With the success of his first novels, some of his early short fiction was collected in *Learning to Swim, and Other Stories* (1982). Swift's short stories offer in microcosm a number of themes and techniques subsequently explored in his novels; indeed, they often constitute excerpts from novels in progress. For example, "About the Eel" appeared in *Granta* in 1983 and subsequently became a chapter in *Waterland*; similarly, "Plastic," published in *Granta* in

1991, was incorporated into *Ever After*. Swift has also published a few nonfiction essays, but he has in general devoted his writing career almost exclusively to long fiction.

ACHIEVEMENTS

Graham Swift's work has been recognized with a number of the most prestigious international literary awards and has been translated into more than twenty languages. Although some of his contemporaries are more prolific, few have achieved Swift's status in the literary world. In 1983, Swift was identified by the literary journal *Granta* as one of twenty of the best young British novelists, in the company of such writers as Martin Amis, Kazuo Ishiguro, and Salman Rushdie. His second novel, *Shuttlecock*, won the Geoffrey Faber Memorial Prize. With his third novel, *Waterland*, Swift won numerous accolades, including the Guardian Fiction Prize, the Winifred Holtby Memorial Prize, and Italy's Premio Grinzane Cavour. *Waterland* was also nominated for the Booker Prize, the most prestigious literary award presented to novelists from Britain and the Commonwealth, and it is widely viewed as the best novel of the 1980's not to win the award. A year later, Swift was elected a fellow of the Royal Society of Literature. In 1992, his novel *Ever After* was awarded France's Prix du Meilleur Livre Étranger, and with his sixth novel, *Last Orders*, Swift won the Booker Prize that had eluded him thirteen years earlier. Several of Swift's novels have been transformed into films notable for the prestigious actors they have attracted. *Waterland* (1992), for example, stars Jeremy Irons and Ethan Hawke, and *Last Orders* (2001) includes such actors as Michael Caine, Tom Courtenay, and Bob Hoskins.

BIOGRAPHY

The son of Sheila Swift and Allan Swift, a former World War II navy pilot turned civil servant, Graham Colin Swift was born near London in 1949. Early on, his parents moved to south London, where Swift continued to make his home in adulthood. As a schoolboy, Swift earned a scholarship to the prestigious Dulwich College (alumni include P. G. Wodehouse and Michael Ondaatje) before being admitted to Cambridge University's Queen's College, from which he earned his B.A. in 1970

and an M.A. in 1975. From 1970 to 1973 Swift attended York University, ostensibly working on a doctoral dissertation titled "The City in Literature"; however, he spent his time refining his creative prose skills, producing the draft of a novel that he subsequently abandoned. While at York, Swift met the woman who would become his longtime partner—then an undergraduate English major—writer Candice Rodd.

Having exhausted funds from the British Academy, Swift taught for a year in Greece, and during most of the 1970's he was a part-time teacher or lecturer in and around London. With the success of *Waterland*, Swift was able to devote his professional life to writing. Typically he averages four or five years between novels, but, as he has established on numerous occasions, much of that time is taken up with book tours, lectures, presentations, and other promotional activities expected by publishers. Swift has often expressed discomfort at this aspect of his writing life. At the same time, he is no recluse; when, for example, Iran's Ayatollah Khomeini issued a fatwa calling for the death of author Salman Rushdie in 1989 for the publication of his novel *The Satanic Verses* (1988), Swift quickly and publicly defended his close friend. He also cofounded the International Committee for the Defense of Salman Rushdie. In general, however, Swift has refused to discuss his personal life in any detail; consequently, few biographical details are available on the author.

ANALYSIS

Graham Swift is one of a number of British writers who emerged in the early 1980's to revitalize the English novel by experimenting with new thematic concerns without sacrificing the genre's roots in realism. Among these are Peter Ackroyd, Julian Barnes, A. S. Byatt, and Penelope Lively. Swift's work shares with theirs a concern for the relationship between fiction and history, between memory and the reconstruction of the past. His novels almost exclusively employ one or more first-person perspectives, and the reader is left to contemplate the "gap" between what one might consider objective reality and how that reality is constructed or refracted by the respective narrators. These narrators are not so much unreliable as they are both the creators and the products of their own pasts. Swift's novels as a whole are marked by the absence of communication, and it is never clear to the reader to whom the narrators' words are directed. In this sense, they often read as internal and reluctant confessions, marked in many instances by the desire for personal exculpation.

THE SWEET SHOP OWNER

Swift's early work draws on a number of modernist techniques, such as stream of consciousness, shifting perspectives, and a concern for the experience and passing of time. This is particularly true of Swift's first novel, *The Sweet Shop Owner*, which offers a single June day in the life of Willy Chapman. The allusion to Virginia Woolf's *Mrs. Dalloway* (1925), and more distantly to James Joyce's *Ulysses* (1922), is no accident. *The Sweet Shop Owner* opens with Chapman contemplating a letter from his daughter severing ties between them. Subsequently, it develops in two directions: following Willy through this, the last day of his life, and tracing the events of the previous forty years leading up to this point. As in

subsequent novels, Swift is concerned here with the breakup of family structure and the barrenness of modern life, isolation punctuated occasionally by poignant connections and missed connections.

SHUTTLECOCK

These themes are taken up in *Shuttlecock*, in a rather more pointed way, particularly in terms of epistemology (the way in which we understand or make sense of the world). The narrator, Prentis, works in an obscure government archive office under the watchful eye of his boss, who often requests files and reports that are missing or incomplete. The paranoia this creates in the narrator reaches a climax when these requests seem to bear on the past of Prentis's own father, known to all as a war hero. Ultimately Prentis is, like the reader, faced with two profound and contemporary questions in terms of the problems of knowledge and textuality: Is his father's heroic memoir fictional or true? Given the opportunity to discover the truth, should he do so or not?

Graham Swift. (Getty Images)

THE LIGHT OF DAY *and* TOMORROW

The questions raised in Swift's second novel are reminiscent of those posed by detective fiction, which is preeminently concerned, of course, with epistemological certainty, with solving mysteries, with determining the truth. Similar elements are found in Swift's later novel *The Light of Day*, in which the narrator is a detective. In typically Swiftian fashion, however, the structural components of the detective-story genre are thoroughly subverted, to the extent that solving the apparent crime is one of the least significant of the novel's concerns; rather, the narrator of *The Light of Day* fuses past and present to create an extended meditation on the nature of love and human relationships. *Tomorrow* also generates suspense toward some unstated (until the end) climactic event; the narrator reflects late one night on a family secret that will, when revealed to the children in the morning, profoundly affect their lives and the family as a whole. Notably, Swift employs a female narrator-interior monologuist for the first time in *Tomorrow* and, again, his ability to create a genuine and credible narrative voice is evident.

OUT OF THIS WORLD *and* EVER AFTER

If in *Shuttlecock* the narrator is confronted with a profound dilemma—to know or not to know the truth—Swift's ensuing novels explore the characteristic postmodernist epistemological concern of whether such knowledge is even possible. In *Out of This World* and *Ever After* this issue is taken up through examination of the relationship between reality and its representation—in the former case through photographic representation (the primary narrator is a photojournalist) and in the latter through the textual representation of a nineteenth century geologist's memoirs (the narrator is a novelist-historian working on a biography of the memoirs' author). Simply put, in a world in which representations proliferate, the distinction between the fake and the real, the false and the true, history and fiction, becomes increasingly difficult to define. Swift's novels as a whole record the often devastating consequences of this dissolution.

WATERLAND

With his third novel, Swift achieved "breakout" success. *Waterland*, arguably Swift's most sophisticated novel, has achieved numerous accolades. Significantly, the bulk of scholarly work on Swift's fiction has focused on *Waterland*, and the novel has been selected in Britain as a "set text" on national high school examinations in English literature.

Told from the perspective of a history teacher, Tom Crick, the novel thoroughly explores questions of contemporary historiography and knowledge. Faced with a number of pressures, Tom switches from the official focus of his class—the French Revolution—to stories of his own childhood in the half-real, half-magical Fenlands of East Anglia, in Britain. In doing so, and seeking to provide an explanation for certain profound events in his past—the murder of a schoolmate and a primitive abortion endured by his future wife—he finds he is forced to provide contexts that ripple out in ever-widening circles. To understand what happened, Cricks suggests, one must understand the families involved and the folklore of the Fens. To understand those, one needs to understand the ancestry of the families and the history of the region. Including, among many other things, a geological and geographical explanation of how this reclaimed land came into being, a history of brewing in the area, and a (historically accurate) biological history of the eel, *Waterland*'s scope is immense and allusive.

The many digressions, prevarications, contradictions, and narrative shifts in Tom's account may be seen as an ironic reflection on the historian's positivist ideal of exhaustiveness, on the desire to know and fix the truth. This apparently Sisyphean quest explains the generic juxtapositions of Tom's narrative, drawing on the rhetorical approaches not only of biology and social history but also of folklore and detective fiction, for example. Even the language itself is unstable: References to the eel—snake, fish, phallic symbol, source of food, consumer of the aborted fetus, and source of the name of the Fenland town of Ely—offer only one example of the slipperiness of language; thus the desire for a pure and transparent language to represent reality on the part of historians and scientists is undermined throughout the novel.

Such is the power and vivid detail of *Waterland* that many readers have assumed that Swift must have grown up in or at least have intimate personal knowledge of the Fens in order to re-create so powerfully the world of the Fenlanders and their culture. In fact, apart from his time in the city of Cambridge, virtually all that he presents in *Waterland* derives from what he learned through extensive reading on the subject.

LAST ORDERS

Swift's sixth novel is often considered his best, although many would argue that *Waterland* holds that position. On the surface *Last Orders* unfolds a deceptively simple plot: Three aging south Londoners, accompanied by their deceased friend's estranged son, travel to Margate to carry out the friend's last wish that his ashes be cast into the sea off the Kentish coast. Where Swift's previous narrators (a history teacher, a photojournalist, a university fellow) reflect quite articulately on the problems of representation and knowledge raised in their narratives, *Last Orders* presents the reader with the working-class neighborhood of Bermondsey in London, the world of a grocer, an insurance clerk, a used-car salesman, and a butcher. Structurally, however, the novel is as complex as anything Swift has written. *Last Orders* comprises seventy-five sections and employs seven narrators; seventeen of the sections move the plot forward in the narrative present as the men drive toward Margate, while the remainder constitute interior monologues in which characters recall moments when their lives intersected, creating a sort of amorphous collective memory stretching back to World War II. The narrative structure creates a spatial and temporal movement: Its labyrinthine quality mirrors the many detours on the way to Margate and also the elaborate network of intersections wherein past meets present.

Whereas elsewhere in Swift's work the isolation of individuals is emphasized by their interior monologues, in *Last Orders* the effect is, in part, to create a sense of the social world inhabited by these working-class characters and of the slender but strong threads that tie them together. True, this world is marked by a complex pattern of absences and substitutions, but it is maintained nonetheless. Another central theme of the novel is chance or coincidence, which reflects ironically on the cause-and-effect pattern established by definition in all narrative forms. This is apparent in Ray Johnson's success at betting on horses. While Ray himself claims this is simply the result of careful analysis, the names of the horses reflect what their victories represent: Ray's tip "Shady Lady" pays off for Vince, a used-car salesman whose

daughter becomes a prostitute; when Ray makes love with his friend's wife, "Conquistador" is the victor; and the long-shot outsider whose victory provides Ray's friend's informal life insurance on the day of the friend's death is, most appropriately, "Miracle Worker."

The awarding of the Booker Prize to *Last Orders* was not without controversy, primarily generated by the popular press. Months after the announcement, an Australian professor pointed out what to those familiar with William Faulkner's work is quite obvious: that Swift's novel draws on the themes and techniques of Faulkner's Deep South gothic *As I Lay Dying* (1930). Amid accusations of plagiarism in the press, Swift received support from previous Booker winners, including Kazuo Ishiguro and Salman Rushdie. In fact, Swift had a year earlier brought attention to his having drawn on Faulkner in a magazine interview, but the news media—and one member of the five-member Booker committee—were not interested in the nuances of allusiveness or other common literary techniques. The furor died down very quickly, however, as is almost always the case with the British popular press, and *Last Orders* remains probably Swift's most widely read novel.

John L. Marsden

OTHER MAJOR WORKS

SHORT FICTION: *Learning to Swim, and Other Stories*, 1982.

EDITED TEXT: *The Magic Wheel: An Anthology of Fishing in Literature*, 1985 (with David Profumo).

BIBLIOGRAPHY

Craps, Stef. *Trauma and Ethics in the Novels of Graham Swift: No Short Cuts to Salvation*. Sussex, England: Sussex Academic Press, 2005. Presents a thorough and scholarly analysis of Swift's fiction.

Higdon, David Leon. "Double Closures in Postmodernist British Fiction: The Example of Graham Swift." *Critical Survey* 3, no. 1 (1991): 88-95. Examines the ways in which Swift's novels are both open-ended and closed-ended, creating ambiguity that renders distinctions between past and present ambiguous.

Janik, Del Ivan. "History and the 'Here and Now': The Novels of Graham Swift." *Twentieth Century Literature* 35, no. 1 (Spring, 1989): 74-88. Explores the distinction between moments in the novels that are contained by narrative ("history") and those that cannot be contained or accounted for by narrative ("here and now").

Lea, Daniel. *Graham Swift*. Manchester, England: Manchester University Press, 2006. An excellent place to start for an analysis of each of Swift's novels through

The Light of Day. Accessible to advanced high school and undergraduate students.

Pedot, Richard. "Dead Lines in Graham Swift's *Last Orders*." *Critique* 44, no. 1 (Fall, 2002): 60-71. Discusses *Last Orders* as a complex meditation on life and death; focuses on that theme as perceived and experienced by various characters in the novel.

JONATHAN SWIFT

Born: Dublin, Ireland; November 30, 1667
Died: Dublin, Ireland; October 19, 1745

PRINCIPAL LONG FICTION

A Tale of a Tub, 1704
Gulliver's Travels, 1726 (originally titled *Travels into Several Remote Nations of the World, in Four Parts, by Lemuel Gulliver, First a Surgeon, and Then a Captain of Several Ships*)

OTHER LITERARY FORMS

Jonathan Swift's oeuvre includes a large and important body of verse, best assembled in *The Poems of Jonathan Swift* (1937, 1958), edited by Harold Williams. His letters may be found in *The Correspondence of Jonathan Swift* (1963-1965), also edited by Williams. Outstanding among a variety of political writings are Swift's contributions to *The Examiner* (1710-1711), the treatise called *The Conduct of the Allies and of the Late Ministry, in Beginning and Carrying on the Present War* (1711), and the important *The Drapier's Letters to the People of Ireland* (1735).

His prose writings have been published together in *The Prose Works of Jonathan Swift* (1939-1968), a fourteen-volume collection edited by Herbert Davis.

ACHIEVEMENTS

It is generally conceded that Jonathan Swift is the greatest satirist among English-language writers, possibly the most brilliant ironist and acerb wit in any lan-

guage. The force of his satiric barbs has rendered him controversial, however, and many critics have retaliated against his potent quill by claiming that Swift is reckless, uncontrolled, spiteful, insensate, heathenish, and insane. Such rash responses merely demonstrate the powerful effects of his writing.

Swift is not an overt lampooner, diatribe-monger, or name-caller. Curiously, he never utilizes the direct approach; he almost always speaks through a defective mouthpiece, a flawed, self-incriminating persona who forges a case against himself. Indeed, Swift is to be remembered as a grand satiric mimic, finely shaping and generating the voices of knaves and fools alike (the "modern" hack writer in *A Tale of a Tub*, the ignorant serving-woman Frances Harris, the idiot astrologer Isaac Bickerstaff, the callous and mathematical Modest Proposer, the proud but demented simpleton Lemuel Gulliver).

Swift's ear for clichés and inflections of dullness is almost perfect, and authors such as Herbert Read (in *English Prose Style*, 1928) have hailed Swift as the inevitable and clear master of "pure prose" style. Swift is, without doubt, the major satirist in prose, yet he is also a first-rate light poet (in the manner of Horace and the coarser Samuel "Hudibras" Butler), and, if anything, his reputation as a poet is rising. Furthermore, Swift wrote political pamphlets with ruthless force, and his prose in sermons, letters, and treatises is virile and direct. Finally, Swift should not be forgotten as wit and jester. He invented a child-language when corresponding with Stella, wrote mock-Latin sayings, devised wicked epigrams, created paraphrases of Vergil and Ovid, and could even toy with versifying when devising invitations to dinner. In a word, Swift is the all-around expert in English in straightforward exposition—especially when it is bent to provoke savage mockery and the *jeu d'esprit*.

BIOGRAPHY

Jonathan Swift was born in Dublin, Ireland, on November 30, 1667, after the death of his father, a lower-middle class Anglo-Irishman. His grandfather, the Reverend Thomas Swift, had been a vicar in Herefordshire. His father, also named Jonathan, had settled in Ireland to work as a steward of the King's Inns in Dublin. His mother was Abigail Erick, the daughter of a Leicestershire clergyman. Swift's mother entrusted her young son to a nurse, who spirited the infant Swift away from Ireland for several years; he was eventually returned, and he was peculiarly linked with Ireland throughout his life. In any case, it was his fancy to picture himself a lonely outcast amid barbarians.

Swift attended Kilkenny School in his youth and Trinity College, Dublin, obtaining a bachelor's degree in 1686. He spent most of the following decade at Moor Park, Surrey, in the household of Sir William Temple, the distinguished Whig statesman. It was at Moor Park that Swift met, in 1689, the child of Esther Johnson (whom Swift later immortalized as "Stella"), the daughter of Temple's widowed housekeeper. Swift helped in supervising her education and inaugurated a lifelong (and little understood) relationship, for Stella later immigrated to Dublin and spent her life near the Anglican Dean Swift. Naturally, under Temple's aegis, Swift hoped for introductions and advancement, but little came of promises and possibilities, and in 1694 he returned to Dublin long enough to be ordained an Anglican priest (in 1695). He subsequently was reunited with Temple until the latter's death in 1699. Thereafter, he returned to Ireland as chaplain to the Earl of Berkeley. His reputation for talent and wit was rapidly growing.

Swift's great political period took place in London from 1708 to 1714. He became the chief spokesman, apologist, and pamphleteer for the powerful Tory leaders then in power, Robert Harley and Henry St. John, first Viscount Bolingbroke. Their fall and disgrace ushered in a lengthy era of Whig dominance that permanently drove Swift back to what he must have considered exile in Ireland. Swift had been finally rewarded (although he would have perceived it as a paltry recognition) with the deanery of St. Patrick's Cathedral in Dublin, where he served for the remainder of his life. His powerful satires had earned him powerful enemies, and significant advancement in the Anglican Church or in England was never permitted to him.

In any event, Swift served with precision, justness, and rectitude as a clergyman and continued throughout his career to be an admirable satirist and wit. He even elected to champion the rights of the maltreated Irish, and he came to be admired as their avatar and protector, a "Hibernian Patriot." In his last years, Swift suffered increasingly from deafness and vertigo (the results of a lifelong affliction by Ménière's syndrome, a disease of the inner ear), which resulted in senility and, most likely, a stroke. Guardians were appointed to oversee his affairs in his last years, and he died in 1745, shortly before his seventy-eighth birthday.

Swift played his last ironic jest on humankind in his will, which committed the bulk of his estate to the founding of a "hospital" for fools and madmen, just as he had pronounced the plan in his *Verses on the Death of Dr. Swift, D.S.P.D.* (1739):

> He gave the little Wealth he had,
> To build a House for Fools and Mad;
> And shew'd by one satyric Touch,
> No Nation wanted it so much

ANALYSIS

It must be noted that Jonathan Swift's "fictions" are nothing like conventional novels. They seldom detail the "adventures" of a hero or even a protagonist and never conclude with a character's romantic achievement of goals or fulfillment of desires. Indeed, Swift is the great master of fictionalizing nonfiction. His satires always purport to be something factual, humdrum, diurnal, unimaginative: a treatise, a travel diary, an annotated edition, a laborious oration, a tendentious allegory, a puffed-out "letter to a friend." Extremist Protestant sects condemned fiction, and "projectors" and would-be investigators in the dawning age of science extolled

Jonathan Swift. (Library of Congress)

the prosaic, the plodding, the scholarly, the methodical, and the factual. At the same time, urban population growth and the rise of the middle class created a growing new audience, and printing presses multiplied in accordance with demand. Many "popular" and best-seller art forms flourished: sermons, true confessions, retellings (and second parts) of hot-selling tales and political harangues, news items, hearsay gossip, and science all became jumbled together for public consumption, much of which led to spates of yellow journalism. Throughout his life Swift rebelled against such indelicacies and depravities, and his satiric procedure included the extremist parody of tasteless forms—*reductio ad absurdum*. It was by such means that Swift secured his fame as an author.

A TALE OF A TUB

Doubtless his most dazzling prose performance of this kind was his earliest, *A Tale of a Tub*, which appeared anonymously in 1704. (Swift, in fact, published most of his satires anonymously, although his work was usually instantly recognized and acclaimed.) *A Tale of a Tub* is actually a "medley" of pieces imitating the penchant for an author's combining fiction, essays, letters, verse, fragments, or anything else to enable him to amass a book-length manuscript. It contains "The Battle of the Books," a wooden allegorical piece in the manner of *Aesop's Fables*, detailing the "quarrel of ancients versus moderns," and a fragmentary treatise titled "The Mechanical Operation of the Spirit," trussed up in the inept form of a casual letter to a friend.

The treatise mocks the new "scientific" trend of reducing all things to some species of Cartesian (or Newtonian) materialism. Rather comically, it deploys in a blasé manner the language of ancient Greek and Roman atomists—Democritus and Epicurus—as if they were contemporary modernists. Indeed, one pervasive theme throughout this volume is the ridiculousness of the modernist position of "independence"—although the moderns might be ignorant of the past, the ideas and genres of classical antiquity keep recurring in their works, a fact that belies their supposed originality (even while demonstrating that, as a result of solipsism, their form and control disintegrate into chaos).

Clearly, the titular piece, "A Tale of a Tub," is Swift's early masterpiece and one of the great (and most difficult) satires in any language. In its pages, an avowed fanatic "modern" aspires to "get off" an edition, to tout and sell himself, to make money, to demonstrate his uniqueness and, however evanescently, tyrannically to be "the latest modern." He seeks to reedit an old tale of three brothers and their adventures. Naturally, he decorates and updates such a version to give it the latest cut and fashion, the style and wit and jargon of the moment. (It is perhaps an accident that this tale of the dissensions of Peter, Martin, and Jack parallels the vicissitudes of the history of Christianity, as it splinters into differing and quarreling religious sects. The modern appears ignorant of historical sense.)

The new version of the old story, however, is fragmented: Every time the modern's imagination or his fancy supplies him with a spark, he promptly follows his rather meandering muse and travels into an elaboration, an annotation, or a digression. In fact, the opening fifty pages of the work are cluttered with the paraphernalia of "modern" publishing: dedications, publisher's comments, introductions, apologies, notes to the second edition, acknowledgments, prefaces, and forewords. Thereafter, when such a cloud of ephemeral formalities would seem to have been dispensed with, the author still manages to interject a plethora of digressions—afterthoughts, asides, cute remarks apropos of nothing, commentary, snipings at critics, obsequious snivelings for the reader, canting pseudophilosophy for the learned, and pity and adoration for himself. In no time at all, the entire tale is awash in detours, perambulations, and divagations.

This modern storyteller is nothing if not effervescent, boorish, and chronically self-indulgent. He claims that his pipe dreams and diversions are in essence planned excursions and in fact deliberately philosophical meditations, rich with allegorical meanings. The opposite is also true, and the modern's tub is like an empty cart—rattling around most furiously in its vacuity, making the most noise. Furthermore, the digressions become unwieldy. The tale is disrupted more and more frequently, and the digressions become longer and longer. The modern is his most penetrating in the trenchant section IX—a digression in praise of madness—as he coyly confesses that his reason has been overturned, his intellect rattled, and that he has been but recently confined. The continued multiplication of digressions (until they subvert sections of the tale) and the finale, when the modern loses his notes and his ramblings give out entirely, are easily understood as the wanderings of a madman—a modern who suppresses the past, memory, reason, and self-control. If Swift's warning about the growing taste for newness, modernity, and things-of-the-moment appears madcap and farcical, it is nevertheless a painfully close nightmare preview of future fashions, fantasms, and fallacies that subsequently came to be real.

A Tale of a Tub clearly demonstrates several of Swift's most common fictional ploys and motifs. Some representative of the depraved "moderns" is usually present, always crass, irreligious, ignorant, arrogant, proud, self-adulatory, concerned with the events of the moment. Indeed, Swift was fond of scrupulously celebrating every April 1 as All Fools' Day, but he also recognized April 2: All Knaves' Day. He doubtless felt that both halves of humankind deserved some token of official recognition. Swift also favored mixing the two, however: He frequently shows readers that a man who is manipulator, con man, and knave in one set of circumstances is himself conned, befooled, and gulled in another. As such, the modern reveals an unexpected complexity in his makeup; he also illustrates the era (as Swift imagines it) that he inhabits—a period overfull of bad taste and poor writing, which are the broad marks of cultural decadence.

In the work of a satirist, the world is regularly depicted as cyclic in historic periods, and usually in decline. Swift and Sir William Temple both stressed some trend toward decay in the modern era and spoke often of barbarians and invasions; it was a type of satiric myth suitable to the disruptive fictions that the satirist envisions. In section IX of *A Tale of a Tub*, the modern vacillates between viewing all humankind as "curious" or "credulous," as busy probers, analysts, and excavators or as superficial and inert: knaves versus fools. As is typical of Swift, the fool and knave personas are infused with enough familiar traits to suggest that all people partake of either. Further, Swift entraps his reader by implying that there are no other categories: One is either fool or knave or both. His irony is corrosive and inclusive, capturing the reader in its toils. In that sense, Swift is deliberately disruptive; he seeks to startle and to embroil the reader in his fictions about stupidity and depravity. To such an end, he tampers with logic to make his case appear substantial and manipulates paradox to keep his readers off balance. Such techniques lend Swift his volatile force.

These strategies are to be found in Swift's best verse; the same may be said for his two great ironic short-prose pieces: *Argument Against Abolishing Christianity* (1708) and *A Modest Proposal for Preventing the Children of Poor People of Ireland from Being a Burden to Their Parents or the Country, and for Making Them Beneficial to the Public* (1729). Both of these works seek to shock the reader and to propose the discomforting, the alarming, the untenable.

GULLIVER'S TRAVELS

Swift's undisputed masterpiece is *Gulliver's Travels*, originally titled *Travels into Several Remote Nations of the World, in Four Parts, by Lemuel Gulliver, First a Surgeon, and Then a Captain of Several Ships*. This fictional work accommodates all of Swift's perennial themes and does so effectually. First, the work is perhaps the definitive study of new middle-class values, specifically the preoccupation with slang, cash, smug self-righteousness, self-assertion, and self-congratulation. Second, it might not be considered a "novel" in the conventional sense of the term, but it is a delightfully fact-filled simulation of adventure fiction, and it stems assuredly from the satiric picaresque tradition (in Spain and France) that greatly contributed to the formulation of modern novelistic techniques and themes.

Swift's Lemuel Gulliver (a mulish gull) is a model representative of the fool and the knave: He aspires to befool others but nevertheless befuddles himself. His medium is the very popular literary genre of the travelogue, or record of a "voyage of discovery." The genre grew popular through its Cartesian emphasis on an inductive observer-self and the Romantic subject of adventures in far-off lands. Such a travelogue format allows the narrator to take his readers on a vicarious journey of adventure and concludes by suggesting that the traveler has fulfilled the pattern of the bildungsroman and has attained education, growth, experience, and Aristotelian *cognitio* (insight, maturation, the acquisition of new knowledge). As might be expected in an exemplary case manipulated by Swift, Gulliver is anything but the apt learner. He is a crass materialist for whom experiences consist of precise measurements of objects observed, a tedious cataloging of dress, diet, and customs, and an infinite variety of pains in note taking, recording, transcribing, and translating. He is superficiality and rank objectivity incarnate. Naturally, therefore, his everyday mean density prevents his acquisition of any true understanding.

Gulliver is a minor physician, the mediocre little man, anxious, like Daniel Defoe's Robinson Crusoe, to make sightseeing tours and to acquire cash. His first of four voyages carries him to the land of six-inch mites, the Lilliputians, and his second voyage to the land of gargantuan giants, the Brobdingnagians. Gulliver remains myopic in both locations, for he can hardly consider that tiny creatures can (and do) perpetuate monstrous deeds, and, once he perceives that the giants are rather tame, he leaps to the conclusion that they are infinitely superior to other human types (even though their political and social institutions are no better than they should be, given the

quirks and flaws of human nature). In sum, the tour from very small to very large merely stimulates in Gulliver a sense of wondrous contrast: He expects in these different worlds wondrous differences.

Amusingly, what the reader finds is much the same—that is, the uneven and imperfect human nature. Equally amusing, Gulliver behaves much the same himself in his attempts to ingratiate himself with his "superiors": He aspires to become a successful competitor in all worlds as a "titled" nobleman, a "nardac," a "courtier" with "connections" at court. Like many middle-class people, he is a man in the middle, aspiring above all for upward mobility, mouthing the commonplaces of the day, utterly incapable of judging people and events. He is also the worst sort of traveler; he is a man who sees no further than his own predilections and preconceptions and who imitates all the manners that he sees around him. Actually, the realms of big and little are merely distortions of the real world. Here, one of the work's central ironies is found in the fact that Gulliver could have learned as much, or as little, if he had stayed at home.

The world of sizes is replaced in Gulliver's third voyage by the world of concepts: The muddled peoples he visits are victims of mathomania and abstraction-worship. At the same time, it is revealed that the world of the past, like the world of the present, has been tainted and corrupt. Even the potentially ideal Struldbruggs, who live forever, are exposed as being far from lucky. They are, rather, especially accursed by the afflictions of impotence, depression, and senility. Swift has, with cartoon facility, carted Gulliver all around the world, showing him the corrosive face of fallen humanity, even among the various robbers, cowards, pirates, and mutineers that had beset him as he traveled in European ships—but Gulliver does not see.

The stage is properly set for the fourth voyage. Utilizing his favorite ploys of reversal and entrapment, Swift puts Gulliver into a land of learned and rational horses (the Houyhnhnms) and debauched hairy, monkeylike beasts (the Yahoos). Once again, there is no middle ground: All in this world is rational horse or wolfish (and oafish) bestiality. Obviously, Gulliver chooses the equestrian gentlemen as his leaders and masters. (Indeed, throughout all the voyages, Gulliver the conformist is in quest of a staid position and "masters" who will tell him what to do and grant him praise and sustenance for his slavish adulation.)

Slowly it is revealed, however, that the Yahoos are men: Gulliver *is* a debased, gross, and deformed member of the Yahoo tribe; as Swift sweetly and confoundingly phrases it, Gulliver is a "perfect yahoo." The horses themselves rebuff this upstart, and Gulliver, who has undergone every other sort of ignominy in the course of his travels, is finally evicted as an undesirable alien from the horsey paradise. At last, Gulliver thinks he has learned a lesson; he aspires to be a horse, and, back in Europe, he shuns the human species and favors the environs of straw and stables. He has hardly acquired the rationality of his leaders and appears quite mad. Swift's ultimate paradox seems to imply that people can "know" about reason and ideals but can never master or practice them. Even here, however, Swift cruelly twists the knife at the last moment, for Gulliver, several years later, is revealed as slowly forgetting his intense (and irrational) devotion to the Houyhnhnms and slowly beginning to be able to tolerate and accept the lowly human race that he had earlier so intransigently spurned. Gulliver cannot even stick to a lesson painfully and rudely learned during many years; he lacks the brains, drive, ambition, and consistency necessary to keep him on any course. Gulliver's travels eventually get him nowhere.

In sum, *Gulliver's Travels* makes a huge tragicomical case for the absurdity of pretentious humankind. Gulliver is fool enough to believe that he is progressing and knave enough to boast about it and to hope to gain some position and affluence from the event. At his proudest moments, however, he is little more than a driveler, a gibbering idiot who is raveningly insane. Gulliver's painful experiences and the brute instruction his readers acquire are a caustic finale to much of the heady and bold idealism of the Renaissance and a cautionary plea for restraint in an era launched on celebrating reason, science, optimism, and enlightenment. Time has shown that Swift was largely right: Blithe superconfidence in people, their sciences, and their so-called progress is very likely to come enormously to grief. *Gulliver's Travels* speaks to everyone because it addresses crucial issues about the human condition itself.

John R. Clark

OTHER MAJOR WORKS

POETRY: *Cadenus and Vanessa*, 1726; *On Poetry: A Rapsody*, 1733; *Verses on the Death of Dr. Swift, D.SP.D.*, 1739; *The Poems of Jonathan Swift*, 1937, 1958 (3 volumes; Harold Williams, editor).

NONFICTION: *A Discourse of the Contests and Dissensions Between the Nobles and the Commons in Athens and Rome*, 1701; *The Battle of the Books*, 1704; *The Accomplishment of the First of Mr. Bickerstaff's Predictions*, 1708; *Argument Against Abolishing Christianity*, 1708 (first published as *An Argument to Prove That the Abolishing of Christianity in England May, as Things Now Stand, Be Attended with Some Inconveniences, and Perhaps Not Produce Those Many Good Effects Proposed Thereby*); *Predictions for the Year 1708*, 1708; *A Project for the Advancement of Religion, and the Reformation of Manners by a Person of Quality*, 1709; *A Vindication of Isaac Bickerstaff, Esq.*, 1709; *The Conduct of the Allies and of the Late Ministry, in Beginning and Carrying on the Present War*, 1711; *A Proposal for Correcting, Improving, and Ascertaining the English Tongue, in a Letter to the Most Honourable Robert Earl of Oxford and Mortimer, Lord High Treasurer of Great Britain*, 1712; *The Public Spirit of the Whigs, Set Forth in Their Generous Encouragement of the Author of the Crisis*, 1714; *A Letter from a Lay-Patron to a Gentleman, Designing for Holy Orders*, 1720; *A Proposal for the Universal Use of Irish Manufacture*, 1720; *A Modest Proposal for Preventing the Children of Poor People of Ireland from Being a Burden to Their Parents or the Country, and for Making Them Beneficial to the Public*, 1729; *The Drapier's Letters to the People of Ireland*, 1735; *A Complete Collection of Genteel and Ingenious Conversation, According to the Most Polite Mode and Method Now Used at Court, and in the Best Companies of England, in Three Dialogues*, 1738; *Directions to Servants in General . . .* , 1745; *The History of the Four Last Years of the Queen, by the Late Jonathan Swift DD, DSPD*, 1758; *Journal to Stella*, 1766, 1768; *Letter to a Very Young Lady on Her Marriage*, 1797; *The Correspondence of Jonathan Swift*, 1963-1965 (5 volumes; Harold Williams, editor).

MISCELLANEOUS: *Miscellanies in Prose and Verse*, 1711; *Miscellanies*, 1727-1733 (4 volumes; with Alexander Pope and other members of the Scriblerus Club);

The Prose Works of Jonathan Swift, 1939-1968 (14 volumes; Herbert Davis, editor).

BIBLIOGRAPHY

Barnett, Louise. *Jonathan Swift in the Company of Women*. New York: Oxford University Press, 2007. Focuses on Swift's relationships with the women in his life and his attitudes toward the fictional women in his texts. Explores Swift's contradictory views and illustrates how he respected and admired individual women yet loathed the female sex in general. Offers a critical, nonjudgmental discussion of the misogynistic attitude Swift displays in his writing when he expresses contempt and disgust for the female body.

Connery, Brian A., ed. *Representations of Swift*. Newark: University of Delaware Press, 2002. Collection of essays examines, among other topics, Swift's treatments of gender, class, and Ireland. Includes an analysis of *A Tale of a Tub*.

Ehrenpreis, Irvin. *Swift: The Man, His Works, and the Age*. 3 vols. Cambridge, Mass.: Harvard University Press, 1962-1983. Monumental biography rejects long-held myths about Swift and provides much previously unavailable information about the author and his works. Relates Swift to the intellectual and political currents of his age.

Fox, Christopher, ed. *The Cambridge Companion to Jonathan Swift*. New York: Cambridge University Press, 2003. Collection of essays about Swift's life and work includes analysis of *A Tale of a Tub* and *Gulliver's Travels* and discussions of Swift's religion, the language and style of his works, and his representation of women.

Fox, Christopher, and Brenda Tooley, eds. *Walking Naboth's Vineyard: New Studies of Swift*. Notre Dame, Ind.: University of Notre Dame Press, 1995. Collection of essays opens with an introduction that discusses Swift in relation to Irish studies, and the subsequent essays all consider aspects of Swift as an Irish writer.

Glendinning, Victoria. *Jonathan Swift: A Portrait*. New York: Henry Holt, 1998. Biography serves to illuminate Swift's nature as a proud and intractable man.

Investigates the main events and relationships of Swift's life, which may be viewed as a tapestry of controversy and paradox.

Hunting, Robert. *Jonathan Swift*. Boston: Twayne, 1989. Good source of biographical information as well as insightful, if general, analysis of Swift's art. Devotes one chapter to *Gulliver's Travels*. Includes chronology, notes and references, bibliography, and index.

Kelly, Ann Cline. *Jonathan Swift and Popular Culture: Myth, Media, and the Man*. New York: Palgrave, 2002. Chronicles the creation of Swift's literary legend in his own time and in succeeding generations. Swift realized that in "a print-contracted world, texts create authors, not the other way around," and Kelly demonstrates how the writer constructed a print persona that differed from the "real" individual.

Nokes, David. *Jonathan Swift, A Hypocrite Reversed: A Critical Biography*. New York: Oxford University Press, 1985. Offers a good introduction for the general reader seeking information about Swift's life and works, drawing heavily on Swift's writings. Nokes views Swift as a conservative humanist.

Palmieri, Frank, ed. *Critical Essays on Jonathan Swift*. New York: G. K. Hall, 1993. Collection of essays is divided into sections on Swift's life and writings, *Gulliver's Travels*, *A Tale of a Tub* and eighteenth century literature, and his poetry and nonfiction prose. Includes index.

Quintana, Ricardo. *The Mind and Art of Jonathan Swift*. 1936. Reprint. New York: Oxford University Press, 1953. One of the standards of Swift criticism, concentrating on the public Swift. Examines his political activities and writings, tracing the intellectual sources of his thought. Includes synopses of his major works and provides historical background.

Rawson, Claude. *The Character of Swift's Satire: A Revised Focus*. Newark: University of Delaware Press, 1983. Presents eleven essays by Swift scholars, including John Traugatt's excellent reading of *A Tale of a Tub*, Irvin Ehrenpreis on Swift as a letter writer, and F. P. Lock on Swift's role in the political affairs of Queen Anne's reign.

T

AMY TAN

Born: Oakland, California; February 19, 1952
Also known as: Amy Ruth Tan

PRINCIPAL LONG FICTION

The Joy Luck Club, 1989
The Kitchen God's Wife, 1991
The Hundred Secret Senses, 1995
The Bonesetter's Daughter, 2001
Saving Fish from Drowning, 2005

OTHER LITERARY FORMS

Although she is best known for her novels, Amy Tan has also published short essays, short stories, and two children's books—*The Moon Lady* (1992) and *The Chinese Siamese Cat* (1994). In addition, Tan cowrote the screenplay for the 1993 film adaptation of her novel *The Joy Luck Club*, and in 2003 she published a memoir, *The Opposite of Fate: A Book of Musings*.

ACHIEVEMENTS

Amy Tan is one of the best-known and most popular Asian American writers and, like Maxine Hong Kingston, is considered a guide to the landscape of the Asian American experience. Gracing the best-seller lists and translated into thirty-five languages, Tan's novels have earned critical and popular acclaim; *The Joy Luck Club* was made into a major motion picture. Tan won the Commonwealth Gold Award and the Bay Area Book Reviewers Award for *The Joy Luck Club*, which was also nominated for the National Book Award and the National Book Critics Circle Award. Three of her works have been included on *The New York Times* "Notable Books" list, two have been Booklist Editors Choices, and two—*The Hundred Secret Senses* and *The Bonesetter's Daughter*—were nominated for the Orange Prize for Fiction; *The Hundred Secret Senses* was a finalist for that prize.

Tan's novels contribute to the dialogue about the meanings of "Asian" and "American" by portraying the intercultural conflict threatening many Asian American immigrant families. Her strong storytelling ability ensures the accessibility of her fiction to general readers; moreover, her work appeals to feminist readers and critics because, as Sau-ling Cynthia Wong has pointed out, Tan's novels belong to significant "discursive traditions," including "mainstream feminist writing; Asian American matrilineal literature; quasi ethnography about the Orient; Chinese American 'tour-guiding' works."

BIOGRAPHY

Amy Ruth Tan was born to Daisy and John Tan, both of whom had emigrated—separately—from China to the United States in the late 1940's. They had met some years earlier but were separated by two things: Daisy was still married to her first husband, and John left for the United States, where he intended to study at the Massachusetts Institute of Technology. Fate intervened—Daisy was divorced from her abusive husband, and John sent for her. They were married in California and had three children; Amy was the middle child. Acutely conscious that she was different from her classmates, Tan recalls pinching her nose with a clothespin in an effort to reshape that appendage to look more Caucasian. Like her Asian American peers, Tan was American at school and Chinese at home. Although her mother spoke to her in Chinese, Tan responded in English. The tensions and conflicts produced by her dual heritage eventually found their way into her fiction, which often portrays the generational conflicts in immigrant families.

At fifteen, Tan lost first her older brother and then her father; both died of brain tumors within months of each other. Her mother reacted by leaving California with the remaining children, moving first to the East Coast and then to the Netherlands and Germany, and finally to Switzerland, where Tan graduated from high school.

After returning to the United States, Tan attended several colleges before earning degrees in English and linguistics from San Jose State University. She married Louis DeMattei, a tax lawyer, after graduation, and enrolled at the University of California at Berkeley to work toward a doctorate in linguistics, but she soon abandoned her studies to become a freelance business writer. After several successful years, Tan realized that, despite a lucrative career, she was both overworked and unsatisfied, and she attempted therapy to overcome her workaholism. When therapy failed (the therapist fell asleep during their sessions), Tan decided to follow a childhood dream—to write fiction. Joining the Squaw Valley Community of Writers, where she met author Molly Giles, Tan commenced work on the short stories that became the nucleus of her first book.

Tan's first novel, *The Joy Luck Club*, published in 1989, was a critical and popular success, catapulting the author into the ranks of significant American novelists and establishing her as a chronicler of cultural and generational conflicts. *The Kitchen God's Wife* followed two years later, garnering high praise and another berth on the best-seller lists. In 1995, Tan published her third novel, *The Hundred Secret Senses*, an exploration of the nature of memory and love. The most overtly autobiographical of Tan's novels, *The Bonesetter's Daughter*, was published in 2001 after her mother's death prompted the author to rewrite completely a manuscript that had been five years in the writing. With her fifth novel, *Saving Fish from Drowning*, Tan refocused her storytelling away from the nuclear family to the dynamics of a group of friends traveling together under difficult circumstances.

ANALYSIS

Like the works of many late twentieth and early twenty-first century writers, Amy Tan's books are difficult to classify into a single fictional genre. Although Tan's works are indisputably novels, readers and critics agree that her fiction fuses several narrative genres: memoir and autobiography, mythology and folktale, history and biography. Moreover, like Maxine Hong Kingston, Tan appropriates and deploys Chinese talk

story—a combination of narrative genres from Chinese oral tradition expressed in a local vernacular—to give shape and a distinctive voice to her novels.

Tan's fictional landscape is both geographically vast and spatially confined. In her first four novels, the American spaces embrace San Francisco and the Bay Area, while the Chinese locations include a large territory from Guilin to Shanghai and encompass time from feudal China to the twentieth century. In her fifth novel, she ventures into new territory—Myanmar, which she calls Burma in the narrative. Between her protagonists' ancestral homeland and their adopted country, between the United States and Burma, lies the Pacific Ocean, symbolically crossed by the woman and the swan in the tale that begins *The Joy Luck Club* and traversed in the other direction by the travelers in *Saving Fish from Drowning*. Nonetheless, the crucial events in Tan's novels are contained within definitive boundaries: a circumscribed Chinatown neighborhood, the tiny village of Changmian, one-room accommodations for Chinese pilots and their wives, a stuffy apartment crammed with elderly Mah-Jongg enthusiasts, an isolated Karen encampment in the jungle, the remote hamlet of Immortal Heart.

Enclosed by framing narratives set in the late twentieth and early twenty-first centuries, the embedded stories in Tan's novels are set in earlier eras, transporting readers to nineteenth century rural China, war-ravaged Nanking (Nanjing) during World War II, or cosmopolitan Shanghai between the wars. Juxtaposing events separated by decades, Tan parallels the dislocations experienced by immigrants from a familiar culture into an alien one with their daughters' painful journeys from cultural confusion to acceptance of their dual heritage.

Tan's protagonists—members of that diasporic community called Asian Americans—represent two groups: Chinese-born immigrants, imperfectly acculturated despite decades of life in the United States, and American-born women of Chinese ancestry, uncomfortably straddling the border between their ethnic heritage and the American milieu that is their home. Enmeshed by their shared histories in California's ethnic neighborhoods, the women in Tan's novels struggle to create personal identities that reflect their lives, needs, and desires.

With *Saving Fish from Drowning*, Tan reworks her themes, developing them through the interactions of characters whose primary identity is as American citizens despite their varied ethnic backgrounds. In this novel, cultural conflict is played out in the experiences of well-meaning Western travelers whose assumptions about the world lead them to manifest disrespect and misunderstanding in their interactions with their Chinese guides and later the Karen tribespeople who kidnap them.

Through her fiction, Tan examines identity—its construction, boundaries, assumptions, and contexts. Indelibly branded by their visible ethnicity, many of Tan's characters daily negotiate the minefields of cultural disjunction and tensions between Chinese tradition and Americanization, family connections and individual desires. These tensions inevitably surface, causing intergenerational conflict and the disintegration of family relationships as members of the older generation look back to China while their daughters remain firmly connected to California, triggering international incidents when traveling Californians fail to see that the rest of the world is different from their home.

Amy Tan. (Robert Foothorap)

THE JOY LUCK CLUB

The Joy Luck Club tells the stories of four mother-daughter pairs: Suyuan and Jing-mei Woo, An-Mei and Rose Hsu Jordan, Lindo and Waverly Jong, and Ying-ying and Lena St. Clair. Implicit in the generational conflicts that erupt between the women is the bicultural angst separating the Chinese-born mothers from their American-born, assimilated daughters. Initially unable to discover common ground, the two groups of women speak different languages, embrace different values, aspire to different ambitions, and lead divergent lives.

The social club of the title binds together the lives of these eight women. As the novel opens, Jing-mei Woo prepares to take her dead mother's place at the Mah-Jongg table that anchors the club's activities. During Jing-mei's first game, the older women beg her to go to China on her mother's behalf, and their pleas trigger in Jing-mei painful memories of her Chinatown childhood. Jing-mei's first narrative introduces the other narrators, and, except for Suyuan, whose story emerges through Jing-mei's, each woman tells her own story.

Representing the immigrant generation that fled China after World War II, the mothers have had difficult early lives: Suyuan Woo is driven to abandon twins to give them a chance to survive, An-Mei Hsu's mother commits suicide to force her husband to acknowledge An-Mei as his child, Lindo Jong endures an arranged marriage at twelve to an even younger child, and Ying-ying St. Clair, deserted by her first husband, experiences a decade of poverty. In the United States, the mothers must negotiate the traumas of leaving a war-ravaged homeland, starting over in an alien country, and trying to learn a strange language. Through their vicissitudes, they cling to memories of China and to fading traces of their ancestral culture, and they eventually establish stable new lives for themselves.

In contrast with their mothers, the daughters have had good lives—with plenty to eat, comfortable homes, intact families, music lessons, and college educations. Nevertheless, the daughters are discontented and unhappy: Jing-mei is single and aimless, Rose is separated from her husband, Waverly is already divorced, and Lena has summoned up the courage to examine her dysfunctional marriage. Each daughter feels detached from herself, her family, and her community; none of them knows how to reconnect.

The novel traces the evolution of understanding between the mothers and daughters, who are, at the end, finally able to articulate the depth of their caring for each other. The novel concludes when Jing-mei travels to China to meet her two half sisters—the women who were the infants that Suyuan lost in wartime China.

THE KITCHEN GOD'S WIFE

The Kitchen God's Wife also explores the dynamics of the mother-daughter relationship in the context of cultural and ethnic disjunctions, albeit in less detail than does *The Joy Luck Club*. This novel focuses on a woman's journey to wholeness after an eventful life that replicates the Chinese immigrant experience in microcosm. The novel's title refers to Winnie Louie's version of the story of the Kitchen God who achieves deity status when he proves to be capable of shame upon discovering that the wife he has mistreated still cares about his welfare. Unfortunately, according to Winnie, the Kitchen God's wife is denied membership in the Chinese pantheon of deities despite her fidelity.

The novel tells two stories: the sketchy framing narrative involving the widening rift between Winnie and her daughter, Pearl, and the fully developed chronicle of Winnie's life in China. Through her story, Pearl contextualizes Winnie's reminiscences, describing a series of events and revelations that ultimately changes their relationship. Required by family obligations to attend the funeral of an ancient "aunt" and the engagement party of a "cousin," Pearl spends more time with Winnie than she has in many months, and the enforced companionship prompts the younger woman to examine the roots of their estrangement. Winnie, goaded to action by a letter from China that closes a painful chapter in her past, decides to tell Pearl about her life in China.

Save for the early chapters, in which Pearl speaks, and the epilogue, in which Winnie and Pearl deify the Kitchen God's wife as Lady Sorrowfree, the novel chronicles the eventful life of Jiang Weili—Winnie's Chinese name—as she negotiates the difficult journey from a privileged childhood through an abusive marriage and the tragedy of war, and ultimately to a secure life in the United States.

The daughter of a wealthy Shanghai merchant, Jiang Weili marries the dashing Wen Fu only to discover after the wedding that he has misrepresented his family's wealth and status. Worse yet, he turns out to be an adulterer, abuser, and pathological liar. Forced to follow her pilot husband as he is posted to different cities during the war, Weili tries to be a good wife and mother, laboring to establish a home wherever they happen to be assigned. She must spend her dowry for family expenses when Wen Fu gambles away his pay or squanders it on a mistress. After silently enduring her miserable existence and the deaths of her two children, Winnie finally escapes to the United States and a new life with Jimmy Louie.

THE HUNDRED SECRET SENSES

Unlike Tan's first two novels, which examine the dynamics of the mother-daughter dyad, *The Hundred Secret Senses* explores the psychological and emotional bonds between sisters. Still, the novel displays several characteristics common to Tan's fiction: conflict between generations in immigrant families, multiple points of view, a strong grounding in Chinese culture and history, and compelling narratives.

Although *The Hundred Secret Senses* is Olivia's story, Kwan is central to every narrative in the novel. One of Tan's most stunningly original creations, Kwan is an energetic woman who is Chinese at the core despite having adopted Western dress and American slang. Kwan claims to have *yin* eyes, which she describes as an ability to see and converse with the dead, whom she calls "*yin* people."

Central to the novel is the uncomfortable relationship between American-born Olivia and her Chinese sister, Kwan, who arrived in San Francisco at eighteen. Although sharing a father, the two women are markedly different: Olivia, whose mother is American, is completely Westernized; Kwan, born to a Chinese first wife, never completely assimilates, remaining predominantly Chinese. Embarrassed by Kwan's exuberant Chineseness, Olivia resists her sister's attempts to form a close relationship. She declines invitations, evades contact, and refuses all overtures of friendship. Despite Olivia's coolness, Kwan continues her friendly attempts to be a real sister to Olivia, whose unhappiness is palpable.

Maneuvering Olivia and Olivia's estranged husband, Simon, into a trip to the hills beyond Guilin in China, Kwan engineers a situation that forces Olivia and Simon to reassess their relationship and take tentative steps toward reconciliation.

Paralleling Olivia's story and embedded in the novel are Kwan's puzzling narratives about a previous life when—she claims—she was a woman called Nunumu, a Chinese servant to a group of missionaries. In that household, Nunumu was befriended by Nelly Banner, a young American woman whose passion for a deceitful adventurer imperils the group and whose love for a half-breed results in death for herself and Nunumu. The intertwined stories of Nunumu and Nelly Banner are set against the backdrop of the nineteenth century Taiping Rebellion, led by a charismatic leader who claimed to be Jesus' younger brother.

As in her first two novels, Tan establishes clear parallels between past and present, between historical events and contemporary problems, between East and West, China and the United States. Constantly relaying messages from her *yin* friends, who seem inordinately interested in Olivia's marital problems, Kwan manages to manipulate Olivia to the brink of believing that she, Olivia, has somehow participated in Nunumu's life, has experienced fear of approaching rebel soldiers, and has faced death on a rainy hillside. Whether Olivia truly had a previous life and once was Nelly Banner is never made clear—what is certain at the end of the novel is Olivia's understanding of the unbreakable ties of love and affection that exist between sisters, friends, and lovers.

THE BONESETTER'S DAUGHTER

With its two parallel narratives, *The Bonesetter's Daughter* adds a layer of complexity to Tan's ongoing analysis of the relationships between mothers and daughters. Structured in three parts, the novel introduces Ruth Young, a successful Chinese American ghostwriter who specializes in self-help books although her personal life is a failure: Her ten-year relationship with her live-in boyfriend, Art, is deteriorating, and she is struggling with her mother, Luling, who is increasingly forgetful and erratic. When Luling's doctor diagnoses a form of dementia, Ruth is catapulted into the realization that family stories as well as her mother's history are in danger of disappearing. Recalling that her mother gave her a copy of her autobiography calligraphed in Chinese, Ruth arranges to have the manuscript translated, hoping to find the key to understanding her mother's fixation with ghosts and the past.

Set in the remote Chinese village of Immortal Heart just prior to and during World War II, the middle of the novel is narrated by Luling, who tells her own story as well as that of Precious Auntie, her nursemaid—and the title character whose suicide defines the rest of Luling's life. Embedded in the story is the mystery of how the once-beautiful Precious Auntie, who was famous for assisting her father in his work as a "bone doctor," has become a mute and horribly disfigured servant who communicates only through sign language and grunts. When Precious Auntie kills herself in despair over Luling's impending marriage, the truth is revealed—she is Luling's real mother. Racked by guilt over her part in the suicide, Luling spends the rest of her life fretting that she never recovered Precious Auntie's body from the deep gorge into which it was thrown.

The final section of the novel focuses on Ruth's new insights into her family history. As a child, she had resented Luling's overprotectiveness and obsession with ghosts, unaware that Luling was trying in her own way to correct the past. Understanding her mother's life provides Ruth with a context for making sense of her own history and its impact on the present, and she is able finally to embrace her life and communicate her desires.

The dominant image in the novel is that of bones—the dragon bones used to heal injuries, the oracle bone that is Luling's legacy from Precious Auntie, the bones of Peking man that draw American scientists to Immortal Heart, the ground-up bones that are a secret ingredient in the ink that Luling's family makes. At the end of the novel, Luling, who is deep in happy memories of the past, finally remembers Precious Auntie's family name: Gu, meaning "bone" but also "character" and "gorge," meanings that resonate with the intertwined narratives of Tan's characters.

Communication is at the heart of *The Bonesetter's Daughter*. In China, Luling translates Precious Auntie's gestures into language; in California, Ruth translates Luling's Chinese into English. Luling is a superb calligrapher, shaping Chinese characters into art; Ruth makes a good living by transforming other people's ideas into best-selling books. Luling is unable to show her love for Ruth, however, and Ruth finds it impossible to communicate her feelings to Art. Baffled by Ruth's wall of silence, Art cannot tell her that he loves her, and their relationship is failing. Significantly, each year during the annual meteor shower, Ruth loses her voice for a week, thus absolving herself from communication with everyone.

SAVING FISH FROM DROWNING

Tan's fifth novel, *Saving Fish from Drowning*, opens with a quote from Albert Camus and a folktale that provides the novel's title. The Camus quote, "The evil that is in the world almost always comes of ignorance, and good intentions may do as much harm as malevolence if they lack understanding," segues neatly into the tale of a pious man who catches fish because he wants to save them from drowning.

In many ways, this novel is a departure from Tan's earlier work: Most of the central characters are Caucasians, nearly all of them are Americans, and some of the notable ones—including the Chinese and Karen—are men. Furthermore, although there are parent-child pairings in the group, the only mother-daughter tension, Bibi's fraught relationship with her stepmother, is in the past tense. Tan's signature focus on cultural conflict is very much a part of the novel, however, albeit in a new form.

Narrated by Bibi Chen, a San Francisco antiques dealer and socialite who died in a bizarre accident, the novel chronicles the adventures of twelve Californians on an art tour on the Burma Road through China and Myanmar. The travelers run the gamut from a nonprofit administrator to a hypochondriac who travels with an arsenal of medications, from a British dog trainer to a Darwinian biologist. Having originally instigated and planned the journey, which she called "Following Buddha's Footsteps," Bibi joins the group as an opinionated ghost who comments on the events as they transpire and occasionally interferes with arrangements.

The China section of the journey is something of a comic travelogue that has serious undertones. The tourists behave much like well-intentioned but unthinking travelers—they desecrate a shrine because they mistake it for a urinal, they romanticize rural landscapes, they judge everything they encounter from a Western per-

spective. Once they cross into Myanmar, however, the reason for the novel's title becomes clearer and the narrative takes on a darker tone.

On a Christmas morning boat trip to see the sunrise, eleven of the travelers are kidnapped by Karen tribesmen who mistake one of the Californians for a Jesus figure, the Younger White Brother for whom they have been waiting for a century. The oblivious travelers are unaware that they are captives, believing that they are trapped in the Karen encampment because a bridge has fallen into a ravine; the tribe's members, meanwhile, fail to realize that their god is merely an American teenager who is singularly adept at card tricks. Left behind because of a hangover when his friends took their sunrise trip, Harry, the celebrity dog trainer, embarks on a picaresque media and public-relations campaign to rescue them from their jungle prison. All eventually ends well, but not until Tan has raised a number of serious issues and questions.

Saving Fish from Drowning turns the spotlight on cultural collisions, not only those created by well-meaning Westerners who travel in the name of "saving" people in developing countries but also those conflicts caused by repressive governments that seek to destroy traditional lifestyles and practices. The travelers find themselves in the middle of both types of conflicts, and they are forced to confront their assumptions and to question the consequences of their actions. If they escape from the jungle camp, what will happen to their captors who have become their friends? Can they save both themselves and the tribe? Tan also questions the role of the news media, particularly in tense situations—does media coverage help to redress a problem, or does it exacerbate tensions to the point of no return? What if good intentions have bad results? Finally, although the novel skirts lightly around the real-world situation in Myanmar, the plight of the Karen tribespeople sets the stage for discussions of moral responsibility and truth telling.

E. D. Huntley

OTHER MAJOR WORKS

SCREENPLAY: *The Joy Luck Club*, 1993 (with Ronald Bass).

NONFICTION: "The Language of Discretion," 1990

(in *The State of the Language*, Christopher Ricks and Leonard Michaels, editors); *The Opposite of Fate: A Book of Musings*, 2003.

CHILDREN'S LITERATURE: *The Moon Lady*, 1992; *The Chinese Siamese Cat*, 1994.

BIBLIOGRAPHY

Adams, Bella. *Amy Tan*. Manchester, England: Manchester University Press, 2005. Provides close readings of Tan's novels through *The Bonesetter's Daughter*, focusing on representations of identity, history, and reality. In addition to a chapter on each novel, presents an introductory chapter that places the works in context and concludes with a critical overview.

Bloom, Harold, ed. *Amy Tan*. Philadelphia: Chelsea House, 2000. Collection of essays pulls together commentary on Tan's work from many different contemporary critics.

Ho, Wendy. *In Her Mother's House: The Politics of Asian American Mother-Daughter Writing*. Walnut Creek, Calif.: AltaMira Press, 1999. Includes two chapters that address Tan's fiction specifically: "Losing Your Innocence But Not Your Hope: Amy Tan's Joy Luck Mothers and Coca-Cola Daughters," and "The Heart Never Travels: The Incorporation of Fathers in the Mother-Daughter Stories of Maxine Hong Kingston, Amy Tan, and Fae Myenne Ng."

Huh, Joonok. *Interconnected Mothers and Daughters in Amy Tan's "The Joy Luck Club."* Tucson: Southwest Institute for Research on Women, 1992. Examines the mother and adult child relationship in Tan's novel. Includes a bibliography.

Huntley, E. D. *Amy Tan: A Critical Companion*. Westport, Conn.: Greenwood Press, 1998. Provides biographical information and analyzes Tan's novels in the context of Asian American literature. Discusses major themes in the work such as the crone figure, food, clothing, language, biculturalism, and relations between mothers and daughters. Includes bibliography.

Ling, Amy. *Between Worlds: Women Writers of Chinese Ancestry*. New York: Pergamon, 1990. Offers a chronological and thematic introduction to prose narratives in English by American women of Chinese or partial Chinese ancestry, helping to place Tan's work within a meaningful context.

Pearlman, Mickey, and Katherine Usher Henderson. "Amy Tan." *Inter/View: Talks with America's Writing Women*. Lexington: University Press of Kentucky, 1990. Provides biographical information on Tan, revealing the sources of some of the stories in *The Joy Luck Club*.

Snodgrass, Mary Ellen. *Amy Tan: A Literary Companion*. Jefferson, N.C.: McFarland, 2004. Readable, engaging work provides an introduction to Tan's life and works. Includes study questions, an extensive bibliography, and a glossary of Chinese terms found in Tan's novels.

Tan, Amy. "Amy Tan." Interview by Barbara Somogyi and David Stanton. *Poets and Writers* 19, no. 5 (September 1, 1991): 24-32. Tan discusses her childhood and her early career as a business writer, her decision to write fiction, her success with *The Joy Luck Club*, and some of that novel's autobiographical elements.

JUN'ICHIRŌ TANIZAKI

Born: Tokyo, Japan; July 24, 1886
Died: Yugawara, Japan; July 30, 1965

PRINCIPAL LONG FICTION

Itansha no Kanashimi, 1917
Chijin no ai, 1924-1925 (serial), 1925 (book; *Naomi*, 1985)
Kōjin, 1926
Tade kuu mushi, 1928-1929 (serial), 1936 (book; *Some Prefer Nettles*, 1955)
Manji, 1928-1930
Yoshinokuzu, 1931 (*Arrowroot*, 1982)
Bushōkō hiwa, 1931-1932 (serial), 1935 (book; *The Secret History of the Lord of Musashi*, 1982)
Sasameyuki, 1943-1948 (serial), 1949 (book; *The Makioka Sisters*, 1957)
Shōshō Shigemoto no haha, 1950 (*The Mother of Captain Shigemoto*, 1956)
Kagi, 1956 (*The Key*, 1960)
Fūten rōjin nikki, 1961-1962 (serial), 1962 (book; *Diary of a Mad Old Man*, 1965)

OTHER LITERARY FORMS

The history of the novel in Japan is quite different from its history in the West, and the distinctions normally observed between the short story and the novel do not apply there. If, arbitrarily, one refers to Japanese works of fewer than one hundred pages of prose fiction as "short stories," Jun'ichirō Tanizaki (tah-nee-zahk-ee) is as famous for his short stories as for his longer works. Typical of his early period, "Shisei" (1910; "The Tattooer," 1963) indicates his early interest in sexual symbolism. "Akuma" (1912; Satan) deals with male masochism, and "Otsuya goroshi" (1913; a springtime case) deals with murder and amorality in Tokyo. Later, Tanizaki wrote such remarkable stories as "Ashikari" (1932; English translation, 1936), "Shunkinshō" (1933; "A Portrait of Shunkin," 1936), "Mōmoku monogatari" (1931; "A Blind Man's Tale," 1963), and the exquisite "Yume no ukihashi" (1959; "The Bridge of Dreams," 1963).

Tanizaki also wrote a number of plays, including

Aisureba koso (pb. 1921; all because of love), *Okumi to Gohei* (pb. 1922), and *Shirogitsune no yu* (pb. 1923; *The White Fox*, 1930). In 1932, he began translating Murasaki Shikibu's *Genji monogatari* (c. 1004; *The Tale of Genji*, 1936-1941, 1951-1954) into modern Japanese; over the years, he produced several revisions of it. *Bunshō tokuhon* (1934; a manual of style), in which he outlined his craftsmanlike attitude toward composing fiction, is often called a minor masterpiece of criticism. Although he published several highly accomplished reviews and essays, he seldom was persuaded to undertake them, believing that he ought to concentrate on his fiction.

ACHIEVEMENTS

Jun'ichirō Tanizaki was recognized as a remarkable talent even in his twenties and continued to be so recognized throughout a long and prolific career, which outlasted several publications of his complete works. At first, he was considered shockingly Western by his contemporaries; during the 1920's, however, he gradually began to incorporate more conservative Japanese literary elements, implicitly warning his readers of the dangers of being overly Westernized. Late in his career, his characters are not endangered by Western culture, enjoying, for example, Western clothes and houses as everyday realities in modern Japan.

Tanizaki's mastery of a carefully composed style and his insight into the psychology of his characters place him among the great writers of twentieth century world literature. A slow, careful writer, Tanizaki argued that one of the most important elements of Japanese is its "vagueness" in comparison to other languages, a vagueness that allows the Japanese author to suggest motives, feelings, and details in delicate strokes rather than in precise exposition. Considering the imagination crucial, Tanizaki often dealt with sensational material and abnormal states of mind; by controlling his style, he did not allow his intensity to become hysterical. Despite their bizarre aberrations, his characters rarely become unbelievable as human beings, because of the objective manner in which he treats them. Like many great writers, Tanizaki was also able to assimilate opposing elements such as tradition and innovation, imagination and realism, and the influences of West and East.

BIOGRAPHY

Jun'ichirō Tanizaki was born in the heart of downtown Tokyo. For generations, his ancestors had lived there as members of the merchant class engaged in rice-brokering and printing and had little of the traditional samurai-class interest in affairs of state. Despite the traditional male-dominated culture of Japan, Tanizaki's grandfather and father were considered feminists, his father nearly worshiping Tanizaki's mother. The boy, as a result, was drawn to his mother very strongly, thus establishing the reverential attitude toward women seen in so many of his works. Tanizaki was also a handsome boy, but not a strong one, and, consequently, was often bullied by older classmates, perhaps encouraging a masochistic streak.

During Tanizaki's primary education, a young teacher noticed the boy's talents and gave him special instruction in Japanese and Chinese classics. It is often reported that Tanizaki became known as the brightest student ever to graduate from the First Municipal Secondary School of Tokyo. He entered Tokyo Imperial University in 1908, where he studied Japanese classical literature. He helped found the literary magazine of the university, *Shinshicho*, in which he published several short stories that received praise from older writers such as Mori Ogai and Nagai Kafu. After only a year, however, because he did not pay his fees, he left the university without finishing his degree.

Tanizaki's unfinished education did not hinder him unduly, because he was becoming known as a writer. A notorious frequenter of the "Bluff," or foreign sections of Yokohama, he wore checked suits and gaudy ties and was strongly under the influence of Decadent Western writers such as Edgar Allan Poe, Charles Baudelaire, and Oscar Wilde; Tanizaki translated Wilde's *Lady Windermere's Fan* (1892) in 1919. This lifestyle changed when he moved to Okamoto in 1923 after the Great Earthquake. In the Hakone mountains south of Yokohama, during the disaster, he first was delighted that all he despised of the old Japan had been destroyed. He predicted a new, modern Tokyo with wide boulevards,

film theaters, and citizens wearing comfortable Western clothing. Yet, as time passed, he began to seek the traditional roots of Japanese literature and went, as is often asserted, from being merely a good author to being a great one.

By 1930, Tanizaki was so famous that his complete works were published. His personal life was almost as sensational as his fiction. After encouraging his wife, Chiyoko, to have an affair with his friend, Sato Haruo, they were divorced in 1930 after fifteen years of marriage. In 1931, he married Furukawa Tomiko, a literary student whom he divorced in 1934. In 1935, he married his last wife, Morita Matzuko, formerly married to an Ōsaka millionaire and patron of several artists and writers, including Tanizaki.

With the rise of militarism in Japan, Tanizaki's work—with its interest in aestheticism and sexuality—was considered improper, and he was forced to suppress the amorous passages of his translation of *The Tale of Genji*, which he had begun in 1935. His longest novel, *The Makioka Sisters*, was not published during the war because of the amorous content, but when it was finally released, it—along with his earlier works—established Tanizaki as possibly the most significant twentieth century Japanese author. In 1949, he received Japan's Imperial Prize for Literature.

During the 1950's and 1960's, Tanizaki returned to some of the themes of his earlier career. The publication of the first episode of *The Key* in the magazine *Chuo koron* in 1956 created a sensation in Japan as customers snatched up copies, partly because of its sexual content. It also became well known in the United States, as did "The Bridge of Dreams" and *Diary of a Mad Old Man*, as a result of a new Western interest in Japanese films (such as Akira Kurosawa's 1951 film of Ryūnosuke Akutagawa's "Rashomon") and literature (notably the works of Yasunari Kawabata and Yukio Mishima). In 1960, a film version of *The Key* was released in the United States as *Odd Obsession*. In 1964, Tanizaki was elected honorary member of the American Academy of Arts and Letters and the National Institute of Arts and Letters. He spent his last few years struggling with various illnesses and living in a Western-style house on the Izu Coast. At the time of his death, Tanizaki was one of the leading candidates for a Nobel Prize.

ANALYSIS

Jun'ichirō Tanizaki's early literary career was characterized by a deep interest in Western literature. Although as a student he studied Japanese literature and had a nostalgia for classical Japanese works, he once commented that about 1918, "I had come to detest Japan, even though I was obviously a Japanese." Assiduously reading Baudelaire, Wilde, and especially Poe, he asserted the supremacy of the imagination in literature, as opposed to the naturalism of many of his contemporaries, arguing that even Gustave Flaubert and Émile Zola could not have produced their naturalistic works without being highly imaginative.

Once using Wilde's aphorism "Nature imitates art" as an epigraph to a story, Tanizaki believed that the representation of reality was not the primary function of literature; it was rather the presentation of truth. "The art-

Jun'ichirō Tanizaki. (The Granger Collection, New York)

ist," he wrote, "justifies his existence only when he can transform his imagination into truth." This truth, in Tanizaki's view, was primarily psychological. Imagination allowed the author to see the subconscious depths of humanity. The writer perceived what people were, not what they could be. There was no need for a writer to justify his (or her) works for social or moral reasons, and Tanizaki was seen as an exponent of aestheticism.

As might be expected, the early influence of the Decadent authors led to intense, macabre works. They are, by turn, gothic, grotesque, hedonistic, diabolic, and erotic. Tanizaki's first important work, "The Tattooer," is typical. Seikichi is a master tattooer who has become so great he only tattoos according to his vision of his client's character. Further, he delights in the suffering his needles cause his clients. His obsession becomes the creation of a masterwork on the skin of a woman who meets his requirements of character as well as beauty. After four years, he sees the foot of a woman disappear into a palanquin, knows instantly that she is the one he has been searching for, but loses the palanquin in the crowd. The next spring, she appears at his house, and after he reveals her true, vampirish nature, he creates an exquisite tattoo of a black widow spider on her back and finds himself the slave of his own creation.

There are several elements characteristic of Tanizaki's work in this story. In most of his works, a man delights in his utter servitude to the woman he adores. Seikichi goes from sadist to masochist as the result of finding his perfect woman, and although Tanizaki devotes this work to the psychological and artistic obsessions of the tattooer, he was generally more interested in his women characters, because they expressed an ideal before which his men groveled. This subservient role has been frequently associated with Tanizaki's attitude toward his mother, who died in 1917. One will also note the foot fetishism implicit in Seikichi's first noticing the young girl. Throughout Tanizaki's career, women's feet play a large role in the sexual relationships between his characters. This is obvious in such works as "Fumiko no ashi" in which an old man is infatuated with the feet of his mistress and dies in ecstasy as Fumiko presses his forehead under her foot, but it reveals itself in other ways as well: Frequently, Tanizaki devotes more detail to his description of a woman's feet than he does to his description of her face.

Despite Tanizaki's interest in Western writers, many elements of his early work were derived from traditional Japanese literature. Throughout his career, he felt no hesitation in setting his stories in the Japanese past. "The Tattooer," for example, occurs in the Tokugawa period of the seventeenth century. In 1919, in the middle of his Decadent interests, the same year as "Fumiko no ashi" and his translation of *Lady Windermere's Fan*, he published a volume of erotic stories in the style of the Japanese 1830's and two novellas in the Chinese style. As they are depicted in works by Tanizaki, women are often portrayed as treacherous, cruel creatures in classical Japanese literature. The seventeenth century novelist Ihara Saikaku wrote many risqué stories, in some of which the heroine's insatiable sexual appetite exhausts the hero. Finally, grotesque and diabolic motifs are very common in classical Japanese literature, and it is perhaps too easy to overemphasize the influence of Poe's and Wilde's content on Tanizaki, when he was more interested in adapting their conception of art in his reaction against naturalism.

There is no doubt, however, that Tanizaki's work changed at the beginning of the 1920's, particularly after he moved from Tokyo to the more conservative Kansai (Kyōto, Ōsaka, and Kōbe) region after the Great Earthquake. Although in his later work he retained his masochistic heroes, characters for whom there are few precedents in traditional Japanese literature, he began to acknowledge more strongly the values and practices of his culture.

NAOMI

Naomi marks the division between Tanizaki's Westernized period and his more tradition-oriented works from the 1920's through the 1940's. Although, like so many of his works, *Naomi* tells of a man's quest for the ideal woman, there is much implied criticism of Japanese worship of the West, despite the fact that the novel seems to have been based on W. Somerset Maugham's *Of Human Bondage* (1915).

Joji, the narrator in *Naomi*, is attracted to a European-looking waitress named Naomi. Her features make him think of Mary Pickford, and he asks her if she would like to go to a film. Instead of the usual polite evasions, she says (like Mildred in *Of Human Bondage*), "I don't mind if I do." Eventually, he takes her home with the intention of remaking her into his ideal of beauty—a woman he will not be ashamed of in front of blond foreigners—and marrying her within a few years. Naomi is given Western clothes, practices playing the piano, speaking English, and dancing. All of this merely encourages her decadent tendencies. He learns she has been unfaithful and attempts to leave her. He discovers he cannot, however, and gives in completely to her. She can do as she wishes, have whatever lover she wishes, as long as she remains his wife.

Joji is a fool as much in his obsessive love of Western things as in his love of the girl. He is ashamed of his racial identity. His shortness, his protruding teeth, his dark complexion, and other typically Japanese features embarrass him, but he is proud of his European-style Yokohama house. He is degraded by his sense of both cultural and sexual inferiority. Often offended by Naomi's crudity, he excuses it because of his fascination with her; to be humiliated by her is an honor. Even when she dresses and behaves like a prostitute, he is filled with masochistic pride that she is his.

SOME PREFER NETTLES

Tanizaki's next major novel, *Some Prefer Nettles*, deals with similar themes. This work tells of a character, Kaname, whose superficial Western tastes are gradually replaced by an appreciation of traditional Japanese culture. Kaname is unhappily married to Misako. He has lost sexual interest in her but is tormented by uncertainty over what to do about it. He encourages her to have an affair while he finds sexual satisfaction with a Eurasian prostitute. There is a superficial resemblance between this plot and certain events in Tanizaki's own life. Bored with his first wife, Chiyoko, one night at dinner he calmly asked Sato Haruo, poet and friend, if he would like to marry her. In 1930, after encouraging the affair, Tanizaki divorced Chiyoko, and she married Sato. Obviously, this arrangement was on his mind during the writing of *Some Prefer Nettles*, and his ambivalence is perhaps reflected by the book itself.

Far more important, however, in assessing the book, is the struggle in Kaname between his appreciation of Western culture and his appreciation of the merchants' culture of old Japan surviving in Ōsaka, particularly represented in this novel by the Bunraku, or puppet theater. At the end of the novel, Kaname confuses a puppet with the Ōsaka beauty O-hisa, showing perhaps that the old way of life is a fantasy that cannot be recaptured. Edward G. Seidensticker, who translated the novel, argues that Kaname (and Tanizaki) is attempting to return to the peace of childhood, although the adult knows the new world is here to stay. In his essay "In'ei raisan" (1934; *In Praise of Shadows*, 1955), Tanizaki wrote "I know as well as anyone that I am dreaming, and that, having come this far, we cannot turn back."

It should also be noted that whatever ambivalence or vagueness readers might find in *Some Prefer Nettles* and other Tanizaki novels is as much a reflection of his aesthetic as of any personal feelings. He always insisted on exploiting the vagueness of Japanese and objected to writers who were too clear. One cannot, for example, know exactly what will happen to Kaname the day after the novel closes. Primary among Tanizaki's goals in writing was to achieve poetic suggestiveness, which the last scene certainly does.

THE MAKIOKA SISTERS

During the late 1930's, Tanizaki continued his rediscovery of traditional Japanese culture by beginning his translation of *The Tale of Genji*, a work that, in many ways, influenced the composition of *The Makioka Sisters*, his longest and, many argue, his greatest novel. Although Tanizaki was always a slow, very careful writer, wartime circumstances forced him to work even more slowly than usual. He spent many years on *The Makioka Sisters*, and censorship prevented complete publication of the work until 1948.

Before Tanizaki began writing the novel, he delineated a precise plan and followed it nearly to the conclusion. Despite this detailed planning, *The Makioka Sisters*—unlike his usual lean, straightforward novels—is a sprawling, indirect novel in the episodic form often favored by Japanese authors. Complex characterization and diverse social forces create many layers of action and emotion to give the book a texture quite different from that of Tanizaki's typical works, which focus on a single character.

In the novel, the four Makioka sisters represent various aspects of Japanese culture during the 1930's. Once a rich Ōsaka merchant family, the Makiokas have declined. Tsuruko, the eldest, is the most conservative, trying to hang on to a way of life they have outlived. Taeko, the youngest, seems the brightest, the most talented, and the most corrupted by the Tokyo-style intelligentsia with its Western fads. Sachiko, with her husband, Teinosuke, holds the family together by mediating between the impulses that tear at it. Yukiko, despite her traditional beauty, is too shy to deal effectively with her sisters or the world about her.

Most of the novel concerns the attempt to find the aging Yukiko a husband; the Japanese title *Sasameyuki* (thin snow) refers to the number of *miai* (marriage arrangements) that fail. Tsuruko generally insists on going through the slow traditional investigation of potential husbands, while Sachiko recognizes the diminishing value of Yukiko as a bride and tries to carry the arrangements out in a reasonable, though not hurried, time. Taeko, who intends to marry a Westernized playboy, must wait for her elder sister's marriage before marrying on her own. Yukiko is so introverted that she often seems indifferent to the whole struggle, except when she rejects another candidate.

This plot, however, is not Tanizaki's main concern. Using details from his wife Tomiko's family history, he re-creates Ōsaka as it was before the war, revealing foreign influences that would inevitably destroy that way of life—the clothing, the foreign films, the German neighbors, the visit to the White Russians, Taeko's desire to go to Paris to learn dressmaking—and the traditional Japanese customs as they were then practiced. Attention is devoted to the cherry blossom festival, Taeko's doll-making, Kabuki, Japanese dance, and the old house of the Makiokas. The elegant Ōsaka dialect is spoken by the main characters and the Tokyo dialect is portrayed as being corrupted. Despite these contrasts, *The Makioka Sisters* is not a didactic work that preaches the superiority of the old ways over the new. It captures a particular way of life at a certain period in a certain place. Free of the grotesqueness that characterizes his early works and of the obsessive characters that populate most of his works, *The Makioka Sisters* is a panoramic view of diverse characters with complex motivations, a work unusual in Tanizaki's oeuvre but indisputably a masterpiece.

Unlike many writers, who, once they have achieved an integrated work such as *The Makioka Sisters*, run out of things to say, Tanizaki remained as creative in the final decades of his life as he had earlier. Entering the third phase of his career, he returned to many of the themes that had occupied him in his youth; with a more detached and sometimes ironic point of view, he dealt with the obsessions of sex in old age. Composed of the parallel diaries of a fifty-six-year-old professor and his forty-five-year-old wife, *The Key* progresses through the former's attempt to expand the sexual abilities of the latter, a woman whom he loves madly but who no longer satisfies him. Once again, one might note the autobiographical resonance of the professor's gradually directing his wife into the young Kimura's arms. One might also note the return of the devouring woman as the wife encourages the eating of beef and incites his jealousy, in spite of her knowledge of her husband's rising blood pressure, which eventually kills him.

THE KEY

The Key created a sensation on its publication, no doubt largely because of its frank treatment of sex; like other works of literature—Gustave Flaubert's *Madame Bovary* (1857) and D. H. Lawrence's *Lady Chatterley's Lover* (1928)—which achieved notoriety before their literary merits were admitted, *The Key*'s craftsmanship can now be assessed more objectively. Presenting one diary in the *katakana* script and the other in the *hiragana* script, Tanizaki exploits the differences between the two characters' perceptions of the situation. Further, he complicates the ostensibly sincere presentations of the diaries by having each character aware that the other may be reading what is written. This complex treatment of point of view turns an apparently simple, short work into a multilayered psychological study.

DIARY OF A MAD OLD MAN

Tanizaki's last novel, *Diary of a Mad Old Man*, also consists mainly of a diary, but by a man even older than the protagonist of *The Key*. Also suffering from high blood pressure, he is sexually impotent as well. Nevertheless, he is attracted to his daughter-in-law, Satsuko, estranged from her husband and having an affair with another man. As in many of Tanizaki's works, the narrator devotes much attention to Satsuko's feet as sexual objects, and he thinks often of his mother. He compares

Satsuko's feet many times with those of his mother, and he delights in kissing Satsuko's feet and biting her toes when she comes from the shower. Her feet also become associated with the Buddhist goddess of mercy, and the old man plans for his daughter-in-law's footprints to be carved on his tombstone.

Objectively treated, *Diary of a Mad Old Man* is a great deal less sensational than it would appear from a plot summary. The artistic coolness that Tanizaki worked so hard to achieve saves the work from any pornographic content. Further, the novel is comic in its attitude toward the main character, satirizing the high intensity of Tanizaki's early works. Several of his works have comic elements—he was fond of cats and often wrote of them in a lighthearted vein—and Tanizaki seems to have ended his career looking back on his extraordinary achievements with a whimsical detachment.

J. Madison Davis

OTHER MAJOR WORKS

SHORT FICTION: "Kirin," 1910; "Shōnen," 1910; "Shisei," 1910 ("The Tattooer," 1963); "Hōkan," 1911; "Akuma," 1912; "Kyōfu," 1913 ("Terror," 1963); "Otsuya goroshi," 1913; "Haha o kouruki," 1919 ("Longing for Mother," 1980); "Watakushi," 1921 ("The Thief," 1963); "Aoi Hano," 1922 ("Aguri," 1963); "Mōmoku monogatari," 1931 ("A Blind Man's Tale," 1963); "Ashikari," 1932 (English translation, 1936); "Shunkinshō," 1933 ("A Portrait of Shunkin," 1936); *Hyofu*, 1950; "Yume no ukihashi," 1959 ("The Bridge of Dreams," 1963); *Yume no ukihashi*, 1960 (collection); *Kokumin no bungaku*, 1964; *Tanizaki Jun'ichirō shu*, 1970; *Seven Japanese Tales*, 1981; *The Gourmet Club: A Sextet*, 2001 (Anthony H. Chambers and Paul McCarthy, translators).

PLAYS: *Aisureba koso*, pb. 1921; *Okumi to Gohei*, pb. 1922; *Shirogitsune no yu*, pb. 1923 (*The White Fox*, 1930); *Mumyō to Aizen*, pb. 1924; *Shinzei*, pb. 1949.

NONFICTION: *Bunshō tokuhon*, 1934; "In'ei raisan," 1934 ("In Praise of Shadows," 1955); *Kyō no yume, Ōsaka no yume*, 1950; *Yōshō-jidai*, 1957 (*Childhood Years: A Memoir*, 1988).

TRANSLATION: *Genji monogatari*, 1936-1941, 1951-1954 (of Murasaki Shikibu's medieval novel).

MISCELLANEOUS: *Tanizaki Jun'ichirō zenshu*, 1930

(12 volumes); *Tanizaki Jun'ichirō zenshu*, 1966-1970 (28 volumes).

BIBLIOGRAPHY

Chambers, Anthony Hood. *The Secret Window: Ideal Worlds in Tanizaki's Fiction*. Cambridge, Mass.: Harvard University Press, 1994. Chambers analyzes seven of Tanizaki's novels and novellas, focusing on the characters' attempts to create "ideal worlds" and the elements of fantasy in these works. Includes notes and a bibliography.

Gessel, Van C. *Three Modern Novelists: Soseki, Tanizaki, Kawabata*. New York: Kodansha International, 1993. The sixty-five-page chapter on Tanizaki concentrates on his approach to modernism. Includes detailed notes but no bibliography.

Golley, Gregory L. "Tanizaki Junichiro: The Art of Subversion and the Subversion of Art." *Journal of Japanese Studies* 21 (Summer, 1995): 365-404. Examines the "return to Japan" inaugurated by Tanizaki's *Some Prefer Nettles*. Discusses themes and images in the work and suggests that Tanizaki's traditionalist fiction both championed and undermined the idea of an essential Japanese traditional culture.

Ito, Ken K. *Visions of Desire: Tanizaki's Fictional Worlds*. Stanford, Calif.: Stanford University Press, 1991. A critical biography, with chapters arranged in chronological order of Tanizaki's life and work. Ito primarily focuses his analysis on Tanizaki's best-known works that have been translated into English, and pays special attention to Tanizaki's language, narrative style, and his male characters' projection of their desires upon women. Includes notes, a bibliography, and a section on names and sources.

Keene, Donald. *Dawn to the West: Japanese Literature of the Modern Era—Fiction*. New York: Holt, Rinehart and Winston, 1984. A massive study of the fiction produced since the Japanese enlightenment of the nineteenth century. Chapter 20 is devoted exclusively to Tanizaki, and he is discussed in the introduction and in several other chapters in association with other writers and literary movements.

_____. *Five Modern Japanese Novelists*. New York: Columbia University Press, 2003. Keene devotes a chapter to Tanizaki in his tribute to five twentieth-century Japanese novelists. Includes his personal recollections of Tanizaki, with whom he was acquainted, and discusses the writer's works.

_____. *Japanese Literature: An Introduction for Western Readers*. New York: Grove Press, 1955. Unlike the comprehensive treatment in *Dawn to the West*, this is a brief introduction to Japanese literature. Tanizaki is briefly mentioned in the introduction and chapter 4, "The Japanese Novel," but is discussed throughout chapter 5, "Japanese Literature Under Western Influence."

Lippit, Noriko Miuta. *Reality and Fiction in Modern Japanese Literature*. White Plains, N.Y.: M. E. Sharpe, 1980. Lippit considers the struggle of several Japanese writers to define the function of art and literature, both socially and personally. The sections on Tanizaki deal with his aesthetic preference for fantasy and complex structure, with a comparison to Edgar Allan Poe. Includes notes.

Suzuki, Tomi. *Narrating the Self: Fictions of Japanese Modernity*. Stanford, Calif.: Stanford University Press, 1996. Two of the chapters are devoted to Tanizaki: "Allegories of Modernity in Tanizaki Jun'ichirō's *Fool's Love*" (also known as *Naomi*) and the epilogue, "Tanizaki's Speaking Subject and the Creation of Tradition." Includes notes and a bibliography.

Ueda, Makoto. "Tanizaki Jun'ichirō." In *Modern Japanese Writers and the Nature of Literature*. Stanford, Calif.: Stanford University Press, 1976. Discusses Tanizaki as one of the eight major writers who make up the majority of modern Japanese fiction familiar to Western readers. Provides an introduction to major literary theories underlying Japanese novels and stories. Supplemented by source notes, a bibliography, and an index.

Yamanouchi, Hisaaki. *The Search for Authenticity in Modern Japanese Literature*. New York: Cambridge University Press, 1978. Discusses twelve modern Japanese writers, analyzing the ways each dealt with difficult personal, social, and intellectual questions in art. The sections on Tanizaki focus on the concept of eternal womanhood in his works. Includes notes, a bibliography, and an index.

BOOTH TARKINGTON

Born: Indianapolis, Indiana; July 29, 1869
Died: Indianapolis, Indiana; May 19, 1946
Also known as: Newton Booth Tarkington

PRINCIPAL LONG FICTION

The Gentleman from Indiana, 1899
Monsieur Beaucaire, 1900
The Conquest of Canaan, 1905
His Own People, 1907
The Flirt, 1913
Penrod, 1914
The Turmoil, 1915
Penrod and Sam, 1916
Seventeen, 1916
The Magnificent Ambersons, 1918
Ramsey Milholland, 1919
Alice Adams, 1921
Gentle Julia, 1922
Growth, 1923 (includes *The Turmoil*, *The*
    Magnificent Ambersons, and *The Midlander*
    [*The Midlander* renamed *National Avenue*])
The Midlander, 1923
Penrod Jashber, 1929
Young Mrs. Greeley, 1929
Presenting Lily Mars, 1933
Little Orvie, 1934
The Fighting Littles, 1941
The Heritage of Hatcher Ide, 1941
Kate Fennigate, 1943
Image of Josephine, 1945

OTHER LITERARY FORMS

Although best known as a novelist, Booth Tarkington also enjoyed some success as a playwright, with such works as the stage versions of his novels *Monsieur Beaucaire* (*Beaucaire*, pr. 1901, with Evelyn Greenleaf Sutherland; adaptation of his novel *Monsieur Beaucaire*), *The Gentleman from Indiana* (pr. 1905), as well as *The Man from Home* (pr. 1907). Tarkington also enjoyed considerable success as a writer of short stories. Two of his stories, "The One-Hundred Dollar Bill" and "Stella Crozier," were honored with the O. Henry Award in

1923 and 1926, respectively. In addition, Tarkington's short-story collection *"Mr. White," "The Red Barn," "Hell," and "Bridewater"* (1935) is one of his most respected. Tarkington also published many magazine pieces in the genres of reminiscences and literary criticism. Chief among these are "As I Seem to Me," "Mr. Howells," and "The World Does Move."

ACHIEVEMENTS

Few authors have enjoyed such critical and popular esteem as Booth Tarkington experienced during his lifetime. Tarkington won two Pulitzer Prizes, the first in 1918 for *The Magnificent Ambersons* and the second in 1921 for *Alice Adams*. In 1933, he received the National Institute of Arts and Letters Gold Medal, and in 1945 he received the William Dean Howells Medal, presented by the American Academy of Arts and Letters. Tarkington was awarded so many honorary doctorates that he began declining them. He did, however, accept an honorary degree in 1940 from Purdue University, which he attended for one year. Tarkington did not explore new modes of fiction, but he excelled at subtle depictions of character in the realistic mode established by William Dean Howells and Henry James, both of whom he greatly admired.

BIOGRAPHY

Newton Booth Tarkington was born in Indianapolis, Indiana, on July 29, 1869, lived most of his life there, and passed away in his hometown on May 19, 1946. He took for his material the characters and concerns of his home city and home state, using the region to highlight the eternal concerns of humanity. He was raised in an upper-middle-class family and received a superior education, particularly at Phillips Exeter Academy. A year spent at Purdue in 1890-1891 brought him into contact with another Hoosier writer, George Ade, and with the illustrator John T. McCutcheon. Tarkington spent the years of 1891-1893 at Princeton University, although he did not take a degree. Although his education did not follow the usual pattern, it did energize him and afford him the opportunity to explore his literary talents.

After leaving Princeton, Tarkington played the part of the struggling writer for five years; however, with the publication of *The Gentleman from Indiana* in 1899, Tarkington was recognized as a major new writer. The novel became a best seller, and Tarkington, a prolific writer throughout his career, followed it with short stories, novels, and plays. Established as a major young writer, Tarkington married Louisa Fletcher in 1902. That same year, he was elected to the Indiana House of Representatives. He served in that capacity for only two sessions before resigning due to ill health—he had contracted typhoid in a southern Indiana resort. His bout with typhoid initiated what was to become a lifelong practice of spending the summers in Kennebunkport, Maine. Tarkington's only child, Laurel, was born in 1906. The Tarkingtons divorced in 1911. The couple's rift was due in part to Tarkington's heavy drinking; he eventually realized he was an alcoholic.

Tarkington soon recovered from depression and divorce, gave up alcohol, and married Susanah Robinson in 1912. The next decade witnessed the burst of creativity that produced his masterworks *Penrod*, *The Magnificent Ambersons*, and *Alice Adams*. The last two works won Pulitzer Prizes, and Tarkington found himself occupying the very pinnacle of American letters. Following this great success, however, was yet another dark period. Tarkington's father, with whom the writer had enjoyed a close relationship, died in January, 1923. This bereavement was followed by the harder blow that came in April: the death of his daughter, Laurel.

With the Great Depression, Tarkington's preoccupation with social concerns increased, but his popularity and success rested mainly on his earlier achievements. He became more socially active and lobbied for the adoption of the United Nations charter. He died on May 19, 1946.

ANALYSIS

A realist in the mode of his mentor, writer Howells, Booth Tarkington excelled at characterization and the integration of moral dilemma with character and plot. In his most successful novels, Tarkington focused on regular people facing complex situations. The people he selected for his subjects were most often Hoosiers, and the setting was nearly always Indiana. Typically, the di-

Booth Tarkington. (Library of Congress)

lemmas faced by his characters highlight flaws marring otherwise sympathetic individuals. Always charming, Tarkington's characters are never entirely lost souls; there exists always the possibility of ethical growth and development.

THE GENTLEMAN FROM INDIANA

Tarkington's first success, *The Gentleman from Indiana*, won for him a national readership and propelled him to a place of prominence in American letters. This novel contains the themes and characters typical of Tarkington's later works, but with far less attention to psychological insight and a greater reliance on romance. The protagonist, John Harkless, is drawn in rather stereotypical fashion as a crusading newspaperman fighting racism and mob violence. The novel is compelling, but it lacks the kind of substantive, complex development of character typical of Tarkington's more mature work. The heroes and villains are clearly drawn, and readers view the action rather than participate in it. In later works, such as *Alice Adams*, Tarkington replicates the dilemmas of his characters within the minds of his readers. Still, the rudiments of Tarkington's concern for characterization and moral dilemma are fleshed out in *The Gentleman from Indiana*.

PENROD

The first volume of a trilogy, *Penrod* was followed by *Penrod and Sam* and *Penrod Jashber*. The title character and protagonist is a young boy who bears a striking resemblance to Mark Twain's Tom Sawyer. Like Tom, Penrod tells lies, often with hilarious results. Caught daydreaming in class, Penrod tells his teacher he has been distracted by his uncle's alcoholism. The yarn spins out beyond the boy's ability to control it, and trouble ensues. Similarly, when cast as an unwilling Launcelot in an amateur theatrical, Penrod is mortified that the tights he has to wear are made from his father's long underwear. At the last minute, he dons the janitor's capacious overalls, ruining the serious tone the director had attempted to instill. Although *Penrod* is often compared to Twain's *Adventures of Huckleberry Finn* (1884), it bears greater similarity to the earlier *The Adventures of Tom Sawyer* (1876). Tarkington's book is related from an omniscient point of view, like Twain's earlier work, and Penrod occupies a position within society, as does Tom. The point of view is particularly appropriate and fits the nostalgic air pervading the novel.

Penrod was wildly popular during Tarkington's life, and it marks an important development of his artistry. With *Penrod*, Tarkington perfected his notable ability to connect plot and character; Tarkington himself observed that "Tom and Huck are realistic only in character. He [Twain] gave 'em what boys don't get when it came to 'plot.'" Tarkington's protagonist is no more "real" than Twain's Tom or Huck, but the incidents Penrod participates in are arguably more typical than what Twain relates. As Tarkington approached his more mature work, he still insisted on the accurate depiction of character and plot.

THE MAGNIFICENT AMBERSONS

Tarkington had achieved commercial success with his earlier work, but it was with *The Magnificent* *Ambersons* that he achieved true critical success. It was for this novel that Tarkington received his first Pulitzer. Critics recognized that the story of the Amberson family was at once a story about one midwestern family, but at the same time it was as universal a story as that of Aeschylus's tragic house of Atreus or of Leo Tolstoy's *Anna Karenina* (1875-1877). Tarkington's novel chronicles the fall of the Amberson family in the years after the American Civil War. Major Amberson had managed to establish himself as a rich and powerful man through hard work in manufacturing, but the third generation scion of the family, George Amberson, wishes only to live the life of a gentleman. He rejects any suggestion that he should work, for he believes work is beneath a gentleman. The privilege enjoyed by the younger Ambersons born into wealth exerts a negative influence on character that militates against the preservation of wealth. Spoiled, George suffers financial losses that derive from his character; he is described as "reckless" financially and is also "arrogant and conceited and badtempered."

The story of the Amberson family, then, is the American success story rewritten. Tarkington explores the Horatio Alger myth of rags to riches and finds it wanting in a family that finds itself unable to sustain the success of its founder. After seeing that even the name of Amberson Boulevard has been changed to Tenth Street, George realizes how low the family has fallen. "The city," readers are told, "had rolled over the Ambersons and buried them under to the last vestige." The novel does not conclude on such a somber note, however, and George seems to muster some inner resources left over from the old major. When he finally does go to work, he does so vigorously. In a somewhat sentimental vein more typical of Tarkington's earlier work, the novel ends with George's reunion with his true love, Lucy, in a hospital room. George had been struck by a car, just as the family as a whole had been "rolled over" by the city.

ALICE ADAMS

With *Alice Adams*, Tarkington returned to the theme of the American success story. This novel won for Tarkington his second Pulitzer, and it is also widely regarded as Tarkington's greatest achievement. His heroine reminds the reader of other characters in literature who test the American myth of success expressed best by the Horatio Alger stories. Like Alger's Ragged Dick, Alice Adams strives to lift herself up into another social realm from the one in which she was born. As Tarkington's novel begins, Alice's family occupies a tenuous position in the midlevel manufacturing class of post-World War I Indiana. Their position affords them a modicum of respect, but they have slowly felt the pinch of declining fortune. They just manage to keep a cook, for example, but they can only afford to hire the surly specimens no other, more respectable, families will employ.

Intent on improving the family fortunes, Alice's mother browbeats her husband, Virgil, into leaving his position with Lamb and Company, where he is respected for his work ethic, honesty, and loyalty. She insists he leave the "old hole," as she calls it, to start his own manufacturing company. Virgil's ethical dilemma revolves around his knowledge of a secret glue formula, the rights to which are owned by Mr. Lamb. However, since Mr. Lamb has done nothing with the formula for years, Virgil allows himself to be convinced by his wife to steal it, quit his position, and open his own glue factory.

Mr. Adams's ethical dilemma and subsequent fall parallel his daughter's attempt to lift herself up socially, also through unethical means. Alice's head is filled with romance, and she begins lying in a futile attempt to deny the grim reality of the family's declining stature. In this pursuit, she is encouraged by her mother, whose mending of old dresses so they will appear to be new is a benign example of how Alice begins by shading the truth and ends by lying outright. Tarkington masterfully illustrates the process whereby economic emulation gradually becomes pernicious dishonesty. In a famous scene, Alice meets Mr. Arthur Russell and tries to impress him by lying that she has been to the tobacconist to procure cigars for her father, who never, she assures him, smokes a pipe; this petty lie grows into a larger claim that her father occupies an almost aristocratic position of wealth and power. The lies grow as Alice and Mr. Russell fall in love, but the lies are ultimately unable to sustain the fiction of the upper-class life she has created.

Three strands of the narrative come together when Mr. Russell comes to dinner at the Adamses' home. The behavior of Alice's family clearly demarcates their social class, undercutting all the things Alice said about them to her beau. Moreover, her brother Walter's embezzlement from Lamb and Company comes to light, even as the glue factory established by Mr. Adams fails. Alice knows when Arthur Russell leaves her house that she will never see him again.

Alice Adams is Tarkington at his most brilliant. Selecting the coming-of-age of an adolescent girl as his ostensible subject, Tarkington establishes the novel's main theme as the much larger issue of America's coming-of-age in the years after the Great War, World War I. The central themes are all developed around Alice's search for her own identity in a culture that seeks to impose identity based on class and economic position. Tarkington also includes some pointed jabs at romance as both an aesthetic movement and as a philosophical outlook. Alice has believed the romantic fictions she has been told, and she tells a few more of her own to Mr. Russell. Only at the end does she give up her romantic illusions and become realistic. As she approaches Frincke's Business College, Alice recalls "a French romance" she had once read and begins to grow sentimental over her own "destiny." Then, as if shaking off the idea, she mounts the stairs, turning her back on the romantic fictions that had led her astray.

Joe B. Fulton

OTHER MAJOR WORKS

SHORT FICTION: *In the Arena*, 1905; *The Fascinating Stranger, and Other Stories*, 1923; "Mr. White," "The Red Barn," "Hell," and "Bridewater," 1935.

PLAYS: *Beaucaire*, pr. 1901 (with Evelyn Greenleaf Sutherland; adaptation of his novel *Monsieur Beaucaire*); *The Gentleman from Indiana*, pr. 1905 (adaptation of his novel); *The Guardian*, pb. 1907 (with Harry Leon Wilson); *The Man from Home*, pr. 1907 (adaptation of his novel); *Mister Antonio*, pr. 1916; *Clarence*, pr. 1919; *The Gibson Upright*, pb. 1919 (with Wilson).

NONFICTION: *The World Does Move*, 1928 (reminiscence).

BIBLIOGRAPHY

Fennimore, Keith J. *Booth Tarkington*. New York: Twayne, 1974. An excellent introduction to Tarkington, with a brief biography and analysis of his major works. A volume in Twayne's United States Authors series.

Jacobson, Marcia Ann. *Being a Boy Again: Autobiography and the American Boy Book*. Tuscaloosa: University of Alabama Press, 1996. Booth Tarkington's work is examined in this study of the "American boy book," which "flourished between the Civil War and World War I." This genre, Jacobson argues, is "an autobiographical form that concentrates on boyhood alone."

LeGates, Charlotte. "The Family in Booth Tarkington's Growth Trilogy." *Midamerica: The Yearbook of the Society for the Study of Midwestern Literature* 6 (1979): 88-99. LeGates's discussion of "the family," which occupies the center of Tarkington's world, is exemplary.

Mallon, Thomas. "Hoosiers." *The Atlantic Monthly*, May, 2004. Mallon takes a close look at Tarkington's oeuvre, finding that his few good works have been "suffocated" by the majority of the mediocre ones. Mallon asks how the once ubiquitous Tarkington could "disappear so completely."

Mayberry, Susanah. *My Amiable Uncle: Recollections About Booth Tarkington*. West Lafayette, Ind.: Purdue University Press, 1983. Tarkington's niece recollects her personal experiences with the writer, providing an important contribution to Tarkington's biography. Includes family photographs.

Noverr, Douglass A. "Change, Growth, and the Human Dilemma in Booth Tarkington's *The Magnificent Ambersons*." *Society for the Study of Midwestern Literature Newsletter* 11 (1981): 14-32. This article treats primarily one novel, but it has value in making clear the major themes of Tarkington's work.

Woodress, James. *Booth Tarkington: Gentleman from Indiana*. 1955. Reprint. New York: Greenwood Press, 1969. This full-scale biography of Tarkington offers some analysis of the novels. The book is considered the standard biography by many critics.

Yardley, Jonathan. "Attaboy! Booth Tarkington's Rascals." *The Washington Post*, August 7, 2004. Yardley reread *Penrod* and *Penrod and Sam*, two books he enjoyed as a child, and discusses his observations about these novels, Tarkington's career, and the demise of the writer's reputation. "We live in an unjust world," Yardley writes, "one of the many injustices of which is that Tarkington is pretty much forgotten now outside Indiana, his native state."

WILLIAM MAKEPEACE THACKERAY

Born: Calcutta, India; July 18, 1811
Died: London, England; December 24, 1863
Also known as: M. A. Titmarsh; George Savage Fitz-Boodle; Ikey Solomons, Jr.

PRINCIPAL LONG FICTION

Catherine: A Story, 1839-1840 (as Ikey Solomons, Jr.)

The History of Samuel Titmarsh and the Great Hoggarty Diamond, 1841 (later as *The Great Hoggarty Diamond*, 1848)

The Luck of Barry Lyndon: A Romance of the Last Century, 1844 (serial), 1852 (book; commonly known as *Barry Lyndon*)

Vanity Fair: A Novel Without a Hero, 1847-1848 (serial), 1848 (book)

The History of Pendennis: His Fortunes and Misfortunes, His Friends, and His Greatest Enemy, 1848-1850 (serial), 1849-1850 (book)

Rebecca and Rowena: A Romance upon Romance, 1849-1850 (as M. A. Titmarsh)

The History of Henry Esmond, Esquire, a Colonel in the Service of Her Majesty Q. Anne, 1852 (3 volumes)

The Newcomes: Memoirs of a Most Respectable Family, 1853-1855 (serial), 1855 (book)

The Virginians: A Tale of the Last Century, 1857-1859 (serial), 1858-1859 (book)

Lovel the Widower, 1860

The Adventures of Philip on His Way Through the World, Shewing Who Robbed Him, Who Helped Him, and Who Passed Him By, 1861-1862 (serial), 1862 (book)

Denis Duval, 1864

OTHER LITERARY FORMS

William Makepeace Thackeray's career as a satirist and journalist contributed to his novelistic style. His works appeared in a number of periodicals, including *The National Standard*, which he owned; *The Constitutional*, for which he was Paris correspondent; and *The New Monthly Magazine*. More important, however, the bulk of his writing appeared in *Fraser's Magazine* and in *Punch*, until, in 1860, he became editor of the *Cornhill Magazine*. In many of his reviews, short stories, burlesques, and travel writings, he adopts facetious pen names that reveal the snobbish preconceptions of his personae. "The Yellowplush Correspondence" appeared in *Fraser's Magazine* in 1837-1838 as the supposed diary of Charles James Yellowplush, an illiterate footman who betrays all of the social prejudices of his employers. The story was later published as *Memoirs of Mr. Charles J. Yellowplush* in 1856.

Thackeray assumed two pseudonyms for some of his comic pieces. As M. A. Titmarsh, Thackeray published *A Legend of the Rhine* (1845), *Mrs. Perkin's Ball* (1847), and *The Rose and the Ring: Or, The History of Prince Giglio and Prince Bulbo* (1855) among others, in addition to some nonfiction works such as *The Paris Sketch Book* (1840; 2 volumes), *The Irish Sketch Book* (1843; 2 volumes), and *Notes of a Journey from Cornhill to Grand Cairo* (1846). As George Savage Fitz-Boodle, an aging and susceptible bachelor, Thackeray wrote *The Fitz-Boodle Papers* (1852), *The Confessions of George Fitz-Boodle, and Some Passages in the Life of Major Gahagan* (1841-1842), and *Men's Wives* (1843). "Punch's Prize Novelists," which appeared in *Punch* magazine, was a series of parodies of popular novelists of the day, such as Benjamin Disraeli and James Fenimore Cooper, and was perhaps even more effective than the burlesque *Catherine* (which he wrote as Ikey Solomons, Jr.). Thackeray's other achievements include *The English Humourists of the Eighteenth Century* (1853)

and *The Four Georges: Sketches of Manners, Morals, Court and Town Life* (1860); a number of tales and short stories, including *A Shabby Genteel Story, and Other Tales* (1852); and a series of ballads and verses, such as the nostalgic "The Ballad of Bouillabaisse" (1849).

ACHIEVEMENTS

Long remembered as a social satirist par excellence, William Makepeace Thackeray wrote more in the manner of Henry Fielding than of Samuel Richardson and more in the realistic vein than in the style of the novel of sensibility, that production of the early nineteenth century that sought to achieve heightened emotional effects at the expense of believable plot and characterization. Both in his miscellaneous writings and in his first great novel, *Vanity Fair*, Thackeray sought to counter the kind of melodramatic and pretentious entertainment provided by such authors as Edward Bulwer-Lytton, William Harrison Ainsworth, and even the early Charles Dickens. He attempted, instead, to make his readers see through the social and literary hypocrisy that, as he believed, characterized the age. To this end, he adopted a number of pseudonyms in his early essay writing, pseudonyms that can be said to foreshadow the personae he used in his fiction.

In reviewing both art and literature for such magazines as *Fraser's Magazine* and *The New Monthly Magazine*, Thackeray adopted the Yellowplush and Titmarsh signatures; he was thus able to ridicule in a lively way what he found false. His reviews were no less devastating to the current trend of idolizing criminals and rogues, as seen in the series of popular Newgate Novels. As Solomons, Jr., he produced *Catherine*, the tale of a murderer, but even here, his attempt to deglamorize the account was mitigated by his growing sympathy for his created characters. Again, *A Shabby Genteel Story* attempted to deal with the middle class in unvarnished terms. His first sustained narrative, *Barry Lyndon*, features an Irish adventurer recounting his own life; the novel follows the rise and fall of its picaresque hero to illustrate the specious nature of worldly success. Perhaps most telling in his ten-year preparation for fiction writing were two series that appeared in *Punch*. "The Snobs of England" was a series of verbal portraits of social types, most drawn for their pretension; "Punch's Prize

Novelists" was a collection of parodic rewritings of popular novelists' works.

In his sustained works, however, Thackeray leaves his readers not with a collection of isolated vignettes but with a panoramic study of humankind under the guidance of a witty persona whose satiric bent is tempered by the realization that he himself partakes of the foibles of his own characters. Thackeray's characteristic persona derives from not only Fielding and his prefaces to the various books of *The History of Tom Jones, a Foundling* (1749) but also Samuel Johnson, who ends *Rasselas, Prince of Abyssinia* (1759) by suggesting that since an ideal world is impossible, a wise individual will stoically accept the one that exists. Thackeray's experimentations with the persona in *The History of Henry Esmond, Esquire, a Colonel in the Service of Her Majesty Q. Anne*—commonly known as *Henry Esmond*—a novel written in the memoir form, laid the groundwork for such masters of psychological realism and irony as Henry James and James Joyce. In addition, Thackeray's experimentations with the generational form, in which several novels are melded together through the familial relationships of their characters, look forward to such productions as John Galsworthy's *The Forsyte Saga* (1922). In presenting the affairs of Henry Esmond's grandsons and the development of the beautiful Beatrix Esmond into a worldly old woman in *The Virginians*, he was also implicitly exploring the kind of genetic and environmental influence that the naturalists defined as determinism.

While many modern readers are perhaps not as comfortable as their nineteenth century forebears with the conception of the authorial voice as a constant, even necessary factor in the plot, Thackeray nevertheless remains noteworthy, especially in his early novels, both for the realistic renderings of individuals in all social walks and for his moral standpoint, best expressed in the preface to *Vanity Fair* as a charitable outlook on human foibles.

BIOGRAPHY

William Makepeace Thackeray was born on July 18, 1811, in Calcutta, India. His father, Richmond Thackeray, pursued a family career in the East India Company; his mother, Anne Becher, traced her ancestry back to a sixteenth century sheriff of London. The senior William Makepeace Thackeray and John Harman Becher had extensive interests in India. After his father's death in 1815, Thackeray's mother married Major Henry Carmichael-Smith, a former suitor. As was the custom, Thackeray was sent to England at the age of five for reasons of health and education. His unhappy, early experiences at the Arthurs' school and at Chiswick were later rendered in "Dr. Birch and his Young Friends" (1849).

At Cambridge, as a member of a privileged class, Thackeray was trained in the standards and preconceptions that he later pilloried in *The Snobs of England, by One of Themselves* (1846-1847; later published as *The Book of Snobs,* 1848, 1852) and many other works. He was left with a distaste for bullying and with a distrust of his own intellectual abilities. After two years at Cambridge, Thackeray abandoned the pursuit of academic

William Makepeace Thackeray. (Library of Congress)

honors. Although he believed that his education had, on the whole, served him ill, it nevertheless had given him a background in history and culture, a double appreciation that is well evidenced in *Henry Esmond*; it also convinced him of his social status, although his expensive aristocratic habits were to prove difficult to control.

The gentle satire evident in *Vanity Fair's* Pumpernickel chapters reflect Thackeray's happy six-month tour of Germany before he undertook to study law in London. While the discipline soon proved not to his taste, his life as a gentleman of fashion (a life that included large gambling debts) was congenial, at least until the collapse of many of the Indian commercial houses reversed his inheritance prospects. Almost relieved to be forced to make his own way, Thackeray decided to develop his talent for drawing, making friends with Daniel Maclise and being tutored by George Cruikshank. While in Paris studying art, he met and married Isabella Shawe, the daughter of a colonel in the Indian army. He endeavored to support his family through journalistic activities, even offering to illustrate Dickens's *Pickwick Papers* (1836-1837, serial; 1837, book). His friendship with Daniel Maginn made his "Yellowplush Papers" welcome in the columns of *Fraser's Magazine*, whose readers were regaled with the malapropisms of a rascally footman. In addition, he wrote for *The Times* of London and for a number of obscure journals. His first long attempt at fiction was *Catherine*, a parody of the Newgate Novel; in quick succession he produced *A Shabby Genteel Story, and Other Tales* (1852) and *The Paris Sketch Book*.

In 1840, Thackeray was visited by domestic calamity; upon the birth of their third daughter, his wife, Isabella, went insane and required institutionalization. The child-rearing was assumed by Thackeray's parents, leaving him to recoup his writing career, initially with *The History of Samuel Titmarsh and the Great Hoggarty Diamond* and soon with contributions to *Punch* and the *Morning Chronicle*. During these middle years, Thackeray solaced himself for the want of domestic connections with a series of friendships with old Cambridge acquaintances such as Alfred, Lord Tennyson and W. H. Brookfield, as well as with journalistic brethren such as Francis Sylvester Mahoney (the "Father Prout" of *Fraser's Magazine* fame) and with Dickens himself, whom

Thackeray could, however, never accept as a "gentleman." His travel literature was published at this time.

Thackeray's connection with *Punch*, begun in 1842, was an important one. From contributing fillers, he went on to write a number of series; moreover, Thackeray's rivalry with the other principal writer, Douglass Jerrold, was to affect the course of *Punch's* publishing history, turning the tide from radicalism and democracy to a Whiggish conservatism of which Dickens himself much disapproved.

The year 1847 was crucial for Thackeray. He began to parody novels for *Punch* in the Punch's Prize Novelists series, he began a long platonic affair with Jane Brookfield, and he published *Vanity Fair*, the novel that has achieved abiding interest for its panoramic social view and its narrator's satirical viewpoint. His four-year relationship with Jane Brookfield certainly affected his writing; much of the nostalgia and agonizing provoked by the affair are reproduced in *Henry Esmond*. Just as important was his entreé into aristocratic circles, for he, along with his daughters Anny and Minnie, with whom he had set up an establishment in Kensington, were welcome at not only Holland House but also in the demirep world of Lady Blessington. Leaving his daughters was the only blight on his first American tour in 1852, when he lectured about "English Humorists of the Eighteenth Century" and marveled at the way in which the nouveau riche mingled with the best society.

Upon his return, Thackeray entered the height of the London social season and visited his daughters in Paris. He began *The Newcomes*, a novel much interrupted by illness but, even as its title suggests, much influenced by his social experiences. His work on the "Four Georges," an indictment of the House of Hanover as well as of the monarchy and the upper classes, indicated his changed attitudes. After his second American tour (undertaken, like the first, to provide stipends for his daughters), Thackeray not only published *The Virginians* but also became editor of the *Cornhill Magazine*, a project that allowed him to move "out of novel-spinning back into the world" of the essay. The periodical was an immediate success, publishing such authors as Anthony Trollope and George Henry Lewes. Although Thackeray retired as editor in 1862, he continued to publish his "Roundabout Papers" there until the year after. Indeed, his last unfinished novel, *Denis Duval*, appeared in the *Cornhill Magazine* posthumously in 1864, after Thackeray had died on December 24, 1863, in London.

ANALYSIS

While William Makepeace Thackeray may indeed be best known as the author of *Vanity Fair*, to examine all of his novels is to understand why his contribution to the history of the novel is singular. His use of the intrusive narrator, although presaged by Henry Fielding, was developed so carefully that it became a new form of fiction, a "genuine creation of narrative experiment," as critic Alexander Welsh calls it. In addition, his panoramic realism—although creating that anathema of Henry James, the novel that is "a loose and baggy monster"—explored, both seriously and satirically, a number of topics from which other Victorian writers shied away, such as married life and the development of the middle-class gentleman.

Quite aside from the interest generated by the story line, many of Thackeray's novels offer explanations of the art of creating fiction as well as criticism of some of his contemporaries' inadequacies. When Amelia in *Vanity Fair*, for example, tries to visualize George's barracks, the doors are closed to her, for the romantic imagination is in all respects inadequate to the exigencies of real life. In *The Newcomes*, Thackeray compares his method of character-building to the work of the paleontologist who discovers a series of bones and who must construct the habits, behavior, and appearance of his subject from a mere skeleton. He thereby suggests that any such "reality" is merely an illusion, for like the paleontologist, the author must work with probabilities. Insofar as his characters follow a probable course of events, they are true to life and, in a sense, interact without the help of the author.

That Thackeray meant his novels to be something more than believable illusionary worlds is clear when his conclusions are examined. In *The Newcomes*, for example, Thackeray retreats at the end from Pendennis's narrative to suggest that the sentimental world he has created has no basis in fact, although the reader may believe so if he (or she) wishes to delude himself. Furthermore, in the well-known ending to *Vanity Fair*, Thackeray puts his "puppets"—his characters—back into their box.

Rather than following Samuel Taylor Coleridge's idea of "willing suspension of disbelief," Thackeray is philosophical, inviting the reader into a reconsideration of his own or of conventional beliefs and preconceptions. Certainly, Thackeray's satire is operative here, particularly in his *Punch* series, in *Catherine*, and in *Barry Lyndon*, in which he deliberately spoofed popular historical, crime, and romantic novels, respectively. The reader is asked to look at more than literary conventions, however; he (or she) is asked to examine his own degree of hypocrisy and snobbery. In so doing, the reader is reminded again and again that if he laughs at his neighbors, he condemns himself. Thackeray's work is thus truly homiletic, both in a literary and in an extraliterary sense.

Unlike many of his predecessors, Thackeray examined in detail the difficulties occasioned not only by marriage but also by other personal relationships; rather than assuming that a novel should end with marriage, he makes it his subject. Certainly, his personally tragic domestic situation and his affair with Jane Brookfield are reflected in Rachel Esmond's trials with her reckless husband in Henry Esmond's growing love for her. In the family chronicle *The Newcomes*, Thackeray looks at the misery occasioned by parental marriage choices; Mrs. Mackenzie (known as the Campaigner), a strongminded virago who runs her daughter's life, is modeled on Mrs. Shawe, Isabella's termagant mother. Finally, in *The Virginians*, he traces the development of family characteristics and family ties.

Another one of the many senses in which Thackeray's novels are educative is the way in which he redefines the word "gentleman" to apply not to a member of a particular social class, but rather to one who possesses a set of personal characteristics, such as clear-sightedness, delicacy, generosity, and humanitarianism. His upperclass upbringing in India as well as his Cambridge education coupled with his love of the high life would seem to militate against such a redefinition, but, in fact, it is the greengrocer's son, Dobbin, in *Vanity Fair* who is the gentleman, rather than the pompous and vain George Osborne, and it is Colonel Newcome who, despite his misguided attempts to settle his son Clive's happiness, emerges as the paradigmatical enemy to snobbery and to greed.

VANITY FAIR

Vanity Fair, the title of which is taken from John Bunyan's *The Pilgrim's Progress* (1678, 1684), proved to be Thackeray's most successful novel. Indeed, its attention to realistic detail and its panoramic sweep, to say nothing of the constant presence of the author-cum-narrator, caused many reviewers to label Thackeray "the Fielding of the nineteenth century." While neither the initial reviews nor the sales were immediately promising, interest in the serial grew steadily until the publication of the volume guaranteed the author a financial as well as a critical success. Rivaling Thackeray at the time was Dickens, whose *Dombey and Son* (1846-1848, serial; 1848, book) appealed to a wide audience; even Thackeray himself, upon reading the passage describing little Paul's death, despaired about writing "against such power." Thackeray, however, had his own power, that of the satirist who created "A Novel Without a Hero" and thus ran counter to his readership's expectations, and that of the moralist who included his reader and himself in his reflective view of society.

The hero that *Vanity Fair* must do without is the typically romantic hero. George Osborne (whose first name conjures up the dandified Regency court) is handsome, dashing, and well loved, but he is also vain, shallow, and pompous. After Joseph Sedley has gone bankrupt, George marries the pining Amelia Sedley only at the urging of his friend, William Dobbin; during their honeymoon, George engages in a flirtation with Becky Sharp, herself newly married to Rawdon Crawley. Killed at the battle of Waterloo, George is cherished as a hero only by Amelia. Dobbin is at the other extreme: Gangly, awkward, and low in social standing, he is nevertheless possessed of compassion and understanding, yet he is so blinded by his selfless love for Amelia that he does not see until the end of the novel on how slight a character he has set his affection. Even Rawdon, who develops from a typical "heavy dragoon" who lives by his gambling into an affectionate father for his neglected son, lacks intellectual acumen and, after his separation from Becky, accepts the post that her prostitution to Lord Steyne earned him.

As A. E. Dyson suggests, Thackeray is indeed writing "an irony against heroes"—and against heroines as well. Amelia and Becky are as different as George and Dobbin. Initally, Amelia seems to be a conventional heroine, but the reader who views her in that light will be shocked to discover that he is idealizing the passivity, self-sacrifice, and hero worship that are the earmarks of neuroticism, the three characteristics well seen in her treatment of her son, Georgy, who is absurdly spoiled despite Amelia's and her parents' penury. No wonder, then, that readers preferred "the famous little Becky puppet" for her wit and ambition.

From the moment Becky rides away from Miss Pinkerton's finishing school, leaving Dr. Johnson's dictionary lying in the mud, her energy in making a place for herself in society is impressive. Failing to entangle Amelia's brother, Jos, she eventually marries Rawdon, the favorite of his wealthy aunt, and only repines when Lord Crawley himself proposes—too late. She turns her very bohemianism into an asset as she gains entry into the best society, and while she claims that she too could be a "good woman on £5000 a year," her energy in luring dupes to Rawdon's card table, wheedling jewels from Lord Steyne, being presented to the king, and playing charades at a social affair, belies her claim. As John Loofbourow shows, as Becky comes into social ascendancy, Amelia declines into obscurity. Amelia lacks Becky's energy, while Becky lacks Amelia's morality. In the end, when Dobbin has won his prize, Becky has devolved into a female picaresque rogue, traveling across the Continent from disreputable gaming table to questionable boarding house. Neither she nor Amelia qualifies as a heroine.

It is Thackeray's preface that reveals the moral purpose behind his satire. Posing as the "Manager of the Performance," Thackeray reminds his readers that they are embarked on a fictional journey through an emblematic Vanity Fair, an evocation related only partly to the original in Bunyan's work. Vanity Fair, for Thackeray, is a representation of the human condition; it is not for the reader, like Bunyan's Christian, to pass through and eschew its lures, but rather to experience it "in a sober, contemplative, not uncharitable frame of mind," for the reader and author alike are part of the fair. Thackeray's comments throughout serve the purpose of distancing the reader from the characters and forcing him or her to judge not only the created "puppets" but also his or her own preconceptions. If everyone is indeed part of the fair, to condemn the booth owners' hypocrisy, or social climbing, or snobbery, or mendacity, is to condemn one's own failings. To be possessed of "charity"—to be able to pity others with the same care one has for oneself—this, Thackeray suggests, is the best that can be expected when the puppets are put back in the box.

THE HISTORY OF PENDENNIS

The subtitle of *The History of Pendennis—His Fortunes and Misfortunes, His Friends, and His Greatest Enemy*—gives ample indication that the novel is a bildungsroman. As Juliet McMaster points out, however, it is also a *Künstlerroman*; that is, a tale about the development of an artist. It is perforce autobiographical, detailing as it does the way in which a young man learns enough about the world and himself to become a writer of "good books." The novel is important in a study of Thackeray's technique, presenting, as it does, the background for the persona who was to narrate *The Newcomes* and showing Thackeray's struggles with Victorian prudery. Indeed, in his preface he complains that his readers, unlike those of Fielding, are unwilling to accept a truthful portrayal of human beings unless they are given "a conventional simper."

Thackeray's reviewers, however, welcomed the novel, their only complaint being the cynicism with which he endowed Pen. Such cynicism refutes the remark of Henry James, Sr., that Thackeray "had no ideas," for Thackeray's wryness results from a consideration of political and religious turmoil, from the "skepticism" brought about by the 1848 French Revolution, and from the controversy occasioned by the Oxford movement and Cardinal John Henry Newman's conversion from Anglicanism to Catholicism. Clearly, one reason for Thackeray's contemporary appeal was that he reflected the very doubts of his own readers, for whom belief was an exercise in paradox.

The tension between the heart and the world that animates *The History of Pendennis* is well represented by the frontispiece to the first volume, in which a youthful figure is clasped on one side by a woman representing marital duty and on the other by a mermaid representing the siren lure of worldly temptations. Within the dictates of the plot, the same tension is demonstrated by the demands of Pen's sentimental mother, Helen Pendennis, who urges her son to marry the domestic, Laura, her

ward, and those of his uncle, Major Pendennis, who is willing to blackmail his acquaintance, Sir Francis Clavering, so that Pen can have a seat in Parliament and the hand of Clavering's wealthy but artificial daughter, Blanche. Between the two, Pen must, as McMaster points out, find his own reality; he must acquire "his uncle's keen perception without the withering selfishness" and participate in his mother's world of emotions without engaging in "romantic illusion." Pen's education progresses primarily through his amours but also through his choice of career, for to be a writer, he must determine the relationship between fact and fiction.

Pen's abiding interest in the nature of experience makes his involvement with an actor allegorical in nature. His first affair is with Emily Costigan (known as the Fotheringay), an Irish actor older than he and one who plays her parts serenely unconscious of their philosophical implications; her ignorance Pen passes off as "adorable simplicity." Extricated by his uncle, who "lends" Emily's father a small sum in return for Pen's love letters, Pen next enters Oxbridge, and then, influenced by his roommate, George Warrington, determines to study law and to become a writer. His affair with Fanny Bolton, the daughter of his landlady, is again one of an attraction to adorable simplicity, and his consequent illness a kind of purgation. His attachment to Blanche Clavering is more serious and more dangerous, for Blanche is a social "actress" with whom Pen plays the role of world-weary lover. With her he believes he has matured because he is willing to compromise with disillusionment. His real moment of maturity comes, however, when he finds that he cannot put up with his uncle's worldliness, for in discovering that Clavering's second marriage is bigamous and that the baronet is paying blackmail money to his wife's first husband, the major in turn blackmails Clavering to give up his seat in Parliament to Pen and to cede his estate to Blanche.

Pen's responsible decision to honor his proposal to Blanche despite the resultant scandal is, in fact, unnecessary, for she jilts him for a more suitable match, freeing him to marry Laura, whose steadfast, honest devotion represents the alternative to Blanche's sham affection. Laura, in fact, is Pen's muse, his living "laurel wreath"; she has insight and a critical faculty that force Pen to come face-to-face with himself. With her, Pen finally frees himself from both romantic illusion and worldly disillusionment.

HENRY ESMOND

Like Dickens, who turned from the largely unplotted "loose and baggy monsters" of his novelistic apprenticeship to produce the tightly controlled *Dombey and Son*, Thackeray moved from the looseness occasioned by serial publication to the careful construction of *Henry Esmond*. While the novelist Anthony Trollope agreed with Thackeray that the book was his "*very* best," initial critical reaction was mixed, ranging from high praise for Thackeray's realism to a scandalized outcry against what Gordon Ray calls the "emotional pattern" of the work—Esmond's marriage to Lady Castlewood, his cousin and senior by eight years. All agreed, however, that the novel was profoundly moving. Much of its power is owing to its genesis: Written when Thackeray was recovering from his alienation from Jane Brookfield, the novel reflects his own emotional current, his nostalgia, his suffering, and his wish fulfillment. In addition, *Henry Esmond* may be read on many levels—as historical fiction, as novel of manners, and as romance.

Superficially, Thackeray might seem an unlikely figure to write a historical novel, inasmuch as he composed a series of parodies of "costume dramas" (as he called them) for *Punch* and inasmuch as the historical novel was going out of fashion by 1852. Nevertheless, because Thackeray was steeped in seventeenth century history, the work has a verisimilitude that, in the view of some critics, allowed him to outstrip even Sir Walter Scott. The point of view he adopts, that of the first-person narrator, adds to the illusion. This tour de force is accomplished with a success that even James, the master of psychological realism, might envy.

The entire story is presented from the limited point of view of Esmond, the cheated heir of the Castlewood estate, who is adopted by his cousins, falls in love with the beautiful but irresponsible Beatrix Esmond, and for her sake joins the Jacobite cause. Then, when Beatrix becomes the Pretender's mistress, he realigns himself on the side of the Stuarts, marries Beatrix's mother, and immigrates to America.

That Thackeray could, through a limited narrator, represent the complexity of Lady Castlewood's growing love for the innocent and unconscious Henry is remark-able in its own right. Thackeray's own memories of his boyhood helped him to re-create Henry's loneliness; his relationship with Jane Brookfield shaped his characterization of Lady Castlewood. As John Tilford points out, Thackeray prepares carefully for the marriage, doubtless aware that it challenged many readers' expectations and moral assumptions. Through nuances of dialogue, Rachel Castlewood's awareness of her feelings and of Henry's is revealed. A number of crucial scenes prepare for the denouement: Rachel's hysterical reaction to Henry's early affair with the blacksmith's daughter, an affair that brings smallpox to the family; her vituperation of Henry as he lies in prison for his involvement in a duel that killed Lord Castlewood, whose drinking, gambling, and hunting had contributed to a loveless marriage; and, finally, her overwhelming joy when she sees Henry after his long period of military service.

One early criticism of the novel was recorded by William Harrison Ainsworth, with whom Thomas Carlyle joined in objecting to the exultation of "sentiment above duty" in the novel; other critics found the comparison between the excitement of romantic love and marital unhappiness to be dangerous. The more sophisticated analysis of McMaster registers an "ironic tension" between "Rachel's moral rectitude and . . . the psychological damage" it can cause.

Like James's *Mme de Mauves*, Rachel is possessed of a cool virtue based on a conviction of moral and intellectual superiority; as McMaster suggests, she may indeed welcome evidence of her husband's coarseness as a way of rationalizing her affection for Henry and may therefore be responsible for exacerbating her husband's untoward behavior. Thackeray does give both sides: While Castlewood, like Fielding's Squire Western, is rough and careless, pursuing a prodigal, adulterous life once his wife has lost her beauty to smallpox, he accuses her of pride and of a blighting coldness, and pleads for "the virtue that can forgive." Even Beatrix complains that her mother's saintliness provided so impossible a model that she was driven to ambitious selfishness. Such complaints themselves sound like rationalizations, however, for at the end of the novel, Rachel has undergone a long period of repentance. Having sent her temptation—Henry—away, she lives with the renunciation of happiness while he matures. Upon his return, then, she is no longer an angel, but, as he says, "more fondly cherished as woman perhaps than ever she had been adored as divinity."

THE NEWCOMES

Subtitled *Memoirs of a Most Respectable Family*, *The Newcomes* is a novel of manners that explores the way in which four generations of a nouveau riche family acquire social respectability. The novel, the first third of which is densely packed with background material and consequently slow-moving, is a deliberate return to the serial format that Thackeray had abandoned in *Henry Esmond*. While some modern critics object to the pace of this "monster," nineteenth century reviewers believed that, with this novel, Thackeray had outstripped even Dickens, whose anti-utilitarian manifesto, *Hard Times* (1854), was running concurrently. To be sure, a number of reviewers noted some repetition in theme and characters, a charge against which Thackeray defended himself in the "Overture" but admitted to in private, acknowledging a failure of invention because of sheer exhaustion. One such "repetition," which is, in fact, a way of extending the scope of the novel, is that Pendennis is the "editor" of the Newcome memoirs. This device allows Thackeray not only to assume an objective stance from which his satire is more telling but also to criticize the very social punctiliousness that Pendennis reveals, thereby achieving an advanced form of psychological analysis.

What provides the novel's "unifying structural principle," as McMaster notes, is "the repetition of the mercenary marriage and its outcome between various couples." This theme, however, is a manifestation of the larger examination of the nature of "respectability," as the subtitle implies. For Barnes Newcome, the banker, for the aristocratic Lady Kew, and even for her granddaughter, Ethel Newcome, affection and generosity are weighed against wealth and social position and found wanting. The touchstone figure is Colonel Thomas Newcome, Barnes's half brother; unworldly, honest, and loving, he is seen by Gordon Ray as a model of Christian humility. The underlying cynicism of the novel is underscored by the inability of the characters to gain happiness, whether they satisfy their acquisitiveness or rebel against such a value, for Thackeray reminds his readers that real fulfillment only exists in "Fable-land."

To pursue the marriage theme is to understand that in Thackeray's world even the best intentions go awry. Certainly, the unhappiness that accrues in some relationships seems self-created: While the joining of money and class in Barnes's marriage to Lady Clara Pulleyn satisfies the dictates of the marriage market, Barnes's brutality drives his wife to elope with a former suitor. In contrast, Clive Newcome, the Colonel's son, is forbidden by Lady Kew to marry Ethel because his profession as an artist is unacceptable. Even Clive himself is infected by the view, for he neglects his modest muse to devote himself to society. For his part, the Colonel, seeing Clive's unhappiness, schemes to marry him to the sweet but shallow Rosey Mackenzie, the niece of his old friend James Binnie. The loveless though well-intentioned match is unhappy, for Clive longs for Ethel's companionship and the couple is tormented by the dictatorial Mrs. Mackenzie after the Colonel's bankruptcy.

Ethel, like Becky Sharp and Beatrix Esmond, is a complex heroine, one who, through much trial and error, weans herself from the respectable avarice she was reared to accept. In love with Clive despite her relations' objections, she nevertheless admits that she delights in admiration, fine clothes, and jewelry, and, although she despises herself for it, that she enjoys being a coquette. Her fine sense of irony about the marriage market, however, prompts her to wear a "sold" ticket pinned to her dress, much to the annoyance of her respectable relatives. At first affianced to Lord Frank Kew, she breaks the engagement; then, capitulating to social pressure, she pursues the feebleminded Lord Farintosh, only to repent at the last moment when the devastation of Barnes's marriage, on which her own is to be patterned, is borne in upon her. In revulsion from her family's values, she devotes herself to Barnes's children and manages to divert some of the Newcome fortune to the impoverished Colonel and his son.

Ethel's "conversion" and Rosey's death do not, however, lead necessarily to a happy ending, for in the years of following Ethel hopelessly, of neglecting his painting, and, finally, of engaging in a loveless marriage, Clive has become less resilient, more demoralized. Indeed, a conventional ending to *The Newcomes* would be as unwieldy as the happy denouement that Dickens was persuaded to tack on to *Great Expectations* (1860-1861, serial; 1861, book). All Thackeray does promise is that in "Fable-land . . . Ethel and Clive are living most comfortably together." As McMaster points out, "poetic justice does not operate in life, however it operates in romance and fairytale." In the end, Thackeray refuses to cater to weak sentimentality.

THE VIRGINIANS

Written while Thackeray was fighting a lingering illness, *The Virginians* is a long, formless novel, many of whose characters appear in earlier works. The weight of critical opinion, both contemporary and twentieth century, implies that Thackeray, as he well suspected, was at the end of his fictional powers. To Walter Bagehot, the novelist merely presented an "annotated picture" and, indeed, many complained about the plethora of details that substituted for imaginative creation. Thackeray's habit of digressing grew more pronounced, aided by his failure to preserve a distance between himself and his persona for the second half of the novel, the sardonic George Warrington. Connected with such digressions was Thackeray's increasing propensity to justify himself in the eyes of his critics; such justification introduced in a work of fiction was as gratuitous, many felt, as the air of mordant rumination that colored the novel.

On the other hand, Thackeray's supporters cited his adept portraiture of character and his classical style. Geoffrey Tillotson's suggestion that all of Thackeray's works are like one long novel well represents this point of view. In reviving earlier characters and in introducing their descendants, Thackeray studies the development of character traits as well as repetitive familial situations. Beatrix Esmond, for example, having been mistress to the pretender and the king and having buried two husbands, one a bishop, reappears as a fleshy old woman with a caustic tongue and piercing black eyes. The enigmatic George Washington in *The History of Pendennis* reappears in the person of his namesake; George and Henry Warrington are twin sons of Rachel, Henry Esmond's daughter.

Thackeray was unable to pursue his original plan, which was to place the brothers on opposite sides in the Revolutionary War and to insert real-life sketches of such figures as Oliver Goldsmith and Dr. Samuel Johnson. The American section was foreshortened, although Thackeray's prodigious reading in American history lends it a remarkably realistic air—so realistic that some American readers were initially incensed that George Washington should be portrayed in so commonplace a light. The book falls into halves, the first reserved for the English adventures of the innocent, gullible Henry. As Gordon Ray points out, the theme, although difficult to discern, is "the contrast between American innocence and Old World corruption."

Henry becomes involved with his cousins at Castlewood, who welcome him as the heir of the Virginia estates, on the supposition that George has died in the battle of Fort Duquesne. Enticed into a proposal by the elderly Maria and encouraged to dissipate his fortune by his infamous cousins, Henry is rescued from debt by his twin, who had not died but was taken prisoner by the French. Deceived by his fortune-seeking relatives, Henry returns to Virginia to marry the housekeeper's daughter. The second half, narrated by George, details his adventures in London. Kept on short funds by his mother, he marries Theo Lambert, the daughter of the gentlemanly General Lambert, a figure much like Colonel Newcome.

Even a brief plot outline of *The Virginians* reveals a number of Thackeray's recurring themes. The attraction of young men to older women is one: Just as Henry Esmond married Rachel, many years his senior, so his grandson becomes attached to Maria, and, conversely, so his mother, Mrs. Esmond Warrington, becomes attached to a much younger suitor. The dogmatic and clinging nature of the parent-child relationship is another, much-explored theme: Hetty Lambert gives up her love for Harry to nurture the general, who is loath to let either of his daughters leave; Mrs. Esmond Warrington throws impediments in the way of George's marriage to Theo; even George himself meditates on his fear that his own daughters will eventually marry. In the final analysis, while *The Virginians* is justly faulted for its digressiveness, Thackeray's treatment of character and his mellow, pure style grant to this work what Gordon Ray calls "a modest vitality."

Overshadowed in modern assessments by his great contemporaries, Dickens and George Eliot, Thackeray is an essential figure in the history of the English novel, and his masterpiece, *Vanity Fair*, is among the great novels in the language. It is with this work that Thackeray is assured a place among the great authors in British literature.

Patricia Marks

OTHER MAJOR WORKS

SHORT FICTION: *The Yellowplush Papers*, 1837-1838; *Some Passages in the Life of Major Gahagan*, 1838-1839; *Stubb's Calendar: Or, The Fatal Boots*, 1839; *Barber Cox and the Cutting of His Comb*, 1840; *The Bedford-Row Conspiracy*, 1840; *Comic Tales and Sketches*, 1841 (2 volumes); *The Confessions of George Fitz-Boodle, and Some Passages in the Life of Major Gahagan*, 1841-1842 (as George Savage Fitz-Boodle); *Men's Wives*, 1843 (as Fitz-Boodle); *A Legend of the Rhine*, 1845 (as M. A. Titmarsh); *Jeames's Diary: Or, Sudden Wealth*, 1846; *The Snobs of England, by One of Themselves*, 1846-1847 (later published as *The Book of Snobs*, 1848, 1852); *Mrs. Perkin's Ball*, 1847 (as Titmarsh); *A Little Dinner at Timmins's*, 1848; "*Our Street*," 1848 (as Titmarsh); *Doctor Birch and His Young Friends*, 1849 (as Titmarsh); *The Kickleburys on the Rhine*, 1850 (as Titmarsh); *A Shabby Genteel Story, and Other Tales*, 1852; *The Rose and the Ring: Or, The History of Prince Giglio and Prince Bulbo*, 1855 (as Titmarsh); "*Memoirs of Mr. Charles J. Yellowplush*" and "*The Diary of C. Jeames De La Pluche, Esqr.*," 1856.

PLAY: *The Rose and the Ring*, pb. 1854.

POETRY: *The Chronicle of the Drum*, 1841.

NONFICTION: *The Paris Sketch Book*, 1840 (2 volumes; as M. S. Titmarsh); *The Irish Sketch Book*, 1843 (2 volumes; as Titmarsh); *Notes of a Journey from Cornhill to Grand Cairo, by Way of Lisbon, Athens, Constantinople and Jerusalem, Performed in the Steamers of the Penninsular and Oriental Company*, 1846 (as Titmarsh); *The English Humourists of the Eighteenth Century*, 1853; *Sketches and Travels in London*, 1856; *The Four Georges: Sketches of Manners, Morals, Court and Town Life*, 1860.

BIBLIOGRAPHY

Bloom, Harold, ed. *William Makepeace Thackeray*. New York: Chelsea House, 1987. A collection of thirteen essays discussing various aspects of Thackeray's fiction, including his use of humor, realism, characterization, point of view, and irony. Includes a bibliography and an index.

Clarke, Micael M. *Thackeray and Women*. DeKalb: Northern Illinois University Press, 1995. Clarke examines Thackeray's life, novels, and other works from the perspective of feminist sociology to analyze his treatment of female characters, demonstrating how his writings critique the position of women in Western culture. Includes bibliographical references and an index.

Dodds, John Wendell. *Thackeray: A Critical Portrait*. 1941. Reprint. New York: Russell & Russell, 1963. This scholarly study of Thackeray's genius and the art of his fiction includes assessments of his novels, short satirical sketches, and stories. The thorough index is useful. An important book in the canon of Thackeray criticism.

Fisher, Judith L. *Thackeray's Skeptical Narrative and the "Perilous Trade" of Authorship*. Burlington, Vt.: Ashgate, 2002. An analysis of Thackeray's narrative techniques, discussing how he sought to create a "kind of poised reading which enables his readers to integrate his fiction into their life."

Harden, Edgar F. *Thackeray the Writer: From Journalism to "Vanity Fair."* New York: St. Martin's Press, 1998.

_____. *Thackeray the Writer: From "Pendennis" to "Denis Duval."* New York: St. Martin's Press, 2000. Two-volume biography chronicles Thackeray's development as a writer, beginning with his experiences as a book reviewer and culminating in the creation of his works of long fiction. Traces how Thackeray became an increasingly perceptive social observer.

Mudge, Isadore Gilbert, and M. Earl Sears. *A Thackeray Dictionary: The Characters and Short Stories Alphabetically Arranged*. 1910. Reprint. New York: Humanities Press, 1962. An essential reference book for students of Thackeray's works. The "Chronological List of Novels and Stories" clarifies and lists the individual and collected works titles under which many of Thackeray's short sketches and stories were published and republished. "Synopses" provides invaluable annotations on the contents of all Thackeray's works. The main "Dictionary" section is an alphabetical reference for Thackeray's characters.

Peters, Catherine. *Thackeray's Universe: Shifting Worlds of Imagination and Reality*. New York: Oxford University Press, 1987. A thorough, fresh, intelligent, and readable twelve-chapter study. In defining what Thackeray's writings owed both to his life and to his particular genius, Peters provides invaluable insights. Includes a thorough index.

Shillingsburg, Peter. *William Makepeace Thackeray: A Literary Life*. New York: Palgrave, 2001. An excellent introduction to the life of the great novelist. Thorough and scholarly, but accessible. Includes a chapter on reading *Vanity Fair* as well as notes and an index.

Taylor, D. J. *Thackeray: The Life of a Literary Man*. New York: Carroll & Graf, 2001. A lengthy biography that argues for Thackeray's preeminence among nineteenth century English novelists. A comprehensive study that sheds much light on Thackeray's work.

Welsh, Alexander, ed. *Thackeray: A Collection of Critical Essays*. Englewood Cliffs, N.J.: Prentice-Hall, 1968. Thirteen essays by a selection of the foremost Thackeray scholars. Includes analysis of some of the novels and of Thackeray's irony, Thackeray as a preacher and a social critic, and his "mother-in-law" characters.

PAUL THEROUX

Born: Medford, Massachusetts; April 10, 1941
Also known as: Paul Edward Theroux

PRINCIPAL LONG FICTION

Waldo, 1967
Fong and the Indians, 1968
Girls at Play, 1969
Murder in Mount Holly, 1969
Jungle Lovers, 1971
Saint Jack, 1973
The Black House, 1974
The Family Arsenal, 1976
Picture Palace, 1978
The Mosquito Coast, 1981
Half Moon Street: Two Short Novels, 1984
O-Zone, 1986
My Secret History, 1989
Chicago Loop, 1990
Millroy the Magician, 1994
My Other Life, 1996
On the Edge of the Great Rift: Three Novels of Africa, 1996 (includes *Fong and the Indians*, *Girls at Play*, and *Jungle Lovers*)
Kowloon Tong, 1997

The Collected Short Novels, 1999
Hotel Honolulu, 2001
Blinding Light, 2005
The Elephanta Suite, 2007

OTHER LITERARY FORMS

In addition to a steady stream of novels, Paul Theroux (thuh-REW) has published collections of short stories such as *Sinning with Annie, and Other Stories* (1972), *World's End* (1980), and *The Stranger at the Palazzo d'Oro, and Other Stories* (2003). He has also published a volume of criticism, *V. S. Naipaul: An Introduction to His Work* (1972); a memoir, *Sir Vidia's Shadow: A Friendship Across Five Continents* (1998); and two collections of children's stories, *A Christmas Card* (1978) and *London Snow: A Christmas Story* (1979). He is well known as the author of many travel books, including *The Great Railway Bazaar: By Train Through Asia* (1975), *The Old Patagonian Express: By Train Through the Americas* (1979), and *Dark Star Safari: Overland from Cairo to Cape Town* (2002). In addition to his books, Theroux has written numerous reviews and articles, many of them based on his perceptions of events in the non-Western world; these have appeared in newspapers and periodicals such as *The New Yorker, The New York Times Magazine*, the *Sunday Times* (of London), *Harper's*, and *Encounter*.

ACHIEVEMENTS

It is in the quirky nature of fame that Paul Theroux, a prolific writer of novels, should be better known for his travel writing than for his fiction. *The Great Railway Bazaar*, which was a Book-of-the Month Club main selection, became a best seller in 1975, gaining for Theroux both popular and commercial success. A second travel book, *The Old Patagonian Express*, published four years later, firmly established his popular reputation. Both offer the reader elegant and humane examples of a genre widely practiced between the world wars that began returning to vogue in the later decades of the twentieth century. Theroux served as guest editor for the 2001 edition of *The Best American Travel Writing*.

In the long run, however, Theroux's literary reputation will rest upon his fiction. He has won a small share of awards for his work, including four Playboy Editorial Awards for fiction (1972, 1976, 1977, and 1979), the Literature Award from the American Academy of Arts and Letters (1977), and the Whitbread Prize for Fiction (for *Picture Palace*, 1978). In 1982, the *Yorkshire Post* recognized *The Mosquito Coast* with its Best Novel of the Year Award. The novel also won the James Tait Black Memorial Prize, one of the oldest literary awards in Britain. In 1984, Theroux was inducted into the American Academy and Institute of Arts and Letters. He was also made a fellow of Britain's Royal Society of Literature and the Royal Geographic Society in London.

A number of Theroux's novels have been adapted for the screen. *Saint Jack*, directed by Peter Bogdonavich, appeared in 1979; Theroux cowrote the film's screenplay. *The Mosquito Coast*, released in 1986, was directed by Peter Weir and starred Harrison Ford; the film adaptation of *Half Moon Street*, directed by Bob Swaim and starring Sigourney Weaver and Michael Caine, also appeared in 1986. *Chinese Box* (1997), a film depicting the British government's handover of Hong Kong to the People's Republic of China, was inspired by Theroux's 1997 novel *Kowloon Tong*.

Theroux writes in the best tradition of English literature, demonstrating a mastery of fictional conventions

as well as a willingness to grapple with some of the thornier issues of modern life. Critics have compared him to, among others, Charles Dickens, Joseph Conrad, W. Somerset Maugham, Graham Greene, and Evelyn Waugh. Interested in neither the splashy innovations of a Donald Barthelme nor the lurid headline material of a Norman Mailer, Theroux is nevertheless a novelist whose body of work deserves serious critical attention.

BIOGRAPHY

Paul Edward Theroux was born of French Canadian and Italian parentage in Medford, Massachusetts, in 1941, the third of the seven children of Albert and Anne Theroux. Literature and writing were important aspects of his early life. Albert Theroux, a leather salesman, read daily to the family from the classics and encouraged the publication of family newspapers. For his efforts, he was rewarded with two novelists among his children: Paul and his brother Alexander.

After conventional public schooling and a B.A. in English from the University of Massachusetts, Theroux volunteered for the Peace Corps in 1963 to escape the draft. He taught English in Malawi for two years until he was expelled for his unwitting involvement in the convolutions of African politics. From Malawi, Theroux went to Makerere University in Kampala, Uganda, where he lectured on seventeenth century English literature and maintained a careful political stance during the beginnings of Idi Amin's rise to power. At Makerere, Theroux met V. S. Naipaul, who became for a time his literary mentor. Theroux left Uganda in 1968 after being trapped in a street riot and went to Singapore, where he spent the next three years lecturing at the university.

Throughout this period, Theroux was writing prodigiously, both fiction and reportage, which he published in a variety of African and European journals. In 1967, he married Anne Castle, then also a teacher, and fathered two sons, Louis and Marcel. In 1972, judging himself able to earn his living by his pen alone, Theroux gave up teaching and moved his family to London. After he and his wife divorced, he returned to the United States, making his home in Massachusetts. Never one to settle down completely, he continued his travels around the globe, gathering materials for his fiction and nonfiction. Theroux divorced Anne Castle in 1993, and two years

Paul Theroux. (Courtesy, Houghton Mifflin Company)

later he married Sheila Donnelly. Still maintaining a residence on Cape Cod, Theroux bought a second home in Hawaii, where he took up beekeeping while continuing his career as a writer.

The Catholic background, the leftish political interests, the ten years in Africa and Asia, the friendship with V. S. Naipaul—these heterogeneous influences all have left their mark on Theroux's fiction. At the same time, one notes how Theroux secularizes, liberalizes, and makes contemporary the Catholic ethic, turns the experience of living in other cultures into a metaphor for all social experience, and absorbs and makes his own the lessons of Naipaul.

ANALYSIS

Paul Theroux approaches his major theme—the ethical behavior of people in society—by way of the experiences of characters, many of them foreigners, in places such as postcolonial Africa and Southeast Asia, in stories that explore cultural interaction and the meaning of civilization. His three early African novels, *Fong and the Indians*, *Girls at Play*, and *Jungle Lovers*, set the scene,

as it were, and suggest the terms for nearly all of his later fiction. These African novels offer not only a fictional portrait of the developing world struggling toward independence but also a metaphor for all modern society and social ethics. In the apparently simpler world of East Africa, where white expatriate confronts black African, where Chinese meets Indian meets German meets American meets Australian, Theroux explores the ways in which individuals interact to form social units and the results, often absurd, of attempts to impose foreign values and ideas of civilization on the primitive life of the jungle.

Although by the 1970's Theroux had begun to make use of other locales in his work, the novels continue to explore the theme of civilization versus jungle, expanding in particular on the moral and ethical implications of certain kinds of social behavior. *The Family Arsenal* and *Saint Jack* provide instructive examples. In the former, Valentine Hood, an American former diplomat from Vietnam living in London, is struck by the domesticity displayed by the members of the terrorist band with which he lives: It is like a family. From this insight develop both the central theme of that novel and its plot structure. In *Saint Jack*, Jack Flowers creates a secular religion out of "giving people what they want."

In a number of his novels Theroux explores the role of the artist in society. In some instances the protagonist bears striking similarities to Theroux, although it would be wrong to read these works as disguised autobiography. Frequently, as in works such as *The Black House* and *The Mosquito Coast*, Theroux separates his protagonists from society to explore the meaning of exile, foreignness, and individualism. The same can be said of later novels as well, including *Kowloon Tong*, in which the story of the central figure symbolizes the internal conflicts and contradictions that invariably arise between colonists and the colonized. Underlying all of these fictions, however, is found the basic assumption that every human experience, from death to redemption, from fear to loneliness, from love to murder, must be understood in a social context.

FONG AND THE INDIANS

Fong and the Indians, the first of Theroux's African novels, is the witty tale of the business partnership between Sam Fong, a Chinese grocer, and Hassanali

Fakhru, the Indian entrepreneur who rents him the store, supplies his goods, and, when business is poor, even becomes his customer. Fakhru dominates Fong's economic life, manipulating it for his own benefit by taking advantage of Fong's innocent incompetence as a businessman. As the plot unfolds, however, it becomes clear that the relationship between Fong and Fakhru is far from one-sided. Moreover, it also becomes clear that this association is representative of all social and economic relationships. Each individual in a society suffers limitations of understanding that arise both from his or her own prejudices and from cultural heritage. When two people meet to do business, they may well be speaking different languages, either literally or metaphorically. Misunderstandings are unavoidable, and the outcome of any action is unpredictable: Good intentions may or may not result in good consequences; the same is true of bad intentions. Chaos and absurdity reign when no one quite understands what anyone else is doing.

The plot of *Fong and the Indians* is an intricate comedy of errors involving Fong, the unwilling grocer; Fakhru, the capitalist swindler; and two agents of the U.S. Central Intelligence Agency (CIA) on a mission to convert suspected Communists. The fiction works as both a satirical portrait of postcolonial African society and an allegory in which the grocery business, the swindles, and the "goodwill" mission—artifices of civilization—are, in the context of African reality, revealed to be absurd. In *Fong and the Indians*, Theroux explores "civilization"; in the later books *Jungle Lovers*, *Girls at Play*, *The Black House*, and *The Mosquito Coast*, he explores the meaning of "the jungle"—a metaphor for the world outside the comfortable First World civilization with which most of Theroux's readers are all too familiar. At no time does Theroux become an apologist for the developing world, elevating primitive civilization over modern. Rather, he turns "jungle" into a metaphor for humanity's natural environment: The jungle is both dangerous and nurturing; it demands that its inhabitants concentrate on basic human needs. Although the metaphor is most easily understood when Theroux sets his story in the literal jungle of Africa or Central America, there is "jungle" too in South London, in an English village, even in Florida, Chicago, Hong Kong, or Hawaii.

In *Fong and the Indians*, Fakhru swindles Sam Fong by convincing him that canned milk represents a victory of civilization. In Africa, however, canned milk makes no sense. Africans do not need it, and Europeans prefer the fresh milk from Nairobi. Fong's only hope of becoming rich rests on the wild improbability that the milk train will one day be wrecked. Aware of the absurdity, Fong accepts both the hope and the improbability of its fulfillment. Fong triumphs because he learns to love what he does not understand. He has the patience to submit, to accommodate his life to the requirements of survival. His change of diet, from the traditional Chinese cuisine he has maintained for all his thirty-seven years in Africa to a free, native one based on bananas and fried locusts, is at once a measure of his economic decline and an assurance of his ultimate triumph.

SAINT JACK

A reader's first impression is liable to be that Theroux's ethic is based on the virtue of inaction. Because human understanding is limited, all events appear ambiguous. Even innocently motivated attempts to improve the lot of humanity may prove unexpectedly destructive, such as Marais's attempt to bring revolutionary ideals to Malawi in *Jungle Lovers*, Valentine Hood's murder to rid the world of Ron Weech in *The Family Arsenal*, or even Maud Coffin Pratt's photographs of the pig feast and of her brother and sister in the mill in *Picture Palace*. Because all events are ambiguous, it is impossible to predict which actions will prove evil and which will prove good. Therefore, the only possible moral strategy is to take no action at all, to be patient and accommodate oneself to the unknowable mystery of the jungle.

Inaction, however, should not be confused with selfish laziness; rather, it is an active, morally motivated inaction akin to the traditional Christian virtue of patience. Patience redeems the absurdity of the modern world, protecting humankind from despair and leading ultimately to a triumph of innocence and virtue that will in turn redeem society. This is the lesson of *Saint Jack*.

A middle-aged, balding, American expatriate, muddled, afraid, and lonely, Jack Flowers jumps ship in Singapore. A stranger and a misfit, Jack sees no hope of rescue; he does not believe in miracles. He is a modern man making a realistic appraisal of his chances in an unfriendly and dangerous world. Yet Jack wrests from this vision of despair an ad-lib ethic based on fulfilling the desires of others. He becomes what others would have him be. Condemning no one, pardoning all, Jack participates in each person's unique fantasy. In the public world, he is called a pimp—he may even be a spy—but in his own private world, Jack is a saint, thoroughly reliable and incapable of cultural misunderstanding. He gives to each what everyone needs—pleasure, security, and forgiveness—and stands ready with whatever else is required to meet even an unexpected desire, be it pornographic pictures, the kind attentions of a good girl, or a game of squash. Jack shapes his own needs to match his companion's—he is the perfect friend and protector.

Jack's tattooed arms, emblazoned with Chinese obscenities and curses disguised as flowers, symbolize the way he eases the pain of human loneliness and fear by providing an illusion of hope and friendship and the reality of a temporary pleasure taken in safety. Pity, compassion, and a stubbornly innocent vision of human needs save Jack himself from doing evil and redeem the actions of all those he takes care of, even General Maddox himself.

The terms of this novel are coyly religious—Saint Jack, the manager of Paradise Gardens—but God is not really present in Singapore. What might in a Christian fiction be termed grace is here good luck, and even Jack's redeeming power itself results, in the end, from his own fantasy. The effect is, on the one hand, tongue in cheek, and on the other, quite serious. Theroux appears to be walking the delicate line between a modern recognition that, in this absurd world, good and evil are meaningless categories and a commonsense realization that people need moral categories and at least an illusion of meaning in order to survive relatively sane.

THE FAMILY ARSENAL

The search for meaning and moral categories provides both the theme and the structure of *The Family Arsenal*. When the story opens, Valentine Hood has come to live with a group of unrelated people in South London. Their domesticity makes them a parody of the typical middle-class family: Mayo, the mother, a thief; Valentine, the father, a murderer; and Murf and Brodie, the teenage children, terrorist bombers. Early in the novel, many odd characters are introduced: Ralph Gawber, an accountant with a fondness for puzzles and a doomsday foreboding; Araba Nightwing, a radical actor who

plays Peter Pan; Ron Weech, the hoodlum whom Hood chases and murders; Lorna Weech, Ron's wife; Rutter, a gunrunner; and Lady Arrow. Initially, the relationships among these characters appear obscure if not irrelevant, but as the plot develops, groupings take shape until the reader discovers, with Valentine Hood, that all are inextricably bound together by all sorts of dirty secrets, making them, in the words of one character, like one big family no one can quit.

The puzzlelike structure of this novel parodies the conventional thriller plot. Its purpose is, however, not action-packed adventure but rather the slow revelation that, as Hood has suspected all along, inaction is best because all seemingly heinous events turn out to be morally ambiguous. Thus, Hood changes from social avenger to listener. He develops an innocent vision of pity and love akin to Jack Flowers's that not only reveals the human bonds among all members and classes of society but also redeems his own guilt and saves at least some from the dangers that threaten them. By the end of the story, all is discovered, and characters are regrouped into more pleasing families based on love rather than convenience.

Paralleling the revelation of relationships in the plot of *The Family Arsenal* is Hood's changing perception of the artistic organization of the stolen painting by Rogier van der Weyden that hangs in Mayo's closet. Mayo stole the painting believing that its theft would signal the beginning of social revolution. It does not: The world cares little about stolen artworks except as an interesting excuse for a headline. In an unexpected and very personal way, however, the painting does, in the end, play a revolutionary role in the story. It becomes the symbolic focus for the way art can organize seemingly disparate shapes and colors into a single beautiful whole. The painting, like the tattoos on Jack's arms, suggests the resemblance between the personal vision of innocence that can redeem through pity and love and the vision of the artist that is capable of changing brutal reality into beauty.

PICTURE PALACE

Theroux's most extensive development of this theme occurs in *Picture Palace*, which becomes less a song of triumph for the artist's vision than a warning of the danger that arises when that vision becomes separated (as it necessarily must) from its real social context. Civilization versus the jungle, art versus reality—in Theroux's fiction these themes become almost versions of each other. The ethical effects of efforts by either art or civilization to improve human society are always unclear, dependent as much on luck as on fantasy. Instinctively, Maud Coffin Pratt seems to realize this tenet and locks away her photograph of Phoebe and Orlando in an incestuous embrace. To her, the picture represented love and innocent fulfillment, but when her brother and sister find it, they see only their own guilt and death. Unlike Jack Flowers (who can grab back his photographs of General Maddox) or Valentine Hood (whose revelations of family secrets save them in the end), Maud finds that her personal vision of innocence redeems no one; indeed, it backfires completely, and she is left alone at the end of her life, famous but anonymous.

THE MOSQUITO COAST

In *The Mosquito Coast*, Theroux returns to the jungle milieu to explore further the consequences of extreme individualism, the separation of self from society and environment. With his perpetual-motion ice machine, Allie Fox expends a mad energy trying to produce ice in order to impress the Indians with the superiority of his civilized genius. Needless to say, whether he floats the ice downstream to a native village or carries it by sledge across the mountains, the ice melts: The impressiveness of civilization disappears in the heat of the sun. Relying completely on his own creativity, Fox, the Yankee inventor, may be seen as a type of artist. His attempt to impose his personal vision of utopia on the brutal reality of the jungle fails utterly; his story reads as a warning of the danger of art without social context.

Like Sam Fong's canned milk in *Fong and the Indians*, Fox's ice machine in *The Mosquito Coast* represents an absurd attempt to civilize the jungle; yet Fong is rewarded with riches (the milk train does wreck), while Fox dies mad and beaten on a Central American beach. Both may be seen as emblems of the modern world, alone in strange lands, possessing nothing, trying to shape their lives out of events that are mysterious, ambiguous, possibly dangerous, and probably absurd. Their differing responses to the jungle environment determine their different ends and provide the reader with a key to Theroux's view of social ethics.

Allie Fox rejects patience and accommodation; he rejects the mystery and the ambiguity of the jungle. He is determined to build a bugless outpost of civilization; he would rather starve than eat a banana. In Theroux's world, it is poetic justice that Fox should misinterpret events and bring about the ruin of all that he has built. With true tragic irony, Fox learns from his failure not the value of accommodation but only the need for an increased purity, an increased separation from the jungle, a separation doomed to failure. If Fong is the comic face of humanity, then Fox must be the tragic face.

MY SECRET HISTORY

Critics of *My Secret History* have pointed out that the narrative takes the first third of the book to begin. A long novel that is really six novellas grouped together, it follows a young man from Massachusetts who moves to Africa and, from there, to England. Andrew Parent (who changes his first name to "Andre" while in college) starts out as an altar boy in Boston, becoming first a Peace Corps volunteer in one African country and then a teacher in another African country before finally deciding to become a writer, ultimately moving to London. Eventually, Andre becomes an international womanizer as well as a successful writer, and the last chapter/novella concentrates on his facing the consequences of what he has done to his life.

Theroux's cosmopolitan experiences are what fuel his characters, and that he draws from his own life is only natural for a writer. Some critics have asserted that this work is too self-referential—that it is thinly disguised autobiography. Pointing to his mentor V. S. Naipaul's 1987 autobiographical novel *The Enigma of Arrival*, they have wondered whether *My Secret History* is a midlife crisis roman à clef.

Theroux's work, however, cannot be so easily categorized or dismissed. The progression of Theroux's novels demonstrates a marked coherence of interest and an increasing complexity of thematic and structural development. Although Theroux draws freely from the modern storehouse of pornography, violence, and antiheroism, he displays at the same time a real if not profound interest in some of the classic themes of Western literature—the source of good and evil, the use of pity and love in society and art, and the nature of reality. Technically, his work shows a similar melding of popular fiction (the gothic horror story, the thriller) with the structure and conventions of the classic novelists.

MY OTHER LIFE

Just as he resists any preconceived notions of a foreign culture he is about to enter, Theroux expects the same of readers who immerse themselves in his writings. "My secret is safe," he states in his introduction to *The Collected Stories* (1997). The secret is his identity as a writer. To assign him to a category is to overlook the sense of separation that drives him in all directions in life. He is the consummate explorer who not only delights in discovery but also observes and records in imaginative detail. Yet as Theroux asks readers not to label him, he also reminds them that "my stories are the rest of me" and "I inhabit every sentence I write," statements that could be directed to his novel *My Other Life*. Written as a companion piece to *My Secret History*, the novel reflects what the author considers his "need to invent." In this case it is an "imaginary memoir" designed to portray his life as a series of short stories, a device that led one critic to refer to the work as another example of a Theroux novel being better for its parts than its whole.

HOTEL HONOLULU

In *Hotel Honolulu* Theroux combines a number of interests that appear in his earlier novels, most notably his fascination with the role of the writer. The narrator of this novel is a successful and modestly well-known writer (who shares many features of Theroux himself) who has traveled to Hawaii partly as an attempt to overcome writer's block. Through a quirk of circumstances, he ends up managing the Hotel Honolulu, modest in size and located off the beach and outside the circle of glitzy establishments that draw the majority of tourists.

Rather than having a conventional plot, the novel consists of a loose collection of stories about the various hotel guests and other islanders and visitors the narrator meets. Though some of the stories are interconnected, the unifying element is really the hotel itself, which serves as a setting for much of the action or the catalyst that brings the narrator into contact with the people whose tales he relates, often with wry detachment. In fact, one of Theroux's principal interests is in this writer-narrator who seems to be a passive receptacle into which the adventures of others are deposited and through which they are refined. His brief accounts, delivered with exceptional wit and often laced with irony, are reminiscent of similar collections such as Giovanni Boccac-cio's *Decameron: O, Prencipe Galeotto* (1349-1351; *The Decameron*, 1620) or Geoffrey Chaucer's *The Canterbury Tales* (1387-1400), or the twentieth century novels *Ship of Fools* (1962), by Katherine Anne Porter, and *Hotel Savoy* (1924; English translation, 1986), by Joseph Roth.

Many of the disparate tales are humorous, but in the same way Theroux uses humor in *The Mosquito Coast* to hook readers and reel them in to the tale, the amusing anecdotes eventually give way to more serious matters. In the running story of the narrator's relationship with the hotel's owner, a larger-than-life character given to practical jokes and bawdy adventures, Theroux explores the condition of contemporary people whose appetites for sensual pleasure and instant gratification seem to empty their lives of any real meaning. Thus, despite the novel's comic overtones, few truly likable characters appear in *Hotel Honolulu*. On the other hand, there is much for readers to ponder about the multiple ways in which people attempt to give meaning to lives that seem little more than subjects for clever vignettes that offer brief amusement to outsiders who are not invested in other people's joys and sorrows.

BLINDING LIGHT

The figure of the artist is at the center of *Blinding Light*, a novel in which Theroux explores the nature and costs of creativity. His protagonist, Slade Steadman, is a writer living off the reputation and residual sales of his first book, a travelogue titled *Trespassing*. Like the protagonist of *Hotel Honolulu*, Steadman seeks to jump-start his creative juices by traveling from the United States to Ecuador. In his case, the purpose of the trip is to obtain a special drug—distributed only by the Native American shamans in the Ecuadoran jungle—that is rumored to have amazing powers to raise a person's consciousness. Steadman is part of a group in search of this hallucinogen, and among the other travelers is his mistress, from whom he plans to separate, and a journalist with whom Steadman instantly develops a bad relationship that lasts throughout the journey. The journalist encourages Steadman to try a different and even more potent drug than the one they have all come to take. Steadman does so, and although it apparently has little effect initially, he soon discovers that it produces a euphoric state in which he seems to have a clear vision of both the past and the future. The drug has a notable side effect, however: It causes temporary blindness.

Back in the United States, Steadman finds that under the influence of this drug he is able to begin writing again, so he takes the drug regularly and remains blind. In that condition he is able to create a novel that explores the depths of his consciousness—and the many ways in which he is able to stimulate his senses through sexual encounters with his mistress, who has remained with him to care for him while he is blind, and a young woman who joins them at Steadman's beach house at the invitation of the mistress. When the novel, which Steadman titles *The Book of Revelation*, receives only tepid reviews despite its initially good sales, Steadman begins to question the value of the drug yet finds himself unable to stop using it. Becoming reclusive and paranoid, Steadman is suddenly confronted by the journalist, who has come to Steadman's home to take vengeance on him for the way Steadman treated him in Ecuador. After their encounter, in which Steadman is almost killed, Steadman returns to Ecuador to see if he can find a way to gain release from the hold that the drug has over him.

Woven into this bizarre story of intrigue, sex, and novel writing is an examination of the creative process. Theroux seems to be asking, What is the nature of creativity? From where does it emerge? Is it something that can be induced? One of the most intriguing questions, and one that allows Theroux room for considerable irony, deals with the nature of the artist's vision. While blind, Steadman seems to see clearly into the depths of his own consciousness and develop great insight into human nature. When he is sighted, he is little more than a washed-up hack writer living off the reputation he earned as a young, adventuresome traveler. Nevertheless, there is a hint that the costs Steadman has paid are too high. His Faustian bargain to reclaim his powers as an artist eventually drives away all his friends, including the mistress, and leaves him a broken man. In *Blinding Light*, Theroux seems to say that there are limits in how one can be aided to achieve life's ambitions and achieve real happiness. By implication, it is better to be passive and let life happen—a theme that runs through many of Theroux's novels.

Linda Howe; William Hoffman
Updated by Laurence W. Mazzeno

OTHER MAJOR WORKS

SHORT FICTION: *Sinning with Annie, and Other Stories*, 1972; *The Consul's File*, 1977; *World's End*, 1980; *The London Embassy*, 1982; *The Collected Stories*, 1997; *The Stranger at the Palazzo d'Oro, and Other Stories*, 2003.

PLAY: *The Autumn Dog*, pr. 1981.

SCREENPLAY: *Saint Jack*, 1979 (adaptation of his novel; with Peter Bogdanovich and Howard Sackler).

NONFICTION: *V. S. Naipaul: An Introduction to His Work*, 1972; *The Great Railway Bazaar: By Train Through Asia*, 1975; *The Old Patagonian Express: By Train Through the Americas*, 1979; *Sailing Through China*, 1983; *The Kingdom by the Sea: A Journey Around Great Britain*, 1983; *Patagonia Revisited*, 1985 (with Bruce Chatwin; expanded as *Nowhere Is a Place: Travels in Patagonia*, 1992); *Sunrise with Seamonsters: Travels and Discoveries, 1964-1984*, 1985; *The Imperial Way*, 1985 (with Steve McCurry); *Riding the Iron Rooster: By Train Through China*, 1988; *To the Ends of the Earth: The Selected Travels of Paul Theroux*, 1990; *The Happy Isles of Oceania: Paddling the Pacific*, 1992; *Travelling the World: The Illustrated Travels of Paul Theroux*, 1992; *The Pillars of Hercules: A Grand Tour of the Mediterranean*, 1995; *Sir Vidia's Shadow: A Friendship Across Five Continents*, 1998; *Fresh-Air Fiend: Travel Writings, 1985-2000*, 2000; *Nurse Wolf and Dr. Sacks*, 2001; *Dark Star Safari: Overland from Cairo to Cape Town*, 2002; *Ghost Train to the Eastern Star: 28,000 Miles in Search of the Railway Bazaar*, 2008.

CHILDREN'S LITERATURE: *A Christmas Card*, 1978; *London Snow: A Christmas Story*, 1979.

BIBLIOGRAPHY

Beecroft, Simon. "*Sir Vidia's Shadow:* V. S. Naipaul, the Writer, and *The Enigma of Arrival.*" *Journal of Commonwealth Literature* 35, no. 1 (2000): 71-85. Presents a structural analysis of Theroux's book on the breakdown of his long friendship with Naipaul, comparing it with Naipaul's own book *The Enigma of Arrival*.

Bell, Robert F. "Metamorphoses and Missing Halves: Allusions in Paul Theroux's *Picture Palace.*" *Critique* 22, no. 3 (1981): 17-30. Discusses Theroux's use of the concepts of the interchangeability of identities, the double image, and the gap existing between art and life.

Coale, Samuel. *Paul Theroux*. Boston: Twayne, 1987. Provides a comprehensive look at Theroux's work as well as a chronology of events in the author's life. Includes bibliographies and index.

Fujii, Hikaru. "Journey to the End of the Father: Battlefield of Masculinity in *The Mosquito Coast*." *Critique* 48, no. 2 (Winter, 2007): 168-183. Presents detailed analysis of one of Theroux's most important novels. Applies theories of masculinity and of power relationships to explain the motivations of both the protagonist and the narrator.

Glaser, Elton. "The Self-Reflexive Traveler: Paul Theroux on the Art of Travel and Travel Writing." *Centennial Review* 33 (Summer, 1989): 193-206. In-depth profile of the author provides insight into what motivates his writing and traveling.

Kerr, Douglas. "A Passage to *Kowloon Tong:* Paul Theroux and Hong Kong, 1997." *Journal of Commonwealth Literature* 34, no. 2 (1999): 75-84. Discusses Theroux's representation in his novel of the transfer of power over Hong Kong from Britain to China and also addresses the response to the novel in Hong Kong and China.

Mowat, John. *Strangers Ourselves: The Adventures of Paul Theroux*. Mumbai, India: Frog Books, 2006. Presents critical analysis of some of Theroux's novels in addition to information about his life that sheds light on his literary influences.

J. R. R. TOLKIEN

Born: Bloemfontein, South Africa; January 3, 1892
Died: Bournemouth, England; September 2, 1973
Also known as: John Ronald Reuel Tolkien

PRINCIPAL LONG FICTION

The Hobbit: Or, There and Back Again, 1937
The Fellowship of the Ring, 1954
The Two Towers, 1954
The Return of the King, 1955
The Lord of the Rings, 1955 (collective title of
    previous 3 novels)
The Silmarillion, 1977
The Children of Húrin, 2007

OTHER LITERARY FORMS

The novels that J. R. R. Tolkien (TAHL-keen) produced represent only a small part of the complicated matrix from which they evolved. During Tolkien's lifetime, he published three volumes of novellas and short stories, *Farmer Giles of Ham* (1949), *Tree and Leaf* (1964), and *Smith of Wootton Major* (1967). Some of these tales had originally been bedtime stories for his own children, such as those in the posthumously published *The Father*

Christmas Letters (1976) and *Roverandom* (1998). *The Silmarillion* and *Unfinished Tales of Numenor and Middle-Earth* (1980) both contain stories Tolkien composed early in his life, material that sets the stage for the events in his novels. His poetry collections, *Songs for the Philologists* (1936), *The Adventures of Tom Bombadil* (1962), and *The Road Goes Ever On: A Song Cycle* (1967), link Tolkien's poetic formulations of Middle-earth's themes with the historical and linguistic themes of which both his professional work and much of his dreams were made, "the nameless North of Sigurd of the Völsungs, and the prince of all dragons." Tolkien's academic publications dealt with the history of the English language and Middle English literature: *A Middle English Vocabulary* (1922) and editions of *Sir Gawain and the Green Knight* (1925; with E. V. Gordon) and the *Ancrene Wisse* (1962). His seminal essay "Beowulf: The Monsters and the Critics" (1936) and his only play, *The Homecoming of Beorhtnoth Beorhthelm's Son* (pb. 1953), offer fresh interpretations of ancient English epic poems.

Tolkien's novels have been adapted for cinema and television, and many, though not all, of his fragmentary stories, articles, and letters have been published since his death. His histories of Middle-earth, a remarkable invented mythology comprising chronicles, tales, maps, and poems, were edited as a series by his son, Christopher Tolkien. Volumes include *The Book of Lost Tales*, *The Lays of Beleriand*, *The Shaping of Middle-Earth*, and *The Lost Road, and Other Writings*.

ACHIEVEMENTS

J. R. R. Tolkien's fiction dismayed most of his fellow scholars at the University of Oxford as much as it delighted most of his general readers. Such reactions sprang from their recognition of his vast linguistic talent, which underlay both his professional achievements and his mythical universe. Tolkien led two lives at once, quietly working as an Oxford tutor, examiner, editor, and lecturer while concurrently Middle-earth and its mythology were taking shape within his imagination.

For twenty years after he took first-class honors in English language and literature at Oxford, Tolkien's teaching and linguistic studies buttressed his scholarly reputation. Editing the fourteenth century text of *Sir Gawain and the Green Knight* with E. V. Gordon helped bring Tolkien the Rawlinson and Bosworth Professorship of Anglo-Saxon at Oxford in 1925. His lecture "Beowulf: The Monsters and the Critics" approached the Anglo-Saxon epic poem from an entirely new perspective and is considered a landmark in criticism of Western Germanic literature. As he was shaping his linguistic career, however, Tolkien was also formulating an imaginary language that, as early as 1917, had led him to explore its antecedents, its mythology, and its history, all of which he molded into the tales of *The Silmarillion*. Over the years, he shared these stories with friends, but he never finished putting them into a unified structure.

His preoccupation with Middle-earth and the practical demands of his teaching distracted Tolkien from scholarship, and between his celebrated essay *On Fairy Stories* in 1939 and his edition of the Middle English *Ancrene Wisse* in 1962, Tolkien published only fiction, a circumstance acknowledged with polite forbearance by most of Oxford's scholarly community, although his novels eventually met with astonishing popular success. *The Hobbit*, originally a children's story, was published in 1937 after a six-year gestation, and by 1949, *The Lord*

of the Rings was complete. Its sales, though steadily increasing after its publication in 1954-1955, did not soar until 1965, when an unauthorized American printing proved a disguised blessing, resulting in a campus cult responsible for the sale of three million copies by 1968.

Most critics of *The Lord of the Rings* have not achieved moderation. As W. H. Auden observed, "People find it a masterpiece of its genre, or they cannot abide it." Auden himself and C. S. Lewis, Tolkien's Oxford friend, headed the "masterpiece" faction, while Edwin Muir in England and Edmund Wilson in the United States deplored Tolkien's style and aims.

Honorary fellowships, an honorary doctorate of letters from Oxford, and the honor of being made a Commander of the Order of the British Empire by Queen Elizabeth II all descended on Tolkien with the unexpected wealth of his last years, which were nevertheless darkened by his reluctance to complete *The Silmarillion*. His reputation rests not on his academic talent or his scholarly production, or even on his brilliant linguistically oriented "mythology for England," but on the novels that began as tales for his children and blossomed into a splendid imaginative tree of fiction whose roots feed on the archetypes of northern European civilization and whose leaves shelter its finest aspirations.

BIOGRAPHY

John Ronald Reuel Tolkien was born in Bloemfontein, South Africa, on January 3, 1892. The piano-manufacturing firm of his father's family, originally descended from German aristocracy, had gone bankrupt, and the elder Tolkien had taken a South African bank position in the hope of improving his shaky finances. Tolkien's mother, Mabel Suffield, joined her husband at Bloemfontein, but when the climate strained Ronald's health, she took their two sons home to England in 1895. Less than a year later, Arthur Tolkien died in South Africa, leaving his widow and children nearly penniless.

In the summer of 1896, Mabel Tolkien rented a rural cottage at Sarehole Mill, close to Birmingham, and for the next four years she taught her boys French, Latin, drawing, and botany, to save school expenses. Much later, Tolkien called these "the longest-seeming and most formative part" of his life. Mabel Tolkien's attraction to Roman Catholicism led to her conversion in

1900, and she moved to a Birmingham suburb from which Ronald attended one of England's then leading grammar schools, King Edward's, on a scholarship. Already, he was demonstrating the fascination with ancient languages that was to determine his career. He was involved in learning such northern European languages as Norse, Gothic, Finnish, and Welsh, as well as the Old and Middle English in which he achieved his academic reputation. He later claimed this philological bent dated from the time he was five or six years old.

In 1904, his mother died at the age of thirty-four, leaving her children in the care of Father Francis Morgan, her friend and pastor. Tolkien's devotion to his mother was inextricably intertwined with his own Catholic faith, and both played vital roles in the development of his fiction. Thus at sixteen, Ronald Tolkien looked back on a series of grievous losses: his father, whom he considered as "belonging to an almost legendary past"; the Sarehole countryside he loved; his mother, whom he considered a martyr to her faith. Not surprisingly for a lonely boy, Tolkien fell in love early when he met Edith Bratt, another orphan, in his Birmingham boarding-house. She was three years older than he, and she had just enough inheritance to support herself modestly while she dreamed of becoming a musician. Recognizing the boy's scholarly talent and fearing for his future, Father Morgan finally stopped all communication between Ronald and Edith until Ronald was twenty-one. Tolkien himself commented thirty years later, "Probably nothing else would have hardened the will enough to give such an affair (however genuine a case of true love) permanence." When he and Edith were reunited in 1913, they seemed to have little in common, but on the eve of his military departure to France in 1916, they were married.

By this time Tolkien had won a scholarship to Oxford University and had graduated with first-class honors in 1913. He enlisted in the Lancashire Fusiliers in 1915, embarking for France in 1916. He survived the Battle of the Somme but was invalided back to England suffering from trench fever. While in a military hospital in 1917, Tolkien began *The Book of Lost Tales*, the genesis of *The Silmarillion*, although he dated the original ideas for the complete oeuvre from as early as 1910 and the original story of Beren and Tinuviel back to 1913. By 1918 he had read a version of "The Fall of Gondolin" to a college group.

After demobilization, Tolkien gained employment working on the new *Oxford English Dictionary*, until in 1921 he was appointed to the University of Leeds in Yorkshire to lecture in Old English. While there he began to establish his academic reputation with *A Middle English Vocabulary* and an edition of *Sir Gawain and the Green Knight* done with Professor E. V. Gordon. On the strength of these and his connections back at Oxford, he was appointed the Rawlinson and Bosworth Professor of Anglo-Saxon Studies at Oxford in 1925, a post he held until 1945, when he was appointed Merton Professor of English Language and Literature at the same university. He held this

J. R. R. Tolkien. (Courtesy, Houghton Mifflin Company)

post until his belated retirement in 1959. Various honorary degrees were bestowed on him, and in 1938 he was Andrew Lang Lecturer at the University of St. Andrews, where he gave his famous lectures on fairy stories.

The central part of Tolkien's life, however, lay in his secret creation of the mythology of Middle-earth. It was initially the demands of his growing family (three sons and a daughter) that brought any of this to light, particularly in *The Hobbit*, which was first drafted, according to his close friend and science-fiction novelist C. S. Lewis, by the beginning of 1930. Then it was through the influence of the Inklings, a group of like-minded university friends that included Lewis and Tolkien, that *The Hobbit* was reformulated and sent for eventual publication in 1937. The importance of the Inklings cannot be stressed enough, especially the friendship of Lewis, who encouraged Tolkien's work on *The Lord of the Rings* during World War II and immediately after, and who reviewed it in glowing terms. In a sense, Lewis was repaying the enormous debt he owed Tolkien for his conversion to Christianity. The Inklings continued until Lewis's death in 1963, though the two men had drifted apart somewhat by then.

Even so, the vast bulk of Middle-earth mythology lay in a constant state of revision, expansion, and rearrangement, and despite the best efforts of friends and publishers, it was unpublished at his death. In fact, after the publication of *The Lord of the Rings* in 1956, he concentrated again on his academic work, and only after retirement did he make any serious inroads again into the mythology. In the end, it was left to his third son, Christopher, also an academic, to order the material and have it published, as he did with a number of incomplete academic studies. Tolkien's death in 1973 had been preceded by his wife's in 1971. They were both buried outside Oxford, their graves suitably inscribed with the names Beren and Lúthien. The year before his death he had been made a Commander of the Order of the British Empire by Queen Elizabeth II.

ANALYSIS

Looking back on his Middle-earth around 1951, J. R. R. Tolkien commented, "I do not remember a time when I was not building it . . . always I had the sense of recording what was already 'there,' somewhere: not of

inventing." He conceived of fantasy as a profound and powerful form of literature with intense philosophical and spiritual meaning, serious purposes, and eternal appeal. He believed the imagination, the mental power of making images, could be linked by art to "subcreation," the successful result of image making, and so he regarded the genuine artist as partaking in the Creator's divine nature.

Three major factors of Tolkien's personality and environment combined to shape the theory of fantasy underlying his novels, as first enunciated in the essay "On Fairy-Stories" (1938). His love of language for its singular rewards, his delight in the English countryside, and his shattering experience of trench warfare during World War I all provided the seeds for his three longest pieces of fiction. They also contributed to the points of view, astonishingly nonhuman and yet startlingly convincing, of *The Silmarillion*, *The Hobbit*, and *The Lord of the Rings*, where Elves and Hobbits illuminate the world of Men.

Even as a boy, Tolkien had been enchanted by Welsh names on railway coal cars, a sign of his unusual linguistic sensitivity, and as a mature scholar, he devoted himself to the mystery of the word in its northern manifestations. In "On Fairy-Stories," he wrote that "*spell* means both a story told, and a formula of power over living men." Tolkien cast his spells in the building blocks of words drawn from the imaginary languages he had been constructing as long as he could remember. The two languages he formulated for his Elves, the Elder Race, both derived from a common linguistic ancestor as human languages do, and this "nexus of languages" supplied the proper names for his fiction, so that despite their considerable length and complication they possess "cohesion, consistency of linguistic style, and the illusion of historicity." The last was possibly the greatest achievement of Tolkien's mastery of language in his novels, fostering vital credence in his imaginary world. He felt that the finest fairy stories "open a door on Other Time, and if we pass through . . . we stand outside our own time, outside Time itself, maybe." In his own childhood, a "troublous" one Tolkien said, he had "had no special 'wish to believe'"; he instead "wanted to know," as, perhaps, do his readers, aided by the resonance of his masterful use of words.

The memory of his years at Sarehole, the happiest of

his boyhood, gave Tolkien an abiding love of nature, "above all trees," which formed the basis for one of his principal concepts, "the inter-relations between the 'noble' and the 'simple.'" He found "specially moving" the "ennoblement of the ignoble," a theme that recurs throughout his fiction. Tolkien's Elves practice love and respect toward nature, as do his Hobbits, "small people" connected closely to "the soil and other living things" who display both human pettiness and unexpected heroism "in a pinch." The Elves, Hobbits, and good Men are countered in Tolkien's Middle-earth by the threat of the machine, by which he meant "all use of external plans or devices," as opposed to "the development of inner powers or talents." The evil of the machine in Tolkien's eyes (he did not own a car after World War II) derived from the misguided human desire for power, itself a rebellion against the Creator's laws, a Fall from Paradise, another recurring theme in his fiction.

The horrors of World War I must have struck Tolkien as evil incarnate, with new military technology that devastated the countryside, struck down the innocent, and left no place for chivalry, heroism, or even common decency. Unlike Andrew Lang, an early Scottish collector of fairy tales, who felt children most often ask, "Is it true?," Tolkien declared that children far more often asked him of a character, "Was he good? Was he wicked?" Tolkien shared G. K. Chesterton's conviction that children "are innocent and love justice; while most of us are wicked and naturally prefer mercy." The child's stern perception of right and wrong, as opposed to the "mercy untempered by justice" that leads to "falsification of values," confirmed Tolkien's long-held inclination toward the steely world of the northern sagas, where human heroism faces inevitable defeat by the forces of evil, and the hero, according to Edith Hamilton, "can prove what he is only by dying." From his basic distrust of the machine and his firsthand memories of the Somme, Tolkien drew one of the major lessons of his fiction: "that on callow, lumpish and selfish youth peril, sorrow, and the shadow of death can bestow dignity, and even sometimes wisdom."

Reconciling this harsh northern *Weltbild* with his Roman Catholic faith did not seem to be difficult for Tolkien. An indispensable element of his theory of fantasy is the "sudden joyous 'turn'" of a "eucatastrophic" story, a moment in fiction accompanied by "a catch of the breath, a beat and lifting of the heart, near to (or indeed accompanied by) tears." By inserting the "turn" convincingly into his tale, the subcreator "denies universal final defeat" and gives "a fleeting glimpse of Joy, Joy beyond the walls of the world, poignant as grief." Hence, Tolkien believed that such a joy was the "mark of the true fairy story," the revelation of truth in the fictional world the subcreator built. It might even be greater, "a far-off gleam or echo of *evangelium* in the real world." Tolkien was able to see the Christian Gospels as "the greatest and most complete conceivable eucatastrophe," believing that in fantasy the human subcreator might "actually assist in the effoliation and multiple enrichment of creation."

Tolkien's *The Silmarillion*, *The Hobbit*, and *The Lord of the Rings* form, as he always hoped, one coherent and archetypal whole. His "creative fantasy" effectively shows the three dissimilar faces his theory demanded: "the Mystical towards the Supernatural; the Magical towards Nature; and the Mirror of scorn and pity toward Man." Humanity's "oldest and deepest desire," the "Great Escape" from death, is satisfied in Tolkien's major fiction, not by denying Mortality but by accepting it gracefully as a gift from the Creator, a benefit to humankind that Tolkien's immortal Elves envied. The Elves' own magic is actually art, whose true object is "subcreation" under God, not domination of lesser beings whose world they respectfully share. Scorn for fallen people (and fallen Elves and Hobbits as well) abounds in Middle-earth, but pity, too, for guiltless creatures trapped in the most frightful evil Tolkien could envision, evil that he believed arises "from an apparently good root, the desire to benefit the world and others—speedily—and according to the benefactor's own plans." Middle-earth lives forever in Tolkien's novels, and with it an affirmation of what is best, most true, and most beautiful in human nature.

For almost fifty years, mostly in the quiet academic atmosphere of Oxford, Tolkien built his resounding tales of "a body of more or less connected legend, ranging from the large and cosmogonic, to the level of romantic fairy-story." He consciously dedicated the work simply "to England; to my country." The intellectual absorption with language he had always enjoyed gave him the starting place for his mythology, which he implemented in

The Silmarillion, whose unifying theme is the Fall of Elves and Men. His happiness in the English countryside seems to have provided him the landscape from which *The Hobbit* grew, perhaps his most approachable "fairy-story" for both children and adults, illustrating the happiness to be gained from simplicity and the acceptance of the gift of mortality. The chivalric dreams of noble sacrifice shattered for Tolkien's generation by World War I were redeemed for him by his realization that the humble may effectively struggle against domination by the misguided technological values of modern civilization. The heroic legend of *The Lord of the Rings* best illustrates Tolkien's resolution of the conflict between the northern values he had admired from youth and the Roman Catholic religion of hope and consolation to which he was devoted. Tolkien wanted to illuminate the simplest and the highest values of human existence, found in a human love that accepts and transcends mortality. Tolkien's "mythology for England," a unique gift of literature and language, has earned its immense popular success by appealing to humanity's eternal desire to understand its mortal lot. As Hilda Ellis Davidson commented of the great northern myths, so like Tolkien's own, "In reaching out to explore the distant hills where the gods dwell and the deeps where the monsters are lurking, we are perhaps discovering the way home."

THE SILMARILLION

Both in Tolkien's life and in the chronology of Middle-earth, the tales of *The Silmarillion* came first, but the book was not published until four years after his death. The volume called *The Silmarillion* contains four shorter narratives as well as the "Quenta Silmarillion," arranged as ordered chronicles of the Three Ages of Tolkien's Middle-earth by his son Christopher, following his father's explicit intention.

Tolkien began parts of *The Silmarillion* in 1917 after he had been invalided home from France. The work steadily evolved after more than forty years, and, according to Christopher Tolkien, "incompatibilities of tone" inevitably arose from his father's increasing preoccupation with theology and philosophy over the mythology and poetry he had originally favored. Tolkien himself never abandoned his work on *The Silmarillion*, even though he found himself unable to complete it. As Christopher Wiseman had suggested to Tolkien, "Why these

creatures live to you is because you are still creating them," and so Tolkien painstakingly revised, recast, and polished these stories, unwilling to banish their characters from his imagination.

The Silmarillion opens with "Ainulindalë," a cosmogonical myth revealing the creation of Middle-earth by God ("Iluvatar") in the presence of the Valar, whom Tolkien described as angelic powers. He wanted "to provide beings of the same order . . . as the 'gods' of higher mythology" acceptable to "a mind that believes in the Blessed Trinity." The universe to which Middle-earth belonged was set in living motion by music, "beheld as a light in the darkness."

The short "Valaquenta" enumerates the individual Valar, whose personal responsibilities covered all created things of Middle-earth, stopping short of the act of creation itself. One of the Valar, Melkor, rebelled in the First Age; Tolkien believed that "there cannot be any 'story' without a fall." Melkor "began with the desire of Light, but when he could not possess it for himself alone, he descended . . . into a great burning." One of Melkor's servants was Sauron, who later embodied evil in the Third Age of Middle-earth.

The twenty-four chapters of the "Quenta Silmarillion" recount the legendary history of the immortal Elves, the First-Born of Iluvatar, whom Tolkien elsewhere called "rational incarnate creatures of more or less comparable stature with our own." After writing *The Lord of the Rings*, Tolkien clearly indicated that the Elves were "only a representation of an apprehension of a part of human nature" from which art and poetry spring, but, he said, "that is not the legendary mode of talking." The Elves originally share the Paradise of the Valar, Valinor, but the Elves suffer a fall from that grace in the "Quenta Silmarillion," the rebellion and exile to Middle-earth of one of the great families of Elves, led by their chief, the artificer Fëanor, who has captured the primal light of Iluvatar in the three Silmarils. Tolkien described these great jewels as aglow with the "light of art undivorced from reason, that sees things both scientifically (or philosophically) and imaginatively (or subcreatively) and 'says that they are good'—as beautiful." Fëanor's lust to possess the Silmarils for himself leads to their capture by Melkor, and in the struggle to redeem them, splendid deeds are performed by Beren, a Man of

Middle-earth beloved of the Elvish princess Lúthien. Tolkien called this "the first example of the motive (to become dominant in Hobbits) that the great policies of world history . . . are often turned . . . by the seemingly unknown and weak." The union of Beren and Lúthien is the first between mortal Man and immortal Elf; they win Paradise together, and eventually Earendil the Elven Mariner closes the "Quenta Silmarillion" by bringing the gem Beren painfully rescued from Melkor to the land of the Valar. His Silmaril was set into the sky as its brightest star, while the others were lost in the depths of the earth and sea, and the First Age of Middle-earth came to its end.

Tolkien saw the Second Age of Middle-earth as dark, and he believed "not very much of its history is (or need be) told." The Valar continued to dwell at Valinor with the faithful Elves, but the exiled Elves with Fëanor were commanded to leave Middle-earth and live in the lonely Isle of Eressëa in the West. Some of them, however, ignored the order and remained in Middle-earth. Those Men of Middle-earth who had aided the Elves to redeem the Silmarils were given the Atlantis-like realm of Númenor as their reward, as well as life spans three times the normal age of Men. Though Melkor was chained, his servant Sauron remained free to roam Middle-earth, and through his evil influence, both Men of Númenor and the Delaying Elves came to grief.

The decay of Númenor is told in the *Akallabeth*, a much briefer illustration of Tolkien's belief that the inevitable theme of human stories is "a Ban, or Prohibition." The long-lived Númenoreans were prohibited by the Valar from setting foot on "immortal" lands in the West. Their wrongful desire to escape death, their gift from Iluvatar, causes them to rebel and bring about their own watery destruction through the worship of Sauron, Melkor's servant. At the same time, the Elves who delayed in Middle-earth suffered the painful consequences of their flawed choice. Tolkien said they "wanted to have their cake without eating it," enjoying the perfection of the West while remaining on ordinary earth, revered as superior beings by the other, lesser races. Some of them cast their lot with Sauron, who enticed them to create three Rings of Power, in the misguided hope of making Middle-earth another Valinor. Sauron secretly made another ring himself, one with the power to enslave all the

others. The ensuing war between Sauron and the Elves devastated Middle-earth, but in the Last Alliance of Elves and Men against Sauron, the One Ring was lost. Tolkien calls this the "catastrophic end, not only of the Second Age, but of the Old World, the primeval age of Legend."

The posthumous collection called *The Silmarillion* ends with Tolkien's résumé "Of the Rings of Power and the Third Age," which introduces the motives, themes, and chief actors in the next inevitable war between Sauron and the Free Peoples of Middle-earth. Although *The Hobbit* and *The Lord of the Rings* have proved vastly more popular, and both can be enjoyed without the complicated and generally loftily pitched history of *The Silmarillion*, its information is essential to a thorough understanding of the forces Tolkien set at work in the later novels. Even more important, *The Silmarillion* was for Tolkien, as his son Christopher has said, "the vehicle and depository of his profoundest reflections," and as such, it holds the bejewelled key to the autobiography Tolkien felt was embedded in his fiction.

THE HOBBIT

Around 1930, Tolkien jotted a few enigmatic words about "a hobbit" on the back of an examination paper he was grading. "Names always generate a story in my mind," he observed, and eventually he found out "what hobbits were like." The Hobbits, whom he subsequently described as "a branch of the specifically *human* race (not Elves or Dwarves)," became the vital link between Tolkien's mythology as constructed in *The Silmarillion* and the heroic legend that dominates *The Lord of the Rings*. Humphrey Carpenter, Tolkien's official biographer, has written that Bilbo Baggins, hero of *The Hobbit*, "embodied everything he [Tolkien] loved about the West Midlands." Tolkien himself once wrote, "I am in fact a hobbit, in all but size," and beyond personal affinities, he saw the Hobbits as "rustic English people," small in size to reflect "the generally small reach of their imagination—not the small reach of their courage or latent power."

Tolkien's Hobbits appear in the Third Age of Middle-earth, in an ominously quiet lull before a fearful storm. Sauron had been overthrown by the Elflord Gil-galad and the Númenorean King Elendil, but since evil is never completely vanquished, Sauron's creatures lurk in the margins of Middle-earth, in the mountain-enclosed region of Mordor, while a few Elves keep watch on its borders. Descendants of a few Númenoreans were saved from their land's disaster (Atlantean destruction was a recurrent nightmare for both Tolkien and his son Christopher), and they rule in the Kingdoms of Arnor in the North of Middle-earth and Gondor of the South. The former Númenoreans are allies of the Homeric Riders of Rohan, whose human forefathers had remained in Middle-earth when Númenor came to be. The three Elven Rings of Power secretly guard Rivendell and Lothlórien, which Tolkien called "enchanted enclaves of peace where Time seems to stand still and decay is restrained, a semblance of the bliss of the True West."

The Hobbits live in the Shire, in "an ordered, civilised, if simple rural life." One day, the Hobbit Bilbo Baggins receives an odd visitor, Gandalf the Wizard, who sends Bilbo off with traveling dwarves, as a professional burglar, in search of Dragon's Gold, the major theme of the novel. In the process, Tolkien uses the humble Hobbit to illustrate one of his chief preoccupations, the process by which "small imagination" combines with "great courage." As he recalled from his months in the trenches, "I've always been impressed that we are here, surviving, because of the indomitable courage of quite small people against impossible odds."

Starting from the idyllic rural world of the Shire, *The Hobbit*, ostensibly a children's book, traces the typical quest of the northern hero about whom Tolkien himself had loved to read in his youth. Gandalf shares certain characteristics with the Scandinavian god Odin, said to wander among people as an "old man of great height," with a long grey cloak, a white beard, and supernatural powers. Gandalf, like Odin, understands the speech of birds, being especially fond of eagles and ravens, and his strange savage friend Beorn, who rescues the Hobbits at one critical point, recalls the berserkers, bearskin-clad warriors consecrated to Odin who fought with superhuman strength in the intoxication of battle. The Dwarves of Middle-earth distinctly resemble their Old Norse forebears, skilled craftsmen who made treasures for the gods. Smaug the Dragon, eventually slain by the human hero Bard, is surely related to "the prince of all dragons" who had captured Tolkien's boyish imagination and who would reappear in *Farmer Giles of Ham*. The Germanic code of the *comitatus*, the warrior's fidelity unto death, celebrated in the tenth century Anglo-Saxon poem "The Battle of Maldon," inspired Tolkien's only play and applies to *The Hobbit*, too, since Bilbo's outward perils are overshadowed by the worst threat of all to the northern hero, the inward danger of proving a coward.

Bilbo's hard-won self-knowledge allows him to demonstrate the "indomitable courage of small people against great odds" when he saves Dwarves, Men, and Elves from suicidal war against one another, after the Dragon has been slain and its treasure freed. *The Hobbit* far exceeded its beginnings as a bedtime story for Tolkien's small sons, since it is also a fable about the child at the heart of every person, perceiving right and wrong as sternly as did the heroes of the North.

In late 1937, at the suggestion of his British publisher, Stanley Unwin, Tolkien began a sequel to *The Hobbit*. To the East, a malignant force was gathering strength in the Europe that even the mammoth sacrifices of World War I had not redeemed from oppression, and while Tolkien often cautions against interpreting his works allegorically, the apprehensive atmosphere of prewar England must have affected his own peace of mind. He described his intention in *The Lord of the Rings* as "an attempt to . . . wind up all the elements and motives of what has preceded." He wanted "to include the colloquialism and vulgarity of Hobbits, poetry and the highest style of prose." The moral of this novel, not a "trilogy" but, he stressed, "conceived and written as a whole," was "obvious": "that without the high and noble the simple and vulgar is utterly mean; and without the simple and ordinary the noble and heroic is meaningless."

THE LORD OF THE RINGS

The Lord of the Rings is a vast panoramic contest between good and evil played out against the backdrop of Tolkien's mythology as presented in *The Silmarillion*. The One Ring of Sauron, long lost, was found by little Bilbo Baggins, and from him it passed to his kinsman Frodo, who becomes the central figure of the quest-in-reverse: Having found the Ring, the allied Men, Elves, Dwarves, and Hobbits must destroy it where it was forged, so that its power can never again dominate Middle-earth. Another quest takes place simultaneously in the novel, as the mysterious Strider who greets the

Hobbits at Bree on the first stage of their perilous journey is gradually revealed as Aragorn, son of Arathorn and heir to Arnor in the North, descendant of Elendil who kept faith with the Valar; he is the human King of Middle-earth who must reclaim his realm. Sauron's minions rise to threaten the Ringbearer and his companions, and, after many adventures, a great hopeless battle is fought before the Gates of Mordor. As Tolkien stated in "Of the Rings of Power and the Third Age," "There at the last they looked upon death and defeat, and all their valour was in vain; for Sauron was too strong." This is the paradoxical defeat-and-victory of the northern hero, whose glory is won in the manner of his death. As a practicing Christian, however, Tolkien had to see hope clearly in the ultimate struggle between right and wrong, "and help came from the hands of the weak when the Wise faltered." Frodo the Hobbit at last manages to carry the Ring to Mount Doom in spite of Sauron, and there it is destroyed, and "a new Spring opened up on Earth." Even then, Frodo's mission is not completed. With his three Hobbit companions, he has to return to the Shire and undo the evil that has corrupted the hearts, minds, and landscape of that quiet region. Only after that may Frodo, with the Elves, depart for the far west.

In retrospect, Tolkien acknowledged that another central issue of *The Lord of the Rings* is "love in different modes," which had been "wholly absent from *The Hobbit.*" Tolkien considered the "simple 'rustic' love" between Sam, Frodo's faithful batman, and his Rosie was "*absolutely essential*" both to the study of the main hero of the novel and "to the theme of the relation of ordinary life . . . to quests, to sacrifice, causes, and the 'longing for Elves,' and sheer beauty." The evidence of Tolkien's own life indicates the depth of his ability to love, like Beren, always faithful to his Lúthien. Such love that makes all sacrifice possible forms the indestructible core of *The Lord of the Rings*, which moved C. S. Lewis to speak of "beauties which pierce like swords or burn like cold iron . . . a book that will break your heart."

Love exemplified in two important romances softens the necromancy and the battles of *The Lord of the Rings*: the poignant "mistaken love" of Eowyn for Aragorn, as Tolkien described it, and the novel's "highest love-story," the tale of Aragorn and Arwen, daughter of Elrond, leader of the Elves of Middle-earth. Eowyn is niece to Theoden, King of Rohan, the land of the horsemen that Tolkien patterned on ancient Anglo-Saxon tribes, which he first encountered through William Morris's *The House of the Wolfings* (1888). In Theoden's decline, the shield-maiden Eowyn gives her first love to the royalty-in-exile she senses in Aragorn, and although he in no sense encourages her, Eowyn's tragedy is one only he can heal once he is restored as King. In contrast, Tolkien merely alludes to the love of Aragorn and Arwen in *The Lord of the Rings*, since it seems almost too deep for tears. Arwen must forsake her Elven immortality and join Aragorn in human death, paralleling the earlier story of Beren and Lúthien. Like Tolkien's own love for Edith, Aragorn's for Arwen is temporarily prevented from reaching fruition until he can return to her in full possession of his birthright. The shadow of her possible loss lends stature to the characterization of Aragorn, the hero of *The Lord of the Rings*.

In 1955, Tolkien observed that "certain features . . . and especially certain places" of *The Lord of the Rings* "still move me very powerfully." The passages he cited sum up the major means by which the novel so strongly conveys love, redemption, and heroism achieved in the face of overwhelming odds. "The heart remains in the description of Cerin Amroth," he wrote, the spot where Aragorn and Arwen first pledged their love and where, many years later at the beginning of his fearful quest, "the grim years were removed from the face of Aragorn, and he seemed clothed in white, a young lord tall and fair." Tolkien magnifies this small epiphany of love through the eyes of the Hobbit Frodo. Another key episode, the wretched Gollum's failure to repent because Sam interrupts him, grieved Tolkien deeply, he said, for it resembled "the *real* world in which the instruments of just retribution are seldom themselves just or holy." In his favorite passage, however, Tolkien was "most stirred by the sound of the horns of the Rohirrim at cockcrow," the great "turn" of *The Lord of the Rings*, a flash of salvation in the face of all odds that comes beyond hope, beyond prayer, like a stroke of unexpected bliss from the hand of the Creator.

The "turn" that makes *The Lord of the Rings* a "true fairy-story" in Tolkien's definition links fidelity to a vow, a Germanic value, to the Christian loyalty that animated many of the great Anglo-Saxon works Tolkien had spent his scholarly life studying. By weaving the immensely complex threads of Elves, Hobbits, Men, and Dwarves into his heroic legend of the last great age of Middle-earth, he achieved a valid subcreation, sharing in the nature of what for him was most divine.

THE HISTORY OF MIDDLE-EARTH

Tolkien's son Christopher undertook the massive task of editing and commenting on the many drafts and manuscripts Tolkien left unpublished. These volumes, grouped under the title *The History of Middle-Earth*, became commentary of a painstaking, scholarly kind, such as Tolkien himself would have enjoyed, no doubt, though it leaves the average reader rather befuddled. Each volume reprints, compares, and comments on original draft material in chronological order. One interesting feature is the emergence of the *Annals*, running alongside the stories; another is the evolution of the Elvish languages and etymologies. Tolkien's original attempt to make this a mythology of England through the character of Aelfwine, an Anglo-Saxon who had somehow reached Middle-earth and then translated some of its material into Old English, can also be seen. *The Lost Road* (1937) emerges as a fragment produced as part of an agreement with C. S. Lewis for a science-fiction story on time travel that would complement a story by Lewis on space. The latter produced *Out of the Silent Planet* (1938), but Tolkien gave up on his, though the attempt to connect it to the *Akallabeth* can be seen clearly.

Christopher Tolkien also edited the childhood stories and poetry; others have dealt with Tolkien's drawings, illustrations, and mapmaking predilections. The production of such works is perhaps in some danger of overshadowing the myth that gave them life. Tolkien saw all of his writings as unfinished and imperfect. As C. S. Lewis saw too in his *Chronicles of Narnia* (1950-1956), our myths can only ever be the first page of the Great Myth that goes on forever.

Mitzi M. Brunsdale
Updated by David Barratt

OTHER MAJOR WORKS

SHORT FICTION: *Tree and Leaf*, 1964 (revised 1988); *Unfinished Tales of Numenor and Middle-Earth*, 1980 (Christopher Tolkien, editor).

PLAY: *The Homecoming of Beorhtnoth Beorhthelm's Son*, pb. 1953.

POETRY: *Songs for the Philologists*, 1936 (with E. V. Gordon et al.); *The Adventures of Tom Bombadil*, 1962; *The Road Goes Ever On: A Song Cycle*, 1967 (music by Donald Swann); *Poems and Stories*, 1980.

NONFICTION: *A Middle English Vocabulary*, 1922; *The Letters from J. R. R. Tolkien: Selection*, 1981 (Humphrey Carpenter, editor); *The Monsters and the Critics, and Other Essays*, 1983.

TRANSLATIONS: *"Sir Gawain and the Green Knight," "Pearl," and "Sir Orfeo,"* 1975; *The Old English Exodus*, 1981; *Finn and Hengest: The Fragment and the Episode*, 1982.

CHILDREN'S LITERATURE: *Farmer Giles of Ham*, 1949; *Smith of Wootton Major*, 1967; *The Father Christmas Letters*, 1976; *Roverandom*, 1998.

EDITED TEXTS: *Sir Gawain and the Green Knight*, 1925 (with E. V. Gordon); *Ancrene Wisse: The English Text of the Ancrene Riwle*, 1962.

MISCELLANEOUS: *The Tolkien Reader*, 1966; *The History of Middle-Earth*, 1983-1996 (Christopher Tolkien, editor; includes *The Book of Lost Tales I*, 1983; *The Book of Lost Tales II*, 1984; *The Lays of Beleriand*, 1985; *The Shaping of Middle-Earth*, 1986; *The Lost Road, and Other Writings*, 1987; *The Return of the Shadow: The History of "The Lord of the Rings,"* Part One, 1988; *The Treason of Isengard: The History of "The Lord of the Rings,"* Part Two, 1989; *The War of the Ring: The History of "The Lord of the Rings,"* Part Three, 1990; *Sauron Defeated, the End of the Third Age: The History of "The Lord of the Rings,"* Part Four, 1992; *Morgoth's Ring*, 1993; *The War of the Jewels*, 1994; *The Peoples of Middle-Earth*, 1996).

BIBLIOGRAPHY

Carpenter, Humphrey. *Tolkien: A Biography*. Winchester, Mass.: Allen & Unwin, 1977. Standard biography was written with access to Tolkien's unpublished letters and diaries; the mostly chronological narrative traces the development of the world of Middle-earth from Tolkien's philological work. Includes an extensive section of black-and-white photographs, a detailed bibliography, a family genealogy, and an index.

Clark, George, and Daniel Timmons, eds. *J. R. R. Tolkien and His Literary Resonances: Views of Middle-Earth.* Westport, Conn.: Greenwood Press, 2000. Collection of fourteen essays is devoted to Tolkien's Middle-earth works. Includes an examination of Tolkien's images of evil, discussion of his use of medieval allegory, and comparisons of his works to those of John Milton and C. S. Lewis.

Crabbe, Katharyn W. *J. R. R. Tolkien.* Rev. ed. New York: Continuum, 1988. Study of Tolkien's writings is unified by a vision of "the quest." After a brief biographical chapter, Crabbe considers Tolkien's use of languages to delineate character in his major works.

Curry, Patrick. *Defending Middle-Earth: Tolkien, Myth, and Modernity.* New York: HarperCollins, 1997. Examines the relevance of Tolkien's mythological creation, especially in terms of its depiction of the struggle of community, nature, and spirit against state. Includes discussion of politics, ecology, and spirituality in Tolkien's works.

Dickerson, Matthew T., and Jonathan Evans. *Ents, Elves, and Eriador: The Environmental Vision of J. R. R. Tolkien.* Lexington: University Press of Kentucky, 2006. Focuses on Tolkien's view of the natural world and environmental responsibility, arguing that the lifestyles of his fictional creations anticipated many of the tenets of modern environmentalism and agrarianism.

Drout, Michael D. C., ed. *J. R. R. Tolkien Encyclopedia: Scholarship and Critical Assessment.* New York: Routledge, 2007. Comprehensive reference volume contains five hundred entries on a wide range of subjects, including Tolkien's biography, characters, influence, and critical reception. Also addressed are the topics of scholarship about the writer and adaptations of his writings to the screen and other media.

Foster, Robert. *The Complete Guide to Middle-Earth: From "The Hobbit" to "The Silmarillion."* Rev. ed. New York: Ballantine, 1978. Alphabetical annotated compendium includes entries on each of the proper names in Tolkien's major works, including persons, places, and things, with page references to standard editions of the works. This invaluable reference guide, written from a perspective within the world created by Tolkien, also provides translations of Middle-earth tongues, chronologies as appropriate, and masterful summaries of complex events.

Haber, Karen, ed. *Meditations on Middle-Earth.* New York: St. Martin's Press, 2001. Collection of essays by a number of fantasy writers, including Ursula K. Le Guin, provides discussion of Tolkien's influence. Also offers an overview of the novelist's work by Tolkien scholar Douglas Anderson.

Johnson, Judith A. *J. R. R. Tolkien. Six Decades of Criticism.* Westport, Conn.: Greenwood Press, 1986. Thorough and well-annotated bibliography of Tolkien scholarship treats all phases of Tolkien's work. Well-indexed volume is especially informative regarding the more obscure periodicals dealing with Tolkien's work.

Lobdell, Jared. *The Rise of Tolkienian Fantasy.* Chicago: Open Court, 2005. Examines Tolkien's fantasy fiction, discussing the writers who influenced him, the elements of his fantasy literature, and his literary heirs, including writers Ursula K. Le Guin, Stephen King, and J. K. Rowling.

Rosebury, Brian. *Tolkien: A Cultural Phenomenon.* 2d ed. New York: Palgrave Macmillan, 2003. Traces the development of Tolkien's writing over several decades, devoting a lengthy analysis to *The Lord of the Rings.* Also addresses Tolkien scholarship in general and discusses director Peter Jackson's film adaptation of *The Lord of the Rings.*

Shippey, T. A. *J. R. R. Tolkien: Author of the Century.* Boston: Houghton Mifflin, 2001. Critical review of Tolkien's work argues that the writer is deserving of both popular and critical acclaim. Demonstrates how, although Tolkien produced fantasy fiction, he addressed real twentieth century issues in his works.

LEO TOLSTOY

Born: Yasnaya Polyana, Russia; September 9, 1828
Died: Astapovo, Russia; November 20, 1910
Also known as: Leo Nikolayevich Tolstoy; Lev
 Tolstoy

PRINCIPAL LONG FICTION

Detstvo, 1852 (*Childhood*, 1862)
Otrochestvo, 1854 (*Boyhood*, 1886)
Yunost', 1857 (*Youth*, 1886)
Semeynoye schast'ye, 1859 (*Family Happiness*,
 1888)
Kazaki, 1863 (*The Cossacks*, 1878)
Voyna i mir, 1865-1869 (*War and Peace*, 1886)
Anna Karenina, 1875-1877 (English translation,
 1886)
Smert' Ivana Il'icha, 1886 (novella; *The Death of
 Ivan Ilyich*, 1887)
Kreytserova sonata, 1889 (*The Kreutzer Sonata*,
 1890)
Voskreseniye, 1899 (*Resurrection*, 1899)
Khadzi-Murat, 1911 (wr. 1904; *Hadji Murad*,
 1911)

OTHER LITERARY FORMS

The works of Leo Tolstoy (TAWL-stoy), like those of
many Russian writers, cannot be divided neatly into long
fiction and short fiction. Tolstoy wrote only three full-
length novels: *War and Peace*, *Anna Karenina*, and
Resurrection. *Family Happiness*, *The Cossacks*, *The
Kreutzer Sonata*, *Hadji Murad*, and the trilogy comprising *Childhood*, *Boyhood*, and *Youth* could be termed
novellas or short novels; the distinction between the two
is often not well defined, but most readers would classify
The Cossacks—the longest of this group—as a short
novel. More problematic are the works that exceed the
length of the traditional short story (as defined by English-language criticism) but not by a large margin. One
such work is *The Death of Ivan Ilyich*, which may be regarded either as a novella (although it is about half the
length of *Hadji Murad*, for example) or as a long short
story. In turn, such well-known stories as "Khozyain i
rabotnik" ("Master and Man"), "Dyavol" ("The Devil"),

and "Otets Sergy" ("Father Sergius") are only slightly
shorter than *The Death of Ivan Ilyich*.

The point of the foregoing is not to split terminologi-
cal hairs but rather to emphasize the fact that the term
"story," often loosely applied to Tolstoy's fiction, can be
misleading. Tolstoy wrote relatively few "short stories"
in the classic sense of the term; among those, some of
the best known are "Nabeg" ("The Raid"), "Mnogo li
cheloveku zemli nuzhno?" ("How Much Land Does a
Man Require?"), and the stories collected in *Sevastopolskiye rasskazy* (1855-1856; *Sebastopol*, 1887). Finally,
Tolstoy published a number of very short, moralistic
tales, largely inspired by the religious reorientation that
he experienced in the 1870's.

In addition to his fiction, Leo Tolstoy published a
substantial body of nonfiction, particularly after his
"conversion" to a new—and, in Orthodox terms, heretical—type of Christianity based on his idiosyncratic interpretation of the Gospels. In *Ispoved'* (1884; *A Confession*, 1885), he undertook a penetrating and negative
self-evaluation, continued in *V chom moya vera* (1884;
What I Believe, 1885), while detailing the tenets of this
newfound faith. He began to dissect all around him, and
specifically the world of art, which led to his two most
famous literary essays: *Chto takoye iskusstvo?* (1898;
What Is Art?, 1898) and *O Shekspire i o drame* (1906;
Shakespeare and the Drama, 1906), in which Tolstoy attacked the world of Western art. Tolstoy is also the author of a voluminous correspondence stretching from his
early adolescence to his death. His collected works appeared in Russia over a thirty-year period (1928-1958),
in ninety volumes.

ACHIEVEMENTS

Leo Tolstoy's literary career spanned sixty years of
the most productive period in Russian literary history.
Tolstoy was a "realist," in the sense that he focused
chiefly on the outward physical aspects of human life.
He was a master of the psychophysical—that is, the depiction of the inner selves of his characters through carefully honed descriptions of their physical beings. From
the first words of his diary to the very last, he perfected

a style extraordinary for its logical precision and prosaic, unpoetic tone. His was a world of gray tones and pale colors rather than the black and white of his equally famous contemporary Fyodor Dostoevski. Tolstoy's fiction oscillates between the poles of memoir and invention, war and peace, moralism and neutrality. He is never lighthearted. His moralism, moreover, has frequently been misunderstood. He did not—as his great contemporary Ivan Turgenev thought—abandon fiction for moralism and moralistic essays. Rather, after 1880, he simply changed the emphasis in his fiction. He remained throughout his life a great artistic creator.

Tolstoy's influence has been enormous: By destroying Romantic conventions, he depoeticized the literary universe and gave it a sharpness, even a coarseness, that it theretofore had not known. One sees Tolstoy's influence in the stories of his contemporaries Nikolai Leskov and the great Anton Chekhov, and even in lesser figures such as Maxim Gorky. Tolstoy's impact, however, has been worldwide—in the Thomas Mann of *Buddenbrooks: Verfall einer Familie* (1901; English translation, 1924), in Marcel Proust, in James Joyce, in the ugliness of Stephen Crane's war, in the Saul Bellow of *The Adventures of Augie March* (1953), in the architectonic fiction of Mario Vargas Llosa. More than 180 years after his birth, Tolstoy remains a vital force in world literature.

BIOGRAPHY

Leo Nikolayevich Tolstoy's life was long and eventful, at times even overwhelming his work. Born the fourth child of a noble family, at its estate of Yasnaya Polyana in 1828, he was reared by a nanny, an aunt, a grandmother, and a succession of tutors. Tolstoy's mother—who, before her marriage, was Princess Marya Nikolayevna Volkonsky—died before his second birthday, leaving him only with idealized memories; his father, who died in 1837, left a much more distinct impression. Tolstoy's father, Nikolay Ilyich, a retired lieutenant-colonel, was very much the country gentleman, with a passion for hunting and little interest in literature. From his youth, Tolstoy himself had an extraordinary appetite for physical exercise, especially hunting. He was a gifted linguist, and when he went to Kazan University, he entered as a student of Far Eastern languages but

left without a degree. A voracious reader, he inclined toward moral dissatisfaction and self-analysis even as a young man; his diary, which he began on March 17, 1847 (he was then eighteen years old), reveals a constant battle between his reason and his soul.

Once he inherited the family estate, Tolstoy attempted in vain to help the peasants through social reform: He was always at war with the conventions of the world around him. Frustrated by his failure as a reformer, he went to St. Petersburg, then to Moscow, leading the dissipated life of the young noble he was. Despite his considerable social exploits, he managed to earn a degree in literature and philosophy from the University of St. Petersburg. His first work, written in 1851 but not published until many years after its completion, was "A History of Yesterday," an attempt to re-create in verbal detail a simple day in his life. It illustrates the central preoccupation of his literary existence: How can one transform the reality of events and the fantasy of dreams into words? This initial effort began an outpouring of fiction and nonfiction that dwarfs in volume the writing of any other Russian to this day.

In 1851, Tolstoy entered the army and traveled in the Caucasus—for him, as for many other Russian writers, a paradise on earth. Having become an officer, he became preoccupied with war and the behavior of the soldier during battle; he is said to have looked into the eyes of a soldier firing a gun to attempt a reading of his soul. After the siege of Sebastopol and the fall of the city late in 1855, Tolstoy's active military career was effectively at an end, although he did not officially resign his commission until September, 1856.

By the time of his marriage in 1862, Tolstoy had already achieved a substantial reputation in Russian literary circles. His wife was Sophia Andreyevna Behrs, the daughter of a court physician; at the time of their marriage, Tolstoy was thirty-four, Sophia only eighteen. Their first son was born in 1863; they were to have thirteen children in all. Happy and inspired, Tolstoy began thinking of a great cyclic novel, which was to become *War and Peace*. No sooner was it finished, however, than Tolstoy suffered a letdown: He plunged into a reading of the pessimistic German philosopher Arthur Schopenhauer, and he began to moralize on the great issues of life and death. This produced his second great novel, *Anna Karenina*, clearly a much more pessimistic work than *War and Peace*. Both books were immensely successful and made him world-famous.

As early as 1870, Tolstoy had begun to study Greek. In the years that followed, he read the Gospels as if for the first time. He began to believe that the Orthodox Church—and Christendom in general—had misinterpreted and distorted the teachings of Christ, and he advanced a revolutionary interpretation of Christianity based on his reading of Christ's own words. *A Confession* made him more than a literary figure; he became a prophet of sorts, preaching a religion the kernel of which is nonviolent resistance to evil. His passion for reform led him to visit slums, provide food for starving peasants, and appeal to the czar for mercy for condemned terrorists. He openly associated with social outcasts; his family and relatives came to feel that he had betrayed them, and he was placed under police surveillance.

Concluding that the impulse to do good is killed by civilization and modern culture, Tolstoy asserted the sanctity of the Russian peasant. His outspoken views attracted a following of disciples, among the most prominent of whom was Vladimir Grigoryevich Chertkov, who was soon managing Tolstoy's literary affairs. This led to bitter and prolonged conflict between Chertkov and Tolstoy's wife over the copyrights to Tolstoy's books. Sophia Andreyevna wanted them for the children, while Tolstoy wished to give them up entirely. Meanwhile, Tolstoy sought to practice what he was preaching: He dressed as a peasant, worked in the fields, and gave up wine, meat, and tobacco, although not sex—despite his assault on sexual love in *The Kreutzer Sonata*.

Tolstoy's last full-length novel, *Resurrection*, was written to raise money to send a pacifist sect, the Dukhobors, to Canada. In the novel, Tolstoy continued his criticism of the Orthodox Church, which finally excommunicated him in 1901. His greatest artistic work of his final years, *Hadji Murad*, took Tolstoy back to the Caucasus he so loved. When the Revolution of 1905 shook Russia, he publicly condemned both sides. Angry at his wife, he willed control of his literary estate, without his wife's knowledge, to his daughter Alexandra. His last years were troubled: He had become a sort of world-

Leo Tolstoy. (Library of Congress)

conscience, and he was tortured by the fact that his life did not live up to his ideals; the almost constant hysteria of his wife added to his misery. Still, he retained a surprising vigor; he was planning a new novel shortly before his death. The manner of his death was indeed characteristic: Sick with pneumonia and confined to bed, he escaped, ostensibly to reach his beloved Caucasus, only to die in the Astapovo railroad station on November 20, 1910.

ANALYSIS

Leo Tolstoy's literary works may be viewed as repeated assaults on Romantic conventions. His view, expressed numerous times throughout his diary, was that such conventions blind both writer and reader to reality. Thus, his goal was to construct a new style, prosaic, matter-of-fact, but sharp and full of contrasts, like life itself. To depict all in motion, the inner world of people and the life surrounding them, is the basic creative method of Tolstoy. He sought to reveal the reality underneath by removing the veneer of custom. Precisely for that reason, Tolstoy was able to write *War and Peace*, a work depicting the ordinary life of an entire period of history in all of its movements, contradictions, and complexity.

Tolstoy, ever the moralist, sought to attain truth through art. In his conception, art is the great unmasker; as he wrote in his diary on May 17, 1896, "Art is a microscope which the artist aims at the mysteries of his soul and which reveals these mysteries common to all." The microscope focuses attention on the telling detail, the apparently meaningless gesture, the simplest expression. To Tolstoy, every inner thought, sense, and emotion was reflected in some physical detail; the resulting psychophysical method was to have a profound influence on later writers. Throughout Tolstoy's fiction, characters are reduced to one or two physical features; the palpable, the perceptible, the visible—this is the universe of Tolstoy.

Tolstoy believed that the literary patterns inherited from the Romantics did not get to the essence of meaning and were thus obsolete. His task: to destroy them. In his diary, he began a series of literary experiments: He made lists, he drew up columns, he numbered propositions in sequence. He was seeking a rational creative method— he wanted to construct narratives that were both factual, that is, true to experience, and aesthetically right.

Tolstoy's first artistic work, "A History of Yesterday," is telling in this respect. It is simply an account of uninteresting things that happen in the course of a day. Tolstoy's problem was to write down an accurate account of a full day: He verges on stream of consciousness as he follows his mental associations and perceives how one thing leads to another. To explain something, one must go back in time to explain its causes; this is Tolstoy the rational analyst. Moreover, there is the problem of what verbal expression does to what it describes. Thus, Tolstoy becomes a dual creator: He is not only the writer writing but also the analyst observing the writer writing. He continually makes remarks, interrupts them, questions himself. Tolstoy the analyst is also a creator, one who is attempting to impose rational order on a series that is nothing more than a random succession of human

acts. He pushes analysis to extremes, and because he realizes that there is no limit in time to causation and that he could theoretically go back all the way to the beginning of history, he arbitrarily stops himself and leaves the fragment unfinished.

Thus, even at the beginning of his career, Tolstoy was experimenting with point of view and the literary recreation of consciousness. This acute self-awareness runs through his oeuvre. As he said in his diary on February 29, 1897, a life that goes by without awareness is a life that has not been lived: "The basis of life is freedom and awareness—the freedom to be aware." To promote such awareness, Tolstoy sought to present things in a new way. To do so, he was obliged to distort, to make the familiar strange. It is no accident that when the Russian Formalist critic Viktor Shklovsky wanted to illustrate the technique he called *ostranenie* ("making strange," or "defamiliarization"), he turned first to the works of Tolstoy, perhaps the supreme practitioner of this device—as in the famous opera scene in *War and Peace* or the church service in *Resurrection*. In such passages, the reader sees familiar experiences as if for the first time. Art has become a path to truth: Tolstoy dissects reality and reconstructs it verbally in a new, more palpable form.

Tolstoy never abandoned this way of looking at reality: He portrayed cause and effect, in sequence. First he selected the facts to be described; then he arranged them. Before him, and even in a novelist such as Dostoevski, the artist's method was to show the result and then explain how it came to be—that is, to go back into the past after depicting the present. Tolstoy's method was the reverse: to show the cause and then the result. Show the wickedness of Napoleon and the strength of Mikhail Kutuzov, for example, and the reader can understand why Russia triumphed against the French.

Of Tolstoy's three full-length novels, only the last, *Resurrection*, is not representative of his distinctive method. This novel, which tells the tale of a repentant noble who seeks to resurrect the life of a young girl whom he once seduced, is full of moral strictures. Precisely because Tolstoy frequently forgot his psychophysical method, the novel fails as a work of art, in contrast to his two earlier and greater novels, which are examples of his method at its best.

WAR AND PEACE

If a conventional novel is a novel with a linear plot focused on one or two central characters, then *War and Peace* is a very unconventional novel. It has no single plot, and it includes more than 550 characters, some fifty of whom play important roles. *War and Peace* is like a gigantic epic, and while it may be called a historical novel, it is not a historical novel in the vein of Sir Walter Scott: There is no great historical distance between the time of composition of the book and the period depicted. It is a book of enormous contrasts, as suggested by the title: war and peace, hate and love, death and life, hero and ordinary person, city and country. For Tolstoy, the world of peace, love, life, and country was the ideal world, but the world of war is the world of *War and Peace*.

The novel began as a story of the ill-fated Decembrist revolt, which took place after the death of Czar Alexander I, in 1825, and before the accession to power of his successor, Czar Nicholas I. Tolstoy seeks to explain the events of 1825. Ever the rationalist, he realizes that to explain 1825, one must examine 1824; to explain 1824, one must examine 1823; and so on. This reasoning (as in "A History of Yesterday") would have carried Tolstoy back to the beginning of time. Arbitrarily, he stopped in 1805 and began his novel there. He never reached 1825: The book covers the period from 1805 to 1812, followed by a twelve-year hiatus, after which the epilogue continues through 1824 to the eve of the 1825 Decembrist revolt. Tolstoy's original plan was to write a family novel rather than a historical novel, with history the scenic decor in which families lived. He completed five versions of the novel: The first, titled "1805," does not resemble the fifth at all.

The book, rather than focusing on individual characters, concentrates on family blocks: Tolstoy used the same contrast technique in portraying the families that he used in treating ideas and events. The main backdrop of the action is the Napoleonic invasion of Russia. From the opening pages in the Moscow salon where Tolstoy first gives a glimpse of his major noble figures, the echoes of the coming Napoleonic invasion can be heard. The reader will watch it develop throughout the novel and will see it ultimately crumble as the great French army is conquered by the Russian climate and expanse.

The book poses two major questions, to both of which it gives answers. First, under what circumstances do people kill one another and expose themselves to death? Tolstoy answers that they do so out of self-preservation and duty. Second, in the battle between life and death, who wins? Life wins, Tolstoy answers, despite the ravages of time. Underlying the whole narrative is a gigantic theory of history based on the idea that the world spins not on the movements of single individuals (heroes) but rather on the movements of masses of people. Thus, the Russian mass will overwhelm the French army and its "hero," Napoleon. It will do this because its commanding officer, Kutuzov, understands that it is the movement of the people that determines the course of history; he is wisely passive. Tolstoy is uncompromisingly a fatalist: Events occur as they do because they are fated to do so; nothing that any single individual does can alter the course of fate. Thus, it is the fate of Russia to undergo the great trials and tribulations of the Napoleonic horror, as it is the fate of Napoleon to lose the crucial battle on Russian soil. Indeed, to underline the importance of this theory, Tolstoy includes, at the end of his novel, a famous epilogue in which he discusses the movements of masses. (Much has been made of this epilogue, but it should be borne in mind that Tolstoy himself omitted it from the 1873 edition of the novel and that the evidence for it is in any case given in the book itself.) *War and Peace* is thus a book with a thesis.

The novel, completely static, in which scenes replace one another but do not flow in a continuous stream, unfolds on two planes: the historical and the familial. Tolstoy writes as if he were composing a massive history of the period. There is an omniscient narrator with a severe national bent. Instead of descriptions of personalities, the reader is given, as in Homer's *Iliad* (c. 750 B.C.E.; English translation, 1611), the everyday facts of human life: birth, marriage, family life, death, and so on. There are no heroes; there is, rather, a sweeping vision of human life, moving one critic to call the book an "encyclopedia of human existence." The novel is characterized by sheer bulk: It presents so much material in such large blocks that the material itself seems to go on after the story has ended. Because of the nontemporal scheme, the reader secures less a feel of artistic framework imposed on all material than a sense of the vivid disconnectedness of real life. Memorable and important as some of the characters may be, no single character dominates the book. Only one is involved from beginning to end: Pierre Bezukhov, the fat, awkward, and bespectacled illegitimate son of a very rich nobleman. His personal quest, to find the meaning of his life, unfolds with the book's events, but in no sense is the novel his story.

The reader looking for great "heroic" characters had best look elsewhere. Heroic characters are a dishonest Romantic convention. The novel contains no great sympathetic or unpleasant figures, none who is extraordinarily beautiful and extraordinarily appealing at the same time. Indeed, the two main contrasting families are combinations of good and bad. The Bolkonskys are a tense mixture of sensibility, intelligence, and narrow-mindedness. Andrey is a hero without a battle who claims to seek peace even though he is at home only at war. Maria—unattractive, mystical, totally devoted—exemplifies almost unjustifiable self-sacrifice. Both characters are dominated by an outwardly detestable father whose peace comes only through his own inner rage. The Rostovs, considerably steadier of mind and background, are a mixture of openness, altruism, and ignorant fear. Natasha is not beautiful, exceptionally intelligent, or extraordinarily adept, but she has unending charm and great possibilities of love. Her parents are wonderful, warm, loving, and foolish. Her brother Nicholas is handsome, intelligent, and dangerously narrow-minded. That Andrey and Natasha eventually come together and almost marry makes no sense, but then history does not have to make sense. That Pierre and Natasha do come together at the end of the novel does, however, make sense, for they share an openness common to virtually no one else in the book. Even the Kuragin family, so attractive and so given to extremes of behavior, is unheroic: The handsome Anatole, who almost marries Natasha, is last seen dying, his leg amputated; his sister Helen, the most beautiful woman in Russia, who marries Pierre and who seems so self-centeredly evil, is redeemed by her apparent willingness to realize that she is restless and can cause only misery to others.

Tolstoy does not write in black and white: All of his characters come in shades of gray, and all wind up fighting Tolstoy's own inner duel, the duel between reason and emotion. Tolstoy was convinced that a natural exis-

tence is the best; thus, Pierre and Natasha survive because they are natural, while Andrey perishes because he is not. Kutuzov triumphs over Napoleon because he is more natural.

Tolstoy exploits to the utmost his famous psychophysical technique of showing people through various gestures and traits. Numerous characters come equipped with single predominant features that forever identify them: the upper lip of Lise, the beautiful wife of Andrey, who dies in childbirth; the beautiful white shoulders of Helen; Pierre's habit of looking out over his glasses; the thick, little white hands of Napoleon; the dimpled chin of the French prisoner; the pimple on the nose of the man who leads the merchant delegation that meets Napoleon as he invades Moscow; the round face and composure of Platon Karatayev, the peasant whom Pierre meets in prison, whose roundness is a symbol of his moral completeness and of his ability to accept the world as it is.

Tolstoy rips away conventions: He redraws the world by changing the point of view of the observer. Just as he identifies characters by physical traits and cuts them down to size by knocking the hero out of them, so he destroys conventional perceptions of other elements of life. The battle of Austerlitz, in Tolstoy's description, consists only of a strange little sun, smoke, two soldiers in flight, one wounded officer, and finally Napoleon's little white hand. To Tolstoy, this was the real battle as seen by the soldier. In Tolstoy's view, battle as depicted by the likes of Scott had nothing to do with the real world: It was a result of conventions, and so Tolstoy deconventionalized it, as he did with opera. In placing Natasha, who has never before seen an opera, in an opera house, Tolstoy destroys the essence of opera by refusing to accept its conventions: Thus, a piece of cardboard on which a tree is painted is exactly that.

Tolstoy has rewritten the novel. It is not the form that existed before him; rather, it is a brand-new one that combines philosophy, ordinary people, and large masses and blocks of time. Curiously, *War and Peace* is frequently read to be an affirmation of life, but in fact it is all about death. It is death at the end, leaving the reader on the eve of the brutish Decembrist revolt, where death awaits those, like Pierre, who will be involved. Moreover, the life that will be led as married couples by Pierre and Natasha, and Maria and Nicholas, is not a happy life:

It is a life of conventions in which the wives will bear children, the husbands will supply the finances, and so on.

As Tolstoy was completing *War and Peace*, he began to read more and more philosophy and more and more of the Bible. The cycle of pessimism that began in *War and Peace* and turned darker as the book wound toward its end culminated in the gloomy and tragic *Anna Karenina*.

ANNA KARENINA

Written between 1873 and 1877, *Anna Karenina* at first appears to be a completely different novel. The title immediately suggests that the book is centered on one dominant personality around which the book spins its plot. Anna's is the story of the fallen woman. Her fall is intertwined with moral and social questions of behavior, and like an expanding pool, the novel becomes all-encompassing of the Russian society of its day. What the book achieves is no less original than what *War and Peace* achieved: It is the classic story of the fallen woman, but it is combined as never before with the burning moral and social questions of the author's day.

The book begins with the pessimistic note with which *War and Peace* ended. It is a book about disorder. There are no happy couples and there are no happy events. Everything is discordant, as if fate had intended the world not to harmonize. Thus, Anna, who is married to a man whom she does not love, falls in love with a man, Vronsky, who cannot satisfy her. Because the story is contemporaneous with Tolstoy's time, he is able to introduce character types of his day that would not have appeared in *War and Peace*. Chief among them is Stiva Oblonsky, Anna's brother, a shameless opportunist and careerist; he exemplifies much of the evil in the Russian bureaucracy. It is he and his suffering family whom the reader sees first: The Oblonsky family introduces the themes of adultery (Stiva is a philanderer) and contemporary society.

From its opening lines, *Anna Karenina* is a serious and critical book. It develops many of the same contrasts that animate *War and Peace*—city and country, good and evil—but it also adds new conflicts: between sex and love, between guilt and truth. Sex, Tolstoy explains, as did Gustave Flaubert in *Madame Bovary* (1857; English translation, 1886), is a path to trouble. Anna follows her sexual instincts, and as those instincts are pro-

duced by modern society, they lead her to her doom. In *War and Peace*, everything seemed logical and sequential, as Tolstoy the rationalist led us from one event to another; in *Anna Karenina*, everything is irrational.

The world has become a system of irrational correspondences. Consider the scene in which Anna first meets Vronsky: Fate operates through signs. Vronsky and Anna look at each other and sense a curious bond. The reader is never told why, as would have been the case in *War and Peace*. The stationman is accidentally crushed to death: This is an omen that will culminate many pages later in the famous and gruesome suicide of Anna, when she throws herself beneath a train. Almost unconscious on her way to the station, she reviews her life and her affair with Vronsky in a long passage of stream of consciousness in which readers sense doom, in the form of the dead stationman, pulling her on. Tolstoy, always given over to interior monologues, now goes one step further and gives the free associations of a character bent on self-destruction. Unlike *War and Peace*, this book is unconscious mystery.

Anna Karenina is a long series of emotional collisions. Various pairs of people line up and contrast with one another: Anna-Vronsky, Stiva-Dolly (Stiva's suffering wife), Kitty-Levin. The latter pair is curious. Kitty, Dolly's younger sister, who is originally engaged to Vronsky, is a superficial version of Natasha, with all the playfulness and none of the true openness. Levin, long considered a mouthpiece for the author, is a continuation of a long line of such Tolstoyan moral spokesmen. At the end of the novel, however, one is left with a Levin who senses but a yawning gap in his existence. Nothing is resolved. Everything will go on as before—but in the absence of Anna, now dead.

Every one of the characters is seriously blemished. Anna has a capacity for genuine love, but she also uses people and ultimately cannot bear what fate has in store for her. Vronsky is honest and honorable but lacks real spirit and is not truly perceptive. Stiva is a foolish, fat bureaucrat, content to live in a class structure he does not understand. Anna's husband, Aleksei (note that both he and Vronsky have the same first name, another mysterious correspondence), is shallow and cold but at the death of Anna shows a magnanimity of spirit foreign to Vronsky. Kitty is romantic and playful but in the end conventional; she accepts what fate has done to her. Levin is well meaning and open, but he is a dead generalization, put in the book to make the case for living close to nature (which, in any case, bores him).

The book's tension is extreme. By contrasting the Anna-Vronsky story with that of Kitty-Levin, Tolstoy plays with the reader's perception, as he does in the opera scene in *War and Peace*. In the famous scene in which Anna's husband discusses divorce with a lawyer who keeps trying (unsuccessfully) to catch a moth, the tension becomes almost unbearable. Humans are alive in a world that simply does not care. Thus, the details that in *War and Peace* make up the tapestry of history appear here to form a set of incomprehensible correspondences. Since *Anna Karenina* is focused so clearly on one intrigue, however, it is considerably more conventional in form than *War and Peace:* Its aura of moral gloom is thus directly communicated. The world, Tolstoy is saying, is not worth preserving.

It is no wonder, then, that Tolstoy's next burst of creative energy was given over to nonfiction. In *Anna Karenina*, Tolstoy had blasted not only the Russian bureaucracy but also the school system, the Orthodox Church, and even the peasantry; in his later work, he fully assumed the role of a social critic. Immediately following the completion of *Anna Karenina*, he burst forth in a fit of moral fervor with *A Confession*. As one critic put it, Tolstoy came under the power of his own method, and art retreated before the pressure of self-observation and analysis; his own soul became material for exposition and clarification. Tolstoy changed the proportions in his creative work and became more the moralist than ever before, but he never ceased being an artist, as any reader of *The Death of Ivan Ilyich* or even *Resurrection* well knows.

Philippe Radley

OTHER MAJOR WORKS

SHORT FICTION: *Sevastopolskiye rasskazy*, 1855-1856 (*Sebastopol*, 1887); *The Kreutzer Sonata, The Devil, and Other Tales*, 1940; *Notes of a Madman, and Other Stories*, 1943; *Tolstoy Tales*, 1947; *Tolstoy's Short Fiction*, 1991; *Divine and Human, and Other Stories*, 2000.

PLAYS: *Vlast tmy: Ili, "Kogotok uvyaz, vsey ptichke propast,"* pb. 1887 (*The Dominion of Darkness*, 1888;

better known as *The Power of Darkness*, 1899); *Plody prosveshcheniya*, pr. 1889 (*The Fruits of Enlightenment*, 1891); *I svet vo tme svetit*, pb. 1911 (*The Light Shines in Darkness*, 1923); *Zhivoy trup*, pr., pb. 1911 (*The Live Corpse*, 1919); *The Dramatic Works*, 1923.

NONFICTION: *Ispoved'*, 1884 (*A Confession*, 1885); *V chom moya vera*, 1884 (*What I Believe*, 1885); *O zhizni*, 1888 (*Life*, 1888); *Kritika dogmaticheskogo bogosloviya*, 1891 (*A Critique of Dogmatic Theology*, 1904); *Soedinenie i perevod chetyrekh evangeliy*, 1892-1894 (*The Four Gospels Harmonized and Translated*, 1895-1896); *Tsarstvo Bozhie vnutri vas*, 1893 (*The Kingdom of God Is Within You*, 1894); *Chto takoye iskusstvo?*, 1898 (*What Is Art?*, 1898); *Tak chto zhe nam delat?*, 1902 (*What to Do?*, 1887); *O Shekspire i o drame*, 1906 (*Shakespeare and the Drama*, 1906); *The Diaries of Leo Tolstoy, 1847-1852*, 1917; *The Journal of Leo Tolstoy, 1895-1899*, 1917; *Tolstoi's Love Letters*, 1923; *The Private Diary of Leo Tolstoy, 1853-1857*, 1927; *"What Is Art?" and Essays on Art*, 1929; *L. N. Tolstoy o literature: Stati, pisma, dnevniki*, 1955; *Lev Tolstoy ob iskusstve i literature*, 1958; *Last Diaries*, 1960.

CHILDREN'S LITERATURE: *Azbuka*, 1872; *Novaya azbuka*, 1875 (*Stories for My Children*, 1988); *Russkie knigi dlya chteniya*, 1875; *Classic Tales and Fables for Children*, 2002 (includes selections from *Azbuka* and *Novaya azbuka*).

MISCELLANEOUS: *The Complete Works of Count Tolstoy*, 1904-1905 (24 volumes); *Tolstoy Centenary Edition*, 1928-1937 (21 volumes); *Polnoye sobraniye sochinenii*, 1928-1958 (90 volumes).

BIBLIOGRAPHY

Bayley, John. *Tolstoy and the Novel*. London: Chatto & Windus, 1966. Influenced by Henry James's organic conception of the novel, Bayley concentrates on trenchant analyses of *War and Peace* and *Anna Karenina*. He also perceptively examines *Family Happiness*, *The Kreutzer Sonata*, and *The Devil*.

Benson, Ruth Crego. *Women in Tolstoy: The Ideal and the Erotic*. Urbana: University of Illinois Press, 1973. Interesting and provocative piece of feminist criticism concentrates on Tolstoy's changing vision of the role and importance of family life. Suggests that Tolstoy struggled most of his life with a dichotomous view of women, regarding them in strictly black-and-white terms, as saints or sinners, and analyzes the female characters in the major and several minor works in terms of such a double view.

Christian, R. F. *Tolstoy: A Critical Introduction*. New York: Cambridge University Press, 1969. Clearly written work by a leading Tolstoyan who is knowledgeable about his subject's sources and influences. Provides particularly helpful interpretations of *Family Happiness* and *The Kreutzer Sonata*.

Gustafson, Richard F. *Leo Tolstoy, Resident and Stranger: A Study in Fiction and Theology*. Princeton, N.J.: Princeton Univ. Press, 1986. Gustafson seeks to rescue Tolstoy from those who would classify him solely as a realist. By focusing on what he sees as the inherently and uniquely Russian attributes of Tolstoy's writing, Gustafson reunites the preconversion artist and the postconversion religious thinker and prophet. Includes a bibliography divided into two sections: books devoted to Tolstoy and books focusing on Eastern Christian thought.

McLean, Hugh. *In Quest of Tolstoy*. Boston: Academic Studies Press, 2008. Essays by a longtime Tolstoy scholar examine Tolstoy's writings and ideas and assess his influence on other writers and thinkers.

Orwin, Donna Tussig. *Tolstoy's Art and Thought, 1847-1880*. Princeton, N.J.: Princeton University Press, 1993. Attempts to trace the origins and growth of the Russian master's ideas. Focuses on the first three decades of Tolstoy's literary career, first examining his initial creative vision and then analyzing, in depth, his principal works.

_____, ed. *The Cambridge Companion to Tolstoy*. New York: Cambridge University Press, 2002. Collection of essays includes analyses of *War and Peace*, *Anna Karenina*, and *Resurrection* as well as discussions on topics such as Tolstoy as a writer of popular literature, the development of his style and theme, his aesthetics, and Tolstoy in the twentieth century.

Rowe, William W. *Leo Tolstoy*. Boston: Twayne, 1986. Offers a concise introduction to Tolstoy's life and work, with special emphasis on the major novels and later didactic writings. Discusses, briefly, most of Tolstoy's major concerns, and presents excellent treatment of individual characters in the major novels. Includes bibliography.

Shklovsky, Viktor. *Energy of Delusion: A Book on Plot*. Translated by Shushan Avagyan. Champaign, Ill.: Dalkey Archive Press, 2007. English-language translation of the book that some scholars have called the greatest critical work on *War and Peace*. Shklovsky, a prominent Soviet literary critic who died in 1984, examines the form of the novel, what it was like to read the book in the 1980's, and many other aspects of the epic work.

Tolstaia, Sophia Andreevna. *The Diaries of Sophia Tolstoy*. Translated by Cathy Porter, edited by O. A. Golinenko et al. New York: Random House, 1985. This massive personal record of Tolstoy's wife, detailing their life together, spans the years 1862-1910. Sophia Tolstoy kept an almost daily account of her husband's opinions, doubts, and plans concerning his literary activity and social ventures as well as of his relationships with other writers and thinkers. Her notes give a fascinating and intimate view of the Tolstoy family and of the extent to which it served as background for many of her husband's literary episodes. Illustrated.

Wasiolek, Edward. *Tolstoy's Major Fiction*. Chicago: University of Chicago Press, 1978. Superb study concentrates on thorough analyses of ten of Tolstoy's works, including *Family Happiness*, *The Death of Ivan Ilyich*, and "Master and Man." Provides a close and acute reading that is influenced by Russian Formalists and by Roland Barthes. Includes an illuminating brief chronicle of Tolstoy's life and work.

Wilson, A. N. *Tolstoy*. New York: W. W. Norton, 1988. A long but immensely readable biography, breezy, insightful, and opinionated, by a highly regarded British novelist. Includes illustrations and a useful chronology of Tolstoy's life and times as well as notes, bibliography, and index.

GIUSEPPE TOMASI DI LAMPEDUSA

Born: Palermo, Italy; December 23, 1896
Died: Rome, Italy; July 23, 1957
Also known as: Giuseppe Tomasi

PRINCIPAL LONG FICTION

Il gattopardo, 1958 (*The Leopard*, 1960)

OTHER LITERARY FORMS

A lifelong voracious reader, Giuseppe Tomasi di Lampedusa (toh-MAH-see dee lahm-pay-DEW-zah) became a writer late in his intellectual career. His first public writings were a series of lectures begun in the fall of 1953 on the development of English and, later, French literature. The audience was a select company of young students, and only one of the lessons has been published to date: the "Lezioni su Stendhal" (lesson on Stendhal), which appeared in the April, 1959, issue of *Paragone*. This literary discussion offers as much critical insight into Lampedusa as it does into its subject, Stendhal. The amateur critic presents the French novelist as an exemplary narrator whose "thin" style requires the reader's active participation in deciphering the implicit, as well as the explicit, text. Lampedusa's own narrative style lacks this Stendhalian simplicity and pregnant silence he so admired; *The Leopard* is a "fat" book, prone to lushness and descriptive delineation. Nevertheless, Lampedusa shared Stendhal's interpretation of the narrative voice and his concept of realism: Events are presented through the subjective filter of a protagonist's perceptions and sensibilities. Lampedusa imitates this Stendhalian procedure somewhat erratically, identifying primarily with his novel's hero, Don Fabrizio Corbera, prince of Salina. Author and character occasionally merge as the prince becomes an autobiographical mouthpiece.

This lesson on Stendhal, as well as the other unpublished lectures, helped direct Lampedusa's thoughts to the techniques of writing, the formal construction of the novel, the function of the artist ("a fellow who knows how to express himself"), and the value of art. Apparently, this organized meditation on culture awoke the hibernating author in Lampedusa. In mid-1955, he began to produce the memoirs of his childhood as a means of preserving the past for himself and others. These memoirs proved to be the inspirational impetus for his only novel, which he began writing early the following year. The memoirs, which center on the places of Lampedusa's youth (the same locales that reappear as the backdrops of *The Leopard*), alongside three short stories produced later form a slight volume titled *Racconti* (1961; partial translation *Two Stories and a Memory*, 1962). The language and motifs of the stories connect them to the more justly famous novel. "Lighea" is a particularly moving, surreal tale about an old professor's recollections of his youthful affair with a siren; its meditations on life and nothingness and immortal versus human love echo Don Fabrizio's courtship of Death in *The Leopard*. Both the short stories and the "Lezioni su Stendhal" are read primarily because of their connection to Lampedusa's novel.

ACHIEVEMENTS

Giuseppe Tomasi di Lampedusa's only novel appeared posthumously in 1958, having received rejections during the brief period between its completion and the author's death. Once published, *The Leopard* exploded onto the Italian literary scene, attaining two or three printings per month in early 1959 and selling a record total of more than one million copies in Italy alone; it also left political, ideological, and literary controversies in its wake. The 1950's witnessed the growth of the experimental novel and a continuing emphasis on socially committed art. In this context, *The Leopard* was an anomaly. Its style was reminiscent of the nineteenth century novel; critics viewed it as an anachronistic descendant of such Sicilian realists as Giovanni Verga, Federico De Roberto, and Luigi Pirandello. Politically, its ideology was suspect. Ironically, in a period that mourned the death of the novel as a genre, Lampedusa's book obtained incredible public approbation and the stature of an international best seller, which further fanned the critical controversies.

Opinions varied immensely on the merit, importance, structure, and significance of the novel. Lampedusa was alternately accused of being an aristocratic reactionary and a subtle opponent of the old guard; some declared him deficient in historical vision, whereas others viewed him as the voice of Italy's postwar crisis. Aesthetically, the critics were also divided, finding the novel very difficult to categorize and contradictory in its formal structure. Was it a historical novel or a psychological study? Was it naturalist, realist, decadent, or lyric? Had the writer been influenced by Marcel Proust, Stendhal, or the Italian *veristi*? The avant-garde criticized the book's lack of linguistic experimentation, considering it a throwback to the past; the traditionalists disliked its hybrid nature and ambiguous narrative voice. In fact, *The Leopard* is a complex work, containing elements of all the above, woven into a rich stylistic and thematic fabric.

Lampedusa's narrative operates within an internal duality. What appears superficially to be a historical novel about the unification of Italy is actually a psychological study that centers on the protagonist Don Fabrizio. The chronological setting—the arrival of Giuseppe Garibaldi in Sicily in 1860 and the resulting fall of the Bourbon monarchy—is a background against which the Prince lives out his personal crises. He is a man caught in transitions he cannot control. Read in this manner, *The Leopard* offers a very modern message composed in a classical form. Don Fabrizio is an intelligent, cultivated, and eloquent Everyman seeking meaning in an unstable world, an Everyman trying to survive change without the benefit of any absolutes, devoid of any unshakable beliefs or ready answers, alone with his inner torments, facing the internal enemies of middle age and death while attempting to survive the invasion of a new social order. In his nineteenth century dress, Don Fabrizio is a contemporary student of his inner being, given to bouts of alienation, guilt, and depression.

Through this fictional creation, Lampedusa masterfully depicts the dichotomous nature of the human being, drawn to life with a pagan vitality yet susceptible to the poetry of death and cognizant of the fragility of all things, searching for an elusive sense of eternity to fill a spiritual void. Through his use of a narrative style that is by turns realistic and subjective, the novelist is able to convey subtle states of mind, existential contradictions, personal commentary, a feeling for the ephemeral beauty of life, and a pervasive historical pessimism

without resorting to the linguistic obscurations of the experimentalists or the political stances of the ideologists. *The Leopard* is both poetic and philosophical, but it is also a good story with interesting characters. Because of this, the novel continues to appeal to readers everywhere.

BIOGRAPHY

Giuseppe Tomasi, duke of Palma and prince of Lampedusa, was born into the Sicilian aristocracy described in his novel. During his childhood and youth, the family retained much of its wealth and prestige; Lampedusa led the privileged existence of a noble scion, being the last male descendant of an ancient line. His time was divided between the country estate and the great house in Palermo, both of which are lovingly treated in his memoirs and provide the models for the princely dwellings in *The Leopard*. The young noble's schooling was private, in keeping with aristocratic tradition, and stressed the humanities and a refined cultural sensibility. He read voluminously and avidly, aided by his knowledge of a variety of languages and his firsthand acquaintance with other cultures.

It was a relatively uneventful existence: artillery service in World War I, followed by two escapes from prisoner-of-war camps; a law degree from the University of Torino, which was never put to use; numerous trips abroad, during which he met his future wife, the Baltic baroness Alexandra Wolff-Stomersee, a noted psychoanalyst; military service as a captain in World War II; the destruction of his beloved house and library by Allied bombs; the lessons on English and French literature; and the adoption of Gioacchino Lanza, one of his pupils, late in life—the young man served as the model for the character of Tancredi in *The Leopard*. It was a quiet existence, devoted to a rich and adventurous intellectual life. Lampedusa was extraordinarily well read in history and European literature, but his knowledge was acquired solely for personal enrichment. By nature a reserved, intelligent, proudly aristocratic man, he shied away from the intellectual and literary environment of his day.

Preferring his solitary routine, Lampedusa made only one contact with the Italian world of letters: In 1954, he attended a literary conference with his cousin, the poet

Lucio Piccolo. Although all of his writing was concentrated in the last two years of his life, Lampedusa had spent more than twenty-five years thinking about writing a historical novel about his great-grandfather, the astronomer Prince Giulio. Early in 1956, he completed the first draft of the novel. At the time of his death, in July, 1957, the original manuscript had been revised, expanded, and polished. Sadly, the novel was rejected by a publisher five days prior to its author's death. Fifteen months later, another publisher, Feltrinelli, issued a version lovingly edited by writer Giorgio Bassani. It was an immediate and sensational success, soon followed by a film adaptation by one of Italy's greatest directors, Luchino Visconti (*Il gattopardo*, 1963), and an operatic version by Angelo Musco and Luigi Squarzina.

ANALYSIS: THE LEOPARD

The title of Giuseppe Tomasi di Lampedusa's novel, *The Leopard*, was inspired by the Lampedusas'—and fictional Salinas'—coat of arms, which functions as a recurring symbol within the text and as a bond connecting the author to his creation. This feline emblem of position and power represents the best qualities of the aristocracy, in contrast to the jackals and hyenas destined to replace it in a new social order. The leopard is the pride and essence of the Salinas, embodied spiritually and physically in the prince of Salina, Don Fabrizio Corbera. Its origins are in the history and consciousness of an ancient family and in the traditions of a ruling caste. Like the nobility, the leopard comes face-to-face with its vulnerability and mortality as an individual, a family, a social group, and a way of life. Clearly, the novel's point of view, generally expressed through the character of Don Fabrizio, is aristocratic.

PLOT AND CHARACTERS

The story begins in 1860. It is the Italian Risorgimento; General Garibaldi and his Red Shirts have landed in Sicily with the intent of unifying the peninsula and ending the Bourbon monarchy. Here and elsewhere in the text, the historical events function as a backdrop to the incidents in the life of Don Fabrizio and his family. Chronologically, the eight chapters composing the novel are unevenly divided. The first covers only twenty-four hours in the life of Don Fabrizio, concurrent with the arrival of Garibaldi in Marsala, an event that is mentioned

but not stressed. The following three chapters are dated later the same year; chapter 5 is dated 1861; chapter 6, 1862; the final divisions leap to 1883 and, last, 1910—a total span of fifty years. A day in the life of Don Fabrizio introduces the reader to many of the personalities who inhabit the novel—the slightly neurotic princess, the seven Salina children, the beloved and ambitious nephew Prince Tancredi Falconeri, the family priest, Father Pirrone, and the friendly dog Bendicò—and to the environment of aristocratic life: the daily rosary, family meals and conversations, the palace and gardens, the casual administration of the estate.

Very little actually occurs; the first chapter develops characterizations, introduces relationships, paints an atmosphere, and renders a lifestyle. Tancredi announces his decision to join the Red Shirts, not out of revolutionary fervor but to protect the standing of the Sicilian ruling class during the inevitable political upheavals, because "everything must change so that everything remains the same." His words appear prophetic some months later as the family members travel to one of their summer estates; they are surrounded by the same feudal respect as in the past, but times have changed somewhat. A plebiscite joins Sicily to the Kingdom of Italy, and the local mayor, Calogero Sedàra, has amassed a fortune almost equal to that of the prince.

Tancredi, who is shrewd and bold, decides to marry the mayor's voluptuously beautiful daughter Angelica, thus uniting her wealth with his impoverished title, to the proud but quiet despair of Concetta, one of the Salina girls. The remaining chapters center on the sensually agitating courtship of the new fiancés, on Father Pirrone's visit to his peasant family (a section that has often been criticized as irrelevant to the plot), on a fashionable ball that seems to celebrate the survival and continuity of the nobility, and on the death of Don Fabrizio, the last true Leopard. The episode dated 1910 functions as an epilogue about the fate of the remaining Salinas.

The preceding outline does a great injustice to Lampedusa's novel, which is a subtle, poetic work and not an adventure story. Such a summary also points out the error of defining *The Leopard* as a traditional historical novel. Historical events take place in the story's background, whereas the protagonists experience the resulting sociopsychological changes in their daily existence.

The marriage of Tancredi and Angelica is the most prominent example, the first union of blood and money, aristocracy and nouveaux riches. Others are less dramatic but equally significant: the entrance of former peasant Sedàra in a tuxedo; a lowering in public respect for Don Fabrizio when he demonstrates excessive, nonfeudal friendliness; the switch from the Red Shirt of the guerrillas to the uniform of the regular Piedmontese army; and an offer the prince receives to become a senator in a constitutional parliament.

ISSUES AND THEMES

While history moves in the novel's background, historical discussion dominates the foreground. Don Fabrizio's conversations often enter into current affairs, touching on many of the issues crucial to postunification Italy: the failure of the ideals of the Risorgimento because of personal egotisms and mismanagement; the impossibility of channeling the southern part of the peninsula into a modern, progressive, and democratic state; and the continuing class divisions. Salina, as the voice of Lampedusa, judges history negatively. One king replaces another; one government is substituted for another, while people continue to live and die. Things change and remain the same. The prince's vision of history is not new; rather, it continues a tradition of humanistic pessimism. The actions of human beings are interpreted as futile; the destinies of individuals are insignificant in the eternal flow of time, which they are impotent to alter or stop.

A symbol of this impotence and history's indifference to the individual is Sicily, where millennia of political shifts and invasions have had little influence on the people, who reject the possibility of real change and choose apathy, desiring immobility or, more exactly, death. Sicily, as a landscape and a state of mind, dominates *The Leopard*. In fact, the novel presents two Sicilies: on one hand, the exquisitely beautiful and sensuous land of sea, sun, vegetation, and overpowering scents; on the other, the arid, desolate interior of hunger and pain. The light and the dark Sicilies are actually the same Janus-land of the mind, with its inherent dichotomies. Life, with its vigor, hides the promise of death. The natural settings in the novel possess dual personalities, such as the garden of chapter 1, the olfactory excesses of which denote this complementary contradiction of death in

life—the musky perfume of the roses mingling with the acrid stench of the decaying corpse of a Bourbon soldier. Lampedusa's Sicilian landscapes are signs not of a specific time or object but of the human condition, outside historical demarcations, in which an eternal and indifferent Nature (Fate) engulfs all.

Don Fabrizio explains the Sicilian tendency toward violence or its opposite, apathy, as a desire for immobility, which is another synonym for death. The attraction and pursuit of death is a constant theme throughout *The Leopard*, from its very first sentence: "Nunc et in hora mortis nostrae. Amen." ("Now and in the hour of our death. Amen.") The truncated Latin quotation from the conclusion of the Hail Mary initiates a long meditation on death and dying on the part of both the main protagonist and the narrator. As in his description of Sicily, the author offers a dual image of death: It can be ugly and repellent but also serene and spiritual. Don Fabrizio regularly encounters the former while courting the latter. Painfully aware of the presence of death in all living things, he is nevertheless attracted to its promise of never-ending tranquillity. It is this perpetuity he seeks in the stars, distant and all-powerful yet subject to his calculations.

Astronomy is Don Fabrizio's occupation but also his bond with something greater than his own mortality. The search for continuity in a transient world likewise underlies the protagonist's attachment to his homes and lands, to the pride in traditions and the desire to preserve himself and the ancestral past in his descendants. When death comes for Salina, it is in the guise of a beautiful woman inviting possession. However trite, the image once again links vitalism and annulment in a sensual union typical of the novel. The positive elements of life are also expressed in sensory terms, ranging from eroticism to the joys of the table and the pleasures of the hunt.

Love in *The Leopard* is primarily instinct, as embodied in the feral beauty of Angelica and in the fountain representing a lustful Neptune embracing a willing Amphitrite, an effigy that evokes melancholy regret in the prince. What distinguishes him from the youthful lovers is not a lesser attachment to the joys of life but a greater knowledge of the inherent temporality of all matter. At the ball, he waltzes with the charming Angelica and loses his mature awareness in the pleasure of the music and her young body, yet a few minutes earlier he had been contemplating a mournful painting representing a deathbed scene, meditating on his own inevitable demise. Attracted to the handsome young couple, he nevertheless pities them, for they are doomed to disappointment and awareness similar to his own. The knowledge of the ephemeral nature of life animates Lampedusa's fictional universe. Everything is destined to disappear, to flow into nothingness, for everything contains the seed of mortality.

STYLE

What saves *The Leopard* from maudlin sentimentality or elegiac pessimism is the constant presence of an omniscient narrator who balances the novel's lyricism with an infusion of irony and comedy. The author conducts an ongoing dialogue with his audience—filling in gaps, making pungent asides, shifting times from the narrated past to the narrating present—remembering, commenting, informing, judging, and involving. This is only one aspect of a relatively complex style employed by Lampedusa in his novel, which has been declared a fragmentary book by some critics, whereas others have compared it to a film montage. The text does present a variety of voices and tones. From the traditional historical novel, it borrows a fairly straightforward third-person narrative—realism if not naturalism—that includes descriptions and dialogue depicting the environment, events, and characters.

Because the novel is also a psychological study, a Stendhalian attempt to narrate through the eyes and viewpoint of a protagonist, Lampedusa experiments with the interior monologue, moving the plot forward through mental rather than temporal associations. To complete the stylistic picture, there is a strong lyric vein present in the author's descriptive passages and meditations. Structurally, *The Leopard*'s chapters are somewhat uneven, a roughness caused in part by Lampedusa's death before the book was accepted for publication; it can be presumed that some changes would have been made. It is known that the novelist had doubts about introducing the chapter centering on Father Pirrone's visit to his peasant family, although it does function as a lower-class version of the Tancredi-Angelica love story. Other inclusions have been challenged as well: The romance is overextended, detracting from the main character; the death of

Don Fabrizio is superfluous and somewhat banal; the epilogue serves no valid purpose in the plot development. Binding together all the chapters of *The Leopard* are the recurring voice of the omnipresent narrator—his humor, irony, and consciousness collecting all the disparate threads of his tale—and, on a more thematic level, an unrelenting sense of loss.

Lampedusa's novel resembles a threnody that not only sings the pleasures and beauty of life but also remarks on their evanescence. Nothing survives the corrosive passage of time, a fact known through the comments of the narrator if not through the development of the plot. Nothing is truly immortal in this fictional universe; the author takes pains to inform his readers of the loss of emotions, people, ideals, and places. For example, Angelica and Tancredi's brief season of sensual love changes into an unsatisfactory marriage and a series of adulterous affairs, a fate shared by Father Pirrone's plebeian niece and her virile hunk; the Salina descendants grow to resemble the children of the Sedàras and other hyenas and jackals rather than their ancestors, the lions and leopards; members of the middle class, in turn, lose their survival skills and take on the vulnerability of the aristocracy, the price paid for gentrification; the numerous children of Don Fabrizio are reduced to three old maids collecting false relics; the beautiful palaces are sold or destroyed by bombs in World War II. Even strong emotions, such as Concetta's repressed hatred for her father, dissolve in time, losing all consistency.

What remains is a painful state of lucid awareness that unites the maturing prince, the old Concetta of chapter 8, and the pervasive narrator, creating skepticism and impotence. It is not incidental that Don Fabrizio allows his wealth to be siphoned off as he observes the disintegration of his class and the decay of his family with mixed feelings of loss and vindication. It is the same desire for immobility—or death—that afflicts his Sicily. Don Fabrizio suffers from alienation, not only from the common people but also from his own caste, and estrangement from his environment and family: anger at his wife's neurotic possessiveness, an autocratic detachment from his children, displeasure with the pettiness of the nobility. He searches poignantly for absolutes on which to base his existence: The aristocracy subsists as an ideal, although individual aristocrats are judged as inept, boring, unintelligent, even unattractive inbred "monkeys"; the family heritage is venerated but is reduced to his pompously silly heir; the stars are a symbol of an idealized death, but the reality of death is a carload of butchered animals and dirty sheets.

In this context, Don Fabrizio is brother to the existentialist heroes—or antiheroes—found in the pages of Jean-Paul Sartre, Albert Camus, Luigi Pirandello, and Søren Kierkegaard, men possessed of the human angst of having been born and "being" for death. It is a realization that occasionally produces reactions of disgust or Sartrean nausea for the act of living. But the prince, like Lampedusa's text itself, is a complex creation whose cosmic pessimism is moderated by an instinctual passion for life and a spiritual quest for eternity, however dubious.

Were the novel to conclude with the ball episode (as chosen by Visconti for the finale of his brilliant film rendition), which ends with the vision of the morning star, promising Don Fabrizio a rendezvous with eternal truth, or with the death of the protagonist, with its erotic suggestions of union with Death as Beauty, Lampedusa would have left his text open to positive interpretations. However, the episode dated 1910 destroys these hopeful readings. Little is left of the aristocracy, the Salina family, or the prince's memory. The youths have aged or died, becoming cynical, childlike, or hardened. As they ironically prepare to celebrate the fiftieth anniversary of Garibaldi's invasion, Concetta is forced to meditate on the past, only to recognize that it was her own thoughtless pride rather than her father's opposition that destroyed her chance to marry Tancredi. This realization shatters her interpretation of the past and nullifies the ancient resentments and emotions that had sustained her.

The narrator comments on the unknowability of truth as Concetta prepares to dispose of her personal history, emptied of any true vital involvement. The objects in her old-maid's room speak of a time no longer present and of a life ill spent: family photographs, the locked trunks of her dowry filled with musty linens, and the remnants of the beloved dog Bendicò, his carcass transformed into a rug. Lampedusa's final image is poetically powerful and thematically relevant: Concetta's maid throws out the mangy hide, which takes on the shape of a dancing quadruped, cursing with his right paw, before it decomposes

into a pile of ashen dust. It is a final sign of decay, loss, and death: the last leopard.

Fiora A. Bassanese

OTHER MAJOR WORKS

SHORT FICTION: *Racconti*, 1961 (partial translation *Two Stories and a Memory*, 1962).

NONFICTION: "Lezioni su Stendhal," 1959.

BIBLIOGRAPHY

Bondanella, Peter, and Andrea Ciccarelli, eds. *The Cambridge Companion to the Italian Novel*. New York: Cambridge University Press, 2003. Tomasi di Lampedusa and *The Leopard* are mentioned in a number of essays in this volume, but the majority of the discussion is found in two chapters: "Alessandro Manzoni and Developments in the Historical Novel," by Olga Ragusa, and "The Italian Novel in Search of Identity: Lampedusa and Pasolini," by Manuela Bertone.

Cowart, David. "The Turning Point." In *History and the Contemporary Novel*. Carbondale: Southern Illinois University Press, 1989. Scholarly examination of *The Leopard* is part of a larger discussion of historical novels published after World War II. Cowart points out similarities between historical and narrative fiction and assigns historical novels to four categories; he places *The Leopard* in the "turning point" category, his term for a novel that pinpoints the precise moment when the modern age, or some aspect of it, came into being.

Cupolo, Marco. "Tomasi di Lampedusa's *Il gattopardo* and Postwar Italian Political Culture." In *Risorgimento in Modern Italian Culture: Revisiting the Nineteenth-Century Past in History, Narrative, and Cinema*, edited by Norma Bouchard. Madison, N.J.: Fairleigh Dickinson University Press, 2005. Cupolo's study of *The Leopard* is included in a collection of essays that examine cultural responses to the Risorgimento, the period of history from 1859 through 1870 when Italy became a unified and independent nation.

Della Coletta, Cristina. *Plotting the Past: Metamorphoses of Historical Narrative in Modern Italian Fiction*. West Lafayette, Ind.: Purdue University Press, 1996. Analysis of *The Leopard* and two other Italian historical novels written in the twentieth century begins with a discussion of Alessandro Manzoni's essay "On the Historical Novel" and then describes how the three novelists accepted and adapted Manzoni's ideas.

Donadio, Rachel. "*The Leopard* Turns Fifty." *The New York Times Book Review*, July 13, 2008. Takes a fresh look at *The Leopard* on the fiftieth anniversary of its original publication with a review of a new American edition published to commemorate the event.

Gilmour, David. *The Last Leopard: A Life of Giuseppe di Lampedusa*. New York: Pantheon Books, 1988.

The only biography of Tomasi di Lampedusa available in English provides an incisive portrait of the author, depicting him as a deeply skeptical man, similar to his fictional counterpart, Don Fabrizio in *The Leopard*. Also discusses *The Leopard* in its historical and aesthetic context, recounting the controversy surrounding its publication.

Pacifici, Sergio. "Giuseppe Tomasi di Lampedusa: The View from Within." In *The Modern Italian Novel: From Pea to Moravia*. Carbondale: Southern Illinois University Press, 1979. Analyzes *The Leopard* within the wider context of the Italian literature of its time.

MICHEL TOURNIER

Born: Paris, France; December 19, 1924
Also known as: Michel Édouard Tournier

PRINCIPAL LONG FICTION

Vendredi: Ou, Les Limbes du Pacifique, 1967 (revised 1978; *Friday: Or, The Other Island*, 1969)

Le Roi des aulnes, 1970 (*The Ogre*, 1972; also known as *The Erl-King*)

Les Météores, 1975 (*Gemini*, 1981)

Gaspard, Melchior, et Balthazar, 1980 (*The Four Wise Men*, 1982)

Gilles et Jeanne, 1983 (*Gilles and Jeanne*, 1987)

La Goutte d'or, 1985 (*The Golden Droplet*, 1987)

Eléazar: Ou, La Source et le buisson, 1996 (*Eleazar, Exodus to the West*, 2002)

Le Bonheur en Allemagne, 2004

OTHER LITERARY FORMS

In addition to long fiction, Michel Tournier (tewr-NYAY) produced a one-act play, the monologue *Le Fétichiste* (pr. 1974; *The Fetishist*, 1983), the title of which reveals a great deal psychologically about many of Tournier's fictional characters. It was followed by a travel journal, *Canada: Journal de voyage* (1977; Canada: travel journal), about a country that symbolizes a sort of promised land in some of his stories, as well as by

Le Vent paraclet (1977; *The Wind Spirit*, 1988), a volume of essays that are not up to the level of his novels. Thirteen short stories and Tournier's one play were published under the title *Le Coq de bruyère* (1978; *The Fetishist, and Other Stories*, 1983). In his short stories, Tournier explores briefly, pointedly, and often amusingly areas treated at greater length in his novels. Equally interesting is the group of what he calls "images and prose," a sort of intellectual autobiography titled *Des clefs et des serrures: Images et proses* (1979; some keys and some locks: images and prose).

Tournier has also published in two other areas, both of which illuminate aspects of his fiction. The first is children's literature. Under the title *Vendredi: Ou, La Vie sauvage* (1971; *Friday and Robinson: Life on Esperanza Island*, 1972), Tournier adapted his interpretation of the story of Robinson Crusoe to a form suitable for young readers. He also adapted two of the stories in *The Fetishist, and Other Stories*—"L'Aire du muguet" ("The Lily of the Valley Rest Area") and "Que ma joie demeure" ("Jesu, Joy of Man's Desiring")—for young readers in the volumes *L'Aire du muguet* (1982) and *Que ma joie demeure* (1982). In a series of what he calls *enfantimages*, Tournier has published, among other stories, *Barbedor* (1980), an adaptation of the chapter "Barbedor" ("King Goldenbeard: Or, The Problem of Succession") from his novel *The Four Wise Men*.

Tournier's children's literature abounds in opposites—good and evil, beauties and beasts—as well as in ogres, secrets, storms, and miraculous adventures, all of which are to be found in his novels for more mature readers as well.

Another important aspect of Tournier's books for children is the close alliance between the pictorial and the verbal, the image and the word. That talent undoubtedly has been sharpened by the author's hobby, which is photography. In this second area, he has written text to accompany photographs by well-known photographers such as Édouard Boubat and Arthur Tress. Titles such as *Miroirs, autoportraits, photographies* (1973; with Boubat; mirrors, self-portraits, photographs) and *Vues de dos* (1981; with Boubat; views from behind) indicate that Tournier looks at the world as in a mirror but views it from behind, the perspective of many of his works. For Tournier, whatever view one takes of the world is but a dream that threatens at every moment, as it often does in his novels, to turn into a nightmare.

ACHIEVEMENTS

Tournier's first great literary achievement was a work of nonfiction. With his intimate knowledge of the German language, he published, between 1950 and 1953, four volumes of French translations of the secret archives of the German Ministry of Foreign Affairs (located on the Wilhelmstrasse in Berlin during the years 1937 to 1939) as *Les Archives secrètes de la Wilhelmstrasse*. The volumes contain more than twenty-five hundred pages of text on the subject of the Ministry from the tenure of Konstantin von Neurath to that of Joachim von Ribbentrop, covering Germany's relations with Czechoslovakia, the Spanish Civil War, and the aftermath of the Munich Accords.

Born in 1924, Tournier belongs to the generation of Robert Pinget (born 1919), Alain Robbe-Grillet (born 1922), and Michel Butor (born 1926). His colleagues began to publish in the 1950's and were soon grouped together loosely, along with others, as the New Novelists, not because their works resembled one another but because their novels represented a radical departure from the traditional form of the genre. Unlike the New Novelists, however, Tournier did not begin to publish until 1967. In his first novel, *Friday*, Tournier returned to a

much more traditional form, in which he combined the omniscient narrator with excerpts from Robinson's logbook—unlike Daniel Defoe, who recounted his tale of Robinson Crusoe entirely in the first person, although he did include pages from the protagonist's journal. This device permitted Tournier to tell his story with a great deal more freedom from two points of view, the third and first persons. The title hints, however, that Tournier will turn the story of Robinson Crusoe upside down, so that within a traditional form he will create something surprisingly new. Indeed, Tournier's achievement was so striking that the novel was awarded the Grand Prix of the Académie Française in 1967, thus assuring it and its author a much wider readership.

As Tournier used a well-known English novel as a point of departure for his first novel, so in his second novel he took a character from a celebrated poem in German literature as a symbol for the hero. The poem is Johann Wolfgang von Goethe's "Erlkönig" (1782), which becomes in French "Le Roi des aulnes" and is known in English as "Erl-King" or "The King of the Alders." In his novel *The Ogre*, Tournier recounts the adventures of a French prisoner of war within Adolf Hitler's Third Reich during World War II. Again, the technique includes first- and third-person narratives, and this time the results were so impressive that for the first time in its seventy-four-year history, the Académie Goncourt awarded the novel the prestigious Prix Goncourt by unanimous vote in 1970. In only three years, then, Tournier's first works were crowned with the prizes of two of France's most prestigious academies, and as a result, Tournier's career as a novelist and man of letters was firmly established. In addition, he was elected one of the ten French members of the Académie Goncourt in 1972. In 1975, he was named a knight in the Légion d'Honneur, and in 1993 he was the recipient of the Goethe Medal.

BIOGRAPHY

Michel Édouard Tournier was born in Paris on December 19, 1924, to parents who were both specialists in the German language, a fact that undoubtedly influenced their son's career. He studied law and philosophy at the Sorbonne in Paris with well-known thinkers such as the philosopher Gaston Bachelard and the ethnologist Claude Lévi-Strauss, as well as at the University of

Tübingen in Germany. He earned the equivalent of master's degrees in both letters and law but failed the enormously difficult *agrégation*, the examination required for entry into university teaching, in 1949. After this failure, Tournier gave up the idea of an academic career and became a director and producer for the French radio and television network from 1949 to 1954. During those years, he also published the translations from German already mentioned. Beginning in 1955, he spent three years as a journalist and then became the director of literary services for the publishing house Plon. That was to prove to be his last employment in the business world. With the success of *Friday* in 1967, Tournier left Plon in 1968, after ten years with that firm, to devote himself to full-time writing.

Tournier's achievements as a novelist are particularly impressive in view of the fact that he published his first novel (actually his fourth, in the order in which he wrote them) at the comparatively late age of forty-three.

Michel Tournier. (Jacques Sassier/Editions Gallimard)

His novels have continued to intrigue readers, and his reputation seems assured. Tournier resides in the picturesque Chevreuse Valley, a few miles southwest of Paris.

ANALYSIS

Like most educated Frenchmen of his generation, Tournier was influenced by the Surrealist movement of the 1920's, by the existentialist philosophy of Jean-Paul Sartre and Sartre's German predecessors in the 1940's, and by the Theater of the Absurd of Samuel Beckett and Eugène Ionesco of the 1950's. Certainly one of the greatest influences on many French writers of Tournier's age was that of novelist André Gide, whose *récits*, or narratives, say much in little space. Tournier also experienced World War II at an impressionable age, and his profoundly Christian upbringing colors all of his works.

FRIDAY

Few Englishmen and Americans realize how popular Defoe's *The Life and Strange Surprizing Adventures of Robinson Crusoe, of York, Mariner, Written by Himself* (1719; commonly known as *Robinson Crusoe*) has been with the French since it was first translated (1720-1721). In *Friday*, Tournier uses many of the details Defoe recounts in *Robinson Crusoe*, but he very quickly begins to create a myth rather than simply reproduce the story told by Defoe. Tournier replaces Defoe's forty pages of introduction, which tell the reader whence Robinson has come, with an eight-page scene aboard the ill-fated ship in which the captain predicts Robinson's future with tarot cards, thus symbolically revealing the adventures that lie ahead.

Tournier shifts the date of the shipwreck from 1659 to 1759, to the very heart of the Age of Enlightenment. Robinson, in his despair, is first tempted to return to the primeval slime, but reason soon prevails, and he becomes the logical, thinking man who will make every effort to realize progress by turning his desert island into a replica of civilization as he knows it. Through the cards, Robinson has learned that he is a born organizer who will struggle to conquer disorder only to find his work an illusion. He will wield absolute power with piety and purity, but his austerity will appear to be an affectation. In his efforts to analyze the phenomenon of solitude, he will search for his own origins and, in so doing, become a different man. He will have to fight against chaos in the form of a fiery monster while being turned upside down psychologically.

Tournier's greatest divergence from Defoe comes with the introduction of the tarot card Gemini, the twins, which will prove to be Robinson's dual self as well as Robinson and Friday. This is Tournier's first mention of the phenomenon of twins, which haunts almost all of his subsequent novels. In *Robinson Crusoe*, Defoe passes quietly over the problem of sex, whereas in *Friday*, the captain maintains that the twins will live in childish innocence in their solar city, having arrived at an androgynous solar sexuality. Robinson will be in great danger but will be saved by a golden child born of the entrails of Earth, who will give him the keys to the solar city. Thereupon the ship is wrecked, and all but Robinson are lost. The irony here, as in Defoe's novel, is that if the crew had remained aboard instead of abandoning ship, most of them might have been saved.

Robinson's predecessor dubbed his island the Island of Despair. In like manner, Robinson at first calls his the Island of Desolation, but with incurable optimism he soon changes the name to Speranza, from the Italian *speranza*, meaning "hope." He slowly but surely brings order out of chaos, with only his Bible and his dog Tenn to keep him company. The introduction of the Bible follows Defoe's example, but it also announces Tournier's preoccupation with theology, which permeates all of his novels. Tournier's Robinson indulges in a great deal of philosophizing, an occupation totally uncharacteristic of Defoe's hero. The modern Robinson comes to the startling realization that the absence of others has caused him to doubt his own existence. In his efforts to analyze the relation between the knower and the known, he finally understands that human beings have two types of knowledge of themselves: that which comes from within and that which comes from others. Up to this point, Robinson seems to be a faithful exponent of existentialism as propounded by Jean-Paul Sartre. Contrary to Sartre's vision, however, Robinson does not fall into the dualism of the self as subject and the other as object. Because his being depends on the existence of others and because the being of others depends on his being, he concludes that the knowledge he has of an object is identical with the object itself, so that in the end the subject and object are one and the same. He is the world, an element in the world.

Concomitant with this regression toward the sources of himself, Robinson descends into the bowels of the island as if returning to the womb of Speranza, only to realize that one cannot be born again. He emerges to seek other means of union and reunion with the world. He finds that he can exist only by fleeing from himself toward others, but the only "other" that exists is the island Speranza herself. He eventually locates a receptive spot and there has sex with the earth. It is almost as if Robinson has heeded John Donne's exhortation in his poem "Song" (1633)—"Go, and catch a falling star,/ Get with child a mandrake root"—because from this insemination spring pure white mandrakes. The mandrake is a plant whose forked roots were once believed to have magical human attributes, and Robinson discovers that the roots of these mandrakes have indeed taken on the form of a little girl. While Robinson is convinced that a stronger and more powerful link now attaches him to Speranza and that he has succeeded in humanizing the island, he is also aware that he has taken the first step in abandoning his own humanity. The fact is proved when he awakens the next morning to discover that his beard has taken root in the earth.

Defoe did not introduce the character of Friday into his story until two-thirds of the way through the novel. Tournier brings him in at midpoint because Robinson has arrived at the stage where his story can continue only with the appearance of the other. We must all choose, as Albert Camus put it and as Tournier's Robinson repeats after him, between the side of the victim and that of the executioner. When Robinson sees Friday fleeing his would-be executioners in a ritual sacrifice, he chooses the side of the stronger, the executioner, and takes aim at the victim. At that moment, his dog Tenn bumps his arm, and, by mistake, Robinson kills one of the pursuers and Friday is saved. From this accident stems the rest of Robinson's story.

At first, Friday seems to be the perfect servant, doing more or less exactly as his master commands and suffering any punishment more or less silently. Little by little, Robinson observes, however, that Friday has an elemental knowledge of the world that his master, with all of his knowledge and skills, has never acquired. At one point, Friday innocently opens the sluice gates of the rice paddy, thus inundating Robinson's plantation with a virtually biblical flood and ruining the crop. Then, when he is almost caught having a forbidden smoke with Robinson's pipe, he throws the pipe to the rear of the cave to escape detection. Robinson has stored the dynamite saved from the ship in the depths of the cave, and the lighted pipe ignites the explosives, creating the fiery monster the captain had foretold. All of Robinson's work is completely undone; hence, because the master no longer has the support of his props, the roles are reversed.

Friday now shows Robinson how to live in fundamental and peaceful union with the earth, while he himself observes the benefits of civilized living. Thus, when deliverance arrives, Friday elects to sail away to civilization while Robinson remains on Speranza, where he will hunt for his salvation in communion with the elements, having become elemental himself. He will not be alone, however, for a young Estonian who was being mistreated aboard the rescue ship sneaks ashore and remains with Robinson, who will call him Thursday, which is the day of Jupiter, the god of the sky.

In this comic and cosmic novel, the reader encounters the familiar adventures of Robinson Crusoe only to see them metamorphose into the myth of Tournier's Robinson, in which the solidarity with humanity of Defoe's novel becomes a study of solar and solitary dehumanization. If Tournier's Robinson seems at times to be a twentieth century French intellectual rather than an eighteenth century English merchant's son, his adventures recapitulate the efforts of contemporary human beings to define themselves in their relationships with others and with the objects of this world. To become one with the world, Tournier seems to be saying, an individual must first become one with him- or herself. Luckily for most of us, a little Estonian lurks nearby who, by his "otherness," reminds us that our true being continues to depend on the existence of others.

THE OGRE

In his isolation, Robinson risks becoming a kind of ogre. Tournier takes the ogre, the Erl-King of Goethe's poem, and makes of him *le roi des aulnes* of his second novel, *The Ogre*. According to Goethe, the Erl-King lures innocent children to their deaths; in Goethe's poem, the Erl-King leaves a father with a dead son in his arms. The book is dedicated to one of the early twentieth century's most famous ogres, Grigori Yefimovich Rasputin,

whose reputation, according to Tournier, has been unjustly defamed. The novel's hero is Abel Tiffauges, whose Christian name, Abel, evokes all the overtones of the biblical story of Cain and Abel. The story begins with Tiffauges's "Sinister Writing," a double play on words: the Latin *sinister*, meaning "on the left side" (consequently unlucky and inauspicious), and the French *sinistre*, meaning "a fire." Tiffauges has injured his right hand and therefore must—and can—write as well with his left. Unlucky Tiffagues will be saved twice by calamitous conflagrations.

Tournier's novel is loaded (some might say overloaded) with symbols. Tiffauges attends a Catholic school named after Saint Christopher, the saint who carried the Christ child across a river and as a result became the patron saint of travelers, which links the saint with the Erl-King, because in Goethe's poem the father is traveling with his son on horseback. The adult Tiffauges becomes an automobile repairman, which also links him to the idea of travel. In the opening sentence of the novel, Tiffauges's Jewish mistress calls him an ogre because of his inept lovemaking. The story of Tiffauges will be the revelation of how he becomes a true ogre under the aegis of the Erl-King, Rasputin, and Saint Christopher.

Tiffauges was early alienated psychologically from society, as Robinson was isolated physically from others; both were therefore forced to ponder the problem of being. When Rachel calls Tiffauges an ogre, he reacts with the nostalgic exclamation "Ô saisons, ô châteaux!"—the first line of a poem by Arthur Rimbaud, which can be freely translated as "Other times, other places!"; the second line asks, "Whose soul is without faults?" The most important event in Tiffauges's childhood occurs when he is unjustly accused of having started a small fire in the school chapel. Although innocent, he sneaks home to avoid punishment, only to be returned to school the next day. Upon his arrival, he finds that the school has been seriously damaged by a fire that began in the basement. Tiffauges has been saved by fire, but it makes little difference, because he fails the *baccalauréat* examinations anyway.

Tiffauges takes up Tournier's hobby, photography. He particularly enjoys photographing children as they pour forth from school. He narrows his attentions to a young girl, who accuses him of rape. Again, Tiffauges is innocent; while the judge does not believe that Tiffauges is guilty, he lets him go only because World War II has begun. Tiffauges is thus saved by fire a second time, this time a worldwide fire. He is drafted by the army and sent to the eastern front to help set up a telegraphic center. The Germans soon reveal that they know almost more about the center than the French themselves. One officer then hits upon the ridiculous idea of communicating by carrier pigeon from the same position. The area is quickly overrun by the Germans, revealing the abysmal state of the French military mentality of the period. Tiffauges is taken prisoner and sent to East Prussia. His journey has only begun, however, as the reader has only arrived at the midpoint of the novel.

Because of his knowledge of pigeons and automobiles, Tiffauges is assigned as an assistant to a forest ranger in the great wildlife preserve of Rominten. There he is provided with a horse, which he immediately names Bluebeard. The horse brings him ever closer to the poem of the novel's title in this land of alders. The master of Rominten, dubbed the "Ogre of Rominten," turns out to be the notorious Nazi Hermann Göring, who, from Tiffauges's point of view, appears to be nothing much more than a capricious, greedy fat man interested mainly in animal phallology and coprology, the latter of which fits in with Tiffauges's fecal fetish. The reader must keep in mind that Tiffauges is witnessing Nazi Germany from behind, so to speak, or from the viewpoint of a French prisoner who has been lucky enough to find that his prison and its labor are not too oppressive. As the Russian campaign grinds on, Göring has less and less time to spend at Rominten. When Tiffauges learns that he is to be returned to the prison camp, he manages to have himself assigned to the fortress of Kaltenborn, one of the forty training camps where four hundred of Germany's finest youth are indoctrinated physically and mentally into the Nazi philosophy, only to be swallowed up by the war machine.

Tiffauges rapidly becomes the "Ogre of Kaltenborn." With his unfailing eye, he is adept at locating in the surrounding countryside and taking by force the recruits necessary to keep the camp at full complement. Tiffauges is the name of a château belonging to one of the most famous ogres of France, Gilles de Rais. The reader learns that the name can be rendered in German as *tief*

Auge, "deep eye," which is almost too clever a touch on Tournier's part. Tiffauges has reached Kaltenborn too late. The year is 1944, and Germany's eastern front is collapsing. Tiffauges saves a Jewish child from the columns of concentration camp victims being marched to the west ahead of the advancing Russians, which takes the reader back to the beginning of the novel, in which Tiffauges's Jewish mistress Rachel is the first to call him an ogre. Tiffauges, with little Ephraïm on his shoulders, escapes from Kaltenborn and the invading Russian soldiers when the quick-thinking Ephraïm identifies Tiffauges and himself as French prisoners. They slowly disappear into a swamp surrounded by alder trees.

Tiffauges thus realizes his destiny as Saint Christopher carrying the Christ child on his shoulders; as Rasputin, who was apparently successful at alleviating the suffering of the Russian czar's hemophiliac young son; but also as the Erl-King, who kills the young. As an old German aristocrat points out to Tiffauges, in Germany "everything that passes is a symbol, everything that happens is a parable." Like Robinson before him, Tiffauges has made a trip, much shorter in distance but profound in its human resonance. From symbol and parable, one must be able to decipher true meaning. Tiffauges realizes that ability, but too late to save him from the hidden reality.

GEMINI

In *Friday*, Robinson reveals his fascination with twins as exemplified by the zodiacal constellation Gemini, calling them "beings fallen from the sky like meteors," which again echoes Donne's line "Go, and catch a falling star." Tiffauges adds to the allegory when he finds twin pigeons while serving in the army and twin boys whom he recruits for Kaltenborn. Like meteorites fallen to the earth, the pigeons are roasted and eaten; the twins are impaled on heraldic Prussian lances. The references illuminate the connection Tournier sees between meteors and twins and explains why the title of his third novel, *Les Météores*, was translated into English as *Gemini*. The identical twins Jean and Paul are so alike that they are given the collective name Jean-Paul. The story is told from several points of view, that of the omniscient narrator, the twins' uncle Alexandre, the twins themselves, Jean's fiancé Sophie, and others. What the novel loses in formal structure in comparison with

Tournier's first two novels it gains in a much greater variety of characters, many more than in the earlier works. While the points of view are easily distinguished, the "voices" of the characters tend to be, with a few exceptions, equally intelligent, equally intellectual, and equally literate and literary.

The plot can be reduced in part to the role of the existential third—the outsider, the stranger. Alexandre, the shocking uncle, a flamboyant homosexual, suddenly finds himself the heir to his older brother's garbage-disposal service, the name of which, SEDOMU, suspiciously echoes the word "sodomy." Alexandre becomes convinced that a civilization can be characterized best by its detritus. During his peregrinations, he encounters a couple, Eustache and the young Daniel, but when Daniel attempts to join Alexandre, almost as if lured by an ogre, he is caught in a storm and killed by the rats in Alexandre's garbage dump. Alexandre the outsider remains the outsider. He also interferes in the marriage of two aristocrats with the result that the bride goes off to Venice on her honeymoon by herself. Alexandre the bourgeois is still the outsider. Later, Alexandre encounters his twin nephews, and when he realizes that he is forever excluded from their company, he commits suicide by venturing onto the docks of Casablanca at night. Alexandre thus becomes the ultimate outsider.

When Jean's desire to marry Sophie is frustrated by Paul, who would thus become the third, Jean goes off to Venice to honeymoon by himself. Roughly the last half of the novel recounts Paul's pursuit of his absolute other to Venice, then Tunisia, Iceland, Japan, and across Canada from west to east, only to end in failure and catastrophe in Berlin at the moment the Berlin Wall is erected, a wall that separates human beings from themselves. If the voyage risks degenerating into a guided tour or travelogue, the reader encounters along the way a splendid cast of characters and a series of exceptional experiences. The reader also witnesses Tournier's magic in transforming the soft and humid west-southwest breeze of the opening paragraph into the calm and clear, dry and cold east-northeast wind of the conclusion, all recounted in an incomparable human speech that, if it is "situated halfway between the mutism of the beasts and the silence of the gods," is nevertheless the feature that differentiates human beings from both. By means of such meta-morphoses, Tournier more than compensates the reader for the endurance necessary to reach the end of this lengthy novel.

THE FOUR WISE MEN

The connection between meteors and the Star of Bethlehem is evident. The English title of Tournier's fourth novel, *The Four Wise Men*, unfortunately reveals the conceit concealed in Tournier's French title, *Gaspard, Melchior, et Balthazar*. Each of the Three Wise Men follows the star as the symbol of a personal and private obsession, only to find that obsession satisfied in the person of the Christ child. The fourth Wise Man, Taor, is simply hunting for the best recipe for the candy known in English as Turkish Delight. He arrives in Bethlehem too late to see the Christ child. He learns the recipe, but at a great cost. In order to spare a mother and her children, he sacrifices himself by taking the place of the father as a laborer in the salt mines of Sodom for a symbolic thirty-three years. Upon his release, he searches for the house of Joseph of Arimathea and again arrives too late, this time for the Last Supper. Dying of hunger, he eats the scraps of bread, drinks the last drops of wine, and is wafted away by angels, thus becoming the first to receive the Eucharist and the first Christian martyr after John the Baptist, demonstrating again that "the last shall be first and the first shall be last."

In this novel, even the donkey and bull in attendance on the Christ child speak, adding amusing and unexpected sidelights to this scene central to the Christian religion. Taor's story reveals Tournier's inventive imagination in retelling an oft-told tale whose renditions frequently seem stale when compared to Saint Matthew's incomparable version.

Tournier's short novel *Gilles and Jeanne* recounts the story of Beauty and the Beast: Saint Joan of Arc and the ogre Gilles de Rais, who fought together to deliver France from the English. That Gilles's encounter with the saintly Joan should have driven him to commit his evil deeds is hardly convincing, and the novel therefore does not rise to the heights of Tournier's earlier works. Tournier's oeuvre nevertheless demonstrates its author's marvelous ability to reveal all the anguish and exaltation that comes with, as he has put it, "the metamorphosis of life into destiny."

F. C. St. Aubyn

OTHER MAJOR WORKS

SHORT FICTION: *Le Coq de bruyère*, 1978 (*The Fetishist, and Other Stories*, 1983); *Le Médianoche amoureux: Contes et nouvelles*, 1989 (*The Midnight Love Feast*, 1991).

PLAY: *Le Fétichiste*, 1974 (*The Fetishist*, 1983).

NONFICTION: *Canada: Journal de voyage*, 1977; *Le Vent paraclet*, 1977 (*The Wind Spirit*, 1988); *Des clefs et des serrures: Images et prose*, 1979; *Le Vol du vampire: Notes de lecture*, 1981; *Le Vagabond immobile*, 1984 (with Jean-Max Troubeau); *Le Tabor et le Sinai: Essais sur l'art contemporain*, 1988; *Le Miroir des idées: Traité*, 1994 (*The Mirror of Ideas*, 1998); *Le Pied de la lettre: Trois cents mots propres*, 1994; *Célébrations: Essais*, 1999; *Journal extime*, 2002.

TRANSLATION: *Les Archives secrètes de la Wilhelm-strasse*, 1950-1953 (4 volumes; of the secret archives of the German Ministry of Foreign Affairs).

CHILDREN'S LITERATURE: *Vendredi: Ou, La Vie sauvage*, 1971 (adaptation of his novel *Friday*; *Friday and Robinson: Life on Esperanza Island*, 1972); *Barbedor*, 1980; *L'Aire du muguet*, 1982; *Que ma joie demeure*, 1982; *Les Rois mages*, 1983 (adaptation of his novel *The Four Wise Men*).

BIBLIOGRAPHY

Cloonan, William. *Michel Tournier*. Boston: Twayne, 1985. Provides an introductory overview, with biographical information and critical responses to Tournier's major works. Includes bibliography and index.

Davis, Colin. *Michel Tournier: Philosophy and Fiction*. New York: Oxford University Press, 1988. Reliable, comprehensive study demonstrates that despite his statements to the contrary, Tournier shares many of the assumptions of the French New Novelists about the role of literature. Includes analyses of his major novels and considerations of his theory of reading and his attitudes toward language.

Edwards, Rachel. *Myth and the Fiction of Michel Tournier and Patrick Granville*. Lewiston, N.Y.: Edwin Mellen Press, 1999. Examines the use of myth in the works of the two French writers. Discussion of Tournier's novels focuses on *Friday* and *The Ogre*.

Ferrigan, Mark. "Dispossessing the Father in the Fiction of Michel Tournier." In *Paternity and Fatherhood:*

Myths and Realities, edited by Lieve Spaas and Trista Selous. New York: St. Martin's Press, 1998. Examination of Tournier's fictional depiction of fathers is included in a collection of essays that explore the dichotomy between the biological function of paternity and the cultural concept of fatherhood.

Gascoigne, David. *Michel Tournier*. Washington, D.C.: Berg, 1996. Analysis of Tournier's fiction focuses on its reinterpretation of mythology and its attack on Western cultural norms and assumptions. Places Tournier within the context of the French intellectual tradition.

Maclean, Mairi. *Michel Tournier: Exploring Human Relations*. Bristol, England: Bristol Academic Press, 2003. Addresses the various human relationships in Tournier's fiction, including homosexuality, heterosexuality, relationships between parents and children, twinship, and the relationship of humankind to nature.

Petit, Susan. *Michel Tournier's Metaphysical Fictions*. Philadelphia: J. Benjamins, 1991. Offers analyses of Tournier's works, including his novels *Friday*, *The Ogre*, *Gemini*, *The Four Wise Men*, and *The Golden Droplet*. Also contains an interview with Tournier titled "I Write Because I Have Something to Say."

Platten, David. *Michel Tournier and the Metaphor of Fiction*. New York: St. Martin's Press, 1999. Focuses on the use of metaphor in Tournier's fiction, demonstrating how he combines the fantastic with the real to create new perspectives on the Robinson Crusoe myth, Nazism, and the nature of education.

Spaas, Lieve, and Brian Stimpson, eds. *Robinson Crusoe: Myths and Metamorphoses*. New York: St. Martin's Press, 1996. Features several interpretations of Tournier's novel *Friday*: "Myth as Microscope: Michel Tournier's *Vendredi: Ou, Les Limbes du Pacifique*," by Lorna Milne; "'Skilful in the Usury of Time': Michel Tournier and the Critique of Economism," by Anthony Purdy; and "*Vendredi: Ou, Les Limbes du Pacifique*: Tournier, Seduction, and Paternity," by Emma Wilson.

Worton, Michael, ed. *Michel Tournier*. New York: Longman, 1995. Collection of essays about the writer includes examinations of his depictions of relationships between the sexes and his use of history and legend. Also contains an interview with Tournier.

ROSE TREMAIN

Born: London, England; August 2, 1943
Also known as: Rosemary Jane Thomson

PRINCIPAL LONG FICTION

Sadler's Birthday, 1976
Letter to Sister Benedicta, 1979
The Cupboard, 1981
The Swimming Pool Season, 1985
Restoration, 1989
Sacred Country, 1992
The Way I Found Her, 1997
Music and Silence, 1999
The Colour, 2003
The Road Home, 2007

OTHER LITERARY FORMS

Although Rose Tremain is most highly recognized as a novelist, she has also published acclaimed collections of short stories, including *The Colonel's Daughter, and Other Stories* (1984), *Evangelista's Fan, and Other Stories* (1994), and *The Darkness of Wallis Simpson* (2005). She wrote the popular 1985 children's book *Journey to the Volcano* and has written plays as well as scripts for television and radio. Her early writings also include works of nonfiction.

ACHIEVEMENTS

Rose Tremain is considered to be an important contemporary British novelist, and she is also one of the most celebrated of her generation. In 1983, *Granta* magazine named her one of its twenty "Best Young British Novelists" along with Martin Amis, Salman Rushdie, and Ian McEwan. Tremain's 1985 novel *The Swimming Pool Season* won the Angel Literary Award, as did her 1989 work *Restoration*, which also was named the *Sunday Express* Book of the Year and was short-listed for the Booker Prize for Fiction. An award-winning film adaptation of *Restoration*, starring Robert Downey, Jr., Sam Neill, and Meg Ryan, was released in 1995.

Tremain's 1992 novel *Sacred Country* won the James Tait Black Memorial Prize and the Prix Femina Étranger, and in 1999 *Music and Silence* won the

Whitbread Award. *The Colour* was short-listed for the 2004 Orange Prize for Fiction, an honor that Tremain received again for *The Road Home* in 2008. In addition, Tremain was named as a judge for the Booker Prize for Fiction in 1988 and in 2000. In 2000, she was awarded an honorary Litt.D. by the University of East Anglia, and in 2007 she received the prestigious honor of being named a Commander of the Order of the British Empire.

BIOGRAPHY

Rose Tremain was born Rosemary Jane Thomson on August 2, 1943, in London. Her parents, Keith Nicholas Thomson and Viola Thomson, separated when she was ten years old, and she became estranged from her playwright father. Before attending the Sorbonne in Paris, where she received a diploma in literature in 1962, she was educated at a variety of boarding schools, including Crofton Grange School. She graduated from the University of East Anglia with a B.A. in English studies in 1965. While a student there, she took classes with novelist Angus Wilson; later, she taught creative writing there herself (from 1988 to 1995). She also worked for two years as an elementary school teacher and for two years as an editor at the British Printing Corporation. In 1973 her first published work appeared: *The Fight for Freedom for Women*, a nonfiction work about the woman suffrage movement.

In 1971, she secretly married Jon Tremain, her college boyfriend, and they had one daughter, Eleanor, who was born in 1972. The couple divorced after five years. In 1982 Tremain married Jonathan Dudley, a theater director. That marriage also ended in divorce, and in 1992 Tremain began a longtime relationship with the well-known biographer Richard Holmes.

ANALYSIS

Rose Tremain is a historical novelist who latches on to, as one critic has put it, "unglamorous outsiders" for her protagonists. These characters invariably evoke great compassion from her readers. She couples these alienated characters with historical characters. For instance, in *Restoration*, the young, sensuous, but common doctor

Merivel becomes part of the court of Britain's King Charles II. In *Silence and Music*, the lovelorn musician Peter Claire plays his lute at the court of King Christian IV of Denmark.

Tremain's creative method, in conjunction with her elaborate descriptions of religious attitudes, medical practices, social customs, and so forth, helps bring the historical era in question to life. In addition, by destabilizing readers' assumptions, Tremain keeps them surprised—and thus fascinated. More than anything, she creates highly sensual, and sexual, characters who long for something or someone with great intensity but sadly, with little chance of ever achieving what they long for. For instance, in *Restoration*, Merivel longs for the king's mistress, the haughty Celia. Harriet, in *The Colour*, longs to build a life for herself in the wilds of New Zealand. In *Letter to Sister Benedicta*, Amanda longs desperately for her brother while her mother, Ruby, longs for reconciliation with both her children. In *Silence and Music*, the king longs for his boyhood friend and to hear once more an elusive piece of music before he dies.

In addition to compelling characters, Tremain uses fascinating settings such as New Zealand in *The Colour* and Denmark in *Silence and Music*, and different times, such as 1660 England in *Restoration*, to lure her readers into accepting and anticipating that anything can, and will, happen. Tremain also uses humor and irony to heighten readers' enjoyment of her novels. In *The Road Home*, the main character, Lev, forgets to turn off his cell phone at a musical performance, and when it rings, the orchestra conductor turns around to glare at him. Ironically, Lev is out of place, and the call is from his home in Eastern Europe, where he belongs and to which he returns in the end.

Perhaps in an effort to separate herself from the label of "historical novelist," Tremain has tended to set her later novels in more recent times. *The Road Home*, for instance, tells the story of modern-day immigrants from Eastern Europe and their integration into Western Europe.

LETTER TO SISTER BENEDICTA

The protagonist of Tremain's 1978 novel *Letter to Sister Benedicta* is Ruby Constad. At age fifty, Ruby feels lost and so begins an intermittent letter to a favorite nun she knew as a child in India, Sister Benedicta. The letter turns into a journal in which Ruby juxtaposes the happy time in her life when she knew the sister with her present enormously sad situation. It is the Christmas season, and Ruby's husband, Leon, a successful divorce lawyer whom she married against her family's wishes, lies in a nursing home recovering from a stroke. Ruby's daily visits to him are the focus of her life. Ruby and Leon's daughter remains out of touch, and their son has left Cambridge and gone missing. Ruby's only bit of company during this dreary holiday season is her husband's former partner, with whom she had an affair of sorts, and his new wife.

As Ruby continues her letter to Sister Benedicta (who is aptly named, as the book is indeed a request for benediction), we learn how dysfunctional Ruby's family really is. After ending an incestuous affair, her children have separated not only from each other but from their parents as well. Undoubtedly, Ruby is writing a letter to

Rose Tremain. (Getty Images)

a dead woman that will never be mailed, but invoking the spirit of Sister Benedicta enables her to achieve some modicum of serenity. The character of Ruby makes an appearance as one of the residents of the nursing home featured in Tremain's 2007 novel *The Road Home*.

RESTORATION

Set in London during the reign of England's flamboyant Charles II, *Restoration* tells the story of the bawdy Robert Merivel, an on-again, off-again medical student with a disregarded gift for medicine who comes to the king's court to provide treatment for Charles's favorite spaniel. While there, he meets and falls in love with Celia, the king's mistress. Soon, the king singles out the hard-drinking Merivel to marry Celia, as the king wants to be rid of her. He makes Merivel a lord and sets him up on his own estate. It would appear that Merivel is set for life, but he is rebuffed by the scorned Celia and sinks into depression.

The title of the novel refers to Charles II's restoration to the British throne, but it also refers to the spiritual restoration of the young Merivel, who has an uncanny gift for healing. When he once again takes up his medical practice, serving to help victims of the plague and subsequently as a physician in an insane asylum, Merivel meets a beautiful female patient, as different from Celia as can be imagined, and manages to fulfill his destiny and become a brilliant doctor.

THE COLOUR

Set in New Zealand during the 1860's gold rush, *The Colour* revolves around newlyweds Joseph and Harriet Blackstone, who emigrate from England to New Zealand. After they arrive, Harriet finds herself once more disheartened after Joseph takes off for the goldfields, leaving her in Christchurch with his mother, Lillian. Harriet feels angry because she has always dreamed of a challenge that would involve her physical strength and presence of mind and, after serving twelve years as a governess in England, she believed she had been given the opportunity to face such a challenge when she married Joseph and traveled to New Zealand. Now, however, she finds her new life just as frustrating as her old one, as she cares for her husband's mother, who does not like her.

After Joseph finds gold in a creek, he hides the discovery from his wife and mother, and when he hears of even better new goldfields on the other side of New Zealand, he abandons his family once again to chase the elusive "colour." Harriet decides to set out after the colour herself, however, and on the way she encounters Pare, a Maori nurse, and the stoic Chinese market-gardener Pao Yi, with whom she falls in deeply in love. The title of this novel refers to the term the gold miners use for the seductive gleam of gold, which they give up their sanity and many times their lives to chase.

MUSIC AND SILENCE

Music and Silence is set in the seventeenth century ruined Danish court of Christian IV, where the king is outraged over his financial losses and his wife's adulterous affair, which she takes no pains to cover up. Depressed, Christian recedes into dreams and the music provided by his royal orchestra, the members of which sit playing underneath the king's own warm *vinterstue* (winter room) in the castle's icy basement. The king seeks succor in music, but Queen Kristen simply cannot stand it. Peter Claire, a handsome young English musician hired to play the lute at Christian's court, arrives in Copenhagen in 1629. He attempts to disregard the cold and concentrates instead on the sublime music that rises through a series of tubes reminiscent, in an architectural sense, of a musical instrument. In the manner of a musical composition, Tremain interweaves throughout the novel other fascinating tales that support and enlighten the main story: the tale of Christian's miser mother, the tale of tragic young Bror, and the tale of Claire's romance with Emilia Tilsen, the queen's faithful lady-in-waiting.

Like the king, Claire, who suffers over the lost love of a beautiful Irish countess, is depressed. Claire reminds Christian of his lost boyhood friend, Bror, and the king imagines his new musician as an angel come to save him. The characters thus suffer from unrequited love, which remains the novel's major thematic construct. The masterful storyteller Tremain ends the novel on a happy musical note, however.

THE ROAD HOME

Loss, separation, and the desire to go home again interplay thematically in Tremain's *The Road Home*, which is set in present-day England. Forty-two-year-old Lev is a depressed Eastern European immigrant, an outsider forced to leave his village and travel by bus to London in search of a job to support his jewelry-maker mother and his five-year-old daughter, Maya. He has lost his wife, Marina, to leukemia, and the former lumberyard worker knows no one in London except another immigrant named Lydia, who befriended him on the bus. Barely able to make himself understood, Lev spends a few nights sleeping on the street before he manages to land a dishwashing job in a gourmet restaurant and begin a new life. Soon, hope replaces hopelessness as Lev works hard, sends money home, and falls in love with the pixieish assistant chef, Sophie. He becomes particularly fascinated with the dishes prepared at the restaurant, takes copious notes, and begins another job cooking at a nursing home.

Things could have continued favorably for Lev, who by the middle of the book has captured the reader's heart, but he bungles his new life when Sophie falls for an arrogant artist. After a drunken night on the street and a visit to the police station, Lev is fired from his job and has to find work on a farm. From another immigrant he learns that his home village is to be flooded as part of a national dam project. At this point, Lev somehow manages to shift his life into high gear—hope springs eternal—and he manages to slave away at two jobs, gain a legacy from a nursing-home patient he befriended, and open a restaurant back home in his own newly prospering country.

M. Casey Diana

OTHER MAJOR WORKS

SHORT FICTION: *The Colonel's Daughter, and Other Stories*, 1984; *The Garden of the Villa Mollini, and Other Stories*, 1987; *Evangelista's Fan, and Other Stories*, 1994; *Collected Short Stories*, 1996; *The Darkness of Wallis Simpson*, 2005.

PLAYS: *Mother's Day*, pr. 1980; *Yoga Class*, pr. 1981.

TELEPLAYS: *Halleluiah, Mary Plum*, 1979; *A Room for the Winter*, 1981; *Findings on a Late Afternoon*, 1981.

RADIO PLAYS: *The Wisest Fool*, 1976; *Blossom*, 1977; *Dark Green*, 1977; *Don't Be Cruel*, 1978; *Leavings*, 1978; *Down the Hill*, 1979; *Half Time*, 1980; *Temporary Shelter*, 1984; *The Kite Flyer*, 1989; *Music and Silence*, 1992; *Who Was Emily Davison?*, 1996; *The End of Love*, 1999; *One Night in Winter*, 2000.

NONFICTION: *The Fight for Freedom for Women*, 1973; *Stalin*, 1975.

CHILDREN'S LITERATURE: *Journey to the Volcano*, 1985.

BIBLIOGRAPHY

Field, Trevor. *Form and Function in the Diary Novel.* London: Macmillan, 1989. Discusses Tremain's *Letter to Sister Benedicta*, which Field refers to as a "borderline" diary novel, as it takes the form of an autobiographical letter.

Parker, Emma, "The Real Thing: Transsexuality and Manhood in Rose Tremain's *Sacred Country*." *Women: A Cultural Review* 18, no. 3 (Winter, 2007): 303-326. Scholarly article focuses on gender issues in Tremain's early novel *Sacred Country*, in which six-year-old Mary Ward discovers that she was meant to be a boy.

Rustin, Susanna. "Costume Dramatist." *The Guardian*, May 10, 2003. Interesting article provides information on Tremain's life and her various approaches to teaching as well as insights into her works. Also discusses her successful students.

Sceats, Sarah. "Appetite, Desire, and Belonging in the Novels of Rose Tremain." In *The Contemporary British Novel Since 1980*, edited by James Acheson and Sarah Ross. New York: Palgrave Macmillan, 2005. Discusses Tremain's major works of fiction, with a focus on the various kinds of desires that motivate her protagonists.

Tremain, Rose. "Tremain's Terrain." *History Today* 49, no. 10 (October, 1999): 62-63. Tremain reveals how her fascination with the seventeenth century was the key that unlocked the world of her acclaimed historical novels.

WILLIAM TREVOR

Born: Mitchelstown, county Cork, Ireland; May 24, 1928

Also known as: William Trevor Cox

PRINCIPAL LONG FICTION

A Standard of Behaviour, 1958
The Old Boys, 1964
The Boarding-House, 1965
The Love Department, 1966
Mrs. Eckdorf in O'Neil's Hotel, 1969
Miss Gomez and the Brethren, 1971
Elizabeth Alone, 1973
The Children of Dynmouth, 1976
Other People's Worlds, 1980
Fools of Fortune, 1983
Nights at the Alexandra, 1987
The Silence in the Garden, 1988
Juliet's Story, 1991
Two Lives, 1991
Felicia's Journey, 1994
Death in Summer, 1998
The Story of Lucy Gault, 2002
My House in Umbria, 2003

OTHER LITERARY FORMS

In addition to novels, William Trevor has written numerous short stories, many of which have appeared in collections such as *The Day We Got Drunk on Cake, and Other Stories* (1967), *Angels at the Ritz, and Other Stories* (1975), *The News from Ireland, and Other Stories* (1986), and *Outside Ireland: Selected Stories* (1995); his short fiction has also been published in *The New Yorker* and other periodicals. Most critics recognize Trevor as a master of both the short story and the novel. His works of nonfiction include his memoir *Excursions in the Real World* (1993), and he has also written many plays for the stage, radio, and television. Several of his television plays have been based on his short stories.

ACHIEVEMENTS

Considered one of the most important storytellers in the English-speaking world, William Trevor is a mem-ber of the Irish Academy of Letters. His books have won numerous awards: *The Children of Dynmouth*, *Fools of Fortune*, and *Felicia's Journey* each won the Whitbread Award; *The Silence in the Garden* won the *Yorkshire Post*'s Book of the Year Award; *Reading Turgenev* (a novella included in *Two Lives*) was short-listed for the Booker Prize; *My House in Umbria* (the other novella in-cluded in *Two Lives*) was short-listed for the Sunday Ex-press Prize; and *The Story of Lucy Gault* was short-listed for both the Booker Prize and the Whitbread Award. Trevor has received the O. Henry Award for four of his short stories: "Sacred Statues" (2003), "The Dress-maker's Child" (2006), "The Room" (2007), and "Folie à Deux" (2008). In 2008, he was awarded the Bob Hughes Lifetime Achievement Award in Irish Litera-ture. In addition, a bronze sculpture of Trevor's image by Liam Lavery and Eithne Ring was unveiled in his home-town, Mitchelstown, in 2004. Always aware of a moral vision, Trevor is known for his ability to combine this vi-sion with sometimes chilling stories, usually about the psychology of eccentrics and outcasts of society.

BIOGRAPHY

Born William Trevor Cox in Mitchelstown, county Cork, Trevor spent his childhood in provincial Ireland. After attending a number of Irish schools, and later Trin-ity College in Dublin, he began his career as an instructor and sculptor, teaching history and art in Northern Ireland and England. He married Jane Ryan in 1952, and in 1960 they moved to London, where Trevor worked as an ad-vertising copywriter. In describing this period of his life (1960-1965), he has noted the boredom he experienced as well as the rewards of the job: The company had given him a typewriter to work on, thus offering him the impe-tus to start writing stories.

Trevor then moved to Devon, England, to write full time in his home, an old mill surrounded by forty acres. Often described as an Anglo-Irish writer, Trevor actu-ally transcends that label, having once said that the ad-vantage of living in England is that "it is sometimes eas-ier to write about your own people from a foreign country," and having developed the pattern of spending half the year traveling in Italy or in Ticino, the nub of Switzerland that juts down into Italy, and visiting Ireland during the other half of the year.

ANALYSIS

William Trevor began to write fiction in his thirties and soon became one of the most revered and prolific writers in the English language. Influenced by the popular Irish writer James Joyce and the English writer Charles Dickens—writers from the two countries in which Trevor has lived—he is known for his lyrical and psychologically rich fiction, in which a moral vision shines through with unusual clarity. With a wry and often macabre sense of humor, he develops characters who are social outsiders and eccentrics, putting them into situations in which they must make decisions that irreversibly affect their lives and the lives of others. The story is always at the heart of Trevor's work, for he is a consummate narrator who weaves tales that capture readers in his fictional webs.

THE OLD BOYS

The Old Boys, Trevor's second novel, opens with the meeting of a group of "old boys," a committee of an alumni association of an English public school that is five hundred years old. As it is a tradition of the association that members do not serve on the committee until they are very senior and that all members of the committee during a two-year term of office should have been at the school at the same time, these individuals are indeed appropriately described as "old boys." This small group of men, all between seventy and seventy-five years old, includes Mr. Turtle, Mr. Nox, Mr. Swabey-Boyns, Mr. Jaraby, General Sanctuary, Sir George Ponders, Mr. Sold, and Mr. Cridley. United by their memories, jealousies, anecdotes, and dislikes, they are holding an important meeting to decide the next chairman of the Old Boys' Association. The setting is contemporary London.

Mr. Jaraby wants the job. Mr. Nox does not want Jaraby to have it, and to prevent him from getting the position, he hires a detective to watch Jaraby, whom he suspects of frequenting prostitutes, and then gets a prostitute to approach Jaraby. Meanwhile the other old boys meet, talk, and reminisce. A number of events complicate the election process, including a visit that the committee makes to the school for Old Boys Day, and Turtle dies

there. This death does not perturb the others, however, since they have become accustomed to the deaths of their old friends.

While the plot line of the novel is not completely unexpected—Jaraby is clearly an unpleasant character who gets what he deserves—the development of the characters is a rare accomplishment. Eccentric geriatrics, they offer Trevor the opportunity to explore old age with the skills that have become his trademarks: humor and compassion. The story is written largely in stylized dialogue, which some have criticized as artificial; however, it is consistent with the satiric tone of this novel as well as with its message about the persistence of smug, insular, superficial—and perhaps artificial—groups of old boys at every level of society and within every country.

THE CHILDREN OF DYNMOUTH

At the heart of *The Children of Dynmouth* is an aimless, sadistic fifteen-year-old named Timothy Gedge, a

William Trevor. (Getty Images)

virtual orphan who wanders about the seaside town of Dynmouth trying to connect himself with other people. In his desperate quest for connections, he goes to funerals, knocks on people's doors, and greets everyone he meets on the street. To fulfill his dream of participating in a talent show, and thus launching a career as a comic impersonator, he enlists the assistance of several people, all of whom he tries to blackmail: an aging homosexual whose marriage he almost destroys, an adulterer who has been having an affair with Timothy's mother, and a twelve-year-old boy and his stepsister.

Timothy is unmasked at the end of the novel, and he surrenders his hope of becoming a famous comedian. He does not surrender everything, however; instead, he takes on the fantasy of being the son of a couple more attractive than his own parents.

As in other Trevor novels, the characters are the focus of *The Children of Dynmouth*. United in a town that is a veritable failure, they likewise share another unity: a dislike of Timothy, whose menacing omnipresence is unnerving and ominous. Although nothing is neatly resolved at the conclusion of the novel, there is the suggestion of redemption insofar as the vicar's wife, unable to have a son, sees Timothy as that son. In his characteristic way, Trevor leaves a trail of memorable characters and unanswered questions, both developed with humor and compassion.

TWO LIVES

The title of *Two Lives*, which contains two novellas, seems straightforward and simple. In fact, this book does trace the lives of two women, both captives of their own lives and both attempting to find escape through literature. The first, *Reading Turgenev*, is a sorrowful love story about a woman trapped in Ireland; the second, *My House in Umbria*, is a kind of thriller about a woman trapped in Italy. Though different in style and setting, the two stories have thematic similarities, including the complexity of being human and the ways in which humanity can encourage or discourage love and life.

Mary Louise Quarry is the heroine of *Reading Turgenev*, which opens with the following understated description:

A woman, not yet fifty-seven, slight and seeming frail, eats carefully at a table in a corner. Her slices of but-

tered bread have been halved for her, her fried egg mashed, her bacon cut. . . . She's privileged, the others say, being permitted to occupy on her own the bare-topped table in the corner. She has her own salt and pepper.

This apparently "privileged" woman, who has been institutionalized for more than half her life, is preparing to leave the institution that has been both her confinement and her security. The authorities have decided that the patients currently in the institution will be better off in the community, and thus Mary Louise is facing a return to her husband, Elmer, and his two maiden sisters, Matilda and Rose. This trio has been getting along quite nicely without Mary Louise—just as they had before Elmer courted this unwanted intruder.

Moving back and forth in time, Trevor tells the story of Mary Louise Dallon, the twenty-one-year-old daughter of a poor Irish Protestant farmer, who tries to escape the boredom of country life by marrying tradesman Elmer Quarry, almost twice her age. He also tells the story of Mary Louise Quarry, the anguished wife whose husband is unable to consummate their marriage and whose sisters-in-law make daily life a living hell for her. Elmer retreats into alcoholism, and Mary Louise retreats into books. She enters into a chaste relationship with her invalid cousin Robert, who reads to her from the novels of nineteenth century Russian writer Ivan Turgenev. This dual relationship—with Robert and with Turgenev—allows her to escape the harsh reality of life with Elmer and his sisters. When Robert dies, Mary Louise plunges deep into herself and into literature, eventually to be institutionalized and, as described in the opening lines, eventually to be released. Past and present, as well as reality and fantasy, converge in Mary Louise's life until they create a blurry universe within which she survives.

Her counterpart in Italy and in *My House in Umbria* also deals with this blurry convergence and, like Mary Louise Quarry, holds on to literature as a ballast amid the storms of memory and reality. Emily Delahunty, also in her mid-fifties, has lived a life that is even more fantastic than the formulaic romances she has begun to write in her middle age. Sold at birth by her natural parents, she was sexually abused at an early age by her adoptive father, and eventually she becomes a prostitute in Africa, where she saves enough money to buy a villa in Italy and begin writing her novels. On a trip to Milan, she travels in a railway carriage in which a terrorist bomb has been planted. She is not harmed by the explosion, but nonetheless she is hurt in another way, for she develops writer's block, which prevents her from continuing her next novel, a work she has planned to call *Ceaseless Tears*.

Deciding to offer shelter to the other victims of the bombing, Emily also chooses to write about these survivors, intending to write about reality instead of romance. Just as the distinction between these two views of life is a literary blur, however, so it becomes ambiguous for Emily. As she narrates her story, and as she tries to write the stories of the others, she layers numerous scenes: from her past, her dreams, her romances, films, biblical stories, her fan mail from readers. The result is what she describes as the writer's challenge—and her own: "pieces of a jigsaw jumbled together on a table . . . that higgledy-piggledy mass of jagged shapes." Trying to assemble this mass, trying to write the story of her life and the lives around her, compels Emily to state what may be the moral of all of Trevor's fictions: "Survival's a complicated business."

The complications within these two novellas are testimony to Trevor's insistence that there are no neat resolutions to messy situations, no neat conclusions to fictions that resound with the complexities of human behavior. Even the obvious similarities between the novellas, including the focus on two middle-aged women who escape into literature, are deceptively complicated, for Trevor has said that he did not plan to write a book comprising a pair of novellas about two women. In his words, "They just seemed to belong together. They seemed instinctively to contain echoes and reflections of each other. Most things in art of any kind happen by accident, and this is a case in point." That two lives should intersect by accident, and that two novellas should complement each other by accident, is just one more mystery to add to the numerous other inexplicable dimensions of Trevor's fiction in general and *Two Lives* in particular.

DEATH IN SUMMER

Three deaths occur in the summer of *Death in Summer*. Like many of Trevor's novels, including *Felicia's*

Journey, which immediately precedes *Death in Summer*, this novel reads like a thriller, a mystery story that begins with one premature demise and ends with another. In between, Trevor explores the complex psychology of characters, some of whom live on the fringes of society, others of whom appear to be privileged but who are nonetheless also disconnected internally and externally.

At the heart of *Death in Summer* is Thaddeus Davenant, an emotional cripple who is scarred by a lonely childhood. His short-lived marriage was for money, and it leaves him with a daughter to care for, a mother-in-law who moves in to help with this care, and potential nannies who apply for a position within the household. One rejected applicant, Pettie, reveals herself as a person as troubled and lonely as Thaddeus, and their two social classes—his the privileged elite and hers the economically deprived—clash and collide. This collision course is complicated by still other factors: an older woman with whom Thaddeus had a brief affair and who reenters his life, seeking financial help; the kidnapping of Thaddeus's daughter; and minor characters who are intriguing and critical to the ultimate outcome of the novel.

The novel's ending does not provide solutions to all the mysteries in this fiction. Indeed, Trevor concludes this book characteristically—with unanswered questions as chilling as the events he chronicles. Like Emily Delahunty in *My House in Umbria*, Thaddeus Davenant and the other survivors in *Death in Summer* learn that survival is a complicated business, one that is dependent on connections with others while at the same time threatened by those connections.

THE STORY OF LUCY GAULT

In the heartrending novel *The Story of Lucy Gault* Trevor recounts the tale of a young girl whose Protestant family is forced to leave turbulent Catholic Ireland in 1921. Lahardane is the name of the house where the eight-year-old Lucy, an only child, lives in edenic happiness with her adoring mother and British army captain father until one night when an attempt is made to burn it down. Lucy does not want to leave her idyllic life next to the sea, so before moving day she runs away in an effort to make her parents change their minds. A piece of Lucy's clothing is found on the beach, and her heartbroken parents, believing Lucy to be dead, leave Ireland for the Continent in the hope of forgetting the past.

Lucy is not dead, however. After breaking her leg, she manages to crawl to a derelict cottage and is almost dead when a servant discovers her and returns her to Lahardane. Now a pariah in the village, Lucy spends her lonely childhood in the company of childless servants, waiting for her parents to return. Meanwhile, the boy who attempted to set the fire that caused Lucy's parents to want to leave Ireland is filled with guilt and sinks into madness. Unable even to talk about the life they lived in Ireland, Lucy's parents move disconsolately from place to place, attempting to forget their daughter. As in many of Trevor's other novels, the characters go to grave lengths to avoid the truth and manage, despite unfathomable odds, to achieve forgiveness.

Marjorie Smelstor
Updated by M. Casey Diana

OTHER MAJOR WORKS

SHORT FICTION: *The Day We Got Drunk on Cake, and Other Stories*, 1967; *The Ballroom of Romance, and Other Stories*, 1972; *The Last Lunch of the Season*, 1973; *Angels at the Ritz, and Other Stories*, 1975; *Lovers of Their Time, and Other Stories*, 1978; *Beyond the Pale, and Other Stories*, 1981; *The Stories of William Trevor*, 1983; *The News from Ireland, and Other Stories*, 1986; *Family Sins, and Other Stories*, 1990; *Collected Stories*, 1992; *Ireland: Selected Stories*, 1995; *Marrying Damian*, 1995 (limited edition); *Outside Ireland: Selected Stories*, 1995; *After Rain*, 1996; *The Hill Bachelors*, 2000; *A Bit on the Side*, 2004; *The Dressmaker's Child*, 2005; *Cheating at Canasta*, 2007.

PLAYS: *The Elephant's Foot*, pr. 1965; *The Girl*, pr. 1967 (televised), pr., pb. 1968 (staged); *A Night Mrs. da Tanka*, pr. 1968 (televised), pr., pb. 1972 (staged); *Going Home*, pr. 1970 (radio play), pr., pb. 1972 (staged); *The Old Boys*, pr., pb. 1971; *A Perfect Relationship*, pr. 1973; *Marriages*, pr. 1973; *The Fifty-seventh Saturday*, pr. 1973; *Scenes from an Album*, pr. 1975 (radio play), pr., pb. 1981 (staged).

RADIO PLAYS: *Beyond the Pale*, 1980; *Autumn Sunshine*, 1982.

NONFICTION: *A Writer's Ireland: Landscape in Literature*, 1984; *Excursions in the Real World*, 1993.

EDITED TEXT: *The Oxford Book of Irish Short Stories*, 1989.

BIBLIOGRAPHY

Bloom, Jonathan. *The Art of Revision in the Short Stories of V. S. Pritchett and William Trevor*. New York: Palgrave Macmillan, 2006. Focuses on Trevor's short fiction (and that of Pritchett) but provides fascinating insights into Trevor's method of transforming actual events and people into fiction and the critical role of fantasy in all of Trevor's fiction.

Bonaccorso, Richard. "William Trevor's Martyrs for Truth." *Studies in Short Fiction* 34 (Winter, 1997): 113-118. Discusses two types of Trevor characters: those who try to evade the truth and those who gravitate, often in spite of themselves, toward it. Argues that the best indicators of the consistency of Trevor's moral vision may be his significant minority, those characters who find themselves pursuing rather than fleeing truth.

Fitzgerald-Hoyt, Mary. *William Trevor: Re-imagining Ireland*. Dublin: Liffey Press, 2003. Examines Trevor's fiction in the light of the great social and economic changes that have taken place in Ireland, including its growing cultural diversity. Discusses all of Trevor's major works, including *The Story of Lucy Gault*.

MacKenna, Dolores. *William Trevor: The Writer and His Work*. Dublin: New Island, 1999. Offers interesting biographical details that help explain the influences on Trevor's fiction. Includes bibliography and index.

Morrison, Kristin. *William Trevor*. New York: Twayne, 1993. Presents a good general introduction to Trevor's work, focusing on a conceptual "system of correspondences" often manifested in the fiction by a rhetorical strategy of "significant simultaneity" and a central metaphor of the Edenic garden. Examines the overall unity of Trevor's fiction through close readings of his major works.

Schirmer, Gregory A. *William Trevor: A Study in His Fiction*. New York: Routledge, 1990. Excellent study, one of the first book-length examinations of Trevor's fictional writings, notes the tension in Trevor's works between morality and the elements in contemporary society that make morality almost an impossibility, with lonely alienation the result. Discusses Trevor as an outsider, both in Ireland and in England. Includes bibliographical references.

ANTHONY TROLLOPE

Born: London, England; April 24, 1815
Died: London, England; December 6, 1882

PRINCIPAL LONG FICTION

The Macdermots of Ballycloran, 1847
The Kellys and the O'Kellys, 1848
The Warden, 1855
Barchester Towers, 1857
Doctor Thorne, 1858
The Three Clerks, 1858
The Bertrams, 1859
Castle Richmond, 1860
Framley Parsonage, 1860-1861 (serial), 1861
   (book)
Orley Farm, 1861-1862 (serial), 1862 (book)
The Small House at Allington, 1862-1864
   (serial), 1864 (book)
Rachel Ray, 1863
Can You Forgive Her?, 1864-1865 (serial), 1864,
   1865 (book)
Miss Mackenzie, 1865
The Belton Estate, 1865-1866 (serial), 1866
   (book)
The Claverings, 1866-1867 (serial), 1867 (book)
The Last Chronicle of Barset, 1867
Phineas Finn, the Irish Member, 1867-1869
   (serial), 1869 (book)
He Knew He Was Right, 1868-1869 (serial), 1869
   (book)
The Vicar of Bulhampton, 1869-1870 (serial),
   1870 (book)
The Eustace Diamonds, 1871-1873 (serial), 1872
   (book)
Phineas Redux, 1873-1874 (serial), 1875 (book)
The Way We Live Now, 1874-1875 (serial), 1875
   (book)
The Prime Minister, 1875-1876 (serial), 1876
   (book)
The American Senator, 1876-1877 (serial), 1877
   (book)
Is He Popenjoy?, 1877-1878 (serial), 1878 (book)
John Caldigate, 1878-1879 (serial), 1879 (book)

The Duke's Children, 1879-1880 (serial), 1880
   (book)
Dr. Wortle's School, 1880
Ayala's Angel, 1881
The Fixed Period, 1881-1882 (serial), 1882 (book)
The Landleaguers, 1882-1883 (serial), 1883
   (book)
Mr. Scarborough's Family, 1882-1883 (serial),
   1883 (book)

OTHER LITERARY FORMS

The novels of Anthony Trollope (TRAHL-uhp) were frequently first published in serialized form in various periodicals such as the *Cornhill Magazine* and *The Fortnightly Review*. They appeared subsequently in a two- or three-volume format. Trollope wrote several books of cultural reportage that were more than mere travelogues: *The West Indies* (1859), *North America* (1862), *Australia and New Zealand* (1873), and *South Africa* (1878), along with the more impressionistic *Travelling Sketches* (1865-1866). Three volumes of short stories appeared: *Lotta Schmidt, and Other Stories* (1867), *An Editor's Tales* (1870), and *Why Frau Frohmann Raised Her Prices, and Other Stories* (1882). He wrote sketches of clerical men in *Clergymen of the Church of England* (1865-1866) and detailed biographies of William Makepeace Thackeray, a longtime friend (*Thackeray*, 1879), and Lord Palmerston, the prominent politician (*Lord Palmerston*, 1882). His *Autobiography* appeared posthumously in 1883. He tried his hand at classical translation in an edition of *The Commentaries of Caesar* (1870). Many of Trollope's letters were collected in a 1951 volume edited by Bradford A. Booth, but a number of complete and fragmentary letters remain unpublished at Princeton University.

ACHIEVEMENTS

Anthony Trollope was acknowledged during his lifetime as a prominent though not necessarily a weighty or enduring writer. He wished to entertain and he did so, at least until the late 1860's, when *He Knew He Was Right* turned out to be a failure. His posthumous reputation was harmed by his *Autobiography*, which claimed that he wrote automatically, that his characters were imitations of commonly observed types, that he transcribed reality without much aesthetic control, and that he forced his production by his methodical habits of composition whatever the circumstances. These admissions brought upon him the wrath of the next generation of writers in the 1880's and 1890's who were imbued with more aesthetic doctrines of carefully contrived and consistent viewpoints, detailed representation of interior states, a conscious interplay of ideas, and a complex style to suit a more complex method of storytelling.

Later, Trollope suffered from those who deemed him a pedestrian realist padding his work with creaking plots, flat characters, prosaic situations, and dull prose. He was, and still is for much of the public, the novelist of a single work, *Barchester Towers*, but other writers and critics have not forgiven him for writing more than thirty novels and setting himself a goal to exceed in quantity if not in quality. Despite what seems to be a simple theory of fiction—the writer tries as closely as possible to make the reader's experience approximate his own, to make his characters and events appear to parallel actual life—Trollope was more sophisticated than many have allowed.

According to scholar Walter Kendrick, before *He Knew He Was Right*, Trollope's works do not distinguish inner thought from outer events, consciousness is presented chronologically, and characters, at least by implication, appear without authorial intervention. After *He Knew He Was Right*, character becomes "a zone of space on a canvas" with changes of age, feeling, and appearance even while outside the narrative. Various linear plots create a spatial unity for the reader, and they become a mosaic on which the character exists. Fiction writing becomes a subject in the novel, and the characters are a warning against efforts to define their existence with the narrative. This view sees the characters as a complex interplay between narrative and reader. Nathaniel Hawthorne had a very different view of Trollope, equating him to a giant hewing a great lump out of the earth as the earth's inhabitants go about the business of putting it under a glass case. This comment leads, unfortunately, in the direction of Henry James's evaluation, made after Trollope's death, that Trollope had "a great

deliberate apprehension of the real" but that his "great fecundity is gross and importunate."

Trollope is a mixture of several kinds of writer, sometimes realistic in the sociological way of Honoré de Balzac, analyzing class and caste, sometimes a comedian of manners and mores like Henry Fielding, at times a sentimental melodramatist like Charles Dickens, fairly often an ironist deliberately breaking fictional illusions like Thackeray, often introspective if not as equally learned as George Eliot, and periodically a brilliant chronicler of dementia like Joseph Conrad. This mixture is what creates havoc with critical response. Trollope is a master of convincing and accurate dialogue, good at retrospective interior analysis, and gifted with varieties of ironic voices. The building of his reputation, aided by Michael Sadleir's biography in the 1920's, was materially assisted by *The Trollopian* (now *Nineteenth-Century Literature*), a journal devoted to studies of his novels, further work by scholars, such as Ruth apRoberts, Robert M. Polhemus, and James R. Kincaid, and new critical techniques, which have given Trollope his present reputation as a leading English novelist.

BIOGRAPHY

Anthony Trollope, born on April 24, 1815, in London, seems to have owed his boisterous energy, booming voice, quarrelsome touchiness, and reticent sensitivity to a childhood of offhanded upbringing. C. P. Snow refers to him as "weighed down by 20 years of neglect and humiliation." His father was a tactless and impractical barrister who had pretensions about being a landowner in Harrow. There, he established his family in an elegant though quickly declining farm, Julians, later the model for the experimental Orley Farm in the novel of that name. Trollope's mother, Frances, was the driving force of the family; she was closer to Trollope's oldest brother, Tom, than to Anthony: Anthony received neither much encouragement nor much regular affection from her. After starting his education at Sunbury School, with a brief stint at Harrow, Anthony was sent to Winchester, his father's old school, for three years. In 1827, the family was forced to move into a smaller house in Harrow for financial reasons.

Meanwhile, his mother made the acquaintance of a zealous utopian reformer, Fanny Wright, and went with her and three of her children—Henry, Cecilia, and Emily—to the United States. Their experiences there border on black comedy. Among other misfortunes, Frances, without past experience or common sense, started a fancy emporium or bazaar in Cincinnati; the building evolved into a grand structure modeled on an Egyptian temple. The enterprise only succeeded in making the family penniless. Through the efforts of a painter friend, her husband, and son Tom, they managed to piecemeal their way home to England.

Anthony was removed from Winchester in 1830, which deprived him of the chance to enter Oxford University, from which he might have entered into the clergy, the usual course at that time. He returned as a day student to Harrow School, where the intense and entrenched snobbery made the shabby boy the butt of ridicule and persecution, and perhaps began his lifelong pattern of irritability. Also at that time, Trollope's father sank into petty miserliness and self-pitying moroseness, becoming more obsessively preoccupied with his scholarly work, an ecclesiastical encyclopedia.

The success of Frances's *Domestic Manners of the Americans* (1832), a book adversely critical of American society, temporarily kept the family from bankruptcy, but her husband's financial mismanagement created more debts. To prevent his arrest for bankruptcy in 1834, the family, without Anthony, went to Bruges, Belgium. Any possible happiness they might have found was destroyed by tuberculosis, which killed Anthony's father, brother Henry, and sister Emily between 1834 and 1836. Frances Trollope was obviously too occupied with nursing to pay much attention to Anthony, but she did get him a tutoring position in Belgium for a short time. He returned to England, where he survived in squalid lodgings in Marylebone, London, at a clerk's job in the main post office for seven years. At age twenty-six, he got the chance that changed his life, obtaining the post of deputy surveyor, the overseer of mail service, in western Ireland.

At Banaghar, he found a comfortable social milieu for the first time, though his manner with carriers and postmasters was brusque and his temper was at times violent. Trollope became a man jovial with companions, truculent with superiors, bullying with inferiors, and tender with close friends and family. In 1842, he married Rose Heseltine, an Anglo-Irish woman. Her

Anthony Trollope. (Library of Congress)

bank-manager father, like one of Trollope's own shady characters, was an embezzler. A trusted partner, Rose handled Trollope's financial affairs, edited his manuscripts, and accompanied him on his journeys around the world. The portraits of solid, sensible, and compassionate wives and mothers found throughout his work, such as Lady Staveley in *Orley Farm*, suggest the type of woman Trollope had found in Rose.

Irish scenery and politics, and the models of his mother and his brother, Tom, led Trollope to his own fiction writing. Thus, not coincidentally, his first two novels have an Irish theme. In these years, Trollope also began rearing a family, two sons. Henceforth, Trollope's career ran on a dual path, pursuing his duties for the postal service and his writing.

Posted to southwest England in 1851 to correct faults in rural delivery, Trollope and his family led a roving existence for three years until he became his own boss as full surveyor in Belfast, at age thirty-nine. The experience of sleepy country towns and a current topic—the Anglican Church's misuse of endowed charity funds to create sizable incomes for administrators—resulted in the writing of *The Warden*, finished in Belfast and published in 1855; it was his first major success. When Trollope moved his family to Dublin, he established a daily routine of writing. The successor to *The Warden*, *Barchester Towers*, his best-known novel, is a social comedy in the eighteenth century mock-heroic vein of Henry Fielding or Oliver Goldsmith.

During a visit to see his mother and brother in Italy, Trollope met a young American woman, Kate Field, and began a long and close friendship, mostly carried out by correspondence. C. P. Snow thinks that Trollope was impressed by the independent and self-assertive woman, who was rather unlike English women. Intrigued by Kate's advocacy of female freedom, in *Orley Farm*, Trollope presents a woman who affronts social and moral conventions by an act of forgery to save the inheritance of her infant son. The motivation is a bit slick, but the fact that the resolute heroine succeeds against a determined male antagonist suggests that Kate's independence was sympathetically perceived.

Trollope went to North America during the early years of the American Civil War (1861-1862), a trip that resulted in a travel book. Like his mother's work, the book took a negative stance toward American institutions. He then published, among others, *Rachel Ray*, *The Last Chronicle of Barset*, and *The Claverings*, which gained Trollope his biggest sales price ever. His works were also being serialized in various periodicals, such as *The Fortnightly Review*. It became obvious, however, that Trollope's continued output led him to repeat themes and recycle characters.

Immersed as he was in writing and somewhat resentful of his position at the post office, Trollope resigned in October, 1867, after receiving the offer of the editorship of a new journal, *St. Paul's Magazine*. He continued to do some work on behalf of the post office, however; he went to Washington, D.C., to negotiate a postal treaty in 1868. Trollope ran *St. Paul's Magazine* for three years before it went under financially. He was not temperamentally suited to deal with authors.

In his own writing, Trollope tended, as Walter Kendrick has noted, to turn toward more sensational materials that other authors had discarded, but he was also experimenting in the psychological novel. In *He Knew He Was Right*, Trollope treats the subject of insanity and he presents a fascinating study of psychosis. Ruth

apRoberts has praised the novel for its economy and the supporting relationships among its closely knit characters. Trollope's work began to command less popular attention, however, and he increasingly turned to the political world. He created Phineas Finn, an Anglo-Irish politician, who appears in the novel of that name in 1869 and reappears in *Phineas Redux*, part of the loose series sometimes referred to as the Palliser novels. Trollope, however, did not give up what is really his chief subject: conflict between the sexes.

In 1871, having sold Waltham House and given up his editorship, Trollope and his wife embarked on an eighteen-month visit to New Zealand and a stay with their son, Fred, a relatively unprosperous sheep-farmer in Australia. Trollope continued to write during their stay in the primitive sheep-station. A travel commentary and materials for *John Caldigate* were the result of the voyage, as well as further work on the novel *The Eustace Diamonds*. The Trollopes then settled in London, where he wrote on the current topic of "the condition of England" in *The Way We Live Now* and *The Prime Minister*. Trollope presented his skeptical views about the ability of a democratic society to govern itself effectively.

The final stage of Trollope's life was a restless one in his sixties. He took another trip to Australia for eight months in 1875, returning through the United States and meeting with Kate Field. Then, he immediately went to South Africa to inspect the Boer territory with the encroaching British settlement based on gold and diamond exploitation. The Trollopes again returned to the land by moving into a refined farmhouse at Hartung, near Hastings, where Trollope worked on his autobiography. Along with other fiction, he wrote a mystery novel, *Mr. Scarborough's Family*, which was serialized before his death but published posthumously in 1883. Farm living aggravated Trollope's asthma and thus drained his energy, causing him to return to London. He was enjoying club life, dinners, and letters to his son, Henry, who was also a writer, when Trollope suffered a sudden stroke in the fall of 1882 that left him paralyzed. A month later, on December 6, 1882, he died, at the age of sixty-seven.

ANALYSIS

Twentieth century criticism of Anthony Trollope acknowledged his affinity with comic satirists of the eighteenth century, and this affinity is reflected in his best-known work, *Barchester Towers*. There are two distinct worlds in the novel: that of London vanity, represented by Mr. Slope, the London preacher who comes to Barchester as the protégé of Mrs. Proudie; and that of the smaller, conservative rural world, represented by Arch-deacon Grantly of Barchester Cathedral, who opposes Mr. Slope with "high and dry" Anglicanism. At the end, Slope is rejected but so is the siren of the comic interlude, Signora Madeleine Vesey Neroni, daughter of the gentlemanly but parasitic, self-indulgent Dr. Vesey Stanhope, canon of the cathedral.

BARCHESTER TOWERS

The novel is concerned with the pursuit of Eleanor Bold, a young prosperous widow and daughter of Mr. Harding, by Obadiah Slope, a brash and unctuous social climber. The newly vacant position of warden provokes a struggle between the Grantly forces and the Proudie forces (including Mr. Slope), with Mrs. Proudie at the head. In this strand of the plot, the mock-heroic or mock-epic combat parodies the Miltonic epic tradition, with Grantly and his supporters as the rebel angels struggling against the tyrant Mrs. Proudie, with Slope as a kind of fallen angel. Slope is first supported by Mrs. Proudie in his efforts to prevent the return of the vacant post to Harding, but Slope, in his effort to attain favor with Eleanor Bold, eventually gets the position for Harding.

Slope is emasculated by Signora Neroni, who trans-fixes him with her bright eyes and silvery laughter during rural games and festivities at Ullathorne, the ancient seat of the Thornes and center of a static pastoral world. Seduced by her witchery, he is humiliated by this demo-niac Eve and defeated by the godlike rebuff of Eleanor, who slaps his face as he presses his suit upon her. Further, he incurs the wrath of his patroness, Mrs. Proudie, with his attentiveness to Signora Neroni, who, although crippled, rules from a couch where she resides in state like Cleopatra. In this world of sham battles, Grantly celebrates his triumph, including a dean's position for Mr. Harding in a solemn conclave of the clergy.

The disputants in these mock exercises practice their feints around innocent third parties: Bishop Proudie between Slope and Mrs. Proudie; Quiverful, the other candidate for the wardenship, a pathetically comic father of numerous children, between his determined wife and

Slope; and Harding between Slope and Grantly. In this formally ordered structure, it is appropriate that Eleanor and Frances Arabin, the naïve Oxford academician, be matched by Miss Thorne, reaffirming the power of the old order, yet still contending with Proudies. The marriage of Eleanor and Arabin asserts the two worlds, old and new, country and city, innocent and corrupt.

The novel has a rich galaxy of minor characters. For example, there is Bertie Stanhope, the dilettante sculptor, who is pressed into proposing to Eleanor, but he undermines his own courtship by the candid admission of his motives; Mr. Harding, the unwilling tool of both Slope and Grantly, who takes such delight in the cathedral music that he mechanically saws an imaginary cello during moments of partisan plots and counterplots; and Mrs. Quiverful, who functions like a wailing chorus in a Greek tragedy, piteously reminding the world and Mrs. Proudie of the cruel difficulties of pinched means and a large family. Although Trollope did write important novels on more serious themes, *Barchester Towers* remains his best known, with its effective comic scenes, the balletlike entrances and exits, the lively irony, and the mock-heroic bathos. The orchestration of speaking styles ranging from the pomposity of the Archdeacon to the vacuity of Bertie Stanhope is another example of the buoyancy and playful wit that Trollope achieved only intermittently thereafter.

ORLEY FARM

Orley Farm was written during Trollope's middle period. Its central situation revolves around the plight of Lady Mason, the second wife of a rich man, who, twenty years earlier, forged a codicil to her dying husband's will so that it leaves Orley Farm, her sole economic support, to her and her young child, Lucius. The possession of the farm has become a matter of regret, as the suspicions of the legitimate heir, Joseph Mason, otherwise the inheritor of considerable wealth, eventuate in a trial to break the will. The effort fails only because Lady Mason commits perjury. Using the omniscient viewpoint, Trollope shows both her guilt and her anguish in trying to provide security for her infant son. Lucius, as the novel opens, is a proud, priggish young man given to notions of scientifically reforming agricultural practice; he is well educated, theoretical, and self-righteous.

The novel's unusual perspective poses two main

themes: first, how justice can be accomplished, and second, whether justice can actually be achieved. In setting human rights against legal rights, Trollope portrays Lady Mason's crime in the light of vested interests and the selfish motives of various people. Like C. P. Snow in a novel such as *The Masters* (1951), Trollope displays in *Orley Farm* an abstract ideal distorted and transformed by human emotions, calculations, and egotism. Joseph Mason is more concerned with defeating Lady Mason than with enjoying the actual property; Sir Peregrine Orme, a highly respected landowner, proposes marriage to Lady Mason in order to extend the protection of his name, but even he is forced to realize the stain on his honor if the truth should come out, and after Lady Mason refuses his offer, he, having been told the damning truth, keeps his promise to support her in her new trial. Another perspective is provided through Mr. Dockwrath, the country lawyer who discovers the evidence that necessitates the new trial and hopes it will prove lucrative and will enhance his legal reputation. Lady Mason's solicitor, Mr. Furnival, carefully avoids definite knowledge of her guilt, though he suspects it, while also wishing she were proven guilty so that he might forgive her with pleasure. A less selfish attitude is seen in Edith Orme, Sir Peregrine's widowed daughter-in-law, who recognizes with compassion the necessity for Lady Mason's crime and the suffering it has entailed for her.

Trollope reveals some of his other typical thematic concerns in the subplots of *Orley Farm*. He explores various attitudes toward marriage and money in the romances of Peregrine, Jr., Lucius Mason, and Felix Graham, a poor barrister, with a variety of modern young women. The women's responses to the gentlemen's advances run from prudent calculation of worldly advantages to prudent reticence in acknowledging love until family wisdom approves it. Also, Trollope's impulses toward indulgence of children are exemplified in Lord and Lady Staveley, who, having made their way without worldly advantages, are willing to offer the same chance to their children by permitting the engagement of a daughter to Felix Graham, whose success has been impeded by his honesty. Trollope's conservatism is revealed through the reluctance of these young people to avow their love until they have consent from the Staveleys.

With regard to the central theme of moral and legal justice, purely through the oratorical skills of the trial lawyer, Lady Mason is found innocent of perjury, a finding wholly incorrect. The trial frees the guilty, turns the truthful into villains, makes the innocent bear the burden of deceit, challenges the loyalty of lawyers, and implicates the idealists' posturings. The system has turned Lady Mason's desperate chicanery into heroism. It is somewhat anticlimactic that Trollope has the pure Edith Orme take Lady Mason to her heart and, from a sense of Christian charity, refuse to render judgment against her.

Meanwhile, Lady Mason's greatest trial has been alienation from Lucius, who, unaware of her guilt, has attempted vigorous countermeasures to defend her honor rather than respecting her dignified silence. His discovery of the truth cuts deeply into his priggish pride, destroys his dreams of becoming a gentleman-farmer, and makes him restore the farm to Joseph Mason before departing abroad with his mother. Again, Trollope makes an ambivalent statement through this conclusion. Although forgiveness implies repentance and restitution, Lady Mason has not been, at least in public, repentant, and the restitution is as much a matter of pride as of justice. The effect is a tacit denial of Lady Mason's innocence and thus the aborting of the whole effort to save her reputation.

CAN YOU FORGIVE HER?

If the power of money, or the distortions of human choice and desire that money brings, is Trollope's major concern, the warfare of the sexes and the frustrations that warfare brings are secondary themes in his novels. *Can You Forgive Her?*, the first of the Palliser series—which includes *Phineas Finn*, *Phineas Redux*, and *The Prime Minister*, each grounded in politics—raises the issue of what sort of love a woman wishes in marriage or indeed whether marriage is a suitable institution. The novel presents the case of Alice Vavasour, a "new woman" who does not know what she wants in life but resents the demands of social propriety. She especially resents the expectation that she accept the marriage proposal of John Grey, whom she really does love, merely because everyone knows him to be a suitable partner. Her cousin, the heiress Lady Glencora McCluskie, has married Plantagenet Palliser, the dull younger son of a ducal family, to support his Liberal political career with her money;

but she has fallen in love with the handsome Burgo Fitzgerald, an unconventional, ruinous, yet passionate charmer. Alice reinstitutes her former affection for her cousin George Vavasour, another charmingly irresponsible man who needs her money to campaign to keep his seat in Parliament. For Alice, the masculine excitement of politics makes George attractive, although she honestly admits his desire for her money.

The novel has low-comedy relief in Alice's aunt, Arabella Greenow, and her two suitors, a grocer with money and a retired military officer without it. Arabella means to have her own way, giving her lovers only as much liberty as she desires, choosing the officer because of "a sniff of the rocks and the valleys" about him. The comedy underscores the desire of Alice and Glencora, who, if they had a choice, would put themselves at the mercy of weak men.

In a melodramatic turn of the main plot, George knocks down his sister, Kate, for refusing to assist him in overturning their grandfather's will, which had left all the family property to her. This turn of the plot demonstrates, through George's furious masculine rage, the falsity of the normal economic subjugation of women, which has been reversed in Kate's case. Arabella Greenow, for her part, is also financially independent and can bargain her way into a satisfactorily romantic liaison balancing "rocks and valleys" against "bread and cheese."

Glencora, aware of being sold into matrimony, almost runs off with Burgo but is dissuaded at the last minute by the vigilance of Alice, who makes clear to Plantagenet the temptation he has given to his wife by his conduct. In an improbable reversal that displays Trollope's own romanticism, Plantagenet sacrifices his political hopes for a cabinet appointment in order to take her away from the scenes of her misery after she has confessed her infatuation. Indeed, he is even willing to provide Burgo, who becomes a frequenter of gambling tables, with an allowance at her behest when they encounter him abroad.

Plantagenet can make a sacrifice for Glencora because he has money and social position; George Vavasour, by contrast, is defeated in politics and exiled for lack of money. John Grey, meanwhile, has interposed himself in Alice's arrangement with George so that her

fortune is not at stake. This conduct, chivalrous in one sense, paternalistic in another, results in George's challenging him to a duel. The Victorian world is not that of Regency rakes, however, and George's blustering challenge is physically rebuffed, and he is sent away degraded. Alice finally accepts John Grey in a contrite mood. Although Grey has kindly intentions, Alice's undefined longings for autonomy anticipate those Henrik Ibsen made memorable through Nora Helmer in *Et dukkehjem* (1879; *A Doll's House*, 1880), where Nora sacrifices love in the effort to mold her own destiny.

If the future of his heroines seems to lie within conventional marital arrangements or respectable spinsterhood secured by inherited money, Trollope's questioning title for the novel seems to turn the issue of feminine aspiration somewhat ambivalently to the reader. He has shown women challenging the decorum of prudent emotions and affections based on money, but only the ungenteel Mrs. Greenow succeeds in mastering her destiny through financial manipulation.

THE EUSTACE DIAMONDS

In *The Eustace Diamonds*, Trollope shows the psychologically damaging effects of survival in an upperclass and aristocratic hierarchy, a society that channels affections and loyalties in terms of property and money, where people struggle for ascendancy, domination, and power while subscribing to Romantic illusions of unfettered expression and creative self-development. The narrator ironically undercuts the Romantic pretensions as the novel delineates the unrealistic strategies of men and women coping with the moral corruption of social ambition. They seek security, status, prestige, and elegance while evincing pretentiousness, snobbery, envy, and parasitism. Trollope takes an anarchic pleasure in those egotistical characters who subvert institutions by undermining the rules of conduct, stretching them to the point of fatuity.

In the novel, Lizzie Eustace appropriates the diamonds without specific authority from her late husband, Sir Florian, and uses them as weapons against the respectable family lawyer, Mr. Camperdown, and the man she intends as her second husband, the morally honorable Lord Fawn. The diamonds become a symbol of Lizzie's inner rage against the world, a rage arising from self-doubt prompted by the excessive demands of her own idealized views of herself. While denying that ownership of the necklace gives her any pleasure, Lizzie simultaneously insists that she will throw the diamonds away while guarding them zealously. When the box in which she ostentatiously houses them is stolen, Lizzie claims that the necklace has been stolen as well. The lie is psychologically predictable. The diamonds exemplify her attitudes toward herself, toward Lord Fawn whom she despises for his complete disdain of the diamonds, and toward Frank Greystock, her champion before the world, whom she has lured away from his serious attentions to Lucy Morris. The supposed theft is Lizzie's symbolic punishment for a guilt that will be lessened if the diamonds are believed stolen, but it is also an aggrandizement of her own self-esteem since secretly she knows they are still in her possession. The diamonds, however, are stolen in a second robbery, which ends Lizzie's control of the situation.

Lizzie's desire for social domination gains dimension through the narrator's ironic moral judgment and through the close-ups of the omniscient viewpoint that reveal her own rationalizations and fears. Seeking support, Lizzie confesses to Lord George, hoping that he will be cynically brutal, but instead she receives his weak acknowledgment of her supposed cunning. When the police discover the truth, Lizzie prefers the illusion of submitting to the police administrator to the reality of confronting her own self-destructive behavior. Lizzie then tries desperately to reestablish control by triumphing over someone: She reproaches Mrs. Carbuncle, her friend; breaks her engagement with Lord Fawn, ignoring his earlier efforts to end the relationship and pretending to be heartlessly jilted; offers herself to Lord George, who also refuses her; and finally bids for the attentions of Frank Greystock through his need for money, yet Frank is simply provoked into promising he will abandon her utterly if she persists.

Yielding to a fantasy logic, Lizzie entertains a marriage proposal from Mr. Emilius, an impudent and sanctimonious popular preacher whom she had once refused. She deliberately accepts him knowing that he is a fraud and admitting that his bogus qualities attract her. Lizzie's limited knowledge of how the world operates is supported by Emilius's brazen effrontery, which will offer her a new chance for social domination.

The secondary characters are drawn with an equal sense of psychological aberration. For example, there is the cynical honesty of Lord George, which conceals a fearful vacillation that abhors responsibility yet is resolute in pushing his companion, Sir Griffin Tewett, into marriage with Lucinda Roanoke. Alternately submissive and aggressive, he turns vindictive in denouncing Lizzie for the damage she has caused his reputation by creating suspicions of his complicity in her concealment of the necklace. He is also forgiving, on the other hand, of Mrs. Barnacle, his former mistress, for her good intentions in encouraging her niece, Lucinda, to marry for money. Lord George appears cognizant of obligations assumed by others though irresolute in taking them upon himself. Further, he shows the unreality of Lizzie's dreams, but his own conduct is the model of a romantic neurosis. Other examples of psychologically crippled characters are Lucinda, who suffers from strong sexual repression and emotional sterility, and Sir Griffin, cool, vindictive, and arrogant, who is repelled by anyone who would love him.

These characters are set up in contrast to the more conventional ones, such as Mrs. Hittaway, who reflect the pathological tendencies that a materialistic society encourages. The baffled efforts of Lizzie, Lord George, Sir Griffin, and Lucinda to deal with destructive self-deception reflect the results of social forces inhibiting real creative growth in understanding. V. S. Pritchett criticized Trollope for being "a detailed, rather cynical observer of a satisfied world" and has asserted that "we recognize that he [Trollope] has drawn life as people say it is when they are not speaking about themselves." C. P. Snow commented that an exploratory psychological writer such as Trollope "has to live on close terms with the blacker—including the worse—side of his own nature." *The Eustace Diamonds* is the record of Trollope's endurance of a mental nature that was divided.

Pritchett accused Trollope of not capturing or presenting the depth of moral experience. This may reflect a demand for a more complex style, a more intensive depiction of the intricacies of moral struggle, and a more insistent emphasis on values. Snow, however, perceived the simple, direct style as cutting out everything except the truth. Trollope was not temperamental or self-advertising, but as a novelist he covers the wide range of social, institutional, and religious issues and controversies constituting the fabric of Victorian society. He dramatizes the moral and intellectual dilemmas often arising from them and has considerable insight as well as the ability to present the sheer flux of mental life, which anticipates later developments in the work of James Joyce, Virginia Woolf, and Dorothy Richardson.

Roger E. Wiehe

OTHER MAJOR WORKS

SHORT FICTION: *Tales of All Countries*, 1861, 1863; *Lotta Schmidt, and Other Stories*, 1867; *An Editor's Tales*, 1870; *Why Frau Frohmann Raised Her Prices, and Other Stories*, 1882.

NONFICTION: *The West Indies*, 1859; *North America*, 1862; *Clergymen of the Church of England*, 1865-1866; *Travelling Sketches*, 1865-1866; *Australia and New Zealand*, 1873; *South Africa*, 1878; *Thackeray*, 1879; *Lord Palmerston*, 1882; *Autobiography*, 1883; *The Letters of Anthony Trollope*, 1951 (Bradford A. Booth, editor).

TRANSLATION: *The Commentaries of Caesar*, 1870.

BIBLIOGRAPHY

Bridgham, Elizabeth A. *Spaces of the Sacred and Profane: Dickens, Trollope, and the Victorian Cathedral Town*. New York: Routledge, 2008. Describes how Trollope and Charles Dickens use the setting of Victorian cathedral towns to critique religious attitudes, business practices, aesthetic ideas, and other aspects of nineteenth century English life.

Bury, Laurent. *Seductive Strategies in the Novels of Anthony Trollope, 1815-1882*. Lewiston, N.Y.: Edwin Mellen Press, 2004. Presents a study of seduction in Trollope's novels. Argues that seduction was a survival skill for both men and women in the Victorian era and demonstrates how Trollope depicted the era's sexual politics.

Felber, Lynette. *Gender and Genre in Novels Without End: The British Roman-Fleuve*. Gainesville: University Press of Florida, 1995. Examination of multivolume works of British fiction focuses on Trollope's Palliser novels, Dorothy Richardson's *Pilgrimage*, and Anthony Powell's *A Dance to the Music of Time*. Includes notes and index.

Glendinning, Victoria. *Anthony Trollope*. New York: Alfred A. Knopf, 1993. Perceptive, witty biography focuses on Trollope's relationships with his parents and siblings, his wife, and his lovers. Uses incidents from Trollope's novels and other works to tell the writer's story.

Hall, N. John. *Trollope: A Biography*. Oxford, England: Clarendon Press, 1991. Discussion of Trollope's life draws heavily on the great Victorian's own words. Pays particular attention to Trollope's travel writing and the final decade of his life.

_____, ed. *The Trollope Critics*. New York: Macmillan, 1981. Critical anthology provides a good introduction to Trollope. Contains essays by twenty Trollope critics who cover a wide range of topics. Includes bibliography.

Markwick, Margaret. *New Men in Trollope's Novels: Rewriting the Victorian Male*. Burlington, Vt.: Ashgate, 2007. Examines Trollope's novels to trace the development of his ideas about masculinity. Argues that Trollope's male characters are not the conventional Victorian patriarchs and demonstrates how his works promoted a "startlingly modern model of manhood." Markwick also has published an examination of Trollope's female characters, *Trollope and Women* (London: Hambledon Press, 1997).

Mullen, Richard, and James Munson. *The Penguin Companion to Trollope*. New York: Penguin Books, 1996. Comprehensive guide describes all of Trollope's novels, short stories, travel books, and other works; discusses plot, characters, background, tone, allusions, and contemporary references and places the works in their historical context.

Pollard, Arthur. *Anthony Trollope*. Boston: Routledge & Kegan Paul, 1978. Seeks to put all of Trollope's novels and a variety of miscellaneous works within the context of his life and time. Emphasizes Trollope's evocation of his age and his guiding moral purpose. Includes index.

Wright, Andrew. *Anthony Trollope: Dream and Art*. New York: Macmillan, 1983. Brief study of fifteen of Trollope's novels sees them as contemporary fictions, transfiguring life in a certain way. Includes bibliography and index.

IVAN TURGENEV

Born: Orel, Russia; November 9, 1818
Died: Bougival, France; September 3, 1883
Also known as: Ivan Sergeyevich Turgenev

PRINCIPAL LONG FICTION

Rudin, 1856 (*Dimitri Roudine*, 1873; better
known as *Rudin*, 1947)
Asya, 1858 (English translation, 1877)
Dvoryanskoye gnezdo, 1859 (*Liza*, 1869; also
known as *A Nobleman's Nest*, 1903; better
known as *A House of Gentlefolk*, 1894)
Nakanune, 1860 (*On the Eve*, 1871)
Pervaya lyubov, 1860 (*First Love*, 1884)
Ottsy i deti, 1862 (*Fathers and Sons*, 1867)
Dym, 1867 (*Smoke*, 1868)
Veshniye vody, 1872 (*Spring Floods*, 1874;
better known as *The Torrents of Spring*,
1897)
Nov, 1877 (*Virgin Soil*, 1877)
The Novels of Ivan Turgenev, 1894-1899
(15 volumes)

OTHER LITERARY FORMS

The literary reputation of Ivan Turgenev (tewr-GYAYN-yuhf) rests primarily on his narrative prose works, which, aside from his novels, include novelettes, novellas, and short stories, the latter a genre in which he excelled and became prolific. In 1847, he began putting together a collection of stories that was published in 1852 bearing the title *Zapiski okhotnika* (*Russian Life in the Interior*, 1855; better known as *A Sportsman's Sketches*, 1932), highly admired by Leo Tolstoy, which includes many of Turgenev's well-known pieces. Turgenev's naturalism was well adapted to the portrayal of the life of poor countryfolk—enough to evoke compassion while inciting indignation at their lot.

Turgenev tried his hand at drama, too, achieving reasonable success with *Gde tonko, tam i rvyotsya* (pr. 1912; *Where It Is Thin, There It Breaks*, 1924), *Kholostyak* (pr. 1849; *The Bachelor*, 1924), *Provintsialka* (pr. 1851; *A Provincial Lady*, 1934), and especially *Mesyats v derevne* (pb. 1855; *A Month in the Country*,

1924), a play whose innovations in many ways adumbrate those of Anton Chekhov.

Turgenev began writing poetry as a student and had some verses published in 1838. Toward the end of his life, he assembled a collection of his poetic works titled *Senilia* (1882, 1930; better known as *Stikhotvoreniya v proze; Poems in Prose*, 1883, 1945). The total profile of Turgenev's literary activities encompasses other forms as well, including opera libretti, essays, articles, autobiographical pieces and memoirs, and even a semiscientific study on nightingales.

ACHIEVEMENTS

In the world of letters, Ivan Turgenev stands out as a naturalist, although not in the hammering manner of Émile Zola, the depressing manner of Thomas Hardy, or the milder, veristic manner of Giovanni Verga. Even if the words "idealization" and "sentimentality" are often used in connection with Turgenev, his "Nature school" tonality has neither the idealizing tendency of Sergei Aksakov nor the sentimental tendency of Dmitrii Vasil'evich Grigorovich, both of whom were his compatriots and contemporaries. On the surface, these qualities are there; when one digs further, they are not. If, on one hand, the reader luxuriates in Turgenev's intensely felt descriptions of nature, he or she is, on the other hand, struck by Turgenev's devastating irony (especially as applied to the upper classes) and by the uncompromising realism of his portrayals (of all classes, including the peasantry). Turgenev's worldview—more exactly, the view of his Russia, whose social history his novels chronicle for two decades—is not optimistic. His most famous hero, the controversial Bazarov in *Fathers and Sons*, is a nihilist; otherwise, his "heroes" are nonheroes, that is, "superfluous men." His heroines appear affirmative only in the perhaps important but not exhilarating sense of loyalty and self-sacrifice. Turgenev's sentimental hue coats a tragic substance, and his instinctive idealism is pared by a naturalistic objectivity.

One reason for the initial positive flavor is the constant appearance of the love motif and the delicate treatment of that special aspect of it, its awakening. Another is the sensual way in which nature fits Turgenev's creative scheme, particularly landscapes, which may or may not shape a background to events but reflect, along with his compassion for the serfs, what may well be the author's most genuine inspiration of all. Finally, there is the softening effect produced by a manicured style; a sense of language and its need for immediate communication at the proper level; the use of several adjectives to enhance descriptiveness, individualizing it through incorrectness or strange words or French phrases; and the author's care not to allow an idea to become so involved that it mars the basic tenet: clarity (Turgenev liked the short sentence as much as he disliked the metaphor). He was a craftsman.

Turgenev profited from his many and admired Western friends and writers, Alphonse Daudet, George Sand, Gustave Flaubert, Prosper Mérimée, and Henry James among them. Despite his preoccupation with things Russian, he is the most "Western" of Russian authors and among the most tempered, the least given to extremes, even when he presents the peasants as far more human than their masters. To speak of his friends' influence, however, would be to stretch the point, for, in his homeland, there were also Alexander Pushkin, Mikhail Lermontov, Tolstoy, Aleksandr Herzen, and Fyodor Dostoevski (who hated Turgenev, as shown by the character Karmazinof in Dostoevski's *Besy*, 1871-1872; *The Possessed*, 1913)—to mention but a few Russian writers. Turgenev unquestionably felt an aesthetic and cultural affinity with the West, and he surely believed in the Europeanization of Russia, but he was his own artist, and he wrote his own way as a creator who could see and say more through his personal optic than through varied imitation.

Turgenev's irony notwithstanding, moderation shaped this optic, a moderation that could come down hard on both sides of an issue (why else were both conservatives and radicals outraged at the portrayal of Bazarov?). It was a moderation that implied that, whatever the desirability of Romantic idealism and the rationality of what is reasonable, there are no answers to life's problems. The important thing is to maintain a balanced, liberal altruism. In his speech titled "Gamlet i Don Kikhot" (1860; "Hamlet and Don Quixote," 1930), Turgenev showed that Don Quixote's accomplishments are sec-

ondary to the way he feels about people, to his sense of ideal and of sacrifice, his ability to act on indignation, although his fantasy makes him appear a madman. Hamlet, on the other hand, is the total egocentric, doubting, hesitating, and calculating, more concerned with his situation than with his duty. Only the Fates "can show us whether we struggled against visions, or against real enemies." The Knight of the Woeful Countenance made more of an impact on society than did the Prince of Denmark. Turgenev tended to emphasize the social over the human side of things, though one must be cautious in accepting this observation without qualification.

BIOGRAPHY

Ivan Sergeyevich Turgenev was born in Orel, Russia, and spent his early childhood on his mother's estate in Spasskoye. His father, Sergey Turgenev, a former cavalry officer, belonged to the nobility—the fallen nobility—and had acquired solvency with his marriage to a rich heiress, Varvara Petrovna Lutovinova. Unfortunately, this lady was unhappy, matching energy with despotism, loveless toward her husband and harsh toward her servants and three sons. Ivan's passion for reading sometimes managed to keep him out of the reach of her capricious cruelty. German and French tutors taught him their languages, and he listened eagerly when an old servant read to him from Gavriil Derzhavin, Lermontov, Pushkin, and others.

He began the study of philosophy at the University of Moscow, but after his father's death, when the family moved to St. Petersburg and he transferred to the university there, his literary inclinations began to take hold. He met P. A. Pletnev, the new editor (after Pushkin's death) of the journal *Sovremennik*, and published some poetry. Even after he made poetry secondary to prose, he never discarded its sense, either in his lyric view of life (not merely in his descriptions of nature) or in his refinement of style.

In 1838, Turgenev headed westward, first to Berlin, where his attendance at the university (in the faculty of philosophy) was incidental to the various friendships he made with "Westernizers" such as Nikolai Stankevich, Herzen, Timofei Nikolaevich Granovsky, Mikhail Bakunin, and other "progressives," who believed, as opposed to the more orthodox "Slavophiles," that Russia's cultural future lay in emulating the best of Western civilization. Turgenev became one of them ideologically, especially after wider travels in Europe that took him as far south as Rome and Naples. Indeed, after returning to his homeland in 1841, trying his hand at civil service and deciding on a career in writing, he returned to the West in 1847.

Despite the encouragement of Vissarion Belinsky, Turgenev had known more failures than successes in composing verse (much in the Romantic tradition) and came to see realistic narrative prose as his likely avenue as a creative writer. His mother expressed her dissatisfaction with his expressed vocation, as she did in response to his infatuation with the widowed French singer Pauline Viardot (with whom, and with whose family, he formed a strange but close lifetime relationship), by withdrawing financial support, but in 1847 Turgenev proved his point with his first literary success, the short story "Khor and Kalinych." As his short stories contin-

Ivan Turgenev. (Library of Congress)

ued to appear with consistent success, he became confirmed in his decision and in his Western thrust.

In 1850, Turgenev inherited a large fortune. By his mother's seamstress, he had an illegitimate daughter, who was reared by Pauline and named Paulinette and about whom he was very sensitive (he challenged Tolstoy to a duel—unfought—over an uncomplimentary remark about her). With Pauline providing the music, he also wrote some libretti for light opera. He never married the French diva, but clearly she meant much to him: "Oh, thou, my only friend, oh thou whom I love so deeply and so tenderly," he wrote of her in a poem.

A Sportsman's Sketches was published in 1852. Turgenev, while following in the footsteps of Nikolai Gogol, Lermontov, and the early Dostoevski, aimed at accurate portrayal of the serfs, without idealizing them and without highlighting the negative side; this was well in the tradition of Honoré de Balzac, Sand, and especially Berthold Auerbach, whose *Schwarzwälder Dorfgeschichten* (1843-1860; *Black Forest Village Stories*, 1869), complete with local language, explored the lives and traditions of the German peasants. It is believed that Czar Alexander II was influenced by Turgenev's stories on the occasion of the emancipation of the serfs in 1861. The stories, however, had also displeased the censors under Alexander II's predecessor, Nicholas I, and as a result of an article on Gogol's death, Turgenev was arrested, detained in St. Petersburg, and then forced to reside for eighteen months on his Spasskoye property. He left it in 1853, and a few years later also left Russia—almost for good.

It was then that Turgenev the novelist emerged; his first novel, *Rudin*, appeared in 1856. He was already well known in Russia, France, and Germany, as well as England and Italy. The novels that followed, like the first, all written abroad but all concerned with the social and political problems of Russia, were awaited and discussed—and polemically debated, because, rather than engage in philosophical flights and metaphysical views of the human condition, Turgenev engaged immediate, recognizable issues realistically. In addition, the usual controversy between Westernizers (including Nikolay Dobrolyubov and Nikolay Chernyshevsky) and Slavophiles (including Aleksey Khomyakov, Ivan Vasil'evich Kireevsky, Yuri Samarin, the Aksakovs, and even, though with greater circumspection, Dostoevski) continued to rage, to the point that *Fathers and Sons* was deemed by some a criticism of the new generation. The fact was that at that time, because of the rapid interactions of shifting events and cultural conditions, opinions could change monthly. Hence, the intellectual points of reference in Turgenev's earlier novels are different from those in later novels.

When critics overstress the social importance of Turgenev's novels, they siphon off a good part of his vitality as an artist, for it is not only the social commentary that makes Balzac, Alessandro Manzoni, or Jane Austen great writers. Turgenev's handling of nature and character development alone—without elevating his works' psychological attributes to the level of Dostoevski or James—together with his sense of style and structure, are enough to welcome him to the writers' pantheon. His ability in character portrayal is evident in his comedies, so well interpreted by the young actor Maria G. Savina, with whom he fell madly in love in his twilight years. In his novels, short stories, and plays, however, he remained ultimately the poet rather than the social critic, as his deep and private interest in collecting his prose poems near the end of his life, with no intention of publishing them, suggests—indeed, symbolizes. It is fitting that he returned briefly to Russia in 1880 to deliver a telling lecture in honor of the poet Pushkin, whose monument was being unveiled. Turgenev died of cancer at the home of Pauline Viardot, to whom he had dictated his last story, "An End," in 1883.

ANALYSIS

The idealistic generation of the 1830's and 1840's, the so-called superfluous men and victims of the Russia of Nicholas I, comes to the fore in Ivan Turgenev's first novel, *Rudin*. It is a philosophically articulate generation, little given to action.

RUDIN

Dmitri Rudin fascinates and charms the household of Daria Mikhailovna Lasunskaia with his poetic linguistic abilities and his brilliant capacity for discussion drawing on keen aphorisms and on German Transcendentalists (including Georg Wilhelm Friedrich Hegel), so that instead of staying overnight, he remains for several months. In time, he declares his love for the young Natasha, yet,

as the vainglorious human figure he is (something her "lioness" mother and patroness of the arts comes to discern), he withdraws spinelessly, though aware that his love is returned, when he learns of Lasunskaia's opposition. He departs, leaving Natasha hurt.

The story is told by his friend Leznev, not always sympathetically, and it is probable that Turgenev originally wanted to satirize the budding anarchist Bakunin (the novel's original, satiric title was "The Genius"). As such, Rudin would have emerged not as a superfluous man but simply as an unsavory boaster. Events in Russia changed quickly, however: Bakunin's arrest, the death of the admired historian Granovsky, who liked the rebel, and other circumstances invited an "Epilogue" (1855-1856) and finally a last paragraph (1860). Here Rudin dies in the Paris barricades of 1848 in a kind of hero's apologia, in which, from a vain failure, he becomes a tragic failure, a true superfluous man, full of remorse over his treatment of Natasha and conscious that he is "sacrificing [himself] for some nonsense in which [he does not] believe." Now the Russian radicals protested (again the events were changing) against what they believed was an ideological acquiescence to older values. This was a typical Turgenevian situation: the incarnation of a problem in a hero by the writer and the argumentative reaction to it by society.

A HOUSE OF GENTLEFOLK

One answer to the plight of the superfluous man is the return to the soil, to the Russian homeland, "tilling it the best way one can," a task that can be accomplished with a deep sense of religion. *A House of Gentlefolk*, published in 1859—a Slavophile novel that was enormously well received and stirred no polemics—provides this answer. The European-educated nobleman Fedor Ivanovich Lavretsky has remained spiritually Russian and returns to his homeland from Paris when his frivolous wife, Varvara Pavlovna Korobine, beguiled by the delights of the French capital, is unfaithful to him. His goal is to organize his lands with humility, seeing to the well-being of the serfs. He comes across a distant cousin, the serious, religious, and dutiful Liza Kalitina, one of Turgenev's most idealized portrayals—recalling Pushkin's Tatyana in *Evgeny Onegin* (1825-1832, 1833; *Eugene Onegin*, 1881)—of Russian womanhood. Although the shadow of Varvara cannot be dispelled, they fall in love. The impossible union appears briefly possible when a newspaper account reports Lavretsky's wife's death; the story is incorrect, however, and Varvara appears at his home in Russia, only to leave the country estate and move on to the social pleasures of St. Petersburg, where she acquires a new lover. Lavretsky becomes a model landlord, and Liza retires to a convent.

While the plot is typically sparse, the characterization is typically rich: Vladimir Nikolaevich Panshin, the deceptively charming and egotistical young careerist (a pro-Western foil to Lavretsky), who courts Liza before Lavretsky's appearance; her wealthy and widowed provincial mother, Maria Dmitrievna Kalitina; her old German music teacher, Christopher Lemm, a man of unrecognized talent reluctantly living in Russia; Lavretsky's despotic and narrow-minded father; his harsh and fierce Aunt Glafira; his idealistic and poor university friend, Mikhyalevich, who speaks nobly about the duties of landed gentry toward the country and the peasants—these figures and others are to be added to the characters of Lavretsky, Varvara, and above all Liza herself, an array of portraits that pleased the artistic reader and an espousing of ideas that pleased the social forces of the time (the model landlord for the radicals, the Russian consciousness for the Slavophiles, the profound faith and devotion, rectitude, and determination of Liza for those seeking a sociomoral message, like Turgenev's good, religious friend Countess Elizabeth Lambert).

ON THE EVE

On the Eve is also relatively plotless yet sensitive in its drawing of characters; it turns one's eyes back to the West, though the heart of the story throbs in Bulgaria through the most ideal pair of lovers Turgenev ever conceived. There is a contrast between the trifling pedantry of young Russians and the vital commitment of youth elsewhere: The elegant and superficial Pavel Yakovlich Schubin, a fine-arts student, represents the French leaning, while the awkward but good and learned Andrei Petrovich Bersenyev represents the German. Both pursue the superior and beautiful Elena Nikolaevna Strahof, an ardent and noble-minded daughter of a dissipated aristocrat and a faded society belle. Her willpower is no match for her wooers, and it is not surprising that when the Bulgarian patriot Dmitri Insarov passes through (his cause is the liberation of Bulgaria from the Turks), she

falls in love with him. Both of his parents having been victims of the Turks, Insarov, though not of sound health, is regarded as the leader of the coming revolt. (The "eve" of the revolt could be the approaching Crimean War and the forthcoming reforms of Alexander II that followed that war.)

Because he returns her love, Insarov fears on the eve of the conflict that Elena is distracting him from his mission and leaves her, but she seeks him out and tells him that her idealism will make her forsake everything for him and his cause. They marry and leave for Bulgaria but get only as far as Venice before he dies. Elena follows the coffin to Bulgaria, where, having no country now, she joins the Sisters of Mercy, who act as army nurses. Turgenev said that he derived the plot outline from a manuscript handed to him by one V. V. Karataev, who left for Crimea at the outbreak of the war in 1853. It would be reading something into the novel that is not there to see in the Bulgarian Insarov a forerunner of the Russian revolutionary hero, as it would be incorrect to see in the self-sacrificing and idealistic Elena, who is reminiscent of Anita, the wife of the famous Italian patriot Giuseppe Garibaldi, whom Turgenev much admired, a prototype of the revolutionary heroine. In their own way, one religious and one secular, Liza and Elena are the same. At first, the novel disappointed the public, which expected to see the willful Russian man dedicated to a noble cause; the protagonists pointed Westward, as it were, the way Ivan Goncharov's active Stolz, a German, pointed away from the dreamy Russian Oblomov. Here again, however, the value of the work is better sought less in the ideological orientation than in the series of types it presented—in other words, in the characterization (for example, of Uvar Ivanovich).

FATHERS AND SONS

Time and again, discussion of Turgenev's novels focused on his social concerns, relegating the artistic side of his endeavors, characterization (which, to be sure, is central to the communication of these concerns), to a secondary plane. Hence, his most famous novel, *Fathers and Sons*, completed in 1861, around the time of the emancipation of the serfs, and published with some modifications supposedly prompted by publisher M. N. Katkov in 1862, aroused widespread polemics about the ideological facets of the characters, particularly Bazarov, rather than about the balanced objectivity of the characterizations themselves. There is no doubt that Turgenev liked what his "nihilist" (a term that, while not coined by the author, gained currency through this novel) protagonist stood for, but there is equally no doubt that he did not like the way that he stood for it.

Evgeni Bazarov, a medical student, and his friend, Arkadi Kirsanov, stop at the latter's provincial home after a three-year absence. The widowed father, who has taken up with a peasant girl and is a mismanaging member of the landed gentry, especially after the emancipation, lives with Arkadi's uncle, a frustrated and intolerant ex-officer of the guard. In this sedentary, conservative atmosphere, the ineffectualness of which represented everything that the younger generation—the materialistic and utilitarian "new men and women" that Chernyshevsky (in his novel *Chto delat'?*, 1863; *What Is to Be Done?*, c. 1863) and Dobrolyubov (in his essay "Chto takoye Oblomovshchine," 1859-1860; "What Is Oblomovism?," 1903) praised with such ingenuous dullness—could not stand, the insolently cynical and aggressive libertarian views of Bazarov, let alone his uninhibited manner, are hardly received with smiles. In the words of his less militant friend Arkadi, Bazarov "bows before no authority and accepts no principle without examination."

His intellectually cold and antiromantic attitude toward women shocks the old Kirsanov brothers. When the students leave the estate, however, Bazarov meets a widow at a ball, Ana Odintsova, and falls in love withher, despite much self-struggle, in the sentimental, unmaterialistic way he most despised. She eludes him; Arkadi's admiration for his friend cools as he, too, leaves him, preferring to shape his life according to more traditional values. Now Bazarov goes to his own provincial parents (a former army doctor and an uneducated daughter of the lower nobility), lovable if rather naïve, who both love him and fear him. Through an infection sustained in a finger while performing an autopsy on a tubercular body, left unattended because of a lack of cauterizing medication as well as his own apathy, young Bazarov dies.

In the contrast between two generations, the novel divided Russia between "fathers" and "sons." Neither group liked what it read, and both forgot about the fine lines of character, the accurate descriptions of milieus,

and the impressive landscapes. The two generations looked at rebellion or not, authority or not, tradition or not, the need to live (to Live) or not, the necessity for change (progress) or not, and in so doing betrayed their desire to have things stated in black-and-white terms: The revolutionaries were scum or could do no wrong; the conservatives were dangerous regressives or the sole pillars of moral strength. Turgenev made Bazarov not sufficiently satanic for the "sons" and not sufficiently godly for the "fathers."

Turgenev appreciated the social-minded impetus of Bazarov's ideas, and at times he gave his protagonist moving, human touches, but he also gave the character offensive, elitist attitudes toward the "oafs" he would use to do the dirty work. Bazarov's quixotic integrity and relentless single-mindedness under the banner of a social cause are not enough to offset his brash intemperance and lack of rational circumspection. Turgenev, like all true creators of types, drew from life synthetically, making his characters composites of what they represented. Bazarov's brutal cynicism and his anticlimactic end, almost making him a pointless victim of his "new realism" founded on science, encouraged the interpretation that Turgenev had parodied Chernyshevsky and Dobrolyubov by caricaturing the revolutionary—an act of faithlessness in the "new men and women." Such had not been his intent, however. Rather, his purpose had been to demonstrate the gap between generations, but more than that, on a more universal level that his immediate reading public by and large missed, to suggest the transience of all ideology—social, political, economic, even moral—in the light of the eternal and fundamental realities of love and death.

SMOKE

This same stress on milieu and characterization examined at arm's length (except for the author's mouthpiece Potúgin), but now with an even more intensified appreciation of the natural setting, obtains in *Smoke*, and the same displeasure on the parts of both radicals and conservatives ensued. Turgenev's idea of putting together a simple love story outside the homeland, in Baden-Baden, Germany, the meeting spot of the European international set, merged with a desire to follow up his observations on postreform Russia, on the biases interfering with the reform itself, the lack of depth of both revolutionaries and aristocracy, and the continuing controversy between Slavophiles and Westernizers. Too many things to say, perhaps, between the covers of one book, but Turgenev, whose career had already peaked, tried it anyway.

The love story involves the protagonist Grigóry Mikhailovich Litvinov and his former fiancé, Irína Pavlovna. Shortly before their wedding was to take place, Irína, embarrassed by her impoverished situation, and after a successful appearance at a high-society ball, jilted Litvinov and married for rank a fatuous and unattractive young general, Ratmírov. Now in Baden-Baden, Litvinov awaits the arrival of his new betrothed, his cousin Tátiana Petrovna Shestova, whose mother will accompany her. Irína is there, too, and the old love is rekindled; she and Litvinov plan to run away together—a plan that Litvinov divulges to the saddened Tátiana— but at the last moment, the general's wife changes her mind, thus disrupting Litvinov's life for a second time. Disconsolate, the latter returns to Russia, where his dedication to work succeeds in bringing about a reconciliation with Tátiana—unconvincing as this happy ending (unusual for Turgenev) sounds.

Innocent and naïve enough as a story, and whatever its autobiographical innuendos (the author had almost married his cousin Olga Turgeneva after a parting from Pauline Viardot in 1850), the novel hits hard at two groups of people: the hypocritical, mercenary, rabble-rousing intellectuals who call themselves radicals, and the vapid, narrow-minded bosses—the "planters"—who do not mend their ways after the emancipation as far as the serfs are concerned. In addition, a good part of the book deals with arguments quite extraneous to the story line: the long discourses by Potúgin, who upholds intransigently the Westernizing ideology as opposed to the cultural distinctiveness of Russia in which the Slavophiles believed. Aleksandr Herzen, with whom Turgenev had crossed swords and who could not embrace the Potúgin-Turgenev philosophy, ultimately seemed sympathetic to the novel (unlike publisher Katkov, who found this occasion to break away from the outspoken author), but the spiritualistically and nationalistically irritable Dostoevski found reason to be thoroughly vexed by it. The point, however, had been made: Matters Russian were enveloped in a symbolic smoke, whether in the cultural ineffectiveness inside the homeland or in its citizens' flavorless lives in Germany. Superfluous men abounded. Turgenev had lived too long away from this homeland to understand what was going on there—this became the facile charge, obviously a weak one, since what he had to say aroused such furor and such partisan passions.

VIRGIN SOIL

Without relinquishing his interest in portraying types, Turgenev turned to depicting the new (post-Alexander II) Russia in his longest and most complex novel, *Virgin Soil*, about the "going to the people" period of the mid-1870's. At the University of St. Petersburg, there is a student, the revolutionary Nezhdánov, the illegitimate son of a nobleman. Nezhdánov earns his living as preceptor at the home of a high dignitary and self-fancying though cautious liberal, Sipyágin. There Nezhdánov meets Sipyágin's crafty and attractive wife and a pair that shares his political persuasion: Sipyágin's poor niece Marianna and his fanatical brother-in-law Markélov, who loves the niece, though his love is unrequited. In fact, Marianna, who dislikes the Sipyágin couple, is drawn in her quest for freedom to Nezhdánov and his revolutionary goals. He, however, is too introspective for action and unsure of those goals, even of loving Marianna. A manager of a paper factory, Solómin, an active, progressive, but practical man, shields Nezhdánov and Marianna (they have fled the Sipyágin household) from the authorities. While Markélov tries to incite insurgency, Nezhdánov distributes pamphlets and attempts ineffectually to stir up revolution, and Marianna does her share by teaching the peasants' children. Attempts are aborted, the intellectuals are suspected by the peasants themselves, Markélov is arrested, and Nezhdánov, dramatically facing his besetting weakness—his inability to decide and to act, whether in a political or a personal context (as Leonard Schapiro has aptly said, "the tragedy of a Hamlet who longs to be a Don Quixote"—escapes arrest through suicide. Solómin and Marianna go into hiding and marry.

Turgenev's message was not revolution, as some of his contemporaries sought to demonstrate, but rather the Solómin brand of compassionate and sober evolution, constantly, efficiently, and practically working toward a diminishing of inequality. Only the educated class, not the well-intentioned and liberal gentry, will bring about reform, unless the gentry develop a true capacity for action and self-sacrifice. Around Solómin, the novel's hero, and the other frontline characters drift a host of secondaries—as usual, as important in the Turgenevian scheme as the primaries, for the message would lack both formation and relief without them: the homely and poor student revolutionary Mashurina, the lively but spineless Páklin (who speaks the author's mind), the wealthy and illiberal landlord Kollomietsev, the old aristocrats Fimushka and Fomushka, Sipyágin's beautiful man-eating wife, and many more. Again, Turgenev drew from reality, and his fundamental greatness continues today to lie in his naturalistic characterizations (alongside his stylistic and descriptive powers), without which he could not feel any confidence in his own ideas. He himself once wrote,

When I do not have concrete figures before my eyes I am immediately disoriented and don't know where to go. I always feel that an idea opposite to my own could be affirmed with equal reason. But if I speak of a red nose or of a white hair, then the hair is white and the nose is red. No dialectics will be able to alter this state of things.

Jean-Pierre Barricelli

OTHER MAJOR WORKS

SHORT FICTION: *Zapiski okhotnika*, 1852 (*Russian Life in the Interior*, 1855; better known as *A Sportsman's Sketches*, 1932); *Povesti i rasskazy*, 1856; *First Love, and Other Stories*, 1989.

PLAYS: *Neostorozhnost*, pb. 1843 (*Carelessness*, 1924); *Bezdenezhe*, pb. 1846 (*A Poor Gentleman*, 1924); *Kholostyak*, pr. 1849 (*The Bachelor*, 1924); *Zavtrak u predvoditelya*, pr. 1849 (*An Amicable Settlement*, 1924); *Razgovor na bolshoy doroge*, pr. 1850 (*A Conversation on the Highway*, 1924); *Provintsialka*, pr. 1851 (*A Provincial Lady*, 1934); *Mesyats v derevne*, pb. 1855 (wr. 1850; *A Month in the Country*, 1924); *Nakhlebnik*, pb. 1857 (wr. 1849; *The Family Charge*, 1924); *Vecher v Sorrente*, pr. 1884 (wr. 1852; *An Evening in Sorrento*, 1924); *Gde tonko, tam i rvyotsya*, pr. 1912 (wr. 1851; *Where It Is Thin, There It Breaks*, 1924); *The Plays of Ivan Turgenev*, 1924; *Three Plays*, 1934.

POETRY: *Parasha*, 1843; *Senilia*, 1882, 1930 (better known as *Stikhotvoreniya v proze*; *Poems in Prose*, 1883, 1945).

NONFICTION: "Gamlet i Don Kikhot," 1860 ("Hamlet and Don Quixote," 1930); *Literaturnya i zhiteyskiya vospominaniya*, 1880 (*Literary Reminiscences and Autobiographical Fragments*, 1958); *Letters*, 1983 (David Lowe, editor); *Turgenev's Letters*, 1983 (A. V. Knowles, editor).

MISCELLANEOUS: *The Works of Iván Turgenieff*, 1903-1904 (6 volumes); *The Essential Turgenev*, 1994.

BIBLIOGRAPHY

Allen, Elizabeth Cheresh. *Beyond Realism: Turgenev's Poetics of Secular Salvation*. Stanford, Calif.: Stanford University Press, 1992. Attempts to expose the unique imaginative vision and literary patterns in Turgenev's work and argues that readers should not turn to Turgenev merely for transparent narratives of nineteenth century Russian life.

Bloom, Harold, ed. *Ivan Turgenev*. Philadelphia: Chelsea House, 2003. Collection of critical essays about Turgenev's work includes discussion of *Fathers and Sons*. Other essays compare Turgenev's works to those of Ernest Hemingway, Willa Cather, and Sherwood Anderson.

Costlow, Jane T. *Worlds Within Worlds: The Novels of Ivan Turgenev*. Princeton, N.J.: Princeton University Press, 1990. Focuses on four of Turgenev's early novels: *Rudin*, *A House of Gentlefolk*, *On the Eve*, and *Fathers and Sons*. Includes bibliographical references and index.

Dessaix, Robert. *Twilight of Love: Travels with Turgenev*. Washington, D.C.: Shoemaker & Hoard, 2005. Provides insights into Turgenev's life, particularly concerning the writer's experience of love. Dessaix, an Australian writer and scholar of Russian literature, traveled to Turgenev's homes and conducted research at the Moscow Library to locate the "soul" of the Russian writer.

Knowles, A. V. *Ivan Turgenev*. Boston: Twayne, 1988. Excellent introductory study offers a brief biographical sketch and chapters on the start of Turgenev's literary career, the establishment of his reputation, his individual novels, his letters, his final years, and his place in literature. Includes chronology, notes, and annotated bibliography.

Lowe, David A., ed. *Critical Essays on Ivan Turgenev*. Boston: G. K. Hall, 1989. Collection of essays on Turgenev's literary works presents many analyses of his novels, including discussions of *Fathers and Sons*, *On the Eve*, and *First Love*. Includes bibliography and index.

Magarshack, David. *Turgenev: A Life*. London: Faber & Faber, 1954. Illustrated biography by Turgenev's translator concentrates on the events that shaped the author's life, his relationships with Russian and foreign writers, and the factual circumstances surrounding his works. A useful introduction to Turgenev and his opus.

Seeley, Frank Friedeberg. *Turgenev: A Reading of His Fiction*. New York: Cambridge University Press, 1991. Thorough study of Turgenev's fiction is prefaced with an outline of Turgenev's life and a survey of his poetry and plays. This volume incorporates later findings and challenges some established views, especially the traditional notion of the "simplicity" of Turgenev's works. Seeley stresses the psychological treatment that Turgenev allotted to his characters.

Waddington, Patrick, ed. *Ivan Turgenev and Britain*. Providence, R.I.: Berg, 1995. Essays on Turgenev's reputation in England and the United States include reviews by distinguished critics such as Frank Harris, Virginia Woolf, and Edmund Gosse. Waddington provides a comprehensive introduction, explaining the historical context in which these reviews appeared. Includes extensive notes and bibliography.

Yarmolinsky, Avrahm. *Turgenev: The Man, His Art, and His Age*. 1959. Reprint. New York: Collier, 1962. Reliable short biography is useful as an introduction to Turgenev. Addresses all the important stages in his life and discusses the origins of his works, their salient features, and their overall significance for Turgenev and for Russian and world literature. Concludes with a useful chronology and a good bibliography.

SCOTT TUROW

Born: Chicago, Illinois; April 12, 1949
Also known as: Scott Fredrick Turow; L. Scott Turow

PRINCIPAL LONG FICTION

Presumed Innocent, 1987
The Burden of Proof, 1990
Pleading Guilty, 1993
The Laws of Our Fathers, 1996
Personal Injuries, 1999
Reversible Errors, 2002
Ordinary Heroes, 2005
Limitations, 2006

OTHER LITERARY FORMS

Early in his career, while an undergraduate at Amherst College, Scott Turow (tuh-ROH) published short stories. In 1977, he published *One L: An Inside Account of Life in the First Year at Harvard Law School*, a compelling nonfiction account of his first year as a law student. *One L* became required reading for prospective law students and eventually sold more than three million copies. Turow has continued to write and publish various works of nonfiction, including book reviews, articles for legal journals, and newspaper articles on topics ranging from politics to sports.

ACHIEVEMENTS

Scott Turow received the Crime Writers' Association Silver Dagger Award in 1988 for *Presumed Innocent*. Paperback rights to *Presumed Innocent* sold for a record three million dollars, and Turow was paid one million dollars for the motion-picture rights, an unprecedented amount for a first novel. Turow's remarkable success with *Presumed Innocent*, coupled with his determination to remain a practicing lawyer, started an interest in legal fiction written by lawyers, especially Turow and novelist John Grisham. Turow's success helped to create a new market for courtroom drama, and scores of lawyers and law students began tinkering with writing fiction. Turow is often hailed as having transcended his genre, producing consistently literary works with mass audience appeal.

BIOGRAPHY

The eldest of two children, Scott Fredrick Turow was born into an upper-middle-class Jewish family in Chicago, the son of a physician and a former public school teacher. When he was in his teens, his family moved from a largely Jewish neighborhood in the city to the suburbs. Turow's father, a former U.S. Army doctor, treated depression and devoted most of his time to his work, so Turow's relationship with him was somewhat strained. Largely inspired by his mother, who had written unpublished short stories and novels and published a self-help book, Turow decided to pursue a career as a writer. He enrolled in Amherst College in Massachusetts in 1966, where he majored in English and studied with Tillie Olsen, a noted writer of Jewish and feminist short stories. Turow graduated summa cum laude and in 1970 entered the master's program in creative writing at Stanford University, where he continued to study with Olsen as well as with the well-known novelist Wallace Stegner.

In 1971, Turow married Annette Weisberg, a painter and teacher who also had grown up in the suburbs of Chicago; the couple would eventually have three children. Turow was awarded the appointment of E. H. Jones Lecturer in Creative Writing at Stanford, but after three years as a teacher he began to feel that life in academia kept him too far removed from the real world. Turow had become interested in the law, intrigued by research into legal matters he had done for his first novel, "The Way Things Are" (which was eventually rejected by twenty-five publishers). He was accepted into Harvard Law School in 1975. Turow felt that the legal system was to some degree taking on the role once played by organized religion in American culture; he saw practitioners of the law as vital modern-day arbiters of truth and defenders of right against wrong. Receiving his law degree in 1978, he accepted a job as an assistant U.S. attorney in the U.S.

Court of Appeals in Chicago. There, he became involved with "Operation Greylord," an investigation into corruption in the court system, and helped prosecute police officers, lawyers, and judges.

Often noted for his remarkable discipline, Turow successfully juggled his legal career, growing family, and literary pursuits, writing *Presumed Innocent* during the hours he traveled on a commuter train between his office and his suburban home. Realizing that he could not both maintain his grueling work schedule and complete the book, on his wife's advice Turow resigned his job with the U.S. Attorney's Office and accepted a position with Sonnenschein Nath and Rosenthal, a private Chicago law firm. Before starting work there, he took three months off to finish *Presumed Innocent*.

Presumed Innocent's record-breaking success made Turow a wealthy man. Although he continued to work as a lawyer and was determined to maintain his two careers, soon after the publication of *Presumed Innocent* he asked Sonnenschein Nath and Rosenthal to allow him to work part time. He still does legal work with the firm as well as pro bono legal work while writing his bestselling novels.

ANALYSIS

Typically, Scott Turow draws on his own firsthand experiences of the courtroom, of police procedures, and of political maneuvering and corruption to create realistic and gripping characters and scenes. He tends to return to several compelling themes: the technical and moral intricacies of legal practice, the elusive quality of truth and how well truth can be revealed by the legal process, and the notions that anyone can be corrupted and that everyone has at least one dark secret. Heroes can be quite flawed, and even villains act because of understandable human motives. These ideas are central to all of Turow's fiction, although each work takes a different approach to exploring these themes. Turow's later novels introduce a greater range of characters, examine these characters' failures in greater depth, and address more convoluted aspects of courtroom tactics, crime, and criminal behavior. Each book features a corpse, but the mystery of "whodunit" has increasingly become secondary to Turow's delight in legal maneuvering and his concerns with larger questions of character.

Scott Turow.

PRESUMED INNOCENT

Upon its publication, *Presumed Innocent* was an astonishing critical and popular success. Drawing on Turow's experiences as a prosecutor in the U.S. Attorney's Office in Chicago, the novel presents a detailed, realistic portrait of Rusty Sabich, a chief deputy prosecutor in the fictional midwestern Kindle County. The particularity of this world, especially the rendition of the murder trial central to the book, figures heavily in its appeal.

As the novel opens, Sabich's beautiful, ambitious colleague, Carolyn Polhemus, has just been raped and murdered, apparently by someone she trusted. Her murder embarrasses Sabich's boss, chief prosecuting attorney Raymond Horgan, who is up for reelection, so Horgan asks Sabich to head the investigation. When Sabich fails to uncover the murderer and Horgan loses the election, Horgan conspires to frame his deputy for the murder. Sabich, who had had a brief affair with Polhemus and pursued her obsessively for months afterward, is charged with her murder and brought to trial,

with attorney Alejandro "Sandy" Stern defending him. The courtroom scenes and Sabich's consultations with his lawyer offer fascinating insights into real-world legal tactics and explore a theme that Turow revisits in later works: the ambiguity and simple human recalcitrance that plague the search for the truth.

A long-past bribery scam and Polhemus's affairs with Horgan and the judge, Andrew Lyttle, complicate everyone's motives, and Horgan testifies against Sabich to hide his own connection to Polhemus. When Stern discredits prosecution witnesses, suggests that Sabich might have been framed for Polhemus's murder, and lets the judge know indirectly that he is willing to bring in the judge's connection to Polhemus, the case is dismissed. Thus, *Presumed Innocent* creates a many-layered world where motives and perceptions shift depending on point of view and current knowledge, with nearly every noble act countered by the reprehensible.

Even after the murderer's identity is revealed, what really happened remains unknowable as Sabich and his friend Lipranzer disagree about the murderer's intentions. The final revelation of the killer is deeply satisfying and thematically apropos, as the title signals: There is no real innocence, only "the presumption of innocence," a legal term acknowledging the ineffability of human motive and thus the impossibility of establishing clear-cut culpability. Trials may or may not end in justice, but they rarely reveal the full truth. Truth in *Presumed Innocent* emerges not from Sabich's trial but from his first-person meditations, revealing his brooding, philosophical temperament, and readers must repeatedly re-examine thoughts and actions based on new pieces of the whole. This disturbing moral ambiguity indicates that readers are not in hackneyed thriller country but rather in literature territory.

THE BURDEN OF PROOF

The Burden of Proof opens with the suicide of defense lawyer Alejandro "Sandy" Stern's wife of thirty-one years, Clara. In the rest of the novel, Stern, Rusty Sabich's defense attorney in *Presumed Innocent*, unravels the reasons for Clara's death and comes to terms with his own life. Stern soon learns that Clara had been unfaithful, acquired a venereal disease, and wrote a check to an unknown payee that almost depleted her estate. He fails to connect his wife's suicide with the troubles of his brother-in-law, Dixon Hartnell, the owner of a brokerage house and Stern's most significant client (Stern is defending Hartnell on charges of illegal trading).

In this novel Turow explores the psyche and the complex family ties of the hero as this reserved, formal, middle-aged Argentine immigrant and Jew returns to society, engages in a reinvigorated sex life, and finds love with the married, pregnant federal prosecutor investigating Hartnell's case. Stern's strained relationships with his three children eventually lead him to understand the death of his wife and the burden of proof—in both the technical legal sense and as the weight he must carry by unraveling his wife's inexplicable behavior.

PLEADING GUILTY

A detective story about human greed written in a modern epistolary style—in the contents of six Dictaphone tapes—*Pleading Guilty* is the first-person narrative of McCormack "Mack" Malloy, a policeman turned lawyer, tasked with finding a missing law partner, star litigator Bert Kamin. Kamin might have absconded with more than five million dollars, the settlement for a class-action suit and the funds intended to be shared as profits. The tapes are Malloy's report to the Management Oversight Committee, but they are also an indictment of the law firm that pays him. The narrative provides a kaleidoscope view of actions whose nature changes as the point of view shifts and professional integrity yields to self-interest and betrayal of public trust.

THE LAWS OF OUR FATHERS

Turow's fourth novel, *The Laws of Our Fathers*, continues his move away from the page-turning intensity of *Presumed Innocent*. Ghetto gang leader and drug dealer Ordell Trent, known as Hardcore, meets a white woman who comes to his neighborhood to see him for unclear reasons; before she can explain, she is gunned down, and a teenage girl wounded. The murdered woman is June Eddgar, ex-wife of State Senator Loyall Eddgar. Hardcore turns state's evidence to reduce the sentence for his own seeming involvement in the murder, claiming that June Eddgar's son Nile set up the meeting and conspired to have his mother killed.

The murder and Nile's trial reintroduce a secondary character from an earlier work, just as *The Burden of Proof* does with *Presumed Innocent*'s defense attorney Sandy Stern. Here, Sonia "Sonny" Klonsky, a prosecut-

ing attorney and love interest for Stern in *Burden of Proof*, has moved on: Several years later, she is divorced from her poet husband, struggling with single motherhood, and sitting as a state court judge in Kindle County, feeling out of place even among her clerical staff.

The trial also reunites Sonny with several people from the late 1960's, when Sonny and the Eddgars, then leftist revolutionaries, lived in the same apartment building. Seth Weissman was Sonny's uneasy boyfriend, trying to wring some kind of commitment out of a determinedly distant Sonny. Seth's best friend Hobie Tuttle, an African American who has become a successful defense attorney representing Nile Eddgar, once flirted with black separatism, while Seth now writes a syndicated column about the faded 1960's idealism.

Hobie's showboating defense (despite indignant screaming by prosecuting attorney Tommy Molto, who first appeared in *Presumed Innocent*) drags the proceedings into theatrics, and Sonny declares a mistrial. Three-quarters through the novel, the trial is suddenly over, but it has been simply a vehicle for reuniting the Eddgars, Seth, Sonny, and Hobie and examining the people they have become, told from either Seth's or Sonny's point of view, shifting backward and forward from the 1960's to 1995. No one knows the full truth about the Eddgars and Hardcore, neither judge nor journalist; the legal process has not uncovered the events that led to June Eddgar's death. The book's last few chapters cut quickly to interior points of view of Hardcore, Nile, Loyall Eddgar, and June Eddgar, allowing the reader to learn why June met Hardcore and why she was killed. Much of this novel is devoted to the characters' struggles—not always successful—to leave behind the legacies of their parents and find happiness by improving on or rejecting the past.

PERSONAL INJURIES

In *Personal Injuries* Turow draws on his experiences as a federal prosecutor in Operation Greylord, creating the fictionalized Project Petros, a federal investigation of Kindle County judges suspected of bribery. U.S. Attorney Stan Sennett, who heads the investigation, has evidence against personal injury attorney Robert "Robbie" Feaver, who failed to report a slush fund. To escape a long prison term for tax fraud, Feaver reluctantly agrees to assist in a sting operation against the judges, with agent Evon Miller of the Federal Bureau of Investigation as his watchdog. When Feaver hires defense attorney George Mason, who understands the contrasting roles of prosecution and defense and, like Feaver, sees the law in shades of gray rather than in the black-and-white divisions of Sennett's conception, he has an ally.

The operation has Feaver bringing fake personal injury cases before key judges and then offering them bribes to rule in his supposed clients' favor. The novel makes clear the difficulty of gathering evidence of corruption sufficient to survive defense challenges, as video surveillance fails, recordings are muddled, and judges prove cautious. Feaver's beautiful wife, Rainey, is dying of Lou Gehrig's disease, and a jail sentence will leave her without care and protection. Miller, a lesbian from a Fundamentalist Christian religious background, is attracted to the charming Feaver despite his cynicism, relativism, lies, and borderline criminality (he does not really have a law degree). Turow's point is that people do not fit into the narrow legal categories on which Sennett insists; rather, they are complex beings, mixtures of good and bad, more gray than any black or white extreme. Sennett cannot make his case because of the rigidity of his outlook and is to some degree responsible for Feaver's death. In contrast, Miller learns to see the gray areas of life and acts humanely to assist Rainey.

Reversible Errors

In *Reversible Errors*, Turow fictionalizes the discussion of capital punishment that he raises in his nonfiction work *Ultimate Punishment: A Lawyer's Reflections on Dealing with the Death Penalty* (2003) to make his case against capital punishment and to show precisely how easily justice can miscarry. Corporate attorney Arthur Raven has been assigned the final appeal of Rommy Gandolph, convicted of murdering a popular restaurateur based on circumstantial evidence and a confession produced under pressure. Despite Gandolph's marginal developmental disability and disagreeable nature, Raven comes to believe him innocent. To prove his case, he must face detective Larry Starczek, who was responsible for Gandolph's confession, and Muriel Wynn, the prosecutor, both of whom seem unbending. These two were once lovers, and a continuing attraction affects their professional judgment. They do not question their own behavior and are skeptical about defense ploys; they

believe they have acted justly and take pride in the conviction.

Ironically, the former judge who sentenced Gandolph, Gillian Sullivan, was herself imprisoned for taking bribes and now helps Raven's defense. Her vulnerability brings out the best in Raven, who begins an affair with her. Turow thus shows personal and emotional states affecting both prosecution and defense: Wynn permits Starczek great leeway in his conduct of the investigation, and Raven more zealously defends Gandolph to show his new lover his masculine power. Ultimately, it is revealed that the true culprit and motive were never a part of the original investigation. In this novel, Turow captures the complexity of human behavior and motive so well, describing the best efforts of highly competent and basically honorable people, that the reader remains unsure. While many errors can be reversed, death by execution cannot. In this case, only random happenstance—the illness of the true culprit—brings justice.

Ordinary Heroes

Ordinary Heroes departs physically and thematically from Kindle County, although the action begins and ends there and briefly returns. The premise is that reporter Stewart Dubinsky, a very minor character in *Presumed Innocent*, is wrestling with his feelings about his recently deceased father, David Dubin, a judge advocate general (JAG) lawyer in World War II Europe who has been closed-mouthed about his war service. (The son has resurrected the original Russian family name that his father had Americanized.) Stewart, now retired early and searching for a freelance writing project, discovers love letters his father wrote home to a fiancé, Grace Morton, a WASP-ish fellow student he met at Easton College in Kindle County who is very different from Gilda Dubin, Stewart's mother, rescued by his father from a German concentration camp while he was on JAG assignment in the war. Shocked by this unknown and out-of-character fiancé, Stewart realizes how little he really knows about his father. His mother claims ignorance of David's life before she met him, and Stewart is further shaken to learn from documents that his father was court-martialed toward the end of the war. His father's defense attorney, "Bear" Leach, is aged but still lucid and in possession of a long manuscript of David's describing the events leading up to the court-martial. The novel shifts to David's story of his 1944 European experiences, returning occasionally to Stewart in the early 2000's. Stewart plans to publish his father's memoir and is rewriting parts, so we hear the father's tale as edited by the son. As in *The Laws of Our Fathers*, the action shifts back and forth in time and place, but the difference is more than fifty years and on two continents.

The theme of stories is central to *Ordinary Heroes*, which deals with stories told and stories withheld, the latter especially by parents being less than totally candid with their children. In fact, the layers of tales is even greater than one generation, since some of the best yarns were told to a youthful Scott Turow by his father David D. Turow, a field surgeon commanding a military medical company, notably of parachuting at low altitude at night into a Bastogne under German siege and losing excretory control out of sheer terror. (Turow insists that though the stories and travels around the front are his father's, David Turow is in no way David Dubin.) The last line of the book, "And when we tell our parents' tales to the world, or even to ourselves, the story is always our own," addresses both Turow's retelling of his father's history and Stewart's reworking of his fictional father's narrative.

David Dubin feels guilty to be avoiding combat as a JAG lawyer but also relieved. He is conducting courts-martial in France just behind General George S. Patton's advance, punishing American soldiers who have abused French civilians. His investigation of an American expatriate, Robert Martin, a former union organizer on the French railways who now works for the Office of Strategic Services (OSS), the secret operations agency that became the Central Intelligence Agency (CIA), and who is suspected of being a communist with Soviet sympathies, aims at ascertaining Martin's true loyalties. In fact, he finds his own understanding of himself so altered that he begins to question his role as a JAG lawyer. A love triangle intensifies his self-doubts as the pursuit continues. Dubin finds out later that even Martin's London OSS handler is not quite sure whether Martin is a patriot or a double agent. This is classic Turow—characters filled with passionate obsession but clouded by an indeterminate truth. Dubin witnesses the Battle of the Bulge, the brotherhood that combat creates, and the liberation of a Nazi concentration camp. The large-screen scope of *Ordinary Heroes* makes the exactitude of Turow's courtroom novels impossible to sustain, producing a fine read, but short of the author's past successes.

LIMITATIONS

Limitations, which was serialized in sixteen issues of *The New York Times Magazine* beginning April 23, 2006, has a tightness of plot, a highly focused central theme, and an economy of telling that set it apart from Turow's more expansive novels. It ends abruptly, leaving readers wishing for more about its attractive central character. George Mason, first seen as a defense attorney in *Personal Injuries*, representing Robbie Feaver and crossing swords with federal prosecutor Stan Sennett, is the perfect counter to Sennett's prosecutorial zeal, a transplanted Virginian distantly related to the original George Mason of colonial times, a Founding Father and Bill of Rights originator. Mason's philosophy perceives reality in shades of gray, finding human motive complex and even unfathomable, in utter contrast to prosecutor Sennett's insistence on the polar opposites: guilty or not.

At fifty-nine, Judge Mason has done very well, landing an appeals court position in which he has thrived, raising a happy family, and earning the respect of his superiors, his peers, and his court staff. He faces three problems, however, which intermingle: His wife, Patrice, is undergoing treatment for a cancer on her thyroid; he has received e-mailed death threats escalating in intensity; and a sexual assault case before his court, *Warnovits et al.*, in which a high school ice hockey team raped an unconscious girl, recalls a personal sexual encounter, Mason's first, in which the young woman was helplessly drunk. Mason's term of service as judge is up shortly, and he must commit to standing for an assured reelection even as he doubts his right to sit in judgment of a crime he may well have committed himself, no matter that standards of the time were different. Mason is no longer sure who he is, and he even asks Rusty Sabich, the defendant in *Presumed Innocent* but now chief judge, "Who are we to judge?"—an unpromising question for a distinguished senior jurist up for reelection.

The plot unfolds neatly, with several candidates introduced as possible origins of the death threats, sharp and convincing portraits of Mason's staff and coworkers, an assault that rings of authenticity for any urban resident, and nuanced meditations on culpability and how it can be sorted out by the all-or-nothing force of the law: Should the rapists be freed because the statute of limitations period has passed? How can real justice be served without resort to simply ignoring the rule of law and exercising personal judgment, as some of Mason's appeals court colleagues seem to do? The title *Limitations* resonates with meanings: that of the statutory period but also the more general sense of human constraints and insufficiencies. Mason's age allows Turow to present a retrospective of changing sexual mores in the last half of the twentieth century and the ways in which the law has attempted to adapt to new attitudes.

Andrew F. Macdonald

OTHER MAJOR WORKS

NONFICTION: *One L: An Inside Account of Life in the First Year at Harvard Law School*, 1977; *Ultimate Punishment: A Lawyer's Reflections on Dealing with the Death Penalty*, 2003.

EDITED TEXTS: *Guilty as Charged: A Mystery Writers of America Anthology*, 1996 (also known as *Guilty as Charged: The Penguin Book of New American Crime Writing*); *The Best American Mystery Stories, 2006*, 2006.

BIBLIOGRAPHY

Diggs, Terry K. "Through a Glass Darkly: John Grisham and Scott Turow Lay Down the Law for Millions of Americans." *American Bar Association Journal* 82 (October, 1996): 72-75. Compares the realities of the legal life with its representation in the novels of Turow and John Grisham.

Gray, Paul. "Burden of Success: As a High-Powered Lawyer and Novelist, Scott Turow Has Become the Bard of the Litigious Age." *Time*, June 11, 1990. Discusses aspects of Turow's legal fiction and Turow's influence on public perceptions of the legal system.

Lundy, Derek. *Scott Turow: Meeting the Enemy*. To-

ronto, Ont.: ECW Press, 1995. Presents an admiring examination of Turow's background, his work, and his personal views on life, authorship, fame, and the law. Also provides analysis of his early short stories and his first three novels.

Macdonald, Andrew, and Gina Macdonald. *Scott Turow: A Critical Companion*. Westport, Conn.: Greenwood Press, 2005. Provides an examination of Turow's life and literary influences as well as discussion of his major works, including the topics of characterization, themes, and plot structure. Includes bibliography and glossary.

_____. "Scott Turow's *Presumed Innocent*: Novel and Film—Multifaceted Character Study Versus Tailored Courtroom Drama." In *It's a Print! Detective Fiction from Page to Screen*, edited by William Reynolds and Elizabeth Trembley. Bowling Green, Ohio: Bowling Green State University Popular Press, 1994. Discusses the differences between the novel and its film adaptation, focusing in particular on the film's failure to capture the psychological complexity of the novel.

Turow, Scott. "Building a Legal Thriller: Scott Turow Finds Compelling Stories in the Gray Areas Between What's Legal and What's Moral." Interview by Elfrieda Abbe. *Writer* 188 (May, 2005): 18-22. Turow discusses his approach to the creation of a legal thriller.

_____. "Scott Turow: Nothing Is More Moving to Me than What Happens in the Average Life." Interview by Nancy Bunge. In *Master Class: Lessons from Leading Writers*. Iowa City: University of Iowa Press, 2005. Turow addresses his writing methods and techniques.

Watson, Jay. "Making Do in the Courtroom: Notes on Some Convergences Between Forensic Practice and Bricolage." *Studies in Law, Politics, and Society* 14 (1994): 119-137. Discusses how the American judicial process is portrayed in works of fiction, including in Turow's *Presumed Innocent*.

AMOS TUTUOLA

Born: Abeokuta, Nigeria; June 20, 1920
Died: Ibadan, Nigeria; June 8, 1997

PRINCIPAL LONG FICTION

The Palm-Wine Drinkard, 1952
My Life in the Bush of Ghosts, 1954
Simbi and the Satyr of the Dark Jungle,
    1955
The Brave African Huntress, 1958
Feather Woman of the Jungle, 1962
Ajaiyi and His Inherited Poverty, 1967
The Witch-Herbalist of the Remote Town,
    1981
The Wild Hunter in the Bush of Ghosts, 1983
    (wr. c. 1948)
Pauper, Brawler, and Slanderer, 1987

OTHER LITERARY FORMS

Excerpts from the novels of Amos Tutuola (tew-tew-OH-lah) have appeared in numerous anthologies of African literature, but only a handful of short stories have been published. Most of these stories were, until the 1980's, either earlier or later versions of tales included in the novels. These stories include "The Elephant Woman" (in *The Chicago Review*, 1956), "Ajaiyi and the Witchdoctor" (*The Atlantic Monthly*, 1959), "The Duckling Brothers and Their Disobedient Sister" (*Présence africaine*, 1961), "Akanke and the Jealous Pawnbroker" (*Afriscope*, 1974), and "The Pupils of the Eyes" (*Confrontation: A Journal of Third World Literature*, 1974). In 1984, two new stories about a character called Tort, the Shell Man, were published in a popular fantasy anthology in the United States, indicating the possibility of an entirely new audience in the 1980's. Those stories, "The Strange Fellows Palm-Wine Tapster" and "Tort and the Dancing Market Woman," published in *Elsewhere* in 1984, reprise themes found in Tutuola's earliest writings.

ACHIEVEMENTS

Amos Tutuola, who was unknown to both African and Western readers at the time of the publication of *The Palm-Wine Drinkard*, occupies a unique place in the literary world. While his novels have been praised by serious writers and literary critics, he is, quite literally, one of a kind. Despite a limited command of Standard English (which, coupled with his depictions of a "backward" and "superstitious" Africa, has drawn the wrath of many educated Africans), he produced a body of work that stands at the very beginning of the increasingly impressive body of anglophone African literature. Combining the rich folkloric traditions of his Yoruba people with a powerful imagination, his stories supply the Nigerian Bushman with heroes and heroines who face television-handed ghosts, half-bodied babies, bloodthirsty satyrs, and witch-mothers.

Few writers have achieved such serious attention while remaining as unsophisticated in their literary style as did Tutuola. There is no question that Tutuola is, in the truest sense of the word, a "natural," yet he is more than a literary curiosity. In a number of ways, he is a crossroads figure. He succeeded as a writer not by imitating the West but by depending on local sources (mixed with a number of influences from the West but never overwhelmed by them). This helped create a climate in which other Africans could write about the African experience and be accepted both in their own nations and abroad. His dependence on Yoruba folk stories, and such Yoruba-language writers as Chief Daniel O. Fagunwa, continues to draw attention to the richness and variety of African folk traditions.

The depth of Tutuola's debt to those folk stories and the writings of Fagunwa has yet to be fully explored. Extensive passages in several of Tutuola's books appear to be in large part translated or paraphrased from Fagunwa's *The Forest of a Thousand Daemons: A Hunter's Saga* (1950), a title that in itself suggests both Tutuola's second published novel, *My Life in the Bush of Ghosts*, and his first-written novel, *The Wild Hunter in the Bush of Ghosts*. It cannot be said, however, that Tutuola was merely plagiarizing. In a sense, he continued—on paper—the time-honored storytellers' practice of drawing on existing and remembered material to make the old tales new again. Moreover, Tutuola's stories are possessed of a human warmth that makes them more than simply entertaining embellishments of the folk heritage. Despite hardships—which sometimes make the sufferings of Job appear insignificant—his men and women persevere and eventually triumph against all odds. Like all great cultural heroes, they stand up to a potentially destructive universe and struggle to preserve themselves and their people. Their mythic successes are rather like Tutuola's own achievement—wildly unexpected and strangely gratifying.

BIOGRAPHY

There was little in Amos Tutuola's early life to indicate that he would be a world-famous author. Born in 1920, in Abeokuta, Nigeria, in the township of Iporo-Ake, he eagerly listened to the folktales told to him in the evenings by his mother and his aunt. At the age of ten, he was enrolled in the nearby Salvation Army school, where he first began to study English. English is the official language of Nigeria (whose people speak many different African languages), but Tutuola's first language was Yoruba. Furthermore, the everyday English spoken by uneducated Nigerians is either pidgin or affected by West African idiom. Like many other Nigerians, Tutuola combined the deep grammar of his native language with English surface grammar. "I had no other work more than to drink," for example, the statement made by the Palm-Wine Drinkard at the start of his story, is typical Yoruba syntax.

When his family could no longer afford to send him to school, Tutuola began to work as a houseboy for a government clerk. In return for his services, the clerk enrolled Tutuola in Ake Central School and, later, in Lagos High School. There, Tutuola became familiar with the Yoruba writings of Fagunwa and simplified versions of such classics as John Bunyan's *The Pilgrim's Progress* (1678, 1684). Apparently he was not an outstanding student, for he decided to leave school and learn the trade of blacksmith, finding a job as a metalworker for the Royal Air Force at Oshodi. When this job ended, the only work Tutuola could find was as a junior messenger for the labor department in Lagos in 1946. Much of his time was spent sitting in the offices, waiting for messages to carry. To combat his boredom, he began scribbling down stories on scraps of paper. Around 1948, he sent his first completed manuscript, *The Wild Hunter in the Bush of Ghosts*, to a photography publisher in London, the Focal Press. The book, he explained to them in a letter, was written to accompany a collection of photographs of ghosts. Those photographs, he said, would follow shortly. The photographs turned out to be of drawings of ghosts, and Focal Press dumped both text and "ghost photos" into their files. There they remained for more than thirty years.

Although Tutuola may have been discouraged by that early failure (which he did not mention to anyone for decades), he continued to write. Upon seeing an advertisement for books from the United Society for Christian Literature in a newspaper, he decided to send to that organization a manuscript, the first draft of which had been written in lead pencil over the course of several days. After three months of enlarging the story, he made a copy of it in ink and sent it off. The society did not publish books but, making one of those small decisions that have unexpectedly large effects, it sent the manuscript to the publishing house Faber and Faber. Slightly more than one year later, in 1952, it was published as *The Palm-Wine Drinkard*. Three months after its publication, Faber and Faber received a second Tutuola manuscript. After a small amount of editing by Geoffrey Parrinder, it was published as *My Life in the Bush of Ghosts*. It is clear now that it drew freely on Tutuola's memories of his first, "lost" manuscript.

Enchanted by his fresh West African idiom, critics praised the book and went so far as to urge other African writers to follow Tutuola's example—a difficult task; indeed, Tutuola himself found it hard to do. He continued for a time to work as a messenger (who was visited now and then by distinguished white scholars, to the disapproving surprise of his employers) but was now concerned about his own shortcomings. He acknowledged that his English was imperfect, so he attended night school to improve it. His renown brought him a great deal of attention, but he remained a shy, retiring person. A job working as a storekeeper for the Nigerian Broadcasting Corporation was given to him in 1956, and in 1957, he arranged to be transferred to the Ibadan offices of the corporation so that he could work with Professor Collis at the University of Ibadan in producing a play version of *The Palm-Wine Drinkard*. This version was translated into Yoruba and successfully staged throughout West Africa in the early 1960's.

Married in 1947 and the father of several children, Tutuola was never comfortable playing the part of a celebrity. He had little to say to interviewers and did not like to go on lecture tours or even have much to do with other writers (though he was a self-effacing charter member of the Mbari Club, a seminal writers' and publishers' group in Nigeria). A six-month scholarship was offered to him in 1963 by West Germany, but he did not accept it.

By the time Tutuola's third novel was published, there was some improvement in his standard of English, but there also was a growing disenchantment with his work. Africans continued to criticize both his bad habits and his borrowings, and Europeans intimated that his "improvement" had a negative effect on his work, which they also criticized for being repetitive. To some, he was now deliberately childish, whereas before he had been pleasingly childlike.

By the 1970's, however, Tutuola was again receiving praise from both African and European critics, who were beginning to see his writings for what they were: not true novels, but linked stories in the monomythic tradition. Some see him as the equivalent for world literature of the *akpala kpatita* (professional storyteller) of Nigeria. (Jorge Amado, the popular Brazilian writer, shows the influence of Tutuola in his own writing.) This renewed and more balanced attention directed toward Tutuola is surely one of the factors that led to his publishing a book in 1981, the first in more than a decade, and an extended tour of the United States in the 1980's, during which he spoke and took part in symposia. Thanks to some fine scholarly detective work by Bernth Lindfors, the handwritten original manuscript of what was to be Tutuola's first novel, *The Wild Hunter in the Bush of Ghosts*, was found; it was then published in 1983. As a result, both scholars and biographers of the Yoruba writer had to do considerable backtracking. Published by Three Continents Press with a typeset script facing photocopies of the original handwritten pages, it is significant as a minor work at an early stage of Tutuola's development. Furthermore, as Lindfors puts it in his introduction to the book, it is "the first long piece of prose fiction written for publication in English by a Nigerian author."

ANALYSIS

Although it is certainly possible to enjoy Amos Tutuola's novels on their own merits—merits that include economy of language, a strong storytelling voice, a marvelous self-assurance on the part of his narrators (almost always in the first person), fantastic imagination, and virtually nonstop action—it is useful to look at him within the context of Yoruba culture. The Yorubas are a people of western Nigeria who both have embraced Western culture and have remained intensely connected to traditional ways. The Yoruba people make up about 20 percent of the population of Nigeria, Africa's most populous nation and one of its best educated. Although Christianity is the religion of virtually all Yoruba people, there is a deep undercurrent of animism.

As with Tutuola's narrators, contemporary Yoruba people see nothing unusual in a world where churches coexist with magical charms (*juju*) and the deepest and most impassable jungles (the bush) are filled with spirits, both those of the dead and those of nonhuman beings. Yoruba folklore is characterized by a belief in a distant but benevolent supreme deity and the presence on the earth of numerous smaller "gods" and powers, often anthropomorphic. It is still common practice for both adults and children to sit around in the evening and listen to folk stories much like those in Tutuola's books. In some cases, they do so while drinking palm wine, a mildly alcoholic beverage made from the sap of palm trees.

Inexpensive or "free" primary education in British-style schools, often run by churches, was common when Tutuola was a child, and this exposure, from his tenth year until his late teens, provided Tutuola with the necessary tools—literacy and a knowledge of literary forms (from simplified classics in the schools to books published in Yoruba)—to begin his career as a writer. One thing those schools did not give him, however, was the confidence of one who knows a good story and is not afraid to tell it. It was that self-assurance (so clearly echoed in the gentle strength of all of his various protagonists) that led a junior clerk, a man in a lowly position in an extremely class-conscious colonial society, to dare to send his first writings to a publisher.

THE PALM-WINE DRINKARD

The Palm-Wine Drinkard begins with the narrator telling us a bit about himself. "I was a palm-wine drinkard since I was a boy of ten years of age. I had no other work more than to drink palm-wine in my life." These first words hardly prepare readers for the mythic dimensions of the character seen later in the book, but the prodigious amounts of palm wine he consumes (225 kegs every twenty-four hours) give us the hint that he is no ordinary human. When his palm-wine tapster falls from a tree and dies, the Drinkard sees that the only thing he can do is seek out his tapster in the land of the Dead. This sets the mythic tone of the book and all the rest of Tutuola's work. The Drinkard enters the bush, a netherworld inhabited by spirits and strange creatures. His first encounter, with an old man who sets him the Herculean task of capturing Death, reveals to us the Drinkard's superhuman powers. His other name, he tells us, is "Father of gods who could do everything in this world," and his success in capturing Death (who then escapes, which is why "we are hearing his name about in the world") proves that his title is no idle boast. The Drinkard's next exploit is to rescue his wife-to-be from a skull who has borrowed body parts to masquerade as a "Complete Gentleman." Thereafter, he and his wife continue on his quest, but not before she becomes pregnant (in her thumb) and gives birth to a miraculous and dangerous half-bodied child who must be destroyed before they can continue on their way. They do eventually reach the town of the Dead, despite the menace of such beasts as a Spirit of Prey with eyes like searchlights and with the help of the Drinkard's powerful jujus and such beings as the Faithful Mother, whose servants buy the Drinkard's death and rent his fear.

Novelistic plot development in the conventional sense does not exist in this or Tutuola's other romances; the various episodes are almost interchangeable. The Drinkard, however, does learn a lesson at the end of the novel. His tapster has now (like a student in a European school or an apprentice blacksmith) "qualified" as a full dead man. He cannot return to the living. Instead, he gives the Drinkard and his resourceful wife, who has developed into something of a Sibyl, a miraculous egg. The Drinkard and his wife return to the land of the living. There he finds a famine and, sending a sacrifice to Heaven, brings rain to the people—an ending that seems to recapitulate the conclusion of a traditional creation story.

In one of the best analyses of Tutuola's style, Lindfors concludes that his books are not novels at all; instead, they are, in content, structure, and style, concatenated folktales. Both African and English critics have noted the structure of the quest and the rite of passage that also characterize Tutuola's extended narratives. They always begin with the introduction of a main character; the sending out of that character into the world, where many hardships are encountered; the overcoming of all obstacles; and the return of the hero or heroine in triumph. This structure is both that of *The Pilgrim's Progress* and that of the epic stories of Yoruba (and other African) cultural heroes as they overcome death, use their personal magic to change themselves into animals or objects, and travel through a world fully as hostile as real life. To describe either Tutuola's stories or African folklore as escapism, in fact, is quite inaccurate. The worlds of Simbi, of the Brave Huntress, and of the Drinkard are graphically horrifying. They are no more an escape than would be a series of vivid nightmares.

The flavor of the stories is that of the naïve tall tale. Almost anything is possible in such accounts, even turning oneself into a stone and then throwing oneself to escape. The reader (or the listener, for the voice in Tutuola is that of an oral storyteller) is carried along by the headlong rush of events, the total acceptance of this illogical world by the narrators (who always live well within this world, playing and winning by its rules), the humor and humanity that are among the author's greatest virtues. Furthermore—and here both Tutuola's Christian faith (which is very real) and the folktale tradition come into play—these are moral tales. There are always lessons to be learned. No one commits a foolish action without having to pay the consequences. Good is always eventually rewarded; evil is always strong but eventually defeated.

There is a clear structure to each of Tutuola's books, a beginning and an end that are carefully linked. The Drinkard's search for his tapster ends with his finding him and learning a lesson as a result of all of his efforts— a lesson that was unexpected on the protagonist's part but that the reader responds to and understands. *My Life in the Bush of Ghosts* begins with the central character not knowing what "good" or "bad" or hatred is. It ends, after twenty-four years of trials and wandering in the bush, with these words: "This is what hatred did."

A cornucopia of horrifically memorable menaces confronts Tutuola's protagonists in each of the books. Indeed, this may be one of the more serious of Tutuola's failings, the very abundance of monsters and fabulous encounters in each of his stories (although those monsters are invariably memorable and individually characterized with surprising economy). After a certain point, especially when one reads a series of Tutuola's novels in a short space of time, events and characters begin to blur and one feels overwhelmed. It was probably with this overabundance in mind that the dramatic version of *The Palm-Wine Drinkard* was created out of only eight of the twenty episodes found in the book. In his essay "Amos Tutuola: A Nigerian Visionary," Gerald Moore characterizes the first two novels as quest romances and ties them to the monomyth of Joseph Campbell's *The Hero with a Thousand Faces* (1949). Considering that Tutuola's stories follow the pattern of Yoruba storytelling sessions, only a bit more extended, and those stories often relate creation myths, it is not surprising that Moore should find that pattern.

MY LIFE IN THE BUSH OF GHOSTS

It is difficult to use conventional critical apparatus in dealing with Tutuola. It is equally difficult to summarize easily any of his books, for they consist, like his first book, of a loosely organized, helter-skelter collection of fantastic events that have their own logic.

My Life in the Bush of Ghosts presents its readers with another character like the Drinkard, but possessed of less magic. He is, however—like the Drinkard—resourceful, plucky, and often very shrewd. He is not fortunate enough to have a wife like the Drinkard's, but Tutuola makes up for that in the characters of both Simbi and the Brave African Huntress in his later books. They are women of purpose, wonderfully self-reliant, and as capable as his male heroes. Simbi engages in heroic combat with a "Satyr" (Tutuola's names for his mythic creatures are often drawn from Western mythology but have nothing at all to do with the original beings in Western myth) who is ten feet tall, covered with blood and feathers, "an impatient and ill-tempered, impenitent and noxious creature." The Brave African Huntress vows death to all the "pygmies" (small creatures that resemble the various dwarflike forest creatures of African myth rather than human beings) who have either killed or "de-tained" her four brothers. She proceeds to do so with bloodthirsty efficiency, burning the pygmy town, blowing it up with gunpowder, and then picking off the pygmies one by one with her gun as they run from the ruins. After rescuing her brothers, she proceeds to sell the minerals found in the Jungle of the Pygmies and becomes wealthy.

The world that is inhabited by the characters in all of Tutuola's writing is an interesting one in another way. It contains no Caucasians. Aside from one brief reference to a set of footprints made in the rocks near Ife by "the first white men who had traveled from heaven through that rock to the earth," one finds no Europeans in his books. Instead, the books are set in an African Africa, albeit an Africa affected by Western inventions and institutions such as newspapers, gunpowder, the Methodist Church, and airplanes. Though it may be unintentional, certain sections of Tutuola's novels—such as the description of the Dead Cousin who has become a Methodist bishop in the "10th Town of Ghosts"—seem to be parodies of real events in Nigerian history. More often than not, Western objects appear in Tutuola's similes—as when he compares the sound of the skulls chasing the Drinkard to "a thousand petrol drums pushing along a hard road." His is thus not an ideal Africa, but one rather like the West Africa of the early nineteenth century, when the influence of the slave trade had deepened rivalries between such African states as Oyo and Dahomey and created a climate of continual warfare and uncertainty. In this world, Tutuola's heroes and heroines are much like many Yoruba people of today, men and women who deal with an increasingly complicated world with pragmatism, shrewdness, and even humor.

Joseph Bruchac

OTHER MAJOR WORKS

SHORT FICTION: "The Elephant Woman," 1956; "Ajaiyi and the Witchdoctor," 1959; "The Duckling Brothers and Their Disobedient Sister," 1961; "Akanke and the Jealous Pawnbroker," 1974; "The Pupils of the Eyes," 1974; "The Strange Fellows Palm-Wine Tapster," 1984; "Tort and the Dancing Market Woman," 1984; *Yoruba Folktales*, 1986; *The Witch Doctor, and Other Stories*, 1990.

NONFICTION: *Tutuola at the University: The Italian Voice of a Yoruba Ancestor*, 2001 (lectures; Alessandro Di Maio, editor).

BIBLIOGRAPHY

Achebe, Chinua. "Work and Play in Tutuola's *The Palm-Wine Drinkard*." In *Hopes and Impediments: Selected Essays*. New York: Doubleday, 1989. Novelist Achebe's perceptive article about Tutuola's novel *The Palm-Wine Drinkard* is included in this collection of essays examining art and literature.

Afolayan, A. "Language and Sources of Amos Tutuola." *In Perspectives on African Literature*, edited by Christopher Heywood. New York: African Publishing, 1971. Afolayan's essay assesses Tutuola's contribution to Yoruba literature from a Yoruba perspective.

Ajayi, Jare. *Amos Tutuola: Factotum as a Pioneer*. Ibadan, Nigeria: Creative Books, 2003. Ajayi, a Nigerian journalist, spent sixteen years researching and writing this first English-language biography of Tutuola, which discusses, among other subjects, the novelist's motivations for creative writing and how he was exploited by publishers. Also includes interpretations of Tutuola's work.

George, Olakunle. *Relocating Agency: Modernity and African Letters*. Albany: State University of New York Press, 2003. George examines writings by Tutuola and three other Nigerian writers—Daniel O. Fagunwa, Wole Soyinka, and Chinua Achebe. He uses several modern critical theories, including poststructuralism and postcolonialism, to interpret these writers' works.

Gera, Anjali. *Three Great African Novelists: Chinua Achebe, Wole Soyinka, and Amos Tutuola*. New Delhi, India: Creative Books, 2001. Gera's examination of Tutuola—along with novelists Chinua Achebe and Wole Soyinka—focuses on the use of the Yoruba and Igbo storytelling traditions in his work. Gera describes how Tutuola adapts these traditions to define himself and his society.

Irele, Abiola. "Tradition and the Yoruba Writer: Daniel O. Fagunwa, Amos Tutuola, and Wole Soyinka." In *Perspectives on Wole Soyinka: Freedom and Complexity*, edited by Biodun Jeyifo. Jackson: University Press of Mississippi, 2001. Irele's essay compares Tutuola's work with that of two other Yoruba writers. The essay should be read with Afolayan's essay in *Perspectives on African Literature*.

Lindfors, Bernth, ed. *Critical Perspectives on Amos Tutuola*. Washington, D.C.: Three Continents Press, 1975. This collection of essays, edited by a respected Tutuola scholar, provides critical insight into Tutuola's individual novels. Includes a bibliography.

Onyeberechi, Sydney E. *Critical Essays: Achebe, Baldwin, Cullen, Ngugi, and Tutuola*. Hyattsville, Md.: Rising Star, 1999. Essays on African and African American literature, featuring critical commentary on Tutuola, Chinua Achebe, Ngugi wa Thiong'o, Countee Cullen, and James Baldwin.

_____. "Myth, Magic, and Appetite in Amos Tutuola's *The Palm-Wine Drinkard*." *MAWA Review* 4 (1989): 22-26. Often cited as one of the best studies of Tutuola's masterpiece. A brief but comprehensive study.

Owomoyela, Oyekan. *Amos Tutuola Revisited*. New York: Twayne, 1999. An excellent introduction to Tutuola's life and works, written by a Yoruba writer and scholar. Owomoyela argues that Tutuola symbolizes the African tradition from the time of colonialism to postcolonialism. Includes notes, references, a selected bibliography, and an index.

Quayson, Ato. "Treasures of an Opulent Fancy: Amos Tutuola and the Folktale Narrative." In *Strategic Transformation in Nigerian Writing: Orality and History in the Work of Rev. Samuel Johnson, Amos Tutuola, Wole Soyinka, and Ben Okri*. Bloomington: Indiana University Press, 1997. A sound treatment of the element of orality in fiction by Tutuola and three other Nigerian writers. Quayson focuses on Tutuola's novels *The Palm-Wine Drinkard* and *My Life in the Bush of Ghosts*.

MARK TWAIN
Samuel Langhorne Clemens

Born: Florida, Missouri; November 30, 1835
Died: Redding, Connecticut; April 21, 1910
Also known as: Samuel Langhorne Clemens

PRINCIPAL LONG FICTION

The Gilded Age, 1873 (with Charles Dudley
    Warner)
The Adventures of Tom Sawyer, 1876
The Prince and the Pauper, 1881
Adventures of Huckleberry Finn, 1884
A Connecticut Yankee in King Arthur's Court,
    1889
The American Claimant, 1892
Tom Sawyer Abroad, 1894
The Tragedy of Pudd'nhead Wilson, 1894
Personal Recollections of Joan of Arc, 1896
Tom Sawyer, Detective, 1896
A Double-Barrelled Detective Story, 1902
Extracts from Adam's Diary, 1904
Eve's Diary, Translated from the Original Ms,
    1906
A Horse's Tale, 1906
*Extract from Captain Stormfield's Visit to
    Heaven*, 1909
The Mysterious Stranger, 1916 (revised as *The
    Chronicle of Young Satan*, 1969, by Albert
    Bigelow Paine and Frederick A. Duneka)
Report from Paradise, 1952 (Dixon Wecter,
    editor)
Simon Wheeler, Detective, 1963
Mark Twain's Mysterious Stranger Manuscripts,
    1969 (William M. Gibson, editor)

OTHER LITERARY FORMS

In addition to his novels, Mark Twain wrote a great deal of short fiction, which can be divided, although often only arbitrarily, into short stories, tales, and humorous sketches. One of the best examples of his short stories is "The Man That Corrupted Hadleyburg," and one of the best examples of his humorous sketches is the jumping frog story. Somewhere between the story and the sketch are tales such as "Captain Stormfield's Visit to Heaven."

Twain also wrote speeches and essays, both humorous and critical. Representative of his best satiric essays, which range from the very funny to the very sober, are "Fenimore Cooper's Literary Offenses" and "To the Person Sitting in Darkness." The first of these is a hilarious broadside against Cooper's style and invention in which Twain is obviously enjoying himself while at the same time continuing his ongoing war against the romanticizing of the past. "To the Person Sitting in Darkness," considered by some to be his finest piece of invective, is his attack on what he saw as the exploitation of the Philippines following the Spanish-American War by, in his words, "The Blessings-of-Civilization Trust."

Early in his career, Twain wrote the travel sketches and impressions *The Innocents Abroad* (1869), *Roughing It* (1872), and *A Tramp Abroad* (1880), and later, *Following the Equator* (1897). Two of his most important books are autobiographical, *Life on the Mississippi* (1883) and *Mark Twain's Autobiography*, published in various editions in 1924.

ACHIEVEMENTS

The coincidental appearance of Halley's comet in the years of Mark Twain's birth and death, 1835 and 1910, has been much remarked. A historical event, however, in contrast to the cosmic one, occurring very near the midpoint of his life, provides a better symbol for his career and his achievement than does the mysterious, fiery comet. In 1869, at Promontory Point, Utah, a golden spike was driven to complete the first North American transcontinental railroad. The subsequent settling of the great midwestern center of the continent and the resulting transformation of a frontier society into a civilized one, a process people thought would take hundreds of years, was to be effected in several decades. Twain's life spanned the two Americas, the frontier America that produced so much of the national mythology and the emerging urban, industrial giant of the twentieth century. At the heart of Twain's achievement is his creation

Mark Twain. (Library of Congress)

represent on the personal, the literary, and the cultural planes.

On the personal plane, Tom and Huck represent aspirations so fundamental to Twain's life as to make them seem rather the two halves of his psyche. Like good and bad angels, they have been taken to represent the contending desires in his life: a strong desire for the security and status of material success on one hand set against the deeply ingrained desire for freedom from conventional social and moral restraints on the other. It has been conjectured that steamboat piloting was perhaps the most satisfying of Twain's occupations because it offered him high degrees of both respectability and freedom. Although the character of Tom, the symbol of perennial boyhood, can be easily overburdened by this perspective, there is in him the clear outline of the successful, settled, influential man-of-affairs-to-be. If Tom had grown up, he—like Twain himself—might well have made and lost a fortune in the publishing business and through investments in the Paige typesetter. He almost certainly would have been a successful professional or businessman. He would most likely have traveled abroad and would have been eager to associate with nobility at every opportunity. It is relatively easy to imagine Tom growing up. It is instructive to realize that it is almost impossible to imagine Huck's doing so.

On the literary plane, the two may also be seen as representing contending forces, those of the two principal literary schools of the period, the Romantic and the realistic. Surely, Twain's pervasive attacks on Romantic literature are somewhat compulsive, reminiscent of Nathaniel Hawthorne's preoccupation with the Puritans. Both protest too much. Twain is one of America's foremost Romantics, even if he did see himself as a realist and even if he did engage much of his time in puncturing the sentimental balloons of the disciples of Sir Wal-

of Tom Sawyer and Huck Finn, who embody that mythic America, midway between the wilderness and the modern super-state.

Tom and Huck, two of the nation's most enduring characters, give particular focus to Twain's turbulent, sprawling, complex career as journalist, humorist, entrepreneur, and novelist. The focus is dramatic because the two characters have made their way into the popular imagination with the abiding vitality of legend or folklore. They have been kept before generations of Americans in motion pictures, television, cartoons, and other popular art forms as well as in their original form in the novels. The focus is also symbolic because of the fundamental dualism that the two characters can be seen to ter Scott, Cooper, and the graveyard poets. He was both Romantic and realist, and Tom and Huck emerge almost allegorically as symbols of the two major literary schools of the late nineteenth century.

Tom as the embodiment of socially conforming respectability and as a disciple of Romantic literature contrasts illustratively with Huck as the embodiment of the naturally free spirit, who is "realistic" in part because of his adolescent honesty about such things as art, royalty, and the efficacy of prayer. It is the symbolic dualism on the historical plane, however, that brings into sharpest focus the nature of Twain's central and most enduring achievement. On the historical plane, his two central characters reflect most clearly Twain's principal legacy to posterity: the embodiment in fiction of that moment in time, a moment both real and imaginary, given some historical particularity by the driving of the golden spike at Promontory Point in 1869, when America was poised between the wilderness and the modern, technological state. In this context, Tom represents the settlements that were to become the towns and cities of the new century, and Huck represents the human spirit, freer, at least in the imagination, in the wilderness out of which the settlements were springing. At the end of *Adventures of Huckleberry Finn*, Twain sends Huck on that impossible mission that has been central to the American experience for centuries, when he has him decide to "light out for the territory" before Aunt Sally can "adopt" and "civilize" him.

Twain the humorist and satirist, the silver-mining and typesetting entrepreneur, the journalist, the family man, the anguished, skeptical seeker after religious faith—all must be taken into consideration in accounts of the nature of his achievements. Without Tom Sawyer and Huck Finn, he would have made his mark as a man of his time, a man of various and rich talents. Most likely, his reputation would rest today largely on his talents as a humorist and satirist, and that reputation still figures largely in assessments of his overall achievement. With Tom and Huck, however, his achievement is given the depth and dramatic focus of a central contribution to the national mythology. Huck's "voice" is frequently compared to the voice of Walt Whitman's "Song of Myself" (1855). Such comparisons rest in part on rhetorical similarities between the two voices, similarities in what has

been called the "vernacular mode." More significantly, they derive from the similarities of the achievements of the poet and the novelist in the establishing of historically and culturally distinctive American "voices" in poetry and fiction. Tom Sawyer and Huck Finn loom large on the nineteenth century literary horizon. They stand, along with James Fenimore Cooper's Natty Bumppo and Chingachgook, Hawthorne's Hester Prynne and Arthur Dimmesdale, and Whitman's persona in "Song of Myself," as the principal characters of the emerging national literature. Twain's contribution to that body of literature is at the deepest center of his achievement as a major American writer.

BIOGRAPHY

Mark Twain was born Samuel Langhorne Clemens in Florida, Missouri, in 1835. He first used the pen name Mark Twain, taken from the leadsman's cry for two fathoms of water, in 1862. Twain's father was a Virginia lawyer, and the family was of poor but respectable southern stock. In 1839, the family moved to Hannibal, Missouri, the Mississippi River town that provided the source material and background of some of Twain's best-known fiction. After his father died in 1847, Twain left school to become an apprentice in the printing shop of his brother, Orion. From 1853 to 1856, Twain worked as a journeyman printer in St. Louis, New York, Philadelphia, Keokuk, and Cincinnati.

Between 1857 and 1860, Twain acquired much of his knowledge of the Mississippi River as a pilot, beginning that short though richly productive career under the tutelage of a senior pilot, Horace Bixby. He was a Confederate volunteer for several weeks after the American Civil War began. In 1861, he left for the Nevada Territory with Orion, where he drifted into prospecting and journalism, beginning his career as a reporter with the *Virginia City Territorial Enterprise* and continuing it with the *San Francisco Morning Call*.

Twain's literary career and the beginning of his fame might be said to have begun in 1865 with the publication in the *New York Saturday Press* of "Jim Smiley and His Jumping Frog" (later known as "The Celebrated Jumping Frog of Calaveras County"). As a journalist, he went to the Sandwich Islands in 1866 and to Europe and the Holy Land in 1867. The latter of the two provided him with the experiences that he shaped into his first book, *The Innocents Abroad*. His narrative of pioneers striving to establish civilization on the frontier, *Roughing It*, appeared in 1872, and his first novel-length fiction, *The Gilded Age*, written with Charles Dudley Warner, came in 1873.

In 1870, Twain married Olivia Langdon. After beginning their married life in Buffalo, New York, they resettled in Hartford, Connecticut, in 1871. Their infant son, Langdon, died in 1872, the year Susy, their first daughter, was born. Her sisters, Clara and Jean, were born in 1874 and 1880, respectively. Twain's most productive years as a novelist came in this middle period when his daughters were young and he was prospering. *The Adventures of Tom Sawyer*, *The Prince and the Pauper*, *Adventures of Huckleberry Finn*, and *A Connecticut Yankee in King Arthur's Court* were all written during this highly productive period.

By 1890, Twain's financial fortunes were crumbling, mostly owing to bad investment in his own publishing firm and in the Paige typesetter. In 1891, he closed the Hartford mansion, sold the furniture, and went to Europe to economize. In 1896, after he completed a round-the-world lecture tour, his daughter, Susy, died, and his wife shortly afterward suffered a nervous collapse from which she never recovered. Twain blamed himself for bringing on his beloved family the circumstances that led to both tragedies. His abiding skepticism about human nature deepened to cynicism and found expression in those dark stories of his last years, such as "The Man That Corrupted Hadleyburg," "The Mysterious Stranger," and the essay "What Is Man?" Twain died in 1910 at the age of seventy-four in Redding, Connecticut.

ANALYSIS

It is instructive to note that the most pervasive structural characteristic of Mark Twain's work, of his nonfiction as well as his fiction, is dualistic. That observation is not worth much without detailed application to specific aspects of particular works, but even before turning to particulars, it is useful to consider how many "pairs" of contending, conflicting, complementary, or contrasting characters, situations, states of being, ideas, and values run through Twain's work. One thinks immediately of Tom and Huck, of Huck and Jim, of Huck and Pap,

of Aunt Sally and Miss Watson, of the prince and the pauper, of the two sets of twins in *The Tragedy of Pudd'nhead Wilson*. One thinks of boys testing themselves against adults, of youth and adulthood, of the free life on the river contrasted with the settled life of the river towns, of the wilderness and civilization, of the promises of industrial progress against the backdrop of the humbler, traditional rural setting, of Eden and everything east of Eden, and, finally, of good and evil.

The tonal quality of Twain's works is also dualistic. The jumping frog story is almost pure fun. "The Mysterious Stranger," first published in bowdlerized form after Twain's death, is almost pure gloom. Most of Twain's fiction comes between the two, both chronologically and thematically. Except for *The Gilded Age*, which he wrote with Warner, the novels, from *The Adventures of Tom Sawyer* to the final two, *The Tragedy of Pudd'nhead Wilson* and *Personal Recollections of Joan of Arc*, fall within the thematic and tonal extremes established by the short fiction. That is, Tom's adventures take place in the hallowed light of innocence and virtue beyond the reach of any truly effective evil forces, while Roxy's adventures in *The Tragedy of Pudd'nhead Wilson* are of almost unrelieved gloom. *Adventures of Huckleberry Finn* is midway between the extremes, with its blending of the light and affirmation that shine so brightly in Twain's childhood idyll with the darkened vision of the later years.

THE ADVENTURES OF TOM SAWYER

Nearly everyone agrees that *The Adventures of Tom Sawyer*, Twain's second novel, is an American classic, and nearly everyone agrees that there is no accounting for its success. It is at the same time a novel of the utmost simplicity and of deep complexity. The novel is a marvelous boy's adventure story, a fact given perspective by Twain's observation that "it will be read only by adults." That is, the essence of childhood can be savored only after the fact, only after one has passed through it and can look back on it. Popularizations of Tom's adventures are produced for children, but the continuing vitality of the novel depends on the adult sensibility and its capacity and need for nostalgic recollection. Twain plays on all the strings of that sensibility as he guides the reader through Tom's encounters with the adult world, represented by Aunt Polly and Judge Thatcher, through Tom's romance with Becky, and finally to the adventurous triumph over evil in the person of Injun Joe.

Aunt Polly is the perfect adult foil for a perfect boyhood. Not only does she provide the emotional security that comes from being loved in one's place, but she also serves as an adult Tom can challenge through his wits, thereby deepening his self-confidence about his place in the adult world. The fence whitewashing episode is surely one of the best known in American literature. In it, Tom not only outwits his friends, whom he persuades to whitewash the fence for him, but also successfully challenges the adult world, which, through Aunt Polly, assigned the "boy's chore" to him in the first place. The episode also provides Twain an opportunity to exercise his irony, which, in contrast to much that was to come in the later fiction, is serenely gentle here. Judge Thatcher represents the secure, if somewhat pompous, authority of the adult world beyond the domestic circle. The much desired recognition of that authority is achieved with decisive pomp when the Judge makes the treasure found in the cave legally Tom's and Huck's.

The romance with Becky is almost pure idyll, although the young lovers' descent into the cave inevitably raises speculations about deeper implications. While Injun Joe as evil incarnate is believable enough to raise the hair along the back of the necks of adults as well as children, especially when the last candle burns out in the cave, there is never any doubt that Tom and Becky will be saved, that good will triumph—never any doubt, that is, for the adult sensibility, secure beyond the trials and tribulations of adolescent infatuation and terror.

The book as childhood idyll is really a simple matter, but that does not diminish the significance of that dimension of the work. Rather, it affirms an understanding of the book's success on that level. There is more to be considered, however, especially in terms of the companion piece to come, *Adventures of Huckleberry Finn*. The poignancy of *The Adventures of Tom Sawyer* is attributable in part to its being an imaginative reconstruction of youthful experience from the perspective of early middle age. The actual historical frame of the re-creation adds its own deeply poignant dimension to the book. The American national experience was clearly in the transitional state between frontier and modern society when the novel was published in 1876. Twain's idyll of boy-hood is set in a time and place in history calculated to deepen the significance of the adult's backward recollection of a time of innocence and joy. The American wilderness was never Eden, but that image has haunted the American imagination from at least the time of Cooper's creation of his frontiersman, Natty Bumppo, down to at least the time of Robert Frost's creation of his travelers through the dark, lonely woods.

Finally, in part because it is one of those many pairings of characters so pervasive in Twain's work, Tom's relationship with his half brother, Sid, should be noted. The relationship is instructive in that it foreshadows that of the later Tom-Huck relationship. Sid is the model boy who serves as Twain's foil for Tom's adventuresome independence. While Tom is never good in the subservient, lap-dog sense that Sid is, there is a kind of lateral movement of his character from the early to the later novel; in *The Adventures of Tom Sawyer*, Tom plays off the foil of Sid's pious "respectability," while in *Adventures of Huckleberry Finn*, Tom has moved over to provide a similar foil for Huck's freedom.

THE PRINCE AND THE PAUPER

Unlike its predecessor, *The Prince and the Pauper* is a "children's book" that has remained simply that, a book for children. Twain professed to have taken great joy in the writing of it, probably in part because of the relief he felt upon completing the troublesome *A Tramp Abroad*. His wife and children admired the book, as did William Dean Howells and the reviewers for the *New York Herald*, the *Boston Transcript*, *The Atlantic Monthly*, and *Century*. Nevertheless, the novel holds little interest for the mature reader except in terms of its relationship to the two superior novels that preceded and followed it.

Its plot hinges on one of Twain's most explicit pairings, that of Prince Edward with the pauper Tom Cantry. The switching of these look-alike adolescents in the England of Henry VIII allows the prince to learn what poverty and hardship are like in the alleyways of his kingdom and the pauper to satirize, through his innocence, the foibles of royalty and court life. Neither the satire nor the compassion, however, ring true. It is almost as if Twain were finding his way from his first classic to his second through this experiment, set in a time and place far removed from his native Mississippi River valley.

With that contrast in mind, it is perhaps reasonable to see the prince and the pauper as another Sid and Tom, another Tom and Huck, all of the sets representing at various removes those two basic drives of Twain's nature for respectability and freedom. Huck and Tom Cantry, the pauper, are "freer" than are Tom and Prince Edward, although the relationships are not that simple, since the members of each pair are attracted like magnetic opposites to their mates. This attraction is made most explicit in *The Prince and the Pauper*, where the two actually exchange places. Later in his career, in *The Tragedy of Pudd'nhead Wilson*, Twain made a comparably explicit exchange with wholly tragic consequences. In *The Prince and the Pauper*, it is all play with little consequence at all except for the exigencies of a contrived, melodramatic plot. Twain's truest pairing, that of Huck and Jim, was yet ahead of him.

ADVENTURES OF HUCKLEBERRY FINN

Adventures of Huckleberry Finn is almost universally hailed as Twain's best book, as well as one of the half dozen or so American classics of the nineteenth century. This is not to say that the novel is without defects. The ending, in particular, presents some very real problems, structurally, thematically, and rhetorically. The very high place of the novel, however, is generally conceded. This success depends on several considerations. In the first place, the novel continues the mythic idyll of American boyhood begun with *The Adventures of Tom Sawyer*. That connection and that continuation by itself would have ensured the book a place in the National Archives if not the national heart. Most agree, however, that its success derives from even deeper currents.

Adventures of Huckleberry Finn is Twain's best book because, for whatever reasons, he brought together in it, with the highest degree of artistic balance, those most fundamental dualities running through his work and life from start to finish. The potentially destructive dualities of youth and age, of the need for both security and freedom, of the wilderness and civilization, of innocence and corruption, all are reconciled by means of an aesthetic transformation. Historical, realistic dualities as well as psychological and moral dualities are brought into an artistic synthesis, into a novel, the most distinctive feature of which, finally, is its own modal duality, played out in the terms of a delicate balance between lyricism and satire.

Huck's relationship with Jim, the runaway slave, is central to the novel's narrative, to its structure, and to its theme. Escaping "down" the river, a cruel irony in itself, provides the episodic structure, which is the narrative thread that holds together the developing relationship between the two runaways on the raft. The escape, the quest for freedom, is literal for both Huck and Jim as they flee from Pap and Jim's owner, Miss Watson. It may also be seen as symbolic on several planes: historical, philosophical, and moral. The historical setting of the novel is that pivotal era in American history when the new nation was being carved out of the wilderness. The flight down the river is a flight from the complexities of the ever-expanding, westward-moving settlements of the new civilization. The continuing vitality of the novel depends in part on the survival in the present day of the need for that imaginative escape. Like Henry David Thoreau's Walden Pond, Huck's Mississippi River, originally an escape from what may now seem some of the simpler strictures of society, continues to serve the American psyche as an imaginative alternative to modern civilization.

The philosophical dimensions of the rapidly disappearing frontier are those of nineteenth century Romanticism. Celebrating their freedom on the raft from the legal and social strictures of the town along the river, Huck and Jim are at the same time affirming the central Romantic thesis concerning people's need to return to nature and to the natural self. There are two kinds of Romanticism in the novel: that which Tom espouses in his adolescent preoccupation with adventure and that which Huck practices on the river under the stars and, most significantly, in the final resolution of the problem of Jim as a runaway slave. Twain holds up Tom's bookish Romanticism as childish at best and, for the most part, as silly. This attack on Romanticism—a secondary theme in *Adventures of Huckleberry Finn*, where Twain sends the derelict steamer the *Walter Scott* to its destruction on a rock—was one of Twain's lifelong preoccupations. It was continued with vehemence later in *A Connecticut Yankee in King Arthur's Court*, but its deep-running, destructive potential for Twain is harnessed in *Adventures of Huckleberry Finn*. The satire is there, but it is in the largely playful terms of the antics of the king and the duke, their mangling of William Shakespeare, and the graveyard art and poetry of Emmeline Grangerford. This playful treatment of one of his serious themes results in part from the fact that Twain is here working a deeper vein of Romanticism in the person of his supreme fictional creation, Huck.

The moral climax of the novel comes in chapter 31, when Huck decides that he will "go to hell" rather than turn in Jim. The difficulties with the ending of the book derive largely from that relatively early resolution of its central theme. Shortly thereafter, Huck is reunited with Tom, who is responsible for all the preposterous plans to save Jim, who, ironically, no longer needs to be saved. There are real problems here with the plot, with motivation, and with the prose itself, which is no longer sustained by the lyricism of Huck's accounts of life on the raft. The artistic achievement of the climax, however, makes such problems pale into relative insignificance. Twain embodies in Huck and dramatizes in his decision a principal line of American political and moral thought that has its roots in Thomas Jefferson and Thomas Paine, its "philosophical" development in Ralph Waldo Emerson and Thoreau, and its aesthetic transformation at the hands of Twain and Whitman. Huck is the embodiment of both the political and the Romantic ideals of common humanity, with no past or roots, whose principal guide is experience rather than tradition. He is one of the principal literary symbols of that fundamental American mythical dream of moral rejuvenation in the edenic wilderness of the "new" continent. He stands at the center of nineteenth century American literature and at the center of Twain's achievements.

A CONNECTICUT YANKEE IN KING ARTHUR'S COURT

In *Adventures of Huckleberry Finn*, Twain's attack on the Romantic glorification of the past is a peripheral theme. In *A Connecticut Yankee in King Arthur's Court*, it is central and devastating, both in the novel itself and in its signaling of the direction in which Twain's thought and creative energies were heading. Although this, too, is a child's book of a kind, there is about it none of the idyllic radiance of *Adventures of Tom Sawyer* nor the harmonious balancing of opposites of *Adventures of Huckleberry Finn*. Rather, there is finally outright war between the forces of the feudal past and those of the progressive present, with considerable ambiguity

about which is to be considered the good and which the evil.

There is no doubt that the reader's sympathies at the outset are with the Yankee mechanic, Hank Morgan, who, after a blow on the head, wakes up in King Arthur's England of 528 C.E. After saving himself from execution as a witch by "commanding" a total eclipse of the sun, he vies successfully with Merlin for power and prestige at court. He is like Huck in his commonsense responses to life in general, and in particular to the romantic claims of the feudal society in which he finds himself. He is unlike Huck in his vigorous progressivism, in his determination to bring the fruits of nineteenth century democracy and technology to feudal England. He introduces explosives, sets up schools to train workers in the mechanical arts, gives instruction in journalism to his page with an eye to a national press, and stretches telephone lines haphazardly across the countryside. His talents, taken for magic for the most part, earn for him the title "the Boss," and the abiding enmity of Merlin, whom he replaces at court. He plans to declare a republic after Arthur's death, and the sixth century kingdom enjoys all the fruits of progress: schools, trains, factories, newspapers, the telephone and telegraph.

The end of the story, however, just before Hank returns to his own century, pictures anything but the envisioned utopia. Arthur dies in a battle with Lancelot, Camelot is reduced to shambles, and Hank fortifies himself in a cave against the surviving chivalry of England. One of his final concerns is with the pollution caused by the dead bodies piled in the trenches around his fortress. The repressive, superstitious nightmare of feudal society has been compounded by the fearful efficiency of nineteenth century technology.

The ambiguity of the ending of the novel is symptomatic. The artistic balance of *Adventures of Huckleberry Finn* is no longer in evidence. Twain, always something of an allegorist, was by 1889 becoming more and more a polemicist, increasingly more interested in conflicts between abstract ideas and values than in the development and portrayal of human characters in all their complexities. Hank can be identified with Huck in terms of their common sense and their human values, but the big difference between them is that Huck's chief concern is with another human being while Hank's is with an abstraction called feudalism.

THE TRAGEDY OF PUDD'NHEAD WILSON

Twain was to do some of his most important writing in the last two decades of his life, including short fiction and social and moral criticism. His best novels, however, were completed in 1875 and in the 1880's. Of those coming after 1889, *The Tragedy of Pudd'nhead Wilson* is the most readable and the most consistent with the principal direction of his deepening cynicism about the "damned human race." The novel's only really interesting character is Roxy, a slave woman who switches her son with that of her owner, Percy Driscoll, to save her child from eventually being sold "down river." The whole of the dark tale that follows indicates, in Maxwell Geismar's words, how much "irony and tragedy have taken over the center stage in [Twain's] comic proscenium of life."

Lloyd N. Dendinger

OTHER MAJOR WORKS

SHORT FICTION: *The Celebrated Jumping Frog of Calaveras County, and Other Sketches*, 1867; *Mark Twain's (Burlesque) Autobiography and First Romance*, 1871; *Mark Twain's Sketches: New and Old*, 1875; *Punch, Brothers, Punch! and Other Sketches*, 1878; *The Stolen White Elephant, and Other Stories*, 1882; *Merry Tales*, 1892; *The £1,000,000 Bank-Note, and Other New Stories*, 1893; *The Man That Corrupted Hadleyburg, and Other Stories and Essays*, 1900; *King Leopold's Soliloquy: A Defense of His Congo Rule*, 1905; *The $30,000 Bequest, and Other Stories*, 1906; *The Curious Republic of Gondour, and Other Whimsical Sketches*, 1919; *The Complete Short Stories of Mark Twain*, 1957 (Charles Neider, editor); *Letters from the Earth*, 1962; *Mark Twain's Which Was the Dream? and Other Symbolic Writings of the Later Years*, 1967 (John S. Tuckey, editor); *Selected Shorter Writings of Mark Twain*, 1962; *Mark Twain's Satires and Burlesques*, 1967 (Franklin R. Rogers, editor); *Mark Twain's Hannibal, Huck, and Tom*, 1969 (Walter Blair, editor); *Mark Twain's Fables of Man*, 1972 (Tuckey, editor); *Life as I Find It*, 1977 (Neider, editor); *Early Tales and Sketches*, 1979-1981 (2 volumes; Edgar Marquess Branch and Robert H. Hirst, editors); *A Murder, a Mystery, and a Marriage*, 2001 (Roy Blount, Jr., editor).

PLAYS: *Colonel Sellers*, pr., pb. 1874 (adaptation of his novel *The Gilded Age*); *Ah Sin*, pr. 1877 (with Bret Harte); *Is He Dead? A Comedy in Three Acts*, pb. 2003 (Shelley Fisher Fishkin, editor).

NONFICTION: *The Innocents Abroad*, 1869; *Roughing It*, 1872; *A Tramp Abroad*, 1880; *Life on the Mississippi*, 1883; *Following the Equator*, 1897 (also known as *More Tramp Abroad*); *How to Tell a Story, and Other Essays*, 1897; *My Début as a Literary Person*, 1903; *What Is Man?*, 1906; *Christian Science*, 1907; *Is Shakespeare Dead?*, 1909; *Mark Twain's Speeches*, 1910 (Albert Bigelow Paine, editor); *Europe and Elsewhere*, 1923 (Paine, editor); *Mark Twain's Autobiography*, 1924 (2 volumes; Paine, editor); *Mark Twain's Notebook*, 1935 (Paine, editor); *Letters from the Sandwich Islands, Written for the Sacramento Union*, 1937 (G. Ezra Dane, editor); *Mark Twain in Eruption*, 1940 (Bernard De Voto, editor); *Mark Twain's Travels with Mr. Brown*, 1940 (Franklin Walker and Dane, editors); *The Love Letters of Mark Twain*, 1949 (Dixon Wecter, editor); *Mark Twain to Mrs. Fairbanks*, 1949 (Wecter, editor); *Mark Twain of the Enterprise: Newspaper Articles and Other Documents, 1862-1864*, 1957 (Henry Nash Smith and Frederick Anderson, editors); *Traveling with the Innocents Abroad: Mark Twain's Original Reports from Europe and the Holy Land*, 1958 (letters; Daniel Morley McKeithan, editor); *Mark Twain-Howells Letters: The Correspondence of Samuel L. Clemens and William D. Howells, 1872-1910*, 1960 (Smith and William M. Gibson, editors); *The Autobiography of Mark Twain*, 1961 (Neider, editor); *Mark Twain's Letters to His Publishers, 1867-1894*, 1967 (Hamlin Hill, editor); *Clemens of the Call: Mark Twain in San Francisco*, 1969 (Edgar M. Branch, editor); *Mark Twain's Correspondence with Henry Huttleston Rogers, 1893-1909*, 1969 (Lewis Leary, editor); *A Pen Warmed-Up in Hell: Mark Twain in Protest*, 1972; *Mark Twain's Notebooks and Journals*, 1975-1979 (3 volumes); *Mark Twain Speaking*, 1976 (Paul Fatout, editor); *Mark Twain Speaks for Himself*, 1978 (Fatout, editor); *Mark Twain's Letters*, 1988-2002 (6 volumes; Branch et al, editors); *Mark Twain's Own Autobiography: The Chapters from the "North American Review,"* 1990 (Michael J. Kiskis, editor); *Mark Twain's Aquarium: The Samuel Clemens Angelfish Correspondence, 1905-1910*, 1991 (John Cooley, editor); *The Bible According to Mark Twain: Writings on Heaven, Eden, and the Flood*, 1995 (Howard G.

Baetzhold and Joseph B. McCullough, editors); *Mark Twain: The Complete Interviews*, 2006.

MISCELLANEOUS: *The Writings of Mark Twain*, 1922-1925 (37 volumes); *The Portable Mark Twain*, 1946 (Bernard De Voto, editor); *Collected Tales, Sketches, Speeches, and Essays, 1853-1891*, 1992 (Louis J. Budd, editor); *Collected Tales, Sketches, Speeches, and Essays, 1891-1910*, 1992 (Budd, editor); *Who Is Mark Twain?*, 2009.

BIBLIOGRAPHY

Camfield, Gregg. *The Oxford Companion to Mark Twain*. New York: Oxford University Press, 2003. Collection of about three hundred original essays on individual works, themes, characters, language, subjects that interested Twain, and other topics. Includes an appendix on researching Twain, which lists useful secondary sources, and an annotated bibliography of more than seventeen hundred of Twain's novels, plays, poems, and other writings.

Emerson, Everett. *Mark Twain: A Literary Life*. Philadelphia: University of Pennsylvania Press, 2000. A complete revision of Emerson's *The Authentic Mark Twain* (1984), this masterful study traces the development of Twain's writing against the events in his life and provides illuminating discussions of many individual works.

Fishkin, Shelley Fisher. *Lighting Out for the Territory: Reflections on Mark Twain and American Culture*. New York: Oxford University Press, 1996. A broad survey of Twain's influence on modern culture, including the many writers who have acknowledged their indebtedness to him. Discusses Twain's use of Hannibal, Missouri, in his writings, and charts his transformation from a southern racist to a committed antiracist.

Kaplan, Justin. *Mr. Clemens and Mark Twain*. New York: Simon & Schuster, 1966. This Pulitzer Prize-winning biography is a superior general work on Twain's life after 1861. Skillfully places Twain's life and work within the historical context of America's Gilded Age.

Leonard, James S., ed. *Making Mark Twain Work in the Classroom*. Durham, N.C.: Duke University Press, 1999. Collection of essays by leading Twain scholars

designed for students and teachers. Special attention is given to *A Connecticut Yankee in King Arthur's Court*, *Joan of Arc*, *Innocents Abroad*, and *Adventures of Huckleberry Finn*.

Messent, Peter B. *Mark Twain*. New York: St. Martin's Press, 1997. Messent, a leading British scholar of Twain, provides a useful introduction to Twain's life and works. His book contains chapters on many of the individual novels and on Twain's late writings.

Paine, Albert Bigelow. *Mark Twain: A Biography*. 3 vols. 1912. Reprint. Philadelphia: Chelsea House, 1997. Often reprinted, this immense study by Twain's authorized biographer and editor remains the fullest study of Twain's life and benefits from Paine's close personal acquaintance with Twain and his access to sources that no longer exist.

Powers, Ron. *Mark Twain: A Life*. New York: Free Press, 2005. A massive, engrossing, and updated biography by a Pulitzer Prize-winning author who grew up in Hannibal. Powers examines Twain's life and work, placing them within their historical context. Includes a bibliography and an index.

Railton, Stephen. *Mark Twain: A Short Introduction*. Malden, Mass: Blackwell, 2004. A useful guide to some of Twain's major works by the scholar who maintains the Mark Twain in His Times Web site. Includes a bibliography and an index.

Rasmussen, R. Kent. *Critical Companion to Mark Twain: A Literary Reference to His Life and Work*. 2 vols. New York: Facts On File, 2007. A revised and significantly expanded edition of Rasmussen's *Mark Twain A to Z* (1995), with alphabetically arranged entries about the plots, characters, places, and other subjects relating to Twain's writings and life. Features extended analytical essays on Twain's major works, an expanded and fully annotated bibliography of books about Twain, and a glossary explaining unusual words in Twain's vocabulary.

Sloane, David E. E. *Student Companion to Mark Twain*. Westport, Conn.: Greenwood Press, 2001. General guide to Twain's life and writings designed to assist students. Features individual chapters about some of the novels, as well as discussions of the short fiction, travel narratives, and his career and contributions to American literature.

Twain, Mark. *Mark Twain: The Complete Interviews.* Edited by Gary Scharnhorst. Tuscaloosa: University of Alabama Press, 2006. Collection of interviews with Twain dating from 1871 to 1910, presented in chronological order. The interviews paint a vivid picture of Twain, bringing to life his speech patterns and idiosyncracies, his likes and dislikes, and his philosophies on life and writing. Scharnhorst makes the book easily accessible to those unfamiliar with Twain by providing annotations to clarify the historical and biographical references.

Ward, Geoffrey C., and Dayton Duncan. *Mark Twain: An Illustrated Biography.* New York: Alfred A. Knopf, 2001. A heavily illustrated companion to the PBS television documentary. More than a picture book, however, this volume provides ample biographical information that is well researched and thoughtfully presented.

ANNE TYLER

Born: Minneapolis, Minnesota; October 25, 1941

PRINCIPAL LONG FICTION

If Morning Ever Comes, 1964
The Tin Can Tree, 1965
A Slipping-Down Life, 1970
The Clock Winder, 1972
Celestial Navigation, 1974
Searching for Caleb, 1976
Earthly Possessions, 1977
Morgan's Passing, 1980
Dinner at the Homesick Restaurant, 1982
The Accidental Tourist, 1985
Breathing Lessons, 1988
Saint Maybe, 1991
Ladder of Years, 1995
A Patchwork Planet, 1998
Back When We Were Grownups, 2001
The Amateur Marriage, 2004
Digging to America, 2006

OTHER LITERARY FORMS

In addition to her novels, Anne Tyler has published many short stories, including several in such periodicals as *Harper's*, *Mademoiselle*, *The New Yorker*, *Seventeen*, and the *Southern Review*. Her stories have not yet been published in any collected form, but two stories appeared in the *O. Henry Prize Stories* volumes for 1969 and 1972 and others have been included in such anthologies as *The Best American Short Stories* (1977), *Stories of the Modern South* (1978, 1981), *New Women and New Fiction* (1986), and *Louder than Words* (1989) as well as in several anthologies of American literature published by major publishing houses for use in college and university courses. Tyler has also written several autobiographical and personal essays, one for *The Washington Post* in 1976 and another for *The Writer on Her Work* (1980), edited by Janet Sternburg. Her reviews of current fiction, criticism, and biography have appeared in many major newspapers and magazines, including the *Boston Globe*, the *Chicago Sun-Times*, the *Chicago Tribune*, the *Detroit News*, *The New Republic*, *The New York Times Book Review*, *USA Today*, and *The Washington Post*.

ACHIEVEMENTS

Despite praise for the truth of her characterizations and her eye for detail, Anne Tyler did not receive much national recognition for her fiction until the publication of her sixth novel, *Searching for Caleb*, in 1976. Before that time, the largest segment of her audience was in the South, although her short stories appeared in prestigious national magazines throughout the 1960's and 1970's. All of her novels except *A Slipping-Down Life* have been published abroad. In addition to English editions, translations into Danish, French, German, Italian, and Swedish have appeared. Still, the American academic and critical communities were slow to appreciate Tyler's work. Her strong supporters include John Updike, who favorably reviewed her novels for *The New Yorker*, beginning with *Searching for Caleb*, and Reynolds Price, Tyler's professor at Duke University, who also reviewed her work.

In 1976, Tyler began to receive increasing recognition. In 1977, the American Academy and Institute of Arts and Letters cited her as a novelist of excellence and promise. *Earthly Possessions* and *Morgan's Passing* also received largely favorable national reviews. While a few critics, including Updike, expressed some disappointment in *Morgan's Passing*, the Writers Workshop of the University of Rochester awarded it the 1980 Janet Heidinger Kafka Prize for fiction by an American woman.

With the publication of *Dinner at the Homesick Restaurant*, her first novel to make the best-seller lists, Tyler at last acquired full national stature. Benjamin DeMott's front-page notice in *The New York Times Book Review* pointed to the novel's wit and the depth of Tyler's psychological insight and characterizations. DeMott saw the book as clear evidence of Tyler's having joined the ranks of major novelists. Updike reiterated this praise, citing *Dinner at the Homesick Restaurant* as a work of considerable power. As a result of this increasing recognition and praise, scholarly studies of Tyler's work, including her early novels, began to appear. Tyler's reputation as a major contemporary American novelist was fixed with the publication of *The Accidental Tourist*, which won the 1985/1986 National Book Critics Circle Award for fiction. The successful film version of the novel, released in 1988, increased Tyler's popularity with the reading public. *Breathing Lessons* was nominated for the National Book Award and won the 1989 Pulitzer Prize for fiction.

BIOGRAPHY

Anne Tyler was born in Minneapolis, Minnesota, on October 25, 1941, to Phyllis Mahon Tyler, a social worker, and Lloyd Parry Tyler, an industrial chemist. She was the eldest of four children, the only girl. Both of her parents were Quakers dedicated to finding an ideal community, a quest that produced the theme of frustrated idealism in Tyler's fiction. As a consequence of her parents' idealism, Tyler spent most of her early years, from infancy until age eleven, in various rural

Quaker communes scattered throughout the midwestern and southern United States. When she was six, the family settled in Celo, North Carolina—a large, isolated, valley commune virtually independent of the outside world and unquestionably the setting for Tyler's short story "Outside," which appeared in the *Southern Review* in 1971.

Tyler later wrote of the impact of her early years on her fiction. Unable to sleep at night and needing to amuse herself, she began telling herself stories at age three. Furthermore, her isolation in the rural communes in which she lived as a child contributed to the themes of isolation and community dominant in her novels. Growing up in North Carolina, where she spent summers tying tobacco, Tyler listened carefully to the stories of the tobacco handlers and tenant farmers. Later, she was able to capture the cadences of everyday speech in her fiction, realizing that the stories these workers told could form the basis for literature. She also relied heavily on the North Carolina tobacco country as the setting for her early novels, especially *The Tin Can Tree* and *A Slipping-Down Life*.

When Tyler was eleven, she and her family moved to Raleigh, North Carolina, where they finally settled into an "ordinary" middle-class existence. There, Tyler attended Broughton High School and received encouragement in her writing. She also discovered the work of Eudora Welty, which was to have great influence on Tyler's own fiction.

In September, 1958, Tyler entered Duke University as an Angier Duke Scholar majoring in Russian. She was encouraged by Reynolds Price, who taught her freshman composition and later introduced her to his literary agent. At Duke, Tyler helped edit the *Archive* (the student literary magazine), published three early stories, acted in several productions of the Wesley Players, and learned a great deal about the craft of fiction from reading Leo Tolstoy and the other major Russian novelists. She twice received the Anne Flexner Award for creative writing at Duke. In 1961, she graduated Phi Beta Kappa, just three years after entering Duke.

In September, 1961, Tyler began work on a master's degree in Russian at Columbia University, an experience that provides some of the background for *If Morning Ever Comes*. She completed the course work for the de-

Anne Tyler. (Diana Walker)

later that same year in its entirety by Alfred A. Knopf. Between *The Tin Can Tree* and *A Slipping-Down Life* she wrote an additional book—"Winter Birds, Winter Apples"—that was not published. A second daughter, Mitra, was born in November, 1967, in Baltimore. A dedicated mother and a productive, organized writer, Tyler managed her dual careers for years by writing in the mornings while her children were at school. Although eventually Tezh moved to New York and Mitra to San Francisco, Tyler and her husband continued to live in Baltimore. Taghi Modarressi died there of lymphoma in April, 1997, at age sixty-five. Tyler continues to reside in, and set her fiction in, Baltimore.

ANALYSIS

In her essay "Still Just Writing" (in *The Writer on Her Work*, edited by Janet Sternberg, 1980), Anne Tyler discusses the importance of her having lived as a child in "an experimental Quaker community in the wilderness." For her, this early experience of isolation and her later effort "to fit into the outside world" provided the "kind of setting-apart situation" the writer requires for aesthetic distancing. Tyler's early isolation and struggle to belong also provided both the style and material for her fiction: the ironic distance characteristic of her prose as well as the subject of the individual's relationship to the community, particularly to other members of one's own household and family. Most of Tyler's short fiction and all of her novels published to date, from *If Morning Ever Comes* to *Digging to America*, concern the intricacies of family relationships and the isolation of the individual within the family. For Tyler, families clearly provided not only her major source for learning about the world as a child but also fertile ground for studying how people endure the pain of loss and disappointment of life, adjust to living with others, and yet continue to love. All of the major conflicts and central themes of her novels have evolved from this concern with the family and the individual's relationship to the community.

In this regard, Tyler falls clearly within the southern literary tradition, with its emphasis on family life and

gree but quit before writing her thesis. The following summer she spent in Maine, supporting herself by working on a schooner and proofreading for a local newspaper.

In 1962, Tyler returned to Duke University as the library's Russian bibliographer. That fall, she met her future husband, Taghi Modarressi, an Iranian student in child psychiatry at the Duke Medical Center. The couple married in May, 1963, three months after the publication of Tyler's first short story in a national magazine. That spring, they moved to Montreal, Canada; during their four years there, Tyler wrote her first novel, taught herself Persian in anticipation of living in Iran, and worked as a librarian at the McGill University law library. In September, 1965, she gave birth to her first daughter, Tezh. The publication of *The Tin Can Tree* followed the next month.

In June, 1967, Tyler and her family moved to Baltimore, Maryland. While Tyler's short stories continued to appear frequently in national publications between 1965 and 1970, her third novel was not published until January, 1970, first in condensed form in *Redbook* and history. As Paul Binding has pointed out, Tyler, like her mentor Reynolds Price, relies on interaction and "badinage between members of a family or between people who know one another well in order to illuminate personality." Tyler does not, however, evoke or write of a regional past. She focuses on the present, narrating the past to provide a personal or familial, not a regional, history. Nor are her characters and families symbolic figures—they are, instead, idiosyncratic personalities, truthfully depicted, memorable, yet atypical. In all but her first three novels and, to an extent, *Ladder of Years*, Tyler's setting has not been that of the small towns and rural landscapes so often considered synonymous with southern life. Rather, her terrain is the border city of Baltimore and the decay and transience of modern urban life. Price, in fact, has said that Tyler is the closest thing the South has to an urban novelist, indicating her somewhat unusual position among late twentieth and early twenty-first century American writers: a southerner with a traditional interest in family, community, and the past; a modern woman fascinated with change and drawn to urban life; a writer with faith in humankind's ability to love and endure; and yet an individual keenly aware of the difficulties of contemporary life, particularly the failure of communication within the family.

In her concern for familial relationships, Tyler raises the existential issues of freedom and commitment. Significantly, hers is a compassionate art without explicit moral judgment—an absence of judgment for which some critics have faulted her. The effect of this gentle portrayal of serious themes is ironic: The disturbing failure of Tyler's characters to understand fully and to be understood by those they love is counterbalanced by a witty, carefully detailed style. Violence is usually absent from her work as well, and so are the grotesques found in the fiction of Flannery O'Connor and Carson McCullers. The most disfigured character in Tyler's work—Evie Decker, the overweight teenager in *A Slipping-Down Life* who carves a local rock singer's name in her forehead—is compassionately portrayed. Like Eudora Welty, Tyler populates her novels with ordinary people, all of whom, she has noted, are mildly eccentric in some way and "have something unusual" at their centers, something "funny and strange" and "touching in unexpected ways." From Ben Joe Hawkes

in *If Morning Ever Comes*, who reads texts upside down to relieve boredom, to the elusive and difficult black sheep of her fictional families—Caleb and Duncan Peck, Morgan Gower, Cody Tull, and Barnaby Gaitlin—Tyler warmly and humorously portrays a wide spectrum of fascinating yet ordinary human beings.

Tyler's view of human nature, her talent for realistically capturing generations of squabbling families, her keen ear for dialogue, and her interest in character and the isolation of the individual within the family derive from various sources. Her own "setting-apart" experience in the North Carolina wilderness, her early childhood habit of telling herself bedtime stories for rest and amusement, and her long periods listening to tenant farmers' stories contributed substantially to her art. Shy, quiet, and keenly observant, she listened carefully to the stories the workers told. Later, she could call up the words of her own characters. "Having those voices in my ears all day," she has written, "helped me to summon up my own characters' voices."

Images also serve as an impetus for her writing. In an interview with Jennifer Morgan Gray, Tyler indicated that watching a family in an airport contributed substantially to her novel *Digging to America*: "It [the image of the family waiting for their adopted child] hung on my mind for several years, germinating in the dark the way seeds for novels often do." Additionally, with Reynolds Price as her teacher and Eudora Welty as a model, Tyler saw early in her career the rich source of literary materials offered by commonplace experience. Paul Binding has also noted the influence of Tyler's study of the Russian masters, particularly Ivan Turgenev and Anton Chekhov, as a basis for her tolerant and warm portrayal of multiple generations of entangled and eccentric families.

Finally, and perhaps most prominent, is Tyler's own witness to her parents' idealism, their quest for a perfect community throughout her youth, and later their apparently easy adjustment to an ordinary existence in a middle-sized southern city. Like her own father, whom she describes in "Still Just Writing," the heroes of Tyler's novels are those who are "infinitely adapting" and always "looking around . . . with a smile to say, 'Oh! So this is where I am!'" They are complex people, enriched and deepened by experience—Elizabeth Abbott in *The*

Clock Winder, Justine Peck in *Searching for Caleb*, Charlotte Emory in *Earthly Possessions*, Jenny Tull in *Dinner at the Homesick Restaurant*, Maggie Moran in *Breathing Lessons*, Delia Grinstead in *Ladder of Years*, and Rebecca Davitch in *Back When We Were Grownups* best represent the type—and able to enjoy life because they view themselves and others with tolerance and wit.

IF MORNING EVER COMES

In an interview with Clifford Ridley for the *National Observer*, Tyler commented that she did not particularly "like either" of her "first two books" because "they seem so bland." Ben Joe Hawkes, the hero of *If Morning Ever Comes*, is "a likable guy; that's all you can say about him." While it is true that Ben Joe lacks the zaniness and interest that some of Tyler's later characters exhibit, his struggle to deal with his family, to recognize both his own independence and theirs, and to come to terms with the past and the psychological distance that isolates people even within an intimate group provides a basis for understanding Tyler's later work and her place within the southern literary tradition. *If Morning Ever Comes* had its origins in two short stories: "I Never Saw Morning," which appeared in the April, 1961, issue of *Archive* and was later collected in *Under Twenty-five: Duke Narrative and Verse, 1945-1962* (1963), edited by William Blackburn; and "Nobody Answers the Door," which appeared in the fall, 1964, issue of the *Antioch Review*. Both involve incidents suggested by the novel but occurring prior to the time of its opening. With the novel, they indicate Tyler's strong sense of the continuity of her characters' lives.

As in Tyler's later novels, the plot and subject of *If Morning Ever Comes*, Ben Joe's five-day journey home to Sandhill, North Carolina, from Columbia University, where he is a law student, evolve from family conflict. The family of women Ben Joe has left behind—six strikingly independent sisters, a proud mother, and a spry, seventy-eight-year-old grandmother, the first of Tyler's zanies—fail to tell him what is happening at home. Jenny, the family letter writer, is all business. No one mentions the illegitimate son whom Ben Joe's father left behind with a mistress when he died, or the support payments Ben Joe personally delivered for years before he left for New York. The family treats lightly even the fact that Ben Joe's oldest sister, Joanne, has left her husband

of seven years and returned home with her child. The family's behavior and their failure to understand Ben Joe's concern and worry point clearly to the theme of the individual's isolation within the family, here the only male in a family of women.

On the surface, *If Morning Ever Comes* is a simply structured novel covering less than a week in the life of its hero. As one critic has observed, however, going home is "only partly a spatial relocation." Ben Joe, like other southern literary heroes, "from Quentin Compson to Jack Burden," must return home "to embrace the spiritual crisis" created by an unsettled past and attempt to forge a future shaped by that very past. In this regard, *If Morning Ever Comes* is clearly a southern novel. That it draws on a sharp contrast between the peaceful North Carolina setting and the briskness of New York, as well as the hero's discomfort and sense of dislocation in the North, is also suggestive of Tyler's southern literary roots.

THE TIN CAN TREE

Although not widely reviewed or acclaimed, *The Tin Can Tree* is a moving novel that expands and deepens Tyler's treatment of family relationships and the individual's struggle to remain committed in the face of significant loss and change. Just as Ben Joe Hawkes in *If Morning Ever Comes* remains committed to his family despite their pride and reticence, and to his father's memory despite the elder Hawkes's unfaithfulness, so do the characters in *The Tin Can Tree*, the members of three separate families sharing one house—the Pikes, the Greens, and the Potters—deal with their commonly experienced grief at the death of the Pikes' six-year-old daughter, Janie Rose. Tyler's achievement here is that she captures eight different characters' varying responses to grief while avoiding the sentimental and maudlin. She begins the novel at the close of the funeral service, thus deliberately focusing on life and the resumption of the tasks of everyday living rather than on the death itself.

In addition to this theme of grief, *The Tin Can Tree* explores the background and interactions of James and Ansel Green and Joan Pike, Janie Rose's cousin. The study of James's commitment to his ailing brother Ansel, the two brothers' alienation from their family, and Joan's distance from her own elderly parents, as well as her unresolved romantic involvement with James, give the novel a depth lacking in *If Morning Ever Comes*, with its heavy focus on one central character. As one reviewer noted, *The Tin Can Tree* illustrates Tyler's talent for bringing "into focus a remarkable range of human traits and emotions." Lou Pike's depressive withdrawal and immobility after her daughter's death, her husband's worried yet practical concern, their son Simon's sense of rejection and neglect, Joan's uncertainty and anger at James and his brother Ansel—all acquire full portraiture. A love of detail permeates the book, from the Potter sisters' eccentric way of wearing hats and gloves even when visiting only at the other end of the porch to the details of Janie Rose's quirky behavior: her "tin can tree" made in honor of God during a religious period and her wearing layer upon layer of underwear on "her bad days." Such details make the characters realistic and give Janie Rose's death more immediate poignancy.

The Tin Can Tree is also the first Tyler novel to draw explicitly on the author's tobacco-field experience. Joan Pike, a school secretary, spends part of her summers handling tobacco in the warehouses, as Tyler herself did as a teenager. Aside from providing elements of plot and characterization, the "*Tobacco Road* landscape" mirrors the sterility of the characters' lives following Janie Rose's death and provides a spokesman for the novel's theme. "Bravest thing about people, Miss Joan," one of the tobacco handlers says, "is how they go on loving mortal beings after finding out there's such a thing as dying." Unlike Erskine Caldwell, whose stereotypical white-trash characters are often farcical grotesques, Tyler deepens the *Tobacco Road* landscape by adding a compassionate, detailed account of the grief of several families at the death of a child. Hers is a fiction of psychological insight, not a document for social change. *The Tin Can Tree*, as one critic observed, is "a novel rich in incident that details the closing of a family wound and the resumption of life among people stunned by the proof of mortality."

A SLIPPING-DOWN LIFE

In her third novel, *A Slipping-Down Life*, Tyler returns to the existential themes of the individual's isolation, the struggle for identity, and the lack of understanding and meaningful communication among people living closely together. Set in the fictional towns of Pulqua and Farinia, North Carolina—suspiciously similar to the actual town of Fuquay-Varina near Raleigh—this is the last of Tyler's books set entirely in North Carolina but also the first to portray the barrenness of familial relationships in a clearly modern setting. While most of *If Morning Ever Comes* and all of *The Tin Can Tree* are set in peaceful, remote areas where family life, though troubled, seems unaffected by distinctly modern problems, *A Slipping-Down Life* draws heavily on the impact of modern American culture and media on family life. Also, where Tyler's first two novels cover only a few days in the lives of the principal characters, *A Slipping-Down Life* chronicles one full year in the life of its heroine—an overweight, dowdy teenage girl named Evie Decker—indicating an evolution in Tyler's ability to depict one character over an extended period of time.

Originating in a "newspaper story about a fifteen-year-old girl in Texas who'd slashed 'Elvis' in her forehead," the novel traces Evie's sterile interactions with her father, her only living relative, as well as the development and dissolution of a relationship with a local rock singer named Bertram "Drumstrings" Casey, the first of Tyler's unworthy yet likable antiheroes. Though exploitative and selfish, Drumstrings is also touchingly shy and dependent on his parents and Evie. Evie's entanglement with him, leading eventually to their marriage, is initiated by her carving the name "Casey" in her forehead with a pair of nail scissors and ends with the couple's separation, the death of Evie's family, and her discovery of Casey's infidelity. Throughout, Evie thinks of herself as an actor on a stage set, taking her cues from the soap operas she watches daily with Clotelia, the Deckers' sullen maid and Evie's sometimes chiding surrogate mother. Like Joan Pike in *The Tin Can Tree* and later Tyler heroines—Justine Peck in *Searching for Caleb*, Charlotte Emory in *Earthly Possessions*, and Rebecca Davitch in *Back When We Were Grownups*—Evie is an only child faced with growing up alone in a dark, stifling household and creating an identity without the companionship and aid of siblings or understanding parents.

In addition to its characterizations, *A Slipping-Down Life* is noteworthy for capturing part of the American experience in the 1960's: the lonely world of teenagers, the generation gap, the high school student's unending quest for popularity and romance, as well as a small town's tawdry local rock scene, featuring the chilled air of a roadside tavern, painfully loud music, necking couples, and the smell of stale beer. As one reviewer observed, *A Slipping-Down Life* captures "a *way* of life, a way that is tacked upon teenage bulletin boards, sewn to dresses 'decorated with poodles on loops of real chain,' enclosed in high-school notebooks containing *Silver Screen* magazine."

THE CLOCK WINDER

Tyler's first three novels all involve some type of journey home during which a central character confronts both the distance between self and family and the difficulties of unresolved past conflicts. Ben Joe's journey from New York to Sandhill in *If Morning Ever Comes* fits this pattern, as do James Green's trip to Caraway, North Carolina, in *The Tin Can Tree* and Evie Decker's return to her father's house after his death in *A Slipping-Down Life*. A similar trip occurs in *The Clock Winder*. A novel characterized by Sarah Blackburn as having all the "virtues" of southern writing—"an easy, almost confidential directness, fine skill at quick characterization, a sure eye for atmosphere, and a special nostalgic humor"—*The Clock Winder* was at the time of its publication Tyler's most ambitious work, tracing the intricate relationships of a large cast of characters over an entire decade. It was also her first novel set in Baltimore.

The diverse, eccentric, eight-member Emerson family of Baltimore and their one adopted member, Elizabeth Abbott, clearly form one of those "huge, 'loving-bickering'" southern families Tyler told Clifford Ridley she hoped to create in writing *If Morning Ever Comes*. Mrs. Emerson—a skinny, fragile widow—unrelentingly nags her children about their neglected duties to her. She is, consequently, estranged from all but one: Timothy, a pressured medical student. Timothy and his twin, Andrew, are two of the most neurotic and disturbed characters in Tyler's novels. Into this entangled, crisis-prone family, Elizabeth Abbott brings the very skills she is unable to practice with her own family in Ellington, North Carolina. Tolerant, practical, dexterous, and witty—the first of Tyler's "infinitely adapting" heroines based on her own father—Elizabeth is a handyman and a godsend for the nervous Mrs. Emerson. In her own birth family, however, Elizabeth is a "bumbler," a rebellious college dropout, and a painful reminder of failure to her minister father. Her life at home is bleak, ordinary, and restricted. Elizabeth's commitment to the Emersons, despite their family feuds, offers her an opportunity for real interaction as well as freedom from her own family's dicta, giving her an opportunity to form a new identity and a life free of reminders of past mistakes.

In addition to expanding character, setting, and time frame, *The Clock Winder* is unusual among Tyler's first four works for its use of violence and its experimentation with point of view. Timothy Emerson commits suicide by shooting himself in Elizabeth's presence, sending her home to her family for several years. Later, after her return to Baltimore, Andrew Emerson shoots her, though he causes only a flesh wound. Also, where in earlier novels Tyler used omniscient point of view focusing largely on one major character—the exception is *The Tin Can Tree*, in which Joan Pike and James Green serve alternately as centers of consciousness—*The Clock Winder* shifts perspective among many characters, some of them minor. In one chapter, the reader witnesses the succession of disconnected thoughts, the confusion of physical sensations, and the temporal disorientation accompanying Mrs. Emerson's stroke. Another chapter presents the views of the youngest Emerson, Peter, who appears only in the final section of the novel. These shifts in point of view result in an intimate portrait not only of the novel's central character, Elizabeth, but also of the Emersons—a varied, contrasting family of idiosyncratic individuals.

CELESTIAL NAVIGATION

With *Celestial Navigation*, Tyler moved her novels to a totally urban landscape. Eight months after the novel's publication, Tyler told a Duke University audience that she "could no longer write a southern novel" since she had lived away from the South too long to capture realistically the "voices" and behavior of the people who live there. Set almost exclusively in a seedy Baltimore boardinghouse "smack in the middle" of a deteriorating inner-city neighborhood, *Celestial Navigation* is Tyler's portrait of the artist. It covers thirteen years in the central character's life, expanding the study of character development found in her earlier novels and illustrating her increasing skill in handling point of view. The various boarders narrate firsthand their experiences and relationships to other residents.

Additionally, since the novel focuses largely on

boarders rather than kin—somewhat like *The Tin Can Tree*, with its three families unrelated by blood—and since it includes the common-law marriage of its hero, *Celestial Navigation* redefines the meaning of family ties as characterized in Tyler's novels. Also, because Jeremy Pauling, the artist-hero protagonist of the novel and the owner of the rooming house, is so reclusive that for years he has not left the city block where he lives, the novel intensifies Tyler's theme of the isolation of the individual within the community. Jeremy's principal ties are not with his two sisters in Richmond, neither of whom is very understanding of his peculiar artistic temperament, but with the boarders with whom he lives.

The caring family of boarders the novel studies, however, is essentially composed of other equally isolated strangers living in private rooms. They are mostly older people with severed family connections or no remaining kin. Ironically, they exhibit more tolerance and unquestioning respect for the peculiarities and privacy of one another than do many blood-related members. Mrs. Vinton, an aged spinster who works in a bookstore, stays on to care for Jeremy years after the others move out or die, yet she never interrupts his trancelike states or work. Mrs. Vinton and the other boarders—the elegant widow Mrs. Jarrett, the nubile Mary Tell, the young Olivia, and the fractious old Mrs. Somerset, shuffling about in slippers—serve as testaments to Tyler's talent for realistically capturing a gallery of idiosyncratic yet identifiably ordinary people.

The real achievement of *Celestial Navigation*, however, is Jeremy Pauling. He is one of Tyler's minor grotesques. A pale, pudgy sculptor, he rarely speaks and withdraws for days at a time to his secluded bedroom-studio. The novel works as Jeremy's story partly because Tyler gives him a full range of emotions—including sexual attraction to several female boarders and a love for the children he has with his common-law wife. Tyler also views him with both compassion and humor and lets the reader see him from several points of view, shifting to third-person point of view to narrate Jeremy's chapters, since Jeremy himself is incapable of communicating his impressions in the coherent manner of the other characters. Tyler has said that she based the character of Jeremy in part on a shy, easily flustered little man she helped one day in the library where she worked, but she added several of her own traits to the character: a dread of telephones and doorbells (something retained from her isolated childhood) and, most important, her own artistic vision, an eye for the "smallest and most unnoticed scenes on earth," very much like those details Tyler captures in *Celestial Navigation*.

SEARCHING FOR CALEB

Searching for Caleb marked a turning point in Tyler's career. It was her first novel to receive national recognition, and its publication coincided with the time when Tyler's own reviews began to appear in national publications. As Walter Sullivan commented in 1977 when reviewing *Searching for Caleb* for the *Sewanee Review*, Tyler "retained" in her work "a kind of innocence . . . a sense of wonder at all the crazy things in the world and an abiding affection for her own flaky characters." *Searching for Caleb* was also evidence that Tyler had retained her southern literary roots and her delight in huge families and the range of human characters those families produce.

Something of a combined family history and detective story, the novel is one of Tyler's most ambitious works, tracing five generations of one large, dichotomous, and extremely long-lived clan, the Pecks of Baltimore, from the 1880's through 1973. As in *The Clock Winder* and *Celestial Navigation*, Tyler shows her strong fascination with urban life, a result perhaps of her own early life in remote areas. She also returns to Roland Park, one of Baltimore's oldest residential neighborhoods and the main setting of *The Clock Winder*.

As the title suggests, *Searching for Caleb* involves a quest for the vanished Caleb, the great-uncle of the novel's protagonists, the married first cousins Duncan and Justine Peck, and the half brother of their grandfather, Daniel Peck. Representing one side of the family, Caleb, Justine, and Duncan are outcasts of a sort: talented, imaginative, and free-spirited individuals unable or unwilling to live as typical family rules dictate. Caleb becomes a musician, Justine a fortune-teller. Duncan leads an unsettled life as a mechanic and jack-of-all-trades, foreshadowing Morgan Gower, the hero of *Morgan's Passing*. Like Morgan and, later, Barnaby Gaitlin of *A Patchwork Planet*, Duncan dismays his family.

The other side of the family, the Pecks of Roland Park, headed by Daniel, are uniformly humorless and restricted. The women, though educated, are unthreatening; the men, all attorneys educated at Johns Hopkins University, drive black Fords and dress in Brooks Brothers suits. They are, above all, clannish, living side by side in similar Roland Park houses. For them, family tradition and training—in effect, the past—are inescapable. Even Daniel's late-life quest for his half brother evolves from his ties to family and an unsettled conflict. It represents a delayed response to the question frequently asked in his childhood: "Daniel, have you seen Caleb?"

Searching for Caleb, like Tyler's earlier novels, also illustrates the author's belief in the need for human adaptability, tolerance, and love. Justine epitomizes this philosophy. She weathers a dark and uncertain childhood with a depressive mother, frequent moves with her restless husband, the death of both parents and her grandfather, and the loss of her one daughter, who marries a milquetoast minister, yet she remains spirited and continues to love her family, embracing change more than stability. She insists on visiting Roland Park, a longing Duncan cannot understand, and she is committed to finding Caleb, not only out of a love of travel and adventure but also to share the experiences with her grandfather and to find her own roots. With its focus on community and family and its delineation of the impacts on the present of the unsettled conflicts of the past, *Searching for Caleb* indicates Tyler's own roots in the family of southern literature.

EARTHLY POSSESSIONS

When it appeared in 1977, *Earthly Possessions* was Tyler's most unfavorably received novel. Among disapproving reviewers, Roger Sale in *The New York Times Review of Books* saw the book as "a cartoon" of sorts, with the life of Charlotte Emory, the protagonist, "reduced . . . by her own hand" until all "possible anguish is . . . lost." The reason for this response is no doubt the sardonic nature of Charlotte herself, an entrapped housewife who sets out to leave her husband but gets kidnapped instead in a bungled bank robbery. Such reversals characterize Charlotte's life and have led her to "loosen" her hold so that she sees everything from an ironic distance. Charlotte, moreover, is the novel's only narrator, and she tells her life story and the story of her experiences with Jake Simms, her kidnapper, in alternating chapters. Detailing Jake and Charlotte's trip south from Clarion, Maryland, Charlotte's hometown, Tyler captures the fragmentation and transience of modern life, reflected in a string of drive-in restaurants, banks, and films. The triumph of the novel is not, as in earlier Tyler works, characterization, but the panorama of contemporary American life that the book captures during this journey of both hostage and kidnapper.

With its contrapuntal chapters, *Earthly Possessions* is Tyler's most highly structured novel, the first to be told entirely in the first person by one narrator. The result is an artificial, temporal arrangement and a restricted focus, one lifetime as compared with those of eight or nine Emersons or five generations of Pecks. Also, the reader is always in the presence of two somewhat unlikable characters: a nail-biting, minor-league criminal and a stoic, cynical woman. All of the characters might have come from the pen of Flannery O'Connor, but for the touchingly human flaws Tyler includes.

Neither Jake nor Charlotte is morally culpable, despite the fact that both have failings. What they share is a common, impractical desire for freedom from the entanglements of life: for Charlotte, marriage complete with a house full of relatives and in-laws, rooms of furniture (earthly possessions), even sinners from the mourner's bench at her husband's church; for Jake, jail for a petty crime and a pregnant girlfriend. Heading south to rescue Mindy Callendar, Jake's Kewpie-doll girlfriend, from a home for unwed mothers, Jake, Charlotte realizes, is actually like her, "criss-crossed by strings of love and need and worry." Even Charlotte and Jake's relationship grows into a type of commitment. Eventually the two share the driving as well as their troubles. Any "relationship," Tyler told Marguerite Michaels in an interview for *The New York Times Book Review*, even one "as bizarre as" that of "a bank robber and hostage could become . . . bickering [and] familiar. . . . Anything done gradually enough becomes ordinary."

Earthly Possessions, despite its problems, shares with *The Tin Can Tree* and *Celestial Navigation* a redefinition of family ties. As with Tyler's other novels, it also illuminates the problems and conflicts of the individual within a close relationship, whether familial or not, and focuses on the eccentric nature of ordinary lives and the ordinariness of the bizarre.

MORGAN'S PASSING

In her eighth novel, Tyler returned to the heart of Baltimore for her setting and to a central character, Morgan Gower, who is strikingly eccentric. Critics have compared Morgan with Saul Bellow's Henderson and Joseph Heller's Major Major. He also resembles Duncan Peck as well as other Tyler protagonists. Like those heroes, Morgan is in conflict with his family. In Morgan's case, his family consists of seven daughters who find him embarrassing, a slovenly though good-natured wife, a senile mother, and a depressed, inert sister. Like Ben Joe Hawkes, Morgan feels trapped and misunderstood in a house cluttered with "the particles of related people's unrelated worlds" and full of women with whom he is unable to communicate satisfactorily.

While his family insists on going about life unconsciously, Morgan, spirited and highly inventive, faces a midlife crisis that calls for a change. He must also come to terms with his past, the consequences of marrying Bonny for her money as well as his father's inexplicable suicide when Morgan was a teenager. Like Duncan Peck, Morgan is a kind of mechanical mastermind who takes up various projects and then drops them—"a tinkering, puttering, hardware sort of man." Like the renegade Pecks, he eventually abandons his Baltimore family to take up a new life and identity with a traveling amusement company.

Despite these resemblances to other Tyler heroes, Morgan is a unique creation, the product of Tyler's maturing vision of life. Her understanding of his sexual attraction to a young puppeteer and her portrayal of his frustration with his wife suggest a depth of insight into the problems of marriage, a depth lacking in the early *If Morning Ever Comes*. Morgan is also a complex character, a genuine impostor who tries on identities complete with appropriately matching costumes. At times he is "Father Morgan, the street priest of Baltimore"; at other times, he is an immigrant with family still abroad, a doctor who delivers a baby in the backseat of a car—any role in which people will accept him. Though most of this role-playing is harmless, Morgan is an antihero lacking a firm identity, a modern eccentric who revels in the anonymity and emptiness of decaying city neighborhoods and also a man who assumes a false identity to take up life with another man's wife without benefit of divorce.

Not surprisingly, reviewers found it difficult to like Morgan, but few found him unbelievable.

Tyler's increasing skill in capturing and making believable such a character testifies to her maturation as a writer. As John Leonard commented in *The New York Times* when reviewing the novel, readers "are obliged to care" about Tyler's "odd people" "because their oddities are what we see at an angle in the mirror in the middle of a bad night." Drawing from selected everyday scenes covering twelve years in Morgan's life, Tyler roots her novel firmly in the here and now. Morgan becomes believable because he is not always posing. He reads the morning paper over coffee, affectionately slaps his wife on her rear end, smokes too much, attends a daughter's wedding, despairs over a quarrel-filled family vacation, works in a hardware store, and comes down with a terrible cold. Tyler's is a realistic art illuminating family conflict and solidly based in the ordinary details of life.

DINNER AT THE HOMESICK RESTAURANT

Of all Tyler's novels, *Dinner at the Homesick Restaurant* most inspires comparison with the work of Flannery O'Connor. The title is reminiscent of O'Connor's wit and irony, and the mood of the novel, as one reviewer noted, is that of "O'Connor's Gothic South," with its "sullen, psychic menace." At her best, as in *Celestial Navigation*, Tyler captures the pain, anxiety, and isolation beneath the surface of ordinary lives. At times, however, particularly in *Earthly Possessions* but also in *Morgan's Passing*, she treats this pain lightly, thus denying a sense of genuine struggle. In *Earthly Possessions*, Charlotte is flippant and ironic; in *Morgan's Passing*, Morgan is zany, the mood quick and light. *Dinner at the Homesick Restaurant*, representing what John Updike called a "darkening" of Tyler's art, presents the other side of the coin from *Morgan's Passing*, not only in mood but also in story line. Its focus is not the husband who abandons his family to find a new life but the family he leaves behind. It is a stunning psychological portrait of the Tulls, Pearl and her three children, and the anger, guilt, hurt, and anxiety they feel growing up in an uncertain world without a husband and father. All carry their pain through life, illustrating more profoundly than any of Tyler's earlier books the past's haunting influence on the present.

Covering thirty-five years and three generations of Tulls, the novel opens with Pearl on her deathbed. This first chapter, reminiscent of Katherine Anne Porter's short story "The Jilting of Granny Weatherall" (1930), depicts Pearl as a stoic, frightened woman who has weathered a youth filled with dread of being an old maid, a quick marriage, and a lonely struggle to rear three "flawed" children: Cody, the oldest boy, a troublemaker from childhood, "prone to unreasonable rages"; Jenny, the only girl, "flippant" and "opaque"; and Ezra, his mother's favorite, a gentle man who has not "lived up to his potential" but instead has become the ambitionless owner of the Homesick Restaurant. Not one of Pearl's children has turned out as she wished. Consequently, she, like other Tyler characters, feels "closed off" from her family, the very children to whom she has devoted her life. Later chapters reveal why, focusing on each of the children in turn and tracing the evolution of their lives as well as their fear of their mother's rages. All, like their mother, end up in some way "destroyed by love."

Tyler's compassionate portrayal of her characters and her distinctive humor help to mitigate the darkness of this novel. Although Pearl, her forehead permanently creased from worry, verbally and physically abuses her children, Tyler lets the reader understand the reasons for Pearl's behavior, even though one may not forgive her, and shows a far mellower Pearl in old age. Jenny, after struggling through medical school, two marriages, and a nervous breakdown, is nursed back to health by her mother. Cody spares no expense in caring for his family, even though he is unable to forgive Pearl for mistreating him as a child. The teenager Cody plays cruel but funny tricks on his brother Ezra—partly out of resentment at Ezra's being the favorite, but also because of Cody's own pain and sense of rejection. Taking slats from Ezra's bed, Cody strews the floor with pornographic magazines so Pearl will think Ezra the kind of disappointment she finds Cody to be. Later, after stealing Ezra's sweetheart, Cody recognizes not only his guilt but also his love for his brother. These tales fill in the dark psychological portrait Tyler draws, making *Dinner at the Homesick Restaurant*, like many of Tyler's earlier books, a confirmation of life's difficulties as well as of the value of love.

The Accidental Tourist

A mood of dark comedy pervades *The Accidental Tourist*. It is the only Tyler work in which a murder oc-

curs, and a sense of the inexplicable, tragic nature of reality moves the plot and forms a backdrop for the novel. The book opens with Macon and Sarah Leary returning from a truncated beach vacation and Sarah's sudden announcement that she wants a divorce. Macon, the central character, is a forty-four-year-old writer of guidebooks for businessmen who find themselves in foreign places but prefer the familiarity of home. The logo for the series of guidebooks, titled Accidental Tourist, is a winged armchair, a motif suggesting Macon's attitude toward the disruptions of travel.

In the opening pages of *The Accidental Tourist*, the reader learns of the death of Macon and Sarah's twelve-year-old son, Ethan, who was killed in a robbery at a burger stand. Aside from their grief at the death of their son, Macon and Sarah must confront the permanent jarring of their world by the random nature of the crime: The robber shot Ethan as an afterthought; Ethan and his friend had impulsively stolen away from a summer camp to be there. With Sarah's leaving, Macon's life tailspins, yet he strives desperately to maintain control, to reduce life to its simplest terms. He sleeps in one sheet sewn together like a body bag and showers in his shirt to save on laundry. In a spirit of fun, Tyler gives Macon an alter ego, a Welsh corgi, Edward, who becomes increasingly surly as Macon's life disintegrates. By including Edward as a troubled dog, Tyler can introduce the unpredictable Muriel Pritchett, a dog trainer intent on finding a father for her sickly son, Alexander.

Told from a limited third-person point of view, *The Accidental Tourist* displays Tyler's art at its best: her eye for idiosyncratic behavior and the accidental quality of reality, as well as her focus on family as the center of life's triumphs and tragedies. The family here is not only Macon and Sarah but also Macon's siblings: his sister, Rose, whose romance with Julian Edge, Macon's publisher, forms a dual plot to Macon's romance with Muriel, and his two brothers, Charles and Porter. For part of the novel, Tyler centers on the Leary siblings, all marred somewhat by their mother's carefree abandonment of them. Both Charles and Porter are divorced, and Rose maintains her grandparents' home for her brothers. What is striking about the house is its orderliness—every item in the kitchen is shelved in alphabetical order—and its changelessness. When Macon breaks a leg in a freak accident, he returns to his siblings and resumes life just as if he had never been married, had a child, and lived away for years. The characteristics of families, Tyler suggests, are permanently etched; only the occurrences of life constantly shift.

BREATHING LESSONS

In *The Accidental Tourist*, Tyler depicts the dissolution of a twenty-year marriage following the violent death of the Learys' son. In *Breathing Lessons*, she presents the opposite: the duration of Ira and Maggie Moran's marriage for twenty-eight years despite challenges. Told primarily through flashbacks as the couple journeys to the funeral of a friend, the novel covers nearly thirty years in one September day and contrasts the Morans' courtship and marriage with the relationship of their son, Jesse, and his former wife, Fiona. From its beginning, *Breathing Lessons* concerns not only Ira and Maggie's bickering, love, and tolerance for each other but also Maggie's struggle to reconcile Jesse and Fiona.

Set in Pennsylvania and Baltimore, the novel has three principal divisions, each told from a restricted third-person point of view. The first and third sections focus on Maggie's consciousness, while the middle section, which constitutes something of an interlude, centers on Ira's thoughts. The first section wittily depicts the music and mores of the 1950's. The second part delineates a side trip in which Ira and Maggie temporarily become concerned with an elderly black man who has separated from his wife of more than fifty years. This section also provides Ira's family history and his response to his wife and children. Tyler reveals here a masterful handling of exposition through internal thought sequences and flashbacks. The novel's third section, which introduces the characters of Fiona and Leroy, Jesse and Fiona's daughter, returns to Maggie's thoughts and her memories of Jesse and Fiona's relationship. A return to Baltimore with Fiona and Leroy completes the section, suggesting the cyclical nature of experience, a central theme in the novel.

In *Breathing Lessons*, Tyler continues to balance a lighthearted view of human nature with a depth of insight into the darker side of marriage. Maggie and Ira's marriage, while offering a sound balance of two contrasting personality types who can bicker and then rec-

oncile, has its dark side also: a "helpless, angry, confined feeling" that Maggie experiences "from time to time." Ira, too, realizes that marriage involves "the same old arguments, . . . the same old resentments dragged up year after year." The joyful side of Tyler's fiction is her fondness for zany characters, her keen eye for the bizarre in human behavior, which she observes with amused detachment, and her finely tuned ear for human speech. *Breathing Lessons* offers many examples, beginning with the zesty, lower-class names of her characters: Serena, Fiona, and Duluth. Maggie herself belongs to a long line of lively, unpredictable Tyler heroines—most of whom are expert caretakers—beginning with Granny Hawkes in *If Morning Ever Comes*. In fact, in both her acute observations of others and her repeated attempts "to alter people's lives," Maggie resembles her creator, the fiction writer who manipulates the lives of her characters to fill her plot.

SAINT MAYBE

The "darkening" of Tyler's work continues in *Saint Maybe* despite its lovably offbeat characters and unambiguously happy ending. Possible marital infidelity, child neglect, and suicide set the novel moving. The Bedloes are an "ideal, apple-pie" family, determined to be happy and "normal." Trouble invades their Eden in the form of Lucy, a sexy single mother who marries the elder son, Danny, bringing along two young children and, most likely, another she was carrying when she met her new groom. She also brings an insatiable restlessness. The Bedloes welcome the addition to the fold, proclaiming their son fortunate to have found "a ready-made family." It is the seventeen-year-old protagonist Ian, Danny's younger brother, who questions Lucy's virtue, a query with lethal consequences: Danny's suicide when he sees himself a cuckold and Lucy's when she forfeits a bleak future with an overdose of pills.

Guilt over the double tragedy he believes he has caused drives Ian to join the Church of the Second Chance, a congregation of born-again Christians who pursue active atonement for their failings. Obsessively seeking forgiveness, Ian drops out of college at nineteen to raise his brother's orphaned stepchildren. Christ-like, he forswears sexual activity and pursues carpentry. He leads a martyred, though by no means solitary, existence over the next twenty-three years. Like many of Tyler's heroes, Ian lacks self-awareness: He cannot recognize his own goodness and does not understand that he has paid any debt in full. When, at forty-two, he marries Rita diCarlo, a character reminiscent of Muriel Pritchett, Macon Leary's freewheeling lifeline in *The Accidental Tourist*, Ian is surprised and delighted to realize that he has not spent his years paying a penance; rather, he has been leading a rich—if unorthodox—life.

LADDER OF YEARS

Ladder of Years tells the story of forty-year-old Cordelia Grinstead's circular flight from her upper-middle-class life in Baltimore. Until she simply walks away from her husband and teenage children during a vacation, Delia has never left home. Having passively married her father's assistant, who chose her as a helpmate in assuming the family medical practice, Delia lives her married life in her girlhood home, where she suffocates under the weight of domesticity. Her presence is defined by the demands of the family she nurtures, yet her children's increasing self-sufficiency threatens her with obsolescence. Fleeing home, Delia embarks on a journey toward self-discovery, a quest reminiscent of Charlotte Emory's in *Earthly Possessions*. She initially revels in her spare new existence in a small Maryland town, but, like others among Tyler's would-be renegades from the hearth, she finds that her caregiver's habits of heart and mind reassert themselves. Realizing that she has re-created the very role she believed she had shed, Delia embraces her identity as a nurturer and returns home, aware finally of her family's genuine, though unvoiced, appreciation.

A PATCHWORK PLANET

A Patchwork Planet revisits *Saint Maybe*'s theme of debt and repayment. Black sheep Barnaby Gaitlin is a former juvenile delinquent who, to the shame of his affluent parents, was arrested in his youth for breaking into the homes of their wealthy Guilford neighbors. To keep her son out of jail, Margot Gaitlin (born Margo Kazmerow, "just a Polish girl from Canton") swallowed her pride to beg and buy her neighbors' silence. Barnaby's freedom cost $8,700, a sum his embittered mother continually holds over him. Although Barnaby eventually repays this debt, he learns that self-respect cannot be purchased.

A handyman who performs odd jobs for an assort-ment of crotchety and colorful senior citizens, Barnaby stumbles across a client's "Twinform" while tidying her attic. The mannequin—shaped and painted to resemble the owner—was invented by the client's great-grandfather as an aid to foolproof dressing: By first modeling an outfit on a "double," one could gauge and adjust the effect of the intended apparel. Barnaby is intrigued by this premise of the "trial run," and he imputes his many mistakes to his failure to hold metaphoric dress rehearsals for his life. He is convinced that he lacks necessary information for successful living, a need that prompted the boyhood burglaries during which he would examine his victims' photographs and diaries for clues to how they managed their lives. He remains rudderless at thirty, wavering between intentionally disappointing his parents through exaggerated irresponsibility and straining to please them, nearly marrying the unsuitably staid Sophia Maynard because she lends him the respectability he lacks.

Barnaby sinks to an emotional low when he is wrongly accused of theft, a crime Sophia believes him guilty of and a charge that he feels he vicariously deserves. However, in the homemade blanket alluded to in the novel's title, Barnaby finds the expansive perspective from which to accept the love and faith that his clients rightly place in him. On an elderly woman's quilt he sees that Earth is "makeshift and haphazard, clumsily cobbled together, overlapping and crowded and likely to fall into pieces at any moment." He is moved to accept and forgive his own failings as a universal condition of his humanity. The novel ends with his resolute good-bye to the girlfriend who doubted his goodness: "Sophia, you never did realize. I am a man you can trust."

BACK WHEN WE WERE GROWNUPS

Rebecca Davitch, the protagonist of *Back When We Were Grownups*, shares with earlier Tyler heroines a desire to flee the isolating and often confusing and limiting dynamics of a large, needy family in order to explore the possibilities of a less encumbered life. Unlike Charlotte Emory of *Earthly Possessions* and Delia Grinstead of *Ladder of Years*, however, Rebecca does not have to leave an existing family physically in order to explore her alternate self. Instead, at fifty-three, widowed, with three grown stepdaughters, one grown daughter, numerous grandchildren, and a befuddled elderly great-uncle-in-law all relying on her to maintain the psychic connections that hold the family together, Rebecca embarks on a mostly internal journey to re-create the life she began as the only child in a sterile household.

The novel, told entirely from Rebecca's limited omniscient perspective, tracks her initial mental retreat from the family as she finds her self-contained college sweetheart Will Allenby and they begin where they left off before she unexpectedly eloped with Joe Davitch. Except, of course, Rebecca cannot entirely disentangle herself from her real family despite her wishes to do so. Like many of Tyler's characters who are members of autonomous families in which organization and reserve are the norm—such as Charlotte Emory in *Earthly Possessions*, Elizabeth Abbott in *The Clock Winder*, and Emily Meredith in *Morgan's Passing*—Rebecca feels drawn to her mostly adopted, unruly family members, largely because of the magic of their laughter and their constant movement, regardless of how fractious family gatherings might become. As she begins to explore the alternative, she soon realizes that despite her feelings to the contrary, she has changed irrevocably into a more expansive person who needs and provides love to those in her evolving family.

THE AMATEUR MARRIAGE

In *The Amateur Marriage*, Tyler interrogates the foibles, peculiarities, and passions of a marriage. Though this theme has appeared in Tyler's fiction in many guises, such as the disintegrating marriage at midlife of Morgan and Bonny Gower in *Morgan's Passing* and the sustained marriage of Maggie and Ira Moran in *Breathing Lessons*, in previous novels she has not purposefully followed the trajectory of one marriage from its beginning to its demise, and even beyond.

The novel opens from a third-person omniscient narrator's perspective that seems to speak for the tight-knit Polish community of St. Cassian's in Baltimore's inner city in a recounting of how the main characters, Pauline and Michael Anton, met in 1941. This opening segment presents not only their initial meeting but also the social and cultural milieu of that time and place. The novel then follows the couple through the post-World War II movement to the suburbs, through the turbulent 1960's and 1970's, and into the more historically complacent years after. These kinds of cultural markers, which are rare in

Tyler's fiction, keep the characters in the novel grounded in real time.

From varying perspectives, *The Amateur Marriage* depicts pivotal scenes from Michael and Pauline's life together: Pauline's near affair with a man in the neighborhood; their daughter Lindy's vanishing from a facility for drug treatment in San Francisco; their discovery of Lindy's son Pagan, whom they help raise when Lindy disappears; their separation and ultimate divorce after their thirtieth anniversary party; and, eventually, the recombining of the family with the reappearance of Lindy after Pauline's death. These scenes highlight the public differences between the two main characters as friends and relatives watch them fight and make up in consistently volatile and public ways. The two often argue loudly, with "tears and shouting and slamming and painful, obvious silences." Because the point of view shifts between chapters, the characters also convey their own perspectives on their marriage: Pauline's admonition to her potential lover that the "anxiety committee" is always waiting on her when she is gone from home; Michael's fear that he can love Pauline and "dislike her" at the same time.

More than in any of her other novels, Tyler focuses here on the thin line of marriage and how this central relationship within a family can be maintained despite personality differences, can be destroyed by the slightest word, and can be resurrected even after its loss. Though the children in this novel are influenced by their parents' life, Tyler does not explore in any depth the ramifications of the marriage for the children; rather, the exploration stays centered on the volatile relationship at the core of the work, including the enduring love between those so connected.

DIGGING TO AMERICA

One of Tyler's recurring themes concerns the individual's sense of displacement within his or her own family. Whether it be Ben Joe Hawkes in *If Morning Ever Comes* or Rebecca Davitch in *Back When We Were Grownups*, Tyler's characters often describe themselves as outsiders within the one community where they should feel a sense of familial belonging. In *Digging to America*, Tyler uses the trope of the outsider to show this disconnection, extending it by creating not simply a metaphoric "foreignness" in these characters but also a literal foreignness. Although Tyler has included foreign-born characters in earlier novels, such as the Middle Eastern students who live on Waverly Street in *Saint Maybe*, she has never before created such a range of foreign-born characters: The Iranian Yazdan family, which includes Sami and Ziba, Sami's mother Maryam, and their adopted daughter Susan, who is from Korea, as well as Ziba's extended family, provide some of the perspective of the novel. They are juxtaposed with the members of the Donaldson family, natives of Baltimore: Brad and Bitsy; their adopted daughters, Jin-Ho from Korea and Xiu-Mei from China; and Bitsy's parents, Connie and Dave.

The novel opens on the night when both families are sitting in the airport waiting for their adopted Korean daughters to arrive. After realizing that the two families are experiencing this life change, the more outgoing and including family, the Donaldsons, essentially invite the more reserved Yazdans to become a part of their extended family. As in other Tyler novels, such as *Celestial Navigation*, where ostensibly disconnected, nonfamilial characters find strength in each other, these two families debunk the idea that difference can prevent connectedness. However, the conjoining of the two families also highlights how estranged any one individual can feel at times, how a sense of foreignness—whether it be literal or metaphoric—continues to create gaps despite familiarity.

Although the focus of the book shifts to the potential relationship between Bitsy's widowed father, Dave, and Sami's widowed mother, Maryam, the cross-cultural mistakes and misunderstandings that take place are not as problematic for them as the distinct differences in their abilities to be open to change. By illustrating their problems of personal and familial connection in this way, Tyler indicates how a character's recognition of foreignness can provide a basis for bonding rather than disassociation.

Stella A. Nesanovich; Theresa M. Kanoza
Updated by Rebecca Hendrick Flannagan

OTHER MAJOR WORKS

SHORT FICTION: "The Common Courtesies," 1968; "Who Would Want a Little Boy?," 1968; "With All Flags Flying," 1971; "The Bride in the Boatyard," 1972; "The Base-Metal Egg," 1973; "Spending," 1973; "Half-Truths and Semi-Miracles," 1974; "A Knack for Languages," 1975; "The Geologist's Maid," 1975; "Some Sign That I Ever Made You Happy," 1975; "Your Place Is Empty," 1976; "Average Waves in Unprotected Waters," 1977; "Foot-Footing On," 1977; "Holding Things Together," 1977; "Uncle Ahmad," 1977; "Under the Bosom Tree," 1977; "Linguistics," 1978; "Laps," 1981; "The Country Cook," 1982; "Teenage Wasteland," 1983; "Rerun," 1988; "A Woman Like a Fieldstone House," 1989; "People Who Don't Know the Answers," 1991.

CHILDREN'S LITERATURE: *Tumble Tower*, 1993 (illustrations by Mitra Modarressi); *Timothy Tugbottom Says No!*, 2005 (illustrations by Modarressi).

BIBLIOGRAPHY

Bail, Paul. *Anne Tyler: A Critical Companion*. Westport, Conn.: Greenwood Press, 1998. Provides biographical information, a discussion of Tyler's literary influences, and analysis of twelve of her novels. Among the topics addressed are Tyler's approaches to plot, characters, themes, literary devices, historical settings, and narrative points of view as well as how the novels fit into southern regional literature, women's literature, and popular culture.

Carson, Barbara Harrell. "'Endlessly Branching and Dividing': Anne Tyler's Dynamic Causality." *Soundings* 85, nos. 3/4 (Fall/Winter, 2002): 301-321. Focuses on Tyler's ambiguity concerning the question of fate versus free will in her novels.

Coleman, Cheryl Devon. "Metaphorical Redemption in Anne Tyler's *The Clock Winder* and *Dinner at the Homesick Restaurant*." *Christianity and Literature* 49, no. 4 (Summer, 2000): 511-532. Examines Tyler's realistic portrayals of flawed humans who are still capable of moments of grace.

Evans, Elizabeth. *Anne Tyler*. New York: Twayne, 1993. Good introduction to Tyler's work includes biographical information and an overview of her novels up to the early 1990's. Includes a useful bibliography of primary and secondary sources.

Jansen, Henry. "Houses and Foreigners: Anne Tyler." In *Laughter Among the Ruins: Postmodern Comic Approaches to Suffering*. New York: Peter Lang, 2001. Presents discussion of the juxtaposition of humor and suffering in Tyler's work, as part of a larger examination of the approaches to human tragedy taken by novelists including Tyler, Iris Murdoch, and John Irving.

Kissel, Susan S. *Moving On: The Heroines of Shirley Ann Grau, Anne Tyler, and Gail Godwin.* Bowling Green, Ohio: Bowling Green State University Popular Press, 1996. Compares the heroines in the fiction of the three authors, with discussion of Tyler's heroines focusing on the author's identity as a southern writer. Includes bibliography and index.

Robertson, Mary F. "Anne Tyler: Medusa Points and Contact Points." In *Contemporary American Women Writers: Narrative Strategies*, edited by Catherine Rainwater and William J. Scheick. Lexington: University Press of Kentucky, 1985. Discussion of the narrative form of Tyler's novels focuses on her disruption of the conventional expectations of family novels.

Salwak, Dale, ed. *Anne Tyler as Novelist.* Iowa City: University of Iowa Press, 1994. Collection of essays addresses topics such as Tyler's development, attainments, and literary reputation.

Town, Caren J. "'Three Meal a Day Aftermaths': Anne Tyler's Determined Adolescents." In *The New Southern Girl: Female Adolescence in the Works of Twelve Women Authors.* Jefferson, N.C.: McFarland, 2004. Discussion of the portrayal of adolescents in Tyler's works is part of a larger exploration of the depiction of teenage girls in the works of authors such as Tyler, Lee Smith, Jill McCorkle, and Dorothy Allison.

Voelker, Joseph C. *Art and the Accidental in Anne Tyler.* Columbia: University of Missouri Press, 1989. The first book-length study of Anne Tyler's fiction, this volume focuses on the development of Tyler's aesthetics and her treatment of character, particularly her view of selfhood as mystery and of experience as accidental.

U

MIGUEL DE UNAMUNO Y JUGO

Born: Bilbao, Spain; September 29, 1864
Died: Salamanca, Spain; December 31, 1936

PRINCIPAL LONG FICTION

Paz en la guerra, 1897 (*Peace in War*, 1983)
Amor y pedagogía, 1902
Niebla, 1914 (*Mist: A Tragicomic Novel*, 1928)
Abel Sánchez: Una historia de pasión, 1917
  (*Abel Sánchez*, 1947)
Tres novelas ejemplares y un prólogo, 1920
  (*Three Exemplary Novels and a Prologue*,
  1930)
La tía Tula, 1921 (*Tía Tula*, 1976)
San Manuel Bueno, mártir, 1931 (*Saint Manuel
  Bueno, Martyr*, 1954)
Dos novelas cortas, 1961 (James Russell Stamm
  and Herbert Eugene Isar, editors)

OTHER LITERARY FORMS

Miguel de Unamuno y Jugo (ew-nah-MEW-noh-ee-KEW-goh) wrote extensively in all genres (novel, poetry, short story, drama, and essay). Manuel García Blanco has compiled Unamuno's works under the title of *Obras completas* (1959-1964), a collection numbering sixteen volumes, edited with prologues and notes. Only a few articles are missing from this collection, published in Madrid by Vergara Editorial, by special concession of Afrodisio Aguado. A later edition, in ten volumes, has appeared since, but neither edition is definitive.

ACHIEVEMENTS

Miguel de Unamuno y Jugo achieved distinction as a philosopher, a novelist, a poet, and a scholar. Fluent in many languages, active in public life, he was indeed a protean figure, and his achievements are still being assimilated. Unamuno had important and influential admirers, particularly among French scholars and writers, such as Jean Cassou, Marcel Bataillon, and Pierre Emmanuel. Martin Heidegger read and admired him. Though studies of existentialism done in English have largely neglected him, Unamuno was among the first to recognize the greatness of Søren Kierkegaard and to adapt his ideas to his own philosophy.

For Hispanists, Unamuno stands among the greatest of Spanish writers. That does not mean that he is without detractors. Pío Baroja, a famous contemporary of Unamuno, predicted that Unamuno's works would not endure. Ramón José Sender, a generation removed from Unamuno, made a similar prediction, and José Ortega y Gasset later added that if Unamuno's virtues are gigantic, so are his defects. Nevertheless, more than a century after Unamuno's birth, scholars are still filling volumes in homage to his works, with a circumspect nod at his idiosyncracies.

BIOGRAPHY

Miguel de Unamuno y Jugo was born in Bilbao, Spain, an important industrial center of the Basque province, on September 29, 1864, the third of six children. His father died when he was six years old. Womanhood exerted a great influence on his work. His early religious training shaped his mind toward a career as a priest, but other influences won out, not the least of which was his childhood sweetheart, Concepción Lizárraga (Concha), who seems never to have had a rival, before or after matrimony, for Unamuno's loyalty.

In *Recuerdos de niñez y de mocedad* (1908; memories of childhood and adolescence), Unamuno recalls highlights of his early years, especially the bombardment of Bilbao in 1874 during the Carlist War. These memories find further development in his first novel,

Peace in War, and provide a great deal of insight into young Unamuno's state of mind during the four years he spent at the University of Madrid, beginning in 1880. Francisco (Pachico) Zabalbide, a youthful character in the novel, parallels that of Unamuno in his intellectual appetites, his shyness, dreaminess, and the decay in his religious resolve.

Unamuno received his licentiate degree in 1883, and one year later he was awarded the doctorate. That same year (1884), he returned to Bilbao, taught part time, and began publishing in regional newspapers. Following several unsuccessful attempts to obtain posts at the Instituto Viscaíno (Basque Institute), he was appointed the chair of Greek at the University of Salamanca in 1891. In that same year, he married Concha.

Whether writing of current political problems, religion, or professional issues at the university, Unamuno was always outspoken. Yet in 1900, he was named rector of the University of Salamanca. His writing always reflected the agony of the loss of his childhood faith and the struggle to find solutions to the insoluble problems of identity and immortality. A short story, "Ver con los ojos" (using the eyes to see), was published in *El noticiero bilbaíno* in 1886, wherein the introspective young protagonist reflects Unamuno's own questioning of the value of life and his antagonism toward prevailing beliefs.

In 1897, one of Unamuno's children, a son born the previous year, contracted meningitis, which resulted in a terminal hydrocephalic condition. This precipitated a spiritual crisis in Unamuno, and the experience rooted itself so deeply in his thoughts and feelings that it surfaced repeatedly in scenes throughout his works. Following this crisis, Unamuno attempted a return to the religious pursuits of his childhood, but he found that he could not shake himself free of his uncertainties. His life and his works thereafter reflect in varying degrees the agony of tension between his nostalgic attachment to traditional faith and the rending doubts that would not die.

In 1914, for no formally explained reason, Unamuno was relieved of the rectorship at Salamanca. In 1920, he accepted the appointment of vice rector, which he held until 1924, when his open criticism of Primo de Rivera resulted in the loss of his post and his subsequent exile.

He went to Fuerteventura, in the Canary Islands, then fled to Paris, then later to Hendaye, France, where he settled for the rest of his exile. Primo de Rivera's dictatorship fell in 1930, and Unamuno returned triumphantly to Spain in February of that year. In 1931, he was reappointed rector at Salamanca.

In May, 1934, death claimed the quiet, unpretentious Concha, his "habit," who had represented the spiritual strength and stability of motherhood for Unamuno and his nine children. In July of that same year, a married daughter, Salomé, also died. A few months later, Unamuno retired from his teaching duties at the university, but he was named lifetime rector, an appointment far more temporary than it promised, notwithstanding the little time left to him. His criticism of Francisco Franco prompted his dismissal, and he was confined to his home, where he died on December 31, 1936.

ANALYSIS

Miguel de Unamuno y Jugo described himself as a man of contradiction and struggle. The intensity of his

Miguel de Unamuno y Jugo. (Library of Congress)

pursuit of autonomy against a doubtful backdrop of twentieth century dehumanization amounts almost to monomania. The quantity of his output betrays his comfortless conviction that the only immortality he could expect would come from his legacy to the world, either his physical offspring, the children of his body, or his spiritual offspring, the children of his mind. Scholarly attention to his works and personal idiosyncrasies thus at least fulfills his hope that his works would keep his name alive.

Unamuno's consciousness is structured by the inevitable life-death cycle and the problem of immortality. He often portrays motherhood as a symbol of immortality and uses, conversely, the barrenness of the womb as a representation of the futility of a life without meaning. His men are reminiscent of Adam in a nonparadisiacal wilderness or of a modern Ishmael in an existential desert. Unamuno constantly wraps the vast limits of his universe about himself like a security blanket, making existence his hobby, profession, and obsession.

In Unamuno's characters, the differentiation between the opposites of good and evil is rarely, if ever, clear-cut. The Good Mother or Earth Mother possesses some of the qualities of the Terrible Mother; the Soul Mate reveals also the aspects of the femme fatale; the hero is also in some respects the antihero.

Mist

Unamuno's *Mist* is the story of Augusto Pérez, an individual whose spirit has never matured and whose personality consequently remains unaffirmed. In his struggle to establish his identity, Augusto feels drawn toward Eugenia, a piano teacher, and he seeks to assert his existence by establishing a vital relationship with her. She, in turn, agrees to marry him but immediately elopes with her former lover. She further plays Augusto for a fool by taking advantage of his willingness to pull her out of economic straits and even to arrange for a comfortable position for her lover in a distant province. On the verge of suicide, Augusto seeks the advice of a certain Miguel de Unamuno, who informs him that he is but a fictitious entity and cannot of his own will work out his own destruction. At this point, Augusto's resolution to kill himself completely dissolves; face-to-face with his creator, he asserts that his existence is as real as Unamuno's own, whereupon Unamuno irascibly retorts that Augusto will die, not because Augusto wills it, but because he, the author, so wills.

In keeping with this typically Unamunian inversion is the fact that Augusto's mother, genuinely concerned with Augusto's welfare, has so smothered him with solicitude that she has absorbed his will, his power to assert himself—his identity. At the moment of her death, her advice to Augusto to look for a wife who will mother him is a recognition of the fact that he is still unable to take care of himself. In her genuine concern, she deprives him of real existence, while Eugenia in her indifference is the agent who brings about the one great assertion in his otherwise meaningless life. Thus, the mother figure is in a sense the femme fatale, while the fatal woman gives him life.

Abel Sánchez

The love of paradox evident in *Mist*, characteristic of Unamuno's philosophy as well as of his fiction, animates the novel that many critics regard as his greatest, *Abel Sánchez*. This novel also offers Unamuno's most striking treatment of one of his favorite motifs: the double. In Unamuno's treatment of the archetypal Cain-Abel relationship, "the other one" represents a second self that reminds the Unamunian man of his finiteness. Unamuno sees the sibling rivalry as the battle of man with his alter ego. The "hero" of the novel is not Abel Sánchez but Joaquín Monegro. He is the point-of-view character, but the title gives the story to Abel. Joaquín, it seems, must yield everything to his alter ego, Abel.

Abel's death is the culmination of many events. Abel and Joaquín have known each other since infancy; Abel, an artist, has been the more popular of the two, Joaquín, a doctor, the more intellectual. Joaquín has long been jealous of Abel's attainments, but the jealousy begins to turn to a bitter hatred when Abel steals the affection of Joaquín's sweetheart, Helena. Abel is complacent and easygoing; Heaven seems to smile on him. He paints a portrait of Helena that becomes famous, thus immortalizing her. Joaquín's envy consumes him. With all of his medical training and intellect, Joaquín can only temporarily preserve life; he cannot immortalize it. This idea is shown clearly when one of Joaquín's matronly patients dies, despite his efforts to save her life. Hanging in her living room is a large, stunning portrait: She has been immortalized by Abel.

Fostering his intense hatred for Abel, Joaquín marries Antonia, a motherly woman who pities him. His envy of Abel reaches new proportions when he learns that Helena has given birth to Abel's son, Abelín. When his own wife, Antonia, conceives, she bears a daughter, whom they name Joaquina.

Abel and Joaquín discuss a picture Abel plans to paint—a representation of the Old Testament version of the first murder. The subject tantalizes Joaquín. In addition to the Bible, he reads Lord Byron's *Cain* (1821) and finds himself inexorably identifying with Cain. Abel completes the painting and triumphs again. Joaquín swallows his bitterness and gives a banquet in Abel's honor, making a speech so eloquent that he increases Abel's fame considerably.

As Abelín and Joaquina grow up, the young Abelín decides to study medicine and eventually joins Joaquín as an assistant in his medical office. Joaquín takes heart when he learns that Abelín has little love for his father, whom he regards as a self-contained, rather selfish person. Eventually, Abelín and Joaquina marry. Their first child is a son, whom they name Joaquín. Joaquín tries incessantly to win the affections of his grandson, but as the child grows older, he seems to prefer Abel. Finally, Joaquín, desperately longing for the love of his grandson, approaches his old friend and begs him not to take the boy's love from him, as he has taken everything else during their lifetime. At Abel's cold response, Joaquín angrily grips him by the throat to choke him, but he does not kill him. In that instant, Abel suffers a heart attack. The horror of the moment is intensified as Joaquín realizes that his grandson, too young to comprehend fully the situation, has watched the "murder" from the doorway. The child flees, as if from a madman.

Joaquín is a reflection of the first rebel, the first to fall from grace—Satan himself. His surname, Monegro, insinuates into the reader's consciousness the suggestion of "Monseigneur de Negro"—the Prince of Darkness. This parallel is established in a conversation between Joaquín and Helena. Joaquín confesses to her that he plans to find a mate and get married, but he fears his inability to love. "That's what Don Mateo, the priest, says of the devil—that he can't love," observes Helena.

The devil, then, is the antithesis of God. If God is love, the devil is the negation of love; hence, Joaquín speaks bitterly of the "eternal hatred" that freezes his breast (his reference to the "dragón de hielo," or "ice dragon," recalls Dante's ninth circle of Hell, reserved for those who had committed some act of treachery against love). On his deathbed, Joaquín's last confession consists of an open admission to his wife, Antonia, that he has never loved her; love, he grants, would have saved him, but he has been incapable of loving. Joaquín's life is cankered by envy, the vice that caused the devil's downfall.

SAINT MANUEL BUENO, MARTYR

If Joaquín is a devil figure, Don Manuel in *Saint Manuel Bueno, Martyr* is diametrically opposite. Manuel Bueno, the priest of the village of Valverde de Lucerna, with tremendous personal magnetism, draws the entire village into a faith in life and Christ while he himself agonizes in the conviction that there is nothing after death: no life, no hope, nothing.

The archetype for this work, especially the life-death cycle, is first established in the author's choice of proper names. Manuel (from Immanuel, meaning "God with us") is clearly a Christ figure, his name identifying his function from the outset. Angela Carballino's name betokens at once her angelic tenderness and the fact that she, as the narrator, brings the story to the reader (*Angel*, from the Greek meaning "messenger"). Moreover, she represents the Good Mother or Soul Mate, for she is a life-giver. The reader knows of Manuel only through her; hence, his achievements live on through her instrumentality. Lázaro becomes a foil for Manuel's power for creating "new life" in the irony of the Unamunian way. Manuel raises Lázaro from the deathbed of skepticism to the "new life" of awareness—the awareness of utter death.

The source for the name Blasillo is less readily apparent. Antonio Sánchez Barbudo (in *Estudios sobre Unamuno y Machado*, 1959) sees in the name a reflection of Unamuno's opinion regarding one of Blaise Pascal's *Pensées* (1670). Blasillo (Blas being the equivalent of Blaise), the simple believer, reflects a simple philosophy: "Drink holy water, and it will make you a believer." More plausible, perhaps, is the theory advanced by James Russell Stamm and Herbert Eugene Isar, editors of two short novels by Unamuno, who hold that Blas is typically the name of the credulous rustic, the "rube" of Spanish tradition. He is referred to, they indicate, as a *pobre idiota* (poor idiot) in the novel. Unamuno has pointed out that the word "idiot" in its original Greek means simply a common or ignorant person, or, by extension, a villager. Thus, in the largest sense, Blasillo, with pitiful limitations on his awareness, symbolizes the abandonment from which all the characters suffer. Finally, with greatly compressed irony, Unamuno sets the story in a village named Valverde de Lucerna, which suggests "green valley of eternal light" (*valle verde de luz eterna*)—a paradise that is paradisiacal only through the villagers' ignorance of the dark truth that Manuel hides in his bosom.

The archetypal intent of the novel is further evident in Unamuno's treatment of the setting. Valverde de Lucerna lies "like a brooch" between the lake and the lofty mountain reflected in it. Angela continually links Manuel with the countryside, the mountain, and the lake. To her, "everything revolved around Don Manuel: Don Manuel, the lake and the mountain." Later, alluding to the climactic moment when Lázaro receives Holy Communion, she describes Don Manuel as "white as January snow on the mountain, and moving like the surface of the lake when it is stirred by the northeasterly wind." Water (the lake) is a symbol of the mystery of creation, as well as the source of life, the element of the security of prenatal confinement. It is also, according to Carl Jung, the most common symbol of the unconscious. Earth (the mountain) symbolizes the harvest, productivity, and—by contrast to the water symbol—consciousness. Reflecting on life, Don Manuel observes, "Have you seen, Lázaro, a greater mystery than the snow falling on the lake, and dying there, while it covers the mountain with a hood?" Snow represents death, enshrouding everything except the lake. Beneath this shroud, conscious life and achievements disappear, yet death itself disappears in the mystery of creation. Moreover, Don Manuel is torn between his conscious desire to act and the agonizing urge to return to the source of creation.

The setting provides still another symbol for the life-death cycle in the magnificent walnut tree that, even after it has dried up, continues to give life to the village—in the form of toys for the children and wood for the poor. Manuel calls the tree a matriarchal tree and fashions his coffin out of the wood of its trunk, for in his suffering, he longs to return to the primordial womb, or the origin of creation. The tree is a symbol of the Earth Mother, who gives life, harbors and protects her "children." Manuel's longing is repeated in his attraction for the lake, toward which he is drawn irresistibly. The lake here represents the peace of prenativity, the urge to return to the womb, the source of life.

Don Manuel seems to find in the lake the secret of his spiritual agony. Village tradition has it that after death, fortunate souls go to dwell in a city at the bottom of the lake—a city identical to their own. Part of Manuel's "sacrificial punishment" (he suffers so that his village may be free from suffering) is that he must carry inside himself the knowledge that the heaven the people see for themselves is but a reflection of their own lives. The only life after death, as Manuel envisions it, is the essence created by the individual—that pitiful portion of one's identity that he leaves behind in others. His mission is to keep this awful secret to himself and let the villagers dream their lives as the lake dreams the heavens.

Manuel's yearning for the maternal confines of prenativity, reflected in both his attraction for the lake and his fascination with the walnut tree, suggests the motherhood motif, a motif elaborated more fully and literally in the two principal female figures, Don Manuel's mother and Angela, both of whom function as Christian symbols of the life-giving, almost divine Mother. They provide an absorbing influence for Manuel's overriding anguish. When he reaches the climactic moment of his Good Friday High Mass, his personal suffering overflows in his cry, "My God, My God, why hast thou forsaken me?" At that moment, the people believe they are hearing the Lord Jesus Christ himself, his voice springing from the ancient Crucifix. On one such occasion, Manuel's mother, hearing his words and sensing his anguish, cries out to him, "My son," and it is as if her cry has issued from the lips of the Mater Dolorosa, "her heart transfixed by seven swords."

Don Manuel, with the power and trust to absolve the town's citizens of their sins, is the spiritual father of them all, but Angela, even from the beginning, senses a deeper participation in Manuel's life and struggles than is typical of the generic body of his "flock." She yearns for his personal protection and feels the need of his personal influence. Her opening words:

I want to leave in writing my testimony . . . of all that I remember of that matriarchal man who pervaded the most secret life of my soul, who was my true father, the father of my spirit, the spirit of myself, Angela Carballino.

Then, following her first confession with Don Manuel, an inversion begins to take place in their relationship. Her original feelings of awe become compassion and intuitive understanding. She has already begun to fill the need for him that she originally felt was her own. She observes that, even though only a girl, she has felt the flow and stirrings of maternity, and finding herself in the confessional next to the priest, she senses his own quiet confession in the submissive murmur of his voice. As her feelings deepen, she sees herself with qualities that the reader can identify with the Good Mother, for she longs to absorb Don Manuel's sorrow, sensing his need for solace and refuge. She says:

I missed my Don Manuel, as if his absence called to me, as if he were endangered by my being so far away, as if he were in need of me. I began to feel a kind of maternal affection for my spiritual father; I longed to help him bear the cross of birth.

Finally, in her ultimate role as the redeeming Good Mother, she hears the echo of Manuel's own mother's voice within her, crying, "My son!" He, at last, is unable to withhold from her his awful secret, and he begs her to absolve him from blame for his pious deceit. She assumes a matriarchal priesthood that invests her with the voice of the whole village, and she absolves her confessor "in the name of the Father, the Son, and the Holy Ghost." As they leave the church, she again feels the tremblings of maternity within her.

It is in her role as both spiritual daughter and mother that she reflects the angelic qualities that her name suggests. In her relationship with Don Manuel there are also clear resonances of the Virgin Mary. Angela, who remains a virgin all of her life, becomes the immaculate spiritual mother to the Savior of Valverde de Lucerna, Don Manuel, thus assuming the same ironic qualities of deification that Unamuno vouchsafes to Manuel. She fills the function reserved in more orthodox theology for the Holy Ghost. As Manuel administers his last Communion, he whispers to Angela while giving her the Host,

"Pray, my child, pray for us . . . and pray also for Our Lord Jesus Christ." Angela is the earthly version of the Virgin Mother, a Mother of Sorrows, to whom the tormented priest turns in his need.

Unamuno calls his hero a martyr, and so he is. A martyr gives his life for what he believes. Manuel believes in his mission: to give solace, consolation, and faith to others. He does not believe in the Resurrection or in life everlasting. On the traditional expectation that a priest should be personally engaged in that faith, a champion of his own convictions, rests the Unamunian irony: Manuel gives his life for what he does not believe. Martyrs create faith, says Unamuno; faith does not create martyrs.

Unamuno styled himself a man of contradiction and struggle, and so he proved to be. The struggle that characterized his own life finds reflections in the lives of all of his fictional offspring. Absolutes, like mirages, disappear as one draws close enough to them to feel that they are within one's grasp. Unamuno's characters reflect the lonely condition of humankind without God, and in this respect, Unamuno's message has never ceased to be timely.

Harold K. Moon

OTHER MAJOR WORKS

SHORT FICTION: *El espejo de la muerte*, 1913; *Soledad y otros cuentos*, 1937; *Abel Sánchez, and Other Stories*, 1956.

PLAYS: *La esfinge*, pr. 1909 (wr. 1898); *La difunta*, pr. 1910; *La princesa doña Lambra*, pb. 1913; *La venda*, pb. 1913 (wr. 1899); *Fedra*, pr. 1918 (wr. 1910; *Phaedra*, 1959); *El pasado que vuelve*, pr. 1923 (wr. 1910); *Raquel encadenada*, pr. 1926 (wr. 1921); *Sombras de sueño*, pr., pb. 1930; *El otro*, pr., pb. 1932 (wr. 1926; *The Other*, 1947); *El hermano Juan: O, El mundo es teatro*, pb. 1934 (wr. 1927); *Soledad*, pr. 1953 (wr. 1921); *Teatro completo*, pb. 1959.

POETRY: *Poesías*, 1907; *Rosario de sonetos líricos*, 1911; *El Cristo de Velázquez*, 1920 (*The Christ of Velázquez*, 1951); *Rimas de dentro*, 1923; *Teresa*, 1924; *Romancero del destierro*, 1928; *Poems*, 1952; *Cancionero: Diario poético*, 1953 (partial translation as *The Last Poems of Miguel de Unamuno*, 1974).

NONFICTION: *Nicodemo el fariseo*, 1899; *De la enseñanza superior en España*, 1899; *Tres ensayos*,

1900; *En torno al casticismo*, 1902; *De mi país*, 1903; *Vida de Don Quijote y Sancho según Miguel de Cervantes Saavedra, explicada y comentada por Miguel de Unamuno*, 1905 (*The Life of Don Quixote and Sancho According to Miguel de Cervantes Saavedra Expounded with Comment by Miguel de Unamuno*, 1927); *Recuerdos de niñez y de mocedad*, 1908; *Mi religión, y otros ensayos breves*, 1910; *Soliloquios y conversaciones*, 1911 (*Essays and Soliloquies*, 1925); *Contra esto y aquello*, 1912; *Del sentimiento trágico de la vida en los hombres y en los pueblos*, 1913 (*The Tragic Sense of Life in Men and in Peoples*, 1921); *La agonía del Cristianismo*, 1925 (in French as *L'Agonie du Christianisme*; in Spanish 1931; *The Agony of Christianity*, 1928, 1960); *Cómo se hace una novela*, 1927 (*How to Make a Novel*, 1976); *La ciudad de Henoc*, 1941; *Cuenca ibérica*, 1943; *Paisajes del alma*, 1944; *La enormidad de España*, 1945; *Visiones y commentarios*, 1949; *Tratado del amor de Dios*, 2005 (wr. 1905-1908; *Treatise on Love of God*, 2007).

MISCELLANEOUS: *De Fuerteventura a París*, 1925; *Obras completas*, 1959-1964 (16 volumes).

BIBLIOGRAPHY

Ellis, Robert Richmond. *The Tragic Pursuit of Being: Unamuno and Sartre*. Tuscaloosa: University of Alabama Press, 1988. Ellis compares and contrasts the existential ideas revealed in the works of Unamuno and Jean-Paul Sartre. Includes a bibliography and an index.

Evans, Jan E. *Unamuno and Kierkegaard: Paths to Selfhood in Fiction*. Lanham, Md.: Lexington Books, 2005. Evans examines how Unamuno was influenced by the ideas of Danish philosopher Søren Kierkegaard. Analyzes three of Unamuno's novels—*Mist, Saint Manuel Bueno, Martyr*, and *Abel Sánchez*—from a Kierkegaardian perspective.

Franz, Thomas R. *Unamuno's Paratexts: Twisted Guides to Contorted Narratives*. Newark, Del.: Juan de la Cuesta, 2006. Focuses on paratextual material, such as epigraphs, prefaces, postlogues, epilogues, and notes, in Unamuno's novels and novellas. Franz argues these materials are an integral part of the narra-

tives and describes how Unamuno makes use of these devices.

Hansen, Keith W. *Tragic Lucidity: Discourse of Recuperation in Unamuno and Camus*. New York: Peter Lang, 1993. Hansen examines the political and social views of Unamuno and Albert Camus, as evidenced in their literary works, to arrive at a twentieth century definition of tragedy. Includes a bibliography.

Jurkevich, Gayana. *The Elusive Self: Archetypal Approaches to the Novels of Miguel de Unamuno*. Columbia: University of Missouri Press, 1991. Jurkevich examines Unamuno's work from the perspective of Jungian analytical psychology and discusses the writer's psychological portrayal of his characters. Includes bibliographical references and an index.

Nozick, Martin. *Miguel de Unamuno*. New York: Twayne, 1971. An introductory overview, featuring a biography and discussion of Unamuno's works. Includes a bibliography. One of the volumes in the Twain World Authors series.

Olson, Paul R. *The Great Chiasmus: Word and Flesh in the Novels of Unamuno*. West Lafayette, Ind.: Purdue University Press, 2003. Examines Unamuno's use of chiasmus—parallel phrases in which there is a reversal in the order of words or parts of speech. Olson demonstrates how this word order transforms things that appear to be contrary by making them easily reversible and therefore identical.

Rubia Barcia, José, and M. A. Zeitlin, eds. *Unamuno: Creator and Creation*. Berkeley: University of California Press, 1967. A collection of transcripts of lectures from a program commemorating the centennial of the birth of Unamuno. Contains valuable biographical material and critical studies. Includes bibliographical references.

Sinclair, Alison. *Uncovering the Mind: Unamuno, the Unknown, and the Vicissitudes of Self*. New York: Manchester University Press, 2002. An examination of the fictional works of Unamuno, including the novels *Mist* and *Tía Tula*, that focuses on his portrayal of the self. Includes a bibliography and an index.

SIGRID UNDSET

Born: Kalundborg, Denmark; May 20, 1882
Died: Lillehammer, Norway; June 10, 1949

PRINCIPAL LONG FICTION

Fru Marta Oulie, 1907
Fortaellingen om Viga-Ljot og Vigdis, 1909
  (*Gunnar's Daughter*, 1936)
Jenny, 1911 (English translation, 1921)
Varen, 1914
Kransen, 1920 (*The Bridal Wreath*, 1923; also
  known as *The Wreath*, 1997)
Husfrue, 1921 (*The Mistress of Husaby*, 1925;
  also known as *The Wife*, 1999)
Korset, 1922 (*The Cross*, 1927; previous 3 novels
  collectively known as *Kristin Lavransdatter*,
  1929)
Olav Audunssøn i Hestviken and *Olav Audunssøn
  og hans børn*, 1925-1927 (*The Master of
  Hestviken*, 1928-1930, 1934; includes *The
  Axe*, 1928; *The Snake Pit*, 1929; *In the
  Wilderness*, 1929; and *The Son Avenger*, 1930)
Gymnadenia, 1929 (*The Wild Orchid*, 1931)
Den brændende busk, 1930 (*The Burning Bush*,
  1932)
Ida Elisabeth, 1932 (*Ida Elizabeth*, 1933)
Den trofaste husfru, 1933 (*The Faithful Wife*,
  1937)
Madame Dorthea, 1939 (English translation,
  1940)
Sigurd og hans tapre venner, 1955 (in German as
  *Die Saga von Vilmund Vidutan und seiner
  Gefährten*, 1931; *Sigurd and His Brave
  Companions*, 1943)

OTHER LITERARY FORMS

The literary works of Sigrid Undset (UHN-seht)
include short stories, poetry, drama, essays, and autobiographies. In her youth, Undset favored shorter forms,
following her first novel with a one-act play, *I graalysningen* (wr. 1908; in the grey light of dawn); a volume of
lyrics, *Ungdom* (1910; youth); and four collections of
short fiction, *Den lykkelige alder* (1909; the happy age),

Fattige skjæbner (1912; humble existences), *Splinten av
troldspeilet* (1917; *Images in a Mirror*, 1938), and *De
kloge jomfruer* (1918; the wise virgins). She wrote in
German and English as well as in her native Norse, and
her numerous articles, essays, and speeches reflected
the major social and spiritual concerns from which
her fiction grew, such as her *Samtiden* article "Nogen
kvindesaks-betragtninger" ("Reflections on the Suffragette Movement") in 1912 and the collection *Et kvindesynspunkt* (1919; a woman's point of view).

The passionate interest in medieval Scandinavian
history that had inspired Undset's sagalike *Gunnar's
Daughter* not only led to her mammoth mature novels
Kristin Lavransdatter and *The Master of Hestviken* but
also merged with her conversion to Roman Catholicism,
to which she testified fervently in the essays collected in
Kimer i klokker (1924; the bells are ringing), *Katolsk
propaganda* (1927; Catholic propaganda), *Begegnungen
und Trennungen: Essays über Christentum und Germanentum* (1931; meetings and partings: essays on Christianity and Germanism), and *Etapper I and II* (1929,
1933; *Stages on the Road*, 1934). In *De søkte de gamle
stier* (1936; they sought the ancient paths) and *Norske
helgener* (1937; *Saga of Saints*, 1934), she explored the
lives of great European defenders of the faith. As one of
Nazi Germany's first and strongest opponents, Undset
assailed totalitarian aims in "Fortschritt, Rasse, Religion"
("Progress, Race, Religion"), an essay that appeared in
*Die Geföhrdung des Christentums durch Rassenwahn
und Judenverfolgung* (1935), an anti-Nazi anthology
published in Switzerland. Later, from the United States,
she continued to attack Nazism and all other forms of
modern paganism in the collections *Selvportretter og landskapsbilleder* (1938; *Men, Women, and Places*, 1939),
Tillbake til fremitiden (1942; *Return to the Future*, 1942),
and *Artikler og taler fra krigstiden* (1953; wartime articles and speeches). Her warm friendship with the United
States and the American people is also reflected in
her essays "Skjønne Amerika" ("Beautiful America"),
"Amerikansk litteratur" ("American Literature"), and
"Common Ground," all of which were written during
World War II.

Sigrid Undset. (© The Nobel Foundation)

Toward the end of her life, Undset published several autobiographical fragments, of which the most detailed are *Elleve år* (1934; *The Longest Years*, 1935) and *Lykkelige dager* (1947; *Happy Times in Norway*, 1942). Her last works, like her first, dwell on her Christian Scandinavian heritage, and her last theoretical and historical essays, "Scandinavia and the New World," "Brotherhood," and "Scandinavian Literature," written in the early 1940's, all stress the peculiarly Scandinavian response to life she celebrated in her novels: the "preference for the realities of life . . . [the] interest in the innate disparities which condition our development."

ACHIEVEMENTS

The reality of Sigrid Undset's early life was the necessity of leaving school and earning her living in an Oslo law office; the innate disparities between Undset

and her office-mates were her ambition to write about the Middle Ages and her ability to comprehend all that she observed around her. When the draft of *The Master of Hestviken* that she completed in 1905 was rejected, Undset turned to the contemporary situations of working women with *Fru Marta Oulie. Jenny*, a novel depicting a woman defeated both in love and in artistic vocation, aroused indignant tirades from suffragettes. Undset attended one such meeting and noted "the essence of comedy. . . . [I] waited for them to start beating one another about the head with their handbags, but unfortunately it never got so far." Undset's bold realism offended some readers, but according to Andreas H. Winsnes, even more upsetting was her characterization of her heroine Jenny as more closely dependent on her sexual nature than are the men in the novel, a view that seemingly reduced woman's claim to equality. Despite this objection, Einar Skavlen and other Norwegian critics praised the novel's painstaking revelation of the "slow process of change" in Jenny's thoughts and feelings.

Ten years later, Undset's *Kristin Lavransdatter* and *The Master of Hestviken*, two multivolume novels treating the Norway of the thirteenth and fourteenth centuries with no less vital realism, received the highest critical acclaim and were translated into every major European language. Undset received the Nobel Prize in Literature in 1928 for these novels, and on them her reputation beyond Norway largely rests. In *Kristin Lavransdatter*, European critics recognized a new dimension of historical fiction, with insights into love and marriage realistically portrayed in the context of an essentially moral universe. With *The Master of Hestviken*, Undset achieved a still greater triumph, a profound insight into the psychological ramifications of guilt that Sigurd Hoel has compared favorably with Fyodor Dostoevski's portrait of Raskolnikov in *Prestupleniye i nakazaniye*, 1866 (*Crime and Punishment*, 1886).

By 1945, Undset was exhausted from her own battles against Nazi Germany. She returned to Norway to find her home at Lillehammer sadly devastated by the wartime occupation, but on her sixty-fifth birthday, King Haakon awarded her Norway's highest honor, the Grand Cross of the Order of Saint Olav, "for eminent services to literature and to the nation."

BIOGRAPHY

Sigrid Undset was born in Kalundborg, Denmark, on May 20, 1882. Her father, Ingvald Undset, a famous Scandinavian archaeologist, had reacted against the provincial surroundings of his rural boyhood at Østerdal in Norway and the confining atmosphere of Norwegian Lutheranism. Undset's beautiful and intellectual mother, Anna Charlotte Gyth, had been reared by an indulgent Danish aunt and retained both the air of a grande dame and a rationalistic outlook after her marriage to Ingvald Undset, already not a well man. Not surprisingly, Sigrid Undset received only perfunctory religious training as a child.

In 1884, the Undsets moved to Christiania (now Oslo), where Undset's liberal parents allowed her to follow her own precocious interests. Her father's illness often shadowed the childhood memories she recorded in *The Longest Years*, which ends at his death when she was eleven, but her home was filled constantly with the atmosphere of the Middle Ages. She often read aloud to her father from medieval texts, perhaps only half understanding but wholly spellbound by the stern power and the splendor of Old Norse poetry, as in the Hávarðar Saga, which she read to him the day before he died:

> Drag Þú mér af hendi
> hring enn rauða,
> faer Þú enni engu
> Ingibjorgu.
> Sá mun henni
> hugfastr tregi,
> er ek eigi kem
> til Uppsala.
>
> (Draw from my arm
> the ring so red,
> carry it back
> to Ingibjorg.
> It will be to her
> a deep-set grief,
> when I return not
> to Uppsala.)

At sixteen, Undset began to support herself and her family. Her ten years in an Oslo office made her familiar at first hand with the day-to-day struggles of ordinary women. She educated herself by reading voraciously, not only of Norway's past but also of the history of all Western Europe; in addition, she read widely in English literature. Her first literary attempt, a long medieval novel that later evolved into *The Master of Hestviken*, was rejected, and she turned to the problems of modern women, opening *Fru Marta Oulie* with the theme of marital conflict that she never abandoned in her fiction: "I have been unfaithful to my husband."

The first phase of Undset's literary activity extended through World War I as she unflinchingly portrayed women torn between their desire for independence and their yearning to be fulfilled in love and marriage. In 1912, she had married the divorced artist Anders C. Svarstad in Belgium. Despite his impetuosity, he was highly sensitive to color and artistic technique, a quality he shared with Undset. While rearing their three children and Svarstad's three from his former marriage, Undset wrote continuously, describing herself occasionally as "a bad housewife" and criticizing the egotistic materialism of the times that led to the evasion of responsibility. She saw the unwed, self-sufficient woman as abnormal: "A woman can become nothing better than a good mother, and nothing much worse than a bad one." The moral position she was developing by 1918 depended on woman's traditional role: "The normal human being . . . has always had a central shrine, the fireside of his home, and from there he has kindled all his altar-fires."

As she worked on her great medieval novels, Undset was increasingly drawn to the altar of the Roman Catholic Church, which she already considered in 1918 "the bearer of those ideals which cannot die." Her marriage was disintegrating under insurmountable stresses, and in 1925, shortly before her formal conversion, it was annulled: "I had nothing else to do but . . . ask to be instructed in all that the Catholic Church taught as true."

Between the two world wars, Undset firmly fixed her criticism of contemporary culture on her religious ideals. Many commentators feel the fiction she wrote during this time was impaired by her attempts to solve all human problems through the Catholic faith alone, but her essays reveal a concurrent preoccupation with the incommensurability of God and humans, the basic theme of all of her writing. By 1938, she was also able to acknowledge and praise D. H. Lawrence's recognition of "the consequences of the mechanisation of our existence—a slow death from the loss of our vital warmth."

Nazism for Undset was only one manifestation of that menace, and in her last novel, *Madame Dorthea*, she concentrated on the eighteenth century in the rationalistic spirit she had inherited from her mother. On her way to the United States during World War II, Undset traveled across the Soviet Union, which she later assessed as "a nationalist and imperialist state . . . under the thumb of Josef Stalin." One of Undset's last works was the deceptively childlike memoir *Happy Times in Norway*, a celebration of traditional, home-centered Norwegian culture. Upon Undset's death in 1949, she was hailed as a Christian universalist, a relentless enemy of pseudo-liberalism and irresponsible individualism.

ANALYSIS

From Sigrid Undset's first work to her last, the central issue of her fiction is loyalty. At first, she depicted the loss of a wife's loyalty in *Fru Marta Oulie*, then Jenny's loss of faith in herself that led to suicide. In her epic medieval novels, Undset analyzed the development of the sense of loyalty to others, to self, and finally to God, which motivates all lesser relationships in Christian morality. Once she had accepted her religion, Undset could write, "The history of the Church is like a paradigm which illustrates the fate of the divine when it comes into human hands." Her later novels reflect contemporary concerns in her basic religious context, for, as Winsnes has observed, she invariably judges the human torments of conscience that stem from disloyalty by the standard of her Catholic faith.

At the beginning of her career, Undset felt that William Shakespeare's Brutus was "the noblest figure in all literature," because when he saw he had lost everything on the field at Philippi, he "found no man but he was true to me." Undset commented in 1914, "Brutus feels such triumphant joy . . . because he can now say for certain that disloyalty, which is for him the ugliest sin, has never come near him." Such perfect idealism, she knew, could not be found in the life she saw around her, but she developed the typical situation of her fiction from oaths, pacts, vows, and covenants upheld or abused. From the outset, she linked the abstract concept of fidelity to one of humankind's most powerful and bedeviling drives,

the urge for sexual fulfillment. In "Fru Hjelde" ("Mrs. Hjelde"), one of her earliest short stories, Undset framed her message lyrically: "in the brief moment when love's caresses are new and make the blood flutter, you must understand and take control of all your life." A companion story, "Fru Waage," more realistically stresses the human need to make reparation: "better to pay for a precious hour of happiness with a whole lifetime of penance and prayer than to go on fretting oneself into grey hairs and bitterness."

The pagan Scandinavia to which her father's work drew Undset had worshiped gods who knew they themselves would die in flaming *Götterdämmerung*. Because the eventual defeat of good by evil was inevitable, only the manner in which the northern hero died could matter, and the old Nordic tales resound with the song of two-handed battle swords carving bitter destiny into the personal immortality of the saga. As she immersed herself in Scandinavian folklore and history in preparation for *Kristin Lavransdatter*, her reading of the thirteenth century *Njáls saga* became a turning point in Undset's life, she said, because she recognized there the intense psychological pressure exerted on the individual by the old pagan familial society. She came to believe, as she wrote in *Saga of Saints*, that the thirst for loyalty engendered by the ancient Germanic code, however noble its individual exemplifications, was fatally limited by the lack of "a door which leads to freedom for the soul of every human being, even though his deeds . . . have their inevitable consequences and defeat here on earth."

Undset's ideal gradually changed from the pagan moralist Brutus to the Christian humanist Sir Thomas More, who served his God before his king even unto death. In *De søkte de gamle stier*, a collection of sketches of "almost forgotten soldiers of Christ," Undset declared that the eventual victory of the good depends on "whether the wills of individual men and women are directed into an effort to do God's will—even if in life they have not been able to . . . without wavering, deviation and interruption."

KRISTIN LAVRANSDATTER

Undset's *Kristin Lavransdatter* traces the life of a well-born woman of medieval Norway through youth in *The Bridal Wreath*, maturity in *The Mistress of Husaby*, and old age with *The Cross*. As in all of Undset's fiction, the characters are developed in an immensely detailed social and cultural milieu. By the time she wrote *Kristin Lavransdatter*, Norwegian scholars such as Magnus Olsen and Sigurður Nordal had applied modern research methods to Scandinavian history, and Undset praised their respect for medieval documents as "examples of literary art," the basis for her re-creation of medieval Nordic life.

In *The Bridal Wreath*, Undset simultaneously depicted youthful love and mature marriage, both impeded by the tragic consequences of broken vows. Kristin's father, Lavrans Björgulfsson, all of his life had been devoted to doing the will of God, but the wife he took at his family's wish came to him secretly flawed by a previous affair. That hidden sin had to be faced and overcome before Lavrans and Ragnfrid could die at peace with God and each other. Kristin herself is betrothed to the good though dull Simon Darre, but she forces her father to break the vow and weds instead the dashing Erlend Nikulausson, a breach of faith that haunts them the remainder of their lives.

As *The Mistress of Husaby*, Erlend's manor, Kristin bears son after son in mounting frustration at Erlend's apparent lack of concern for their future. As she labors to rear their children and improve their estate, Erlend is drawn into a gallant yet abortive attempt to free Norway from the Swedish throne. Because Erlend fails and loses his inheritance, he must live on Kristin's land; his innate nobility, however, allows him to forget old injuries to an extent that Kristin, fatally, cannot.

In *The Cross*, Kristin's unwillingness to forgive causes Erlend's needless death. They are separated, and he is living at his last holding, a little hut on the mountain at Haugen, when she visits him there briefly and conceives their last child. At its birth, the countryfolk accuse her of adultery, and in returning to defend her honor, Erlend is killed. Kristin's sons grow away from her, and she at last accepts the pilgrim's road to faith, dying of bubonic plague after she has nursed the poor and outcast as a lay sister in a convent not far from the road where she last saw the houses at Haugen, "high on the topmost mountain ridge."

In the story of Kristin Lavransdatter and Erlend Nikulausson, Undset championed the new, emerging Norway against the old. Kristin slowly and painfully wins her Christian faith, but Erlend perishes, unshriven, through the violence of his Scandinavian warrior's values. The old code of the sagas required the individual himself to execute the justice that he was due, but Undset's traditionally Christian orientation insisted on the will of God before the will of people. Upon secretly plighting their troth, Erlend swears to Kristin, "May God forsake me if woman or maid ever rests in my arms, before I can possess you with law and honour." Kristin, however, replies, "May God forsake me if ever I take another man in my arms as long as I live." To Erlend, people's law and honor are tragically uppermost; to Kristin, even though she does not fully understand until she bears her own cross, God's law is finally all.

THE MASTER OF HESTVIKEN

Despite the great success of *Kristin Lavransdatter*, Undset considered the tetralogy *The Master of Hestviken* her masterpiece. Set in a slightly earlier historical period, *The Master of Hestviken* hinges on the conflict between ancient family honor and the new code in which church and state, rather than the individual, must defend the law. Whereas Kristin's redemption is earned through her overcoming the pride that injures others, the long saga of Olav Audunssøn of Hestviken strikes inward to the tender spot of conscience, where a person stands loneliest before God. Olav's revolt demonstrates the special Norse meaning of contrition as a power for rejuvenation. Henrik Ibsen hints at such pagan redemption in his play *Rosmersholm* (pb. 1886; English translation, 1889), when Rebecca West recognizes that "What I have sinned—it is fit I must expiate," as she goes "gladly" to her death with Rosmer. Undset carries Olav's redemption to its Christian extreme beyond physical death: "here on earth it would never be his to see the radiance of a standard under which he might fight."

The Axe, the first volume of the tetralogy, exposes the bloody family feuds that underlie Olav's exile from Norway and Ingunn, to whom he was betrothed as a child. Olav is nominally Christian, but when Ingunn's relatives deny their marriage, he kills one of them and must flee to Denmark. While waiting for Olav, Ingunn is trapped by a clever young rogue by whom she becomes pregnant; she confesses to Olav on his return. To preserve his own reputation, Olav secretly kills the youth who seduced Ingunn.

In *The Snake Pit*, Olav returns with Ingunn to Hestviken on the Oslo-fjord, where his life comes to resemble the old carving on the hall doorpost of Gunnar of the *Volsunga saga*, stricken by the one snake he could not charm. Olav's human loyalty to Ingunn and to Duke Haakon, whom he follows on an expedition to Norway, helps him restore his estate, but this is a pale shadow of his loyalty to God as Lord, which to Olaf only confirms the old morality. He still takes no account of the man he secretly killed: "He had had to kill so many a better man in battle, and never taken it to heart." At Ingunn's death, Olav thinks of confession, but he draws back, not knowing whether something prevents him or whether "after all he dared not come forward."

Olav's middle years are spent *In the Wilderness*, as he now knows that he has chosen the path of Cain. Leaving Hestviken, he at last visits London and wins some respite from the snake gnawing at his breast: "It was not that he now thought less of his sin, but that he himself bulked far less in his own eyes." After he returns to defend Hestviken against marauding Swedes, the snake ceases to tear at his heart: "He saw now it was not his suffering that destroyed the happiness of his life . . . sufferings that are of some *avail*, they are like the spearpoints that raise the shield on which the young king's son sits when his subjects do him homage."

The final act of Olav Audunssøn's divine comedy is *The Son Avenger*, in which Olav reaches the end of his human resources and places himself, helpless, at the mercy of God. In solemn irony, Ingunn's illegitimate son Eirik helps Olav to contrition. Olav "must stand forth and could not declare one deed that he had performed from full and unbroken loyalty," but in a final ecstatic vision, "the very rays from the source of light" high on the hill above the fjord "broke out and poured down over him." Olav's loyal spirit had bowed at last before its true Lord.

Darker in spirit than *Kristin Lavransdatter* but no less evocative, *The Master of Hestviken* displays the essentially conservative theological position Undset adopted toward the psychological complex of guilt. Other views of Olav's tragic life are possible, as Sigurd Hoel noted in 1928—both the psychological theory of dangerously suppressing one's emotions and the biological explanation that certain minds are "disposed to melancholia, remorse, and all that is tragic." Hoel concluded, however,

that Undset regarded Olav's "fixed ideas of sin and guilt" strictly from the religious viewpoint: "Olav's fate is the fate of one who disobeys the voice of God."

The twin purposes of Christianity and realism animated all of Undset's work. Inspired by the intense attention to detail, the concentration on personal loyalty, and the breadth of background of the Scandinavian family saga, she joined to these the considerable insight she achieved through her acceptance of Catholic tradition. She felt herself more at home in the Middle Ages than in modern civilization, and through her vividly realized characterizations of Kristin Lavransdatter and Olav Audunssøn and the wealth of their environments, no less than by her contemporary novels, she achieved a moral refuge for all who seek the personal relationship of faith, the only fellowship she thought worthwhile: the fellowship of individual souls in God.

Mitzi M. Brunsdale

OTHER MAJOR WORKS

SHORT FICTION: *Den lykkelige alder*, 1909; *Fattige skjæbner*, 1912; *Splinten av troldspeilet*, 1917 (*Images in a Mirror*, 1938); *De kloge jomfruer*, 1918; *Four Stories*, 1969.

PLAY: *I graalysningen*, wr. 1908 (one act).

POETRY: *Ungdom*, 1910.

NONFICTION: *Et kvindesynspunkt*, 1919; *Kimer i klokker*, 1924; *Katolsk propaganda*, 1927; *Etapper I and II*, 1929, 1933 (*Stages on the Road*, 1934); *Begegnungen und Trennungen: Essays über Christentum und Germanentum*, 1931; *Elleve år*, 1934 (*The Longest Years*, 1935); *De søkte de gamle stier*, 1936; *Norske helgener*, 1937 (*Saga of Saints*, 1934); *Selvportretter og landskapsbilleder*, 1938 (*Men, Women, and Places*, 1939); *Tillbake til fremtiden*, 1942 (*Return to the Future*, 1942); *Lykkelige dager*, 1947 (*Happy Times in Norway*, 1942); *Caterina av Siena*, 1951 (*Catherine of Siena*, 1954); *Artikler og taler fra krigstiden*, 1953; *Sigrid Undset on Saints and Sinners*, 1993 (Deal W. Hudson, editor).

MISCELLANEOUS: *The Unknown Sigrid Undset: Jenny, and Other Works*, 2001 (novel, short fiction, and letters).

BIBLIOGRAPHY

Bayerschmidt, Carl F. *Sigrid Undset*. New York: Twayne, 1970. Introductory study presents discussion of Undset's life as well as her early works, her social novels, and her later novels. Includes notes and bibliography.

Brunsdale, Mitzi. *Sigrid Undset: Chronicler of Norway.* New York: Berg, 1988. Provides a useful introduction to Norwegian culture and literature, a short biography of Undset, analysis of her early novels and later masterpieces, and a final chapter assessing her achievement. Includes chronology, notes, and a bibliographical essay.

Harbison, Sherrill. "Sigrid Undset and Willa Cather: The Uses of Catholicism." In *Nordic Experiences: Exploration of Scandinavian Cultures,* edited by Berit I. Brown. Westport, Conn.: Greenwood Press, 1997. Comparison of works by the two authors was originally presented as a paper at a conference on Scandinavian culture held at Hofstra University in 1993.

Hudson, Deal W., ed. *Sigrid Undset on Saints and Sinners: New Translations and Studies—Papers Presented at a Conference Sponsored by the Wethersfield Institute, New York City, April 24, 1993.* San Francisco, Calif.: Ignatius Press, 1993. Collection includes essays titled "A Life of Sigrid Undset," "Sigrid Undset: Holiness and Culture," and "In the Blood: The Transmission of Sin in *The Master of Hestviken.*"

Lytle, Andrew. *"Kristin": A Reading.* Columbia: University of Missouri Press, 1992. Lytle, a novelist and critic, aims to recover an appreciation for *Kristin Lavransdatter,* which he deems a neglected twentieth century classic. Provides an especially sensitive—indeed a model—reading of this complex literary work.

Maman, Marie. *Sigrid Undset in America: An Annotated Bibliography and Research Guide.* Lanham, Md.: Rowman & Littlefield, 2000. Useful resource for English-speaking students of Undset. Compilation of bibliographies of American publications featuring information about Undset places the works into four categories: reviews and articles about Undset's novels set in the Middle Ages, materials about Undset's contemporary novels, other articles, and book chapters about the writer. Also includes a bibliography of autobiographical material found in Undset's own works.

Naess, Harold S., ed. *A History of Norwegian Literature.* Lincoln: University of Nebraska Press, 1993. Survey of Norwegian literature includes a chapter titled "The Epic Novelists: Undset, Duun, Uppdal, Falkberget," which is devoted to analysis of Undset's works within the broader context of Norwegian epic fiction.

Solbakken, Elisabeth. *Redefining Integrity: The Portrayal of Women in the Contemporary Novels of Sigrid Undset.* New York: Peter Lang, 1992. Examines Undset's feminism and treatment of female characters in her novels. Takes issue with critics who charge that Undset's work was antifeminist after she converted to Catholicism and demonstrates how Undset's contemporary novels feature female protagonists who are stronger and of greater integrity than their male counterparts.

Whitehouse, J. C. *Vertical Man: The Human Being in the Catholic Novels of Graham Greene, Sigrid Undset, and Georges Bernanos.* London: Saint Austin Press, 1999. Examines the depiction of human beings and their relationship with God in the works of Undset and two other twentieth century Catholic novelists.

JOHN UPDIKE

Born: Shillington, Pennsylvania; March 18, 1932
Died: Danvers, Massachusetts; January 27, 2009
Also known as: John Hoyer Updike

PRINCIPAL LONG FICTION

The Poorhouse Fair, 1959
Rabbit, Run, 1960
The Centaur, 1963
Of the Farm, 1965
Couples, 1968
Bech: A Book, 1970
Rabbit Redux, 1971
A Month of Sundays, 1975
Marry Me: A Romance, 1976
The Coup, 1978
Rabbit Is Rich, 1981
Bech Is Back, 1982
The Witches of Eastwick, 1984
Roger's Version, 1986
S., 1988
Rabbit at Rest, 1990
Memories of the Ford Administration, 1992
Brazil, 1994
In the Beauty of the Lilies, 1996
Toward the End of Time, 1997
Bech at Bay: A Quasi-Novel, 1998
Gertrude and Claudius, 2000
Seek My Face, 2002
Villages, 2004
Terrorist, 2006
The Widows of Eastwick, 2008

OTHER LITERARY FORMS

From the time he published his first story in *The New Yorker* in 1954, John Updike truly became a man of letters, publishing in virtually every literary genre—poetry, short fiction, novel, essay, drama, art criticism, and autobiography. His first short-story collection, *The Same Door*, appeared in 1959; many more followed, including *The Afterlife, and Other Stories* in 1994. Updike's play *Buchanan Dying* was published in 1974. His poetry has appeared in many volumes of his own, be-

ginning with *The Carpentered Hen, and Other Tame Creatures* (1958), as well as in anthologies. Updike published his first nonfiction prose collection in 1965; most of his nonfiction works are collections of essays and criticism, but the autobiographical *Self-Consciousness: Memoirs* appeared in 1989 and the single-themed *Golf Dreams: Writings on Golf* was published in 1996.

ACHIEVEMENTS

One of the major figures to emerge in American fiction after World War II, John Updike is widely acclaimed as one of the most accomplished stylists and prolific writers of his generation. Showing remarkable versatility and range, his fiction represents a penetrating chronicle in the realist mode of the changing morals and manners of American society. Updike's work has met with both critical and popular success. His first novel, *The Poorhouse Fair*, received the Rosenthal Award of the National Institute of Arts and Letters in 1960. In 1964, Updike received the National Book Award for *The Centaur*, and he was elected the same year to the National Institute of Arts and Letters. A number of his short stories have won the O. Henry Prize for best short story of the year and have been included in the yearly volumes of *The Best American Short Stories*. In 1977, Updike was elected to the prestigious American Academy of Arts and Letters. In 1981, his novel *Rabbit Is Rich* won the Pulitzer Prize for fiction and the American Book Award. That same year, he was awarded the Edward MacDowell Medal for literature. Along with an honorary doctoral degree from alma mater Harvard University, Updike received numerous honors throughout his career, including another Pulitzer Prize for fiction, the National Arts Club Medal of Honor, the National Book Foundation Medal, and the National Medal for the Humanities.

While Updike's novels have continued the long national debate on the American civilization and its discontents, perhaps more significant is their depiction of restless and aspiring spirits struggling within the constraints of flesh, of time and gravity—lovers and battlers all. As Updike wrote about the novel in an essay, "Not to be in love, the capital N novel whispers to capital W western man, is to be dying."

BIOGRAPHY

The only child of Wesley Updike and Linda Grace Updike (née Hoyer), John Hoyer Updike spent the first thirteen years of his life living with his parents and grandparents in his maternal grandparents' home in Shillington, Pennsylvania, in rather strained economic conditions. In 1945, the Updikes had to move to the family farm in Plainville, ten miles away from Shillington. Updike's father supported the family on his meager salary as a mathematics teacher at the high school. His mother had literary aspirations of her own and later became a freelance writer. A number of Updike's short stories, such as "Flight," and the novels *The Centaur* and *Of the Farm* drew upon this experience. As a youth, Updike dreamed of drawing cartoons and writing for *The New Yorker*, an ambition he fulfilled in 1955. Updike went to Harvard University in 1950 on a full scholarship, majoring in English. He was editor of the *Harvard Lampoon* and graduated in 1954 with highest honors. In 1953, he married Radcliffe student Mary Pennington, the daughter of a Unitarian minister; they were to have four children.

After a year in Oxford, England, where Updike studied at the Ruskin School of Drawing and Fine Art, he returned to the United States to a job offered him by E. B. White as a staff writer with *The New Yorker*, for which he wrote the "Talk of the Town" column. In April of 1957, fearing that the city scene would disturb his development as a writer, Updike left New York for Ipswich, Massachusetts, where he and his family would live for the next seventeen years and which would serve as the model for the settings of a number of stories and novels. During this time, Updike was active in Ipswich community life and regularly attended the Congregational church.

During the late 1950's and early 1960's, Updike faced a crisis of faith prompted by his acute consciousness of death's inevitability. The works of such writers as Søren

Kierkegaard and, especially, Karl Barth, the Swiss orthodox theologian, helped Updike come to grips with this fear and to find a basis for faith. Religious and theological concerns pervade Updike's fiction. In a real sense, like Nathaniel Hawthorne's writing more than one hundred years earlier, Updike's fiction explores for his time the great issues of sin, guilt, and grace—of spiritual yearnings amid the entanglements of the flesh.

Updike's success as a writer enabled him to travel under government auspices. In 1964-1965, he traveled to Russia, Romania, Bulgaria, and Czechoslovakia as part of the U.S.S.R.-U.S. Cultural Exchange Program. In 1973, he traveled and lectured as a Fulbright lecturer in Ghana, Nigeria, Tanzania, Kenya, and Ethiopia. Updike's Bech novels and *The Coup* reflect those journeys.

In 1974, Updike and his first wife divorced. In 1977, Updike remarried, and he and his new wife, Martha Bernhard, settled in Georgetown, Massachusetts. Through the ensuing decades, he distinguished himself by writing works of nearly every genre, concentrating

John Updike. (Davis Freeman)

his attention on novels, short stories, reviews, and essays. He continued to work until his death from lung cancer in January, 2009.

ANALYSIS

A writer with John Updike's versatility and range, whose fiction reveals a virtually symphonic richness and complexity, offers readers a variety of keys or themes with which to explore his work. The growing and already substantial body of criticism that Updike's work has engendered, therefore, reflects a variety of approaches. Alice and Kenneth Hamilton were among the first critics to give extensive treatment to the religious and theological elements in Updike's fiction. Rachel Burchard explores Updike's fiction in terms of its presentations of authentic quests for meaning in our time, for answers to age-old questions about humanity and God, and in terms of its affirmation of human worth and hope despite the social and natural forces threatening defeat of the human enterprise. Considering technique as well as theme, Larry Taylor treats the function of the pastoral and antipastoral in Updike's fiction and places that treatment within a long tradition in American literature. British critic Tony Tanner discusses Updike's fiction as depicting the "compromised environment" of New England suburbia—the fear and dread of decay, of death and nothingness, and the dream of escaping from the complications of such a world. Edward Vargo focuses on the recurrence of ritualistic patterns in Updike's fiction, the struggle to wrest something social from an increasingly secularized culture. Joyce Markle's thematic study of Updike's fiction sees a conflict between "Lovers," or life-givers, and the embodied forces of convention, dehumanizing belief, and death.

In a 1962 memoir titled "The Dogwood Tree: A Boyhood," Updike discusses his boyhood fascination with what he calls the "Three Great Secret Things: Sex, Religion, and Art." Critic George W. Hunt contends that "these three secret things also characterize the predominant subject matter, thematic concerns, and central questions found throughout his adult fiction." Detailing Updike's reliance on the ideas of Søren Kierkegaard and Karl Barth, Hunt's study is interested in the religious implications of Updike's work. A more sociological interest informs Philip Vaughan's study of Updike's fiction, which, to Vaughan, provides readers with valid depictions of the social conditions—loneliness, isolation, aging, and morality—of today's world. David Galloway sees Updike's fiction in existential terms, viewing Updike's protagonists as "absurd heroes" seeking meaning in an inhospitable universe. More impressionistic but quite suggestive is Elizabeth Tallant's short study of the fate of eros in several of Updike's novels. Believing that a thesis or thematic approach does not do full justice to Updike's work, Donald J. Greiner examines Updike's novels more formalistically in order to "discuss the qualities that make Updike a great writer."

Using a comparative approach, George Searles discusses Philip Roth and Updike as important social realists whose work gives a true sense of life in the last half of the twentieth century. To Searles, Updike's overriding theme is cultural disintegration—questing but alienated protagonists confronting crises caused by a breakdown of the established order. Jeff Campbell uses Updike's long poem *Midpoint* (1969) as a key to an analysis of Updike's fiction. Seeing Updike as an "ironist of the spiritual life," Ralph C. Wood discusses Updike's fiction—along with the fiction of Flannery O'Connor, Walker Percy, and Peter Peter De Vries—as depicting the "comedy of redemption," a study deeply indebted to the theology of Barth.

In a compendious study of American fiction since 1940, Frederick R. Karl offers a useful overview of Updike: "Updike's fiction is founded on a vision of a compromised, tentative, teetering American, living in suburban New England or in rural Pennsylvania; an American who has broken with his more disciplined forebears and drifted free, seeking self-fulfillment but uncertain what it is and how to obtain it." While this rather global description fairly represents the recurring condition in most of Updike's novels, it does not do justice to the complex particularities of each work. Nevertheless, it does point to the basic predicament of nearly all of Updike's protagonists—that sense of doubleness, of the ironic discrepancy of the fallen creature who yet senses, or yearns for, something transcendent. Updike's people are spiritual amphibians—creatures in concert with two realms, yet not fully at home in either. Updike employs an analogous image in his novel *The Centaur*— here is a creature that embodies the godly with the bestial, a fitting image of the human predicament in Updike's fiction. His fiction depicts the ambiguity of the "yes-but" stance toward the world, similar to the paradox of the "already and the not-yet." In his fine story "The Bulgarian Poetess" (1966), Updike writes: "Actuality is a running impoverishment of possibility." Again there is a sense of duplicity, of incompleteness. In such a world, problems are not always solved; they are more often endured if not fully understood. Yet even the curtains of actuality occasionally part, unexpectedly, to offer gifts, as Updike avers in his preface to *Olinger Stories: A Selection* (1964)—such gifts as keep alive a vision of wholeness in an often lost and fragmented world.

THE POORHOUSE FAIR

Updike's first novel, *The Poorhouse Fair*, may seem anomalous in comparison with the rest of his work. In fact, the novel depicts a collision of values that runs throughout Updike's work. As in so much of Updike's fiction, the novel is concerned with decay, disintegration, a loss or abandonment of vital traditions, of values, of connection to a nurturing past. This opposition is embodied in the two principal characters: ninety-four-year-old John Hook, former teacher and resident of the poorhouse, and Stephen Conner, the poorhouse's prefect. The novel is set in the future, sometime in the late 1970's, when want and misery have virtually been eliminated by a kind of humanistic socialism. Such progress has been made at a price: sterility, dehumanization, spiritual emptiness, and regimentation. In a world totally run by the head, the heart dies. Hook tells Conner, in response to the prefect's avowed atheism: "There is no goodness, without belief." Conner's earthly paradise is a false one, destroying what it would save. The former prefect, Mendelssohn, sought, as his name would suggest, to fulfill the old people's spiritual needs in rituals and hymn singing.

Out of frustration with Conner's soulless administration, the old people break into a spontaneous "stoning" of Conner in the novel's climax. In effect, Conner is a corrupt or perverted martyr to the new "religion" of godless rationalism. The incident symbolizes the inherent desire and need for self-assertion and individualism. Conner's rationalized system is ultimately entropic. The annual fair is symbolic of an antientropic spirit in its celebration of the fruits of individual self-expression—

patchwork quilts and peach-pit sculptures. In its depiction of an older America—its values of individuality, personal dignity, and pride—being swallowed up by material progress and bureaucratic efficiency, the novel is an "old" and somber book for a young author to write. In effect, Updike depicts an America become a spiritual "poorhouse," though materially rich. It is Hook, one of the last links to that lost America, who struggles at the end for some word to leave with Conner as a kind of testament, but he cannot find it.

THE CENTAUR

In a number of stories and the novels *The Centaur* and *Of the Farm*, Updike draws heavily on his experiences growing up in Shillington, Pennsylvania. Both novels—though very different from each other—concern the reckoning of a son with a parent, in the case of *The Centaur* with his father and in *Of the Farm* with his mother, before he can proceed with his life. This is emotional and spiritual "homework" necessary for the son's passage to maturity, to freedom from the past, yet also to a new sense of responsibility. As in all Updike's fiction, this passage is difficult, complex, and ambiguous in its resolution.

The Centaur is arguably Updike's most complex novel, involving as it does the complicated interweaving of the myth of Chiron the centaur with the story of an adolescent boy and his father one winter in 1947. Although the novel won the National Book Award, its reception was quite mixed. A number of reviewers thought the use of myth to be pretentious and not fully realized, while others praised the author's achievement. The novel is part bildungsroman, a novel of moral education, and part *Künstlerroman*, a novel of an artist seeking his identity in conflict with society and/or his past. Operating on different levels, temporally and spatially, the nine chapters of the novel are a virtual collage, quite appropriate for the painter-narrator, nearly thirty, self-described as a "second-rate abstract expressionist," who is trying to recover from his past some understanding that might clarify and motivate his artistic vocation. Peter Caldwell, the narrator, reminisces to his black mistress in a Manhattan loft about a three-day period in the winter of 1947, fourteen years earlier. On the realistic level, Peter tells the story of his self-conscious adolescence growing up an only child, living on a farm with his parents and Pop

Kramer, his grandfather. His father is the high school biology teacher and swim coach, whose acts of compassion and charity embarrass the boy. On the mythic level, the father is depicted as Chiron the centaur, part man and part stallion, who serves as mentor to the youthful Greek heroes. As such, he suffers for his charges. By moving back and forth between the mythic and the realistic levels, Peter is able to move to an understanding of his father's life and death and to a clarification of his own vocation.

Just as Chiron sacrifices his immortality—he accepts death—so that Prometheus may be free to live, so too does George give his life for his son. While George is obsessed with death, it is doubtful that his sacrifice takes the form of death. Rather, his sacrifice is his willingness to go on fulfilling his obligations to his family. In reflecting upon this sacrifice by his father, Peter, feeling a failure in his art, asks: "*Was it for this that my father gave up his life?*" In the harsh reappraisal his memory provides, Peter is learning what he could not know as an adolescent. Love, guilt, and sacrifice are somehow inherent in the very structure of life. It is this that his mythicized father reveals to him in the very act of his narrating the story. For many critics, George Caldwell's sacrificial act frees the son to resume his artistic vocation with courage. For others, the novel is a mock epic showing in Peter the artist, the son of a scientist father and the grandson of a preacher, a loss of the metaphoric realm that makes great art possible and that leaves Peter diminished by his confinement to the earth alone. However the end is taken, the mythic element of the narrative richly captures the doubleness of human existence so pervasive in Updike's fictions.

OF THE FARM

A short novel, *Of the Farm* is another tale of the intricacy of love, guilt, sacrifice, and betrayal. In *The Centaur*, Peter Caldwell, stalled and failing in his artistic vocation, goes home through a creative act of the memory and imagination to recover his lost vision, a basis to continue his work. Peter can fulfill his Promethean charge because his father was Chiron. In contrast, *Of the Farm*'s Joey Robinson goes home to get his mother's blessing on his recent remarriage. Joey seeks forgiveness of the guilt he bears for the acts of betrayal that have constituted his life. He betrays his poetic aspirations by be-

coming an advertising executive and betrays his marriage to Joan and his three children through adultery and divorce. Bringing home for his domineering mother's approval his sensuous new wife, Peggy, sets the stage for more betrayals and recriminations. As the weekend progresses, Peggy and Joey's mother vie for Joey's soul. Joey cannot please both women or heal the wounds of his past betrayals. For Joey, Peggy is the "farm" he wishes to husband. At the end, failing to win his mother's blessing, Joey and Peggy return to their lives in the city, leaving Joey's mother to die amid the memorials of her own unrealized dreams. If the novel is an exploration of human freedom, as the epigraph from Jean-Paul Sartre would suggest, the reader sees that freedom escapes all the characters, bound as they are by conflicting desires, guilt, and obligation.

RABBIT, RUN

In 1960, when Updike published *Rabbit, Run*, a story of an ex-basketball player and his floundering marriage set in the late 1950's, he had no intention of writing a sequel, but he returned to Harry "Rabbit" Angstrom once every ten years for four novels—*Rabbit Redux* (1971), *Rabbit Is Rich* (1981), and *Rabbit at Rest* (1990)—as a kind of gauge of the changes occurring in American culture. This series of novels is among the most popular of his work.

For *Rabbit, Run*, Updike uses a quote from Blaise Pascal for an epigraph: "The motions of Grace, the hardness of heart; external circumstances." Updike later commented that those three things describe our lives. In a real sense, those things also describe the basic movements and conflicts in the Rabbit novels. From *Rabbit, Run* to *Rabbit at Rest*, as the titles themselves suggest, Rabbit's life is characterized by a series of zigzag movements and resistances and yearnings, colliding, often ineffectually, with the external circumstances of a fast-paced and changing world.

Rabbit, Run takes place in the late 1950's, when Harry Angstrom, a former high school basketball great nicknamed Rabbit, at twenty-six finds himself in a dead-end life: with a job selling items in a dime store and a marriage to a careless and boozy woman. Wounded by the stifling boredom of everyday life and the cloying pressures of conforming and adapting to his environment, so characteristic of the 1950's, Harry wonders, confusingly, what has happened to his life. The disgust he feels about his present life is aggravated by his memories of when he was "first-rate at something" as a high school basketball great. Out of frustration, Rabbit bolts from his life-stifling existence, feeling that something out there wants him to find it.

The novel is the study of this nonhero's quest for a nonexistent grail. Rabbit's zigzagging or boomeranging movements from wife Janice to mistress Ruth, the part-time prostitute, wreaks havoc: Janice accidentally drowns the baby; Ruth is impregnated and seeks an abortion. Pursued by the weak-faithed, do-gooder minister Eccles and failed by his old coach Tothero, Rabbit has no one to whom he can turn for help. Rabbit, like so many of Updike's protagonists, is enmeshed in the highly compromised environment of America, locked in the horizontal dimension yet yearning for something transcendent, the recovery of the vertical dimension. For Rabbit, the closest he can come to that missing feeling is sex, the deep mysteries of a woman's body replacing the old revelations of religion. Rabbit, though irresponsible, registers his refusal to succumb to such a world through movement, his running replacing the lost territories of innocent escape.

RABBIT REDUX

Ten years later, in *Rabbit Redux*, Rabbit has stopped running. He is back home with Janice and works as a typesetter. It is the end of the 1960's, and Rabbit watches the Moon landing on television as well as the upheavals of the Civil Rights movement, campus demonstrations, and the Vietnam War. Rabbit feels that the whole country is doing what he did ten years earlier. As Janice moves out to live with her lover Stavros, Rabbit and his son Nelson end up as hosts to Jill, a runaway flower-child, and a bail-jumping Vietnam veteran and black radical named Skeeter. This unlikely combination allows Updike to explore the major cultural and political clashes of the 1960's. This time Rabbit is more a passive listener-observer than an activist searcher.

Skeeter's charismatic critiques of the American way of life challenge Rabbit's unquestioning patriotism and mesmerize him. As a result, Rabbit is helpless when disaster comes—his house is set on fire and Jill dies inside. Rabbit helps Skeeter escape. Fearing for her lover's heart, Janice returns to Rabbit. Unlike the restless figure

of the first novel, Rabbit now seems to have capitulated or resigned himself to those powerful "external circumstances" from which he once sought escape. Rabbit bears witness, numbingly, to a disintegrating America, even as it puts a man on the Moon. America's spiritual landscape is as barren as that on the Moon. The novel ends with Rabbit and Janice asleep together. Perhaps they can awake to a new maturity and sense of responsibility for what they do in the world.

RABBIT IS RICH

In the first two Rabbit novels, Rabbit was out of step with the times—running in the placid 1950's, sitting in the frenetic 1960's. In *Rabbit Is Rich*, he is running again, but this time in tune with the rhythms of the 1970's. Rabbit now jogs, which is in keeping with the fitness craze that began in the 1970's. He and Janice are prospering during the decade of inflation and energy crises. They own a Toyota agency and are members of a country club. Rabbit plays golf and goes to Rotary Club lunches. Instead of newspapers, as in *Rabbit Redux*, he reads *Consumer Reports*, the bible of his new status. The ghosts of his past haunt him, however: the drowned baby, the child he did or did not have with Ruth, memories of Jill and Skeeter. The chief reminder of the sins of his past is his son Nelson, returning home, like something repressed, to wreak havoc on the family's new affluent complacency.

Like his father of old but lacking Rabbit's conscience and vision, Nelson has a quest for attention that practically wrecks everything that he touches: his father's cars, his relationships. Rabbit can see himself in Nelson's behavior and tries to help him avoid making the same kinds of mistakes, but communication is difficult between them. With Skylab falling and America held hostage by Iranians, the present is uneasy and anxious, the future uncertain. Characteristically, Rabbit turns to sex to fill the spiritual void. He and Janice make love on top of their gold Krugerrands. Rabbit lusts for the lovely Cindy, but in the wife-swapping escapade during their Caribbean holiday, Rabbit gets Thelma Harrison instead and is introduced to anal sex—for Updike a fitting image of the sense of nothingness pervading American culture at the end of the "Me Decade." Updike does not end there. He leaves Rabbit holding his granddaughter, "another nail in his coffin" but also another chance for renewal, perhaps even a motion of grace, a richness unearned.

RABBIT AT REST

The sense of exhaustion—of a world "running out of gas" in so many ways—that pervades *Rabbit Is Rich* becomes more serious, even terminal, in *Rabbit at Rest*. The fuzzy emptiness and mindlessness of the 1980's pervade the novel, even as so much is described in such vivid detail. Rabbit and Janice now winter in Florida, and Nelson runs the car dealership. Rabbit sustains himself on junk food and endless television viewing, images of the emptiness of American life under Ronald Reagan. He suffers a heart attack and undergoes an angioplasty procedure. His son's cocaine addiction and embezzlement of $200,000 from the business shock the family. Yet this often coarse and unsympathetic man continues to compel the reader's interest. He wonders about the Dalai Lama, who is then in the news. As the Cold War dissipates, Rabbit asks: "If there's no Cold War, what's the point of being an American?"

The man called "Mr. Death" in *Rabbit, Run* now must face death in his own overblown body and contemplate it in relation to a world he has always known but that now is no more. Can such a man find peace, an acceptance and understanding of a life lived in such struggle and perplexity? In *Rabbit Is Rich*, Harry confesses to Janice the paradox of their lives: "Too much of it and not enough. The fear that it will end some day, and the fear that tomorrow will be the same as yesterday." In a hospital intensive care unit in Florida, at the end of *Rabbit at Rest*, Rabbit says, "Enough." Is this the realization and acceptance of life's sufficiency or of its surplus? A confession of his own excesses and indulgences, or a command of sorts that he has had enough? These are only a few of the questions raised by the Rabbit novels.

MARRY ME

Many critics have praised Updike as the premier American novelist of marriage. Nearly all of his fiction displays the mysterious as well as commonplace but ineluctable complexities and conflicts of marriage. It is one of Updike's major concerns to explore the conditions of love in the present-day world. His fiction is his updating and reworking of the Tristan and Isolde myth, about which Updike commented in his review of Denis de Rougement's book *Love in the Western World*

(1956)—lovers whose passion is enhanced by the obstacles needed to be overcome to fulfill it; the quest for an ideal lover who will assuage the fear of death and the longing for the infinite; the confusions of eros and the death wish. Many of Updike's male protagonists are aspects of both Tristan and Don Juan in their quests for life-enhancing or death-denying passion. Such are the ingredients in the novels *Couples*, *Marry Me*, and *The Witches of Eastwick*.

All these novels are set in the 1960's—the spring of 1962 to the spring of 1963 in *Marry Me*, the spring of 1963 to the spring of 1964 in *Couples*, and probably 1969 for *The Witches of Eastwick*. In their various ways, all try to answer the question, "After Christianity, what?" Human sexuality is liturgy and sacrament of the new religion emerging in the United States in the 1960's—a new end of innocence in a "post-pill paradise." The three novels make an interesting grouping because all deal with marriages in various states of deterioration, and all explore the implications of "sex as the emergent religion, as the only thing left," Updike says. While not published until 1976, *Marry Me* was actually written before *Couples*. In fact, one story seems to lead right into the other. *The Witches of Eastwick* explores the theme from a woman's perspective.

Both Jerry Conant of *Marry Me* and Piet Hanema of *Couples* are educated professionals, married with children, and live in upper-middle-class suburbs of great cities. They are both suffering spiritually, longing for affirmation from outside themselves, for some sort of blessing and certainty. As Jerry says, "Maybe our trouble is that we live in the twilight of the old morality, and there's just enough to torment us, and not enough to hold us in." The mortal fear that such an insight inspires leads each man to a desperate quest for a love that will mend or heal his spiritual brokenness or emptiness.

Marry Me takes place during the second year of John F. Kennedy's presidential administration, when the charm of the Camelot myth still captivated Americans. Significantly, Updike calls *Marry Me* a "romance" rather than a novel, suggesting an attempt to use the freer form to explore the ambiguities of love, marriage, and adultery. The novel ends in ambiguity, with no clear resolution. In fact, there are three possible endings: Jerry with his lover, Sally, in Wyoming; Jerry with his wife,

Ruth, in France; and Jerry in the Virgin Islands alone, on the island of St. Croix, symbolizing perhaps Jerry's self-immolation.

COUPLES

Couples takes place during the last year of Kennedy's presidency, including his assassination; it is a much more cynical book, harsher and darker than *Marry Me*. A certain light has gone out in the land; death and decay haunt the imagination. In contrast to *Marry Me*, choices are made and lives reconstitute themselves in a kind of cyclical way at the end of *Couples*. These two rather weak men fail at their quests to find in the flesh what they have lost in the spirit. Both men are believers and churchgoers, and both face a crisis in their faith. The church, committed to secularity and worldliness, fails them. Their respective wives are naturalistic and feel at home on earth and offer them little surcease to their anxiety.

In *Marry Me*, Jerry must contend with Sally's husband, Richard, an atheist with one blind eye, who insists on clear-cut decisions. For Jerry, however, every choice involves a loss that he cannot tolerate. In *Couples*, Piet is pitted against Freddy Thorne, the self-proclaimed priest of the new religion of sensuality. To Freddy, it is their fate to be "suspended in . . . one of those dark ages that visits mankind between millennia, between the death and rebirth of gods, when there is nothing to steer by but sex and stoicism and the stars."

The many adulteries among the ten couples of *Couples* lead finally to divorce and disintegration of the secular paradise of Tarbox, the fictional suburb of the novel. Piet leaves his unattainable but earthbound wife, fittingly named Angela, for the sensuous Foxy Whitman, whose abortion of Piet's child Freddy arranges. When his church is destroyed by fire, Piet is freed from his old morality and guilt and the tension inherent in his sense of fallenness. Yet the satisfaction obtained with Foxy is a foreclosure of the vertical hope and is a kind of death. Both novels depict the failure of sex as a religion as well as the profound disappointment with love in its romantic or secular forms. Such may be Updike's answer to the question he posed: "After Christianity, what?"

THE WITCHES OF EASTWICK

The setting of *The Witches of Eastwick* is a small town in Rhode Island during the first year or so of Rich-

ard Nixon's presidency, an era of protest and discontent. Three divorcées—Alexandra Spofford, Jane Smart, and Sukie Rougemont—discover the power of sisterhood and femininity and become witchlike in their powers. The delicate balance of their friendship is upset by the entrance of the apparently demoniac Darryl Van Horne, who takes them all as his lovers. The novel's three parts, "The Coven," "Malefica," and "Guilt," suggest a progression from the women's newfound power and independence through an encounter with the demoniac to a rediscovery of responsibility through an awareness of guilt.

Like Updike's many male protagonists, the three women must come to grips with death before they can reconstitute a meaningful life. Van Horne is a satanic figure whose machinations lead to a dissipation of the women's powers. When he chooses the young Jennifer Gabriel for his wife, the women employ their powers to create a curse to bring about Jennifer's death. When she does die, the women feel guilt, even though it is not clear that their curse caused her fatal cancer. Van Horne preaches a sermon on the evilness of a creation saturated with disease and leaves town with Jennifer's brother, Christopher. The three women disband and find their way into suitable marriages.

The use of witchcraft allows Updike to explore the nature of evil and its connections with nature, history, and technology. The ambiguities of feminism are examined in *The Witches of Eastwick* in the context of the moral and social confusions of the late 1960's and efforts to break down the destructive and outmoded polarities of the patriarchal tradition.

BECH *and* THE COUP

The first two Bech books—*Bech: A Book* and *Bech Is Back*—and *The Coup* are novels and stories resulting from Updike's travels to Eastern Europe and to Africa. Each work offers the author an opportunity to develop a very different persona from those of his domestic novels, as well as the chance to explore another aspect of "otherness" and "difference." *Bech: A Book* is a collection of seven stories about a middle-aged and very successful Jewish novelist, Henry Bech, and his various experiences both abroad and in America. The collection is framed by the fiction of Updike writing about an actual person contemporary with him. The book has a foreword by the putative author as well as two appendixes. Such devices afford Updike an opportunity for humorous satire of the literary life in America. Bech emerges as a strong and believable character struggling with the failure of his success as a writer in a success-plagued culture. In *Bech Is Back*, Updike creates seven more stories about Bech's travels and his wrestling with the ambiguities of fame, fortune, and human worth, the protagonist's success with women an index of his success and worth as a writer. He must struggle with the question of whether he has sold out his talent for the marketplace, defiling both.

Felix Ellellou, the protagonist of *The Coup*, is a bold creation for Updike, a black Islamic Marxist whose memoirs constitute the novel. Now in exile, the former president of the fictional sub-Saharan nation of Kush recounts the story of his rise and fall and of his perpetual struggle to avoid the ambiguous gifts of American aid. He fears not only the junk food but also the forces of secularity and materialism that will ultimately make of his beloved Kush a spiritual wasteland. He virtually stands alone in his resistance to the so-called benefits of American civilization, toward which he admits ambivalence. In Ellellou, one can see an African version of Updike's body-spirit conflict so prevalent in his fiction. For Ellellou, freedom must be freedom from material possessions, yet he anguishes over his people's poverty-stricken plight. He believes that it is better to die in poverty than from spiritual loss. In privation, he believes, the spirit will soar. Despite Ellellou's stoicism, his faith is plagued by doubts. He suspects that the new world religion will be godless and entropic. Updike's African novel is a replay of the author's critical interrogation of the moral and spiritual failures of the West.

A MONTH OF SUNDAYS, ROGER'S VERSION, and S.

Updike's concerns with love, marriage, and adultery in so much of his fiction link him to Nathaniel Hawthorne's great novel *The Scarlet Letter* (1850), America's first great treatment of the complex social and religious consequences of adulterous love. Three novels in particular address different dimensions of that adulterous triangle of Hawthorne's novel—*A Month of Sundays*, *Roger's Version*, and *S.* Hawthorne's Dimmesdale is updated in the figure of the Reverend Tom Marshfield,

the exiled protagonist of *A Month of Sundays*. Roger Lambert of *Roger's Version*, the professor of theology specializing in heresies, is Updike's treatment of Hawthorne's Roger Chillingworth. Sarah Worth of *S.* is a contemporary depiction of Hawthorne's Hester, the truly noble and strong character of *The Scarlet Letter*.

Hawthorne's Dimmesdale is crushed by his inability to integrate the body-and-soul division. So, too, does Updike's Marshfield suffer from this split in a novel with many allusions to *The Scarlet Letter*. Marshfield marries the former Jane Chillingworth, whose father was Marshfield's ethics instructor. The retreat center is managed by Ms. Prynne, who reads the diary entries of Marshfield and his fellow clerical exiles. The novel traces Marshfield's integration of body and spirit, a mending of Marshfield's fragmented self, enabling him to return to his ministry as a true helper to the faithful. Roger Chillingworth in *The Scarlet Letter* was the cuckolded husband seeking revenge for his wife's adultery. In *Roger's Version*, Roger Lambert imagines that his wife Esther is having an affair with Dale, the computer science graduate student trying to prove God's existence by computer. Dale is a kind of innocent, a fundamentalist seeking technological support for his faith. By the end, Dale's project has failed, as Roger believed it would, and Dale returns to Ohio, his faith demolished. Yet Dale's project provoked Roger to revivify his own faith and to engage his world more responsibly than he has.

Updike's Sarah Worth of *S.* is certainly one possible version of a late twentieth century Hester Prynne. Sarah is a woman who has taken her life fully into her own hands without shame or illusion. After bolting from her faithless but wealthy physician husband, Sarah goes to an ashram in Arizona for spiritual renewal. That proves to be a false endeavor, but Sarah survives intact (and with much of the cult's money). Loving and compassionate yet willful and worldly, Sarah Worth dares to follow her own path.

TOWARD THE END OF TIME

Ever the chronicler of societal obsessions, Updike in 1997 provided his readers with a millennial book, *Toward the End of Time*. The year is 2020, and a Sino-American nuclear war has recently destroyed the North American infrastructure and the U.S. government. In a universe of two moons and new life-forms, the "metallobioforms" that rose up out of the nuclear slime, the normal order of things seems to have come undone. Updike's protagonist, Ben Turnbull, seems at times to assume the identities of such disparate entities as an ancient Egyptian tomb robber and a medieval monk, and he is having an affair with a dark-eyed young woman whom he suspects is also a doe. Updike spends considerable time mulling over the mysteries of quantum mechanics and string theory, implying that such abstractions may contain the key to the enigma of time. In the end, though, the drama of Ben's postmillennial existence seems an elaboration of the sublunary obsessions of other Updike protagonists. The story of this sixty-six-year-old retired financial adviser could almost serve as a coda to the *Rabbit* books.

BECH AT BAY

With *Bech at Bay*, Updike ended the saga of another of his favorite alter egos, the now septuagenarian Henry Bech. Like its predecessors, this "quasi-novel" consists of a series of linked stories concerning the crabbed but accomplished—and now superannuated—Jewish novelist. *Bech at Bay* finds Bech at the heart of late twentieth century American literary life; however, that life, like Bech himself, seems to have lost nearly all its vitality. The mood is set in the book's opening section, "Bech in Czech," in which Bech finds himself on a book tour in the gloom of Prague, haunted by the uneasy feeling that he is no more than a character in someone else's book. In another episode, Bech is tapped to head an elite artistic organization called "The Forty"—a group not unlike the American Academy of Art and Letters, which Updike served as chancellor—but finds himself presiding over its demise when the elderly existing members refuse to admit any new blood.

Nonetheless, Bech has not lost all his imaginative powers. In "Bech Noir," he fantasizes the murders of critics who have abused him. Then, in the volume's finale, Bech is awarded the Nobel Prize. Delivering his acceptance speech before the Swedish Academy, Bech asserts his vitality by holding aloft his newborn daughter for the audience's edification. The gesture is, if nothing else, life affirming. Exactly how Bech—a "semi-obscure" writer with a slim body of work—arrived at this pinnacle of literary recognition is no clearer than the import of Bech's entire literary saga. Updike may be saying that

for his fictional counterpart, this jaded urban Jew with writer's block, life and sex trump art. As the title of the book tells the reader, this last installment of the Bech series is a quasi-novel, and Henry Bech seems often to be merely a mask for his creator. The epigraph, "Something of the unreal is necessary to fecundate the real," which Updike borrows from Wallace Stevens, points to the correspondence between creator and creation.

GERTRUDE AND CLAUDIUS

Returning once more in 2000 to a central subject of so many of his novels and short stories—that is to say, adultery and its pleasures, pains, ensuing entanglements, and consequences—yet with an original use for it, Updike creates a tale that has as its takeoff point not only William Shakespeare's *Hamlet* (pr. c. 1600-1601) but also two ancient sources that the Bard of Avon drew upon when writing the play. Here Updike focuses reader attention on these versions not in order to recast or refurbish the existing plot of a storied revenge tale but to add depth to two characters Shakespeare placed on his second tier—namely, Queen Gertrude and her second husband, Claudius, whose rule is made possible by the latter's murder of Hamlet's father, the king.

Like many other couples in Updike, Gertrude and Claudius have shared an intense affair that has led them to the precipice, and yet they are ignorant of their peril. In this case, their ill-conceived adulterous coupling will lead Hamlet, as readers of Shakespeare know, from a stunned realization of what has happened to his father to hatred of the murderers and to thoughts of revenge, which, as a wronged son, in turn will lead to matricide and the murder of a detested, conniving uncle—his own form of justice. This progression is not the subject of this book, however, for Updike chooses to take us only as far as midway into the first act of Shakespeare's play, and here Gertrude and Claudius share the spotlight, with Hamlet for the most part only a presence discussed by them rather than himself being "onstage." Readers know, for example, that Hamlet has a close tie with a clown named Yorick as well as with the "fair Ophelia," but they get to know Hamlet only from the words of others—that is, until he finally turns up at book's end.

Those whom readers do get to know are Hamlet's mother, his uncle, and, to some extent, his father, that stern warlord devoid of emotional connection to wife and son. Unlike Shakespeare's rendition of the ancient saga, Updike's Queen Gertrude is not simply a whorish woman or a murderous one—she is shown more as a lonely person who gets little attention from her husband and thus is ripe for male conquest once Claudius makes his pitch for her affections. Claudius, for his part, is only doing what comes naturally when he woos Gertrude straight into his bed; no grand villain, he seems more the conniver and opportunist. What readers discover here is an arrestingly plausible romance that serves to fill in gaps and answer the questions left in Shakespeare's version of things.

SEEK MY FACE

Just as he did with *Gertrude and Claudius* in 2000, John Updike demonstrated with *Seek My Face* in 2002 that he could take chances and explore new literary terrain in his old age. As with the earlier novel, however, several reviewers found *Seek My Face* both singular when compared with the typical works in the Updike canon, which tend to focus on everyday East Coast suburbs and the ordinary people who live there, and yet disappointing, in this case because they found the novel to be less a literary breakthrough than a tired retelling of the life story of one of the modern art world's most celebrated painters, the so-called drip artist, abstract expressionist Jackson Pollock. Some critics, however, have nevertheless found in this celebrity memoir a new direction for Updike's prose.

Here one finds the free-ranging recollections of Hope Ouderkirk, a woman once married to artist Zach McCoy (read "Pollock"), whose loutish behavior, epic drinking bouts, and general unpredictability ultimately lead to his demise. Her second husband, Guy Holloway—no accident in his name—is ultimately a derivative, vapid artist whose art follows the fashions of the times and who cannot depose McCoy in Hope's life and memories. As for McCoy, he finds women mysterious and worthy of pursuit, but, like his real-life model, he also finds them emotionally elusive. They in turn are fascinated and sometimes repelled by him and the puzzling conflicts that churn within him.

VILLAGES

Updike loyalists who possibly feel a bit dislocated by his two previous works are likely to feel at home in this 2004 novel *Villages*, which is, as many have noted, a return to much the same suburbs found in the author's Rabbit series of works—to Tarbox or any of the other middling-sized Updike upscale communities—and the adulterous lives of their residents. Instead of young or even middle-aged virile characters, however, *Villages* has the virile—yet precariously so—Owen MacKenzie in his dotage living out the end of his romantically tangled days in Haskells Crossing, Massachusetts, and remembering what it was like to be young and in love or lust or both. MacKenzie, a man whose early interest in computers and their creation at the Massachusetts Institute of Technology eventually makes him a fortune, has many opportunities to meet women, many of them married. Here once again is an archetypal Updike male "lead"—a rather unlikable and rather ordinary individual who, by means of the author's impressive poetic gift, becomes someone to whom attention must be paid.

TERRORIST

With *Terrorist*, Updike, though not abandoning the American East Coast or his predilection for depicting with high accuracy the mundane and the everyday, does strike out into what constitutes more new territory—the inner life of a highly conflicted and desperate young Muslim man named Ahmad who is growing up angry in the northern New Jersey city of Prospect. Ahmad eventually becomes so obsessed by fanatical thoughts that he embarks on a mission to kill as many supposedly free-thinking infidels as he can with the assistance of explosives. Taking far more chances with subject, setting, and genre than he had for some time previously in his fiction, Updike crafts a fast-paced and credible suspense novel that also functions as a critique of culture in the United States in the years following the terrorist attacks of September 11, 2001.

As a counterweight to the angry Muslim fanatic is his unlikely mentor, hedonistic sixty-three-year-old Jewish schoolteacher Jack Levy, whose inner life is as focused on making love as Ahmad's is on eliminating the enemies of Islam. A further use of a counterweight comes as Updike introduces the evil Lebanese terrorist Charlie, a man who inflames his mind with hatred of the West just as Levy would soothe it with his "take life as it comes and appreciate it" preachments. Charlie goes further than simply encouraging Ahmad's prejudices—he offers him a concrete way to get revenge on the United

States and on those among his fellow teenagers who give him a hard time. The journey Ahmad undertakes is memorable and, at times, thrilling.

With the astonishing variety and richness of his narratives, Updike created novels that constitute a serious exploration and probing of the spiritual conditions of American culture in the late twentieth and early twenty-first centuries. In Updike's fiction, the fate of American civilization is seen in the condition of love—its risks and dangers as well as its possibility for gracious transformation.

John G. Parks; Lisa Paddock
Updated by John D. Raymer

OTHER MAJOR WORKS

SHORT FICTION: *The Same Door*, 1959; *Pigeon Feathers, and Other Stories*, 1962; *Olinger Stories: A Selection*, 1964; *The Music School*, 1966; *Museums and Women, and Other Stories*, 1972; *Problems, and Other Stories*, 1979; *Three Illuminations in the Life of an American Author*, 1979; *Too Far to Go: The Maples Stories*, 1979; *The Chaste Planet*, 1980; *The Beloved*, 1982; *Trust Me*, 1987; *Brother Grasshopper*, 1990 (limited edition); *The Afterlife, and Other Stories*, 1994; *Licks of Love: Short Stories and a Sequel, "Rabbit Remembered,"* 2000; *The Complete Henry Bech: Twenty Stories*, 2001; *The Early Stories, 1953-1975*, 2003; *My Father's Tears, and Other Stories*, 2009.

PLAYS: *Three Texts from Early Ipswich: A Pageant*, pb. 1968; *Buchanan Dying*, pb. 1974.

POETRY: *The Carpentered Hen, and Other Tame Creatures*, 1958; *Telephone Poles, and Other Poems*, 1963; *Dog's Death*, 1965; *Verse*, 1965; *The Angels*, 1968; *Bath After Sailing*, 1968; *Midpoint, and Other Poems*, 1969; *Seventy Poems*, 1972; *Six Poems*, 1973; *Cunts (Upon Receiving the Swingers Life Club Membership Solicitation)*, 1974; *Query*, 1974; *Tossing and Turning*, 1977; *Sixteen Sonnets*, 1979; *Five Poems*, 1980; *Jester's Dozen*, 1984; *Facing Nature*, 1985; *Mites, and Other Poems in Miniature*, 1990; *Collected Poems, 1953-1993*, 1993; *A Helpful Alphabet of Friendly Objects*, 1995; *Americana, and Other Poems*, 2001; *Endpoint, and Other Poems*, 2009.

NONFICTION: *Assorted Prose*, 1965; *Picked-Up Pieces*, 1975; *Hugging the Shore: Essays and Criticism*, 1983; *Just Looking: Essays on Art*, 1989; *Self-Consciousness: Memoirs*, 1989; *Odd Jobs: Essays and Criticism*, 1991; *Golf Dreams: Writings on Golf*, 1996; *More Matter: Essays and Criticism*, 1999; *Still Looking: Essays on American Art*, 2005; *Due Considerations: Essays and Criticism*, 2007.

EDITED TEXT: *The Best American Short Stories of the Century*, 2000.

BIBLIOGRAPHY

Boswell, Marshall. *John Updike's Rabbit Tetralogy: Mastered Irony in Motion*. Columbia: University of Missouri Press, 2001. Offers a comprehensive examination of Harry Angstrom's literary journey through life.

Broer, Lawrence R., ed. *Rabbit Tales: Poetry and Politics in John Updike's Rabbit Novels*. Tuscaloosa: University of Alabama Press, 1998. Collection of essays demonstrates that Updike's Rabbit novels are a carefully crafted fabric of changing hues and textures, of social realism and something of grandeur. Includes bibliographical references and index.

De Bellis, Jack, ed. *John Updike: The Critical Responses to the "Rabbit" Saga*. Westport, Conn.: Praeger, 2005. Collection of thirty-four scholarly essays examines Updike's "Rabbit" novels, providing a historical view of the works' critical reception.

Detweiler, Robert. *John Updike*. Rev. ed. Boston: Twayne, 1984. Offers an excellent introductory survey of Updike's work through 1983, with biographical information and analyses of individual works. Includes chronology, select bibliography, and index.

Miller, D. Quentin. *John Updike and the Cold War: Drawing the Iron Curtain*. Columbia: University of Missouri Press, 2001. Focuses on the influence of Cold War society and politics in forming Updike's worldview.

Newman, Judie. *John Updike*. New York: St. Martin's Press, 1988. Covers Updike's long fiction with facility and insight and offers a solid foundation for understanding the author's primary concerns throughout his writing.

Olster, Stacey, ed. *The Cambridge Companion to John Updike*. New York: Cambridge University Press, 2006. Comprehensive resource contains a fine chronology and bibliography plus major critical analyses of Updike's works, the former representing a global perspective concerning what he got right about American life and popular culture and what he may have misconstrued.

Pritchard, William H. *Updike: America's Man of Letters*. South Royalton, Vt.: Steerforth Press, 2000. Examines Updike's novels, short fiction, and other works and argues that Updike belongs to the tradition of such American storytellers as William Dean Howells and Henry James.

Schiff, James A. *John Updike Revisited*. New York: Twayne, 1998. Good introductory work surveys all of Updike's work up to 1998 but focuses on his fiction of the late 1990's.

Updike, John. "The Art of Fiction: A Conversation with John Updike." Interview by Sanford Pinsker. *Sewanee Review* 104 (Summer, 1996): 423-433. Updike discusses the visual artists who have inspired him, how his academic experiences helped to shape his writing, and how he regards criticism of his work.

HONORÉ D'URFÉ

Born: Marseille, France; February 11, 1568
Died: Villefranche-sur-Mer, France; June 1, 1625
Also known as: Marquis de Valbromey, Count de Châteauneuf, and Sieur de La Bastie

PRINCIPAL LONG FICTION

L'Astrée, 1607-1628, 1925 (5 volumes; *Astrea*, 1657-1658; volume 4 is fragmentary and was published posthumously. The fifth volume was written by Balthazar Baro, d'Urfé's secretary, and is based on notes left by d'Urfé)

OTHER LITERARY FORMS

The first literary work of Honoré d'Urfé (dur-FAY) was a series of philosophical meditations, *Epistres morales* (1598). *Le Sireine*, a pastoral poem begun in 1583, was published in 1606. Between 1599 and 1609, d'Urfé composed a heroic poem in nine books, *La Savoysiade* (a fragment of this work appears in *Nouveau Recueil des plus beaux vers de ce temps*, 1609). At the request of Marie de Médicis, d'Urfé wrote a long pastoral play in five acts titled *La Sylvanire* (pb. 1627). *Les Tristes Amours de Floridon* (1628) contains two shorter pastoral works, "Les Fortunez Amours de Poliastre et de Doriane" and "Le Berger désolé."

ACHIEVEMENTS

In spite of Honoré d'Urfé's numerous other works, his fame rests on his five-volume novel *Astrea*. *Astrea* was one of the most prodigious successes of the period and became the most widely read novel in seventeenth century France, influencing the life of the time as well as the literature that succeeded it. The appearance of *Astrea* coincided with the end of the political and social unrest caused by the religious wars from 1562 to 1598.

The period following the Ligue was one in which heroic individuals tried to mold themselves to a courtly and therefore civilized pattern. The warrior became attuned to social requirements and the polite conversation of the salons. *Astrea*, with its refined dialogue and its bucolic setting, spoke directly to a psychological need for calm and order after years of civil strife. It quickly became a manual of courtly love for the aristocracy. It was through *Astrea* and the courtly texts of the Italian Renaissance, Torquato Tasso's *Aminta* (1587; English translation, 1591) and Baldassare Castiglione's *Il cortegiano* (1528; *The Book of the Courtier*, 1561), that the nobility became versed in the code of Neoplatonic love.

From 1607 to the middle of the seventeenth century, Celadon, Astrea, Silvandre, Diane, and the code of *amour honnête* that they exemplified enjoyed a great vogue. *Astrea* was read at court, in the salons of the *précieuses*, at the home of Cardinal de Retz, and by Madame de La Fayette. At the reunions of the Académie des Parfaits Amants and in the park of the Hôtel de Rambouillet, noble ladies and gentlemen disguised themselves as the heroines and heroes of d'Urfé's pastoral. Around the middle of the century, it became the fashion to have one's portrait painted in pastoral costume. It is quite possible that Marie Antoinette had *Astrea* in mind when she decided to build the Hamlet, a pastoral retreat in the park of the Trianon.

Astrea's success can be measured not only by its effect on seventeenth century French society but also by its influence on writers such as Pierre Corneille, Jean de La Fontaine, Jean Racine, Madame de Sevigné, Jean-Jacques Rousseau, and George Sand. D'Urfé's novel continues to attract the attention of modern writers. Suzanne Poirier notes the influence of *Astrea* on *The Magus* (1965, 1977), John Fowles's labyrinthine tale of love and adventure.

H. C. Lancaster points out that *Astrea* influenced the French stage for almost fifty years. The numerous secondary episodes as well as the central intrigue of Celadon and Astrea provided ample material for the many pastoral plays that were popular at the time. Critics such as Henri Bochet (in *"L'Astrée": Ses origines, son importance dans la formation de la littérature classique*, 1967) and Maurice Magendie (in *De Nouveau sur "L'Astrée,"* 1927, and *Le Roman français au XVIIe siècle: De "L'Astrée" au "Grand Cyrus,"* 1932) see d'Urfé's novel as a precursor of French classicism. The psychological and historical realism of the novel and its examination of illusion and reality paved the way for the emergence of more realistic novels, such as La Fayette's *La Princesse de Clèves* (1678; *The Princess of Clèves*, 1679), in the second half of the seventeenth century.

BIOGRAPHY

Honoré d'Urfé, Marquis de Valbromey, Count de Châteauneuf, and Sieur de La Bastie, was born in Marseilles on February 11, 1568. His mother, Renée, was descended from the powerful House of Savoy, and his father, Jacques, was a lieutenant general in the government of Forez, a region in central France in the Loire department. D'Urfé's parents were married in 1554, and they had twelve children. D'Urfé's father, Jacques, was the

eldest son of Claude d'Urfé, an influential nobleman who was ambassador to Rome and to the Council of Trent under Francis I of France, while his older brother authored several books of poetry.

While the family was influential, it was always short of funds and encouraged d'Urfé, at the age of thirteen, to join the Knights of Malta. After following his parents' wishes, he returned to the family castle at La Bastie and entered the College of Tournon, a Jesuit school. The education he received at Tournon strongly influenced the young d'Urfé and gave him a good foundation in Humanist and classical studies. The intellectual atmosphere at his home of La Bastie, with its renowned library, great works of art, and frequent visitors, also seems to have contributed to d'Urfé's interest in literature. At the age of twenty-two, d'Urfé followed the example of his brother, Anne, and fought in the Ligue during the religious wars. He was twice taken prisoner, once at Feurs in 1595, and several years later at Montbrison. In the prison at Montbrison, he wrote his first major work, *Epistres morales*.

After the victory of Henry IV, d'Urfé went to live in Savoy. When Anne decided to join a religious order, d'Urfé married his brother's wife, Diane de Châteaumorand, in 1600. The couple separated amicably some fourteen years later; critics have speculated that it was the beautiful Diane who inspired the story of Celadon and Astrea. D'Urfé spent the rest of his life in Savoy, in Paris, and at his properties of Châteauneuf and Virieu-le-Grand. In 1625, he fought a battle on the side of the duke of Savoy against Genoa and was taken afterward to the town of Villefranche-sur-Mer near the Italian border. At Villefranche he became ill and died on June 1, 1625.

ANALYSIS: ASTREA

The setting of *Astrea* is the Forez, in which Honoré d'Urfé lived and with which he was very familiar. He situates his novel during the fifth century, a time that witnessed the invasion of barbaric tribes. Nevertheless, the Forez shepherds, under the benevolent rule of Queen Amasis and the guidance of the high priest Adamas, enjoy a life of abundance and tranquility. When the novel opens, Celadon, the shepherd hero, is in love with the beautiful sheepherder Astrea. Astrea mistakenly believes that Celadon loves Aminthe and has been unfaithful to her. In her jealousy, she orders him not to appear before her again unless it is by her express command. Like the knights in chivalric romances that precede *Astrea* and that influenced it, Celadon vows never to disobey the wishes of his beloved. He despairs at incurring her wrath and throws himself into the currents of the Lignon River. His suicide attempt fails, and he is rescued by a group of nymphs, who look after him until he has recovered.

Keeping in mind Astrea's interdiction never to appear before her, Celadon decides that he will live the life of a hermit in the forest. There he builds a temple to Astrea and renders homage to her by an austere existence. Celadon continues to grow progressively weaker until he is discovered by Adamas, a high priest and one of the principal figures in the novel. Adamas tells Celadon that his appearance has changed so much that Astrea will never recognize him. He convinces him to disguise himself as a woman in order to be near Astrea again. Celadon dons the garments of a woman and takes the name of Alexis, thereby rejoining Astrea and living in her company without her knowing it. The long episode of Celadon's disguise is one of the central intrigues of the novel and occupies several volumes. At the novel's end, and with the help of Adamas and various shepherds, Astrea orders Celadon to appear before her. Celadon finally reveals his identity and the lovers are reconciled. D'Urfé's tragicomedy ends with the marriage of the hero and heroine.

The story of Celadon and Astrea is interspersed with lengthy digressions, stories, and numerous secondary episodes involving a multitude of characters. The five volumes of the novel form a lengthy narrative catalog of fine points in love, honor, etiquette, and courtly devotion. Critics have frequently noted that the stories in *Astrea* are marked by the ideology of Neoplatonic love inherited from the writers of the Italian Renaissance; they also recall the love dialogues of Marguerite de Navarre's *L'Heptaméron* (1559; *The Queene of Navarres Tales*, 1597; also known as *The Heptameron*, 1959), the writings of Marsilio Ficino, and the pastoral romances of Jorge de Montemayor.

Honoré d'Urfé. (Roger Viollet/Getty Images)

Astrea presents two fundamentally diverging conceptions of love. The first position is represented by the jovial shepherd Hylas; he finds his pleasure in a carefree *inconstance*, or infidelity, to his lady. According to Hylas, his changing affections conform to the fundamental instability of the natural world that surrounds him. Hylas almost never experiences misfortune in love; he erases any threat of unhappiness by simply giving his affections to a different lady. The love interests of Hylas change as quickly as his whims. In Hylas's view, the lover is a rather passive personality; the lover conforms to worldly flux rather than trying to go against it. The underlying merit of this position is that the lover conforms to the movement of the world, symbolized in the novel by the recurring figure of the Wheel of Fortune. In this Baroque vision, the body, the intellect, and love itself are caught in a constant state of evolution. Harmony between the universe and the individual is the desired result of this *Weltanschauung*; infidelity is seen as a logical way to achieve harmony.

The opposite view, taken by Celadon, Silvandre, and the majority of the Forez shepherds, holds that man should not be submerged in unnecessary change and movement. Celadon, Silvandre, and their ladies advocate fidelity and introduce the role of self-discipline and the will in love. The philosophy of the faithful lovers is closely tied to the Neoplatonism of Ficino, Pietro Bembo, and León Hebreo. Here love is not a state that results from a momentary attraction, but rather is a choice freely made and carefully considered. As Celadon and Silvandre commit themselves to the service of their ladies, they engage in a quasi-spiritual quest that recalls the chivalric romances. Their quest delivers them from worldly concerns and becomes a fixed point in a chaotic world. They realize that although the body is subject to living in the world, the intellect need not be totally subjected to it and may escape through contemplation.

This position echoes the teachings of Ficino, who counsels the soul to retire from the body and withdraw into the mind (see *Supplementum Ficinianum*, 1937, edited by Paul Kristeller). The detachment produced by the will makes the love of the faithful shepherds relatively independent of the beloved. In his mind's eye, the lover retains the image of his lady as he contemplates, through her beauty, the static qualities of beauty and virtue. As one of the shepherds notes, "The lover desires nothing outside of himself." The end of love is thus a type of spiritual meditation that escapes the movement of Fortune's wheel. For Hylas's life of physical pleasures, Celadon substitutes a life of contemplation.

The opposition between inconstancy (Hylas) and constancy (Celadon) may also be seen as representative of the clash between two different aesthetic systems, the Baroque and the classical. For Hylas, art, like nature and love, is marked by change. The musician and the painter, in their arrangement of notes and colors, incorporate diversity into their work. Hylas's philosophy and the aesthetics of change it advocates are closely tied to certain categories that Jean Rousset (*La Littérature de l'âge baroque en France: Circé et le paon*, 1954) has identified as Baroque. After studying certain characteristics of German and Italian art and architecture, Rousset applied his discoveries to French literature from 1580 to the mid-seventeenth century, the period of *Astrea*. His work did much to establish the existence of the literary period known as the Baroque. Scholars who had theretofore seen *Astrea* as a preclassical or a post-Renaissance text were forced to contend with the new movement that Rousset had identified—a movement characterized by an emphasis on the themes of change, movement, inconstancy, disguise, metamorphosis, death, and life as spectacle. Later critics applied Rousset's findings specifically to *Astrea* and claimed that it was clearly a Baroque text.

Other critics, notably Bochet, have emphasized the classical aspects of d'Urfé's text: his realism, his style, his attention to historical facts. The Neoplatonism of Celadon and Silvandre, with its tendency toward transcendence and constancy, is seen as having much in common with the static qualities of French classicism. Yet other critics, such as Herbert De Ley, underline the coexistence of both Renaissance and classical tendencies in *Astrea*; in this view, the presence of both Hylas and Celadon attests the influence of Renaissance writers such as Michel Eyquem de Montaigne and prefigures the intellectual discipline of Cartesian thought.

Astrea's five volumes thus reflect a diversity of aesthetic viewpoints and literary periods, inviting readers to pursue, along with the faithful shepherds, a contemplative love quest. The Forez shepherds create for themselves an inner quest tied to devotion to the lady; their withdrawal to a pastoral setting and their initiation to higher forms of beauty and virtue are signs of spiritual goals. *Astrea* has been and continues to be an influential work, not only in terms of the role models it gave to French society but also in terms of the novelists and critics whom it has inspired.

Carole Deering Paul

OTHER MAJOR WORKS

SHORT FICTION: *Les Tristes Amours de Floridon*, 1628.

PLAY: *La Sylvanire*, pb. 1627.

POETRY: *Le Sireine*, 1606; *La Savoysiade*, 1609 (fragment in *Nouveau Recueil des plus beaux vers de ce temps*).

NONFICTION: *Epistres morales*, 1598.

BIBLIOGRAPHY

Hembree, James M. *Subjectivity and the Signs of Love: Discourse, Desire, and the Emergence of Modernity in Honoré d'Urfé's "L'Astrée."* New York: Peter Lang, 1997. An analysis of the novel *Astrea* and its significance to the history of French philosophy. Hembree argues that the novel is a bridge between Michel Eyquem de Montaigne's ideas about the nature of being and René Descartes's more modern and subjective ideas about self-knowledge.

Hinds, Leonard. *Narrative Transformations from "L'Astrée" to "Le Berger extravagant."* West Lafayette, Ind.: Purdue University Press, 2002. A comparison of d'Urfé's idealist, pastoral romance with Charles Sorel's *The Extravagant Shepherd—The Anti-Romance*, a realistic parody of d'Urfé's novel published in 1627. Demonstrates how Sorel altered d'Urfé's language and other aspects of the pastoral genre to create his satire.

Horowitz, Louise K. *Honoré d'Urfé.* Boston: Twayne, 1984. A volume in the Twayne World Authors series, Horowitz's book is an introductory overview of d'Urfé, with biographical information and discussion of *Astrea* and other writings. Includes a bibliography and an index.

_____. "Honoré d'Urfé: Bellwether Beginnings." In *Beginnings in French Literature*, edited by Freeman G. Henry. Amsterdam: Rodopi, 2002. Horowitz's examination of the sources and origins of *Astrea* is included in this collection of essays about French literature. A scholarly essay, appropriate for advanced students.

Wine, Kathleen. *Forgotten Virgo: Humanism and Absolutism in Honoré d'Urfés "L'Astrée."* Geneva: Librairie Droz, 2000. An analysis of *Astrea*, in which Wine discusses how d'Urfé altered the traditional genres of pastoral and epic to create myths about personal and literary autonomy that would resonate throughout French literature.

LEON URIS

Born: Baltimore, Maryland; August 3, 1924
Died: Shelter Island, New York; June 21, 2003
Also known as: Leon Marcus Uris

PRINCIPAL LONG FICTION

Battle Cry, 1953
The Angry Hills, 1955
Exodus, 1958
Mila 18, 1960
Armageddon, 1964
Topaz, 1967
QB VII, 1970
Trinity, 1976
The Haj, 1984
Mitla Pass, 1988
Redemption, 1995
A God in Ruins, 1999
O'Hara's Choice, 2003

OTHER LITERARY FORMS

Leon Uris (YEWR-ihs) is known primarily for his novels, but he wrote for films as well. He wrote the screenplay adaptation of his first novel, *Battle Cry*, in 1955, and he wrote the screenplay for the 1957 American Western classic *Gunfight at the OK Corral*. He also wrote the script for the short documentary film *Israel*, which was released in 1959.

ACHIEVEMENTS

Perhaps Leon Uris's greatest achievement was the novel for which he is most remembered, *Exodus*. Published in 1958, *Exodus* was an international sensation. It was translated into more than fifty languages, and millions of copies were sold. Hailed as Uris's best work, it was on the *New York Times* best-seller list for more than a year, staying at number one for five months. Inside the Soviet Union, where it was forbidden reading, smuggled copies of the 599-page paperback edition of *Exodus* were translated and then typed by hand because citizens were not allowed access to copy machines or duplicating equipment. The 1960 film adaptation of *Exodus*, directed by Otto Preminger and starring Paul Newman, was a blockbuster success.

BIOGRAPHY

Leon Marcus Uris was born in Baltimore, Maryland, to William and Anna Uris in 1924. His father, a paperhanger by trade, had immigrated to the United States from Poland after having spent a year in Palestine. The author once said of his father, "He went from failure to failure." Leon Uris was a failure himself in high school, having failed English three times. He dropped out of high school and joined the U.S. Marine Corps at the age of seventeen.

Uris served in World War II as a radioman in Tarawa, Guadalcanal, and New Zealand. After his service, while recovering from malaria in San Francisco, Uris met the first of his three wives, Betty Beck. Uris used his war experiences extensively, especially in his first novel, *Battle Cry*. Before he became a successful writer, Uris was employed in California as a newspaper delivery driver for the *San Francisco Call-Bulletin* in the late 1940's.

Battle Cry was written when Uris was twenty-nine years old, after he had a story published in *Esquire* and was encouraged by the editors to write a novel. After 1950, Uris was a full-time writer. Living in California, he also became a screenwriter, penning *Gunfight at the OK Corral*, a film directed by John Sturges. Uris could be a difficult man to work with, and he often found himself at odds with Hollywood directors, including Sturges. Later he fought with two directors who filmed adaptations of his novels: Otto Preminger, who directed *Exodus* (1960), and Alfred Hitchcock, who directed *Topaz* (1969).

In 1958, *Exodus* made Uris's reputation as a writer. Having served as a war correspondent during the Arab-Israeli conflict of 1956, Uris once again turned to his personal experience for the basis of his next novel. In only his third book, Uris displayed a tremendous work ethic and attention to detail, sending an unlikely epic about the founding of the state of Israel to the top of the best-seller lists. Uris's career as a writer centered on the block-

buster, the large, sweeping saga that brings history to life; examples include *Mila 18*, which centers on the Warsaw ghetto uprising, and *Trinity*, an epic novel that focuses on Ireland under English rule and covers generations.

Hard to live with as well as to work with, Uris admitted to being difficult and sometimes ruthless. His first marriage ended in divorce in 1965 after twenty years and three children. Uris married Margery Edwards in 1968 and she died in 1969, apparently a suicide. Uris married for a third time, to Jill Peabody, in 1970, when Uris was forty-six and his bride was twenty-four. They had two children before divorcing in 1989. Uris died of congestive heart failure in June, 2003, in his home in Shelter Island, New York, at the age of seventy-eight.

ANALYSIS

The historical novel is neither strictly history nor strictly novel. The best writers in this genre, of which Uris was certainly one, are skilled enough to blur the lines between fiction and history. If all one knows about the founding of Israel or life in Ireland under English occupation is what one has read in Uris's *Exodus* or *Trinity*, then one has only a rudimentary understanding of the subject, and that understanding is likely to be biased by the author's own prejudices.

It is a testament to Uris's power as a writer and thoroughness as a researcher that he was able to present his works in such a convincing light as to persuade his readers that they have gained a useful knowledge of the subject at hand. Literary critics, whose job it is to dissect works of fiction, point out Uris's complete lack of objectivity. For example, Uris spoke on behalf of Jewish interests around the world, raising money for Jewish causes during his career, and his portrayals of Jewish soldiers and settlers in works such as *Exodus* must be accepted as the products of a man who was a devout Zionist. This observation, however, is not really criticism as much as truth. Uris was a Jew, and he sympathized with the plight of European Jews especially, and his novels reflect this.

Uris was a great storyteller, if somewhat overly melodramatic at times. He did not graduate from high school, and he earned his writer's reputation on the job. The lack of polish, the brute force of his prose, shines through at times. His treatment of women characters

Leon Uris. (Time & Life Pictures/Getty Images)

in his novels, for example, is a product of his lack of sophistication. Women in his early novels, such as Kitty Fremont and Jordana Ben Canaan in *Exodus*, struggle with the role of the feminine. Jordana wants to be the equal of any man, but she resents Kitty's frilly dresses, cosmetics, and demure attitude in the company of men. Kitty, meanwhile, resents Jordana and Dafna, Ari Ben Canaan's first wife, for their strength and uncompromising personalities. In later novels, Uris moved away from this dichotomy and presented women as more modern, less inhibited, and more likely to engage men on a level playing field.

EXODUS

Exodus is the story of the founding of the state of Israel, including almost one hundred years of history before the Jewish state was founded in 1948. Full of great detail, this work is typical and the best example of Uris's historical novels. The amount of background work that Uris invested and his extensive research into the supporting documents that went into the writing of *Exodus* are impressive.

While *Exodus* is a famous novel, it must be viewed in the context of its time. Published only ten years after the founding of the state of Israel, *Exodus* was particularly significant in its day because it gave Jewish people a

sense of their history and chronicled their struggles, not only in Nazi Germany and Eastern Europe but also around the world. In the year of its publication, Israeli prime minister David Ben-Gurion has been quoted as saying about *Exodus*, "As a piece of propaganda, it's the greatest thing ever written about Israel."

Exodus presents Jewish characters in a light that up to the time of its publication was unusual—one of heroic stature. The novel's main character, Ari Ben Canaan, is a sort of Jewish superman. Tall, dark, handsome, fearless, decisive, bold, and daring, Ari is a far cry from the Jewish stereotype presented in previous popular fiction. Uris addresses this difference in his foreword to the novel, noting that the characters in *Exodus* do not include shrewd businessmen, intelligent doctors, or humorous, self-deprecating Jewish men who have been in therapy for years.

This sweeping epic begins on the island of Cyprus only a couple of years after the end of World War II. The refugee problem, the issue of where to resettle millions of displaced Jews, many of them survivors of Nazi concentration camps, is vexing Europe. For generations, Jews have been slowly returning to Palestine; however, the large number of Jews needing relocation could overwhelm the resources of the Middle East and aggravate Arabs who already live there. Great Britain has control of the region and must walk a tightrope between appeasing Arab interests and allowing Jewish settlement in Palestine. In the meantime, Cyprus serves as a holding pen for tens of thousands of displaced persons.

Since the end of the war, Jewish financiers in the United States and Europe have paid to have ships outfitted for the purpose of transporting illegal immigrants to Palestine. Jewish underground agents, including Ari Ben Canaan, have been secreting Jews aboard ships, evading British barricades, and grounding their crafts on the beaches of Palestine. Ben Canaan's latest idea is to smuggle thousands of children out of Cyprus on a ship the Jews have named *Exodus*. This time, however, the aim is not to run the British blockade but to gain worldwide sympathy for the plight of displaced Jews and win the battle of public opinion. To accomplish his mission, Ben Canaan must be willing to risk the lives of the children to bluff the British and embarrass them on the world's stage so that the ship *Exodus* will be allowed to sail to Palestine without conflict.

Aside from Ari Ben Canaan, other important characters in *Exodus* include Katherine "Kitty" Fremont, an American nurse from Indiana who is falling in love with Ben Canaan and who dotes on a young Jewish girl named Karen Clement Hansen. Karen, who has lost her family in the Holocaust, was smuggled out of Germany by her parents before the war and was raised in Denmark. She has come to Palestine to find her father, who was an important German scientist and professor before the war. Karen has a fondness for young Dov Landau, a survivor of a Polish concentration camp and the Warsaw ghetto uprising. He has been emotionally scarred by his horrid past and withdraws from everyone except Karen. *Exodus* also explores the story of Ari Ben Canaan's family, including his father and uncle, who have conflicting ideas about how Jews should bring about the state of Israel. The stories of Ari's family, of Karen Clement Hansen, of Kitty Fremont, and of Dov Landau are all told through long flashbacks. These four people and their intertwining relationships serve as the pattern that carries the novel's story.

The novel has been criticized for its sexism and for its blatant anti-Arab bias as well as for what many critics contend are oversimplified themes, unrealistic portrayals, trite dialogue, and shoddy sentence structure. Although it is perhaps not a great work of literature, *Exodus* stands as an important document in the history of Israel and in the world's understanding of Jews and their passion for a Jewish state. In a way that no pure historical work could convey, *Exodus* gives readers a feeling for how Jews were treated by the world after World War II and how they responded with great persistence, bravery, and ingenuity.

QB VII

One of the main characters of Uris's 1970 novel *QB VII* is Abe Cady, an American Jew who has written a best-selling book titled *The Holocaust*. Some of Cady's family members died in Jadwiga, a Nazi concentration camp in Poland that was known for the medical experiments performed there on twins, including Jews. In adHdition to the Nazi doctors in the camp there were also some prisoner-surgeons, including a Pole named Adam Kelno. In 1947, at Poland's insistence, Kelno became a wanted man for his part in the war crimes committed at the camp. Kelno was living in England by this time, however, and the British were reluctant to send a physician, even one accused of war crimes, to Communist Poland. The evidence against Kelno had to be overwhelming to speed his extradition to Poland. After spending two years in an English prison awaiting evidence, Kelno was finally brought face-to-face with an accuser. At a legal hearing, the accuser could not pick Kelno out of a lineup of suspects, and Kelno was set free. Shortly thereafter he left England with his wife and young son, bound for Borneo in the South Pacific.

The novel moves to the past to relate Kelno's life in Borneo, which is above reproach. For seventeen years he fights to improve the living conditions of the local tribespeople, introducing medicines, working to change dangerous customs that are based on tribal superstitions, altering the diet of the tribe and improving nutrition—single-handedly saving the lives of a generation of Borneo natives. Word spreads of his accomplishments, and scientific papers are written on his work. Finally, the world learns about the British doctor performing miracles in the farthest reaches of the empire.

Kelno is afraid of returning to Western civilization, afraid of the accusations that might have been lying dormant through the years. He feels that he cannot risk his hard-earned good name, and he does not want to bring shame upon his family. The groundswell of recognition proves too much, however, and Kelno moves his family back to England. He is knighted for his service to the Crown and its subjects. Kelno avoids the spotlight as much as he can, preferring to run his clinic in London's poorest neighborhood. His instincts tell him to keep a low profile. Kelno's son Stephan and his apprentice Terrence are in awe of Kelno's work and aspire to be like him. This admiration means everything to Kelno, who believes that Jews hate him and will not rest until he is punished for crimes he never willingly committed. After all, he was a prisoner, the same as they were.

Cady's book, an in-depth chronicling of Nazi atrocities, has become a worldwide best seller. Kelno learns of the book, and he is particularly disturbed by one paragraph in it that identifies him as a butcher, a killer of innocents. Kelno brings a libel suit against Cady in the English courts, and the trial is heard by a jury in a courtroom designated Queen's Bench VII (QB VII).

This is a novel about forgiveness and redemption. Are there some human acts that are beyond the pale, that can never be forgotten or forgiven, no matter how many years have passed or what circumstances may have prevailed or what good deeds may have been performed in the interim? Is there a limit to the power of denial and self-delusion? Is there an ultimate accountability for one's actions, even those performed under the most extreme duress?

Randy L. Abbott

OTHER MAJOR WORKS

SCREENPLAYS: *Battle Cry*, 1955 (adaptation of his novel); *Gunfight at the OK Corral*, 1957.

NONFICTION: *Exodus Revisited*, 1959 (photographs by Dimitrios Harissiadis; also known as *In the Steps of Exodus*); *Ireland, a Terrible Beauty: The Story of Ireland Today*, 1975 (photographs by Jill Uris); *Jerusalem: Song of Songs*, 1981 (photographs by Jill Uris).

BIBLIOGRAPHY

Cain, Kathleen Shine. *Leon Uris: A Critical Companion.* Westport, Conn.: Greenwood Press, 1998. Provides biographical information and presents critical analysis of each of Uris's novels, discussing plot, characterization, and major themes.

Gonshak, Henry. "Rambowitz Versus the Schlemiel in Leon Uris' *Exodus*." *Journal of American Culture* 22, no. 1 (Spring, 1999): 9-16. Offers in-depth discussion of the characterization of Jews in Uris's *Exodus*.

Salt, Jeremy. "Fact and Fiction in the Middle Eastern Novels of Leon Uris." *Journal of Palestine Studies* 14, no. 3 (Spring, 1985): 54-63. Examines the historical accuracy of Uris's novels, particularly *Exodus* and *The Haj*.

Weissbrod, Rachel. "*Exodus* as a Zionist Melodrama." *Israel Studies* 4, no. 1 (Spring, 1999): 129-153. Discusses *Exodus* in its capacity as a historical novel—a work of fiction that is more easily digested than actual histories or sacred works that include a history of Palestine.

Whitfield, Stephen J. "Necrology: Leon Uris, 1924-2003." *Jewish Quarterly Review* 94, no. 4 (Fall, 2004): 666-671. Traces Uris's writing career, including *Exodus*, which Whitfield terms a propaganda novel.

V

JUAN VALERA

Born: Cabra, Spain; October 18, 1824
Died: Madrid, Spain; April 18, 1905
Also known as: Juan Valera y Alcalá Galiano

PRINCIPAL LONG FICTION

Mariquita y Antonio, 1861
Pepita Jiménez, 1874 (*Pepita Ximenez*, 1886)
Las ilusiones del doctor Faustino, 1875
El comendador Mendoza, 1877 (*Commander Mendoza*, 1893)
Pasarse de listo, 1878 (*Don Braulio*, 1892)
Doña Luz, 1879 (English translation, 1891)
Juanita la larga, 1896
Genio y figura, 1897
Morsamor, 1899

OTHER LITERARY FORMS

The first edition of the collected works (*Obras completas*, 1905-1935) of Juan Valera (vah-LEHR-ah) came to fifty-three volumes. In addition to his nine novels, he published poetry, drama, and short stories. He composed short stories early in his career, worked again in the genre in midcareer, and returned to the form more assiduously during the last decade of his life.

Valera also was a notable literary critic, with a number of volumes to his credit, among them *Disertaciones y juicios literarios* (1878; literary discourses and judgments), *Apuntes sobre el nuevo arte de escribir novelas* (1887; notes on the new art of writing novels), *Nuevos estudios críticos* (1883; new critical studies), and *Cartas americanas* (1889; American letters). If his criticism were to be faulted, it would be on the grounds of unwarranted benevolence toward some of his less gifted contemporaries and occasionally hastily conceived, shallow reviews; if it is to be especially praised, it is for opening the public's eyes to the then largely unknown field of Latin American literature. In general, his point of view was classically conservative.

Finally, there is Valera's five-volume edition of the *Florilegio de poesías castellanas del siglo XIX* (1902-1903; anthology of nineteenth century Spanish poetry) and his translation into Spanish of Adolf F. Schack's *Poesie und Kunst der Araber in Spanien und Sicilien* (1865) as *Poesía y arte en los árabes en España y Sicilia* (1867, 1868, 1871). In addition to almost every form of literature, critical and creative alike, Valera wrote on matters political and social and left a large body of well-crafted letters, of which more than a thousand have already turned up, addressed to his many friends in Spain and abroad.

ACHIEVEMENTS

Although today Juan Valera is remembered mainly for the ever-popular *Pepita Ximenez* (and perhaps to a lesser extent for *Juanita la larga*), during the latter part of the nineteenth and into the twentieth century, he ranked high among the great Spanish novelists and even among the better Spanish critics of his day. His complete works in fifty-three volumes appeared in Madrid from 1905 to 1935, and the widely disseminated Aguilar compact series devoted to him a three-volume set of virtually the same material. Only Benito Pérez Galdós, the dominant Spanish novelist of that time, stood preeminently above him. Because Pérez Galdós himself and other potential rivals, such as Emilia Pardo Bazán, Leopoldo Alas (Clarín), and José María de Pereda, wrote in the realistic or naturalistic vein, the one serious competitor in Valera's chosen field was probably Armando Palacio Valdés, whose *La hermana San Sulpicio* (1889; *Sister San Sulpicio*, 1890), in subject, treatment, and acclaim, bears favorable comparison to the best of Valera's work.

Valera was also an excellent critic of the literature of

his day and was largely responsible for popularizing with the Spanish public the works of the then quite ignored Latin American writers from across the sea, especially the Nicaraguan poet Rubén Darío. Indeed, Valera's early election into the Spanish Academy was principally the result of his criticism rather than of his (rather slim) accomplishments as a poet. His career as a novelist was still in the future. It might be added that his short stories and plays come to no more than should be expected from any major writer in a related genre.

Valera's long diplomatic career did not prevent an impressively large literary output: Forty works bear his name, including works he not only wrote but also edited and translated. Only in a country such as Spain, proverbial for the abundant output of its writers (Lope de Vega Carpio reputedly penned more than two thousand plays, of which more than four hundred are indisputably his; Pérez Galdós wrote some one hundred novels and dramas), could Valera be considered slothful. By any other national standard, his production is impressive.

BIOGRAPHY

Juan Valera, whose full name is Juan Valera y Alcalá Galiano, was born on October 18, 1824, in Cabra, a hill town some thirty-five miles southeast of Córdoba, Spain. His parents were distinguished if not affluent, his mother of the Spanish nobility, his father a naval officer, and his maternal uncle the famous orator and politician Antonio Alcalá Galiano. Valera attended a good secondary school in Málaga from 1837 to 1840, studied law in Granada's Colegio del Sacro Monte and in Madrid, and—back in Granada—graduated in 1844. Though an avid reader of literary classics, he was not a diligent student. It might be noted that many nineteenth century Spanish undergraduate law majors never intended a career in jurisprudence. Such degrees were closer to what would be considered today as the bachelor of arts. Valera, however, despite predictable excursions into the field of literature (a few poems in magazines and a volume of verses whose publication was subsidized by his father as a graduation present), actually attempted to practice law in Madrid.

Valera's family connections gave him entrée into high society. It was a pleasant but unremunerative existence; he soon had to think of correcting his course. Diplomacy appeared a more likely choice, and, after a slow start, it proved a good one. He obtained an unofficial post in Naples, working for his friend the great Romantic author the Duque de Rivas, at the time Spanish Ambassador, from 1847 to 1849. Valera was sent to Lisbon in 1850 and to Rio de Janeiro in 1851. There followed a post in Dresden (1855) and a visit to Russia (1856).

Returning to Spain, Valera ran for the office of deputy (similar to the position of congressman) in 1858, an office he held during two not very outstanding terms. In 1865, he received his first really important diplomatic appointment as minister in Frankfurt. In 1868, Isabel II lost her throne; Valera became undersecretary of state for most of one year. He even helped choose Amadeo of Savoy as the new king of Spain in 1870 and was made director of public instruction, if only for a very short time. The king soon abdicated, leaving Valera out of political favor. For seven years, Valera devoted himself to writing.

During previous lulls in his public career, Valera had already managed to produce a volume of poetry in 1858, helped found two satiric literary magazines in the two succeeding years, and was editor in chief for the middle-of-the-road *El contemporáneo* (where his first, unfinished, novel *Mariquita y Antonio* appeared in 1861). Although he had only one book to his credit, the 1858 volume of poetry (an earlier one in 1844 had sold so poorly that he had had it withdrawn from the market), he was elected in 1861 into the Spanish Academy, whose standards, it must be admitted, were somewhat less strict than those of its sister institution in France.

Valera's first collection of essays—*Estudios críticos sobre literatura, política, y costumbres de nuestros días* (critical studies on contemporary literature, politics, and customs)—appeared in 1864. In 1867, by then in his early forties, he married Dolores Delavat, a daughter of a career diplomat, whom he had first known in Rio de Janeiro in 1851. She was half his age, stubborn, and extravagant; he was usually strapped for funds, given to sarcasm, and notably fond of affairs of the heart (an early addiction still catered to long after his marriage). It was not an especially happy union, although they never separated, and the last few years proved somewhat calmer.

From 1881 to 1883, needing funds to support a growing family along with his extravagant wife, Valera ac-

Juan Valera. (The Granger Collection, New York)

cepted a post as minister in Lisbon, where the accusation of certain financial and political improprieties almost led to a duel. He resigned the position, supposing that his career was ruined but, on the contrary, the next year he was appointed minister to the United States in Washington, D.C. His wife stayed in Spain with the children.

Washington, D.C., like almost all of his appointments, seemed a mixed blessing. He was forever impugning the climate, the manners, the dress, or the tastes of the places—European or American—where he served his country. American men he termed dull money-grubbers; as always, however, he enjoyed the women. One of them, Katherine Lee Bayard, the twenty-eight-year-old daughter of the U.S. secretary of state, loved him deeply enough to commit suicide in 1886, on hearing that he was to return to Spain. Despite her death and that of his eldest son from typhoid, he seems to have enjoyed his transatlantic stay. Besides his usual active social life, he found time to read generously from American literature, even translating a few poems by James Russell Lowell and John Greenleaf Whittier with an eye

to adding fifty or so more to make up a whole book, a project that died aborning.

Valera's last two diplomatic posts were as minister in Brussels, from 1886 to 1887, and, after a six-year lapse, in Vienna, from 1893 to 1895. There ended his diplomatic career, rendered untenable by questionable health and increasing blindness. Returning to Madrid, he resumed his pursuit of literature. Even in government harness, he had produced *Cartas americanas* and *Nuevas cartas americanas* (1890; new American letters), discussing Latin American writers such as the Nicaraguan *Modernismo* poet Rubén Darío. Full-time commitment allowed for three more novels—*Juanita la larga* (shrewd Juanita), usually considered his best after *Pepita Ximenez*; *Genio y figura* (the title a shortened version of "genio y figura hasta la sepultura," an expression signifying "what's bred in the bone will be with you until you die"); and his historical novel, *Morsamor*—as well as short stories, essays, polemics, and an extensively annotated five-volume anthology of nineteenth century Spanish poetry. Valera died peacefully on April 18, 1905, while composing a discourse to be delivered before his beloved Spanish Academy.

The author-cum-diplomat was a proud man, at times even haughty, a chronic complainer, occasionally belligerent. He was often guilty of provincialism, not above denigrating foreign writers who dared pass judgment on things Spanish. He could be superficial and flighty, traits he exhibited all of his adult years. That he utilized some dozen publishers during his writing career is somewhat unusual, though the large body of his oeuvre may to some extent justify what seems to indicate a difficult personality. He was quite outspoken, a characteristic not always found among professional diplomats. Yet, despite his thorniness, he was normally kind to writers of his own generation in Spain (even too kind, some critics have objected), and he encouraged young writers and scholars. The public tends to expect social and moral perfection in its famous men. Valera might fail his critics, but he remains basically someone to honor and respect.

ANALYSIS

Juan Valera's constant preoccupation with language and form (not merely in a restricted but also in a spiritual sense); his knowledge of and deep respect for the classics, which he doubted modern authors could surpass; his demand for balance and moderation; his belief in absolute ideals; his rejection of Romantic excesses and imperfections—all bespeak a latter-day classicist. Where he diverges somewhat from classicism is in what could be called the pleasure principle. The aim of art is to please; it has no intrinsic end, moral or instructive. Its goal is beauty alone. Valera derided the ancient Roman Horace's famous precept that art should be at once useful and delightful. Valera's demand, so often heard from nineteenth century writers, was "art for art's sake," a phrase capable of various interpretations and inevitably given them, as often occurs with aesthetic theories.

Valera's most famous pronouncement on his concept of the ideal novel is to be found in the preface to *Pepita Ximenez*:

A pretty novel cannot be a servile, prosaic, common representation of life; a pretty novel should be poetry, not history; it should depict things, not as they are, but more beautiful than they are, casting upon them a light with a certain magical charm.

He disliked the prevailing doctrine of naturalism, enunciated by Émile Zola in France and taken up in Spain by Pardo Bazán and Clarín, which to Valera justified wallowing in things filthy and unpleasant, sexually degraded, morbid, and diseased, in an attempt to show what life was really like, especially for the great masses of the poor.

Valera's word *bonita* (pretty), as opposed to the naturalists' seeming preference for the ugly, must not, however, be understood to justify insipidity or smothering the reader in sweetness and light. Even the rather idyllic *Pepita Ximenez* hints strongly at seduction and presents a sixteen-year-old heroine forced to marry an unlovable old man in his eighties, as well as a bastard hero who breaks his religious vows to marry her. Furthermore, Valera confessed that this early novel echoed his benevolent view of life at the time. His later novels often describe more unpleasant events, tragic failures, broken loves—one novel even features a prostitute as protagonist. Valera knew the seamier side of life and could on occasion depict it. Some of his uncharacteristic short stories (in the 1898 collection *Cuentos y chascarrillos andaluces*) are actually pornographic, but normally, with good classicist reticence, he chose to select aspects of life refined through the sieve of artistry. If the expression "pretty novel" must be taken with a grain of salt, Valera still remains far from Zolaesque naturalism.

Finally, Valera's psychological acumen warrants mention. More than his rather conventional, occasionally clumsy plots and as much as his fine eye for the accurate physical detail, it is his knowledge of the human psyche that lends depth and credibility to his fiction. His characters convince because their creator accurately sounds the wellsprings of their actions. His long life and his experiences around the world served him well.

What term, then, best fits his literary theory and practice? "Neoclassicism" as well as any, yet his predilection for heroes that mirror, if imperfectly, his own character and events from his own life, heroines who embody his ideals of womanhood, his love of outer nature, his sensuous side—all indicate Romanticist. His mocking, detached, worldly, rational attitude toward life suggests eighteenth century rationalism. He can reflect paganism and Christianity in turn. He really is not like any other Spanish writer of his day: a genius unto himself. Many critics have foundered trying to categorize the elusive quality of his literary production.

Valera, who was seemingly born to write, who took up the career of diplomacy as a livelihood rather than as a vocation, who published a volume of poetry at age twenty, who, in high school, read extensively from such literary masters as Voltaire, William Shakespeare, and Sir Walter Scott, still failed to compose anything in the field of the novel—his one real claim to greatness—until well into maturity. He had written criticism since 1853 and a second volume of poetry in 1858, helped found two literary reviews, and edited a newspaper between 1859 and 1863, but his first novel began to appear in 1861 in the literary section of his own newspaper. Even then, he abandoned it in midstream. Its main importance lies in its foreshadowing of many of the characteristics of his later fiction, from 1874 on.

To understand what Valera was offering his public, it is necessary to say a word about the status of the nineteenth century Spanish novel. In the 1830's and 1840's, Spain was copying the Romantic novel of the school of Scott, but not the social novels of Charles Dickens or William Makepeace Thackeray. Eighteenth century Spanish literature had not enjoyed the richness of French and English literature of the period, particularly in the field of the novel. Miguel de Cervantes' *Don Quixote de la Mancha* (1605, 1615), often termed the first modern novel and a unique masterpiece, had had no worthy off-spring. Hence, Spain's reentry into the mainstream of the European novel came about by a different route.

In the 1830's, a popular literary form was a little local-color sketch describing regional customs—a country fair, peasant dances, a religious holiday, and the like—which in Spain is called *costumbrismo* (*costumbres* meaning "customs" in Spanish). The *costumbrista* format permitted realism but downplayed reality's drab side. In 1849, the writer Fernán Caballero was the first to combine a group of related *costumbrista* sketches with a story line into a novel, *La gaviota* (1856; *The Seagull*, 1864). From this badly flawed effort, the Spanish regional novel of the second half of the nineteenth century was born, destined to produce a distinguished group of practitioners: Pereda, Pérez Galdós, Pedro Antonio, and Valera himself, among others.

MARIQUITA Y ANTONIO

Mariquita y Antonio is such a regional novel, a genre to which Valera was to turn again and again. The beautiful, capable heroine Mariquita is the niece of the keeper of the pension (depicted realistically, even humorously) where the law student, Antonio, is staying. The latter is hardly the serious type. He gambles, indulges in love affairs, composes poetry. He is, in short, the amorous Valera as young law student (1840-1844), in the same city (autobiographical elements do not prove uncommon in Valera's later work). Improbably, Mariquita is kidnapped, and the story breaks off before one learns whether Antonio, for all of his taking her disappearances to heart, really loved her. Originally, his aim simply had been to seduce this woman whom he considered beneath him socially.

Valera lost interest in or could not find time to continue the work. The reader cannot feel any deep sense of loss: The novel, at least in the chapters at hand, is not well developed; the heroine, who is, as usual with Valera, the principal character, is not clearly defined; there is on the face of it no good reason for the melodramatic kidnapping. It would not have been easy to rectify these flaws in

the unfinished section, as perhaps Valera realized in abandoning his project.

PEPITA XIMENEZ

Valera's next attempt at full-length fiction, *Pepita Ximenez*, almost certainly his finest work, became an immediate success and has remained a staple of Spanish literature ever since. The author was almost fifty; he had spent more than thirty years polishing his craft when he sent his first completed novel to press. He had lived in Madrid, Lisbon, Rio de Janeiro, Dresden, St. Petersburg, and Frankfurt; he was an experienced diplomat; he had had several love affairs and had already been married for six years. This novel was hardly the first fruit of an apprentice in literature or in the business of life itself.

The setting is once again Andalusia. The structure is classically tight, almost too intricate. Section 1 is titled "Letters from My Nephew," given the reader by the dean of a religious seminary, the uncle of the protagonist, Luis. Section 2, "Paralipómenos" ("Supplementary Revelations"), is followed by the coda "Letters from My Brother." The Greek title for section 2, many occasional phrases in the text itself, references in the preface and elsewhere in his writings approving of an idealized depiction of reality, and his meticulous attention to form and style all hint at Valera's leanings toward classicism. He shows an equal love and appreciation for and knowledge of the sixteenth century Spanish mystics, such as Saint Teresa de Ávila and Saint John of the Cross. Robert Lott, in his *Language and Psychology in "Pepita Jiménez"* (1970), has revealed the extent of Valera's debt to both of these mystics, from whom he borrowed many ideas and much religious terminology (here sometimes used profanely). Lott has also analyzed Valera's style, a carefully balanced mixture of Spanish Golden Age turns of phrase, archaisms, and grammar with nineteenth century refinements.

Luis de Vargas, twenty-two years of age, reared by his uncle in the relative seclusion of a religious seminary, returns to visit his worldly-wise father, a local political power and small-town leader, before taking his final vows as a priest. He happens to be illegitimate and as a result experiences a sense of guilt mixed with pride in the brilliant future he envisages for himself, converting heathens in faraway lands. Valera suggests that Luis is only falsely devout; he intends to achieve union with God through effecting salvation for others, not by mortifying himself before Him. In short, he is a dubious candidate for the rigors of missionary life.

This proud, naïve young man meets the irresistible Pepita Ximenez, one in a long line of Valera's vivacious Andalusian heroines, beautiful, charming, clever, an idealized version of most men's concept of the perfect wife. The formula may vary on occasion: mistress, not wife, her perfection perhaps flawed, not merely clever but scheming. Rarely, however, are these women actually antipathetic, Pepita least of all. She had already been married at the age of sixteen to a very elderly, unprepossessing moneylender and is now a widow of only twenty. Luis, as is clearly shown in letters to his uncle, gradually becomes infatuated with her. The uncle warns him to break short his visit. Obviously, Luis will not. His attempts to explain away his newfound attraction for Pepita are scarcely convincing (nor are they meant to be), and his naïveté in failing to diagnose his love borders on the incredible, but he is such a likable chap, she so desirable, that from the very start the reader wants him to abandon his priestly vocation and opt for marriage. Thus, his growing worldliness, his pleasure in the sensual beauty of the Andalusian countryside, his pride in finding that he can ride a horse well, his gradual if reluctant feeling of congeniality with his father, and his final spiritual downfall (which outraged certain Spanish religious conservatives) are all quite palatable.

This downfall, fittingly occurring on Saint John's Eve—that is, Midsummer's Eve, from time immemorial devoted to merrymaking and amorous escapades the world over—is spectacular. Luis announces to Pepita his decision to give her up and return to the seminary. There is a tearful scene in her parlor; she runs into her bedroom; he follows her; and when he emerges some time later, he has obviously succumbed. The language—Valera is rarely crude, and certainly not in this novel—is oblique but realistic, the whole scene effective, even somewhat humorous. Neither author nor reader thinks Heaven has lost a sinner. Rather, an innocent young man has grown up. Now considering himself in a position to retaliate more properly, he returns to the casino where he had earlier been forced to endure insults to Pepita's morals uttered by a rejected suitor, challenges him to a duel, and nearly kills him. The former seminarian's transforma-

tion is now complete. He becomes his father's son and marries Pepita. The obligatory *costumbrista* village wedding scene concludes the novel.

This bare outline cannot do more than hint at the felicities of style, the charm of the local color (if not as pronounced here as in some of Valera's later novels, still quite in evidence), the author's psychological perspicacity, and his feeling for the beauty of outer nature used to symbolize Luis's increasingly secular love. There may be countless novels more powerful than this one, but few more captivating or better crafted. The reader's joy echoes the writer's own; as Valera said, it came when he felt most healthy, optimistic, and warm toward the whole world. He added, "Unfortunately, it will not happen again."

LAS ILUSIONES DEL DOCTOR FAUSTINO

No sooner had Valera published *Pepita Ximenez* serially in the distinguished *Revista de España* than the first installments of his next novel, *Las ilusiones del doctor Faustino*, started to appear in the same magazine, in October, 1874. Much longer than any of his other novels, it is at the same time philosophically his most ambitious. Valera fully intended the allusive name he bestowed on his protagonist. "Although," he wrote,

I am not very fond of symbols or allegories . . . Dr. Faustino has something of the symbolic or allegorical about him . . . a man for a whole contemporary generation . . . Dr. Faust in miniature, without magic, without a devil . . . a composite of the vices, ambitions, dreams, scepticism, disbelief, and longings that afflicted the youth of my day.

In a word, Faustino is a Romantic, one of those who embodies "useless knowledge, political ambitions, aristocratic prejudices," according to Valera, who considered his creation his most real literary achievement. It is nevertheless debatable whether this petty Faust is strong enough to support so lofty a philosophical superstructure, even if Christopher Marlowe's original was equally lightweight. It is Johann Wolfgang von Goethe's later incarnation that possesses the grandeur more naturally inviting comparison.

Clarín, Valera's fellow novelist and a percipient critic as well, considering the novel one of the most important in nineteenth century Spanish literature, compared it to Gustave Flaubert's *L'Éducation sentimentale* (1869; *A Sentimental Education*, 1898). Frédéric, like Faustino, is indeed a Romantic weakling, buffeted by the fates of his time, but Flaubert did not ask him to stand for a Romantic Everyman as Valera expected of Faustino. Few critics today would rank Valera's novel very high, much less in a class with Flaubert's counterpart.

The plot involves most of Faustino's life. It begins with his days as a young law student at the University of Granada (another of the autobiographical details so numerous in Valera's fiction), from which he is graduated without having burned much midnight oil.

He hopes for an important career in Madrid in law, the government, or perhaps journalism, but realizes that his talents are not matched by the necessary wealth. Marriage with his rather well-to-do cousin, Costanza, fails to materialize. Back in his small hometown, he takes up with Rosita, though considering her beneath him. They spend a night together, but he abandons her for María, who turns out to be the illegitimate daughter of a bandit by whom Faustino is later kidnapped. In all fairness to Valera, it should be noted that this bit of melodrama is to an extent necessary for the plot, and capture by highwaymen was a recurrent nightmare for Spanish travelers at the time, but the author is never especially felicitous in his handling of action scenes. They rarely ring true or seem well motivated. This one at least keeps the hero out of town long enough to let Rosita, the woman scorned, have her father foreclose on the property of Faustino's mother, who dies from worry and sorrow.

Faustino moves to Madrid and, by now middle-aged, is eking out a living as a subordinate government bureaucrat. María arrives in the city with a sixteen-year-old daughter; María and Faustino marry. He should at last find success and happiness with the only woman who really loves him, but he dissipates his opportunities and, worse, resumes his old affair with cousin Costanza. Rosita, ever vindictive, avenges herself on the man who jilted her by telling his wife. María dies of sorrow; Faustino kills himself. This weak Romantic, suffering from what a later generation of Spanish writers at the turn of the twentieth century came to call *abulia* ("lack of willpower," "apathy," after the psychological term "aboulia"), a disease afflicting the whole country in their eyes, falls victim to his own flawed character and the faults of his day: bad education, political chaos, aristocratic social climbing.

Is Faustino really Valera's alter ego? They had the same education, the same trouble in deciding on a career. Valera eventually became internationally famous, but in 1874 he was only beginning to find himself as a writer, and successes in his diplomatic career were balanced by some notable failures. He quite likely saw himself in many ways as another Romantic Faustino. At the least, his is a cautionary tale, with himself an example for those who could read between the lines.

Some of the early parts of the story recall the unfinished *Mariquita y Antonio*, while Cyrus C. DeCoster, in *Bibliografía crítica de Juan Valera* (1970), notes a similarity between the theme and the character of Faustino and those of a projected novel Valera titled "Currito the Optimist," about a spendthrift who tried to make a pact with the Devil. DeCoster dates the few extant pages of the manuscript as probably early 1850's. Valera's plots tend toward repetition; his male characters are often himself as a youth or idealized, while his women are cast much in the same mold. His early creation, Pepita, for example, is replicated in *Juanita la larga* near the very end of his career. Regardless of its originality, the novel is at best only moderately successful. The plot suffers from imbalance: Most of the book deals with a very few months; the next twenty years are merely summarized; then the story again slows to set the stage for Faustino's suicide. Finally, the philosophical contents do not fit comfortably into the dimensions of the plot, and Faustino seems ill at ease carrying them.

COMMANDER MENDOZA

Commander Mendoza started to appear serially in 1876. Unlike Valera's other long fiction, with the exception of his one historical novel, it lacks a contemporary setting. The novel is set in the eighteenth century; Mendoza is a sort of French *philosophe*; a rationalistic Deist; a skeptic; a believer in the infinite perfectibility of humans, in freedom and justice; a sensualist with Condillac; and perforce, another persona of his author. Middle-aged, now wealthy, and disgusted with Spanish atrocities that he has seen committed against the Indians in Peru, where he has made his fortune, he goes to Paris but runs into the French Revolution, equally marred by inhuman excesses. He returns to his native Andalusia, to

Villabermeja, the same small fictional town in which Valera had located some of the action of *Las ilusiones del doctor Faustino*. This place, under one name or another, turns up in most of Valera's novels, being an idealization of Doña Mencía, a hill-town where the author had spent a good part of his early life.

An equally strong role in the novel is played by the formidable Doña Blanca, seduced many years before in Peru by Mendoza himself. Soon after this affair, she married; with her husband, she has also returned to Villabermeja, leading a life of exemplary expiation in a world she views as cursed with moral evil, a cross to be borne on the road to eventual salvation. She has reared her daughter, Clara, strictly, in an effort to shelter her from a mistake like her own. The daughter is Mendoza's, though the husband does not suspect.

Insistent that Clara should not unjustly inherit her husband's estate, Doña Blanca plans to marry her off to his rightful heir, an elderly, undesirable cousin. Mendoza sees through her plan and, though admitting that Clara should not inherit unjustly, still cannot bear to see her married to the old cousin (compare Pepita's old husband in Valera's earlier novel). Clara meanwhile decides to enter a convent, because she cannot have the man whom she really loves. Mendoza solves the dilemma by posing as the father of the woman whom the cousin is currently courting, giving her a generous dowry that the cousin will receive in lieu of Clara's inheritance. Before these improbable subterfuges can be effected, Mendoza must soften Doña Blanca's indomitable will, for she remains adamant, at first that Clara and her cousin wed, then—when that solution proves untenable—that she enter the convent. Doña Blanca suffers a stroke; on her deathbed, she forgives Mendoza and releases Clara from her vows so that she can marry Carlos, the young man whom she has loved all along.

Doña Blanca, though absent in person from most of the story, remains a spiritual force throughout, and when she does appear, she easily bests her antagonists. The only likely solution was to have her removed from the stage, as Valera did. The story ends with the marriage of Clara and Carlos and, less credibly, with Mendoza, who has been having many long discussions of family problems with his young niece, Lucía, finding that they share a mutual affection. The concept of the union of old age with youth, already found in *Pepita Ximenez* and in the aborted marriage of Clara and her cousin, reappears in Valera's next novel, *Don Braulio*, and in *Juanita la larga* almost twenty years later.

The plot complications in *Commander Mendoza* are badly contrived, the happy ending is barely convincing, and the long contest of wills between a stubborn, overly possessive, dominant woman and a tolerant yet persistent male adversary is the sort of thing that Spaniards perhaps even more than other European readers of that day accepted but that today seems childish at best and at worst risible. It must be remembered, however, that those drawn battles between moral imperatives were a commonplace of Victorian fiction.

If the plot is handled somewhat clumsily, the characters come off better. Mendoza is attractive and credible. Doña Blanca, though shown to be harsh and domineering, is treated nobly. Mendoza's friend, the village priest, Jacinto, is admirably humanistic, acting as a worthy foil for the skeptical protagonist. Lucía represents Valera's usual vivacious and charming young female lead. The story possesses a tragic undertone that lends depth, although the contrived happy ending mitigates it, as do the obligatory bits of local color that Valera almost always inserts. The considered judgment of most of the modern critics gives *Commander Mendoza* qualified approval as a good novel but certainly not a great one.

DON BRAULIO

The following season, Valera produced another novel, *Don Braulio*. The original title, *Pasarse de listo*, is a colloquial Spanish idiom meaning something like "to be too clever for one's own good." The protagonist, Braulio, another study in frustration, has indeed outsmarted himself. Talented, bright, and lazy (compare *Las illusiones del doctor Faustino* only three years before), Braulio remains in his mediocre position with the Department of the Treasury. Valera, as the omniscient narrator, observes that his hero is mistaken: Brains are not enough to ensure success in government positions; it takes drive and character as well. Braulio unjustly suspects his beautiful young wife (not half his age—a recurring theme with Valera) of having an affair with a nobleman and commits suicide. Actually, the Count is courting Braulio's sister-in-law, whom he later weds. Braulio's widow remarries, to a childhood friend. Though all the principal characters act irresponsibly, all but Braulio achieve a measure of happiness.

Although this is Valera's shortest novel, it is still fleshed out with authorial digressions. There are also *costumbrismo* sketches (the bullfight, for example, a common set piece with many Spanish novelists). Andalusian country life is compared with the mores of Madrid, to the detriment of the latter. Valera paints a black picture of the capital, the idle-rich Count, and his coterie of friends.

DOÑA LUZ

In the late 1870's, Valera was averaging a novel a year, and *Doña Luz* appeared on schedule. The author complained that serial publication had hurt his previous work, *Don Braulio*, a fact that writers as great as Dickens and Honoré de Balzac had already learned. The demands of story segments that can stand on their own, with enough excitement to hold reader interest and satisfy magazine editors bent on increasing circulation, force compromises, pander to lowered standards of taste, and control the flow of the story line, often to its disadvantage. Valera had expensive tastes, however, as well as family obligations: *Doña Luz* began in *Revista contemporánea*, in the fall of 1878.

With this story, Valera returns to the problem of secular versus religious love. Doña Luz, the proud but illegitimate daughter of a Madrid nobleman, elects to remain a spinster and live as her poverty prescribes. She strikes up a warm Platonic friendship with Enrique, an older priest, who has come back to Andalusia to regain his health, shattered while he was a missionary in the Philippines. Late in the story, her mother dies, and she is suddenly rich. She is courted by a local politician, marries him only to find that he was after her money, and leaves him. The priest, meanwhile, realizes that he actually loves Doña Luz. His health further undermined by the ravages of his concealed passion, he takes to his bed, finally in a coma. Sitting beside him, Doña Luz bestows a kiss. He dies soon after. As one of his heirs, she is privileged to read his private diary, in which he confesses his criminal love. Remorseful for having unintentionally aroused his passion, yet flattered, she will name her unborn child after him.

In his preface, Valera claimed that the novel teaches a lesson: to guard against the possibility of erotic sin. Was he serious, or was he merely attempting to avoid the kind of criticism that Roman Catholic conservatives heaped on *Pepita Ximenez* four years earlier? His sympathies undeniably lay with Doña Luz and her priest, facing a love whose only solution was the latter's death, but in none of his books did he ever go so far as to depict a priest actually succumbing to sexual temptation, as Anatole France was to do in *Thaïs* (some ten years later and as Zola had already done in 1875 with *La Faute de l'abbé Mouret* (*Albine: Or, The Abbé's Temptation*, 1882; better known as *The Sin of Father Mouret*, 1904, 1969). If Luis opted for the secular life in *Pepita Ximenez*, he had not taken his final vows. Conscience permitting, he was free to break them and marry. Enrique was not. Nevertheless, Valera consistently preached the basic rightness of earthly love.

A larger point involves the matter of "preaching" in the first place. Like many European novelists of his day, Valera professed avoidance of didacticism, yet *Doña Luz* comes rather close to preaching. To be sure, the many nineteenth century novelists who abjured preachments in favor of art for art's sake did not always follow their own advice strictly. Indeed, their favorite technique of the omniscient narrator favors commentary and judgment. Valera is really following a tradition at least as ancient as Vergil: the writer as seer, bringer of light to the public. The particular subject he chooses, priestly versus secular love, has long been a mainstay of Catholic Spanish fiction and drama, from the seventeenth century plays of Pedro Calderón de la Barca and Tirso de Molina to the twentieth century existentialist novels of Miguel de Unamuno y Jugo. The reading public was conditioned to expect it, whatever stand Valera might choose to take.

Luckily, the heavy religious moral tone of the book is leavened with greater than usual attention paid by Valera to descriptions of village life. Next to *Juanita la larga*, not destined to appear until seventeen years later, *Doña Luz* is Valera's most strongly costumbristic novel, with its detailed scenes of the life, dwellings, customs, and character of the villagers. The town is here named Villafría, but as always, it remains a composite of the places where Valera lived out his younger years.

In the doomed priest Enrique, Valera created one of his few really fine male protagonists, a truly tragic figure deeply appealing to the reader; his *Doña Luz* is an interesting, well-rounded portrait as well. Among secondary characters, her father's former overseer and Enrique's uncle, the unscrupulous Don Acisclo, is a minor masterpiece, a picturesque old scoundrel whose clever financial schemes have drained Luz's father dry and filled his own coffers. Any artistic problems with the novel involve Valera's usual shortcomings. He narrates and describes well, his style is admirable, his characters incisively drawn, his psychology penetrating, but his plots are artificial and contrived. Events occur because the plots demand them.

JUANITA LA LARGA

Improbably, *Juanita la larga* (the word *larga* also suggesting something of the Amazon), which appeared serially, like his earlier novels, had the verve and charm of Valera's youthful period. Indeed, the novel is almost as fine a production as *Pepita Ximenez*, though Valera was in his early seventies at the time of its publication. It is another idyll of life in his beloved small-town Andalusia. His earlier depictions of this milieu are often darkened by thematic profundities—religious, economic, and social clouds on the horizon. It is a simple love story, grinding no ideological axes. In outlook, intent, tone, and conclusion, it compares with *Pepita Ximenez*, his first great work, dating back twenty years. It might seem to differ in one substantial respect in that Pepita and Luis face the formidable barrier of the latter's priestly vocation. Actually, the reader knows very well that the barrier is paper-thin. No one really expects Luis to withstand for long Pepita's charms or to be shorn of his prize. The novels that follow, however, turn more somber. Their problems of religion and social ambition and their character flaws raise truly resistant walls. Happy outcomes are no longer certain. With *Juanita la larga*, once again, and for one last time, the weather turns fair.

Juana and her daughter, Juanita, live in the little southern town of Villalegre. Significantly, the name Valera has coined for it means "Happytown" (in contrast to Villafría, "Coldtown," his name for the locale of the more somber *Doña Luz*). Like the Villabermeja ("Redtown") of several of his other stories, it is modeled on the Doña Mencía of his earliest days. There is something of the Edenic myth, the withdrawal from Paradise into the evil big city and the return, sometimes unrealiz-

able, sometimes fatally too late, in Valera's longing, not only novelistically but in real life as well, for the simple country life of his youth. The old Valera manages to return home through the persona of Paco López, fifty-three years old and in love with Juanita, thirty-six years his junior.

Juanita, as is so common with Valera's characters, is illegitimate. She and her mother, Juana, are of the less favored class, the latter earning a good living as cook, seamstress, and midwife. Juanita is proud for all of her lowly birth, beautiful, energetic, sturdy, and sufficiently strong-willed that when she realizes her love for the older Paco, nothing will prevent her getting him, even if she has to knock another suitor down, kneel on him, and choke him until he agrees to support her own suit. Nor is she above using the same suitor to make Paco jealous. There are complications, however spurious. Paco's daughter, Inés, a snob married into one of the town's upper-crust families, opposes her father's wedding out of his own class. She is domineering, a meddler into the affairs of the whole town, miserly, and speciously mystical. This unsympathetic woman is in league with a narrowly orthodox priest (the first time Valera has presented a basically unlikable man of the cloth). Another repugnant character is Inés's immoral, profligate nobleman husband, given his just deserts at the story's end when he becomes senile. No force, no characters, however evil or mean, will prevail against the marriage. Juanita and Paco are happily wed at the conclusion of the book.

No more than in his other novels is Valera's success in this one primarily the result of a strong story line. The plot is reasonably credible, simple enough not to detract from the reader's joy in cheering for the protagonists. Inés's opposition is determined but destined for failure. The plot is adequate, no more, but things work out satisfactorily. Valera himself, in the dedicatory preface, writes of his concept of the novel in general and of *Juanita la larga* as well, "I do not know whether this book is a novel or not. I have written it very artlessly, combining recollections of my earliest youth." In all fairness, his novel is not merely a series of costumbristic sketches or youthful personal reminiscences held together by a narrative thread, for all of its heavy burden of *costumbrismo*.

Even more oddly, in the selfsame preface, Valera characterizes his novel, which most would call something close to a pastoral idyll, as a true copy of reality. He even goes on to speak of it as a photographic reproduction and calls himself more historian than novelist. He would seem to be breaking bread with the naturalistic school of Zola, who called himself a literary scientist and recorder of truths, or at least to be enlisting in the ranks of realists such as Flaubert and Balzac. Could Valera be saying that reality and the realists' method need not be applied exclusively to scenes of brutality, unpleasantness, stark passion, and the like, or is he simply using the term "reality" in a different sense? *Juanita la larga* contains more *costumbrismo* than any of his other novels. Country life, the many local dishes, lovingly and accurately described, local deformations of the Spanish language, the wines, legends, festivals, the Holy Week procession—all of these and more take up a good part of the novel. This attention to the details of regional peculiarities and distinctions necessarily helps bind the characters and their actions to their environment, a fact in keeping with the general tenets of realism and naturalism. Nevertheless, the tone of the book remains determinedly antirealist.

A word, too, must be said about the author's charmingly light, humorous touch. Valera always displays an ironic temper, a distancing of writer from the problems of his own characters, the double vision that allows the creator, even one given, like Valera, to autobiographical incidents and to characters who to some extent represent himself, to mock, however gently, their trials, tribulations, and shortcomings. It is what keeps him from falling into the Romantics' solipsistic trap. Never is his touch lighter than in this novel of his late years. He can let Juanita make fun of the very relationship he has made possible: her youth and Paco's middle age. He can write a wonderful scene in which the despondent lover escapes to the hills and contemplates suicide but fills his knapsack with meat and bread to avoid starving. Valera's customary mockery has become true humor.

Juanita la larga and *Pepita Ximenez* are the works on which Valera's reputation will continue to rest—his contribution to the impressive reemergence of the novel in Spain in the later years of the nineteenth century.

Armand E. Singer

OTHER MAJOR WORKS

SHORT FICTION: *Cuentos y diálogos*, 1882; *Algo de todo*, 1883; *Cuentos, diálogos y fantasías*, 1887; *Cuentos y chascarrillos andaluces*, 1898 (with Narciso Campillo, Conde de las Navas, and Doctor Thebussem); *De varios colores*, 1898.

PLAYS: *Tentativas dramáticas*, pb. 1879; *Teatro*, pb. 1908.

POETRY: *Ensayos poéticas*, 1844; *Poesías*, 1858; *Canciones, romances, y poemas*, 1885.

NONFICTION: *De la naturaleza y carácter de la novela*, 1860; *Estudios críticos sobre literatura, política, y costumbres de nuestros días*, 1864; *Crítica literaria*, 1864-1871; *Disertaciones y juicios literarios*, 1878; *Nuevos estudios críticos*, 1883; *Apuntes sobre el nuevo arte de escribir novelas*, 1887; *Carta al señor don Juan Valera*, 1888; *Cartas americanas*, 1889; *Nuevas cartas americanas*, 1890; *Las mujeres y las academias*, 1891; *Ventura de la Vega: Estudio biográfico crítico*, 1891; *Ecos argentinos*, 1901.

TRANSLATION: *Poesía y arte en los árabes en España y Sicilia*, 1867, 1868, 1871 (of Adolf F. Schack's nonfiction study *Poesie und Kunst der Araber in Spanien und Sicilien*).

EDITED TEXTS: *Florilegio de cuentos, leyendas y tradiciones vulgares*, 1860; *Florilegio de poesías castellanas del siglo XIX*, 1902-1903 (5 volumes).

MISCELLANEOUS: *Obras completas*, 1905-1935 (53 volumes); *Obras completas*, 1947-1958 (3 volumes).

BIBLIOGRAPHY

DeCoster, Cyrus Cole. *Juan Valera*. New York: Twayne, 1974. An informative biography. Contains an overview of Valera's life and literary career and analyzes the literary characters and themes of his fiction. Includes a bibliography.

Ford, J. D. M. *Main Currents of Spanish Literature*. 1919. Reprint. New York: Biblio and Tannen, 1968. In these critical lectures delivered at the Lowell Institute in Boston, Valera's novels are considered high points of Spanish American literature. Includes a bibliographical note.

Franz, Thomas R. *Valera in Dialogue = In Dialogue with Valera: A Novelist's Work in Conversation with That of His Contemporaries and Successors*. New

York: Peter Lang, 2000. Chronicles the debate between Valera and his contemporaries and chief rivals, Benito Pérez Galdós and Leopoldo Alas, over the aesthetics of Spanish realist fiction, and how this debate influenced the later writing of Miguel de Unamuno y Jugo and Ramón María del Valle-Inclán.

Lott, Robert E. *Language and Psychology in "Pepita Jimenez."* Urbana: University of Illinois Press, 1970. A well-regarded study of language and psychology in the novel *Pepita Ximenez*. The first part is an analysis of language, style, and rhetorical devices. The second section is a psychological examination of characters.

Taylor, Teresia Langford. *The Representation of Women in the Novels of Juan Valera: A Feminist Critique*. New York: Peter Lang, 1997. Taylor's feminist literary critique of Valera's novels focuses on his representation of women and the underlying patriarchal ideology of his works. Includes bibliographical references and an index.

Trimble, Robert. *Chaos Burning on My Brow: Don Juan Valera in His Novels*. San Bernardino, Calif.: Borgo Press, 1995. A critical study of Valera's novels. Includes an index and a bibliography.

Turner, Harriet, and Adelaida López de Martínez, eds. *The Cambridge Companion to the Spanish Novel: From 1600 to the Present*. New York: Cambridge University Press, 2003. Numerous references to Valera in this historical survey of the Spanish novel, but the most extensive consideration of his work is found in two chapters: "The Regional Novel: Evolution and Consolation" by Alison Sinclair and "The Realist Novel" by Harriet Turner.

Valle, José del. "Historical Linguistics and Cultural History: The Polemic Between Rufino José Cuervo and Juan Valera." In *The Battle over Spanish Between 1800 and 2000: Language Ideologies and Hispanic Intellectuals*, edited by Valle and Luis Gabriel-Stheeman. New York: Routledge, 2002. Valle's essay recounts the debate between Valera and Rufino José Cuervo, a nineteenth century Colombian writer and linguist, over issues pertaining to the Spanish language. The debate among intellectuals of the time shaped national identity and Hispanic culture.

RAMÓN MARÍA DEL VALLE-INCLÁN

Born: Villanueva de Arosa, Spain; October 28, 1866

Died: Santiago de Compostela, Spain; January 5, 1936

Also known as: Ramón José Simón Valle Peña

PRINCIPAL LONG FICTION

Cara de Dios, 1899

Sonatas, 1902-1905 (*The Pleasant Memoirs of the Marquis de Bradomín: Four Sonatas*, 1924; includes *Sonata de otoño*, 1902 [*Autumn Sonata*]; *Sonata de estío*, 1903 [*Summer Sonata*]; *Sonata de primavera*, 1904 [*Spring Sonata*]; *Sonata de invierno*, 1905 [*Winter Sonata*])

Flor de santidad, 1904

La guerra carlista, 1908-1909 (includes *Los cruzados de la causa*, 1908; *El resplandor de la hoguera*, 1909; and *Gerifaltes de antaño*, 1909)

Tirano Banderas: Novela de tierra caliente, 1926 (*The Tyrant: A Novel of Warm Lands*, 1929)

El ruedo ibérico, 1927-1958 (includes *La corte de los milagros*, 1927; *Viva mi dueño*, 1928; and *Baza de espadas*, 1958 [serialized 1932])

OTHER LITERARY FORMS

Ramón María del Valle-Inclán (BAHL-yay-eeng-KLAHN) was a highly innovative dramatist as well as an accomplished novelist. His best-known and most influential plays include the three *comedias bárbaras*—*Águila de blasón* (pb. 1907), *Divinas palabras* (pb.

1920; *Divine Words*, 1968), and *Luces de Bohemia* (pb. 1924; *Bohemian Lights*, 1967)—and the three plays that are included in *Martes de carnaval* (1930; Shrove Tuesday carnival). He also published several collections of short stories, among them *Femeninas* (1895; feminine vignettes), *Corte de amor* (1903; court of love), *Jardín umbrío* (1914; garden of shadows), and three volumes of poetry that were collected and republished in 1930 as *Claves líricas* (lyrical clues).

Other work includes *La lámpara maravillosa* (1916; *The Lamp of Marvels*, 1986), an aesthetic statement written in poetic prose; translations from the Portuguese and Italian; and numerous critical essays and prologues. Many of these short pieces have been collected and republished by individual scholars, but there is not yet a complete edition of Valle-Inclán's writing, one that would contain all of his essays, letters, and interviews, as well as the variants of the many works that were serialized in contemporary newspapers and magazines before their publication as books. The series of his collected works that Valle-Inclán initiated in 1913 (*Opera omnia*, 1913-1930) is not complete, nor is the two-volume edition *Obras completas*, which was first published posthumously in 1944. Espasa Calpe in Madrid has begun to publish critical editions of Valle-Inclán's major plays and novels in the Cla icos Castellanos series; *Bohemian Lights*, *The Tyrant*, and *La guerra carlista* have appeared.

ACHIEVEMENTS

Ramón María del Valle-Inclán's life and work have occasioned considerable controversy, much of it provoked by his eccentric personal manner, but there is no doubt about his reputation as one of Spain's greatest authors: He is highly respected as a brilliant, versatile writer who was able simultaneously to ridicule and renovate Spanish prose, thereby linking an acute awareness of Spain's diminished historical position with the quality of its language and literature.

Especially at the beginning of his career, his careful attention to form and style led many critics to place Valle-Inclán's work with that of the Spanish-American *Modernismo* poets rather than with that of his Spanish contemporaries. These Spanish writers (including Miguel de Unamuno y Jugo, Pío Baroja, Azorín, Jacinto Benavente y Martínez, and Antonio Machado), who are usually referred to as the *generación del 1898*, or Generation of '98, seemed more explicitly concerned with revitalizing Spain's literature and self-esteem. The richness of Valle-Inclán's early stories and novels was recognized and praised, but he was reprimanded by critics such as José Ortega y Gasset, who found the work overly precious and wished that it were less mannered and more concerned with human, down-to-earth themes.

As Valle-Inclán matured as a writer, his work did, in fact, change considerably. The primacy of his aesthetic considerations never lessened, but his use of irony intensified and redirected itself; in the *esperpentos*, his moral, social, political, and historical preoccupations became increasingly explicit. After World War I, he was recognized as a highly committed writer, and he has come to be considered one of the most significant writers of the Generation of '98. This recognition did not, however, mean that his work was fully comprehended and accepted during his lifetime. On the contrary, for both political and aesthetic reasons, much of it was not accessible to the general public. His theater, for example, was not widely represented; some of his plays were banned for their satiric content, and others were thought to be unpresentable because of their experimental, avant-garde nature. For the most part, this inaccessibility continued through the Spanish Civil War and the Francisco Franco years until 1966, when, with Valle-Inclán's centennial, a serious reevaluation of his work began in Europe and the United States as well as in Spain. There remains a great deal of editorial and interpretive work awaiting Valle-Inclán scholars.

Valle-Inclán's plays have been edited and performed in Spain and abroad, his presence in contemporary Spanish literature is increasingly evident, and the overall unity of his work is becoming more and more apparent. Because only a few of his books have been translated into English, his North American reputation is limited, but his influence on modern Spanish American literature, especially on the novel, is considerable.

BIOGRAPHY

Ramón María del Valle-Inclán was born Ramón José Simón Valle Peña in Villanueva de Arosa, Pontevedra, Galicia, Spain, on October 28, 1866. His father, Ramón

Valle Bermúdez, was an amateur writer and a seaman. Both of his parents belonged to distinguished families; it was from their names that he created his authorial name and the aristocratic titles he bestowed on himself: Ramón María del Valle-Inclán y Montenegro, Marqués del Valle, Vixconde de Viexín, and Señor del Caramiñal. These were names that also reflected his ties to Galicia, a region that is still known for its myths and legends, for the survival of its Celtic, pagan substratum, and for the rural, medieval ambience that characterizes both the many tiny farms of its mountainous interior and the small ports—such as Villanueva de Arosa—that dot its rocky coast. The landscape and the culture are often likened to those of Ireland and northern England, and their stamp on Valle-Inclán's work was strong and lasting. From his earliest writing, he seemed to identify both with Galicia's rural, oral tradition and with that of its declining aristocracy.

Ramón María del Valle-Inclán. (Roger Viollet/Getty Images)

The Galician language also survives in Valle-Inclán's work, for although he wrote only a few poems in his regional tongue, he infused Spanish with the Galician vocabulary, syntax, and tone. Like other writers of his generation who were not born in central Spain, he brought a critical vision to bear on the crisis confronting the nation; unlike most of his contemporaries, however, his harshness toward Castile never softened. He lived a large part of his life outside Galicia but continued to return and to stay for varying lengths of time.

Valle-Inclán first left Galicia in 1890, when he went to Madrid. He had studied law for two years in Santiago de Compostela, but he left the university after the death of his father. Although he had published a few short stories as a student, and he published a few others while he was in Madrid, it was during a trip to Mexico in 1892 that his career as a writer truly began, with the stories and newspaper articles that he wrote and published there. In 1895, after a period of several years in Pontevedra, where the library of one of his father's friends enabled him to read widely in contemporary European literature, he published his first book, *Femeninas*. The following year, he went back to Madrid, where he began to establish himself as a writer. He frequented artists' cafés; made friends with artists, critics, and writers (including the Nicaraguan poet Rubén Darío); and soon acquired a singular reputation for his extravagant bohemian appearance; his highly articulate, witty, and forthright opinions; and his famous lisp.

Because there is no definitive biography of Valle-Inclán and because he deliberately elaborated a complicated and at times contradictory series of anecdotes about his experiences, it is difficult to speak with certainty about many of the details of his life. It is certain, however, that he lived in Madrid from 1896 until 1912. During those years, he lost his right arm after a skirmish with another writer, Manuel Bueno. He published extensively, both fiction and drama, and was active in the theater. There he met the actor Josefina Blanco, whom he married in 1907. In 1910, he accompanied his wife's theater company to South America and in Buenos Aires delivered a series of lectures about aesthetics.

In 1912, Valle-Inclán decided to move his family to Galicia; the first two of his six children had been born, and despite his publications and growing literary reputation, his financial situation was precarious. He continued to live in the north until 1924, although on many occasions he left to travel. In 1916, for example, as a correspondent for the Madrid newspaper *El imparcial*, he journeyed to France and the Allied war fronts. In 1921, at the invitation of the Mexican government, he made his second trip to Mexico, to participate in the centennial celebration of Mexican independence. While he was there, he created no small consternation among the representatives of "Official Spain" by publicly supporting a popular land reform designed to break up large estates, many of which were held by wealthy Spaniards. This outspokenness was consistent with Valle-Inclán's lifelong articulation of his convictions, which were often both controversial and apparently contradictory. His opinions, which would be echoed directly in *The Tyrant*, reflect the increasingly social and political nature of his writing in the years following the trip to France. These were years of intense creative work; in 1920 alone he published four plays, two of which, *Divine Words* and *Bohemian Lights*, are among his finest.

In 1924, Valle-Inclán returned once again to Madrid, where for nearly all the next decade he continued to write prolifically and develop as a writer. Although he was never wealthy, for a time his writing brought economic security as well as considerable esteem. His outspoken comments continued, in particular his opposition to the military dictatorship of General Miguel Primo de Rivera; three of Valle-Inclán's plays were banned by the censors, and in 1929 he spent several days in a Madrid jail. After the dictatorship ended, Valle-Inclán tried unsuccessfully for a seat in the constituent Cortes, representing one of Galicia's districts as a member of one of the newly founded republican parties. The republican government, however, was to honor him with an appointment as director of the Spanish Academy of Fine Arts in Rome, a position he held for almost two years, between 1933 and 1935. During this time, both his financial position and his personal life were difficult; he had divorced his wife, and he was quite ill with health problems that had plagued him for many years. In 1935, he returned to Galicia, where he continued to work on *El ruedo ibérico* and to receive friends at the sanatorium where he was hospitalized until his death from cancer on January 5, 1936.

ANALYSIS

"We are no longer a race of conquerors and theologians, and that fiction always breathes in our ballads and our popular speech." This statement, from *The Lamp of Marvels*, is central to an understanding of Ramón María del Valle-Inclán's novels, for it suggests and synthesizes his most important ideas about the potential of fiction and its position in contemporary Spanish literature and culture. In the first place, there is an unmasking of Spain's self-image, which is described as a false expression frozen in the pretense that Spain is still the imperialist world power it was at the time of the Catholic kings. Such self-deception is dangerous, according to the wise old poet who narrates *The Lamp of Marvels*, particularly because of its effect on Spanish sensibility, which—because of its egotism and lack of perspective—refuses to grapple with significant spiritual and historical issues.

In the second place, the fiction of Spain's importance is shown to be closely linked to its language and literature; instead of expanding to include the linguistic changes it has undergone in the New World, Spanish is rigid and brittle. It insists on the fiction of its own purity, which implies an inappropriate, warped perception of integrity. Furthermore, the literature that could work to renovate language and open perspective is also locked in a dead rhetoric that maintains the lie of Spanish sovereignty: Both popular speech and the ballads, the traditional repositories of spontaneous popular expression, reveal the deterioration of language and an obsessive national pride.

For Valle-Inclán, then, the writer of fiction is linked to the poet as a "visionary" who can break the limits of his or her own sensory perceptions. Although this vision, as it is presented in *The Lamp of Marvels*, does not unlock the secrets of the future, it is able to recognize the complexity of the present, to perceive and present an incident—or an instant—from multiple points of view. It is clearly linked to the irony that characterizes Valle-Inclán's work from his earliest stories, as well as to the aesthetic and artistic perspectives that he enumerated in the three *esperpentos* of *Martes de carnaval*.

The world, Valle-Inclán explained, can be witnessed with reverence, on one's knees, as if events and characters were larger than life; it can also be seen eye-to-eye; and it can be watched from above, with distance and even with disdain. Although each of these attitudes can be said to predominate at one time or another in Valle-Inclán's work, the aesthetics presented in *The Lamp of Marvels* suggest that the ideal fiction has something of each: A certain distancing is necessary to break free of traditional perspective, but in the same way that an excess of awe leads one to "wallow" in emotions, extreme distancing can lead to overabstraction and a lack of feeling. The nature of language, which is always rooted in the "earth" of human feelings, is, when perfected by poetry, a link between the two extremes that hold them both in a kind of dynamic stillness or insight, which the poet calls "aesthetic quietism."

This aesthetic experience or principle is valid for both Valle-Inclán's fiction and his theater, for even though he was well aware of their differences and distinct possibilities, he continually explored the boundaries and relations between them. In his early work, this exploration includes the use of dramatic settings in his novels whereby characters and situations are presented in a series of tableaux, as if they were on stage. Ambience, gesture, and the spoken word are always important, and even in the first-person narrative of *The Pleasant Memoirs of the Marquis de Bradomín*, the reader becomes acquainted with the narrator through his poses and highly selected "confessions," not through the "inner workings" of his thoughts. This absence of psychological development remains constant in Valle-Inclán's fiction; in fact, individual characters became less important as Valle-Inclán strove to encompass Spanish society and create a collective protagonist.

As the novels and plays developed, the perfected vision he described for Spanish fiction in *The Lamp of Marvels* became increasingly linked, for both forms, with the absence of any true Spanish collectivity and with the distortion and deformation Valle-Inclán perceived around him. As Max Estrella, the blind poet-protagonist of *Bohemian Lights*, explains, old literary forms are inappropriate for contemporary Spain; a new aesthetic genre is necessary, one that—like the distorting mirrors found in a fun house—will mathematically distort an already deformed society and sensibility. Estrella names this genre the *esperpento* (literally, "absurdity" or "nonsense"), a term that Valle-Inclán used to label some of his own plays. Hence, to capture the distortions of

reality, Valle-Inclán peopled his dramatic works with unheroic, grotesque characters presaging the Theater of the Absurd. Although Valle-Inclán does not label his novels *esperpentos*, he does discuss them in terms of the *esperpentos* and indicates ways in which their fragmented structure is "almost theater."

This deliberate fusion of genres mirrors the careful way in which Valle-Inclán controlled the story of his own life, intentionally mixing fact and artifice and elaborating a fiction that welded those two ingredients. His "real" life was not a particularly exciting one: He frequently lived in poverty, he was often ill, and he had few adventures. He nevertheless was able to declare himself "an aesthetic adventurer": He knew how to make his own life a supple fiction by continually experimenting and taking risks as a writer, by rethinking and restating his opinions, by publishing fictional autobiographies and giving conflicting interviews, and by encouraging multiple versions of the events of interest that did happen to him (among them, the loss of his arm and his trips to South America). In other words, in the same way that his fiction and drama were developed as interlocking forms, fiction and history were seen and lived as interchangeable rather than mutually exclusive.

Thus it was especially appropriate when in June of 1981, Spain's king Juan Carlos created the marquisate of Bradomín, a hereditary title that he bestowed on Carlos Luis del Valle-Inclán, the writer's eldest living son. During his lifetime, Valle-Inclán had petitioned to have the nobility of his self-defined titles recognized. That petition was denied, but after his death, in recognition of his contribution to Spain's fiction, his heirs were awarded the title he had created for his best-known fictional character, a most controversial being who appeared in both plays and novels, who both does and does not resemble his creator.

The Marquis de Bradomín made his definitive appearance in 1902 as the narrator of *Autumn Sonata*, Valle-Inclán's first major work of fiction, but he had been prefigured earlier in some short stories and articles. There is also a hint of him in *Cara de Dios* (the face of God), a long novel that, although it was published in 1899, is generally considered Valle-Inclán's first because it was a serialized adaptation of a play by the Madrid dramatist Carlos Arniches. Although Valle-Inclán never hid the fact that he began his novelistic career by writing fiction in installments, he did not include *Cara de Dios* in his *Opera omnia*, and for a long time it remained out of print and virtually forgotten. All of this early work was important to the development of Valle-Inclán's later novels, for in it he experimented with different styles and themes, and much of it he reworked for incorporation into his later books. It was, however, the publication of *Autumn Sonata* that established him as one of Spain's most talented and promising writers, at the same time that influential and innovative novels were also published by Azorín, Baroja, and Unamuno.

THE PLEASANT MEMOIRS OF THE MARQUIS DE BRADOMÍN

Autumn Sonata is the first of four novels of *The Pleasant Memoirs of the Marquis de Bradomín*. The title character is an aging dandy who defines himself as "ugly, Catholic and sentimental." He begins his narrative in the autumn of his life and moves "backward" to summer, spring, and, finally, winter. The novels can also be read according to the calendar, for in *Spring Sonata*, the marquis is a young man who proceeds to age as the seasons progress. Each novel has a different setting and, to some extent, a different tone: *Autumn Sonata* is set in Galicia; *Summer Sonata*, in Mexico; *Spring Sonata*, in Italy; and *Winter Sonata*, in Navarre.

The four novels are unified, however, by the personality and the prose of the marquis and by the fictional purpose that Valle-Inclán had in mind for them as a whole. As he explained himself, in these novels he wanted to work with an "eternal" Spanish theme, the legend of Don Juan. For Valle-Inclán, Don Juan was a complex figure, and in addition to presenting him as a great seducer of women, Valle-Inclán believed that it was necessary to examine Don Juan's lack of respect for religion and the dead, along with his willingness to satisfy his own desires by trampling on the rights of others. Valle-Inclán's "Don Juan," the marquis, defines himself in terms of those three themes—the trinity of the World, the Flesh, and the Devil—presenting his exploits and conquests in a tongue-in-cheek manner that is at once sentimental and stoic. As if fully aware of the ironic self-portrait he is drawing, the marquis speaks proudly of his aristocratic lineage, his participation in the Carlist War, his ability to resist pain, and the great attraction he has for

women. At the same time, he is conscious of the various elements of decadence that characterize his life: the excessive sentimentality of his writing; the morbid, even macabre nature of some of his experiences; the fact that Carlism has become a lost cause.

The irony and ambiguity is what makes *The Pleasant Memoirs of the Marquis de Bradomín* fascinating; thanks to the richness and precision of "his" writing, the Marquis de Bradomín seems to breathe life into the decadent figure whose death he exemplifies. His prose is elegant and highly refined; its musicality and suggestiveness reveal Valle-Inclán's reading of fin de siècle writers from Spanish America, France, and Italy. His sensuous descriptions are highly visual, and each sonata evokes its different setting. On the other hand, there is something too precious about the writing, the descriptions are complex but static, the Marquis repeats his images of regret, and his laments of lost youth and the absence of further adventures grow tiring. His reader is likely to recognize long before the Marquis does that he is—as he fears—like a god whose cult has died out and that the greatest loves of his life have not led to enduring relationships but to melancholy, resentment, and even death.

Although Valle-Inclán eventually referred to the *Sonatas* as "trivial tunes for the violin," the Marquis de Bradomín continued to appear throughout his work (in *La guerra carlista*, *Bohemian Lights*, and *El ruedo ibérico*). This reappearance and the many similarities between novelist and character (for example, a noble Galician birth, journeys to Mexico, the loss of an arm) have prompted much speculation about the extent to which Valle-Inclán's stories about the Marquis and his adventures are autobiographical. It is clear that the *Sonatas* are, in many ways, "writer's novels" (for example, the Marquis is a highly self-conscious narrator who continually refers to himself as a confessional writer, constantly examines the possibilities and power of language, and alludes frequently to other autobiographical works), which suggests that Valle-Inclán was using the Marquis to write about his own aesthetic development. The links between them are, however, highly fictionalized: Valle-Inclán was interested not in telling his own personal "story" but in personifying his thoughts about fiction and legend in such a way that the reader could also experience, simultaneously, decadence and virtuosity—the end of a legend and the process of its re-creation. That he succeeded is proved by the popularity of the *Sonatas*, which continue to prompt new critical studies and are perhaps his most widely read novels.

THE TYRANT

In 1926, fifteen years after his previous novel, Valle-Inclán published *The Tyrant*. This first novel after a long break was an immediate success, and it has continued to be one of Valle-Inclán's most influential and popular books; indeed, many critics consider it his masterpiece. Although he was sixty years old when this novel was published, Valle-Inclán himself called it his "first" work and said that his labor as a writer was only beginning.

The Tyrant does signal the ambitious and innovative novelistic undertaking that would occupy the final decade of Valle-Inclán's life. It incorporates in a work of fiction the perspective and techniques that Valle-Inclán had recently perfected and exemplified in the *esperpentos*. *The Tyrant* also brought to fruition the theme of Spain in the New World, which had been present in Valle-Inclán's work since his first trip to Mexico. It was in Mexico, he believed, that the truest or purest essence of Spain could be found, although—as he shows in *The Tyrant*—that essence was not so much a living influence as a deathly presence. It was apparently this deathly presence that he wanted to explore, for, as he wrote to Alfonse Reyes in 1920, the *gachupines* (or Spaniards) in Mexico owned seventy percent of the land and were the "quintessence of Iberian barbarity." True revolution, he said, would involve a change in the position of the Indian, not merely "a shuffling of viceroys."

The Tyrant is set in Santa Fe de Tierra Firme, the capital of an imaginary republic on the eve of a revolutionary uprising. Death is indeed a central presence in the novel; the action spans three days during the feasts of All Saints and All Souls, and the uprising is responsible for the demise of the tyrant Santos Banderas and the end of his dictatorship. The plot of *The Tyrant* can be stated briefly: Valle-Inclán was not concerned with chronicling the entire history of an attempted revolution but in presenting—from many perspectives—the instant of its explosion: On the eve of the rebellion, the interests and aspirations of the republic's three racial groups (Indians, Creoles, and *gachupines*) are detailed, and the links and antagonisms among them are revealed or suggested.

Santos Banderas is first seen after he has impassively squelched an insurrection in another town; at the end of the novel, he just as impassively kills his own daughter to protect her from the revolutionaries, before he himself is riddled with bullets.

The victorious uprising, which is only one of several quite disparate revolutionary efforts, is led by Filomeno Cuevas, a Creole rancher, and Domiciano de la Gándara, a former military officer who has his own ambitions for power. The participation and motivation of their Indian troops is pivotal to their success, just as the Indians' role in New World society is pivotal to most of the novel's discussions of social change. This role is examined from various points of view by politicians who hope to inspire revolution, by the Diplomatic Community, and by the Spanish Colony, whose economic ties to the dictatorship make any genuine sympathy for the Indians virtually impossible. Many aspects of the novel's historical and political situation, its landscape, and its characters are reminiscent of Mexico and the revolution that overthrew Porfirio Díaz, but there are also suggestions of other Central and South American nations, and the novel is clearly not confined within the boundaries of any one country.

The structure of *The Tyrant* has been studied in detail and praised for the exemplary manner in which it fuses Valle-Inclán's constant attention to form and his thoughts about society and change in Spanish America. As in the trilogy *La guerra carlista*, *The Tyrant* is composed of short (often very short) fragments. In this later work, however, their ordering conforms to a stricter and more meaningful pattern. The novel itself is framed by a brief prologue and a brief epilogue; the prologue presents Filomeno Cuevas, Domiciano de la Gándara, and their rebel Indians as they prepare to march on the former convent where the Tyrant has his headquarters; the epilogue takes place within the Tyrant's headquarters as the uprising succeeds.

Suspended between the prologue and epilogue, the novel's plot unfolds not as a linear series of events but as three concentric circles. The central part, which is also the longest, contains the most developed story in the novel, that of the Indian Zacarías San José, who joins Filomeno Cuevas's insurgents in order to wreak vengeance on the *gachupín* Quintín Pereda, a miserly pawnbroker who was responsible for the imprisonment of Zacarías's wife and, indirectly, for the fact that their young son was killed by pigs. This circular structure is closely related to the ideas about Gnostic and Christian time, history, and poetic vision that are presented in *The Lamp of Marvels*; it also reflects Valle-Inclán's interest in theosophy and the occult, which is linked to his aesthetics. The recurrence of the numbers three and seven in the novel's structure and action, for example, is not coincidental but highly symbolic, as is the fact that Santa Fe's three social "circles" revolve around a center of mutual responsibility that may explode but will not change.

Although this artificial structure and, in particular, the compactness of the short chapters or fragments—the events of which often occur simultaneously—link *The Tyrant* to Valle-Inclán's dramatic work of the years immediately preceding, it is in the development and description of the novel's characters that the aesthetics perfected in his plays become most evident. Like the characters of the *esperpentos*, many of the inhabitants of Santa Fe are puppet figures who are not described psychologically but are presented externally, by means of their gestures and grotesque appearance and through their dialogue. Aside from the Tyrant, who is often referred to as a mummy or skull and identified by his dark glasses and his grimace (which is green because his saliva is discolored from chewing coca leaves), the most grotesque characters are the *gachupines*.

Their most extreme representative is the Spanish minister, a gay drug addict who is shunned by other foreign ministers and referred to alternately as the Plenipotentiary Minister of His Catholic Majesty and as Isabelita, the name given him by his lover, a former bullfighter. As puppets of their own maliciousness and hypocrisy, these characters are thoroughly dehumanized. Described with reference to masks, animals, parts of the body, or articles of clothing, they become objects; at times, some of the objects and animals in the novel take on more life than its characters. That is not to say, however, that all of the characters are deformed or distorted. Some of them, such as the Indian Zacarías, are presented as dignified, almost epic figures. Filomeno Cuevas and Roque Cepeda—the latter a popular apostle of the Revolution, a spiritual figure who offers a striking contrast to the Tyrant and in many ways resembles the precipitator of the Mexican Revolution, Francisco Madero—are presented as noble men, even though, for different reasons, their efforts to alter society will not be effective in a lasting way. Like Cepeda, many of the characters are based to varying degrees on historical personages, a resemblance that reveals Valle-Inclán's careful documentation and great familiarity with Mexican history; even so, like the situation itself, which seems to take place simultaneously in 1873 and during the Mexican Revolution, the characters differ significantly from the models they synthesize and re-create.

Although it is difficult to say which aspect of *The Tyrant* has proved to be most innovative and influential, certainly one of the more admirable elements of the novel is its language. In the same way that the landscape suggests various South American countries and the characters are both historical and fictional, the language of *The Tyrant* is created from a highly artificial vocabulary that draws on Spanish as it is spoken in all parts of the New World. This synthesis makes for difficult reading for Spanish speakers unfamiliar with the dialects of their Hispanic counterparts, but it creates a fascinating phenomenon that is almost an antidote to the death of Spanish that the novel chronicles in so many other ways. As the narrator presents the brief, condensed, allusive descriptions (which are more like the stage directions of the *esperpentos* than like traditional novelistic passages) and as the characters strut grotesquely, uttering their short, telegraphic outbursts, a rebirth of the Spanish language does, indeed, occur. As the boundaries of strict discourse are broken down, the possibility of a new language is suggested; the message is one of discouragement and death, but in the words that convey that message there are signs of life.

EL RUEDO IBÉRICO

At the time of his death, Valle-Inclán was working on an ambitious project, which he hoped would "bring to the novel Spanish sensibility as presented in its reaction to events of importance." He believed that "a nation's sensibility is reflected in and can be measured by the way it reacts to those events." The historical period that he chose for his "measurement" was much the same one that had interested him in *La guerra carlista* and *The Tyrant*; this time, however, he would focus on the entire Spanish nation. There were to be nine novels, which would span the years 1868 to 1885 in three cycles of three novels each; only the first three were written.

Collectively titled *El ruedo ibérico*, Valle-Inclán presents in them the multiplicity of revolutionary schemes, monarchical abuses, and social injustices that filled the seven months immediately preceding the "Glorious" Revolution of September, 1868, and Isabel II's flight into exile. Later novels were to include the period of the first Spanish Republic and the Bourbon Restoration, and they were to end with the death of Alfonso XII. Valle-Inclán knew that he would not be able to complete the entire project, but he worked on it steadily during the last decade of his life, writing and rewriting the novels that were to make up the first cycle.

The first novel, *La corte de los milagros* (the court of miracles), appeared in 1927; the second, *Viva mi dueño* (hurrah for my master), in 1928. In 1931 and 1932, these two novels were republished in serial form, with alterations, in the Madrid newspaper *El sol*. In the spring of 1932, the same newspaper published five sections of *Baza de espadas* (military tricks), a novel that was never completed but was published posthumously in book form in 1958. Since Valle-Inclán's death, several additional fragments of *El ruedo ibérico* have been published, and scholars have linked other fragments published during his lifetime to its theme and plots; at least one of its characters appeared in some of his early articles.

Although the novels of *El ruedo ibérico* are much more extensive than *The Tyrant* (as Valle-Inclán indicated himself), his novelistic techniques, his perspective on Spain, and his use of historical documentation were established with that earlier novel. Like *The Tyrant*, the first cycle of *El ruedo ibérico* studies the end or death of an era; as *The Tyrant* explores the fiction of Spain's heroic posture in the New World, the first novels of *El ruedo ibérico* expose the "eternal duality" of its "soul" and its "deceptive national unity." This notion is explained quite clearly in *Viva mi dueño*:

In those amens, once the bonfires of the Holy Office had been extinguished, the unity of a religious creed, which for three dark centuries managed to serve as a political bond, began to slacken, for it could no longer sustain its fiction.

Once again, as he had done before in *La guerra carlista* and *The Tyrant*, Valle-Inclán documented his novels by reading voluminously in nineteenth century history. He also studied exhaustively the popular press and popular literature; as a result, *El ruedo ibérico* reiterates the link between popular songs, language, and Spain's "finest hours" that was suggested in *The Lamp of Marvels*. As in his earlier works, however, Valle-Inclán's use of his historical material is highly original; his intention was not to recount history but to reorder it by altering Spain's traditional historical perspective. To do so, he employed (as he had in *The Tyrant*) a highly artificial structure and language, as well as new renditions of many well-known historical figures. The result is a rich but highly demanding narrative, for in order to appreciate fully Valle-Inclán's new focus on Spanish sensibility the reader must be thoroughly familiar with Spain's history.

The work's title illustrates the integral way in which Valle-Inclán's vision of history was related to the actual form of the novels, for in addition to "arena" or "bullring," the word *ruedo* means "rotation." Although the events in the three novels move forward chronologically, each book is structured circularly, with a long, pivotal section at its center. The narrative is broken into sections, which are further divided into chapters of varied lengths. To some of Valle-Inclán's early critics, the arrangement of the chapters appeared arbitrary, but recent scholars have discovered a careful patterning in each of the novels.

The first impression is indeed one of confusion and fragmentation, but attentive readers learn that this fragmentation coherently suggests hidden links between characters and intrigues. It also clearly suggests that in the jumble of revolutionary schemes and plots that existed throughout Spain in 1868, those at the top (the upper or outer circles) were the least revolutionary—that in order for lasting social change to occur, it would be necessary to focus on the nation's true center, the peasants and workers, who are at the center of *El ruedo ibérico*. The message inherent in this concentric structure could not help but remind Spanish readers of the conflicts of their own era.

In much the same way that *El ruedo ibérico*'s relatively short time span is crowded with events and intrigues, those events and intrigues are peopled with a large cast of characters; as Valle-Inclán himself said, the cycle of novels was not to have a traditional protagonist, because "its major protagonist is its social milieu, its ambience." Within this milieu, some characters are more prominent than others, but the effect is one of a complex world of interwoven stories in which the characters move into the spotlight for varying lengths of time but none dominates it. This complexity can be confusing, for at times a subtle allusion or small detail is the only clue provided to a character's motive or identity. Readers are, moreover, expected to be familiar with Valle-Inclán's earlier novels, some of whose characters (such as the Marquis de Bradomín) reappear.

In addition, the novels of *El ruedo ibérico* are peopled with many historical figures, whose significance depends to a large degree on the reader's recognition of them. These historical characters include the inept and scandalous Queen Isabel II and her weak and effeminate husband; Sor Patrocinio, a nun on whom the queen relied almost fanatically; Father Claret, the Royal Confessor; General Juan Prim, one of the revolution's leading figures; the anarchist Michael Bakunin; and numerous military officers, revolutionaries, ministers, advisers, and aristocrats. Many of these figures are presented as ridiculous, grotesque, and culpable; as in *The Tyrant*, Valle-Inclán's descriptions are at times scathing. Not all of the characters are reflected in the distorting lens of *esperpento*, but those who are—particularly the figures of "official" Spanish history—are shown to be egotistical, deceitful, and corrupt.

Given Valle-Inclán's intention to make an entire society the protagonist of these novels, it was necessary that the language of this collective character contain the speech patterns of the whole nation. *El ruedo ibérico* presents exactly this kind of spectrum, and the language of the novels is one of Valle-Inclán's greatest accomplishments. His own vocabulary is a synthesis of Spanish as spoken throughout the Iberian Peninsula, and as his many characters speak (which they do continually—there is a great deal of dialogue in these novels), they exemplify Spanish as spoken, from that of the queen's bed-chamber to the slang of workers and peasants.

To render some of this jargon, particularly the speech of the Andalusian bandits and gypsies, Valle-Inclán consulted cultural studies and reference works, encrusting the dialogue with authentic vocabulary. These passages are highly artificial, but they do accomplish an important goal, one that is closely linked to the purpose of *El ruedo ibérico*. The fiction of a pure and elegant Spanish language is destroyed, but the language itself expands to include the speech of all of Spain's inhabitants. In *El ruedo ibérico*, Valle-Inclán realized his most complete simultaneity of language destruction and re-creation. His achievement, however, surpasses the boundaries of a single genre: *El ruedo ibérico* is a culmination of his work in all genres, a synthesis of narrative, poetry, and theater confirming Valle-Inclán's lifelong preoccupation with the fictions of Spain.

Carol S. Maier

OTHER MAJOR WORKS

SHORT FICTION: *Femeninas*, 1895; *Corte de amor*, 1903; *Jardín umbrío*, 1914.

PLAYS: *Cenizas*, pr., pb. 1899; *El marqués de Bradomín*, pr. 1906; *Águila de blasón*, pb. 1907; *Romance de lobos*, pb. 1908 (*Wolves! Wolves!*, 1957); *El yermo de las almas*, pb. 1908; *La cabeza del dragón*, pr. 1910 (*The Dragon's Head*, 1918); *Cuento de abril*, pr., pb. 1910; *Voces de gesta: Tragedia pastoríl*, pb. 1911; *La marquesa Rosalinda*, pr. 1912; *El embrujado*, pb. 1913; *Divinas palabras*, pb. 1920 (*Divine Words*, 1968); *Farsa de la enamorada del rey*, pb. 1920; *Luces de Bohemia*, pb. 1920 (in French), pr. 1971 (in Spanish; *Bohemian Lights*, 1967); *Los cuernos de don Friolera*, pb. 1921 (in Italian), pr. 1936 (in Spanish; *The Grotesque Farce of Mr. Punch the Cuckold*, 1991); *Cara de Plata*, pb. 1922; *Farsa y licencia de la reina castiza*, pb. 1922; *Las galas de difunto*, pb. 1926; *La hija del capitán*, pb. 1927; *Retablo de la avaricia, la lujuria, y la muerte*, pb. 1927; *Obras completas de don Ramón del Valle-Inclán*, 1944 (2 volumes); *Las "comedias bárbaras": Historicismo y expresionismo dramático*, 1972 (includes *Águila de blasón*, *Wolves! Wolves!*, and *Cara de Plata*); *Plays*, 1993; *Savage Acts: Four Plays*, 1993.

POETRY: *Aromas de leyenda*, 1907; *La pipa de kif*, 1919; *El pasajero*, 1920; *Claves líracas*, 1930 (includes the three earlier collections).

NONFICTION: *La lámpara maravillosa*, 1916 (*The Lamp of Marvels*, 1986); *La media noche*, 1917.

MISCELLANEOUS: *Opera omnia*, 1913-1930; *Obras completas*, 1944.

BIBLIOGRAPHY

Almeida, Diane M. *The Esperpento Tradition in the Works of Ramón del Valle-Inclán and Luis Buñuel.* Lewiston, N.Y.: Edwin Mellen Press, 2000. Almeida takes a close look at *esperpento*—a Spanish style of black comedy—in the novels of Valle-Inclán and in the films of Luis Buñuel. Includes a bibliography and an index.

Andrews, Jean. *Spanish Reactions to the Anglo-Irish Literary Revival in the Early Twentieth Century: The Stone by the Elixir.* Lewiston, N.Y.: Edwin Mellen Press, 1991. Andrews examines the search for spiritual and aesthetic fulfillment in the works of Valle-Inclán and Juan Ramón Jiménez and contrasts them to contemporary Anglo-Irish works. Includes a bibliography and an index.

Flynn, Gerard C. *The Aesthetic Code of Don Ramón del Valle-Inclán.* Huntington, W.Va.: University Editions, 1994. An extensive analysis of the aesthetics of Valle-Inclán's works. Includes a bibliography and an index.

Lima, Robert. *Valle-Inclán: The Theater of His Life.* Columbia: University of Missouri Press, 1988. A full-length biography of Valle-Inclán, covering his life and works. Includes a bibliography and an index.

LoDato, Rosemary C. *Beyond the Glitter: The Language of Gems in Modernista Writers Rubén Darío, Ramón del Valle-Inclán, and José Asunción Silva.* Lewisburg, Pa.: Bucknell University Press, 1999. LoDato examines the use of gems and jewelry as symbols in the works of Modernista writers Valle-Inclán, Rubén Darío, and José Asunción Silva. Includes a bibliography and an index.

Longhurst, Alex. "The Survival of Genre: Cervantine Paradigms in Unamuno, Valle-Inclán, and Pérez de Ayala." In *"Never-Ending Adventure": Studies in Medieval and Early Modern Spanish Literature in Honor of Peter N. Dunn,* edited by Edward H. Friedman and Harlan Sturm. Newark, Del.: Juan de la Cuesta, 2002. This collection of essays about medieval and early modern Spanish literature includes Longhurst's examination of the influence of Miguel de Cervantes on the work of Valle-Inclán and two other Spanish writers.

Schoolfield, George C. "Spain: Ramón María del Valle-Inclán." In *A Baedeker of Decadence: Charting a Literary Fashion, 1884-1927.* New Haven, Conn.: Yale University Press, 2003. Schoolfield's study of thirty-two Decadent writers devotes a chapter to the works of Valle-Inclán, which includes an examination of the Sonatas.

CARL VAN VECHTEN

Born: Cedar Rapids, Iowa; June 17, 1880
Died: New York, New York; December 21, 1964

PRINCIPAL LONG FICTION

Peter Whiffle: His Life and Works, 1922
The Blind Bow-Boy, 1923
The Tattooed Countess, 1924
Firecrackers, 1925
Nigger Heaven, 1926
Spider Boy, 1928
Parties, 1930

OTHER LITERARY FORMS

Carl Van Vechten (van VEHK-tehn) had three major careers in the arts; he was a critic, a novelist, and a photographer. His music criticism includes *Music After the Great War* (1915), *Music and Bad Manners* (1916), and *The Music of Spain* (1918). His involvement with major American and European writers and artists of the 1920's and 1930's is chronicled in his autobiographies, *Sacred and Profane Memories* (1932) and *Fragments from an Unwritten Autobiography* (1955).

ACHIEVEMENTS

The spirit of the Jazz Age, the Roaring Twenties, and the lost generation is nowhere better depicted than in the saucy and irreverent novels of Carl Van Vechten. Van Vechten moved deftly through three careers: he began as a music, dance, and drama critic, producing several volumes of wide-ranging, urbane essays; then, he devoted himself to fiction, writing seven well-received novels in a decade that saw the first publications of Ernest Hemingway, F. Scott Fitzgerald, and John Dos Passos; finally, he became a noted photographer, specializing in portraits of writers and artists.

In all his diverse endeavors, Van Vechten was witty, cosmopolitan, and above all, unconventional. He publicized the work of such writers as William Faulkner, Ronald Firbank, and especially Gertrude Stein, who remained his close friend until her death, and who assigned him as her literary executor. He was among the first critics to recognize the exciting cultural renaissance flourishing in Harlem and devoted much effort to helping establish the careers of Countée Cullen, Langston Hughes, James Weldon Johnson, Bessie Smith, Ethel Waters, and other black artists. He saw himself as a popularizer and supporter of avant-garde artists, and with a clear eye and self-assurance, he brought to the attention of the American public figures ranging from Wasław Nijinsky to Erik Satie, from Mary Garden to Igor Stravinsky.

Van Vechten, more than many of his contemporaries, lived the literary life with seemingly boundless enthusiasm. His verve animates all of his writing, including the essays he frequently contributed to such journals as *Trend*, *The Smart Set*, and *Vanity Fair*. This effervescent spirit informs his novels as well. His wide interests, diverse friendships, and tireless pursuit of the new, the brilliant, and the innovative make Van Vechten a fascinating guide to America's cultural life in the first decades of the twentieth century.

BIOGRAPHY

Carl Van Vechten was born in Cedar Rapids, Iowa, on June 17, 1880. His father was a banker turned insurance company executive; his mother was a college graduate, suffragette, and for her time, a political and social activist. Born when his parents were in their forties, Van Vechten had two siblings much older than he and so spent his childhood surrounded by four adults. Predictably, this atmosphere nurtured a precocious child. By the time he was an adolescent, Van Vechten had thoroughly immersed himself in whatever cultural offerings could be found in Cedar Rapids—opera, theater, concerts that stopped in the city on tour—and began to apply his own talents to amateur theatrical productions and family piano recitals. Physically he was an awkward youth—too tall too early, with large buck teeth—and his omnivorous appetite for culture made him feel socially awkward among his peers. Longing to escape from the complacent bourgeois existence of Cedar Rapids, he enrolled at the University of Chicago and, in 1899, took his first steps East, a direction that would eventually lead to New York and then to Paris.

At college, Van Vechten studied with Robert Morss Lovett and William Vaughn Moody. He also began writing passionately and composing music. After he graduated, he took a job with the *Chicago American*; he was assigned to write short news pieces and collect photographs to illustrate news stories. He soon decided, however, that, for his purposes, Chicago was little better than Cedar Rapids. In 1906, he left for New York.

Van Vechten's first writing assignment in New York was an opera review for Theodore Dreiser, then editor of *Broadway Magazine*. Soon, Van Vechten joined the staff of *The New York Times* as assistant to the music critic. From 1908 to 1909, he served as Paris correspondent for *The New York Times*, a post that brought him into close contact with leading European dancers, sculptors, artists, and writers. When he returned to New York in the spring of 1909, he resumed his job as music critic, but he longed to return to Europe. He was back in Paris in 1914.

By then, Van Vechten had, in many ways, left his Cedar Rapids days behind him. In 1912, he was divorced from Anna Elizabeth Snyder, a childhood sweetheart he had married just five years before. Shortly after the divorce, he met the Russian-Jewish actor Fania Marinoff, an attractive woman whom he would soon marry. In 1913, he met Mabel Dodge, the irrepressible center of her own vibrant salon; in 1914, at the second performance of Stravinsky's *Sacre du Printemps* in Paris, he met Gertrude Stein, at whose rue de Fleurus home he would soon encounter the leading figures of Parisian cultural life.

From 1915 to 1932, Van Vechten wrote an astonishing number of books—first several volumes of essays on music and the arts, then seven novels. He preferred the experimental; the daring; the works of young artists being performed, written, and conducted in America and on the Continent; and the enthusiasm with which he greeted such works helped earn their acceptance by his readers. He predicted the enduring greatness of Stravinsky at a time when some wondered if what they were hearing was, indeed, music. He approached his task as critic with "curiosity and energy," he said, and his tastes, idiosyncratic as they were, reflected his certainty in empathizing with the aims of modern artists.

In 1928, Van Vechten's brother died, leaving him with a substantial bequest that allowed for financial independence. This event coincided with, and perhaps made possible, Van Vechten's new career: photographer. He had his first show in 1934, and he became a portrait photographer of such writers and artists as Stein, Truman Capote, George Gershwin, Leontyne Price, and William Faulkner.

Carl Van Vechten. (Carl Van Vechten/Library of Congress)

Van Vechten was the founder of several libraries and archives, including the James Weldon Johnson Memorial Collection (black art and literature) at Yale, the George Gershwin Memorial Collection (music) at Fisk University, the Rose McClendon Memorial Collection (photographs of famous blacks) at Howard University, and the Florine Stettheimer Memorial Collection (fine arts) at Fisk.

ANALYSIS

In his first novel, *Peter Whiffle*, Carl Van Vechten's hero expounds on the art of criticism, Van Vechten's vocation in the decade before he wrote fiction. Recalling Remy de Gourmont, Peter Whiffle asserts, "Criticism is perhaps the most suggestive of literary forms; it is a perpetual confession; believing to analyze the works of others, the critic unveils and exposes himself to the public." So, he continues, one learns more about the critic than about the object of his (or her) observations. "Criticism should open channels of thought and not close them; it should stimulate the soul and not revolt it. And criticism can only be wholesome and sane and spiritually stimulating when it is contradictory." Van Vechten, above all, believed that life itself was contradictory, that appearances often deceived, that absurdity ruled more often than logic. Nevertheless, he exulted in strong, creative, exciting personalities, and believed that such strength could overcome the inherent absurdity of life. If there were no truth, no unalterable facts, there could at least be style, anecdote, spirit—those qualities that Whiffle said readers looked for in "the old critics"—and there also could be enthusiasm and joy.

Given Van Vechten's notions about literary criticism, it is no wonder that he gravitated toward fiction, where characters might easily express contradictory ideas and where the writer's style, spirit, and personality are expected to pervade the text. In his novels, Van Vechten emerges as an observant and perceptive critic of his own society and his particular time. His novels, as Donald Pizer notes, "Chronicle either in authorial asides or miniature essays the taste and interests of the decade from the conventional to the avant garde." His friends and acquaintances often made appearances, sometimes under pseudonyms, and current music, books, and paintings are evoked vividly.

Aiming to analyze his world, Van Vechten also reveals his own particular point of view: that of the tolerant but wiser and older participant (he was nearly forty-two years old when he published his first novel), one who looks with bemused sympathy on the antics around him. He accepts—as his characters often do not—that the world is absurd; he is not shocked or dismayed by the suffering, unhappiness, and anguish beneath the glittering life of cosmopolitan high society because he knows that life offers joy and satisfaction, if only one knows where to look. He is aware of the conflict between the sensitive artist and a world that would deny him, but he believes that strength of personality and self-assertion can overcome many obstacles. In his acceptance of absurdity and his belief in the capacity of the artist to survive emotionally and psychologically, he stands apart from some of the younger writers of his time: Sherwood Anderson, Hemingway, Fitzgerald, Sinclair Lewis. Though he shares many of their artistic problems, he does not share their anger, and this ability to delight and be delighted distinguishes Van Vechten's fiction.

PETER WHIFFLE

Peter Whiffle, in this novel about writing a novel, is a would-be writer, searching for self and inspiration in a troubling world. He encounters Van Vechten, who reappears in the novel to meet Peter at several stages of his artistic development; Peter confides his theories of life and art to the patient older man, and reveals the confusions faced by the artist as a young man. At first, Peter announces that he plans to write a book, and Van Vechten asks him what it will be about. Peter replies,

That is what it is to be about, about three hundred pages, three hundred pages of colour and style and lists, lists of objects, all jumbled artfully. There isn't a

moral, or an idea, or a plot, or even a character. There's to be no propaganda or preaching, or violence, or emotion, or even humour.

Art, Peter says, is necessarily abstract—never concrete; art is the pattern that emerges from artful juxtaposition. Some sixty pages later, Peter has discarded these notions and come to another conclusion: art "has nothing to do with style or form or manner. . . . The *matter* is what counts. . . . No style, no form, just *subject*."

Obsessed now with political and social revolution, Peter decides that he must opt for realism over expressionism; Dreiser—and not, for example, Georg Kaiser—must be his model. Again, some sixty pages later, Peter is thoroughly confused: "Never did I feel less sure of the meaning of art than I do here," he confesses. He has immersed himself in the world of literature, music, and painting, only to discover that no theory or formula will explain art. Finally, he decides that the personality of the artist and his ability to convey his impressions might yield a masterpiece of art. "I think a great book might be written if everything the hero thought and felt and observed could be put into it," he says, adding,

These ideas, impressions, objects, should all be set down. Nothing should be omitted, nothing! One might write a whole book of two hundred thousand words about the events of an hour. And what a book! What a book!

That book will never be written by Peter Whiffle, however, nor would it be written by Van Vechten. Peter observes that one might be able to create a work of art from one's life, merely by living well. "I wanted to write a new Comedie Humaine," Peter says. "Instead," he adds,

I have lived it. And now, I have come to the conclusion that that was all there was for me to do, just to live, as fully as possible. Sympathy and enthusiasm are something, after all. I must have communicated at least a shadow of these to the ideas and objects and people on whom I have bestowed them.

He is disillusioned with the idea that the successful artist is a fulfilled human being. "All expression lifts us farther away from simplicity and causes unhappiness," he concludes. Of his own search for the meaning of art, he finds, "Everybody is striving to do something *new*, instead of writing or painting or composing what is natural. . . . The great secret is . . . to do what one *has* to do."

This paean to individuality and self-knowledge is the theme not only of *Peter Whiffle* but also of many other Van Vechten novels. Indeed, *Peter Whiffle* is an example of what Van Vechten, in *Nigger Heaven*, calls a propaganda novel: His message is the celebration of self-awareness and a love of life.

THE TATTOOED COUNTESS

Peter Whiffle leaves the provinciality of his native Toledo, Ohio, for the cultural capitals of the world. In *The Tattooed Countess*, Van Vechten reverses the process: Countess Ella Nattatorrini returns from an urbane European life to her childhood home, Maple Valley, Iowa. Maple Valley is as stifling as Carol Kennicott's Gopher Prairie, but unlike Carol, the Countess does not intend to enlighten the town. Instead, she decides to run from it, taking with her the only artist Maple Valley has spawned: Gareth Johns. Moreover, unlike Sinclair Lewis, Van Vechten does not depict small-town life with bitterness or rancor; instead, he is sympathetic toward the repressed characters of Maple Valley, just as he empathizes with the dreams of Ella and Gareth Johns.

The Countess, like Hester Prynne in *The Scarlet Letter* (1850), openly displays a symbol of nonconformity, of sexuality, of freedom: a tattoo on her arm. The "curious emblem" consists of a butterfly perched on a skull, with the phrase "*Que sais-je?*" beneath. Fragile, elusive beauty can distract humans from a preoccupation with their own mortality, but the butterfly must be taken for what it is, and not elevated into theories of art or into doctrines by which one decides to live. During a passionate love affair, Ella had the design tattooed on her arm, and it recalls for her not only her lost love—a sad reminder—but her ability to live fully, a notion she celebrates. Her sister is aghast: Surely, even if one were foolhardy enough to be tattooed, one would do it in a discreet place. "That is the sort of thing we keep hidden here," she tells the Countess, but Ella Nattatorrini cannot live a hidden life. It is not Van Vechten's intention to flaunt Ella's quest for freedom and self-fulfillment, but only to allow her a world in which she, as well as the inhabitants of Maple Valley, can live as she must.

NIGGER HEAVEN

Nigger Heaven reflects Van Vechten's intense interest in black culture, an interest that went far beyond Pablo Picasso's fascination with African art or Stein's interest in the Baltimore community on which she drew for her story "Melanctha." Impressed with the vitality of the arts in Harlem, Van Vechten befriended many black writers and musicians and brought them to the attention of cultural leaders downtown. Without becoming politically or socially active in support of civil rights, Van Vechten managed to become a significant spokesperson for an oppressed people through *Nigger Heaven*, a novel that, despite its blatant propaganda, is a vivid and sympathetic study of New York blacks of the 1920's.

The book centers on the relationship between Mary Love and yet another aspiring writer (surely Van Vechten had many models, black and white, from which to choose), Byron Kasson. Both are educated (Byron is a University of Pennsylvania graduate, Mary a librarian), articulate, sensitive young people, but their love and Byron's dreams are doomed to failure. Byron refuses to "see" Harlem and the real lives of blacks as suitable material for his stories; his insistence on his separateness leaves him isolated. Both the black and white communities look upon him as a misfit. Mary is willing to work within the limitations placed on her and urges Byron to approach his own people with compassion and even humility. When he tells her he will use the prejudice against his people as a plot for a story, she cautions him against "becoming melodramatic, cheap even. Unless such a story is written with exquisite skill, it will read like a meretricious appeal to the emotions arising out of race prejudice." Ultimately Byron fails, not only in his story but also in his effort to propel himself out of a culture that threatens to undermine all his hopes. Yet Van Vechten suggests that it is Byron himself—as Peter Whiffle had done before him—who causes his own downfall.

Van Vechten, like his writer-protagonist, faced the problem of seeming melodramatic in a novel that is in large part, as he put it, propaganda. He was, in 1926, anticipating the anger of James Baldwin and Richard Wright; for Van Vechten, "Nigger Heaven" (a black phrase, he explains, for the Harlem community) was ready to explode. Rarely is Van Vechten as sedate, controlled, and carefully paced as he is in this novel, and rarely is his authorial presence so discreet. *Nigger Heaven* is his most serious novel, his only attempt to deal with social issues in a culture and class different from his own; the book is a reflection of a deep commitment to social change.

PARTIES

Parties, Van Vechten's last novel, is an intense portrait of a dissolute and frenzied decade. David and Rilda Westlake, characters based on Van Vechten's friends F. Scott and Zelda Fitzgerald, move throughout the novel in a series of parties where they argue, drink, attempt seductions, gossip, toss off jaded remarks, and drink more, and still more. Vividly sketching his dissipated cast of characters, Van Vechten manages to portray their physical and emotional instability and the emptiness of their lives. Van Vechten's characters are often grotesque rather than enviably attractive.

When the reader first meets David Westlake, he is a "distorted figure" with blood drying on his lips, crying "I've killed a man or a man has killed me." Rilda's entrance is by telephone: She claims to have committed suicide. An alleged murder victim appears alive, if not completely well, finally to be killed as the plot spirals. Among these living dead cavorts a sprightly seventy-year-old European aristocrat, the Grafin Adele von Pulmernl und Stilzernl, whose lively interest in parties places her in the company of the young Americans driven to drink and misery. She alone, unable to perceive the real meaning of the whirlwind social life, enjoys the parties and finds them amusing. "It is so funny," she tells David Westlake after he summarizes "the life of our times in words of two syllables. . . . We're here because we're here, and we should be extremely silly not to make the worst of it." The Grafin, delighted with David's pronouncement, has the last words of the book: "I love your country."

Though it was poorly received by critics, Van Vechten's novel succeeds in taking the prototypal Fitzgerald characters and spinning them in a mindless maelstrom. These are the damned, who spent a decade in drunken revelry, only to wake up, forced to confront a new decade and a new spirit. With *Parties*, Van Vechten's role as a social critic ended. He had chronicled an age, and written its epitaph.

Linda Simon

OTHER MAJOR WORKS

NONFICTION: *Music After the Great War*, 1915; *Music and Bad Manners*, 1916; *Interpreters and Interpretations*, 1917; *The Merry-Go-Round*, 1918; *The Music of Spain*, 1918; *In the Garret*, 1920; *Interpreters*, 1920; *The Tiger in the House*, 1920; *Red*, 1925; *Excavations*, 1926; *Sacred and Profane Memories*, 1932; *Fragments from an Unwritten Autobiography*, 1955; *Keep A-inchin' Along: Selected Writings of Carl Van Vechten About Black Art and Letters*, 1979 (Bruce Kellner, editor); *The Letters of Gertrude Stein and Carl Van Vechten, 1913-1946*, 1986 (Edward Burns, editor); *Letters of Carl Van Vechten*, 1987 (Kellner, editor); *Remember Me to Harlem: The Letters of Langston Hughes and Carl Van Vechten, 1925-1964*, 2001 (Emily Bernard, editor); *The Splendid Drunken Twenties: Selections from the Daybooks, 1922-1930*, 2003 (Kellner, editor).

BIBLIOGRAPHY

Burke, Flannery. "Carl Van Vechten's Place." In *From Greenwich Village to Taos: Primitivism and Place at Mabel Dodge Luhan's*. Lawrence: University Press of Kansas, 2008. Van Vechten was a frequent visitor at Mabel Dodge Luhan's home in Taos, New Mexico, and, like other guests, he was inspired by the American Indians of the area. Burke examines Van Vechten's concepts of "primitivism."

Coleman, Leon. *Carl Van Vechten and the Harlem Renaissance*. New York: Garland, 1998. Essentially a biography of Van Vechten, emphasizing his interest and influence in the arts. Contains much valuable background on Van Vechten and his relations with fellow writers, artists, and dancers during the 1920's. Includes a bibliography, an index, a chronology, and photographs.

Dowling, Robert M. "*Nigger Heaven*: Carl Van Vechten, Claude McKay, and the Construction of Mythic Harlem." In *Slumming in New York: From the Waterfront to Mythic Harlem*. Urbana: University of Illinois Press, 2007. Dowling discusses the use of New York City's working-class, ethnic neighborhoods and their marginalized residents as subjects in the making of a "mythic" Harlem by "mainstream" writers, including Van Vechten.

Lueders, Edward. *Carl Van Vechten*. New York: Twayne,

1965. A critical study of Van Vechten's fiction and other works. A knowledgeable, sympathetic study by Leuders, who defends Van Vechten from critics who argue his work is superficial and pointless. Includes an afterword, a chronology, and a bibliography.

Smalls, James. *The Homoerotic Photography of Carl Van Vechten: Public Face, Private Thoughts*. Philadelphia: Temple University Press, 2006. Van Vechten, who was gay (or bisexual), was a successful photographer. This study features sixty black-and-white, homoerotic photographs shot by Van Vechten in the 1930's and 1940's. These images, including those

presented in this volume, were released to the public by the Beinecke Library in 1989. The book also includes critical discussion of Van Vechten's photographic work.

Van Vechten, Carl. *Letters of Carl Van Vechten*. Edited by Bruce Kellner. New Haven, Conn.: Yale University Press, 1987. An intimate portrait of Van Vechten, as seen through his letters to friends, fellow authors, publishers, artists, biographers, and family members. The letters have been selected from private collections as well as private and public institutions.

MARIO VARGAS LLOSA

Born: Arequipa, Peru; March 28, 1936
Also known as: Jorge Mario Pedro Vargas Llosa

PRINCIPAL LONG FICTION

La ciudad y los perros, 1962 (*The Time of the Hero*, 1966)
La casa verde, 1965 (*The Green House*, 1968)
Los cachorros, 1967 (novella; *The Cubs*, 1979)
Conversación en la catedral, 1969 (*Conversation in the Cathedral*, 1975)
Pantaleón y las visitadoras, 1973 (*Captain Pantoja and the Special Service*, 1978)
La tía Julia y el escribidor, 1977 (*Aunt Julia and the Scriptwriter*, 1982)
La guerra del fin del mundo, 1981 (*The War of the End of the World*, 1984)
Historia de Mayta, 1984 (*The Real Life of Alejandro Mayta*, 1986)
El hablador, 1987 (*The Storyteller*, 1989)
¿Quién mató a Palomino Molero?, 1986 (*Who Killed Palomino Molero?*, 1987)
Elogio de la madrastra, 1988 (*In Praise of the Stepmother*, 1990)
Lituma en los Andes, 1993 (*Death in the Andes*, 1996)

Los cuadernos de don Rigoberto, 1997 (*The Notebooks of Don Rigoberto*, 1998)
La fiesta del Chivo, 2000 (*The Feast of the Goat*, 2001)
El paraíso en la otra esquina, 2003 (*The Way to Paradise*, 2003)
Travesuras de la niña mala, 2006 (*The Bad Girl*, 2007)

OTHER LITERARY FORMS

In addition to his novels, Mario Vargas Llosa (VAHR-gahs YOH-sah) has written a number of works of literary criticism. Two of his best-known critiques are *Gabriel García Márquez: Historia de un deicidio* (1971) and *La orgía perpetua: Flaubert y "Madame Bovary"* (1975; *The Perpetual Orgy: Flaubert and "Madame Bovary,"* 1986). In 2004, he published *La tentación de lo imposible: Victor Hugo y "Los miserables"* (*The Temptation of the Impossible: Victor Hugo and "Les Misérables,"* 2007), in which he extols Hugo as a timeless author. He has also written several works of short fiction, most of which are included in the collection *Los jefes* (1959; *The Cubs, and Other Stories*, 1979). In 1981, he published his first play, *La señorita de Tacna*. His other works of drama include *La Chunga* (pb. 1987; English translation, 1990) and *El loco de los balcones* (pb.

1993). In *Cartas a un joven novelista* (1997; *Letters to a Young Novelist*, 2002), Llosa outlines novelistic structure using examples from James Joyce's *Ulysses* (1922) and from the fiction of Marcel Proust. His other works of nonfiction include *Claudio Bravo: Paintings and Drawings* (1997; with Paul Bowles), about the Chilean-born painter, and *Making Waves* (1996), a collection of essays on a wide variety of topics. In 1993, he published a memoir primarily concerning his campaign in 1990 for the Peruvian presidency, *Pez en el agua* (*A Fish in the Water: A Memoir*, 1994).

ACHIEVEMENTS

In the course of an energetic life, Mario Vargas Llosa has created an image of the writer as activist, and both his works and his life conform to his perception of that role. A prolific writer, he is also a constant traveler as a member of literary juries, newspaper commentator, peripatetic professor of Latin American fiction at English and North American universities, soccer enthusiast, and investigator of Amazonian texts. During the years spanned by his career, Vargas Llosa's fiction has outlived the theory that the sudden explosion of vitality in Latin American fiction in the 1960's was a mere "boom."

Vargas Llosa explores new areas of reality in each successive novel. The enthusiasm that characterizes his appreciation for Gustave Flaubert, William Faulkner, the novels of chivalry, and the fiction of his peer Gabriel García Márquez has developed new affinities within the cultural milieu of Latin America, a continent not always open to such influences in the past. Vargas Llosa eloquently decries the pejorative influence of politics on literature, and he simultaneously articulates political opinions that are not always the most popular; he has both supported and excoriated the Cuban Revolution. The Sartrean formulation of praxis could find no clearer illustration than the adventurous life of Vargas Llosa.

Vargas Llosa was a fellow at the Woodrow Wilson Center and has been the recipient of numerous awards, including the Premio de la Crítica Española (1963 and 1967), the Ritz Paris Hemingway Award (1985), the Cervantes Prize for literature (1994), the Planeta Prize (1994), the Jerusalem Prize (1995), El Sol de Peru (2001), the Nabokov Prize (2002), and the Roger Caillois Prize (2003).

BIOGRAPHY

Jorge Mario Pedro Vargas Llosa was born in Arequipa, Peru, in March of 1936. As a child, he endured an unstable family life, his mother compensating for his having been abandoned by his father. The family moved to Bolivia and later to Piura, a city in northern Peru that would later figure importantly in *The Green House* and in *Captain Pantoja and the Special Service*. Eventually, they moved to Lima, where Vargas Llosa was enrolled in the Leoncio Prado Military Academy. The trauma related to his schooling at this military institution found its later expression in Vargas Llosa's first novel, *The Time of the Hero*.

In 1951, Vargas Llosa began to work for the newspaper *La crónica*; he would later employ his insight into the journalistic life in *Conversation in the Cathedral, Aunt Julia and the Scriptwriter*, and *The War of the End of the World*. He studied at the San Miguel School in Piura, and the student strike that he organized there is reflected with unusual immediacy in his short story "Los jefes" ("The Leaders"). He participated more seriously in the literary milieu, collaborating on newspapers and literary magazines, and he, Luis Loayza, and Abelardo Oquendo edited the journals *Cuadernos de composición* and *Literatura*. He married Julia Urquidi and saved the delicious parody of his own romance for *Aunt Julia and the Scriptwriter*.

The short story "El desafío" ("The Challenge") earned for Vargas Llosa a trip to France in 1958. A scholarship to the University of Madrid gave him the opportunity to study the novel of chivalry, prototype of the modern novel, a form that has continued to interest him. After his collection *The Cubs, and Other Stories* was published in Barcelona in 1959, Vargas Llosa returned to Paris. He completed the first draft of *The Time of the Hero* while he was working at Berlitz, at Agence France-Presse, and at the French Radio-Television Network (ORTF). His work for the ORTF provided the necessary entrée to the many Latin American writers in Paris, where Vargas Llosa met Julio Cortázar, Jorge Luis Borges, and Carlos Fuentes; it also took him to Cuba, where he met Carlos Barral, whose publishing house in Barcelona would subsequently issue all of Vargas Llosa's novels.

In 1962, Vargas Llosa entered *The Time of the Hero*

in the competition for the Biblioteca Breve Prize. The following year, he won that prize as well as the Premio de la Crítica Española. He began work on *The Green House* and on the novella *The Cubs*. The extraordinary critical reception that *The Time of the Hero* received was amplified in 1965, when he published *The Green House*. He moved to London to take a professorship at Queen Mary College. In 1967, *The Cubs* appeared, but its reception was overshadowed by the three prizes won by *The Green House*, the most important of which was the Rómulo Gallegos Novel Prize. He traveled to Caracas for the awarding of the Gallegos, and in a ceremony that was an international event, he delivered the speech in which he clearly assumed the role of artist as public conscience. He met García Márquez at the ceremony, thereby initiating a friendship that would have both literary and personal significance. Vargas Llosa's confrontation with the fiction of García Márquez produced

Mario Vargas Llosa. (© Jerry Bauer)

the *Historia de un deicidio* (history of a deicide), an explication of his as well as of García Márquez's aesthetics, and it would later encourage the gift for satire that he suppressed until *Captain Pantoja and the Special Service*.

Vargas Llosa traveled extensively in 1968, including a stint as writer-in-residence at Washington State University. At that time, he was revising *Conversation in the Cathedral*, which he would publish in 1969. He moved to Barcelona in 1970 and continued his exploration of García Márquez's fiction. Two screenplays and *Captain Pantoja and the Special Service* were finished in 1973. In 1974, Vargas Llosa returned to Lima, where he worked on the correspondence and fiction of Flaubert, a preoccupation that resulted in the publication of *The Perpetual Orgy: Flaubert and "Madame Bovary"* in 1975. In this second volume of literary criticism, Vargas Llosa both celebrated the achievement of Flaubert and developed his own concept of the art of fiction. As president of the International Association of Poets, Playwrights, Editors, Essayists, and Novelists (PEN Club), Vargas Llosa spent much of 1976 and 1977 traveling. In 1977, he lectured at the University of Oklahoma during an international symposium, was a visiting fellow at Cambridge University, and published *Aunt Julia and the Scriptwriter. Texas Studies in Literature and Language* devoted a special issue to Vargas Llosa's fiction, and the winter, 1978, issue of *World Literature Today* presented the papers of the Oklahoma symposium.

In the fall of 1980, Vargas Llosa, Fuentes, and Juan Goytisolo were the subjects of a symposium organized by José Miguel Oviedo at the University of Indiana. The essays from the symposium were later published in two issues of *Revista iberoamericana*. During this period, Vargas Llosa was at work on a vast novel set in Brazil, which he published in 1981 as *The War of the End of the World*. In 1984, he declined an offer of the premiership in Peru, and in 1990, he mounted an ultimately unsuccessful campaign for the Peruvian presidency, running for the Liberty Movement Party. He lost to Alberto Fujimori, an agricultural engineer and son of Japanese immigrants.

Vargas Llosa received Spanish citizenship in 1993 and became a member of the Real Academia Española (Royal Spanish Academy) in 1994. He lives and works primarily in London but spends about three months each year in Peru.

ANALYSIS

The fictional world of Mario Vargas Llosa is one of complex novels, of murals of characters, of actions whose significance the reader must determine, of vast edifices that aspire to become total realities. Vargas Llosa's vision of reality is consistently binary, as can be seen from the titles of some of his works. The tension created by the opposition between the two realities is felt both by the characters within the novels and by the reader, and it is the prime factor in the dramatic nature of Vargas Llosa's style. In his early short stories and in his first novel, he focused the narrative on existential gestures, those acts or words that irrevocably set into action the course of a character's fate. As his novels grew more complex, Vargas Llosa concentrated on long dialogues that gave the intricate structures their cohesion. When he turned to humor and satire, he reverted to the emphasis on gestures, tag words, and brief but revealing verbal interchanges between characters. *The War of the End of the World* resembles those massive descriptions of entire epochs that characterized fiction in the nineteenth century (which is precisely the period that gives life to the novel's plot). Vargas Llosa, then, has never contented himself with one style; rather, he has continued to adjust his narrative procedure to the subject at hand.

The influences to which Vargas Llosa has submitted himself for apprenticeship are, with the exception of the Peruvian José María Arguedas, either European or North American. This aspect of his development, in combination with an original use of cinematic techniques, gives his fiction its distinctive flavor. Beneath the glittering surface of technique there are constants within Vargas Llosa's novels. The murals of characters always present doubles, characters whose fates are connected and whose ends always provide moral points of reference for the society configured in the novels. Insofar as the real or psychic death of one of the doubles is significant for society as a whole, these characters function as scapegoats, those generally unfortunate beings who must atone for the sins of their society. The marginality of these figures sometimes obscures the tragic nature of their fates and of Vargas Llosa's concept of fic-

tion itself. In his exploration of Flaubert's *Madame Bovary* (1857; English translation, 1886), Vargas Llosa provides the most succinct explication of his aesthetics: "The greatest satisfaction that a novel can provide is to provoke my admiration for an act of nonconformity." As one considers his canon, it becomes clear that, no matter how complex the fictional structure becomes, the vital spark for the novel's action is the act of nonconformity.

THE TIME OF THE HERO

In his first novel, *The Time of the Hero*, Vargas Llosa was already the narrative perfectionist that his readers have come to expect. He had outgrown the personal trauma produced by his experiences in the Leoncio Prado, gaining the maturity to make of that terrifying institution a microcosm for the corruption of society as a whole. The military hierarchy and those secret hierarchies that the cadets (the "dogs") form give him the structure that houses the plot, which, set in motion by a dice game, works itself out with the irrevocability of a classical tragedy. In this most Sartrean of his novels, Vargas Llosa uses multiple narrators. Each of the significant characters has his moment on the stage, a moment that Vargas Llosa explores dramatically as the character converses with himself and as he comes into conflict with other characters.

The crisis of adolescence is the natural subject for a bildungsroman, and it is a theme to which Vargas Llosa returned in *The Green House, Conversation in the Cathedral*, and *Aunt Julia and the Scriptwriter*. *The Time of the Hero* concentrates on the moment in adolescence when one's roles suddenly become limited, when the mask freezes to the face, when the violence of the games becomes mortal—the moment Jean-Paul Sartre termed the time of election, when one becomes the self one has chosen to be. Vargas Llosa explores the moment when desire becomes reality, not only for the adolescents but also for their officers and for the power structure of Peru. By stressing the limited options available to the cadets and by revealing the hideous strength of the social hierarchies into which they must blend, he creates a narrative web of tragic intensity. Character is fate, and the adolescents' furious attempts to enter adult reality only bring about disaster.

The cadets at the Leoncio Prado are from varying social strata, thereby providing Vargas Llosa with the perfect mechanism for including the structure of the entire country within his range of vision. The cadets form a small cell (the "Circle") to ensure their survival. The cell selects an emissary to carry out the members' desires, and, through a series of mistakes, the cell is implicated in the complete subversion of the rules of the school and even in the death of a cadet. The guilt associated with the responsibility for the cadet's death spreads through the school like a cancerous growth. The moral implications of the cadet's murder can be realized most clearly in the reactions of three characters: Gamboa, the perfect officer; Alberto, the author of pornographic novels and the typical bourgeois; and the Jaguar, the invincible strongman who created the Circle. Each of them comes to terms with the harsh reality of the Leoncio Prado and with the even harsher reality of death itself. The defeat suffered as a result of the confrontation with the Leoncio Prado indelibly marks each of them: Gamboa's career is ruined because he disputes his superior officers' decisions, Alberto returns to the artificial paradise of the bourgeois suburb instead of becoming the writer he should have been, and the Jaguar escapes through his love for Terry, but his life is constantly threatened by the corruption surrounding it. The fragmented conversations, the disjointed interior monologues, the sudden connections between disparate events, the constant tension between adolescent and adult realities—all of these aspects create a dramatic field on which the battles for honor are lost.

The Green House

The Green House is a more complex novel than *The Time of the Hero*, but it is built on the same binary concept found in the earlier work. The Peruvian jungle and the desert city of Piura are the contrasting environments that reiterate the hellish milieu of the Leoncio Prado. The social hierarchies are as solidly in place in the jungle as they are in Lima, and the "heroic" characters who succeed in forming their private paradise eventually recreate the same infernal structures. Five plots are interwoven in *The Green House*: the tale of the Indian child Bonifacia; the life of the Indian chief, Jum; the career of Anselmo and his romance with the blind deaf-mute Antonia; the fortunes of the multinational bandit Fushía; and the tragedy of Sergeant Lituma. *The Green House* initiated the period of Vargas Llosa's exploration of

Faulknerian themes and techniques; it has the alternating plots, the sudden character metamorphoses, the insistence on fate in the manipulation of the plot, and the exploration of the perverse precincts of the human soul that are Faulkner's hallmarks. *The Green House* was also the first novel in which Vargas Llosa revealed his fondness for the chivalric romance, as the careers of Fushía and Anselmo illustrate. Flaubert's influence is also evident here, particularly in the character of Bonifacia, who might be termed the Madame Bovary of the Peruvian jungle.

The theme of exploitation connects the five plots and is the basis for the interaction of all the characters; Vargas Llosa builds a multilayered society based on exploitation on physical, material, and moral levels. Only two of the novel's many characters escape appropriation by others for ends that they cannot control. Anselmo, who calculatedly installs a bordello (the Green House of the title) in the desert near Piura, is capable of the most courtly romance, and he spends his life after the destruction of the Green House wondering if Antonia did, indeed, reciprocate his love. After his infamous career as robber baron and absolute ruler of an island of pleasure, Fushía is reduced to utter dependence on his friend Aquilino, who ferries him by boat to the leper colony where he will end his ignoble life. The conversation between Aquilino and Fushía during the course of their river journey is pure metaphysics, and it provides the poetic thread that prevents the fragmentation that the novel's multiple plots would otherwise create.

Anselmo's Green House is destroyed by fire, only to rise again like the phoenix. Each of the plots ends in the utter defeat of the characters, but the characters themselves never give up. Although all are severely embattled by the structures in which they are trapped, the characters nevertheless persist in being themselves, in exploiting the possibilities of their roles to the limits of their potential ramifications. Although Vargas Llosa rarely allows his creatures to become heroic, in their stubborn election of selves in conflict with all other selves and with society itself, his characters do forge an active role in a narrative realm that would demand their complete domination. Considered as a whole, the novel's entire cast is making the same trip as Fushía, down the slow river of death. Some of them—including

Fushía himself, Anselmo, and Aquilino—are fortunate enough to enjoy the supreme gift in Vargas Llosa's fiction: the pleasures of friendship.

CONVERSATION IN THE CATHEDRAL

Conversation in the Cathedral presents Vargas Llosa's bleakest enactment of the strategies of nonconformity. Lima at all levels is the stage for an endless struggle that Vargas Llosa symbolizes in the conflict between fathers and sons. The nefarious career of the political strongman Cayo Bermádez infects and eventually destroys the life of every character in the novel. The most vital of the many interwoven plots is the one that concerns a young newspaperman, Santiago Zavala, and his discovery that his ostensibly bourgeois father is the infamous Bola de Oro. Vargas Llosa constructs this enormous novel's edifice upon the running dialogue between Santiago and his father's former chauffeur, a dialogue that takes place in a seedy dive called the Cathedral.

The atmosphere of the prose resembles that of Faulkner's *Sanctuary* (1931); there is even a character named Popeye. The vast nature of the reality configured in the narrative once again reminds the reader of Flaubert and his eye for re-creating the minutiae of mundane existence; at the same time, the novel is a kind of allegory of an oppressive political situation all too common in Latin America. Coming to realize just how pervasive Bermádez's influence is throughout Lima, Santiago must acknowledge that his father's capitalistic gambling provides significant sustenance for Bermádez's power, that his father's moral decay is the real field on which the family's honor is lost. His anagnorisis does not lead to the triumph typical of Greek drama but instead to the deliberate election of mediocrity; Santiago will forever hide himself in the gray streets and mean bars of Lima's underside.

Whereas Vargas Llosa captures the definitive gestures of adolescence in *The Time of the Hero* and those of maturity in *The Green House*, he captures in *Conversation in the Cathedral* the desperate grimace of a society in need of a complete revolution. Like Faulkner's *Absalom, Absalom!* (1936), the novel suggests that humanity's design, no matter how grand or intricate, only attracts destruction from the gods. Santiago comes to know his father, and thereby to know himself, only to understand that his life was destroyed even before it began.

CAPTAIN PANTOJA AND THE SPECIAL SERVICE

In *Captain Pantoja and the Special Service*, military hierarchies supply the structure upon which Vargas Llosa weaves the tragicomic career of Pantaleón Pantoja, the archetypal military man whose perfectionism is his downfall. Although the thematic preoccupation is much like that of *The Time of the Hero*, the tone is radically different. Vargas Llosa treats injustice, corruption, and defeat, but he presents them with humor and satire rather than as the components of tragedy. Captain Pantoja is given the curious task of devising a system to provide "ladies of the night" to the Peruvian military forces stationed at hardship posts in the jungle. He attacks his task with gusto and rigor, and he succeeds beyond the greatest expectations of his officers. The fact that his family is destroyed and his life completely changed restrains Pantoja not at all.

Although Vargas Llosa abandons his usual practice of avoiding a protagonist in this novel, he does provide Pantoja with the customary double that has characterized his plots. The jungle also harbors a religious fanatic, Brother Francisco, whose career holds up a dark mirror to Pantoja's and whose death at the hands of his followers reflects the danger inherent in Pantoja's success. In this novel, Vargas Llosa extends the use of dream sequences as vehicles for the expression of the subconscious, and Pantoja's surreal nocturnal voyages eloquently reveal the distress caused by his new life.

Pantoja's downfall is engineered by the radio announcer Sinchi, an egomaniac who cannot tolerate competition from Pantoja's kingdom of pleasure. Vargas Llosa deftly uses the cliché-ridden texts of Sinchi's radio broadcasts to exaggerate the boredom of daily life in the towns lost in the jungle. Sinchi's delirious diatribes are, however, no match for the monomaniacal military reports in which Pantoja marshals ever-increasing statistics to convince his officers in Lima of the success of his system. These parodies were anticipated in the pornographic novels of Alberto in *The Time of the Hero*, and they are carried to a hyperbolic extreme in *Aunt Julia and the Scriptwriter*.

Pantoja is eventually defeated by the very numbers he has assembled to validate his reports. His moral decay becomes evident to the whole region as he enjoys a brief but intense affair with an irresistible Brazilian, one of his fleet of "visiting ladies." Rather than make of Pantoja the tragic figure that Gamboa is in *The Time of the Hero*, Vargas Llosa makes him the pawn of even more comic generals, thereby implying that the most powerful institution in Peru can be reduced to a hierarchy of absurd buffoons.

AUNT JULIA AND THE SCRIPTWRITER

In counterpoint closely resembling the structure of Faulkner's *The Wild Palms* (1939), *Aunt Julia and the Scriptwriter* alternates the story of a young writer, Mario Varguitas (whose name clearly echoes that of the author), with the fortunes of Pedro Camacho, a writer of radio serials. As he serves his apprenticeship as a writer, Varguitas gradually explores the mysteries of love with his "Aunt" Julia, the recently divorced sister-in-law of his Uncle Lucho. His success in both endeavors parallels the decline of Camacho.

An obvious difference of tone characterizes the two modes of narration. Varguitas recounts his experiences with humor, and as his romance progresses, that humor is extended to hyperbole. Both the texts of Camacho's serials and the episodes concerning Camacho in Varguitas's narration are marked by ferocious satire. Varguitas narrates the episodes of his romance in a linear fashion, but the history of Pedro Camacho is presented obliquely, through the texts of increasingly alienated soap operas. The characters in Camacho's texts exhibit all the repressed elements of his seething unconscious. Inasmuch as his texts are connected thematically rather than by the characters, they provide the opportunity for Vargas Llosa to bring back former characters and favorite subjects—Sergeant Lituma reappears and undergoes an apotheosis, and a savage is once again confronted with the modern city, recapitulating one of the major themes of *The Green House*.

The desperate isolation of Pedro Camacho and the subsequent sublimation of that loneliness into the texts of his soap operas carry the same import as does the radical isolation of Quentin Compson in Faulkner's *The Sound and the Fury* (1929). Unlike Quentin, however, Camacho does not kill himself; instead, he becomes even more mediocre than before, becoming as invisible as Santiago Zavala in *Conversation in the Cathedral*. In his last appearance in the novel, he is a completely changed man, and his magnificent voice is all that re-

mains of his former personality. Varguitas does not become invisible; rather, he perfects himself by perfecting his craft, constantly rewriting his short stories, and his escape from the grimy world of second-class journalism is assured. After all, he becomes the author of the novel the reader is reading.

THE WAR OF THE END OF THE WORLD

After the writing of *The Green House*, Brazil hovered on the horizon of Vargas Llosa's fiction as a potential paradise for adventurers. After the relatively lighter novels *Captain Pantoja and the Special Service* and *Aunt Julia and the Scriptwriter*, Vargas Llosa returned to the novel of massive complexity in *The War of the End of the World*, a work based on the same historical events that form the background for Euclides da Cunha's influential novel *Os sertões* (1902; *Rebellion in the Backlands*, 1944)—indeed, Vargas Llosa dedicated his novel to Cunha. In a manner reminiscent of Leo Tolstoy, Vargas Llosa recounts the military campaign of the Brazilian government to obliterate the utopian community established at Canudos. The unrest in the north of Brazil at the end of the nineteenth century provides the stage for the war of wills and of concepts of reality, and the struggle between gigantic forces threatens the very fabric of society itself. Canudos is established by a religious zealot, Antonio the Counselor, as a refuge for those citizens whose reality is consistently denied by the modern state.

Vargas Llosa's analysis of the problems of the state demands an excursion into the eighteenth century, and the character of the Barón de Cañabrava conveys the unresolved problems that century bequeathed to the nineteenth. The pilgrims following Antonio take over land owned by the Barón de Cañabrava as a site for their city, so that the struggle extends even beyond that between the modern government and the military to encompass the fundamental disagreement between owners of vast tracts of land and the humble masses who own nothing. Only gradually does the government come to understand the desperate nature of the military campaign to expel the religious community from Canudos; the two principal antagonists in the struggle, Antonio the Counselor and the military commander Moreira Cesar, suffer from no such illusions. Each of them understands that this is a battle to the death, a war of the end of the world. Although the struggle is protracted and both leaders are killed, there is never any doubt as to which side will emerge triumphant. The victory of the status quo gives an additional poignancy to the sacrifices of the individual characters, created with Vargas Llosa's customary vividness.

Just as Faulkner in *Absalom, Absalom!* uses several distinct literary styles to capture the distinct worldviews of various narrators, so Vargas Llosa employs a variety of styles to create the complex community of Canudos. The rational eighteenth century life of the Barón de Cañabrava, the picaresque world of the reformed thieves and murderers who form the army of the Counselor, the chivalric romances of the enigmatic beauty Jurema on the way to Canudos—all are narrated in styles appropriate to the interior worlds of the characters. Galileo Gall, the ludicrous phrenologist seduced by the idea of revolution, is one of the most bizarre characters. As Gall ineffectively attempts to transplant the European mystique of revolution à la Pierre Joseph Proudhon and Mikhail Bakunin to an environment already leavened by the Counselor's revolution of the interior world, Vargas Llosa produces the necessary vehicle for a thorough examination of the apocalypse, a subject latent in his fiction since *The Green House*.

The character of a myopic journalist whose constant sneezing interrupts even the most serious moments of the campaign against Canudos serves Vargas Llosa as a roving camera, one whose lens analyzes and freezes the vast scope of the action. The journalist functions as the conscience of the society embattled by the alternative reality of Canudos. He constantly meditates on the secret motivations of the deadly campaign to exterminate the community. His glasses are shattered during a skirmish, and he is reduced to helpless dependence on his friends. Without the use of his eyes, the journalist must gather information on the actions around him with his other senses, and he moves like an amoeba through the frightful violence of the last days of Canudos. Because the journalist sees events no one else can see, he serves as a bridge between characters and events. His role gives continuity and a sense of completion to a novel that might otherwise become too diffuse.

In *The War of the End of the World*, Vargas Llosa returns to the epic style that he forged in *The Green House* and *Conversation in the Cathedral*. He lightens the somber atmosphere with the antics of Galileo Gall and the nearsighted journalist, but the novel's tone is ultimately dark and despairing. The concept of individual honor is swallowed up by the larger struggles of the military hegemony and religious fanaticism. Even the war of the end of the world, the apocalypse itself, does not change the fundamental structure of society or the future of the hapless individuals trapped within it.

Seen as a whole, Vargas Llosa's fictions center on a set thematic structure organized around bipolar opposites. Clearly established in his first novel, his style has nevertheless evolved to include humor, satire, and the exploration of the subconscious. Vargas Llosa's world is one of male domination. The feminine characters serve primarily as bridges to other characters or as sporadic amusements for the more vital males. Although certain women—Bonifacia in *The Green House*, the Brazilian in *Captain Pantoja and the Special Service*, and the vivacious Aunt Julia—escape their roles and reveal aspects of themselves beyond their stereotypes, these are temporary phenomena.

The incorporation of symbolic space has increased in Vargas Llosa's fiction; from the foggy precinct of the Leoncio Prado, he has proceeded to incorporate the jungle, the desert, and Lima itself, with all of its infernal layers. *The War of the End of the World* makes concrete the Brazil that previously in his fiction existed only as a region of dreams. No matter how complex the stage becomes, however, Vargas Llosa's characters are condemned to being themselves and to carrying out individual acts of nonconformity against the rigid hierarchies that would otherwise annihilate them. Even as they are defeated, Vargas Llosa's characters find a way to affirm themselves.

THE REAL LIFE OF ALEJANDRO MAYTA

The Real Life of Alejandro Mayta is based on the Trotskyite revolutionary Alejandro Mayta, who led an uprising against the Peruvian government in 1958. The novel is a reconstruction and fictionalization of Mayta's life. Vargas Llosa uses his story in the context of modern Peru and its social unraveling. He opens and closes the novel on the garbage dumps outside Lima, a clear reference to the detritus that threatens the culture's ability to sustain its humanity.

WHO KILLED PALOMINO MOLERO?

In *Who Killed Palomino Molero?* Vargas Llosa returns to the themes of injustice, political corruption, and defeat of *The Time of the Hero* and *Captain Pantoja and the Special Service*. Although the novel is not a fictional re-creation of Vargas Llosa's own experience as a member of the investigatory commission that attempted to enlighten the public about a horribly brutal massacre of eight journalists during the Sendero Luminoso uprising in the Peruvian Andes, the work reflects influences of the incident and the strong impression it made on Vargas Llosa as well as the criticism he received for the conclusions drawn by the commission.

The novel begins with the discovery of the terribly mutilated remains of Palomino Molero both hanging from and impaled on a tree. Vargas Llosa incorporates elements of mystery and detective fiction as Sergeant Lituma and Lieutenant Silva, members of the Guardia Civil, investigate the murder. They conduct interviews and piece evidence together. It appears at first that the murder was a crime of passion, then it appears to be a crime of revenge or perhaps a cover-up of a smuggling operation.

The novel presents an ironic depiction of the futility of efforts to solve a crime and the difficulties of finding a truth that will satisfy public opinion. The townspeople accuse Lituma and Silva of not really trying to solve the murder in order to protect powerful individuals. Rumors run rampant about why Palomino was murdered. Lituma and Silva are determined to solve the crime and continue to investigate even when their superiors and the military oppose the investigation. They are rewarded for their efforts with transfers to remote stations where they will stagnate, their careers ruined.

The social order portrayed in the novel is one of prejudice, oppressive power, and resentment. The airmen live on a base not far from Talara, within a private fenced enclosure with a guard stationed at the gate, inaccessible to the townspeople and even to the Guardia Civil. The base commander, Colonel Mindreau, repeatedly informs Silva that he does not want to waste time with him and that Silva has no authority over the airmen. The gringo employees of the International Petroleum Company live in a compound, in their big houses with their swimming pools. Mindreau speaks disparagingly of Molero as a cholo, a lower-class person. He reiterates that a common soldier was not an acceptable boyfriend for a colonel's daughter and that Molero's being a cholo made it even more unthinkable. The townspeople explain everything as being caused by the big guys. There is no truth, no honesty, no fairness—everything is manipulated for the advantage of the big guys.

Vargas Llosa also addresses the complexity of life in his treatment of sexuality in this novel. Palomino's mutilation murder and the alleged incestuous rape of Alicia by her father, the colonel, are the result of sexual desire. The meaningless encounters in the whorehouse and Silva's obsession are motivated by sexual desire. Palomino and Alicia's love and the love songs he plays are motivated by sexual desire. Yet how different all of these are. It is as Lituma says of the howling cats—they may be fighting or mating.

The harsh reality portrayed in the novel, in the graphic description of the murdered Palomino and in the ever-present exercise of corrupt power and oppression, is lightened by Vargas Llosa's portrayal of Lituma's ironic naïveté and Silva's sexual obsession with Doña Adriana, which is reminiscent of the comically satirical portrayal of sexual attraction dating to the Middle Ages. Lituma, who has only recently joined the Guardia Civil, is highly impressed by his superior's expertise in interviewing techniques—he remarks that Silva knows how to get people to tell the truth. They never really solve the crime, however.

IN PRAISE OF THE STEPMOTHER

In Praise of the Stepmother offers a detached, cold view of sexuality and its perversities through the story of the aging insurance executive Don Rigoberto, his second wife, sexy Doña Lucretia, and his young son, Alfonso. Aware of the possibility that Alfonso may resent her replacement of his mother, Lucretia attempts to gain his favor; however, the two become sexually involved. "Fonsito" later writes an essay detailing his seduction of Lucretia and lets his father read it. Don Rigoberto appears to accept the liaison between his new wife and son until the maid discovers that Alfonso has set out from the beginning to seduce his stepmother as a way of ridding himself and the household of her presence. He claims that his goal was to restore the household's original order: his father and the maid all to himself.

THE NOTEBOOKS OF DON RIGOBERTO

The Notebooks of Don Rigoberto, a sequel to *In Praise of the Stepmother*, is set in Lima, where Don Rigoberto fills ledgers with descriptions of his fantasies and sexual obsessions. Vargas Llosa purposely plays with the division between fiction and reality as Rigoberto's entries are soon confused with details of Lucretia's attempts to resist her stepson's advances. Rigoberto describes high-flown scenes with his wife, such as having her portray the subjects of famous, sexually titillating paintings. The portrayal of Alfonso is one of a sexually astute wolf in sheep's clothing. Barely on the cusp of adolescence, he visits his outcast stepmother to show her his drawings and discuss artist Egon Schiele, whose own art reflects a certain perversity and lustiness. She feigns outrage at his impudence after he "tricks" her into a sexual liaison. The scene ends with the boy leaving, Lucretia masturbating on the bidet, and then, unexpectedly, Don Rigoberto giving scrupulous instructions to the architect of his new house on how to accommodate his art and book collection. Vargas Llosa clearly takes pleasure in creating such juxtapositions of Lucretia's carnal weaknesses and her husband's near-obsessive attention to his art and literature, as he skillfully weaves together Lucretia's erotic experiences, Schiele's life and art, and Rigoberto's sensual musings.

THE BAD GIRL

In *The Bad Girl*, Vargas Llosa creates a structure of dichotomy by employing a motif of opposites and contrasts. *The Bad Girl* is the story of a love affair between a bad girl (Lily) and a good boy (Ricardo). It alternates between ecstasy and despair, between abandonment and reconciliation. In the characterization of Lily and Ricardo, Vargas Llosa creates a polar opposition that permeates the entire intrigue of the novel. Lily comes from a poor Peruvian family, Ricardo from an upper-middle-class milieu. Lily is always disguising herself and assuming false names. Ricardo is simply Ricardo Somocurcio. Lily needs adventure, danger, and an extravagant lifestyle; Ricardo is satisfied with a quiet, peaceful, restrained life. The motif of contrasts is repeated in the unfolding of Lily's life. As Lily ascends in social status and wealth, she descends in dignity and freedom. The political subplot of the love reveals the contradiction between the idealistic beliefs of the Peru-

vian revolutionaries in their power to change Peru and the reality of failure and death that is their fate. The lives of the minor characters also play out in a series of contrasts that are often ironic.

In his literary criticism, Vargas Llosa has stated that fiction creates its own reality and that good fiction convinces the reader to accept this fictional reality even though it may contrast sharply with everyday reality. *The Bad Girl* accomplishes this feat. By creating an ambience of destiny, Vargas Llosa is able to use chance and coincidence repeatedly to bring Lily and Ricardo back together and keep the reader convinced of the tale's reality. Lily and Ricardo are fated to be together, so naturally they will be reunited in Paris, in England, in Japan, and in Spain. Wherever one is, the other will eventually appear.

Vargas Llosa concludes his tale of tragic nonconformist love with the death of the bad girl. She loves Ricardo but requires so much that he cannot give her that she will always leave him. Her death unites her with him forever. The death of the unfaithful heroine is a traditional ending, but Vargas Llosa adds an innovative aspect to it: Ricardo has always wanted to write a novel, and, before she dies, Lily tells him she has given him that novel.

Mary E. Davis; Nika Hoffman
Updated by Shawncey Webb

OTHER MAJOR WORKS

SHORT FICTION: *Los jefes*, 1959 (*The Cubs, and Other Stories*, 1979).

PLAYS: *La señorita de Tacna*, pr., pb. 1981 (*The Young Lady from Tacna*, 1990); *Kathie y el hipopótamo*, pr., pb. 1983 (*Kathie and the Hippopotamus*, 1990); *La Chunga*, pb. 1987 (English translation, 1990); *Three Plays*, 1990; *El loco de los balcones*, pb. 1993.

NONFICTION: *La novela en América Latina: Dialogo*, 1968; *Literatura en la revolución y revolución en literatura*, 1970 (with Julio Cortázar and Oscar Collazos); *Gabriel García Márquez: Historia de un deicidio*, 1971; *La historia secreta de una novela*, 1971; *El combate imaginario*, 1972; *García Márquez y la problemática de la novela*, 1973; *La novela y el problema de la expresión literaria en Peru*, 1974; *La orgía perpetua: Flaubert y "Madame Bovary,"* 1975 (*The Perpetual Orgy: Flaubert* and *"Madame Bovary,"* 1986); *José María Arguedas: Entre sapos y halcones,* 1978; *La utopia arcaica,* 1978; *Entre Sartre y Camus,* 1981; *Contra viento y marea, 1964-1988,* 1983-1990 (3 volumes); *A Writer's Reality,* 1991 (Myron I. Lichtblau, editor); *Fiction: The Power of Lies,* 1993; *Pez en el agua,* 1993 (*A Fish in the Water: A Memoir,* 1994); *Making Waves,* 1996; *Cartas a un joven novelista,* 1997 (*Letters to a Young Novelist,* 2002); *Claudio Bravo: Paintings and Drawings,* 1997 (with Paul Bowles); *El lenguaje de la pasión,* 2001 (*The Language of Passion: Selected Commentary,* 2003); *La verdad de las mentiras,* 2002; *La tentación de lo imposible: Victor Hugo y "Los miserables,"* 2004 (*The Temptation of the Impossible: Victor Hugo and "Les Misérables,"* 2007); *Wellsprings,* 2008.

BIBLIOGRAPHY

Booker, M. Keith. *Vargas Llosa Among the Postmodernists.* Gainesville: University Presses of Florida, 1994. Provides one of the most comprehensive treatments of Vargas Llosa's work available in English. Includes discussion of topics such as "the reader as voyeur."

Castro-Klarén, Sara. *Understanding Mario Vargas Llosa.* Columbia: University of South Carolina Press, 1990. Offers insightful analysis of Vargas Llosa's major works of fiction, placing them within their political and cultural contexts.

Gerdes, Dick. *Mario Vargas Llosa.* Boston: Twayne, 1985. Collection of critical essays examines Vargas Llosa's fiction. Supplemented with a chronology of the events of the author's life and a bibliography.

Guillermoprieto, Alma. "The Bitter Education of Vargas Llosa." In *Looking for History: Dispatches from Latin America.* New York: Pantheon, 2001. Focuses on Vargas Llosa's political career as part of a larger examination of Latin American political history.

Kerr, R. A. *Mario Vargas Llosa: Critical Essays on Characterization.* Potomac, Md.: Scripta Humanistica, 1990. Discusses Vargas Llosa's techniques of characterization and the interrelationships of his characters with other components of his narratives. Examines individual novels as well as recurring modes of characterization across works.

Köllmann, Sabine. *Vargas Llosa's Fiction and the Demons of Politics.* New York: Peter Lang, 2002. Explores the influence of Vargas Llosa's political involvement on his work as a writer.

Kristal, Efra'n. *Temptation of the Word: The Novels of Mario Vargas Llosa.* Nashville: Vanderbilt University Press, 1999. Discusses the overarching reasons for Vargas Llosa's political passions and divides Vargas Llosa's writing career into sections corresponding to the results of his ideas on capitalism and the decline of the Cuban Revolution.

Lutes, Todd Oakley. *Shipwreck and Deliverance: Politics, Culture, and Modernity in the Works of Octavio Paz, Gabriel García Márquez, and Mario Vargas Llosa.* Lanham, Md.: University Press of America, 2003. Presents a comparative study of the fiction of three of the most important Latin American writers of the twentieth century.

Moses, Michael Valdez. "Vargas Llosa: Apocalyptic History and the Liberal Perspective." In *The Novel and the Globalization of Culture.* New York: Oxford University Press, 1995. Discussion of the cultural context of Vargas Llosa's major works of fiction is part of a larger examination of the emergence of the modern "global novel."

Muñoz, Braulio. *A Storyteller: Mario Vargas Llosa Between Civilization and Barbarism.* Lanham. Md.: Rowman & Littlefield, 2000. Presents a sociotheoretical consideration of Vargas Llosa as a writer and a political activist.

GIOVANNI VERGA

Born: Catania, Kingdom of the Two Sicilies (now in Sicily, Italy); September 2, 1840

Died: Catania, Sicily (now in Italy); January 27, 1922

PRINCIPAL LONG FICTION

Amore e patria, 1857

I carbonari della montagna, 1861-1862

Sulle lagune, 1863 (serial), 1975 (book)

Una peccatrice, 1866 (*A Mortal Sin*, 1995)

Storia di una capinera, 1871 (*Sparrow: The Story of a Songbird*, 1994)

Eva, 1873

Eros, 1874

Tigre reale, 1875

I malavoglia, 1881 (*The House by the Medlar Tree*, partial translation, 1890, 1953; complete translation, 1964)

Il marito di Elena, 1882

Mastro-don Gesualdo, 1889 (English translation, 1893, 1923)

OTHER LITERARY FORMS

Giovanni Verga (VAYR-gah) was a writer of short stories and a playwright as well as a novelist. "Nedda" is the story of a Sicilian peasant girl who harvests olives and suffers the buffets of bad fortune until at length she thanks the Virgin Mary that her baby has been taken and will no longer suffer on earth. This story, written in 1874, prompted Luigi Capuana to predict that Verga had opened "a new seam in the mine of Italian literature." In *Primavera ed altri racconti* (1876; springtime and other stories), Verga attempts a certain realism by occasionally reproducing the Milanese dialect of his characters. *Vita dei campi* (1880; *Cavalleria Rusticana, and Other Stories*, 1928; also known as *Life in the Country*, 2003) contains some of his finest stories, such as "La lupa" ("The She-Wolf"), in which a woman drives her son-in-law to kill her as the result of her continual sexual prodding. Verga transformed this story into the play *La lupa* (1896).

Also notable in *Cavalleria Rusticana, and Other Stories* is "Fantasticheria" ("Reverie"), in which a man and a woman compare the merits of the world of high society with the unsullied world of the peasant, and the man in the story argues eloquently for the superiority of the latter. The collection also includes Verga's "Cavalleria rusticana" (literally meaning "rustic chivalry" but known in English only by its Italian name), the tragedy of Turiddu at the hands of the cuckolded Alfio, each one cooperating with fate to work out the other's destruction.

Novelle rusticane (1883; translated by D. H. Lawrence in 1925 as *Little Novels of Sicily*) explores in its twelve stories the peasant's struggle to survive and his victimization by nature and society. In "La libertà" ("Liberty"), for example, in which the peasants rebel and slaughter their oppressors, they are immediately cowed by the enormity of their vengeance and are soon made into willing victims by those who execute the law. "Pane nero" ("Black Bread"), more a short novel than a story, is striking for the contrast its peasants provide to the idealism of the Malavoglia family; the fear of poverty in these peasants drives them to ignore all scruples in their search for material necessities. In *Per le vie* (1883; through the streets), Verga writes of the struggles of the urban Milanese poor; these stories seem to lack the brilliance of his stories set in Sicily. In "Camerati" ("Buddies"), Verga takes a dim view of the Socialist ideas that were coming into vogue in Northern Italy on the grounds that they merely complicate the problems that they are out to solve.

All of his life, Verga dreamed of being a successful playwright; although he did not write many plays, some of them were successful. In 1883, he rewrote "Cavalleria rusticana" as a one-act tragedy, which was performed the next year in Turin with Eleanora Duse, Cesare Rossi, and Tebaldo Checchi, the finest actors in Italy at the time. It was published the same year and marks the greatest success of Verga's career as a writer; in 1889, the play was transformed into an opera by composer Pietroc Mascagni. The play was translated into English and published in 1893. "The She-Wolf," rewritten into a two-act tragedy, premiered as *La lupa* in Turin in 1896 with some success, and for a time Mascagni considered using it also as the basis of an opera. *In portineria* (pb. 1884; the porter's lodgings) is a stage adaptation in two acts taken from a story in *Per le vie*; when it premiered in Milan in 1885, it was a failure. *La caccia al lupo* (pr. 1901; *The Wolf Hunt*, 1921) and *La caccia alla volpe* (pr. 1901; the fox hunt) are companion pieces that explore instances of marital infidelity among the poor and among the rich; predictably, Verga is more successful portraying the story set in the world of the Sicilian peasant than the one set in the empty world of high society. *Dal tuo al mio* (pr. 1903; what's yours is mine), which deals with a confrontation between sulfur miners and the barons who own the mines, and which puts forth the self-interest motive as the source of all actions, was later reconstructed by Verga as a less effective short novel in 1906. There is no complete edition of the plays of Verga, although the one-volume *Teatro*, published by Mondadori in 1912, is a valuable collection of the better ones.

ACHIEVEMENTS

Giovanni Verga is generally viewed as the second greatest novelist Italy has produced, after Alessandro Manzoni. His objectivity, his efforts to infuse new life into the petrified, tradition-shackled Italian language, his compassion for humanity, and his conception of society as controlled by immutable economic laws have made an indelible impression on the Italian writers who followed him, especially on the neorealists. One of the landmark works of the neorealist cinema is Luchino Visconti's *La terra trema* (1948), based on Verga's novel *The House by the Medlar Tree*. The tragic vision elaborated in his best novels, however, has less appeal than his short stories.

Abroad, Verga is best known as the source of the libretto *Cavalleria rusticana* (1884), and his stories, such as "The She-Wolf," "Conforti" ("Consolation"), "Black Bread," "Liberty," and "Cos'è il re" ("So Much for the King"), are frequently anthologized. Furthermore, he is among the few modern Italian writers included with any regularity in textbooks of literature published in the United States.

Although his dramatic works were not many, Verga was the only fully successful writer of tragedy in Italian theater between Count Vittorio Alfieri and Luigi

Pirandello. *Cavalleria rusticana* is a work of monumental importance in the history of Italian theater, for it ushered in a new age of realistic drama dealing with contemporary problems after centuries of plots based on medieval themes.

In his best novels, Verga achieved a perfect synchronization of style and story and created a language capable of conveying the feelings of his Sicilian peasant characters that his Italian readers could understand. Verga steeped himself in the customs and the psychology of Sicily and then proceeded to convert the Sicilian dialect of his characters into a crystalline and "unartificial" Italian. Generally remaining within the bounds of standard Italian, Verga preserved successfully syntactic features of his native dialect, such as the tendency to repeat the verb at the end of a sentence, as in "Per voi tirerei tutta la casa, tirerei" ("For you I would lift the whole house up, I really would") from "Cavalleria rusticana." Gabriele D'Annunzio would later imitate this feature of Verga's language in his own short stories.

BIOGRAPHY

Giovanni Verga was the eldest of five children born to Giovanni Battista Verga Catalano and Caterina di Mauro. The Vergas were upper middle class, descended from a Spaniard, Lajn Gonzalo de Vergas, who came to Sicily in the thirteenth century. The elder Giovanni Verga was cultured and well read, and he dabbled in the occult; Verga's mother was an intellectual and was a cousin of Domenico Castorina, a local writer. Both of Verga's parents were cautiously liberal in that they opposed the Bourbon monarchy that held a tyrannical sway over southern Italy at that time. Although born and reared in Catania, Verga spent much of his life in Vizzini, where his father owned considerable property. There the family sought refuge in summers to avoid outbreaks of cholera and political violence.

In 1850, Verga went to a secular school directed by Antonino Abate. There he read Dante, Petrarch, Torquato Tasso, Ludovico Ariosto, Ugo Foscolo, and Manzoni, as well as the bombastic writings of Catania's own Castorina.

Although Abate favored the union with Italy, unlike some Sicilians, who desired an independent Sicily, he wished to see an Italian republic rather than a monarchy.

Giovanni Verga. (Library of Congress)

His student, Verga, on the other hand, was so grateful when the troops of Giuseppe Garibaldi made a unified Italy possible that he accepted the idea of a monarchy easily. A unified Italy, however, did not bring all it had seemed to promise. When the new leaders began to break up the ancient feudal estates, as the land-hungry peasants had hoped, the fragmented estates were purchased by members of the middle class, who by this means were able to elevate themselves, to the total exclusion of the peasants, who no longer had even the rights of use that they had enjoyed under the previous system. There occurred savage attacks on the gentry by an embittered and defrauded peasantry, and although Verga himself had to flee their unleashed wrath, somehow there took root deep within him a remarkable compassion for the plight of this unfortunate class of people, and it was precisely this empathy that led him to greatness as a writer.

To please his father, Verga entered the University of Catania to study law, but he soon was bored and began to

apply himself to writing fiction. Because these first literary efforts were mildly successful, he decided to move to the Italian mainland to perfect his Italian and his literary style. Following the tradition of writers such as Alfieri, Foscolo, and Manzoni, who purified their Italian by taking up residence in the country's linguistic capital, Verga chose to move to Florence, which in 1865 was also the country's interim political capital. He mastered Italian, as was his goal, but skillfully preserved the rhythms and syntax of the dialects and, although he used outright idioms that had to be italicized within his texts less and less frequently as he matured as a writer, he succeeded in substituting Italian words for dialect in such a way as to preserve even the lexical flavor of the original speech.

In Florence, Verga renewed his acquaintance with Luigi Capuana, from Mineo, and Mario Rapisardi, from Catania; he also became acquainted with Francesco Dall'Ongaro, a respected critic and writer. At the Dall'Ongaro residence, Verga met Giselda Fojanesi, soon to be Rapisardi's wife and subsequently Verga's mistress. Verga saw her during his frequent visits to Catania, where she and her husband returned to live, until December, 1883, when Rapisardi discovered the infidelity and sent Giselda back to Florence, whereupon Verga ended the liaison.

Verga published *Sparrow* in 1871, and in November, 1872, he moved to Milan, where he associated with members of the Scapigliatura literary group, making friends with Giuseppe Giacosa, Giacomo Puccini's foremost librettist, and with Arrigo Boito, who wrote libretti for Verdi. The *scapigliati* (the "disheveled," or those against the establishment) reacted against bourgeois traditions and sought greater originality, subjectivity, and immediacy in their writing. Although Verga probably did not ever consider himself a member of this group, it is in the impulse that they gave to him that much of their own historical importance lies. Verga enjoyed his years in Milan, where he wrote several trivial novels featuring erotic escapades among the rich, usually set in Florence or Milan; only the publication of "Nedda" in 1874 gave an inkling of his potential greatness. The decade 1880 to 1890 was a glorious one for Verga; during this period, he published two great novels, *The House by the Medlar Tree* and *Mastro-don Gesualdo*, in addition to a number of masterpieces of short fiction. Still, the critical reception of his works was not enthusiastic, and this depressed him.

In 1889, Giovanni Targioni-Tozzetti and Giovanni Menasci took Verga's "Cavalleria rusticana" and turned it into a libretto for the then-unknown Pietro Mascagni. Verga was consulted beforehand and gave his consent without specifying what share of the royalties he wished. When the opera proved successful, Verga initiated a lawsuit that ended in 1893 with the court awarding him the onetime sum of 143,000 lire. A few years later, Verga brought suit again, claiming that his agreement to the 1893 terms had been fraudulently induced. The litigation, at great cost to Verga, dragged on until 1915. It was said invidiously that Verga lost interest in his writing because he enjoyed litigating more; if the assertion is untrue, certainly the fact of the litigation served to take his personal focus away from his writing to worldly matters.

Disillusioned by what he viewed as the failure of his literary career and moved by nostalgia for the Sicilian countryside, Verga left Italy for Catania in 1893. From Sicily he continued to travel, especially to Milan, but he no longer maintained an apartment there and stayed instead in hotels. The return home failed to revitalize Verga's interest in the cycle of five novels that he was planning; although the plot of the third novel, "La duchessa di Leyra" (the duchess of Leyra), was already worked out, he never finished it. In the last decades of his life, he had the consolation of his friendship with the younger Federico De Roberto, author of the historical novel *The Viceroys* (1894), who came to play Boswell to Verga's Johnson. De Roberto published a series of newspaper articles on Verga after his death that left no doubt that Verga had been considered the most important person in De Roberto's life.

In Rome in 1881, Verga had met Dina Castellazzi, wife of the count of Sordevolo, and the relationship that developed between them was to last the rest of Verga's life. The more than seven hundred letters he wrote to her from Catania serve as the primary sources of information on the last two decades of his life. Although she became a widow in 1891 and wanted Verga to marry her, he was unwilling and remained a bachelor.

As he became more withdrawn in old age, Verga became more politically conservative. His stance against demonstrations that could disrupt the political order of Italy hardened. When Luigi Capuana and De Roberto publicly faulted the Italian government for its inefficiency in handling the aftermath of the earthquake that destroyed Messina and Reggio di Calabria in 1908, Verga, afraid of triggering a secession movement in Sicily, remained silent. His inability to understand the march of time began to interfere with his art. In his play *Dal tuo al mio*, about the suppression of a strike at a sulfur mine and the turncoat loyalties of the mine's foreman, his message that greed is the incontrovertible source of evil in a world devoid of idealism had become doctrinaire and boring. Politics as such interested Verga only sporadically, but in 1920, Prime Minister Giovanni Giolitti made him a senator of the kingdom, following a tradition begun in 1860 when Alessandro Manzoni was similarly invested.

Verga died on the morning of January 27, 1922, having suffered a cerebral hemorrhage three days earlier. De Roberto scarcely left Verga's bedside those three days; afterward he made a thorough search for the manuscript of "La duchessa di Leyra," which everyone expected to appear as a finished product, but he found only the first chapter and a few pages of the second. In a letter in 1899, Verga had complained of difficulties ("May God help me with this Duchess!") he was having with the duchess's language, the international, stilted, and pretentious language of the upper classes. For the novelist who had mastered the medium used by the peasants, the medium of his own class was an insurmountable obstacle; whereas in his prematurity novels, he had openly permitted himself to react against the false world of this privileged group, his self-imposed adherence to verism kept him, at this point, from expressing his unutterable disdain and thus from completing a possible masterpiece.

ANALYSIS

Giovanni Verga's first novels were romantic, predictable, and superficial. His masterpieces of verism were written between 1880 and 1890, and for the last thirty years of his life, though full of good intentions, he produced relatively little. In one of his earliest novels, *A Mortal Sin*, which could be called an autobiography of wish fulfillment (in the story, a young Sicilian, footloose in the big city, both achieves literary fame and wins the beautiful woman he loves), the author strives for a veneer of realism by claiming that his story comes from authentic documents that have come into his possession. Although Verga in his maturity would disown this novel, the writer's task to re-create reality is already taken seriously in it. *Sparrow* tells the story of a young girl forced to become a nun against her will, in the manner of Denis Diderot's *The Nun* (1796). For years Verga's most widely read novel, *Sparrow* consists of letters allegedly written by the girl herself. The blackcap of the title is a fragile bird Verga claims to have seen once and been reminded of later when he learned the girl's story.

In the preface to *Eva*, Verga again asserts the veracity of what he writes, although this time not insisting that it is true, but rather that it could have happened. Although the character of Eva is lost in the bombast of the novel's conventionalities, Eva's speech is precise and reflects her personality. Further, Eva's decision to leave Enrico for a rich lover stems from Verga's firm belief that love, without the social coercion afforded by marriage or without the nostalgia caused by separation, cannot survive routine when lovers live together. Also emphasized is the incontestable power of financial security to nurture art and love.

Hardly an advance over *Eva*, *Tigre reale* (royal tigress) concerns a consumptive Russian lady who lives in Florence and falls in love with a young Sicilian. Despite its title, another early novel, *Eros*, is the most complex of this group and the one least trammeled by the unreality of the dreamlike eroticism that fascinated the early Verga. The aristocratic Alberto, a type Verga never again explored in his novels, grows up without a family, searches for love, makes many mistakes, and ends his life with a gunshot. Although the often realistic and colloquial language coincides with character, Verga as author obtrudes upon the reader his strong dislike for the aristocratic world he is portraying.

The appearance in 1874 of the short story "Nedda" marked the point at which Verga abandoned his autobiographical theme of aristocrats searching for love and began to seek a commoner world apparently closer to his heart, the world of the Sicilian "primitive." It was at this point that Verga joined the literary movement known as Verism, the Italian equivalent of the realistic and naturalistic schools in France. Verga had long followed French literary trends closely and admired Émile Zola, Gustave Flaubert, and Guy de Maupassant. The views of Maupassant, whose success did much to stimulate interest in the short story in Italy, were especially compatible with Verga's concept of good writing. In fact, there developed between the two a mutual respect, and Maupassant even offered at one time to write a preface for *Little Novels of Sicily* when it appeared in French translation.

Verga's cardinal rules of good writing were in the process of emerging: The story must tell itself without evidence of or interference from the author, and language must coincide in every way with the characters who are speaking. The spare narrative style that Verga achieved in his best work, however, did much to alienate the critics, who were also put off by his pessimism and the harshness of his vision. The characteristics of the Italian novel had been set by Manzoni thirty years earlier, and it was unacceptable for a novelist to deviate from this norm. Certainly Manzoni had written of the harshness of real-life situations, but the harshness of Manzoni is balanced by his deep religious belief, a feeling absent in Verga's writing.

Verga's intent, expressed as early as 1878 and clearly based on the inspiration of Honoré de Balzac's *The Human Comedy* (1829-1848) and Zola's *The Rougon-Macquart Family* (1871-1893), was to compose a cycle of five novels to be called "La marea" (the tide)—later changed to "I vinti" (the doomed)—that would scrutinize successive stages in people's struggle for material security. The first novel of the cycle, *The House by the Medlar Tree*, would involve the struggle of a Sicilian family for minimal needs alone. The search would evolve to outright greed for riches typified by a middle-class character, Mastrodon Gesualdo, in the second book of the series. "La duchessa di Leyra" (begun in 1907), still with a Sicilian setting, would explore aristocratic vanity in Palermo, and "L'onorevole Scipioni" (the honorable Scipioni) would study political ambition in Rome. Finally, "L'uomo di lusso" (the man of wealth) would portray a character who possesses all these desires and is consumed by them. These last two titles were only projected works; Verga never completed his planned five-volume series.

THE HOUSE BY THE MEDLAR TREE

The first book of the cycle, "Padron 'Ntoni" (Master 'Ntoni), was to be named after its main character, but Verga decided at the last minute to name the novel after the family, *I malavoglia* (an emphasis lost in the title of the English translation). The tragic error of the Malavoglias, a family of fishermen, is their speculation in a shipload of lupine (a forage crop), to be paid for from profits yet to be made. A storm at sea sinks their boat, the *Provvidenza*, and causes the loss of the lupine cargo and the death of Master 'Ntoni's son, Bastianazzo. Because the debt must be paid, their cherished house by the medlar tree is lost and the family risks disintegration. The tragedy pervades the book, but the poetic psychology of their moral code, especially their family ties, raises the book far beyond the commonplace and gives it a rare dignity. True to Verga's belief that an author must not interfere in his or her story, the major characters do all the narrating, and the minor characters act as a chorus for the reader, commenting on events in a colloquial style that sounds more like spoken than written speech.

The story is told from the inside by all the characters rather than by a single voice. There is little description per se, and what there is seems as if it were spoken by some unidentified villager using the same language as the other speakers. Verga does not furnish the reader with character descriptions; instead, he gives only names and gestures. Those events that are not witnessed, such as the sinking of the *Provvidenza*, are left to the reader's imagination through the subsequent conversation of the villagers.

Consistent with Verga's aim of precision and factuality, the reader knows exactly when each event in the novel takes place. Master 'Ntoni was born in 1801 and the youngest of his grandchildren in 1864. The setting is Aci-Trezza, ten miles north of Catania in eastern Sicily, where nearly the entire plot unfolds and whose pervasive atmosphere serves a function not unlike that of Egdon Heath in Thomas Hardy's *The Return of the Native* (1878). When Master 'Ntoni's grandson, also named 'Ntoni, is inducted into the Italian navy, he is sent to Naples, the former capital of the Kingdom of the Two Sicilies, which the new Kingdom of Italy has recently incorporated and superseded; there he is struck by the many sensations and temptations of the metropolis. Although these years of unification were exciting ones in the history of the Italian nation, the villagers here are ignorant of current events. The military service that is required by the new Italian government imposes a terrible drain of human power on a hardworking family such as the Malavoglias. When Master 'Ntoni, in his attempts to gain an exemption for his grandson, speaks with Don Franco, the town pharmacist and one of the few villagers who knows anything about politics, the pharmacist blames conscription on the monarchy and speaks in favor of the republic, whereupon Master 'Ntoni begs him to start his republic soon, "as though Don Franco kept a republic up his sleeve."

Master 'Ntoni's character is revealed in his frequent use of proverbs (which in Italian are used more freely than in modern colloquial English), such as "To pull an oar, the five fingers must work together" and "Before you can be a Pope, you must learn to be a sacristan." Master 'Ntoni is the "thumb" (the only indispensable finger) and "Pope" of these metaphors, and his son, Bastianazzo, though big and burly, takes orders from his father, the patriarch. Bastianazzo's wife, Maruzza, called "La Longa," is good at bearing and rearing their five children: 'Ntoni, a big oaf of twenty; Luca, who has more sense but who is killed in military service at the naval Battle of Lissa in 1866; Alessi, who resembles grandfather 'Ntoni and who will carry on the family name and honor; Mena, an industrious young woman; and Lia, who is not yet "fish, flesh nor fowl."

After the loss of the lupine, the moneylender, Uncle Crucifix, demands his money. Uncle Crucifix is a tyrant who reappears with amplifications as Mazzaro in the story "La Roba" ("Property") in *Little Novels of Sicily* and as Mastro-don Gesualdo, the most complex and the most tragic of the three. Tyrant that he is, however, Uncle Crucifix is respected in the village, because he is rich and because he "sticks to his trade." Master 'Ntoni, after exhausting all honest methods open to him to repay the debt, agrees to surrender his beloved house by the medlar tree. The sunken *Provvidenza* has been recovered and will be repaired so that eventually the Malavoglia family will be able to buy back the house. At this point, the story becomes less that of a debt that must be paid, and more a story of personal heroism, a story in which Master

'Ntoni looms like a giant, strong in his faith that he will be able to recover the house and unswerving in his courage.

The grandson 'Ntoni, who is not a bad person and who does genuinely love his family, cannot see the sense in fighting a losing battle when there are opportunities elsewhere and soon gets involved in smuggling coffee, sugar, and silk kerchiefs. When the local customs official, Don Michele, catches up with him, 'Ntoni knifes him in the chest and is brought to trial. When he sees his namesake brought to trial as a criminal, Master 'Ntoni has a stroke and, just as his grandson, Alessi, brings him word that the house by the medlar tree is about to be theirs again, he dies. Alessi is destined to carry on the family name and is Verga's reaffirming symbol of faith in tradition and hard work.

The defense lawyer at the trial argues that there had been no smuggling and that young 'Ntoni wished only to restore the family honor, because Don Michele had seduced his sister, Lia. This does irreparable damage to Lia's reputation; to avoid dishonor, she is forced to leave home and is actually forced into prostitution by the very villagers who claim to abominate sexual promiscuity. Because no self-respecting man in the village would marry a prostitute's sister, this also condemns Mena to spinsterhood. Mena will take a room in the attic and wait to help rear Alessi's children when they come. Young 'Ntoni must go away as well, but Alessi and Mena carry on in the same house almost as if nothing had happened. Although many of their number have been lost, the disasters that have befallen the Malavoglia family have not destroyed their faith in life.

Despite its fatalism, the book is filled with irony and humor. The very name Malavoglia, which suggests both "ill-will" and "sloth," has little application to the family members themselves; the boat, *Provvidenza*, is hardly providential for the family; and there is little redemption in the undisguised greed of Uncle Crucifix. There is humor in some of the marriages that occur in the course of the novel: Uncle Crucifix meets his nemesis when he marries La Vespa, who blithely squanders the money that he has amassed in his long career, and Brasi Cipolla, who feels he can no longer marry Mena because of the family's reputation, is stuck with the worthless Mangiacarrube.

MASTRO-DON GESUALDO

Mastro-don Gesualdo, Verga's other masterpiece, the second of his projected cycle of novels and the last one completed, is the epic of a self-made man impelled toward the acquisition of greater and greater wealth. The title is applied to him sarcastically by the villagers in order to remind him of his humble origins, since "Mastro" (master craftsman; in this case, stonemason) and "don" (landowning gentleman) are sociologically incompatible ideas.

Everyone in the novel is obsessed by greed, but Gesualdo also sees his wealth as a means to power. As in Verga's earlier masterpiece, the use of proverbs underscores the philosophies of the characters: "The world belongs to those who have money" and "Everyone works in his own interest." Gesualdo's goal is to be admitted into the bourgeoisie, a class that would not tolerate him if it were not for his riches. He marries the aristocratic but penniless Bianca Trao—even though she has already been seduced by her cousin, Baron Ninì Rubiera—simply for the prestige the marriage will give him in business deals. *La roba* (property) is an obsessive symbol for Gesualdo, and it is significant that on his wedding night he applies this very word, in its second sense of "stuff," to Bianca ("Fine stuff you are!").

After his marriage to Bianca, Gesualdo must give up his mistress, the faithful Diodata, by whom he has fathered two children and for whom he provides a dowry to ensure her subsequent marriage. Count Ninì Rubiera, who, unbeknown to Gesualdo, is the father of his "daughter," Isabella, falls in love with an actor and applies to Gesualdo for a loan. Gesualdo obliges happily, seeing in this still another way to acquire property. Later he forces Isabella to marry the duke of Leyra from Palermo, who has an illustrious name but who is badly in need of Isabella's dowry.

The specter of death haunts the last quarter of the book. The tubercular Bianca is dying. The peasants rebel against the rich, who in order to save their own property try to divert the attention of the furious crowds to the upstart Gesualdo. Once his own cancer-like disease is diagnosed, Gesualdo fights furiously against the thought of death. He is finally taken to Palermo by the duke of Leyra, where, under surveillance, he will not be able to rewrite his will in favor of his illegitimate children. Because Gesualdo never loses awareness of the great price his riches have cost him, because his own interest has often included interest in many other people, and because of the detachment from his riches that he achieves while in Palermo, he is a character with whom the reader can ultimately sympathize: "I want to clear my accounts with God" are his last words.

For many years after the appearance of *Mastro-don Gesualdo*, critics argued over which of the two Verga masterpieces was the greater. It is now generally agreed that *The House by the Medlar Tree* is the more powerful narrative, yet in content rather than style and for the stature of its hero, *Mastro-don Gesualdo* deserves to be appreciated in its own right.

Jack Shreve

OTHER MAJOR WORKS

SHORT FICTION: "Nedda," 1874 (English translation, 1893); *Primavera ed altri racconti*, 1876; *Vita dei campi*, 1880 (*Cavalleria Rusticana, and Other Stories*, 1928; also known as *Life in the Country*, 2003); *Cavalleria Rusticana, and Other Tales of Sicilian Peasant Life*, 1893; *Under the Shadow of Etna: Sicilian Stories*, 1896; *Novelle rusticane*, 1883 (*Little Novels of Sicily*, 1925); *Per le vie*, 1883; *Vagabondaggio*, 1887; *I ricordi del capitano D'Arce*, 1891; *Don Candeloro e C'.*, 1894; *Dal tuo al mio*, 1905 (adaptation of his play); *The She-Wolf, and Other Stories*, 1958; *The Defeated: Six Sicilian Novellas*, 1996.

PLAYS: *Cavalleria rusticana*, pr., pb. 1884 (adaptation of his short story; English translation, 1893); *In portineria*, pb. 1884 (adaptation of his short story "Il canario del N. 15"); *La lupa*, pr., pb. 1896 (adaptation of his short story); *La caccia al lupo*, pr. 1901 (adaptation of his short story; *The Wolf Hunt*, 1921); *La caccia alla volpe*, pr. 1901; *Dal tuo al mio*, pr. 1903; *Teatro*, pb. 1912; *Rose caduche*, pb. 1928 (wr. 1873-1875).

NONFICTION: *Lettere al suo traduttore*, 1954; *Lettere a Dina*, 1962, 1971; *Lettere a Luigi Capuana*, 1975.

BIBLIOGRAPHY

Alexander, Foscarina. *The Aspiration Toward a Lost Natural Harmony in the Work of Three Italian Writers: Leopardi, Verga, and Moravia*. Lewiston, N.Y.: Edwin Mellen Press, 1990. Compares the work of Verga, Giacomo Leopardi, and Alberto Moravia, three Italian writers who lived in different periods but whose work shared a common desire for harmony. Discusses how the writers' works expressed the often tragic quest to attain this desire. Includes biographical notes and a bibliography.

Amatangelo, Susan. *Figuring Women: A Thematic Study of Giovanni Verga's Female Characters*. Madison, N.J.: Fairleigh Dickinson University Press, 2004. A study of Verga's representation of women in his novels that places his female characters within the social and cultural context of nineteenth century Italy. Includes a bibliography and an index.

Bergin, Thomas Goddard. *Giovanni Verga*. 1931. Reprint. Westport, Conn.: Greenwood Press, 1969. Although dated, this well-organized and still-useful study traces a definite line of development from Verga's first published work to his last. Includes a bibliography and an informative commentary on Verga's style.

Carsaniga, Giovanni. "Literary Realism in Italy: Verga, Capuana, and *Verismo*." In *The Cambridge Companion to the Italian Novel*, edited by Peter Bondanella and Andrea Ciccarelli. New York: Cambridge University Press, 2003. An examination of Italian realism, called Verism, focusing on the works of Verga and Luigi Capuana.

Cecchetti, Giovanni. *Giovanni Verga*. Boston: Twayne, 1978. An extensive study of Verga's life and work, providing an overview of the most complex characteristics of the author's writing. Includes a bibliography and an index.

Lane, Eric. Introduction to *Short Sicilian Novels*, by Giovanni Verga, translated by D. H. Lawrence. London: Daedalus Books, 1984. Lane's introduction provides the reader with an accurate historical overview and with perspicacious critical observations.

Pagano, Tullio. *Experimental Fictions: From Emile Zola's Naturalism to Giovanni Verga's Verism*. Madison, N.J.: Fairleigh Dickinson University Press, 1999. A close study of major novels by the two writers, focusing on questions of ideology in their works. Pagano seeks to challenge many of the traditional assumptions about Verga and Zola.

Patruno, Nicholas. *Language in Giovanni Verga's Early*

Novels. Chapel Hill: University of North Carolina Press, 1977. An excellent study that examines, analyzes, and determines the linguistic norm of the early works of Verga, namely the novels *A Mortal Sin*, *Eva*, *Tigre reale*, and *Eros*. Particular attention is given to Verga's Florentine period, between 1866 and 1875. This work contains a historical introduction and an explanation of phonology and the lexicon used by Verga in his early novels.

Tench, Darby. *Fictive Mediation and Mediated Fiction in the Novels of Giovanni Verga*. Lewiston, N.Y.: Edwin Mellen Press, 2005. An examination of Verga's novels, particularly *The House by the Medlar Tree*, focusing on his use of immediacy and mediation as rhetorical strategies. Includes a bibliography and an index.

Wood, James. "Giovanni Verga's Comic Sympathy." In *The Irresponsible Self: On Laughter and the Novel*. London: Jonathan Cape, 2004. This essay examining humor in Verga's work is included in a collection of pieces about "the comedy of forgiveness," Wood's term for a form of humor that is more disposed to sympathy than to the ridicule and moral strictness of satire.

JULES VERNE

Born: Nantes, France; February 8, 1828
Died: Amiens, France; March 24, 1905
Also known as: Jules Gabriel Verne

PRINCIPAL LONG FICTION

Cinq Semaines en ballon, 1863 (*Five Weeks in a Balloon*, 1876)

Voyage au centre de la terre, 1864 (*A Journey to the Centre of the Earth*, 1872)

Voyages et aventures du capitaine Hatteras, 1864-1866 (2 volumes; includes *Les Anglais au pôle nord*, 1864 [*English at the North Pole*, 1874], and *Le Désert de glace*, 1866 [*Field of Ice*, 1876]; also known as *Adventures of Captain Hatteras*, 1875)

De la terre à la lune, 1865 (*From the Earth to the Moon*, 1873)

Les Enfants du capitaine Grant, 1867-1868 (3 volumes; *Voyage Round the World*, 1876-1877; also known as *Captain Grant's Children*; includes *The Mysterious Document*, *Among the Cannibals*, and *On the Track*)

Vingt mille lieues sous les mers, 1869-1870 (*Twenty Thousand Leagues Under the Sea*, 1873)

Autour de la lune, 1870 (*From the Earth to the Moon . . . and a Trip Around It*, 1873)

Une Ville flottante, 1871 (*A Floating City*, 1876)

Aventures de trois russes et de trois anglais, 1872 (*Meridiana: The Adventures of Three Englishmen and Three Russians in South Africa*, 1873)

Le Tour du monde en quatre-vingts jours, 1873 (*Around the World in Eighty Days*, 1873)

L'Île mystérieuse, 1874-1875 (3 volumes; includes *Les Naufrages de l'air*, *L'Abandonné*, and *Le Secret de l'île*; *The Mysterious Island*, 1875)

Le Chancellor, 1875 (*Survivors of the Chancellor*, 1875)

Michel Strogoff, 1876 (*Michael Strogoff*, 1876-1877)

Hector Servadac, 1877 (English translation, 1878)

Les Cinq Cents Millions de la Bégum, 1878 (*The Begum's Fortune*, 1880)

La Maison à vapeur, 1880 (*The Steam House*, 1881; includes *The Demon of Cawnpore* and *Tigers and Traitors*)

La Jangada, 1881 (2 volumes; *The Giant Raft*, 1881; includes *Down the Amazon* and *The Cryptogram*)

Mathias Sandorf, 1885 (English translation, 1886)

Robur le conquérant, 1886 (*The Clipper of the Clouds*, 1887)

Sans dessus dessous, 1889 (*The Purchase of the North Pole*, 1891)

Le Château des Carpathes, 1892 (*The Castle of the Carpathians*, 1893)

L'Île à hélice, 1895 (*Floating Island*, 1896; also known as *Propeller Island*, 1965)

Face au drapeau, 1896 (*For the Flag*, 1897)

Le Sphinx des glaces, 1897 (*An Antarctic Mystery*, 1898; also known as *The Mystery of Arthur Gordon Pym*)

Le Superbe Orénoque, 1898 (*The Mighty Orinoco*, 2002)

Le Village aérien, 1901 (*The Village in the Treetops*, 1964)

Maître du monde, 1904 (*Master of the World*, 1914)

L'Invasion de la mer, 1905 (*Invasion of the Sea*, 2001)

La Chasse au météore, 1908 (*The Chase of the Golden Meteor*, 1909; also known as *The Meteor Hunt*, 2006)

Les Naufragés du Jonathan, 1909 (*The Survivors of the Jonathan*, 1962)

Le Secret de Wilhelm Storitz, 1910 (*The Secret of Wilhelm Storitz*, 1965)

L'Étonnante Aventure de la mission Barsac, 1920 (2 volumes; *Into the Niger Bend*, 1919; *The City in the Sahara*, 1965)

Paris au XXe siècle, 1994 (*Paris in the Twentieth Century*, 1996)

OTHER LITERARY FORMS

Jules Verne's initial ambition was to be a playwright, and several of his plays and operettas were produced in Paris during the 1850's. The first was *Les Pailles rompues*, produced by Alexandre Dumas, *père*, in 1850, which also appeared in print. Others were the librettos *Colin Maillard* (pb. 1853) and *Les Compagnons de la*

Marjolaine (pr. 1855). A number of Verne's short stories appeared in periodicals during the same period; some were collected along with the novelette "Une Fantasie du docteur Ox" in 1874. A collection of later stories was assembled for publication by Verne's son, Michel Verne, appearing under the title *Hier et demain* (1910; *Yesterday and Tomorrow*, 1965). Verne also wrote various nonfictional works on the history of exploration and took over from Théophile Lavellée a multivolume project called *Géographie illustrée de la France et de ses colonies*, which was issued in the period 1867-1868. Many of his novels were adapted to dramatic form and were usually represented as collaborations when produced or subsequently published as plays. Of his early articles, the most important is an essay on Edgar Allan Poe that he published in 1864 in the journal *Musée des familles*.

ACHIEVEMENTS

Jules Verne is remembered today chiefly as one of the two most notable writers of science fiction in a time before that term existed. I. O. Evans has described Verne as the "founder" of science fiction, and Peter Costello has called him the "inventor" of science fiction. The claim is justified, but it should be remembered that Verne did not see himself in this way—he was quite sincere in seeing no real literary relationship between his own work and that of H. G. Wells, with whom he was frequently compared during the last decade of his life. What Verne actually set out to do, consciously and methodically, was to use geography as an ideative resource in the same way that Alexandre Dumas, *père*, had used history. Only a fraction of his work can be described as science fiction, yet all of it fits into a single pattern that is suggested by his use of the term *les voyages extraordinaire* as a kind of series title for his oeuvre. The medium that Verne invented and developed might more appropriately be called "the novel of imaginary tourism"; the science-fiction element in his work arose out of his occasional ambitions to send his tourists to places never before visited by humans (the North Pole, the moon, and cave systems beneath the earth's surface). In some instances, he had to devise new modes of travel—Barbicane's space-gun and Robur's flying machine—but, for the most part, he was content to employ conventional means of transport or slightly more luxurious versions of already existing machines (balloons and submarines).

There is a sense in which Verne's reputation has been distorted by the emphasis on his achievements as a precursor of modern science fiction. He has been described by Franz Born as "the man who invented the future" and by Peter Haining as "the master of prophecy," but these descriptions are plainly absurd. Apart from two whimsical essays and his last, most somber, short story, "L'Eternel Adam" (written c. 1900 and included in *Yesterday and Tomorrow*; "The Eternal Adam"), Verne wrote nothing set in the future. Many of his novels deal with achievements not yet accomplished in the real world, but they were all achievements that Verne believed to be perfectly possible in the context of his own times. Even in his own day, Verne was hailed as the inventor, in his imagination, of technological devices later realized, but Verne always disclaimed any such achievement. In relation to the most commonly quoted example—the submarine described in *Twenty Thousand Leagues Under the Sea*—Verne pointed out, when questioned, that there had been submarines around for at least sixty years (he had probably seen *Le Plongeur*, built in 1864, on display at the Paris Exhibition of 1867) and that all the innovations he had attributed to the *Nautilus* actually remained unrealized.

Verne's real achievement was simply to notice the impact that the revolution in transportation was having on the world. When he saw the *Great Eastern* under construction in London in 1859, he had the wit to realize what a difference steamships would make to the business of travel and to the accessibility of distant parts of the world. He realized that a revolution in exploration was under way quite as important as the great navigations of the fifteenth and sixteenth centuries, and that new technologies would shrink the world very dramatically. If his novel *Around the World in Eighty Days* seemed sensational, it was only because of the ignorance of the audience; Thomas Cook had already advertised the first tour around the world for anyone who cared to go, and a Bostonian named George Francis Train had already gone around the world in eighty traveling days, though his total journey time was extended by a few sojourns in foreign jails.

Verne's enthusiasm for the Industrial Revolution was undoubtedly based on a one-sided view of its consequences; the same might be said, however, of the many writers who saw and bemoaned the social consequences of the revolution—the growth of the industrial poor—without realizing the historical significance of technological advancement. Verne had little to say about the future of technology, but he was aware of the fact that the process of innovation would continue and would be important in its impact on human affairs. This makes him a wiser man than most of the political economists of the day—including Karl Marx—who grossly underestimated, or even mistook, the significance of technological change.

Verne has never been taken very seriously as a novelist. Partly this is because he was considered popular, and thus vulgar—all the more so because Pierre-Jules Hetzel, his publisher, dealt mainly in juvenile fiction. In Britain, Verne's books were published in butchered translations as "boys' books," and it is only in recent years that unmutilated translations of a few of his more famous works have become available. In France, interest in Verne has revived. Michel Butor wrote an excellent essay titled "The Golden Age in Jules Verne" (1960), and even Roland Barthes paid wry homage to Verne in one of the brief essays in *Mythologies* (1957; English translation, 1972). The contribution made by Verne to nineteenth century consciousness is now openly acknowledged, if not universally admired. The literary skills displayed in Verne's novels are limited, and the very processes of change that he was celebrating have robbed his stories of their excitement and conviction, leaving to them only historical interest and a certain naïve charm. For these reasons, modern readers have great difficulty in reading Verne for pleasure; his appeal is anchored in a lost past from which today's reader is far removed. Nevertheless, his achievements, seen in their appropriate historical context, should not be underestimated.

BIOGRAPHY

Jules Gabriel Verne was born in 1828, the son of Pierre Verne, a lawyer, and Sophie, née Allotte de la Fuye. He was born in Nantes, on the Île Feydeau, an island in the Loire River that has since been connected to the bank. His family appears to have been a bastion of middle-class respectability, desperately concerned with keeping up appearances. This fact appears to have had a profound effect on Verne's life, a subtle but important influence on his work, and to be the cause of some misrepresentation in the biographies written by members of his family—even the one published in 1973 by Jean Jules-Verne (his grandson).

Verne's life story seems to have been one of constant and unsuccessful rebellion against the standards and lifestyle that his family tried to impose on him. He never escaped the clutches of middle-class respectability and seems to have spent the last forty years of his life maintaining a facade for the sake of the expectations of his family. Under such circumstances, it is perhaps not surprising that he took full advantage of the opportunity to become a voyager in the imagination—a champion escapist.

Verne studied law in his father's office for a while before going to Paris, ostensibly to continue his studies there. Actually, he wanted to be a playwright, and he threw himself into the bohemian life of the student quarter of the Left Bank, where he met Victor Hugo and Alexandre Dumas, *père*. Dumas encouraged his literary endeavors and produced Verne's first one-act comedy at the Théâtre Historique. Verne's attempts to establish himself in the literary world were, however, less than wholly successful. While he wrote plays, short stories, and operettas in the early 1850's, he was for three years secretary of the Théâtre Lyrique, but by the end of 1855, he had had enough. In 1856, he planned to marry a young widow, Honorine Morel, and in order to be able to support her, he asked his father to buy him a share in a stock-broking business.

This business provided Verne with an income, but he still had other ambitions and began collecting articles that he hoped might help him to carve out a niche for himself as a novelist exploiting geography in the same way Dumas had exploited history. He traveled extensively, visiting Britain in 1859 and Scandinavia in 1861, and produced more light plays with music. His son Michel was born in August, 1861.

Around this time, Verne appears to have become partly estranged from his wife. They had no more children and occupied separate beds, but they continued

to maintain the appearance of a happy marriage. Verne retreated more and more frequently to his club—the Cercle de la Presse Scientifique—where he met and became friendly with Félix Tournachon, a photographer and aeronaut who used the pseudonym "Nadar." Out of the interest in aeronautics inspired by this association came a documentary novel about ballooning, which Verne took to the publisher Hetzel (who himself wrote, under the pseudonym P. J. Stahl) in 1862. Hetzel suggested sweeping revisions, which Verne carried out in only two weeks. Verne put to Hetzel, soon after the publication of *Five Weeks in a Balloon*, his idea for an extended series of *les voyages extraordinaires*, and Hetzel encouraged him to go ahead. By September, 1863, when the Verne family moved to Auteuil, Verne was well established as a novelist. He was, however, apparently under great personal strain. He suffered a good deal from stress-related facial paralysis, which eventually had to be relieved by electric shock treatment.

Verne seems to have been grateful to Hetzel, and his first biographer, Marguerite Allotte de la Fuÿe (his niece), alleges that Hetzel treated him with the utmost generosity. In fact, Hetzel's financial records reveal that Hetzel made about five times as much from Verne's books as Verne did and, although Verne eventually became quite well-off, his family certainly struggled for a while in the 1860's and may have suffered mild financial embarrassments later in his career, when his sales fell off dramatically.

In 1870, Ferdinand de Lesseps solicited the Légion d'Honneur for Verne; it was awarded in 1870 immediately before the fall of the Third Republic. He was honored by the Académie Française in August, 1872, but was never elected to it. During the Franco-Prussian War, Verne set up a coast-guard unit at Crotoy, where he had been living for some years, and afterward had to return to the Bourse for a while because of the effect of the war on the book trade. This did not last long, however, and in 1872, he settled permanently in Amiens, devoting himself from then on to full-time writing.

Verne's son Michel proved a great disappointment to him. As a boy, Michel was a delinquent, and he was estranged from his parents for a long time, living a turbulent personal life. When he finally settled down, however, he and his father were reconciled. Michel's third son, Jean Jules-Verne, eventually became one of Verne's biographers.

Verne's main relaxation during his years at Amiens was his involvement with a series of small boats, all of which he called *St. Michel*, the third and last of which he bought in 1877. He spent a great deal of time on these boats, and the third one was actually large enough to allow him to undertake some voyages of his own. He visited Britain and Scandinavia in 1877, went cruising in the Baltic in 1880, and toured parts of the Mediterranean in 1884. On the last trip, in particular, he was exposed to a great deal of publicity and was hailed as a celebrity wherever he went. He tried to avoid this, but his wife reveled in it and frustrated his attempts to remain unnoticed. He sold the third *St. Michel* in 1886, possibly because of financial problems—throughout the 1880's, sales of his new books plummeted. Whereas, at the peak of his career, *Around the World in Eighty Days* had sold more than a hundred thousand copies in the trade edition, by 1880, his new works frequently sold less than twenty thousand copies, and the books he wrote in the last decade of his life sold less than ten thousand copies.

In March, 1886, Verne was shot in the foot by a would-be assassin—his nephew Gaston. Gaston was confined to an asylum; the incident was so shocking to the family that, according to Peter Costello's 1978 Verne biography, no one in the family would discuss the matter almost one hundred years later. Verne remained lame for the rest of his life, but that did not prevent him from going into local politics the following year. This represented a modest emergence from his shell, in that he stood as a radical, undoubtedly offending his staunchly conservative family. It is interesting that Verne's political radicalism is occasionally evident in his wry asides but is never given free expression in his works. The same is true of his religious beliefs. Though his family was staunchly Catholic (and the family biographers maintain that Verne was also), Verne appears to have become an agnostic, if not an atheist, as early as the 1850's. Religiosity was part of the facade that he maintained throughout his life, and his novels do very little to suggest his true opinions, except in certain sly remarks. This self-conscious hypocrisy is, at times, willfully sub-

Jules Verne. (Library of Congress)

verted by the author, as in *The Village in the Treetops*, in which a token denial of belief in Darwinism is then made to look absurd by a story about apes with quasi-human intelligence—living "missing links." The difficulty of penetrating this facade was increased when Verne, in 1898, burned a number of his personal papers, including manuscripts and account books.

Even after Verne's death, the business of keeping up appearances continued. Michel became his father's literary executor and seems to have taken a hand in revising one or two of his manuscripts for posthumous publication. The authorship of the novel translated into English in two volumes as *Into the Niger Bend* and *The City in the Sahara*, in particular, is rather dubious. A ghostwriter named Georges Montignac may well have been involved, as well as Michel. Certain other works published under Jules Verne's name are most likely the work of Michel, although this may apply only to shorter pieces.

What is remarkable about Verne's life, insofar as it affected his literary career, was the extent to which everything that really mattered to him remained private. He was a man whose "real" life was lived inside his head, quite disconnected from the daily routine of going through the motions of respectable middle-class life. Even in his books, his innermost thoughts remain covert, peeping out only occasionally, and then in disguise. The best of his fantasies concern ordinary people snatched by circumstance into isolation and imprisonment, which they accept with relief and guilty joy. He was the archetypal armchair traveler, a man who found solace in his dreams and worked to add a special verisimilitude to those dreams, researching indefatigably to fill in their background. He pretended to be satisfied with his lot in life, but his stories are the work of a deeply disappointed and frustrated man.

ANALYSIS

Most of Jules Verne's novels, including the ones for which he is best known, are imaginary travelogues whose initial appeal to readers is that they will provide access to the remote regions of the world and allow readers to participate in adventures that could take place only there. In the first ten years of his career, Verne's imaginary travels took him to all the most inaccessible corners of the globe: Captain Hatteras went to the North Pole; the children of Captain Grant circumnavigated the Southern Hemisphere; and the protagonists of *Five Weeks in a Balloon* and *Meridiana* crossed darkest Africa at a time when "darkest" still meant obscure and unknown. Other characters undertook still bolder voyages: Axel and Professor Lidenbrock never did reach the center of the earth, but they did get under its skin, and though Barbicane and his companions failed to land on the moon (mercifully, as they had no means of return), they did get a trip around it.

We know today that all these stories are unrealistic, but Verne's audience could not know that, and they were compelled to be impressed by the elaborate methods Verne used to create an atmosphere of verisimilitude. His attention to detail, particularly the detail of scientific instrumentation and measurement, gives his travelers a vital sense of purpose. They are researchers, collecting information with the same intellectual curiosity and ded-

ication that guided Verne's collecting of research materials. It may well be that the scientifically minded heroes have less serious companions who are along for the ride (and who usually provide comic relief), but there is no doubt as to where the real value of the works is located.

A JOURNEY TO THE CENTRE OF THE EARTH

The best of the early works is *A Journey to the Centre of the Earth*, because it is at once the most painstaking, the most imaginative, and the most elegantly plotted. The notion of an enclosed world inhabited by primeval monsters is one that has been copied many times since, and though it is the kind of wild invention of which Verne rather disapproved (he never did anything similar again), it seems perfectly appropriate to this particular literary exercise. Significantly, however, *A Journey to the Centre of the Earth* was not the most popular of the early works, and it does not enjoy the highest reputation—that distinction goes to *Twenty Thousand Leagues Under the Sea*.

TWENTY THOUSAND LEAGUES UNDER THE SEA

There are many reasons for the popularity of *Twenty Thousand Leagues Under the Sea*. The undersea world that it displays is bound to seem meager, and sometimes laughable, to modern readers who have seen and become familiar with films made by Jacques Cousteau. The contemporary reader knows what a strange and wonderful world it is, and how many bizarre inhabitants it has. In 1870, however, there was no underwater photography, the first skin-diving equipment had not yet been designed, and the undersea world was as alien as the planet Mars. The mysterious menace of the sea was legendary and had been spectacularly recalled to the public attention in 1861, when the French naval vessel *Alecton* encountered a so-called giant octopus (actually a giant squid), which the crew nearly succeeded in harpooning and hauling aboard.

In fact, *Twenty Thousand Leagues Under the Sea* is the least reliable of all Verne's novels as far as its informational content is concerned. Almost every invention in it, no matter how modest, missed the mark. Although the illustrations imply that the diving suits in the novel are rather like the pressurized suits that later became widespread, in reality the ones Verne describes would be lethal. Despite the credit given to Verne for "inventing" the modern submarine, the *Nautilus* is rather an absurd vessel, in terms of its scientific plausibility. All of this, of course, would not have affected the contemporary reader, who could quite easily swallow the whole story, hook, line, and sinker.

Quite apart from these considerations, however, the book offers powerful attractions. Captain Nemo and the *Nautilus* may not be particularly realistic, but they are most certainly charismatic. They are only disguised as rational creations; in fact, they are myth figures whose significance reveals a good deal about the spirit of Verne's work.

Barthes, in *Mythologies*, claims that what Verne's characters are always seeking is seclusion and that the many vessels employed in Verne's stories are to be seen not so much as the means of reaching faraway destinations but as microcosmic private worlds where "claustrophilic" heroes can live in comfort, safe from the chaotic and confusing world that flows by outside the windows. In this respect, the *Nautilus* is by far the best of the Verne ships. It has every possible comfort—Nemo not only has the best of everything, but his best also reaches a standard unknown to the aesthetes of Paris. It is also sealed tight; Aronnax is so completely enclosed that he is a helpless prisoner—even the power of self-determination has been taken away from him, so that he can relax utterly and completely into a security greater than anything he has undergone since the womb.

This desire for seclusion and the retreat into a private microcosm is by no means all there is to Verne—it is often the case that his characters cannot seclude themselves and are forced to fight a dogged battle for survival—but it is something that shows up strongly in his romantic and most personal stories. The fantasy of being held prisoner by a benevolent captor, maintained in luxury, and removed from the hurly-burly of the actual world is a common one, and in *Twenty Thousand Leagues Under the Sea*, it finds almost perfect expression. The wonders and dangers of the undersea world are most important here as a kind of emphatic counterpoint, standing in for the uncertainties of life. Nemo's obsessive crusade against the world's shipping is basically a strategy of rejection and retreat that, though it can be admired, envied, and temporarily shared, must ultimately be refused as a viable mode of conduct. The real world, after all, does have to be faced; one cannot help but deal with it even if one's dealings constitute a facade and one's heart is elsewhere.

THE MYSTERIOUS ISLAND

It is significant that Captain Nemo makes his reappearance in Verne's own favorite among his novels—the long and languid *The Mysterious Island*. This was the first and best of Verne's several robinsonades, in which the island on which the protagonists are cast away becomes an ideal microcosm where (with a little help from an unknown friend) they carefully reconstruct a world of middle-class comfort. Significantly, it is an all-male world strongly reminiscent of a gentlemen's club. The discovery, late in the novel, that the *Nautilus* is hidden deep in the bowels of the island is a magnificently naïve emphasis of the fact that, in terms of Verne's private mythology, the island and the submarine are really the same in terms of their function.

The Mysterious Island belongs to the second decade of Verne's career, a decade in some ways very different from the first. It commenced with the most popular of his nonfantastic works, *Around the World in Eighty Days*, which constitutes a travelogue rather different from his earlier ones in that the emphasis is on speed rather than leisurely seclusion. Significantly, it is from the closed world of a Victorian club that Phileas Fogg emerges, and to which he intends to return in the minimum possible time, once he has demonstrated that the world can be encircled (and therefore, in a sense, brought under control) on an unexpectedly tight schedule.

The travelogues that Verne wrote after *Around the World in Eighty Days* are markedly different in character from those that he wrote before. The emphasis on scientific research is largely abandoned, though the characters are always subject to occasional lapses into careful observation of odd phenomena and debates about their significance. There are no more expeditions of the kind undertaken by Professor Lidenbrock—Verne takes care to provide his characters with more urgent and more personal motives for travel and thus begins to rely more and more on shipwreck and catastrophe as motive forces.

It may be significant that the highly self-indulgent *The Mysterious Island* was followed by the grim horror story *Survivors of the Chancellor*, the story of a ship beset by a chain of catastrophes leaving the survivors to face further appalling ordeals. The contrast reflects the tension in Verne's work to which Barthes does not do full justice—the author was quite well aware of the cozy romanticism that occasionally dominated his stories, and he shared with Barthes the suspicion that there was something unhealthy about it and that it might even be something to be despised. It is almost as if, after 1874, Verne made a conscious effort to distance his work from his own daydreams, to free himself from dependence on their emotional charge in order to become a genuine literary craftsman. He went on after *Survivors of the Chancellor* to write the adventure story *Michael Strogoff*, the plot of which is built around a journey but which can under no circumstances be accounted a novel of imaginary tourism. When, in *Hector Servadac*, he made a conscious return to imaginative territory similar to that covered in *From the Earth to the Moon . . . and a Trip Around It*, he was noticeably halfhearted about it and allowed the novel to decay into confusion. Not until 1881, when he published *The Giant Raft*, did he really recapture something of the spirit of his early travel-adventure novels.

THE BEGUM'S FORTUNE

One of the most interesting experiments of this second decade was *The Begum's Fortune*, an exercise in social speculation in which an enormous inheritance split between two legatees is used to build two very different cities—the utopian Frankville and the militaristic Stahlstadt. In imagining this sharp contrast between the ideals of a French social scientist and a German militarist, Verne was reflecting on the intellectual legacy of the Franco-Prussian War, but his vision of Stahlstadt proved to be rather more prophetic than he would have wished. Verne was, in reality, interested in politics and in town planning—there was a streak of authentic utopianism in him—but that was one of the few occasions when he allowed his interest to affect his literary work, and it does so only in a rather stylized manner; both Frankville and Stahlstadt are deliberately oversimplified almost to the point of caricature, as if to emphasize the fact that Verne had no wish to deal in serious speculations about the possible future developments in French or German society. He seems to have believed that there would be a kind of impropriety in so doing, and this belief may be connected with his curiously hostile reaction to the idea that he belonged in the same literary category as Wells.

For the whole of his career as a novelist, Verne maintained a steady productivity. His books were released at the rate of one or two a year, and he left behind enough of a stockpile for the publishers to maintain this schedule for five years after his death. The decline in his popularity in the 1880's, however, reflected a genuine decline in the appeal of his work. He might with justification have wondered at that, believing himself to be demonstrating much greater versatility in his work, but it is ironically true that he echoed his earlier vitality only when he was virtually plagiarizing himself. Many of his later works are interesting, for one reason or another, but few of them are really memorable. *The Clipper of the Clouds* and its sequel, *Master of the World*, are effective pastiches of *Twenty Thousand Leagues Under the Sea*, reduced dramatically in effect by virtue of the fact that the skies patrolled by the flying machine are no substitute for the submarine world of the *Nautilus*. A rather more interesting "microcosmic fantasy" is provided in *Propeller Island*, but Verne deliberately does not treat the notion too seriously.

Interesting for a different reason is *The Castle of the Carpathians*, in which Verne set out to write a gothic romance, albeit of a rationalized nature. Because of his association with science fiction and his use of scientific apparatus in assuring the verisimilitude of his early travelogues, Verne's interest in Romantic fiction of a more exotic character is often overlooked entirely, though he was a great admirer of Edgar Allan Poe and E. T. A. Hoffmann. In *An Antarctic Mystery*, Verne provided a continuation of Poe's classic *The Narrative of Arthur Gordon Pym* (1838), and the best of his own early works of short fiction—"Maître Zacharius: Ou, L'Horloger qui a perdu son âme" (1854; "Master Zacharius," 1874) and "Une Fantaisie du Docteur Ox" (1872; "Dr. Ox's Experiment," 1874)—are plainly a pastiche of Hoffmann. Both *The Castle of the Carpathians* and *An Antarctic Mystery*, however, show how difficult Verne found it to create any real sense of supernatural threat. Both stories are rationalized, but they are pedestrian and mundane even before the climactic "explanations." The fact that Verne could be interested in this kind of fantasy and yet be incapable of writing it is symptomatic of the fact that his work became steadily more detached from any real core of personal feeling; it became gradually more self-conscious and artificial, a product of intellectual craftsmanship, with no real roots in his own beliefs and feelings. By the 1880's, if not earlier, Verne seems to have made a decision that his writing was to be a commercial activity, a way of making a living, rather than a mode of self-expression. Only his works published before 1875—and not all of those—really show any measure of imaginative vigor. For all of its carefulness and frequent cleverness, all the later work is rather lifeless.

LATER WORKS

In the work of Verne's last years, a certain bleakness becomes gradually more evident. The misanthropy glimpsed in some of his earlier novels (in the character of Captain Nemo, for example) also gained rather freer expression. Members of the ape race in *The Village in the Treetops*, with their primitive caricature of religion, offer a challenge to human vanity, and a much more explicit condemnation of human traits is to be found in the criticisms of materialism that occur in several of the posthumous novels as satirizations of gold lust. This censure is most evident in *The Chase of the Golden Meteor*, which has a very moral ending in which the scientist-hero sinks the golden meteor rather than allow any of his greedy rivals in the pursuit to get their hands on it. It is perhaps more telling, however, in *The Survivors of the Jonathan*, in which the anarchist hero's attempts to found a utopian community are confounded by the discovery of a vicinity of gold. This novel is one of the few in which Verne's radical political sympathies are made unmistakably explicit. A rather different kind of bitterness is seen in *The Secret of Wilhelm Storitz*, in which a jilted lover uses unusual means in order to get back at the woman who rejected him. This downbeat streak in Verne's last period culminated in the short story "The Eternal Adam," a tale of historical cycles of decline and fall that gives voice to an almost Spenglerian pessimism. This is pure science fiction, but it is the work of a very different man from the young Verne who wrote *A Journey to the Centre of the Earth*.

It seems odd to write of a man whose work has been read by millions—a man who is possibly the most translated French writer of all time—that he kept very much to himself. Despite his involvement in a closely knit web of family relationships (which he seems to have re-

garded as a burdensome oppression), he was essentially a loner. His heroes are mostly independent and detached men who escape into situations in which they enjoy the undemanding companionship of tolerable acquaintances, but in which they have abundant opportunity to be by themselves, observing and meditating on the world around them. Verne's main appeal is to the reader's longing to "get away from it all," and the key to his great popularity as a writer is that it is precisely that impulse toward escape that drives many people to the activity of reading.

It is by no means surprising that a man with such a personality should have been so interested in science and technology, because it is very often men of such temperament who find contemplation of the abstract world of knowledge congenial. Painstaking research and attention to detail are the prerogatives of individuals willing and able to withdraw habitually from the routines of human intercourse. One may regret that Verne did not "put himself into" his works to any great extent, with the exception of *Twenty Thousand Leagues Under the Sea* and *The Mysterious Island*. One may also regret, especially if one values Verne primarily for his contribution to the emergent genre of scientific romance, that he kept such a disciplined rein on his imagination after the early extravagances of *A Journey to the Centre of the Earth* and *From the Earth to the Moon . . . and a Trip Around It*. These, however, are facets of the man's character, which undeniably has its puzzling aspects.

Verne was not a great writer, but he was a unique and interesting one. He is a literary phenomenon who remains even today something of an enigma despite the fact that his books are straightforward tales of adventure, mostly lacking in depth. Though his work was wide enough in its appeal to generate many imitations, there remains something inimitable about his best books—and not merely the naïveté that the passage of time has rendered impossible to duplicate. There is a Vernean esprit that remains his alone.

Brian Stableford

OTHER MAJOR WORKS

SHORT FICTION: *Le Docteur Ox*, 1874 (*Dr. Ox's Experiment, and Other Stories*, 1874); *Hier et demain*, 1910 (*Yesterday and Tomorrow*, 1965).

PLAYS: *Les Pailles rompues*, pr. 1850; *Colin Maillard*, pb. 1853 (libretto); *Les Compagnons de la Marjolaine*, pr. 1855 (libretto).

NONFICTION: *Géographie illustrée de la France et de ses colonies*, 1867-1868 (with Théophile Lavellée); *Histoire des grandes voyages et grand voyageurs*, 1870-1873 (3 volumes; with Gabriel Marcel; *Celebrated Travels and Travellers*, 1879-1881).

BIBLIOGRAPHY

Butcher, William. *Jules Verne: The Definitive Biography*. New York: Thunder's Mouth Press, 2006. Exhaustive examination of Verne is large in scope and reveals rich—and sometimes controversial—details of his life. Presents a portrait of Verne that is very different from the somewhat stodgy character depicted in Herbert Lottmann's biography (cited below).

_____. *Verne's Journey to the Centre of the Self: Space and Time in the Voyages Extraordinaires*. London: Macmillan, 1990. Presents a comprehensive discussion of Verne's science fiction, supplemented by detailed notes and a comprehensive bibliography.

Costello, Peter. *Jules Verne: Inventor of Science Fiction*. New York: Charles Scribner's Sons, 1978. Readable biography places Verne's works of fiction within their historical context. Includes a bibliography.

Jules-Verne, Jean. *Jules Verne*. New York: Taplinger, 1976. Entertaining biography by Verne's grandson draws on material in the family archives to explore Verne's methods and the experiences that led to his novels and stories. Provides a good portrait of the times in which Verne lived and wrote. Includes detailed bibliography and index.

Lottmann, Herbert. *Jules Verne: An Exploratory Biography*. New York: St. Martin's Press, 1996. Graceful study by a veteran biographer of many French subjects. Describes the difficulties in Verne's life that made the writer a disillusioned man. Includes detailed notes that reflect extensive new research.

Lynch, Lawrence. *Jules Verne*. New York: Twayne, 1992. Reliable introductory study discusses Verne's early life, his early fiction, his period of masterpieces, and his final works of fiction. Includes an appendix listing film adaptations of Verne's works, detailed notes, a chronology, and an annotated bibliography.

Martin, Andrew. *The Mask of the Prophet: The Extraordinary Fictions of Jules Verne*. Oxford, England: Clarendon Press, 1990. Attempts to recapture Verne for modern readers, focusing on his fictions of subversion and law and disorder and on the prophetic nature of fiction itself.

Saint Bris, Gonzague. *The World of Jules Verne*. Translated by Helen Marx, illustrated by Stephane Heuet, with a preface by Arthur C. Clark. New York: Tuttle Point Press, 2006. Blends biographical material with anecdotes, extracts from Verne's novels, and illustrations in an attempt to re-create the settings and characters of Verne's visionary fiction.

Smyth, Edmund J., ed. *Jules Verne: Narratives of Modernity*. Liverpool, England: Liverpool University Press, 2000. Collection of essays by Verne scholars examines, among other topics, Verne's science fiction in relation to modernity and Verne's place in the French literary canon.

Unwin, Timothy. *Jules Verne: Journeys in Writing*. Liverpool, England: Liverpool University Press, 2005. Reexamines Verne's fiction, comparing his work with that of Gustave Flaubert and other nineteenth century French authors. Argues that Verne was a skillful creator of self-conscious, experimental novels.